THE

HOME CYCLOPEDIA,

OR

LIBRARY OF REFERENCE.

IN EIGHT VOLUMES,

EACH COMPLETE IN ITSELF.

I. HISTORY AND CHRONOLOGY. The World's Progress. By G. P. PUTNAM.
II. GENERAL LITERATURE AND THE FINE ARTS. By GEORGE RIPLEY and BAYARD TAYLOR.
III. THE USEFUL ARTS—including Agriculture, Domestic Economy, &c. By DR. ANTISELL.
IV. UNIVERSAL BIOGRAPHY—a Record of the Names of Eminent Persons. By PARKE GODWIN.
V. UNIVERSAL GEOGRAPHY—a Comprehensive Gazetteer of the World. By T. C. CALLICOTT.
VI. SCIENCE—including Natural History, Botany, Geology, Mineralogy, &c. By Professor SAMUEL ST. JOHN, of Western Reserve College. *In Press.*
VII. ARCHITECTURE—Historical, Descriptive, Topographical, Decorative, Theoretical, and Mechanical. By ROBERT STUART.
VIII. CYCLOPEDIA OF EUROPE—a Manual of European Geography—embracing valuable Statistics concerning every important place. By F. L. UNGEWITTER.

*** These volumes are intended to comprise a comprehensive view of the whole circle of human knowledge—in other words, to form a General Cyclopedia in a portable shape, for popular reference, for Family Libraries, for Teachers and School Libraries, and for the general reader.

NEW YORK:
A. S. BARNES & CO., 51 JOHN-STREET.
CINCINNATI:—H. W. DERBY.
1854.

BOBBETT & EDMONDS. Sc. N.Y.

ARCHITECTURE.

(Norman Interior.) p. 426

THE HOME CYCLOPEDIA.

CYCLOPEDIA

OF

LITERATURE AND THE FINE ARTS;

COMPRISING

COMPLETE AND ACCURATE DEFINITIONS OF ALL TERMS EMPLOYED IN BELLES-LETTRES, PHILOSOPHY, THEOLOGY, LAW, MYTHOLOGY, PAINTING, MUSIC, SCULPTURE, ARCHITECTURE, AND ALL KINDRED ARTS.

COMPILED AND ARRANGED BY

GEORGE RIPLEY AND BAYARD TAYLOR.

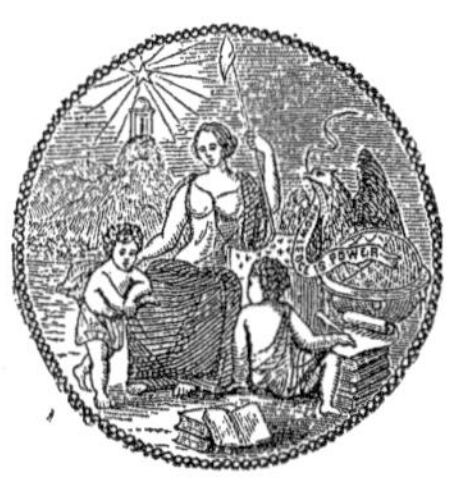

NEW YORK:

A. S. BARNES & CO., 51 JOHN-STREET.

CINCINNATI:—H. W. DERBY & CO.

1854.

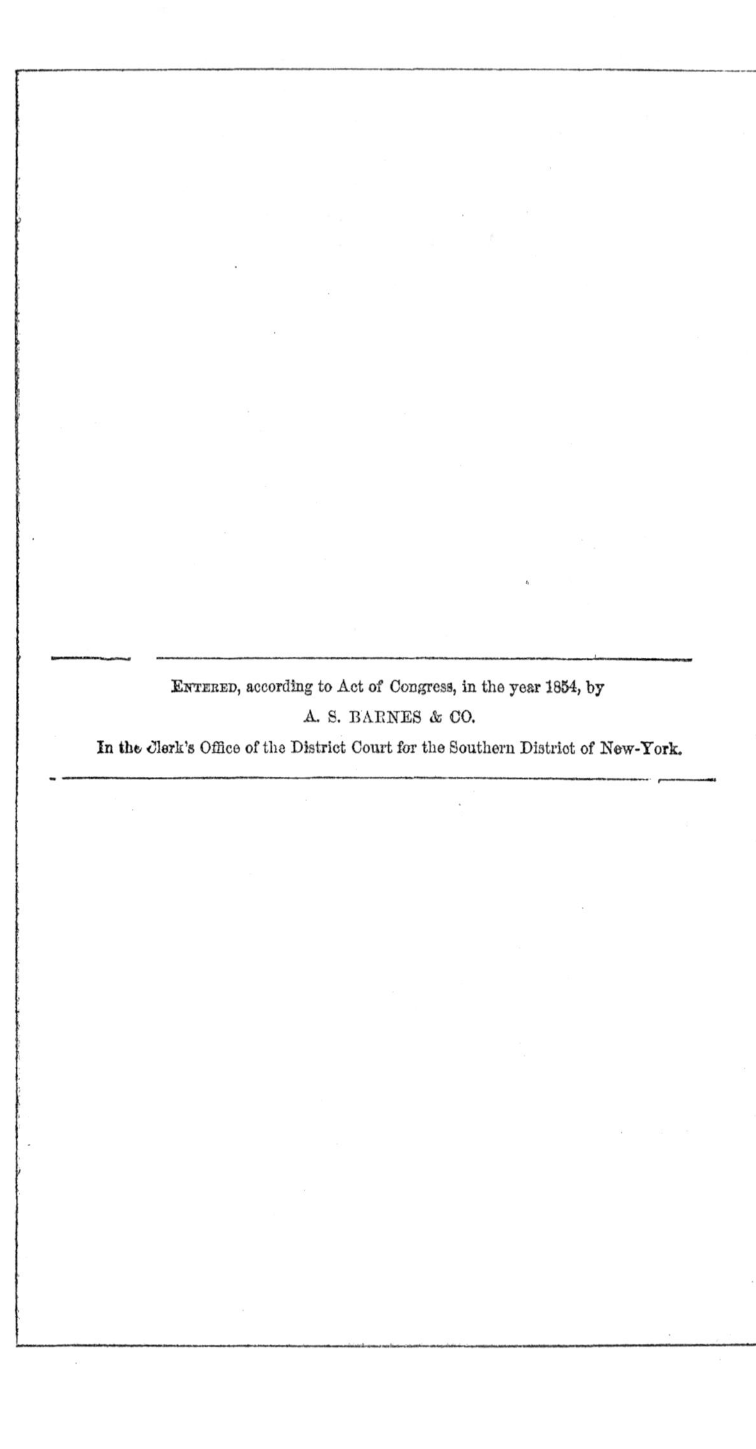

PREFACE.

THE character of this work is fully set forth in the title-page, yet a few words of introduction still seem necessary, further to elucidate its general scope and aim. The design of the compilers has been to furnish the reading community, and more especially the large class of students in our colleges and seminaries of learning, with a comprehensive handbook or lexicon of all branches of Literature and Art. A work of this kind has long been needed. The great aim of all modern systems of instruction is to present knowledge in as concise and accessible a form as possible, and bring the results of many different theories and systems into forms of practical convenience. In this respect the present work will be found adapted to the purposes of the author, the artist, the student of any learned profession, and the reader. No technical term of general use in any of the departments it includes will be found wanting, while many words, which in a strict sense belong neither to literature nor art, have been added on account of some peculiar association or application.

In Literature, the work embraces all terms of logic and rhetoric, criticism, style, and language; sketches of works which stand as types of their age or tongue; reviews of all systems of philosophy and theology, both of ancient and modern times; and a complete series of the history of literature among all nations, made up wholly from original sources. All the most important terms of common and international law, all technical words and phrases employed in theology and philosophy, and a number of scientific and historical phrases, which have become familiarized in literature, have been included. The explanations are not confined to mere definitions; whereever it has been found necessary, illustrative woodcuts have been introduced, which will greatly assist the reader in his knowledge of architectural terms.

In Art, the department of painting, sculpture, and architecture, have been treated as fully and carefully as the nature and limits of the work would permit. While a mere technical array of terms has been avoided, care has been taken to explain all the words; and phrases of art-criticism have been defined at some length, as of interest and value to the general reader, especially since criticism has been recognized as a distinct department of literature. All words relating to the art and practice of music have been likewise retained.

In compiling the work, liberal use has been made of *Maunder's Literary and Scientific Treasury*, and *Brande's Dictionary of Science and Art*. The *Imperial Dictionary*, the Leipzig *Conversations-Lexicon*, the *Art-Journal* Dictionary, and a number of other works have been consulted; while the article entitled "Literature," comprising sketches of the rise and progress of literature among ancient and modern nations, has been prepared expressly for the present work. The definitions copied from the above-named authorities have been adapted to the usages of the United States, and much that was irrelevant, on account of its application to the local laws or customs of foreign nations, has been purposely omitted. The work, therefore, as it now stands, is intended to furnish a thorough vocabulary of Art and Literature, specially designed for the use of schools, colleges, and the great reading community of the United States.

NEW-YORK, Sept. 1851

Cyclopedia of Literature and the Fine Arts.

A is the first letter, and the first vowel, of the alphabet in every known language, except the Ethiopic; and is used either as a word, an abbreviation, or a sign. If pronounced *open*, as in FATHER, it is the simplest and easiest of all sounds; the first, in fact, uttered by human beings in their most infantile state, serving to express many and even opposite emotions, according to the mode in which it is uttered. A has therefore, perhaps, had the first place in the alphabet assigned to it. In the English language it has four different sounds: the *broad* sound, as in FALL; the *open*, as in FATHER; the *slender*, or *close*, as in FACE; and the *short* sound, as in FAT. Most of the other modern languages, as French, Italian, German, &c., have only the *open*, or Italian *a*, pronounced short or long.—Among the Greeks and Romans, A was used as an arithmetical sign: by the former for 1; by the latter for 500; or with a stroke over it for 5,000. The Romans also very extensively used it as an abbreviation; which practice we still retain, as A.M., *artium magister;* A.D., *anno domini, &c.*—A, *a*, or *aa*, in medical prescriptions, denotes *ana*, or equal parts of each.—A, in music, is the nominal of the sixth note in the diatonic scale; in algebra, it denotes a known quantity; in logic, an universal affirmative proposition; in heraldry, the *dexter chief*, or chief point in an escutcheon; and it is the first of the dominical letters in the calendar.

AAN'CHE, is a term applied to wind instruments with reeds or tongues, as the clarionet, hautboy, &c.

AA'NES, the tones and modes of the modern Greek music.

AB, is the 11th month of the civil year, and the 5th of the ecclesiastical in the Hebrew calendar. In the Syriac calendar, it is the last of the summer months. The eastern Christians called the first day of this month *Suum Miriam*, the fast of Mary, and the 15th, on which day the fast ended, *Fathr-Miriam.*

ABACIS'CUS, in ancient architecture, the square compartments of Mosaic pavements.

AB'ACUS, in architecture, is the superior member of the capital of a column, to which it serves as a kind of crown. In its origin, it was intended to represent a square tile laid over a basket; it still retains this form in the Tuscan, Doric, and Ionic orders; but in the Corinthian and Composite, its four sides are arched inwards, having some ornament in the middle.—ABACUS, among ancient mathematicians, was a table strewed over with dust, or sand, on which they drew their figures.—ABACUS, in arithmetic, an ancient instrument for reckoning with counters. It is used in various forms; but the most common arrangement is made by drawing parallel lines distant from each other at least twice the diameter of a counter; which placed on the lowest line, signifies 1; on the second 10; on the third, 100; on the fourth, 1000; and so on. In the intermediate spaces, the same counters are estimated at one half of the value of the line immediately superior.

AB'BE, a French word, literally meaning an *abbot;* but the character denoted by it, has long ceased to be of any official nature. Before the Revolution, the term designated a body of persons, who had little connection with the church, but who followed a course of theological study, in hopes that the king would confer on them a real abbey, that is, a part of the revenues of a monastery. They were employed in various literary pursuits, and exerted an important influence on the character of the country. Either in the capacity of a friend or spiritual counsellor, an abbe was found in almost every distinguished family in France.

AB'BESS, the superior of a nunnery, or other religious community of women. She has the same authority as an abbot, but cannot exercise any of the spiritual functions.

AB'BEY, a religious house governed by a superior, under the title of an abbot or abbess. The abbeys of England, at their dissolution under Henry VIII., became lay-sees; when no less than 190 were dissolved, the yearly revenue of which has been estimated at 2,853,000*l*. At present, an abbey is, in general, the cathedral or episcopal church of the see or diocese in which it stands.

AB'BOT, was originally the name of every aged monk; but, since the 8th century, it denotes the head of a monastery. In most countries, they held a rank next to that of bishop, and had votes in the ecclesiastical councils. At present they are chiefly distinguished into regular and commendatory; the former being real monks or religious, and the latter only seculars.

ABBREVIA'TION, a contracted manner of writing words so as to retain only the initial letters. Such abbreviations were in common use with the Romans, as they are with us, to save time and space. —Abbreviation, in music, one dash, through the stem of a minim or crotchet, or under a semibreve, converts it into as many quavers as it is equal to in time: two dashes into semiquavers; three into demisemiquavers; and so on. When minims are connected together like quavers, semiquavers, &c., they are to be repeated as many times as if they were really such notes. An oblique dash through the 2d, 3d, and 4th lines after an arpeggio, signifies that it is to be repeated; for quavers, a single dash being used; for semiquavers, a double one; and so on.

ABBRE'VIATORS, officers who assist the vice-chancellor in drawing up the Pope's briefs, and reducing petitions into proper form, to be converted into bulls.

ABDICA'TION, properly speaking, is a *voluntary* resignation of a dignity, particularly a regal one; and if he in whose favor the abdication was made, dies, or declines the offered dignity, the right of the abdicated prince is reverted. Involuntary resignations are, however, also termed *abdications*, as in the case of Napoleon's abdication at Fontainebleau.

ABDITA'RIUM, or ABDITO'RUM, in archæology, a secret place for hiding or preserving valuables.

ABDUC'TION, the crime of unlawfully taking away, either by force, or fraud and persuasion, the person of another, whether of child, wife, ward, heiress, or woman generally.

ABE'LIANS, or A'BELITES, a Christian sect which sprung from the Gnostics. They abstained from matrimony, but adopted the children of others, and brought them up in their own principles.

ABEY'ANCE, in law, the expectancy of an estate, or possession: thus, if lands be leased from one person for life, with reversion to another for years, the latter estate is in abeyance till the death of the lessee. It is a fixed principle of law, that the fee-simple of all lands is in somebody, or else in abeyance.

A'BIB, the first month of the Hebrew year, more generally known by the Chaldean name of *Nisan*. It is first mentioned in the 4th verse of the 13th chapter of Exodus.

ABJURA'TION, a forswearing, or renouncing by oath: in the old law it signified a sworn banishment, or an oath taken to forsake the realm forever. In its modern, and now more usual signification, it extends to persons, and doctrines, as well as places.

AB'LATIVE *case*, the sixth case of the Latin nouns implied in English by the preposition *from*.

ABLEC'TI, in ancient Rome, a chosen band of foreign troops, selected from the *extraordinarii sociorum*.

ABLEG'MINA, in Roman antiquity, choice parts of the entrails of victims, called also *proficiæ*, *porriciæ*, *prosecta*, and *prosegmina*. The ablegmina were sprinkled with flour, and burnt on the altar; the priests pouring some wine on them.

ABLU'TION, a religious ceremony of washing the body, still used by the Turks and Mohammedans. It originated in the obvious necessity of practising cleanliness, for the prevention of diseases in hot countries; for which purpose it was made a religous rite; and by an easy transition of idea, the purity of the body was made to typify the purity of the soul: an idea the more rational, as it is perhaps physically certain that outward wretchedness debases the inward mind.

ABNOR'MAL, contrary to the natural condition. In Art, the term *abnormal* is applied to everything that deviates from the rules of good taste, and is analogous to *tasteless*, and *overcharged*.

ABOL'LA, a kind of military garment worn by the Greek and Roman soldiers.

ABORI'GINES, a name given to the original or first inhabitants of any country; but more particularly used for the ancient inhabitants of Latium, when Æneas with his Trojans came into Italy.

ABOR'TION, in a *figurative* sense, any production that does not come to maturity, or any design or project which fails before it is properly matured.

AB'RACADAB'RA, a term of incantation, formerly used as a spell or charm, and worn about the neck as an amulet against several diseases. In order to give it the more virtue, it was to be written as many times as the word contains letters, omitting always the last letter of the former, and so forming a triangle. But charms and incantations have had their day; and *abracadabra*, if used at all, now serves as a word of jest, like *hocus pocus*, and other unmeaning gibberish.

ABRAX'AS, or ABRASAX', in church-history, a mystical term expressing the supreme God, under whom the Basilidians supposed 365 dependent deities. It was the principle of the Gnostic hierarchy.—ABRAXAS, or ABRASAX STONES, are very numerous, and represent the human body, with the head of a cock, and the feet of a reptile. The name of *Abrasax stone* is, in modern times, applied to a variety of gems that exhibit enigmatical compositions, but have not the true characteristics of the Basilidians.

ABRIDG'MENT, the bringing the contents of a book within a short compass. The perfection of an abridgment consists in taking only what is material and substantial, and rejecting all superfluities, whether of sentiment or style: in which light, abridgments must be allowed to be eminently serviceable to all whose occupations prevent them from devoting much time to literary pursuits.

ABSCIS'SION, in rhetoric, a figure of speech, whereby the speaker stops short in the middle of his discourse, and leaves his hearers to draw their own inferences from the facts he has stated.

ABSENTEE', a word of modern times, applied to land-owners and capitalists, who expend their incomes in another country.

AB'SOLUTE, whatever is in all respects unlimited and uncontrolled in its own nature: it is opposed to the *relative*, and to whatever exists only conditionally. Thus the absolute is the principle of entire completion, the universal idea and fundamental principle of all things. The question of absolute beauty, *i. e.* the prototype of the beautiful, is the most important within the reach of Art, involving the foundation of Æsthetics, and of the philosophy of the beautiful.

ABSOLU'TION, a ceremony practised in various Christian churches. In the Roman Catholic, the priest not only declares absolution to the repentant sinner, but is believed to have the power of actually releasing him from his sins: and this authority is declared by the council of Trent to belong to him in its full extent. The Church of England, in the Order for the Visitation of the Sick, has retained nearly the same words; but her authorities seem not to be exactly agreed as to the force and effect of the absolution so conferred. In the daily service, the words of the absolution are merely declaratory.

ABSORB'ED, in Italian, *Prosciugato;* in French, *Embu.* When the oil with which a picture is painted has sunk into the ground or canvas, leaving the color flat or dead, and the touches indistinct, it is said to be *absorbed.*

ABSORBENT-GROUNDS are picture-grounds prepared in distemper upon either panel or canvas; they have the property of imbibing the redundant oil with which the pigments are mixed, of *impasting*, and are used principally for the sake of expedition.

AB'SIS, or AP'SIS, in architecture, a word used by ecclesiastical authors to signify that part of the church wherein the clergy were seated, or the altar was placed. The apsis was either circular or polygonal on the plan, and domed over at top as a covering. It consisted of two parts, the altar and the presbytery, or sanctuary: at the middle of the semicircle was the throne of the bishop; and at the centre of the diameter was placed the altar, towards the nave, from which it was separated by an open balustrade, or railing. On the altar was placed the cibarium and cup.

AB'STINENCE, the abstaining or refraining from what is either useful, agreeable, or pernicious; but more especially, from eating and drinking. In the Romish church there are "days of abstinence," as well as "fast days;" the former importing a partial, and the latter, almost a total abstinence from food.

AB'STINENTS, a sect of Christians who appeared in France about the end of the third century, professing celibacy, and abstinence from particular kinds of food, &c.

AB'STRACT, a concise but general view of some large work; in which sense it differs from an *abridgment* only as being shorter, and its entering less minutely into particulars; and from an *extract*, as this last is only a particular view of some part or passage of it.

ABSTRAC'TION, in logic, that operation of the mind whereby it forms abstract ideas. The faculty of abstraction stands directly opposite to that of compounding. By composition we consider those things together, which, in reality, are not joined together in any one existence. And by abstraction, we consider those things separately and apart, which in reality do not exist apart. In its passive sense it implies occupation with one's self to the exclusion of other objects.

ACADEM'ICS, certain philosophers who followed the doctrine of Socrates and Plato, as to the uncertainty of knowledge and the incomprehensibility of truth. Academic, in this sense, amounts to much the same with Platonist; the difference between them being only in point of time. They who embraced the system of Plato, among the ancients, were called Academici; whereas those who did the same since the restoration of learning, have assumed the denomination of Platonists.

ACAD'EMY, in Grecian antiquity, a large villa in one of the suburbs of Athens, where the sect of philosophers called Academics held their assemblies. It took its name from Academus, a celebrated Athenian, who resided there, and became celebrated from its being the place in which Plato taught philosophy. —ACADEMY, in the modern acceptation, is a society of persons united for the pursuit of some objects of study and application, as the Royal Academy of Arts of London, and the Royal Academy of Sciences of Berlin. The first academy of science, in modern times, was established at Naples, by Baptista Porta, in 1560.

ACAD'EMY FIGURE, in painting, a drawing usually made with black and white chalk, on tinted paper, after the living model. Sometimes Academy-figure is understood to be one in which the action is constrained, and the parts without mutual connection with each other, as frequently happens to those who model from a study which was only intended to exhibit the development of certain muscles or members of the body.

ACAN'THUS, the bear's claw, a plant used in Greece and Italy on account of its beautiful indented leaves and graceful growth for garden plots and also in works of Art for the borders of embroidered garments, the edges of vases, for wreaths round drinking cups; and in architecture, for ornamenting the capitals of columns, particularly those of the Corinthian order, and the Roman, or Composite, which sprang from it. The type of the Corinthian capital may be found on numerous Egyptian capitals.

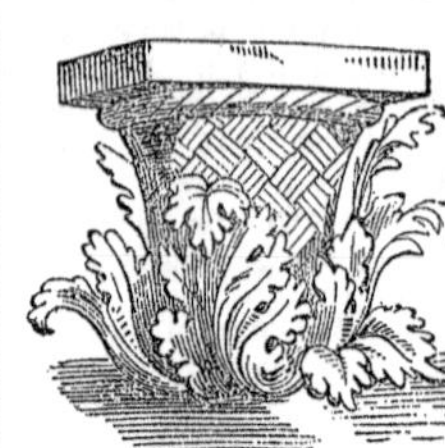

ACAT'ALEPSY, (*acatalepsia*,) among ancient philosophers, the impossibility of comprehending something; uncertainty in science.

ACCA'LIA, in Roman antiquity, solemn festivals held in honor of Acca Laurentia, the nurse of Romulus: they were also called *Laurentalia*.

ACCENDEN'TES, or ACCENSO'RES, in the church of Rome, an inferior rank of ministers, whose business it is to light, snuff, and trim the candles and tapers.

ACCEN'DONES, in Roman antiquity, officers in the gladiatorial schools, who excited and animated the combatants during the engagement.

ACCEN'SI, in Roman antiquity, certain supernumerary soldiers, designed to supply the place of those who should be killed, or anywise disabled.—ACCENSI also denoted a kind of inferior officers, appointed to attend the Roman magistrates.

AC'CENT, a modification of the voice in pronouncing certain words or syllables: also, the marks on the words or syllables; as, the acute accent, marked thus (´), the grave accent thus (`), the circumflex thus (ˆ). This is called grammatical accent, but there is also a rhetorical accent or emphasis, which is designed to give to a sentence distinctness and clearness. In a sentence, therefore, the stress is laid on the most important word, and in a word on the most important syllable. When the accent falls on a vowel, that vowel has its long sound, as in *po'rous;* but when it falls on a consonant, the preceding vowel is short, as in *pot'ter.* Accents also not only give a pleasing variety and beauty to the modulation of the voice, but often serve to ascertain the true meaning of the word.—In music, accent denotes a certain modulation or warbling of the sounds, to express passions, either naturally by the voice, or artificially by instruments. Every bar or measure is divided into the accented and unaccented parts; the former being the principal, on which the spirit of the music depends.

ACCEPT'ANCE, in commerce, is when a man subscribes, signs, and makes himself a debtor for the sum contained in a bill of exchange, or other obligation, drawn upon, or addressed to him; which is done by his writing the word "Accepted" on it, and signing his name.

ACCEPT'OR, the person who accepts a bill of exchange by signing it, and thereby becoming bound to pay its contents.

AC'CESSARY, in law, a person who aids in the commission of some felonious action. There are two kinds of accessaries, *viz.* before the fact, and after it. The first is he who commands and procures another to commit an offence; who, though he be absent when it is committed, is now regarded as much a principal as the actual offender. The accessary after the fact is one who receives, comforts, or assists the offender, knowing him to be such. In the highest crimes, as high treason, &c., and the lowest, as riots, forcible entries, &c., there are no accessaries, but all concerned are principals.

AC'CESSORIES, objects and materials independent of the figure in a picture, and which, without being essential to the composition, are nevertheless useful, whether under the picturesque relation, to fill up those parts that without them would appear naked, to establish a balance between the masses, to form the contrast, to contribute to the harmony of colors, and so add to the splendor and richness of a picture; or, under the relation of poetic composition, to facilitate the understanding of the subject, recalling some one of the circumstances which have preceded, or which will follow the action; to make known the condition and habits of the figures; to characterize their general manners, and through them the age and country in which the action takes place, &c.; such are draperies variously adjusted, trophies affixed to the walls, devices, sculptured divinities, furniture, carpets, lamps, groups of vases, arms, utensils, &c.

ACCIACATU'RA, in music, a sweeping of the chords of the pianoforte, and dropping sprinkled notes usual in accompaniments.

AC'CIDENCE, a display of the variations of words according to their government or sense.

AC'CIDENS, or PER ACCIDENS, a term applied to the operations of natural bodies, in distinction from *per se;* thus fire is said to burn *per se,* but a heated iron *per accidens.*

AC'CIDENT, that which belongs accidentally, not essentially, to a thing, as sweetness, softness, &c.

ACCIDEN'TAL, in philosophy, a term applied to effects which result from causes occurring by accident.

ACCIDEN'TAL COLORS, colors depending on some affection of the eye, and not belonging to light itself, or any quality of the luminous object. If we look for a short time steadily with one eye upon any bright-colored spot, as a wafer on a sheet of paper, and immediately after turn the same eye to another part of the paper, a similar spot will be seen, but of a different color. If the wafer be red, the imaginary spot will be green; if black, it will be changed into white; the color thus appearing being always what is termed the complementary color of that on which the eye was fixed.

ACCIDEN'TAL LIGHT, secondary lights, which are not accounted for by the prevalent effect.

ACCIDEN'TAL POINT, in perspective, the point in which a straight line drawn from the eye, parallel to another straight line, cuts the perspective plane

ACCIDEN'TALS, in painting, are those fortuitous or chance effects, occurring from luminous rays falling on certain objects, by which they are brought into stronger light than they otherwise would be, and their shadows are consequently of greater intensity. This sort of effect is to be seen in almost every picture by Rembrandt, who used them to a very great extent. There are some fine instances of accidentals in Raphael's Transfiguration, and particularly in the celebrated picture, the *Notte* of Coreggio, in which the light emanates from the infant Christ.—ACCIDENTALS, in music, are those flats and sharps which are prefixed to the notes in a movement, and which would not be considered so by the flats and sharps in the signature.

ACCLAMA'TION, in Roman antiquity, a shout raised by the people, to testify their applause, or approbation of their princes, generals, &c. In ages when people were more accustomed to give full utterance to their feelings, acclamations were very common, whenever a mass of people was influenced by one common feeling. We find, therefore, acclamations in theatres, senates, ecclesiastical meetings, elections, at nuptials, triumphs, &c. In the early times of Christianity, the bishops were elected by acclamation. The first German emperors were elected in the same way; and at the present day, wherever the forms of civilized life are least regarded, approbation or disapprobation of proposed public measures is shown by acclamations of the assembled multitude.

AC'COLA, among the Romans, signified a person who lived near some place; in which sense it differed from *incola*, the inhabitant of such a place.

ACCOLADE', the ancient ceremony of conferring knighthood, by the king's laying his arms about the young knight's neck, and embracing him. This familiar expression of regard appears to have been exchanged for the more stately act of touching, or gently striking, with the royal sword, the neck of the kneeling knight. The present ceremony of conferring the honor of knighthood is evidently derived from it.

ACCOM'PANIMENT, an instrumental part added to a musical composition by way of embellishment, and in order to support the principal melody. When the piece may be performed with or without the accompaniment at pleasure, it is called *accompaniment ad libitum;* but when it is indispensable, *accompaniment obligato.*

ACCOM'PLICE, in law, a person who is privy to, or aiding in, the perpetration of some crime.

ACCOM'PLISHMENT, in a general sense, denotes the perfecting, or entirely finishing and completing any matter or thing; but it more expressly describes the acquirement of some branch of learning, useful art, or elegant amusement.—ACCOMPLISHMENT is also particularly used for the fulfilment of a prophecy; in which sense, we read of a literal accomplishment, a mystical accomplishment, &c.

ACCORDATU'RA, an Italian word, to express the tuning of an instrument.

ACCOR'DION, a new musical instrument, of German invention, but now also made in this country, consisting of a double series of vibrating tongues, acted on by a current of air from a sort of bellows, and producing tones very similar to those of the organ.

ACCOUNT'ANT, or ACCOMPT'ANT, in a general sense, denotes one whose business it is to compute, adjust, and range in due order accounts in commerce. In a more restricted sense, the term is applicable to a person appointed to keep the accounts of a public company or office: thus, we say the accountant of the India Company, the Custom-house, the Excise, &c.

ACCOU'TREMENTS, the necessaries of a soldier, as belts, pouches, cartridge-boxes, &c.

ACCRE'TION, the increase or growth of a body by an external addition of new parts; thus shells, stones, and various other substances are formed.

ACCUBA'TION, the posture used among the Greeks and Romans at their meals, which was with the body extended on a couch, and the head resting on a pillow, or on the elbow, supported by a pillow. This practice was not permitted among soldiers, children, and servants; nor was it known until luxury had corrupted manners. Their couches were called ACCUBITA.

ACEPH'ALI, a sect of Christians, so called because they admitted no head, or superior, either lay or ecclesiastic.

ACER'RA, in Roman antiquity, was a small altar erected near the bed on which a dead person was laid out. Incense and perfumes were burnt upon it, till the time of the funeral. The real intention, probably, was to prevent or overcome any offensive smells that might arise about the corpse.

A'CHERON, the river of sorrow which flowed round the infernal realms of Hades, according to the mythology of the ancients. There was a river of Thesprotia, in Epirus, of the same name, and also one in Italy, near which Alexander, king of the Molossi, was slain; both of which from the unwholesome and foul nature of their waters, were supposed to communicate with the infernal stream.

AC'ME, in rhetoric, the extreme height, or farthest point of pathos, or sentiment, to which the mind is judiciously conducted by a series of impressions gradually rising in intensity.

ACOLY'THI, in ecclesiastical history, denotes candidates for the ministry, so called from their continually attending the bishop. It is also an appellation given to the Stoics, on account of their steady adherence to what they had once resolved.

ACOUSMAT'ICI, in Grecian antiquity, such disciples of Pythagoras, as had not finished their five years' probation. The *acousmatici* were instructed by bare positive precepts and rules, without reasons or demonstrations, and these precepts they called *acousmata*.

ACROAT'IC, in the Aristotelian schools, a denomination given to such lectures as were calculated only for the intimate friends and disciples of that philosopher; being chiefly employed in demonstrating some speculative or abstruse part of philosophy. The acroatic lectures stood contradistinguished from the exoteric ones, which were adapted to a common auditory.

ACRO'LITHOS, in sculpture, a statue whose extremities are of stone, the body being made of wood. According to Vitruvius, there was a temple at Halicarnassus dedicated to Mars, and built by Mausolus, king of Caria, wherein was an acrolithan statue of the god. And from Trebellius Pollio we learn that Calpurnia set up an acrolithan statue of Venus, which was gilt.

ACROMONOGRAMMAT'ICUM, a poetical composition, wherein each subsequent verse commences with that which the verse preceding terminates.

ACROP'OLIS, the citadel of Athens. It was formerly the whole city, and at first called Acropia, from Acrops the founder; but, after the inhabitants were greatly increased in number, the whole plain around it was filled with buildings, and the original city became the centre, under the denomination of Acropolis, or the upper city.

ACROS'TIC, a poem, the lines of which are so contrived, that the first letters of each, taken together, will make a proper name or other word.

ACROSTO'LIUM, in the naval architecture of the ancients, the extreme part of the ornament used on the prows of their ships. It was usual to tear the *acrostolia* from the prows of vanquished ships, as a token of victory.

ACROTE'RIA, in architecture, small pedestals, upon which globes, vases, or statues stand at the ends or middle of pediments. It also denotes the figures themselves placed in such situations.

ACT, in a general sense, denotes the exertion, or effectual application, of some power or faculty. Act is distinguished from power, as the effect from the cause, or as a thing produced, from that which produces it.—ACT, among logicians, more particularly denotes an operation of the human mind; in which sense, comprehending, judging, willing, &c. are called acts.—ACT, in law, is used for an instrument or deed in writing, serving to prove the truth of some bargain or transaction. Thus, records, certificates, &c. are called acts.—ACT is also used for the final resolution, or decree of an assembly, senate, council, &c.—ACTS of parliament are called statutes; acts of the royal society, transactions; those of the French academy of sciences, memoirs; those of the academy of sciences at Petersburg, commentaries; those of Leipsic, *acta eruditorum*; the decrees of the lords of session, at Edinburgh, *acta sederunt*, &c.—ACT, in the universities, is the delivery of orations, or other exercises, in proof of the proficiency of a student who is to take a degree. At Oxford, the time when masters or doctors complete their degrees, is called the *act*. At Cambridge, the same period is called the *commencement*.—ACT, in a dramatic sense, is the name given to certain portions of a play, intended to give respite both to the spectators and the actors. In the ancient drama, five acts were required both in tragedy and comedy; and in what is termed the regular drama that rule is still observed, the acts being divided into smaller portions, called *scenes*.

AC'TA CONSISTO'RII, the edicts or declarations of the council of state of the emperors.

AC'TA DIUR'NA, was a sort of Roman gazette, containing an authorized narrative of the transactions worthy of notice, which happened at Rome.

AC'TA PUB'LICA, in Roman history, the journal of the senate. It seems to have resembled the votes of the English House of Commons, wherein a short account was given to the public of what passed in the senate-house.

AC'TIAN GAMES, or LUDI ACTIACA, were instituted in commemoration of the victory obtained by Augustus over Antony at Actium. They returned every fifth year, according to the general opinion, and were sacred to Apollo, who was then called Actius Apollo. Actian years became an era, commencing from the battle of Actium, called also the era of Augustus. The Actian games consisted of shows of gladiators, wrestlers, and other exercises, and were kept generally at Nicopolis, a city built by Augustus, near Actium, for that purpose, with a view to perpetuate the fame of his victory.

AC'TION, in ethics, something done by a free or moral agent, capable of distinguishing good from evil. The essence of a moral action consists in its being done knowingly and voluntarily: that is, the agent must not only be able to distinguish whether it be good or bad in itself; but he must likewise be entirely free from compulsion of any kind, and at full liberty to follow the dictates of his own understanding.—ACTION, in rhetoric, may be defined, the accommodation of the voice, but more especially the gesture of an orator, to the subject he is upon.—ACTION, in a theatrical sense, is nearly the same with action among orators; only the actor adapts his action to an assumed character, whereas the orator is supposed to be in reality what his action expresses.—ACTION, in painting and sculpture, denotes the posture of a statue or picture, serving to express some passion, &c.—ACTION, in the military art, is an engagement between two armies, or between different bodies of troops belonging thereto.

AC'TIVE, in a general sense, denotes something that communicates motion or action to another, in which sense it stands opposed to passive.—ACTIVE, among grammarians, an appellation given to words expressing some action, as I write, I read, &c.—ACTIVE POWER, in metaphysics, the power of executing any work or labor; in contradistinction to speculative powers, as those of seeing, hearing, reasoning, &c.

AC'TOR, in a dramatic sense, is a man who enacts some part or character in a play. It is remarkable with what difference actors were treated among the ancients. At Athens they were held in such esteem, as to be sometimes sent on embassies to foreign powers; whereas, at Rome, if a citizen became an actor, he thereby forfeited his freedom. Actors in the present day have little to complain of, in regard to the treatment they receive: according as they contribute to the gratification of the public so are they rewarded; and if their moral conduct be irreproachable, no persons are more esteemed or lauded.

AC'TRESS, a female dramatic performer. They were unknown to the ancients, among whom men always took the parts of women. Nor were they introduced on the English stage till the days of the Stuarts.

ACTUA'RIUS, or ACTA'RIUS, in Roman antiquity, an officer, or rather notary, appointed to write down the proceedings of a court.—ACTUARII were also officers who kept the military accounts, and distributed the corn to the soldiers.

AC'TUARY, the chief clerk, or person, who compiles minutes of the proceedings of a company in business.

ACU'MEN, mental sharpness, or quick discernment; great intellectual capacity. In ancient music, *acumen* denotes a sound produced by raising the voice to a high pitch.

ACUTE', an appellation given to such things as terminate in a sharp point, or edge: thus, we say, an acute angle, acute-angled triangle, &c.—ACUTE, in music, an epithet given to sharp or shrill sounds, in opposition to those called grave.

ACYROLO'GIA, in grammar, denotes an improper word, phrase, or expression: it differs a little from the catachresis.

AD, a Latin preposition, expressing the relation of one thing to another. It is frequently prefixed to other words: thus, AD HOMINEM, among logicians, an argument drawn from the professed belief or principles of those with whom we argue. —AD LUDOS, in Roman antiquity, a kind of punishment, whereby the criminals entertained the people, either by fighting with wild beasts, or with each other.—AD VALOREM, in commerce, according to the value.—AD INFINITUM, indefinitely, or to infinity.

ADA'GIO, a degree quicker than grave time, in music, but with graceful and elegant execution.

A'DEPT, a distinctive term applied to those alchemists who were supposed to have attained the great object of their researches, or to have discovered the philosopher's stone.

ADHE'RENCE, the effect of those parts of a picture which, wanting relief, are not detached, and hence appear adhering to the canvas or surface.

AD'JECTIVE, in grammar, that part of speech which is annexed to substantives, to define more accurately the conceptions intended to be denoted by them.

ADJOURN'MENT, the putting off a court or other meeting till another day. In parliament, adjournment differs from prorogation, the former being not only for the shorter time, but also done by the house itself, whereas the latter is an act of royal authority.

AD'JUNCT, some quality belonging either to body or mind, either natural or acquired. Thus, thinking is an adjunct of the mind, and growth of the body. It also denotes something added to another, without being any necessary part of it.

Thus water absorbed by a sponge is an adjunct, but no necessary part of that substance.

ADJUST'MENT, in a picture, is the manner in which draperies are chosen, arranged, and disposed.

AD'JUTANT, a military officer, whose duty it is to carry orders from the major to the colonel and serjeants. When detachments are to be made, he gives the number to be furnished by each company or troop, and assigns the hour and place of rendezvous. He also places the guards, receives and distributes the ammunition to the companies, &c.

AD'JUTANT-GEN'ERAL, an officer of distinction, who assists the general, by forming the several details of duty of the army with the brigade majors.

ADLOCU'TION, or ADLOCU'TIO, in Roman antiquity, the address made by generals to their armies, in order to rouse their courage before a battle.

AD'MIRAL, the commander of a fleet of ships of war; having two subordinate commanders, as vice-admiral and rear-admiral; and distinguished into three classes, by the color of their flags, as white, blue, and red. The admiral carries his flag at the main-top-mast head; the vice-admiral, at the fore-top-mast head; and the rear-admiral, at the mizen-top-mast head.

AD'MIRALTY, the Board of Commissioners for executing the office of Lord High Admiral, and having authority over naval affairs generally.—ADMIRALTY, COURT OF, in law, is a court of record, of which the proceedings are carried on, at least to a certain extent, according to the course of the civil law; although, as the judge may have in some cases the assistance of a jury, it has also a resemblance to the courts of common law. It has jurisdiction principally for the determination of private injuries to private rights arising at sea, or intimately connected with maritime subjects; and in most cases, to which its authority extends, it has concurrent jurisdiction, either with the common law courts, or those of equity.

ADONA'I, one of the names of God used in the Scriptures, and properly signifying *my lords*, in the plural, as ADONI does *my lord*, in the singular number.

ADO'NIA, solemn feasts in honor of Venus, instituted in memory of her beloved Adonis, and observed with great solemnity by the Greeks, Phœnicians, Lycians, Syrians, Egyptians, &c. They lasted two days, during the first of which the women carried about images of Venus and Adonis, weeping, tearing their hair, beating their breasts, and using every token of grief. On the second, they sung his praises, and made rejoicings, as if Adonis had been raised to life again.

ADO'NIC, a species of verse consisting of a dactyle and a spondee. It was invented by Sappho, and derived its name from being principally sung at the festivals in memory of Adonis.

ADO'NIS, in mythology, a beautiful youth, son of Cinyras, king of Cyprus, beloved by Venus, and killed by a wild boar, to the great regret of the goddess. It is, also, the name of a river of Phœnicia, on the banks of which Adonis, or Thammuz, as he is called in the East, was supposed to have been killed. At certain seasons of the year this river acquires a high red color, by the rains washing up particles of red earth. The ancient poets ascribed this to a sympathy in the river for the death of Adonis. This season was observed as a festival in the adjacent country.

ADORA'TION, a mode of reverence or worship anciently shown to the gods, by raising the right hand to the mouth, and gently applying it to the lips; also, in general, any outward sign of worship, by kissing the hand or feet, walking barefoot, or the like. Among the Jews, adoration consisted in kissing the hands, bowing, kneeling, and even prostration. But the posture of adoration most common in all ages and countries, is kneeling.

ADO'REA, in Roman antiquity, grain, or a kind of cakes made of fine flour, and offered in sacrifice; a dole or distribution of corn, as a reward for some service; whence, by metonymy, it is put for praise or rewards in general.

A'DRIAN, ST., in Christian art is represented armed, with an anvil at his feet or in his arms, and occasionally with a sword or an axe lying beside it. The anvil is the appropriate attribute of St. Adrian, who suffered martyrdom, having his limbs cut off on a smith's anvil, and being afterwards beheaded. St. Adrian was the chief military saint of northern Europe for many ages, second only to St. George. He was regarded as the patron of soldiers, and the protector against the plague. He has not been a popular subject with artists. St. Adrian is the patron saint of the Flemish brewers.

ADULTERA'TION, in a general sense, denotes the act of debasing, by an improper mixture, something that was pure and genuine. Thus, adulteration of coin, is the casting or making it of a metal inferior in goodness to the standard, by using too great a portion of alloy.

ADUL'TERY, a violation of the nuptial bed; a crime which has been regarded by all civilized nations with abhorrence, and in ancient times was punished as a capital offence. By the Jewish law, the penalty was death.

AD'VENT, the coming of our Saviour; also the festival commemorative of the Advent, which falls about a month before Christmas.

AD'VERB, a word so called from its signification and connection with verbs; though they are also frequently joined with adjectives and other parts of speech to modify their meaning.

ADVERSA'RIA, a memorandum-book, journal, or common-place book.

ADVER'TISEMENT, any printed publication of circumstances, either of public or private interest, particularly that inserted in the newspapers.

AD'VOCATE, the original pleaders of causes at Rome were the Patricians, who defended gratuitously their clients; but even before the downfall of the republic, the class had degenerated into a profession, its members receiving rewards for their services, although still among the most honorable of employments. In the later ages of the empire, the advocati appear to have formed a distinct class from the jurisconsulti, or chamber-counsel, and to have much declined in reputation. In France, the avocats, or counsel, form a separate order, of which each member is attached to a particular local court. The lord advocate, in Scotland, is a public officer, who prosecutes crimes before the court of justiciary.

ADVOW'SON, properly, the relation in which a patron stands towards the living to which he presents, i. e. the patronage of a church. The earliest provision for divine worship, in England and in other countries, was derived from the offerings of the laity, which were distributed by the bishop of each diocese among his clergy, whom he sent from place to place to preach and administer the sacraments. By degrees he was enabled, by the bequests of the faithful, and the customary offering of tithes, to subdivide his diocese, or parochia, as it was originally called, into various districts, and to build churches and establish permanent ministers in each. At the same time it became a common practice among the nobles to build and endow churches for the benefit of themselves and their own dependents; in which case they were allowed to present to the benefice, subject to the licensing power of the bishop and the canons of the church.

AD'YTUM, the most retired and secret place of the heathen temples, into which none but the priests were allowed to enter. The adytum of the Greeks and Romans answered to the sanctum sanctorum of the Jews, and was the place from whence oracles were delivered. The term is purely Greek, signifying inaccessible.

ÆACE'A, in Grecian antiquity, solemn festivals and games in honor of Æacus, who, on account of his justice upon earth, was thought to have been one of the judges in hell. At the end of the solemnity, the victors in the games used to present a garland of flowers.

Æ'DES, in Roman antiquity, besides its more ordinary signification of a house, or the internal part of a house, where the family used to eat, likewise signified an inferior kind of temple, consecrated indeed to some deity, but not by the augurs.

ÆDIC'ULA, a small ædes or temple, which was erected in every village or parish.

ÆDI'LES, a Roman magistrate, whose chief business was to superintend buildings of all kinds, but more especially public ones, as temples, aqueducts, bridges, &c.; and to take care of the highways, weights, and measures, &c.

Æ'GIS, a shield, particularly the shield of Jupiter.

ÆNE'ID, the title of Virgil's epic poem, in which he celebrates the adventures of Æneas, one of the bravest among the Trojan heroes. The author introduces him as sailing from Troy, after its destruction, in search of the shores of Italy, on which it had been promised by the gods that he should found an empire destined to be immortal; and the poem ends with the complete success of Æneas over Turnus, king of the Rutuli, whose dominions he had invaded, and who falls by his hand. The unrivalled force, elegance, and beauty of Virgil's style have been the theme of admiration in every succeeding age, and given him an indisputable right to a niche in the temple of Apollo, second only to that of Homer.

ÆO'LIAN HARP, an arrangement of strings placed in a window and played upon by the wind. It produces the effect of a distant choir of music in the air, sweetly mingling all the harmonic notes, and swelling or diminishing its sounds according to the strength or weakness of the blast.

ÆʹRA, or EʹRA, a fixed historical period whence years are reckoned: as the building of Rome, or the birth of Christ. Era and Epoch are not exactly synonymous. An *era* is a point fixed by a particular people or nation; an *epoch*, one determined by chronologists and historians. The idea of an era, also, comprehends a certain succession of years, proceeding from a fixed event; and an epoch is that event itself.

AEʹRIAL, in painting, a term applied to the diminishing intensity of color on objects receding from the eye. Aerial perspective is the relative apparent recession of objects from the foreground, owing to the quantity of air interposed between them and the spectator, and must accompany the recession of the perspective lines.

AERʹOMANCY, a kind of divination amongst the Greeks, and from them adopted by the Romans, whereby they pretended to foretell future events from certain spectral phenomena or noises in the air. By aeromancy, in the present day, is meant the art of foretelling the changes and variations of the air and weather, by means of meteorological observations.

AʹERONAUT, one who sails in the air in a balloon.

AERONAUʹTICS, or AEROSTAʹTION, the art of navigating the air, by employing air-balloons, or silken globes, filled with gas lighter than atmospheric air.

ÆSTHETʹICS, a term derived from the Greek, denoting *feeling*, sentiment, imagination, originally adopted by the Germans, and now incorporated into the vocabulary of Art. By it is generally understood "the science of the beautiful" and its various modes of representation; its purpose is to lead the criticism of the beautiful back to the principle of reason. In beauty lies the soul of Art. Schelling declares that the province of Æsthetics is to develop systematically the manifold beautiful in every Art, as the one idea of the beautiful.

ÆSʹTIVA, summer encampments for the Roman soldiers, in distinction from the *hibernia*, or winter quarters.

ÆSʹTIVAL, in a general sense, denotes something connected with, or belonging to summer. Hence we say æstival point, æstival sign, æstival solstice, &c.

AFFECTAʹTION, in the Fine Arts, an artificial show arising from the want of simplicity either in coloring, drawing, or action. Also, the overcharging any part of a composition with an artificial or deceitful appearance.

AFFETUOʹSO, *affetto*, Ital., in a tender and affecting style; a term employed in music-books, at the beginning of a movement.

AFFIʹANCE, in law, denotes the mutual plighting of truth, between a man and a woman; to bind one's self to the performance of a marriage contract.

AFFIDAʹVIT, an oath in writing, taken before some person who is legally authorized to administer the same.

AFFINʹITY, in civil law, the relationship in which each of the parties married stands to the kindred of the other.

AFFIRʹMATIVE, an epithet used by logicians for a species of proposition wherein any predicate is affirmed of its subject; as, "a dog is a quadruped;" here "*quadruped*" is affirmed of a dog.

AFʹFIX, in grammar, a particle added at the close of a word, either to diversify its form, or alter its signification.

AFFLAʹTUS, in a general sense, a divine influence communicating to the receiver supernatural powers, particularly the gift of prophecy. Among heathen mythologists and poets, it denotes the actual inspiration of some divinity. Tully, however, extends the meaning of the word farther, by attributing all great actions to a divine *afflatus*.

A FORTIOʹRI, a term implying that what follows is a more powerful argument than what has been before adduced.

AFTER, modelled or drawn *after* the antique, after Raphael, or some other great master. It is to copy an antique statue, or some work of the great masters.

AGʹAPÆ, love-feasts kept by the ancient Christians, as a token of brotherly charity and mutual benevolence. In course of time abuses crept in, and rendered the abolition of them necessary.

AGAPEʹTÆ, a society of unmarried women among the primitive Christians, who attended on and served the clergy. At first there was nothing improper in these societies, though they were afterwards charged with gross immoralities, and were wholly abolished by the council of Lateran, in 1139.

AGʹATHA, St., when represented as a martyr, is depicted crowned, with a long veil, and bearing the instruments of her cruel martyrdom, a pair of shears, with which her breasts were cut off. As patron saint, she bears in one hand a palm branch, and holding with the other a plate or salver, upon which is a female breast. The subject of her martyrdom has been treated by Sebastian del Piombo, Van Dyck, Parmigiano, and others.

AGE, a certain period or limit of time, marked for the convenience of chronology and history by some remarkable events. Chronologers usually reckon seven such ages, namely, 1. From the creation to the deluge. 2. From the deluge to the birth of Abraham. 3. From the birth of Abraham to the departure of the Israelites out of Egypt. 4. From the departure of the Israelites to the building of the temple by Solomon. 5. From the laying the foundation of the temple to the reign of Cyrus in Babylon. 6. From the reign of Cyrus to the coming of Christ. 7. Since the birth of our Saviour.—Among ancient historians, the duration of the world was also subdivided into three periods, or ages: the first, reaching from the creation to the deluge which happened in Greece during the reign of Ogyges, is called the obscure or uncertain age; the second, called the fabulous or heroic, terminates at the first olympiad; where the third, or historical age, commences. The poets also distinguished the period of the world into four ages: the *golden age*, or the age of simplicity and happiness; the *silver age*, which was less pure than the golden age, and in which men began to till the ground for their sustenance; the *brazen age*, when strife and contentions began; and the *iron age*, when justice and honor had left the earth.

AGEN'DA, small books are now published under this title, in which individuals may set down, under their proper heads, the things to be daily attended to.

A'GENT, in a general sense, denotes anything which acts, or produces an effect. Agents are either *natural* or *moral*. Natural agents are all such inanimate bodies as have a power to act upon other bodies, in a certain and determinate manner: such is fire, which has the invariable property or power to warm or heat. Moral agents, on the contrary, are rational creatures, capable of regulating their actions by a certain rule.

A'GIO, in commerce, a term chiefly used in Holland and at Venice, to signify the difference between the value of bank-stock and the current coin.

AG'NES, St., this saint is represented as a martyr, holding the palm-branch in her hand, with a lamb at her feet or in her arms, sometimes crowned with olives, and holding an olive-branch as well as the palm-branch.

AGNO'MEN, in Roman antiquity, was the fourth or honorary name bestowed on account of some extraordinary action, virtue, or accomplishment. Thus the agnomen *Africanus* was given to Publius Cornelius Scipio, on account of his exploits in Africa.

AG'NUS DEI, (Lamb of God,) the oval medallions, which are made either from the wax of the consecrated Easter candles or of the wafer dough. They are also sometimes made of silver, and have on one side the Lamb, with the banner of Victory, or St. John, and on the other the picture of some saint. They were first made about the fourteenth century.

A'GON, in the public games of the ancients, a term used indifferently for any contest or dispute, whether respecting bodily exercises, or accomplishments of the mind. Thus poets, musicians, &c., had their *agones*, as well as the athletæ.—Agōn was also used for one of the ministers employed in the heathen sacrifices, whose business it was to strike the victim.

AGONA'LIA, festivals in Rome, celebrated in honor of Janus, or Agonius, three times a year.

AGONOTHE'TÆ, officers appointed at the Grecian games to take care that all things were performed according to custom, to decide controversies amongst the antagonists, and adjudge the prizes.

AGRA'RIAN LAWS, statutes, which forbid the possession of more than a certain extent of land by any single individual. That law of the Romans, called, by way of eminence, *the agrarian law*, was published by Spurius Cassius, about the year of Rome, 268, enjoining a division of the conquered lands, in equal parts, among the citizens, and limiting the number of acres that each might enjoy.

AIR, in music, signifies the *melody*, or treble part of a musical composition. The word is also used for a tune, or song itself, that is, for a series of sounds whose movement is regular and graceful.—Air, in painting, the medium in nature through which every object is viewed, and hence to be transferred to the imitation on canvas. The effects which it produces are an indispensable part of the knowledge of every artist. It affects the sizes and color of objects according to their distance.

AL, an Arabian particle, answering to the English *the*, and employed in the same manner to mark anything indefinitely.

AL'ABASTER, a well-known sulphate of lime, forming a soft, granular, imperfectly transparent marble; used for ornaments in houses, and by statuaries. It is found in Germany, France, and Italy.

A LA GRECQUE, (Fr.) an architectural ornament resembling a variously twisted ribbon, when it is merely a narrow continuous stripe, forming right angles, either raised or cut in, and sometimes only painted. This ornament, called also a labyrinth, may be used for rectilineal mouldings. If it be only *one* stripe, it is called the simple labyrinth; but if two stripes be twisted into one another it is called the double labyrinth.

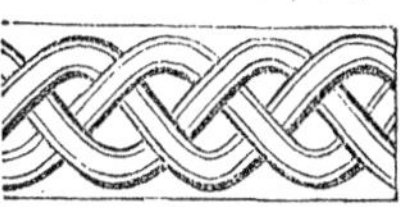

ALB, or ALBE, (*alba*,) in the Romish church, a vestment of white linen, hanging down to the feet, and answering to the surplice of the Episcopal clergy. In the ancient church, it was usual with those newly baptized, to wear an alb, or white vestment; and hence the Sunday after Easter was called *dominica in albis*, on account of the albs worn by those baptized on Easter-day.

AL'BAN, St., in Christian art, is represented (as also is St. Denis), carrying his head between his hands. His attributes are a sword and a crown.

AL'BATROSS, or Man-of-War Bird, the *Diomedes* of Linnæus, a large and voracious bird, which inhabits many countries between the tropics.

ALBIGEN'SES, a name common to several sects, particularly the Cathari and Waldenses, who agreed in opposing the dominion of the Romish hierarchy, and endeavoring to restore the simplicity of primitive Christianity. They endured the severest persecutions, and after the middle of the 13th century, the name of Albigenses altogether disappeared; but fugitives of their party formed, in the mountains of Piedmont and in Lombardy, what is called the *French Church*, which was continued through the Waldenses, to the era of the Reformation.

ALBI'NOS, or Leucæ'thiops, a variety of the human species, that frequently occurs in Africa. The Portuguese first gave the name of Albino to the white negro, and they formerly described them as a distinct race; but modern naturalists have discovered them in various countries of Europe, viz., in Switzerland, among the Savoyards in the valley of Chamouni; in France, in the tract of the Rhine; in Tyrol, &c.

AL'BUM, a white table or register, whereon the Roman prætors had their decrees written. There were many of them in use, and they received their appellations from the various magistrates whose names were thereon entered; as the *album judicum*, the *album decurionum*, &c.—The fashionable Albums of the present day are derived from the practice adopted in many foreign countries of having a white paper book, in which strangers of distinction or literary eminence were invited to insert their names, or any observation in prose or verse, as a memorial of their visit.

ALCA'ICS, a term given to several kinds of verse, from their inventor, the poet Alcæus.

AL'CAIDE, or AL'CALDE, a Spanish or Portuguese magistrate, or officer of justice, answering nearly to the French provost, and the British justice of peace. Both the name and office are of Moorish origin.

AL'CORAN, or the Koran, the name of the volume containing the revelations, doctrines, and precepts of Mahomet, in which his followers place implicit confidence. The general aim of the Alcoran was to unite the professors of the three different religions then followed in Arabia, Idolaters, Jews, and Christians, in the knowledge and worship of one God, under the sanction of certain laws, and the outward signs of ceremonies, partly of ancient, and partly of novel institution, enforced by the consideration of rewards and punishments, both temporal and eternal, and to bring all to the obedience of Mahomet, as the prophet and ambassador of God, who was to establish the true religion on earth.

AL'DINE EDITIONS, those editions of the Greek and Roman classics which were printed by the family of Aldus Manutius, first established at Venice about 1490.

ALEXAN'DRIAN, or ALEXAN'-DRINE, in poetry, a kind of verse, consisting of twelve, or of twelve and thirteen syllables alternately, the pause being always on the sixth syllable. It is so called from a poem on the life of Alexander, written in this way, by some French poet.

ALEXAN'DRIAN LIBRARY, this celebrated library was founded by Ptolemy Soter, for the use of an academy that he instituted in Alexandria; and, by continual additions by his successors, became at last the finest library in the world, containing no fewer than 700,000 volumes. The method followed in collecting books for this library, was, to seize all those which were brought into Egypt by Greeks or other foreigners. The books were transcribed in the museum by persons appointed for that purpose, the copies were then delivered to the proprietors, and the originals laid up in the library. It was eventually burnt by order of the caliph Omar, A.D. 624.

ALEXAN'DRIAN MANUSCRIPT, or CODEX ALEXANDRINUS, a famous copy of the Scriptures, consisting of four volumes, in a large quarto size; which contains the whole Bible, in Greek, including the Old and New Testaments, with the Apocrypha, and some smaller pieces, but not quite complete. This manuscript is now preserved in the British Museum. It was sent as a present to king Charles I., from Cyrillus Lucaris, patriarch of Constantinople, by Sir Thomas Rowe, ambassador from England to the grand seignior, about the year 1628.

ALEXAN'DRIAN SCHOOL, an academy for literature and learning of all kinds, instituted at Alexandria by Ptolemy, son of Lagus, and supported by his successors. The grammarians and mathematicians of this school were particularly celebrated. In the former class occur the noted names of Aristarchus, Harpocration, and Aristophanes; and among the latter were numbered the astronomer Ptolemy, and geometer Euclid. The grammarians of Alexandria exercised a universal literary jurisdiction, publishing canons of those who were to be considered standard authors, and revised editions of ancient writers.

ALEX'IS, ST., the patron saint of beggars and pilgrims. In Christian art, he is usually represented in a pilgrim's habit and staff; sometimes as extended on a mat, with a letter in his hand, dying. St. Roch is also represented as a pilgrim, but he is distinguished from St. Alexis by the plague spot on his body, and in being accompanied by a dog.

AL'GUAZIL, the title of one of the lower orders of Spanish officers of justice, whose business is to execute the orders of the magistrate.

A'LIAS, in law, a Latin word signifying otherwise; often used in describing the accused, who has assumed other names beside his real one.

AL'IBI, in law, a Latin word signifying, literally, elsewhere. It is used by the accused, when he wishes to prove his innocence, by showing that he was in another place when the act was committed.

AL'IMONY, in law, the maintenance sued for by a wife, in case of a legal separation from her husband, wherein she is neither chargeable with elopement nor adultery.

AL'LAH, the Arabian name of God.

ALLA'-PRIMA, (*Ital.*) AU PREMIER COUP, (*Fr.*) a method of painting in which the pigments are applied all *at once* to the canvas, without impasting or retouching. Some of the best pictures of the great masters are painted in at once by this method, but it requires too much knowledge, skill, and decision to be generally practised.

ALLEGOR'ICAL PICTURES are of two kinds: the one comprehends those in which the artist unites allegorical with real persons, and this is the lower rank of allegorical painting. Such are those of Rubens, in the Gallery of the Luxembourg, representing the stormy life of Mary de Medicis. The other, those in which the artist represents allegorical persons only; and by the position of single figures, the grouping of many and the composition of the whole, conveys to the mind of the spectator one thought or many thoughts, which he cannot convey by the common language of his art: this is allegorical painting in the true sense of the term.

AL'LEGORY, a series or chain of metaphors continued through a whole discourse. The great source of allegory, or allegorical interpretations, is some difficulty, or absurdity, in the literal and obvious sense.

ALLE'GRO, an Italian word used in music, to denote that the part is to be played in a brisk and sprightly manner. The usual distinctions succeed each other in the following order: *grave, adagio, largo, vivace, allegro, presto.* Allegro time may be heightened, as *allegro assai* and *allegrissimo*, very lively; or lessened, as *allegretto* or *poco allegro*, a little lively. *Piu allegro* is a direction to play or sing a little quicker.

ALLEMAN'NIC, in a general sense, denotes anything belonging to the ancient Germans. Thus we meet with Allemannic history, Allemannic language, Allemannic law, &c.

ALL-HAL'LOWS, or ALL-SAINTS, a festival observed by many denominations of Christians, in commemoration of the saints in general. It is kept on the first of November, Gregory IV. having in 835 appointed that day for its celebration

ALLITERA'TION, a figure or embellishment of speech, which consists in the repetition of the same consonants, or of syllables of the same sound, in one sentence. The Greek and Roman literature afford many instances of this; and in English poetry there are also many beautiful specimens of alliterations; though it must be confessed that it is too often used without the requisite skill, and carried too far. In burlesque poetry it is frequently used with excellent effect; though even there the sense should never be sacrificed to the sound. Tastefully used, it is a most enchanting ornament, and will equally contribute to softness, to energy, and to solemnity.

ALLU'SION, in rhetoric, strictly, a covert indication, as by means of a metaphor, a play of words, &c., of something not openly mentioned and extrinsic to the principal meaning of the sentence.

AL'MAGEST, the name of a celebrated book, composed by Ptolemy; being a collection of many of the observations and problems of the ancients, relating both to geometry and astronomy.

AL'MA MA'TER, a title given to the universities of Oxford and Cambridge by their several members who have passed their degrees in either of these universities.

AL'MANAC, a calendar or table, containing a list of the months, weeks, and days of the year, with an account of the rising and setting of the sun and moon, the most remarkable phenomena of the heavenly bodies, the several festivals, and fasts, and other incidental matters.—The Nautical Almanac, a most valuable work for mariners, is published in England two or three years in advance. It was commenced in 1767, by Dr. Maskelyne, the astronomer royal, and has been regularly continued ever since.

AL'PHABET, the natural or customary series of the several letters of a language. The word is formed from *alpha* and *beta*, the first and second letters of the Greek alphabet. It is undoubtedly the most important of all inventions, for by means of it sounds are represented, and language made visible to the eye by a few simple characters. The five books of Moses are universally acknowledged to be the most ancient compositions, as well as the most early specimens of alphabetical writing extant; and it appears that all the languages in use amongst men which have been conveyed in alphabetical characters, have been the languages of people connected, ultimately or immediately, with the Hebrews. Hence a most energetic controversy has existed amongst learned men, whether the method of expressing our ideas by visible symbols, called letters, be really a human invention; or whether we ought to attribute an art so exceedingly useful, to an immediate intimation of the Deity.

ALPHON'SINE TABLES, astronomical tables made in the reign of Alphonsus X., king of Arragon, who was a great lover of science, and a prince of rare attainments; but though these tables bear his name, they were chiefly drawn up by Isaac Hazan, a learned Jewish rabbi.

ALSEG'NO, in music, a notice to the performer that he must recommence from that part of the movement to which the sign or mark 𝄋 is prefixed.

ALT, in music, that part of the great scale lying between F above the treble cliff note, and G in *altissimo*.

AL'TAR, a place upon which sacrifices were anciently offered to the Almighty, or some heathen deity. Before temples were in use, altars were erected sometimes in groves, sometimes in the highways, and sometimes on the tops of mountains; and it was a custom to engrave upon them the name, proper ensign, or character of the deity to whom they were consecrated. Thus St. Paul observed an altar at Athens, with an inscription, *To the unknown God.* In the great temples of ancient Rome, there were ordinarily three altars: the first was placed in the sanctuary, at the foot of the statue of the divinity, upon which incense was burnt, and libations offered; the second was before the gate of the temple, and upon it they sacrificed the victims; and the third was a portable altar, upon which were placed the offerings and the sacred vessels. The principal altars of the Jews were those of *incense*, of *burnt-offerings*, and the *altar* or *table*, for the *show-bread*.—Altar is also used among Christians, for the communion-table.

ALTIS'SIMO, in music, an Italian epithet for notes above F in alt.

ALTIS'TA, in music, an Italian name for the vocal performer who takes the *alto primo* part.

AL'TO, or AL'TO TENO'RE, in music, is the term applied to that part of the great vocal scale which lies between the *mezzo soprano* and the tenor, and which is assigned to the highest natural adult male voice. In scores, it always signifies the counter-tenor part.

AL'TO RELIE'VO, in sculpture, a representation of figures and other objects against a flat surface; differing from *basso relievo* only in the work being much more brought forward.

AMATEUR', a person having a taste for a particular art, yet not professing, nor being dependent on it.

AM'BER, a hard, brittle, tasteless substance, mostly semi-transparent, or opaque, and of a glossy surface. This curious production of nature is inflammable, and, when heated, yields a strong and bituminous odor. Its most extraordinary properties are those of attracting after it has been exposed to a slight friction, straws, and other surrounding objects; and of producing sparks of fire, visible in the dark. Many thousand years before the science of electricity had entered the mind of man, these surprising qualities were known to exist in amber, and hence the Greeks called it *electrum*.

AM'BIDEXTER, a person who can use both hands with equal facility, and for the same purposes that the generality of people do their right hands.—In law, a juror who takes money for giving his verdict.

AM'BITUS, in music, signifies the particular extent of each tone, or modification of grave and sharp.

AM'BO, in architecture, the elevated place, or pulpit, in the early Christian churches, from whence it was usual to address the congregation, and on which certain parts of the service were chanted.

AM'BROSE, St., the patron saint of Milan: but few works of art exist, in which he is so represented. The finest is the painting that adorns his chapel in the Frari at Venice, painted by Vivarini, towards the end of the fifteenth century, a work of the highest excellence. St. Ambrose is usually represented in the costume of a bishop.

AMBRO'SIA, in heathen antiquity, denotes the food of the gods. Hence, whatever is very gratifying to the taste or smell has been termed *ambrosial*.

AMBRO'SIAN CHANT, in music, so called from St. Ambrose, archbishop of Milan, who composed it for the church there in the fourth century: it is distinguished from the Gregorian chant by a great monotony and want of beauty in its melody.

AMEN', in Scripture language, a solemn formula, or conclusion to all prayer, signifying *verily*, or *so be it*.

AMENDE HONORABLE, (French,) an infamous kind of punishment formerly inflicted in France on traitors, parricides, or sacrilegious persons, who were to go naked to the shirt, with a torch in their hand, and a rope about their neck, into a church or a court, to beg pardon of God, the court, and the injured party.—The modern acceptation of the term indicates that an open apology is made for an offence or injury.

AMER'ICANISM, any word or phrase in general use among the inhabitants of the United States, which deviates from the English standard. Of these, a great proportion are mere vulgarisms and technical words of local character, originally taken from different counties in England, by the first emigrants; others are words formerly used by the English writers, but which have become obsolete; while many are of modern coinage, and owe their origin to the caprice of inventors. Every living language is subject to continual changes; and it is not to be expected that a large community, in a state of social and political activity, who are daily developing new and characteristic features, will fail to exercise their share of influence upon that which they naturally consider as a part of their inheritance.

AM'ETHYST, a rock crystal of a purple color. Many ancient vases and cups are composed of this mineral, and the finer varieties are still much in request for cutting into seals and brooches.

AM'MON, the title under which Jupiter was worshipped in Libya, where a temple was erected to him, from which oracles were delivered for many ages.

AMMUNI'TION, all warlike stores, and especially powder, ball, bombs, guns, and other weapons necessary for an army.

AM'NESTY, an act by which two parties at variance promise to pardon and bury in oblivion all that is past. It is more especially used for a pardon granted by a prince to his rebellious subjects.

AMPHIBO'LIA, or AMPHIBOL'OGY, in rhetoric, ambiguity of expression, when a sentence conveys a double meaning. It is distinguished from an equivocation, which lies in a single word.

AMPHIC'TYONS, in Grecian antiquity, an assembly composed of deputies from the different states of Greece. The amphictyons at first met regularly at Delphi, twice a year, viz. in spring and autumn; but in latter times they assembled at the village of Anthela, near Thermopylæ; and decided all differences between any of the Grecian states, their determinations being held sacred and inviolable.

AMPHITHE'ATRE, in antiquity, a spacious edifice, built either round or oval, with a number of rising seats, upon which the people used to sit and behold the combats of gladiators, of wild beasts, and other sports. Some of them, as the Coliseum at Rome, were capable of containing from 50,000 to 80,000 spectators. The principal parts of the amphitheatre were the *arena*, or place where the gladiators fought; *cavea*, or hollow place where the beasts were kept; *podium*, or projection at the top of the wall which surrounded the arena, and was assigned to the senators; *gradus*, or benches, rising all round above the podium; *aditus*, or entrances; and *vomitoriæ*, or gates which terminated the aditus.

AM'PHORA, in antiquity, a liquid measure in use among the Greeks and Romans. The Roman amphora contained forty-eight sextaries, and was equal to about seven gallons one pint, English wine-measure; and the Grecian, or Attic amphora, contained one third more.—Amphora was also a dry measure in use among the Romans, and contained three bushels.

AMPHORI'TES, in antiquity, a sort of literary contest in the island of Ægina, where the poet who made the best dithyrambic verses in honor of Bacchus was rewarded with an ox.

AMPLIFICA'TION, in rhetoric, part of a discourse or speech, wherein a crime is aggravated, a praise or commendation heightened, or a narration enlarged, by an enumeration of circumstances, so as to excite the proper emotions in the minds of the auditors.

AMPUL'LA, an ancient drinking vessel; and among ecclesiastical writers it denotes one of the sacred vessels used at the altar. The ampulla is still a distinguished vessel in the coronation of the kings of England and France. The vessel now in use in England is of the purest chased gold, and represents an eagle with expanding wings standing on a pedestal, near seven inches in height, and weighing about ten ounces. It was deposited in the Tower by the gallant Edward, surnamed the Black Prince.

AM'ULET, a superstitious charm or preservative against mischief, witchcraft, or diseases. They were made of stone, metal, animals, and, in fact, of everything which fancy or caprice suggested. Sometimes they consisted of words, characters, and sentences, ranged in a particular order, and engraved upon wood, &c., and worn about the neck, or some other part of the body. At other times they were neither written nor engraved; but prepared with many superstitious ceremonies, great regard being usually paid to the influence of the stars.

A'NA, a name given to amusing miscellanies, consisting of anecdotes, traits of character, and incidents relating to any person or subject.

ANAB'ASIS, the title of Xenophon's description of the younger Cyrus's expedition against his brother, in which the writer bore a principal part.

ANA'CHRONISM, in literature, an error with respect to chronology, whereby an event is placed earlier than it really happened; in which sense it stands opposite to parachronism.

ANACOLU'THON, in grammar or rhetoric, a want of coherency, generally arising from inattention on the part of the writer or orator.

ANACREON'TIC Verse, in ancient poetry, a kind of verse, so called from its being much used by the poet Anacreon. It consisted of three feet, generally spondees and iambics, sometimes anapæsts, and was peculiarly distinguished for softness and tenderness.

ANADIPLO'SIS, a figure in rhetoric and poetry, in which the last word or words of a sentence are repeated at the beginning of the next.

ANAGLY'PHIC, in antique sculpture, chased or embossed work on metal, or anything worked in relief. When raised on stone, the production is a cameo. When sunk or indented, it is a diaglyphic or an intaglio.

AN'AGRAM, the change of one word or phrase into another, by the transposition of its letters. They were very common among the ancients, and occasionally contained some happy allusion; but, perhaps, none were more appropriate than the anagram made by Dr. Burney on the name of the hero of the Nile, just after that important victory took place: Horatio Nelson, "*Honor est a Nilo.*" They are frequently employed satirically, or jestingly, with little aim beyond that of exercising the ingenuity of their authors.

ANALEC'TA, a collection of extracts from different works.

ANAL'OGY, a certain relation and agreement between two or more things, which in other respects are entirely different. Or it may be defined an important process of reasoning, by which we infer similar effects and phenomena from similar causes and events. A great part of our philosophy has no other foundation than analogy.

ANAL'YSIS, among grammarians, is the explaining the etymology, construction, and other properties of words.—Analysis is also used for a brief, but methodical illustration of the principles of a science; in which sense it is nearly synonymous with what is termed a synopsis.

ANAMNE'SIS, in rhetoric, an enumeration of the things treated of before; which is a sort of recapitulation.

ANAMORPHO'SIS, in perspective and painting, the representation of some image, either on a plane or curved surface, deformed, or distorted; which in a certain point of view appears regular and in just proportion.

AN'APÆST, a foot in Greek and Latin metre, consisting of two short syllables followed by a long, being the name of the dactyle.

ANAPH'ORA, a rhetorical figure, which consists in the repetition of the same word or phrase at the beginning of several successive sentences.

AN'ARCHY, a society without a government, or where there is no supreme governor.

ANASTA'SIA, St., is represented with the attributes, a stake and fagots; and with the palm as a symbol of her martyrdom.

ANASTAT'IC, a word derived from the Greek signifying "*reviving*." A recently invented process, by which any number of copies of a printed page of any size, a wood-cut, or a line-engraving, can be obtained. The process is based upon the law of "the repulsion of dissimilar, and the mutual attraction of similar particles," and is exhibited by oil, water, and gum arabic. The printed matter to be copied is first submitted to the action of diluted nitric acid, and, while retaining a portion of the moisture, is pressed upon a sheet of polished zinc, which is immediately attacked by the acid in every part except that covered by the printing-ink, a thin film of which is left on the zinc; it is then washed with a weak solution of gum arabic; an inked-roller being now passed over the zinc-plate, the ink adheres only to that portion which was inked in the original; the impressions are then taken from the zinc-plate, in the same manner as in lithographic printing.

ANAS'TROPHE, in rhetoric, the inversion of words in a sentence, or the placing them out of their natural order.

ANATH'EMA, among ecclesiastical writers, imports whatever is set apart, separated, or divided; but the word is most usually intended to express the cutting off a person from the privileges of society, and from communion with the faithful.

AN'CHOR, in Christian art, is the symbol of hope, firmness, tranquillity, patience and faith. Among those saints, of whom the anchor is an attribute, are Clement of Rome and Nicolas of Bari.

AN'CHORITE, more properly, anachoret, a hermit, or person who has retired from the world with the purpose of devoting himself entirely to meditation and prayer. Such was the case with many of the early Christians, beginning perhaps with such as fled from the persecutions of Decius and Diocletian, and retired into forests and deserts, at first with a view to security merely, and afterwards continued, from religious motives, the mode of life they had there adopted.

AN'CIENTS, in the more general sense of the term, means those who lived long ago, or before the *Moderns*. But the term is now usually employed to designate the Greeks and Romans; and if any other people be meant, it is customary to specify them, as the ancient Germans, the ancient Jews, &c.

ANCY'LE, or ANCI'LE, in antiquity, a small brazen shield which fell, as was pretended, from heaven in the reign of Numa Pompilius, when a voice was heard, declaring that Rome should be mistress of the world as long as she should preserve this holy buckler.

ANDAN'TE, in music, the Italian term for exact and just time in playing, so as to keep the notes distinct from each other.—Andante largo, signifies that the music must be slow, the time exactly observed, and each note distinct.

ANDANTI'NO, in music, an Italian word for gentle, tender; somewhat slower than *andante*.

ANDREW, St., the patron saint of Scotland; also of the renowned order of the Golden Fleece of Burgundy, and of the order of the Cross of St. Andrew of Russia. The principal events in the life of this apostle chosen for representation by the Christian artists are, his Flagellation, the Adoration of the Cross, and his Martyrdom. He is usually depicted as an old man, with long white hair and beard, holding the Gospel in his right hand, and leaning upon a transverse cross, formed sometimes of planks; at others, of the rough branches of trees. This form of cross is peculiar to this saint, and hence it is termed St. Andrew's Cross.

AN'GEL, the name given to those spiritual, intelligent beings, who are supposed to execute the will of God, in the government of the world. It is sometimes used in a figurative, and at others in a literal sense.—ANGEL, the name of an ancient gold coin in England, so called from the figure of an angel upon it. It weighed four pennyweights.

AN'GLICISM, an idiom of speech, or manner peculiar to the English.

ANGLO-SAX'ON, the name of the people called Angles, who with the Saxons and some other German tribes, flourished in England after it was abandoned by the Romans, about the year 400; and who introduced their language, government, and customs.—ANGLO-SAXON LANGUAGE. After the conquest of England by the Angles and Saxons, the Saxon became the prevalent tongue of that country; and after the Norman conquest, the English language exhibits the peculiar case, where languages of two different stocks are blended into one idiom, which, by the cultivation of a free and active nation and highly-gifted minds, has grown to a powerful, organized whole.

AN'IMA, among divines and naturalists, denotes the soul, or principle of life in animals.—ANIMA MUNDI, a phrase formerly used to denote a certain pure ethereal substance or spirit which is diffused through the mass of the world, organizing and actuating the whole and the different parts.

AN'IMAL, a living body endued with sensation and spontaneous motion. In its limited sense, any irrational creature, as distinguished from man.

AN'IMUS, in metaphysics, the mind or reasoning faculty, in distinction from *anima*, the being or faculty in which the faculty exists.

AN'NALS, a species of history, in which events are related in the exact order of chronology. They differ from perfect history in this, that annals are a bare relation of what passes every year, as a journal is of what passes every day; whereas history relates not only the transactions themselves, but also the causes, motives, and springs of actions.

AN'NO DOM'INI, abbreviated A.D., the year of our Lord; the computation of time from our Saviour's incarnation. It is used as the date for all public deeds and writings in England and this country, on which account it is called the "Vulgar Era."

ANNOTA'TION, a brief commentary, or remark upon a book or writing, in order to clear up some passage or draw some conclusion from it.

AN'NUAL, an epithet for whatever happens every year, or lasts a year: thus we say, the annual motion of the earth, annual plants, annual publications, &c.

ANNU'ITY, the periodical payment of money, either yearly, half-yearly, or quarterly; for a determinate period, as ten, fifty, or a hundred years; or for an indeterminate period, dependent on a certain contingency, as the death of a person; or for an indefinite term, in which latter case they are called perpetual annuities. As the probability of the duration of life at every age is known, so annuities may be purchased for fixed sums during the life of the party. An annuity is said to be in *arrear* when it continues unpaid after it is due, and in *reversion*, when it is to fall to the expectant at some future time.

AN'NULET, in architecture, a small square member in the Doric capital, under the quarter-round. Also a narrow flat moulding, encompassing other parts of the column, as in the base, capital, &c., which is variously termed *fillet*, *cincture*, *&c.*

ANNUNCIA'TION, the delivery of a message, particularly the angel's message to the Virgin Mary, concerning the birth of our Saviour. The festival in commemoration of that event is called Lady-day, and falls on the 25th of March.

ANOM'ALOUS, in a general sense, is applied to whatever is irregular, or deviates from the rule observed by other things of the like nature.—ANOMALOUS VERBS, in grammar, such as are irregularly formed, of which the Greek language furnishes numerous examples.

ANON'YMOUS, in literature, works published without the name of the author. Those published under a false name are termed *Pseudonymous*. The best catalogue of anonymous works is that of Barbier (*Dictionnaire des Œuvrages Anonymes et Pseudonymes*, 3 vols. Paris, 1822–1824.) There is also the great work of Placcius, *Theatrum Anonymorum et Pseudonymorum*, t. fol. Hamburg, 1708.

AN'TA, Æ. plur., in architecture, a pilaster or square projection attached to a wall. When they are detached from the wall, Vitruvius calls them parastatæ. They are not usually diminished, even when accompanying columns from whose capitals, in all Greek works, they vary.

ANTANACLA'SIS, in rhetoric, a figure which repeats the same word, but in a different sense; as, "dum vivimus, vivamus."

ANTECE'DENT, in grammar, the word to which a relative refers: thus, "God whom we adore," the word *God* is the antecedent to the relative *whom*.—ANTECEDENT, in logic, is the first of the two propositions in an enthymeme.

ANTECLE'MA, in oratory, is where the whole defence of the person accused, turns on criminating the accuser.

ANTEDILU'VIAN, whatever existed before the deluge; thus, the inhabitants of the earth from Adam to Noah are called the antediluvians.

ANTEPENUL'TIMA, ANTEPENUL'TIMATE, or ANTEPENULT', in grammar, the third syllable of a word from the end, or the last syllable but two.

ANTEPOSI'TION, a grammatical figure, whereby a word, which by the ordinary rules of syntax ought to follow another, comes before it.

AN'THEM, a piece of music performed in cathedral service by choristers who sing alternately. This manner of singing is very ancient in the church; some suppose it to have descended from the practice of the earliest Christians, who, according to Pliny, were accustomed to sing their Hymn to Christ in parts or by turns.

ANTHOL'OGY, a collection of choice poems, particularly a collection of Greek epigrams so called. The word in its original sense simply means a collection of flowers.

ANTHONY, ST., the events in the life of this saint form a very important class of subjects in Christian Art. Among the most frequent are his Temptation, and his Meeting with Saint Paul. St. Anthony has several distinctive attributes by which he is easily recognized: as the founder of monachism he is depicted in a monk's habit and cowl, bearing a crutch in the shape of a T, called a *tace*, as a token of his age and feebleness, with a bell suspended to it, or in his hand, to scare away the evil spirits by which he was persecuted; a firebrand in his hand, with flames at his feet, a black hog, representing the demons Gluttony and Sensuality, under his feet; sometimes a devil is substituted for the hog.

ANTHROPOL'OGY, the science which treats of human nature, either in a physical or an intellectual point of view.

ANTHROPOMOR'PHITE, one who ascribes a human figure and a bodily form to God.

ANTHROPOPH'AGI, or cannibals persons who eat the flesh of men as well as animals. Abhorrent and unnatural as the practice is, there is no doubt that whole nations have been addicted to this practice, and that it still prevails in the South Seas.

AN'TI, a Greek particle, which enters into the composition of several words, both Latin, French, and English, and signifies opposite or contrary to, as in *antiscorbutics*.

ANTI-CLI'MAX, in literary composition and oratory, when a writer or speaker suddenly descends from the great to the little.

AN'TIDOTE, a counter-poison, or any medicine generally that counteracts the effects of what has been swallowed.

ANTIL'OGY, an inconsistency between two or more passages of the same book.

ANTIMETAB'OLE, in rhetoric, a setting of two things in opposition to each other.

ANTIMETATH'ESIS, in rhetoric, an inversion of the parts or members of an antithesis.

ANTIPHO'NA, or ANTIPH'ONY, in music, the answer made by one choir to another, when the psalm or anthem is sung verse for verse alternately.

ANTIPH'RASIS, in rhetoric, a figure of speech, or kind of irony, whereby we say a thing by denying what we ought rather to affirm it to be; as when we say, "he is no fool," we mean "he is a man of sense."

AN'TIQUARY, a person who studies and searches after monuments and remains of antiquity. There were formerly in the chief cities of Greece and Italy, persons of high distinction called antiquaries, who made it their business to explain the ancient inscriptions, and give every other assistance in their power to strangers who were lovers of that kind of learning.—The monks who were employed in making new copies of old books were formerly called *antiquarii*.

ANTI'QUE, in a restricted sense, pieces of ancient art, and by artists usually confined to such as were made by the Greeks and Romans of the classical age.

ANTIQ'UITIES, all such documents of ancient history as industrious and learned men have collected; genealogies, inscriptions, monuments, coins, names, etymologies, archives, mechanical instruments, fragments of history, &c. Antiquities form a very extensive science, including an historical knowledge of the ancient edifices, magistrates, habiliments, manners, customs, ceremonies, religious worship, and other objects worthy of curiosity, of all the principal nations of the earth. In England, there are British, Roman, Saxon, and Norman antiquities, many of which are highly interesting, and serve to throw a light on the manners and customs of the people.

ANTIS'TROPHE, the alternate verse in ancient poetry, which was divided into the *strophe* and *antistrophe*. In reciting their odes the chorus turned from the left to the right at the antistrophe, and *vice versa*.

ANTITH'ESIS, in rhetoric, a figure of speech, by which two things are attempted to be made more striking, by being set in opposition to each other. "Antitheses, well managed," says Bohours, "give infinite pleasure in the perusal of works of genius; they have nearly the same effect in language as lights and shadows in painting, which a good artist distributes with propriety: or the flats and sharps in music, which are mingled by a skilful master." The beautiful antithesis of Cicero, in his second Catilinarian, may serve as an example: "On the one side stands modesty, on the other impudence; on the one fidelity, on the other deceit; here piety, there sacrilege; here continency, there lust," &c.

AN'TITYPE, among ecclesiastical writers, denotes a type corresponding to some other type or figure. In the Greek church it is also an appellation given to the symbols of bread and wine in the sacrament.

ANTONOMA'SIA, a mode of speaking in which a person is addressed or described by some appropriate or official designation, but not by his surname; as, in the House of Lords, "the noble lord," in the House of Commons, "the honorable gentleman."

ANU'BIS, in mythology, an Egyptian deity. The seventh, according to the astronomical Theology, of their eight gods of the first class. The Greeks identified him with Mercury. In Egyptian painting and sculpture he is represented as a man with the head of a dog.

A'ORIST, that inflection of the verb which leaves the time of the action denoted uncertain.

AP'ANAGE, an allowance to younger branches of a sovereign house out of the revenues of the country; generally together with a grant of public domains. A district with the right of ruling it, when thus conferred, is termed paragium. An apanage, in ordinary cases, descends to the children of the prince who enjoys it.

AP'ATHY, a term expressive of an utter privation of passion, and an insensibility of pain. Thus, the Stoics affected an entire apathy, so as not to be ruffled, or sensible of pleasure or pain.

APHÆRE'SIS, in grammar, the taking away a letter or syllable from a word.

APH'ORISM, a maxim or principle of a science; or a sentence which comprehends a great deal in a few words. The aphoristic method has great advantages, as containing much matter in a small compass; sentiments are here almost as numerous as expressions; and doctrines may be counted by phrases.

APLUS'TRE, or APLUS'TRIA, in the naval architecture of the ancients, an ornament resembling a shield fixed in the poop of a ship, in which case it differed from the acrostolium.

APOC'ALYPSE, the Greek name of the last book of the New Testament, so called from its containing revelations concerning several important doctrines of Christianity.

APOC'OPE, in grammar, a figure by which the last letter or syllable of a word is cut off.

APOC'RYPHA, in theology, certain books of doubtful authority which are not received into the canons of holy writ.

APODIC'TICA, in rhetoric, an epithet for arguments which are fitted for proving the truth of any point.

APODIOX'IS, in rhetoric, a figure whereby we either pass over a thing slightly, or reject it as unworthy of notice.

APODIX'IS, in rhetoric, an evident demonstration.

APOD'OSIS, in rhetoric, the latter part of a complete exordium, or application of a simile.

AP'OGRAPH, a copy or transcript of some book or writing. It is opposed to *autograph*.

APOLLINA'RES LU'DI, or APOLLINA'RIAN GAMES, in Roman antiquity, were instituted U. C. 542. They were celebrated in honor of Apollo, by a decree of the senate, in consequence of a prediction of the prophet Marcius relative to the battle of Cannæ.

APOL'LO, or PHŒBUS, a heathen divinity, son of Jupiter and Latona, in Homeric times the god of archery, prophecy, music, and medicine. Later poets represent him also as the god of day and the sun. The statues of Apollo represent a young man in the perfection of manly strength and beauty, with unshorn curling locks, and a bow or lyre in his hand.

APOL'LO BEL'VIDERE, an ancient marble statue of Apollo most exquisitely finished. It was found in the ruins of Antium, in the 15th century, and placed in the Belvidere gallery of the Vatican palace at Rome.

APOLLO'NIA, in antiquity, an annual festival celebrated by the Ægialians in honor of Apollo.

APOLLONIA, St., of Alexandria, the events in the life of this saint form the subjects of some fine pictures, of which one of the best, painted by Domenichino, is in the Gallery of the Library at Mayence. She is usually represented as holding the martyr's palm in one hand, and a pair of pincers, with a tooth, in the other, illustrating her martyrdom, during which all her teeth were pulled out.

AP'OLOGUE, a poetical fiction, the purpose of which is the improvement of morals. Some writers are of opinion, that this term ought to be confined to that species of fable in which brute or inanimate things, as beasts or flowers, are made to speak; but this distinction, so far from being followed, is generally reversed. It is, in reality, more usual to give the name of apologue where human actors only are introduced.

APOL'OGY, in literature, a defence, or answer to an accusation. The two pieces of Xenophon and Plato, each commonly termed Apologia Socratis, differ in character: the first being a defence supposed to be pronounced by the philosopher himself; the last, a narration of his last hours and discourses. Treatises in defence of the Christian religion, in its early period, were denominated Apologies by their writers; as those of Justin Martyr, Tertullian, and others, both preserved and lost. The title has been retained by some writers in modern times: as by Robert Barclay, in his Apology of Quakerism, and by Bishop Watson, in his Apologies for the Bible and for Christianity.

APOPH'ASIS, a figure of speech in which the orator briefly alludes to, or seems to decline stating, that which he wishes to insinuate.

AP'OPHTHEGM, or AP'OTHEGM, a short, sententious, and instructive remark, especially if pronounced by a person of distinguished character.

APOPH'YGE, in architecture, the part of a column where it springs out of its base.

A POSTERIO'RI, in logic, a mode of reasoning from the effect to the cause.

APOS'TLE, a person sent forth upon any business: hence applied, by way of eminence, to the twelve elect disciples of Christ, who were sent forth by him to convert and baptize all nations. In the first century, the apostles assumed the highest office in the church; and the term apostle during that period was equivalent to bishop in after-times.

APOS'TLES' CREED, a confession of faith, supposed anciently to have been drawn up by the apostles themselves, and deriving the title "Creed" from the word with which it begins in Latin (credo, *I believe*). With respect to its antiquity, it may be affirmed, that the greater part of its clauses is quoted by the apostolic father Ignatius; and that the whole, as it now stands in the liturgy, is to be found in the works of St. Ambrose, in the fourth century.

APOSTOL'IC FATHERS, the writers of the Christian Church, who lived in the apostolic age, or were during any part of their lives contemporary with the apostles. They are five: Clement of Rome, Barnabas, Hermas, Ignatius, and Polycarp; of whom the last suffered martyrdom, A. D. 147.

APOS'TROPHE, in rhetoric, a figure of speech by which the orator or writer suddenly breaks off from the previous method of his discourse, and addresses himself in the second person to some person, or thing, absent or present.

APOTHE'OSIS, deification, or the ceremony of placing among the gods, which was frequent among the ancients. It was one of the doctrines of Pythagoras, which he had borrowed from the Chaldees, that virtuous persons, after their death, were raised into the order of the gods. And hence the ancients deified all the inventors of things useful to mankind, and who had done any important service to the commonwealth. This honor was also conferred on several of the Roman emperors at their decease.

APOT'OME, in music, the difference between the greater and the less semitone, being expressed by the ratio of 128 to 125.

APPEL'LATIVE, in grammar, a noun or name applicable to a whole species or kind, as, a man, a horse.

APPEN'DIX, in literature, a treatise or supplement added at the end of a work, to render it more complete.

APPOGIATU'RA, in music, a small note inserted by the practical musician, between two others, at some distance; or a note inserted by way of embellishment.

APPOSI'TION, in grammar, the placing two or more substantives together, without any copulative between them, as Wellington, the conqueror.

APPREHEN'SION, in logic, the first or most simple act of the mind, whereby it perceives, or is conscious of some idea: it is more usually called perception.

A'PRIL, the fourth month of the year. The name is probably derived from Lat. aperire, *to open*, either from the opening of the buds, or of the bosom of the earth in producing vegetation.

A PRIO'RI, a mode of reasoning from the cause to the effect.

AQUATIN'TA, a style of engraving, or rather etching, by which an effect is produced similar to that of a drawing in Indian ink.

AQ'UEDUCT, a conduit of water, is a construction of stone or timber, built on uneven ground, to preserve the level of water, and convey it, by a canal, from one place to another. There are aqueducts under ground, and others raised above it supported by arches. The Romans were very magnificent in their aqueducts. In the time of the Emperor Nerva there were nine, which emptied themselves through 13,594 pipes of an inch diameter. That constructed by Louis XIV. for carrying the Bucq to Versailles, is 7000 fathoms long. The Croton aqueduct, 40 miles long, supplying the city of New York with water, is probably the greatest work of the kind in ancient or modern times.

AR'ABESQUE, or MORESQUE, a style of ornament in painting and sculpture, so called from the Arabians and Moors, who rejected the representation of animals.

AR'ABIC FIGURES, the numeral characters now used in our arithmetic, which were borrowed from the Arabians, and introduced into England about the eleventh century.

ARABO-TEDES'CO, a style of architecture, in which the Moorish and Gothic are combined.

A'RÆOSTYLE, in architecture, a sort of intercolumniation, in which the columns are at a distance from each other.

AR'BOR SCIEN'TIÆ, a general distribution or scheme of science, or knowledge.

ARCADE', in architecture, a series of arches crowned with a roof or ceiling, with a walk or passage thereunder. The piers of arcades may be decorated with columns, pilasters, niches, and apertures of different forms. The arches themselves are turned sometimes with rock-worked and sometimes with plain rustic arch stones or voussoirs, or with a moulded archivolt, springing from an impost or platband, and sometimes,—though that is not to be recommended,—from columns. The key-stones are generally carved in the form of a console, or sculptured with some device.

ARCA'NUM, among physicians, any remedy, the preparation of which is industriously concealed, in order to enhance its value.

ARCH, a concave building with a mould bent in form of a curve, erected to support some structure. Arches are either circular, elliptical or straight, as they are improperly called by workmen. Elliptical arches consist of a semi-ellipsis, and have commonly a key-stone and imposts; they are usually described by workmen on three centres. Straight arches are those used over doors and windows, and having plain straight edges, both upper and under, which are parallel, but both the ends and joints point towards a centre. The term arch is peculiarly used for the space between the two piers of a bridge, for the passages, of water, vessels, &c.—TRIUMPHAL ARCH, a stately gate of a semicircular form, adorned with sculpture, inscriptions, &c. erected in honor of those who had deserved a triumph.—ARCH, as a syllable prefixed to another word, denotes the highest degree of its kind, whether good or bad; as *archangel, archduke, archbishop, arch-fiend*, &c. Many of the highest offices in different empires have this syllable prefixed to them.

ARCHÆOL'OGY, in general, means the knowledge of antiquity, but in a narrower sense, the science which inquires into and discovers the mental life of ancient nations from their monuments, whether literary, artistical, or mechanical. Artistic Archæology treats of remains as works of the Fine Arts, in those two nations which were models in Art, the Greeks and Romans; besides these the artistic productions of the Indians, Egyptians, Babylonians, and Persians, take an honorable place in the Archæology of Art.

AR'CHAISM, any antiquated word or phrase. The use of archaisms, though generally objectionable, occasionally add to the beauty and force of a sentence.

ARCHBISH'OP, a metropolitan prelate, having several suffragan bishops under him. In England there are two archbishops—the archbishop of Canterbury, who is primate of *all* England; and the archbishop of York, who is only styled primate of England. The first establishment of archbishops in England, according to Bede, was in the time of Lucius, said to be the first Christian king in Britain; but the first archbishop of Canterbury was Austin, appointed A.D. 598, by Ethelbert, when he was converted. An archbishop consecrates the inferior diocesans, as those ordain priests and deacons, and when invested with his dignity, he is said to be enthroned; a term which probably originated with that period of English history, in which the archbishop of Canterbury had some of the privileges of absolute royalty.

ARCHDEA'CON, an ecclesiastical officer, next in rank below a bishop. Every diocese has one, and the generality more. They are usually appointed by their diocesans; but their authority is independent. They visit the clergy, and have courts for the punishment of offenders by spiritual censures, and for hearing all other causes that fall within ecclesiastical cognizance.

ARCH'ERY, the art of shooting with the bow and arrow. Since the introduction of gunpowder, the arrow has ceased to be employed as an offensive weapon: but in former times it was reckoned of the utmost importance to the military strength of England. The practice of archery was followed both as a recreation and a service, and Edward III. prohibited all useless games that interfered with the practice of it on holidays and other intervals of leisure. By an act of Edward IV. every man was to have a bow of his own height, to be made of yew, hazel, or ash, &c.; and mounds of earth were to be made in every township for the use of the inhabitants. Indeed, it appears from the use made of the bow by the English at the battles of Cressy, Agincourt, and Poictiers, that their claim to be considered the best of modern archers can scarcely be disputed.

AR'CHETYPE, the first model of a work, which is copied after to make another like it. Among minters it is used for the standard weight by which the others are adjusted.—The *archetopal world*, among Platonists, means the world as it existed in the idea of God, before the visible creation.

AR'CHITECT, one who is skilled in architecture. The architect forms plans and designs for edifices, conducts the work, and directs the artificers employed in it.

AR'CHITECTURE, the art of inventing and drawing designs for buildings, or the science which teaches the method of constructing any edifice for use or ornament. It is divided into *civil*, *military*, and *naval*; according as the erections are for civil, military, or naval purposes; and for the sake of convenience, other divisions are sometimes introduced. Architecture appears to have been among the earliest inventions, and its works have been commonly regulated by some principle of hereditary imitation. Whatever rude structure the climate and materials of any country have obliged its early inhabitants to adopt for their temporary shelter, the same structure, with all its prominent features, has been afterwards in some measure kept up by their refined and opulent posterity. To Greece we are indebted for the three principal orders of architecture, the *Doric*, (Fig. 1.) the *Ionic*, (Fig. 2.) and the *Corinthian*, (Fig. 3.); Rome added two others, both formed out of the former, the *Tuscan*, (Fig. 4) and the *Composite*, (Fig. 5.) Each of these has a particular expression; so that a building, or different parts of a building, may be rude, solid, neat, delicate, or gay, accordingly as the Tuscan, the Doric, the Ionic, the Corinthian, or the Composite are employed. The columns of these several orders are easily distinguishable to common observers, by reason of the ornaments that are peculiar to their capitals; but the scientific difference consists in their proportions. The Tuscan order is characterized by its simplicity and strength. It is devoid of all ornament. The Doric (Fig. 1.) is enlivened with ornaments in the frize and capital. The Ionic is ornamented with the volute scroll, or spinal horn: its ornaments are in a style of composition between the plainness of the Doric, and the richness of the Corinthian. The Corinthian order is known by its capital being

Fig. 1.

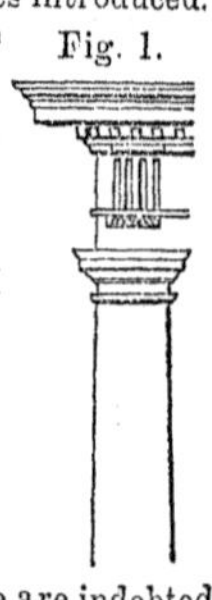

Fig. 2.

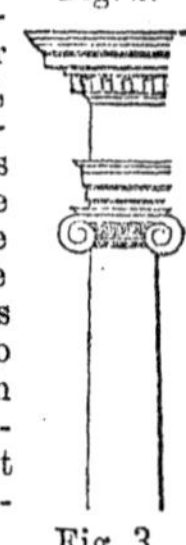

Fig. 3.

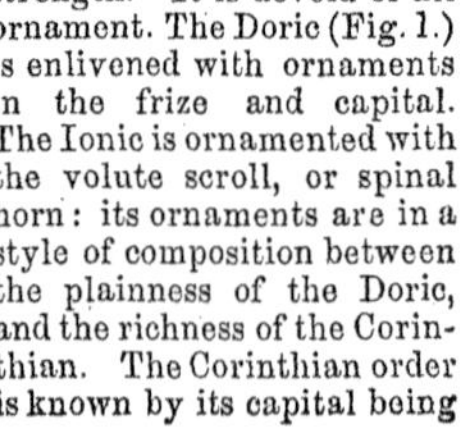

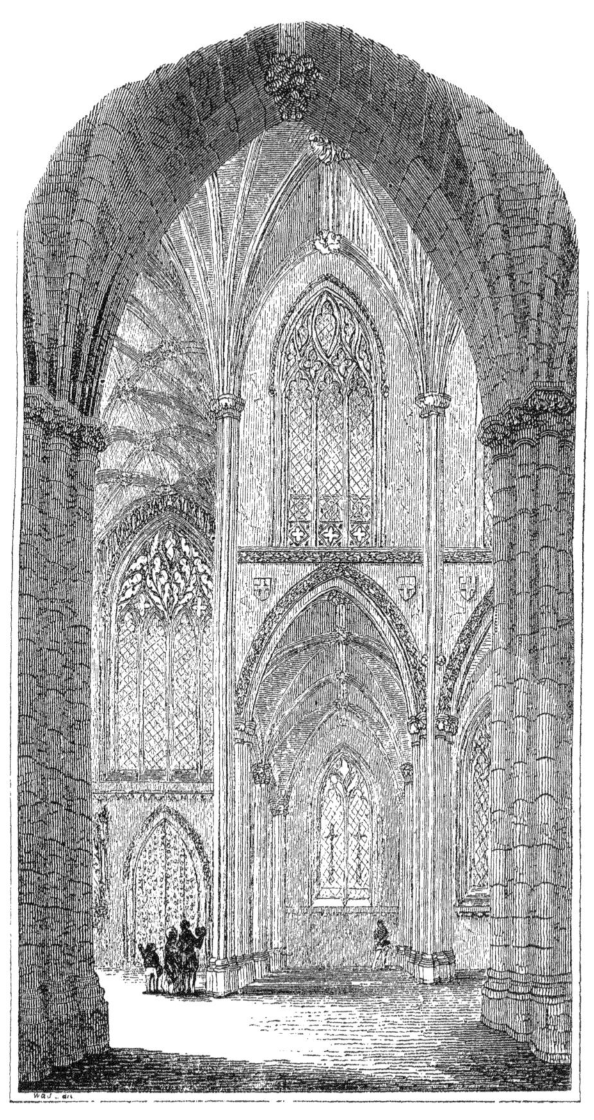

ARCHITECTURE,

(Interior of Grace Church, N. Y.)

Fig. 4.

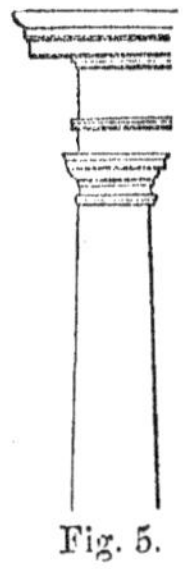

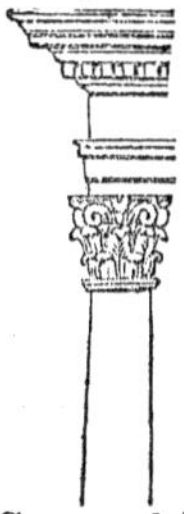

adorned with two sorts of leaves; between these rise little stalks, of which the volutes that support the highest part of the capital, are formed. The Composite is nearly the same as the Corinthian, with an addition of the Ionic volute. In their private buildings the Roman architects followed the Greeks; but in their public edifices they far surpassed them in grandeur. During the dark ages which followed the destruction of the Roman empire, the classic architecture of Greece and Rome was lost sight of, but was again revived by the Italians at the time of the restoration of letters. The *Gothic style* was so called because it was first used by the Visigoths; but at first it was vastly inferior to that which we now call Gothic, and which exhibits grandeur and splendor, with the most accurate execution. The *Saxon* and *Norman styles* were so called because they were respectively used by the Saxons before the Conquest, and by the Normans after, in the building of churches. The Saxon style was distinguished by the semicircular arch, which they seem to have taken partly from the Romans, and partly from their ancestors on the continent. The Norman was distinguished by the following particulars: the walls were very thick, generally without buttresses; the arches, both within and without, semicircular, and supported by very plain and solid columns. These two styles continued to be the prevailing modes of building in England until the reign of Henry II., when a new mode was introduced, which was called *modern Gothic*. Whether this was purely a deviation from the other two modes, or whether it was derived from any foreign source, is not known. It is, however, supposed to be of Saracenic extraction, and to have been introduced by the crusaders. The style is distinguished by its numerous buttresses, lofty spires and pinnacles, large and ramified windows, with a profusion of ornaments throughout. In the fifteenth and sixteenth centuries the taste for Greek and Roman architecture revived, and brought the five orders again into use, although for sacred edifices the Saxon and Gothic styles still maintain the pre-eminence.

Fig. 5.

AR'CHITRAVE, in architecture, that part of a column, or order of columns, which lies immediately upon the capital; being the lowest member of the entablature. Over a chimney, this member is called the mantle-piece; and over doors or windows, the hyperthyron.

AR'CHIVAULT, in architecture, the inner contour of an arch, or a frame set off with mouldings, running over the faces of the arch stones, and bearing upon the imposts.

AR'CHIVES, ancient records, or charters which contain titles, pretensions, privileges, and prerogatives of a community, family, city, or kingdom.

AR'CHON, the chief magistrates of the city and commonwealth of Athens.

ARE'NA, in Roman antiquity, that part of the amphitheatre where the gladiators fought; so called from its being always strewed with sand, to conceal from the view of the people, the blood spilt in the combat.

AREOP'AGUS, a sovereign tribunal at Athens, famous for the justice and impartiality of its decrees. It was in the town, on a rock or hill opposite to the citadel. There are some remains of the areopagus still existing in the middle of the temple of Theseus, which was heretofore in the middle of the city, but is now without the walls.

AR'GONAUTS, in Grecian antiquity, a company of illustrious Greeks, who embarked along with Jason in the ship Argo, on an expedition to Colchis with a design to obtain the golden fleece. Some writers imagine, and foremost among them is Sir Isaac Newton, that this expedition was really an embassy sent by the Greeks, during the intestine divisions of Egypt, in the reign of Amenophis, to persuade the nations upon the coasts of the Euxine and Mediterranean seas to take that opportunity of shaking off the yoke of Egypt, which Sesostris had laid upon them: and that fetching the golden fleece was only a pretence to cover their true design.

AR'GUMENT, in rhetoric and logic, an inference drawn from premises, the truth of which is indisputable, or at least highly probable. In reasoning, Mr. Locke observes that men ordinarily use four sorts of arguments. The first is to allege the opinions of men, whose parts and learning, eminency, power, or some other cause, have gained a name, and settled their reputation in the common esteem, with some kind of authority; this may be called *argumentum ad verecundiam*. Secondly, another way is to require the adversaries to admit what they allege as a proof, or to assign a better; this he calls *argumentum ad ignorantiam*. A third way is, to press a man with consequences, drawn from his own principles or concessions; this is known by the name of *argumentum ad hominem*. Fourthly, the using proofs drawn from any of the foundations of knowledge or probability; this he calls *argumentum ad judicium;* and observes, that it is the only one of all the four, that brings true instruction with it, and advances us in our way to knowledge.—ARGUMENT, in literature, denotes also the abridgment, or heads of a book, history, chapter, &c.

ARIO'SO, in musical composition, the Italian word for the time of a common air.

ARISTOTE'LIAN, something relating to Aristotle: thus we read of the Aristotelian philosophy, school, &c. The Aristotelians were also designated Peripatetics, and their philosophy long prevailed in the schools, till it gave place to the Newtonian.

AR'MOR, a name for all such habiliments as serve to defend the body from wounds, especially of darts, a sword, a lance, &c. A complete suit of armor anciently consisted of a casque or helm, a gorget, cuirass, gauntlets, tasses, brassets, cuishes, and covers for the legs, to which the spurs were fastened. This they called armor *cap-a-pie;* and was worn by cavaliers and men-at-arms. The infantry had only part of it, viz., a pot or headpiece, a cuirass and tasses; but all of them made light. Lastly, the horses themselves had their armor, wherewith to cover the head and neck. Of all this furniture of war, scarcely anything is now retained except the cuirass.

ARMOR-BEARER, the person who was formerly employed to carry the armor of another.

ARMS, in military phraseology, all kinds of weapons, whether used for offence or defence.—ARMS, in a legal sense, extend to anything that a person wears for his own defence, or takes into his hand, and uses, in anger, to strike or throw at another.—ARMS denote also the natural weapons of beasts, as claws, teeth, beak, &c.

ARMS, COATS OF, family insignia or distinctions, which had their rise from the painting of the shields used in war before the invention of gunpowder.

AR'MY, in a general sense, is taken for the whole armed force raised for the defence of the country by land. In a limited sense, it denotes a large body of soldiers, consisting of horse and foot, completely armed, and provided with artillery, ammunition, provisions, &c., under a commander-in-chief, having lieutenant-generals, major-generals, brigadiers, and other officers under him. An army is generally divided into a certain number of corps, each consisting of brigades, regiments, battalions, and squadrons; when in the field, it is formed into lines; the first line is called the vanguard, the second the main body, the third the rearguard, or body of reserve. The middle of each line is occupied by the foot; the cavalry forms the right and left wing of each line, and sometimes squadrons of horse are placed in the intervals between the battalions. The *materiel* of an army, as the French term it, consists of the horses, stores, provisions, and everything necessary for service. *Armies* are moreover distinguished according to their service, into *blockading army, army of observation, army of reserve, &c.*

ARPEG'GIO, in music, is a term implying that the tones should be sounded distinctly, as they are heard on the harp.—ARPEGGIO ACCOMPANIMENT consists chiefly of the notes of the several chords taken in returning successions.

ARRANGE'MENT, in the plastic Arts, and in painting, Invention and Arrangement are the groundwork of every composition. ARRANGEMENT is the placing together of *parts* in a manner conformable to the character and aim of the work; it relates entirely to the form, in which the subject must be worked out so as to produce an intuitive perception of its individuality. Artistic arrangement belongs not only to the object as a whole, but to each part specially, to groups as well as to single figures, and to the position and contrast of their limbs. In painting, it refers to the distribution of colors, and the disposition of light and shade, all of which require a peculiar artistic arrangement; light, shade, and coloring, being the soul of all painting.

AR'RIS, in architecture, the intersection or line formed by the meeting of the exterior surfaces of two bodies, answering to what is called the edge.—ARRIS FILLET, a small piece of timber, of a triangular section, used in raising the slates against a wall that cuts obliquely across the roof.

AR'SIS and THESIS, in music, terms used in composition, as when a point is inverted or turned, it is said to move *per arsin et thesin*, that is, when it rises in one point and falls in another; properly speaking, it is the rise and fall of the hand in beating time.

ART, a system of rules, serving to facilitate the performance of certain actions; in which sense it stands opposed to science, or a system of merely speculative principles.—*Terms of Art*, are such words as are used in regard to any particular art, profession, or science.

AR'TICLE, in grammar, a particle in most languages, that serves to express the several cases and genders of nouns, when the languages have not different terminations to denote the different states and circumstances of nouns.

ARTICULA'TION, in painting and sculpture, the movable connection of the bones, in the representation of which by the artist the greatest skill and knowledge of anatomy is required.

ARTIL'LERY, a collective name denoting engines of war, but particularly cannon, mortars, and other large pieces, for the discharge of shot and shells. It is also employed to denote the science which teaches all things relating to the artillery, as the construction of all engines of war, the arrangement, movement, and management of cannon and all sorts of ordnance, used either in the field, or the camp, or at sieges, &c. The same name is also given to the troops by whom these arms are served, the men being, in fact, subsidiary to the instruments.—*Park of artillery*, a place set apart in a camp for the artillery, and large fire-arms.—*Train of artillery*, a set or number of pieces of ordnance mounted on carriages.—*Flying artillery*, a sort of artillery, so called from the celerity with which it can be moved. Seats are contrived for the men who work it, and a sufficient force of horses is applied to enable them to proceed at a gallop; each horse being rode by a separate driver.

AR'TIST, a proficient in the liberal arts, in distinction from ARTISAN, or one who follows one of the mechanic arts.

AR'TS, in the most general sense of the word, means any acquired skill. They are usually divided into *fine* and *useful;* comprising under the former, all those, the direct object of which is not absolute utility, as painting, sculpture, music, poetry, &c., in distinction from the arts called *useful*, or such as are essential to trade and commerce.

ART-UNIONS are societies formed for the encouragement of the Fine Arts by the purchase of paintings, sculptures, &c. out of a common fund raised in small shares or subscriptions; such works of art, or the right of selecting them, being distributed by lot among the subscribers or members. They appear to owe their origin to M. Hennin, a distinguished amateur of Paris, who about forty years ago organized a little society for the purpose of bringing together the unsold works of artists, exhibiting them, and with the exhibition money, and other subscriptions, purchasing a selection from among them, which was afterwards distributed by lot to the subscribers. In 1816 this company merged into the "Société des Amis des Arts." Art-Unions have been extensively organized in most of the German states. The Art-Union of Berlin was established in 1825. The first Art-Union formed in Great Britain was in Scotland, in the year 1834. The Art-Union of London was established in 1837, and since that period similar societies have been established in Ireland, and in many of the principal towns in England. The American Art-Union of New York has exhibited the most remarkable instance of rapid growth and prosperity of any similar societies. It was founded in 1839, and at the close of 1850 the number of members was 16,310, to whom were distributed as prizes, 433 paintings selected by a committee, 27 statuettes, 30 sets of prints, from Col. Trumbull's celebrated pictures of the *Battle of Bunker Hill*, and *Death of Montgomery*, measuring 30 inches by 20 inches, 50 sets of *Outlines and Sketches* by Washington Allston, 250 "Trumbull" medals, and 250 "Stuart" medals.

ARUNDE'LIAN MARBLES, called also the Parian Chronicle, are ancient stones, on which is inscribed a chronicle of the city of Athens, supposed to have been engraven in capital letters in the island of Paros, 264 years before Christ They take their name from the earl of Arundel, who procured them from the East, or from his grandson, who presented them to the University of Oxford.

ARUS'PICES, or HARUS'PICES, an order of priesthood among the Romans, who pretended to foretell future events by inspecting the entrails of victims killed in sacrifice. They were introduced by Romulus, and abolished by Constantine, A.D. 337.

AS, a weight used by the ancients, consisting of 12 ounces: it was also used as a coin, and as an integer divided into 12 parts.

A'SAPHEIS, defective utterance.

ASARO'TA, in antiquity, a pavement or floor laid in dining-rooms, and composed of very small tiles inlaid in different colors.

ASBES'TOS, or ASBES'TUS, an inflammable mineral substance, of which *amianthus* is one of its principal species. This consists of elastic fibres, somewhat unctuous to the touch, and slightly translucent. The ancients manufactured cloth from the fibres of the asbestos for the purpose, as is said, of wrapping up the bodies of the dead when exposed on the funeral pile; it being incombustible in its nature.

ASCEND'ANT, in architecture, an ornament in masonry or joiner's work, which borders the three sides of doors, windows, and chimneys.

ASCET'ICS, in ecclesiastical history, such Christians in the primitive church as inured themselves to great degrees of abstinence and fasting, in order to subdue their passions. In short, every kind of uncommon piety laid claim to the name *ascetic*.

ASCLE'PIA, a Grecian festival, held in honor of Æsculapius. It was also called the sacred contest, because poets and musicians contended for victory there.

ASCLEPIADÆ'AN VERSE, a kind of poetic measure so called from Æsclepias, the inventor of it.

ASCO'LIA, in Grecian antiquity, a festival celebrated by the Athenian husbandmen, in honor of Bacchus, to whom they sacrificed a he-goat, because that animal destroys the vines.

ASCRIPTI'TII, in ancient history, supernumerary soldiers, who served to supply the losses in the legions. Also, in later times, foreigners or aliens newly admitted to the freedom of a city.

ASH'LAR, in architecture, common freestones, as they are brought rough and chipped or detached from the quarry, of different lengths and thicknesses. Their usual thickness is nine inches.

ASH'LERING, in architecture, the upright timber or quarters towards the rooms or inwards in garrets by which the slope of the roof is concealed—sometimes it is only two or three feet high, and sometimes the whole height of the room.

ASH-WEDNES'DAY, the first day in Lent, so called from the ancient custom of fasting in sackcloth and ashes.

A'SIARCH, in Grecian antiquity, a governor of the provinces, who used to preside over the public games.

ASIDE', a term in plays for what is to be said on the stage without being heard by the other performers.

ASINA'RIA, a festival anciently held in Sicily, in commemoration of the victory obtained over the Athenians, when Demosthenes and Nicias were taken prisoners; and was so called from the river Asinarius, near which it was fought.

AS'PECT, in architecture, the direction towards the point of the compass in which a building is placed. The aspectus is also used by Vitruvius to denote the external distribution of a temple. Thus he describes seven sorts of aspects of temples.

ASPHAL'TUM, a bituminous or inflammable substance, found in abundance in different countries, especially near the Dead Sea, and in Albania; but nowhere in such quantities as in the island of Trinidad, where there is a large plain of it, called the Tar Lake, which is three miles in circumference and of an unknown depth. It is also found in France, Switzerland, and some other parts of Europe.

AS'PIRATE, in grammar, a character in the Greek (marked thus, ʽ) to denote that the vowel must be sounded with a breathing. In English, the letter *h* is called aspirate, when it is sounded, in distinction to *h* mute.

AS'SAI, a musical term, which indicates that the time must be accelerated or retarded; as *allegro*, quick; *allegro assai*, still quicker; *adagio assai*, still slower.

ASSAS'SIN, one who kills another, not in open combat, but privately, or suddenly. The name is generally restrained to murderers of princes or other political characters; or, to speak perhaps more explicitly, to where the murder is committed from some sentiment of hatred, but in a private and dastardly manner.

ASSIGNAT', the name of the national paper currency in France during the Revolution. Four hundred millions of this paper money were first struck off by the constituent assembly, with the approbation of the king, April 19, 1790, to be redeemed with the proceeds of the sale of the confiscated goods of the church. They at length increased, by degrees, to forty thousand millions, and after awhile they became of no value whatever.

ASSIGNEE', in law, a person appointed by another to do an act, transact some business, or enjoy a particular privilege.—The person to whom is committed the management of a bankrupt's estate.

ASSIGN'MENT, in law, the act of assigning or transferring the interest or property a man has in a thing; or of appointing and setting over a right to another.

ASSI'ZES, a meeting of the English royal judges, the sheriff, and juries, for the purpose of making jail-deliveries, and trying causes between individuals; generally held twice in the year. The assizes are *general* when the justices go their circuits, with commission to take all assizes, that is, to hear all causes; and they are *special* when special commissions are granted to hear particular causes.

ASSOCIA'TION OF IDEAS, by this phrase is understood the connection between certain ideas which causes them to succeed each other involuntarily in the mind. To the wrong association of ideas made in our minds by custom, Mr. Locke attributes most of the sympathies and antipathies observable in men, which work as strongly, and produce as regular effects, as if they were natural, though they at first had no other origin than the accidental connection of two ideas, which either by the strength of the first impression, or future indulgence, are so united, that they ever after keep company together in that man's mind as if they were but one idea.

AS'SONANCE, in rhetoric or poetry, is where the words of a phrase or verse have nearly the same sound, or termination, but make no proper rhyme.

ASSUMP'SIT, in law, a voluntary promise by which a man binds himself to pay anything to another, or to do any work.

ASSUMP'TION, a festival in the Romish church, in honor of the miraculous ascent of the Virgin Mary into heaven.—ASSUMPTION, in logic, is the minor or second proposition in a categorical syllogism. It is also used for a consequence drawn from the propositions whereof an argument is composed.

AS'TERISK, in diplomatics, a sign in the figure of a star, frequently met with in ancient Latin manuscripts, and seeming to serve various purposes; sometimes to denote an omission, sometimes an addition, sometimes a passage which appeared remarkable on any account to the copyist.

AS'TRAGAL, in architecture, a little round moulding, in form of a ring, serving as an ornament at the tops and bottoms of columns.

ASY'LUM, in antiquity, a place of refuge for offenders, where they were screened from the hands of justice. The asyla of altars and temples were very ancient. The Jews had their asyla; the most remarkable of which were, the temple, the altar of burnt-offerings, and the six cities of refuge. A similar custom prevailed both among the Greeks and Romans, where temples, altars, and statues, were places of refuge for criminals of every description. They had an idea, that a criminal who fled to the temple or altar, submitted his crime to the punishment of the gods, and that it would be impiety in man to take vengeance out of their hands. In former times the like immunities were granted by the pope to churches, convents, &c.

ASYN'DETON, in rhetoric or composition, the omission of conjunctions, or other connecting particles of speech, in order to render the sentence more lively and impressive.

AT'ABAL, a kind of tabor used among the Moors.

ATARAX'IA, or AT'ARAXY, a term used to denote that calmness of mind which secures us from all emotions arising from vanity or self-conceit. In this consisted the *summum bonum*, or sovereign good of the Stoics.

AT'AXY, in a general sense, the want of order: with physicians it signifies the irregularity of crises and paroxysms of fevers.

ATE'LIER, a term derived from the French, and applied specially to the workroom of sculptors and painters, which are also called STUDIOS. The Dutch and Flemish painters have delighted to portray their Ateliers.

A-TEM'PO, in music, Italian for 'in time,' employed when the regular measure has been interrupted.

ATHENÆ'UM, in antiquity, a public school wherein the professors of the liberal arts held their assemblies, the rhetoricians declaimed, and the poets rehearsed their performances. These places, of which there were a great number at Athens, were built in the manner of amphitheatres, encompassed with seats called *cunei*. The three most celebrated Athenæa were those at Athens, at Rome, and at Lyons, the second of which was built by the emperor Adrian.

ATHLE'TÆ, in antiquity, men of remarkable strength and agility, disciplined to perform the public games. This was a general term, under which were comprehended wrestlers, boxers, runners, leapers, throwers of the disk, and those who practised in other exercises exhibited in the Olympic, Pythian, and other solemn sports, wherein there were prizes allotted for the conquerors.

ATLAN'TES, TELAMONES, PERCES, GIGANTES, are the athletic male statues which we find as supports of parts of ancient buildings; female figures for the same purpose were called CARYATIDES; they are not exact imitations of nature, but their use is sufficiently justified by the antique. They were only employed when pillars were too insignificant for the erections; they are suitable to a rich style, to small screens, fountains, for supporting a gallery, and for the upper rows of pillars: these should not appear so heavy as to excite compassion, but the expression should be one of graceful freedom.

ATLAN'TIS, an island mentioned in Plato's Dialogue entitled Limæus, as having once existed in the Atlantic Ocean opposite to the Pillars of Hercules. It was said to have exceeded Europe and Africa jointly in magnitude; and after existing for 9000 years, during which period its inhabitants extended their conquests throughout the known quarters of the globe, to have been uprooted by prodigious earthquakes and inundations, and submerged in the ocean. The question of the reality and site of this island has been frequently discussed by modern geographers.

AT'LAS, in geography, a collection of maps; more properly, a book containing maps of the whole world; so called from Atlas, who was fabled to have borne the world on his shoulders. It is also the name of a chain of high mountains in Africa, extending from the coast of the Atlantic to the border of Egypt.

AT'OM, in philosophy, a particle of matter, so minute as to admit of no division. Atoms are the *minima naturæ*, and are conceived as the first principle or component parts of all physical magnitude. From the earliest times of antiquity, down to the present day, two opinions directly opposed to each other, have divided the world on this subject; the one, that matter is composed of an assemblage of minute particles, or atoms, incapable of farther division; the other that there is no limit to its divisibility, the smallest conceivable portion still consisting of an infinity of parts. The first of these theories, which is commonly distinguished by the name of the ATOMIC PHILOSOPHY, was originated in Greece by Leucippus; it was supported by Democritus, and subsequently improved by Epicurus and his disciples. The Epicureans professed to account for the origin and formation of all things by supposing that these atoms were endued with gravity and motion, and thus come together into the different organized bodies we now see.

ATTACH'MENT, in law, the taking or apprehending a person, by virtue of a writ or precept. It differs from an arrest, inasmuch as it lays hold of the goods, as well as the person; and also from a distress, which seizes on lands, tenements, and goods; but an attachment on the goods and body.

ATTAIN'DER, the name of a law by which the estate and life of a traitor are forfeited. A Bill of Attainder is a bill for attainting persons convicted of high treason. A person attainted of high treason forfeits all his lands, tenements, and hereditaments; his blood is corrupted, and he and his posterity rendered base; and this corruption of blood cannot be taken off but by act of parliament.

ATTAINT', in law, a writ that lies after judgment against a jury of twelve men that are charged with having given a false verdict.

AT'TIC, in architecture, a sort of building, in which there is no roof or covering to be seen, as was usual in the houses of the Athenians.—The ATTIC, or ATTIC STORY, is the upper story of a house.—The ATTIC BASE is a peculiar kind of column, or support, employed both in the Doric and Ionic orders.

AT'TICISM, an elegant or concise form of expression. Milton, in his Apology for Smectymnuus, thus uses it: "They made sport, and I laughed: they mispronounced, and I misliked; and, to make up the atticism, they were out, and I hissed." The term *Sal Atticum* was employed by the Romans at once to characterize the poignancy of wit and brilliancy of style peculiar to the Athenian writers, and to designate the liveliness, spirituality, and refined taste of the inhabitants of that city, which formed the focus and central point of all the eloquence and refinement of the Greeks.

AT'TITUDE, in painting and sculpture, the position and gesture of a figure or statue, or such a disposition of their parts, as shall best display some grace or beauty, or serve to express the action and sentiments of the person represented.

ATTOR'NEY, one who is appointed by another to do a thing in his absence. A *public* attorney is one who acts in the courts of law, and is a lawyer by profession.

AT'TRIBUTES, in theology, the several qualities or perfections of the divine nature, or such as we conceive to constitute the proper essence of God; as his wisdom, power, justice, goodness, &c.—ATTRIBUTES, in logic, are the predicates of any subject, or what may be affirmed or denied of anything.—ATTRIBUTES, in painting and sculpture, are symbols added to a figure or group, which are characteristic of the principal subject. Thus the eagle is an attribute of Jupiter; a peacock, of Juno; a caduceus, of Mercury; a club, of Hercules, &c.

AU'DIENCE, the persons assembled at a theatre, or other public place to see and hear the performances.—AUDIENCE, a ceremony used in courts at the admission of ambassadors or other public ministers to a hearing. In England, audience is given to ambassadors in the presence chamber; and to envoys and residents in a gallery, closet, or any place where the king happens to be.—AUDIENCE is also the name of an ecclesiastical court, held by the archbishop of Canterbury, wherein differences upon elections, consecrations, institutions, marriages, &c., are heard.

AU'DIT, a regular examination of accounts by officers appointed for that purpose.

AU'DITOR, an officer of any corporate body, appointed annually to examine accounts.

AU'GUR, an officer among the Romans, appointed to foretell future events, by the chattering and feeding of birds. The augurs bore an augural staff or wand, as the ensign of their authority, and their dignity was so much respected, that they were never deposed, nor any substituted in their place, though convicted of the most enormous crimes.

AU'GURY, a species of divination, or the art of foretelling future events, practised by the ancients. It was distinguished into five sorts, viz., augury from appearances in the heavens; from birds; from chickens; from quadrupeds; and from portentous events. This, like other human errors, appears to have arisen from ideas tolerably rational at first. The regular appearance and disappearance of the birds, and the precision that is observable in almost their whole proceedings, might naturally impress an ignorant race of men with a belief that they either inherently possessed, or from time to time received, supernatural information. Accustomed to regulate by these monitors their rural occupations, the shepherd and the husbandman were led, by the most excusable association of ideas, to consult the same advisers in the few other concerns of life that fell to their lot: and on the foundation laid by superstition, imposture subsequently raised a fantastic structure.

AUGUS'TAN HISTORY, a series of history of the Roman empire from the year 157 A.D. to 285 A.D., written by the following six authors: Æl. Spartianus, J. Capitolinus, Æl. Lampridius, Vulcatius Gallianus, Trebellius Pollio, and Flavius Vopiscus.

AUGUS'TINE AGE, a term used to designate the reign of Augustus, the most brilliant period in the literary history of Rome. The civil wars that had long distracted the Roman empire had stifled the cultivation of literature and the arts; and when the battle of Actium had terminated internal commotion, nothing, it was supposed, could so effectually celebrate and adorn the restoration of peace and the happy reign of Augustus, as the appearance of great national poets, who might supply the chief defect in the literature of their country, and create a body of classical works, in which the ancient Roman traditions might be transmitted to posterity. To accomplish this object, men of genius were flattered, courted, and enriched, in an unexampled manner, by the liberality of Augustus; and after a brief interval, the verses of Virgil, Horace, Propertius, Ovid, and Tibullus resounded throughout the empire in their respective epic, lyric, and elegiac strains. The science of jurisprudence then received its full development: and the boundaries of strict law on the one hand, and equity on the other, were respectively ascertained. In this age, too, Rome became the seat of universal government and wealth; and so numerous and splendid were the architectural decorations with which it was embellished, as to justify the saying of Augustus—that he found Rome of brick, and left it of marble.

AUGUS'TINES, a religious order, so called from St. Augustine, their founder, and vulgarly called Austin friars, or

Christian hermits. Before the Reformation they had 32 houses in England. Among other things, this rule enjoins to have all things in common, to receive nothing without the leave of the superior; and several other precepts relating to charity, modesty, and chastity. There are likewise nuns of this order. The Augustines are clothed in black, and at Paris are known under the name of the religious of St. Genevieve, that abbey being the chief of the order.

AUGUSTIN'IANS, a religious sect of the 16th century, who maintained that the gates of heaven would not be opened till the general resurrection.

AU'LIC, an epithet given to certain officers in the *ci-devant* German empire, who composed a court which decided, without appeal, in all judicial processes entered in it. This court, which was proverbial for the slow administration of justice, had not only concurrent jurisdiction with the court of the imperial chamber, but, in many cases, exclusive jurisdiction. The right of appeal, possessed by the estates, existed also in regard to the judicial decisions of the aulic court.

AURE'OLA, in its original signification, denotes a jewel, which is proposed as a reward of victory in some public dispute. Hence, the Roman schoolmen applied it to the reward bestowed on martyrs, virgins, &c., on account of their works of supererogation; and painters use it to signify the crown of glory with which they adorn the heads of saints, confessors, &c.

AU'RUM MOSA'ICUM, a combination of tin and sulphur, used by statuaries and painters, for giving a gold color to their figures.

AUS'PICES, a kind of soothsaying among the Romans, by the flight or singing of birds.

AUTHENTIC MEL'ODIES, in music, such as have their principal notes contained between the key-note and its octave. This term is applied by the Italians to four of the church modes or tones in music which rise a fourth above their dominants, which are always fifths above their finals, that is, rise to complete their octaves, thus distinguished from plagal melodies, which fall a fourth below their finals.

AUTOBIOG'RAPHY, this word is of Greek origin, and signifies literally *the life of a person written by himself.* These memoirs may be divided into two classes: those in which the chief object of the writer is to illustrate the history of his own mind and heart, and the manner in which these were swayed by the destinies of his life; and those in which his purpose is merely to give a sketch of the scenes and events which have occurred within his own experience, and of characters with which he has been brought in contact. Of the first class of writings, from the Confession of Saint Augustine down to the Confessions of Rousseau, and the many works which have since been produced in imitation of the latter, it may be said that the general defect is a morbid spirit of exaggeration. Of the more narrative class of memoirs, it is sufficient to say, that where the writer was himself a prominent actor in passing events, they are usually little better than apologies or self-justifications, such as the famous Memoirs of the Cardinal de Retz, and, in our own times, the various fragments of autobiography which have been published from the hand of Napoleon.

AUTOCH'THONS, the Greek term for the aboriginal inhabitants of a country, implying that they were sprung from the soil. The Athenians, whose territory had been held by the same race from time immemorial, chiefly on account of its sterility, which offered no incitement to foreign aggression, particularly laid claim to this title, in memorial of which they wore the emblematic grasshopper as part of their head-dress.

AUTO-DA-FE, properly AUTO-DE-FE, a public solemnity held by the Court of the Inquisition in Spain and Portugal. It was a jail delivery, at which extracts from the trials of offenders, and the sentences pronounced by the judges, were read; after which absolution was conferred on those who were penitent, and discharged: after which, those condemned to death (relaja dos) were transferred to the secular authority: and here the auto, properly so called, ended; the execution of the victims taking place immediately afterwards, under the authority of the civil judge, a secretary to the inquisition attending.

AU'TOGRAPH, an epithet, applied to whatever is written in a person's own hand-writing, as an autograph letter, a letter of one's own writing.

AU'TUMN, the third season in the year, which begins in the northern hemisphere, on the day when the sun enters Libra, that is, on the 22d of September. It terminates about the same day in December, when the winter commences. Autumn is represented, in painting, by a man of mature age, clothed and girt with a starry girdle; holding in one hand a pair of scales equally poised, with a globe in each; and in the other a bunch of grapes and other fruit. His age denotes the perfection of this season; and the balance, that sign of the zodiac which the sun enters when our autumn begins.

AUXIL'IARY VERBS, in grammar, are such verbs as help to form or conjugate others; as, in English, the verbs "to have," and "to be."

AVA'TAR, a term used by the Hindoos to express an incarnation or descent of Vishnu, their deity: nine of which are believed to be passed, and the tenth yet to come.

A'VE MARI'A, the name given to the angel Gabriel's salutation to the Virgin Mary. Also, the chaplets and rosaries of the Romish church, which are divided into ave-marias and pater-nosters.

AVER'NUS, a lake of Italy 10 miles west of Naples, celebrated in antiquity as the entrance to the infernal regions. This place continued to be the favorite haunt of superstition till the time of Augustus, who violated its sanctity, and dispelled the impenetrable darkness in which it had hitherto been enshrouded, by cutting down the surrounding wood, and connecting it with the Lucrine lake, then an arm of the sea. This lake still exists under the name Lago d'Averno; it is about a mile and a half in circumference, and in many places 190 feet deep.

AWARD', in law, the judgment of an arbitrator, or of one who is not appointed by the law a judge, but chosen by the parties themselves for terminating their differences.

AX'IOM, in philosophy, is such a plain, self-evident proposition, that it cannot be made more plain and evident by demonstration; because it is itself better known than anything that can be brought to prove it. By axioms, called also maxims, are understood all common notions of the mind, whose evidence is so clear and forcible, that a man cannot deny them without renouncing common sense and natural reason.

AZ'URE, the blue color of the sky. Among painters, this word originally signified *lapis-lazuli*, and the blue color prepared from it. At present it is called *ultra-marine;* and the blue glass made from the earth of cobalt and other vitrifiable matters, which, when in masses, is called *smalt*, is, in the state of fine powder, known by the name of *azure*. Azure being employed to color starch, is also called *starch-blue*.

AZ'YMITES, in church history, Christians who administer the eucharist with unleavened bread. This appellation was given to the Latin by the Greek church, and also to the Armenians and Maronites.

B.

B, the second letter, and first consonant, in the alphabet, is formed in the voice by a strong and quick expression of the breath, and a sudden opening of the lips; it is therefore called a *labial*, and its pronunciation differs but slightly from *p* and *v*. It is often used as an abbreviation for *Bachelor*, as B.A. Bachelor of Arts, B.D. Bachelor of Divinity, &c., and for *before*, as B.C., Before Christ. B, as a numeral among the Romans, stood for 300, and with a dash over it for 3000. B, in chronology, stands for one of the dominical letters, and in music for the seventh note in the gamut.

BA'AL, an idol among the ancient Chaldeans and Syrians; supposed to represent the sun, and to be the same as the Bel or Belus of the Greeks. The word signifies also lord or commander; and the character of the idol was varied by different nations, at different times.

BABYLON'ICA, in antiquity, a species of rich weaving so called from the city of Babylon, where the art of weaving hangings with a variety of colors was first invented.

BABYLON'ICS, in literary history, a fragment of the ancient history of the world, ending at 267 years before Christ; and composed by Berosus, a priest of Babylon, about the time of Alexander.

BAC'CHÆ, the priestesses of Bacchus, who, crowned with vine and ivy leaves, and clad in the skins of wild beasts, celebrated the orgies of their god with frantic cries and gestures. They were also called *Mænades*, *Bassarides*, and *Thyades*.

BACCHANA'LIA, feasts celebrated in honor of Bacchus by the ancient Greeks and Romans. Their times of celebration were spring and autumn: the former in the city, and the latter in the fields. The company personified Silenus, Pan, Fauns, Satyrs, &c.; and in this manner appeared in public, night and day, counterfeiting drunkenness, dancing obscenely, committing all kinds of licentiousness and debauchery; and running over the mountains and forests, with horrible shrieks and howlings, crying out *Evoe Bacche*, or *Io Bacche*. Livy informs us, that during the Bacchanalian feasts at Rome, such shocking disorders were practised under the cover of the night, and those who were initiated were bound to conceal them by an oath attended with horrid imprecations, that the senate suppressed them first in Rome, and afterwards throughout all Italy.

BACH'ELOR, in its primitive sense, means a man who has not been married: and in all its various senses it seems to include the idea of youth or immaturity.—Bachelor, in universities, is one who has attained the first degree in the liberal arts and sciences, or the first degree in the particular study to which he devotes himself. This degree of honor is called the *baccalaureate*. At Oxford and at Cambridge, to attain the degree of bachelor of arts, a person must have studied there four years: after three more, he may become master of arts; and at the end of another series of seven, bachelor of divinity.

BACK'GROUND, in painting, is the space behind a portrait or group of figures. The distance in a picture is usually divided into the foreground, middle-distance, and background. In portrait-painting, the nature and treatment of backgrounds have varied in the hands of almost every master, yet there are certain recognized methods which are more worthy of imitation and study than others. In most of the portraits of Titian, Vandyke, and Rembrandt, the backgrounds represent only *space*, indicated by a warm brown gray tone, and this treatment is the most effective.

BACK-PAINTING, the method of painting mezzotinto prints pasted on glass with oil colors.

BADGE, an exterior ornament of a coat of arms, originally worn by the retainers or attendants of the nobility. It fell into disuse in the reign of queen Elizabeth.—In naval architecture, an ornament placed on the outside of ships near the stern, containing either a window, or the representation of one.

BAD'GER, a quadruped of the *genus ursus*.

BAG'PIPE, a musical wind instrument used chiefly in Scotland and Ireland. It is of high antiquity, and consists of two parts: namely, a leathern bag, and pipes for admitting and ejecting the air. One of the pipes called the drone, with which the bass part is played, never varies its tone. The third pipe is played on by compressing the bag under the arm.

BAIL, in law, sureties given for the appearance, when required, of a person in custody. *Common Bail* is in common cases, where any sureties may be taken; but *Special Bail* is necessary in matters of greater importance, where special surety of two or more persons must be taken according to the value of the cause.—*To admit to bail*, is to release upon security given by bondsmen.—*To justify bail*, is to prove by the oath of the person that he is worth the sum for which he is surety beyond his debts.

BAILEE', in law, the person to whom the goods of the one that is bailed are delivered. The party who delivers the goods is termed the Bailor.

BAL'CONY, in architecture, a projection from the front of a house, surrounded by a balustrade or open gallery. In large buildings they are susceptible of considerable elegance of decoration, and may be made highly ornamental to the edifices to which they are attached.

BALD'ACHIN, in architecture, a kind of canopy erected over an altar.

BAL'LAD, a short lyric composition, or tale in verse, of a simple and popular character; set to music, and generally in most esteem by the lower classes. It originally meant a solemn song of praise.

BAL'LET, a theatrical representation of actions, characters, sentiments, and passions, by means of mimic movements and dances, accompanied by music. The ballet is divided into three kinds—historical, mythological, and allegorical; and consist of three parts—the entry, the figure, and the retreat.

BAL'USTER, (often improperly written *bannister*,) in architecture, a small turned column usually introduced between piers, on the upper parts of large buildings under windows, and on balconies, &c.

BALUSTRADE', a series or row of balusters, joined by a rail: serving as well for rest to the elbows, as for a fence or inclosure to balconies, altars, staircases, &c.

BAN, (*bannum*,) in the feudal law, a solemn proclamation or publication of anything. Hence the custom of asking, or publishing the bans, before marriage.—Ban, in military affairs, a proclamation made in the army, by beat of drum, sound of trumpet, &c., requiring the strict observance of discipline, either for the declaring a new officer, or punishing an offender.—The word Ban also means an edict of interdiction or proscription. Thus, to put a prince under the *ban* of the empire, is to divest him of his dignities, and to interdict all intercourse and all offices of humanity with the offender.

BAND, in architecture, a term used to denote what is generally called a face or fascia. To speak correctly, it signifies a flat, low, square, profiled member without respect to its place. That member in a cornice on which modillions or dentils are cut is called the modillion band in the former, and the dentil band in the latter case.

BANDOLEER', a large leathern belt, thrown over the right shoulder, and hanging under the left arm, worn by ancient musketeers, for sustaining their fire-arms and musket-charges.

BANDIT'TI, a term peculiarly denoting companies of armed robbers, formerly common in Italy and France; but sometimes also used, in a more general sense, for robbers, pirates, outlaws, or others, united for nefarious purposes.

BANGUE, the name of an opiate used in the East, made from the leaf of wild hemp. It is used by the Mahometans for the same purpose as wine and spirits are by the Christians.

BAN'IAN-DAYS, a proverbial expression, imported from the Asiatic colonies, used for a short or indifferent dinner, or days on which no animal food is eaten: in allusion to the Banians described below.

BAN'IANS, a caste of the Hindoos, whose profession is trade and merchandise; and, in India and Asia, they are the great factors and bankers, as the Jews are in the West. They believe in the transmigration of souls, and not only abstain from eating the flesh of animals, but endeavor to release even the most noxious from the cruelty of others. They are mild in temper, and honest in their dealings; and are so cautious of having communication with any but their own caste, that if any of another nation or tribe has drunk out of or touched their cup, they break it.

BAN'IAN-TREE, one of the greatest wonders of the vegetable kingdom. It never dies, and continually extends itself; for every branch shoots downward, and, striking into the ground, becomes itself a parent tree, whose branches, in like manner, spread. One of them, the Cubbeer Burr, has 350 stems, equal to large oaks, and more than 3000 smaller ones, covering space sufficient to shelter 7000 persons. Its branches are crowded with families of monkeys, and with birds of every description, and also with enormous bats, all of which find luxurious subsistence upon the rich scarlet figs that grow upon it.

BANK, in commerce, an establishment for the receiving of moneys and letting them out on interest. It may likewise be defined, a place used as a common repository of the money of individuals or companies. Also, a company of persons concerned in a private bank; or the directors of an incorporated one. The basis of all banking is the profitable use to which the banker or company can apply the capital which is deposited. The first bank was established at Venice about 1157, and the name of Banco was given to it in Italian, from the bench which the money-changers or bankers used to sit upon in their burses or exchanges.

BANK'ER, a person who traffics in money, by receiving the current cash of individuals free of interest, and negotiating with it, either in the discount of bills, or the advance of money on sufficient securities. The moneyed goldsmiths in the reign of king Charles II. first acquired this name.—The Romans had two sorts of bankers, whose office was much more extensive than that of the bankers among us; theirs being that of public affairs, in whom were united the functions of a broker, agent, banker, and notary, managing the exchange, taking in money, assisting in buying and selling, and drawing the writings necessary on all these occasions.

BANK-NOTE, or BANK-BILL, a promissory note, issued by a banking company, properly signed and countersigned, payable to the *bearer* in the current coin of the realm, on demand.

BAN'NER, a square flag, or the principal standard belonging to a prince or state.

BAN'NERET, an ancient order of knights or feudal lords, who, possessing several large fees, led their own flag or banner. As the spirit of the feudal system declined, persons came to be created bannerets, and hence the institution must have become merely titular. The last knight of this description was Sir John Smith, on whom the honor was bestowed after Edgehill fight, for rescuing the standard of Charles I. On the day of battle, the candidate presented his flag to the king or general, who cutting off the train or skirt, and making it a square, returned it again. Hence, bannerets are sometimes called knights of the square flag.

BAP'TISM, a rite of the Christian religion, by which the members of its church are received into the communion. Almost all sects of Christians style baptism a sacrament, and consider its use as important; but the manner in which it ought to be performed, and the effects to be derived from it, have been subjects of much controversy.

BAP'TISTERY, in ecclesiastical writers, a place in which the ceremony of baptism is performed. In the ancient church, it was one of the *exedræ* or buildings distinct from the church itself, and consisted of a porch or ante-room, where the persons to be baptized made their confession of faith, and an inner room where the ceremony of baptism was performed. Thus it continued till the sixth century, when the baptisteries began to be taken into the church-porch; and afterwards into the church itself.

BAP'TISTS (a contraction of ANABAPTISTS), a Christian sect who practise the baptism of adults instead of that of children.

BAR, the partition which separates the members of a court of justice from those who have to report or hear. It is also applied to the benches, where the lawyers are seated, because anciently there was a bar to separate the pleaders from the attorneys and others. Hence those who are called to the bar, or licensed to plead, are termed *barristers*, an appellation equivalent to *licentiate* in other countries.—BAR, in music, a stroke drawn perpendicularly across the lines of a piece of music, including between each two a certain quantity or measure of time.

BARALYP'TON, in logic, an indirect mode of syllogism, consisting of two universals and one particular affirmative proposition: as, "Every animal is endued with sense; every man is an animal; therefore something endued with sense is man."

BARA'THRUM, in antiquity, a deep pit, with sharp spikes at the top and bottom, into which condemned persons were cast headlong, at Athens.

BAR'BARA, in logic, an arbitrary term for the first mode of the first figure of syllogisms, consisting of three universal propositions: as, "All animals are endued with sense: all men are animals; therefore, all men are endued with sense."

BAR'BARA, ST., the patron saint of those who might otherwise die impenitent. Her attributes are, 1. The cup, given her as a sign that those who honored her could not die without the sacrament. 2. A tower, her father having shut her up in one when a child. 3. The sword by which she was beheaded. 4. A crown which she wears as a symbol of victory and reward. St. Barbara, who was the patron saint of Mantua, was a favorite subject with the artists of the middle ages.

BARBA'RIAN, a name given by the ancient Greeks and Romans to all who were not of their own country, or were not instituted in their language, manners, and customs. In this sense the word signified with them no more than foreigner, not signifying, as with us, a wild, rude, or uncivilized person.

BAR'BARISM, in a general sense, a rudeness of language or behavior.—In grammar, an offence against the purity of style or language; or a mode of speaking or writing contrary to the true idiom of any particular language.

BAR'BITON, the name given to the lyre of Apollo.

BARD, the name given to those individuals of semi-barbarous tribes, whose genius or imagination enabled them to describe events in elevated or measured language. Homer was one of these bards among the early Greeks; Ossian another among the ancient Irish; and their rhapsodies were the foundations of the art of poetry, which has been cultivated with success by all civilized nations. In the first stages of society, in all countries, bards have made a conspicuous figure; and the "light of the song" has been the morning-beam that first broke upon the darkness of ignorance: but nowhere does it appear, did ever verse and its professors receive so much public regard as under the druidical establishment; a regard with which they continued to be honored long after that system had perished. In battle the bards of the Celtic tribes raised the war-cry, and in peace they sung the exploits of their heroes, celebrated the attributes of their gods, and chronicled the history of their nation. Originally spread over the greater part of western Europe, they seem to have been the heralds, the priests, and the lawgivers of the free barbarians who first occupied its ancient forests, until, by the gradual progress of southern civilization and despotism, they were driven back into the fastnesses of Wales, Scotland, and Ireland, where the last echoes of their harps have long since died away.

BARGE, in naval affairs, a boat of state and pleasure, adorned with various ornaments, having bales and tilts, and seats covered with cushions, and carpets, and benches for many oars; as a company's barge, an admiral's barge, &c. It is also the name of a flat-bottomed vessel employed for carrying goods on a navigable river, as those upon the river Thames, called west country barges.

BAR'NABAS, St., representations of this saint are seldom to be met with, except in the works of the Venetian artists. He is usually depicted as a venerable man, of majestic mien, holding the Gospel of St. Matthew in his hand. The subjects are chiefly taken from the Acts of the Apostles, and from the life of St. Paul.

BAR'ON, a degree of nobility next below a viscount, and above a baronet. Originally, the barons being the feudatories of princes, were the proprietors of land held by honorable service: hence, in ancient records, the word *barons* comprehends all the nobility.—Barons of the Exchequer, the four judges to whom the administration of justice is committed, in causes between the king and his subjects, relating to matters concerning the revenue. They were formerly barons of the realm, but of late are generally persons learned in the laws.

BARON AND FEMME, a term in law for husband and wife, who are deemed but one person; so that a wife cannot be witness for or against her husband; nor he for or against his wife, except in cases of high treason.

BAR'ONET, the lowest degree of honor that is hereditary, being next below a baron, and above a knight. The order was founded by king James I. at the suggestion of Sir Robert Cotton, when 200 baronets were created at once: to which number it was intended that they should be always restrained: but it is now enlarged at the royal pleasure, without limitation.

BAR'RACKS, large buildings erected for the security and accommodation of soldiers, whether infantry or cavalry.

BAR'RATOR, in law, a common mover, or maintainer of suits and quarrels, either in courts or elsewhere; an encourager of litigation.

BARRICADE', or BARRICA'DO, a fortification made in haste, of trees, earth, palisades, wagons, or anything that will obstruct the progress of an enemy, or serve for defence or security against his attack.

BAR'RISTER, a counsellor learned in the law, admitted to plead at the bar, and there to take upon him the protection and defence of clients.

BARTHOL'OMEW, St., the Apostle, generally depicted with a knife, and his skin in his hand. The horrible scene of his being flayed alive, by order of the chief magistrate of Albanopolis, who condemned him also to be crucified, has been painted by some artists.

BAR'YTONE, in music, a male voice the compass of which partakes of the common bass and the tenor, being lower than the one and higher than the other.

BASAL'TES, or BASALT', a stone supposed to be of volcanic origin, black or green in color, and found in pillars in the prismatic form. Columns of basalt form the Giant's Causeway, the Isle of Staffa, and Fingal's Cave, and are always found near great volcanoes, as Hecla, &c. It is remarkably hard and heavy, will not strike fire with steel, and is a fine touch-stone.

BASE, in architecture, is used for any body which bears another, but particularly for the lower part of a column and pedestal. The base of columns is differently formed in different orders: thus, the Tuscan base consists only of a single torus, besides the plinth; the Doric has an astragal more than the Tuscan; the Ionic has a large torus over two slender scotias, separated by two astragals; the Corinthian has two toruses, two scotias, and two astragals: the Composite has an astragal less than the Corinthian; the Attic base has two toruses and a scotia, and is proper for either the Ionic or Composite columns.

BASHAW', Pasha', or Pacha', a dignity under the Turkish government. *Bashaw*, used absolutely, denotes the prime vizier; other bashaws, which are generally governors of provinces or cities, being distinguished by the name of the place under their command. The appellation is given by way of courtesy to almost every person of any figure at the Grand Signior's court. Their degrees of dignity were marked by their bearing one, two, or three horses' tails.

BASIL, St., representations of this saint, who was Bishop of Cesarea, are very rare. He is represented in Greek pontificals bareheaded, with an emaciated appearance.

BASIL'ICÆ, anciently, public halls or courts of judicature, where princes and magistrates sat to administer justice. They were at first the palaces of princes, but were finally converted into churches. Hence *basilic* now means a church, chapel, cathedral, or royal palace.

BASS, (sometimes written *base*, which is the correct English word for *basso*, low:) the lowest or fundamental part in mesic, and important as the foundation of harmony.—*Thorough bass* is that which includes the fundamental rules of composition.—*Ground bass* is that which commences with some subject of its own that is continually repeated throughout the movement, whilst the upper parts pursue a separate air.—*Counter bass* is a second or double bass, where there are several in the same concert.

BAS'SO, in music, the Italian for *bass*. Thus, *Basso concertante*, is the bass of the little chorus; *basso repieno*, the bass of the grand chorus; and *basso continuo*, that part of a composition which is set for the organ, &c.

BASSOON'. a musical wind instrument, consisting of a very long tube, with a reed for the mouthpiece.

BAS'SO RELIE'VO, or BASS RELIEF, sculpture in which the figures are represented as projecting not far above the plane on which they are formed. Figures cut are said to be done in *relief*, and when the work is low or flat it is called *bass relief*, or *basso relievo*, in distinction from *alto relievo* and *mezzo relievo*.

BASS VIOL, a stringed musical instrument of the same shape as a violin, but much larger.

BASTILE', a noted fortress in Paris, which was used as a state prison, and in which many persons who had incurred the resentment of the French monarchs, or their ministers, had been immured for life. It was built at the latter part of the 14th century; and was demolished by the enraged populace at the commencement of the revolution in 1789.

BASTINA'DO, a mode of punishment used among the Turks, of beating the offender on the soles of the feet.

BATH, (KNIGHTS OF THE) a military order of knighthood in England, supposed to have been instituted by Richard II., who limited the number of knights to four; but his successor, Henry IV., on the day of his coronation increased them to forty-six. This order received its denomination from a custom of bathing before the knights received the golden spur. The badge or symbol of the order is a sceptre, rose, thistle, and three imperial crowns conjoined within a circle, upon which is the motto, "Tria juncta in uno," alluding to the three cardinal virtues—faith, hope, and charity. The order of the bath, after remaining many years extinct, was revived under George I., by a solemn creation of a great number of knights.

BA'TON', in music, a term denoting a rest of four semibreves.

BATOON', in architecture, a moulding in the base of a column.

BAT'TEL, an ancient mode of trial by single combat, which was introduced into England by William the Conqueror. The contest was had before the judges, on a piece of ground enclosed, and the combatants were bound to fight until the stars appeared, unless the death of one party or victory sooner decided the contest. It is but of late years that this barbarous law has been abolished.

BAT'TERING-RAM, a military machine, with which the ancients made breaches in fortifications. These engines were variously constructed, and of different sizes; but in general the battering-ram consisted of a vast beam suspended to a frame, and armed at one end with a head of iron, resembling that of a ram; from the butting of which animal the idea was doubtless derived. This being equally balanced, and furnished with a number of ropes, at the extremity opposite to the ram's head, a great number of men threw it forward with violence, and thus, by a repetition of the strokes, demolished the wall against which it was directed.

BAT'TERY, in the military art, a parapet thrown up to cover the gunners and men employed about the guns from the enemy's shot. This parapet is cut into embrasures for the cannon to fire through. A *battery of mortars* is sunk in the ground, and has no embrasures.—BATTERY, in law, the striking, beating, or offering any violence to another person, for which damages may be recovered. It is distinguished from an *assault*, inasmuch as the latter does not necessarily imply a hitting or blow. There may be an assault without battery, but battery always implies an assault.

BAT'TLE-AXE, a kind of halberd, first introduced into England by the Danes, and much used in the early part of the middle ages.

BAT'TLEMENTS, in architecture, are indentures or notches in the top of a wall, or other building, in the form of embrasures.

BATTOL'OGY, in grammar, a superfluous repetition of some words or things.

BAY, or BAY TREE, the female laurel tree, an evergreen which grows wild in Italy and France.—BAYS, in the plural, an honorary garland or crown, bestowed as a prize for victory or excellence, anciently made of laurel branches.

BAY'ONET, a short pointed instrument or triangular dagger, make to fix on the muzzle of a firelock or musket.

BAZAR', or BAZAAR', a kind of exchange or market-place among the Turks and Persians. Some of these buildings are remarkable, not only for their extent, but for their magnificence.—This name has of late years been in use to denote certain large buildings containing a collection of shops or stalls, let to different persons, and in which a great variety of "fancy goods" are exposed for sale.

BDEL'LIUM, a gummy resinous juice, produced by a tree in the East Indies, of which we have no satisfactory account. It is brought into Europe from the East Indies, and from Arabia.

BEA'CON, a signal erected on a long pole, upon an eminence, consisting of a pitch-barrel or other combustible matter, to be fired at night, to notify the approach of an enemy. Also, any object serving as an occasional signal, or as a constant seamark, by means of which ships may be warned of danger, or assured of their port.

BEAD, in architecture, a round moulding, commonly made upon the edge of a piece of stuff, in the Corinthian and Roman orders, cut or carved in short embossments, like beads in necklaces.

BEATIFICA'TION, an act of the Pope, by which he declares a person beatified or blessed after death, and is the first step towards canonization, or the raising of one to the dignity of a saint; but no person can be beatified till fifty years after his death.

BEAT'INGS, in music, the regular pausative swellings of sound, produced in an organ by pipes of the same key, when not in unison, and their vibrations not simultaneous or coincident.

BEAT'ING TIME, in music, that motion of the hand or foot by which some person marks and regulates the movements of the performers.

BEAU IDE'AL, in painting, that beauty which is freed from the deformity and peculiarity found in nature in all individuals of a species. All the objects which nature exhibits to us have their blemishes and defects, though every eye is not capable of perceiving them; and it is only by long habit of observing what any objects of the same kind have in common that it acquires the faculty of discerning what each wants in particular. By such means the artist gains an idea of perfect nature, or what is called the *Beau Ideal.*

BEAU'TY, a general term for whatever excites in us pleasing sensations or causes our admiration. Or it may be defined to be an assemblage of graces or properties which please the eye and interest the mind. The proportion and symmetry of parts, the regularity and symmetry of features, the expression of the eye, and the complexion, are among the principal properties which constitute *personal* beauty. This kind is said to be *intrinsic*, and immediately perceptible; but when reflection is requisite to comprehend the utility of an object, it is said to be *relative:* for instance, the beauty of a machine is not perceived till we understand its uses and adaptation to its purpose. Thus, an object may please the understanding without interesting the sense; and on the other hand, we perceive agreeable sensations, excited by some objects, whose ideas are not related to anything that is praiseworthy.—BEAUTY, in architecture, painting, and other arts, is the harmony and justness of the whole composition taken together.

BEL-ESPRIT', a term formerly naturalized in England, applied to those individuals whose conversation or writings display an agreeable sprightliness or vivacity.

BELLES-LET'TRES, or POLITE LITERATURE, in its most obvious sense, is that description of literature which has a peculiar reference to matters of taste: but according to many writers, the term has a much more extensive signification, and is made to comprehend not merely every elegant acquirement, but nearly every branch of knowledge.

BEL'LEVUE, a name given in France to small country-seats, or to arched bowers at the end of a garden or park, intended for the enjoyment of fresh air in the shade.

BELLONA'RII, in Roman antiquity, the priests of Bellona, who, in honor of that goddess, used to make incisions in their bodies; and after having gathered the blood in the palm of their hand, give it to those who were partakers of their mysteries.

BEL-META'LO DI VOCE, in music, an Italian expression for a clear and brilliant-toned *soprano* voice.

BEL'VEDERE, a name given in Italy

to the cupolas on palaces or large houses, which are ascended for the enjoyment of a fine prospect and the advantage of a pure air. This is the name also of a part of the Vatican, where the famous statue of Apollo is placed, and which, on this account, is called the *Apollo Belvedere.*

BENCH, in law, a seat of justice, as the Queen's Bench at Westminster. Also, the persons sitting on a bench, as a bench of magistrates.

BENCH'ER, a lawyer of the oldest standing in the inns of court.

BENEDIC'TINES, a celebrated order of monks, who profess to follow the rules of St. Benedict. They wear a loose black gown with large white sleeves, and a cowl on the head, ending in a point. They are the same that are called *Black-friars.*

BENEFIT OF CLERGY, a privilege, originating in a superstitious regard for the church, whereby the clergy were either partially or wholly exempted from the jurisdiction of the lay tribunals. It extended in England only to the case of felony; and though it was intended to apply only to clerical felons or clerks, yet as every one who could read was by the laws of England, considered to be a clerk, when the rudiments of learning came to be diffused almost every person became entitled to this privilege.

BE'NE PLA'CITO, in music, an Italian term, denoting that the performer is to exercise his own taste.

BENZOIN', a solid balsam, yielded from incisions made in a tree which grows in Sumatra, called the Styrax Benzoin. It is hard, friable, with an agreeable fragrant odor, soluble in alcohol, ether, and oil of turpentine. It has been employed as an ingredient in spirit varnishes by the Italians and Spaniards, but does not appear to have been an ingredient in oil varnishes.

BER'NARDINES, an order of monks, founded by Robert, abbot of Moleme, and reformed by St. Bernard. They wear a white robe with a black scapulary, and when they officiate they are clad in a large white gown, with great sleeves, and a hood of the same color.

BE'TA, the second letter in the Greek alphabet.

BEY, among the Turks, signifies a governor of a country or town. The Turks write it *begh*, or *beg*, but pronounce it *bey*. The word is particularly applied to a lord of a banner, whom they call sangiac-beg or bey. Every province in Turkey is divided into seven sangiacs, or banners, each of which qualifies a bey, and these are all commanded by the governor of the province, whom they also call begler-beg, that is, lord of all the beys of the province.

BI'BLE, (THE BOOK,) a name given by way of eminence to the Sacred Writings. The Old Testament consists of the five books called the Pentateuch; the Historical, Poetical, and Prophetic books: the New Testament, of the four Gospels, the Acts, and the Epistles. The earliest version of the Bible is a Greek translation called the Septuagint, and from this other translations have been made. It was first printed in English in 1535. The present authorized version of the Holy Scriptures was completed in the reign of James the First, about the year 1603.

BIBLIOG'RAPHY, the knowledge of books as to their several editions, time of being printed, and other information tending to illustrate the history of literature.

BIBLIOM'ANCY, a kind of divination, performed by means of the Bible, by selecting passages of Scripture at hazard, and drawing from them indications concerning future events.

BIBLIOTHE'CA, in its original and proper sense, denotes a library, or place for depositing books. In matters of literature, it means a treatise giving an account of all the writers on a certain subject; thus, we have bibliothecas of theology, law, philosophy, &c. There are likewise universal bibliothecas, which treat indifferently of books of all kinds.

BIG'AMY, double marriage, or the marrying of two wives or two husbands while the first is living.

BIGA'RIUS, in antiquity, the charioteer of a *biga*, or two-wheeled chariot. Money or medals stamped with this emblem were called *biga'ti.*

BIG'OT, a person who is obstinately and unreasonably wedded to a particular religious creed, practice, or opinion; or one who is illiberally attached to any opinion or system of belief.

BI'NARY MEASURE, in music, that in which the raising the hand or foot is equal to that of falling, usually called common time. The Italians are accustomed after a recitative to use the phrase *a tempo giusto*, to indicate that the measure is to be beat true and correct, which is otherwise conducted in the recitative in order to express passion, &c.

BIOG'RAPHY, the life of one or more individuals whose actions are deemed worthy of record. No species of history can be more entertaining or instructive than the lives of eminent men, who by their private virtues or public deeds, by the efforts of genius or the impulses of philanthropy, excite our admiration, and afford examples for posterity to emulate.

BIRD'S-EYE VIEW, in the Fine Arts, a term used to denote a view arranged according to the laws of perspective, in which the point of sight or situation of the eye is placed at a very considerable height above the objects viewed and delineated. In architectural representations, it is used chiefly for the purpose of exhibiting the disposition of the different courts or quadrangles and roofs of a building. It is a useful method of representing battles, as also of giving a general notion of a small district of a country.

BIS, in music, a word placed over passages which have dots postfixed to one bar, and prefixed to a subsequent bar, signifying that the passage between the dots is to be twice played.

BIS'CUIT, a kind of white, unglazed, baked porcelain-clay, much employed in the manufacture of statuettes, &c., but for this purpose, a much finer and more suitable material is the so-called PARIAN. Biscuit is the term generally applied to articles of clay, which have gone through only one "baking" or "firing" in the oven, and which have not received the glaze. In this state it is porous, and is used for wine-coolers, and for other purposes.

BISH'OP, a prelate, or person consecrated for the spiritual government of a diocese. In Great Britain, bishops are nominated by the sovereign, who, upon request of the dean and chapter for leave to elect a bishop, sends a *conge d'elire*, or license to elect, with a letter missive, nominating the person whom he would have chosen.

BISSEX'TILE, or LEAP-YEAR, a year consisting of 366 days, and happening every fourth year, by the addition of a day in the month of February, which that year consists of 29 days. And this is done to recover the six hours which the sun takes up nearly in his course, more than the 365 days commonly allowed for it in other years.

BIS'TRE, or BIS'TER, the burnt oil extracted from the soot of beech-wood, which is used as a brown pigment by painters.

BLACK, a well-known color, supposed to be owing to the absence of light, most of the rays falling upon black substances being not reflected but absorbed. There are several species of blacks used in painting; as *Frankfort black*, of which there are two sorts, one a natural earth inclining to blue; and the other made from the lees of wine burnt, washed, and ground with ivory, bones, &c.; *lamp black*, the smoke of resin, prepared by melting it in iron vessels; *ivory black*, made of burnt ivory, and used in miniatures; *Spanish black*, made of burnt cork, and first used by the Spaniards.

BLACK LETTER, is the name now applied to the old English or modern Gothic letter, which was introduced into England about the middle of the fourteenth century, and became the character generally used in MS. works before the art of printing was publicly practised in Europe. On the application of that art to the multiplying of books, about the middle of the fifteenth century, the block books, and subsequently those written with movable types, were in this character, to imitate writing, and were disposed of as manuscripts; and so perfect was the imitation, that it required great discrimination to distinguish the printed from the written. The first printed Bible, known as "the Mentz Bible without date," was an instance of this.

BLACK'-MAIL, a certain rate of money, corn, or cattle, anciently paid, in the north of England, to certain persons connected with the moss-troopers, or robbers, to be by them protected from pillage.

BLANK, a void space in any writing or printing. This word is applied to various objects, usually in the sense of destitution, or emptiness.

BLANK-VERSE, in poetry, that which is composed of a certain number of syllables, without the assistance of rhyme.

BLOCKADE', in military affairs, the blocking up a place, by posting troops at all the avenues leading to it, to keep supplies of men and provisions from getting into it; and by these means proposing to starve it out, without making any regular attacks.—To *raise a blockade*, is to force the troops that blockade to retire.

BLUE, one of the seven primitive colors into which they are divided when refracted through a glass prism. Blue, as a color in painting, is distinguished into *ultra-marine*, from the azure stone, called *lapis lazuli*; *Prussian blue*, a color next to ultra-marine for beauty; *blue ashes*, used in limning, fresco, and miniature; *blue verditer*, a blue somewhat inclining to a green; and *bice*, which is the palest of all the bright blues. In dyeing, the principal ingredients for giving a blue color are *indigo* and *woad*.

BODY, in matters of literature, denotes much the same with system, being a collection of everything belonging to a particular science or art, disposed in proper order: thus we say, a body of divinity, law, physic, &c.

BOLD'NESS, that quality which distinguishes the artist, who, educated in the soundest principles of art, designs and executes with fearlessness and decision. When under proper control, it imparts to all his productions a vigor that is sure to charm. It is exhibited in the highest degree in the works of Rubens.

BOLOGNESE' SCHOOL, in painting, sometimes called the *Lombard school* of painting. It was founded by the Caracci, and its object was to unite the excellencies of the preceding schools; hence it is occasionally called the *Eclectic school*. Among the principal painters which it numbered were Domenichino, Lanfranco, Corregio, Guido, Schidone, Caravagio, Zampieri, Primaticcio, &c.

BOMB, a large shell or ball of cast iron, round and hollow, with a vent to receive a fusee, which is made of wood, and filled with combustible materials of all kinds. This being done, and the fusee driven into the vent, the fusee is set on fire, and the bomb is thrown from the mortar, in such a direction as to fall into a fort, city, or enemy's camp, when it bursts with great violence, and often with terrible effect, blowing into pieces whatever may be in its way.

BOM'BAST, in literary composition, an inflated style, by which, in attempting to raise a low or familiar subject beyond its rank, the writer seldom fails to be ridiculous.

BONA DEA, in Roman mythology, a goddess concerning whom a great diversity of opinion prevails, even among the writers of antiquity. She is represented by Macrobius, who treats at length upon her nature and worship, as synonymous with the Grecian Rhea or Cybele. The Bona Dea had two temples at Rome; but her rites were generally solemnized in the house of the consul or prætor. In the celebration of these rites only women participated, thereby indicating the peculiar chastity of the goddess. But a perusal of the ancient writers will convince the most skeptical that the exclusion of men from the solemnities of the Bona Dea was purely nominal, and that in the course of time the grossest licentiousness was practised during their celebration.

BOND, in architecture, the connection of one stone or brick with another by lapping them over each other in carrying up work, so that an inseparable mass of building may be formed, which could not be the case if every vertical joint was over that below it.—BOND, in law, a deed whereby the obligator, or party binding himself, obliges himself, his heirs, executors, and administrators, to pay a certain sum of money, called the penalty, to another (the obligee) at a day appointed.—BOND, ENGLISH, in architecture, that disposition of bricks in a wall wherein the courses are alternately composed of *headers*, or bricks laid with their heads or ends towards the faces of the wall, and in the superior and inferior courses of *stretchers* or bricks, with their lengths parallel to the faces of the walls, as in the margin, in which the upper is called the heading, and the lower the stretching course.—BOND, FLEMISH, in architecture, that disposition of bricks in a wall wherein each course has headers and stretchers alternately, as in the margin.—BOND OR LAP OF A SLATE, in architecture, the distance between the nail of the under slate and the lower edge of the upper slate.

BOND STONE, in architecture, a stone running through the whole thickness of a wall at right angles to its face, for the purpose of binding the wall together in the direction of its thickness.

BOND TIM'BER, in architecture, timber worked in with a wall as it is carried up, for the purpose of tying it together in a longitudinal direction while the work is setting.

BONZE, an Indian priest, who wears a chaplet of beads about his neck, and carries a staff, having a wooden bird at one end. The bonzes of China are the priests of the Fohists, or sects of Fohi; and it is one of their established tenets, that there are rewards allotted for the righteous, and punishments for the wicked, in the other world; and that there are various mansions, in which the souls of men will reside, according to their different degrees of merit. The number of bonzes in China is estimated at fifty thousand, and they are represented as idle, dissolute men.

BOOK, a literary composition, designed to communicate something which the author has invented, experienced, or collected, to the public, and thence to posterity; being printed, bound in a volume.

and published for that purpose.—The five books of Moses are doubtless the oldest books now extant; and there are none in profane history extant anterior to Homer's poems. A great variety of materials were formerly used in making books: plates of lead and copper, the bark of trees, bricks, stone, and wood, were among the first materials employed to engrave such things upon, as men were desirous to transmit to posterity. Josephus speaks of two columns, the one of stone, the other of brick, on which the children of Seth wrote their inventions and astronomical discoveries: Porphyry makes mention of some pillars, preserved in Crete, on which the ceremonies practised by the Corybantes in their sacrifices, were recorded: Hesiod's works were originally written upon tables of lead, and deposited in the temple of the Muses, in Bœotia: the ten commandments, delivered to Moses, were written upon stone; and Solon's laws upon wooden planks. Tables of wood, box, and ivory, were common among the ancients: when of wood they were frequently covered with wax, that people might write on them with more ease, or blot out what they had written. The leaves of the palm-tree were afterwards used instead of wooden planks, and the finest and thinnest part of the bark of such trees, as the lime, the ash, the maple and the elm; from hence comes the word *liber*, which signifies the inner bark of the trees: and as these barks were rolled up, in order to be removed with greater ease, these rolls were called *volumen*, a volume; a name afterwards given to the like rolls of paper or parchment. With regard to the use of books, it is indisputable that they make one of the chief instruments of acquiring knowledge; they are the repositories of the law, and vehicles of learning of every kind; our religion itself is founded on books, and "without them, (says Bartholin) God is silent, justice dormant, physic at a stand, philosophy lame, letters dumb, and all things involved in Cimmerian darkness." Yet, with all the well-merited eulogies that have been bestowed on them, we cannot overlook the fact that many are frivolous, and some pernicious. It will therefore be well to bear in mind the opinion of the learned Selden, who says that the characteristics of a good book are solidity, perspicuity, and brevity.

BOR'DER, that which limits or ornaments the extremities of a thing. FRAMES in a picture, is a border of carved wood, sometimes painted or gilt, and of copper-gilt. on which the picture is placed. The frame is not only a luxurious ornament, but it is necessary to circumscribe the composition, and to figure the opening through which the spectator perceives the painted objects, which an illusion of perspective leads him to think are beyond the wall on which the picture is placed. TAPESTRIES, in imitation of paintings, have also BORDERS, worked in the tapestry: as these must be proportionate to the size of the picture, which in tapestry are usually very large, they may be ornamented with Arabesques, Masks, Cameos, &c. The greatest painters have not disdained this style of composition; the borders of many of the tapestries in the Vatican were executed after designs by Raffaelle.

BO'REAS, in Grecian mythology, the son of Astræus and Aurora, and usually worshipped as the god of the north wind. There are few of the minor Grecian divinities of whom so strange and multifarious exploits are recorded as of Boreas; and it is interesting to trace to its source the allegory of all his adventures and achievements, and thence to elucidate the causes of his deification. The assiduity, for instance, with which the worship of Boreas was cultivated at Athens proceeded from gratitude, the north wind having on one occasion destroyed the fleet of the Persians when meditating the invasion of Athens. A similar cause induced the inhabitants of Megalopolis to consider Boreas as their guardian divinity, in whose honor they instituted an annual festival. With his usual partiality for mythological allusion, Milton has given Boreas a place in his *Paradise Lost*:—

> Now from the north
> Of Norumbega, and the Samoed shore,
> Bursting their brazen dungeon, armed with ice,
> And snow and hail, and stormy gust and flaw,
> Boreas and Cæcias and Argestes loud,
> And Thruscias rend the woods and seas upturn.

Boreas was usually represented with the feet of a serpent, his wings dripping with golden dew-drops, and the train of his garment sweeping along the ground.

BOR'OUGH, this word originally denoted a fortified city or town; but at present it is given to such town or village as sends burgesses or representatives to parliament. Boroughs are equally such whether they be incorporate or not; there being several boroughs that are not incorporated, and, on the contrary, several corporations that are not boroughs.

BOR'RELISTS, in church history, a sect of Christians in Holland, (so called from Borrel, their founder,) who reject the use of the sacraments, public prayer, and all external worship; yet they lead a very austere life.

BORS'HOLDER, among the Anglo-Saxons, one of the lowest magistrates, whose authority extended only over one tithing, consisting of ten families. Each tithing formed a little state of itself, and chose one of its most respectable members for its head, who was called a borsholder, a term derived from two words signifying a "surety" and a "head."

BOSS', this term describes sculptured objects in their full forms in contradistinction to those which are in RELIEF, or attached more or less to a plane or ground.

BOS'SAGE, in architecture, a term used for any stone that has a projecture, and is laid rough in a building, to be afterwards carved into mouldings, capitals, coats of arms, &c.—*Bossage* is also the name for what is otherwise called *rustic work*, consisting of stones that seem to project beyond the level of the building, by reason of indentures or channels left in the joinings. These are chiefly in the corners of edifices, and are there called *rustic quoins*.

BOSS'ES, are projecting ornaments used in architecture in various situations, such as ceilings, to cover the points of intersection of the ribs, &c. They consist variously of foliage, heads, armorial shields, &c., and embrace a great variety of fanciful shapes.

BOTAN'IC GARDEN, a garden devoted to the culture of a collection of plants, with reference to the science of botany. The legitimate object of gardens of this description appears to be to collect and cultivate, at the public expense, all the species and varieties of plants that can be cultivated in the given climate, with or without the aid of glass; and then to distribute these to private individuals throughout the district by which the botanic garden is supported. The most complete system of this kind ever established appears to have been that of France soon after the revolution. All the botanical articles that could be procured from other countries were sent to the botanic garden at Paris; and after they had borne seeds or been propagated there, the progeny was distributed among the provincial botanic gardens, of which there is one or more in every department. After being propagated in the provincial botanic gardens, the seeds or progeny were given out, free of expense, to whoever in the district to which the garden belonged thought fit to apply for them. As the useful species and varieties were as much attended to in these gardens as those which were cultivated only in a scientific point of view, the greatest facilities were thus given to the spread of every useful grain, pulse, culinary vegetable, and fruit, over the whole of France.

BOTANOMAN'CY, an ancient species of divination by means of plants, especially sage and fig leaves. Questions were written on leaves, which were then exposed to the wind, and as many of the letters as remained in their places were taken up, and, being joined together, contained an answer to the question.

BOT'TOM RAIL, in architecture, a term used for denoting the lowest horizontal rail of a framed door.

BOT'TOMRY, in commercial law, is in effect a mortgage of a ship, being an agreement entered into by an owner or his agent, whereby, in consideration of a sum of money advanced for the use of the ship, the borrower undertakes to repay the same, with interest, if the ship terminate her voyage successfully; and binds or hypothecates the ship for the performance of the contract.

BOU'DOIR, in architecture, a small room or cabinet, usually near the bed-chamber and dressing-room, for the private retirement of the master or mistress of the house.

BOUL'TIN, in architecture, a name given to a moulding whose section is nearly a quadrant of a circle, whose diameter being horizontal, the contour is convex in respect of a vertical to such diameter. It is more usually called the egg or quarter round, placed next below the plinth in the Tuscan and Doric capital.

BOUN'TY, in commerce and the arts, a premium paid by government to the producers, exporters, or importers of certain articles, or to those who employ ships in certain trades, when the profits resulting from these respective branches of industry are alleged to be insufficient.

BOUSTROPHE'DON, a word descriptive of a mode of writing common among the early Greeks until nearly the middle of the fifth century before Christ; viz. in alternate lines from right to left and from left to right, as fields are ploughed in furrows having an alternate direction, from whence the derivation.

BOUTS-RIMES, a term for certain rhymes disposed in order, and given to a poet, together with a subject, to be filled up with verses ending in the same word and same order.

BOWL'DER, or BOWL'DER-STONE, a roundish stone found on the sea-shore, or in the channels of rivers, &c., worn smooth by the action of water.

BOWL'DER WALL, a wall, generally on the sea-coast, constructed of large pebbles or bowlders of flint, which have been rounded by the action of water.

BOWLS, a game played upon a fine smooth grassy surface, used solely for the purpose, and denominated a bowling-green.

BOX'ERS, a kind of athletæ, who combat or contend for victory with their fists. Among the Romans they were called *pugiles;* hence the appellation of *pugilists* to the boxers of the present day.

BRACE, in architecture, a piece of timber framed in with bevel joints, to keep the building from swerving either way. When the brace is framed into the principal rafters, it is sometimes called a *strut.*

BRACE'LETS, were with the Ancients, and are still with the Moderns, the symbol of marriage. They were generally in the form of a serpent, and some were round bands fastened by two serpent's heads like the girdle of warriors. The number of golden and bronze bracelets found at Herculaneum and Pompeii, show that these ornaments, particularly those in the form of serpents, were articles of luxury among the females of ancient times. Antique bracelets are of two kinds, armlets and true bracelets, the one worn on the upper arm and the other on the wrist or lower arm. Smaller bracelets, generally of gold, beautifully worked, and sometimes set with jewels, were worn on the wrist. Bracelets have also been found like twisted bands. The Bacchantes wore real serpents instead of serpent-like bracelets. These ornaments were not worn exclusively by women, for we find that the Roman Consuls wore bracelets in triumphal processions; they were presented by the emperors to soldiers who distinguished themselves (ARMILLÆ.) The ankles had similar ornaments, thence called ANKLETS.

BRACHYG'RAPHY, stenography, or the art of writing in short hand.

BRACHYL'OGY, in rhetoric, the method of expressing anything in the most concise manner.

BRACK'ET, a support suspended from or attached to a wall for the purpose of supporting statuettes, vases, lamps, clocks, &c. The skill of the artist has been frequently employed upon this ornament, which is susceptible of great elegance of form and embellishment.

BRAH'MINS, or BRAM'INS, the caste or hereditary division of Hindoos peculiarly devoted to religion and religious science, in the same manner as, among the Jews, the priesthood was ordained to continue in the tribe of Levi. The families of this caste claim peculiar veneration from the rest, and seem, in their name of *bramins,* to claim the merit of being the more immediate followers of Brahma, their incarnate deity. Some of them, however, are described as very corrupt in their morals; while others live sequestered from the world, devoted to superstition and indolence. To the bramins we are indebted for whatever we know of the Sanscrit, or ancient language of the country, in which their sacred books are written.

BRAVU'RA, in music, an air so composed as to enable the performer to show his skill in the execution of difficult passages. It is also sometimes used for the style of execution.

BREADTH, this term is employed in the language of Art to express that kind of grandeur which results from the arrangement of objects and of the mode of proceeding in delineating them. In painting it is applied both to Design and to Coloring: it conveys the idea of simple arrangement, free from too great a multiplicity of details, following which the lights and shades spread themselves over the prominent parts, without dazzling or interfering with each other, so that the attention of the spectator is arrested and kept fixed, and there is *breadth of effect,* the result of judicious coloring and *chiaro-oscuro.* When a work offers these results, we say it has *breadth;* and "broad touch," and "broad pencil," are terms applicable to this manner of working, when the touches and strokes of the pencil produce *breadth of effect.* In a similar sense, in engraving, we say "a broad burin." But although a work of sculpture is susceptible of breadth, we do not say "a broad chisel."

BREC'CIA, an Italian name for those stones which consist of hard angular or rounded fragments of different mineral bodies, united by a kind of cement, of which the so-called pudding-stone is an example, which consists of flint detritus, cemented by quartz. The ancients used breccia both in architecture and the Plastic Arts. Porphyry breccia, or Egyptian breccia, is one of the most beautiful varieties of this material, of which a fine pillar is contained in the Museo Pio Clementino.

BREED'ING, in a moral sense, denotes a person's deportment or behavior in the external offices and decorums of social life. In this sense, we say, well-bred, ill-bred, a man of breeding, &c. Lord Shaftesbury compares the well-bred man with the real philosopher; the conduct and manners of the one are formed according to the most perfect ease and good entertainment of company; of the other, according to the strictest interest of mankind; the one according to his rank and quality in his private station; the other, according to his rank and dignity in nature. In short, *good-breeding* is politeness, or the union of those qualifications which constitute genteel deportment.

BREVE, in music, a note of the third degree of length. It is equal to two semibreves, or when dotted, to three: the former is called an *imperfect*, the latter, a *perfect* breve.

BREVET', a military term, expressive of nominal promotion without additional pay: thus, a brevet major serves a captain, and draws pay as such. The word is borrowed from the French, signifying a royal act granting some favor or privilege; as *brevet d'invention.*

BRE'VIARY, the book containing the daily service of the church of Rome.

BRIEF, in law, an abridgment of the client's case, made out for the instruction of counsel on a trial at law; wherein the case of the plaintiff, &c., is to be briefly, but completely, stated.—*Brief*, in music, a measure of quantity, which contains two strokes down in beating time, and two up.—*Brief apostolical*, letters or written messages of the pope, addressed to princes or magistrates, respecting matters of public concern.

BRIGADE', a party or division of soldiers, either horse or foot. An army is divided into brigades of horse and brigades of foot: a brigade of horse is a body of eight or ten squadrons; a brigade of foot consists of four, five, or six battalions.

BRIG'ANDINE, a kind of ancient defensive armor, consisting of thin jointed scales of plate, so arranged as to be pliant and easy to the body.

BRIGHT, in painting, shining with light; a term applied to a picture in which the lights preponderate over the shadows.

BRILLAN'TE, in music, prefixed to a movement, denotes that it is to be played in a gay and lively manner.

BRITAN'NIA, the name given by the Romans to the island of Britain, which is represented on their medals under the figure of a female resting her left arm on a shield.

BRITIN'IANS, a body of Augustine monks who received their name from Britini, in Ancona. They were distinguished by their austerities in living.

BROCADE', a stuff of gold, silver, or silk, raised and enriched with flowers, foliages, and other ornaments, according to the fancy of the merchants or manufacturers.

BROGUE, a defective pronunciation of a language, particularly applied to the Irish manner of speaking English.

BRO'KER, a name applied to persons of several and very different professions, the chief of which are exchange-brokers, stock-brokers, pawn-brokers, and brokers who sell household furniture.

BRON'TIUM, in Grecian antiquity, a place underneath the floor of the theatres, in which were kept brazen vessels full of stones and other materials, with which they imitated the noise of thunder.

BRONZE, a mixed metal, composed principally of copper, with a small portion of tin and other metals. The ancients used bronze for a great variety of purposes; hence, arms and other instruments, medals and statues of this metal, are to be found in all cabinets of antiquities. The moderns have also made much use of bronze, particularly for statues exposed to accidents, or the influence of the atmosphere, and for casts of celebrated antiques. Bronze of a good quality acquires, by oxydation, a fine green tint, called *patina antiqua* or *ærugo;* which appearance is imitated by an artificial process, called *bronzing.*

BROWN, or tan-color, was used both in ancient and mediæval times as a sign of mourning; regarded as a compound of red and black, BISTRE, it is the symbol of infernal love and of treason. By the Egyptians Typhon was represented of a red color, or rather of red mixed with black; everything in nature of a brown color was consecrated to Typhon. In the ancient pictures representing the Passion of Jesus Christ, the personages are frequently depicted brown. Several religious orders adopt this color in their costume, as the symbol of renunciation. With the Moors it was emblematic of every evil. Tradition assigns red hair to Judas. Christian symbolism appropriates the color of the dead leaf for the type of spiritual death; the blue, the celestial color, which gives them life, is evaporated—they become of a dark-yellow, hence the term "dead leaf."

BRU'MAL, the winter quarter of the year, beginning at the shortest day.

BRUMA'LIA, in antiquity, a festival celebrated by the Romans in honor of Bacchus twice a-year; viz., on the twelfth of the calends of March, and the eighth of the calends of December.

BRUTE, an animal without the use of reason, or that acts by mere instinct, in which sense it denotes much the same with beast, and comprehends all animals excepting mankind. Philosophers, however, are far from being agreed on this subject; some making brutes mere machines, whilst others allow them not only reason, but immortality. Others take a middle course, and allow brutes to have imagination, memory, and passion; but deny that they have understanding or reason, at least, in any degree comparable to that of mankind. The sagacity of many brutes is indeed admirable; yet what a prodigious difference is there between that sagacity and the reason of mankind!

BUCANIER', or BUCCANEER', a name given to those piratical adventurers, chiefly English and French, who, in the seventeenth century, committed the most excessive depredations on the Spaniards in America. The name had been given to the first French settlers on the island of St. Domingo, whose sole employment consisted in hunting bulls or wild boars, in order to sell their hides and flesh; and as they smoked and dried the flesh of the animals according to the manner of the Indians, which was called *buccaneering*, they thus obtained the name of buccaneers.

BUCCELLA'RII, an order of soldiery under the Greek emperors, appointed to guard and distribute the rations of bread.

BUCCI'NA, an ancient musical and military instrument, somewhat similar to the modern trumpet.—Hence BUCCINATOR, or trumpeter.

BUCEN'TAUR, the name of the large vessel which the Venetians formerly used in the ceremony of espousing the sea.

BUCK'LER, a piece of defensive armor used by the ancients, commonly composed of hides, fortified with plates of metal.—*Bucklers, votive*, were those consecrated to the gods, and hung up in their temples, in commemoration of some hero, or as a thanksgiving for a victory obtained over an enemy, whose bucklers, taken in war, were offered as a trophy.

BUCK'RAM, a sort of coarse cloth made of hemp, gummed, calendered, and dyed of several colors. It is used in drapery, garments, &c., required to be kept stiff to their form.

BUCOL'ICS, the Greek term for pastoral poems, meaning literally the songs of herdsmen. We have considerable remains of this species of poetry in the poems of Theocritus, Bion, and Moschus, and the Eclogues of Virgil. The metre universally employed is the hexameter or heroic; but in pastoral poetry an easier flow of the lines was studied than in epics, and this was generally accomplished by introducing a larger proportion of the metrical feet called dactyls in the former than in the latter; but no rules were laid down on this point. This species of poetry has been cultivated also by most modern nations, and in England, France, and especially in Germany, with great success. Indeed, the last-mentioned country can boast among others of a Gessner, whose Idyls have been pronounced by some modern critics to be models of pastoral poetry, combining the most finished harmony of numbers with a simplicity and tenderness of sentiment and expression worthy of Theocritus himself.

BUDD'HISTS, the followers or worshippers of Buddha, the founder of a very ancient religion in India, which afterwards spread to Japan, Thibet, and China, where it exists at the present day. Buddha, whose historical name was Tshakia-muni, was born under the reign of Tshao-wang, of the dynasty of Tsheu, 1029 B.C., and died under the reign of Mouwang, 950 B.C. His disciple Mahakaya succeeded him, and is the first saint or patriarch of Buddhism; but a regular dynasty of successors filled this important station till A.D. 713. Their history is mixed with the grossest fables; but it is clear that they devoted themselves to religious exercises and constant contemplation, and condemned themselves to the severest abstinence. Besides many other monuments of the ancient worship of Buddha, there are two particularly remarkable—the ruins of the gigantic temple Boro-Budor, in Java, and the five large subterranean halls, called Pantsh-Pandu, on the way from Guzerat to Malwa. Tradition ascribes these astonishing works of ancient Indian architecture and sculpture, which far surpass the skill of the modern Hindoos, to the Pandus, the heroes of Indian mythology.

BUD'GET, in a general sense, means a condensed statement of the income and expenditure of a nation, or of any particular public department. In England, however, the term is usually employed to designate the speech made by the chancellor of the exchequer when he gives a general view of the public revenue and expenditure, and intimates whether government intend to propose the imposition or repeal of any taxes, &c.

BUF'FO, the Italian for a singer, or actor, when he takes the humorous part in comic operas, &c.

BUHL, this word is a corruption of *Boule*, the name of an Italian artisan who first introduced this kind of ornament into cabinet-work. It is used to designate that sort of work in which any two materials of different colors are inlaid into each other, as brass, tortoise-shell, pearl, &c.; it is applied to chairs, tables, desks, work-boxes, &c.

BUL, in the ancient Hebrew chronology, the eighth month of the ecclesiastical, and the second of the civil year; it has since been called Marshevan, and answers to our October.

BULL, PAPAL, an instrument, ordinance, or decree of the Pope, equivalent to the proclamations, edicts, letters patent, or ukases of secular princes. Bulls are written on parchment, to which a leaden seal is affixed, and are granted for the consecration of bishops, the promotion to benefices, and the celebration of jubilees, &c. The publication of papal bulls is termed fulmination; and it is done by one of three commissioners, to whom they are usually addressed.

BUL'LA, in antiquity, a small round ornament of gold or silver, worn about the neck or breast of the children of the nobility till the age of fourteen.

BUL'LETIN, an official account of public transactions or matters of general interest.

BULL'-FIGHT, an entertainment formerly frequent in Spain and Portugal, at which wild bulls are encountered by men on horseback, armed with lances.

BULL'ION, uncoined gold or silver in the mass. Those metals are called so, either when smelted from the native ore, and not perfectly refined; or when they are perfectly refined, but melted down in bars or ingots, or in any unwrought body, of any degree of fineness.

BUR'DEN, in music, the drone or bass in some musical instruments, and the pipe or string that plays it. The bass pipe in the bagpipe is so called. Hence, that part of a song that is repeated at the end of every stanza is called the burden of it.

BUREAU', in its primary sense, is a cloth covering a table; next a writing-table; and afterwards used to signify the chamber of an officer of government, and the body of subordinate officers who labor under the direction of a chief.

BUREAU'CRATIE, or BUREAUCRACY, is the system by which the business of administration is carried on in departments, each under the control of a chief, in contra-distinction to those systems in which the officers of government have a co-ordinate authority.

BUR'GESS, an inhabitant of a borough, or one who possesses a tenement therein. In other countries, burgess and citizen are used synonymously; but in England they are distinguished, burgess being ordinarily used for the representative of a borough-town in parliament.

BURG'LARY, in law, the breaking and entering the dwelling of another in the night, with the intent to commit some felony, whether the felonious intent be put in execution or not. The like offence committed by day, is called house-breaking.

BUR'GOMASTER, the chief magistrate of the great towns in Flanders, Holland, and Germany. The authority of a burgomaster resembles that of the Lord Mayor in London.

BU'RIN, an instrument used for engraving on copper or steel plates.

BURLES'QUE, the Italian poesia burlesca, signifies merely comic or sportive poetry; but the term, in French and English, is more commonly restricted to compositions of which the humor consists in a ludicrous mixture of things high and low: as high thoughts clothed in low expressions; or, vice versâ, ordinary or base topics invested in the artificial dignity of poetic diction. The humor of parody or travestie arises from the burlesque.—*Burletta*, a slight comic musical drama, is derived from the same origin.

BURLET'TA, a light, comic species of musical drama, which derives its name from the Italian *burlare*, to jest.

BUR'SARS, originally clerks or treasurers in convents: in more modern times, persons enabled to prosecute their studies at a university by means of funds derived from endowments. It is a singular circumstance that the latter acceptation of this term originated among the Poles, who, even in the 14th century, were accustomed to supply young men of talent with the means of travelling to Germany, and there studying philosophy under the guidance of the monks. This practice was soon adopted by other nations; and there is now, perhaps, no civilized country in which it does not exist, under the name of bursaries, fellowships, exhibitions, scholarships, &c. These endowments are of two kinds: either furnishing the student with the means of prosecuting his studies during the academical curriculum; or enabling him to devote himself, without distraction, to literary pursuits even after the expiration of this period.

BUR'SCHE, a youth, especially a student at a university.

BUR'SCHEN COMMENT, the code of laws adopted by the students for the regulation of their demeanor amongst themselves, &c.

BUR'SCHENSCHAFT, a league or secret association of students, formed in 1815, for the purpose, as was asserted, of the political regeneration of Germany, and suppressed, at least in name, by the exertions of the governments.

BURSE, BUR'SA, or BASIL'ICA, an exchange, or place of meeting for merchants to consult on matters of trade, and to negotiate bills of exchange.

BUSI'RIS, in Egyptian mythology, a fabulous personage, of whose origin, exploits, and character, Apollodorus, Herodotus, Diodorus Siculus, and other ancient writers, have given a most discrepant account. His history is blended with that of Osiris.

BUS'KIN, a kind of boot, or covering for the leg, of great antiquity. It was part of the costume of actors in tragedy; it is worn by Diana in representations of that goddess, as part of the costume of hunters. In antique marbles it is represented tastefully ornamented. Being laced in front it fitted tightly to the leg. Buskin is used in contradistinction to the sock, (*soccus*) the flat-soled shoe, worn by comedians, &c., and both terms are used to express the tragic and comic drama.

BUST, or BUS'TO, in sculpture, denotes the figure or portrait of a person in relievo, showing only the head, shoulders, and stomach, the arms being lopped off. The stomach and shoulders are, strictly speaking, the bust. The term is also used by the Italians, for the *torso* or trunk of the body, from the neck to the hips.

BUS'TUM, in antiquity, a funeral pile on which the dead bodies of the Romans used to be burnt. Hence, BUSTUA'RII were gladiators who fought about the bustum of any person in the celebration of his obsequies.

BY'-LAWS, or BYE'-LAWS, private and peculiar laws for the good government of a city, court, or other community, made by the general consent of the members. All by-laws are to be reasonable, and for the common benefit, not private advantage of any particular persons, and must be agreeable to the public laws in being.

BYZAN'TINE, a gold coin of the value of 15*l*., so called from being coined at Byzantium. Also an epithet for anything pertaining to Byzantium, an ancient city of Thrace, situated on the Bosphorus.

BYZAN'TINE HISTORIANS, a series of Greek historians and authors, who lived under the Eastern Empire between the 6th and the 15th centuries. They may be divided into three classes: 1. Historians whose works form a continuous history of the Byzantine Empire from the fourth century of the Christian era down to the Turkish conquest of Constantinople. They are nearly thirty in number, with various shades of literary merit; but their works constitute the almost only authentic source of the history of that eventful period. 2. General chroniclers or historians, whose works, embracing a wider range than those of the former, treat chiefly of the chronography of the world from the oldest times. 3. Authors who confined their attention to the politics, statistics, antiquities, manners, &c., of the Romans. These two classes combined amount also to about thirty, and their writings give an excellent illustration of the times of which they treat, whether as historians, chroniclers, antiquaries, or politicians.

C.

C, the third letter and second consonant of the alphabet, is pronounced like *k* before the vowels *a*, *o*, and *u*, and like *s* before *e*, *i*, and *y*. Before *h* it has a peculiar sound, as in chance, chalk; in chord and some other words, it is hard like *k*; but in many French words it is soft before *h*, like *s*, as in chaise, chagrin, &c. As a numeral C stands for 100, and C C for 200, &c.; as an abbreviation it stands for Christ, as A.C. Anno Christi, or Ante

Christum; also for Companion, as C.B. Companion of the Bath. And in music, C after the cliff, is the mark of common time.

CAA'BA, or CAA'BAH, properly signifies a square building; but is particularly applied by the Mahometans to the temple of Mecca, built, as they pretend, by Abraham, and Ishmaël his son. It is towards this temple they always turn their faces when they pray, in whatever part of the world they happen to be. This temple enjoys the privilege of an asylum for all sorts of criminals; but it is most remarkable for the pilgrimages made to it by the devout Mussulmans, who pay so great a veneration to it, that they believe a single sight of its sacred walls, without any particular act of devotion, is as meritorious in the sight of God, as the most careful discharge of one's duty, for the space of a whole year, in any other temple.

CABAL', denotes a number of persons united in some close design, and is sometimes used synonymously with *faction.* This term was applied to the ministry of Charles II., from the initial letters of their respective names, viz., Clifford, Ashley, Buckingham, Arlington, and Lauderdale.

CAB'ALA, a mysterious kind of science pretended to have been delivered by revelation to the ancient Jews, and transmitted by oral tradition to those of our times; serving for the interpretation of the books both of nature and scripture.

CAB'INET, a select apartment set apart for writing, studying, or preserving anything that is precious. Hence we say, a cabinet of paintings, curiosities, &c.—Also, the closet or private room in the royal palace, where councils are held; likewise the ministers of state who are summoned to attend such councils.

CABI'RI, certain deities greatly venerated by the ancient Pagans in Greece and Phœnicia, who were supposed to have a particular influence over maritime affairs. Various opinions have been entertained concerning the nature and origin of the Cabiri; but from the multiplicity of names applied to them, together with the profound secrecy observed in the celebration of their rites, an almost impenetrable veil of mystery has been thrown around their history. They seem to have been men who, having communicated the art of melting metals, &c., were deified by a grateful posterity. Their worship was chiefly cultivated in the island of Samothracia, whence it was afterwards transferred to Lemnos, Imbros, and certain towns of Troas. They were styled the offspring of Vulcan, though their name was derived from their mother Cabera, daughter of Proteus. Their number is variously given. Those who were initiated in their rites were held to be secured against all danger by sea and land. Their distinguishing badge was a purple girdle.

CACOE'THES, an ill habit or propensity; as the *cacoethes scribendi*, an itch for authorship.

CAC'OPHONG, in rhetoric, an uncouth, bad tone of the voice, proceeding from the ill disposition of the organs.

CACOPH'ONY, in rhetoric, a defect of style, consisting in a harsh or disagreeable sound produced by the meeting of two or more letters or syllables, or by the too frequent repetition of the same letters or syllables: *e.g.*

And oft the ear the open vowels tire.—*Pope.*

CACOSYN'THETON, in grammar, an improper selection and arrangement of words in a sentence.

CA'CUS, in fabulous history, the son of Vulcan, a robber of Italy, whose dwelling was in the Aventine wood. His exploits form the subject of a fine episode in the 8th book of the *Æneid.* He was represented as a frightful monster of enormous strength, who, after a long life of crime, was at length slain by Hercules, from whom he had stolen some oxen. To express his gratitude for his victory, Hercules erected the *Ara Maxima;* and Evander, with his infant colony of Arcadians, performed divine honors to Hercules as their benefactor.

CA'DENCE, in grammar, the fall of the voice; also the flow of verses or periods; in music, the conclusion of a song, or of some parts thereof, in certain places of the piece, dividing it as it were into so many numbers or periods. The cadence takes place when the parts fall or terminate on a note or chord naturally expected by the ear, just as a period closes the sense in the paragraph of a discourse. A cadence is either perfect or imperfect. The former when it consists of two notes sung after each other, or by degrees conjointed in each of the two parts, the harmony of the fifth preceding that of the key-note; and it is called perfect, because it satisfies the ear more than the latter. The latter imperfect; that is, when the key-note with its harmony precedes that of the fifth without its added seventh. A cadence is said to be broken or interrupted when the bass rises a major or minor second, instead of falling a fifth.

CADET', one who is trained up for the army by a course of military discipline; such as the cadets at the military colleges of Woolwich, Addiscombe, &c. In England there are three grand institutions for the education of cadets: Sandhurst for the British line; Woolwich for the artillery and engineers; and Addiscombe for the Indian army, both line and artillery. The academy at Sandhurst was instituted by George III., for the purpose of affording general and professional instruction to the sons of private or military gentlemen, with the view of their obtaining commissions in the British army without purchase. Before the commission is conferred, the cadet must undergo an examination before a competent board in the classics, mathematics, military drawing, &c.

The academy at Woolwich was established with the view of qualifying cadets for the artillery or engineers; and to this institution the master-general of the ordnance has the sole right of granting admission. The attention of the cadets is specially directed to geography; general history, ancient and modern; modern languages; military drawing and surveying; mathematics; engineering and fortification. After the lapse of four years, generally, the cadets undergo an examination in the above mentioned branches of science; when the most distinguished are selected for the engineers, the others for the artillery.

The college of Addiscombe is established for the education of officers of the line, artillery, and engineers for the Indian army. The plan of instruction pursued there combines the two systems adopted at Sandhurst and at Woolwich. In order to become a cadet in this institution, it is necessary to have the promise of a commission from a director of the East India Company; and after a prescribed examination, an appointment is obtained in one of the branches of the Indian army, according to the merit or pleasure of the cadet.

In France the academies for cadets which existed previously to the French Revolution have been merged in the Polytechnic schools.

The Dutch possess two institutions of this nature; one at Breda, the other at Delft.

In Germany every small state has a military school; while those at Berlin, Vienna, and Munich are on so extensive a scale as to challenge a comparison with any similar institutions in Europe. In Germany, too, the word cadet has a wider signification than in England, being applied to those persons who, without having frequented a military school, join the army in the expectation of obtaining a commission when they have gained a competent knowledge of the service.

In Russia there is a famous academy for cadets, which was instituted by Ann at St. Petersburg in 1732; and since its foundation has afforded instruction in military science to upwards of 9000 pupils, many of whom have acquired celebrity in the annals of Russian literature.

In the United States there is one at West Point, on nearly the same principle as that at Addiscombe.

CADET'SHIP, the commission given to a cadet to enter the East India Company's service.

CA'DI, a civil judge or magistrate in the Turkish empire.

CADU'CEUS, the staff of Mercury or Hermes, which gave the god power to fly. It was given to him by Apollo, as a reward for having assisted him to invent the Lyre. It was then a winged staff; but, in Arcadia, Hermes cast it among serpents, who immediately twined themselves around it, and became quiet. After this event, it was used as a herald of peace. It possessed the power of bestowing happiness and riches, of healing the sick, raising the dead, and conjuring spirits from the lower world. On the silver coins of the Roman emperors, the Caduceus was given to Mars, who holds it in the left hand, and the spear in the right, to show how peace succeeds war.

CÆLATU'RA, from the Latin *cælum*, the tool used: the art, called also by the Romans, *sculptura*, or chasing, if we mean "raised-work" Cælatura corresponds to the Grecian term *toreutice*, derived from *toros*, which in its true sense means only raised-work. Quintilian expressly limits this term to metal, while he mentions wood, ivory, marble, glass, and precious stones as materials for engraving. Silver was the artist's favorite metal, but gold, bronze, and even iron, were embossed. Closely connected with this art was that of stamping with the punch, called by the Romans *excudere*. Embossings were probably finished by *toreutice*, of which Phidias is called the inventor. The colossal statues of gold and ivory made by him and by Polycletus belong partly to sculpture by the ivory-work, and partly to toreutic art from the gold-work, the embossing of which was essential to their character, as also to castings: the statue of Minerva was richly embossed. Besides Phidias and Polycletus, Myron, Mys and Mentor are mentioned as great toreutic artists. Arms, armor, &c., were adorned in this manner; other articles, such as goblets and other drinking cups, were also embossed, partly with figures in alto-relievo, or with figures standing quite clear: also dishes, the ornaments of which were set in *emblemæ*, or fastened slightly on as *crustæ*. Carriages were ornamented not only with bronze, but even with silver and gold embossings. Other articles of furniture, tripods, disks of candelabra, were thus ornamented. With this *toreutice* or embossing, must not be confounded the art of inlaying, *empaistike*, much practised in antiquity.

CÆRI'TES TAB'ULÆ, in antiquity, tables or registers in which the censors entered the names of those citizens, who for any misdemeanor were deprived of their right of voting at an election.

CÆ'SAR, in Roman antiquity, the family name of the first five Roman emperors, and afterwards adopted as a title by their successors. It was also used, by way of distinction, for the intended or presumptive heir of the empire.

CÆSA'RIANS, in Roman antiquity, officers or ministers of the Roman emperors, who kept an account of their revenues, and took possession in their name of such things as devolved or were confiscated to them.

CÆSU'RA, a figure in prosody, by which a division or separation takes place in a foot that is composed of syllables belonging to different words.

CÆT'ERIS PAR'IBUS, a term often used by mathematical and physical writers; the words literally signifying *the rest, or other things, being alike or equal.* Thus of a bullet, it may be said *cæteris paribus*, the heavier it is the greater the range, supposing the length and diameter of the piece and the quantity and strength of the powder to be the same.

CAI'NITES, a sect of heretics, who appeared about 159 A.D. They probably originated in some of the various schools of Manicheism; and, if their doctrines are truly reported to us, they are said to have asserted that the power which created heaven and earth was the evil principle; that Cain, Esau, Korah, the people of Sodom, and others whom the Old Testament represents as victims of peculiar divine judgments, were in fact children of the good principle, and enemies of the evil. Some of them are said to have published a gospel of Judas on the same principle. The Quintilianists, so called from a lady named Quintilia, of whom Tertullian speaks, were an offset of this sect.

CA IRA, CA IRA, (literally, *it* (the Revolution) *shall go on,*) the burden of a famous revolutionary song, which was composed in the year 1790 in denunciation of the French aristocracy. The tune and sentiments of this song were much inferior to those of the Marseillaise Hymn ("Allons enfans de la patrie,") the object of which was to rouse the French to defend their country against foreign aggression.

CAIRN, a word of Celtic origin, used to denote the piles of stones of a conical form so frequently found on the tops of hills, &c. in various districts; erected probably, for the purpose of memorials, although some have assigned to them a peculiar character, as receptacles for the bodies of criminals burnt in the wicker images of the Druids, &c. According to some antiquaries, *cairn* is distinct from *carnedd*, the Welsh name for heaps of stones on the tops of high mountains, (Carnedd David, Carnedd Llewellyn, &c.,) which are said to have been sacrificial. Some cairns are undoubtedly sepulchral.

CA'ISSON, in architecture, a sunken panel in a flat or vaulted ceiling, or in the soffit of a cornice. In ceilings they are of various geometrical forms, and often enriched with rosettes or other ornaments.

CAL'AMUS, a rush or reed used anciently as a pen to write on parchments or papyrus.

CALAN'TICA, CALVATICA, a kind of head-dress worn by women in ancient times, and known very early in Greece; there were two kinds, nets and cap-like bags. Many varieties of these caps are to be seen upon ancient vases; sometimes they are of a plain material, sometimes having a pattern, and sometimes striped or checked; they are either open behind, so that part of the hair hangs out, or it covers only the two sides of the head.

CAL'ATHUS, the ancient term for the basket in which the spinners kept their wool and their work; it was also called TALARUS, and was made of wicker-work, with a wide opening at top and pointed at bottom. The calathus was a

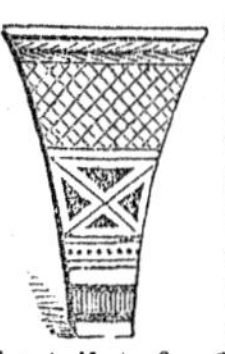

symbol of maidenhood, and in this sense was employed by artists, as is seen in the reliefs representing Achilles among the daughters of Lycomedes. Other antiques show us that these baskets were used for many purposes at the toilet, for flowers, &c. The calathus also appears in the basket-like form of the capitals of Corinthian pillars.

CALA'TOR, in antiquity, was a public servant, and a freeman, such as a bailiff or crier, to summon courts, synods, and other public assemblies. He also attended on the priests in the sacrifices.

CAL'CEUS, a shoe or short boot used by the Greeks and Romans as a covering to protect the feet while walking; the term being used in contradistinction to sandals or slippers, and corresponding to the modern shoes. There were two sorts, the *calcei lunati*, which were worn by the patricians, so called from an ivory crescent with which they were ornamented, and the *calcei mulli*, or red shoes. They came up to the middle of the leg, but only covered the sole of the foot.

CALCOG'RAPHY, an engraving after the manner of a drawing in chalk.

CALCULA'TION, the act of computing several sums by means of addition, subtraction, multiplication, division, &c., or an estimate formed in the mind by comparing the various circumstances which influence its determination.

CALCULATO'RES, accountants among the Romans, who used to reckon by means of little stones or pebbles.

CAL'ENDAR, a distribution or division of time into periods adapted to the purposes of civil life; also a table or register of such divisions, exhibiting the order in which the seasons, months, festivals, and holidays succeed each other during the year. The word is derived from the ancient Latin verb *calare*, to call. In the early ages of Rome, it was the custom for the pontiffs to call the people together on the first day of each month, to apprise them of the days that were to be kept sacred in the course of it. Hence *dies calendæ*, the calends or first days of the different months. The calendars in use throughout Europe are borrowed from that of the Romans. Romulus is supposed to have first undertaken to divide the year in such a manner that certain epochs should return periodically after a revolution of the sun; but the knowledge of astronomy was not then sufficiently advanced to allow this to be done with much precision. The Roman calendar continued in a state of uncertainty and confusion till the time of Julius Cæsar, when the civil equinox differed from the astronomical by three months. Under the advice of the astronomer Sosigenes, Cæsar abolished the lunar year, and regulated the civil year entirely by the sun. The Julian year consisted of 365¼ days, and consequently differed in excess by 11 minutes 10·35 sec. from the true solar year, which consists of 365 d. 5 h. 48 m. 49·62 sec. In consequence of this difference the astronomical equinox, in the course of a few centuries, sensibly fell back towards the beginning of the year. In the time of Julius Cæsar it corresponded to the 25th of March; in the sixteenth century it had retrograded to the 11th. The correction of this error was one of the purposes sought to be obtained by the reformation of the calendar effected by Pope Gregory XIII. in 1582. By suppressing 10 days in the calendar, Gregory restored the equinox to the 21st of March, the day on which it fell at the time of the Council of Nice in 325; the place of Easter and the other movable church feasts in the ecclesiastical calendar having been prescribed at that council. And in order that the same inconvenience might be prevented in future, he ordered the intercalation which took place every fourth year to be omitted in years ending centuries. The Gregorian calendar was received immediately or shortly after its promulgation by all the Roman Catholic countries of Europe. The Protestant states of Germany, and the kingdom of Denmark, adhered to the Julian calendar till 1700; and in England the alteration was successfully opposed by popular prejudices till 1752. In that year the Julian calendar, or *old style*, as it was called, was formally abolished by the act of parliament, and the date used in all public transactions rendered coincident with that followed in other European countries, by enacting that the day following the 2d of September of the year 1752 should be called the 14th of that month.

A new reform of the calendar was attempted to be introduced in France during the period of the Revolution. The commencement of the year was fixed at the autumnal equinox, which nearly coincided with the epoch of the foundation of the republic. The names of the ancient months were abolished, and others substituted having reference to agricultural labors, or the state of nature in the different seasons of the year. But the alteration was found to be inconvenient and impracticable, and after a few years was formally abandoned.

CA'LENDS, in the ancient Roman calendar, were the first days of each month. The Roman month was divided into three periods by the *Calends*, the *Nones*, and the *Ides*. The *Calends* were invariably placed at the beginning of the month; the *Ides* at the middle of the month, on the 13th or 15th; and the *Nones* (*novem*, nine) were the ninth day before the Ides, counting inclusively. From these three terms the days were counted backwards, in the following manner:—Those days comprised between the calends and the nones, were denominated *days before the nones;* those between the nones and the ides, *days before the ides;* and those from the ides to the end of the month, *days before the calends.*

CAL'ICO, cloth made of cotton. It is called *calico*, because originally brought from *Calicut*, a kingdom of India on this side of the Ganges, on the coast of Malabar. These cloths, whether plain, printed, dyed, stained, or painted, chintz, or muslin, are all included under one general denomination.

CAL'IDUCT, in antiquity, a pipe or canal disposed along the walls of a house for conveying heat from a furnace to the various apartments.

CAL'IGA, in antiquity, a sort of sandal worn by the Roman soldiers, whence Caligula derived his name. These *caligæ* were sometimes adorned with gold and silver nails.

CALIG'RAPHY, the art of beautiful writing. The scribes who made a profession of copying manuscripts, before the invention of printing, have been termed Caligraphers. Their art consisted not merely in writing, but also in embellishing their work with ornamental devices, although illumination was also practised as a distinct employment. Among the MSS. of the early part of the middle ages which we possess, there are some sumptuous specimens of the art, written in letters of gold, vermilion, &c., and on leaves of different colors, but that fashion went early out of use; and in general it may be said, that the current writing of caligraphers diminished in beauty and laborious minuteness, especially in Italy, during the centuries immediately preceding the invention of printing.

CA'LIPH, the chief sacerdotal dignity among the Saracens or Mahometans, vested with absolute authority in all matters relating both to religion and policy. It is at this day one of the Grand Signior's titles, as successor of the Prophet; and of the Sophi of Persia, as successor of Ali. The government of the original Caliphs continued from the death of Mahomet till the 655th year of the hegira.

CALK'ING, or CAULK'ING, in painting, the covering of the back side of a design with red chalk, and tracing lines through on a waxed plate or wall, so as to leave an impression of the color there.

CALLI'OPE, in mythology, one of the Muses usually associated with Homer in the statues of antiquity, and thence considered as the patroness of heroic poetry.

CALL OF THE HOUSE, a parliamentary term, implying an imperative call or summons, sent to every member on some particular occasion.

CALOR'IC, the principle or cause of heat, as distinguished from the sensation.

CALOTE', a sort of skull cap worn by the French cavalry under their caps, as a guard against the blows of the sabre.

CAL'UMET, a symbolical instrument of great importance among the Indians of America. It is a smoking-pipe, the bowl of which is generally made of a soft red marble, and the tube of a very long reed, ornamented with feathers. This instrument, the use of which bears a great resemblance to the caduceus of the Greeks, is a pledge of peace and good faith. The calumet of war, differently made, is used to proclaim war.

CAL'VINISM, the theological tenets of John Calvin, who, in the 16th century, flourished at Geneva, where his doctrines still subsist. The doctrinal parts of this system differ from that of other reformers of Calvin's period, chiefly in what regards the absolute decrees of God, by which, according to this teacher, the future and eternal condition of the human race was predetermined.

CALYP'SO, in fabulous history, a daughter of Atlas, according to Homer, but of Oceanus and Thetys, according to Hesiod, was the queen of the island Ogygia. On this island Ulysses suffered shipwreck; and Calypso, by the united influence of her love and spells, prevailed on him to remain and share her sceptre. After the lapse of seven years, however, his desire to revisit his native country became irrepressible, and he resolved to forego his honors in Ogygia. Calypso tried every expedient, offering him even the bribe of immortality, to induce him to remain; but all her efforts proved unavailing, and on his departure she died of grief. The island of Ogygia, placed by Pliny off the Lacinian promontory, between the Tarentine and Sycillian bays, has long since been engulfed in the ocean, along with the famous islands of the Sirens.

CAMAYEU, CAMAIEU, MONOCHROME. By this term we understand painting with a single color, varied only by the effect of *chiaro-oscuro;* we apply this term to painting in gray, which, as well as red, was used by the ancients. Pictures in two or three tints, where the natural hues of the objects are not copied, may also be called *en camayeu;* we speak of brown, red, yellow, green, and blue *camayeu*, according to their principal colors. The pictures of Polidori Caravaggio, for example, by their heavy brown tint, give the impression of monochrome painting, and, with all their perfection, they are but pictures *en camayeu*. Drawings in red or black chalk, lead and other pencils, Indian ink, sepia and bistre, as well as engraving, may be called Camayeux.

CAM'BRIC, a species of fine white linen, made of flax, said to be named from Cambray, in Flanders, where it was first manufactured.

CAM'BER-BEAM, in architecture, a beam cut hollow or archwise in the middle, commonly used in platforms.

CAM'EO, CAMEI, gems cut in *relief*, the most expensive class of cut stones. The custom of ornamenting goblets, cratera, candelabra, and other articles with gems, originated in the East; and was followed at the court of the Seleucidæ, the greatest extravagance being practised with regard to such ornaments. When the image on the stone was not to be used as a seal it was cut in relief, and the variegated onyx was generally selected. Great attention was paid to the different colors of the strata of the stone, so that the objects stood out light from a dark ground. Some of the cameos preserved to us are wonders of beauty and technical perfection, showing the high degree of Art to which the Grecian lapidaries had attained under the luxurious successors of Alexander the Great. The finest specimen now existing is the Gonzaga cameo, formerly at Malmaison, now in the imperial collection of gems at St. Petersburg. Among the remains of the ancient art of stone-cutting, the gems cut in relief, called on account of the different layers of stone camei, are rarer and more valuable than those cut in intaglio. Cameos are not mentioned in the history of mediæval art; they were brought forward again in Italy in recent times. The production of cameos has become an art-manufacture of considerable importance.

CAMERALIS'TICS, the science of finance or public revenue, comprehending the means of raising and disposing of it.

CAM'ERA LU'CIDA, an optical instrument, for the purpose of making the image of any object appear on the wall in a light room, either by day or night.—Also, an instrument for drawing objects in true perspective.

CAM'ERA-OBSCU'RA, or *dark chamber*, an optical machine or apparatus, in which the light being collected, and thrown through a single aperture, external objects are exhibited distinctly, and in their native colors, on any white surface placed within the machine.

CAMISADE', a French term for attacking or surprising an enemy by night. It obtained the name from the soldiers wearing their shirts over their other clothes, that they might be known to each other.

CAM'LET, a sort of stuff originally made of camel's hair and silk mixed, but now of wool and silk.

CAMP, the residence of an army resting in tents; or, the place and order of tents for soldiers in the field. On the continent of Europe tents are abolished, and the armies *bivouac* in the open air, or, if the time will allow it, lodge in huts built of branches, &c. In short, in the progress of the military art, camps have become more slight and simple, even with those who still continue to make use of them.

CAMPAIGN', the space of time during which an army is kept in the field. A campaign is usually from spring to autumn; but sometimes armies make a winter campaign.

CAMPANILE', in architecture, properly a tower for containing a bell or bells. Though the word has been adopted in the English language, and applied to the bell towers of churches, it more properly belongs to those towers near churches, but detached from them, to be seen in many of the cities of Italy. The principal of these are the Campanile of Cremona, which is of the extraordinary height of 396 feet; that of Florence, 268 feet high, built from the design of Giotto;

the Garisendi tower at Bologna, built in 1110, which is 147 feet high, and is 8 feet 8 inches out of an upright; and very near to it in the same city another tower, bearing the name of Asinelli, 327 feet in height, and leaning from the perpendicular 3 feet 8 inches, but which, seen, as it always is, in company with the first, seems to lean but little. The last we shall name is that which is commonly called the leaning tower of Pisa, and perhaps the most remarkable of all. It is 151 feet high, and overhangs 12 feet 9 inches. Its general form possesses elegance, and is that of a cylinder encircled by 8 tiers of columns over each other, and each with an entablature. The columns are all of marble, and the upper tier is recessed back.

CAMPES'TRE, a short garment fastened about the loins, and extending from thence down the legs, nearly to the knees, after the manner of the *kilt.* It was worn by the Roman youths when they exercised in public places, also by soldiers and gladiators for the sake of decency when exercising.

CAM'PUS MAII, an anniversary assembly of our ancestors, held on Mayday, when they confederated together for defence of the kingdom against all its enemies.

CAM'PUS MAR'TIUS, among the Romans, a field, by the side of the Tiber, where the youth exercised themselves in warlike exercises. It was so called, on account of a temple that stood on it, consecrated to the god Mars. The consuls, Brutus and Collatinus, made it the place for holding the comitia or assemblies of people, and, in after times, it was adorned with a great quantity of fine statues.

CANA'BUS, CANE'VAS, CANNE'VAS, the term by which the ancients designated the wooden skeleton covered with clay, or some other soft substance, for modelling larger figures; hence the French word *canevas.* Similar skeletons were used as anatomical studies, by painters and plastic artists.

CANA'RIUM AUGU'RIUM, in antiquity, a sacrifice among the Romans, of a red dog, for the purpose of appeasing the fury of the dog-star on the approach of harvest.

CANCELLA'RIA CU'RIA, in archæology, the court of Chancery.

CANCEL'LI, in architecture, trellis, or lattice-work, made of cross bars of wood or iron. Also, the balusters or rails encompassing the bar of a court of justice.

CANDELA'BRA, were objects of great importance in ancient Art; they were originally used as candlesticks, but after oil was introduced, they were used to hold lamps, and stood on the ground, being very tall, from four to seven or ten feet in height. The simplest candelabra were of wood, others were very splendid both in material and in their ornaments. The largest candelabra, placed in temples and palaces, were of marble with ornaments in relief and fastened to the ground; there are several specimens in the Museum Clementinum at Rome. These large candelabra were also altars of incense, the carving showing to what god they were dedicated: they were also given as offerings, and were then made of finer metals, and even of precious stones. Candelabra were also made of baked earth, but they were mostly of elegantly wrought bronze. They consisted of three parts:—1. the feet; 2. the shaft; 3. the plinth with the tray, upon which the lamp was placed. The base generally consisted of three animals' feet, ornamented with leaves. The shaft was fluted; and on the plinth often stands a figure holding the top, generally in the shape of a vase, on which rests the tray. The branching candelabra are valuable as works of Art, and also those where the shaft is formed by a statue, bearing a torch-like lamp, and each arm holding a plate for a lamp. Another kind of candelabrum was called Lampadarii: these were in the form of pillars, with arms or branches from which the lamps hung by chains. In the Museo Etrusco Gregoriano at Rome, are forty-three candelabra of various forms, which were excavated at Cervetri. Some have smooth, and some have fluted, shafts, on which is represented a climbing animal, a serpent, lizard, weasel, or a cat following a cock. Sometimes these shafts bear a cup, or branch into many arms, be-

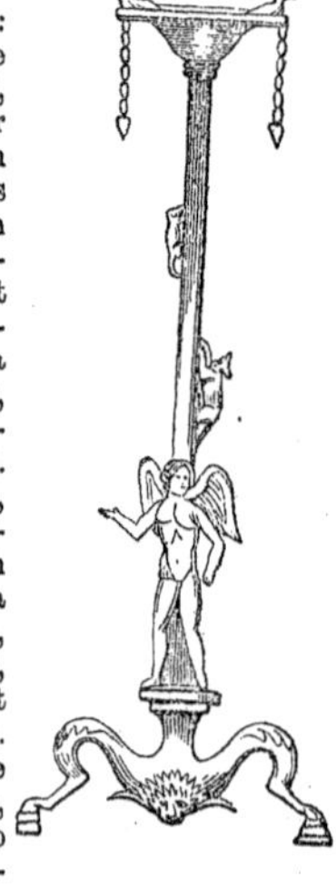

tween which stand beautiful little figures, or they have plates rising perpendicularly above one another. They generally rest on feet of lions, men, or stags, or they are supported by figures of satyrs, &c. Some candelabra are in the form of a human figure, bearing the plate in the outstretched hand, and sometimes the pillar is supported by caryatides. The most curious specimens of candelabra, as respects form, use, and workmanship, are those excavated at Herculaneum and Pompeii. These are all of bronze; and that they were employed for domestic purposes is proved from the representation, on an Etruscan vase, of one which serves to give light to the guests assembled round a banquet table. They are slender in their proportions, and perfectly portable, rarely exceeding five feet in height. It is to be observed, that none of the candelabra hitherto found exhibit any appearance of a socket or of a spike at top, from which an inference of the use of candles could be drawn.

CAN'DIDATE, a person who seeks or aspires to some public office. In the Roman commonwealth, the CANDIDATI were obliged to wear a white robe, during the two years of their soliciting for a place. This garment, according to Plutarch, they wore without any other clothes, that the people might not suspect they concealed money for purchasing votes; and also, that they might the more easily show to the people, the scars of those wounds they had received in fighting for the defence of the commonwealth.

CANDIDA'TI MIL'ITES, an order of soldiers, among the Romans, who served as the emperor's body-guards, to defend him in battle. They were the tallest and strongest of the whole troops; and were called *candidati*, in consequence of being clothed in white.

CAN'DLEMAS DAY, the festival observed on the second day of February, in commemoration of the purification of the Virgin Mary. It is borrowed from the practice of the ancient Christians, who on that day used an abundance of lights both in their churches and processions, in memory, as is supposed, of our Saviour's being on that day declared by Simeon "to be a light to lighten the Gentiles." In imitation of this custom, the Roman Catholics on this day consecrate all the tapers and candles which they use in their churches during the whole year.

CAN'DYS, a kind of gown, of woollen cloth with wide sleeves, worn by the

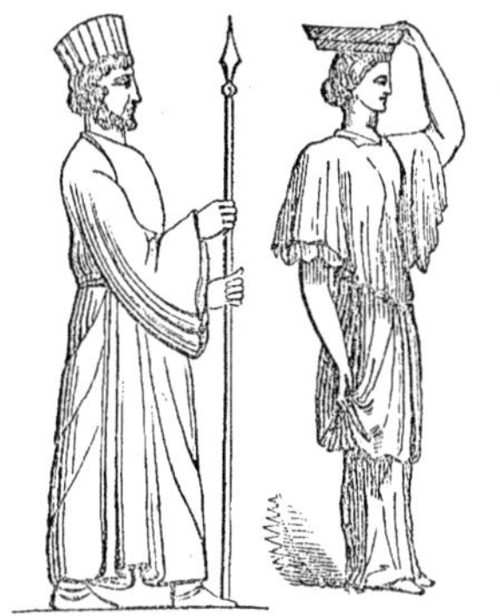

Candys. Canephoros.

Medes and Persians as an outside garment; it was usually of purple or similar brilliant color.

CANEPHO'ROS, the bearer of the round basket containing the implements of sacrifice, in the processions of the Dionysia, Panathenea, and other public festivals. The attitude in which they appear in works of Art, is a favorite one with the ancient artists; the figure elevates one arm to support the basket carried on the head, and with the other slightly raises her tunic.

CANIC'ULAR DAYS, or DOG DAYS, the name given to certain days of the year, during which the heat is usually the greatest. They are reckoned about forty, and are set down in the almanacs as beginning on the 3d day of July, and ending on the 11th of August. In the time of the ancient astronomers, the remarkable star Sirius, called also *Canicula*, or the *Dog Star*, rose heliacally, that is, just before the sun, about the beginning of July; and the sultry heat which usually prevails at that season, with all its disagreeable effects, among which the tendency of dogs to become mad is not one of the least disagreeable, were ascribed to the malignant rage of the star. Owing to the precession of the equinoxes, the heliacal rising of Sirius now takes place later in the year, and in a cooler season; so that the *dog days* have not now that relation to the particular position of the *Dog Star* from which they obtained their name.

CANIC'ULAR YEAR, the ancient solar year of the Egyptians; so called because its commencement was determined by the heliacal rising of the Dog Star. The

Egyptians chose this star for their observations, either on account of its superior brightness, or because its heliacal rising corresponded with the annual overflow of the Nile. At a very early period of history the Egyptians had perceived that the solar year contains 365¼ days; for their common years consisted of 365 days, and every fourth year of 366, as in the Julian Calendar.

CAN'NON, a piece of ordnance, or a heavy metallic gun for a battery, mounted on a carriage. Guns of this kind are made of iron or brass, and of different sizes, carrying balls from three or four to forty-eight pounds' weight. The explosion being directed by the tube, balls and missiles are carried to great distances with destructive force. In a field of battle they are often drawn by horses on light carriages, and are called field-pieces, or flying artillery.

CANOE', a small boat, made of the trunk of a tree, hollowed out by cutting or burning; and sometimes also of pieces of bark joined together. It is impelled by a paddle instead of an oar; and is used by the uncivilized nations in both hemispheres.

CAN'ON, a word of various significations, of which we can only enumerate the principal.

1. In cathedral and collegiate churches there are canons who perform some of the services, and are possessed of certain revenues connected with them. These are, strictly speaking, *residentiary* canons: *foreign* canons are those to whom collegiate revenues are assigned without the exaction of any duty.

2. The laws and ordinances of ecclesiastical councils are called canons.

3. The canon of Scripture signifies the authorized and received catalogue of the sacred books. The canon of the Old Testament, as received by the Catholics, differs from that of the Protestant churches in regarding as inspired those books which they reject under the term Apocrypha. The catalogue received by the Jews themselves, which we adopt, was first enlarged by the Council of Carthage to the extent in which it is held by our opponents, and that decision was formally confirmed by the Council of Trent. In the canon of the New Testament, however, the agreement of Christian churches may be considered unanimous. There exist a series of enumerations of sacred books of the latter covenant in the writings of the first four centuries, the general agreement of which, and the satisfactory reasons which can be assigned in most cases of omission — there are no additions—distinctly mark the universality of the judgment of the early churches in this matter.—In music, a perpetual fugue. This original method of writing this was on one line, with marks thereon, to show where the parts that imitate were to begin and end. This, however, was what the Italians more particularly call *canone chiuso*, (shut) or *canone in corpo*.

CAN'ONESS, a description of religious women in France and Germany. Their convents were termed *colleges*. They did not live in seclusion. The college of Remiremont was the oldest establishment of this order in France. Similar noble monasteries still exist in Germany, and the revenues and dignities of some belong to Protestants.

CANON'ICAL HOURS, stated times of the day set apart, more especially by the Romish church, for devotional purposes. In England the canonical hours are from 8 to 12 in the forenoon, before or after which the ceremony of marriage cannot be legally performed in any parish church.

CANONIZA'TION, a ceremony in the Romish church, by which holy men deceased are enrolled in the catalogue of saints. The privilege of canonizing was originally common to all bishops, and was first confined to the Pope by Alexander III. in 1170. When it is proposed to canonize any person, a formal process is instituted, by which his merits or demerits are investigated. Hereupon the *beatification* of the person in question is pronounced by the Pope, and his canonization follows upon the production of testimony to miracles performed at his tomb or by his remains. The day of his death is generally selected to be kept in his honor, and is inserted as such in the calendar.

CAN'OPY, a covering of velvet, silk, or cloth of gold, extended on a frame, and richly embroidered with suitable devices, supported and carried by four or more staves of wood or silver, borne in procession over the heads of distinguished personages, or over the hearse at the funerals of noble persons. In the religious processions of the Catholic church it is borne over the Host and sacred reliques. According to Roman use they are white, but in the French and Flemish churches they are generally red. In England, the two colors seem to have been used indiscriminately.

CANT, quaint or vulgar language, affected by particular persons or professions, and not authorized by established usage.—In architecture, a term expressing the position of any piece of timber not standing square.—*Cant moulding*, a moulding with a bevelled surface applied to the capitals of columns.

CANTAB'ILE, in music, a term applied to movements intended to be in a graceful and melodious style.

CANTAN'TE, in music, a term to denote the vocal part of the composition.

CANTA'TA, a song, or composition, intermixed with recitatives, airs, and different movements, chiefly intended for a single voice, with a thorough bass, though sometimes with other instruments.

CAN'THARUS, a kind of drinking-cup with handles, sacred to Bacchus, who

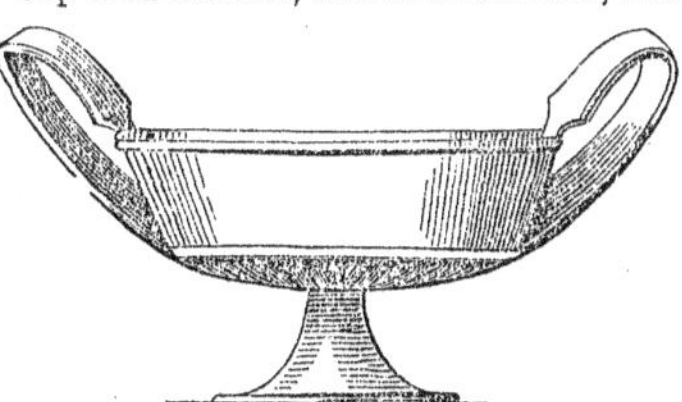

is frequently depicted on antique vases, &c., holding it in his hand.

CAN'TICÆ, ancient dramatic soliloquies, supposed to have been introduced as interludes.

CAN'TICLES, the Song of Songs, in the Bible, supposed to be a marriage song written by Solomon; to be explained by compositions of a similar nature in Eastern countries. By other writers it is supposed to be a series of sacred idols, each distinct and independent of the other.

CANTILE'ENA, in music, the treble melody, or upper part of any composition.

CANTILE'VER, in architecture, a piece of wood framed into the front or side of a house, and projecting from it, to sustain the eaves and mouldings over them.

CAN'TO, a part or division of a poem, answering to what in prose is called a book. In Italian, *canto* is a song; and it signifies also the first treble, or highest vocal part.

CAN'TO-FER'MO, in music, the subject song. Every part that is the subject of counterpoint, whether plain or figured, is called by the Italians *canto fermo*.

CAN'TONED, in architecture, is when the corner of a building is adorned with a pilaster, an angular column, rustic quoins, or anything that projects beyond the level of a wall.

CAN'VAS, a coarse sort of cloth, of which there are several kinds. Among others, are, 1. That worked regularly in little squares as a basis for tapestry: 2. That which is called buckram: 3. The cloth used for pictures: And, 4. That employed for sails of ships, tents, &c. Two kinds are prepared for artists' use; the best is called *ticking*. It is *primed* with a ground of a neutral gray color, or with other colors, according to the fancy of the painter. Certain sizes being in greater request than others, they are kept stretched on frames ready for use; for portraits, these are known by the names of *Kit-cat*, which measures 28 or 29 inches by 36 inches; *Three-quarters*, measures 25 by 30; *Half-length*, 40 by 50; *Bishops' half-length*, 44 or 45 by 56; *Bishops' whole length*, 58 by 94.

CAN'ZONE, or CANZO'NA, in music, a song or air in two or three parts, with passages of fugue and imitation; but it is sometimes used for a kind of lyric poem, in Italian, to which music may be composed in the style of a cantata.

CANZONET', in music, a short song, in one or two parts.

CAP, a part of dress made to cover the head. The use of caps and hats is referred to the year 1449, the first seen in Europe, being at the entry of Charles VII. into Rouen: from that time they began to take place of hoods or chaperons.—CAP, in architecture, the uppermost part of any assemblage of principal or subordinate parts.—*Cap of maintenance*, one of the ornaments of state, carried before the kings of England at the coronation. It is of crimson velvet, faced with ermine. It is also frequently met with above the helmet, instead of wreaths, under gentlemen's crests.—*Cap-a-pie*, (French) from head to foot.

CA'PET, the name of the French race of kings, which has given 118 sovereigns to Europe, viz., 36 kings of France, 22 kings of Portugal, 5 of Spain, 11 of Naples and Sicily, 3 of Hungary, 3 emperors of Constantinople, 3 kings of Navarre, 17 dukes of Burgundy, 12 dukes of Brittany, 2 dukes of Lorraine, and 4 dukes of Parma.

CA'PIAS, in law, a writ of two sorts; one before judgment, to take the defendant; the other after, which is called the writ of execution.

CAP'ITAL, in commerce, the fund or stock, in money and goods, of a merchant, manufacturer, &c., or of a trading company.—*A floating capital* is that which remains after payment is made for all the apparatus and implements of the business.—*Fictitious capital* generally means nothing more or less than excessive credits, which throw the management and disposition of a great deal of property into the hands of persons who are not able to answer for the risks of loss from its bad management, or other causes.—CAPITAL, in architecture, the uppermost part of a column or pilaster, serving as the head or crowning, and placed immediately over the shaft, and under the entablature.

CAPITA'TION, a tax or imposition raised on each person in consideration of his labor, industry, office, rank, &c. It is a very ancient kind of tribute, and answers to what the Latins called *tributum*, by which taxes on persons are distinguished from taxes on merchandise, called *vectigalia*.

CAP'ITOL, a castle, in ancient Rome, on the Mons Capitolinus, where there was a temple dedicated to Jupiter, in which the senate assembled; and on the same spot is still the city-hall or town-house, where the conservators of the Roman people hold their meetings. The foundations of the capitol were laid by Tarquin the elder, in the year of Rome 139: his successor Servius raised the walls, and Tarquin the Proud finished it in 221; but it was not consecrated till the third year after the expulsion of the kings, and establishment of the consulate. The capitol consisted of three parts, a nave, sacred to Jupiter; and two wings, the one consecrated to Juno, and the other to Minerva: it was ascended by stairs; the frontispiece and sides were surrounded with galleries, in which those who were honored with triumphs entertained the senate at a magnificent banquet, after the sacrifices had been offered to the gods. Both the inside and outside were enriched with numerous ornaments, the most distinguished of which was the statue of Jupiter, with his golden thunder-bolt, sceptre, and crown. In the capitol also were a temple to Jupiter the guardian, and another to Juno; with the mint; and on the descent of the hill was the temple of Concord. This beautiful edifice contained the most sacred deposits of religion, such as the ancylia, the books of the sybils, &c.

CAP'ITOLINE GAMES, these were annual games instituted by Camillus, in honor of Jupiter Capitolinus, and in commemoration of the preservation of the capitol from the Gauls. There was also another kind of Capitoline games, instituted by Domitian, and celebrated every five years, at which rewards and crowns were bestowed on the poets, champions, orators, historians, &c.

CAPIT'ULA RURA'LIA, assemblies or chapters held by rural deans and parochial clergy within the precinct of every distinct deanery.

CAPIT'ULARY, the body of laws or statutes of a chapter, or of an ecclesiastical council.

CAPITULA'TION, in military affairs, a treaty made between the garrison of a place besieged and the besiegers, for surrendering on certain conditions. The term is also applicable to troops in any situation in which they are compelled to submit to a victorious enemy.

CAPIT'ULUM, in antiquity, a transverse beam in the military engines of the ancients, wherein were holes for the strings with which they were set in motion.

CAPOTE', a large great coat, with a hood or cowl, which is sometimes worn by sentinels in bad weather.

CAPRIC'CIO, in music, the term for that irregular kind of composition in which the composer, without any restraint, follows the bent of his humor.—CAPRICCIO'SO denotes that the movement before which it is written, is to be played in a free and fantastic style.

CAP'TAIN, in the army, the commander of a company of foot or a troop of horse; and in the naval or merchant service, the commander of a vessel.—A *Captain-lieutenant* is an officer, who, with the rank of captain and pay of lieutenant, commands a company or troop.—A *Post-captain* in the British navy, is an officer commanding any man-of-war, from a ship of the line down to a ship-rigged sloop.—A man eminently skilled in war or military affairs is styled a "*great-captain*," as the Duke of Wellington.

CAP'TION, in law, the act of taking any person by any judicial process.

CAPTIV'ITY, in sacred history, a punishment which God inflicted upon the Jews for their vices and infidelity. The first captivity was that of Egypt, from which the Israelites were delivered by Moses; then followed six captivities during the government of the judges; but the greatest and most remarkable were those of Judah and Israel, which happened under the kings of those different kingdoms.

CAPUCHINS', an order of Franciscan friars in the Romish church, so called from their *capuche* or hood sewed to their habits, and hanging down their backs.

CAP'ULA, in antiquity, a wooden utensil with two handles for taking oil out of one vessel into another. The person who did this office was called the *capulator*.

CAR'ABINE, or CAR'BINE, a short gun used by the cavalry.

CAR'ACOLE, the half wheel which a horseman makes, either to the right or left. The cavalry make a caracole after each discharge, in order to pass to the rear of the squadron.

CA'RAITES, a sect among the Jews who adhere closely to the text and letter of the scriptures, rejecting the rabbinical interpretations and the cabbala.

CAR'AVAN, a company of merchants, travellers, or pilgrims, who associate together in many parts of Asia and Africa, that they may travel with greater security through deserts and other places infested with robbers or exposed to other dangers. The commercial intercourse of Eastern and African nations has from the remotest ages been chiefly carried on by means of caravans, as the governments that have sprung up in those continents have seldom been able, even if they had had the will, to render travelling safe or practicable for individuals. Since the establishment of the Mohammedan faith, religious motives, conspiring with those of a less exalted character, have tended to augment the intercourse between different parts of the Eastern world, and to increase the number and magnitude of the caravans. Mohammed, as is well known, enjoined all his followers to visit Mecca once in their lifetime; and in obedience to a command so solemnly enjoined and sedulously inculcated, large caravans assemble for this purpose in every country where the Mohammedan faith is established. There are four regular caravans which proceed annually to Mecca; the first from Damascus, composed of pilgrims, travellers, and merchants, from Europe and Asia; the second from Cairo, for the Mohammedans of Barbary; the third from Zibith, near the mouth of the Red Sea, where those of Arabia and India meet; the fourth from Babylon, where the Persians assemble. Every caravan is under the command of a chief or aga, who has frequently under him such a number of troops or forces as is deemed sufficient for its defence. When it is practicable they encamp near wells or rivulets, and observe a regular discipline. Camels are almost uniformly used as a means of conveyance, in preference to the horse or any other animal, on account of their wonderful patience of fatigue, and their peculiarity of structure, which so admirably fits them for travelling through desert wastes.

CARAVAN'SERA, a large public building, or inn, appropriated for the reception and lodgment of caravans in the desert. Though serving in lieu of inns there is this essential difference between them, that the traveller finds nothing in the caravansera for the use either of himself or his cattle, but must carry all his provisions and necessaries with him. Caravanseras are also numerous in cities, where they serve not only as inns, but as shops, warehouses, and even exchanges.

CAR'CANET, in archæology, a chain for the neck.

CARCE'RES, in the ancient Circensian games, were inclosures in the circus, wherein the horses were restrained till the signal was given for starting, when, by an ingenious contrivance they all at once flew open.

CARCHE'SIUM, CARCHE'SION, the name of an antique drinking vessel, and also of the goblet peculiar to Bacchus, found on numerous antiques, sometimes in his own hand, as in the ancient representations in which the god is clothed and bearded, and sometimes at the Bacchic feasts. The carchesium has a shallow foot; it is generally wider than it is deep, smaller towards the centre, and with handles rising high over the edge, and reaching to the foot. Its use in religious ceremonies proves it to have been one of the oldest forms of goblets.

CAR'DINAL, which in a general sense signifies principal or pre-eminent, is formed of the Latin word *cardo*, a hinge, agreeably with the common expression, in which it is said of an important matter that everything *turns* upon it: thus Justice, Prudence, Temperance, and Fortitude are called the four *cardinal virtues*.—The *cardinal signs*, in astronomy, are Aries, Libra, Cancer, and Capricorn.—The *cardinal points* of the compass, north, south, east, and west.—*Cardinal numbers*, in grammar, are the numbers, one, two, three, &c., which are indeclinable, in opposition to the ordinal numbers, first, second, third, &c.

CAR'DINAL, in the Roman hierarchy, an ecclesiastical prince and subordinate magistrate, who has a voice in the conclave at the election of a pope, and who may be advanced to that dignity himself. The dress of a cardinal is a red soutanne, a rochet, a short purple mantle, and a red hat; and his title of address, "His eminence."

CA'RET, in grammar, a character in this form ^, denoting that something has been omitted, and is interlined.

CAR'ICATURE', in painting, an exaggerated representation of any object, in which any natural defects are overcharged, so as to make it appear ridiculous.

CAR'ILLONS, a species of chimes frequent in the Low Countries, particularly at Ghent and Antwerp, and played on a number of bells in a belfry, forming a complete series or scale of tones or semitones, like those of the harpsichord and organ.

CAR'MELITES, an order of mendicant friars, very numerous in Italy and Spain. They wear a scapulary, or small woollen habit of a brown color, thrown over the shoulders.

CAR'MEN, a Latin term, used, in a general sense, to signify a verse; but in a more peculiar sense, to signify a spell, charm, form of expiation, execration, &c., couched in few words, placed in a mystic order, on which its efficacy was supposed to depend.

CAR'MINE, a pigment or powder of a deep red or crimson color, procured from cochineal, and used for painting in miniature.

CARNA'TIONS, in painting, the parts of a picture which represent the naked limbs, &c.

CARNE'IA, a festival observed in most of the cities of Greece, and especially at Sparta, in honor of Apollo, surnamed Carneius. The festival lasted nine days, and was conducted in imitation of the method of living in camps; for nine tents were erected, in each of which nine men of three different tribes lived nine days.

CARNE'LIAN, a precious stone, either red, flesh-color, or white. The finest carnelians are those of the East Indies: there are some beautiful ones in the rivers of Silesia and Bohemia; and some of a quality not to be despised in Britain. The use to which they are most generally applied is that of seals.

CAR'NIVAL, the feast or season of rejoicing previous to Lent, celebrated with great spirit throughout Italy, when feasts, balls, operas, concerts, masquerades, &c., abound. The churches are filled with choristers, and the streets with masks. This festival flourishes more particularly at Venice, where it begins on the second holiday in Christmas, and where it boasts to have had at one time seven sovereign princes, and thirty thousand foreigners among its votaries.

CARNIV'OROUS, an epithet applied to animals that feed on flesh.

CAROLOT'IC COLUMNS, in architecture, columns with foliated shafts, decorated with leaves and branches winding spirally around them, or forming crowns and festoons.

CARO'LUS, a gold coin struck in the reign of Charles I., at that time valued at twenty shillings, but afterwards current at twenty-three.

CAR'PENTRY, in building and architecture, an assemblage of pieces of timber connected by framing or letting them into each other, as are the pieces of a roof, floor, centre, &c. It is distinguished from *joinery* by being put together without the use of other edge tools than the axe, adze, saw, and chisel; whereas joinery requires the use of the plane.

CAR'PET, a sort of stuff wrought either with the needle or the loom, and used as a covering for the floor. Persian and Turkish carpets are the most costly; but a variety of other kinds are used, many of which are both elegant and durable.

CAR'RACK, a large armed vessel employed by the Portuguese in the East India and Brazilian trade.

CARRA'GO, in the military art of the ancients, a barricade made by carts and wagons, which the Gauls and other barbarous nations put in the way to impede the progress of an enemy.

CARRA'RA, a hard white kind of marble, somewhat resembling the Parian; so called from the town of Carrara, where it was found.

CARRONADE', a short piece of ordnance, having a large calibre, and a chamber for the powder, like a mortar.

CARRU'CA, in antiquity, a splendid kind of chariot or car on four wheels, which were made of brass, ivory, silver, and sometimes of gold.

CARTE-BLANCHE, a blank paper, signed at the bottom with a person's name, and given to another person with permission to fill it up as he pleases; applied generally in the sense of unlimited terms being granted.

CAR'TEL, an agreement between two states for the exchange of their prisoners of war.—A *cartel-ship*, a ship commissioned in time of war to exchange the prisoners of any two hostile powers; also to carry any particular request from one power to another. The officer who commands her is ordered to carry no cargo, ammunition, or implements of war, except a gun for the purpose of firing signals.

CARTE'SIAN PHILOSOPHY, the philosophical system of René des Cartes, (born 1596,) a native of France, perhaps the most original thinker that country has produced. Des Cartes was the contemporary of Bacon, and exercised an equally powerful influence, though in a manner widely different, on the progress of philosophy in Europe. What Bacon strove to accomplish by calling men's attention to experiment and observation of nature, Des Cartes proposed to attain by the search for a first and self-evident ground of all knowledge. This he finds in the act of consciousness, involving necessarily the idea of self or mind. Consciousness is the act of thought, constitutes the essence of the soul, and is that which distinguishes it from matter. The ideas or objects of consciousness are of three kinds,—acquired, compounded, and innate. All physical phenomena Des Cartes endeavored to account for by his celebrated *vortices*—motions excited by God, the source of all motion.

CARTHAGIN'IAN, a native of ancient Carthage, or something pertaining to that celebrated city, which was situated on the northern coast of Africa, about twelve miles from the modern Tunis. It was founded by the Phœnicians, and destroyed by the Romans.

CARTHU'SIANS, a religious order, founded in the year 1080, by St. Bruno. They received their name from Chartreuse, the place of their institution. They are so remarkable for their austerity, that they never leave their cells except to go to church, nor speak to any person without leave.

CARTOON', a design drawn upon large sheets of paper for the purpose of being traced upon any other substance, where the subject is to be finished. The most celebrated cartoons in existence are those of Raphael, seven of which are at Hampton Court, and were originally designed for tapestry.

CARTOUCH', a case of wood holding about four hundred musket balls, besides iron balls, from six to ten, to be fired out of a howitzer. Also, a portable box for charges.—In architecture, *cartouches* are blocks or modillions used in the cornices of wainscoted apartments: also ornaments representing a scroll of paper.

CAR'TRIDGE, a case of paper or parchment filled with gunpowder, and used in the charging of guns. The cartridges for small arms, prepared for battle, contain the powder and ball: those for cannon and mortars are made of pasteboard or tin. Cartridges without balls are called *blank-cartridges*.—The *cartridge-box* is a case of wood covered with leather, with cells for cartridges, and worn upon a belt thrown over the left shoulder.

CAR'TULARY, or CHAR'TULARY, a register-book, or record, as of a monastery.

CARV'ING, a branch of sculpture usually limited to works in wood and ivory, sculpture, properly so called, being generally applied to carving in stone or marble. Various kinds of wood were used by the ancients, chiefly for images of the gods, to each of which a different or particular kind of wood was appropriated; as, for instance, the images of Dionysia, the God of Figs, were made of the wood of the fig-tree. Ivory was also used to great extent by the ancients in their works of Art; and the Chryselephantine sculpture, or the union of gold with ivory, was adopted by the greatest artists. For a long period prior to the Reformation, there was an immense demand for fine wood-carvings, as the remains in cathedrals, churches, colleges, of screens, canopies, desks, chair-seats; and in baronial halls, of door frames, staircases, chimney-pieces, cabinets, picture-frames, sufficiently show.

CARYATI'DES, in architecture, columns, or pillars shaped like the bodies of women, and in the dress of the Caryan people. They were erected as trophies, and intended to represent the Caryan women who were taken captives by the Athenians. Other female figures were afterwards used in the same manner, but they were called by the same name.

CASCADE', a small waterfall, either natural or artificial. The word is applied to such as are less than a cataract.

CASE, the particular state, condition, or circumstances that befall a person, or in which he is placed. Also, any outside covering which serves to enclose a thing entirely, as packing-cases, or knife-cases. Case, in grammar, implies the different inflections or terminations of nouns, serving to express the different relations they bear to each other and the things they represent.—*Action on the case*, in law, is an action in which the whole cause of complaint is set out in the writ

CASE'MENT, a window that opens on hinges. Also, a hollow moulding.

CASE-SHOT, musket balls, stones, old iron, &c., put into cases and discharged from cannon.

CASH, money in hand, or ready money, distinguished from bills.

CASHIER', a person who is entrusted with the cash of some public company. In a banking establishment the cashier superintends the books, payments, and receipts of the bank: he also signs or countersigns the notes, and superintends all the transactions, under the order of the directors.

CASK'ET, the diminutive of *cask*, a small chest or box, for jewels, &c.

CASQUE, a piece of defensive armor, to cover and protect the head and neck in battle.

CASQUETEL', a small steel cap or open helmet, without beaver or visor, but having a projecting umbril and flexible plates to cover the neck behind.

CASSA'TION, Court of, one of the most important institutions of modern France, which gives to the whole jurisdiction of that country coherency and uniformity, without endangering the necessary independence of the courts. It was established by the first national assembly, and has been preserved, in every essential respect, under all the changes of the revolution and restoration. It properly signifies the annulling of any act or decision, if the forms prescribed by law have been neglected or justice has been perverted.

CAS'SOCK, the vestment worn by clergymen under their gowns.

CAST, among artists, any statue or part of a statue, of bronze, or of plaster-of-Paris. A cast is that which owes its figure to the mould into which the matter of it has been poured or cast while in a fluid state; and thus differs from a model, which is made by repeated efforts with a ductile substance, as any adhesive earth; and from a piece of sculpture, which is the work of the chisel.

CASTANETS', instruments formed of small concave shells of ivory or hard wood, fastened to the thumb and beat with the middle finger. The Spaniards and Moors use them as an accompaniment to their saraband dances and guitars.

CASTE, the general name for the tribes of various employment, into which the Hindoos are divided in successive generations, and generations of families. The first caste is religious; the second warlike; the third commercial; and the fourth laborers. Persons of the religious caste are universally denominated *bramins;* the soldiers or princes are styled *cuttery* or *rajahs;* the traders, *choutres* or *shuddery;* the lowest order, *parias.*

CAS'TELLAIN, in feudal times, the owner, lord, or governor of a castle or fortified place.

CAS'TELLANY, the lordship belonging to a castle; or the extent of its land and jurisdiction.

CAST'ING, with founders, the running of metal into a mould: among sculptors, it is the taking casts or impressions of figures, &c. Plaster-of-Paris is the most usual material employed for this purpose.—In architecture, a term used to denote the bending of the surfaces of a piece of wood from their original state, caused either by the gravity of the material, or by its being subject to unequal temperature, moisture, or the uniform texture of the material. Called also Warping.

CASTING OF DRAPERIES, in painting or sculpture, consists in the proper distribution of the folds of the garments, so that they appear the result of accident rather than of study or labor. The arrangement of draperies sometimes gives the artist much trouble, but this is frequently caused by the material employed in the model being of a different substance to that depicted in the picture.

CAS'TLE, a fortress or place rendered defensible, either by nature or art.—English castles, walled with stone, and designed for residence as well as defence, are for the most part of no higher date than the Conquest. Those previously erected had been suffered to fall into ruin; and many writers have assigned this circumstance as a reason for the facility with which William the Norman made himself master of the country. It was the policy of this able general to build a considerable number: and in process of time the martial tenants of the crown erected them for themselves; so that towards the end of Stephen's reign, we are told that there existed upwards of eleven hundred. At this period castles were an evil of the greatest magnitude to both the sovereign and the subject; considerable struggles appear to have taken place with regard to their continuance; several were demolished; and their general decline commenced. A complete castle consisted of a ditch or moat, an outwork, called a barbican, which guarded the gate and drawbridge; an artificial mount; an outer and inner ballium or inclosure; and the keep, or lofty tower, in which the owner or governor resided, and under which were the dungeons.—*Castle-guard*, a feudal tenure, or knight service, which obliged the tenant to perform service within the realm, without limitation of time.—*Castle-ward*, an imposition laid upon subjects dwelling within a certain distance of a castle, for the purpose of maintaining watch and ward in the castle.

CAS'TOR AND POL'LUX, the name given to a meteor which sometimes appears at sea, attached to the extremities of the masts of ships under the form of balls of fire. When one ball only is seen, it is called Helena. The meteor is generally supposed to indicate the cessation of a storm, or a future calm; but Helena, or one ball only, to portend bad weather.

CAS'UISTRY, the science of resolving cases of doubtful propriety, or of determining the lawfulness or unlawfulness of any act, by rules and principles drawn from the Scriptures, from the laws of society, or from reason.

CA'SUS FŒD'ERIS, the case stipulated by treaty, or which comes within the terms of compact.

CA'SUS OMIS'SUS, in law, where any particular thing is omitted, and not provided for by the statute.

CATACHRE'SIS, in rhetoric, a trope which borrows the name of one thing to express another. Thus Milton, in describing Raphael's descent from the empyreal heaven, says,

"Down thither prone in flight
He speeds, and thro' the vast ethereal sky
Sails between worlds and worlds."

So in Scripture we read of the "*blood* of the grape." A catachresis, in fact, is the abuse of a trope, or when a word is too far wrested from its original signification.

CAT'ACOMB, a grotto or subterraneous place for the burial of the dead. It is generally applied to a vast number of subterraneous sepulchres, in the Appian Way, near Rome; supposed to be the cells in which were deposited the bodies of the primitive Christian martyrs. But there are now many other catacombs, as at Paris, &c.

CATADRO'MUS, in antiquity, the stadium, or place where races were run.

CATAFAL'CO, in architecture, a temporary structure of carpentry, decorated with painting and sculpture, representing a tomb or cenotaph, and used in funeral ceremonies. That used at the final interment of Michael Angelo at Florence was of the most magnificent description, and perhaps unequalled as to the art employed on it by any used before or since.

CATALEC'TIC, in Greek and Latin poetry, a verse wanting one syllable of its proper length: *acatalectic*, a verse complete in length; *hypercatalectic*, having one syllable too many; *brachycatalectic*, wanting two syllables.

CAT'ALEPSY, a disease in which the functions of the organs of sense and motion are suspended, whilst the heart continues to pulsate. The patients are said to be in a *trance;* and in this state they remain for some hours, or even days. Ammoniacal and ethereal stimulants are the most effectual restoratives.

CAT'ALOGUE RAISONNE', in bibliography, a catalogue of books, classed under the heads of their several subjects, and with a general abstract of the contents of works where the title does not sufficiently indicate it; thus serving as a manual, to direct the reader to the sources of information on any particular topic. The want of alphabetical arrangement is supplied by an index at the end. The catalogue of the French *Bibliothèque Royale* (10 vols. fol. 1739–53) is said to be the best work of this description.

CATAPUL'TA, or CAT'APULT, in antiquity, a military engine used for throwing arrows, darts, and stones upon the enemy. Some of these engines would throw stones of a hundred weight. Josephus takes notice of the surprising effects of these engines, and says, that the stones thrown out of them beat down the battlements, knocked off the angles of the towers, and would level a whole file of men, from one end to the other.

CAT'ARACT, a great fall of water over a precipice in the channel of a river, caused by rocks or other obstacles stopping the course of the stream; as that of Niagara, the Nile, the Danube, and the Rhine.

CATAS'TASIS, in poetry, the third part of the ancient drama, being that wherein the intrigue, or action, is supported and carried on, and heightened, till it be ripe for unravelling in the catastrophe.

CATAS'TROPHE, in dramatic poetry, the fourth and last part in the ancient drama, or that immediately succeeding the catastasis; and which consists in the unfolding and winding up of the plot, clearing up difficulties, and closing the play.

CATCH, in music, is defined to be "a piece for three or four voices, one of which leads, and the others follow in the same notes." But perhaps it may be more correctly described as a fugue in the unison, wherein to humor some conceit in the words, or to give them a different meaning, the melody is broken, and the sense is interrupted in one part, and *caught* and supported by another.

CAT'ECHISM, a form of instruction in religion, conveyed in questions and answers. The catechism of the Church of England originally consisted of no more than a repetition of the baptismal vow, the creed, and the Lord's Prayer; but King James I. ordered the bishops to add to it a short and plain explication of the sacraments.

CAT'ECHIST, an officer in the primitive Christian church, whose business it was to instruct the catechumens in the first principles of religion, and thereby prepare them for the reception of baptism.

CATECHU'MENS, a name formerly given in the Christian church to such as were prepared to receive the ordinance of baptism. These were anciently the children of believing parents, or pagans not fully initiated in the principles of the Christian religion; and were admitted to this state by the imposition of hands and the sign of the cross.

CAT'EGOREMAT'IC, in logic, when a word is capable of being employed by itself as a *term*, or predicate of a proposition.

CAT'EGORY, in logic and metaphysics, a Greek word, signifying originally that which may be said or predicated of a thing; a general term in reference to a less general one which is included under it. By Aristotle, from whom the word, and its corresponding Latin term *predicate*, was borrowed by the schoolmen, it was applied to denote the *most general* of the attributes that may be assigned to a subject. Of those he attempted an enumeration, under the name of substance, quantity, quality, relation, place, time, condition, state or habitude, action, and passion. The word has been revived in modern time by Kant, to express the most general of the modes in which a thing can be raised from an object of sense to an object of intellect; or, in other words, the forms or conditions which must pre-exist in the understanding, in order that an act of intelligence may take place. The difference between the categories of Kant and those of Aristotle is this, that the latter are mere generalizations from experience, which may consequently be multiplied indefinitely; whereas the former result from a professedly exhaustive analysis of the human understanding as it is in itself, or formally, that is, apart from all consideration of its object-matter

CATENA'RIAN ARCH, in architecture, an arch whose form is that of a chord or chain suspended from two fixed points at its extremities.

CAT'GUT, the name for the strings made of the intestines of sheep or lambs, used in musical instruments, &c. Great quantities are imported from Lyons and Italy.

CATHE'DRA, in archæology, a term used to denote the pulpit, or the professor's chair. It originally signified any chair.—Among ecclesiastical writers it denotes a bishop's see, or throne. Hence, *ex cathedra* is a phrase which is much used among the clergy of the Romish church, in relation to the solemn decrees of the pope.

CATHE'DRAL, the principal church of a diocese, in which is the throne of the bishop. The term cathedra was originally applied to the seats in which the bishop and presbyters sate in their assemblies, which were held in the rooms in which the worship of the first Christians was also performed before they had liberty to erect temples for that purpose. In after-times the choir of the cathedral church was made to terminate in a semicircular or polygonal apsis; and in the recess thus formed were placed the throne of the bishop in the centre, and seats of an inferior class for presbyters.

CATHER'INE, St., of Alexandria, the patron saint of Philosophy and the Schools. The pictures of her are almost innumerable; as patron saint or martyr, her attributes are a broken wheel set round with knives, and a sword, the instruments of her martyrdom.

CATH'OLIC, an epithet properly signifying universal. Originally this appellation was given to the Christian church in general, but now the Romish church assumes it exclusively to itself; whence the name of Roman Catholics has been applied, since the Reformation, to the followers of the Romish doctrine and discipline.—*Catholic Majesty*, the title given to the king or queen of Spain.—*Catholic Priest*, a clergyman or priest ordained to say mass and administer the sacraments, &c., according to the rites of the Romish church.

CATOP'TROMANCY, a species of divination among the ancients, which was performed for the sick, by letting down a mirror, fastened by a thread, into a fountain before the temple of Ceres, to look at his face in it. If it appeared distorted and ghastly, it was a sign of death; if fresh and healthy, it denoted a speedy recovery.

CAUSAL'ITY, or CAUSA'TION, among metaphysicians, the action or power of a cause in producing its effect.

CAUSE, that from whence anything proceeds, or by virtue of which anything is done: it stands opposed to *effect*. We get the ideas of cause and effect from our observation of the vicissitude of things, while we perceive some qualities or substances begin to exist, and that they receive their existence from the due application and operation of other beings. That which produces is the *cause;* that which is produced, the *effect.*—Causes are distinguished, by the schools, into efficient, material, final, and formal. *Efficient Causes* are the agents employed in the production of anything. *Material Causes*, the subjects whereon the agents work; or the materials whereof the thing is produced. *Final Causes* are the motives inducing an agent to act: or the design and purpose for which the thing was done. Causes are again distinguished into physical and moral; universal, or particular; principal, or instrumental: total, or partial; univocal, equivocal, &c.—*Cause*, among civilians, is the same with *action;* denoting any legal process which a party institutes to obtain his demand, or by which he seeks his supposed right.

CAUTIO'NE ADMITTEN'DA, in law, a writ which lies against a bishop that holds an excommunicated person in prison for contempt, after he has offered sufficient caution or security to obey the orders of the church. On receipt of this writ, the sheriff warns the bishop to take caution.

CAVALCADE' a pompous procession of horsemen, equipages, &c., by way of parade to grace a triumph, public entry, or the like.

CAVALIER', a gallant armed horseman. It was also an appellation given to the party of Charles I. to distinguish them from the parliamentarians, who were called Roundheads.—In fortification, a work raised within the body of a place, above the other works.

CAV'ALRY, a body of soldiers on horseback; a general term for light-horse, dragoons, lancers, and all other troops who are armed and mounted. Their chief use is to make frequent excursions to the disturbance of the enemy, and intercept his convoys; in battle, to support and cover the infantry, and to break through and disorder the enemy. The use of cavalry is probably nearly as ancient as war itself. At the present day the cavalry is divided into *light* and *heavy horse*, which are employed for different purposes. The heavy cavalry, with defensive armor (cuirassiers,) is generally employed where force is requisite; the lighter troops are used in small detachments, where swiftness and continued effort are required.

CA'VEAT, an entry in the spiritual courts, by which the probate of a will, letters of administration, license of marriage, &c., may be prevented from being issued without the knowledge, and, if the reason be just, the consent of the party entering the caveat.

CAV'ERN, a natural cavity, or deep hollow place in the earth, arising either from arches accidentally made, or from streams of water flowing under ground. One of the grandest natural caverns known is Fingal's cave, in Staffa, one of the western islands of Scotland. The grotto of Antiparos, in the Archipelago, is celebrated for its magnificence. In some parts, immense columns descend to the floor; others present the appearance of trees and brooks turned to marble. The Peak Cavern, in Derbyshire, is also a celebrated curiosity of this kind. It is nearly half a mile in length, and, at its lowest part, 600 feet below the surface. Many caves are formed by the lava of volcanoes. In the Cevennes mountains, in France, are caverns and grottoes of great extent, and which abound in objects of curiosity. But the largest we read of is the cavern of Guacharo, in South America, which is said to extend for leagues.

CAVET'TO, in architecture, a hollow member, or round concave moulding, containing the quadrant of a circle; and used as an ornament in cornices.

CECIL'IA, St., the patroness of music, and supposed inventress of the organ; she suffered martyrdom by being plunged into a vessel of boiling oil. She is sometimes depicted with a gash in her neck, and standing in a cauldron, but more frequently holding the model of an organ, and turning her head towards heaven, as if listening to the music of the spheres.

CEIL'ING, in architecture, the upper part or roof of a room, being a lay or covering of plaster over laths, nailed on the bottom of the joists which bear the floor of the upper room, or on joists put up for that purpose where there is no upper room, hence called ceiling joists.

CEL'ARENT, in logic, a mode of syllogism, wherein the major and conclusion are universal negative propositions, and the minor an universal affirmative; as "No man that is a hypocrite can be saved: Every man who with his lips only cries Lord, Lord, is a hypocrite: Therefore, no man, who with his lips only cries Lord, Lord, can be saved."

CEL'EBE, a vase, found chiefly in Etruria, distinguished by its peculiarly shaped handles, which are pillared.

CEL'ERES, in Roman antiquity, a regiment of body-guards belonging to the Roman kings, established by Romulus, and composed of 300 young men chosen out of the most illustrious Roman families, and approved by the suffrages of the curiæ of the people, each of which furnished ten.

CELES'TIAL, in its first and obvious sense, denotes something pertaining to, or dwelling in heaven. In mythology, the term is applied to the residence of the gods, supposed to be in the clouds or stars; and hence the space in which the stars are situated are commonly called the celestial spaces.

CEL'ESTINS, a religious order of Christians, reformed from the Bernardins by Pope Celestin V. The Celestins rise two hours after midnight to say matins; they eat no flesh at any time, except when sick, and fast often. Their habit is a white gown, a capuche, and a black scapulary.

CELEUS'MA, in antiquity, a naval shout serving as a signal for the mariners to ply their oars, or to cease from rowing. It was also made use of to signify the joyful acclamation of vintagers, and the shouts of the conquerors over the vanquished.

CELIB'ACY, an unmarried or single state of life, to which, according to the doctrine and the discipline of the church of Rome, the clergy are obliged to conform.

CEL'TIC, pertaining to the *Celts*, or primitive inhabitants of Britain, Gaul, Spain. Thus we say *Celtic* customs, *Celtic* origin, *Celtic* remains, &c.

CEM'ETERY, a repository for the dead. Among modern improvements, perhaps few are more deserving of commendation than the custom, recently introduced, of appropriating an eligible spot of ground, at a convenient distance from populous towns, for the purpose of human interment.

CEN'OTAPH, a monument erected to a deceased person, but not containing the remains. Originally cenotaphs were raised for those only whose bones could not be found, who had perished at sea, &c., or to one who died far away from his native town. The tomb built by a man during his life-time for himself and family was called a cenotaph.

CEN'SER, in the religious rites of the ancients, was a vase, containing incense to be used in sacrificing to the gods. Censers were likewise in use among the Jews, as we find in the 1 Kings vii. 50. "Solomon, when he prepared furniture for the temple of the Lord, among other things made censers of pure gold."

CEN'SOR, an officer in ancient Rome, whose business it was to reform the manners and to value the estates of the people. At first they were chosen out of the senate, but after the plebeians had got the consulate open to them, they soon arrived at the censorship. Cicero reduces their functions to the numbering of the people, the correction and reformation of manners, the estimating the effects of each citizen, the proportioning of taxes, the superintendence of tribute, the exclusion from the temples, and the care of the public places. The office was so considerable, that none aspired to it till they had passed all the rest.

CEN'SURE, a judgment which condemns some book, person, or action, or more particularly a reprimand from a superior.—*Ecclesiastical censures* are penalties by which, for some striking malconduct, a member of a church is deprived of the communion of the church, or prohibited from executing the sacerdotal office.

CEN'SUS, in Roman antiquity, an authentic declaration made before the censors, by the several subjects of the empire, of their respective names and places of abode. This declaration was registered by the censors, and contained an enumeration of all their estates, lands, and inheritances, their quantity and quality, with the wives, children, domestics, tenants, and slaves of each citizen. The census was instituted by Servius Tullius, and was held every five years. The word *census* is still used to signify an enumeration of the inhabitants of any kingdom or state, taken by order of its legislature.

CENT, from *centum*, "a hundred," is used in commercial concerns to signify a hundred pounds. A profit of 10 *per cent.* is the gain of 10*l.* by the use of 100*l.*

CEN'TAUR, in classic antiquity, a monster, half man and half horse. It is intimated by Virgil, and generally believed, that the Centaurs were a tribe of Lapithæ, who inhabited the city of Pelethronium, adjoining to Mount Pelion, and who first broke and rode upon horses. Nations to whom the sight of a man on horseback was new, believed, as did the Americans of the Spaniards, the horse and his rider made but one animal.

CEN'TENARY, the number of a hundred, or pertaining thereto. Hence the epithet *centennial* for what regularly occurs once in a century.

CENTESIMA'TION, a military punishment, in cases of desertion, mutiny, &c., when every hundredth man is selected for execution.

CEN'TO, in poetry, a work wholly composed of verses or passages, promiscuously taken from other authors, and disposed in a new order.

CENTRAL FIRE, a supposed perpetual fire, which, according to the theory of some philosophers, exists in the centre of the earth, and to which, in ancient times, volcanoes and other similar phenomena were attributed.

CENTUM'VIRI, in Roman antiquity, judges appointed to decide common causes among the people. Three were chosen out of each tribe; and though there were five more than a hundred, they were nevertheless called centumviri, from the round number *centum*.

CENTU'RION, among the Romans, an officer in the infantry, who commanded a century, or a hundred men. The Roman legions were, in fact, divided into *centuries*.

CEN'TURY, in a general sense, denotes a hundred; or anything divided into, or consisting of, a hundred parts. The Roman people, when they were assembled for the electing of magistrates, enacting of laws, or deliberating upon any public affair, were always divided into centuries, and voted by centuries, in order that their suffrages might be the more easily collected; whence these assemblies were called *comitia centuriata*. This mode of dividing the Roman people was introduced by Servius Tullius; the first class contained eighty, to which were added the eighteen centuries of the knights; the three following classes had each twenty centuries, the fifth thirty, and the sixth only one century.—In chronology, it means the space of one hundred years; and this is the most common signification of the word. As we begin our common computation of time from the incarnation of Christ, the word is generally applied to some term of a hundred years subsequent to it.

CEREA'LIA, in antiquity, feasts of Ceres, instituted by Triptolemus of Eleusis, in Attica. These feasts were celebrated with religious purity; but the votaries of the goddess ran about with lighted torches, in commemoration of her search after her daughter Proserpine.—The word also was used to denote all sorts of corn of which bread is made.

CER'EMONY, an assemblage of several actions, forms, and circumstances, serving to render a thing more magnificent and solemn; particularly used to denote the external rites of religious worship, the formality of introducing ambassadors to audiences, &c.—*Master of the Ceremonies*, an officer instituted by James I. for the more honorable reception of ambassadors and strangers of quality, and for the regulation of all matters of etiquette in the assemblies over which they preside.—*Ceremonial of European Powers*, comprises—1. The particular titles due to sovereigns in different states; the imperial title being considered as expressing some sort of superiority over the royal, and having been in consequence assumed by various kings in their public acts (as the king of England since the union of the crowns.) 2. The acknowledgment of sovereign titles, the right to confer which was formerly claimed by the popes as their own prerogative, but they are now assumed by princes, and confirmed by the acknowledgment of other sovereigns. 3. The respective prerogatives of different sovereigns; which species of precedence is that which has occasioned the greatest amount of discussion and dispute when sovereigns, or their representatives, have been brought together. In 1504, Pope Julius II. arranged the rank of European powers in the following order: 1. The Roman emperor; 2. The king of Rome; 3. France; 4. Castile; 5. Aragon; 6. Portugal; 7. England; 8. Sicily; 9. Scotland; 10. Hungary; 11. Navarre; 12. Cyprus; 13. Bohemia; 14. Poland; 15. Denmark; 16. Republic of Venice; 17. Duke of Britanny; 18. Burgundy; 19. Elector of Bavaria; 20. Saxony; 21. Brandenburg; 22. Archduke of Austria; 23. Duke of Savoy; 24. Grand Duke of Florence; 25. Duke of Milan; 26. Bavaria. 27. Lorraine. This arrangement, however, gave birth to repeated contests. At present, where precedence is not considered as established between rulers of equal dignity, each concedes to the other precedence at home; and when they meet on the territory of a third party, they take precedence alternately until some arrangement is effected.

CERIN'THIANS, the followers of Cerinthus, one of the first heresiarchs in the church. They denied the divinity of Christ, but they held that a celestial virtue descended on him at his baptism in the form of a dove, by which he was consecrated and made Christ.

CERO'MA, an ointment made of oil and wax, with which the ancient wrestlers rubbed themselves to render their limbs more pliant.

CER'OMANCY, an ancient mode of divination, by means of dropping melted wax in water, and observing the shapes, &c., it assumed.

CEROPLAS'TIC, the art of modelling in wax, one of very high antiquity. Lysistratus, the brother of Lysippus, was the first that used wax for modelling the human figure. He lived in the time of Alexander the Great, and was a native of Sicyon.

CERTIF'ICATE, in a general sense, a testimony given in writing to declare or certify the truth of anything. Of these there are many which are requisite in almost every profession, but more particularly in the law and in the army.

CERTIORA'RI, a writ issuing out of some superior court, to call up the records of an inferior court, or remove a cause there depending, that it may be tried in a superior court.

CESSA'TION OF ARMS, an armistice or occasional truce, agreed to by the commanders of arms, to give time for a capitulation, or for other purposes.

CESSA'VIT, in law, a writ to recover lands, when the tenant or occupier has *ceased* for two years to perform the service which constitutes the condition of his tenure, and has not sufficient goods or chattels to be distrained.

CES'SION, in a general sense a surrender; but particularly a surrender of conquered territory to its former proprietor or sovereign by treaty.—CESSION, in the civil law, is a voluntary surrender of a person's effects to his creditors, to avoid imprisonment.

CES'TUS, CAESTUS, thongs of leather round the hands and arms, worn by boxers for offence and defence, to render their blows more powerful. The cestus was introduced when athletics were generally practised, and the name is Roman. It was a stronger defence than the *Himantes* of the ancient Greeks; the simple thongs of leather were still used occasionally in boxing, and in the exercises of the Agonistæ, and were called *Melichai*, because the blows they gave were less formidable than those of the cestus. There are many kinds of cestus, in some the thongs of leather are studded with nails. Works of ancient Art abound in which the cestus is represented.—*Cestus*, a girdle said to be worn by Venus, to which Homer ascribes the power of exciting love towards the wearer. It was also a marriage girdle, richly studded, with which the husband girded his wife at the wedding, and loosed again at night.

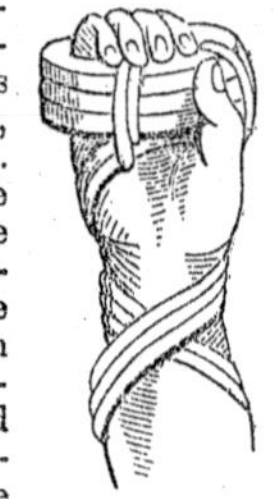

CHACONE', or CIACONE, in music, a kind of dance resembling a saraband, of Moorish origin. The bass of it consists of four notes, which proceed in conjoint degrees, whereon the harmonies are made with the same burden. Some have derived this dance from *cieco*, a blind man, its supposed inventor.

CHAIR, (*cathedra*), was anciently the *suggestum*, or pulpit, whence the priest or public orator spoke to the people. It is still applied to the place whence professors in universities deliver their lectures; thus we say, the professor's chair. It is commonly used for a speaker or president of a public council or assembly, as the *speaker's chair;* and by a metonymy, the speaker himself; as, to address the *chair.*—*Chair*, among the Roman Catholics, certain feasts held anciently in commemoration of the translation of the see or seat of the vicarage of Christ by St. Peter.—*Curule chair*, in Roman antiquity, an ivory seat placed on a car, wherein were seated the chief magistrates of Rome, and those to whom the honor of a triumph was granted.

CHALCED'ONY, a kind of quartz, semi-transparent, of a bluish white, but frequently striped and clouded with other colors. AGATE is a mixture of chalcedony and varieties of quartz, often beautifully tinted. Chalcedony and agate were used for seals and other works of art.

CHALCID'ICUM, in ancient architecture, a magnificent hall belonging to a tribunal or court of justice.

CHALCOG'RAPHY, a modern term for engraving on copper.

CHALDEE', or CHALDA'IC, the *language* spoken by the Chaldeans, or people of Chaldea: it is a dialect of the Hebrew.

CHAL'ICE, the communion cup, or vessel used to administer the wine in the sacrament of the eucharist. The form has undergone many variations in different ages, always preserving, however, its cup-like shape. Chalices are made of gold, but more commonly of silver, either

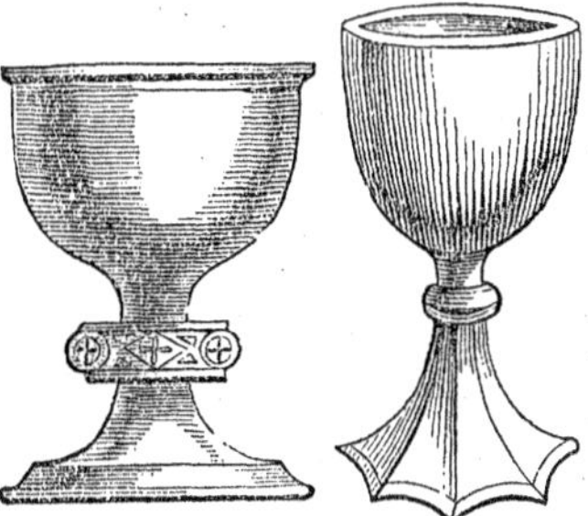

whole, or parcel gilt and jewelled. They have sometimes been made of crystal, glass, and agate, but these materials are now prohibited on account of their brittle nature.

CHALI'ZA, in Hebrew antiquity, the ceremony whereby a woman, left a widow, pulled off her brother-in-law's shoes, who should have espoused her; after which she was at liberty to marry whom she pleased.

CHAL'LENGE, in a general sense, a summons to fight, whether in a duel or in a pugilistic contest. In law, an exception to jurors, made by the party put on his trial: or the claim of a party that certain jurors shall not sit in trial upon him or his cause. The right of challenge is given both in civil and criminal trials, and extends either to the whole panel, or only to particular jurors. In criminal cases, a prisoner may challenge twenty jurors, without assigning a cause; which is called a *peremptory* challenge.

CHALYB'EATE, an epithet for waters in which iron forms the principal ingredient, as the waters of Tunbridge Wells. Chalybeates act chiefly as absorbents and deobstruents. The action of the particles of a chalybeate, by their elasticity, together with the momentum they give the blood by their ponderosity, makes it not only preferable to most other deobstruents, but also proper in other cases; especially where there is a viscidity of the juices, the blood impoverished, or the circulation languid.

CHAM, or KHAM, the title of the sovereign prince of Tartary. It is likewise applied to the principal noblemen of Persia.

CHAMADE', in war, a signal made by beat of drum or sound of trumpet, for a conference with the enemy, either to invite to a truce, or to propose a capitulation.

CHAM'BER, in building, any room situated between the lowermost and uppermost rooms. *Chamber*, in polity, the place where certain assemblies are held; also the assemblies themselves. Of these some are established for the administration of justice, others for commercial affairs. In many languages, *chamber* is used to designate a branch of government whose members assemble in a common apartment. — *Privy-chamber*. Gentlemen of the privy-chamber are servants of the king, who are to wait and attend on him and the queen at court.

CHAM'BERLAIN, a high officer in all European courts. Originally the chamberlain was the keeper of the treasure-chamber; and this meaning of the word is still preserved, in the usages of the corporations of London and other places, where the chamberlain is the officer who keeps the money belonging to the municipal body. But in modern times, the court officer styled chamberlain has the charge of the private apartments of the sovereign or noble to whom he is attached. In England, the lord great chamberlain, or king's chamberlain, is one of the three great officers of the king's household. He has the control of all the officers above stairs, except the precinct of the bedchamber, which is under the government of the groom of the stole. Under him are the vice-chamberlain, lord of the bedchamber, &c.; the chaplains, officers of the wardrobe, physicians, tradesmen, artisans, and others retained in his majesty's service are in his department, and sworn into office by him. He is commonly one of the highest nobility of the country; in virtue of his situation he precedes dukes. The emblem of office appropriated to the chamberlain in European courts is a gold key, generally suspended from two gold buttons.—The LORD GREAT CHAMBERLAIN OF ENGLAND (not of the household) is the sixth great officer of state. This office belonged for many centuries to the noble family of De Vere, Earls of Oxford; afterward to that of Bertie, Lords Willoughby de Eresby and Dukes of Ancaster. In that line it became vested in coheiresses, by whom the present deputy chamberlain (Lord Gwydir) is appointed.

CHAM'BRE ARDENTE, in French history, a name given to the tribunal which was instituted by Francis I. for the purpose of trying and burning heretics; and also the extraordinary commissions established under Louis XIV. for the examination of prisoners, and under the regent Duke of Orleans against public officers charged with certain offences against the revenues, and those guilty of fraud in the matter of Law's bank.

CHAM'BRE DES COMPTES, (Chamber of Accounts,) in French history, a great court established for various purposes; as for the registration of edicts, ordinances, letters patent, treaties of peace, &c. The sovereign chambre des comptes was at Paris: there were also inferior courts in ten provincial cities.

CHAM'FER, in architecture, the edge of anything originally right-angled cut aslope or bevel, so that the plane it then forms is inclined less than a right angle to the other planes with which it intersects.

CHAMP DE MARS, in French history, the public assemblies of the Franks, which were held in the open air.

CHAM'PERTY, in law, a bargain made with either plaintiff or defendant in any suit, for giving part of the land, debt, &c., sued for, to the party who undertakes the process at his own expense.

CHAM'PION, a person who undertakes a combat in the place of another: sometimes the word is used for him who fights in his own cause. In ancient times, when two champions were chosen to maintain a cause, it was always required that there should be a decree of the judge to authorize the combat: when the judge had pronounced sentence, the accused threw a gage or pledge, originally a glove or gantlet, which being taken up by the accuser, they were both taken into safe custody, till the day of battle appointed by the judge. Before the champions took the field, their heads were shaved to a kind of crown or round, which was left at the top: they then made oath that they believed the person who retained them to be in right, &c. They always engaged on foot, and with no other weapon than a club and a shield, and they always made an offering to the church, that God might assist them in the battle.—*Champion of the King (or Queen,)* an officer who rides armed into Westminster Hall on the coronation, while the sovereign is at dinner, and by herald makes proclamation, "That if any man shall deny the king's (or queen's) title to the crown, he is there ready to defend it in a single combat:" which being done, the sovereign drinks to him, and then presents him with a cup for his fee.

CHANCE, a term applied to events that are supposed to happen without any known or necessary cause; or, rather, of which the cause is such that they may happen in one way as well as another. Thus, when a piece of money is tossed up in the air, as no reason can be given why it should fall on one side rather than on the other, it is said to be an even chance which of the sides shall turn up.

CHAN'CEL, that part of the choir of a church between the altar and the balustrade that incloses it, where the minister is placed at the celebration of the communion. The *chancel* is also the rector's freehold and part of his glebe, and therefore he is obliged to repair it; but where the rectory is impropriate, the impropriator must do it

CHAN'CELLOR Under the Roman emperors, a chancellor signified a chief notary or scribe; but in England it means an officer invested with high judicial powers.—*The Lord High Chancellor of Great Britain* is one of the principal officers of the civil government, created without writ or patent, by the mere delivery of the king's great seal into his custody. He is a privy counsellor by his office, and prolocutor of the House of Lords by prescription. He also appoints all the justices of the peace throughout the kingdom. Persons exercising this office in former times having been ecclesiastics, and superintendents of the royal chapel, the Lord Chancellor is still styled *keeper of the king's conscience*, and for the same reason he is visitor, in right of the king, of all hospitals and colleges of the king's foundation; and patron of all the king's livings under the value of 20*l.* per annum in the king's books. He is the general guardian of all infants, idiots, and lunatics; has a control over all public charities; and a jurisdiction of vast extent, as the head of the law in his Court of Chancery; where he decides without the assistance of a jury, but from which there is an appeal to the House of Lords.—*Chancellor of a Diocese*, a lay officer under a bishop, versed in the canon and civil law, who is judge of his court.—*Chancellor of a Cathedral*, an officer who hears lessons in the church, inspects schools, hears causes, writes letters, and applies the seal of the chapter, keeps the books, &c.—*Chancellor of a University*, an officer who seals the diplomas, or letters of degree, &c. The chancellors of Oxford and Cambridge are selected from among the prime nobility; the former holds his office for life; the latter is elected every three years.—*Chancellor of the Exchequer*, an officer who presides in that court, and takes care of the interests of the crown. He has power with the lord treasurer to lease the crown lands, and with others to compound for forfeiture of lands, on penal statutes: he has also great authority in managing the royal revenues, and in all matters relating to the finances of the state.

CHANCE-MEDLEY, in law, the accidental killing of a person, not altogether without the killer's fault, though without any evil intention.

CHAN'CERY, the grand court of equity and conscience, instituted to moderate the rigor of the other courts that are bound to the strict letter of the law.

CHAN'CES, a branch of mathematics, which estimates ratios of probability.

CHANT, in music, an ecclesiastical song usually adapted to the psalms and litanies. There have been several sorts, of which the first was the Ambrosian, invented by St. Ambrose, bishop of Milan. The Gregorian chant, which was introduced by Pope Gregory, is still in use in the Roman church, and is the foundation of all that is grand and elevated in music.

CHAN'TRY, a little chapel or altar, commonly in some church endowed (before the Reformation) with revenues for the maintenance of a priest to perform prayers for the soul of the founder and others.

CHA'OS, that confusion in which matter is supposed to have existed before the world was produced by the creative power of Omnipotence; or, in other words, the unformed primeval matter of which everything was made. The ancient poets, and Ovid in particular, represent *chaos* thus: that there was neither sun to make the day, nor moon to enlighten the night; that the earth was not yet hung in the circumambient air, nor the sea bounded by any shore; but that earth, air, and water, were one undigested mass.

CHAP'EL, a place of divine worship, served by an incumbent under the denomination of a chaplain. There are various kinds of chapels; as *parochial chapels*, distinct from the mother church; *chapels of ease*, built in large parishes for the accommodation of the inhabitants; *free chapels*, which were founded by different kings; *chapels* belonging to particular *colleges; domestic chapels*, built by noblemen or gentlemen for the use of their families.

CHAP'ELRY, the precinct belonging to a chapel, in distinction from a parish, or that belonging to a church.

CHAP'LAIN, an ecclesiastic who performs divine service in a chapel; but it more commonly means one who attends upon a king, prince, or other person of quality, for the performance of his clerical duties in the private chapel.

CHAP'LET, in a general sense, a garland or wreath to be worn on the head.—In architecture, a little moulding, carved into round beads, pearls, &c.—*Chaplet*, a string of beads used by the Roman Catholics, by which they count the number of their prayers, and are called *paternosters*. This practice is believed to have been introduced by Peter the Hermit into the church on his return from the Holy Land, the Orientals using a kind of chaplet called a chain, and rehearsing one of the perfections of God on each link or bead.

CHAP'TER, in ecclesiastical polity, is an assembly for the transaction of such business as comes under its cognizance. Every cathedral is under the superintendence of the dean and *chapter* of its canons. A meeting of the members of an order of knighthood is also called a *chapter*.

CHAP'TER-HOUSE, in architecture, the apartment (usually attached) of a cathedral or collegiate church, in which the heads of the church or the chapter meet to transact business.

CHAR'ACTER, that which distinguishes each species of being in each genus, and each individual of each species. In man, character consists of the form of the body, stature, and gait, which distinguish him from other animals. In mankind, the natural or accidental peculiarities resulting from sex, temperament, age, climate, the exercise of the passions, the position of the individual in the social scale, and his mode of living. These peculiarities and differences are, after the study of the human figure in general, the most important subjects of the study of the painter and sculptor, since upon these peculiarities and differences depend all the significance of their compositions. Each genus, each family of animals, has also its general and particular character. So also in the inanimate productions of nature, trees, rocks, fields, and meadows, which vary in reality as well as in appearance, according to the climate, season, time of day, accidental condition of the sky, and also according to the modifications they receive at the hands of man, the effect of time, or by the effect of natural accidents. If all these things, observed with sagacity and selected with taste, are faithfully represented in a picture, we say that the animals, the trees, the rocks of the picture have good character.

CHARACTERIS′TIC, in a general sense, a peculiar mark or character, whereby a person or thing is distinguished from all others.

CHARADE′, a syllabic enigma, so named from its inventor, made upon a word the two syllables of which, when separately taken, are themselves words. It consists of three parts; the two first describing the syllables separately; the second alluding to the entire word. A charade can only be called complete if the different enigmas which it contains are brought into a proper relation to each other, and as a whole unite in an epigrammatic point. The following charade, which we borrow from the *Dictionnaire de l'Academie Française*, may be regarded as a good specimen of this species of riddle:—"My first makes use of my second to eat my whole;" the solution being *chien-dent*, (*dog-tooth*,) or dog's grass. The word *charade* has been applied to this sort of amusement, from the name of its inventor.

CHARGE, in a general sense, is that which is enjoyed, committed, intrusted or delivered to another, implying care, custody, oversight, or duty to be performed by the party intrusted. *Charge*, in civil law, the instructions given by the judge to the grand jury.—In ecclesiastical law, the instructions given by a bishop to the clergy of his diocese.

CHAR′IOT, in antiquity, a car or vehicle used formerly in war, and called by the several names of *biga*, *triga*, *quadriga*, &c., according to the number of horses which drew them. When the warriors came to encounter in close fight, they alighted and fought on foot; but when they were weary they retired into their chariot, and thence annoyed their enemies with darts and missive weapons Besides this sort, we find frequent mention of the *currus falcati*, or chariots armed with hooks or scythes, with which whole ranks of soldiers were cut off together: these were not only used by the Persians, Syrians, Egyptians, &c., but we find them among our British ancestors.—The Roman *triumphal chariot* was generally made of ivory, round like a tower, or rather of a cylindrical figure; sometimes gilt at the top and ornamented with crowns; and, to represent a victory more naturally, they used to stain it with blood. It was usually drawn by four white horses, but oftentimes by lions, elephants, tigers, bears, leopards, &c.

CHARIS′IA, a Roman nocturnal festival and dance kept in honor of the Graces, when sweetmeats, called *charisia*, were distributed among the guests.

CHARIS′TIA, a solemn festival among the Romans kept in the month of February. It was well worthy the imitation of Christians; for at this time the relations of each family compromised any differences that had arisen between them, and renewed their former friendships upon the principles of pure benevolence and good-will.

CHAR′ITY, in a general sense, that disposition of heart which inclines men to think favorably of their fellow-men, and to do them good; or liberality and benevolence, either in alms-giving or in contributing towards public charitable institutions.—In a theological sense, supreme love to God, and universal good-will to men.

CHAR′LATAN, one who makes unwarrantable pretensions to skill, and prates much in his own favor. The original import of the word was an empiric, or quack, who retailed his medicines on a public stage, and drew the people about him by his buffooneries.

CHARM, some magical words, characters, verses, &c., imagined to possess some occult and unintelligible power: by which, with the supposed assistance of the devil, witches and sorcerers have pretended to do wonderful things. The word, in its more modern acceptation, is used to describe that which delights and attracts the heart.

CHA′RON, in mythology, the ferryman of hell, who conducted the souls of the departed in a boat across the Stygian lake to receive judgment from Œacus, Rhadamanthus, and Minos, the judges of the infernal regions. He received an obolus from every passenger, for which reason the ancients used to put that piece of money in the mouths of the dead. He was said to be the son of Erebus and Night.

CHAR'TA, MAG'NA, in English history. The "Great Charter of the Realm" was signed by King John in 1215, and confirmed by his successor Henry III. It is reported to have been chiefly drawn up by the Earl of Pembroke and Stephen Langton, Archbishop of Canterbury. Its most important articles are those which provide that no freeman shall be taken or imprisoned or proceeded against, "except by the lawful judgment of his peers or by the law of the land," and that no scutage or aid should be imposed in the kingdom (except certain feudal dues from tenants of the crown) unless by the common council of the kingdom. The remaining and greater part of it is directed against abuses of the king's power as feudal superior.

CHARTE, in French history, originally used to indicate the rights and privileges granted by the French kings to various towns and communities; but recently to the fundamental law of the French monarchy, as established on the restoration of Louis XVIII. in 1814. The *Charte* consisted of 69 articles, and was founded on principles analogous to those of the British constitution, as embodied originally in the Magna Charta, and subsequently extended in the Bill of Rights.

CHAR'TER, in law, a written instrument, executed with usual forms, whereby the king grants privileges to towns, corporations, &c.; whence the name of Magna Charta, or the Great Charter of Liberties granted to the people of the whole realm.

CHA'RTER-PARTY, in mercantile law, is defined to be a contract, by which the owner or master of a ship hires or lets the whole or a principal part of it to a freighter for the conveyance of goods, under certain specified conditions, on a determined voyage to one or more places. A charter-party is generally under seal; but a printed or written instrument signed by the parties, called a memorandum of a charter-party, is binding if no charter-party be executed. A voyage may be performed in part under a charter-party, and in part under a parol agreement; but the terms of a charter-party cannot be altered by parol evidence, although they may be explained by mercantile usage. The instrument expresses the freight to be paid, and generally, but not necessarily, the burden of the ship; together with some usual covenants, and others at the discretion of the parties.

CHAR'TULARY, in diplomatics, a collection of the charters belonging to a church or religious house.

CHARYB'DIS, a much-dreaded vortex at the entrance of the Sicilian straits, celebrated for its engulfing perils, by the ancient writers. It is, however, no longer dreadful to navigators, who, in a quiet sea, and particularly with a south wind, cross it without danger.

CHASE, in law, a part of a forest for game, which may be possessed by a subject: though a forest cannot. The word *chase* has also several meanings in maritime language; as, *chase-guns*, that lie at the head, to fire on a vessel that is pursued, in distinction to *stern-chasers*, which fire on the pursuer.—With huntsmen, the *chase* is a figurative expression for their sport in general.

CHA'SING, in sculpture, the art of embossing on metals, or representing figures thereon by a kind of *basso-relievo*, punched out from behind, and carved on the front with small gravers. The metals usually chased are gold, silver, and bronze, and among the ancients, iron also. The remains of ancient art show to what a degree of perfection it was carried; and in our own times, some very fine works have been executed.

CHASSEURS', a French term for a select body of light infantry, formed on the left of a battalion, and who are required to be particularly light, active, and courageous.—*Chasseurs à cheval*, a kind of light horse in the French service.

CHA'SUBLE, Chesable, Chesible, called also a vestment, the upper or last vestment put on by the priest before celebrating the mass. In form it is nearly circular, being slightly pointed before and behind, having an aperture in the middle for the head to pass through, and its ample folds resting on either side upon the arms. It is richly decorated with embroidery and even with jewels.

CHA'TEAU, a French word, formerly used for a castle, or baronial seat in France; but now simply for a country seat.

CHEF-D'ŒU'VRE, a work of the highest excellence in itself, or relatively to the other works of the same artist. Thus the *Apollo Belvedere*, or the *Trans-*

figuration of Raffaelle, are chef-d'œuvres of sculpture and painting.

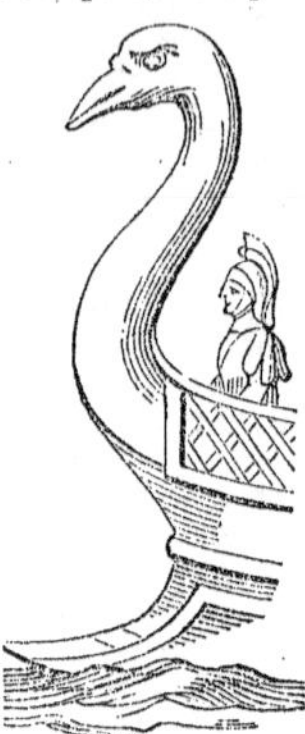

CHENIS'CUS, in works of ancient art, ships are seen with ornamental prows, shaped to represent the head and neck of a goose, or other aquatic bird; this part was called cheniscus, and was constructed of bronze and other materials.—Sometimes, but rarely, the cheniscus is affixed to the stern of a ship.

CHER'UBIM, in Christian Art, a higher class of angels, the nearest to the throne of God, of which they are the supporters. Their forms are known by the poetical writings of the Old Testament. They appear first as guardians of Paradise, whence our first parents were expelled by a cherub with a flaming sword. Jehovah rested between the wings of the cherubim on the cover of the ark; and in the history of Ezekiel they are represented with four wings, two of which covered the body and drew the chariot of the Lord through the air. In the heavenly hierarchy the cherubim form one of the three high angel choirs—seraphim, cherubim, and angels, which constitute the first and upper order of angels; they rank next to the seraphim.

CHER'SONESE, a tract of land, of any indefinite extent, which is nearly surrounded by water, but united to a larger tract by a neck of land or isthmus.

CHEVAL-DE-FRISE, (generally used in the plural, CHEVAUX-DE-FRISE, Fr. pron. *shevo de freez*,) spikes of wood, pointed with iron, five or six feet long, fixed in a strong beam of wood, and used as a fence against cavalry, or to stop a breach, &c.

CHIARO OSCU'RO, (an Italian phrase, meaning *clear-obscure*,) is the art of distributing lights and shadows in painting. The aim of paintings is to form a picture by means of light and shade, and by colors and their gradations; the more truly painting accomplishes this end, the more artistic it will be. Correggio and Rembrandt are famous for their chiaro-oscuro. According to the common acceptation of the term in the language of art, chiaro oscuro means not only the mutable effects produced by light and shade, but also the permanent differences in brightness and darkness.

CHICA'NERY, mean or unfair artifices to perplex a cause or to obscure the truth; applied either in a legal sense, by which justice is somehow intended to be perverted; or to disputatious sophistry.

CHIEF, a term signifying the head, or principal part of a thing or person. Thus we say, the chief of a party, the chief of a family, &c.

CHIEF''TAIN, a captain or commander of any class, family, or body of men: thus, the Highland chieftains, or chiefs, were the principal noblemen or gentlemen of their respective clans.

CHIL'IAD, the sum or number of one thousand. Hence *chiliarch* denotes the military commander or chief of a thousand men: *chiliarchy*, a body consisting of 1000 men: *chiliahedron*, a figure of 1000 equal sides: and *chiliagon*, a figure of 1000 angles and sides.

CHILL'ED. When a cloudiness or dimness appears on the surface of a picture that has been varnished, it is called blooming, and we say the varnish has chilled. This defect arises from the presence of moisture, either on the surface of the picture, or in the brush, or in the varnish itself, and can easily be avoided by making the former thoroughly dry, and the latter hot before it is applied.

CHIMÆ'RA, a misshapen monster in Grecian mythology, described by Homer as having a lion's head, a goat's body, and the tail of a dragon. The chimæra appears in Art as a lion, except that out of the back grow the head and neck of a goat, and gigantic carvings of it are found on rocks in Asia Minor, according to Homer the native country of the monster. There are innumerable small antique statues of chimæra, and Bellerophon, by whom the chimæra was killed, of which one of the most remarkable is in the Uffigi palace at Florence. In Christian Art, the chimæra is a symbol of cunning. It is frequently seen on the modillions and capitals of architectural works executed in the eleventh and twelfth centuries, and again in the fifteenth and sixteenth centuries.

CHIMES, the musical sounds of bells struck with hammers, arranged and set in motion by clock-work.—In a clock, a kind of periodical music, produced at certain hours by a particular apparatus.

CHIM'NEY, in architecture, a body of brick or stone erected in a building, containing a funnel to convey smoke and other volatile matter through the roof from the grate or hearth. How far the Greek and Roman architects were acquainted with the construction of chimneys is a matter of dispute. No traces of them have been discovered in the ruins of Pompeii, and Vitruvius gives no rules for erecting them. The first certain notice of chimneys, as we now build them, is believed to be that contained in an in scription of Venice, over the gate of an edifice, which states that in 1347 a great many chimneys were thrown down by an earthquake.

CHI'NA-WARE, the most beautiful of all kinds of earthenware, takes its name from China, whence the Dutch and English merchants first brought it into Europe. It is also called *porcelain*, from the Portuguese *porcellana*, a cup or vessel. The Japan china is considered superior to all other of oriental manufacture, in its close and compact granular texture, its sonorosity when struck, its extreme hardness, its smooth and shining appearance, and its capability of being used to boil liquids in. With the Chinese potters, the preparation of the clay is constantly in operation; and usually remains in the pits from ten to twenty years prior to being used; for, the longer it remains there, the greater is its value. The Dresden china has some qualities which render it decidedly superior to the oriental. Its texture exhibits a compact, shining, uniform mass, resembling white enamel, while it possesses firmness, solidity, and infusibility by heat.

CHI'NESE WHITE, an empirical name given to the white oxide of zinc, a valuable pigment recently introduced into the Arts as a substitute for the preparations of white lead. It is little liable to change, either by atmospheric action or by mixture with other pigments. Its only defect appears to be a want of *body*, as compared with white lead.

CHI'ROGRAPH, among the Anglo-Saxons, signified any public instrument of gift or conveyance, attested by the subscription and crosses of witnesses. Any deed requiring a counterpart was engrossed twice on the same piece of parchment, with a space between, on which was written *chirograph*, through which the parchment was cut, and one part given to each party. It was also anciently used for a fine: the manner of engrossing the fines, and cutting the parchment in two pieces, is still retained in the chirographer's office, in the Court of Common Pleas.

CHIROL'OGY, the art or practice of communicating thoughts by signs made by the hands and fingers; as a substitute for language.

CHIR'OMANCY, a species of divination, drawn from the different lines and lineaments of a person's hand; by which means, it is pretended the inclinations may be discovered. The modern word is *palmistry*.

CHIRON'OMY, in antiquity, the art of representing any past transaction by the gestures of the body, more especially by the motions of the hands: this made a part of liberal education: it had the approbation of Socrates, and was ranked by Plato among the political virtues.

CHIS'LEU, the ninth month of the Jewish year, answering to the latter part of November and the beginning of December.

CHI'TON, the under-garment of the Greeks, corresponding to the tunic of the Romans, mentioned as early as Homer; it was made of woollen cloth. After the Greek migration it was called *chitoniscos*, while the light loose garment or himation was also called *chlania*, or chlanis. The Doric chiton, worn by men, was short and of wool; that of the Athenians and Ionians, of linen, in earler times worn long, but with the former people, after the time of Pericles, it was shorter.

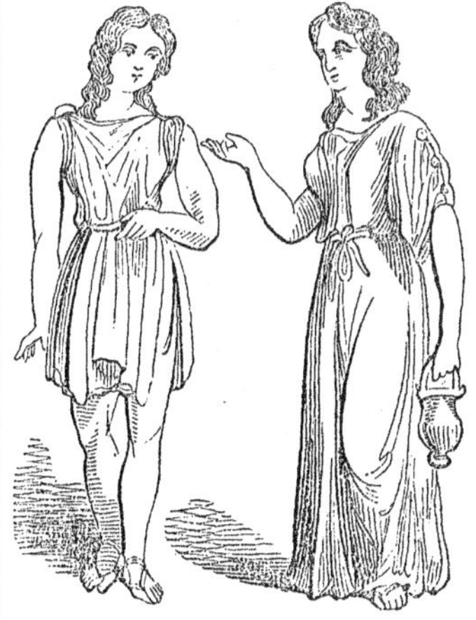

The chiton, worn by freemen, had two sleeves, that of workmen and slaves only one. A girdle (called, when worn by men, zoma) was required when the garment was long, but that of the priests was not girded. The Doric chiton for women was made of two pieces of stuff sewn together, and fastened on the shoulders by clasps. In Sparta it was not sewn up the sides, but only fastened, and had no sleeves. The chiton appears to have been generally gray or brown. Women fond of dress had saffron-colored clothing; and the material (cotton or fine linen) was striped, figured, or embroidered with stars, flowers, &c. With regard to statues, we need only remark that Artemis, as a huntress, wears a girdle over the chiton, which is fastened on the shoulders and folds over the bosom. Pallas Athene often wears a double chiton, reaching to the feet, and leaving the arms free. On the statues of amazons the chiton is sleeveless, clasped up in two places, leaving the breast uncovered, and drawn up sufficiently to show even above the knee.

CHIV'ALRY, the name anciently given to knighthood, a military dignity; also the martial exploits and qualifications of a knight. Chivalry, as a military dignity, is supposed by some to have taken its rise soon after the death of Charlemagne, and by others as arising out of the crusades, because in these expeditions many chivalrous exploits were performed, and a proud feeling of heroism was engendered. The general system of manners and tone of sentiments which the institution of knighthood, strictly pursued, was calculated to produce, and did in part produce, during the middle ages in Europe, is comprehended in ordinary language under the term of chivalry. This imaginary institution of chivalry, such as it is represented in the old romances, had assuredly no full existence at any period in the usages of actual life. It was the ideal perfection of a code of morals and pursuits, which was in truth only partially adopted; and bore the same relation to the real life of the middle ages, which the philosophical excellence aimed at by the various sects of antiquity bore to the real conduct of their professors. But, in both instances, a system of abstract perfection was propounded in theory, which, although the defect of human nature prevented it from being reduced into practice, yet exercised a very important influence in modelling the minds, and even controlling the actions, of those who adopted it. The vivifying principle of ancient philosophy was ideal virtue; that of chivalry, the ideal point of honor. The origin of chivalry has often been traced to the German tribes; nor has its spirit ever penetrated very deeply into the usages of any country in which these tribes have not either produced the ancestors of the great body of the nation, or at least the conquering and governing class, which transfused its habits and sentiments into that body. Thus Germany and France, and England, whose gentry derive their origin from both, have been the countries most distinguished for the prevalence of this institution. The martial spirit of the Spaniards was, indeed, partly animated by it; but in their country it always bore something of the character of a foreign importation, modified by the circumstances of their juxtaposition with the Arab race. In Italy, it existed only among those classes which imitated the manners of France and Germany, and never entered into the general character of the natives, notwithstanding the popularity of the romances of chivalry. Among the Slavonic nations it has never prevailed extensively; although the feudal constitution of Polish society derived a certain tincture from it, it never penetrated into Russia. It has often been remarked, that it is only within the last two or three generations that the nobility of that country, by their intercourse with the nations of Western Europe, have derived something of the spirit of the chivalrous code, so far as it still subsists among ourselves: the point of honor, and its peculiar concomitant the usage of the duel, were scarcely known in Russia before the present century. It is to the 14th century, and especially to that part of its chronicles preserved by the true annalist of chivalry, Froissart, that we must look for the period when the line between real society and that represented in romances was most nearly broken down. When the usages of chivalry were most flourishing, all men of noble birth, (except the highest) were supposed to pass through three orders or gradations. They first lived as pages in the train of nobles and chiefs of high rank; next, as esquires, they attached themselves to the person of some individual knight, to whom they were bound by a strict law of obedience, and for whom they were bound to incur every danger, and, if necessary, sacrifice their lives; and, thirdly, they were promoted to the rank of knighthood. However great the distinction might be between knights in point of rank and wealth, custom established a species of equality among all of the same order, which may be said to subsist among gentlemen of the present day. They formed, all over Europe, a common corporation, as it were, possessing certain rights, and owing each other certain mutual duties and forbearances. They were united, not by the ties of country, but by those of feudal obedience, which attached every knight to the banner of his liege lord, from whom he held his fee; but little or rather no dishonor attached to knights who were under no such feudal tie, if they chose their own chieftain wherever they thought fit: they were free adventurers, whose order was a passport in every service; and in the actual conflict, the hostility of knights was moderated by usage. Thus, it was dishonorable in any knight to take a knight's life if disarmed, and not set him free when a prisoner on receiving a fitting ransom. With regard to the point of honor, which forms the most important feature in the usages of chivalry, the principal objects were religious belief; fealty to the feudal superior; devotion to some one selected lady; and, finally, the general character for honor and courtesy which it was incumbent on a knight to maintain; for although his imaginary duties, as a knight errant, to avenge wrong and succor the oppressed on every occasion, were not of course very strictly put in practice, yet his vow to perform those duties attached to his character a certain degree of sacredness which it was necessary to maintain. Chivalrous honor was chiefly supported in two ways: first, by the single combat or duel, whether on account of serious provocation or by way of trial of strength; secondly, by the performance of vows, often of the most frivolous and extravagant nature. These latter were generally undertaken for the honor of the ladies. The commencement of extravagances, however, was rather a sign of the decline of the true spirit of chivalry. It decayed with the progress of mercenary armies and the decline of feudal institutions through the 15th century; in the 16th, it was little more than a lively recollection of past ages, which knights such as Bayard, and sovereigns such as Francis I. and Henry VIII. strove to revive; and finally, it became extinguished amid religious discords, leaving as its only relic the code of honor, which is still considered as governing the conduct of the gentleman.

CHLA'MYS, in antiquity, a military habit worn over the tunica. It belonged to the patricians, and was the same in the time of war, that the toga was in the time of peace. It was a light cloak, or rather scarf, the ends of which were fastened on the shoulder by a clasp or buckle. It hung with two long points as far as the thigh, and was richly ornamented with purple and gold. When the *fibula* was unclasped the chlamys hung on the

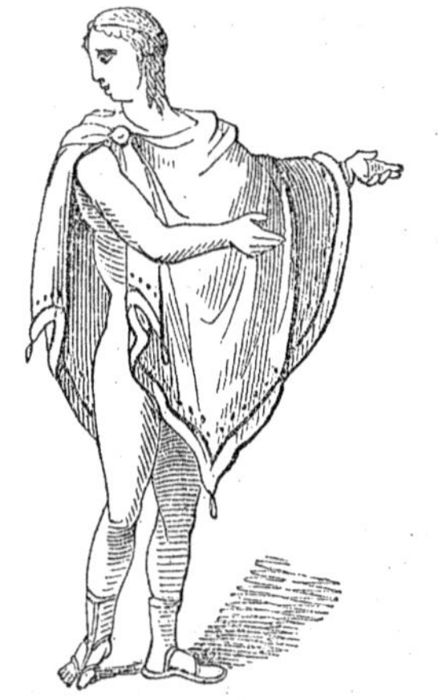

left arm, as with Hermes, or served as a kind of shield, as Poseidon, on the old coins, protects his arm with the chlamys. It is fastened on the right shoulder, in the statues of Theseus and the heroic Ephebes, in a wrestling attitude, covering the breast and enveloping the left arm, which is somewhat raised. The figures of Heracles and Hermes, are quite covered by the chlamys, even below the body, whence the Hermes pillar tapers; the right hand lies on the breast under the chlamys, and the left arm, covered to the wrist, hangs by the side; in the centre of the breast depends a lion's claw at the opening of the scarf. In the Hermes' statues, the chlamys, when fastened on the right shoulder, forms a triangle from the neck.

CHOIR, in architecture, the part of a church in which the choristers sing divine service. In former times it was raised separate from the altar, with a pulpit on each side, in which the epistles and gospels were sung, as is still the case in several churches on the continent. It was separated from the nave in the time of Constantine. In nunneries, the choir is a large apartment, separated by a grate from the body of the church, where the nuns chant the service. This term is used also in music to signify a band of singers in different parts.

CHORA'GIC MONUMENTS, the small monuments to which we apply this term originated in the time of Pericles, who built an Odeon at Athens for musical contests, not of single persons, but of choruses. The richest and most respectable man was chosen from the ten Athenian tribes, as choragus, to make the necessary arrangements, in return for which distinction he had to defray the expenses. If his chorus were victorious, he had also the right of placing upon a monument erected at his own cost, the tripod, which was given as the prize. The rich citizens whose chorus conquered in these contests displayed great splendor in their monuments, which were so numerous that at Athens there was a street formed entirely of them called the "Street of the Tripods."

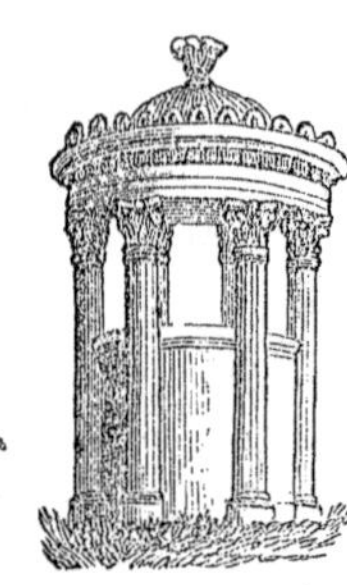

CHORD, in music, the union of two or more sounds uttered at the same time, forming an entire harmony; as a third, fifth, and eighth.

CHOREG'RAPHY, the art of representing dancing by signs, as singing is by notes.

CHORE'US, in ancient poetry, a foot of two syllables; the first long, and the second short; the *trochee*.

CHORIAM'BUS, in ancient poetry, a foot compounded of a trochee and an iambus.

CHOROG'RAPHY, the art of delineating or describing some particular country or province: it differs from *geography* as a description of a particular country differs from that of the whole earth; and from *topography* as the description of a country from that of a town or district.

CHO'RUS, in ancient dramatic poetry, one or more persons present on the stage during the representation, uttering an occasional commentary on the piece, preparing the audience for events that are to follow, or explaining circumstances that cannot be distinctly represented. Several examples may be referred to by the English reader, in the plays of Shakspeare. In tragedy, the chorus was at first the sole performer; at present it is wholly discontinued on the stage.—CHORUS, in music, is when, at certain periods of song, the whole company are to join the singer in repeating certain couplets or verses.

CHREMATIS'TICS, the science of wealth; a name given by Continental writers to the science of political economy, or rather to what in their view constitutes a portion of the science. They consider political economy as a term more properly applicable to the whole range of subjects which comprise the material welfare of states and citizens, and chrematistics as merely a branch of it.

CHRESTOM'ATHY, according to the etymology, that which it is useful to learn. The Greeks frequently formed commonplace books by collecting the various passages to which, in the course of reading, they had affixed the mark χ (χρηστος, *useful*.) Hence books of extracts chosen with a view to utility have received this name.

CHRISM, or CHRIS'OM, in the Romish and Greek churches, an unction or anointing of children, which was formerly practised as soon as they were born.

CHRIS'TENDOM, a word sometimes employed in such a sense as to comprehend all nations in which Christianity prevails: more commonly, all realms governed under Christian sovereigns and institutions. Thus European Turkey, although three fourths of its inhabitants are Christians, is not in ordinary language included within the term Christendom.

CHRIS'TENING, a term particularly applied to infant baptism, denoting the ceremony of admitting a person into the communion of the Christian church by means of baptism, or sprinking with water.

CHRISTIAN'ITY, the religion of Jesus Christ. From the period when the disciples "were called Christians first in Antioch" down to the present day, the main doctrines of the gospel, and the great moral principles which it reveals and confirms, have been preserved without interruption in the church. But notwithstanding this substantial unity, it cannot be denied that the character of the religion has been very materially colored throughout all its history by the circumstances and genius of different nations and ages. The foundation of a Christian's faith and practice, his ultimate, and, in truth, only appeal, must be to the facts, the doctrines, and the precepts of the Scriptures, especially to those of the New Testament.

CHRIST'MAS, the festival observed in the Christian church on the 25th of December, in commemoration of our Saviour's nativity; and celebrated in the church of England by a particular service set apart for that holy day.

CHRIS'TOPHER, St. We frequently meet with this saint in old woodcuts; he is represented as a giant, his staff being the stem of a large tree, and he is carrying the infant Jesus on his shoulders across a river. This was a favorite subject with the artists of the middle ages, and the saint is placed in the side entrances of German churches as the symbol of the transition from heathenism to Christianity. The incidents in the life of this saint chosen for illustration by painters, consist of the passage of the river, the conversion of the heathen at Samos, and his martyrdom.

CHROMAT'IC, in music, an epithet descriptive of that which proceeds by several consecutive semitones.

CHROME GREEN, a beautiful dark-green pigment, prepared from the *oxide of chromium*. Different shades of this pigment are used in porcelain and in oil-painting. Mixed with Prussian blue and chrome yellow it is called green cinnabar.

CHROME RED, the pigment known at present by this name is not prepared from *chrome*, but is a beautiful preparation of red lead. The name chrome red was given to it by speculators, in order to secure a good sale and a high price. Red lead is an *oxide of lead*, while chrome red is a *chromate of lead*, which is a durable pigment, and admissible in oil-painting.

CHROME YELLOW, the most poisonous of the chrome pigments, and to be entirely rejected in oil-painting: it is not durable. When mixed with white lead it turns to a dirty gray. By itself, and as a water-color pigment, it is less objectionable.

CHRON'IC, an epithet for inveterate diseases, or those of long duration.

CHRON'ICLE, in literature, an historical register of events in the order of time. Most of the historians of the middle ages were chroniclers who set down the events which happened within the range of their information, according to the succession of years.

CHRON'ICLES, the name of two books in the canon scripture. They consist of an abridgment of sacred history from its commencement down to the return of the Jews from the Babylonish captivity, and are called by the Septuagint παραλειπομενα, (lit. things omitted,) because they contain many supplemental relations omitted in the other historical books. It has been generally supposed that the Chronicles were compiled by Ezra, though circumstances are not wanting to diminish the probability of this conjecture. Eichhorn gives as his reasons for attributing them to Ezra their similarity in point of style, idiom, and orthography to the books of Kings and Ezra; while the opponents of this view base their opinion on the discrepancies that occur throughout Chronicles and Kings, in regard to facts, dates, numbers, names, and genealogies.

CHRON'OGRAM, an inscription in which a certain date or epoch is expressed by numeral letters.

CHRONOL'OGY, the science which determines the dates of events, and the civil distinctions of time. The divisions of time are either natural or artificial; the natural divisions of time are the year, month, week, day, and hour, deduced from the motions of the heavenly bodies, and suited to the purposes of civil life: the artificial divisions of time are the cycle or period, the epoch, and the æra or epoch, which have been framed for the purposes of history. In order to ascertain and register the intervals of time between different events, two things must necessarily be assumed: 1st, an epoch or fixed point in time to which all events, whether preceding or succeeding may be referred; and 2d, a measure or definite portion of time, by which the intervals between the fixed epoch and other events may be estimated. Of these the first is entirely arbitrary, and the second arbitrary to a certain extent; for though certain periods are marked out by the recurrence of natural phenomena, yet a choice of these phenomena must be made. It is on account of the arbitrary nature of these two elements, on which all chronological reckoning depends, that so much confusion and uncertainty exist respecting the dates of historical events. The diversity of epochs which have been assumed as the origin of chronological reckoning, is a natural consequence of the manner in which science and civilization have spread over the world. In the early ages the different communities or tribes into which mankind were divided began to date their years each from some event remarkable only in reference to its own individual history, but of which other tribes were either ignorant, or regarded with indifference. Hence not only different nations, but almost every individual historian or compiler of annals, adopted an epoch of his own. Events of local or temporary interest were also constantly occurring in every community which would appear of greater importance than those which were long past, and constantly be adopted as new historical dates. The foundation of a monarchy or a city, or the accession of a king, were events of this class; and accordingly are epochs of frequent occurrence in the ancient annals. Religion also came in to increase the confusion caused by political changes. Soon after the introduction of Christianity, the various sects began to establish eras, commencing with events connected with the appearance of Christ; but no regard was given to uniformity. In like manner, the Mohammedans employ dates having reference to the origin of their faith. All these circumstances have conspired to render it a task of extreme difficulty for modern historians to ascertain the order of the political occurrences of ancient times. But it is not merely the number of chronological epochs and the various origins of eras that have caused the perplexity; the measure by which long intervals were compared varied in different countries, and in different ages, and hence arises another source of confusion in arranging the order of time. In the scripture history, the lapse of time is frequently estimated by generations or reigns of kings. Some of the historians of early Greece reckoned by the succession of the priestesses of Juno; others by that of the ephori of Sparta; and others again by the archons of Athens. Even when the length of the solar year began to be used as the measure of time, uniformity was not obtained. The length of the solar year is a fixed element in nature, and liable to no variation. But neither the commencement or termination of the year is marked by any conspicuous sign. Its precise length can only be ascertained by a long-continued series of astronomical observations. Rude nations were therefore unacquainted with it; and even when it had become known with considerable accuracy, it was still necessary to form a civil year, and adapt it to the seasons, the solar year not being composed of an exact number of days. Most nations had recourse to intercalations for this purpose. For these reasons, and numerous others that might easily be adduced, it is very seldom that the precise interval between the events mentioned in ancient history and modern dates can be determined with any degree of certainty, and great discrepancies exist among the computations of different chronologers.

CHRYSELEPHAN'TINE, religious images of gold and ivory. These, the earliest images of the gods in Greece, were of wood, gilt, or inlaid with ivory, whence were derived acrolites, the heads, arms, and feet of which were of marble, the body still of wood, inlaid with ivory, or quite covered with gold. From this arose the chryselephantine statues, of which the foundation was of wood, covered with ivory or gold, with drapery and hair of thin plates of gold, chased; and the rest of the exterior was of ivory, worked in a pattern by the scraper and file, with the help of isinglass. The ivory portion of these works belongs to sculpture, and the gold part to toreutic art; they were long in favor as temple statues, as marble and brass were used for common purposes.

CHRYS'OCOLLA, (*Gr.* gold green.) The Greek term for a green pigment prepared from copper, (green verditer) and one of the most beautiful ancient greens, Armenian green; it was obtained by grinding varieties of malachite and green carbonate of copper, also by decomposing the blue vitriol of Cyprus, (*sulphate of copper*,) as a secondary form of dissolved copper ore. This pigment is identical in color with our different shades of mountain green; the best was brought from Armenia; a second kind was found near copper mines in Macedonia; the third, and most valuable, was brought from Spain. Chrysocolla, called by ancient painters *pea* or *grass green*, was valued in proportion as its color approached to the color of a seed beginning to sprout.

CHURCH, in religious affairs, is a word which is used in several senses: 1. The collective body of persons professing one and the same religion; or that religion itself: thus, we say, the Church of Christ. 2. Any particular congregation of Christians associating together, as the Church of Antioch. 3. A particular sect of Christians, as the Greek

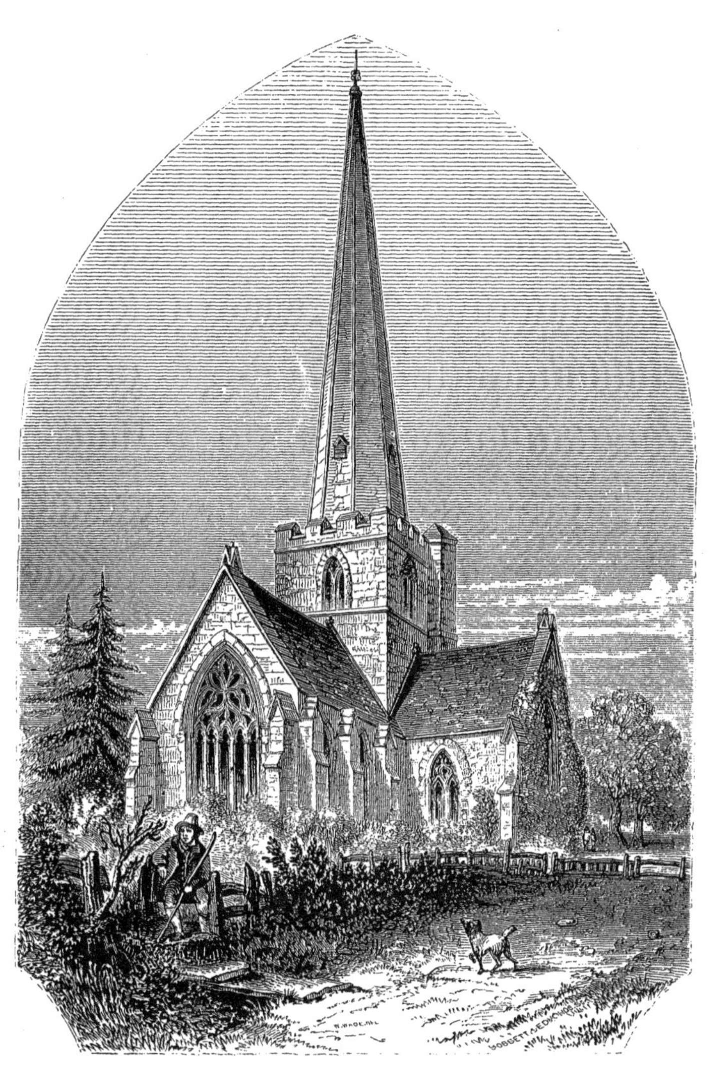

CHURCH ARCHITECTURE.

(Shottesbrook Church. England.) p. 82.

Church or the Church of England. 4. The body of ecclesiastics, in contradistinction to the laity. 5. The building in which a congregation of Christians assemble.—*Church*, in architecture, a building dedicated to the performance of Christian worship. Among the first of the churches was that of St. Peter's at Rome, about the year 326, nearly on the site of the present church; and it is supposed that the first church of St. Sophia at Constantinople was built somewhat on its model. That which was afterwards erected by Justinian seems in its turn to have afforded the model of St. Mark's at Venice, which was the first in Italy constructed with pendentives and a dome, the former affording the means of covering a square plan with an hemispherical vault. The four most celebrated churches in Europe erected since the revival of the arts are, St. Peter's at Rome, which stands on an area of 227,069 feet superficial; Sta. Maria del Fiore at Florence, standing on 84,802 feet; St. Paul's, London, which stands on 84,025 feet; and St. Genevieve, at Paris, 60,287 feet.

CIBA'RIÆ LE'GES, in Roman history, were sumptuary laws, the intention of which was to limit the expense of feasts, and introduce frugality amongst the people, whose extravagance at table was notorious and almost incredible.

CIBO'RIUM, in architecture, an insulated erection open on each side, with arches, and having a dome of ogee form carried or supported by four columns. It is also used to denote the coffer or case which contains the Host. The ciborium is often merely an addition to the high altar, and is then a synedoche. In the early Christian times, the ciborium was merely a protection to the altar table, first a tabernacle, then a baldachin over the altar, of which, the canopy used at solemn processions and under which the priest wears the *casula*, still reminds us. The ciborium was generally supported by four pillars, and is above the altar; between the pillars were curtains, which were opened only while believers made their offerings, but closed in the presence of catechumens or infidels.—*Ciborium* also signifies a vessel in which the blessed Eucharist is reserved. In form it nearly resembles a chalice with an arched cover, from which it derives its name. The most splendid ciboria are those belonging to ancient German art; the finest of these, which was in the cathedral of Cologne in the preceding century, exists no longer. The most remarkable ciboria in Italy are the tabernacle over the high altar of St. Paul's at Rome, that in the cathedral at Milan, and that in the church of the Lateran.

CICERO'NE, a name originally given by the Italians to those persons who pointed out to travellers the interesting objects with which Italy abounds; but applied universally at present to any individual who acts as *a guide*. This application of the term cicerone has probably its origin in the ironical exclamation, "E un Cicerone," (he is a Cicero,) being elicited from the traveller by the well-known garrulity of the Italian guides. A good Cicerone must possess accurate and extensive knowledge, and many distinguished archæologists have undertaken this office, which, while serving others, affords them also an opportunity of making repeated examinations of the works of art, and enabling them to increase their familiarity with them.

CICERO'NIANS, epithets given by Muretus, Erasmus, &c., to those moderns who were so ridiculously fond of Cicero, as to reject every Latin word, as obsolete or impure, that could not be found in some one or other of his works. The word *Ciceronian* is also used as an epithet for a diffuse and flowing style and a vehement manner.

CICISBE'O, a word synonymous with *cavalier servente*, and applied to a class of persons in Italy who attend on married ladies with all the respect and devotion of lovers. Formerly the establishment of a fashionable lady was not considered complete without a cicisbeo, whose duty it was to accompany her to private parties and public amusements, to escort her in her walks, and in short to be always at her side ready for her commands. This practice is now, however, on the decline.

CID, the name given to an epic poem of the Spaniards which celebrates the exploits of their national hero, Roderigo Diaz, Count of Bivar. It is supposed to have been written in the 13th century, about 150 years after the hero's death; but unfortunately the author's name has not been transmitted to posterity.

CID'ARIS, in antiquity, the mitre used by the Jewish high-priests.

CILI'CIUM, in Hebrew antiquity, a sort of habit made of coarse stuff, formerly in use among the Jews in times of mourning and distress. It is the same with what the Septuagint and Hebrew versions call sackcloth.

CIM'BRIC, pertaining to the Cimbri,

the inhabitants of the Cimbric Chersonese, now Jutland.

CIMME'RIAN, pertaining to *Cimmerium*, a town at the mouth of the Palus Mæotis, which the ancients pretended was involved in darkness; whence the phrase "Cimmerian darkness" to denote a deep or continual obscurity. The country is now called the Crimea.

CINCTO'RIUM, a leathern belt worn round the waist, to which the swords worn by the officers of the Roman army were suspended. The common men wore their swords suspended from a balteus, which is worn over the right shoulder.

CINC'TURE, in architecture, a ring, list, or orlo, at the top and bottom of a column, separating the shaft at one end from the base, and at the other from the capital.

CIN'NABAR, one of the red pigments known to the ancients, called also by Pliny and Vitruvius minium; supposed to be identical with the modern vermilion, (the bisulphuret of mercury,) and the most frequently found in antique paintings. The Roman cinnabar appears to have been dragon's blood, a resin obtained from various species of the calamus palm, found in the Canary Isles. It is beyond a doubt that the Greeks applied the term cinnabari, generally meaning cinnabar, to this resin. Cinnabar, as well as dragon's blood, was used in monochrome painting; afterwards ruddle, especially that of Sinopia, was preferred, because its color was less dazzling. The ancients attached the ideas of the majestic and holy to cinnabar, therefore they painted with it the statues of Pan, as well as those of Jupiter Capitolinus and Jupiter Triumphans. It was used upon gold, marble, and even tombs, and also for uncial letters in writing, down to recent times. The Byzantine emperors preferred signing with it. Its general use was for walls, on which much money was spent: in places which were damp and exposed to the weather it became black, unless protected by encaustic wax.

CINQUE CENTO, this generic term, which is a mere abbreviation for *five hundred*, is used to designate the style of Art which arose in Italy shortly after the year 1500, and therefore strictly the Art of the sixteenth century. The characteristics of this style are, a sensuous development of Art as the highest aim of the artist, and an illustration of subjects drawn from classical mythology and history.

CINQUE-FOIL, a figure of five equal segments derived from the leaf of a plant so called, particularly adapted for the

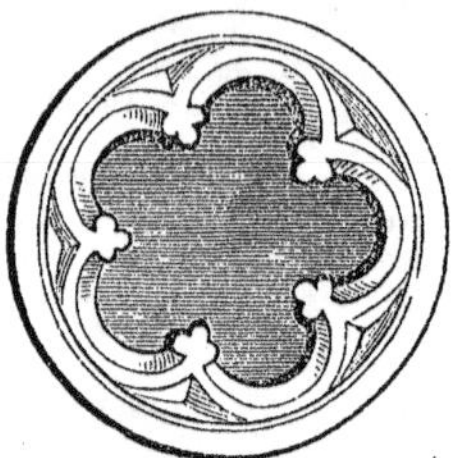

representation of the mysteries of the Rosary. It is frequently seen in irregular windows, one of which is engraved as a specimen.

CINQUE-PORTS, the five ancient ports on the east coast of England, opposite to France, namely, Dover, Hastings, Hythe, Romney, and Sandwich, to which were afterwards added, as appendages, Winchelsea and Rye. As places where strength and vigilance were necessary, and where ships might put to sea in cases of sudden emergency, they formerly received considerable attention from government. They have several privileges, and are within the jurisdiction of the Constable of Dover Castle, who, by his office, is called Warden of the Cinque-Ports.

CI'PHER, or CY'PHER, one of the Arabic characters, or figures, used in computation, formed thus 0. A cipher standing by itself signifies nothing; but when placed at the right hand of a figure, it increases its value tenfold.—By *cipher* is also denoted a secret or disguised manner of writing; in which certain characters arbitrarily invented and agreed on by two or more persons, are made to stand for letters or words.

CIP'OLIN, a green marble from Rome, containing white zones.

CIP'PUS, in antiquity, a low column, with an inscription erected on the highroads, or other places, to show the way to travellers, to serve as a boundary, to mark the grave of a deceased person, &c.

CIRCE'AN, pertaining to Circe, the fabled daughter of Sol and Perseus, who was supposed to possess great knowledge of magic and venomous herbs, by which she was able to charm and fascinate.

CIRCEN'SIAN GAMES, (*Circenses Ludi*,) a general term, under which was comprehended all combats exhibited in the Roman circus, in imitation of the Olympic games in Greece. Most of the feasts of the Romans were accompanied with Circensian games; and the magistrates, and other officers of the republic, frequently presented the people with them, in order to gain their favor; but the grand games were held for five days, commencing on the 15th of September.

CIR'CLE, the circle has always been considered as the emblem of Heaven and Eternity, hence many figures in Christian design are constructed on its principle, such as the Rotation of the Seasons, which are constantly returning; or the Adoration of the Lamb, and other subjects which are found in the great wheel-windows of painted churches.

CIR'CULATING ME'DIUM, a term in commerce, signifying the medium of exchanges, or purchases and sales, whether this medium be gold or silver coin, paper, or any other article; and it is therefore of a more comprehensive nature than the term *money*. All people have a circulating medium of some description, and, accordingly, we find all the tribes of savages hitherto discovered referring to some article in estimating the value of the various commodities which compose their capital. But from the earliest times, the precious metals, where they could be had, have been preferred for this purpose, because they comprised a sufficient value in a small compass and weight to be a convenient medium.

CIRCUMAM'BIENT, an epithet given to anything that surrounds or encompasses another on all sides; chiefly used in speaking of the air.

CIRCUMCI'SION, the initiatory rite of the Jewish covenant; which, as is recorded, was first enjoined to Abraham by God, and after his posterity had neglected it during their wanderings through the desert, was solemnly renewed upon the passage of the Jordan. This custom has been long prevalent among Eastern nations. Herodotus refers to it as the practice of the Egyptians and Ethiopians, and as borrowed from them by the Phœnicians and Syrians. It does not appear, however, to have been considered by these nations in the light of a religious ceremony. It is enforced by the Koran upon all the disciples of Mahomet, whether from an idea of salubrity vulgarly attributed to it in the East, or merely as a distinguishing rite.

CIR'CUMFLEX, in grammar, an accent serving to note or distinguish a syllable of an intermediate sound between acute and grave: generally somewhat long.

CIRCUMFORA'NEOUS, an epithet for wandering about.—*Circumforaneous musicians*, male and female, are daily seen at the doors of hotels in France; and sometimes they enter the room, expecting a few sous for their reward. Nor are characters of a similar description by any means rare in London or New York.

CIRCUMLOCU'TION, a paraphrastical method of expressing one's thoughts, or saying in many words that which might have been said in few.

CIRCUMPOTA'TION, in antiquity, a funeral entertainment which was given in honor of the deceased to the friends that attended. It was afterwards abolished by law.

CIRCUMROTA'TION, the act of rolling or revolving round, as a wheel.

CIRCUMSTAN'TIAL EV'IDENCE, in law, is that kind of evidence obtained from circumstances which necessarily or usually attend facts of a particular nature. It is used to corroborate personal evidence.

CIRCUMVALLA'TION, or *line of circumvallation*, in the art of war, is a trench bordered with a parapet, thrown up round the besieger's camp, by way of security against any army that may attempt to relieve the place besieged, or to prevent desertion.

CIR'CUS, a straight, long, narrow building, whose length to its breadth was generally as five to one. It was divided down the centre by an ornamented barrier called the spina, and was used by the Romans for the exhibition of public spectacles and chariot races. There were several of these at Rome, of which the most celebrated was the Circus Maximus. Julius Cæsar improved and altered the Circus Maximus; and that it might serve for the purpose of a naumachia, supplied it with water. Augustus added to it the celebrated obelisk now standing in the Piazza del Popolo. No vestiges of this circus remain. Besides these were at Rome the circi of Flaminius, near the Pantheon; Agonalis, occupying the site of what is now the Piazza Navona; of Nero, on a portion whereof St. Peter's stands; Florus, Antoninus, and Aurelian, no longer even in ruins; and that of Caracalla, which was 738 feet in length, and is sufficiently perfect in the present day to exhibit its plan and distribution in the most satisfactory manner. The spectacles exhibited in the circus were called the Circensian games, and consisted chiefly of chariot and horse races. The Romans were passionately fond of them, and more particularly of the chariot races, which excited so great an interest in the times of the emperors as to divide the whole population of the city into factions, known by the names of the colors worn by the different charioteers. The disputes of these factions sometimes led to serious disturbances, and even bloodshed.—In modern times, the word is applied to designate a circular enclosure for the exhibition of feats of horsemanship.

CIST, in architecture and sculpture, a chest or basket. It is a term usually applied to the mystic baskets employed in processions connected with the Eleusinian mysteries. They were originally of wicker-work, and when afterwards made of metal the form and texture were preserved in imitation of the original material. When sculptured on antique monuments it indicates some connection with the mysteries of Ceres and Bacchus. The cista found at Preneste, and now in the *Collegio Romano*, is of surpassing beauty; on it is represented the expedition of the Argonauts in a style not unworthy of Grecian art, but by the inscription apparently of Italian workmanship.

CISTER'CIANS, in church history, a religious order founded in the 11th century by St. Robert, a Benedictine.

CITA'TION, in ecclesiastical courts, is the same with *summons* in civil courts.—A *citation* is also a quotation of some law, authority, or passage from a book.

CITH'ARA, in antiquity, a musical instrument, the precise structure of which is not known.

CITHARIS'TIC, an epithet for anything pertaining to or adapted for the harp.

CITH'ERN, an ancient stringed instrument, supposed to bear a resemblance to the guitar.

CITY, a large town, incorporated and governed by particular officers. In Great Britain, it means a town having a bishop's see, and a cathedral; but this distinction is not always observed in common discourse.—War having rendered it requisite that cities should be defensible posts, the smallness of the space they occupied became a consideration of importance. Their inhabitants were taught to crowd themselves together as much as possible; and among the expedients resorted to was that of building apartments over one another, thereby multiplying the number of dwellings without increasing the superficial magnitude of the place. Trade, too, by requiring a multitude of persons upon one spot, has always been the foundation of what we now call cities. Cities usually possess, by charter, a variety of peculiar privileges; and these charters, though they now sometimes appear to be the supporters of a narrow policy, were, in their institution, grants of freedom at that time nowhere else possessed; and by these the spell that maintained the feudal tyranny was broken.—*City*, (*civitas*,) among the ancients, was used in synonymous sense with what we now call an imperial city; or, rather, answered to those of the Swiss cantons, the republics of Venice, Genoa, &c., as being an independent state, with territories belonging to it.

CIVIC CROWN, (*corona civica*,) in antiquity, a crown, or garland composed of oak-leaves, given by the Romans to any soldier who had saved the life of a citizen. Various marks of honor were connected with it: the person who received the crown wore it at the theatre; and when he entered, the audience rose up as a mark of respect.

CIV'IL, an epithet applicable to whatever relates to the community as a body, or to the policy and the government of the citizens and subjects of a state. It is opposed to *criminal:* as a *civil* suit, a suit between citizens alone, and not between the state and a citizen. It is also distinguished from *ecclesiastical*, which respects the church; and from *military*, which includes only matters relating to the army and navy.—The popular and colloquial use of the word *civil*, means complaisant, polite.—*Civil Law*, is properly the peculiar law of each state, country, or city; but as a general and appropriate term, it means a body of laws composed out of the best Roman and Grecian laws, comprised in the Institutes, Code and Digest of Justinian, &c., and, for the most part, received and observed throughout all the Roman dominions for above 1200 years. This law is used under certain restrictions in the English ecclesiastical courts, as also in the university courts and the court of admiralty.—*Civil List*, the revenue appropriated to support the civil government; also the officers of civil government who are paid from the public treasury.—*Civil Death*, in law, that which cuts off a man from *civil* society, or its rights and benefits, as banishment, outlawry, &c.; as distinguished from *natural* death.—*Civil War*, a war between people of the same state, or the citizens of the same city.—*Civil*

Year, the legal year, or that form of the year which each nation has adopted for computing their time by. The civil year in England and other countries of Europe consists of 365 days for the common year, and 366 days for leap year.—*Civil Architecture*, the architecture which is applied to buildings constructed for the purposes of civil life, in distinction from military and naval architecture.

CIVIL'IAN, a doctor or professor of the civil law; or in a more extended sense, one who is versed in law and government.

CLAN, a family or tribe, living under one chief. This appears to have been the original condition of the savages of northern Europe; and from this we ought to trace the germ of the feudal system. All the members of a clan held their lands of the chief, followed him to war, and were expected to obey him in peace. The clans of the Scottish Highlands are tribes consisting of many families all bearing the same surname, which according to tradition descend from a common ancestor. But it is more probable that most clans were formed of an aggregate of different families, the inferior standing to the superior in the same sort of relation as the Roman clients to their patrons, and by degrees assuming the same name. Some clans, however, are divided into branches, each possessing a distinct surname. The chieftainship of every clan descends regularly through heirs male; but in the earliest times of their history the rights of primogeniture were not very distinctly defined.—The word *clan* is also sometimes used in contempt, for a sect or society of persons united by some common interest or pursuit.

CLANG, a sharp, shrill sound, implying a degree of harshness in the sound; as, the *clang* of arms. The words *clank* and *clink* denote a more acute and less harsh sound than *clang*.

CLARE-OBSCURE, CLARO-OBSCURO, Latin; CHIARO-OSCURO, Italian; and CLAIR-OBSCUR, French; a phrase in painting, signifying light and shade. In pictural criticism, it means the relief that is produced by light and shade, independently of color. In the art itself, it denotes that species of painting or design, in which no attempt is made to give colors to the objects represented, and where, consequently, light and shade are everything.

CLAR'ICHORD, or CLAV'ICHORD, a musical instrument sometimes called a *manichord*. It has fifty stops, or keys, and seventy strings; and is in the form of a spinnet. The tone is soft and sweet. Hence it is a favorite instrument with nuns.

CLAR'ION, a kind of trumpet, whose tube is narrower, and its tone more acute and shrill, than that of the common trumpet.

CLAR'IONET, a wooden musical wind instrument, whose mouth partakes of the trumpet form, and is played by holes and keys: said to have been invented about the year 1600 by John Christopher Denner of Leipsic. Like the oboe it is played with a reed mouth-piece though it is of somewhat different form.

CLASS, a term applied to the scientific division or arrangement of any subject; as in the Linnæan system, where animals, plants, and minerals, are divided into classes, each of which is to be subdivided by a regular downward progression, into orders, genera, and species, with occasional intermediate subdivisions, all subordinate to the division which stands immediately above them. Classes are *natural* or *artificial*, according as they are founded on natural relations or resemblances, or when formed arbitrarily.—*Class* also denotes a number of students in a college or school, of the same standing, or pursuing the same studies.

CLASSI'CAL, in the Fine Arts, a term denoting such an arrangement of a subject that all the accessories or parts are suitable to the general design, and such that nothing be introduced which does not strictly belong to the particular class under which it is placed. In antiquity, the Roman people were divided into classes, and the highest order were, by pre-eminence, termed *classical*. Hence the name came to signify the highest and purest class of writers in any language; although, down to a comparatively recent period, the term was used merely to denote the most esteemed Greek and Latin authors. Nothing marks more strongly the increased attention to modern literature, than the now universal application of the term to modern languages also, and the establishment, in this manner, of a line between those authors whom we regard as models and authorities in point of style, and those who are not so highly esteemed. An author is said to be *classical* if public opinion has placed him in the former order; language, or an expression, to be *classical*, if it be such as has been used in a similar sense and under similar rules of construction by those authors. The epithet classical, as applied to ancient authors, is determined less by the purity of their style than by the period at which they wrote. Thus we speak of the classical age of Greek or Latin writing. With respect to the former, the classical age begins with Homer, the earliest Greek writer with whom we are acquainted. The purest age of Greek classical literature may be said to end about the time of the Macedonian conquest, or about 300 B.C.; but, in a wider sense, it extends to the time of the Antonines, and embraces a much larger catalogue of authors; while the centuries subsequent to that time produced a few, who, by the purity of their style, deserve to be ranked with earlier classics. The Latin classical period is shorter; its earliest writer is Plautus, and the language may be said to have lost its classical character about the same time with the Greek, *i. e.* the reigns of the Antonines; although this limit is arbitrary, and some later writers, even down to Claudian, are generally included among classics. Within the Latin classical era there is a more restricted period of the purest Latinity, comprising the age of Cicero and that of Augustus.

CLASS'IFICA'TION, in the Fine Arts, an arrangement by which objects of the fine arts are distributed in classes; as, for instance, in galleries of paintings, the works should be arranged in schools, each school being subject to a chronological order of the masters. In numismatology, the coins should be arranged by countries, and these again in chronological order of the monarchs; and the like of other branches of the Arts.

CLAUSE, in law, an article in a contract or other writing; a distinct part of a contract, will, agreement, charter, &c.—In language, a subdivision of a sentence, in which the words are inseparably connected with each other in sense, and cannot, with propriety, be separated by a point.

CLAUS'TRAL, relating to a cloister or religious house; as, a *claustral* prior.

CLEF, or CLIFF, a character in music, placed in the beginning of a stave to determine the degree of elevation occupied by that stave, in the general claviary or system, and to point out the names of the notes which it contains in the line of that clef.

CLEPSAM'MIA, an ancient instrument for measuring time by sand, like an hour-glass.

CLEP'SYDRA, a Roman and Grecian timepiece, or water clock; an instrument to measure time by the fall of a certain quantity of water.

CLER'GY, a general name given to the body of ecclesiastics of the Christian church, in distinction from the laity. The revenues of the clergy were anciently more considerable than at present. Ethelwulf, in 855, gave them a tithe of all goods, and a tenth of all the lands in England, free from all secular services, taxes, &c. The charter whereby this was granted them, was confirmed by several of his successors; and William the Conqueror, finding the bishoprics so rich, created them into baronies, each barony containing at least thirteen knights' fees.

CLERK, a word originally used to denote a learned man, or man of letters; whence the term is appropriated to churchmen, who were called clerks or clergymen; the nobility and gentry being bred to the exercise of arms, and none left to cultivate the sciences but ecclesiastics. In modern usage, the word *clerk* means a writer; one who is employed in the use of the pen, in an office, public or private, either for keeping accounts, or entering minutes. In some cases *clerk* is synonymous with secretary, but not always. A clerk is always an officer subordinate to a higher officer, board, corporation, or private individual; whereas, a secretary may either be a subordinate officer, or the head of an office or department.

CLICHE', the impression of a die in a mass of melted tin or fusible metal. Medallists or die-sinkers employ it to make proofs of their work, to judge the effect, and stage of progress of their work before the die is hardened. The term cliché is also applied to the French stereotype casts from woodcuts.

CLI'ENT, a person who seeks advice of a lawyer, or commits his cause to the management of one, either in prosecuting a claim, or defending a suit in a court of justice.—Among the Romans, a *client* meant a citizen who put himself under the protection of a man of distinction and influence, who was accordingly called his *patron*. This relation was in many respects similar to that of a serf to his feudal lord, but bore a much milder form. It was the duty of the patron to watch over the interests of his clients and protect them from aggression, and appear for them in lawsuits. He also frequently made them grants of land on lease. In return the client was bound to defend his patron, and contribute towards any extraordinary expenses he might be subject to; as the portioning his daughters, the payment of a fine imposed by the state, &c. He might not appear as accuser or witness against him in judicial proceedings, a prohibition which was reciprocal. If he committed any offence against his patron, he was obliged to submit to him as his judge; and in ancient times it appears that the power of life and death was held by the latter. On the other hand his security against oppression at the hands of his patron lay in the injunctions and authority of religion, which rendered the bond of union inviolably sacred, as that between father and son. The origin of this relation cannot now be traced; but it seems to have existed, with various modifications, throughout Italy and Greece. In Rome it appears at the foundation of the city by Romulus, when every family not included among the patricians was obliged to find itself a patron from their number. The body of clients was afterwards increased by the institution by which foreigners, who, as allies of Rome, had a share in its franchise, might choose themselves patrons on their coming to settle in the city. The obligations of clients were hereditary, and could not be shaken off unless through the decay of the family of the patron. This body alone in earlier times furnished artisans and shopkeepers; they had votes in the Comitia Centuriata; and though generally confounded with the plebeians, were undoubtedly perfectly distinct from them, as we continually meet in history with instances of their joining the patricians in opposition to the former; and when some of the plebeian houses became powerful, they themselves attached bodies of clients.

CLIMACTER'ICAL YEAR, certain years in the life of man have been from great antiquity supposed to have a peculiar importance, and to be liable to singular vicissitudes in his health and fortunes. This superstitious belief is supposed to have originated in the doctrines of Pythagoras. The well-known notice of the climacterical year, sixty-three, supposed to be particularly dangerous to old men, in a letter of Augustus Cæsar preserved by Aulus Gellius, evinces its prevalence among the Romans. This year has been called by some astrological writers "heroicus," as having been peculiarly fatal to great men. The virtue of this year seems to consist in its being a multiple of the two mystical numbers, seven and nine. It is certainly singular that usage should have attached in all countries peculiar distinction to those years which are denoted by compounds of the number seven. Thus fourteen has been fixed for various purposes as the epoch of puberty, twenty-one of full age; thirty-five has been selected by Aristotle as the period when the body is in its highest physical vigor. The same author supposes the vigor of the mind to be perfected at forty-nine: sixty-three is the grand climacterical year; seventy the limit of the ordinary age of man. Bodinus says that seven is the climacterical number in men and six in women. The term *climacteric disease* has more lately been applied to that declension of bodily and vital powers which is frequently observed to come on in the latter period of life, and from which many persons again rally so as to attain extreme old age.

CLI'MAX, a figure in rhetoric, consisting of an assemblage of particulars, rising, as it were, step by step, and forming a whole in such a manner that the last idea in the former member becomes the first in the latter, till the climax, or gradation, is completed. Its strength and beauty consist in the logical connection of the ideas, and the pleasure the mind receives from perfect conviction; as may be perceived in the following example: "There is no enjoyment of property without government; no government without a magistrate; no magistrate without obedience; and no obedience where every one acts as he pleases."

CLIN'ICAL, in its literal sense, means anything pertaining to a bed. Thus, a *clinical lecture* is a discourse from notes taken at the bedside by a physician, with a view to practical instruction in the healing art. *Clinical medicine* is the practice of medicine on patients in hospitals, or in bed. And the term *clinic* was also applied by the ancient church historians, to one who received baptism on his death-bed.

CLI'O, in mythology, the muse who was usually supposed to preside over history, though she sometimes invaded the province of her sister Calliope, the goddess of epic poetry. In his magnificent ode addressed to Augustus, Horace invokes Clio as the patroness of the flute or the lyre, or in other words of lyric poetry.

CLOA'CA, an ancient common sewer.

CLOCK, a machine for measuring time, called, when first invented, a nocturnal dial, to distinguish it from the sun-dial. This machine consists of wheels moved by weights, so constructed that by a uniform vibration of a pendulum, the hours, minutes, and seconds are measured with great exactness; and it indicates the hour by the stroke of a small hammer on a bell. The invention of clocks has been ascribed to Boethius, about the year 510; but clocks, like those now used, were either first invented, or revived, between two and three centuries ago. The clock measures even 24 hours, but the solar day is unequal, according to the situation of the earth in its orbit, and the declination of the sun. Hence the clock is sometimes a few minutes faster or slower than the sun.

CLOIS'TER, the principal part of a regular monastery, consisting of a square, erected between the church, the chapter-house, and the refectory, and over which is the dormitory. In a general sense, *cloisters* mean covered passages, such as were formerly attached to religious houses.

CLYPE'US, part of the armor worn by the heavy infantry of the Greeks, and a portion of the Roman soldiery, consisting of a large shield or buckler, circular and concave on the inside, sufficiently large to cover the body from the neck to the middle of the leg. It was formed of ox-hide stretched upon a frame of wicker-work, and strengthened with plates of metal; sometimes it was formed entirely of bronze.

COACH, a vehicle of pleasure, distinguished from others chiefly from being a covered box hung on leathers. The oldest carriages used by the ladies in England were called *whirlicotes;* and we find that the mother of Richard II., who, in 1360, accompanied him in his flight, rode in a carriage of this sort. But coaches, properly so called, were introduced into England from Germany, or France, in 1580, in the reign of Elizabeth. In 1601, the year before the queen's death, an act was passed to prevent men from riding in coaches, as being effeminate; but in twenty-five years afterwards hackney-coaches were introduced.

COADJU'TOR, in ecclesiastical matters, the assistant of a bishop or other prelate, (in some instances even of a canon or prebendary, but the latter usage was irregular.) These assistants, in France and other countries, were instituted by the pope. A coadjutor was equal in rank to the dignitary whose functions he might on occasion supply; hence the coadjutor of a bishop was himself consecrated a bishop *in partibus infidelium.* The celebrated Cardinal de Retz was known by the title of the Coadjutor of Paris during the most active period of his career, having the administration of the temporalities of that see, which belonged to his uncle the Archbishop de Retz. Coadjutors usually succeeded their principals in their dignities; and hence arose an abuse which tended towards making ecclesiastical dignities hereditary, nephews and other relatives of bishops being named their coadjutors. The institution of coadjutors to bishoprics is preserved by the French concordat of 1801.

COAD'UNATE, two or more parts joined together.

COAT, a garment worn commonly uppermost. Also, a thin covering laid or done over anyth'ng, as a coat of paint, &c.—*Coat of arms,* in the modern acceptation, is a device, or assemblage of devices, supposed to be painted on a shield; which shield, in the language of heraldry, is called the *field.*—*Coat of mail,* a piece of armor made in the form of a shirt, and wrought over with a kind of net-work of iron rings.

COA VES'TIS, THE COAN ROBE, a garment worn chiefly by dancing girls, courtesans, and other women addicted to pleasure, of texture so fine as to be nearly transparent, and through which the forms of the wearers were easily seen.

CO'BALT BLUE, a beautiful pigment compounded of alumina and phosphate of cobalt. It was discovered in 1802 by the French chemist Thénard. There is no reason to doubt its durability, although, when imperfectly prepared, it is subject to change. Cobalt is the coloring matter of smalts.

CO'BALT GREEN, a preparation of cobalt, the green color of which is due to the presence of iron: it works well both in oil and water.

COCH'INEAL, a dried insect in the form of a small, round grain, flat on one side, either red, brown, powdered with white, or blackish brown. This valuable insect was first introduced into Europe about the year 1523. It is imported from Mexico and New Spain. It feeds on several species of cactus. It is small, rugose, and of a deep mulberry color. They are scraped from the plants into bags, killed by boiling water, and dried in the sun. Those are preferred which are plump, of a peculiar silvery appearance, and which yield a brilliant crimson when rubbed to powder. This splendid coloring material is soluble in water. and is used for making the red lake pigments known by the names carmine, Florentine, and other lakes. Cochineal is sometimes adulterated by the admixture of a manufactured article composed of colored dough. This is detected by the action of boiling water, which dissolves and disintegrates the imitation, but has little effect upon the real insect. The principal component of cochineal is a peculiar coloring matter, which has received the names of *carminium* and *cochinelia*.

COCK, this bird is regarded as the emblem of watchfulness and vigilance; and from a very early period its image was placed on the summit of church crosses. A cock, in the act of crowing, is introduced among the emblems of our Lord's passion, in allusion to the sin of St. Peter.

COCKADE', (from *Cocarde*,) a plume of cock's feathers, with which the Croats adorned their caps. A bow of colored ribbons was adopted for the cockade in France. During the French revolution, the tri-colored cockade became the national distinction.

COCK'NEY, a contemptuous appellation of a citizen of London. Various derivations have been assigned to this word, all of which are more distinguished for ingenuity than probability. But whatever may be the origin of the term, its antiquity cannot be disputed, as it is mentioned in some verses generally attributed to Hugh Bagot, Earl of Norfolk, in the reign of Henry II.:—

> Were I in my castle at Bungey,
> Upon the river of Waverney,
> I would not care for the king of Cockeney
> (i. e. of London,)

COCK'PIT, the after part of the orlop deck, or deck below the lower deck, and altogether below the water. Here, in line-of-battle ships, are the cabins of several of the officers. The cock-pit is appropriated to the use of the wounded in time of action. There is also a fore cockpit in the fore part of the ship, and sometimes an after cock-pit.—*Cock-pit* is the name given to the place where gamecocks fight their battles. The room in Westminster in which her Majesty's privy council hold their sittings is called the *cock-pit*, from its having been the site of what was formerly the cock-pit belonging to the palace at Whitehall.

COCY'TUS, in mythology, the river of Lamentations, which was one of the streams that washed the shores of the mythological hell, and prevented the imprisoned souls from returning to the earth. Milton alludes to it thus:—

> Cocytus named of lamentations loud
> Heard on the rueful stream.

CO'DA, in music, the passage at the end of a movement which follows a lengthened perfect cadence. In some cases it consists of merely one phrase, in others it is carried to a great extent. At the conclusion of a canon or fugue, it often serves to end the piece which might otherwise be carried on to infinity.

CODE, (from *codex*, a roll, or volume,) a collection or system of laws. The collection of laws or constitutions made by order of the emperor Justinian is distinguished by the appellation of *code* by way of eminence.—The *Code Napoleon*, or *civil code* of France, proceeding from the French Revolution, and the administration of Napoleon, while consul, effected great changes in the laws of France. It was a work of great magnitude, and will remain a perpetual monument of the state of things as they then existed in that country.

COD'ICIL, a supplement to a will, containing anything which the testator wishes to add; or any explanation, alteration, or revocation, of what his will contains.

CODET'TA, in music, a short passage which connects one section with another, and not composing part of a regular section.

CO'DEX, a manuscript; in its original sense (Latin) the inner bark of a tree, which was used for the purposes of writing. The word was thence transferred by the Romans to signify a piece of writing on whatever material; *e. g.* with the stylus on tablets lined with wax, or on a roll of parchment or paper. In modern Latin a manuscript volume. *Codex rescriptus*, or *palimpsestus*, is a manuscript consisting of leaves, from which some earlier writing has been erased in order to afford room for the insertion of more recent. Many such codices exist; and from the imperfect nature of the erasing process, the earlier writing has, in some instances, been restored. Considerable fragments of classical works, previously considered as lost, have been thus recovered by the Abate Mai from among the contents of the Ambrosian Library at Milan.

CŒ'NA, the principal meal among the Greeks and Romans. The time of the *cœna*, or supper, was the ninth hour, answering to three o'clock in the afternoon with us, and it consisted of three courses

They made a libation both before and after supper, and concluded the evening with much festivity.

CŒNAC'ULUM, in ancient architecture, the eating or supper room of the Romans. In the early periods of the Roman history, the upper story of their houses, which rarely consisted of more than two, seems to have been called by this name.

CŒNA'TIO, in ancient architecture, an apartment for taking refreshment in the lower part of the Roman houses.

CŒN'OBITE, one who lives under a rule in a religious community, as distinguished from an anchoret or hermit, who lives in solitude.

COETA'NEOUS, an epithet denoting of the same age, or beginning with another. The word *coeval* is synonymous with it; *contemporary* implies, existing at the same time.

COF'FER, in architecture, a sunk panel in vaults and domes, and also in the soffit or under side of the Corinthian cornice, usually decorated in the centre with a flower.

COG'NIZANCE, in law, an acknowledgment of a fine, of taking a distress, &c. It also signifies the power which a court has to hear and determine a particular species of suit.

COGNO'MEN, in antiquities, the last of the three names by which all Romans, at least those of good family, were designated. It served to mark the house to which they belonged, as the other two names, viz., the *prænomen* and *nomen*, served respectively to denote the individual and the class to which his family belonged.

COHORT', a military body among the Romans, consisting of the tenth of a legion, or from five to six hundred men.

COIN, a piece of metal stamped with certain marks, and made current at a certain value. Strictly speaking, coin differs from money as the species differs from the genus. Money is any matter, whether metal, or paper, or beads, or shells, &c., which have currency as a medium in commerce. Coin is a particular species always made of metal, and struck according to a certain process called coining. The British *coinage* is wholly performed at the Tower of London, where there is a corporation for the purpose, under the title of the Mint.—*Current coin*, is coin legally stamped and circulating in trade.—*Counterfeit coin*, that which is forged or stamped without authority.

COLIPH'IUM, in antiquity, a sort of coarse bread which wrestlers used to eat in order to make them strong and muscular.

COLISE'UM, an elliptical amphitheatre, at Rome, built by Vespasian, in which were statues representing all the provinces of the empire, and in the middle stood that of Rome, holding a golden apple in her hand. This immense structure was 1612 feet in circumference, contained eighty arcades, and would hold 100,000 spectators. Down to the 13th century, this unrivalled monument of ancient grandeur remained almost uninjured; afterwards Pope Paul II. took all the stones from it which were used for the construction of the palace of St. Mark, and in later times some other palaces were erected from its fragments. At present, care is taken not to touch the ruins of the Coliseum, but it is gradually crumbling away of itself, and in a few centuries, perhaps, nothing more may be seen of its upper part; the lower part, however, may safely bid defiance to the ravages of time. Benedict XVI. caused a cross to be erected in the centre of the arena, where, every Sunday afternoon, Catholic worship is performed. The great object of this magnificent building was to exhibit the brutal spectacles of the gladiators contending with wild beasts. We accordingly read, that on the triumph of Trajan over the Dacians, 11,000 animals were killed in the amphitheatres at Rome; and 1000 gladiators fought during 123 days. The gladiators at first were malefactors, who fought for victory and life; or captives and slaves, who were made to fight for their freedom; but after a time many lived by it as a profession; and these exhibitions continued, with modifications, for above 500 years.—A very large and most ingeniously constructed building, erected in the Regent's Park, London, is called the Coliseum, or Colosseum.

COLLAPSE', to close by falling together; as, the fine canals or vessels of the body *collapse* in old age; or, as a balloon collapses when the gas escapes from it.

COL'LAR, in Roman antiquity, a chain put round the neck of slaves that had run away, after they were taken.—In a modern sense, it denotes an ornament consisting of a chain of gold, enamelled, &c., frequently set with ciphers or other devices, with the badge of the order hanging at the bottom, and worn by the knights of several military orders over their shoulders.

COLLAT'ERAL, in genealogy, signifies descending from the same stock or ancestor, but not in a direct line; and is therefore distinguished from *lineal*.—*Collateral security*, in law, is security for the performance of covenants on the payment of money, besides the principal security.

COLLA'TION, in the canon law, the presentation to a benefice, by a bishop, who has it in his own gift or patronage. When the patron of a church is not a bishop, he presents his clerk for admission, and the bishop institutes him; but *collation* includes both presentation and institution.—*Collation*, in law, the comparison of a copy with its original, to ascertain its conformity; or the report of the officer who made the comparison. Hence, a collator means one who compares copies or manuscripts. And from the same is derived the term *Collating* among printers, by which is meant the examining the whole number of sheets belonging to a book, in order to see if they are all gathered properly.

COL'LECT, a short and comprehensive prayer, particularly such prayers as are appointed with the epistles and gospels in the public service of the Church of England.

COLLECTA'NEA, in literature, notes, observations, or any matter collected from a variety of works.

COLLEC'TIVE, in grammar, an epithet for any noun which comprehends many persons or things; as a *multitude*, a *company*, a *congregation*, an *army*, &c.

COL'LEGE, in its usual, though somewhat limited sense, is a public place endowed with certain revenues, where the several parts of learning are taught, and where the students reside, under a regular discipline. An assemblage of several of these colleges is called a *university*. The establishment of colleges or universities forms a remarkable period in literary history; for the schools in cathedrals and monasteries were confined chiefly to the teaching of grammar; and there were only one or two masters employed in that charge; but in colleges, professors are appointed to teach all the branches of science.—There are colleges of physicians and surgeons, a college of philosophy, a college of heralds, a college of civilians, &c.

COLLE'GIATE CHURCHES, are those that, without a bishop's see, have the ancient retinue of a bishop; such as the church of St Peter's, Westminster. This was anciently a cathedral; but the revenues of the monastery being vested in the dean and chapter by act of parliament, it became a collegiate church.

COLLOCA'TIO, in antiquity, a ceremony at the funerals of the Greeks and Romans, which consisted of placing the corpse, laid on a bier, near the threshold of the house, that all might see whether he had met his death by violence or not.

COLLU'SION, in law, a deceitful agreement or compact between two persons to bring an action one against the other for some fraudulent or unlawful purpose.

COLO'GNE-EARTH, a substance used in painting, much approaching to umber in its structure, and of a deep brown. It is supposed to be the remains of wood long buried in the earth.

CO'LON, in grammar, a point marked thus (:) to divide a sentence.

COLO'NEL, the chief commander of a regiment, whether infantry or calvary.—LIEUTENANT-COLONEL, the second officer in a regiment, who commands in the absence of the colonel.

COLONNADE', a range of pillars running quite round a building.

COL'ONY, a company or body of people removed from their mother country to a remote province or country, where they form a settlement under the sanction of the government. Also, the place where such a settlement is formed, as the colonies belonging to Great Britain in the East and West Indies, North America, &c.

COL'OPHON, in bibliography, the postscript contained in the last sheet of an early printed work (before the introduction of title-pages,) containing the printer's name, date, &c., is so termed, from a fanciful allusion to a Greek satirical proverb, in which the people of Colophon, in Asia Minor, are reproached with being always the hindmost.

COL'OR, the type of color is found in the *prismatic spectrum* or the *rainbow*. In which we discover that a ray of white light in capable of being decomposed into three *primitive* colors—red, blue, and yellow; these, by their mixture, produce three other colors, which are termed *secondary*; thus, the union of red with blue yields, when in varied proportions, the different hues of purple and violet; red, mixed with yellow, yields orange: yellow, with blue, produces green. Every hue in nature is a compound of two or more of the primitive colors in various proportions. Grays and browns are compounds of all three of the primary colors in unequal proportions. Black results from a mixture of blue, red, and yellow of equal intensity and in equal proportions. Of material colors (pigments) there is but one (ultramarine) that approaches the purity of the type in the spectrum—all the others are more or less impure; thus we cannot obtain a pure red pigment, since all are more or less alloyed with blue or yellow. If we could obtain a red and a yellow of the same purity and transparency as ultramarine, we should need no other pigments for our palette, since, by judicious mixture, they would yield every tint in nature.—*Local colors* are those peculiar to each individual object, and serve to distinguish them from each other.—*Complementary colors* are composed of the *opposites* of any given color. If this color is a *primitive*, such as blue, the *complementary* color is composed of the other two primitive colors, viz., red and yellow, or orange; the complementary color to any *secondary* is the other primitive color; thus the complementary to green (composed of blue and yellow,) is red, and so on, for the remainder.—*Harmony of colors* results from an equal distribution of the three primary colors, either pure, or compounded with each other, as grays and browns.—*Contrast of color* is either simple or compound. Each of the primitive colors forms a *contrast* to the other two; thus blue is contrasted by yellow and by red—either of these forms a simple contrast to blue; but by mixing yellow and red together, we produce orange, which is a *compound* contrast, consequently orange, the *complementary* color, is the most powerful contrast that can be made to blue. Colors are regarded as warm or cold, positive or negative; thus blue is a *cold*, and orange a *warm*, color. Red, neither warm nor cold. All *warm* colors are contrasts to *cold* colors.—*Symbolic colors.* Colors had the same signification amongst all nations of remotest antiquity. Color was evidently the first mode of transmitting thought and preserving memory; to each color appertained a religious or political idea. The history of symbolic colors testifies to a triple origin marked by the three epochs in the history of religion—the divine, the consecrated, and the profane. The first regulated the costume of Aaron and the Levites, the rites of worship, &c. Religion gave birth to the Arts. It was to ornament temples that sculpture and painting were first introduced, whence arose the *consecrated* language. The *profane* language of colors was a degradation from the divine and consecrated languages.

COL'ORATURE, in music, all kinds of variations, trills, &c. intended to make a song agreeable.

COLO'RES FLO'RIDI, the name given by the ancients to the expensive and brilliant pigments, as distinguished from the four hard rough principal pigments of earlier times. The colores floridi were supplied by the employer, and often purloined by the artist: they were chrysocolla; indicum (*indigo* introduced into Rome in the time of the emperors;) cæruleum (a blue smalt made at Alexandria, from sand, saltpetre, and copper;) and cinnibaris, which was partly natural and partly artificial vermilion; but also an Indian pigment, procured from the sap of the *pterocarpus draco*, and called also dragon's blood. Other pigments were called colores austeri.

COL'ORIST, a painter whose works are remarkable for beauty of color. Titian, Correggio, Paul Veronese, Rubens, Vandyke, are in the first rank of colorists. The Venetian and the Flemish schools have supplied the greatest number of colorists, as well as the best; always excepting Correggio, the founder of the Lombard school, who is by many regarded equal to Titian. Color being, as well as design, an essential part of a picture, every colorist is, at the same time, more or less a draughtsman. But experience shows, and theory furnishes good reasons for believing, that these two qualities, which many artists possess together in a moderate degree, are rarely found in an eminent degree, united *in the same individual*, and still less in the same picture.

COLOS'SAL, in the Fine Arts, a term applied to any work of art remarkable for its extraordinary dimensions. It is, however, more applied to works in sculpture than in the other arts. It seems probable that colossal statues had their origin from the attempt to astonish by size at a period when the science of proportion and that of imitation were in their infancy. Colossal statues of the divinities were common both in Asia and Egypt. By the description of the palace or temple attributed to Semiramis it abounded with colossal statues, among which was one of Jupiter forty feet in height. In Babylon we learn from Daniel that the palaces were filled with statues of an enormous size, and in the present day the ruins of India present us with statues of extraordinary dimensions. The Egyptians surpassed the Asiatics in these gigantic monuments, considering the beautiful finish they gave to such a hard material as granite. Sesostris, according to history, appears to have been the first who raised these colossal masses, the statues of himself and his wife, which he placed before the temple of Vulcan, having been thirty cubits in height. This example was imitated by his successors, as the ruins of Thebes sufficiently testify. The taste for colossal statues prevailed also among the Greeks. The great Phidias contributed several works of this order. The statue of Apollo at Rhodes, was executed by Cnares, a disciple of Lysippus, who devoted himself to this object during twelve years. It was placed at the entrance of the harbor, with the right foot standing on one side the land and the left on the other. It was of brass, and is said to have existed nearly fourteen centuries, before the period in which it fell by the shock of an earthquake. When the Saracens became possessed of Rhodes, they found the statue in a prostrate state, and sold it to a Jew, by whom 900 camels were laden with the materials. The colossus at Tarentum by Lysippe was no less than forty cubits in height; and the difficulty of removing it, rather than the moderation of the conqueror, prevented Fabius carrying it off with the Hercules from the same city. But the proposition made to Alexander of cutting Mount Athos into a statue, in one of whose hands a city was to be placed capable of holding ten thousand inhabitants, whilst in the other he was to hold a vessel pouring out the torrents from the mountain, exceeds all others in history. Before the time of the Romans colossal statues were frequently executed in Italy. The first monument of this nature set up in Rome was one placed in the capitol by Sp. Carvillius after his victory over the Samnites. This was succeeded in after-times by many others, of which those now on Monte Cavallo, said to be of Castor and Pollux, are well known to most persons. In modern times the largest that has been erected is that of S. Carlo Boromeo at Arona near Milan. This gigantic statue is upwards of sixty feet in height.

COLUMBA, St., this saint is represented with a crown upon her head, and standing on a pile of burning wood, an angel by her side; sometimes she holds a sword. According to the legend, the angel is said to have extinguished the flames with his wings. whereupon she was beheaded by order of the Emperor Aurelian, at Cordova, A.D. 273. The idea that she was of royal blood appears to have arisen from the crown, which, on the contrary, refers to her being a martyr.

COLUMBA'RIUM, in architecture, a pigeon-house or dovecote. From the similarity the arched and square-headed recesses in the walls of cemeteries, which were made to receive the cinerary urns, were also called columbaria.

COLUM'BIAN, an epithet for anything pertaining to America, from its having been discovered by Columbus.

COL'UMN, in architecture, a cylindrical pillar, or long round body of wood, stone, or iron, which serves either for the support or ornament of a building. It consists of a capital, which is the top or head; the shaft, which is the cylindrical part; and the base, or that on which it rests. Columns are distinguished as to their form into the Tuscan, Doric, Ionic, Corinthian, and Composite. The Tuscan is characterized by being rude, simple and massy; the Doric is next in strength and massiveness to the Tuscan; the Ionic is more slender than the Tuscan and Doric; the Corinthian is more delicate in its form and proportions, and enriched with ornaments; and the Composite is a species of the Corinthian. In strictness, the shaft of a column consists of one entire piece; but it is often composed of different pieces, so united as to have the appearance of one entire piece. — The word column has also many other meanings; as, a division of a page, which may contain two or more *columns*. A large body of troops drawn up in order; as, a solid *column*. Any body pressing on its base, and of the same diameter as its base; as, a *column* of water, air, or mercury.

COM'EDY. (From the Greek words κώμη, *village*, and ᾠδή, *a song;* because the original rude dialogues, intermixed with singing and dancing, out of which the early Greek comedy arose, were sung by rustic actors at village festivals.) A species of drama, of which the characteristics in modern usage are, that its incidents and language approach nearly to those of ordinary life; that the termination of its intrigue is happy; and that it is distinguished by greater length and greater complexity of plot from the lighter theatrical piece entitled a farce. The original Attic comedy was a burlesque tragedy in form, in substance a satire on individuals, and founded on political or other matters of public interest. The modern comedy is derived from the new comedy of the Greeks, of which Menander and Philemon were the principal authors, and which has been preserved to us through the Latin imitations of Plautus and Terence. According to Bossu, comedy differs from tragedy in this, that comic writers invent both the names of the persons and the actions which they represent; whereas the tragic writers invent only the latter, taking the former from history. Among us, comedy is distinguished from farce, as the former represents nature as she is, the other distorts and overcharges her; but whether it be to recommend virtue or to render folly ridiculous, the real intention and effect are amusement.

COMI'TIA, in Roman antiquity, an assembly of the people, either in the *Comitium* or *Campus Martius*, for the election of magistrates, or consulting on the important affairs of the republic. The people originally gave their votes *vivâ voce*, but in process of time this was superseded by the use of tablets. The comitia were of three kinds, distinguished by the epithets, *Curiata*, *Centuriata*, and *Tributa*. 1. The comitia curiata were the assemblies of the patrician houses or *populus;* and in these, before the plebeians attained political importance, was vested the supreme power of the state. The name *curiata* was given because the people voted *in curiæ*, each curia giving a single vote representing the sentiments of the majority of the members composing it; which was the manner in which the tribes and centuries also gave their suffrages in their respective comitia. After the institution of the comitia centuriata, the functions of the curiata were nearly confined to the election of certain priests, and passing a law to confirm the dignities imposed by the people. 2. The comitia centuriata were the assemblies of the whole Roman people, including patricians, clients, and plebeians, in which they voted by centuries. By the constitution of the centuries, these comitia were chiefly in the hands of the plebeians, and so served originally as a counterpoise to the powers of the comitia curiata, for which purpose they were first instituted by the lawgiver king Servius Tullius. These comitia quickly obtained the chief importance, and public matters of the greatest moment were transacted in them; as the elections of consuls, prætors, and censors, and the passing laws and trials for high treason. 3. The comitia tributa were the assemblies of the plebeian tribes. They were first instituted after the expulsion of the kings; and in them were transacted matters pertaining to the plebeians alone, as the election of their tribunes and ædiles.

COM'MA, in grammar, a point or character marked thus (,) denoting the shortest pause in reading, and separating a sentence into divisions or members.—In theoretic music, it is a term to show the exact proportions between concords.

COMMANDANT', the commanding officer of a place or of a body of forces.

COMMAND'ER, the chief officer of an army, or one who has the command of a body of men. The commander-in-chief in the British army is he who has the supreme command over all the land forces in Great Britain. In the naval service the chief admiral in any port or station is so called.—The *commander of a ship*, otherwise called the *master*, is an officer next in rank to a post captain, who has the command of a ship of war under 18 guns, a sloop, &c.

COMMENCE'MENT, an annual public assembly of a university, or the day on which degrees are publicly conferred on students who have finished a collegiate education.

COMMEND'AM, in ecclesiastical law, the trust or administration of the revenues of a benefice given to a layman to hold as a deposit for six months, in order to repairs, &c., or to an ecclesiastic to perform the pastoral duties till the benefice is provided with a regular incumbent. In England, the right of granting benefices *in commendam* is vested in the crown by a statue of Henry VIII.—One who holds a living in commendam is called a *commendatory*.—*Commendatory letters*, are letters sent from one bishop to another in behalf of any of the clergy, &c.

COMMENTAC'ULUM, in antiquity, a wand which those who were going to sacrifice held in their hand, to make people stand out of the way.

COM'MENTARY, an explanation of the obscure passages in an author; or an historical narrative, as, the Commentaries of Cæsar.

COM'MERCE, in a general sense, is the intercourse of nations in each other's produce or manufactures, in which the superfluities of one are given for those of another, and then re-exchanged with other nations for mutual wants. Commerce is both *foreign* and *inland*. Foreign commerce is the trade which one nation carries on with another; inland commerce, or inland trade, is the trade in the exchange of commodities between citizens of the same nation. The benefits of commercial intercourse have been felt and admitted from the earliest times; but they have never been so highly appreciated, or carried to such an extent as at present. It gives a stimulus to industry; supplies mankind with enjoyments to which they would otherwise be strangers, tends greatly to obliterate unfounded prejudices between nations; excites a spirit of laudable competition among all classes; enables one country to profit by the inventions of another; diffuses the blessings of civilization to the most remote corners of the earth; enlarges the powers and faculties of the mind; and advances human knowledge by the improvements which it carries into every art and science. On the other hand, it cannot be denied that it has contributed to unjust aggressions, and that the peace and welfare of man have often been made subservient to commercial avarice. Yet much as the evils attributed to commerce have been deplored by some moral writers, we cannot but adopt the sentiments of one who says, "To commerce, with all its mischiefs, with all its crimes, committed upon every shore, its depopulation of fields, and corruption of cities, to commerce we must attribute that growing intimacy between the members of the human race from which great benefits have redounded, and greater still may spring."

COMMISSA'RIATE, the whole body of officers in the commissary's department.

COM'MISSARY, in a general sense, one who is sent or delegated to execute some office or duty, as the representative of his superior.—In military affairs, an officer, who has the charge of furnishing provisions, clothing, &c. for an army. There are various separate duties devolving on commissaries, and they have names accordingly: as the *commissary-general*, who is at the head of the department; *deputy-commissaries*, &c.—In ecclesiastical law, an officer of the bishop who exercises spiritual jurisdiction in distant parts of the diocese.

COMMIS'SION, in law, the warrant, or letters patent by which one is authorized to exercise jurisdiction.—In military affairs, the warrant or authority by which one holds any post in the army: in distinction to the inferior or non-commissioned officers.—In commerce, the order by which any one traffics or negotiates for another; also the per centage given to factors and agents for transacting the business of others.

COMMIS'SIONER, a person authorized by commission, letters-patent, or other lawful warrant, to examine any matters, or execute any public office, &c.

COMMIT'MENT, is the sending a person to prison by warrant or order, either for a crime or contumacy.

COMMIT'TEE, certain persons elected or appointed, to whom any matter or business is referred, either by a legislative body, or by any corporation or society.—A *Committee of the Legislature*, signifies a certain number of members appointed by the house to proceed on some specific business. The whole house frequently resolves itself into a committee, in which case, each member has a right to speak as often as he pleases. When the house is not in committee, each gives his opinion regularly, and is only allowed to speak once, unless to explain himself.—*Standing committees* are such as continue during the existence of the legislature. *Special committees* are appointed to consider and report on particular subjects.

COMMOD'ITY, in commerce, any merchandise which a person deals in.—*Staple commodities*, such wares and merchandises as are the proper produce or manufacture of the country.

COM'MODORE, an officer in the navy, invested with the command of a detachment of ships of war destined for a particular purpose.—The *Commodore of a convoy* is the leading ship in a fleet of merchantmen, and carries a light in her top to conduct the other ships.

COM'MON, a tract of ground, or open space, the use of which is not appropriated to an individual, but belongs to the public, or to a number. The right which a person has to pasture his cattle on land of another, or to dig turf, or catch fish, or cut wood, or the like, is called *common* of pasture, or turbary, of piscary, and of estovers.

COMMON COUN'CIL, the council of a city or corporate town, empowered to make by-laws for the government of the citizens. It is generally used in speaking of a court in the city of London, composed of the lord mayor, aldermen, and a certain number of citizens called common-councilmen. The city of London is divided into 24 wards; the chief magistrate of each ward has the title of alderman; the 24 aldermen, with the lord mayor, form the court of aldermen; and certain inhabitants chosen out of each ward, for the purpose of assisting the aldermen with their advice in public affairs, form the court of *common council.*

COMMON LAW, the law that receives its binding force from immemorial usage and universal reception, in distinction from the *written* or statute law; and which chiefly originated in judicial decisions founded on natural justice and equity, or on local customs.

COMMONPLACE-BOOK, a register of such thoughts and observations as occur to a person of reading or reflection.

COMMON PLEAS, a superior court where pleas or causes are heard between subject and subject.

COMMON PRAYER BOOK, the name given to the collection of all the offices of regular and occasional worship according to the forms of the church of England. The basis of this book is to be found in the King's Primer, set forth in 1546 by Henry VIII., which was intended to convey instruction to the people in the most important parts of the church service; but contained little more than the Creed, Lord's Prayer, Commandments, and Litany. This Primer underwent two revisions and republications under Edward VI., whose second Liturgy approaches very near in its contents to that which exists at present. It was at that review that the Sentences, Exhortation, Confession, and Absolution were prefixed to the Daily Service; the Decalogue was introduced into the Communion Service; and certain remnants of the Romish customs were finally abolished, as the sign of the cross in confirmation and matrimony, the anointing of the sick, and the prayers for the dead. On the accession of Elizabeth, another review of the Liturgy was instituted; but the alterations effected were little more than in the selection of the lessons. At the review in the reign of James I., after the conference with the Presbyterians at Hampton Court, no change of importance was introduced, except the addition of the explanation of the Sacraments in the Catechism. Again, when on the restoration of Charles II. a conference had been held with the dissenters at the Savoy, the subject of the common prayer book was reconsidered in convocation. The services for the 30th of January and 29th of May were then added, as also the form to be used at Sea. A few trifling alterations were made also in the other services; but these were the last that have been effected. On the accession of William III. another revision took place, and a considerable number of alterations were proposed and supported by many of the bishops and clergy; but they were rejected by convocation, and have never since been revived by authority.

COM'MONS, the lower house of Parliament, consisting of the representatives of cities, boroughs, and counties, chosen by men possessed of the property or qualifications required by law. This body is called the *House of Commons;* and may be regarded as the basis of the British constitution. The origin of this assembly ought, perhaps, to be attributed to the necessity under which the first Edward perceived himself of counteracting a powerful aristocracy. The feudal system had erected a band of petty monarchs from whom the crown was in perpetual danger. It is to the struggles of these men with regal authority, in the course of which, in order to strengthen their opposition, they were obliged to make common cause with the people, that the existence of English liberty may be attributed. In a word, the House of Commons arose on the ruins of the feudal fabric, gained ground as that decayed, pressed on its weaker parts, and, finally, levelled it with the dust. Though each member is elected by a distinct body of people, he is, from the moment of his election, the representative, not of those particular persons only, but of the kingdom at large; and is to consider himself not merely as the organ through which his constituents may speak, but as one who, having been intrusted with a general charge, is to perform it to the best of his judgment. In performance of this great function, his liberty of speech is bounded only by those rules of decency of which the house itself is the judge; and while, on the one hand, he is free to propose what laws he pleases, on the other, he is exposed, as a private man, to the operation of the laws he makes. This assembly is composed of six hundred and fifty-eight members; and though many small boroughs were disfranchised by the Reform Bill, the elective franchise was given to several places of rising importance, and a variety of alterations took place by adding to the number of representatives of counties, &c., so that the total number of members remains the same.

COMMONWEALTH', in a general

sense, applies to the social state of a country, without regarding its form of government.—In the usual, though more restricted sense, a republic, or that form of government in which the administration of public affairs is open to all with few, if any, exceptions.

COMMU'NION, the act of communicating in the sacrament of the eucharist, or the Lord's Supper.—*Communion Service*, the office for the administration of the holy sacrament.—*Communion Table*, the table erected at the east end of a church, round which the communicants kneel to partake of the Lord's Supper.

COMMU'NITY, a society of people living in the same place, under the same laws and regulations, and who have common rights and privileges. History shows that the establishment of communities has been one of the greatest advances in human improvement: and they have proved, in different ages, the cradle and the support of freedom.

COMMUTA'TION, in law, the change of a penalty or punishment from a greater to a less; as when death is commuted for transportation or imprisonment.

COM'PACT, a word denoting an agreement or contract, but generally applied in a political sense; as, a compact or agreement entered into between nations and states for any particular object.

COM'PANY, in a commercial sense, a society of merchants, mechanics, or other traders, joined together in a common interest. The term is also applied to large associations set on foot for the purpose of commerce; as, the East India Company; a banking or insurance company, &c. When companies do not trade upon a joint stock, but are obliged to admit any person properly qualified, upon paying a certain fine, and agreeing to submit to the regulations of the company, each member trading upon his own stock, and at his own risk, they are called *regulated companies;* when they trade upon a joint stock each member sharing in the common profit or loss, in proportion to his share in the stock, they are called *joint stock companies.*—In military affairs, a small body of foot, consisting usually of a number from 60 to 100 men, commanded by a captain, who has under him a lieutenant and ensign.—Also, the whole crew of a ship, including the officers.

COMPAR'ISON, in a general sense, the consideration of the relation between two persons or things, when opposed and set against each other, by which we judge of their agreement or difference.—*Comparison of ideas*, among logicians, that operation of the mind whereby it compares its ideas one with another, in regard of extent, degree, time, place, or any other circumstance, and is the ground of relations.—*Comparison*, in rhetoric, a figure by which two things are considered with regard to a third, which is common to them both; as, a hero is like a lion in courage. Here courage is common to hero and lion, and constitutes the point of resemblance.

COMPART'MENT, in architecture, a proportionable division in a building, or some device marked in an ornamental part of the building.

COMPENSA'TION, in civil law, a sort of right, whereby a person, who has been sued for a debt, demands that the debt may be compensated with what is owing him by the creditor, which, in that case, is equivalent to payment.

COMPERTO'RIUM, a judicial inquest in the civil law, made by delegates or commissioners, to find out and relate the truth of a cause.

COMPITA'LIA, a Roman feast celebrated in honor of the Lares and Penates. Under Tarquinius Superbus, it is said that human victims were sacrificed at this solemnity. The gods invoked at it were termed Compitales, as presiding over the streets.

COMPLEX'ION, among physicians, the temperament, habitude, and natural disposition of the body; but, in general use, the word means the color of the skin.

COM'PLEX TERMS, and COM'PLEX IDE'AS, in logic, are such as are compounded of several simple ones.

COMPLU'VIUM, in ancient architecture, an area in the centre of the Roman houses, so constructed that it might receive the waters from the roofs. It is also the gutter or eave of a roof.

COMPO'SING, that branch of the art of printing which consists in taking the types or letters from the cases, and arranging them in such an order as to fit them for the press. The instrument in which they are adjusted to the length of the lines is called a *composing-stick.*

COM'POSITE OR'DER, in architecture, one of the five orders of architecture, and, as its name imports, composed of two others, the Corinthian and the Ionic Its capital is a vase with two tiers of acanthus leaves, like the Corinthian; but instead of stalks, the shoots appear small and adhere to the vase, bending round towards the middle of the face of the capital; the vase is terminated by a fillet over which is an astragal crowned by an ovolo. The volutes roll themselves over the ovolo to meet the tops of the upper row of leaves, whereon they seem to rest. The corners of the abacus are supported by an acanthus leaf bent upwards. The abacus resembles that of the Corinthian capital. In detail the Composite is richer than the Corinthian, but less light and delicate. Its architrave has usually only two fasciæ, and the cornice varies from the Corinthian in having double modillions. The column is ten diameters high. The principal examples of this order are the Temple of Bacchus at Rome, the arch of Septimius Severus, those of the Goldsmiths and of Titus, and that in the baths of Diocletian.

COMPOSI'TION, in a general sense, the putting together, and uniting of several things, so as to form of the whole one mass or compound—*Composition of ideas*, an act of the mind, whereby it unites several ideas into one conception, or complex idea.—In literature, the act of inventing or combining ideas, furnishing them with words, arranging them in order, and committing them to writing.—In logic, a method of reasoning, whereby we proceed from some general self-evident truth, to other particular and singular ones. This method of reasoning is opposed to *analysis*, which begins with first principles, and, by a train of reasoning from them, deduces the propositions or truths sought; but *composition* or *synthesis* collects the scattered parts of knowledge, and combines them into a system, so that the understanding is enabled distinctly to follow truth through its different stages of gradations.—In music, the art or act of forming tunes, either to be performed vocally or instrumentally.—In commerce, an agreement entered into between an insolvent debtor and his creditor, by which the latter accepts a part of the debt in compensation for the whole.—In painting, this word expresses the idea of a whole created out of single parts, and to this idea the whole ought to conform. In the whole there ought never to be too much or too little; all parts must be necessary, and must refer to one another, being understood only under such relationship. This does not imply that every part must be co-ordinate, some parts must be of more importance than others, and all must be subordinate to a centre-point, which raises them, while it is raised by them. This quality, which is seen in natural landscape, we call *organism;* we desire to produce it in art, and require pictures to be *organic*. This is valid as well in simple composition as in compound, which as a composition of compositions, represents many wholes. All this, though not attained, is at least attempted by those who call themselves artists. The following is less acknowledged but not less important, viz., every composition consists of three elements, whose one-sided predominance in painters and connoisseurs produces three schools of error; while the fervent working together of these elements alone makes the work a living whole, and gives it that which is expressed by the Latin word *compositio*—a quieting satisfying effect. The artist's subject furnishes the *first* element. Every subject has its own law of representation, which the artist must clearly understand if he would depict it truly upon the canvas. This comprehension is to be acquired only by his forgetting *himself* in the contemplation of his *subject*. It is the power of doing this which we prize so highly in poetry under the term *objectivity*. By thus treating the subject the artist becomes a splendid organ, through which nature speaks like a history to sentient man: thus followed out, the majesty of Rome in Rubens, and the cheerfulness of nature in Claude, are conveyed to posterity. The *second* element of composition is fixed by the given space which is to be filled by color, form and light, harmonized according to the laws of art; then a history adorning a space becomes the property of art. The *third* element lies in the mind of the artist; as "woman's judgment is tinged by her affections," so the artist who cannot imbue his subject with his own feelings will fail to animate his canvas. For though every legitimate subject dictates the laws of its representation, yet every cultivated man sees objects in his own light, and no one may say that he alone sees rightly. He who knows not how to give that to his pictures, by which they become, not from manner but from subject, *his* pictures, is no artist, but a mere copyist, even could he imitate Phidias or Scopas perfectly. Excess of individualism leads the artist to depict *himself* instead of the *subject*, to sacrifice this is a favorite caprice, and in allegorizing his own dreams to confuse the action as well as the spectator; but if he represent it truthfully, working it with pictorial effect and stamping it with his genius, he has *composed*, and his work is completed, satisfying all requisitions.

COMPO'SITOR, in printing, the workman who arranges the types in lines and pages, and prepares them for being printed off.

COMPURGA'TION, an ancient mode of trial both in civil and criminal cases. In the latter, by the law of the Saxons (which William the Conqueror confirmed in this respect, at least as to its main features,) the accused party was allowed to clear himself by the oath of as many of his neighbors to his innocence as amounted in collective worth, according to the legal arithmetic of the Anglo-Saxons, to one pound if he could in the first instance (being a villein) obtain the testimony of his lord that he had not been previously convicted. If otherwise, he is bound to undergo ordeal, or wage his law with a greater number of compurgators. Compurgation in criminal cases was abolished in general by Henry II.'s assizes, the ordeal being enforced in lieu of it.

CON, in language, a Latin inseparable preposition or prefix to other words. Ainsworth remarks that *con* and *cum* have the same signification, but that *cum* is used separately, and *con* in composition.—In the phrase *pro* and *con*, for and against, *con* denotes the negative side of a question.

CONCATENA'TION, a term chiefly used in speaking of the mutual dependence of second causes upon each other.

CONCEP'TION, in mental philosophy, that faculty or act of the mind by which we combine a number of individuals together by means of some mark or character common to them all. We may observe, for instance, that equilateral, isosceles and scalene triangles all agree in one respect, that of having three sides; and from this perceived similitude we form the conception *triangle*.

CONCERTAN'TE, in music, a term expressive of those parts of a musical composition that sing or play throughout the piece, as distinguished from those that play only occasionally in particular places.

CONCER'TO, in music, a piece composed for a particular instrument, which bears the greatest part in it, or in which the performance is partly alone and partly accompanied by other parts.

CONCES'SION, in rhetoric or debate, the yielding, granting, or allowing to the opposite party some point or fact that may bear dispute, in order to show that even admitting the point conceded, the cause can be maintained on other grounds.

CONCET'TI. (Rendered by English writers on rhetoric, *conceits*.) Ingenious thoughts or turns of expression, points, jeux d'esprit, &c., in serious composition. In the 16th century, the taste for this species of brilliancy, often false and always dangerous, spread rapidly in the poetical composition of European nations, especially in Spain and Italy; where the name of *concetti* was applied rather in a good than in a bad sense, the critical taste being much perverted. Tasso is not free from *concetti*. After his time they became offensively prominent in Italian poetry for a century afterwards: Marino and Filicaia offer strong examples. In France, the mode of concetti was equally prevalent in the 17th century, and was peculiarly in vogue with the fair critics of the Hotel Rambouillet, so well known by Molière's "Précieuses Ridicules." In England, Donne and Cowley are instances of a style full of *concetti*.

CONCIN'NOUS, in music, an epithet for a performance in concerts, which is executed with delicacy, grace, and spirit.

CONCIONATO'RES, in law, the common councilmen of the city of London.

CONCLAMA'TIO, in antiquity, the funeral cry over the body of a deceased person previous to its being burnt; by which it was expected to recall, as it were, the soul of the deceased from everlasting sleep.

CON'CLAVE the place in which the cardinals of the Romish church meet for the election of a pope. It consists of a range of small cells or apartments standing in a line along the halls or galleries of the Vatican.—*Conclave* is also used for the assembly or meeting of the cardinals when shut up for the election of a pope. This begins the day following the funeral of the deceased pontiff. The cardinals are locked up in separate apartments and meet once a day in the chapel of the Vatican, (or other pontifical palace,) where their votes, given on a slip of paper, are examined. This continues until two thirds of the votes are found to be in favor of a particular candidate. The ambassadors of France, Austria, and Spain have each the right to put in a veto against the election of one cardinal, who may be unacceptable to their respective courts.

CONCLU'SION, in logic, that proposition which is inferred from certain former propositions, termed the premises of the argument.

CON'CORD, in music, the union of two or more sounds in such a manner as to render them agreeable to the ear. Concord and harmony are, in fact, the same thing, though custom has applied them differently; for as concord expresses the agreeable effects of two sounds in consonance, so harmony expresses the agreement of a greater number of sounds in consonance.—In grammar, that part of syntax which treats of the agreement of words in a sentence.—In law, an agreement between the parties in a fine, made by leave of the court.

CONCORD'ANCE, a dictionary of the Bible, in which every word is given with references to the book, chapter, and verse, in which it occurs, for the purpose of enabling the student to collate with facility one passage with another in the view of determining its meaning. The importance of this class of works was early appreciated, and a vast deal of labor has been expended in compiling them. Concordances have been made of the Greek Septuagint, the Greek Testament, the Latin Vulgate, and the English Old and New Testaments. The first concordance was compiled by Cardinal Hugues de St. Cher, who died in 1262. The best English concordance is that of Cruden, which appeared in 1737, and still maintains its ground as an authority.

CONCOR'DAT, an agreement or convention upon ecclesiastical matters made between the Pope and some temporal sovereign, as that between Pius VII. and Bonaparte in 1802, by which the Roman Catholic religion was re-established in France; on which occasion the Pope recognized the new division of France into 60 sees, instead of the much greater number which had existed before the revolution, the payment of the clergy from the national revenues, and the appointment of the bishops by the civil authority. Originally the term was applied to agreements regulating mutual rights between bishops, abbots, priors, &c.

CON'CRETE, in architecture and engineering, a mass composed of stone chippings or ballast cemented together through the medium of lime and sand, usually employed in making foundations where the soil is of itself too light or boggy, or otherwise insufficient for the reception of the walls.

CON'CRETE TERM, in logic, is so called when the notion derived from the view taken of any object is expressed with a reference to, or in conjunction with, the object that furnished the notion; as "foolish," or "fool." When the notion is expressed without any such reference, it is called an abstract term; as, "folly."

CONDI'TION, in law, a clause in a bond or other contract containing terms or a stipulation that it is to be performed, and in case of failure, the penalty of the bond is to be incurred.—We speak of a good *condition* in reference to wealth and poverty, or to health and sickness, &c. Or, we say,—a nation with an exhausted treasury is not in a *condition* to make war; religion affords consolation to man in every *condition* of life.—*Conditional propositions*, in logic, such as consist of two parts connected together by a conditional particle.—*Conditional syllogism*, a syllogism where the major is a conditional proposition.

CONDOTTIE'RI, in Italian history, a class of mercenary adventurers in the 14th and 15th centuries, who commanded military bands, amounting to armies, on their own account, and sold their services for temporary engagements to sovereign princes and states. One of the earliest and most famous among those leaders was the Englishman Sir John Hawkwood, who commanded in various Italian wars about the time of Edward III. The bands under command of the condottieri were well armed and equipped. Their leaders had, in many instances, considerable military skill; but as they took no interest in national contests, except to receive pecuniary advantages, the wars between them became a sort of bloodless contest, in which the only object of each party was to take as many prisoners as possible for the sake of the ransom. This singular system of warfare was only put an end to by the more serious military operations of the French, who invaded Italy under Charles VIII.

CON'DUIT, a subterraneous or concealed aqueduct. The ancient Romans excelled in them, and formed the lower parts, wheron the water ran, of cement of such an excellent quality, that it has become as hard as the stone itself which it was employed to join.—*Conduits*, in modern times, are generally pipes of wood, iron, or pottery, for conveying the water from the main spring, or reservoirs, to the different places where it is required.

CONFARREA'TION, in antiquity, a ceremony observed by the Romans in their nuptial solemnities. It consisted of the offering of some pure wheaten bread, and rehearsing, at the same time, a certain formula in presence of the high-priest and at least ten witnesses.

CONFEC'TION, a sweetmeat, or anything prepared with sugar; it also signifies a liquid or soft electuary, of which there are various sorts.

CONFEC'TOR, an officer in the Roman games, whose business was to kill any beast that was dangerous.

CONFED'ERACY, in law, a combination of two or more persons to do some damage or injury to another, or to commit some unlawful act.

CONFEDERA'TION, a league, or compact, for mutual support, particularly of princes, nations, or states.

CONFES'SION, in a legal sense, the acknowledgment of something prejudicial to the person making the declaration. A confession, according to law, must never be divided, but always taken entire; nor must a criminal be condemned upon his own confession, without other concurring proofs.—In theology, a public declaration of one's faith, or the faith of a public body. Also a part of the Liturgy, in which an acknowledgment of guilt is made by the whole congregation.—*Auricular confession*, a private confession or acknowledgment of one's sins made by each individual in the Romish church to the priest or father confessor. It is so called because it is made by whispering in his ear.—Among the Jews, it was a custom, on the annual feast of expiation, for the high-priest to make confession of sins to God in the name of the whole people.

CONFES'SOR, a Roman Catholic priest, who hears confessions, and is empowered to grant absolution to those who confess.—The seat, or cell, wherein the priest or confessor sits to hear confessions, is called the *confessional*.

CONFIRMA'TION, the act or ceremony in the Christian church of laying on of hands, by which baptized persons are confirmed in their baptismal vows. This ceremony is performed by the bishop; and the antiquity of it is, by all ancient writers, carried as high as the apostles, upon whose example and practice it is founded.—*Confirmation*, in law, an assurance of title, by the conveyance of an estate or right *in esse*, from one person to another, by which a possession is made perfect, &c.—*Confirmation*, in rhetoric, the third part of an oration, wherein the orator undertakes to prove the truth of the proposition advanced in his narration.

CONFISCA'TION, in law, the condemnation and adjudication of goods or effects to the public treasury, as the bodies and effects of criminals, traitors, &c.

CON'FLICT OF LAWS, the opposition between the municipal laws of different countries, in the case of an individual who may have acquired rights or become subject to duties within the limit of more than one state.

CONFORM'IST, in ecclesiastical concerns, one that conforms to the established church; the seceders or dissenters from which are called *Non-conformists*.

CON'GE, in architecture, a mould in form of a quarter round, or a cavetto, which serves to separate two members from one another; such as that which joins the shaft of the column to the cincture; called also *apophyge*.

CONGÉ D'ELIRE, (French,) in ecclesiastical affairs, the king's permission to a dean and chapter in the time of a vacancy, to choose a bishop.

CONGE'RIES, a collection of several particles or bodies united into one mass or aggregate.

CON'GIARY, in Roman antiquity, a present of wine or oil, given to the people by their emperors, and so called from the *congius*, wherewith it was measured out to them. Sometimes, however, the congiary was made in money or corn.

CON'GIUS, a liquid measure of the ancient Romans, containing the eighth part of the amphora, or rather more than a gallon.

CONGREGA'TIONALISTS, in church history, a sect of Protestants who reject all church government, except that of a single congregation, which, they maintain, has the right to choose its own pastor and govern itself.

CON'GRESS, an assembly of envoys, commissioners, deputies, &c. from different courts, who meet to concert measures for their common good, or to adjust their mutual concerns. Having exchanged their credentials, the envoys of the different powers carry on their negotiations directly with each other, or by the intervention of a mediator, either in a common hall, or in their own residences by turns, or, if there is a mediator, in his residence. These negotiations are continued either by writing or by verbal communication, until the commissioners can agree upon a treaty, or until one of the powers dissolves the congress by recalling its minister.—*Congress of the United States of America*. The assembly of senators and representatives of the several states of North America, forming the legislature of the United States, is designated, in the constitution of the general governmemt, by this title. It consists of a senate and a house of representatives, each constituting a distinct and independent branch. The house of representatives is chosen every second year, by the people of the several states; and the voters and electors are required to have the same qualifications as are requisite for choosing the members of the most numerous branch of the state legislature of the state in which they vote. The number of representatives is appointed according to the population of each state, and is altered every ten years, when the census is taken by authority. The manner of apportioning the congressional representation was fixed by an act passed May 23, 1850. After March 3, 1853, the House of Representatives, unless otherwise ordained by congress, is to consist of 233 members. The apportionment is made by adding to the number of free persons three fifths of the number of slaves: the representative population, thus found, divided by 233, gives the ratio of apportionment; the representative population of each state, divided by this ratio, shows the number of representatives to which the state is entitled. To the aggregate thus obtained is added a number sufficient to make up the whole number of 233 members; this additional number is apportioned among the states having the largest fractions. It is, however, provided by the constitution that each state shall be entitled to at least one representative. The senate is composed of two members from each state: the senators are chosen for six years by the legislature of the state. The house of representatives chooses its own speaker: the vice-president of the United States is, ex-officio, president of the senate. Bills for revenue purposes must originate in the house of representatives; but are liable to the proposal of amendments by the senate. The senate has the sole power of trying impeachments; but can only convict by a majority of two thirds of the members present, and its sentence extends only to removal from office and incapacitation for holding it. The regular meeting of congress is on the first Monday in December annually. Every bill which passes the two houses is sent to the president for approval or disapproval; in the latter case, he returns it, with his reasons, to the house in which it originated: if, on reconsideration, it is passed again by a majority of two-thirds in each house, it becomes law. The powers of congress are strictly limited, and separated from those of the various state legislatures, by the constitution.

CONISTE'RIUM, in ancient architecture, a room in the gymnasium and palæstra, wherein the wrestlers, having been anointed with oil, were sprinkled over with dust, that they might lay firmer hold of their antagonists.

CON'JOINT DEGREES, in music, a term used of two or more notes which immediately follow each other in the order of the scale.

CON'JOINT TETRACHORDS, in music, two tetrachords or fourths, in which the same note is the highest of one and the lowest of the other.

CONJUGA'TION, in grammar, is to verbs what *declension* is to substantives—the sum total of the inflexions which they admit, corresponding to the various circumstances of time or mood under which an action is conceived to take place.

CONJUNC'TION, in grammar, that part of speech which expresses the relation of propositions or judgments to each other.

CONJUNC'TIVE MOOD, that modification of the verb which expresses the dependence of the event intended on certain conditions.

CONNOISSEUR', a critical judge or master of any art, particularly of painting, sculpture, and the belles lettres. The connoisseur is the true friend of Art; he judges of works from their intrinsic excellence, regardless of the influence or bias of popular names upon the indiscriminating crowd. He is prompt to recognize, seek out, and foster genius in its early struggles and obscurity, and help to occupy that position too frequently usurped by the pretender. The qualities necessary to constitute a connoisseur are—a natural *feeling* for art, a keen perception, and a sound judgment; by study and observation he has become familiar with the technics of art, the manner and method of various schools and masters. He has no prejudices or predilections; hence he is impartial. He can appreciate defects as well as merits, and distinguish an original from a copy.

CON'QUEST, the right over property or territory acquired in war. It presupposes a just war, and is generally admitted as a part of the law of nations. Conquest may respect either persons or things: it may apply to a whole nation, or to a single town or province: and it may be temporary or permanent. Where persons are not found in arms, but are included as inhabitants of a town or province which has surrendered, they are treated generally as subjects. The original allegiance to their own government is suspended, and they come under the implied obligation to the conqueror, to submit to his orders, and to demean themselves, for the time, as faithful subjects. Under such circumstances, the conqueror generally leaves them in possession of their property, and punishes them only for rebellious or traitorous conduct. It is not usual, in modern times, to change the fundamental laws of a conquered country; but the sovereign power of the conqueror so to do is conceded by the law of nations.

CONSANGUIN'ITY, the relation which subsists between persons who are sprung from the same stock or common ancestor, in distinction from affinity or relation by marriage. It terminates in the sixth or seventh degree, except in the succession to the crown, in which case it is continued to infinity. Marriage is prohibited by the church to the fourth degree of consanguinity inclusive.

CON'SCIENCE, in ethics, a secret testimony of the soul, whereby it gives its approbation to things that are naturally good, and condemns those that are evil. Some writers term conscience the "moral sense," and consider it as an original faculty of our nature; others allege that our notions of right and wrong are not to be deduced from a single principle or faculty, but from various powers of the understanding and will.

CON'SCIOUSNESS, the knowledge of sensations and mental operations, or of what passes in one's own mind.

CON'SCRIPT, in Roman antiquity, an appellation given to the senators of Rome, who were called *conscript-fathers*, on account of their names being entered in the register of the senate.—In the French armies, an enrolled soldier, or recruit.

CONSCRIP'TION, the enlisting the inhabitants of a country capable of bearing arms, by a compulsory levy, at the pleasure of the government. The name is derived from the military constitution of ancient Rome. Under the consulship, all persons capable of bearing arms were obliged, under penalty of losing their fortune and liberty, to assemble in the Campus Martius, or near the capitol, where the consuls, seated in their curule chairs, made the levy by the assistance of the legionary tribunes. The consuls ordered such as they pleased to be cited out of each tribe, and every one was obliged to answer to his name, after which as many were chosen as were wanted.—France, in the beginning of the revolution, declared it the duty and honor of every citizen to serve in the army of his country. Every French citizen was born a soldier, and obliged to serve in the army from sixteen to forty years of age: from forty to sixty he belonged to the national guard. Every year the young men of the military age were assembled, and distributed in the different military divisions; and it was decided by lot who, among the able-bodied men of suitable age, should take arms. Thus it was that those prodigious masses were so quickly raised, and sent to the field of slaughter.

CONSECRA'TION, the act of devoting and dedicating anything to the service and worship of God. Among the ancient Christians, the consecration of churches was performed with a great deal of pious solemnity. In England, churches have been always consecrated with particular ceremonies, the form of which was left to the discretion of the bishop.—*Consecration* was also a religious rite among the Romans, by which they set any person or thing apart for sacred purposes, as their high-priests; or made it sacred, or a fit object of divine worship; as the emperors, their wives, or children, who were in this manner enrolled among the number of their gods. This was sometimes called *apotheosis*, but on medals it is distinguished by the word *consecratio*, with an altar or some other sacred symbol.

CONSEN'TIAN GODS, a term by which the Latins distinguished their twelve chief deities—Juno, Vesta, Minerva, Ceres, Diana, Venus, Mars, Mercury, Jupiter, Neptune, Vulcan, and Apollo. The origin of these deities was Italian, and distinct from those of the Greeks; but as the literature of Rome took its tone and color from Greece, so its mythology was mixed up with that of the latter country, those deities whose functions most resembled each other being confounded, till the above names became regarded as nothing more than the Latin appellations of the Greek divinities.

CON'SEQUENCE, that which follows as an inference of truth and reason, from admitted premises or arguments. Thus, "every rational being is accountable to his Maker;" man is a rational being; the *consequence* then must be, that man is accountable to his Maker.

CONSERVA'TOR, an officer appointed for the security and preservation of the privileges of some cities, corporations, and communities. The ancient office of *conservator of the peace* is now performed by all judges and magistrates, but particularly by what we now term *justices of the peace.*

CONSERV'ATORY, a term sometimes used for a green-house. It is, properly, a large green-house for exotics, in which the plants are planted in beds and borders, and not in tubs or pots, as in the common green-house.—In various parts of Italy and France there are musical schools, called *conservatories*, which are expressly intended for the scientific cultivation of musical talents, and from which many first-rate composers, as well as vocalists, have attained their proficiency.

CONSIDERA'TION, in law, the material cause or ground of a contract, without which the party contracting would not be bound. A consideration is either express or implied; *express*, when the thing to be given or done is specified; *implied*, when no specific consideration is agreed upon, but justice requires it, and the law implies it: as when a man labors for another, without stipulating for wages, the law infers that he shall receive a reasonable *consideration.*

CONSIGN'MENT *of goods*, in commerce, is the delivering or making them over to another: thus, goods are said to be consigned to a factor, when they are sent to him for sale, &c. He who consigns the goods is called the *consignor;* and the person to whom they are sent is the *consignee.*

CONSIST'ENCE, or CONSIST'ENCY, that state of a body in which its component parts remain fixed. Also, congruity and uniformity in opinions and actions.

CONSISTO'RIUM, in antiquity, a council-house or place of audience.

CONSIS'TORY, an assembly of ecclesiastical persons; also certain spiritual courts are so called which are holden by the bishops in each diocese. At Rome the consistory denotes the judicial court constituted by the college of cardinals. The representative body of the reformed church in France is styled Consistory; a title and assembly originated by Calvin.

CONSIS'TORY COURT, the place or court in which the session or assembly of ecclesiastical persons is held by the bishop or his chancellor.

CONSOLIDA'TION, in the civil law, signifies the uniting the possession or profit of land with the property, and vice versa. In the ecclesiastical law, it is the uniting two benefices into one by assent of the ordinary, patron, and incumbent.

CON'SOLE, in architecture, a bracket or shoulder-piece: or an ornament cut upon the key of an arch, which has a projecture, and on occasion serves to support little cornices, figures, busts, and vases.

CON'SOLS, in commerce, funds formed by the *consolidation* (of which word it is an abbreviation) of different annuities, which had been severally formed into a capital.

CON'SONANCE, in music, the agreement of two sounds simultaneously produced, the one grave and the other acute

CON'SONANT, a letter so named because it is considered as being sounded only in connection with a vowel. But some consonants have no sound, even when united with a vowel, and others have a very imperfect sound; hence some are called *mutes*, and others *semi-vowels.*

CONSONAN'TE, in music, an Italian epithet for all agreeable intervals.

CONSPIR'ACY, a combination of men for an evil purpose; or an agreement between them to commit some crime in concert; as, a *conspiracy* against the government.—In law, it signifies an agreement between two or more, falsely to indict, or procure to be indicted, an innocent person of felony.

CON SPIR'ITO, in music, an Italian phrase, denoting that the part is to be played with spirit.

CON'STABLE, a civil officer, anciently of great dignity, as the Lord High Constable of England, and also the constables or keepers of castles, &c. It is now the title of an officer under the magistrates for the preservation of the peace, whose duty principally consists in seizing and securing persons guilty of tumultuary offences. In the United States, constables are town or city officers of the peace, with powers similar to those possessed by the constables in Great Britain. They are invested also with powers to execute civil as well as criminal process, and to levy executions. In New England, they are elected by the inhabitants of towns in legal meeting.

CONSTANT WHITE, PERMANENT WHITE, a pigment prepared from the sulphate of barytes, useful in water-color painting, possessing great body. It is very poisonous.

CON'STAT, a certificate given out of the exchequer to a person who intends to plead or move for a discharge of anything in that court. The effect of it is to show what appears upon the record, respecting the matter in question.

CONSTELLA'TION, an assemblage or system of several stars, expressed or represented under the name and figure of some animal or other object, as a bear, a ship, and the like; whence they have derived those appellations which are convenient in describing the stars. The division of the heavens into constellations is very ancient, probably coeval with astronomy itself.

CONSTIT'UENT, in politics, one who by his vote constitutes or elects a member of parliament.—*Constituents*, in physics, the elementary or essential parts of any substance.

CONSTITU'TION, in politics, any form or principle of government, regularly constituted. Constitutions are either democratic, aristocratic, or of a mixed character. They are, 1. *Democratic*, when the fundamental law guarantees to every citizen equal rights, protection, and participation, direct or indirect, in the government, such as the constitutions of the United States of America, and of some cantons of Switzerland. 2. *Aristocratic*, when the constitution establishes privileged classes, as the nobility and clergy, and entrusts the government entirely to them, or allows them a very disproportionate share of it: such a constitution was that of Venice. 3. *Of a mixed character;* to which latter division belong some monarchical constitutions, which recognize the existence of a sovereign whose power is modified by other branches of government, of a more or less populous cast. In the United States, the constitution is paramount to the statutes or laws enacted by the legislature, limiting and controlling its power; and even the legislature itself is created, and its powers designated, by the constitution.—*Apostolic constitutions*, an ancient code of regulations, respecting the doctrine and discipline of the church, pretended by some to have been promulgated by the apostles, and collected by Clemens Romanus. They appear to have been at one time admitted into the canon of scripture. Their authenticity has been a subject of much dispute. They have been printed together with the so-called canons of the apostles.

CONSTRUC'TION, in a general sense, the manner of putting together the parts of a building, or of a machine, &c.—In grammar, syntax, or the proper arrangement of words in a sentence. Also, the manner of understanding the arrangement of words, or of understanding facts: thus we say, "let us give the author's words in a rational and consistent *construction*."

CONSUA'LIA, in Roman antiquity, a festival instituted by Romulus, and dedicated by him to Neptune, whom he termed Consus, or the god of counsel, in consequence of his successful scheme on the Sabine virgins.

CONSUBSTAN'TIAL, in theology, an epithet signifying of the same substance: thus, in the articles of the Church of England, Christ is declared *consubstantial*, or of one substance with the Father.

CONSUBSTANTIA'TION, a tenet of the Lutheran church, the members of which maintain that after consecration of the sacramental elements, the body and blood of our Saviour are substantially present, together with the substance of the bread and wine, which is called consubstantiation, or impanation.

CON'SUL, in the Roman commonwealth, the title of the two chief magistrates, whose power was, in a certain degree, absolute, but who were chosen only for one year. The authority of the two consuls was equal; yet the Valerian law gave the right of priority to the elder, and the Julian law to him who had the greater number of children; and this was generally called *consul major* or *prior*. In the first ages of Rome they were elected from patrician families; but in the year of Rome 388, the people obtained the privilege of electing one of the consuls from their own body, and sometimes both were plebeians.—In modern usage, the name *consul* is given to an officer appointed to reside in a foreign country, to protect the interests of trade, and to aid his government in any commercial transactions with such country. Such officers appear to have been first employed by the Italian republics, to protect their merchants engaged in trade in the cities of the Levant. The consuls of European states in that region, and in Africa, are at the present time officers of more importance than those established in the cities of Christendom: as they exercise, according to treaties, civil jurisdiction over the citizens of their respective states. In general, the consul is not regarded as a minister or diplomatic functionary, and is subject to the civil authorities of the place where he resides.—*Consuls*, in French history, were the persons (Bonaparte, Sieyes, and Ducos) to whom, after the dissolution of the Directory in November 1799, was entrusted the provisional government of the country, and at whose suggestion it was agreed that

France should be permanently subjected to consular authority.

CON'SULARS, the title given to Roman citizens who had been dignified with the office of consul, and consequently were honored with a certain precedence in the senate.

CONSULTA'TION, a council for deliberation; as, a *consultation* of physicians was called.

CONTA'GION, the propagation of specific diseases from person to person. *Contagious poisons* communicate the property of producing similar poisons: the *small-pox* is a characteristically contagious disease. By some writers the term has been limited to diseases requiring *actual contact* for their communication; but contagious matter appears often transmissible by the air, hence the terms *immediate* and *mediate contagion.* Where diseases are propagated through the medium of the air, they are generally called *infectious.*

CONTEMPT', in law, disobedience to the rules, orders, or process of a court of competent authority. Contempt in court is punishable by fine and imprisonment: for contempt out of court attachment may be granted.

CONTENTS', anything or things held, included, or comprehended within a limit or line; as, the contents of a cask or bale, the contents of a book, &c.

CON'TEXT, the parts of a discourse which precede or follow the sentence quoted; for instance, the sense of a passage of Scripture is often illustrated by the *context.*

CON'TINENT, in geography, a great extent of land, not disjoined or interrupted by a sea; or a connected tract of land of great extent, as the Eastern or Western continent.—The *continental* powers, those whose territories are situated on the continent of Europe.

CONTINENT'AL SYSTEM, a term given to a plan devised by Napoleon to exclude England from all intercourse with the continent of Europe; thereby to prevent the importation of British manufactures and commerce, and thus to compel the English government to make peace upon the terms prescribed by the French ruler. The history of Napoleon's continental system begins with the decree of Berlin of Nov. 21, 1806, by which the British islands were declared to be in a state of blockade; all commerce, intercourse, and correspondence were prohibited; every Englishman found in France, or in any country occupied by French troops, was declared a prisoner of war; all property belonging to Englishmen fair prize, and all trade in English goods entirely prohibited. Great Britain immediately directed reprisals against the Berlin decree; prohibiting all neutral vessels from sailing from one port to another belonging to France, or one of her allies, &c. This was met by counter-reprisals; and for a long time a fierce and most annoying system was carried on for the annihilation of British commerce; the effects of which are still felt, from the rival products and manufactures on the continent to which the system gave rise.

CONTIN'GENT, in politics, the proportion (generally of troops) furnished by one of several contracting powers in pursuance of an agreement.

CONTIN'UED BASS, in music, the same as thorough bass. It receives the name from its continuation through the whole of a composition.

CONTORNIA'TI, in numismatics, medals supposed to have been struck about the period of Constantine the Great and his immediate successors: they are of bronze, with a flat impression, and marked with peculiar furrows. (It. contorni, whence their name.) They bear the figures of famous emperors or celebrated men. Their object is uncertain; but they have been supposed to be tickets of admission to the public games of the circus in Rome and Constantinople.

CON'TOUR, in the Fine Arts, the external lines which bound and terminate a figure. The beauty of contour consists in those lines being flowing, lightly drawn, and sinuous. They must be carefully and scientifically drawn, which cannot be effected without a thorough knowledge of anatomy.

CON'TRABAND, in commercial language, goods exported from or imported into a country against its laws. *Contraband of war*, such articles as a belligerent has, by the law of nations, the right of preventing a neutral from furnishing to his enemy. Articles contraband of war are, in general, arms and munitions of war, and those out of which munitions of war are made; all these are liable to be seized: but very arbitrary interpretations have been affixed to the term by powerful states, when able to enforce them by arms. Thus, provisions are held contraband of war when it is the object to reduce the enemy to famine. But with respect to these and other articles not in their nature contraband, it seems to be the practice that the belligerent should purchase them from the neutral for a reasonable equivalent, instead of confiscating.

CONTRABAS'SO, the largest of the violin species of string and bowed instruments, whereof it forms the lowest bass, usually called the double bass.

CON'TRACT, in civil law, the term usually applied to such agreements, whether express or implied, as create, or are intended to create, a legal right, and corresponding liability; such right not attaching to the possession of the subject matter of the contract, except in equity, and that indirectly, but subsisting both in equity and law against the contracting party.

CONTRADIC'TORY PROPOSITION, in logic, are those which having the same terms differ in quantity and in quality. *Contrary propositions* are two universals with the same terms, the one negative and the other affirmative.

CONTRALT'O, in music, the part immediately below the treble; called also the counter tenor.

CON'TRAST, in the fine arts, an opposition of lines or colors to each other, so contrived that the one gives greater effect to the other. By means of contrast energy and expression are given to a subject, even when employed on inanimate forms. All art is indeed a system of contrast: lights should contrast with shadows, figures with figures, members with members, and groups with groups. It is this which gives life, soul, and motion to a composition.

CON'TRATENO'RE, in music, the same as *contralto*.

CONTRIBU'TION, in a general sense, the act of giving to a common stock. In a military sense, impositions upon a country in the power of an enemy, which are levied under various pretences, and for various purposes, usually for the support of the army.

CONTROL'LER, in law, an overseer or officer appointed to control or verify the accounts of other officers.

CON'TUMACY, in law, a refusal to appear in court when legally summoned, or disobedience to its rules and orders.

CONVALES'CENCE, the insensible recovery of health and strength after disease.

CON'VENT, a religious house, inhabited by a society of monks or nuns.

CONVEN'TICLE, a private assembly or meeting, for the exercise of religion; the word was at first an appellation of reproach to the religious assemblies of Wickliffe, in the reigns of Edward III. and Richard II., and is now usually applied to a meeting of dissenters from the established church.—As the word *conventicle*, in strict propriety, denotes an unlawful assembly, it cannot be justly applied to the assembling of persons in places of worship, which are licensed according to the requisitions of law.

CONVEN'TION, in law, an extraordinary assembly of the estates of the realm.—In military affairs, an agreement entered into between two bodies of troops opposed to each other; or an agreement previous to a definitive treaty. —*National convention*, the name of the assembly by which the government of France was conducted during a period of the revolution.

CONVER'SION, in a theological sense, that change in man by which the enmity of the heart to the laws of God, and the obstinacy of the will are subdued, and are succeeded by supreme love to God and his moral government; and a reformation of life.—*Conversion of a proposition*, in logic, is a changing of the subject into the place of the predicate, and still retaining the quality of the proposition.

CON'VERT, a person who changes his religion. Individuals, of what faith soever, who abandon their own creed and embrace Christianity are called *converts*, in contradistinction to *apostates*, applied generally to *Christians* who adopt another religion.

CONVEY'ANCE, in law, a deed or instrument by which lands, &c., are conveyed or made over to another.

CONVEY'ANCER, one who professes to draw deeds, mortgages, and conveyances of estates. This profession requires great knowledge of the law, and a solid and clear understanding; for on conveyancing the security of property greatly depends.

CON'VICT, in law, a person found guilty of a crime alleged against him, either by the verdict of a jury, or other legal decision.

CONVIC'TION, the act of proving guilty of an offence charged against a person by a legal tribunal. Also, the state of being sensible of guilt; as, by *conviction* a sinner is brought to repentance.

CONVIV'IUM, in antiquity, a banquet or entertainment given to a friendly party.

CONVOCA'TION, an assembly of the clergy of England, which at present is merely nominal. Its province is stated to be the enactment of canon-law, subject to the license of the king; and the examination and censuring of all heretical and schismatical books and persons; but from its judicial proceedings lies an appeal to the king in chancery, or his delegates. It is held during the session of parliament, and consists of an upper and a lower house: in the upper sit the bishops, and in the lower the inferior clergy, who are represented by their proctors, and all the deans and archdeacons; in all, 143 divines.

CON'VOY, ships of war which accompany merchantmen in time of war, to protect them from the attacks of the enemy.—By land, any body of troops which accompany provision, ammunition, or other property for protection.

COPE, an ecclesiastical vestment, like a cloak (which it originally was, and used to protect the wearer from the inclemency of the weather,) worn in processions, at vespers, during the celebration of mass, by some of the assistant clergy, at benediction, consecration, and other ecclesiastical functions. Its form is an exact semicircle, without sleeves, but furnished with a *hood*, and is fastened across the breast with a morse or clasp. Copes were ornamented with embroidery and jewels, (apparells,) wrought with elaborate splendor, at a very early period. In the thirteenth century they became the most costly and magnificent of all the ecclesiastical vestments.

CO'PECK, a small Russian coin, equal to about one farthing English.

COPER'NICAN SYSTEM, that system of the universe which was anciently taught by Pythagoras, and afterwards revived by Copernicus, a Polish astronomer. According to this system, the sun is supposed to be placed in the centre, and all the other bodies to revolve round it in a particular order; which theory is now universally adopted, under the name of the Solar System.

CO'PING, in architecture, the upper covering or top course of a wall, usually of stone, and wider than the wall itself, in order to let the rain water fall clear from the wall.

COP'PER-PLATE, a plate of copper on which figures are engraven; also the impression taken from that plate.—*Copper-plate printing*, is performed by means of what is called a rolling-press. The engraved plate is covered with ink, made of oil and Frankfort black, then cleanly wiped on the smooth parts, and laid on wet soft paper; and on being passed between two cylinders with great force, the impression of the engraved part is perfectly transferred to the paper.

COP'PICE, or COPSE, a wood of small growth, cut at certain times, and used principally for fuel.

COP'TIC, the language of the Copts, or anything pertaining to those people, who are the descendants of the ancient Egyptians, and called *Copthi* or *Copts*, as distinct from the Arabians and other inhabitants of modern Egypt.

COP'ULA, the word that connects any two terms in an affirmative or negative proposition; as "God *made* man;" "Religion *is* indispensable to happiness."

COP'ULATIVE PROP'OSITIONS, in logic, those where the subject and predicate are so linked together, by copulative conjunctions, that they may be all severally affirmed or denied one of another. "Science *and* literature enlighten the mind, *and* greatly increase our intellectual enjoyments."

COP'Y, in law, signifies the transcript of any original writing, as the copy of a patent, charter, deed, &c. A common deed cannot be proved by a copy or counterpart, where the original may be procured. But if the deed be enrolled, certifying an attested copy is proof of the enrolment, such copy may be given in evidence.—*Copy*, among printers, denotes the manuscript or original of a book, given to be printed. Also, when we speak of a book, or a set of books, we say a *copy;* as, a copy of the Scriptures, a copy of Sir Walter Scott's works, &c.—*Copy*, in the fine arts, is a multiplication or reproduction of a work, whether painting, statue, or engraving, by another hand than the original. If a master copies his own picture, we call it merely a *repetition*, which the French designate by the term *doublette*. Copies are of three kinds; the most general are those in which the copyist imitates the original with anxious exactitude; in this case the difficulty of copying is but slight. The second kind is where the copyist avoids exact imitation, but renders the original freely in its principal traits. These copies, exact imitations in style and coloring, are soon seen to be apocryphal pictures. The third, and most important kind of copy is, that in which the picture is imitated with the freedom of a skilful hand, but at the same time with a truthful feeling of the original, and with the inspiration of genius, finding satisfaction not in copying, but in an imitation little short of creation.

COP'YHOLD, a tenure of landed property, by which the tenant holds his land by copy of court roll of the manor at the will of the lord, or rather, according to the custom of the manor by which such estate is discernible.

COP'YRIGHT, the exclusive right of printing and publishing copies of any literary performance, either by an author in his own right, or vested in the hands of those to whom he may have assigned that right.

COQUET'TE, a light, trifling girl, who endeavors to attract admiration by making a display of her amatory arts, from a desire to gratify vanity, rather than to secure a lover.

CO'RAL, a marine zoophyte, which, when removed from the water, becomes as hard as a stone. It is of a fine red color, and will take a fine polish. It is much used for small ornaments, but is not so susceptible of a high rank in gem-sculpture, as many precious stones. The islands in the south seas are principally coral rocks covered with earth, which have been formed by them from the bottom of the ocean. The coral fishery is particularly followed in the Mediterranean, on the coast of France. The coral is attached to the sub-marine rocks, as a tree is by its roots, but the branches, instead of growing upwards, shoot downwards towards the bottom of the sea; a conformation favorable to breaking them off, and bringing them up. For this kind of fishing, eight men, who are excellent divers, equip a felucca or small boat, called commonly a coralline; carrying with them a large wooden cross, with strong, equal, and long arms, each bearing a stout bag-net. They attach a strong rope to the middle of the cross, and let it down horizontally into the sea, having loaded its centre with a weight sufficient to sink it. The diver follows the cross, pushes one arm of it after another into the hollows of the rocks, so as to entangle the coral in the nets; when his comrades in the boats pull up the cross and its accompaniments.

COR'BEIL, in fortification, a little basket, to be filled with earth, and set upon a parapet, to shelter men from the fire of besiegers.

COR'BEL, in building, a short piece of timber in a wall, jutting six or eight inches, in the manner of a shoulder piece; sometimes placed for strength under the semi-girder of a platform.

CORDELIER', in church history, a gray friar or monk of the order of St. Francis. The cordeliers wear a white girdle or rope, tied with three knots, and called the *cord of St. Francis;* but the design of it, they say, is to commemorate the bands wherewith Christ was bound.

CORDELIERS'. This word, as we have seen above, originally signified an order of Franciscan monks; but it was afterwards given to a society of Jacobins in France from 1792 to 1794, who were so called from their place of meeting. They were distinguished by the violence of their speeches and conduct, and contributed not a little to the execrable crimes which disgraced the French name and nation during the early periods of revolutionary anarchy.

COR'DON, in fortification, a row of stones jutting before the rampart, and the basis of the parapet. The word cordon is still more used to denote a line or series of military posts; as, a *cordon* of troops. Cordon also signifies a ribbon, as the *cordon bleu*, the badge of the order of the Holy Ghost.

COR'DOVAN, leather made of goat skin, and named from Cordova in Spain.

CORE'IA, in antiquity, a festival in honor of Proserpine.

CORIN'THIAN ORDER, in architecture, one of the five orders of architecture. The capital is a vase elegantly covered with an abacus, and surrounded by two tiers of leaves, one above the other; from among which stalks spring out, terminating at their summits in small volutes at the external angles and centres of the abacus. The capitals of the Tuscan, Doric, and Ionic orders appear added to the tops of the shafts; but the Corinthian capital seems to grow out of the column, varying in height from a diameter and one sixth of the lower part of the shaft to one diameter only; such last being the height of the capitals of the temple at Tivoli. The entablature of this order is variously decorated. The architrave is usually profiled, with three fasciæ of unequal height, though in some specimens there are only two. The frieze is often sculptured with foliage, and the cornice decorated both with modillions and dentils; the former having a sort of baluster front, with a leaf under them; and the latter, which are cut into the body of the band, being occasionally omitted, as are sometimes even the modillions. The principal remaining ancient examples of the order at Rome are in the Temple of Mars Ultor, Portico of Severus, the Forum of Nerva, Temple of Vesta, Basilica of Antoninus, the Pantheon, &c. &c.

COR'IUM, a leathern body armor, cut into scale form, occasionally worn by the Roman soldiers. A specimen is here given from Trajan's column.

CORN. Ears of corn are the attribute of Ceres, and also of Dike (goddess of justice) and Juno Martialis, who is represented on a coin of Trebonianus Gallus with some ears of corn in the right hand. They were also the symbol of the year. The harvest month, September, was represented by a maiden holding ears of corn, and Ceres wore a wreath of them, or carried them in her hand, as did also the Roman divinity *Bonus Eventus*. The ears of corn were also used as a symbol of tillage, fruitfulness, culture and prosperity, and we find on the reverse of a silver coin of Metapontis, an ear of barley, with a field-mouse beside it; the barley alludes to the sacrifice of golden ears at Delphi, and the mouse to Apollo Sminthios.

COR'NET, a commissioned officer in a troop of horse, corresponding in rank with the ensign of a battalion of infantry. His duty is to carry the standard, near the centre of the front rank of the squadron.—*Cornet*, in music, a shrill wind instrument formed of wood, which appears to have been in use in the earliest times, and remained so till about the commencement of the 18th century, when it was displaced by the oboe.

COR'NET-A PISTONS, a brass wind musical instrument, of the French horn species, but capable of much greater inflection from the valves and stoppers (pistons) with which it is furnished, and whence it derives its name.

COR'NICE, in architecture, the upper great division of an entablature, consisting of several members. The cornice used on a pedestal is called the cap of the pedestal.

CORNUCO'PIA, or the HORN OF PLENTY, a source whence, according to the ancient poets, every production of the earth was lavished; a gift from Jupiter to his nurse, the goat Amalthea. In elucidation of this fable, it has been said that in Libya, the ancient name of a part of Africa, there was a little territory, in shape not ill resembling a bullock's horn, which Amnon, the king, gave to his daughter Amalthea, the nurse of Jupiter. Upon medals, the cornucopia is given to all deities, genii, and heroes, to mark the felicity and abundance of all the wealth procured by the goodness of the former, or the care and valor of the latter.

COR'OLLARY, a conclusion or consequences drawn from premises, or from what is advanced or demonstrated.

CORO'NA, in architecture, a large flat member of a cornice, crowning the entablature and the whole order.—A crown or circlet suspended from the roof or vaulting of churches, to hold tapers, lighted on solemn occasions, the number of which is regulated according to the solemnity of the festival. Sometimes they are formed of triple circles, arranged pyramidically.

CORONA'TION, the public and solemn ceremony of crowning, or investing a prince with the insignia of royalty, in acknowledgment of his right to govern the kingdom; at which time the prince swears reciprocally to the people, to observe the laws, customs and privileges of the kingdom, and to act and do all things conformable thereto. The form of the coronation oath of a British monarch is as follows: "I solemnly promise and swear to govern the people of this United Kingdom of Great Britain and Ireland, and the dominions thereto belonging, according to the statues in parliament agreed on, and the laws and customs of the same; to the utmost of my power to maintain the laws of God, the true profession of the gospel, and the Protestant reformed religion established by the law; to preserve unto the bishops and the clergy of this realm, and the churches committed to their charge, all such rights and privileges as by law do or shall appertain unto them or any of them." After this, the king or queen, laying his or her hand upon the holy Gospels, shall say, "The things which I have before promised, I will perform and keep; so help me God."

COR'ONER, the presiding officer in a jury convened to inquire into the cause of sudden deaths.

COR'PORAL, the lowest military officer in a company of foot, who has charge over one of the divisions, places and replaces sentinels, &c.—*Corporal*, in law, an epithet for anything that belongs to the body, as *corporal punishment*. Also, *corporal oath*, so called because the party taking it is obliged to lay his hand on the Bible.

CORPORA'TION, a body politic or corporate, so called because the persons or members are joined into one body, and authorized by law to transact business as an individual. Corporations are either spiritual or temporal: *spiritual*, as bishops, deans, archdeacons, &c., *temporal*, as the mayor, and aldermen of cities. And some are of a mixed nature, being composed of spiritual and temporal persons; such as heads of colleges and hospitals, &c. It has been truly said, that the whole political system is made up of a concatenation of various corporations, political, civil, religious, social, and economical. A nation itself is the great corporation, comprehending all the others, the powers of which are exerted in legislative, executive, and judicial acts.

CORPS, (French, pron. *kore*) a body of troops; any division of an army; as, a *corps de reserve*, the troops in reserve; *corps de bataille*, the whole line of battle, &c.

CORPUS CHRISTI DAY, a festival appointed by the church of Rome in honor of the sacrament of the Lord's Supper.

CORPUSCULAR PHILOS'OPHY, a system of physics, in which all the phenomena of the material world are explained by the arrangement and physical properties of the corpuscules or minute atoms of matter. A doctrine of this sort was anciently taught in Greece by Leucippus and Democritus, and is described in the beautiful poem of Lucretius.

COR'PUSCULE, a minute particle or physical atom. Corpuscules are not the elementary principles of matter, but such small particles, simple or compound, as are not dissolved or dissipated by ordinary heat.

COR'PUS JURIS, the collection of the authentic works containing the Roman law as compiled under Justinian. The Corpus Juris comprehends the Pandects, the Institutes, the Code, and the Novels or Authentics, *i. e.* the latter constitutions of Justinian; to which, in some editions, are added a few issued by his successors.

CORREC'TION, in the fine arts. With the Italians the word, *correzione*, is used to denote an exact acquaintance with the different proportions of the parts of a body or design generally: but with us the term is applied to those emendations of inaccuracies or alterations of first thoughts, which they call *pentimenti*, to be seen under the surface of the finished picture, and which are accounted indications of its originality.

CORREL'ATIVE, an epithet denoting the having a reciprocal relation, so that the existence of one in a certain state depends on the existence of another; as, father and son; light and darkness; motion and rest; all of which are correlative terms.

CORRESPON'DENCE, in the fine arts, the fitting or proportioning the parts of a design to each other, so that they may be correlative, and that the same feeling may pervade the whole composition.

COR'RIDOR, in architecture, a gallery or long aisle round a building, leading to several chambers at a distance from each other.—In fortification, the covered way lying round the whole compass of the fortifications of a place.

COR'SAIR, a pirate or cruiser; a name commonly given to the piratical cruising-vessels of Barbary, which, from the beginning of the sixteenth century to a recent period, infested the Mediterranean.

CORTE'GE, a French word, signifying the train or retinue that accompanies a person of distinction.

CORT'ES, the assembly of the estates of Spain and Portugal; answering, in some measure, to the parliament of Great Britain. These estates were framed, as elsewhere, of nobility, dignified clergy, and representatives of the towns. In Arragon, they were presided over by a high officer, termed Justiza, with powers in some respects sufficient to control the monarch. The origin of popular representation in the cortes of the several kingdoms out of which that of Spain was finally formed, is assigned to a date as early as the 12th century; but the deputies sent by the towns were irregularly summoned, frequently did not attend, and the numbers which appeared for each town frequently bore no proportion to the relative size of the different places. In the 14th century the power of the cortes seems to have been at its height, after which it gradually decayed, and under the government of Ferdinand and Isabella was reduced almost to a nullity.

COR'TILE, in architecture, an open quadrangular of curved area in a dwelling-house, surrounded by the buildings of the house itself.

CORVE'E, in feudal law, the obligation of the inhabitants of a district to do certain services, as the repair of roads, &c., for the sovereign or the feudal lord Some species of corvée were performed gratis: others for a fixed pay, but gener-

8

ally below the value of the labor performed.

CORVET'TE, a French word for any vessel of war carrying less than twenty guns.

CORYBAN'TES, in Grecian mythology, were the priests of Cybele; so called either from Corybas, the son of that goddess, or from the frantic gestures with which their devotions were accompanied; the term corybantes signifying literally "shaking the head violently." They used to beat brazen cymbals in their sacred rites: and their whole religious proceedings were characterized by such extravagant fanaticism as to have enriched the Greek language with several terms expressive of *madness* or *frenzy*.

CORYCE'UM, in ancient architecture, an apartment in a gymnasium whose exact destination is not known.

CORYM'BUS, in ancient sculpture, the cluster of ivy leaves, berries, garlands, &c., with which vases were encircled.

CO'RYPHŒ'US, the leader of the chorus in ancient dramas; by whom the dialogue between the chorus and the other actors of the drama was carried on, and who *led* in the choric song.

COSMOG'ONY, the science which treats of the origin of the universe. If we except the cosmogony of the Indians, the earliest extant is that of Hesiod, which is delivered in hexameter verse. The first prose cosmogonies were those of the early Ionic philosophers, of whom Thales, Anaximenes, Anaximander, and Anaxagoras are the most celebrated. In modern times, a theory of the world has been produced by Burnet. We do not include in this list of cosmogonies the researches of modern geologists, or the systems to which they have led. They may be said to hold the same place in relation to the old cosmogoners, which the astronomer or the chemist occupies in reference to the astrologers and alchemists of ancient times.

COSMOL'OGY, a treatise relating to the structure and parts of creation, the elements of bodies, the laws of motion, and the order and course of nature.

COSMOP'OLITE, a citizen of the world; one who makes himself at home everywhere.

COSMORA'MA, a view or series of views of the world; a comprehensive painting. Properly, a name given to a species of picturesque exhibitions. It consists of eight or ten colored drawings, laid horizontally round a semicircular table, and reflected by mirrors placed diagonally opposite to them. The spectator views them through convex lenses, placed immediately in front of each mirror.

COS'SACKS, the tribes who inhabit the southern and eastern parts of Russia, Poland, the Ukraine, &c., paying no taxes, but performing, instead, the duty of soldiers. They form a kind of military democracy; and have proved highly serviceable, as irregular cavalry, in the Russian campaigns. Their principal weapon is a lance from ten to twelve feet in length; they have also a sabre, a gun, and a pair of pistols, as well as a bow and arrows. The lances, in riding, are carried upright by means of a strap fastened to the foot, the arm, or pommel of the saddle. Those who use bows carry a quiver over the shoulder. Though little adapted for regular movements, they are very serviceable in attacking baggage, magazines, and in the pursuit of troops scattered in flight. They fight principally in small bodies, with which they attack the enemy on all sides, but mostly on the flanks and in the rear, rushing upon them at full speed, with a dreadful hurrah, and with levelled lances.

COS'TUME, in painting and the fine arts generally, the observance of that rule or precept by which an artist is enjoined to make any person or thing sustain its proper character; the scene, dress, arms, manners, &c., all corresponding. The study of costume requires, on the part of the artist, the observance of propriety in regard to the person or object represented; an intimate knowledge of the countries, their history, manners and customs, arts, and natural productions; the vestments peculiar to each class; their physiognomy, complexion, their ornaments, arms, furniture, &c. All should be conformable to the scene of action and historical period. Many of the old masters, and not a few of the modern, have committed some very glaring improprieties in their costume; we may instance Paul Veronese, while, on the contrary, Nicolas Poussin is remarkable for his accuracy in this respect. The observance of correct costume is a great merit in an artist, at the same time, it must be subservient to pictorial effect.

COTERIE', an old French word, supposed to be derived from the Latin quot, *how many*, signifying literally a society or company. In the 13th or 14th century, when merchants were about to embark in any commercial enterprise, they formed a coterie or company, each contributing his *quota* of goods or money, and deriving his *quota* of profit. But the term soon acquired a more extended signification, in which, however, the original meaning is still perceptible, it being applied to any exclusive society in which interesting subjects (chiefly literary and political) are discussed, each member being supposed to contribute his quota or share for the general edification or amusement.

COTHUR'NUS, in antiquity, a kind of high shoes, laced high, such as Diana and her nymphs are represented as wearing. The tragic actors also wore them, in order to give additional height to those who personated heroes; the *cothurnus* used for this purpose differing from the one used in hunting by its having a sole of cork at least four fingers thick.

COUCH, in painting, a term used for each lay or impression of color, either in oil or water, covering the canvas, wall, or other matter to be painted. Gilders use the term *couch*, for gold or silver lace laid on metals in gilding or silvering.

COUN'CIL, in national affairs, an assembly of persons for the purpose of concerting measures of state. In England, that is called the *Privy Council*, wherein the sovereign and privy councillors meet in the palace to deliberate on affairs of state. When the council is composed only of cabinet ministers, it is called a *Cabinet Council*.—*Council of war*, an assembly of the principal officers of a fleet or army, called by the admiral or general to concert measures for requisite operations.

COUN'SEL, in law, any counsellor or advocate, or any number of counsellors or barristers; as, the plaintiff's or defendant's *counsel*.

COUNT, a title of nobility, equivalent to an English earl.—In law, a particular charge in an indictment, or narration in pleading, setting forth the cause of complaint. There may be different *counts* in the same declaration.

COUN'TENANCE, the whole form of the face, or system of features. This word has many figurative applications: thus, by the *light of God's countenance*, we mean grace and favor: so the *rebuke of his countenance* indicates his anger.—To *keep the countenance* is to preserve a calm, natural, and composed look.—To *keep in countenance*, to give assurance to one, or protect him from shame.—To *put out of countenance*, to intimidate and disconcert.

COUN'TER, a term which enters into the composition of many words of our language, and generally implies opposition.

COUNTER-APPROACH'ES, in fortification, lines and trenches made by the besieged, in order to attack the works of the besiegers, or to hinder their approaches.

COUN'TER-DEED, a secret writing either before a notary or under a private seal, which destroys, invalidates, or alters a public one.

COUN'TERDRAWING, in painting, copying a design, or painting by means of lines drawn on oiled paper, or other transparent substance.

COUN'TERFEIT, that which is made in imitation of something, but without lawful authority, and with a view to defraud by passing the false for the true. Thus we say, *counterfeit* coin, a *counterfeit* bond, deed, &c.

COUN'TERGUARD, in fortification, a small rampart or work raised before the point of a bastion, consisting of two long faces parallel to the faces of the bastion, making a salient angle to preserve the bastion.

COUN'TERMARK, a mark put upon goods that have been marked before. It is also used for the several marks put upon goods belonging to several persons, to show that they must not be opened but in the presence of all the owners or their agents.—The mark of the goldsmith's company, to show the metal to be standard, added to that of the artificer.

COUN'TERMINE, in military affairs, a well and gallery sunk in the earth and running underground, to meet and defeat the effect of the enemy's mine; or, in other words, a mine made by the besieged, in order to blow up the mine of the besiegers.

COUN'TERPART, the correspondent part or duplicate. Also, the part which fits another, as the key of a cipher.—In music, the part to be applied to another; as, the bass is the counterpart to the treble.

COUN'TERPOINT, in music, the art of combining and modulating consonant sounds; or of disposing several parts in such a manner as to make an agreeable whole of a concert.

COUN'TERPROOF, is an engraving taken off from another fresh printed, which, by being passed through the rolling press, gives an inverted figure of the former.

COUNTER-REVOLU'TION, a revolution opposed to a former one, and restoring a former state of things.

COUN'TERSCARP, in fortification,

that side of the ditch which is next the camp, and faces the body of the place; but it often signifies the whole covered way, with its parapet and glacis.

COUNTER-SECUR'ITY, security given to one who has entered into a bond, or become surety for another.

COUN'TERSIGN, a military watchword; or a private signal given to soldiers on guard, with orders to let no man pass unless he first names that sign.—Also, to sign, as secretary or other subordinate officer, any writing signed by a principal or superior, to attest the authenticity of his signature.

COUNTER-TEN'OR, in music, one of the middle parts between the treble and the tenor.

COUNT'ING-HOUSE, the house or room appropriated by merchants, traders, and manufacturers, for the business of keeping their books, &c.

COUN'TRY, any tract of inhabited land, or any region as distinguished from other regions; any state or territory; and also any district in the vicinity of a city or town. Thus we say, This gentleman has a seat in the *country;* America is my native *country;* the countries of Europe, Asia, &c.

COUN'TY, originally, the district or territory of a count or earl: one of the ancient divisions of England, which by the Saxons were called *shires.* England is divided into forty counties or shires, Wales into twelve, Scotland into thirty-three. Each county has its sheriff and its court, with other officers employed in the administration of justice and the execution of the laws; and each lord-lieutenant of a county has the command of its militia.—The several states of America are divided by law into counties, in each of which is a county court of inferior jurisdiction; and in each the supreme court of the state holds stated sessions.—*County-corporate,* a title given to several cities or ancient boroughs (as Southampton and Bristol,) on which certain kings of England have thought proper to bestow peculiar privileges; annexing territory, land, or jurisdiction, and making them counties within themselves, with their own sheriffs and other officers.—*County palatine,* a county distinguished by particular privileges, and named from *palatio,* the palace, because the owner had originally royal powers in the administration of justice; these are now, however, greatly abridged. The counties palatine in England are Lancaster, Chester and Durham.

COUP, a French term for a stroke or sudden blow.—*Coup de grace,* the finishing blow.—*Coup de main,* a sudden unpremeditated attack.—*Coup d'œil,* the first glance of the eye, with which it surveys any object at large.—*Coup de soleil,* any disorder suddenly produced by the violent scorching of the sun.

COUPEE', a motion in dancing, when one leg is a little bent and suspended from the ground, and with the other a motion is made forward.

COUP'LE, two of the same species or kind; as a couple of men, a couple of apples, &c. A *pair* is a *couple,* and a *brace* is a *couple;* but a couple may or may not be a pair or a brace.

COUP'LET, the division of a hymn, ode, or song, wherein an equal number or an equal measure of verses is found in each part, called a *strophe.*

COUR'AGE, firmness of mind, inspired by a sense of what is just and honorable; that which, amidst all the dangers and trials to which human life is incident, enables a man steadily to pursue the dictates of conscience and prudence. It includes valor, boldness, and resolution; and is a constituent part of fortitude.

COURAN'TO, a piece of music in triple time; also, a kind of dance.

COU'RIERS, a name given in ordinary language to the bearers of public despatches or private intelligence by express. The institution of persons to convey intelligence with celerity and regularity is coeval with the earliest history of civilized nations. By the Persians they were styled *αγγαροι,* by the Greeks *ἡμεροδρομοι,* and by the Romans *cursores;* and the duties of the ancient couriers seem to have been wholly analogous to those of the moderns, and were performed chiefly on horseback, though the original derivation of the name would lead to an opposite supposition. In the middle ages couriers were known by the appellation trottarii, or *trotters;* and hence perhaps originated the English term *running footmen,* of whom history makes mention in the 17th and 18th centuries.

COURSE, in its general sense, a motion forward, either in a direct or curving line; and may be applied to animals, and to solid or fluid bodies.—Applied to the arts and sciences, *course* denotes a methodical series; as, the author has completed his course of lectures; or the medical student has completed his course in anatomy.—*Of course,* in natural and regular order; as this effect will follow *of course.*—The *course of exchange,* in commerce, the current price or rate at which the coin of one country is exchanged for that of another; which, as it depends upon the balance of trade and the political relations which subsist between the two countries, is always fluctuating.

COURS'ING, the act or sport of pursuing any beast of chase, as the hare, &c. with greyhounds.

COURT, a palace; a place where justice is administered; also the persons or judges assembled for hearing and deciding causes, civil, criminal, &c. Thus we have a *court* of law; a *court* of equity; a *court* martial; an ecclesiastical *court*, &c.

COURT-BAR'ON, a court incident to manorial rights.

COUR'TESY, it was at the courts of princes and great feudatories that the minstrels and troubadours of the middle ages especially delighted to exercise their art; and it was there, also, that the peculiarities of chivalrous life and manners were chiefly exhibited. Hence courtesy was a general term, expressive of all the elegance and refinement which the society of those times had attained; in fact, it was synonymous with all the gentler parts of chivalry itself: and it is in this sense that it is used both by the early trouvères and romancers, and also by poets of a later age, when affecting the use of chivalrous language. The transition from this wider meaning to that in which it is now employed is obvious enough.—*Tenure by courtesy*, in law, is where a man marries a woman seized of an estate of inheritance, and has by her issue born alive, which was capable of inheriting her estate: in this case, on the death of his wife, he holds the lands for his life, as tenant by courtesy.

COURT-LEET', a court of record held once a year, in a particular hundred, lordship, or manor, before the steward of the leet.

COURT-MAR'TIAL, a court consisting of military or naval officers, for the trial of offences within its jurisdiction.

COURT'-ROLL, a roll containing an account of the number, &c. of lands which depend on the jurisdiction of the manor, &c.

COUS'IN, the son or daughter of an uncle or aunt; the children of brothers and sisters being usually denominated *cousins* or *cousin-germans*. In the second generation they are called *second cousins*.

COUS'SINET, in architecture, the crowning stone of a pier, or that which lies on the capital of the impost and under the sweep. Its bed is level below and inclined above, receiving the first rise or spring of the arch or vault. This word is also used for the ornament in the Ionic capital, between the abacus and echinus or quarter round, which serves to form the volute, and is thus called because its appearance is that of a cushion or pillow seemingly collapsed by the weight over it, and bound with a strap or girdle called the baltheus.

COVE, an inlet on a rocky coast. It is a term nearly synonymous with *harbor;* the word cove being generally, though not always, used when the indentation on the coast is too shallow or narrow to admit first class vessels.

COV'ENANT, in history, the famous bond of association adopted by the Scottish Presbyterians in 1638. It was framed on the model of a similar declaration, which had been twice solemnly subscribed in the early period of the Reformation; but in more violent language, and with more specific obligation to support the kirk, together with a prohibition and abjuration of the Anglican liturgy and articles. The founders of the Solemn League and Covenant were Alexander Henderson, leader of the clergy, and Archibald Johnston, of Wariston, an advocate. A new religious covenant between the two kingdoms was framed in 1643, and taken by the English House of Commons and assembly of divines at Westminster. Charles II. subscribed the Scottish covenant on his coronation in 1651; but on his restoration it was declared null by act of parliament, and burned by the common hangman. It formed, however, the watchword and bond of union of the discontented party, or Covenanters, as they were called, in the rebellions of his reign.—*Covenant*, in a theological sense, a promise made by God to man upon certain conditions; the two grand distinctions of which are emphatically designated the Old and New Covenant, or Testament; in each of which certain temporal or spiritual benefits are promised to man upon the performance of duties therein pointed out.—*Covenant*, in law, is an engagement under seal to do or to omit a direct act. Covenants are of many different species, as in fact and in law, implied and express, &c.; and according to their subject matter, or express stipulation, they are binding respectively on the heirs, executors, and assigns, or executors and assigns only, of the covenantor.—*Covenant* is also a form of action, which lies where a party claims damages for breach of a covenant or contract under seal.

COWL, the hoods which protect both head and neck from the cold. St. Basil and St. Anthony commanded their monks to wear them, and latterly they have come into use by travellers, sailors, and huntsmen.

COW'RIES, small shells brought from the Maldives, which pass current as coin in smaller payments in Hindostan, and throughout extensive districts in Africa.

CRANIOL'OGY, the science which investigates the structure and uses of the skulls in various animals, particularly in relation to their specific character and intellectual powers. One who is versed in this science is termed a *craniologist.*

CRANIOM'ETER, an instrument for measuring the skulls of animals. The art of measuring them for the purpose of discovering their specific differences, is called *craniometry.*

CRANIOS'COPY, the science of discovering, by the eminences produced by the brain on the cranium, the particular parts in which reside the organs that influence certain passions or faculties.

CRA'NIUM, the skull; the assemblage of bones which enclose the brain.

CRA'TER, the aperture or mouth of a volcano, from which the fire issues.—In antiquity, a very large wine cup, or goblet, out of which the ancients poured their libations at feasts.

CRAY'ON, a general name for all colored mineral substances, used in designing or painting in pastil; whether they have been beaten and reduced to a paste, or are used in their primitive consistence, after sawing and cutting them into long narrow slips.

CREA'TION, the act of causing to exist, or of shaping and organizing matter so as to form new beings; as the *creation* of man and other animals, of plants, minerals, &c.—Also, the act of investing with a new character; as, the *creation* of peers by the sovereign.

CREDEN'DA, in theology, things to be believed; articles of faith; distinguished from *agenda,* or practical duties.

CREDEN'TIALS, that which gives a title or claim to confidence; as the letters of commendation and power given to an ambassador, or public minister, by the prince that sends him to a foreign court.

CRED'IT, in political economy, is a term used to express the lending of wealth, or of the means of acquiring wealth, by one individual or set of individuals to another. The party who lends is said to give credit, and the party who borrows to obtain credit. Hence credit may be defined to be the acquisition by one party of the wealth of another in loan, according to conditions voluntarily agreed on between them. Very exaggerated notions are commonly entertained of the influences of credit: but, in fact, all operations in which credit is given or acquired resolve themselves into a new distribution of wealth already in existence. The "magical" effect that is every now and then ascribed to credit is imaginary. A party who purchases goods payable at some future date obviously acquires the command of so much of the capital of the seller of the goods as their value amounts to, in the same way that a party who discounts a bill acquires the command of a corresponding portion of the capital of the discounter. Wealth is not created by the issue of bills; and all that their negotiation does is to transfer already existing property from one individual or party to another. In the great majority of cases loans are made by individuals who wish to retire from business, or who have more capital than they can advantageously employ, to individuals entering into business, or who wish to extend their concerns and to acquire a greater command of capital. The probability is, that capital will be more likely to be efficiently employed by the latter than by the former class of persons; and the advantage of credit, in a national point of view, consists in that circumstance. Loans made to prodigals or spendthrifts, or to individuals who expend them on unprofitable undertakings, are, in so far, publicly injurious; but, speaking generally, these bear but a very small proportion to the other class of loans, or those made to individuals by whom they are advantageously expended. Public credit is the phrase used to express the trust or confidence placed in the state by those who lend money to government. The interest or premium paid by the borrowers to the lenders depends on a great variety of circumstances,—partly on the rate of profit that may be made by the employment of capital at the time, partly on the duration of the loan and the security for its repayment, and partly on the facilities given by the law for enforcing payment. The only way, indeed, in which a government can advantageously interfere to encourage credit is by simplifying the administration of the law, and by giving every facility for carrying the conditions of contracts into effect.

CREED, any brief summary of Christian belief; but more especially either of the three confessions commonly called the Apostles', Nicene, and Athanasian. The term is derived from the word credo, *I believe;* in like manner as paternoster, avemaria, &c., are prayers named from the first word of these formulas in the Latin tongue.

CREMO'NA, a general designation of the violins made at Cremona in Italy, during the 17th and 18th centuries, chiefly by the family Amati. Cremona is also a name erroneously given to a stop in the organ; being nothing more than a corruption of krumhorn, an ancient wind instrument, which it was originally designed to imitate.

CRENOPH'YLAX, in antiquity, a magistrate at Athens, who had the inspection of fountains.

CREO'LE, a name given to the descendants of whites born in Mexico, South America, and the West Indies; in whom the European blood has been unmixed with that of other races. The various jargons spoken in the West India islands by slaves, &c. are called Creole dialects.

CREPUN'DIA, in antiquity, a term used to express such things as were worn as ornaments by children, as rings, jewels, &c., which might serve as tokens whereby they afterwards might be recognized, or as an inducement for others to take charge of them.

CRESCEN'DO, in music, an Italian term for the gradual swelling of the notes over which it is placed.

CRES'CENT, the increasing or new moon, which, when receding from the sun, shows a curving rim of light, terminating in points or horns.—The Turkish standard, on which a crescent is depicted; and, figuratively, the Turkish power or empire of the crescent.

CREST, the plume of feathers or other material on the top of the ancient helmet. The crest is considered a greater criterion of nobility than the armor generally, and therefore forms an important subject in the science of heraldry.

CREUX, a French term used in sculpture, where the lines and figures are cut below the surface of the substances engraved, and thus stands opposed to *relievo*, which latter term intimates the prominence of the lines and figures which appear above the surface.

CRIME, the transgression of a law, either natural or divine, civil or ecclesiastic. In the general sense of the word, crimes are understood to be offences against society or morals, as far as they are amenable to the laws. To this we may add, in order more clearly to distinguish between words often esteemed synonymous, that actions contrary to the precepts of religion are called *sins;* actions contrary to the principles of morals are called *vices;* and actions, contrary to the laws of the state, are called *crimes.*

CRIM'INAL, in the sense usually applied, signifies, a person indicted or charged with a public offence, and one who is found guilty.

CRIM'SON. The color known by this name is red, reduced to a deep tone by the presence of blue.

CRI'SIS, in medicine, according to Galen, is a sudden change, either for the better or the worse, indicative of recovery or death. In its more general sense, it denotes that stage of a disorder from which some judgment may be formed of its termination. At the approach of a crisis, the disease appears to take a more violent character. If the change is for the better, the violent symptoms cease with a copious perspiration, or some other discharge from the system. After a salutary crisis, the patient feels himself relieved, and the dangerous symptoms cease.—By a *crisis* is also meant the point of time when an affair is arrived at its height, and must soon terminate or suffer a material change.

CRITE'RION, any established rule, principle, or fact, which may be taken as a standard to judge by, and by which a correct judgment may be formed.

CRITH'OMANCY, a kind of divination by means of the dough of cakes, and the meal strewed over the victims, in ancient sacrifices.

CRIT'IC, a person who, according to the established rules of his art, is capable of judging with propriety of any literary composition, or work of art, particularly of such as are denominated the Fine Arts. To which may be added, as within the province of a critic, that he should be able to explain what is obscure, to supply what is defective, to amend what is erroneous, and to reconcile the discrepancies he may meet with between different authors who have treated on the subject under review.

CRIT'ICISM, has been defined "the art of judging with propriety concerning any object, or combination of objects." In a somewhat more limited, but still extensive meaning, its province is confined to literature, philology, and the fine arts; and to subjects of antiquarian, scientific, or historical investigation. In this sense, every branch of literary study, as well as each of the fine arts, has its proper criticism as an appendage to it. The elements of criticism depend on the two principles of beauty and truth, one of which is the final end or object of study in every one of its pursuits: beauty, in letters and the arts; truth, in history and the sciences. The office of criticism, therefore, is, first to lay down those forms or essential ideas which answer to our conception of the beautiful or the true in each branch of study; and, next, to point out by reference to those ideas the excellences or defects of individual works, as they approach or diverge from the requisite standard in each particular. Thus, historical criticism teaches us to distinguish the true from the false, or the probable from the improbable, in historical works; scientific criticism has the same object in each respective line of science; while literary criticism, in a general sense, has for its principal employment the investigation of the merits and demerits of style or diction, according to the received standard of excellence in every language; and, in poetry and the arts, criticism develops the principles of that more refined and exquisite sense of beauty which forms the ideal model of perfection in each. Taste is the critical faculty; that perception of the beautiful in literature and the arts, for the acquisition of which, perhaps, some minds have superior natural powers than others, but which can in no instance be fully developed except by education and habit. Among the classical ancients, the criticism of beauty was carried to a high degree of perfection. Less encumbered with a multitude of facts and things to be known than ourselves, their minds were more at leisure, and more sedulously exercised in reflecting on their own notions and perceptions; hence the astonishing progress which they made in the fine arts; and hence, in literature, they valued more the beauty of the vehicle in which sentiments were conveyed, and the moral or poetical beauty of those sentiments themselves, than the objective branches of study which it is the principal purpose of literature, in our days, to convey easily and precisely to the mind. And as the criticism which antiquity has left us consists almost wholly of such as relates to the literature and the arts (in history they had, as far as we know, few critical spirits, in the sciences almost none,) the name is still confined, in its most popular signification, to those provinces of research. The criticism of truth is of later growth; but as it is regulated for the most part by similar rules and principles, and as minds which possess the faculty of judgment in a high degree in the one are generally capable, if exercised, of forming right apprehensions in the other, they may be considered as nearly allied in the more essential respects. For although it is true that in scientific investigation great knowledge of the individual subject is required to constitute a critic, and in the fine arts the most gifted mind will require much education and practice to judge of beauty; yet it is equally true in both of these branches of study, however widely differing from each other, that knowledge alone (except perhaps in purely abstract science, in respect of which the name of criticism seems hardly applicable) will not make the critic, and that the habit of discriminating and judging correctly is a distinct faculty or compound of faculties in the mind.—Criticism, in a more limited sense, is a branch of belles lettres. Essays written for the purpose of commending or discommending works in literature or the arts, and pointing out their various merits and defects, are works in the critical department. Thus the term "periodical criticism" is used to express the body of writing contained in the various works under the name of magazines, reviews, &c., which are periodically published in most literary countries.

CRITIQUE′, a skilful examination of the merits of a performance, with remarks on its beauties and faults.

CROCK′ETTS, enrichments modelled generally from vegetable productions, such as vine or other leaves, but sometimes animals and images are introduced, employed in gothic architecture to

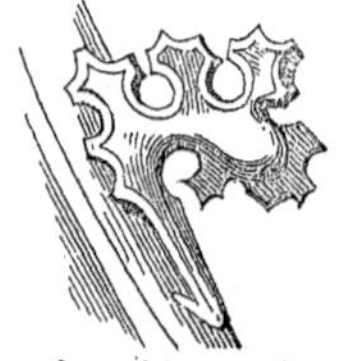

decorate the angles of various parts of ecclesiastical edifices, such as spires, pinnacles, mullions of windows, &c. The forms are infinite, almost every kind of leaf or flower being employed for this purpose, generally with some pointed reference to local circumstances; thus, at Westminster we find a succession of roses and pomegranates; at Magdalen College Chapel, lilies. They only appear in pyramidical and curved lines, never in horizontal.

CROI'SES, in English antiquity, pilgrims bound for the Holy Land, or such as had been there; so called from a badge they wore in imitation of a cross. The knights of St. John of Jerusalem, created for the defence and protection of pilgrims, were particularly called *croises;* and so were all those of the English nobility and gentry, who, in the reigns of Henry II. Richard I. Henry III. and Edward I. were *cruce signati*, that is, devoted for the recovery of Palestine.

CROM'LECH, in British antiquity, large, broad, flat stones raised upon other stones set up to support them. They are common in Anglesea, and are supposed to be remains of druidical altars. Cromlechs are generally supposed by antiquaries to have been constructed to serve as altars. According to some, there is a difference between the cromlechs of the Britons and those of nations of Germanic descent; the former being inclined stones, perhaps for the purpose of allowing the blood shed in sacrifice to run off; the latter thick, round stones, standing on small hillocks and covering caves.

CRO'SIER, the staff of an archbishop, surmounted by a cross, and thereby distinguished from the pastoral staff or crook of a bishop. This staff, according to Polydore Virgil, was given to bishops wherewith to chastise the vices of the people; and was called *baculus pastoralis*, in respect of their pastoral charge and superintendence over their flock, as well as from its resemblance to the shepherd's crook. Many authors contend that the crosier is derived from the *lituus* or augural staff of the Romans.

CROSS, in antiquity, an instrument of ancient vengeance, consisting of two pieces of timber, crossing each other, either in the form of a T or an X. That on which our Saviour suffered, is represented on coins and other monuments to have been of the former kind. This punishment was only inflicted on malefactors and slaves, and was thence called *servile supplicium*. The most usual method was to nail the criminal's hands and feet to this gibbet, in an erect posture; though there are instances of criminals so nailed with their head downward.—*Cross*, the ensign of the Christian religion; and hence, figuratively, the religion itself. Also, a monument with a cross upon it to excite devotion, such as were anciently set up in market places.—In theology, the doctrine of Christ's sufferings and of the atonement. —*Cross*, in Christian Art, the sole and universal symbol of our redemption, and of the person of our Saviour; he is symbolized under this form, as he is also under that of the Fish, the Lion, or the Lamb. The cross is either historic or symbolic, real or ideal; in the one it is a gibbet, in the other an attribute of glory. There are four species of cross. 1. The cross without a summit, in the form of a T; this is the Egyptian cross, the Cross of the Old Testament. Many ancient churches, especially the Basilicas of Constantine, St. Peter and St. Paul at Rome, are, in their ground plan, nearly of this form. 2. The cross with summit; it has four branches; this is the true cross, the cross of Jesus and of the Evangelists. This form of cross is divided into two principal types, which also partake of many varieties; they are known as the Greek and the Latin cross; the first is adopted by the Greek and Oriental Christians, the second by the Christians of the West. The Greek cross is composed of four equal parts, the breadth being equal to the length. In the Latin cross, the foot is longer than the summit or the arms. The Greek cross is an *ideal* cross; the Latin cross resembles the real cross upon which Jesus suffered. 3. The cross with two cross-pieces and summit.

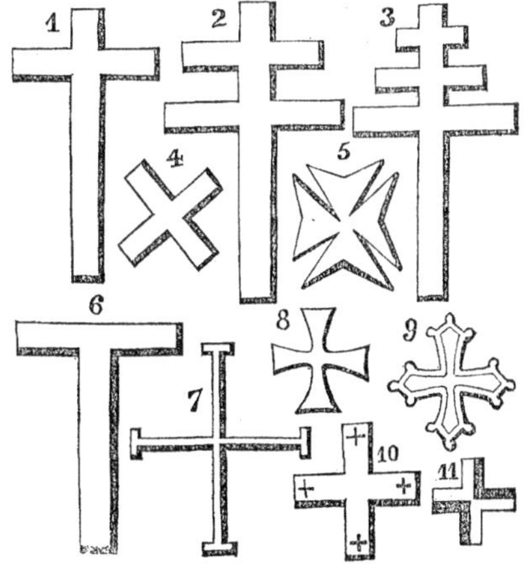

4. The cross with summit and three cross-pieces. When the cross retains its simple form, and is not loaded with attributes or ornaments, we must distinguish the Cross of the Passion from the Cross of the Resurrection. The Cross of the Passion is a real cross, the gibbet upon which Christ suffered. This is the cross in common use in our churches; it is employed by painters and sculptors; and which, in Catholic countries, meets us at every turn; by the roadside, in the street, chapels, and cathedrals. It is also called the Triumphal Cross. The Cross of the Resurrection is the symbol of the true cross; it is that put into the hands of Christ in representations of his resurrection. It is a lance, the staff of which terminates in a cross instead of a pike; it carries a flag or banner, upon which is depicted a cross, which is suspended from the point of intersection of the arms. It is the cross held by the Paschal Lamb; it is that carried at the head of religious processions. It is not a tree, like the Cross of the Passion, but a staff; the first is the Cross of Suffering, the other is the Cross of Victory; they are of the same general form, but the latter is spiritualized; it is the gibbet transfigured.

CROSS-BOW, an ancient weapon, a great improvement on the wooden long-bow, and brought to Europe by the Crusaders. It was made of steel, with a peculiar handle, and the string was stretched by means of a small wheel called a *gaffle*. The bolts or arrows were generally shod with iron, and were either round, angular, or pointed. Burning materials were also discharged from the bow, in order to set fire to buildings and machines of war. Those bows made wholly of iron were called ballisters. The share which Art had in the cross-bows of the middle ages may be seen by a glance into the armories. The most artistic specimen is the bow which Charles V. used for his amusement. It was inlaid with ivory carved by Albert Durer.

CROSS-BAR-SHOT, a bullet with an iron bar passing through it, and standing out a few inches on each side; used in naval actions for cutting the enemy's rigging.

CROSS'ES, STONE, in architectural antiquities, are of various descriptions, according to the occasion or purpose of their erection. They are said to have originated in the practice of marking the Druid stones with a cross, at the period of the conversion of the Celtic tribes to Christianity. *Preaching crosses* are generally quadrangular or hexagonal, open on one or both sides, and raised on steps. They were used for the delivery of sermons in the open air; such was the famous Paul's Cross in London. *Market crosses* are well known. *Weeping crosses* were so called because penances were finished before them. *Crosses of memorial* were raised on various occasions· sometimes where the bier of an eminent person stopped on its way to burial, in attestation of some miracle performed on the spot: such are the well-known crosses of Queen Philippa. Crosses served also as landmarks; they are especially set up for this purpose on the lands of the Templars and Hospitallers.

CROSSET'TES, in architecture, the returns on the corners of door cases or window frames; called also ears, elbows, ancones, prothyrides. In architectural construction, they are the small projecting pieces in arch stones which hang upon the adjacent stones—*a*, *a*, *a*, *a*.

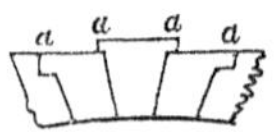

CROSS-EXAMINATION, in law, a close and rigid examination of a witness by the counsel of the adverse party, consisting of cross questions, in order to elicit the truth.

CROTA'LUM, an ancient kind of castanet, used by the Corybantes or priests of Cybele. This instrument must not be confounded with the modern *crotalo*, a musical instrument used chiefly by the Turks, and corresponding exactly with the ancient cymbalum.

CROTCH'ET, in music, half a minim. —In printing, this mark, [ ], to separate what is not the necessary part of a sentence.

CROWN, an ornamental badge of regal power, worn on the head by sovereign princes.—The top of the head; also the top of any elevated object.—In architecture, the uppermost member of a cornice.—Among jewellers, the upper work of the rose diamond.—An English silver coin, of the value of five shillings.—Among the various crowns and wreaths in use among the Greeks and Romans were the following: *Corona aurea* (the golden crown;) the reward of remarkable bravery. *Corona castrensis;* given to him who first entered the camp of an enemy. *Corona civica;* one of the highest military rewards: it was given to him who saved the life of a citizen. *Corona convivialis;* the wreath worn at feasts. *Corona muralis;* given by the general to the soldier who first scaled the enemy's wall. *Corona navalis;* given to him who first boarded and took an enemy's vessel: it was next in rank to the civic crown. *Corona nuptialis;* a crown or wreath worn by brides. *Corona obsidionalis;* a reward given to him who delivered a besieged town, or a blockaded army. It was one of the highest military honors, and very seldom obtained. *Corona triumphalis;* a wreath of laurel which was given by the army to the *imperator*, who wore it on his head at the celebration of his triumph.—In Christian Art, the crown, from the earliest times, is either an attribute or an emblem. It has been employed as an emblem of victory, and hence became the especial symbol of the glory of martyrdom. Its form varied at different periods; in early pictures it is simply a wreath of palm or myrtle,

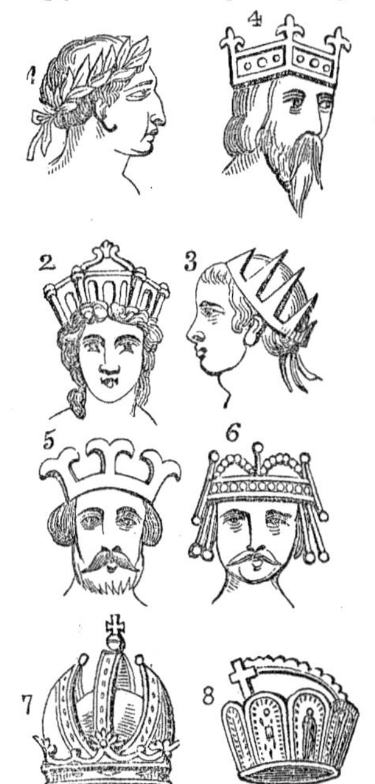

afterwards it became a coronet of gold and jewels. Generally, the female martyrs only wear the symbolical crown of glory on their heads. Martyrs of the opposite sex bear it in their hands, or it is carried by an angel. Sometimes, as in St. Catherine and St. Ursula, the crown is both the symbol of martyrdom, and their attribute as royal princesses. The Virgin, as 'Queen of Heaven,' wears a crown. No. 1, in our cut, represents the Laurel Crown of ancient Rome. No. 2, the Mural Crown worn by Cybele. No. 3, the radiated Crown of its ordinary form. No. 4, the square Saxon Crown. No. 5, the Crown of Edgar. No. 6, the Crown of William the Conqueror. No. 7, the imperial Crown of Germany. No. 8, that worn by Charlemagne.

CROWN-WORK, in fortification, an out-work running into the field, consisting of two demi-bastions at the extremes, and an entire bastion in the middle, with curtains. It is designed to gain some advantageous post, and cover the other works.

CRU'CIFIX, the representation of the Saviour on the cross, but especially that plastic one seen on the altars of Catholic churches, in the centre of which it stands, overtopping the tapers, and only removed at the elevation of the Host. Its intention was to lead the mind back to the cross, which was set up on the altar, or in some convenient spot. It was first known in the time of Constantine, and takes the place of the real crucifix in the Eastern church. The latter was not common till the end of the eighth century. The Greek church never publicly accepted it, although it appears in the quarrel about images, but used the simple cross. It was not general in the Latin church until the Carlovingian era. From the *disciplina arcani* and the early prohibition of images by the Synod of Elvira, (305,) an early use of the crucifix may be supposed, as it referred immediately to the first Christian dogma. At first the simple cross was sufficient—*crux immissa* or *capitata* +; *crux decussata* ✕; and *crux commissa* T—the Lamb standing under a blood-red cross. The addition of the Saviour's bust at the head or foot of the cross while the Lamb lay in the centre, was the next step towards the crucifix; and afterwards Christ himself was represented clothed, his hands raised in prayer, but not yet nailed. At last he appeared fastened to the cross by four nails, (seldom by three,) and on the older crucifixes alive, with open eyes; on the later ones, (from the tenth to the eleventh century,) sometimes dead. Christ was often clad in a robe, having the regal crown on his head; more recently the figure wore only a cloth round the loins, and the crown of thorns. This representation was continued, and the crucifix regarded as an indispensable attribute of churches and altars. The number of them increased, as they were particular objects of veneration; and large ones of wood or stone were placed at the entrances of the church. The altar crucifix was generally of gold or silver, adorned with pearls or precious stones. Later artists have enveloped the Saviour in drapery, leaving the body in its customary position; they have also added the angel by the side, by which addition these crucifixes intended in the spirit of Christian Æsthetics for Protestant churches, become more symbolic representations of Christian ideas. The unpleasant sight of the nailed feet is avoided by their resting free and unbound on the globe, so that only the arms are fastened by nails to the cross. We are now too much accustomed to the naked figure to allow of the innovation of representing Christ after the old custom; we may also question whether the great simplicity of the original crucifix had not more effect.

CRUDE, in painting, a term applied to a picture when the colors are rudely laid on, and do not blend or harmonize.

CRUI'SER, a small armed vessel that sails to and fro in quest of the enemy, to protect the commerce of its own nation, or for plunder.

CRUPELLA'RII, in antiquity, nobility, among the Gauls, who were armed with a complete harness of steel.

CRUSA'DES, the name by which the wars or military expeditions were distinguished, that were carried on by the Christian nations of the West, from the end of the 11th to the end of the 13th century, for the conquest of Palestine. They were called crusades, because all the warriors fought under the banner of the *cross*, and wore that emblem on their clothes. The Christians had long grieved that the Holy Land, where Jesus had lived, taught, and died for mankind, where pious pilgrims resorted to pour out their sorrows, and ask for aid from above at the tomb of their Saviour, should be in the power of unbelievers. The dawn of civilization and mental cultivation had just commenced. They were at that period in a state to receive a strong religious excitement; the spirit of adventure burned within them; and their imaginations were also easily roused by the reports of the riches of the East. The Pope considered the invasion of Asia as the means of promoting Christianity amongst the infidels and of winning whole nations to the bosom of the church; monarchs expected victory and increase of dominion; and their subjects were easily persuaded to engage in the glorious cause! Yet army after army was destroyed; and though some brilliant victories served to exhibit the soldiers of Christendom as heroes of a valorous age, and the holy city of Jerusalem was more than once under their dominion, the Christian empire on the continent of Asia was eventually overthrown, and the dominion of the Mamelukes and Sultans established. But by means of these joint enterprises, the European nations became more connected with each other; feudal tyranny was weakened; a commercial intercourse took place throughout Europe, which greatly augmented the wealth of the cities; the human mind expanded; and a number of arts and sciences, till then unknown by the western nations, were introduced.

CRYPT, a subterranean chapel or oratory; or a vault under a church for the interment of bodies.

CRYPTOG'RAPHY, the art of writing in cipher, or secret characters.

CRYPTOL'OGY, secret or enigmatical language.

CU'BIT, an ancient measure, equal to the length of a man's arm, from the elbow to the tip of the middle finger. Among different nations the length of the cubit differed. The English was 18 inches, the Roman rather less, and the cubit of the Scriptures is supposed to have been 22 inches.

CUE, the last words of a speech, which a player, who is to answer, catches and regards as an intimation to begin. Also, a hint given to him of what and when he is to speak.

CUIRASS', a piece of defensive armor, made of iron plate, well hardened, and covering the body from the neck to the girdle. The cuirass of plate-armor succeeded the hauberk, hacqueton, &c., of mail, about the reign of Edward III.; and from that period the surcoat, jupon, &c., which were usually worn over the coat of mail, began to be laid aside. From that period the cuirass or breast-plate continued to be worn, and was the last piece of defensive armor laid aside in actual warfare. There were cuirassiers in the English civil wars, and in the French service nearly to the end of the 17th century; after this period, the cuirass was generally laid aside, until it was again employed by some of Napoleon's regiments, and it is now, in most services worn by some regiments of heavy cavalry

CUIS'SES, CUIS'SOTS, CUIS'SARTS, &c., in plate-armor, the pieces which protected the front of the thigh.

CUL'DEES, in church history, an order of priests, formerly inhabiting Scotland and Ireland. Being remarkable for the religious exercises of preaching and praying, they were called, by way of eminence, *cultores Dei*. After having exercised a great influence throughout the country, they are said to have been overthrown by the increase of the papal power, and the institution of monasteries, more congenial to the views of the see of Rome.

CUL DE LAMP, in architecture, a term used for several decorations, in vaults and ceilings.

CULI'NA, in antiquity, that part of the funeral pile in which the banquet was consumed.—*Culinæ*, a burial-ground for the poor.

CUL'LIAGE, a barbarous and immoral practice, whereby the lords of manors anciently assumed a right to the first night of their vassals' brides.

CUL'PRIT, in law, a word applied in court to one who is indicted for a criminal offence.

CULTIVA'TION, in a general sense, the art and practice of tilling and preparing land for crops; but it means also the study, care, and practice necessary to the *cultivation* of our talents and the improvement of our minds.

CUL'VERIN, a long slender piece of ordnance, serving to carry a ball to a great distance.

CUME'RUM, in antiquity, a large covered basket, used at weddings for carrying the household stuff, &c., belonging to the bride.

CUNE'IFORM, an appellation given to whatever resembles a wedge; as, in botany, a cuneiform leaf.

CUNE'IFORM LETTERS, the name given to the inscriptions found on old Babylonian and Persian monuments, from the characters being formed like a wedge. This species of writing, as it is the simplest, so it is the most ancient of which we have any knowledge. It is formed of two radical signs—the wedge and the angle—susceptible, however, of about thirty different combinations; and consists of three varieties, distinguished from each other by a greater or less complication of the characters. It is of Asiatic origin; is written from right to left, like the Sanscrit; differs from the ancient Egyptian hieroglyphics, inasmuch as it is alphabetic, not ideographic; and, finally, with a few considerable modifications, forms the basis of most of the Eastern languages.

CU'PID, the Roman name of the Grecian god of love Eros. There were three divinities, or rather three forms of the same deity, with this appellation; but the one usually meant when spoken of without any qualification was the son of Mercury and Venus. Like the rest of the gods Cupid assumed different shapes; but he is generally represented as a beautiful child with wings, blind, and carrying a bow and quiver of arrows, with which he transpierced the hearts of lovers, inflaming them with desire. Among the ancients he was worshipped with the same solemnity as his mother Venus; his influence pervaded all creation, animate and inanimate; and vows and sacrifices were daily offered up at his shrine. Statues of Cupid formed among the ancients great objects of *vertu*. Praxiteles is said to have derived great honor from his statues of this divinity; and in his orations against Verres, Cicero has given celebrity to one statue of Cupid by this artist, which formed an object of peculiar veneration to the Thespians.

CU'POLA, in architecture, a roof or vault rising in a circular form, otherwise called the *tholus* or *dome*. The ancients constructed their cupolas of stone; the moderns, of timber, covered with lead or copper. The finest cupola, ancient or modern, is that of the Pantheon at Rome. Among some of the handsomest modern cupolas, is that on the Bank of England, St. Peter's at Rome, the Hotel des Invalides at Paris, and St. Paul's, London.

CU'RATE, an officiating, but unbeneficed clergyman, who performs the duty of a church, and receives a salary from the incumbent of the living.

CURA'TOR, in a general sense, signifies a person who is appointed to take care of anything. Among the ancient Romans, there were officers in every branch of the public service to whom this application was given: thus we read of *Curatores frumenti*, *viarum*, *operum publicorum*, *Tiberis*, &c. &c., *i. e.* persons who distributed corn, superintended the making of roads and the public buildings, or were conservators of the river.—Curator, in the civil law, is the guardian of a minor who has attained the age of fourteen. Before that age, minors are under a tutor. The guardianship of persons under various disabilities, and of the estate of deceased or absent persons and insolvents is also committed to a curator

This title is derived from the ancient Romans, by whom, as was remarked above, it was given to various officers who acted as superintendents of different departments of the public service. In learned institutions, the officer who has charge of libraries, collections of natural history, &c. is frequently styled curator.

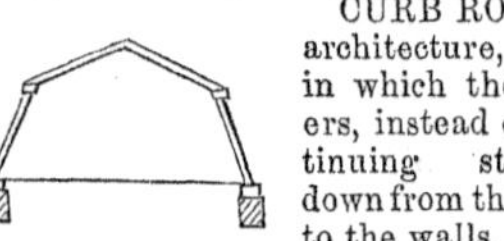

CURB ROOF, in architecture, a roof in which the rafters, instead of continuing straight down from the ridge to the walls, are at a given height received on plates, which in their turn are supported by rafters less inclined to the horizon, whose bearing is, through the medium of the wall-plate, directly on the walls. It presents a bent appearance, as in the diagram, whence it derives its name.

CUR'FEW, a law introduced from Normandy into England by William the Conqueror, that all people should put out their fire and lights at the ringing of a bell, at eight o'clock. The word is derived from the French *couvre-feu.*

CU'RIA, in Roman antiquity, a certain division, or portion of a tribe. Romulus divided the people into thirty *curiæ*, or wards; and there were ten in every tribe, that each might keep the ceremonies of their feasts and sacrifices in the temple, or holy place, appointed for every curia. The priest of the curia was called *curio.*—*Curia*, in law, signifies generally a court, but it was taken particularly for the assemblies of bishops, peers, &c. of the realm, called *solemnis curia*, *curia publica*, &c.

CUR'RENCY, in commerce, bank-notes or other paper-money issued by authority, and which are continually passing current for coin.

CUR'RENTS, in navigation, certain settings of the stream, by which ships are compelled to alter their course, and submit to the motion impressed upon them by the current. The causes of currents are very numerous. The waters may be put in motion by an internal impulse; by a difference of heat and saltness; by the inequality of evaporation in different latitudes; and by the change in the pressure at different points of the surface of the ocean. The existence of cold strata, which have been met with at great depths in low latitudes, prove the existence of a low current, which runs from the pole to the equator. It proves likewise, that saline substances are distributed in the ocean, in a manner not to destroy the effect produced by different temperatures.—It is well known also that there are different *currents of air.*

CUR'SITOR, a clerk belonging to the court of chancery, whose business it is to make out original writs.

CUR'TAIN, in a general sense, a cloth hanging round a bed, or at a window, which may be contracted, spread, or drawn aside at pleasure. Also, a cloth-hanging used in theatres, to conceal the stage from the spectators.—In fortification, the *curtain* is that part of the rampart which is between the flanks of two bastions, bordered with a parapet, behind which the soldiers stand to fire on the covered way and into the moat.

CU'RULE CHAIR, in Roman antiquity, a chair, or stool, adorned with ivory, wherein the chief magistrates of Rome had a right to sit. The curule magistrates were the ædiles, the prætors, censors, and consuls. This chair was placed in a kind of chariot, whence it had its name.

CUSTO'DIA, the shrine or receptacle for the host in Spanish churches. They are frequently constructed of gold and of silver, upon which all the riches of the goldsmith's art were lavished.

CUS'TOM, in law, long established practice or usage, which constitutes the unwritten law, and long consent to which gives it authority.

CUS'TOMS, in political economy, the duties, toll, tribute, or tariff, payable to the government upon merchandise exported and imported, and which form a branch of the perpetual taxes.

CUS'TOS ROTULO'RUM, the keeper of the rolls and records of the sessions of the peace, and also of the commission of the peace itself. He is usually a nobleman, and always a justice of the peace, of the quorum in the county where he is appointed.

CUTA'NEOUS, an epithet for whatever belongs to or affects the skin; as, a *cutaneous* eruption, &c.

CUT'LERY, a term used to designate all kinds of sharp and cutting instruments made of iron or steel, as knives, forks, scissors, razors, &c. The principal seat of the manufacture of British cutlery is Sheffield; and the articles made there are held in the highest estimation in all parts of the world.

CUT'TER, a boat attached to a vessel of war, which is rowed with six oars, and is employed in carrying light stores, passengers, &c.—Also, a vessel with one mast and a straight running bowsprit, which may be run in upon deck.

CYAN'OGEN, carburetted azote, or the blue compound of carbon and azotic gas.

CYATH'IFORM, in the form of a cup or drinking glass, a little widened at the top.

CY'ATHUS, in Roman antiquity, a liquid measure, containing four *ligulas*, or half a pint.—Also, a cup, which the Romans used to fill and drink from as many times as there were letters in the name of their patron or mistress. It is often met with on painted vases in the hands of Bacchus; but the vessel peculiarly sacred to that divinity is the two-handled cup, Cantharus.

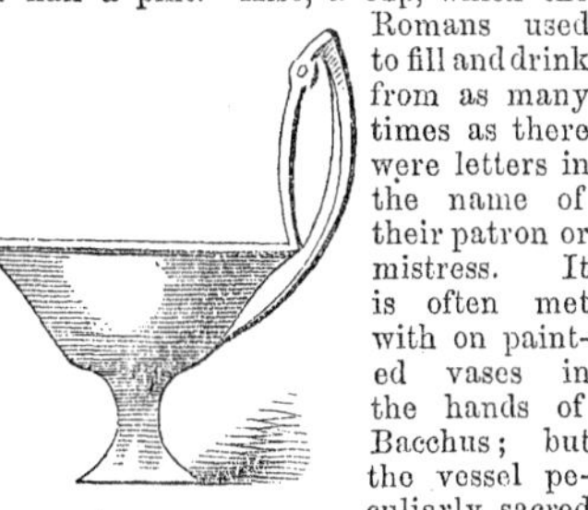

CYBE'LE, in mythology, was originally the Phrygian goddess of the earth. When her worship was introduced among the Greeks, they confounded her with Rhea, as did the Latins with their Ops. Her rites, like those of the Asiatic deities, in general were celebrated with great excitement; her priests, who were called Galli, Corybantes, Curetes, &c., running about with howlings and clashing of cymbals.

CY'CLAS, a large robe of thin texture, with a border embroidered with gold, worn by the Roman women. It was worn in the same manner as the pallium.

CY'CLE, in chronology, a certain period or series of numbers, which regularly proceed from the first to the last, and then return again to the first, and so circulate perpetually.—*Cycle of the sun*, or *solar cycle*, a period of 28 years, in which the Sunday or Dominical letter recurs in the same order.—*Cycle of the moon*, or *lunar cycle*, a period of nineteen years, when the new and full moon recur on the same days of the month.—*Cycle of indiction*, a period of fifteen years, in use among the Romans, commencing from the third year before Christ This cycle has no connection with the celestial motions; but was instituted, according to Baronius, by Constantine.

CY'CLIC CHO'RUS, the chorus which performed the songs and dances of the Dithyrambic odes at Athens. They derived their name from the circumstance of their dancing round the altar of Bacchus in a circle (κυκλος) and were thus distinguished from the square (τετράγωνος) choruses of tragedy.

CY'CLIC POETS. This term was applied to a succession of Epic poets who followed Homer, and wrote merely on the Trojan war and the adventures of the heroes immediately connected with it, keeping, as it were, to one circle of subjects. None of their works have come down to us.

CYCLOPÆ'DIA, a work containing definitions or accounts of the principal subjects in one or all departments of learning, art, or science. Its arrangement may be either according to divisions into the various sciences, &c., or the subjects may be arranged and treated in alphabetical order. The *Encyclopédie Françoise*, or *Dictionnaire Encyclopédique* and the *Encyclopædia Britannica*, have been the most celebrated works of this species; but the earliest appears to be the *Lexicon Technicum* of Harris, published in 1706. The great French work, the *Encyclopédie Methodique*, consists, not of one, but of a series of encyclopedias or dictionaries.

CYCLO'PEAN, an epithet applied to certain huge structures, the remains of which are found in many parts of Greece, Italy, and Asia Minor, the architecture of which was totally different in style from that which prevailed during the historical ages. The epithet originated in the Grecian tradition that assigned these edifices to the gigantic strength of the Cyclops. It is most probable that they were really raised by the Pelasgians, the predecessors or ancestors of the later Greeks; and a gradual progress may be traced in them from the extreme of rudeness to a degree of symmetry that indicates an approach to the elegance of Grecian architecture.

CYCLO'PES, in mythology, a race of gigantic beings fabled by the Greeks to dwell in Sicily, where they assisted Vulcan in forging the thunderbolts of Jupiter. They had only one eye, round, and situated in the centre of the forehead. The most celebrated among them was Polyphemus, whose exploits have formed a prolific theme for the poets of antiquity. His attachment to the nymph Galatea, is happily described in an idyl of Theocritus; and the ninth book of the Odyssey contains a graphic account of his savage propensities, and of the loss of his eye by the stratagem of Ulysses.

CYMA'TIUM, CY'MA, or SI'MA, in architecture, a member or moulding of the cornice, the profile of which is waving, that is, concave at the top and convex at the bottom. When the concave part of the moulding projects beyond the convex part, the *cymatium* is denominated a *sima-recta;* but when the convex part forms the greatest projection, it is a *sima-reversa.*

CYM'BAL, a musical instrument used by the ancients, hollow, and made of brass, supposed to be somewhat like a kettle-drum. The modern *cymbals* used in military bands consist of two concave metal plates, which are occasionally struck together and flourished above the head of the player.

CYN'IC, a man of a surly or snarling temper; a misanthrope.—The *cynics* were a sect of ancient philosophers who valued themselves upon their contempt of riches and state, arts, sciences, and amusements. This sect was founded by Antisthenes, a disciple of Socrates, who sought to imitate his master in carelessness of outward splendor and contempt of riches; but his indifference to these things soon degenerated unhappily into a love of ostentation, shown by a display of poverty. Thus he and many of his followers rejected not only the conveniences but the common decencies of life, and lived in rags and filthiness; while they sneered bitterly at the rest of the world, instead of endeavoring to teach it to cultivate the pure reason of which they professed themselves to be the only followers. Of this sect was the famous Diogenes, whose meeting with Alexander the Great is too well known to require being noticed in this place.

CYNOSAR'GES, a sort of academy in the suburbs of Athens, situated near the Lyceum; so called from the mythological story of a white dog, which, when Diomus was sacrificing to Hercules, the guardian of the place, carried off part of the victim. Besides possessing several temples erected in honor of Hercules, Alcmene, and other mythological personages, it was chiefly famed for its gymnasium, in which foreigners or citizens of half blood used to perform their exercises; and as being the place where Antisthenes instituted the sect of the Cynics, and taught his opinions.

CYN'OSURE, literally the tail of a dog, applied by some philosophers to the constellation Ursa Minor, by which the ancient Phœnicians used to be guided on their voyages: whence it has been borrowed by the language of poetry, in which it signifies "a point of attraction:"

> Where perhaps some beauty lies,
> The cynosure of neighboring eyes.

CYN'THIUS and CYN'THIA, in mythology, surnames given by the ancient poets to Apollo and Diana: from Cynthus, a mountain of the island of Delos, on which they are fabled to have been born.

CY'PHONISM, a species of punishment frequently resorted to by the ancients, which consisted in besmearing the criminal with honey, and then exposing him to insects. This punishment was carried into effect in various ways, but chiefly by fastening the sufferer to a stake, or extending him on the ground with his arms pinioned.

CYRE'NIANS, the philosophers of a school founded at Cyrene, a Grecian colony on the northern coast of Africa, by Aristippus, a disciple of Socrates. They held, with the Epicureans, that pleasure was the only good and pain the only evil, and were not at such pains as the latter to prove that the first could only attend on virtuous conduct; they also differed from them in not considering absence from pain of itself to be a pleasure of the highest order. But though these philosophers held that pleasure should form the ultimate object of pursuit, and that it was only in subserviency to this that fame, friendship, and even virtue are to be desired, still there were many points in their philosophy calculated to command general sympathy. It is impossible not to admit that, with all the defects of the system, its object is to render us happy in relation to ourselves, agreeable and faithful to our friends, and discreet, serviceable, and well-bred in relation to those with whom we are obliged to live and converse. Perhaps the best view of the philosophy of this sect is to be obtained from the Satires and Epistles of Horace, in which the versatility of disposition, politeness of manners, and knowledge of the world that distinguished the Cyrenians are set forth with great clearness, and with all the ardor of an enthusiastic disciple.

CYTHERÆ'A, in mythology, a name given to Venus, from the island Cythera, where she was worshipped with peculiar veneration.

CYZICE'NA, in antiquity, a magnificent sort of banqueting-house, among the

Greeks; so called from Cyzicus, a city famous for its sumptuous buildings.

CZAR, the title assumed by the emperors of Russia. The first that bore this title was Basil, the son of Basilides, under whom the Russian power began to appear, about 1470. The word is of old Sclavonic origin, and is nearly equivalent to *king*.

CZARI'NA, the title of the empress of Russia.

D.

D, the fourth letter in the alphabet, is a dental articulation, having a kind of middle sound between the *t* and *th;* its sound being formed by a stronger impulse of the tongue to the upper part of the mouth, than is necessary in the pronunciation of the *t*. D, as a numeral, denotes 500; as an abbreviation it stands for Doctor, Domini, &c.; as M.D., Doctor of Medicine; D.D. Doctor of Divinity; A.D., Anno Domini. As a sign, it is one of the Dominical or Sunday letters; and in music, it is the nominal of the second note in the natural diatonic scale of C.

DA'ALDER, a Dutch silver coin, of the value of a guilder and a half, or about 35 cents.

DA CAPO, in music, an Italian phrase signifying that the first part of the tune is to be repeated from the beginning. It is also used as a call or acclamation to the musical performer at concerts, &c., to repeat the air or piece which has just been finished.

DAC'TYL, a foot in Latin and Greek poetry, consisting of a long syllable followed by two short ones; as, *dominus*, *carmine*. When combined with the foot called a spondee, consisting of two long syllables, it forms a line of hexameter, or six feet poetry, in which the dactyls and spondees are tastefully intermingled.

DAC'TYLI, priests of Cybele in Phrygia; so called, according to Sophocles, because they were five in number, thus corresponding with the number of the fingers, from which the name is derived. Their functions appear to have been similar to those of the Corybantes and Curetes, other priests of the same goddess in Phrygia and Crete.

DAC'TYLIC, an epithet for verses which end with a dactyl instead of a spondee.

DACTYL'IOGLYPH, in ancient gem sculpture, the inscription of the name of the artist on a gem.

DACTYLIOG'RAPHY, the science of gem engraving.

DACTYLIOM'ANCY, a kind of divination among the Greeks and Romans, which was performed by suspending a ring by a thread over a table, the edge of which was marked with the letters of the alphabet. As the ring, after its vibration ceased, happened to hang over certain letters, these joined together gave the answer.

DACTYLIOTHE'CA, a collection of engraved gems.

DACTYLOL'OGY, or DACTYLON'OMY, the art of communicating ideas or thoughts by the fingers; or the art of numbering on the fingers.

DAC'TYLOS, the shortest measure among the Greeks, being the fourth part of a palm.

DA'DO, the die or that part in the middle of the pedestal of a column between its base and cornice. It is also the name of the lower part of a wall.

DADU'CHI, priests of Ceres, who at the feasts and sacrifices of that goddess, ran about the temple with lighted torches, delivering them from hand to hand, till they had passed through the whole company.

DÆD'ALA, two festivals in Bœotia. One was held by the Platæans in a large grove, where they exposed to the air pieces of boiled flesh; and observing on what trees the crows alighted, that came to feed upon them, they cut them down and formed them into statues called *Dædala*. The other festival, which was much more solemn, was observed in different parts of Bœotia once in sixty years, when they carried about the statue of a female, called Dædala, and every city and every man of fortune offered a bull to Jupiter, and an ox or heifer to Juno, the poorer people providing sheep. These, with wine and incense, were laid upon the altar, and, together with twelve statues which were piled thereon, were set on fire wholly consumed.

DÆD'ALUS, in fabulous history, the great-grandson of Erechtheus king of Athens, is celebrated as the most ancient statuary, architect, and mechanist of Greece To him is ascribed the invention of the saw, the axe, the plummet, and many other tools and instruments; and to such a degree did he excel in sculpture, that his statues are fabled to have been endowed with life. For the alleged murder of his nephew he was obliged to quit Athens, whence he repaired to Crete, then under the sway of Minos, by whom he was favorably received. Here he constructed the famous labyrinth, on the model of the still more famous one of Egypt; but having assisted the wife of Minos in an intrigue with Taurus, he was, by a strange fatality, confined to this very labyrinth along with his son Icarus. By means, however, of wings, which he formed of linen or feathers and wax, Dædalus and his son contrived to make their escape. The former pursued his aërial journey, and arrived safely in Sicily; but the latter having soared too near the sun, in consequence of which the wax that fastened the wing was melted, dropped into and was drowned in the sea (thence called the *Icarian*.) In Sicily Dædalus continued to prosecute his ingenious labors, and lived long enough to enrich that island with various works of art. From the plastic powers of Dædalus, the ancient poets used to regard his name as synonymous with *ingenious*, as in the phrase *Dædaleum opus;* and in a somewhat similar sense Lucretius applies it to the earth, in order to describe its vernal vegetation. A few years ago the name of Dædalus, which had been appropriated by various artists in the history of Grecian art, was assumed by the constructors of some ingenious automata, in memory of the grand impressions which the works of Dædalus had produced.

DAG'GER, a weapon of various sizes,

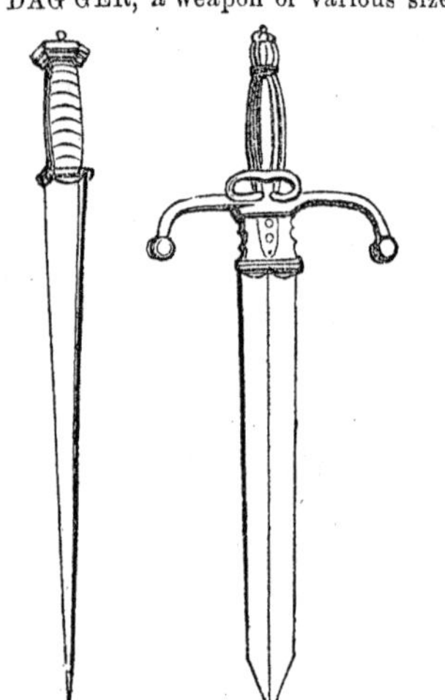

two-edged and pointed, similar in appearance to a sword, but smaller. The cut exhibits two daggers from the armory at Goodrich Court. The first is of the time of Edward III.; the second, which has the more modern improvement of a guard for the hand, is of Italian workmanship, of the latter end of the fifteenth century.

DA'GON, one of the principal divinities of the ancient Phœnicians and Syrians, and more especially of the Philistines. The origin, attributes, and even the sex of this divinity, are all wrapt in the most profound obscurity; but the sacred writers concur in assigning to him such a degree of authority as must place him on a level with the Jupiter of the Greeks and Romans.

DAGUER'REOTYPE, the name applied to a remarkable invention of M. Daguerre, of Paris, by which he fixes upon a metallic plate the lights and shadows of a landscape or figure, solely by the action of the solar light. A plate of copper, thinly coated with silver, is exposed in a close box to the action of the vapor of iodine; and when it assumes a yellow color, it is placed in the dark chamber of a *camera obscura*, where it receives an image of the object to be represented. It is then withdrawn, and exposed to the vapor of mercury to bring out the impression distinctly; after which, it is plunged into a solution of hypo-sulphite of soda, and lastly, washed in distilled water. The process is then complete, and the sketch produced is in appearance something similar to aquatint, but greatly superior in delicacy; and such is the precision of the detail, that the most powerful microscope serves but to display the perfection of the copy.

DA'IS, in architecture, the platform or raised floor at the upper end of a dining hall, where the high table stood; also the seat with a canopy over it for those who sat at the high table.

DALMAT'ICA, a long white gown with sleeves; worn by deacons in the Roman Catholic church over the *alb* and *stole*. It was imitated from a dress originally worn in Dalmatia, and imported into Rome by the emperor Commodus, where the use of it gradually superseded the old Roman fashion of keeping the arms uncovered. A similar robe was worn by kings in the middle ages at coronations and other solemnities.

DAM'AGE-FEAS'ANT, in law, is when one person's beasts get into another's ground, without license of the owner or occupier of the ground, and do damage by feeding, or otherwise, to the grass, corn, wood, &c., in which case the party injured may distrain or impound them.

DAM'AGES, in law, the estimated equivalent for an injury sustained; or that which is given or adjudged by a jury to the plaintiff in an action, to repair his loss.

DAM'ASK, a fabric of silk, linen, wool, also partly or wholly of cotton, woven with large patterns of trees, fruits, animals, landscapes, &c., and one of the most costly productions of the loom. It consists throughout of a body of five or eight shanks, the pattern being of a different nature to the ground. Damask weaving first attained perfection at Damascus, whence this large-patterned fabric derives its name. We find the art flourishing in the mediæval times of Art at Bruges, and other places in Flanders; attempts were also made in Germany and France.

DAMASKEEN'ING, this term, derived from the Syrian Damascus, so renowned in Art, designates the different kinds of steel ornamentation. The first is the many-colored watered Damascus blades; the second kind consists in etching slight ornaments on polished steel-wares; the third is the inlaying of steel or iron with gold and silver, as was done with sabres, armor, pistol-locks, and gun-barrels. The designs were deeply engraved, or chased in the metal, and the lines filled with gold or silver wire, driven in by the hammer, and fastened firmly. This art was brought to great perfection by the French artist Corsinet, in the reign of Henry IV.

DAME, formerly a title of honor to a woman. It is now seldom otherwise applied than to a mistress of a family in the humbler walks of life.

DAM'NIFY, in law, to cause hurt or damage to; as, to *damnify* a man in his goods or estate.

DAMP'ERS, in music, certain parts in the internal construction of the pianoforte, which are covered with soft leather in order to deaden the vibration, and are acted on by a pedal.

DAM'SEL, (from the Fr. *damoiselle*,) a name anciently given to young ladies of noble or genteel extraction. The word is, however, now seldom used, except jocularly, or in poetry.—*Damoisel*, or *damoiseau*, the masculine of the same word, appears to have been applied to young men of rank; thus we read of *damsel* Pepin, *damsel* Louis le gros, *damsel* Richard, prince of Wales. From the sons of kings this appellation first passed to those of great lords or barons, and afterwards to those of gentlemen, who were not yet knights; but, such is the change which language undergoes, that at the present day it is only used (and then rarely) when speaking of young unmarried women. It occurs frequently in the Scriptures, and in poetry.

DANCE OF DEATH. This edifying subject is very frequently met with in ancient buildings, stained glass, and in the decorations of manuscripts, &c. The best known is that by Hans Holbein. It is frequently found in the margins of early printed books. One, from the press of Simon Vostre, in 1502, has a most interesting series, beautifully designed and executed. The earliest representation of this impressive subject dates from the fourth century; but it was rapidly multiplied, and introduced into many English and continental churches.

DAN'CING, may be defined to be a graceful movement of the figure, accompanied by gestures and attitudes indicative of certain mental emotions, and by measured steps in harmony with a piece of music arranged for the purpose. The great antiquity of dancing is attested by history, both sacred and profane. It consisted at first, probably, of nothing more than gesticulation and moving in a procession; in which sense it formed part of the celebration of the religious rites of the ancient Hebrews and Egyptians. But the Greeks, who are confessedly indebted to the Egyptians for the elements of their religion and literature, though these were afterwards refined by them to such a degree as nearly to obliterate all traces of their origin, soon polished and improved these sacred rites, and introduced them into all the festal ceremonies of which their elegant mythology was composed. In this they were, as usual, imitated by the Romans. If we believe Scaliger, the early bishops of the church were styled *præsules*, because (as the word literally implies) they led off the dance at their solemn festivals; and this practice continued in the church till the 12th century. Almost every country can boast of its national dances peculiar to the inhabitants; which it is rare to see so well performed when adopted by others. Of these the best known to us are the *tarantella* of the Neapolitans, the *bolero* and *fandango* of the Spaniards, the *mazourck* and *krakowiaque* of Poland, the *cosaque* of Russia, the *redowac* of Bohemia, the *quadrille* and *cotillon* of France, the *waltz* and *gallopade* of Germany, and the *reel* of Scotland. As an exercise, or amusement, dancing is nothing more than a methodized act instinctive in the human frame. To teach dancing, is to teach the activity of the body to display itself in a manner regulated by the principles of grace, or in imitation of steps and gestures which others have used with approbation. By its mechanical effects on the body, it inspires the mind with cheerfulness; while the music which accompanies it has effect upon the body as well as upon the mind.

DAN'DY, (from *dandiprat*, a little urchin, or probably from the French *dandin*, a ninny;) in modern usage, a male of the human species, who dresses himself like a doll, and who carries his character on his back.

DA'NEGELT, or DA'NEGELD, in England, an annual tax formerly laid on the English nation, for maintaining forces to oppose the Danes, or to furnish tribute to procure peace. It was at first one shilling, and afterwards two, for every hide of land, except such as belonged to the church.

DANGE'RIA, in old English law, a payment of money anciently made by the forest tenants to their lords, that they might have leave to plough and sow in the time of pannage or mast-feeding.

DAPH'NE, in Grecian mythology, a nymph of Diana, the daughter of the river god Peneus. She was beloved by Apollo; but she resisted all his attempts to excite in her a mutual attachment, and at last betook herself to flight. On being hotly pursued by the god, she invoked the earth to swallow her up, when her prayer was granted, and she was immediately changed into a laurel-tree.

DAPHNEPHO'RIA, in antiquity, a novennial festival celebrated by the Bœotians in honor of Apollo, to whom boughs of laurel were offered.

DAP'PLED, variegated with spots of different colors; as, a *dapple-bay* or *dapple-gray* horse.

DARAP'TI, in logic, an arbitrary term expressing the first mood of the third figure of syllogisms, where the first two propositions are universal affirmatives, and the last a particular affirmative.

DA'RIC, in antiquity, a Persian gold coin, said to have been struck by Darius, and supposed to have been equal to 25*s.* sterling.

DASH, in music, a small mark, thus ', denoting that the note over which it is placed is to be performed in a short and distinct manner.

DA'TA, among mathematicians, a term used for such things and quantities as are given or known, in order to find other things therefrom, that are unknown Euclid uses the word for such spaces, lines and angles, as are of a given magnitude, or to which we can assign others equal.

DATE, the notation of the time and place of the delivery or subscription of an instrument. The word is derived from the common formula at the foot of instruments, "datum," or "data," *given* at such a place and time. Dates of time are distinguished into definite and indefinite. The former mark specially the year, and sometimes the month, day, &c. the latter only contain a general reference to some period of time. Thus many instruments of the earlier part of the middle ages are dated only "*Regnante Domino nostro Jesu Christo;*" and very often the date contained only mention of the reigning prince, without reference to the years of his reign. Definite dates are various in ancient charters and deeds The Christian Greeks dated generally, down to the fall of Constantinople, by the year of the world; beginning their year at the 1st of September. The date used in the oldest Latin charters is commonly that of the indiction, which is also frequently added in the Greek. The Christian era (under the several names of year of grace, of the incarnation, of the reign of Christ, of the nativity, &c., &c.,) began to be in common usage in royal charters in France about the reign of Hugh Capet, in Spain and Portugal not until the 13th and 14th centuries. In England, the Saxon kings frequently dated by the incarnation; but deeds and charters under the Plantagenet kings generally bear the year of the reigning prince.

DA'TISI, in logic, an arbitrary term for a mode of syllogisms in the third figure, wherein the major proposition is a universal affirmative, and the minor and conclusion are particular affirmatives.

DA'TIVE, in grammar, the third of the Greek and Latin nouns.

DAU'PHIN, the title of the eldest son of the king of France. It is said that, in 1349, Humbert II., the last of the princes of Dauphiny, having no issue, gave his dominions to the crown of France, upon condition that the king's eldest son should be styled the *Dauphin*.

DAVID'S DAY, (St.) the 1st of March, kept by the Welsh, in honor of St. David, bishop of Miney, in Wales; who at the head of their forces obtained a signal victory over the Saxons. It is the in variable custom of the Welsh to wear leeks in their hats on this day.

DAWN, the commencement of the day, when the twilight appears.

DAY, according to the most natural and obvious sense of the word, signifies that part of the twenty-four hours when it is light; or the space of time between the rising and the setting of the sun; the time which elapses from its setting to its rising again being considered the night. The word day is often taken in a larger sense, so as to include the night also; or to denote the time of a whole apparent revolution of the sun round the earth. The day is also distinguishsd into *civil* and *astronomical*. The civil day is a space of twenty-four hours, reckoned from sunset to sunset, or from sunrise to sunrise, which is different in different parts of the globe. The astronomical day is the space of twenty-four hours, reckoned from twelve o'clock at noon to the noon of the next day.—The *nautical day* ends at the instant the astronomical day begins; so that nautical time in days of the month, is always twenty-four hours in advance of astronomical time, and the civil day is midway between both.—The Babylonians began the day at sun-rising; the Jews at sun-setting; the Egyptians at midnight, as do several nations in modern times, the British, French, Spanish, American, &c.—*Days of grace*, in commerce, a customary number of days allowed for the payment of a bill after it becomes due. *Three* days of grace are allowed in Great Britain and America. In other countries the time allowed is much longer, but the merchants there very rarely avail themselves of the time.

DEA'CON, a minister of religion, holding, in Protestant churches, the lowest degree in holy orders. The first appointment of deacons is mentioned in Acts vi., where the Apostles direct the congregation to look out seven men of honest report, upon whom they may lay their hands. Their office at this time seems to have been chiefly the care of the poor and the distribution of the bread and wine in the love feasts. We learn, however, from the example of Philip, Acts viii., that they also had authority to preach. In the English church it is the lowest of the three orders of clergy (deacons, priests and bishops.) The word is sometimes used in the New Testament for any one that ministers in the service of God; in which sense, bishops and presbyters are styled deacons; but, in its restrained sense, it is taken for the third order of the clergy. In the church of England, the form of ordaining a deacon declares that it is his office to assist in the distribution of the holy communion; in which, agreeably to the practice of the ancient church, he is confined to the administration of the wine to the communicants. A deacon is not capable of any ecclesiastical promotion; yet he may be chaplain to a family, curate to a beneficed clergyman, or lecturer to a parish church.—In the Romish church, the deacon's office is to incense the officiating priest, to incense the choir, to put the mitre on the bishop's head at the pontifical mass, and to assist at the communion.—In Presbyterian and Independent places of worship, the deacons distribute the bread and wine to the communicants.—In Scotland, an overseer of the poor, or the master of an incorporated company, is styled a *deacon*.

DEA'CONESS, a female deacon in the primitive church. This office appears as ancient as the apostolical age; for St. Paul calls Phœbe a servant of the church of Cenchrea. One part of their office was to assist the minister at the baptizing of women, to undress them for immersion, and to dress them again, that the whole ceremony might be performed with all the decency becoming so sacred an action.

DEAD LAN'GUAGE, a language which is no longer spoken or in common use by a people, and known only in writings; as the Hebrew, Greek, and Latin.

DEAN, a dignitary of the church of England, next to a bishop, and head of the chapter, in a cathedral or council.—*Dean and chapter*, are the bishop's council to assist him with their advice in the affairs of religion, and in the temporal concerns of his see.

DEATH, a total and permanent cessation of all the vital functions, when the organs have not only ceased to act, but have lost the susceptibility of renewed action. "Men," says Lord Bacon, "fear death, as children fear the dark; and as that natural fear in children is increased by frightful tales, so is the other. Groans, convulsions, weeping friends, and the like, show death terrible; yet there is no passion so weak but conquers the fear of it, and therefore death is not such a terrible enemy; revenge triumphs over death love slights it; dread of shame prefers it; grief flies to it; and fear anticipates it." The alarms most prevalent among mankind seem to arise from two considerations, viz., the supposed corporeal suffering attending it; and the state that is to succeed it. With respect to the supposed corporeal suffering, it may be observed, that death is a mere passive extinction of the vital fire, unattended with any exertion of the animal functions, and therefore wholly free from pain. The agonies and sufferings incident to sickness or wounds, are the agonies and sufferings of life, not of death; they are the struggles of the body to live, not to die; efforts of the machine to overcome the obstacles by which its functions are impeded. But when the moment of dissolution arrives, all sense of suffering is subdued by an instantaneous stoppage of life, or by a languid insensible fainting.—In law, there is a natural death and a civil death; *natural*, where actual death takes place; *civil*, where a person is not actually dead, but adjudged so by law; as by banishment, abjuration of the realm, &c.

DEATH'-WATCH, a little insect, which inhabits old wooden furniture, and is famous for striking with its head against paper or some other material, and thereby making a ticking noise, like the beat of a watch, which by ignorant and superstitious people is supposed to be a presage of death.

DEBATE', oral contention by argument and reasoning; or a controversy between parties of different opinions, professedly for elucidating the truth.—*Debates in congress*, the published report of arguments for and against a measure, in either house of congress.

DEBEN'TURE, a term used at the custom-house for a certificate signed by an officer of the customs, which entitles a merchant exporting goods to the receipt of a bounty, or a drawback of duties.—It also denotes a sort of bill drawn upon the government.

DEB'IT, a term used in book-keeping to express the left hand page of ledger, to which all articles are carried that are charged to an account.

DEBOUCH', in military language, to issue or march out of a narrow place, or from defiles.

DEBOU'CHEMENT, a French term for the marching of an army from a narrow place into one that is more open.

DEBT, in law, that which is due from one person to another, whether it be money, goods, or services.—In law, used elliptically for an action to recover a debt.—In scripture, sin; that which renders liable to punishment; as, "forgive us our *debts*."—*National debt*, the engagement entered into by a government to repay at a future period money advanced by individuals for public service, or to pay the lenders an equivalent annuity.

DE'BRIS, (pron. *debree*,) ruins or rubbish; applied particularly to the fragments of rocks.—The word *debris* is also used by the French to express the remains or wreck of an army that has been routed.

DEBUT', in its most general acceptation, is applied to the commencement of any undertaking, or to the first step made in a public career; but it is confined more particularly to the language of the theatre, in which it signifies the first appearance of an actor, or his first appearance on any particular stage.

DEC'ACHORD, or DECACHOR'DON, a musical instrument of ten strings.

DEC'ADE, a word used by some old writers in a general sense for the number ten, or an enumeration by tens.

DEC'ALOGUE, the ten commandments or precepts delivered by God to Moses, at Mount Sinai, originally engraved on two tables of stone. The Jews, by way of excellence, call these commandments The Ten Words, whence they afterwards received the name of *decalogue*.

DECAM'ERON, a work containing the actions or conversations of ten days.—*Decameron*, the name given by Boccaccio to his celebrated collection of tales; they are supposed to be narrated in turn, during ten days, by a party of guests assembled at a villa in the country to escape from the plague which raged at Florence in 1348.

DECAPITA'TION, a mode of punishment of great antiquity, having been practised by the Jews, Greeks, and Romans, and some other ancient nations. Among the continental nations of modern times, it has long been the ordinary punishment inflicted on all capitally convicted criminals. During the early period of English history, it was the usual mode of punishing felons; but it afterwards became a punishment appropriated only to criminals of the highest rank, and even to this day it is considered as the most honorable death which a capital offender can undergo. The last instance of the infliction of this punishment in England occurred in 1745, soon after the rebellion in Scotland had been quelled.

DEC'ASTICK, a poem consisting of ten lines.

DEC'ASTYLE, in architecture, a building with an ordnance of ten columns in front.

DECASYL'LABIC, having ten syllables. In the German and English languages the ordinary heroic verse is decasyllabic; but a short syllable is sometimes added at the end by way of a variety, and this, in consequence of the structure of those languages, takes place more frequently in the former than the latter. In the Italian heroic verse the eleventh syllable is almost uniformly added, and hence it is more properly to be termed an *hendecasyllabic*. In French versification the decasyllabic line is appropriated to light compositions, especially tales.

DECEM'BER, the last month of the modern year, consisting of thirty-one days; when the sun enters the tropic of Capricorn, and makes the winter solstice. It was so called from being the tenth month in the Roman year, which began with March.

DE'CEM PRI'MI, or DE'CEM PRIN'CIPES, in Roman antiquity, the ten chief men or senators of every city or borough.

DECEM'VIRI, properly any body of ten men appointed for particular purposes. But that which is especially known by this name was the commission elected from the Roman patricians in the 302d year after the foundation of the city, and invested with all the supreme powers of the state, for the purpose of drawing up a body of laws founded, according to Roman tradition, on the most approved institutions of Greece. They presented to the people a number of laws engraved on ten tables, containing a summary of the privileges to be enjoyed by the people, and the crimes to be punished, &c. At the same time they informed the people that their plan was incomplete; and accordingly a new commission, to which the plebeians were admitted, was appointed for the next year, with the same powers; the result of which was the addition of two more tables to the former ten, thus making up the famous twelve tables, which were the foundation of all Roman law in subsequent times. The second decemvirate did not demean itself with the same moderation as the first, but sought to prolong its power, and at the same time proceeded to some violent acts of despotism, which so exasperated the people as to make its dissolution necessary. Besides these extraordinary commissions, there was a body of decemviri chosen for judicial purposes, to preside over and summon the centumviri, and to judge certain causes by themselves. There were likewise decemviri appointed from time to time to divide lands among the military.

DECEN'NARY, in law, a tithing consisting of ten freeholders and their families. Ten of these decennaries constituted a *hundred*, the origin of which is ascribed to Alfred.

DECEP'TIVE CA'DENCE, in music, a cadence in which the final close is avoided by varying the final chord.

DECIMA'TION, a punishment inflicted by the Romans on such soldiers as quitted their post, or behaved themselves ill in the field. The names of all the guilty were put into an urn or helmet, from which a tenth part only were drawn, whose lot it was to suffer death.

DECK, the planked floor of a ship from stem to stern. Small vessels have only one deck; larger ships have two or three decks. Thus, speaking of the size of a large ship, we say, she is a *two-decker*, or a *three-decker*.

DECLAMA'TION, signified, among the ancients, the art of speaking indifferently upon both sides of a question: a species of intellectual exercise resorted to by the rhetoricians of Greece and Rome, as the best means of acquiring facility in public speaking. In modern times the meaning of *declamation* is different in different countries. In Germany, and in most parts of the Continent, it is often used in a sense nearly synonymous with *recitative*. In France and England, especially the latter, it is sometimes applied to any grand oratorical display, either in the pulpit, at the bar in the senate, or on the stage, in which the voice, gesticulation, and the whole delivery of the speaker are in perfect keeping with the subject matter of his address. But it is employed most usually in a disparaging sense, to indicate the use of forced emphasis, inflated language, and violent gestures, to withdraw the attention of the auditors from the weakness or fallacy of the reasoning.

DECLARA'TION, in law, that part of the process or pleadings in which a statement of the plaintiff's complaint against the defendant is set forth.—*Declaration of war*, a public proclamation made by a herald at arms to the subjects of a state, declaring them to be at war with some foreign power, and forbidding all and every one to aid or assist the common enemy at their peril.

DECLEN'SION, in grammar, the inflection of cases to which nouns are subject. Also, the act of going through these inflections.

DECLI'NATORY PLEA, in law, a plea before trial or conviction, intended to show that the party was not liable to the penalty of the law, or was specially exempted from the jurisdiction of the court.

DECOLLA'TION, a term in frequent use, synonymous with beheading, and used in reference to the decapitation of St. John the Baptist, St. Cecilia, &c.

DECORA'TION, the ornamental parts in an edifice, comprising the columns, pilasters, friezes, bas-reliefs, cornices, festoons, niches, statues, &c., and which form the decorations of the façade of a palace or temple; and the gilding, arabesques, paintings, panellings, carvings, the draperies, &c., which compose the decoration of an interior. The discoveries at Pompeii have furnished some very beautiful interior decorations, quite classical in taste.

DECO'RUM, in architecture, the suitableness of a building, and of its parts and ornaments, to their respective places and uses.

DECOY', in a general sense, any lure that deceives and misleads. Also, a sea term, for a stratagem employed by ships of war, to draw any vessel of inferior force into an incautious pursuit, until she comes within gun-shot. Decoying is also performed to elude the chase of a ship of superior force in a dark night; and this is done by committing to the sea a lighted cask of pitch, which will burn for a considerable time, and misguide the enemy. As soon as the cask is lowered, the ship changes her course, and thus, if at any tolerable distance from the foe, escapes with facility.

DECREE', the order of an authoritative power. In England, the sentence of the judges in the civil courts, and in chancery, is called a decree. In theology, the pre-determined purpose of God, whose plan of operations is, like himself, unchangeable.

DECREET', in the Scotch law, a final decree of judgment of the lords of session, from which an appeal only lies to parliament.

DECRESCEN'DO, in music, the term for gradually decreasing or weakening the sound; as opposed to *crescendo*.

DECRE'TAL, a letter from the pope, determining some point or question in ecclesiastical polity. The *decretals* form the second part of the canon law.

DECU'RIO, in Roman antiquity, a company of ten men under one officer or leader, who was called a *decurion*, their cavalry being divided into centuries, and the centuries subdivided into ten *decuriæ* each.

DECURIO'NES MUNICIPA'LES, a court of judges or counsellors representing the Roman senate in the free towns and provinces.

DEDICA'TION, the act of consecrating, or solemnly devoting, any person or thing to the service of God, and the purposes of religion.—*Feast of dedication*, an anniversary festival among the Jews, in memory of Judas Maccabæus, who repaired and dedicated anew the temple and altar, which had been plundered and profaned by Antiochus Epiphanes. It was observed on the 25th of Chisleu, and continued eight days.—*Dedication*, in literature, a complimentary address to a particular person, prefixed by an author to his work. Dedications arose out of the dependent situation in which authors have too frequently been placed in reference to their powerful or wealthy patrons; and, at no very distant time, were often rewarded by pecuniary presents. The custom of dedicating works was in use at a very early period. The brightest ornaments of Roman literature, Horace, Virgil, Cicero, and Lucretius, were among the number of those who practised it. At the period of the revival of letters in Europe, few works were published without dedications; many of which are remarkable for their elegance and purity of style, and from the interesting matter which they contain are of far more value than the treatises to which they are prefixed. But the practice became gradually perverted: and many of the authors of the succeeding generations employed them chiefly with the view of securing the patronage of the great. Dedications were most abused in France under Louis XIV., and in England from 1670 to the accession of George III. Dryden was a great dedicator, and Johnson wrote dedications for money. Corneille got 1000 louis d'or for the dedication of *Cinna*. Some of the most beautiful dedications with which we are acquainted are those prefixed to the different volumes of the *Spectator*, by Addison; and in more recent times the poetical dedications with which each canto of Sir Walter Scott's *Marmion* is prefaced.

DEDUC'TOR, a client amongst the Romans, who called upon his patron at his lodgings in the morning, waited upon him from thence to the forum, and attended him upon all public occasions.

DEED, in law, a written contract, sealed and delivered. It must be written before the sealing and delivery, otherwise it is no deed; and after it is once formally executed by the parties, nothing can be added or interlined; and, therefore, if a deed be sealed and delivered, with a blank left for the sum, which the obligee fills up after sealing and delivery, this will make the deed void. Every deed must be founded upon good and sufficient consideration; not upon a usurious contract, nor upon fraud or collusion, either to deceive *bona fide* purchasers, or just and lawful creditors; any of which considerations will vacate the deed. It takes effect only from the day of delivery; and, therefore, if a deed have no date, or a date impossible, the delivery will in all cases ascertain the date of it. The delivery of a deed may be alleged at any time after the deed; but unless it be sealed and regularly delivered, it is no deed. And lastly, it must be properly witnessed or attested; which, however, is necessary rather for preserving the evidence, than as intrinsically essential to the validity of the instrument.

DE FAC'TO, in law, something actually in fact, or existing, in contradistinction to *de jure*, where a thing is only so in justice but not in fact; as a king *de facto*, is a person that is in actual possession of a crown, but has no legal right to the same; and a king *de jure* is the person who has a just right to the crown, though he is not in possession of it.

DEFAMA'TION, the malicious uttering of falsehood with a view to injure another's reputation. Defamatory words written and published, constitute a *libel*.

DEFAULT', in law, a non-appearance in court without assigning sufficient cause. —*Defaulter*, one who fails to account for public money entrusted to his care.

DEFEAS'ANCE, in law, a condition relating to a deed, which being performed, the deed is defeated and rendered void. A *defeasance*, or a bond, or a recognizance, or a judgment recovered, is a condition which, when performed, *defeats* it.

DEFEC'TIVE FIFTH, in music, an interval containing a semitone less than the perfect fifth. It is also called semidiapente, and flat, lesser, or diminished fifth.

DEFENCE', in law, the reply which the defendant makes after the declaration is produced.—In military affairs, any work that covers or defends the opposite posts, as flanks, parapets, &c.

DEFEND'ANT, in law, the party that is summoned into court, and *defends*, denies, or opposes the demand or charge, and maintains his own right. It is applied whether the person defends, or admits he claim and suffers a default.

DEFEND'ER OF THE FAITH, a title bestowed on Henry VIII. of England by Pope Leo X., on the occasion of that monarch's publishing his writing against Luther. When at the Reformation Henry suppressed all the monasteries, and convents in England, the pope deprived him of this title; but in the thirty-fifth year of his reign it was confirmed by parliament, and it has been since constantly assumed by the sovereigns of England.

DEFILE', a narrow way, or pass, through which a company of soldiers can march only in file.

DEFINI'TION, the determining the nature of things by words; or a brief description of a thing by its properties. It is generally effected by adding to a generic word the essential and peculiar qualities or circumstances of the thing to be defined; but a strictly accurate definition cannot always be given; and the most simple things are generally the least capable of definition, from the difficulty of finding terms more simple and intelligible than the one to be defined.

DEFIN'ITIVE, a term applied to whatever terminates a process, question, &c. in opposition to provisional and interlocutory.—In grammar, a word used to define or limit the extent of the signification of an appellative or common noun.

DEFORCE'MENT, in law, the holding of lands or tenements to which another person has a right. In Scotland, it denotes a resisting of an officer in the execution of law.

DEGRADA'TION, in ecclesiastical affairs, the depriving a person of his dignity and degree; as the degradation of a clergyman by depriving him of holy orders.—In military affairs, the depriving an officer of his commission.—In painting, a lessening and obscuring of the appearance of distant objects in a landscape, that they may appear as they would do to an eye placed at a distance.

DEGREE', in universities, a mark of distinction conferred on the students or members thereof as a testimony of their proficiency in arts or sciences, and entitling them to certain privileges. This is usually evinced by a diploma. The first degree is that of *Bachelor of Arts;* the second, that of *Master of Arts*. Honorary degrees are those of *Doctor of Divinity*, *Doctor of Laws*, &c. Physicians also receive the degree of *Doctor of Medicine*. The origin of degrees at the universities of Paris and Bologna, the two most ancient in Europe, appears to have been only the necessary distinction between those who taught and those who learnt. The former were styled (such was at least the case at Paris) doctors or teachers, and masters, as a token of respect, indiscriminately. At what time the distinction between these two degrees arose we cannot ascertain; but about the middle of the 13th century we find, at Paris, doctors and masters simply as graduates, and not necessarily connected with the business of teaching; those who were so being called regent masters, or simply regents. The degree of Bachelor, the lowest in the several faculties, is certainly of French origin; from whence it has been argued that the whole system of academical titles is so likewise. Degrees still continue to bear the same names, and, with some variation, the same relative academical rank, in most European countries; but the mode of granting them, and their value at different universities as tokens of proficiency, vary greatly. At Oxford and Cambridge degrees are given in arts, divinity, law, medicine, and music; but among all these the lowest degree in arts, viz. that of bachelor, is the only one conferred on a substantial examination, and the only one which is attained by proceeding through a regular academical course of study. The higher degrees in arts, and those in the other faculties, are attained simply by residence and the performance of a few unimportant exercises. Honorary degrees, in the English universities, are generally conferred in civil law.

DEGREES *of comparison*, in grammar, the inflections of adjectives which express different degrees of the same quality; as, *good*, *better*, *best*.—*Degrees*, in music, the small intervals of which the concords or harmonical intervals are composed.

DE'ICIDE, a term only used for the condemnation and execution of the Saviour of the world, by Pontius Pilate and the Jews.

DEIFICA'TION, the act of deifying, or enrolling among the heathen deities.

DEI GRA'TIA, (*by the grace of God*,) a Latin formula, usually inserted in the ceremonial description of the title of a sovereign. It was used originally by the clergy.

DEI JUDI'CIUM, the old Saxon trial by ordeal, so called because it was supposed to be an appeal to God.

DEIPNOS'OPHIST, one of an ancient sect of philosophers who were famous for their learned conversation at meals.

DE'ISTS, in the modern sense of the word, are those persons who acknowledge the existence of one God, but disbelieve in revealed religion. Taking the denomination in the most extensive signification, a learned theologian has thus divided deists into four classes. 1. Such as believe the existence of an eternal, infinite, independent, intelligent Being, and who teach that this supreme Being made the world, though he does not at all concern himself in the management of it. 2. Those who believe not only the being, but also the providence of God with respect to the natural world, but who not allowing any difference between moral good and evil, deny that God takes any notice of the morally good or evil actions of men; these things depending, as they imagine, on the arbitrary constitutions of human laws. 3. Those who having right apprehensions concerning the natural attributes of God, and his all-governing providence, and some notion of his moral perfections also; yet being prejudiced against the notion of the immortality of the human soul, believe that men perish entirely at death, and that one generation shall perpetually succeed another, without any future restoration or renovation of things. 4. Such as believe the existence of a Supreme Being, together with his providence in the government of the world, as also the obligations of natural religion; but so far only, as these things are discoverable by the light of nature alone, without believing any divine revelation.

DE'ITY, the nature and essence of the Supreme Being; a term frequently used in a synonymous sense with God.—Also, a fabulous god or goddess; as, Jupiter, Juno, Apollo, &c.

DEJEU'NER, a term wholly naturalized in almost all the languages of modern Europe, not excepting the English, signifying the morning meal. The materials of which it is composed vary of course with the climate and usages of different countries; but it is worthy of remark that in France itself this term is rapidly losing, if indeed it has not already lost, its original acceptation, being used, particularly by the fashionable world, as synonymous with the English *luncheon*.

DEL CRED'ERE, a term in commerce expressive of a guarantee given by factors, who for an additional premium warrant the solvency of the parties to whom they sell goods upon credit.

DEL'EGATE, a commissioner of appeal appointed by the king to hear appeal causes from the ecclesiastical court.—

In the United States, a person elected to represent a territory in Congress, who has the right of debate, but not of voting.

DELEGA'TION, in the civil law, the act by which a debtor transfers to another person the duty to pay, or a creditor makes over to a third party the right to receive payment.

DELFT WARE, a coarse species of porcelain, originally manufactured at Delft in Holland, whence its name.

DEL'ICACY, in the fine arts, minute accuracy as opposed to strength or force: slenderness of proportion, great finish, and softness are its characteristics.

DELIR'IUM, a state in which the ideas of a person are wild and irregular, or do not correspond with the truth, or with external objects. Or it may be defined symptomatic derangement, or that which is dependent on some other disease, in distinction from idiopathic derangement or *mania*.

DELIV'ERY, a part of oratory, referring to the management of the voice; as, he has a good or graceful *delivery*.

DEL'PHI, OR'ACLE OF, so called from Delphi, the capital of Phocis, the most famous of all the oracles of antiquity, sacred to Apollo. The origin of the oracle at Delphi is wrapt in obscurity. By some authors it is ascribed to chance; but many incline to believe that it owed its origin to certain exhalations, which, issuing from a cavern on which it was situated, threw all who approached it into convulsions, and during their continuance communicated the power of predicting the future. Be this as it may, these exhalations were soon invested with a sacred character; and as their reputation extended, the town of Delphi insensibly arose around the cavity from which they issued. The responses were delivered by a priestess, called Pythia, who sat upon a tripod placed over the mouth of the cavern; and after having inhaled the vapor, by which she was thrown into violent convulsions, gave utterance to the wished-for predictions, either in verse or prose, which were then interpreted by the priests. Originally the consultation of the oracle was a matter of great simplicity; but in process of time, when the accuracy of the predictions became known, a series of temples, each more magnificent than its predecessor, was erected on the spot. Immense multitudes of priests and domestics were connected with the oracle; and to such a height of celebrity did it attain, that it wholly eclipsed all the other oracles of Greece. The position of the oracle was the most favorable that could well be imagined. Delphi formed at once the seat of the Amphictyonic council and the centre of Greece, and, as was universally believed, of the earth. Hence, in every case of emergency, if a new form of government was to be instituted, war to be proclaimed, peace concluded, or laws enacted, it came to be consulted, not only by the Greeks, but even by the neighboring nations; and thus the temple was enriched by an incredible number of the most valuable presents and the most splendid monuments, and the town of Delphi rose to be one of the most wealthy and important of the cities of Greece.—

DEL'PHIN, an edition of the Latin classics, prepared and commented upon by thirty-nine of the most famous scholars of the day, at the suggestion of Louis XIV., for the benefit of the young prince (in usum Delphini) under the superintendence of Montausier his governor, and his preceptors Bossuet and Huet.

DEL'UGE, an inundation or overflowing of the earth, either wholly or in part, by water.—We have several deluges recorded in history, as that of Ogyges, which overflowed almost all Attica, and that of Deucalion, which drowned all Thessaly, in Greece; but the most memorable was that called the universal deluge, or Noah's flood, from which only Noah and those with him in the ark, escaped. This flood makes one of the most considerable epochas in chronology. Its history is given by Moses in the book of Genesis, ch. vi. and vii., and its time is fixed to the year from the creation 1656. From this flood, the state of the world is divided into "diluvian" and "ante-diluvian."

DEM'AGOGUE, any factious orator who acquires great influence with the populace; whom he flatters, cajoles, or leads into danger, as best suits his purpose.

DEMAIN', or DEME'SNE, in law, a manor-house and the lands thereunto belonging, which the lord of the manor and his ancestors have time out of mind kept in their own occupation. It denotes also all the parts of any manor not in the hands of freeholders; and is frequently used for a distinction between those lands that the lord has in his own hands, or in the hands of his lessee demised at a rack-rent: or such other land appertaining to the manor, which belongs to free or copyholders.

DEMAND'ANT, in law, the pursuer in real actions, in distinction from the plaintiff.

DEMARCA'TION, Line of, every line drawn for determining a border, which is not to be passed by foreign powers, or by such as are at war with each other. The word was first introduced in 1493, when Pope Alexander VI., in order to put an end to the dispute, which prevailed between the crowns of Spain and Portugal, relative to their Indian discoveries and conquests by virtue of his pontifical authority drew through the ocean an imaginary line, by which the dominions of both parties were defined; and thus originated the expression *line of demarcation*. It is only in this phrase that the word is employed to this day in all the languages of Europe.

DEM'I, a half fellow at Magdalen College, Oxford.—Also, a term in composition, signifying half; as, *demigod*, a hero who was enrolled among the gods.

DEM'I-CADENCE, in music, an imperfect cadence, or one that falls on any other than the key-note.

DEM'IDITONE', in music, a minor third.

DEM'IGODS, a general appellation of the inferior divinities of Greece and Rome, more particularly of such of the mixed offspring of divinities and mortals as were afterwards deified. Of these the number was almost incredible; and though their worship was not cultivated with so much veneration or solemnity as that of the superior gods, it prevailed to a greater or less extent in every quarter of the ancient world, and formed a large part of the heathen mythology.

DEM'IQUAVER, in music, a note equal in duration to half a quaver.

DEM'ITINT, in painting, a tint representing the mean or medium between light and shade; by some called a *half* tint.

DEMI'SE, in law, is applied to an estate either in fee, for term of life or years, though most usually the latter.—The death of a king, or a queen regnant, is termed the demise of the crown, by which is implied a transfer of the royal authority or kingdom to a successor.—*Demise and re-demise*, a conveyance where there are mutual leases made from one to another of the same land, or something out of it.

DEMIUR'GUS, *Demiurge*, in the original sense of the word, as used by classical authors, an artificer employed in ordinary handicraft. In the language of Platonist writers, it denotes an exalted and mysterious agent, by whose means God is supposed to have created the universe. Hence the Demiurgus, or Logos, as the same imaginary agent is termed in the *Timæus* of Plato, is identified by the Platonizing Christians with the second person in the Trinity.

DEMOC'RACY, a form of government, in which the supreme power is lodged in the hands of the people collectively, or in which the people exercise the powers of legislation.

DEMOGOR'GON, in mythology, a mysterious divinity of antiquity, of whose origin, attributes, and history no satisfactory account can be given, in consequence of the obscurity in which they are enveloped. By some writers he is regarded as the author of creation; others consider him to have been a famous magician, to whose spell all the inhabitants of Hades were subjected; but all concur in viewing him as an object rather of terror than of worship.

DE'MON, or DÆ'MON, a name used by the ancients for certain supernatural beings, whose existence they supposed They were spirits or genii who appeared to men, either to do them service or to hurt them. The Platonists distinguish between gods, demons, and heroes; the demons being those since called angels Socrates and Tasso spoke, in very distant ages, of being each attended by a demon or familiar. In Tasso, this pretension has been referred to an hypochondriacal state of mind; in Socrates, the matter has given rise to much speculation. From the manner, however, in which the philosopher is said to have described his *demon*, there seems good reason to believe that he spoke figuratively of his natural conscience or intellect: "it directed him how to act in every important occasion of life, and restrained him from imprudence of conduct." The Greeks, from whom we derive the term in Scriptural language, applied it originally to the deified spirits of departed heroes, whom they supposed to have some influence in promoting the good of mankind, and considered therefore as objects of adoration. The manner, however, in which demons are represented in Scripture as evil spirits inflicting injury on men at the suggestion of the Father of Evil, is conformable to the oriental notion upon such points; except, indeed, that in the Scriptures the general supremacy of God, who suffers evil to exist, is maintained, in opposition to the eastern dogma of the eternal and equal conflict of the good and evil principles. The early fathers indulged in much speculation upon these subjects; but in modern times the literal interpretation of the agency of demons as referred to in Scripture has been frequently called in question. The demons, like the fairies and goblins of other mythologies, are represented with various characters of beneficence, malice, and wanton mischief. They were sometimes distinguished by the names Cacodemon and Agathodemon, according as their influence was evil or beneficent.

DEMO'NIACS, persons possessed by or under the influence of demons or devils, of whom mention is made in some passages in the New Testament. Some divines have supposed that such influence was permitted to the powers of evil at one particular time for the greater manifestation of our Lord's authority in rebuking them; but it is certain that the idea of demoniacal possession was very ancient among the oriental nations; and those to whom it seems incredible that it should have been grounded on fact, must be content with interpreting such passages of Scripture as a concession to the opinions and feelings of the Jewish people.

DEMONOL'OGY, the belief in an intermediate race of beings, between deity and humanity, has been a prevalent feature in almost every popular creed; and all tradition or speculation respecting it may be said to fall under the general term of demonology. Among the early oriental nations, especially the Persians and Egyptians, the science of astronomy appears to have been essentially connected with this branch of superstition; the heavenly bodies were honored as dæmons or celestial intelligences. This ancient belief appears to have had much influence on the Jewish rabbinical writers; and out of it connected with what is revealed to us in the Old Testament of the existence and attributes of angels, they framed their peculiar mythology. The Greek word δαιμων, *dæmon*, is said to be derived from δαημων, *knowing* or *intelligent*. In the earliest monuments of the language, its signification is vague and uncertain. In Homer it generally signifies a deity: δαιμονιον is anything godlike, wonderful, which may have been communicated or inspired by a deity; but, in the *Odyssey*, some traces are to be found of the meaning "fortunate" or "unfortunate" attached to the word. In Hesiod, however, we have an express mythological account of the dæmons,—as spirits, in a state between mortality and divinity, peaceful and favorable to man: he describes them as of different orders. The mortals who lived in the golden age have become dæmons of the first rank; those of the silver age have inferior honors, and are mortal, although their life is prolonged to a length of many hundreds of human generations. The heroes form a still inferior class of intermediate spirits. In popular language, when hero-worship became widely spread in Greece, the words hero and dæmon were used without much distinction; but the more recondite difference appears to have been this,—the hero was the departed worthy himself, such as he had once lived on earth; the dæmon was his immaterial part, converted into a sort of abstract principle,—a spiritual agent of good or evil, favorable or unfriendly to mankind. It is in this sense also that the inferior deities themselves are designated as dæmons. Thales is said to have defined more accurately the difference between gods, heroes as the souls of deceased mortals, and dæmons properly so called; and in Plato's theology the dæmons occupy an important place—as intermediate spirits, closely watching over, directing, and recording the actions of mortals. By later writers they were divided into many classes: some ministers of punishment and revenge, some freeing from evils already befallen, some warding off their approach. It was in Egypt and Syria, under the Ptolemies and Seleucidæ, that the Grecian philosophy and mythology came in contact with those of the Rabbis; and from that union a new mixed system of dæmonology took its origin. Hence, in the Greek of the New Testament, the word δαιμονιον is taken, without addition or qualification, as an evil spirit, and rendered by our translators "devil." Analogous to the dæmons of the Greeks were the genii of the Romans; but there were other peculiar and characteristic features about the belief in the latter which show it to be of a different origin, probably derived from the Etruscans, who, as some antiquarians believe, drew their mythology from the ancient source of Samothrace. The genii of the Romans were an innumerable host of spirits: every man, house, or city, had an attendant genius. The genius of every mortal is mortal as himself; accompanies him into life, and conducts him in all its vicissitudes. In this sense, the genius was a favorable companion: to enjoy the good things of life is represented as "indulging" or gratifying the genius; abstaining from them, as "defrauding him. Wine and flowers are appropriate offerings to him. But he is also the companion of the mischances as well as the pleasures of life; unless, as the difficulty appears sometimes to have been solved, the individual had his *pair* of genii good and bad. And this latter should appear to have been the popular belief among the Etruscans, as far as we can collect it, in a subject, where all is vague and indistinct; and it is impossible accurately to separate the abstract creations of philosophers and poets from the substantive objects of general belief. The Etruscans represented the evil genius as a dark and frightful figure, attending a mortal on one side, who is protected or followed on the other by a child or youth—the usual emblem of the good genius. The genius is often represented on vases and in ancient paintings as a winged figure: and a genius holding a torch downwards is the emblem of death. The dæmons of the middle ages were simply fallen angels or devils, according to the sense of the word in the New Testament; and hence demonology, in the language of modern writers, generally signifies the history of the supposed nature and properties of such evil spirits, and of the modern superstition respecting compacts between them and mankind.

DEMONSTRA'TION, a proof of a proposition founded on axioms and intermediate proof; called *a priori* when the effect is proved from the cause, and *a posteriori* when the cause is proved from the effect. It has been remarked that the knowledge acquired by demonstration, though certain, is not so clear and evident as intuitive knowledge. In every step that reason makes in demonstrative knowledge, there is an intuitive knowledge of that agreement or disagreement it seeks with the next intermediate idea, which it uses as a proof; for if it were not so, that yet would need a proof, since without the perception of such agreement or disagreement, there is no knowledge produced.

DEMUR', in law, to stop at any point in the pleadings, and rest or abide on that point in law for a decision of the cause.

DEMUR'RAGE, in commerce, an allowance made to the master of a ship by the merchants, for staying in a port longer than the time first appointed.

DEMUR'RER, in law, a pause or stop put to any action upon some point of difficulty which must be determined by the court before any further proceedings can be had in the suit. A demurrer confesses the fact or facts to be true, but denies the sufficiency of the facts in point of law to support the claim or defence. Demurrers are either *general*, where no particular cause is shown, or *special*, where the causes of demurrer are set forth.

DEMY', the name of paper of a particular size, of which great quantities are used for printing books on.

DENA'RIUS, in Roman antiquity, the chief silver coin among the Romans, worth 8 pence. As a weight, it was the seventh part of a Roman ounce.—*Denarius Dei*, God's Penny, or earnest money given and received by the parties to contracts. It was so called because in ancient times it was given to the church or to the poor.

DENDROPHO'RIA, in antiquity, the carrying of boughs or branches of trees; a religious ceremony so called, because certain priests called from thence *dendrophori*, or tree-bearers, marched in procession, carrying the branches of trees in their hands in honor of Bacchus, Cybele, Sylvanus, or any other god.

DEN'IZEN, in England, an alien who is made a subject by royal letters patent, holding a middle state between an alien and a natural born subject. He may purchase and possess lands, and enjoy any office or dignity; yet it is short of naturalization; for a stranger, when naturalized, may inherit lands by descent, which a denizen cannot do. If a denizen purchase lands, his issue that are born afterward may inherit them, but those he had before shall not; and as a denizen may purchase, so he may take lands by devise.

DENOUE'MENT, a French word, by modern custom nearly anglicized, signifying the development or winding up of any event.

DEN'TIL, in architecture, an ornament in cornices, bearing some resemblance to teeth; used particularly in the Corinthian and Ionic orders.

DE'ODAND, at common law, every personal chattel which has been the immediate occasion of the death of a human being, forfeited to the king on the finding of a coroner's inquest; to be applied as alms by his almoner.

DEONTOL'OGY, the science of duty; a term assigned by the followers of Jeremy Bentham to their own doctrine of ethics, which is founded on the tendency of actions to promote happiness.

DEPART'MENT, either a division of territory, as the *departments* of France; or a distinct class of official duties allotted to a particular person.

DEPLOY', the spreading of troops; a military term.

DEPO'NENT, in law, one who gives written testimony, under oath, to interrogatories exhibited in the court of Chancery.

DEPORTA'TION, a sort of banishment among the Romans, to some island or other place which was allotted to a criminal for the place of his abode, with a prohibition not to leave it, on pain of death.

DEPOS'IT, among civilians, something that is committed to the custody of a person, to be kept without any reward, and to be returned again on demand.

DEPOSI'TION, in law, the testimony given in court by a witness, upon oath.—*Deposition*, the settlement of substances dissolved in fluids; as, banks are sometimes called *depositions* of alluvial matter.—Also, the act of dethroning a king; or divesting any one in authority of his power and dignity.

DEPOT', a French word for a store or magazine for depositing goods or merchandise.

DEPRIVA'TION, an ecclesiastical censure, by which a clergyman is deprived of his dignity.

DEPUTA'TI, in antiquity, persons who attended the army for the purpose of carrying away the wounded from the field of battle and waiting on them. The armorers were also sometimes called *deputati*.

DEP'UTY, in a general sense, signifies a person appointed or elected to act for another; or who is sent upon some business by a community.—In law, a *deputy* is one who exercises an office in another's right; and, properly, the misdemeanor of such deputy shall cause the person he represents to lose his office.—By a *deputation* is generally understood the person or persons authorized and sent to transact business for others, either with a special commission and authority, or with general powers.

DER'ELICTS, in law, such goods as are wilfully relinquished by the owner. It also signifies a thing forsaken, or cast away by the sea; thus, lands which the sea has suddenly left are called *derelict lands;* and vessels forsaken at sea are called *derelict ships*.

DERIV'ATIVE, in grammar, any word derived (*i. e.* taking its origin) from another, called its *primitive*, as *manhood* from *man*, &c.

DEROGA'TION, the act of annulling, revoking, or destroying the value and effect of anything, or of restraining its operation; as, an act of parliament is passed in *derogation* of the king's prerogative.

DEROG'ATORY CLAUSE, in a person's will, is a sentence or secret character inserted by the testator, of which he reserves the knowledge to himself, with a condition that no will he may make hereafter shall be valid unless this clause is inserted word for word. This is done as a precaution to guard against later wills being extorted by violence or otherwise improperly obtained.

DER'VISE, or DER'VIS, a name given to various Mahometan priests or monks. Many of the dervises travel over the whole of the Eastern world, entertaining the people wherever they come with agreeable relations of the curiosities and wonders they have met with. There are dervises in Egypt, who live with their families, and exercise their trades, of which kind are the dancing dervises at Damascus. They are distinguished among themselves by the different forms and colors of their habits; those of Persia were blue; the solitaries and wanderers wear only rags of different colors; others carry on their heads a plume, made of the feathers of a cock; and those of Egypt wear an octagonal badge of a greenish white alabaster at their girdles, and a high stiff cap without anything round it. They generally profess extreme poverty, and lead an ascetic life.

DES'CANT, in music, composition in several parts. It is either *plain*, which consists in the orderly placing of many concords answering to simple counterpoint; *figurate* or *florid*, wherein discords are employed; or *double*, where the parts are so contrived that the treble or any high part may be made the bass, and the contrary.

DESCENT', in a general sense, is the tendency of a body from a higher to a lower place; thus all bodies, unless otherwise determined by a force superior to their gravity, descend towards the centre of the earth.—In law, it means transmission by inheritance; which is either lineal or collateral. Descent is *lineal*, when it proceeds directly from the grandfather to the father, from the father to the son, and from the son to the grandson; *collateral*, when it does not proceed in a direct line, but from a man to his brother, nephew, or other collateral representative.—*Descent*, in genealogy, the order of succession of descendants in a line or family; or their distance from a common progenitor.

DESCRIP'TION, in rhetoric, is used to designate such a strong and lively representation of any object as places it before the reader in a clear and satisfactory light. The execution of this task, as is universally admitted, is attended with great difficulty, and requires no ordinary powers. Indeed, such is the importance which some critics of eminence attach to the possession of this quality, that they have erected it into a standard whereby to estimate the productions of genius in every department of literature; and though such a test may seem somewhat arbitrary, yet when we consider the powers indispensably requisite to form a good description, we shall not be surprised to find that amid the galaxy of brilliant productions in other departments with which our literature is adorned, there are so few authors who have attained eminence in this. A good description, is simple and concise; it sets before us such features of an object as on the first view strike and warm the fancy; it gives us ideas which a statuary or a painter could lay hold of and work after them—one of the strongest and most decisive trials of the real merits of description. Hence among the qualities essentially necessary, and without which, indeed, even mediocrity is unattainable in this walk of literature, are an eye conversant with nature in all her aspects, a strong imagination wherewith to catch her grand and prominent features, and great simplicity and clearness of style to transmit the impression unimpaired to the imagination of others. There is no species of composition, prose or poetical, into which description does not enter in some shape; but the term has been borrowed from literature generally, and applied more particularly to those poetical productions which are devoted exclusively to the description of nature, such as Milton's *Allegro* and Thomson's *Seasons*. Hence, although Shakspeare may with great justice be styled a descriptive poet, from the exquisite descriptions of nature with which his unrivalled plays are interspersed; yet as his chief excellence lies in portraying the character and passions of man, he does not fall, properly speaking, within this category. By no writer, either of antiquity or modern times, was the faculty of description possessed in a more eminent degree than by Sir Walter Scott. All his delineations of natural scenery are executed with an unrivalled fervor of imagination: while at the same time they are marked by such traits of character and truth that every object is brought distinctly before the mind, and might without difficulty be transferred to canvass by the artist's pencil.

DESECRA'TION, a word denoting the very opposite of *consecration*, being the act of divesting anything of a sacred purpose or use to which it has been devoted.

DES'ERT, a large uninhabited tract of land, or extent of country, entirely barren. In this sense, some are sandy deserts, as those of Arabia, Libya, and Zaara: others are stony, as the desert of Pharan, in Arabia Petrea. "The Desert," absolutely so called, is that part of Arabia south of the Holy Land, where the children of Israel wandered forty years. But the term desert may be, and often is, applied to an uninhabited country, covered with wood or overrun with vegetation incapable of affording sustenance to man.

DESER'TER, an officer, soldier, or sailor, who absents himself from his post without permission, and with the intention not to return. The crime of desertion has in all ages and countries been regarded with peculiar detestation. In Greece and Rome, the deserter, during war, suffered death; during peace, was deprived only of civil rights: a sound and enlightened distinction. The military code of Great Britain inflicts "death or such other punishments as may be adjudged by a general court-martial" on deserters; thus leaving a proper discretionary power for the exercise of lenity in cases where the motives to the crime may bear the most favorable construction.

DESIDERA'TUM, is used to signify something wanted to improve or perfect any art or science, or to promote the advancement of any object or study whatsoever. The longitude is a *desideratum* in navigation. A tribunal to settle national disputes without war is a great *desideratum*.

DESIGN', in a general sense, the plan, order, representation, or construction of a building, &c., by an outline or general view of it. The word *design*, in painting, is used for the first draught of a large work, with an intention to be executed and finished in a more elaborate manner. Every work of design is to be considered either in relation to the art that produced it, to the nature of its adaptation to the end sought, or to the nature of the end it is destined to serve; thus its beauty is dependent on the wisdom or excellence displayed in the design, on the fitness or propriety of the adaptation, and upon the utility of the end. The considerations of design, fitness, and utility, have become the three great sources of beauty of form. This beauty frequently arises from the combined power of these expressions. Every work of art supposes unity of design, or some particular end proposed by the artist in its structure or composition. In forms considered simply as expressive of design, the only possible sign of unity of design is uniformity or regularity, by which the productions of chance are distinguished from those of design; and without the appearance of this, variety becomes confusion. In every beautiful work of art, we are not satisfied with mere design,—we must have elegant design, of which the grand feature is variety; it is this which in general distinguishes beautiful from plain forms, and without it uniformity is dull and insipid.

DESIGNA'TOR, in Roman antiquities, a species of master of the ceremonies, whose duty it was to assign to each person his proper place in the theatres and at the other public spectacles. Officers with this appellation were employed among the Romans on every occasion of public display, and in all domestic solemnities, whether of a joyful or mournful character. But the chief occupation of the *designator* consisted in arranging and marshalling the funerals of distinguished persons; and in this capacity he was attended by a troop of inferior officers, all arrayed in black, whose part it was, among other duties, to keep off the crowd, like the lictors of the magistrates.

DESIRE', a wish to possess some gratification or source of happiness which is supposed to be obtainable. It may be either spiritual, intellectual, or sensual; but when directed merely to sensual enjoyment, it differs little from animal appetite.

DES'POTISM, a form of government where the monarch rules by his sole and uncontrolled authority. In popular language, all governments are called despotical that are administered by one individual whose decisions are not controlled by any representative assembly or recognized subordinate authorities. Thus, we are in the habit of saying that the emperors of Austria and Russia and the king of Prussia are despotical or absolute sovereigns; meaning by this, that all legislative and executive measures seem to proceed from their free will. But the abstract idea of despotism goes farther than this; and means a government by a single individual with unlimited power over the lives and fortunes of his subjects. The prophet Daniel, in his description of the Babylonian monarch Nebuchadnezzar, has given what is perhaps the best account of this species of government. "All people, nations, and languages, trembled and feared before him: whom he would he slew, and whom he would he kept alive: whom he would he set up, and whom he would he put down." But though this gives a vivid idea of what is understood by a pure despotism, it can be regarded only as a popular, or rather poetical account, of a government where the sovereign is possessed of great power. The truth is, that a purely despotical government never had, and never can have, any existence in fact. How absolute or despotical soever, all sovereigns must conduct their government so as to procure the concurrence and support of a large, or, at all events, a powerful portion of their subjects. A despot is, after all, merely an individual, and becomes quite powerless when those masses of individuals, in whom the ability to coerce others really resides, disapprove of his proceedings. The prætorian bands in antiquity, the janissaries of Constantinople, and the grenadiers of Petersburg, must, at least, be led by opinion. But though the sanction of the instruments employed in his government be indispensable to the existence of a despot, it is but seldom that he dares trust to it only. The most absolute and tyrannical of the Roman emperors, when they wished to get rid of any obnoxious individual, dared not to order him to be executed, but were obliged to suborn false evidence, and to proceed against him according to legal forms: and so it is in all countries. Were the most absolute sovereign of whom we have any certain accounts openly to seize on the property of any individual in his dominions, or to put him to death, without being able to assign some apparently satisfactory grounds for doing so, the foundations of his power would be shaken to the very centre; and the repetition of such conduct would most likely occasion his deposition. The strength of absolute governments, when they embark in oppressive courses, depends on their being able to conceal or pervert the real facts of the case, so that the victims of their tyranny may be made to appear to be the victims of their justice. We may be assured that no ruler of any country emerged from the merest barbarism ever could, for any considerable period, openly commit on his own responsibility any gross injustice towards any considerable portion of his subjects. Those who have done so have rarely, if ever, failed to expiate their folly and tyranny by some signal punishment. Neither the government of Prussia nor Austria, nor even that of Russia, can be justly called despotical. Their rulers are controlled to a very great extent by the force of public opinion; and are influenced by a much more lively feeling of responsibility than the sovereigns of limited monarchies, or of countries in which the legislative functions are divided. It is this fear of their subjects that makes them so anxious, by laying restrictions on the freedom of the press, to conceal their conduct, or to obtain a favorable judgment upon it. There can be no despotism, nor any considerable approach towards despotical government, where the press is free and the people instructed; and it is to their influence in securing the freedom of the press, and consequently in enlightening public opinion, and making the bulk of the people acquainted with their *real* interests, that the advantage of representative assemblies and of a popular form of government is mainly to be found.

DESSERT′, a word, of doubtful etymology, signifying the last service at dinner, consisting of fruits and confections, &c. The modern dessert is probably equivalent to the *mensæ secundæ* of the Romans. If we believe Congreve, the term came into use among the French about the commencement of the 17th century, and was soon adopted into and naturalized in most of the European languages. In all the countries of Europe the splendor of the dessert has ever since the period of its introduction kept pace with the progress of refinement and civilization, and by many *gastronomes* the qualities and arrangement of a dessert are looked upon as the most valid test of all that is Attic in taste and refined in elegance.

DES′TINY, an inevitable necessity depending upon a superior cause. This doctrine has, under a variety of names, been embodied in almost all the religious systems of antiquity; and even in modern times, with a few modifications, it has been largely adopted by many sects of the Christian church. Destiny was called by the Romans *Fatum*, and by the Greeks Αναγκη, *Necessity*, or Μοιρα, *a Part*, as if it were a chain or necessary series of things indissolubly linked together. According to many of the heathen philosophers, destiny was a secret and invisible power or virtue, which with incomprehensible wisdom regulated all the occurrences of this world which to human eyes appear irregular and fortuitous. The Stoics, on the other hand, understood by destiny a certain concatenation of things, which from all eternity follow each other of absolute necessity, there being no power able to interrupt their connection. To this invisible power even the gods were compelled to succumb. Jupiter and Venus are represented by the poets as vainly attempting to withdraw Cæsar from his impending fate; but, as Seneca observes, it is thus that the Ruler of all things, in writing the book of destiny, has prescribed the limitation of his own power.

DETACH′ED, when figures stand out from the background and from each other in a natural manner, so as to show that there is space and atmosphere between, we say they appear *detached*.

DETACH′MENT, a body of troops selected or drawn out from several regiments or companies, on some special service or expedition. Also, a number of ships, taken from a fleet and sent on a separate service.

DET′INUE, in law, a writ or action that lies against a person who has goods or other things delivered to him to keep, and who afterwards *detains* or refuses to deliver them up.

DEUCE, DUSE, or DEUSE, a demon. A deviling, or little devil. The ancient Germans gave the name of *dusii* to certain demons, and it is supposed that the singular *dusius* is a corruption of Drusus, the son of Tiberius.

DEUTERON′OMY, one of the sacred books of the Old Testament, or the fifth book of the Penateuch. It is so called, because this last part of the work of Moses comprehends a recapitulation of the law he had before delivered to the Israelites himself.

DEVICE′, in painting, an emblem or representation of anything, with a motto subjoined or otherwise introduced. Badges, impresses, and devices, were greatly in vogue in England, from the reign of Edward I. to that of Elizabeth, when they began to be disused.

DEV′IL, the chief of the apostate angels; Satan, the tempter of the human race.

DEVISE', in law, is the disposition of real estate by will; being distinguished from a bequest of personal estate, that being termed a *legacy*. The person to whom a devise is made is called a *devisee*.

DEY, a Turkish title of dignity, given to the governors of Algiers (before the French conquest,) Tunis and Tripoli. The dey is chosen for life from among the chief authorities of the place, with the approbation of the Turkish soldiery. At Tunis the equivalent title of *bey* is more usually substituted for *dey*. This term is admitted by all philologists to be of very great antiquity; though it is impossible to assign any precise date to its introduction.

DIACRIT'IC MARKS, marks used to distinguish letters between the forms of which much similarity exists. Thus *n* and *u* are distinguished in German running hand by the mark ‿ over the latter letter.

DI'ADEM, the frontlet worn by the kings and princes of antiquity, and also by their wives. It was made of silk, wool, or yarn, narrow, but wider in the centre of the forehead, and generally white. Those of the Egyptian gods and kings are adorned with the emblem of the sacred serpent. The Bacchic diadem,

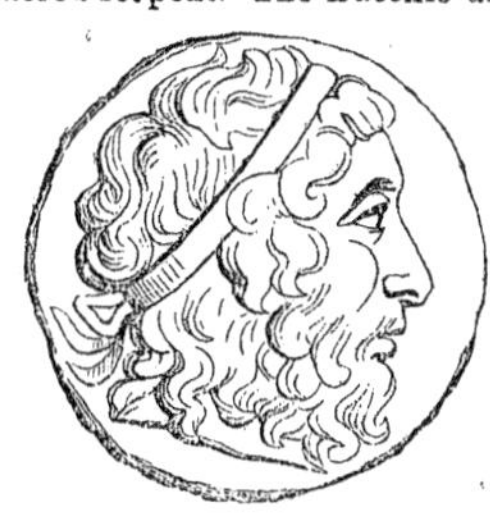

or *credemnon*, which the Indian Bacchus wore, consisted of a folded band encircling the forehead and temples, and fastened behind with hanging ends. With the Parsees (Persians) the diadem was wound round the tiara, and was bluish white. The Greeks presented a diadem to every victor in the public games; and it was also an attribute of priests and priestesses. The real diadem, like the sceptre, is a symbol of power, especially in the representation of Juno, who is thereby designated as the consort of the sovereign of the gods and men, and partaking of his power.

DIÆR'ESIS, in grammar, the resolution of a diphthong, or a contracted syllable into two syllables; as, in Latin, auraï for auræ, &c.; and, in English, the resolution of the last syllable of participles by a sound of the final *e*; belovëd, cursëd, &c.

DIAGNO'SIS, the art of distinguishing one disease from another. The characteristic symptoms of diseases by which they are recognized, are termed their diagnostic symptoms.

DI'AGRAM, the figure or scheme drawn for the illustration of a mathematical proposition, or the demonstration of any of its properties. It is also used in other branches of science, and in the fine arts, for the general purposes of illustration.

DI'AGRAPH, a name given by the French artists to a recently-invented instrument used in perspective.

DI'ALECT, in the philosophical sense of the word, any variety of a common language. Hence, German, English, Swedish, &c., are all strictly said to be dialects, as coming all of them from the same original stock. Commonly, however, we limit the application of the term dialect to the varieties of a national language; and speak of the dialects of English, French, &c. In Greek, the four dialects, Doric, Ionic, Æolic, Attic, were the four written varieties of the language, each possessing a literature of its own. In this respect no modern tongue presents a parallel to the Greek; inasmuch as, in all, one dialect has been arbitrarily adopted as the standard of polite writing and conversation; and the written works which are extant in the other dialects are regarded merely as exceptions to the general rule.

DIALEC'TICS, a name which was originally used by Plato as synonymous with metaphysics, or the highest philosophy. Strictly speaking, it can only be regarded as a preparatory discipline for such investigations, or at most as a scientific method of prosecuting them. The most splendid examples of dialectical subtlety that exist are to be found in the *Dialogues* of Plato, especially in those entitled *Parmenides*, *the Statesman and Sophist*. Aristotle expresses himself with some contempt of dialectics. It is certain, however, that its own logic owes its existence to the dialectical exercises of the Platonic schools; and that it may, in one point of view, be regarded as a body of canons and directions for their legitimate use. In modern times various systems of dialectics have been propounded in different countries; but by no philosophers, either ancient or modern, has this science been more successfully cultivated than by the Germans, who, among a host of other names more or less distinguished, can boast of a Fichte, Kant, Leibnitz, Hegel, Schelling, and Schlegel, as the propounders each of a peculiar dialectical system.

DI'ALOGUE, in literature, a composition or part of a composition in the form of a conversation between two or more persons. The dialogue was the form most generally adopted by the ancients for the conveyance of instruction, and was considered equally applicable to the most grave and philosophical, and to the most ludicrous and comical subjects. Thus it was adopted by Plato, Cicero, and Lucian, with equal success. Plato chose this form for the conveyance of his philosophical sentiments; because real conversation had been the mode by which his master, Socrates, (who left no writing,) gave instruction to the Athenians. In the *Dialogues* of Plato, Socrates is himself introduced as the chief interlocutor. Among modern writers the philosophical dialogue has been frequently employed for the same purpose, more especially by the French, to whose language and mode of thought it should seem to be peculiarly suited. Among other eminent persons of that country who have enriched its literature with this species of composition are, Fenelon; Paschal, in his *Provincial Letters;* Bouhours, in his *Entretiens d'Ariste et d'Eugène;* Fontenelle, in his *Dialogues of the Dead,* and *Plurality of Worlds;* Galiani, *Sur le Commerce des Grains,* &c. In England, this method of composition has been less frequently practised; and, perhaps, with the exception of Berkeley and Hurd, has rarely succeeded in the hands of those who attempted it. Both the Germans and Italians have attempted to impart a knowledge of their different philosophical systems in this manner. Among the latter may be mentioned Machiavelli and Algarotti; and among the former, Lessing, Mendelssohn, Schelling, and Herder; though the labors of none of these distinguished persons in this department of literature are so important as to require any particular notice in this place. The dramatic dialogue differs from the philosophical, inasmuch as its subject is one of action. The whole of modern dramas is dialogue, with the exception of occasional monologue or soliloquy.

DIAL'YSIS, a mark or character, consisting of two points placed over one of two vowels, as *mosaïc,* to separate the diphthong, and show that they must be sounded distinctly.—In rhetoric, *dialysis* is a figure of speech in which several words are placed together, without the aid of a conjunction, as *veni, vidi, vici.*

DI'AMOND, the most valuable and the hardest of gems. When pure, it is perfectly clear and pellucid, and is eminently distinguished from all other substances, by its vivid splendor, and the brightness of its reflections. Though found of different shapes, and sometimes accidentally tinged with several colors, yet it ever carries the same distinguishing characters. Diamonds are generally very small; but a few large ones have been found, for which incredible prices have been given. The largest ever known belonged to the king of Portugal; it weighed 1680 carats, and was valued, although uncut, at 224,000,000*l.* sterling; the one in the sceptre of the emperor of Russia weighs 779 carats, and is valued at upwards of 4,000,000*l.*, but was bought by the empress Catharine for about 135,000*l.* The Pitt diamond, which, at that time was one of the largest, weighed 136 carats, and cost Louis XIV. 130,000*l.* The Mogul diamond, called Koh-i-noor, or Mountain of Light, exhibited at the Great London Exposition of Industry in 1851, weighs nearly 280 carats, and was estimated by Tavernier at 468,959*l.*, or according to the rule proposed by Jeffries, it would be worth 622,000*l.* This diamond formed a part of the spoil taken in the Sikh war, on the defeat of Runjeet Singh, and was presented by the East India Company to Queen Victoria. The places whence diamonds are brought are the island of Borneo, and the king doms of Visapour, Golconda, Bengal, in the East Indies; and the Brazils, in the West Indies. These gems consist of pure carbon, with a specific gravity of 3·5; and the hardest tools making no impression on them, they are cut and ground by the power of their own substance. In the experiments of modern chemists, the diamond has been reduced to ashes by the power both of the furnace and the burning glass.—*Diamonds* are valuable for many purposes. Their powder is the best for the lapidary and gem engraver, and more economical than any other material for cutting, engraving, and polishing hard stones. Glaziers use them for cutting their glass; their diamond being set in a steel socket, and attached to a small wooden handle. It is very remarkable, that only the point of a natural crystal can be used; cut or split diamonds scratch, but the glass will not break along the scratch, as it does when a natural crystal is used. The diamond has also of late years become an article of great value to engravers, particularly in the drawing or ruling of lines, which are afterwards to be deepened by the use of aqua fortis; for which purpose steel points, called etching needles, were formerly used.

DIA'NA, in mythology, the Latin name of the goddess known to the Greeks by the name of Artemis, the daughter of Jupiter and Latona, and sister of Apollo. She was the virgin goddess of the chase, and also presided over health. The sudden deaths of women were attributed to her darts, as those of men were to the arrows of Apollo. In later times she was confounded with various other goddesses, as Hecate, Lucina, Proserpina, and Luna. In the two last of these characters she was said to appear in the nether world and in heaven respectively, while on earth she assumed the character of Artemis; whence she was called the three-formed goddess. She was generally represented as a healthy active maiden in a huntress's dress, with a handsome but ungentle expression of

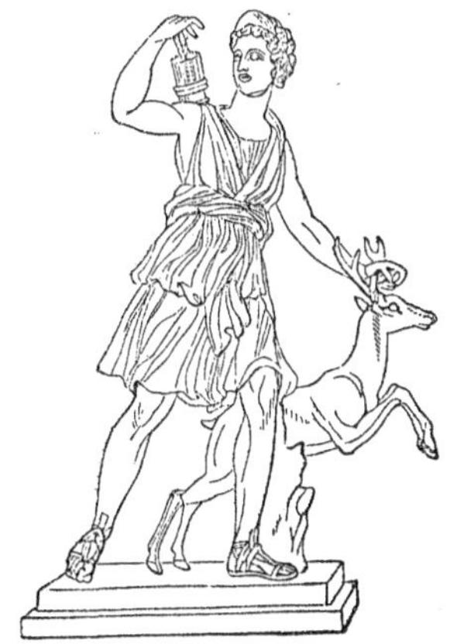

countenance. The homage rendered to Diana was so extensive that the silversmith who remarked that she was worshipped in all Asia and the world, can scarcely be accused of exaggeration. A catalogue of the various places where temples were erected in her honor would comprise every city of note in the ancient world. Among others may be mentioned Ephesus, Abydos, Heraclea, Aulis, Eretria, Samos, Bubastus in Egypt, Delos (whence she was termed Delia,) and Mount Aventine at Rome. But of all her temples, that at Ephesus was the most celebrated. It was erected at the joint expense of all the states of Asia; and according to the accounts of ancient authors, it must have surpassed in splendor all the structures of antiquity, and fully deserved to be regarded as one of the wonders of the world. A small statue of the goddess, or, as she was termed by her votaries, the "Great Diana of the Ephesians," which was commonly supposed to have been sent from heaven, was here enshrined and adorned with all that wealth and genius could contribute. The fate of this temple is well known. On the day that Alexander the Great was born, it was set on fire by Eratostratus, from a morbid desire to transmit his name even with infamy to posterity. This edifice was afterwards rebuilt on a plan of similar magnificence; and it remained in full possession of its wealth and reputation till the year 260, A.D., when it was completely destroyed during an invasion of the Goths.

DIANŒ'A, in rhetoric, a figure of speech by which a correct interpretation is given to a subject suitable to the occasion.

DIAPA'SON, in music, a musical interval, by which most authors, who have written upon the theory of music, use to express the octave of the Greeks. The diapason is the first and most perfect of the concords; if considered simply, it is but one harmonical interval; though, if considered diatonically, by tones and semitones, it contains seven degrees, viz., the three greater tones, two lesser tones, and two greater semi-tones.—*Diapason*, the fundamental or standard scale by which musical instruments are made.

DIAPEN'TE, in music, a fifth; an interval making the second of the concords, and with the diatessaron, an octave.

DI'APER, DIAPER WORK, a kind of ornamental decoration applied to plain surfaces, in which the pattern of flowers or arabesques are either carved or painted. When they are carved, the pattern is sunk entirely below the general surface; when painted they are generally of a darker shade of the same color as the plain surface. The patterns are usually square, and placed close together, but

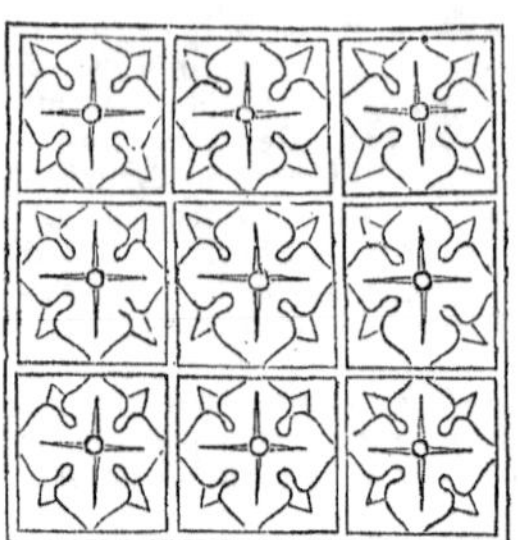

other floriated forms are sometimes met with.

DIAPH'ANOUS, an appellation given to all transparent bodies, or such as transmit the rays of light.

DIAPHO'RA, in rhetoric, a figure of speech, in which a word, when repeated, is taken in a different sense from what it was at first understood.

DIAPORE'SIS, in rhetoric, a figure of oratory, expressive of the speaker's doubt or hesitation as to the manner in which he should proceed in his discourse, the subjects he has to treat of being all equally important.

DI'ARY, signifies properly a note-book or register of daily occurrences, in which the writer has a principal share, or which have come under his own observation, or have happened in his own time. The term *diary* is equivalent to the French *journal*, the Italian *diario* and *giornale*, and the German *Tagebuch*.

DI'ASCHISM, in music, the difference between the comma and enharmonic diesis, commonly called the lesser comma.

DIA'SIA, in Grecian antiquity, a festival kept at Athens in honor of Jupiter the *Propitious*.

DIASTAL'TIC, an epithet given by the Greeks to certain intervals in music, as the major third, major sixth, and major seventh.

DIAS'TEMA, in rhetoric, a modulation of the tones of the voice, by marking with precision the intervals between its elevation and depression.—In *music*, a space or interval.

DIAS'TOLE, in grammar, a figure of prosody, by which a syllable naturally short is made long.

DI'ASTYLE, an edifice in which three diameters of a column are allowed for the intercolumniations.

DIASYR'MOS, in rhetoric, a kind of hyperbole, being an exaggeration of something low and ridiculous; ironical praise.

DIATES'SARON, in music, a concord or harmonic interval composed of a greater tone, a lesser tone, and one greater semitone. Its proportion is as 4 to 3, and it is called a perfect fourth.—In theology, the four Gospels.

DIA'TONI, in ancient architecture, the angle stones of a wall, which were wrought on two faces, and which, from stretching beyond the stones above and below them, made a good bond or tye to the work.

DIATON'IC, an epithet given to music, as it proceeds by tones and semitones, both ascending and descending. Thus we say, a *diatonic* series; a *diatonic* interval; *diatonic* melody or harmony.

DI'ATRIBE, a continued disputation or controversial discourse.

DIAZENET'IC, in the ancient Greek music, a term applied to the tone disjointing two fourths, one on each side of it, and which joined to either made a fifth.

DIAZO'MA, in ancient architecture, the landings or resting places which encircled the amphitheatre at different heights, like so many bands or cinctures; whence the name.

DI'CAST, in ancient Greece, an officer answering nearly to our juryman.

DICASTE'RIUM, in ancient architecture, the name of a tribunal or hall of justice in Athens.

DICE, cubical pieces of bone or ivory, dotted on their face from one to six; and used for gambling purposes. They are said to be of great antiquity, and to have been invented by Palamedes at the siege of Troy, for the amusement of the officers and soldiers.

DICTA'TOR, in ancient Rome, a magistrate created in times of exigence and distress, and invested with unlimited power. He had authority to raise or disband troops, and to make war or peace, and that without the consent either of the senate or people. The ordinary duration of his office was only for six months, during which time all other magistracies cease, the tribuneship excepted. Whenever he appeared in public, he was attended by twenty-four lictors, or double the number allowed a consul. Extensive, however, as his power was, he was nevertheless under some restrictions: he could not, for instance, spend the public money arbitrarily, leave Italy, or enter the city on horseback. The choice of dictator was not, as in the case of other magistrates, decided by the popular voice, but one of the consuls appointed him by command of the senate. A dictator was also sometimes named for holding the *comitia* for the election of consuls, and for the celebration of public games. For the space of four hundred years this office was regarded with veneration, till Sylla and Cæsar, by becoming perpetual dictators, converted it into an engine of tyranny, and rendered the very name odious.

DIC'TIONARY, in its first and most obvious sense, signifies a vocabulary, or alphabetical arrangement of the words in a language, with their definitions. But now, that the various branches of science have become so much extended, the term is also applied to an alphabetical collection of the terms of any art or science, with such explanations or remarks as the writer may deem necessary for their elucidation.

DIC'TUM, a word used in common parlance to signify the arbitrament or award of a judge.

DICTYOTHE'TON, in ancient architecture, masonry worked in courses like the meshes of a net. Also open lattice work for admitting light and air.

DIDAC'TIC, in the schools, signifies every species of writing, whether in verse or prose, whose object is to teach or explain the rules or principles of any art or science. Thus to this class of literature belong the writings of Aristotle on grammar, poetry, and rhetoric; Longinus's Treatise on the Sublime; and the *Institutions* of Quintilian, &c. But the term has been borrowed from scholastic phraseology, and appropriated more exclusively to all poetical writings devoted to the communication of instruction on a particular subject, or of a reflective or ethical character, thence called *didactic poetry*. Among the most celebrated poems of this species may be reckoned in ancient times that of Lucretius, *De Rerum Naturâ*, in which the Epicurean system of philosophy is explained; Virgil's *Georgics*, which has almost always served as a model to the didactic poets of succeeding ages; and Horace's *Art of Poetry;* and in more recent times, Pope's *Essays on Criticism* and *Man;* Du Fresnoy's *Art of Painting;* Vida and Boileau's *Art of Poetry;* Akenside's *Pleasures of the Imagination;* Armstrong's *Art of preserving Health;* Somerville's *Chace;* Dyer's *Fleece;* Young's *Universal Passion*, &c.

DIDASCA'LIA, a term in use among the Greek writers of antiquity, and till within the last century among almost all the nations of modern Europe, applied to the representation of dramatic pieces, or to critical notices of the stage, and of every thing appertaining thereto.

DIDO'RON, in ancient architecture, a brick whose length was one foot, and its breadth one half its length.

DIE, a stamp used in coining, by which a piece of prepared metal is impressed with due force. Coins are generally completed by one blow of the coining-press. The engraver selects a forged plug of the best cast steel of proper dimensions for his intended work, and having carefully annealed it, and turned its surfaces smooth in the lathe, proceeds to engrave upon it the intended device for the coin. When this is perfect the letters are put in, and the circularity and size duly adjusted; it is then hardened, and is termed a *matrix*. Another plug of soft steel is now selected; and the matrix being carefully adjusted upon it, they are placed under a very powerful fly-press, and two or three blows so directed as to commence an impression of the matrix upon the plug; this is then annealed, and the operation repeated till the plug receives a perfect impression of the work upon the matrix. This impression is of course in *relief*, the original work upon the matrix being indented, and produces what is termed the *punch*. This, being duly shaped in the lathe, is hardened, and is employed in the production of impressions in soft steel or *dies*, which, being properly turned and hardened, are exact *fac-similes* of the original matrix, and are used in the process of *coinage*. When a pair of dies are made of good steel duly hardened and tempered, and are carefully used, they will sometimes yield from two to three hundred thousand impressions before they become so far worn or injured as to require to be removed from the coining presses.

DI'ES, (days,) in law, are distinguished into *dies juridici*, days on which the court sits for the administration of justice; *dies non juridici*, days on which no pleas are held in any court of justice; and *dies datus*, a day or time of respite, given by the court to a defendant in the cause.—*Dies caniculares*, in astronomy, the dog-days.—*Dies critici*, in medicine, days in which some diseases are supposed to arrive at a crisis.—Among the Romans, days were distinguished in a variety of ways; the most important of which were *dies nefasti* or *dies atri*, days devoted to religious purposes, on which it was unlawful to do any public business: *dies fasti*, similar to the *dies juridici* of modern times; and *dies feriati*, like our *dies non juridici*, when the courts were shut.

DIE'SIS, the mark ‡; called also a double-dagger, and used as a mark for reference.—*Diesis*, in music, the division of a tone less than a semi-tone; or an interval consisting of a less or imperfect semi-tone.

DI'ET, a name given to the principal national assembly in many countries of modern Europe. By the usage of the *German empire*, two diets were summoned every year by the emperor, besides such as were convoked on extraordinary occasions. There were three chambers—1. That of the electors. 2. That of the sovereign princes, divided into two spiritual and four temporal benches. The counts of the empire voted collectively in four benches or divisions, and not as individuals; the prelates and the abbots in two. 3. The chamber of the imperial cities, divided into the Rhenish and Swabian benches. The diets, together with the emperor, exercised the prerogatives of sovereignty. A decree of the diet was termed a recess of the empire.

DIETET'ICS, the science or philosophy of diets; or that which teaches us to adapt particular foods to particular organs of digestion, or to particular states of the same organ, so that the greatest possible portion of nutriment may be extracted from a given quantity of nutritive matter.

DIEU ET MON DROIT, (French; signifying *God and my right;*) the motto of the royal arms of England, first assumed by king Richard I., to intimate that he did not hold his empire in vassalage of any mortal. It was afterwards taken up by Edward III., and was continued, without interruption, to the time of William III., who used the motto *je maintiendray*, though the former was still retained upon the great seal. After him queen Anne used the motto *semper eadem*, which had been before used by queen Elizabeth, but since queen Anne's time *Dieu et mon droit* has continued to be the royal motto.

DIEU ET SON ACTE, a maxim in law, that the act of God shall not be a prejudice to any man.

DIFFARREA'TION, in Roman antiquity, a ceremony whereby the divorce of the priests was solemnized; or the dissolving of marriage contracted by confarreation.

DIF'FERENCE, in logic, an essential attribute belonging to any species that is not found in the genus; being the idea that defines the species.

DIGAM'MA, so called from its representing two gammas, one set above another, thus, F. The name given to the form of that letter in the ancient Greek alphabet which corresponds in appearance generally to the Latin F. This letter appears to have occupied the sixth place in the alphabet, and was most prevalent in the Æolic dialect; though some grammarians contend that it was common to all the dialects of Greece in their more ancient mode of pronunciation. It has often been expressed by B, and sometimes by Γ, Δ, Θ, Φ, and X; and it is now almost universally considered to have had the force of F, V, or the English W. As the Latin language approximated more nearly to the Æolic than to any of the other Grecian dialects, the use of the digamma is very prevalent in many Latin words.

DI'GEST, in law literature, a collection of the decisions of the Roman lawyers, properly digested or arranged under distinct heads, by order of the emperor Justinian. It is also termed the Pandects, from the Greek words παν, *all*, and δεχεσθαι, *to receive*. The care of this great compilation was entrusted by the emperor to Tribonian, with seventeen associates. It was completed in three years, and published A.D. 533. It contains the best decisions and opinions of former jurists, collected, it is said, from more than two thousand volumes; and follows the same arrangement as the code of the same emperor, which had appeared in 529.

DIG'LYPH, in architecture, a kind of imperfect triglyph, console, or the like, with two channels or engravings, either circular or angular.

DIG'NITARY, in the canon law, an ecclesiastic who holds a dignity, or a benefice which gives him some pre-eminence over mere priests and canons; as a bishop, dean, arch-deacon, prebendary, &c.

DIG'NITY, this word, in a general sense, signifies a nobleness or elevation of mind; and is opposed to *meanness* and *vice*, the true dignity of human nature being based on moral rectitude and religious veneration. In a more extended sense, it means, elevation of deportment; and also an elevated office, civil or ecclesiastical.

DI'GRAPH, a union of two vowels, of which one only is pronounced, as in *bread*. It is essentially different from a diphthong, which consists of two vowels also but produces a sound which neither of the vowels has separately.

DIGRES'SION, signifies any details introduced into a work, which are either altogether foreign from the immediate subjects of which it treats, or not absolutely necessary to the progress or development of the story. It will at once be perceived from this definition that, as a general rule, digressions are to be carefully avoided, from their tendency to withdraw the attention of the reader from the chief points of the story or the question under discussion. There are, however, some departments of literature in which the use of digressions is not only admissible, but even advantageous. On this subject, however, no definite rules can be laid down for the guidance of the author: but there can be little doubt that if introduced properly and without effort, managed with good taste, and confined within reasonable limits, digressions have the effect of relieving the mind from the fatigue of a too long sustained attention, and of imparting life and interest to a subject that may be naturally dry and uninteresting. The Essays of Montaigne exhibit more clearly than any similar productions with which we are acquainted, the admirable uses to which digressions may be turned in the hands of a master. Many of the writings of Sterne, but more especially his *Tristram Shandy*, (which contains an eulogium upon digression,) supply the happiest examples of their effects; and in our times *The Doctor*, by Robert Southey, owes its principal attractions to the digressions with which the story is interlarded.

DILAPIDA'TION, in law, the ruin or damage which accrues to a house in consequence of neglect.

DILEM'MA, in logic, an argument which cannot be denied in any way without involving the party denying in contradictions; or a position involving double choice, each presenting difficulties. A dilemma is usually described, as though it always proved the absurdity, inconvenience, or unreasonableness of some opinion or practice, and this is the most usual design of it. But it is plain, that it may be used to prove the truth or advantage of any thing proposed: as, "In heaven we shall either have desires, or not: if we have no desires, then we have full satisfaction: if we have desires, they shall be satisfied as fast as they arise: therefore, in heaven we shall be completely satisfied." This sort of argument may be composed of three or more members, and may be called *trilemma*. It is also called *syllogismus cornutus*, a horned syllogism; its horns being so disposed, that if you avoid the one, you run against the other.

DILET'TANT, a term wholly naturalized in France, England, and Germany; signifying an amateur, chiefly of music, but also of the kindred sciences. The dilettant is one who treats Art empirically, a lover of art who is not satisfied with looking and enjoying, but must needs criticize without the necessary qualifications for so important a function. The dilettant holds the same relation to the artist, that the bungler does to the artisan, he takes hold of art by the weak end; conscious that art is learned according to rules, he errs in treating its laws as mechanical when they are spiritual. He confounds art with material; he regards neatness and finish, which are mechanical, as the highest excellences. Invention, composition, coloring, being spiritual, are invisible to him. Having no confidence in the application of his *rules*, he applies them empirically, and follows, as nearly as he can, the direction of popular taste. While the aim and endeavor of the artist is the highest in art, the dilettant has no aim: he sees only what is beside him—nothing beyond. Many dilettants are collectors; they are fond, if possessed of the means, of *raking together*, their object being to possess, not to choose with understanding, and be content with a few good things. The dilettants do great injury to artists, by fostering the mechanical, rather than the spiritual, in art, and by bringing them down to their own level. Yet, on the other hand, dilettantism has its advantages; it prevents an entire want of cultivation, and as it is in some sort a necessary consequence of a general extension of art, it may even be the cause of it. Under certain circumstances it may excite and develop a true artistic talent, and substitute a certain idea of art, in place of entire ignorance, and extend it to where the artist would not be able to reach; though few artists can be connoisseurs, many are dilettants.

DIMINU'TION, in architecture, a contraction of the upper part of a column, by which its diameter is made less than that of the lower part. It generally commences from one third of the height of the column.—*Diminution*, in rhetoric, the exaggerating what you have to say by an expression that seems to diminish it.—In music, the imitation of or reply to a subject in notes of half the length or value of those of the subject itself.

DIMIN'UTIVE, in grammar, a word or termination which lessens the meaning of the original word; as, *rivulet*, a small river; *manikin*, a little man.

DIM'ISSORY, dismissing to another jurisdiction.—*A letter dimissory*, is one given by a bishop to a candidate for holy orders, having a title in his diocese, directed to some other bishop, and giving leave for the bearer to be ordained by him.

DIM'ITY, a kind of white cotton cloth, ribbed or figured. It was originally imported from India, but is now manufactured in Lancashire, and various other parts of Britain.

DIO'CESAN, a bishop who has charge of a particular diocese.

DI'OCESE, or DI'OCESS, the district or circuit of a bishop's jurisdiction. The name diocese began first to be used in the fourth century, when the exterior polity of the church began to be formed upon the model of the Roman empire. England, in regard to its ecclesiastical state, is divided into two provinces, viz.: Canterbury and York, and each province into subordinate dioceses; the province of Canterbury contains twenty-one dioceses, and that of York three. The dioceses of the Prot. Epis. Church in the United States are nearly equivalent to the several states in extent.

DIONY'SIA, in ancient history, the festivals of Dionysius or Bacchus, but more particularly those that were celebrated in Attica, which were three in number, distinguished by the following titles:—1. The Country Dionysia. 2. Those in Limnæ, a part of the city of Athens, where they were held, which were also called Lenæan, or Anthesteria; and 3. The Great Dionysia. At all of these festivals the chief amusements consisted in the representation of stage plays; but the last was most celebrated, as then, before the face of all Greece, the great tragic contests were held, no expense being spared to render the decorations and accompaniments as splendid as art could make them.

DIORA'MA, a mode of painting or scenic representation, invented by two French artists, Daguerre and Bouton, and recently brought forward as a public exhibition in all the principal cities of Europe. The peculiar and very high degree of optical illusion produced by the diorama depends upon two principles; the mode of exhibiting the painting, and the manner of preparing it. With respect to the first of these, the spectator and the picture are placed in separate rooms, and the picture viewed through an aperture, the sides of which are continued towards the picture, so as to prevent any object in the picture room from being seen excepting the painting itself. Into the room in which the spectator is placed no light is admitted excepting what comes through this aperture from the picture; he is thus placed in comparative darkness, and also (which contributes to the effect) at a considerable distance from the picture. The picture room is illuminated from the roof, which is glazed with ground glass; and the picture so placed that the light falls on it at a proper angle to be reflected towards the aperture. The roof, which is invisible to the spectator, is provided with an apparatus of folds or shutters, by which the intensity of the illumination may be increased or diminished at pleasure, and so modified as to represent, with great effect and accuracy, the different *accidents* of light and shade, or the changes of appearance depending on the state of the atmosphere; as bright sunshine, cloudy weather, or the obscurity of twilight. The second principle consists in painting certain parts of the picture in transparency, and admitting a stream of light upon it from behind, which, passing through the picture, produces a brilliancy far surpassing what could be obtained by illuminating the picture in the ordinary way, and renders the relief of the objects represented much stronger and more deceptive. Hence, the diorama is peculiarly adapted for representing architectural objects, as the interiors of cathedrals, &c. In order to render the exhibition more attractive, it is usual to present more scenes than one. This may of course be effected by removing one picture and substituting another; but with a view to prevent the illusion from being impaired by the accidents incidental to scene-shifting, a different method is sometimes resorted to.

DIPH'THONG, the union of two vowels pronounced in one syllable. The sound is not simple, but so blended as to be considered as forming but one syllable, as *noise*, *bound*, *joint*, &c.

DIPLO'MA, a written document, conferring some power, privilege, or honor, viz., an instrument or license given by colleges, societies, &c., to a clergyman to exercise the ministerial function, or to a physician to practise the profession, &c., after passing examination, or admitting him to a degree.—Every sort of ancient charter, donation, bull, &c., is comprehended by writers on diplomatics under the name diploma. The term is derived from the earliest charters of donation with which we are acquainted, those of the early Roman emperors having been inscribed on two tablets of copper joined together so as to fold in the form of a book. Writings of earlier date than the fifth century are generally on leaves of the papyrus, or *biblos Ægyptiaca;* those of a later period on parchment. The form and character of the diploma granted by the sovereigns, prelates, nobles, &c. of modern Europe, varied from age to age; and the knowledge of these variations forms an important branch of the science of diplomatics.

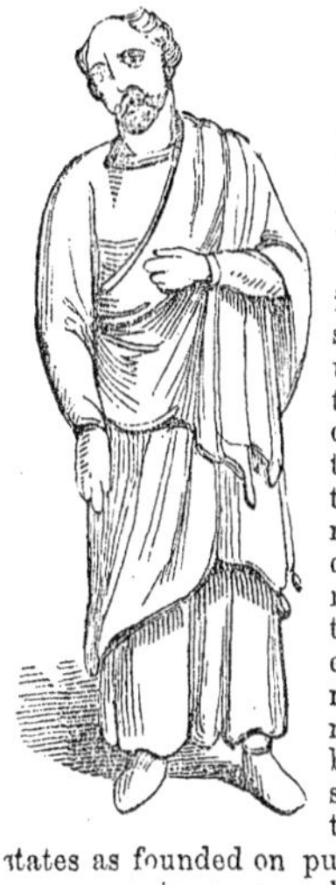

DIP'LOIS, in Grecian costume, a kind of doubled cloak, which, when worn, was folded back in the manner shawls are usually worn.

DIPLOM'ACY, in its most restricted sense, is used to express the art of conducting negotiations or arranging treaties between nations by means of their foreign ministers, or written correspondence; but, in its most extended signification, it embraces the whole science of negotiation with foreign states as founded on public law, positive engagements, or an enlightened view of the interests of each. It has been truly observed, that in times not very distant, it was sufficient to entertain a royal master by the gossip of a capital, the intrigues of ladies and gentlemen of the bed-chamber, and the cabals of rival ministers. Now, the political correspondent of a cabinet is compelled to inquire into the working of the complex machinery of modern society; to observe constantly the pulse of the whole body politic; to keep in view the moral and physical resources of nations; to defend the rights of his country, on the grounds of law and reason; to give information to the minister, from whom he holds his instructions, and to enable his government to profit by the intelligence he imparts, not only in the management of its foreign concerns, but likewise of its internal resources. To be a perfect diplomatist, in fact, in the present state of the world, a man should be well acquainted with the municipal laws of different countries, versed in the sciences, from which industry and art derive their splendor, and a state its strength, and equal to any of the tasks to which those with whom he is brought into contact might put his learning and sagacity.—It was one part of the business of the congress assembled at Vienna, in 1814, to regulate the degrees of rank to which the various *diplomatic agents* were entitled, viz.: 1, ambassadors; 2. envoys extraordinary and ministers plenipotentiary; 3, ministers resident; 4, *chargés d'affaires;* 5, secretaries of legation and *attachés.* Ministers at a court are denominated a *diplomatic* body.

DIPLOMAT'ICS, the science of deciphering ancient writings, assigning their date, &c. The name is derived from *diploma.* Writings of earlier date than the fifth century were mostly on the leaves of the papyrus, or *biblos Ægyptiaca.* Parchment appears to have been first generally used in that century; and the oldest documents bearing the character of diplomas which we possess do not extend to a higher antiquity. Not long after the general adoption of parchment, a variety of substances and colors began to be used in writing, as vermilion, purple, gold and silver; but this sumptuous fashion did not long remain in use. The science of diplomatics teaches the different styles and forms adopted in ancient public documents; the titles, rank, &c., of public officers whose names are subscribed to them; the knowledge of the materials used in writing in different ages, of the different characters used in successive periods and in various countries; and the several kinds of diplomas or public instruments. This science is said to owe its origin to a Jesuit of Antwerp, named Papelroch, who devoted himself arduously to the research and exposition of old diplomas about the year 1675; but the honor of having reduced it to a science, and established it on a sure and more satisfactory foundation, is due to Mabillon, whose learned work, *De Re Diplomatica*, was given to the world in 1681. The principles laid down by Mabillon, however, were more fully developed about the middle of last century, in one of the most elaborate works of which the literature of any nation can boast, the *Nouveau Traité de Diplomatique;* and which has left little to be done by subsequent laborers in this field beyond the duty of translation, compilation, or abridgment. From the above statement of the objects of this science, it will be at once perceived that it is of immense utility. It has greatly facilitated the researches of the historian, the politician, the divine, the political economist; and has contributed to the elucidation of points in the history of nations which might otherwise have been forever buriedin obscurity.

DIP'TERAL, in architecture, a temple which had a double range of columns on each of its flasks.

DIP'TYCHA, or DIP'TYCH, in Roman antiquity, a public register of the names of the consuls and other magistrates. Among the early Christians, they were tablets, on one of which were written the names of the deceased, and on the other those of the living patriarchs, bishops, &c. or those who had done any service to the church. The letters were written inside these tablets, and on the outside were slight reliefs, making the specimens still extant not a little interesting in the history of Art. The whole class of diptycha, together with the triptycha and pentaptycha, belong to the later Roman empire, and are, therefore, curious as the last effort of Antique and also as remnants of Early Christian Art; they are distinguished as *consular*—those presented by the magistrates upon receiving that office; and *ecclesiastical.* They were made of wood as well as of ivory, and some are extant of chased silver. *Diptycha consularia* bore the portraits of the consuls, representations of the games in the circus and scenes of triumph, &c. The *diptycha ecclesiastica* are decorated with scenes from Biblical history. They were very common during the middle ages, and were often most exquisitely wrought.

DI'RÆ, in the Roman divination, signifies any unusual accidents or uncommon appearances, as sneezing, stumbling, strange voices, apparitions, spilling salt or wine upon the table or upon one's clothes, meeting wolves, hares, foxes, &c.

DI'RECT, in music, a character used at the end of a staff, to direct the performer's notice to the succeeding note at the beginning of the following staff.

DIRECT TAX, taxes are distinguished into *direct* and *indirect.* A tax is direct when it is paid by the persons who permanently own, or use, or consume the subject of the tax. An indirect tax falls ultimately on a different person from the one who immediately pays it to the government. Thus the importer of goods pays a duty on them to the government, but reimburses himself by charging the amount of this duty in the price of the goods.

DIREC'TORS, in commerce, the name given to the individuals composing the board of management of a joint stock company.

DIREC'TORY, in French history, the name given by the constitution of 1795 to the executive body of the French republic. It consisted of five individuals, called directors, who were selected by the council of elders from a list of candidates presented by the council of five hundred. One of these directors retired every year, and was succeeded by another elected on the same principle. To the directory was entrusted the superintendence of the home and foreign departments, the finances and the army, and the appointment of the ministers of state and other public functionaries. Its policy was at first moderate and conciliatory; but after a short interval it had recourse to measures which produced wide-spread dissatisfaction, and it was at length overthrown on the ascendency of Bonaparte after an existence of four years.—*Directory*, signifies also a book containing the names of the inhabitants of a town, arranged in alphabetical order, together with their places of abode, &c. It is likewise applied to a book containing directions for public worship, or other religious services.

DIRGE, a song or tune intended to express grief, sorrow, and mourning.

DIS, a prefix or inseparable proposition, which generally has the force of a privative and negative; as, *disarm*, *disallow*, *disoblige.* In some cases, however, it denotes separation, as in *distribute*, *disconnect.*

DISABIL'ITY, in law, an incapacity in a man to inherit or take a benefit which otherwise he might have done, which may happen by the act of any ancestor; by the act of the party himself; by the act of the law; and by the act of God.—*Disability* differs from *inability*, in denoting deprivation of ability; whereas inability denotes destitution of ability, either by deprivation or otherwise.

DISAFFEC'TION, in a political sense, signifies disloyalty; not merely alienation of affection, but positive dislike and enmity.

DISCHARGE', a word of various significations. Applied to *fire-arms*, it means an explosion; to *fluids*, a flowing, issuing, or throwing out, as water from a spring or spout. It also denotes a *dismissal* from office or service; a *release* from debt, obligation, or imprisoment; and the *performance* of any office, trust, or duty.

DISCI'PLE, one who learns anything from another: thus, the followers of any teacher, philosopher, &c., are called disciples. In the more common acceptation, among Christians, the disciples denote those who were the immediate followers and attendants on Christ, of whom there were seventy or seventy-two; but the word is also correctly applied to all Christians, as they profess to learn and receive his doctrines and precepts. The words *disciple* and *apostle* are often synonymously used in the gospel history, but sometimes the apostles are distinguished from disciples as persons selected out of the number of disciples, to be the principal ministers of his religion.

DISCIPLINA'RIAN, one who is well versed in military and naval tactics and manœuvres; and who exacts a strict observance of them from those under his command.

DIS'CIPLINE, signifies, primarily, instruction or government; but it is applied figuratively to a peculiar mode of life, in accordance with the rules of some profession or society. It is also used to designate the punishments employed in convents, and those which enthusiasts undergo or inflict upon themselves by way of mortification.

DIS'CIPLINE, Book of, in the church of Scotland, is a common order, drawn up by the General Assembly in 1650 for the reformation and uniformity to be observed in the discipline and policy of the church. In this book episcopal government is set aside, Kirk sessions are established, the observance of saints' and other holy days is condemned, and other regulations for the internal government of the church are prescribed. It is called the First Book of Discipline.

DISCLAIM'ER, in law, is a plea containing an express denial or renunciation of some claim which has been made upon or by the party pleading. It is more especially taken for the denial, by an alleged tenant, of his tenancy.

DISCOBO'LUS, a thrower of the discus, the attitude of which is rendered

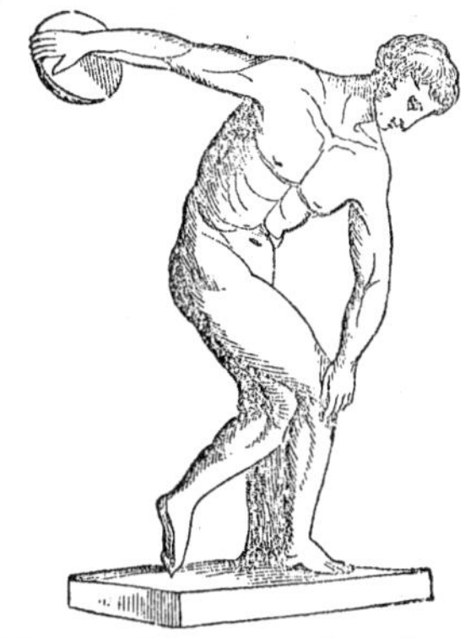

familiar to all by the celebrated statue by the sculptor Myron

DISCONTIN'UANCE, in law, an injury to real property, which consists in the keeping out the rightful owner of an estate by a tenant whose entry was at first lawful, but who wrongfully retains the possession afterwards.

DIS'CORD, in music, a union of sounds which is inharmonious, grating, and disagreeable to the ear; or an interval whose extremes do not coalesce. It is opposed to *concord* and *harmony*. The second, fourth, and seventh. with their octaves, and, in general, all intervals, except those few which precisely terminate the concords, are called discords. There is, notwithstanding, what is termed the *harmony of discords*, wherein the discords are made use of as the solid and substantial part of the harmony; for by a proper interposition of a discord, the succeeding concords receive an additional grace.

DISCOR'DIA, in mythology, a malevolent deity, daughter of Night, and sister of Erinnys, the Parcæ, and Death. She is represented as having been banished from heaven by Jupiter, on account of the broils she perpetually occasioned. This was the goddess who, from disappointment at not being invited to the marriage of Thetis and Peleus, threw into the midst of the assembly the golden apple, with the inscription *detur pulchriori*, (*let it be given to the fairest;*) which, as is well known, occasioned the famed contest between the goddesses Juno, Minerva, and Venus, and ultimately led to the Trojan war, and the destruction of Troy. The ancient poets represent this divinity with a pale and ghastly look, a dagger in her hand, and her hair entwined with serpents.

DIS'COUNT, an allowance made for the payment of money before it is due, and is equivalent to the interest of the principal sum diminished by the discount during the time that must elapse before the money becomes payable.

DISCOURSE', in rhetoric, signifies in its widest acceptation a series of sentences and arguments arranged according to the rules of art, with the view of producing some impression on the mind or feelings of those to whom it is addressed. In logic, this term is applied to the third operation of the mind, commonly called reasoning.

DISCOV'ERY, in a general sense, that which is discovered, found out, or revealed; as, the discovery of America by Columbus; or the properties of the magnet were an important discovery.—*Discovery*, in law, the disclosing or revealing anything by a defendant in his answer to a bill filed against him in a court of equity.

DISCRE'TIVE, in logic, an epithet applied to a proposition expressing some distinction, opposition, or variety, by means of *but*, *though*, *yet*, &c.; as, men change their dresses, *but* not their inclinations.

DISCUM'BENCY, the act of leaning at meals, according to the manner of the ancients.

DIS'CUS, in antiquity, a quoit made of stone, iron, or copper, five or six fingers broad, and more than a foot long, inclining to an oval figure, which they hurled in the manner of a bowl, to a vast distance, by the help of a leathern thong tied round the person's hand who threw it, and put through a hole in the middle.

DISEASE', any state of a living body in which the natural functions of the organs are interrupted or disturbed, either by defective or preternatural action. A disease may affect the whole body, or a particular limb or part of the body; and such partial affection of the body is called a *local* or *topical* disease.

DISFRAN'CHISE, to deprive of chartered rights and immunities; or to deprive of some franchise, as the right of voting in elections, &c.

DISJUNC'TIVE, in grammar, an epithet for conjunctions, which unite sentences, but separate the sense, as *but*, *nor*, &c.—A *disjunctive proposition*, in logic, is one in which the parts are opposed to each other by means of disjunctives; as, "it is either day or night."—A *disjunctive syllogism*, is, when the major proposition is disjunctive; as, "the earth moves in a circle, or an ellipsis; but it does not move in a circle, therefore it moves in an ellipsis."

DISPATCH'ES, in politics, a packet of letters sent by a public officer on some affair of state or public business.

DISPENSA'TION, in ecclesiastical affairs, the granting of a license, or the license itself, to do what is forbidden by laws or canons, or to omit something which is commanded. Also, a system of principles and rites enjoined: as the *Mosaic dispensation*, that is, the Levitical law and rites; the *Gospel dispensation*, or scheme of human redemption by Jesus Christ.

DISPOSI'TION, a word of extensive application, very generally signifying method, distribution, arrangement, or inclination. Thus we speak of the *disposition* of the several parts of an edifice; the *disposition* of the infantry and cavalry in an army; the judicious *disposition* of a person's effects; a *disposition* in plants to grow upwards; a *disposition* in animal bodies to putrefaction; a person's *disposition* to undertake particular work, &c.

DISPUTA'TION, in the schools, a contest, either by words or writing, on some point of learning for a degree, prize, or for an exercise. Also a verbal controversy respecting the truth of some fact, opinion, or argument; as, Paul *disputed* with the Jews in the synagogue.

DISQUALIFICA'TION, that which incapacitates in law; implying a previous qualification, which has been forfeited; and not merely the want of qualification.

DISQUISI'TION, formal or systematic examination into the circumstances of any affair, in order to discourse about it, and so arrive at the truth.

DISSEC'TION, the dividing an animal body into its substantial parts, for the purpose of examining its structures and uses. Le Gendre observes, that the dissection of a human body, even dead, was held a sacrilege till the time of Francis I.; and that he has seen a consultation held by the divines of Salamanca, at the request of Charles V. to settle the question whether or not it were lawful in point of conscience to dissect a human body for the purposes of anatomical science.

DISSEIS'IN, or DISSEIZ'IN, in law, an illegal seizure of a person's lands, tenements, or other incorporeal rights. The person dispossessing is called the *dissei-*

sor, and the person dispossessed, the *disseisee*.

DISSENT'ER, one who separates from the service and worship of any established church. In England, therefore, the word is particularly applied to those who do not conform to the rites and service of its church as by law established. The principles on which dissenters separate from the church of England, are, the right of private judgment, and liberty of conscience. They maintain that Christ, and he alone, is the head of the church, and that they bow to no authority, in matters of religion, but that which proceeds from him.

DIS'SONANCE, in music, inharmonious or discordant sounds.

DISSYL'LABLE, in grammar, a word consisting of two syllables only; as, *kingdom*, *virtue*.

DISSOLU'TION, the separation of a body into its elementary principles; or a cessation of the powers by which it was held together. We speak of the *dissolution* of animal bodies, when the parts separate by putrefaction; and of a reduction of a substance into its smallest parts, by a dissolvent or menstruum. We also say, the *dissolution* of the world, when we refer to its final destruction; and the *dissolution* of government, when it can no longer hold together.

DIS'TAFF, the staff of a spinning-wheel, to which a bunch of flax is tied, and from which the thread is drawn. This implement is of frequent occurrence in ancient Art. It was made out of a cane-stick, of about three feet in length. At the top it was slit in such a manner that it should bend open, and form a receptacle for the flax or wool to be spun. A ring was put over the top as a kind of cap to keep the ends of the cane together. The distaff occurs in representations of the fates, who are engaged in spinning the thread of life. Distaffs of gold were given to goddesses. It was dedicated to Pallas, the patroness of spinning.

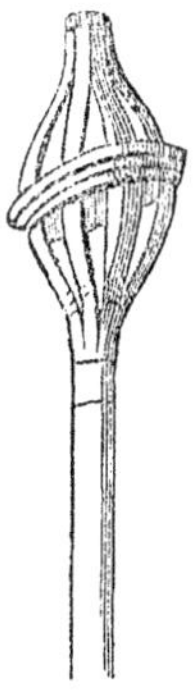

DISTEM'PER, DESTEMPER, DETREMPE (*Fr.*,) TEMPERA (*Ital.*) A kind of painting, in which the pigments are mixed in an aqueous vehicle, such as *size*, and chiefly applied to scene-painting and interior decoration. In former times, when this description of painting was more extensively employed than at present, the vehicles for the pigments were the sap of the fig-tree, milk, and white of egg. Many of the works of the old masters were executed in distemper, and afterwards oiled, by which process they became almost identical with oil-paintings, or pictures executed with an oleaginous vehicle. By many persons, unacquainted with the processes of painting, distemper is regarded as identical with fresco painting. The difference is this—distemper is painted on a *dry* surface, fresco on *wet* mortar or plaster.

DIS'TICH, a couplet, or couple of verses in poetry, making complete sense.

DISTINC'TION, in a general sense means the act of separating or distinguishing. It also denotes elevation of rank or character. Thus we say, of men who hold a high rank by birth or office, as well as of those who are eminent for their talents, services, or moral worth, that they are persons of *distinction*.—*Metaphysical distinction* is the non-agreement of being, whereby *this* entity is not *that*, or one thing is not another.—*Distinction*, or *distinguo*, is also used, in the schools, as an expedient to evade an argument, or to clear up and unfold an ambiguous proposition, which may be true in one sense, and false in another thus they say, "the respondent was hard pressed, but he disengaged himself by a *distinguo*."

DISTRESS', in law, the *distraining* or seizing upon a person's goods for the payment of rent or taxes, &c.

DISTRIBU'TION, the act of dividing or separating; as, the distribution of property among children; or the distribution of plants into genera and species.—In logic, the distinguishing a whole into its several constituent parts.—In medicine, the circulation of the chyle with the blood.—In architecture, the dividing and disposing of the several parts of a building, according to some plan, or to the rules of the art.—In printing, the taking a form asunder, so as to separate the types, and place each letter in its proper cell or box in the cases.—*Distributive justice*, implies, that justice is so administered by a judge, as to give every man his due.—*Distributive*, in grammar, words which serve to distribute things into their several orders, as *each*, *either*, *every*, &c.

DIS'TRICT, a word applicable to any portion of land or country, or to any part of a city of town, which is defined by law or agreement. A governor, a prefect, or a judge may have his *district;* or states and provinces may be divided into *districts* for public meetings, the exercise of elective rights, &c.—*District*, in law, that circuit or territory within which a man may be forced to make his appearance.

DISTRIN'GAS, in law, a writ commanding the sheriff, or other officer, to distrain a person for debt, or for his appearance at a certain day.

DITHYRAM'BUS, a sort of hymn anciently sung in honor of Bacchus, full of transport and poetical rage: any poem written with wildness. The *dithyrambic poetry* was very bold and irregular, for the poets not only took the liberty to coin new words for the purpose, but made double and compound words, which contributed very much to the wild magnificence of this kind of composition.

DI'TONE, in music, an interval comprehending two tones. The proportion of the sounds that form the ditone is 4 : 5, and that of the semi-ditone, 5 : 6.

DIT'RIGLYPH, in architecture, an arrangement of intercolumniations in the Doric order, by which two triglyphs are obtained in the frieze between the triglyphs that stand over the columns.

DIT'TO, in book-keeping, more usually contracted into *do*, signifies *the same* as that which precedes it. It is derived from the Italian word *ditto*, signifying *the said.*

DIT'TY, a word of great antiquity in the English language, signifying most usually a simple or pastoral song. Milton, Shakspeare, Dryden, and many of the old classic English writers, have repeatedly given importance to this word.

DIUR'NAL, is the name given to the book containing those canonical hours of the Roman Catholic breviary which are to be said during the day. It is intended especially for the clergy of the Romish church, and consists generally of four volumes, one for each season of the year.

DIVAN', a council-chamber, or court in which justice is administered, in the eastern nations, particularly among the Turks. There are two sorts of divans, that of the grand seignior, called the council of state, which consists of seven of the principal officers of the empire; and that of the grand vizir, composed of six other vizirs or counsellors of state, the chancellor, and secretaries of state for the distribution of justice.—The word *divan*, in Turkey, also denotes a kind of stage, which is found in all the halls of the palaces, as well as in the apartments of private persons. It is covered with costly tapestry, and a number of embroidered cushions leaning against the wall; and on it the master of the house reclines when he receives visitors. From this, a kind of sofa has obtained the name of divan. It would seem that the earliest acceptation in which this word was employed is that of a muster-roll or military day-book; and we find it used, especially by the ancient Arabs, who borrowed it from the Persians, to signify a collection of poems by one and the same author, arranged in alphabetical order; thus we hear of the divan (*i. e.* the collected poems) of Sadi, the divan of Hafiz, &c.

DIVER'SION, in military tactics, an attack on an enemy, by making a movement towards a point that is weak and undefended, in order to draw his forces off from continuing operations in another quarter.

DIV'IDEND, the part or proportion of profits which the members of a society, or public company receive at stated periods, according to the share they possess in the capital or common stock of the concern. The term is applied also to the annual interest paid by government on various public debts. In this sense, the order by which stockholders receive their interest is called a *dividend warrant*, and the portions of interest unreceived are denominated *unclaimed dividends.* It also signifies the sum a creditor receives from a bankrupt's estate.

DIVINA'TION, the pretended art of foretelling future events, or such as cannot be obtained by ordinary or natural means. The Israelites were always very fond of divination, magic, and interpretation of dreams. It was to cure them of this foolish propensity, that Moses promised them from God, that the spirit of real prophecy should not depart from amongst them; forbade them to consult diviners, astrologers, &c., under very severe penalties; and ordered those to be stoned who pretended to have familiar spirits, or the spirit of divination.—The ancient heathen philosophers divided divination into two kinds, *natural* and *artificial.* Natural divination was supposed to be effected by a kind of inspiration or divine afflatus; artificial divination was effected by certain rites, experiments, or observations, which we have explained under their respective heads. All the ancient Asiatic tribes had modes of divination; the Egyptians and Greeks had their oracles; and, with the Romans, divination and witchcraft were brought into a kind of system, and constituted part of their religion. In truth, there has hardly been a nation discovered, which had advanced beyond the lowest barbarism, that did not practise some kinds of divination; and even in the ages in which reason has most prevailed over feeling, the belief in the power of foreseeing future events has been entertained. At the present day, enlightened as the world is by science, the desire of prying into futurity keeps alive many modes of prognosticating future events; nor is the practice entirely confined to the ignorant and superstitious.

DIVINE RIGHT, THE, OF KINGS, in politics, means the absolute and unqualified claim of sovereigns on the obedience of the people; insomuch that, although they may themselves submit to restrictions on their authority, yet subjects endeavoring to enforce those restrictions by resistance to their unlawful acts are guilty of a sin. This doctrine, so celebrated in English constitutional history, has been asserted on very different grounds. Hobbes deduced the absolute authority of kings from the supposed social contract, whereby men parted absolutely with their natural rights in exchange for protection. But the fashionable political writers and theologians of the times both of Charles I. and II. maintained that government had an existence before property, and before any supposed social contract could take place; that it originated in the patriarchal sway, which was succeeded by the regal, and that no other was authorized by Scripture.

DI'VING, the art of descending under water to a considerable depth, and remaining there for a length of time, as occasion may require. The practice of diving is resorted to for the recovery of things that are sunk, &c.—The most remarkable diver was Nicolo Pesce, who, according to the account given by Kircher, was able to spend five days together in the waves, without any other provisions than the fish which he caught and ate raw. He would swim from Sicily to Calabria carrying letters from the king. At length he met his fate in exploring the depths of Charybdis, at the instance of the king; who, after he had once succeeded in fetching up a golden cup that had been thrown in, ordered him to repeat the experiment.

DIVIN'ITY, a term applied to the Deity or Supreme Being. It also denotes theology; the science which unfolds the character of God, his laws and moral government, the duties of man, and the way of salvation.

DIVIS'ION, the act of dividing or separating any entire bodies into parts.—*Division*, in music, the dividing the interval of an octave into a number of less intervals. The fourth and fifth divide the octave perfectly, though differently: when the fifth is below, and serves as a bass to the fourth, the division is called *harmonical;* but when the fourth is below, it is called *arithmetical.*—*Division*, among logicians, is the explication of a complex idea, by enumerating the simple ideas whereof it is composed.—In rhetoric, it is the arrangement of a discourse under several heads.—A part of an army, as a brigade, a squadron, or platoon.—A part of a fleet, or a select number of ships under a commander, and distinguished by a particular flag or standard.

DIVORCE', a separation, by law, of husband and wife; and is either a divorce *a vinculo matrimonii*, that is, a complete dissolution of the marriage bonds, whereby the parties become as entirely disconnected as those who have not been joined in wedlock, or a divorce *a mensâ et thoro* (from bed and board,) whereby the parties are legally separated, but not unmarried. The Jewish law of divorce is founded on the directions given in the 24th chapter of Deuteronomy; but the permission therein contained is subject to many obstacles and formalities in modern practice. In Greece, in classical times, the practice of divorce seems to have varied in different states; at Sparta it appears to have been unusual, in Athens great facilities were afforded by the law. In republican Rome great strictness in this branch of morals prevailed for a long period, although parties were less impeded in pursuing a divorce by the difficulties imposed by the law than by public opinion. But in the later period of the republic, and under the emperors, divorce became extremely common, and was obtained with equal ease by either sex. Our Saviour's declaration to the Pharisee, in the 19th chapter of St. Matthew, became the foundation of the law on this subject in Christian countries, and divorces were consequently allowed in one particular case only; but after the Roman church had erected matrimony into a sacrament, they became, as they now are in Catholic countries, wholly impossible: the only dissolution of marriage being in cases where it is void ab initio. In most Protestant countries, the facility of divorce has been so much restored in latter times as to approximate to the heathen practice.

DO, is in music, a syllable used by the Italians instead of *ut*, than which it is by them considered more musical and resonant.

DOCE'TÆ, one of the earliest heretical sects; so called from the reality of our Lord's incarnation, and considering him to have acted and suffered only in appearance. Some divines have conceived that the express declarations of the nature of Christ in St. John's writings were specially directed against these opinions.

DOCIMA'SIA, in Greek antiquity, a probation of the magistrates and persons employed in public business at Athens. It was performed publicly in the forum, where they were obliged to give account of themselves and their past life before certain judges.

DOCK'ET, a small piece of paper or parchment, containing the heads of a writing.—Also, a subscription at the foot of letters patent, by the clerk of the dockets.—A bill tied to goods, containing some direction, as the name of the owner or the place to which they are to be sent.—An alphabetical list of cases in a court, or a catalogue of the names of the parties who have suits depending in a court.—In the United States, this is the principal or only use of the word.

DOC'TOR, a person who has passed all the degrees of a faculty, and is empowered to practise and teach it; or, according to modern usage, one who has received the highest degree in a faculty. The title of *doctor* originated at the same time with the establishment of universities; and is either conferred publicly, with certain ceremonies, or by diploma.

DOCTRINAIRES', a party in the French chamber of deputies, on the second restoration of the Bourbons, who would neither rank themselves among the friends of absolute power, nor among the defenders of the revolution. They opposed the ultra royalists, and took a middle course, avowing themselves the supporters of a constitutional monarchy.

DOC'TRINE, a principle or position in any science, that is laid down as true by an instructor therein. Thus, the *doctrines* of the Gospel are the principles or truths taught by Christ and his Apostles. But *any* tenet or opinion is a doctrine; therefore doctrines may be either true or false.

DOC'UMENT, any official or authoritative paper, containing written instructions, or evidence.

DODEC'ASTYLE, in architecture, a building having twelve columns on a front or flank.

DODO'NA, in antiquity, the seat of the most ancient, and one of the most celebrated oracles of Greece, sacred to Jupiter. By some writers its origin is attributed to Deucalion, who is said to have built the town of Dodona where it stood; but according to the traditions of the priestesses of the temple, it was founded by a dove, which, perching on the branch of an oak, recommended, in a human voice, that a temple should be erected to Jupiter in that place. The situation of the oracle was in an extensive forest, the oaks of which are said to have been endowed with the gift of prophecy; and the oracles were most frequently delivered by three priestesses, who expounded the will of the divinity. That the responses of this oracle were received with singular veneration, may be inferred from the number of votaries by whom it was frequented, and the costly presents which adorned the temple and its precincts. This oracle continued to utter responses till the time of Augustus, when it ceased.

DOG, an emblem of fidelity, and generally introduced at the feet of married women in sepulchral effigies with that signification. It also signifies loyalty to the sovereign.

DOG-DAYS, the period between the 24th of July and the 24th of August; so called because the dog star (Sirius) during this period rises with the sun; and the heat, which is usually most oppressive at this season, was formerly ascribed to the conjunction of this star with the solar luminary.

DOGE, formerly the title of the chief magistrate in the republics of Venice and Genoa. The dignity was elective in both places; at Venice it continued for life; at Genoa, only for two years. His power became, by degrees, very limited.

DOG'GEREL, an epithet given to a kind of loose, irregular, burlesque poetry, like that of Hudibras.

DOG'MA, a principle, maxim, tenet, or settled opinion, particularly with regard to matters of faith and philosophy; as, the *dogmas* of the church; the *dogmas* of Aristotle.—In theology, *dogma* has been defined to be a fundamental article of belief derived from acknowledged authority, a d is usually applied to what are considered as the essential doctrines of Christianity, deduced either from the Scriptures or from the fathers of the church. There are, however, many other *dogmas* peculiar to the different sects into which Christianity is divided. Thus the bulls and decretals of the pope, together with all the councils both of earlier and later times, are regarded by the Roman Catholics with as much veneration as the authority of the Scriptures and the holy fathers. The Greek church, on the other hand, acknowledges the authority only of the earlier councils, in addition to that of the Scriptures and the fathers; and the Lutheran and other Protestant churches have embodied their dogmas in their respective confessions of faith and other ecclesiastical standards. *Dogmatic theology*, as this branch of divinity is called, in contradistinction to moral and scholastic theology, forms an important object of study in many of the continental universities. In the Protestant universities of Germany there are chairs set apart for the history of *dogmas*, or, as it is termed, *dogmatik;* in which the origin and nature of the dogmas of the various Christian sects are examined, and the merit of the arguments by which they are supported.

DOG'MATISTS, a sect of ancient physicians, of which Hippocrates was the first. They are also called *logici*, or logicians, from their using the rules of logic on professional subjects. They laid down definitions and divisions, reducing diseases to certain genera, and those genera to species, and furnishing remedies for them all; supposing principles, drawing conclusions, and applying those principles and conclusions to the particular diseases under consideration.

DOIT, the ancient Scottish penny-piece, twelve of which were equal to a penny-sterling. Two of them were equal to the *bodle*, six to the *baubee*, and eight to the *acheson*.

DO'LABRA, CELT, an implement of various forms, extensively used both in ancient and modern times, for similar purposes as our hatchets and chisels. They abound in museums, and are seen depicted on the columns of Trajan and Antoninus at Rome. They are usually formed of bronze and of flint or other hard stone, and to these latter the term celt is usually applied.

DOLCE, in music, an instruction to the performer that the music is to be executed softly and sweetly.

DOLE, in the ancient English customs, signified a part or portion of a meadow, where several persons had shares. It now means a distribution of alms, or a liberal gift made to the people or to some charitable institution.

DOL'LAR, a silver coin of Spain and of the United States, of the value of 4*s*. 6*d*. sterling, or 100 cents. In Germany, the name *dollar* is given to several coins of different values.

DOLL'MAN, a kind of long cassock, worn by the Turks, hanging down to the feet, with narrow sleeves buttoned at the wrist.

DOL'PHIN, an emblem of love and social feeling, frequently introduced as ornaments to coronas suspended in churches.

DOM, in the middle ages, was a title originally possessed by the pope, and at a somewhat later period by the dignitaries of the Roman Catholic church. In more recent times, it formed a distinguishing title of certain monastic orders, such as the Benedictines, &c.; and it appears to have been equivalent to the *don* of the Spaniards, the *von* of the Germans, and the *de* of the French. Mabillon and Calmet are always spoken of as Dom Mabillon and Dom Calmet.

DOME, in architecture, the spherical or other figured concave ceiling over a circular or polygonal building. A *surbased* or *diminished dome* is one that is segmental on its section; a *surmounted dome* is one that is higher than the radius of its base. The forms of domes are various, both in plan and section. In the former, they are circular and polygonal; in the latter, we find them semicircular, and semi-elliptical, segmental, pointed, sometimes in curves of contrary flexure, bell-shaped, &c. The oldest cupola on record is that of the Pantheon at Rome, which was erected under Augustus, and is still perfect.

DO'MESDAY, or DOOMS'DAY-BOOK, a book or record made by order of William the Conqueror, which now remains in the exchequer, and consists of two volumes, a large folio and a quarto; the former contains a survey of all the lands in most of the counties in England, and the latter comprehends some counties that were not then surveyed. The "Book of Domesday" was begun by five justices, assigned for that purpose in each county, in the year 1081, and finished in 1086. It was of such authority, that the Conqueror himself submitted, in some cases wherein he was concerned, to be determined by it. Camden calls it the

Tax-book of king William; and it was farther called *Magna Rolla*. There is likewise a third domesday book, made by command of the Conqueror; and also a fourth, being an abridgment of the other books.

DOM'ICILE, in law, the place where a person has his home. Personal property, on the decease of the owner, is distributable according to the law of the country in which he was domiciled at the time of his death; not according to the law of the country in which the property is situate. Residence for forty days constitutes a domicile as to jurisdiction in Scotland.

DOMICIL'IARY, pertaining to an abode or residence. Hence a *domiciliary visit* signifies a visit to a private dwelling, particularly for the purpose of searching it, under authority.

DOM'INANT, in a general sense, predominant or governing; as the *dominant* party or faction.—In music, the dominant or sensible chord is that which is practised on the dominant of the tone, and which introduces a perfect cadence. Every perfect major chord becomes a dominant chord, as soon as the seventh minor is added to it.

DOM'INIC, St., Dominicus de Guzman, the founder of the Order of Dominicans; he is represented with a sparrow by his side, and with a dog carrying a burning torch in his mouth. The bird refers to the devil, who appeared to the saint in that shape; the dog, to a dream of his mother's, that she gave birth to a black and white spotted dog, who lighted the world with a burning torch. This dog is also said to be the emblem of watchfulness for the true faith, the Dominicans being the first and most zealous enemies of heresy; for to them Spain owes the tribunal of the Inquisition, established for the purpose of kindling funeral piles with the torch of the black and white dog.

DOMIN'ICAL LETTER, for the purpose of exhibiting the day of the week corresponding to any given day of the year, the framers of the ecclesiastical calendar denoted the seven days of the week by the first seven letters of the Alphabet, A, B, C, D, E, F, and G; and placed these letters in a column opposite to the days of the year, in such a manner that A stood opposite the 1st of January or first day of the year, B opposite the 2d, and so on to G, which stood opposite the 7th: after which A returns to the 8th, and so on through the 365 days of the year. Now if one of the days of the week, Sunday, for example, falls opposite to E, Monday will be opposite F, Tuesday G, Wednesday A, and so on; and every Sunday through the year will be represented by the same letter E, every Monday by F, and so on. The letter which represents Sunday is called the *Dominical Letter*, or *Sunday Letter*. As the number of days in the week and the number in the year are prime to each other, two successive years cannot begin with the same day; hence the Dominical Letter changes every year. This mode of representing the days of the week has now fallen nearly into desuetude, and the initial letter of the name of the day is placed in our almanacs opposite the day of the month.

DOMIN'ICANS, called also *Predicants*, or *Preaching Friars*, an order of monks, founded by St. Dominic, a native of Spain, in 1215. The design of their institution was, to preach the gospel, convert heretics, defend the faith, and propagate Christianity. They embraced the rule of St. Augustine, to which they added statutes and constitutions, which had formerly been observed either by the Carthusians or Præmonstratenses. The principal articles enjoined perpetual silence, abstinence from flesh at all times, wearing of woollen, rigorous poverty, and several other austerities. In France they were called *Jacobins*, because the first convent in Paris was in the *Rue St. Jaques*. The *Dominican Nuns*, who were established at the same time, follow similar rules.—A third establishment of St. Dominic was the military order of Christ, originally composed of knights and noblemen, whose duty it was to wage war against heretics. After the death of the founder, this became the order of the penitence of St. Dominic, for both sexes, and constituted the third order of Dominicans. These became extremely influential; and numbered among their fraternity some of the most distinguished scholars, such as Albertus Magnus and Thomas Aquinas. In course of time they were superseded in the schools and courts by the Jesuits; and the order at present flourishes only in Spain, Portugal, Sicily, and South America.

DOMIN'IONS, in Christian Art, an order of celestial spirits disposing of the office of angels; their ensign is a sceptre.

DOM'INO, a long loose cloak of black silk, furnished with a hood removable at pleasure, and worn chiefly at masquerades by persons of both sexes by way of general disguise.

DOM'INUS, in the civil law, signifies one who possesses anything by right of purchase, gift, loan, legacy, inheritance, payment, contract, or sentence.—*Dominus*, in the feudal law, one who grants a part of his estate in fee to be enjoyed by another.

DO'MO REPARAN'DO, a writ which lies for a person against his neighbor, whose house he fears will fall, to the damage of his own.

DON, a Spanish and Portuguese title, which the king, the princes of the blood, and the highest class of the nobility prefix to their names. The ladies of rank have the predicate donna. The title was originally equivalent to that of knight.

DONA'TION, in law, the act or contract by which a person transfers to another either the property or the use of something, as a free gift. In order to be valid, it supposes a capacity both in the donor and donee, and requires consent, acceptance, and delivery.

DO'NATISTS, a religious faction, which arose in Africa in the beginning of the 4th century in oposition to Cecilianus, bishop of Carthage. The Numidian bishops were indignant at a slight received from him at the time of his consecration, and declared him informally appointed, on account of their absence from the ceremony. They also accused him of unworthy conduct during the Diocletian persecution. There are two persons of the name of Donatus celebrated as leaders of this party.

DO'NATIVE, in the canon law, a benefice given by the patron to a priest, without presentation to the ordinary, and without institution or induction.—*Donative*, among the Romans, was properly a gift made to the soldiers, as *congiarium* was that made to the people.

DON'JON, in fortification, signifies a strong tower, or redoubt, into which the garrison of an ancient fortress might retreat, in case of necessity, and capitulate with greater advantage.

DO'NOR, a term of the middle ages, applied to the giver and founder of a work of Art for religious purposes, viz., the giver of a church picture, statue, or painted window, &c., the founder of a church, or an altar. If the gift were a picture, the portraits of the donor and his wife were introduced; the former, attended by his sons, kneels on one side of the Madonna, who is either standing or enthroned, while on the other side are his wife and daughters, all with hands raised, as if in prayer. Royal founders of churches, whose portrait-statues are placed in or on the buildings they have founded, bear in their hands the titular saint and a model of the church, which latter is also found in the monuments of such donors.

DOOM, the old name for the Last Judgment, which impressive subject was usually painted over the chancel arch in parochial churches. In the reign of Edward VI. these edifying representations were effaced, or washed over, as superstitious.

DOR'IC, an epithet for anything belonging to the Dorians, an ancient people of Greece. The *Doric dialect* was broad and rough, yet there was something venerable and dignified in its antique style; for which reason it was often made use of in solemn odes, &c.—The *Doric order* of architecture is the second of the five orders, being that between the Tuscan and Ionic. It is distinguished for simplicity and strength: and is used in the gates of cities and citadels, on the outside of churches, and other situations where embellishment is unnecessary or inappropriate.—The *Doric* mode, in music, was the first of the authentic modes of the ancients; and grave rather than gay.

DOR'MANT, an epithet expressive of a state of inaction or sleep. Hence we speak of *dormant* animals, or such as remain several months in the year apparently lifeless, or, at least, in utter inactivity. The period of long sleep generally begins when the food of the animal grows scarce, and inactivity spreads over the vegetable kingdom. Instinct at this time impels the animals to seek a safe place for their period of rest. The bat hides itself in dark caves, or in walls of decayed buildings; the hedgehog envelops himself in leaves, and generally conceals himself in fern brakes; and the marmot buries himself in the ground. In this period we observe in the animals, first a decrease of animal heat; and secondly, that they breathe much slower and more uninterruptedly than at other times. The digestion is also much diminished; the stomach and intestines are usually empty; and even if the animals are awakened, they do not manifest symptoms of appetite, except in heated rooms. The causes of the dormant state of animals have generally been sought in a peculiar construction of the organs; but the immediate cause producing this torpidity, is mostly, if not entirely, the cold Frogs, serpents, and lizards, kept in artificial cold, may remain for years in this state; hence they have been sometimes found enclosed in stones, in which they have been perhaps for centuries. The other lower animals, as snails, insects, &c., are also subject to a similar torpidity. A state of partial torpor takes place in the case of the common bear, the badger, and the racoon. The bear begins to be drowsy in November, when he is particularly fat, and retires into his den, which he has lined with moss, and where he but rarely awakes in winter.

DOR'MER, or DOR'MENT, in architecture, a window made in the roof of a building.

DOR'NOCK, a kind of figured linen, of stout fabric, manufactured for coarse table cloths. It derives its name from a town in Scotland, where it was first made.

DOR'OTHEA, St., this saint is represented with a rose-branch in her hand, a wreath of red roses on her head, the same flowers and some fruit by her side, or with an angel carrying a basket, in which are three apples and three roses. This angel is a youth barefooted, and clad in a purple garment. St. Dorothea suffered martyrdom in the Diocletian Persecution, A.D. 303, by being beheaded.

DORYPH'ORI, in antiquity, an appellation given to the life-guard men of the Roman emperors.

DO'TAGE, the childishness and imbecility of old age.

DOU'BLE ENTEN'TE, a term applied to a word of two different meanings.—*Double-entendre*, any phrase which has a covert as well as an obvious meaning.

DOUB'LET, among lapidaries, a counterfeit stone composed of two pieces of crystal, with a color between them, so that they have the same appearance as if the whole substance were colored.

DOUB'LING *a cape*, is to sail round or pass beyond it, so that the point of land shall separate the ship from her former situation, or lie between her and any distant observer.

DOUBLOON', a Spanish coin of the value of two pistoles, or 3*l.* 6*s.* sterling.

DOUBT, uncertainty of mind; or the act of withholding our assent from any proposition, on suspicion that we are not thoroughly apprised of the merits or from not being able peremptorily to decide between the reasons for and against it.

DOUCEUR', a present or bribe for the acquirement of any desired object.

DOUCINE', in architecture, a moulding concave above and convex below, serving as a cymatium to a delicate cornice.

DOVE, the dove, in Christian Art, is the symbol of the Holy Ghost; as such, it is represented in its natural form, the body of a snowy whiteness, the beak and claws red, which is the color natural to those parts in white doves. The nimbus, which always surrounds its head, should be of a gold color, and divided by a cross, which is either red or black. A radiance of light invests and proceeds from the person of the dove, and is emblematical of the divinity. It is also sometimes represented, in stained glass, with seven rays, terminating in stars, significant of the seven gifts of the Holy Ghost. The dove has been constantly adopted in Christian iconography as the symbol of the Holy Ghost from the sixth century until the present day. In the tenth and eleventh centuries the human form was also adopted for the same object. In the fourteenth and fifteenth centuries we meet with both together, as the personification of the Holy Ghost in the human form, with the dove as his symbol. The dove is an emblem of love, simplicity, innocence, purity, mildness, compunction; holding an olive-branch, it is an emblem of peace. Doves were used in churches to serve three purposes:—1. Suspended over altars to serve as a pyx. 2. As a type or figure of the Holy Spirit over altars, baptisteries, and fonts. 3. As symbolical ornaments. The dove is also an emblem of the human soul, and as such is seen issuing from the lips of dying martyrs and devout persons. A dove with six wings has been employed as a type of the church of Christ: it has certain peculiarities. The front of the body is of silver, the back of gold. Two of the wings are attached to the head, two to the shoulders, and two to the feet.

DOW'AGER, in law, properly a widow who enjoys a dower; particularly applied as a title to the widows of princes and nobility. The widow of a king is a *queen-dowager*.

DOW'ER, in law, the portion which a widow has of her husband's lands, to enjoy during her life.

DOWN, the softest and most delicate feathers of birds, particularly of geese, ducks, and swans, growing on the neck and part of the breast. The eider duck yields the best kind.—Also the fine feathery substance by which seeds are conveyed to a distance by the wind; as in the dandelion and thistle.

DOWNS, banks or elevations of sand, which the sea gathers and forms along its shore, and which serve it as a barrier.

The term is also applied to tracts of naked land on which sheep usually graze.—*The Downs* is a famous roadstead on the coast of Kent, between the North and South Foreland, where both the outward and homeward bound ships frequently make some stay, and squadrons of men of war rendezvous in time of war. It affords excellent anchorage, and is defended by the castles of Deal, Dover, and Sandwich, as well as by the Goodwin Sands.

DOW'RY, the money or fortune which the wife brings her husband in marriage: it is otherwise called *maritagium*, marriage-goods, and differs from dower.—*Dowry* is also used, in a monastic sense, for a sum of money given with a female upon entering her in some religious order.

DOXOL'OGY, in Christian worship, a hymn in praise of the Almighty. There is the greater and lesser doxology; the angelic hymn, "Glory be to God on high," &c., is the *greater* doxology; the *lesser*, "Glory be to the Father, and to the Son," &c.

DRAFT, in commerce, a bill drawn by one person upon another for a sum of money.—In military affairs, the selecting or detaching of soldiers from an army, or from a military post. Also, the act of *drawing* men to serve in the militia.

DRAG'OMANS, the interpreters attached to European embassies or consulates in the Levant. The dragoman of the Sublime Porte is an important Turkish officer, who forms the medium of communication between his own government and the embassies of foreign countries.

DRAG'ON, in fabulous history, one of the most famous mythological creations of antiquity and the middle ages. The position which this being occupies in fabulous history presents one of the most singular phenomena of the human mind, as its existence was firmly accredited among the ancients of almost every nation, both in the eastern and western regions of the earth. It occurs in the sacred allegories of the Jews, and in the legends of the Chinese and Japanese; and the pages of the classic poets of Greece and Rome teem with representations of the dragon. Thus the dark retreats of their gods and their sacred groves were defended by dragons; the chariot of Ceres was drawn by them; and a dragon kept the garden of the Hesperides. In Scandinavian mysteries, the dragon was the minister of vengeance under their vindictive gods; and the ancient Britons, enslaved in the trammels of Druidic superstition, entertained a similar notion of its nature. The allegory of the Dragon has even found a place among many nations who have embraced Christianity. The dragon plays as important a part in Art as he does in Fiction. We find it upon the shield of the most famous of the early Grecian heroes, as well as on the helmets of kings and generals. It does not appear among the Romans until after their struggle with the Dacians, by which people it was regarded as the sign of warfare; and it remained with the former people a subordinate symbol, as the glorious eagle was not to be displaced from helmets and standards. The dragon was of more importance in German antiquity; as with the early Greeks, it was the symbol of the hero. In the *Nibelungen Lied*, Siegfried killed a dragon at Worms. It is found on English shields after the time of William the Conqueror. In modern heraldry it appears on the shield and helmet; and as a supporter it is called a *lindworm* when it has no wings, and *serpent* when it has no feet; when it hangs by the head and wings it means a conquered dragon.—*Dragon*, in Christian Art, is the emblem of sin. The dragons which appear in early paintings and sculptures are invariably representations of a winged crocodile. It is the form under which Satan, the personification of sin, is usually depicted, and is met with in pictures of St. Michael and St. Margaret, when it typifies the conquest over sin; it also appears under the feet of the Saviour, and under those of the Virgin, as conveying the same idea. Sin is represented in the form of a serpent, sometimes with an apple in its mouth. The dragon also typifies idolatry. In pictures of St. George and St. Sylvester, it serves to exhibit the triumph over paganism. In pictures of St. Martha, it figures the inundation of the Rhone, spreading pestilence and death. St. John the Evangelist is sometimes represented holding a chalice from which issues a winged dragon. As a symbol of Satan, we find the dragon nearly always in the form of the fossil *Icthyosaurus*.

DRAG'ON BEAM, in architecture, an horizontal piece of timber on which the hip or angle rafters of a roof pitch. It is framed into a short diagonal piece, which ties the plates at the internal angles of a roof.

DRAGONNADES', the name given to the persecutions instituted by Louis XIV. and his successors against the French

Protestants, from the coercive measures which were put in force to effect their conversion.

DRAG'ON'S BLOOD, a resin which exudes from a tree growing in India, the *Pterocarpus draco*. It is of a dark blood-red color, formerly used in miniature paintings, but its color is not durable. It is now used principally for coloring varnishes.

DRAGOON', a kind of light horseman, of French origin, trained to fight either in or out of the line, in a body or singly, chiefly on horseback, but, if necessary, on foot also. Experience proving that they did not answer the end designed, they were hardly ever used in infantry service, and now form a useful kind of cavalry, mounted on horses too heavy for the hussars, and too light for the cuirassiers.

DRA'MA, (from the Greek word δρᾶμα, *an action or thing done;* derived from the verb δράω, *I act or do,*) has been defined a species of poem in which the action or narrative is not related but represented. The invention of the drama is one of those which should seem to proceed most naturally from the ordinary customs and feelings of men. There is a species of dramatic action which seems almost instinctive; we naturally imitate the tone and gestures of others in reciting their sayings or adventures, or even in adopting their sentiments. Yet some nations appear never to have taken the farther step of doing, methodically and with design, what all do involuntarily. In the accounts which we possess of the ancient Egyptians, for example, we have no trace of their having possessed dramatic representation. But among a great number of tribes, wholly independent of each other, we find something approaching to the dramatic art intermingled with their common or solemn customs, and generally connected with religious observance. This was especially the case in Greece, whence the name and substance of the drama have been chiefly derived by the modern European nations. The history of the development of the dramatic art in Greece is well known; its elements were found in the religious festivals celebrated from the earliest ages in that country. The feasts of Bacchus in particular had sacred choruses or odes; these were afterwards intermixed with episodic narrations of events in mythological story, recited by an actor in the festival with gesticulation; thence again, the next step was to introduce two actors with alternate recitation; and thus were produced tragedy (τραγῳδιά, *the song of the goat,* from the animal which was led about in those festive processions;) and comedy, (κωμῳδιά, *the village song,*) which differed from the former in that the dialogue of the interlocutors was satirical, and not mythological. The early Greek tragedy was a dramatic representation of some scenes or events recorded in the national traditions, the actors personating those who played a part in these events, together with a chorus or band of singers, representing such persons as might naturally be supposed to have been bystanders at the occurrence (captive women, old men, or counsellors, &c.,) who sang at intervals, during the representations, hymns to the gods, or songs appropriate to the scenes passing in representation; while the Attic comedy, in its first invention, must be regarded as a parody on tragedy, in which the personages were either real characters introduced for the purpose of satire, or ludicrous personifications. Æschylus, the oldest tragic writer, with the exception of Phrynichus, his contemporary, carried the Greek drama at once to nearly its highest state of perfection. Sophocles and Euripides introduced additional actors into the dialogue, which, at first, admitted only two at the same time, and turned the naked recitals of events which form the substance of the plays of Æschylus into something more nearly resembling the modern idea of a plot, with contrasted character and incidents leading to the accomplishment of a main action. Many tragic writers, the whole of whose works have been lost, flourished after Euripides in Athens and Alexandria; but they do not seem to have altered the character of the art which they received from their predecessors. The fate of comedy was different; the old Attic comedy was a political or philosophical satire in action, which in form was a burlesque on the tragedy. Afterwards, passing through the intervening stage of the middle comedy, of which we know little, the art acquired in the new comedy of Menander and Philemon, a character somewhat approaching to that in which it is at present cultivated; a narrative in representation of scenes and incidents in ordinary life of a light or ludicrous character. The dramatic art among the Greeks aimed at producing an impression upon the spectators by three different means; which, according to modern phraseology, we may denominate poetical effect, dramatical effect, and theatrical effect. The poetry of the Greek drama was of the highest order; but it forms a topic to be considered apart. Dramatical effect is the proper subject of the dramatic art; and, in judging of the efforts of the Greek mind in this direction, we are assisted not only by the study of the dramatic poems which we possess, but by the rules of criticism delivered to us by Greek authors, and especially by Aristotle. From these it appears that the parts or characteristics of a tragedy, essentially divided, were held to be the fable or story, the manners, the style, the sentiment, the music, and the diction; that the fable should consist of an entire action, namely one principal event and the auxiliary events; and that the proper emotions to be excited by the action are terror and pity; that its parts of quantity, according to the division of form, were the prologue, being that part of the tragedy which precedes the parode or first entry of the chorus; the episode, being all those several parts which are included between the several choral odes; the exode, the part which follows the last choral ode; and the chorus itself, or the intervening odes, which also admit of various subdivisions. Formally considered, the arrangement of the old comedy nearly resembled that of tragedy; in the new, the chorus was altogether omitted. The unity of action was a remarkable characteristic of the Greek drama, although widely different from that peculiar quality, which modern critics have characterized by the name; it should rather be termed unity of subject, inasmuch as in many of our remaining tragedies, and especially those of Æschylus, there is little or no trace of what we term a plot, *i. e.* a main incident, at which we arrive through subordinate incidents tending to its accomplishment. The unity of time,—viz. that the imaginary duration of the action should not exceed twenty-four hours; and that of place, namely, that the scene in which the events occur should be the same throughout, are inventions of French critics, not warranted by the remains of Greek art, in which both are not unfrequently violated; but, although not rules of Grecian discovery, they are easily rendered applicable to the simple and severe form of the Greek tragedy. In considering the theatrical effect of the Greek drama, we must remember that the tragedies were originally religious solemnities; the theatre, a vast building open at the top, calculated for the accommodation of several thousand spectators; the scene, &c. proportionably large. Dramatic representations were, at Athens, the offering of wealthy men to the people; he who contributed the expenses of the entertainment was said *εἰσάγειν*, to bring in the play; the poet who produced it, *διδάσκειν*, to teach it, *i. e.* teach the actors to perform it. A complete representation consisted of four pieces by the same author; a triology, or three tragedies, narrating successive events in the same series of mythological tradition; and a fourth piece, termed a satyric drama, of which the chorus consisted of satyrs, and the mythological subject was treated in a manner approaching to burlesque.

Chinese Drama.—Before proceeding to the dramatic art of modern Europe, derived as it is from that of Greece, two oriental nations may be noticed which possess a national drama of their own. In China, theatrical entertaiments form one of the most popular amusements, and theatrical writing has been cultivated from a very early period. The Chinese drama comprises pieces which we should term both tragical and historical plays, tragi-comedies, and comedies both of intrigue and of manners; together with abundance of low, pantomimic, and farcical representations. In their regular drama, however, there appears to be less of what we should term connected than of successive action: many of them are, as it were, dramatized memoirs or biographies of individuals, real or fictitious; the representation of some is said to require ten days. It is remarkable that, of all national dramas, the Chinese appears to be the only one in which we can trace no original connection with religious observance.

Hindoo Drama.—The Hindoo plays which now exist are written for the most part in Sanscrit, although not a living language at the period when they were composed; mixed, however, with other dialects, which, according to Hindoo critics, are respectively appropriate to different parts of a play. They seem to have been appropriate to the entertainment of learned persons, and acted only on solemn occasions. They are few in number; about sixty only are known; some containing long mythological narratives, others much complicated incident of a domestic character, in a strain of tragedy, alternating with comedy, like the romantic drama of modern Europe. The dramatic art appears to have flourished in India during a period of several ages, ending about the 14th or 15th centuries of our era. Dramatic criticism was also much cultivated; and the most minute and artificial rules are laid down by Hindoo commentators as to the conduct of a piece, the requisite ethics, the formal arrangement, and the character which must be introduced. The Hindoo drama is so widely different from the Greek or Chinese, that it must be regarded, like them, as a spontaneous offspring of national genius.

Modern European Drama. — For many centuries after the downfall of the Roman empire, the dramatic art appears to have been entirely lost. Its first revival in the middle ages was owing to the solemnities of the church, into which dramatic interludes were introduced in various countries of western Europe, representing at first events in biblical history or the lives of the saints, and afterwards intermingled with allegorical fantasies. The framers of these early pieces were monks, and the monks were the only preservers of classical learning; but whether we can infer from these facts that the idea of these rude representations was suggested, or their details improved by classical associations, it is not easy to pronounce. At the period of the revival of literature, however, the dramatic art was called nearly at once into life in the four principal countries of western Europe; Italy, France, Spain, and England. In the two first of these countries it arose simply classical, and unmixed with any original conceptions, or with the sentiments and fashions of the middle ages; in the two last it partook largely of both, and was also immediately derived from the mysteries and moralities above mentioned: hence, in a historical view, arose the distinction, so elaborately explained by modern critics, between the classical and romantic drama.

Italian Drama.—Originated in close imitation of classical models. The *Sofonisba* of Trissino (1515) is not absolutely the oldest Italian play, but the first which served as a model for subsequent composers. Rucellai and many others followed in the same track; Bibbiena, Michiavel, Ariosto, as closely imitated the model of the Terentian comedy. The pastoral drama of the 16th century, of which Tasso and Guarini were the most celebrated writers, furnished the first novelty in this branch of literature; but these are rather poetical than dramatical compositions. The true national theatre of Italy arose in the 17th century, in the musical drama (opera), to which Metastasio, early in the 18th, communicated all the charms of poetry; but since the period of that writer, the operatic part of the dramatic art has again been wholly disconnected from the literary, and the words only serve as vehicles for the music. While the higher classes were devoted to the opera, the lower found their national amusement in the commedie dell' arte; comedies performed by masqued characters, which gradually became fixed in the well-known persons of Harlequin, Pantaloon, Brighella, &c., who improvised their parts: Goldoni, in the middle of the 18th century, succeeded in establishing a regular comic drama in possession of the stage; while his rival, Gasparo Gozzi, took up the commedie dell' arte as models, and founded upon them a series of amusing extravagances. But since the period of these two spirited writers comedy has fallen almost completely into disrepute. At the end of the 18th century Alfieri, a bold and severe genius, produced tragedies in which the ancient classical form (with the exception of the chorus) was again reverted to, instead of the French imitations of it which had long been current in Italy as well as the rest of Europe; and several dramatic poets have since appeared, who adopted the same model.

French Drama.—The early French tragic writers, from the beginning of the 16th century down to Corneille in the middle of the 17th, produced nothing but unsuccessful and somewhat barbarous imitations of the Greek tragedy. The first pieces of this kind represented on the French stage had prologues and choruses. Corneille had studied and loved the Spanish drama; and without introducing much of its varied form and incident, he transfused a portion of its boldness and romantic sentiment into the French theatre, together with a power of energetic declamation peculiarly his own. Racine, on the other hand, was a pure admirer of antiquity; but with a taste and delicacy of feeling which until his time had been very rarely found to accompany classical knowledge. The French tragedy grew up with these two great writers as models, and Boileau as its legislator. A peculiar and rigorous system of criticism was introduced, affecting both the form and the substance of dramatic writing; and this system became established in the minds of the French public, as the natural and not the conventional rule of beauty. It would be impossible to enter into an examination of the rules of the French drama; suffice it to say, that they banished from the tragic stage all except heroic characters and passion; required perfect simplicity of plot, uniformity of language, and, in addition, the observance of the before-mentioned technical unities of place and time. These rules have ever since been scrupulously followed, without deviation, on the regular French stage, and many of the greatest names in dramatic literature have voluntarily subjected themselves to their restraints. The French comedy, however, is infinitely more national and characteristic than the French tragedy; it originated in that of Spain, and was carried at once to a high degree of perfection by Molière,—rejecting the extravagance of the Spanish drama, confining itself within certain definite limits governed by analogy to those established for tragedy, and retaining satire instead of adventure as its leading principle. Since that period the French comic stage has been, beyond all contradiction, not only the best, but the model from which that of all other nations has been wholly derived. Of the present state of the French drama it is difficult to speak with precision; but the national or regular stage seems to be every day losing in popularity, while the attempts to establish a new one on what is termed in France the romantic model have hitherto met with very partial success.

Spanish Drama.—Spain commenced her literary career more independent of foreign aid than any other country. Her dramatic art appears to have originated as early as the 14th century; which produced satirical pieces in dialogue, and one complete dramatic romance by an unknown author (*La Celestina,*) in addition to the mysteries and miracle plays, which were exhibited in Spain even more plentifully than elsewhere. The early Spanish comedies of the 16th century were conversations, like eclogues, between shepherds and shepherdesses; with occasional interludes of negroes, clowns, and Biscayans, the favorite subjects of popular jest. But the Spanish drama owed to one great author, Lope de Vega, what the English drama owed to his contemporary, Shakspeare,—a rise at a single bound from insignificance to great richness and variety; he created, moreover, nearly all its numerous divisions, and has left examples of each. The name comedy, in the early Spanish stage, implied no ludicrous or satirical representation, but simply a play of adventure. Comedias divinas, or spiritual comedies, were subdivided into lives of saints, and pieces of the holy sacrament: the comedies of human life into heroic, answering to the tragedy of our early English dramatists, although even less regular in form; and comedies of domestic adventure. Besides these, the interludes which were played between the prologue and the piece possess a distinct character as literary compositions. Almost all pieces have one favorite invariable character, the gracioso or buffoon. Calderon, a greater poet than Lope, and his equal in dramatic power, is the only other great name in the Spanish drama. Subsequent writers may all be classed as imitators either of their own older poets, or of the favorite dramatists of the French school.

English Drama.—The semi-religious representations out of which the English drama arose, were called Mystery and Morality. One of the latter, *The New Custom*, was printed as late as 1573; by which time several regular tragedies and comedies, tolerably approaching to the classical model, had appeared. But a third species of exhibition soon took possession of the stage, the historical drama, in which the successive events of a particular reign or portion of history were represented on the stage; and, together with it, arose the English tragedy and comedy. The first dramatic poets of England (those before Shakspeare) were scholars; hence they preferred the form of the ancient drama, the division into acts, &c. But they were also writers, who strove for popularity with the general class of their countrymen; hence, instead of imitating classical simplicity, and confining themselves to a peculiar cast of diction and sentiment removed from the ordinary course of life, they invented a species of composition which intermingled poetical with ordinary life and language. Comedy, again, became in their hands a representation of adventures, differing from those of tragedy only by ending generally in a happy instead of an unhappy exit, and not materially either in the characters or language. Thus the distinctions which they established between tragedy, comedy, and tragi-comedy, are little more than adventitious; and the Shaksperian drama, properly considered, must be looked on as a miscellaneous compound, in which actors, language, and sentiments, of a character far removed from those of ordinary life, alternate with those of a low and even a burlesque character. There is no tragedy in Shakspeare in which comic scenes and characters are not introduced: there is only one comedy (*The Merry Wives of Windsor*) without some intermixture of sentiment approaching to tragic. It continued to be the chief national literature, as well as the favorite national amusement, down to the period of the civil wars, when the opinions and legislation of the prevailing party put a stop to dramatic representations altogether. During the interval thus created the old English art was unlearned altogether, and the new drama, on the model of the French, introduced almost at once on the return of Charles II. and his courtiers from the Continent. The distinction between tragedy and comedy was then first substantially recognized: the former confined to heroic events and language, the latter to those of ordinary life. But tragedy, subjected to foreign rules, ceased entirely to flourish: and Otway, the last writer of the old English drama, who wrote partly on the ancient model, although after the Restoration, is also the last tragic poet of England who still occupies the stage; with the exception of Rowe, and of a few authors of that peculiar species of composition, the domestic tragedy, in which the distresses and melancholy events of common life are substituted for those of an heroic character. Comedy, on the other hand, obtained possession of the national taste and stage; and although the charm of poetry and romantic adventure, which had belonged to the old drama under either name, was denied to the modern comedy, it soon attained a high degree of excellence as well as popularity. The last comedies in verse were written shortly after the Restoration; since which time, with the exception of a few insulated attempts to revive the older form, it has been entirely framed on the French model. The main element of a modern comedy is satire; but it admits of a subdivision into comedy of intrigue and comedy of manners,—the former being chiefly directed to the development of a plot, the latter to the delineation of manners; although these qualities ought, properly speaking, to be united to constitute a good play. The most distinguished English dramatic writers in the former line are, amongst many, Congreve, Vanbrugh, Farquhar, Colman, Sheridan: in the latter, the writings of Shadwell and Foote, perhaps, afford the most remarkable instances of that less popular form of comedy which almost neglects the interest of plot, and confines itself to a satirical representation of prevailing vices and follies.

German Drama.—The modern German drama is founded on the old English model; and, although the last in order of time, has risen to a high degree of excellence, the stage in Germany being incomparably more national and popular at the present time than in other European countries. While France, England, and Spain have to look back two hundred years for those names which form the glory of their dramatic literature, Lessing, Schiller, and Goethe are writers only of the past generation.

DRAMATIS PERSO'NÆ, the characters represented in a drama.

DRAMATUR'GY, the science or art of dramatic poetry and representation; a word used by German writers.

DRA'PERY, in sculpture and painting, the representation of the clothing of human figures; also hangings, tapestry, curtains, and most other things that are not flesh or landscape. Although it is the *natural body*, and not some appendage added by human customs and regulations, that sensibly and visibly represents mind and life to our eyes, and has become the chief object of the plastic arts, yet the requirements of social life demand that the body be clothed; the artist fulfils this obligation in such manner as shall prove least detrimental to his aim. Drapery has, of itself, no determinate form, yet all its relations are susceptible of beauty, as it is subordinate to the form it covers. This beauty, which results from the motion and disposition of the folds, is susceptible of numerous combinations very difficult to imitate; indeed, *casting of draperies*, as it is termed, is one of the most important of an artist's studies. The object is to make the *drapery* appear *naturally* disposed, the result of accident or chance. In ancient Art, the feeling and enthusiasm for corporeal beauty was universal, yet the opportunities for representing it were comparatively rare. Only in gymnastic and athletic figures did nakedness present itself as natural, and become the privileged form of representation to the sculptor; it was soon, however, extended to statues of male deities and heroes. Garments that *concealed* the form were universally discarded; it was sufficient to retain only the outer-garment, and even this was entirely laid aside when the figure was represented in action. In sedent statues, on the contrary, the upper garment is seldom laid aside; it is then usually drawn around the loins; it denotes, therefore, rest and absence of exertion. In this way the drapery, even in ideal figures, is significant, and becomes an expressive attribute. Ancient Art, at the same time, loved a compendious and illusive treatment; the helmet denotes the whole armor; a piece of the chlamys the entire dress of the Ephebos. It was customary at all times to represent children naked; on the other hand, the unrobing of the developed female body was long unheard of in Art, and when this practice was introduced, it required at first a connection with life; here the idea of the bath constantly preserved itself until the eyes became accustomed to adopt the representation without this justification. The portrait statue retained the costume of life, if it also was not raised above the common necessity by the form being rendered heroic or divine.—The draperies of the Greeks, which, from their simple, and, as it were, still undecided forms, for the most part only received a determinate character from the mode of wearing, and, at the same time, furnished a great alternation of smooth and folded parts, were especially calculated from the outset for such purposes; but it also became early an artistic principle to render the forms of the body everywhere as prominent as possible, by drawing the garments close, and loading the skirts with small weights. The striving after clearness of representation dictated to the artists of the best period a disposition into large masses, and a subordination of the details to the leading forms, precisely as is observed in the muscular development of the body.

DRAW, a word used in a variety of situations, and in some of very opposite meanings, but in most of its uses it retains some shade of its original sense—to pull, to move forward by the application of force, or to extend in length. It expresses an action gradual or continuous, and leisurely, yet not requiring the toil and difficulty which its kindred word *drag* implies.

DRAW'BACK, in commerce, a term used to signify the remitting or paying back of the duties previously paid on a commodity, on its being exported; so that it may be sold in a foreign market on the same terms as if it had not been taxed at all. By this device, therefore, merchants are enabled to export commodities loaded at home with heavy duties, and to sell them abroad on the same terms as those fetched from countries where they are not taxed.—In a popular sense, *drawback* signifies any loss of advantage, or deduction from profit.

DRAW'ER, and DRAW'EE, in commerce, the drawer is he who draws a bill of exchange or an order for the payment of money; and the *drawee*, the person on whom it is drawn.

DRAW'ING, the art of representing the appearances of objects upon a flat surface, by means of an outline which describes their form and shadow, situation, distance, &c.

DRAW'ING-ROOM, a room appropriated for the reception of company at court; or to which, in common cases, parties withdraw after dinner. Also, the company assembled at court to pay their respects to the sovereign.

DREAMS, may be defined to be those trains of ideas which occupy the mind, or those imaginary transactions in which it is engaged, during sleep. Dreams constitute some of the most curious phenomena of the human mind, and have in all ages presented to philosophers a subject of most interesting investigation. The theory of dreams embraces two distinct classes of phenomena, *physical* and *psychological*: the former relate to the question as to how the body is affected in a state of sleep, how the body in that state affects the mind, and how this affection operates to the production of the phenomena of dreams; the latter comprehend an inquiry into the laws which regulate the train of ideas that occur during sleep, and the mode in which these laws operate, together with an examination of certain psychological appearances peculiar to that state. To both these classes of phenomena the attention of some of the most distinguished philosophers, both of antiquity and of modern times, has been directed; and much labor and ingenuity have been expended in endeavoring to ascertain the origin and nature of dreams, and to account for the various phenomena by which they are accompanied. Among a multitude of other *efficient* causes, dreams have been ascribed to direct impressions on the organs of sense during sleep,—to the absence of real impressions on the senses,—to a disordered state of the digestive organs,—to a less restrained action of the mental faculties,—to the suspension of volition while the powers of sensation continue,—

and to the succession and unequal relaxation and cessation of the different senses at the commencement and during the time of sleep. From the remotest period of antiquity, dreams have also been ascribed to supernatural agency. The records of history, both sacred and profane, abound in instances of dreams which it has been thought impossible to account for on any other hypothesis than that of a supernatural interposition; and, as has been well observed, though there can be no doubt that many dreams which have been considered supernatural, as revealing facts and scientific truths, may now be explained by means within our own knowledge, it can just as little be doubted that many well-authenticated dreams are utterly inexplicable by ordinary means. This belief in the supernatural character of dreams is common to every nation in a greater or less degree; but it prevails more especially in the countries of the East, where, from time immemorial, there has existed a class of persons whose peculiar occupation consists in the interpretation and explanation of dreams. Those who wish for comprehensive details on this subject may consult the writings of Aristotle, Lucretius, Democritus, &c.; and among modern writers, of Locke, Newton, Hartley, Baxter, Beattie, and Stewart; and still more recently, those of Abercrombie and Macnish, which are extremely valuable for the numerous instances of extraordinary dreams with which their theories are illustrated.

DRESS, clothes worn as the covering or ornament of the body; and generally, though not always, applied to elegant attire.—*To dress*, is a military term for arranging the men in line.

DRESS'INGS, in architecture, mouldings round doors, windows, and the like.

DRIP'PING EAVES, in architecture, the lower edges of a roof wherefrom the rain drips or drops to the ground.

DRIV'ING NOTES, in music, such notes as connect the last note of one bar with the first of the following one, so as to make only one note of both. They are also used in the middle of a measure, and when a note of one part terminates in the middle of the note of another, in which case it is called *binding* or *legature*. Driving notes are also called *syncopation*, when some shorter note at the beginning of a measure or half-measure is followed by two, three, or more longer notes, before any other occurs equal to that which occasioned the driving note to make the number even; for instance, when an odd crotchet succeeds two or three minims, or an odd quaver two or more crotchets.

DROPS, in architecture, the frusta of cones in the Doric order, used under the triglyphs in the architrave below the tœnia. They are also used in the under part of the mutuli or modillions of the order. In the Greek examples they are sometimes curved a little inwards on the profile.

DRUG'GET, a coarse woollen fabric, used for covering carpets, and sometimes as an article of clothing by females of the poorer classes.

DRU'IDS, the priests or ministers of the ancient Britons and Gauls, resembling, in many respects, the bramins of India. The Druids were chosen out of the best families; and were held, both by the honors of their birth and their office, in the greatest veneration. They are said to have understood astrology, geometry, natural history, politics, and geography; they had the administration of all sacred things; were the interpreters of religion, and the judges of all affairs; and, according to Cæsar, they believed in the immortality of the soul, and its transmigration through different bodies.

DRUM, a military musical instrument in form of a cylinder, hollow within, and covered at the ends with vellum, which is stretched or slackened at pleasure by the means of small cords and sliding knots It is beat upon with sticks. Some drums are made of brass, but they are commonly of wood. There are several beats of the drum, as the *chamade*, *reveille*, *retreat*, &c. The drum is supposed to be an eastern invention, and to have been brought into Europe by the Arabians, or perhaps the Moors. The kettle drum, the bass drum, and tambourine, are common in the East.—In architecture, the upright part of a cupola either above or below a dome. The same term is used to express the solid part or vase of the Corinthian and Composite capitals.

DRUNK'ENNESS, intoxication. Physically considered, it consists of a preternatural compression of the brain, and a discomposure of its fibres, occasioned by the fumes or spirituous parts of liquors; so that the drunkard's reason is disordered, and he reels or staggers in walking. Drunkenness appears in different shapes, in different constitutions; some it makes gay, some sullen, and some furious. Hobbes makes voluntary drunkenness a breach of the law of nature, which directs us to preserve the use of our reason.

Paley calls it "a social festive vice;" and says, "The drinker collects his circle; the circle naturally spreads; of those who are drawn within it, many become the corrupters and centres of sets and circles of their own; every one countenancing, and perhaps emulating the rest, till a whole neighborhood be infected from the contagion of a single example." Drunkenness is punishable by fine and imprisonment, and in law is no excuse for any crime committed during the paroxysm.

DRY'ADS, in the heathen theology, a sort of deities or nymphs, which the ancients thought inhabited groves and woods. They differed from the *Hamadryads*, these latter being attached to some particular tree with which they were born, and with which they died; whereas the *Dryads* were goddesses of trees and woods in general.

DRY'ERS, substances, chiefly metallic oxides, added to certain fixed oils, to impart to them the property of *drying* quickly when used in painting. That most commonly employed for this purpose is the oxide of lead; but *white copperas* or *white vitriol*, (sulphate of zinc,) oxide of manganese, ground glass, oxide of zinc, calcined bones, chloride of lime, and *verdigris*, (di-acetate of copper,) have also been used at various periods in the history of Art as dryers.

DRY'ING OIL, Boiled Oil, when linseed oil is boiled with litharge, (oxide of lead,) it acquires the property of drying quickly when exposed in a thin stratum to the air. Its uses as a vehicle and varnish are well known.

DRY'NESS, this term is applied to a style of painting, in which the outline is harsh and formal, and the color deficient in mellowness and harmony. It is not incompatible with good composition and other high qualities, as may be seen in some of the works of Holbein, and the earlier productions of Raphael.

DU'ALISM, a name given to those systems of philosophy which refer all existence to *two* ultimate principles. Dualism is a main feature in all the early Greek cosmogonies, and is that which distinguishes them from the eastern speculations on similar subjects, which mostly regard all things as *emanating* from a single principle. The dualistic hypothesis was, doubtless, originally suggested by the analogy of male and female in animal existence. The earliest forms under which the theory appeared are, as might be expected, rude in the extreme. The Orphic poets made the ultimate principles of all things to be Water and Night; by others Æther and Erebus, Time and Necessity, are severally deemed worthy of this distinction. The ancient Greek and Roman mythology was evidently constructed on this principle. In its more philosophic form, the dualistic theory was maintained among the ancients by Pythagoras and many of the Ionian school; among the moderns, chiefly by Descartes. It may be expressed generally as the assumption of the coeternity and simultaneous development of the formative with the formed, of the *natura naturans* with the *natura naturata*. So the system of philosophy which regards matter and spirit as distinct principles is a species of dualism, as opposed to materialism.—In theology, the doctrine of the two sovereign principles of good and evil is also dualistic; and the high Calvinistic theory may be said to be a species of dualism, viz. that all mankind are divided, in the eternal foreknowledge of God, and by his sovereign decree, into two classes,—the elect and reprobate.

DU'AL NUMBER, in grammar, is the name given to that form of the verb and substantive by which, in the ancient Greek, Sanscrit, and Gothic, and the modern Lithuanian languages, *two* persons or things are denoted, in contradistinction to *plural*, which expresses an indefinite number of persons or things.

DUC'AT, a foreign coin of different values, and which are either of silver or gold. The silver ducat is generally of 4*s*. 6*d*. sterling, and the gold ducat of twice that value.

DUCATOON', a silver coin, struck chiefly in Italy, value about 4*s*. 8*d*. sterling; but the gold ducatoon of Holland is worth twenty florins.

DU'CES TE'CUM, (*bring with thee*,) in law, a writ commanding a person to appear on a certain day in the court of Chancery, and to bring with him some writings, evidences, or other things, which the court would view.

DUE, that which one contracts to pay or perform to another; that which law or justice requires to be paid or done. Also, that which office, rank, station, or established rules of right or decorum, require to be given or performed.

DU'EL, signified originally a trial by battle resorted to by two persons as a means of determining the guilt or innocence of a person charged with a crime, or of adjudicating a disputed right; but in more modern times it is used to signify a hostile meeting between two persons, arising from an affront given by one to the other, and for the purpose (as is said) of affording *satisfaction* to the person affronted. The practice of the duel, as a private mode, recognized only by custom, of deciding private differences, seems to be of comparatively recent date, and descends by no very direct transmission from the ancient appeal to the judicial combat as a final judgment in legal disputes. That it originated with the feudal system is abundantly clear, if it were only from the fact that in Russia, where that system was never known, the custom of the duel was unheard of, until introduced by foreign officers, even within the memory of the present generation. But it is certain that many antiquarian writers have confused together two very different institutions; the *appeal to arms*, as an alternative for the trial by ordeal or by compurgators, appointed by traditionary usage from the earliest periods of Germanic history; and the *voluntary challenge or defiance*, resorted to for the purpose of clearing disputes involving the honor of gentlemen. This last custom was first elevated to the dignity of an established institution by Philip le Bel of France, whose edict regulating the public combat between nobles bears the date of 1308: the best comment on which may be found in the spirited and accurate representation, by Shakspeare, of the quarrel between Mowbray and Bolingbroke.

DUEN'NA, the chief lady in waiting on the queen of Spain. In a more general sense, it is applied to a person holding a middle station between a governess and companion, and appointed to take charge of the junior female members of Spanish and Portuguese families.

DUET', a piece of music composed for two performers, either vocal or instrumental.

DUKE, a sovereign prince in Germany, and the highest title of honor in England next to the Prince of Wales. His consort is called a *duchess*.—In England, among the Saxons, the commanders of armies, &c. were called dukes, *duces*, without any addition, till Edward III. made his son, the Black Prince, duke of Cornwall; after whom there were more made in the same manner, the title descending to their posterity. Duke, at present, is a mere title of dignity, without giving any domain, territory, or jurisdiction over the place from whence the title is taken. The title of duke is said to have originated in the usages of the Lower Empire, where it was given to the military governors of provinces. From thence it was borrowed by the Franks, who adopted, in many respects, the titles and distinctions of the empire. Charlemagne is said to have suffered it to become obsolete, but the emperor Louis created a duke of Thuringia in 847. In course of time, according to the usual progress of feudal dignities, the title became hereditary. In Germany the dukes became the chief princes of the empire; this title being proper to all the secular electors, and to most of the greater feudatories. In other countries their dignity became merely titular. In Italy and France dukes form the second rank in the nobility, being inferior to princes: in England they form the first. The title was not known in the latter country until the reign of Edward III.; and the word dux is used by writers before that period as synonymous with count or earl.

DUL'CIMER, a musical instrument played by striking brass wires with little sticks.

DUMB, the most general, if not the sole cause of dumbness, is the want of the sense of hearing; and nothing is more fallacious than the idea, that the want of speech is owing to the want of mental capacity. The necessity of communication, and the want of words, oblige him who is dumb to observe and imitate the actions and expressions which accompany various states of mind and of feeling, to indicate objects by their appearance and use, and to describe the actions of persons by direct imitation, or pantomimic expression. Hence what has been called the natural sign language has been adopted by instructors of the deaf and dumb, in order to express all the ideas we convey by articulate sounds. This language, in its elements, is to be found among all nations, and has ever been the medium of communication between voyagers and the natives of newly discovered countries. The more lively nations of Europe, belonging to the Celtic race, the French, Italians, &c., make great use of it, in connection with words, and sometimes even without them. The more phlegmatic people of the Teutonic race, in England and Germany, are so little disposed to it, that they regard it as a species of affectation or buffoonery in their southern neighbors. The method of instructing the deaf and dumb, which has been most successfully employed, consists in teaching the pupil the relation between the names of objects and the objects themselves, the analysis of words into letters of the alphabet, and the particular gesture which he is to attach to each word as its distinctive sign—showing to him also the meaning of collective words, as distinguished from those denoting individual objects, or parts of objects.

DUN, of a color partaking of a dull brown and black.—*To dun*, to press for the payment of money by repeatedly calling for it. Hence an importunate creditor is called a *dun*.

DUN'KERS, a Christian sect, which formed itself into a society under peculiar rules in Pennsylvania in the year 1724. The origin of their name is unknown. They practise abstinence and mortification, under the idea that such austerities are meritorious in the sight of God, and effective, first in procuring their own salvation, and further in contributing to that of others. They form a society strictly connected within itself, and hold love feasts, in which all assemble together; but their devotions and ordinary business are carried on in private, nor do they recognize a community of goods. They also deny the eternity of future punishments; conceiving that there are periods of purgation, determined by the sabbath, sabbatical year, and year of jubilee, which are typical of them.

DUN'NAGE, in commercial navigation, loose wood laid in the bottom and against the sides of the ship's hold, in order to prevent the cargo from being injured in the event of her becoming leaky.

DUODE'CIMO, having or consisting of twelve leaves to a sheet; or a book in which a sheet is folded into twelve leaves.

DUPLI'CITY, the act of dissembling one's real opinions for the purpose of concealing them and misleading persons in the conversation and intercourse of life.

DURAN'TE, in law, During; as *durante bene placito*, during pleasure; *durante minore ætate*, during minority; *durante vitâ*, during life.

DU'RESS, in law, is restraint or compulsion; as, where a person is wrongfully imprisoned, or restrained of his liberty, contrary to law; or is threatened to be killed, wounded, or beaten, till he executes a bond, or other writing. Any bond, deed, or other obligation, obtained by duress, will be void in law; and in an action brought on the execution of any such deed, the party may plead that it was brought by duress.

DUSK, a middle degree between light and darkness; as twilight, or the *dusk* of the evening. Hence the words *dusky*, *duskiness*, &c.

DUTCH GOLD, copper, brass, and bronze leaf is known under this name in commerce; it is largely used in Holland for ornamenting toys and paper.

DUTCH SCHOOL, in painting, this school, generally speaking, is founded on a faithful representation of nature, without attention to selection or refinement. The ideas are usually low, and the figures local and vulgar. Its merit lies in coloring and drawing with extreme fidelity what was before the eye of the artist. The pothouse, the workshop, or the drunken revels of unintellectual boors, seem to have furnished its principal subjects. The great appearance of reality infused into its productions induced Hagedora to call it the School of Truth. Notwithstanding its deficiency in all that tends to raise the mind, it has gained an unspeakable lustre from its great head, Rembrandt van Rhyn, to whose name may be added those of De Leide, Heemskirk, Polemburg, Wouvermans, (an exception to our general observations,) Gerard Dow, Mieris, and Vandevelde, &c.

DUTY, in commerce, any tax or excise; a sum of money required by government to be paid on the importation, exportation, or consumption of goods.—In a military sense, the business of a soldier or marine on guard.—In its universal application, *duty* includes any natural, moral, or legal obligation; as, it is the *duty* of every citizen of a state to pay obedience to its laws; obedience, respect, and kindness are the *duties* which children owe their parents.

DUUM'VIRI, in Roman antiquity, a general appellation given to magistrates, commissioners, and officers, where two were joined together in the same function. The office, dignity, or government of two men thus associated, was called a *duumvirate*.—*Duumviri capitales*, were the judges in criminal causes: from their sentence it was lawful to appeal to the people, who only had the power of condemning a citizen to death.—*Duumviri municipales*, were two magistrates in some cities of the empire, answering to what the consuls were at Rome; they were chosen out of the body of the *decuriones;* their office usually lasted five years, upon which account they were frequently termed *quinquinales magistratus*.—*Duumviri navales*, were the commissaries of the fleet. The duty of their office consisted in giving orders for the fitting of ships, and giving their commissions to the marine officers, &c.—*Duumviri sacrorum*, were magistrates created by Tarquinius Superbus, for the performance of the sacrifice, and keeping of the Sibyl's books. They were chosen from among the patricians, and held their office for life: they were exempted from serving in the wars, and from the offices imposed on the other citizens, and without them the oracles of the Sibyls could not be consulted.

DY'NASTY, a race or series of princes who have reigned successively in any kingdom; as the *dynasties* of Egypt or Persia.

DYSPEP'SIA, or DYSPEP'SY, in medicine, difficulty of digestion. Hence those who are afflicted with indigestion are termed *dyspeptic* persons. The disorder of the digestive function is the most frequent and prevailing of the ailments that afflict man in the civilized state; all classes and all ages suffer from its attacks. But in the higher ranks of society, and amongst the luxurious and opulent, it is a common consequence of over eating, or of indulgence in difficultly digestible or over-stimulating food, or of want of due exercise and general bodily and mental exertion. In others it results from mental anxiety and labor associated with a sedentary life; from the fatigues of business or the influence of debilitating passions. In the lower orders it is the constant result of indulgence in spirituous liquors, combined in many instances with want of proper food, the means which ought to be applied to procuring it being disposed of in the dram shop. The symptoms of dyspepsia vary, therefore, in the different grades of life. The epicure loses his relish for the most refined dishes, becomes bloated, plethoric, heavy, and perhaps apoplectic; the lady of fashion suffers from headaches, flatulence, occasional giddiness, and dimness of sight: she becomes indolent, capricious, and full of fancies, or, as the old physicians used to say, she has the *vapors;* the studious man feels the intensity of his mind blunted, loses his appetite, or at least all enjoyment of meals, sleeps ill, and dreams much, gets whimsical and discontented with himself and his friends, and becomes a *hypochondriac;* the lower classes at first take their glass of gin or of rum because they find it a cheap stimulant, little thinking of the misery they are laying up for future years; this stimulant soon becomes habitual, and they not only feel miserable and heartbroken without it, but the single glass soon loses its efficacy, and the dose must be gradually increased till they degenerate into regular tipplers, the aspect and characters of whom it were needless to describe. Complicated as are the symptoms of dyspepsia, and numerous as are the remedies and modes of treatment proposed for its relief or cure, they really resolve themselves into a few simple rules. In the majority of cases, *abstinence* is the first and most essential step; the epicure must abstain from the luxuries of the table, eat and drink with moderation, rise betimes, and use due exercise; the woman of fashion must revert to regular hours, that is, the night and the day must be employed as intended by nature, and not in inverted order; the philosopher and the scholar must occasionally, and often frequently and assiduously, divest themselves of their mental labors, and resort to amusements and occupations of a more trivial character. Those among the lower orders who have once acquired the habit of dram drinking are incurable; for such is the depression of mind and body, and such the gnawing restlessness that want of the accustomed stimulus occasions, that without it they become miserable and inconsolable, and usually fall a sacrifice to mental or bodily disease, or to both combined; here, therefore, prevention is the only cure.

E.

E, the fifth letter in the alphabet, and the second vowel, has different pronunciations in most languages. The French have their *e* open, *e* masculine, and *e* feminine or mute. In English, there are three kinds of *e:* open, as in *wear, bear;* long, as in *here, mere, me;* and short, as in *wet, kept,* &c. As a final letter it is generally quiescent; but it serves to lengthen the sound of the preceding vowel, as in *mane, cane, thine,* which, without the final *e,* would be pronounced *man, can, thin.* In many other words the final *e* is silent, as in *examine, definite,* &c. As a numeral E stands for 250. In sea-charts, E stands for East: E by N. and E by S., East by North, and East by South.—In music, the third note or degree of the diatonic scale, corresponding to the *mi* of the French and Italians. In the bass clef it is that on the third space of the staff, in the tenor on the first space, in the counter tenor on the fourth line, and in the treble clef that on the first line.

EA'GLE, in history, the symbol of royalty; as being, according to Philostratus, the king of birds. Hence, in the Scriptures, a Chaldæan and Egyptian king are styled eagles. The eagle was borne as a standard by many nations of antiquity. The first who assumed it, according to Xenophon, were the Persians, from whom (in all probability through the medium of the Greeks) it was borrowed by the Romans at an early period of their history, but first adopted as their sole ensign in the consulate of C. Marius. Previously to that period they had used as standards wolves, leopards, eagles, and other animals, indifferently, according to the humor of their generals. The Roman eagles were gold or silver figures in relievo, about the size of a pigeon; and were borne on the tops of spears, with their wings displayed, and frequently with a thunderbolt in their talons. When the army marched the eagle was always visible to the legions; and when it encamped, the eagle was always placed before their *prætorium* or tent of the general. The eagle on the summit of an ivory staff was also the symbol of the consular dignity. In modern times an eagle standing with outspread wings, is the military emblem of the United States. During the sway of Napoleon, he caused the tricolor flag, which at the outbreak of the first French Revolution had become the standard of France, to be surmounted with an eagle; and thus constituted it the standard of the consular and imperial armies. From this circumstance, and from the almost unprecedented career of victory so long pursued by the French under this standard, the expression *eagles of Napoleon* is often used metaphorically to designate the *armies* under his command. After the battle of Waterloo the eagle was superseded in France by the fleur de lys, the ancient emblem of the Bourbon race. Eagles are frequently found on ancient coins and medals; where, according to Spanheim, they are emblematic of divinity and providence, but according to all other antiquaries, of empire. They are most usually found on the medals of the Ptolemies of Egypt and the Seleucidæ of Syria. An eagle, with the word *consecratio*, indicates the apotheosis of an emperor. The eagle is also the badge of several orders, as the black eagle and the red eagle of Prussia, the white eagle of Poland, &c.—In Christian Art, an eagle is the attribute of St. John the Evangelist; the symbol of authority, of power, and of generosity; it was regarded by St Gregory as the emblem of contemplative life. It is represented drinking from a chalice, as an emblem of the strength the Christian derives from the Holy Eucharist. The conflict between the "state of nature" and the "state of grace" is represented by an eagle fighting with a serpent, and by an eagle, the body of which, terminating in the tail of a serpent, is turned against the head. A common form for the lectern, constructed of wood or brass, used to support the sacred volume in the choir of churches, is that of an eagle.—Elisha, the prophet, is represented with a two-headed eagle over his head or upon his shoulder, referring to his petition to Elijah for a *double* portion of his spirit.

EARL, a title of British nobility, between a marquis and a viscount; now the third degree of rank. William the Conqueror first made this title hereditary, giving it in fee to his nobles, and allotting them for the support of their state the third penny out of the sheriff's court, issuing out of all pleas of the shire whence they had their title. At present the title is accompanied by no territory, private or judicial rights, but confers nobility, and an hereditary seat in the House of Lords. In official instruments, they are called by the king, "trusty and well-beloved cousins," an appellation as ancient as the reign of Henry IV. For some time after the Norman conquest they were called *counts*, and their wives to the present day are styled *countesses*.—The *Earl's coronet* has no flowers raised above the circle, like that of a duke and a marquis, but only points rising, and a pearl on each of them.

EARL MARSHAL OF ENGLAND, a great officer who had anciently several courts under his jurisdiction, as the court of chivalry, and the court of honor. Under him is also the herald's office, or college of arms. He has some pre-eminence in the Marshalsea court, where he may sit in judgment against those who offend within the verge of the king's court This office is of great antiquity in England, and has been for several ages hereditary in the family of the Howards.

EARN'EST, in commercial law, money advanced by the buyer of goods, to bind the seller to the performance of a verbal bargain.

EAR'RING, an ornament worn at the ear, by means of a ring passing through the lobe, with a pendant of diamonds or

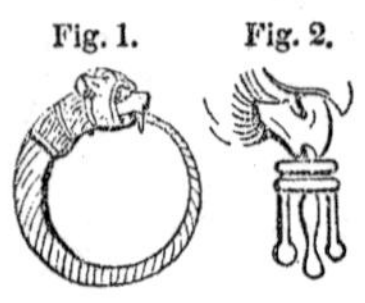
Fig. 1. Fig. 2.

pearls, &c., attached. This ornament has been worn by both sexes, from the earliest times, in oriental countries, but among the Greeks and Romans, its use was confined to females. It was usually constructed of gold, of various forms, very finely wrought, and set with pearls and precious stones. The ears in the statue of the Medicean Venus and other statues are pierced, and probably were at one time ornamented with ear-rings. The cut gives examples of two antique ear-rings. Fig. 1 is an Egyptian one of gold, half an inch in diameter, published by Wilkinson. Fig. 2 is from one of the Syracusan medallions.

EARTH'QUAKE, a concussion or vibration of the ground, usually preceded by a rattling sound in the air, or by a subterraneous rumbling noise; and sometimes accompanied by rents, and by shaking of the surface, so as to swallow up towns and tracts of country. At one time it is hardly perceptible; at another, it is so violent, that it not only demolishes the works of art, but changes the appearance of the ground itself. Sometimes the surface of the ground remains unbroken; sometimes it bursts open into clefts and chasms; and then occasionally appears the phenomenon of the eruption of gases, and also of flames, with the ejection of water, mud, and stones, as in volcanic eruptions. Volcanoes are, indeed, only so many spiracles serving for the discharge of this subterranean fire, when it is thus assembled; and where there happens to be such a structure and conformation of the interior parts of the earth, that the fire may pass freely and without impediment from the caverns therein, it gathers into these spiracles, and then readily and easily gets out from time to time without shaking or disturbing the earth: but where a communication is wanting, or the passages are not sufficiently large and open, so that it cannot come at these spiracles, without first forcing and removing all obstacles, it heaves up and shakes the earth, till it makes its way to the mouth of the volcano; where it rushes forth, sometimes in flames of vast volume and velocity. Earthquakes are sometimes confined to a narrow space, which is properly the effect of the re-action of the fire; and they shake the earth just as the explosion of a powder-magazine causes a sensible concussion at the distance of several leagues. These observations furnish grounds for the conclusion, that earthquakes cannot proceed from external causes, but arise from certain powers operating within the circumference or crust of the earth. The subterranean, thunder-like noises; the shaking, raising, and bursting asunder of the earth; the emission of fire and flames, and the ejection of mineral substances; all occur, occasionally, in earthquakes as well as in volcanic eruptions, even when at a distance from active volcanoes. All the observations, in fact, that have been made, tend to prove, that earthquakes and volcanic eruptions are effects of the same chemical process, (so to speak,) which must have its seat at a great depth beneath the earth's surface. There is no portion of the earth's surface, whether it be land or water, that is not more or less subject to earthquakes; and records of their destructive effects have been transmitted to us through every age. The first earthquake particularly worthy of notice was that which in A.D. 63, destroyed Herculaneum and Pompeii. In the fourth and fifth centuries, some of the most civilized parts of the world were almost desolated by these awful visitations. Thrace, Syria, and Asia Minor, according to contemporary historians, suffered most severely. On the 26th of January, A.D. 447, subterranean thunders were heard from the Black to the Red Sea, and the earth was convulsed without intermission, for the space of six months; and in Phrygia, many cities and large tracts of ground were swallowed up. On the 30th of May, A.D. 205, the city of Antioch was overwhelmed by a dreadful earthquake, and 250,000 of its inhabitants are said to have been crushed in its ruins. In the year 1346, Asia Minor and Egypt were violently shaken; and in the following year severe earthquakes were experienced in Cyprus, Greece, and Italy. In 1692, the island of Jamaica was visited by a terrible earthquake, in which enormous masses of earth were detached from the Blue Mountains; and vast quantities of timber, hurled from their flanks, covered the adjacent sea like floating islands. It was during this earthquake that the city of Port Royal, with a large tract of adjacent land, sunk instantaneously into the sea. In the following year great earthquakes occurred in Sicily, which destroyed Catania and 140 other towns and villages, with 100,000 of their inhabitants. Since the records of history, there have been no earthquakes equal in intensity to those which ravaged different parts of the world in the eighteenth century. Passing over the convulsion which in 1746 nearly laid waste Lower Peru, and those by which in 1750 the ancient town of Concepcion, in Chili, was totally destroyed, we come to 1755, when the city of Lisbon was almost wholly destroyed by one of the most destructive earthquakes which ever occurred in Europe. It continued only six minutes; but such was the violence of the convulsion, that in that short space upwards of 60,000 persons are said to have perished. The phenomena that accompanied it were no less striking. The sea first retired and laid the bar dry; it then rolled in, rising fifty feet or more above its ordinary level. The largest mountains in Portugal were impetuously shaken from their very foundations: and some of them opened at their summits, which were split and rent in a wonderful manner, huge masses of them being thrown down into the subjacent valleys. But the most remarkable circumstance which occurred in Lisbon during this catastrophe was the entire subsidence of the new quay, called Cays de Prada, to which an immense concourse of people had fled for safety from the falling ruins. From this hideous abyss, into which the quay sunk, not one of the dead bodies ever floated to the surface; and on the spot there is now water to the depth of 100 fathoms. This earthquake excited great attention from the incredibly great extent at which contemporary shocks were experienced. The violence of the shocks, which were accompanied by a terrific subterranean noise, like the loudest thunder, was chiefly felt in Portugal, Spain, and northern Africa; but the effects of the earthquake were perceived in almost all the countries of continental Europe, and were even experienced in the West Indies, and on the Lake Ontario in North America. Ships at sea were affected by the shocks as if they had struck on rocks: and even on some of the Scottish lakes, Loch Lomond in particular, the water, without the least apparent cause, rose to the perpendicular height of two feet four inches against its bank, and the subsided below its usual level. During the next twenty years, various earthquakes occurred in different parts of the world, attended with more or less destructive consequences. In 1759, Syria was agitated by violent earthquakes, the shocks of which were protracted for three months, throughout a space of 10,000 square leagues, and levelled to the ground Accon, Saphat, Balbeck, Damascus, Sidon, Tripoli, and many other places. In each of these places many thousands of the inhabitants perished; and in the valley of Balbeck alone, 20,000 men are said to have been victims to the convulsion. In 1766, the island of Trinidad and great part of Columbia were violently agitated by earthquakes In 1772, the lofty volcano of Papanday ang, the highest mountain in Java, disappeared, and a circumjacent area, fifteen miles by six, was swallowed up. In 1783, the north-eastern part of Sicily and the southern portion of Calabria were convulsed by violent and oft-repeated shocks, which overthrew the town of Messina, and killed many thousands of its inhabitants, as well as many persons in Calabria. In the same year, the islands of Japan, Java in 1786, Sicily and the Caraccas in 1790, Quebec in 1791, and the Antilles and Peru in 1797, were violently agitated by convulsions of this kind. Since the commencement of the present century, various earthquakes have occurred both in the Old and New World. In 1811, violent earthquakes shook the valley of the Mississippi, by which lakes of considerable extent disappeared, and new ones were formed. In 1812, Caraccas was destroyed, and upwards of 12,000 of its inhabitants buried in the ruins. In 1815, the town of Tombora, in the island of Sumbawa, was completely destroyed by an earthquake, which extended throughout an area 100 miles in diameter, and destroyed 12,000 persons. In 1819, a violent earthquake occurred at Cutch, in the Delta of the Indus, by which, among other disastrous consequences, the principal town, Bhoog, was converted into a heap of ruins. In 1822, Aleppo was destroyed by an earthquake. In the same year Chili was visited by a most destructive earthquake, from which the coast for 100 miles is stated to have sustained an elevation of from two to four feet, while about a mile inward from Valparaiso, it was raised from six to seven feet. In 1827, Popayan and Bogota suffered severely from earthquakes, during which vast fissures opened in the elevated plains around the latter city. In 1835, the town of Concepcion, in Chili, was entirely demolished by an earthquake. In 1837, the countries along the eastern extremity of the Mediterranean, especially Syria, were violently agitated by an earthquake, which caused great damage to the towns of Damascus, Acre, Tyre, and Sidon, and entirely destroyed Tiberias and Safet. Such are some of the most violent earthquakes that have occurred within the period of authentic history.

EASEL, an apparatus constructed of wood, upon which the panel or canvas is placed while a picture is being painted. EASEL-PICTURE is a term employed to designate a picture of small dimensions,

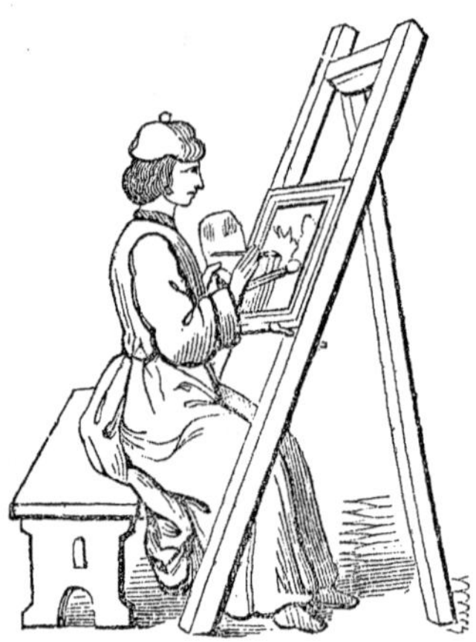

such as render it portable.—In Christian Art, St. Luke is often represented sitting before an easel, upon which is a portrait of the Virgin. Our cut of an artist of the fifteenth century at work at his easel, is from a beautiful Illumination in the famous MS. Romance of the Rose.

EASE'MENT, in law, a privilege or convenience which one man has of another, whether by charter or prescription, without profit; such as a way through his lands, &c.

EAST, one of the four cardinal points of the world; being that point of the horizon where the sun is seen to rise when in the equator.—The word *east* is indefinitely used when we speak of countries which lie eastward of us, as Persia, India, China, &c.—In Christian churches, which are generally built east and west, the chancel stands at the east end, with an emblematic reference to Christ, who is called the Sun of righteousness and the Day-spring.

EAS'TER, a solemn festival observed among Christians, in commemoration of Christ's resurrection. The Greeks and Latins call it *pascha*; a Hebrew word, applied to the Jewish feast of the passover, to which the Christian festival of Easter corresponds. Thus, St. Paul says? "For even Christ our passover is sacrificed for us." This feast was fixed by the council of Nice, in the year 325, to be held on the Sunday which falls upon or immediately after the full moon which happens next after the twenty-first of March; and as such it stands in the rubric of the church of England.—The English name *Easter*, and the German *Ostern*, are supposed to be derived from the name of the feast of the Teutonic goddess *Ostera*, celebrated by the ancient Saxons early in the spring, and for which, as in many other instances, the first missionaries wisely substituted the Christian festival.

EAST'ERLING, a coin struck by Richard II., which is supposed to have given rise to the name of sterling, as applied to English money.

EAST'ER-OF'FERINGS, or EASTER-DUES, small sums of money paid to the parochial clergyman by the parishioners.

EAST-INDIA COMPANY, "the Governor and company of Merchants of London trading to the East Indies," the most celebrated commercial association either of ancient or modern times, which has extended its sway over the whole of the Mogul empire, was incorporated about the 42d of queen Elizabeth, A.D. 1600, and empowered to trade to countries to the eastward of the Cape of Good Hope, exclusive of all others. A variety of causes had been long operating in favor of such an incorporation. Several very valuable East India ships had been taken from the Portuguese and Spaniards by the English fleets, and awakened the cupidity of merchants to the obtaining a share in a traffic which promised such great advantages. At length, in 1593, an armament fitted out for the East Indies by Sir Walter Raleigh, and commanded by Sir John Borroughs, fell in with, near the Azores, the largest of all the Portuguese carracks, a ship of 1600 tons burden carrying 700 men and 36 brass cannon; and, after an obstinate conflict, carried her into Dartmouth. She was the largest vessel that had been seen in England; and her cargo, consisting of gold, spices, calicoes, silks, pearls, drugs, porcelain, ivory, &c., excited the ardor of the English to engage in so opulent a commerce. About the year 1698, application being made to parliament by private merchants, for laying this trade open, an act passed empowering every subject of England, upon raising a sum of money, for the supply of the government, to trade to those parts. A great subscription was accordingly raised, and the subscribers were styled the New East-India Company; but the old establishment being in possession of all the forts on the coast of India, the new one found it its interest to unite; and both, trading with one joint stock, have ever since been known under one name, viz. *The United East-India Company*. Many and severe have been the contests between the advocates of a free trade to India, and the friends of the "incorporated company;" but at length the long-supported monopoly of that powerful body yielded to an act of Parliament passed in 1833, for continuing the charter till 1854, which, in fact, has put a limit to the Company's commercial character, by enacting that its trade to China was to cease on the 22d of April, 1834, and that the Company was, as soon as possible after that date, to dispose of their stocks on hand, and close their commercial business. The functions of the East-India Company are now, therefore, wholly political. She is to continue to govern India, with the concurrence and under the supervision of the Board of Control, till the 30th of April, 1854.

EAVES, in architecture, the lowest edges of the inclined sides of a roof which project beyond the face of the wall so as to throw the water off therefrom, that being their office.

EAVES'-DROPPER, one who skulks under the eaves of houses, for the purpose of listening to what passes within.

E'BIONITES, an ancient sect who believed in Christ as an inspired messenger of God, but considered him to be at the same time a mere man, born of Joseph and Mary. They maintained also the universal obligation of the Mosaic law, and rejected the authority of St. Paul. The origin of their name is uncertain, some deriving it from that of their supposed founder; others deduce it from a Hebrew word signifying *poor*, and suppose the title to be given to them in reference either to the *poverty* of the class to which they mostly belonged, or to the *meanness* of their doctrine.

EB'ONY, a hard, heavy, durable, black wood, which admits of a fine polish. It is the wood of the eben tree, which grows in India, Madagascar, Ceylon, and the Mauritius. It is wrought into toys, and used for mosaic and inlaid work.

EBOU'LEMENT, in fortification, the crumbling or falling away of a wall or rampart.

EBULLI'TION, either the operation of boiling, or the effervescence which arises from the mixture of an acid and an alkaline liquor.

EC'BASIS, in rhetoric, those parts of the proemium, in which the orator treats of things according to their events or consequences.

EC'BOLE, in rhetoric, a digression whereby the speaker introduces some other person speaking in his own words.

EC'CE HO'MO, (Latin;) "Behold the man!" a painting which represents our Saviour, with a crown of thorns on his head, given up to the people by Pilate. The title of it is taken from Pilate's exclamation, John xix. 5.

ECCLE'SIA, in ancient history, the great assembly of the Athenian people, at which every free citizen might attend and vote. This assembly, though nominally possessed of the supreme authority of the state from the earliest times, yet having no fixed times of meeting, was but seldom convened at all; so that the archons, who were elected from the body of nobles or eupatridæ, had virtually the whole management of the state. But the regulations of Solon, which appointed it to meet regularly four times in every period of thirty-five days, besides extraordinary occasions on which it might be convened, called it into active energy. Solon, however, restricted the subjects discussed in the Ecclesia to such as had before passed through the senate of five hundred; but when the democratic spirit of after-times prevailed, this rule was not at all strictly observed. The magistrates who had the management of these assemblies were the Prytanes, the Prohedri, and Epistates. The first of these sometimes convened the people, and hung up in a conspicuous place a programme giving an account of the matters to be discussed. The *Prohedri* proposed to the people the subjects on which they were to decide, and counted the votes. The *Epistate*, who presided over the whole, gave the liberty of voting, which might not be done before his signal was given. The forms of their proceedings were as follow:—First, an expiatory victim was sacrificed, and his blood carried and sprinkled round the bounds of the assembly. Then the public crier demanded silence, and invited all persons above fifty years of age to speak; after that, any one who pleased. After the subject was discussed, they proceeded to vote on the crier's demanding of them, "whether they would consent to the decree proposed to them?" The votes were commonly given by show of hands, but on some occasions by ballot. When the suffrages had been examined and their numbers declared, the *Prytanes* dissolved the assembly. In order to incite the people to attend the Ecclesia, a small pay of one or three oboli was given for early appearance; and a rope, rubbed with vermilion, was carried through the agora, to mark such as lagged behind, who were accordingly fined.

ECCLESIAS'TES, one of the canonical books of the Old Testament, so called from the Greek word signifying a preacher. Solomon is generally supposed to be the author of this book, though various opinions have been entertained on the subject; and indeed the whole question of its author, date, and design is involved in such difficulty, that the labors of critics and commentators serve rather to perplex than to assist the inquirer.

ECCLESIAS'TIC, something pertaining to or set apart for the church: in contradistinction to *civil* or *secular*, which regards the world. Ecclesiastics are persons whose functions consist in performing the service or in maintaining the discipline of the church.

ECCLESIAS'TICUS, an apocryphal book of Scripture; so called from its being read in the church, (*ecclesia*,) as a book of piety and instruction, but not of infallible authority. The author of this book was a Jew, called Jesus the son of Sirach. The Greeks call it the wisdom of the son of Sirach. It was originally written in Syro Chaldaic, and consists chiefly of meditations relating to religion and the general conduct of human life. It displays but little regard for methodical arrangement; but the style is so highly poetical, and the sentiments so profound, that Addison has pronounced it one of the most brilliant moral treatises on record.

E'CHEA, in ancient architecture, sonorous vases of metal or earth in the form of a bell, used in the construction of theatres for the purpose of reverberating the sound of the performer's voice. They were distributed between the seats; and are described in the fifth book of Vitruvius, who states that Mummius introduced them in Rome, after the taking of Corinth, where he found this expedient used in the theatre.

ECHELON', a term in military tactics borrowed from the French, signifying the position of an army with one division more advanced than another, somewhat like the steps of a ladder. A battalion, regiment, &c., marches *en echelon*, if the divisions of which it is composed do not march in one line, but on parallel lines. The divisions are not exactly behind each other, but each is to the right or left of the one preceding, so as to give the whole the appearance of a stairway. This order is used if the commander wishes to bring one part of a mass into action, and to reserve the other. The word *literally* means a ladder or stairway.

ECHID'NA, in Grecian mythology, the daughter of Geryon and the sea-nymph Callirhoe, or of Tartarus and Gaia; a monster that devoured travellers: parents, according to Hesiod, of those well-known terrors of ancient Greece,—Cerberus, the Hydra, the Sphinx, and the Nemean lion. Hence some suppose the name to represent a sort of general type of monsters and terrific phenomena.

ECHI'NUS, the "egg and tongue" or "egg and anchor" ornament, frequently met with in classical architecture, carved

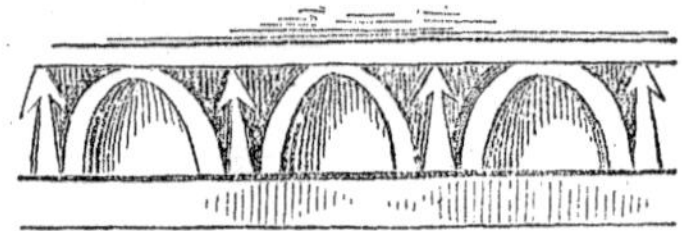

on the ovolo. The type of this ornament is considered to be derived from the chestnut and shell.

ECH'O, a sound reflected or reverberated from some hard surface, and thence returned or repeated to the ear. As the undulatory motion of the air, which constitutes sound, is propagated in all directions from the sounding body, it will frequently happen that the air, in performing its vibrations, will impinge against various objects, which will reflect it back, and so cause new vibrations the contrary way; now if the objects are so situated as to reflect a sufficient number of vibrations back, viz., such as proceed different ways, to the same place, the second will be there repeated, and is called an echo; and the greater the distance of the object is, the longer will be the time before the repetition is heard: and when the sound, in its progress, meets with objects at different distances, sufficient to produce an echo, the same sound will be repeated several times successively, according to the different distances of these objects from the sounding body, which makes what is called a *repeated echo*. Echoes are not, however, caused by a mere repulsion of the sonorous particles of air, for then every hard substances would produce an echo; but it is supposed to require a certain degree of concavity in the repelling body, which collects several diverging lines of sound, and concentrates them in the place where the echo is audible, or, at least, reflects them in parallel lines, without weakening the sound, as a concave mirror collects in a focus the diverging rays of light, or sometimes sends them back parallel. The celebrated echo at Woodstock, in Oxfordshire, repeats the same sound fifty times. But the most singular echo is that near Rosneath, a few miles from Glasgow. If a person placed at a proper distance from this echo plays eight or ten notes of a tune with a trumpet, they are correctly repeated by the echo, but a third lower; after a short pause, another repetition is heard, in a lower tone; and then, after another interval, a third repetition follows in a still lower tone.—*Echo*, in architecture, any vault or arch constructed so as to produce an artificial echo. These are generally of a parabolic or elliptic form; of this kind is the whispering-gallery in St. Paul's cathedral.—*Echo*, in poetry, a sort of verse which returns the sound of the last syllable, the elegance of which consists in giving a new sense to the last words.

ECHOM'ETER, among musicians, a kind of scale or rule, serving to measure the duration and length of sounds, and to find their intervals and ratios.

ECLAIR'CISSEMENT, the clearing up of anything not before understood.

ECLAT', (French,) a burst of applause; renown or approbation following some action or event.

ECLEC'TICS, those philosophers who, without attaching themselves to any particular sect, select whatever appears to them the best and most rational from each.—The *Eclectics* were a sect of Greek philosophers who endeavored to mould the doctrines of Pythagoras and Plato, and blend them with the theology of the Egyptians, and the tenets of Zoroaster. They borrowed many of the principal truths of Christianity from the catechetic school of Alexandria, and blending these with the mysticism of Pythagoras, the errors of Plato, and the superstition of Egypt, they hoped to reconcile the Christians and Pagans to the same opinions. An eclectic spirit, it is evident, can only arise at a period of some maturity in philosophical speculation. Whether or not it is to be regarded as an evidence of the decay of original power in the age in which it appears, must depend on the less or greater coherence in the system when completed. In one sense of the word, Plato and Aristotle may be regarded as eclectics. They both availed themselves largely of the labors of their predecessors. Plato, in particular, comprehended in his scheme of philosophy the whole of more than one foregoing system; as the doctrine of Heraclitus of the perpetual flux of sensible objects, and the consequent uncertainty of sensible impressions. But in the hands of these great thinkers the *discerpta membra* are reunited, and endued with a principle of vitality as constituent parts of a harmonious whole. The same cannot be said of others who have adopted a similar method; especially of most of those to whom the term *eclectic* has been more particularly applied. A far more favorable specimen of the eclectic spirit has been afforded us in modern times in the person of M. Victor Cousin, without doubt the most able and ingenious thinker of modern France. See his *Lectures on the History of Philosophy*, in which eclecticism is presented under its fairest guise, and vindicated with the utmost vigor of style and acuteness of thought.

EC'LOGUE, in the original meaning of the word, the select or choice pieces of an author; or extracts collected out of former works, such as were termed in Latin *excerpta*. It is not known how this title was originally given to the pastoral poems of Virgil; but from the circumstance of their being so named, the word eclogue in modern usage is applied to that species of poetry. The persons who are introduced conversing in eclogues, or whose adventures are recounted in them, are shepherds; that is, for the most part, imaginary personages, whose sentiments, and the external circumstances among which they live, belong rather to an ideal age of gold than to the realities of modern life; and their loves constitute the main and proper subjects of the eclogue. Nevertheless various writers have endeavored, but with little success, to give an air of greater reality to pastoral poetry, and give their rustics more of the costume and diction of actual clowns; but the result has been a species of burlesque, not at all answering to our conceptions of pastoral poetry; nor can we easily imagine that the personages of Theocritus, although the earliest and therefore the simplest of pastoral poets, are correct resemblances of the Sicilian rustics among whom the writer lived. The eclogues of Virgil are of various descriptions: some of them only have the true character of pastorals; others contain occasional poems on public and private events of that day, very slightly enveloped in the pastoral costume. The characteristics of this species of poetry, as assumed by the moderns, are, first, the representation of nature in soft and quiet scenes of cultivation; secondly, a slightly dramatic turn either of action or narration; thirdly, characters whose sentiments and language are confined within certain peculiar limits; thus, any strong emotion, virtue, or vice, would be an unfit topic for a pastoral poet to dwell upon. In English literature, Spenser, Philips, and a few others, may be named as pastoral poets in the strict sense of the word; others, as Milton in his *Lycidas*, have assumed the pastoral costume in order to convey a very different class of ideas. It is worthy of remark, that this species of composition is among those which have wholly disappeared in the present day: the English have had no pastoral poet since Gay and Collins; and Gesner, in Germany, is the latest author who has acquired any degree of celebrity in this line.

ECON'OMY, the frugal expenditure of money, with the prudent management of all the means by which property is saved or accumulated. It also means, a judicious application of time and labor. In a more extended sense, it denotes the regulation and disposition of the affairs of a state or nation, which is called *political economy*. And it is likewise applied to the regular operations of nature in the generation, nutrition, and preservation of animals or plants; as, animal *economy*, vegetable *economy*.

ECOR'CHEE, (ANATOMICAL FIGURE,) this convenient word, for which we have no equivalent in our language, signifies the subject, man or animal, *flayed*, deprived of its skin, so that the muscular system is exposed for the purposes of study. The word skeleton is limited in its application to the *bony* structure. The study of the muscular system is one of the greatest importance to the artist. The difficulties in the way of studying the dead subject are so great, that it has been found necessary to construct models in *papier-mâché* or plaster, in which the prominent muscles are exhibited and colored after nature, which are used in academies and schools by students.

ECPHONE'SIS, in rhetoric, a figure of speech used by an orator to give utterance to the warmth of his feelings.

ECS'TASY, that state of the mind in which the functions of the senses are either suspended or transported with raptures, by the contemplation of some extraordinary object.—In medicine, a species of catalepsy, when the person remembers, after the paroxysm is over, the ideas he had during the fit.

ECSTAT'ICI, a sort of diviners amongst the Greeks, who for a considerable time lay in trances, deprived of all sense and motion, but when they returned to their former state, gave strange accounts of what they had seen and heard during their absence from the body.

EC'TYPE, a word sometimes used by antiquarians, signifying an impression of a medal, seal, or ring, or a figured copy of an inscription or other ancient monument.

ED'DA, the ancient collection of Scandinavian poetry in which the national mythology is contained. There are two Eddas: the older is believed to have been reduced to writing, from oral tradition, in Iceland, between A.D. 1050 and 1133. It was recovered and published in Denmark in 1643. The new Edda, supposed to have been composed 200 years after the former, is an abridgment of it, with a new arrangement of its parts. It was translated by Resenius in 1640, and is thence called the Resenian Edda. The authenticity of these monuments of an early age has been doubted in recent times, but the latest researches of critics (the brothers Grimm and others) seem to go far towards establishing it.

E'DICT, an order issued by a prince to his subjects, as a rule or law requiring obedience. In Roman history we frequently meet with the edicts of the emperors and the edicts of the prætors, containing notices to the people in what manner they intended to execute the laws.—*Edictum perpetuum* was a collection of all the laws which had been yearly published by the prætors in their edicts. It was so called because it was intended to continue in force forever, and serve as a guide and rule in the administration of justice throughout the empire. —The *Edict of Milan* was a proclamation issued by Constantine after the conquest of Italy, A.D. 313, to secure to the Christians the restitution of their civil and religious rites, of which they had long been deprived, and to establish throughout his extended dominions the principles of a wise and enlightened toleration. The most famous edict of modern history is the Edict of Nantes, issued by Henry IV. in 1598, to secure to the Protestants the free exercise of their religion. This act, after continuing in force nearly a century, was repealed by Louis XIV.; and, as is well known, its revocation led to a renewal of the persecutions and bloody scenes which previously, to the issuing of this edict had been enacted against the Protestants. The depopulation caused by the sword was also increased by emigration. Above half a million of her most useful and industrious subjects deserted France, and exported, together with immense sums of money, those arts and manufactures which had chiefly tended to enrich the kingdom. About 50,000 refugees passed over into England; and there can be little doubt that their representations of the cruelties perpetrated by the King of France tended to excite the suspicions of the English against their own Roman Catholic sovereign, and in some degree accelerated the advent of the Revolution of 1688. In the French law, the term *edict* has a wide signification, being applied equally to the most momentous and the most trifling proclamations of the government.

EDI'TION, means simply the (indefinite) number of copies of a work printed at one time, before the types are distributed by the compositor. Any one who prepares for publication the writings of another is said to edit them, and is called the *editor*. In literary language, since the invention of printing, the *editor* of a work revises, adds notes, prepares for the press, &c., &c.: the *publisher* is the bookseller who negotiates the sale of the impression. Sometimes (but especially in classical works) the edition goes generally by the name of the printer or publisher, sometimes by that of the editor. Thus, we have the Aldine and Elzevir Classics, &c., the houses of Aldus and Elzevir having been concerned both in printing and publishing; while *Bentley's Horace, Heyne's Homer*, &c., are so denominated from the name of the *editor*. In bibliographical works, *editio princeps* signifies the earliest printed edition of an author; *editio optima*, that which is generally regarded as the best, &c.

ED'ITORS, are of different species:—1. Those who merely republish a text, or content themselves with adding notes and commentaries to it. 2. Those who superintend the publication of a work, receiving the manuscripts from one or more contributors; seeing that the object of the work is attained, that the language is correct, the illustrations appropriate, and the facts accurately stated, and that all the parts of the work are properly adjusted and made subordinate to each other. 3. Those who furnish the most important matter, and superintend the literary arrangements of a newspaper or other periodical publication.

EDUCA'TION, in its most extended signification, may be defined, in reference to man, to be the art of developing and cultivating the various physical, intellectual, and moral faculties; and may thence be divided into three branches—physical, intellectual, and moral education. This definition is by no means complete; but it is used merely as indicative of the manner in which this subject has generally been discussed. Under physical education is included all that relates to the organs of sensation, and the muscular and nervous system. Intellectual education comprehends the means by which the powers of the understanding are to be developed and improved, and a view of the various *branches of knowledge* which form the objects of instruction of the three departments into which we have divided education. Moral education embraces the various methods of cultivating and regulating the affections of the heart. The influence which education has exercised in humanizing the world is universally acknowledged. Its importance has been recognized by philosophers and legislators in every age; and by all the nations, both of antiquity and modern times, which have become distinguished in history, it has been regarded as the chief element in the attainment and promotion of civilization. The reader will find, in the writings of Plato, Plutarch, and Quintilian, among the ancients, and in modern times of Locke, Rousseau, Basedow, Niemeyer, Rehberg, Cousin, &c., a view of the chief systems that have been proposed or adopted in reference to this subject.—*Education in Greece and Rome*. The education of youth was strictly attended to both amongst the Greeks and Romans. Their minds and bodies were improved at the same time; their minds by every necessary branch of knowledge and learning, and their bodies by the manly exercises of the Campus Martius, or private contests and trials of skill, agility, and strength. It was the chief aim of the Romans, as well as Grecians, to make them shine in the senate and in the field, at the forum and the public games. Oratory was an object which they kept constantly in view; and whatever was their destination, they endeavoured to acquire the arts of elocution and a habit of fluent reasoning. Lacedæmon trained her hardy sons to despise danger, endure fatigue, and seem insensible of pain—to maintain their honor unstained, to love their country, and hold in contempt riches, and all that train of enervating pleasures which are the companions of affluence. So far all this was meritorious in a high degree; but how circumscribed must the space have been which was then allowed for intellectual exertion, when the whole world of science was a *terra incognita*.

EDMUND ST. an Anglo-Saxon king, who in 870 fell a victim to the Danes, by whom England was invaded. He was taken prisoner, scourged, bound to a tree, then killed by arrows; wherefore he, like St. Sebastian, is represented as tied to a tree, with an arrow in his breast, but bearing a crown. The sword, which is also one of his attributes, refers to the legend, that he was afterwards beheaded. As St. Edmund does not always wear the insignia of royalty, his picture is often mistaken for that of St. Sebastian; but the beard on the upper lip, denoting military rank, is the attribute solely of the latter.

EDWARD, THE CONFESSOR, an English king, who died A.D. 1066, is represented in royal garments, and with the symbols of Justice, a Mace, and also his Book of Laws. He sometimes bears a sick person, whom he is said to have healed by carrying him into a church.

EDWARD, THE MARTYR, a king of England. He was stabbed at the instigation of his stepmother, while in the act of drinking, A.D. 978. His attributes are, a goblet, a dagger, and the insignia of royalty.

EFFECT', the consequence of a cause, sometimes simple and visible, sometimes complicated and invisible, but always simultaneous with the cause.—*Effect*, the impression produced upon the mind at the sight of a picture, or other work of Art, at the first glance, before the details are examined. Thus, some bold outlines indicating the principal forms, with the masses of light and shade properly thrown in and the local colors put on, are sufficient to produce a picture which at the first view may appear strikingly brilliant and true, although many of the details proper to the subject are omitted, or the drawing not strictly correct, or the coloring deficient in harmony. Such is the state in which most good sketches or designs are made, by which the ultimate effect of the work when most carefully executed is judged. Effect is also the *result* of all the peculiar excellencies of the true master; the ensemble, which is brilliant and striking, as in the works of Rubens.—The word *effects* signify personal or movable goods.

EFFEC'TIVE, in military language, an epithet for a body of men that are fit for service; as 20,000 *effective* men.

EFFEM'INACY, that softness, delicacy, and weakness, which are characteristic of the female sex, but which in men are considered a reproach.

EFFEN'DI, a Turkish word signifying *lord* or *superior;* applied to legal, ecclesiastical, or other *civil* functionaries, in contradistinction to *aga*, the name by which high *military* personages are designated.

EFFI'CIENT, producing the effect intended. The *efficient cause* is that which produces; the *final cause* is that for which it is produced.

EFFIGY, the literal representation or image of a person. Although the word is sometimes applied to a portrait, it is not synonymous with it, but conveys an idea of a more exact imitation, a more striking and authentic resemblance, as we meet with in *wax-figures*. The ordinary application of the word is to the sculptured figures on sepulchral monuments, and to the heads of monarchs, &c., on coins and medals.

EFFLU'VIA, the small particles perpetually flowing out of mixed bodies in the form of vapors, which are sometimes visible, as in the case of smoke or steam; and sometimes not perceptible, as the noxious exhalations from putrefying animal or vegetable substances. Malignant effluvia are assigned, by physicians, as the cause of the plague and other contagious diseases.

EGYPTIAN-BLUE, a brilliant pigment, which upon analysis is found to consist of the hydrated protoxide of copper, mixed with a minute quantity of iron. It was long supposed that this fine blue was an ore of cobalt.

EISTEDD'FOD, the assemblies or sessions of the Welsh bards were so termed. They were held at different places for the minstrels of their respective neighborhoods; at Caerwys, at Aberfraw in Anglesea, and Mathravel in Powys. The judges were appointed by commissions from the Welsh princes, and after the Conquest from the English kings. The last was issued in 1568. But the Gwynnedigion and Cambrian Societies have lately revived the old custom; and annual meetings for the recitation of prize poems, and for performances on the harp, are now held under the name of Eisteddfod.

EJECT'MENT, in law, a writ or action which lies for the recovery of possession of land from which the owner has been ejected, and for trial of title. Ejectment may be brought by the lessor against the lessee for rent in arrear, or for holding over his term; also by the lessee for years, who has been ejected before the expiration of his term.

ELAB'ORATE, an epithet expressive of great care, diligence, &c., used in the execution of any performance.

EL'DER, a person advanced in life, and who, on account of his age and experience, is selected to fill some important office. In Jewish history, the *elders* were persons the most considerable for age, experience, and wisdom. Of this sort were the seventy men whom Moses associated to himself in the government of his people; such also were those who afterwards held the first rank in the synagogue, as presidents. In the first Christian churches, *elders* were persons who enjoyed offices or ecclesiastical functions, and the word includes apostles, pastors, presbyters, bishops, or overseers; hence the first councils of the Christians were called *presbyteria*, or councils of *elders*. In the modern presbyterian churches, *elders* are officers, who, with the ministers and deacons, compose the sessions of the kirk, and have authority to inspect and regulate matters of religion and discipline.

EL DORA'DO, the name given by the Spaniards to an imaginary country, supposed in the 16th century to be situated in the interior of South America, between the rivers Oronoco and Amazon, and, as the name implied, abounding in gold and all manner of precious stones. After the Spanish conquest of Mexico and Peru, the most exaggerated accounts of the wealth and riches of the newly acquired territory were circulated and believed. A new region was fabled to exist far surpassing the wealth and splendor of Peru; expeditions were fitted out for the purpose of discovering it; and though all such attempts proved abortive, the rumors of its existence continued to be believed down to the beginning of last century. The term then passed into the language of poetry, in which it was used to express a land of boundless wealth and felicity, like the ancient Elysium or the Mohammedan Paradise; until the recent discoveries in California gave that country a fresh claim to the appellation.

ELEAT'IC PHILOS'OPHY, a system owing its origin to Xenophanes, a native of Elea (in Latin *Velia*,) who lived about the year B.C. 530. The most celebrated of his followers were Parmenides and Zeno, also natives of Elea. The dialectical character of the principal systems of antiquity may be said to owe its existence to the Eleatics. The tendency of their speculations was the direct contrary of that which distinguishes the Ionic school. While the latter fixed their attention on outward nature, and strove to discover the laws which regulate its progress, Xenophanes and his disciples confined their thoughts to what they conceived to be the only objects of real knowledge—the ideas of God, or Being as it is in itself. The world of succession and change, which they designated under the title of *that which becomes* (τὸ γιγνόμενον,) they held to be utterly vain and illusory; the very conception of change itself seeming to them to involve a contradiction. Time, space and motion they regarded as mere phantasms, generated by the deceiving senses, and incapable of scientific explanation. They were consequently led to distinguish between the pure reason, the correlative of Being, and in one sense identical with it, and opinion or common understanding, the faculty which judges according to the impressions of sense. Parmenides, in particular, was the author of a philosophical epic, the two books of which treated respectively of these two modes of thinking. For a full account of all that can be gathered from remaining fragments of this rigid system of rationalism, the reader must consult the German writers on the subject: in particular Brandis and Ritter, in their histories of philosophy. Frequent allusion is made both by Plato and Aristotle to the Eleatic doctrines, the authors of which are mentioned by both those philosophers in terms of evident respect and veneration. Plato has made their system the subject of a whole dialogue, entitled the *Parmenides*; perhaps the most striking specimen of dialectic subtlety which Grecian philosophy affords.

ELECT', in theology, among Calvinists, a term for those whom they believe God has chosen, or predestinated to be saved.—*Elect*, in matters of polity, signifies chosen, but not inaugurated. Thus the President of the United States, before his predecessor's term of office has expired, is called the President *elect*.

ELEC'TION, the act of choosing a person to fill an office or employment, by any manifestation of preference; and is applicable to the choice of members of the legislature, which takes place within every seven years; to the choice of parish officers, annually; and to the admission of members into societies. Sometimes it is practised by show of hands; sometimes by ballot, and at others, by every elector giving his vote separately, with an oath in regard to his right and integrity.—*Election* is also the state of a person who is left to his own free will, to take or do one thing or another, which he pleases.—*Election*, in theology, divine choice, by which persons, according to the Calvinistic creed, are distinguished as objects for salvation by the special grace of God, without reference to their good or bad deeds.

ELEC'TIVE GOVERNMENTS are those in which all functionaries, from the highest to the lowest, are chosen by the suffrages of a greater or less number of citizens. Of these the government of Athens in antiquity, and in modern times that of the United States, will serve as examples. When the functionaries of an elective government are chosen by a very great number, it is identical with a democracy; and when by a comparatively small number, either with an aristocracy or an oligarchy.

ELEC'TOR, in law, any one who has the right of giving his vote at an election, particularly at an election of a member of parliament.—*Elector*, in political history, the title of such German princes as formerly had a voice in the election of the emperor of Germany.

ELEC'TORATE, the dignity or territory of an elector in the German empire.

ELEC'TROTYPE, the process by which works in relief are produced by the agency of electricity through which certain metals, such as gold, silver, and copper, are precipitated from their solutions upon moulds in so fine a state of division as to form a coherent mass of pure metal, equal in toughness and flexibility to the hammered metals. The applications of this beautiful Art appear almost unlimited, and as a means of reproducing fac-similes of art it is most invaluable.

ELEC'TRUM, the term is applied in ancient art to amber, and to a compound of gold and silver, which resembled amber in color, and was employed for similar purposes to those metals.

ELEEMOS'YNARY, an epithet for whatever pertains to the use and management of charitable donations, whether intended for the relief of the poor or sick, or appropriated to education. A hospital founded by charity is an *eleemosynary* institution for the sick; a college founded by donation is also *eleemosynary;* and so is the corporation which is entrusted with the care of such institutions.

EL'EGANCE, in a general sense, is that which pleases by its symmetry, purity, or beauty; and is select, as distinguished from what is common.—In literature, *elegance of composition* consists in well-chosen words and phrases, arranged in an appropriate and happy manner. It implies neatness, purity, and perspicuous arrangement; a style calculated to please a delicate taste, rather than to excite admiration or strong feeling.—In speaking, it includes propriety of diction and rich expressions with gracefulness of action.—In painting, it implies a certain manner which embellishes and heightens objects; as in Corregio, where, notwithstanding all the defects as to justness of design, there is an elegance even in the manner of the design itself, as well as in the turn of the attitudes, &c.—In architecture, *elegance* consists in the due symmetry and distribution of the parts of an edifice, or in regular proportions and arrangement.—It is also applied to various works of art or nature remarkable for their beauty of form, &c.

ELE'GIT, in law, a writ of execution, which lies for a person who has recovered debt or damages; or upon a recognizance in any court, against a defendant that is not able in his goods to satisfy his creditors.

EL'EGY, a mournful and plaintive kind of poem. The principal writers of elegiac verse among the Latins, were Propertius, Ovid, and Tibullus; the chief writers of elegy among the Greeks, were Callimachus, Parthenius, and Euphorion. The form of verse in which it was composed was the alternate hexameter and pentameter. In modern times almost all the nations of Europe have practised this species of composition; but if we except the *elegies* of Hammond, Milton's *Lycidas*, and Gray's *Elegy* among the English, and

Matthisson's *Elegie* among the Germans, it does not appear with great success. The noble poem of Tennyson, entitled *In Memoriam*, has, however, recently been placed in the highest rank of this species of compositions by the unanimous verdict of the most enlightened critics.

EL'EMENT, in physiology, a term used to denote the original component parts of bodies, or those into which they are ultimately resolvable. In the ancient and still popular sense of the word, the elements are understood to be four in number; namely, fire, air, earth, and water; but by the researches of modern science it is fully demonstrated that earth is a compound of many earths; air, a compound of at least two gases; water, a compound of hydrogen and oxygen; and fire, only the extrication of light and heat during combustion. Modern chemistry has, in fact, determined that an element is merely the last result of chemical analysis, or that which cannot be decomposed by any means now employed.—*Elements*, in a figurative sense, is used for the principles and foundations of any art or science, as "Euclid's Elements," &c.—*Elements*, in divinity, the bread and wine prepared for the sacrament of the Lord's Supper.

ELEMEN'TARY, an epithet expressive of that which is uncompounded, or having only one principle or constituent part. It also denotes *rudimental*, or *initiatory*; as, an *elementary* treatise.

ELEN'CHUS, in logic, a sophism, or fallacious argument, which deceives the hearer under the appearance of truth.

ELEPHAN'TINE, in Roman antiquity, an appellation given to the books wherein were registered the transactions of the senate and magistrates of Rome, of the emperors or generals of armies, and even of the provincial magistrates, the births and classes of the people, and other things relating to the census. They were so called, perhaps, as being made of ivory.

ELEUSIN'IA, in Grecian antiquity, a solemn and mysterious festival in honor of Ceres, kept every fourth year by the Celeans and Philiasians, and every fifth year by the Athenians, Lacedemonians, Parrhasians and Cretans, at Eleusis, a borough of Attica. It was transferred from thence to Rome by the emperor Adrian. The *Eleusinia* was the most celebrated and mysterious solemnity of any in Greece, and often called by way of eminence *mysteria*. The mysteries were of two kinds, the greater and the less; the less were preparatory to the greater. They consisted of a solemn representation of what was supposed to pass in the regions of Elysium and Tartarus; and their chief design was, by sensible means, to spread among the people a conviction of the immortality of the soul, and of a future state of rewards and punishments. To reveal the secrets of the Eleusinian mysteries was looked upon as a crime that would not fail to draw down the vengeance of heaven. The person who presided at these rites was called Hierophantes, or the revealer of holy truths.

ELEUTHE'RIA, in Grecian antiquity, a festival celebrated at Platæa, in memory of the defeat of Mardonius, the general of Xerxes: and in honor of those who gallantly sacrificed their lives for the liberty of their country. It was held every fifth year, when prizes were contended for.

ELEVA'TION, in its primary sense, denotes exaltation; the act of raising from a lower place to a higher; or, figuratively, the act of exalting in rank; as, the *elevation* of a man to a throne.—In architecture, an orthographic or upright draught of a building.—*Elevation of the Host*, in the Romish church, that part of the ceremony of the mass which consists in the priest's raising the host above his head for the people to adore.

ELF'-ARROWS, a name given to flints in the shape of arrow-heads, vulgarly supposed to be shot by fairies. They are frequently met with in Great Britain, and there is reason to believe they were weapons of offence among the ancient Britons.

ELFS, or FAIRIES, imaginary beings, honored more particularly by the northern nations, in whose mythology they occupy a prominent place. They were divided into two classes—the good and the bad; and their exploits have given rise to a multiplicity of delightful stories.

EL'GIN MAR'BLES, a collection of splendid basso-relievos and fragments of statuary, which were brought from the Parthenon from Athens to England, in 1814, by Lord Elgin, (hence the name.) They are now in the British Museum, having been purchased by the government for £35,000. They are unquestionably some of the finest remains of ancient Art, and offer the richest field for study. They consist chiefly of the Metopes, representing for the most part the combats of the Centaurs and Lapithæ; a portion of the frieze of the cella, representing the Panathenaic procession; and the statues or fragments of them, which ornamented the tympana of the pediments of the Parthenon or temple of Minerva at Athens. The superiority of the Elgin Marbles to all others, consists in this, that they represent the human frame draped and undraped, massive, and beyond the natural size, in nearly every attitude, without the artist having in a single instance degenerated into coarseness, mannerism, or been forgetful of absolute truth—beauty ever kept in view.

ELI'SHA, this prophet is represented with a two-headed eagle over his head, or upon his shoulder; referring to his petition to Elijah for a *double* portion of his spirit. The subjects usually chosen in works of Art in which Elisha appears, are that of the Bears destroying the Children; Elisha seizing Elijah's mantle; his Raising the Child; his Interview with the King's messenger; and his Causing the Axe to Swim.

ELI'SION, in grammar, the cutting off or suppressing a vowel at the end of a word for the sake of sound or measure, when the next word begins with a vowel; as, *th' ensanguined field.*

ELIZABETH'AN ARCHITECTURE, a name given to the impure architect-

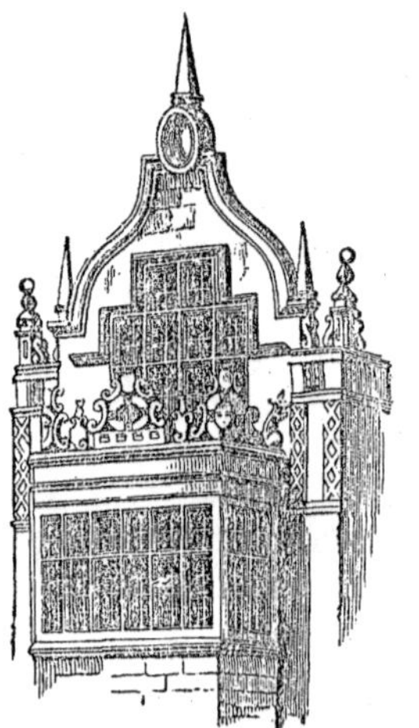

Elizabethan Window, Rushton Hall, cir. 1590.

ure of the times of Elizabeth and James I., when the worst forms of Gothic and debased Italian were jumbled together, producing a singular and absurd heterogeneousness in detail with wonderful picturesqueness in general effect. Its chief characteristics are deeply embayed windows, and galleries of great length.

ELIZ'ABETH, the position which the mother of John, the precursor of the Saviour, occupies in Christian Art, is of importance only in relation to the *Visitation of the Virgin.* She is found in many pictures of the Holy Family, but, like Anne, is inferior to the mother of the Messiah. The pictures of the Visitation are almost innumerable; they consist of the two women—Elizabeth, who is represented as old, and Mary, as youthful, each praising God.

ELLIP'SIS, in grammar, a figure of syntax, by which one or more words are omitted, which the reader may supply; as, the horse I rode, for the horse *which* I rode.—In rhetoric, a figure of speech whereby the orator, through excessive emotion, passes over many things, which, had he been cool, ought to have been mentioned.

ELOCU'TION, in rhetoric, consists of elegance, composition, and dignity: the first comprehends the purity and perspicuity of a language, and is the foundation of elocution; the second ranges the words in proper order; and the last adds the ornaments of tropes and figures, to give strength and dignity to the whole. To which may be added, that there should be a certain musical cadence or intonation, to render it pleasing to the ear.

E'LOGE, a term applied in France to the panegyrical orations pronounced in honor of illustrious deceased persons, and particularly of members of the Royal and other academies. Formerly the secretaries of the various French literary institutions used to compose and pronounce the *éloge;* but this duty is now performed by the new member elected in the room of the deceased. This practice is no doubt open to censure; but it has been the means of giving to the world many interesting biographical sketches, which would never otherwise have appeared. *Eloge* is also applied to any species of biographical writing in which praise predominates over censure, and has been much cultivated by French and Italian authors.

ELOPE'MENT, in law, the voluntary departure of a wife from her husband to go and live with another man. In common acceptation, the secret departure of any female with her lover, either to be married or to live together illicitly.

EL'OQUENCE, the art of clothing the thoughts in the most suitable expressions, in order to produce conviction or persuasion. In its primary signification, eloquence had reference to public speaking alone; but as most of the rules for public speaking are applicable equally to writing, an extension of the term naturally took place; and we find even Aristotle, the earliest systematic writer on the subject whose works have come down to us, including in his treatise rules for such compositions as were not intended for public recitation. A still wider extension of the term was contended for by the ancient rhetoricians, who included under it all kinds of literary productions (such as treatises on law, logic, &c.,) and whatever might be necessary to illustrate and explain them. The invention of eloquence was ascribed by the Egyptians and the fables of the poets to the god Mercury; but no certain account can be given when or by whom this art first began to be cultivated. If we may judge from the eulogiums which Homer pronounced upon Ulysses and Nestor for their attainments in eloquence, it must have been very early in high esteem among the Greeks. But though. from time to time, there arose in Greece many distinguished writers upon eloquence, it does not appear that the practice of the art was combined with the theory for public purposes till the time of Pisistratus, who owed to his rhetorical acquirements his elevation to the throne. Passing from Pericles, (the next in order to Pisistratus,) who was distinguished at once as a general, a statesman, and an orator, we find many eminent names during the Peloponnesian war immortalized for their eloquence by the pen of Thucydides. In the succeeding age arose the school of rhetoricians, or sophists, as they are called, who endeavored to graft upon eloquence the subtleties of logic; and among the earliest and most eminent of this school were Gorgias, Isocrates, and Isæus, of whose publicly delivered orations there are still ten extant. It was in this age that Grecian eloquence attained its highest perfection by the genius of Demosthenes, to whom the palm has been conceded by the unanimous consent of ancient and modern times. Of all human productions, the orations of Demosthenes present to us the models which approach the nearest to perfection. After this period, Grecian eloquence declined rapidly; and though in the following ages there flourished among others Hermagoras, Athenæus, Apollonius, Cæcilius, and Dionysius, their names have been almost without exception rescued from oblivion by a work which may be regarded as the last expiring ray of Grecian eloquence—the incomparable treatise of Longinus on the Sublime. In consequence of the all-absorbing spirit for military glory with which the ancient Romans were animated, it was long before they found leisure to appreciate the advantages of eloquence; and even so late as the year of the city 592, when, by the industry of some Greeks, the liberal arts began to flourish at Rome, the senate passed a decree banishing all rhetoricians from the country. But a few years afterwards, when Carneades, Critolaus, and Diogenes were sent as ambassadors from Athens to Rome, the Roman youth were so charmed with the eloquence of their harangues, that the study of oratory formed thenceforth a branch of a liberal education. Men of the highest rank were now seen teaching and learning respectively the art of eloquence; and such was the impetus given to this study, that it made the most rapid advances, and was at last crowned by the appearance of Cicero, to whom critics have concurred in assigning a rank inferior only to that of Demosthenes. The mighty scale on which everything was conducted at Rome, and the enormous interests so frequently at stake, were never so wonderfully exhibited as in the age of Cicero; and the unparalleled exigency found or created in him a talent for profiting by its advantages or coping with its difficulties. In the succeeding ages of the Roman empire, the despotic character of the government checked the growth of the rhetorical art; but the names of Tacitus, Quintilian, and Pliny are an earnest of what might have been achieved in this arena, had circumstances permitted the development of their talents. With regard to the early history of eloquence in England, there are found, indeed, the names of several distinguished men who in former times directed the resolutions of parliament; but no pains were taken to preserve their speeches; and the authority which they possessed seems to have been owing to their experience, wisdom, or power, more than to their talents for oratory. It was not until the close of the last century that an era arose in the history of British eloquence, which the genius of Chatham, Pitt,

Burke, Fox, and Sheridan has consecrated and immortalized. The little opportunity afforded for a display of forensic or senatorial eloquence by the different governments of Germany has almost entirely checked its growth in that country; and the same remark is applicable to Italy, Spain, and Portugal; all of which, however, have been rich in the eloquence of the pulpit. The only two countries in the world whose orators can be put in competition with those of Britain, are France and America. To the pulpit oratory of the former, the illustrious names of Bossuet, Bourdaloue, and Massillon have given enduring celebrity; while the popular character of their respective institutions has formed a host of forensic and senatorial speakers worthy a prominent place among the orators of antiquity, and modern times.

E'LUL, the name of a Jewish month, answering to part of August.

ELYS'IUM, or ELYS'IAN FIELDS, in heathen mythology, the supposed residence of the blessed after death. The poets describe this region as consisting of beautiful meadows alternated with pleasant groves; where a serene and cloudless sky was spread over them, and a soft, celestial light shed a magical brilliancy over every object. The heroes there renewed their favorite sports; danced to the sound of the lyre from which Orpheus drew the most enchanting tones, or wandered through the most odoriferous groves, where the warbling birds carolled forth their harmony by the side of refreshing fountains. There the earth teemed with plenteous fruits, and the verdure of spring was perpetual; while all cares, pains, and infirmities, were exchanged for the purest bliss.

EMANCIPA'TION, by the ancient Roman law, the son stood in the relation of a slave to the father. By a fiction of that law, the son might be freed from this relation by being three times sold by the father. Hence the enfranchisement of the son derived from this ceremony the name of emancipation. In course of time, various modes of emancipation, both tacit and express, became recognized by the Roman jurisprudence. The word, in countries following that law, signifies the exemption of the son from the power of the father, either by express act, or by implication of law. By the present civil law of France, majority (and with it emancipation) is attained at 21 years of age; and the marriage of a minor emancipates him. In ordinary language, emancipation is used in a general sense to signify the enfranchisement of a slave, or the admission of particular classes to the enjoyment of civil rights.

EMBALM'ING, the opening a dead body, taking out the intestines, and filling the place with odoriferous and desiccative drugs and spices, to prevent its putrefaction. The Egyptians have always been celebrated for their adherence to this practice, and the skill with which they performed it. With some variation, it is still one of the peculiar customs of that nation. It appears to have been a metaphysical notion, inculcated as of their religion, that the soul continued with the body. There naturally followed an affectionate desire to do everything that living creatures can suppose acceptable to the dead. They were even desirous of having the dead bodies of their parents in their houses, and at their tables, and believed, as has been suggested, that their souls were present also; and it was essential to this gratification that those bodies should be preserved in the most perfect manner possible.—Modern chemistry has made us acquainted with many means of counteracting putrefaction, more simple and more effectual than the laborious processes of the ancients.

EMBAR'GO, in commerce, a prohibition of sailing, issued by authority on all shipping, either out of port, or into port. It is generally to restrain ships from leaving a port.

EM'BASSY, the public function or employment of a public minister, whether ambassador or envoy.

EM'BER DAYS, in the Romish calendar, are certain fasts appointed by Pope Calixtus for imploring the blessing of the Almighty on the fruits of the earth, and upon the ordinations performed in the church at these times. They occur four times a year, or once in each of the four seasons; being the Wednesday, Friday, and Saturday after the first Sunday in Lent, after the feast of Pentecost or Whitsunday, after the festival of Holy Cross on the 14th of September, and after the festival of St. Lucia on the 13th of December. The weeks in which the ember days fall are called *ember weeks*. The word *embers* signifies ashes, which the primitive Christians strewed on their heads at these solemn fasts.

EMBEZ'ZLEMENT, the act of fraudulently appropriating a thing to one's own use, which has been intrusted to one's care and management.

EM'BLEM, this word is used frequently as a synonym with Attribute, Symbol, Image, and Allegorical Figure. So indiscriminately are these terms employed, that it becomes a task of great difficulty to point out their special application, and it must be admitted that the shades of difference are so light, that it would be most convenient to regard them all under the general term Symbol. Thus the sceptre is the attribute of royalty, and the emblem or symbol of power. The Paschal Lamb of the Jews figures the Lamb without stain, which has expiated the sins of the world; but as Jesus Christ has been depicted under this emblem in the New Testament, this emblem becomes a symbol. And to remove all uncertainty in depicting this symbol in Christian Art, we give to the Lamb a nimbus upon which is figured a cross; or the *Cross of the Resurrection*, or simply place a cross above its head; these are the attributes which distinguish it from other figures of a lamb, which are neither emblems nor symbols. An emblem is a symbolical figure or composition which conceals a moral or historical allegory; when accompanied with some sententious phrase which determines its meaning, it has the same relation as device.

EMBLEMA'TA, the figures with which the ancients decorated the golden, silver, and even copper vessels, and which could be taken off at pleasure. These belong to toreutic art, and were generally executed in the precious metals, but sometimes carved in amber. The Romans had the Greek term *emblemata*, but applied the word crustæ to the ornaments mentioned above. The Greek term is handed down to us in our word emblem, a sign or symbol.

EM'BLEMENTS, in law, a word used for the produce of land sown or planted by a tenant for life or years, whose estate is determined suddenly after the land is sown or planted, and before a harvest.

EMBONPOINT, (*French*,) a moderate and agreeable fulness of figure.

EMBOSS'ING, the forming or fashioning works in relievo, whether by raising, by carving, or by depression. It is, in short, a kind of sculpture, where the figures project from the plane whereon it is cut; and according as the figures are more or less prominent, they are said to be in *alto mezzo*, or *basso relievo.*—*Embossing wood*, as in picture frames and other articles of ornamented cabinet work, is either produced by means of carving, or by casting the pattern in plaster of Paris, or other composition, and cementing it on the surface of the wood.—*Embossing cloth.* Cotton, woollen cloth, silk, paper, and other fabrics, are embossed by the powerful pressure of revolving cylinders on which the required patterns are engraved.

EMBOUCHURE', signifies a mouth of a river; it is used also for the mouthpiece of a musical instrument.

EMBRA'CERY, in law, the offence of endeavoring to corrupt or influence a jury; punishable by fine and imprisonment.

EMBRA'SURE, in architecture, the enlargement made of the aperture of a door or window, on the inside of the wall. —In fortification, a hole or aperture in a parapet, through which cannon are pointed and discharged.

EMBROI'DERY, the name given to the art of working figures on stuffs or muslins with a needle and thread. All embroidery may be divided into two sorts, embroidery on *stuffs* and on *muslin:* the former is used chiefly in church vestments, housings, standards, articles of furniture, &c., and is executed with silk, cotton, wool, gold and silver threads, and sometimes ornamented with spangles, real or mock pearls, precious or imitation stones, &c.; the latter is employed mostly in articles of female apparel, as caps, collars, &c.; and is performed only with cotton. The art of embroidery was well known to the ancients. As early as the time of Moses we find it practised successfully by the Hebrews; and long before the Trojan war the women of Sidon had acquired celebrity for their skill in embroidery. At a later period, this art was introduced into Greece, probably by the Phrygians, (by some considered as the inventors;) and to such a degree of skill did the Grecian women attain in it, that their performances were said to rival the finest paintings. In our own times the art of embroidery has been cultivated with great success, more especially in Germany and France; and though for a long period it was practised only by the ladies of these countries as an elegant accomplishment, it is now regarded as a staple of traffic, and furnishes employment for a large portion of the population. In England also it appears to have taken deep root, as it now forms an accomplishment of which almost every lady is in possession. A great impetus has been given to the cultivation of this art, both on the Continent and in England, by the invention of a machine which enables a female to execute the most complex patterns with 130 needles, all in motion at once, as accurately as she could formerly do with one.

EMENDA'TION, an alteration made in the text of any book by verbal criticism.—In law, the correction of abuses.

EM'ERALD, a well-known gem of a beautiful green color, somewhat harder than quartz, which occurs in prisms with a regular hexagonal base, and ranks next in value to the oriental ruby and sapphire. It becomes electric by friction, is often transparent, sometimes only translucent, and before the blow-pipe is fusible into a whitish enamel, or glass. The most intensely colored and valuable emeralds are brought from Peru.

EME'RITI, the name given to the soldiers and other public functionaries of ancient Rome, who had retired from their country's service. On these occasions the parties were entitled to some renumeration, resembling *half-pay* in the English service; but whether it was a grant of land or of money has not been accurately ascertained.

EMIGRA'TION, migration is the movement of an individual or a number of people from one place of residence to another; emigration, their abandonment of their former home; immigration, (a word of modern coinage,) their settlement in their new one. Emigration is, in modern times, chiefly regarded in the light of a mode of relieving a country or district laboring under excess of population. Emigration from Europe has for two centuries been chiefly directed to the United States. Of late years, the Cape of Good Hope and Australia have begun to absorb a small portion of the surplus population of Great Britain.

EM'INENCE, an honorary title given to cardinals. They were called *illustrissimi* and *reverendissimi*, until the pontificate of Urban VIII.

E'MIR, a title of dignity among the Saracens and Turks. It was at first given to the caliphs, but when they assumed the title of Sultan, that of Emir remained to their children.

EM'ISSARY, a secret agent sent to ascertain the sentiments and designs of another, and to propagate opinions favorable to his employer.

EMO'TION, in a philosophical sense, an internal motion or agitation of the mind which passes away without desire. When desire follows, the motion or agitation becomes a *passion*.

EMPAIS'TIC, inlaid work, resembling the modern Buhl, Marquetry; next to Toreutic art, (with which it must not be confounded,) that branch most practised by the ancients. It consisted in laying threads, or knocking pieces of different metals into another metal.

EM'PEROR, was originally merely the title of a Roman general; but, on the fall of the republic it was particularly applied to the head of the state. The authority of the Roman emperors was formed principally by the combination of the chief offices of the old republic in a single person; besides which, some extraordinary powers were conferred. Thus, Octavius held the titles of emperor, proconsul, and tribune, pontifex maximus or high priest; and was invested with perpetual consular authority, and also that of the censorship. Besides this, he was termed prince of the senate, and Augustus, which designation descended to his successors; but he was much more moderate in his use of titular dignities than his successors, contenting himself with substantial power. The provinces of the empire were divided between the senate and emperor, who appointed their governors, distinguished by the respective titles of proconsul and proprætor; but this division threw all the armies into the hands of the latter, as he took for his share the frontier provinces. The emperors appointed their own successors, who were dignified with the title of Cæsar, and in later times enjoyed a share in the government. Dioclesian first divided the care of the empire with a second Augustus in the person of Maximian, and each of these colleagues associated with himself a Cæsar. After the court was removed to Constantinople, the old titles and forms of the republic vanished by degrees, and the emperors assumed the style of oriental princes.—Charlemagne assumed the title of emperor after his coronation at Rome; and from his time this title (in German *kaiser*) was claimed exclusively, in western Europe, by the rulers of Germany. On the dissolution of the German empire in 1805, the title passed to the emperor of Austria, and, in the same year, Napoleon assumed it in France; the czars of Russia claimed it in the reign of Alexander.

EM'PHASIS, in rhetoric, a particular stress of utterance, or force of the voice and action, given to such parts or words of an oration, as the speaker intends to impress specially upon his audience.

EM'PIRE, originally the territory or extent of land under the command and jurisdiction of an emperor. The dominions under the sway of ancient Rome were the first to which the term empire was applied: they consisted of two grand divisions,—the Empire of the East, or, as it was afterwards called, the Lower Empire; and the Empire of the West. The former admitted of various subdivisions in reference to the different dynasties to which it was subject; and the latter became, about the end of the 9th century, the German or Holy Roman Empire. In all these cases the sovereign or chief person in the empire was named the emperor. But the term empire has in several instances been employed to designate *a large extent of dominion*, without reference to the title of the ruler or sovereign of a country; thus we hear of the empire of Persia, Hindostan, &c. The dominions of the Queen of England are invariably designated the British Empire; and the epithet "imperial" is officially prefixed to the parliament of the united kingdom. The term empire was applied from 1804 to 1814 to the dominions of France, including all the countries then incorporated with it by the conquests of Napoleon.

EMPIR'IC, one whose knowledge is founded on experience. The empiric school of medicine was opposed to the *dogmatic;* it appears to have originated with Serapion of Alexandria. The empirics considered the foundation of medical science to rest upon experience, derived either directly from experiment or from chance and imitation. They were, however, a pretending, and generally ignorant sect; so that the term empiric is generally applied to quacks and pretenders, without reference to its strict etymology, which should have limited it to the study of medicine, in accordance with the principles of Lord Bacon's philosophy.

EMPO'RIUM, a common resort of merchants for trade; particularly a city or town of extensive commerce, or in which the commerce of an extensive country centres, or to which sellers and buyers resort from different countries.

EMPYRE'UM, or EMPYRE'AN, a term used by divines for the highest heaven, where the blessed enjoy the beatific vision.—Hence we have the word *empyreal*, as pertaining to that region of space which is refined beyond aerial substance, where only pure fire or light is supposed to exist.

ENAM'EL, a kind of colored glass, principally formed by the combination of different metallic oxydes, and used in enamelling and painting in enamel. Enamels have for their basis a pure crystal-glass, or frit, ground up with a fine calx of lead and tin, prepared for the purpose, with the addition usually of white salt of tartar. These ingredients baked together, are the matter of all enamels, and the color is varied by adding other substances, and melting or incorporating them together in a furnace. Enamels are distinguished into transparent and opaque; in the former all the elements have experienced an equal degree of liquefaction, and are thus run into crystal glass, whilst in the others, some of their elements have resisted the action of heat more, so that their particles retain sufficient aggregation to prevent the transmission of light. They are used either in counterfeiting or imitating precious stones, in painting in enamel, or by enamellers, jewellers, or goldsmiths, in gold, silver, and other metals. This art is of so great antiquity, as to render it difficult, if not impossible, to trace to its origin. It was evidently practised by the Egyptians, from the remains that have been found on the ornamented envelopes of mummies. From Egypt it passed into Greece, and afterwards into Rome and its provinces, whence it was probably introduced into Great Britain as various Roman antiquities have been dug up in different parts of the island, particularly in the barrows, in which enamels have formed portions of the ornaments.—*Painting in enamel*, &c. is performed on plates of gold or silver, but more commonly of copper, enamelled with the white enamel; the colors are melted in the fire, where they take a brightness and lustre like that of glass. This painting is prized for its peculiar brightness and vivacity, which is very permanent; the force of its colors not being effaced or sullied by time, as in other painting, and continuing always as fresh as when it came out of the workman's hands. The town of Limoges, in the south of France, has acquired a great name in the history of the art of enamelling; it was particularly distinguished in the twelfth century, and its productions were called *Opus de Limogia* and *Labor Limogiæ*. Many reliquaries of that time are still extant, the sides and sloping roofs of which are composed of plates of copper, covered with etchings and enamel paintings. The most famous artist in enamelling was Leonard Limousin of Limoges, from whom the French works of Art of that period were called Limousins: other masters in this art were Pierre Rexmon, Jean Court, called *Vigier*, J. Laudin, P. Nouaillier, the master J. P., who is known to us only by his cipher, but whose works are excellent, displaying noble ideas, and the master P. C., who is held in high estimation. As regards the technical part of painting, the works of these masters rank far below those produced in more recent times; they are rather illuminated line-drawings, with a glazed transparency of color, or monochrome paintings, the naked figures being well modelled and generally of a reddish tint; the ornaments in gold and the gilded lights make the paintings appear rich and brilliant. In the course of the seventeenth century the technical part of the art of enamel painting improved considerably, progressing from monochrome to that in various colors. Towards the end of the seventeenth and the beginning of the eighteenth centuries, the art arrived at technical perfection, and real pictures were produced with the softest and most delicate gradations of color. But the works of this period were of very small dimensions, the paintings being sometimes on silver, but generally upon gold, and principally portrait medallions, for which the art was now employed. Much that was excellent was produced, but in historical representation the artists followed the degenerate style of the compositions of those days, so that these works, in spite of their technical perfection, must rank below those of the sixteenth century.

ENAMEL PAINTING ON LAVA, a newly-invented style of painting very serviceable for monuments. This invention of enamelling upon stone, discovered in France, and well known in Germany, has produced a kind of painting having all the advantages of color and treatment, and the great recommendation of being nearly indestructible. The material used was discovered by Count Chabrol de Volvic; it consists of volvic stone, and lava from the mountains of Auvergne. The method of painting is a new kind of enamelling, and has been used by Abel du Pujol and others in various works of Art; for example, the altar of the church of St. Elizabeth, at Paris; it has recently been used in architecture by Hittorf of Cologne, for the exterior of buildings. In Paris there are several tablets painted with figures in the Arabesque and Pompeiian styles, which have excited great admiration by the ease and yet preciseness of the treatment, as well as by the firmness of the materials, for a sharp piece of iron might be drawn over them without injuring the painting.

ENCÆ'NIA, in antiquity, anniversary feasts to commemorate the completing or consecrating any new and public work, &c. In modern times, this term is used for any commemorative festival.

ENCAMP'MENT, the act of pitching tents for the accommodation of an army in the open country.

ENCAUS'TIC PAINTING, a peculiar mode of painting in wax, liquefied by fire; by which the colors acquire considerable hardness, brilliance, and durability. Ancient authors often mention this species of painting, but we have no ancient pictures of this description, and, therefore, the precise manner formerly adopted is not completely developed, though many moderns have closely investigated the subject and described their processes. As the thing chiefly regarded in encaustic painting was the securing of permanence and durability, by the application of fire, the word *encaustic* has been applied, in a very general sense, to other processes, in which both the material and the mode of applying the heat, are entirely different from what is conceived to have been the ancient materials and modes. The moderns have used the term for painting on porcelain, and work in enamel; and in the same way it was given to the painting on glass of the middle ages, such as is still seen in the windows of some Gothic churches. It has also been just as erroneously applied to works in metal; where gold and silver were inlaid, melted, or laid on, and of everything which was gilt or silvered by fire; which was called gold or silver encaustic.

ENCHANT'MENT, the use of magic arts and spells, or the invocation of demons, in order to produce wonderful or supernatural effects.

ENCHA'SING, or CHA'SING, the art of enriching and beautifying gold, silver, &c., by some design represented thereon, in low relievo. It is performed by punching, or driving out the metal, to form the figure, from within side, so as to stand out prominently from the plane or surface of the metal.

ENCHYRID'ION, a manual or small volume.

ENCLIT'IC, in grammar, a particle so closely united with any other word as to seem to be part of it, as *que*, in *virumque*.

ENCOMBO'MA, a portion of Greek costume consisting of a kind of apron, fastened loosely round the loins by being gathered into a knot. It was worn chiefly by young maidens; its use appears to have been to keep the tunic clean. The annexed woodcut represents a young female playing on the double pipes, probably an attendant in the scene of some play.

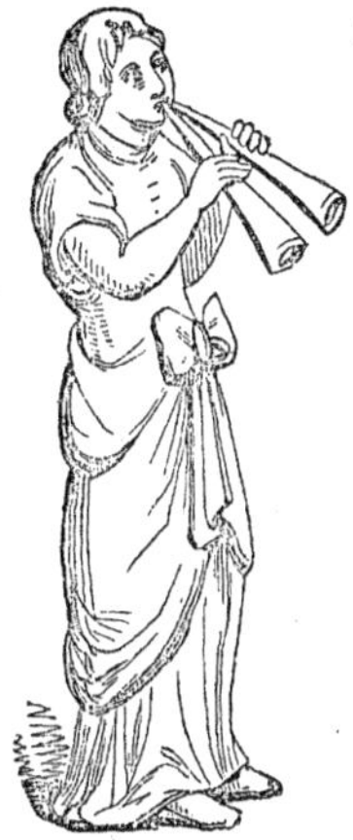

ENCORE', a word signifying *again;* used by the audience at theatres, and other places, when they call for a repetition of a particular song, &c.

ENCRATI'TES, in church history, a sect which appeared towards the end of the second century: they were called *encratites*, or *continentes*, because they abstained from marriage, and the use of wine and animal food.

ENCROACH'MENT, in law, an unlawful intrusion or gaining upon the rights and possessions of another.

ENCYCLOPE'DIA, a general system of instruction or knowledge, embracing the principal facts in all branches of science and the arts, properly digested, and arranged in alphabetical order. *See* CYCLOPEDIA.

ENDEM'IC, a disease peculiar to a certain class of persons, or to a certain district. Thus agues or intermittent fevers are endemic in low countries,—the *goitre* in the Alps, the *plica Polonica* in Poland.

ENDORS'ING, the writing one's name on the back of a bill of exchange or check: by which responsibility for its amount is incurred, if duly presented and not paid.

ENDOW'MENT, in law, the act of giving or assuring a dower to a woman. Also, the assigning certain rents and revenues for the maintenance of a vicar, almshouses, &c.—The word endowment has also a more enlarged signification, implying any quality or faculty bestowed on man by the Creator.

ENDRO'MIS, a cloak made of warm coarse materials like a blanket, used to throw over those who were heated by the foot race; or, after athletic exercises, to protect the wearer from the effects of exposure to cold. In more recent times the name was applied to a luxurious garment worn by women, especially those of Rome. Figures clothed in the Endromis are of frequent occurence in works of Art relating to the exercises of the gymnasium. This word also designates the hunting boots worn by Diana, as being peculiarly suitable for the chase, the toes being left uncovered.

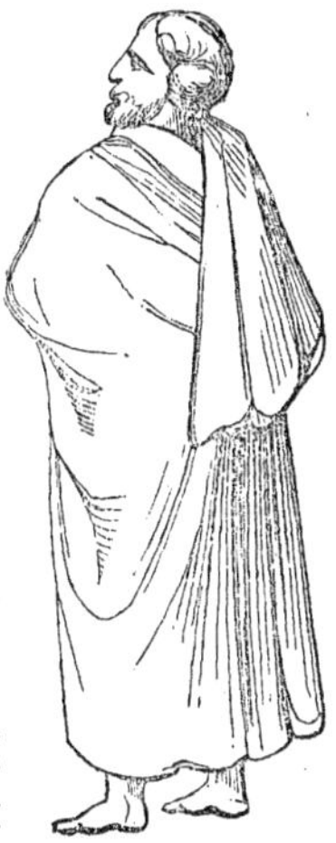

ENDY'MION, according to some, a huntsman, according to others, a shepherd, and according to a third account, a king of Elis. He is said to have asked of Jupiter, whom many have called his father, eternal youth and immortality. His beauty excited passion even in the cold Diana, and hence he has served in all ages as an ideal of loveliness, and Diana's love to him as that of the tenderest affection. He is most generally conceived as sleeping in the wood, where the mild rays of the moon kiss his slumbering eyes.

EN'EMY, in a political sense, any one belonging to a nation with whom our own country is at war.—In law, it denotes an alien or foreigner, who in a public capacity, and with a hostile intention, invades any kingdom.

EN'ERGY, the internal or inherent power, virtue, or efficacy of a thing; as, Danger will rouse our dormant *energies*, into action; the administration of the laws requires *energy* in the magistrate. It also signifies the momentum which any simple or compound body exhibits, by causes obvious or concealed.

ENER'VATE, to deprive of nerve, force, or strength; as, idleness and luxury *enervate* both body and mind.

ENFEOFF'MENT, in law, the act of giving the fee simple of an estate.

ENFILADE′, in military tactics, is used in speaking of trenches, or other places, which may be seen and scoured by the enemy's shot along the whole length of a line.

ENFRAN′CHISEMENT, in law, the incorporating a person into any society or body politic; to admit to the privileges of a freeman.

ENGA′GED COLUMNS, in architecture, columns attached to walls, by which a portion of them is concealed; they never stand less than one half out from the walls.

ENGAGE′MENT, a word used in different senses. Any obligation by agreement or contract, is an *engagement* to perform, &c.; the conflict of armies or fleets is an *engagement;* and any occupation, or employment of the attention, is likewise called an *engagement.*

EN′GLISH, the language spoken by the people of England, and their descendants in India, North America, and the British colonies. The ancient language of Britain is generally allowed to have been the same with that of the Gauls; this island, in all probability, having been first peopled from Gallia, as both Cæsar and Tacitus prove by many strong and conclusive arguments. Julius Cæsar, sometime before the birth of our Saviour, made a descent upon Britain, though he may be said rather to have discovered than conquered it: but, about the year 45, in the time of Claudius, Aulus Plautius was sent over with some Roman forces, by whom two kings of the Britons, Codigunus and Caractacus, were both signally defeated: whereupon a Roman colony was planted at Malden in Essex, and the southern parts of the island were reduced to the form of a Roman province. Britain was subsequently conquered as far north as the friths of Dumbarton and Edinburgh, by Agricola, in the time of Domitian; and a great number of the Britons, in the conquered part of the island retired to the western part, called Wales, where their language continued to be spoken without any foreign admixture. The greatest part of Britain being thus become a Roman province, the Roman legions, who resided in Britain for above two hundred years, undoubtedly disseminated the Latin tongue; and the people being afterwards governed by laws written in Latin, it must have necessarily followed that the language would undergo a considerable change. In fact, the British tongue continued, for some time, mixed with the provincial Latin; but at length, the declining state of the Roman empire rendered the aid of the Roman legions necessary at home, and on their abandoning the island, the Scots and Picts took the opportunity to attack and harass South Britain: upon which, Vortigern, the king, about the year 440, called the Saxons to his assistance, who coming over with several of their neighboring tribes, repulsed the Scots and Picts, and were rewarded for their services with the isle of Thanet, and the whole county of Kent Growing at length too powerful, and not being contented with their allotment they dispossessed the inhabitants of all the country on the east side of the Severn; and thus the British language was in a great measure destroyed, and that of the Saxons introduced in lieu of it. What the Saxon tongue was long before the Conquest, viz. about the year 700, may be seen in the most ancient manuscript of that language, which is a gloss on the Evangelists, by bishop Eadfride, in which the three first articles of the Lord's prayer run thus: "Uren fader thic arth in heofnas, sic gehalgud thin noma, so symeth thin ric. Sic thin willa sue is heofnas, and in eortho, &c." In the beginning of the ninth century, the Danes invaded England, and getting a footing in the northern and eastern parts of the country, their power gradually increased, and in about two hundred years they became its sole masters. By this means the ancient English obtained a tincture of the Danish language: but their government, being of no long continuance, did not make so great an alteration in the Anglo-Saxon, as the next revolution, when the whole land, A D. 1067, was subdued by William the Conqueror, Duke of Normandy, in France: for the Normans, as a monument of their conquest, endeavored to make their language as generally received as their commands: and thereby the English language became an entire medley. About the year 900, the Lord's prayer in the ancient Anglo-Saxon, read as follows: "Thu ure fader the eart on heofenum, si thin nama gehalgod; cume thin rice si thin willa on eorthan swa, swa on heofnum, &c." And, about the year 1160, pope Adrian, an Englishman, thus rendered it in rhyme:

"Ure fader in heaven rich,
Thy name be hayled ever lich,
Thou bring us thy michell blisse:
Als hit in heaven y-doe,
Evar in yearth beene it also, &c."

It continued to undergo various mutations, till the year 1537, when the Lord's prayer was thus printed: "O oure father which arte in heven, halowed be thy name: let thy kingdome come, thy will be fulfiled as well in erth as it is in heven; geve us this daye in dayly bred, &c." Here, it may be observed, the diction is brought almost to the present standard, the chief variations being only in the orthography. By these instances, and many others that might be given, it appears, that the Anglo-Saxon language, which the Normans in a great measure despoiled and rendered obsolete, had its beauties, was significant and emphatical, and preferable to what they substituted for it. "Great, verily," says Camden, "was the glory of our tongue, before the Norman Conquest, in this, that the old English could express, most aptly, all the conceptions of the mind in their own tongue, without borrowing from any." Of this he gives several examples. After the Conquest, it was ordained that all law proceedings should be in the Norman language; and hence the early records and reports of law cases came to be written in Norman. But neither royal authority, nor the influence of courts, could absolutely change the vernacular language. After an experiment of three hundred years, the law was repealed; and since that period, the English has been, for the most part, the official as well as the common language of the nation. Since the Norman invasion, the English has not suffered any shock from the intermixture of conquerors with the natives of England; but the language has undergone great alterations, by the disuse of a large portion of Saxon words, and the introduction of words from the Latin and Greek languages, with some French, Italian, and Spanish words. These words have, in some instances, been borrowed by authors directly from the Latin and Greek; but most of the Latin words have been received through the medium of the French and Italian. For terms in the sciences, authors have generally resorted to the Greek; and from this source, as discoveries in science demand new terms, the vocabulary of the English tongue is receiving continual augmentation. It has, also, a few words from the German and Swedish, mostly terms in mineralogy; and commerce has introduced new commodities of foreign growth or manufacture, with their foreign names, which now make a part of our language. It may then be stated, that the English is composed of, 1st, Saxon and Danish words of Teutonic and Gothic origin. 2nd, British or Welsh, which may be considered as of Celtic origin. 3rd, Norman, a mixture of French and Gothic. 4th, Latin. 5th, French. 6th, Greek. 7th, A few words directly from the Italian, Spanish, German, and other languages of the continent. 8th, A few foreign words, introduced by commerce, or by political or literary intercourse. Of these the Saxon words constitute our mother tongue. The Danish and Welsh also are primitive words, and may be considered as part of our vernacular language.

ENGRA'VING, the art of producing by incision or corrosion designs upon blocks of wood, plates of metal, or other materials, from which impressions or prints upon paper or other soft substances are obtained by pressure. Engraving, as an art, seems to have nearly the same relation to design and painting as typography bears to written language; and its utility and great importance must be obvious to every one from its capability of giving a boundless circulation to representations of the most valuable examples of the arts and of objects connected with science. Xylography, or wood-engraving, was the earliest method practised; but its origin is involved in obscurity. It is possible that it was known in China 1120 years before Christ; though we think its invention is of a much later period, as the Chinese were not acquainted with the art of making paper till 95 B.C. It has been stated that this art was introduced into Europe from China through the intercourse of the Venetian merchants with its inhabitants; for it is proved that engraving on wood had been practised in that part of Italy which borders on the Adriatic as early as the 13th century. The first wood engravings in Europe of which anything is known with certainty, were executed in 1285, by a brother and sister of a noble family of the name of Cunio. They represent the actions of Alexander. But for the accidental discovery by a Venetian architect of the name of Temanza of a decree of the magistracy of Venice, in 1441, we might have been without positive proof of the practice of the art in Italy previous to 1467, and the Germans might still have continued to claim the honor of its introduction into Europe. This decree plainly indicates that wood engraving was practised in Venice as early as the commencement of the fifteenth century. In Germany and the Low Countries, the early block books seem to have existed as early as 1420, and to have given Guttenburg the hint for using movable types. At Rome, in 1467, a work intituled *Meditationes Johannis de Turrecremata* issued from the press of Ulric Han, embellished with wood engravings, in which the design and execution of an Italian artist are evident. The decorations of the work of Valturius by Matteo Pasti, of Verona, published five years afterwards, exhibit considerable spirit and accuracy; and before the end of the fifteenth century the art had been carried to great perfection, as may be proved by the delicacy and purity with which the designs are engraved in the celebrated Hypnerotomachia of Colonna. At this period, however, the discovery of copper-plate engraving had been made, and to this the more ancient art yielded place. Maso Finiguerra, a goldsmith and sculptor of Florence, and pupil of Masaccio, about the middle of the fifteenth century, seems from the most authentic accounts to have been the person to whom the world is indebted for the discovery. Finiguerra was followed by Baccio Baldini, a goldsmith of Florence. His works were numerous, and are of course much sought after by collectors. Botticelli, a painter of eminence as well as an engraver, was a native of Florence, where he was born in 1437. He is spoken of with praise by Vasari, and especially for his picture at San Pietro Maggiore, of the assumption of the Virgin: among the works he engraved from his own designs are subjects illustrative of Dante, and a number of prints of prophets and sibyls. His death occurred in 1515. Contemporary with him flourished Antonio del Pollajuolo, and rather later Gherardo and Robetta, who advanced the art; though it was still dry in execution, and more to be admired for correctness of drawing and design than for any attempt at relief or effect. There can be no doubt that at this period the art was practised at Rome, though the Venetian state and other parts of the north of Italy furnished a more abundant supply of artists. In Germany and the Low Countries the art of engraving had made extraordinary progress during the fifteenth century; and the name of Martin Schoen or Schongauer must not be forgotten. This artist, who was also a painter and goldsmith, was the father of the German school of engraving. He was a native of Culmbach in Franconia, and born about 1420. He began the practice of the art when it was in its infancy, and succeeded in carrying it to a great degree of perfection. His death occurred at Colmar in 1486. Vasari relates that Michael Angelo, when young, was so pleased with a print by Schongauer, representing St. Anthony tormented by devils, that he copied it in colors. Albert Durer, the most celebrated of the early engravers of Germany, was born at Nuremburg, in 1471. Skilled in many arts, and a painter of no ordinary powers, it is astonishing that, in a life not exceeding fifty-eight years, he should have succeeded so eminently in that of engraving that he has even hardly been surpassed. On copper as well as wood his works exhibit specimens of executive excellence, which the experience of centuries has not been able to surpass. Durer is supposed to have been the inventor of the art of etching, at least no etchings are known before those which are extant from his hand. Of the works he has left, which are very numerous, his wood engravings are the most free and masterly. Following Albert Durer were Aldegrever his pupil, Hans Beham and his brother Bartholomew, Altdorfer, Binck, Goerting, Penz, and Solis. Hans Holbein, who, according to some was a native of Basle, and according to others of Augsburg, besides acquiring celebrity as a painter, is known as an engraver on wood, executed many pieces: the best known and most remarkable of which are the fifty-three prints called the "Dance of Death," first published about 1530. Of the Dutch and Flemish schools Lucas van Leyden must be considered the head. Born in 1494, at the place whence he derives his name, he was the contemporary and friend of Albert Durer; to whom, though inferior in design, he was superior in composition. His works, which were both on wood and copper, are few in number. The Low Countries furnished a host of engravers, among whom we think it unnecessary to name more than the Sadelers; Bloemart, who laid the foundation of the principles upon which lines become capable of expressing quality, color and chiaro oscuro, which the French engravers afterwards improved; Goltzius and his pupils; Muller; and Lucas Kiliau: the three last, though they handled the graver with great freedom and dexterity, fell into boundless absurdity and extravagance which, however, were tempered and corrected by Mathieu and Saenredam. In the beginning of the seventeenth century the two Bolswerts appeared, whose style was much improved by the instructions of Rubens. Vosterman, Pontius, and Peter de Jode the younger, were of this school, which is distinguished for the success and correctness with which it transferred the picture to the copper. Rembrandt, notwithstanding all his faults and absurdities, claims a special notice in this place as an engraver. The Descent from the Cross, and the print called "Hundred Guilder Print," are extraordinary efforts of art. His portraits and landscapes are full of nature, expression, and character; and it is difficult to say whether he is more successful in his sunshine effects, than in the sober solemn twilight with which his varied subjects are enveloped. Vandyke has left a few specimens of etchings worthy of his name. Jegher, Lutma, and above all the family of the Vischers, exhibited great excellence in the art, which continued to advance under the hands of Waterloo, Jacob Ruysdael, and Paul Potter; the last of whom, in his etchings of animals, displayed a scientific acquaintance with drawing and anatomy till his time unpractised.

We must now return to close the brief account of the Italian school, in which the appearance of Marc Antonio Raimondi forms the most splendid era. Born at Bologna about 1488, he became the pupil of Raibolini, an artist of that city. His master in the art of engraving is, however, unknown. We first hear of him at Venice, whither Albert Durer went to institute proceedings against him for pirating his prints, which had been copied by Raimondi with such wonderful accuracy that they were sold for the originals. But the proper sphere for Marc Antonio was Rome, whither he soon bent his steps. There his merit soon gained him the friendship and esteem of Raffaelle, then in the plenitude of his glory, by whom he was employed to engrave from his designs. His first plate from a design by Raffaelle was the Lucretia, soon after which he executed the Judgment of Paris. His engravings after this master are very numerous; and though free from the blandishments of style, chiaroscuro, and local color which the art has received since his time, such was his knowledge of drawing, such the beautiful character that pervades his works, that he is entitled to the highest rank in the art to which excellence has ever attained. His school attracted to Rome artists from all parts; among whom may be enumerated Marco de Ravenna, Giulio Bonasoni, Agostino de Musis, Enea Vico, and Nicolo Beatrici. Some of the German artists whom we have named above, viz., Beham, Penz, and James Binck, resorted to Rome for the benefit of his instructions. On the death of Raffaelle, he executed engravings of some of the works of Giullio Romano. His last print, the Battle of the Lapithæ, is dated 1539. Some of the principal pupils of Marc Antonio have already been named; to them may be added Georgio Grisi, commonly called Mantuanus, and others of his family. Many of the Italian painters were extremely successful in engraving, among whom Titian etched many landscapes; but none cultivated the art with more success than Agostino Caracci, who studied under Cornelius Cort, a Dutch engraver, born at Hoorn in 1536. His design and execution are equally to be admired; and had he but concentrated his lights more, and attended to local color, he would have been exceeded by none. In the seventeenth century Della Bella, Callot, who, though born in France, belongs to the Italian school, Guercino, Salvator Rosa, and Claude, continued the reputation of the art. At the latter end of this century was born Antonio Canaletti, originally a scene painter, like his father Bernardo. His etchings opened an entirely new field in architectural engraving, and may be considered almost, if not quite, the first in which fine sparkling effects of light are introduced, and in which the darkest shadows partake of the transparency and clearness which nature herself exhibits. Piranesi, who was born in Venice, and died in 1770, appeared about the middle of that century; he was one of the most surprising architectural engravers that have ever existed, whether we consider the astonishing power or number of his works. His use of the etching needle surpassed all that has been done before or since; and in our own time Volpato of Florence, who, besides his other works, engraved almost all the celebrated performances of Canova with a delicacy, grace, and correctness of the first order.

The French school commenced about the middle of the sixteenth century with Noel Garnier, who was followed by many clever artists; but till the time of Louis XIV. it cannot be said to have been highly distinguished. At that epoch we have Gerard Edelinck, who, though born at Antwerp, belongs properly to the French school, and Gerard Audran. The former of these, who worked entirely with the graver, carried what is called color in engraving to a much greater degree of perfection than had ever before been practised. His facility was amazing, and portrait and history were equally the subjects of his burin. The name of Audran, not less from the circumstance of the family having produced six engravers, than for Gerard Audran, who engraved the well-known battles of Alexander after Le Brun, is conspicuous in the history of the art; his name, however, will descend to posterity with greater lustre from his engravings after the Italian school, and particularly those of Nicolo Poussin. Gerard Audran was born at Lyons in 1640, and died in Paris in 1703. John Audran, the last of the family who exercised the art, and nephew of Gerard, died in 1756. Nanteuil, the three Drevets, of whom Peter was the most eminent, Le Clerc, Chereau, Cochin, Beauvais, Simonneau Dupuis, and many other masters, belong to this period; but Balechon and Wille, towards the middle of the century, outstripped all that had been done by their predecessors. Wille was a German; but his residence having been chiefly at Paris, he is always ranked among the French engravers. His extraordinary powers in imitating the qualities of objects, and particularly of satin, the smoothness of effect he produced, and his extraordinary clearness in the use of the graver, entitle him to a place of the first rank in the French school, which, since the age of Louis XIV., has been more distinguished for its great mechanical skill, than for grace, correctness, and beauty in the higher departments of the art.

Till the middle of the seventeenth century England was indebted to foreign artists for the embellishment bestowed upon the typographical works she produced, as well as for such engravings, either in history, portrait, or landscape, as the taste of the nation required. Among the artists who visited England and made it their permanent or temporary residence were the Passes, Vaillant, Hondius, Vosterman, Hollar, Blooteling, Dorigny, and several others. Payne, who died about 1648, and Faithorne, who executed many historical pieces and portraits in a masterly manner, were the earliest English engravers deserving mention. William Faithorne, son of the last named, was eminent as one of the earliest mezzotinto engravers. This invention, which is usually attributed to Prince Rupert, is claimed by Heineken for Lieutenant Colonel Siegen, who was a Hessian officer, from whom Heineken says Prince Rupert learned the secret, which he brought to England on his return with Charles II. After the two Whites, father and son, appeared Vertue, who was born in 1684. He was the scholar of Vandergucht, and from the numerous works he brought out must have been an artist of great industry and facility. The larger portion of his labors was confined to portraits. The works of Pond and Knapton can only be mentioned as continuing the history, though occasionally they possess some spirit; but Vivares, a Frenchman by birth, belonging, however, to the English school, and indeed the founder of it in landscape engraving, has shown in his engravings from the pictures of Claude, talents, the precursors of that pre-eminence in landscape engraving which the English have not only improved upon but exclusively possessed. Woollett carried execution to a far greater extent than Vivares, uniting with that engraver's spirit all the elegance, clearness, and delicacy of the French school; and to these Woollett superadded every beauty that mechanical skill could effect. John Browne was a contemporary worthy of Woollett, whose works after Salvator, Both, and others, are well executed. Sir Robert Strange distinguished himself by his great mechanical skill, whence resulted beautiful execution, by the breadth he preserved in the effects he copied, and by the delicacy he imparted to flesh in a manner that has never been equalled. His principal engravings are from the Italian painters, especially Titian, Guido, and Corregio, and reflect great honor on the English school, which since his time has never been deficient in producing artists of the first class. Strange was a native of one of the Orkney islands, where he was born in 1721, and died in 1792. Since his time the names of artists of talent might be here supplied to a very great extent: we shall merely mention those of Basire, Bartolozzi, Rooker, Heath, Byrne, Bromley, Lowry, Earlom, Raphael, Smith, &c. In the present day, the demand of prints for the embellishment of books has produced talent both in England and in the United States which, perhaps, might be more nobly employed in works of a higher order.

Engraving on Wood, or *Xylography*.—In this branch of the art the material used is a block of box or pear-tree wood, cut at right angles to the direction of the fibres, its thickness being regulated by the size of the print to be executed. The subject is drawn on the block with a black-lead pencil, or with a pen and Indian ink, taking care that the whole effect is represented in the lines so drawn. The whole of the wood is then cut away, except where the lines are drawn, which are left as raised parts; in which point it is that this mode of engraving differs so essentially from copper-plate engraving, wherein the lines are cut out or sunk in the metal, instead of being raised from it. The impressions from wood blocks are taken in the same manner as from printing types.

Engraving on Copper is performed by cutting lines representing the subject on a copper-plate by means of a steel instrument ending in an unequal-sided pyramidal point, such instrument being called a graver or burin. Besides the graver there are other instruments used in the process: viz., a scraper, a burnisher, an oil stone, and a cushion for supporting the plate. In cutting the lines on the copper the graver is pushed forward in the direction required, being held in the hand at a small inclination to the plane of the copper. The use of the burnisher is to soften down lines that are cut too deep, and for burnishing out scratches in the copper: it is about three inches long. The scraper, like the last, is of steel, with three sharp edges to it, and about six inches' long, tapering towards the end. Its use is to scrape off the burr, raised by the action of the graver. To show the appearance of the work during its progress, and to polish off the burr, engravers use a roll of woollen or felt called a rubber, which is put in action with a little olive oil. The cushion, which is a leather bag about nine inches diameter filled with sand for laying the plate on, is now rarely used except by writing engravers.

Etching is a species of engraving on copper or other metals with a sharp-pointed instrument called an etching needle. The plate is covered with a ground or varnish capable of resisting the action of aquafortis. The usual method is to draw the design on paper with a black-lead pencil; the paper being damped and laid upon the plate, prepared as above, with the drawing next the etching ground, is passed through the rolling press, and thus the design is transferred from the paper to the ground. The needle then scratches out the lines of the design; and aquafortis being poured over the plate, which is bordered round with wax, it is allowed to remain on it long enough to corrode or bite in the lines which the etching needle has made. Etching with a dry point, as it is called, is performed entirely with the point without any ground, the burr raised being taken off by the scraper. Etching with a soft ground is used to imitate chalk or black-lead drawings. For this purpose the ground is mixed with a portion of tallow or lard, according to the temperature of the air. A piece of thin paper being attached to the plate at the four corners by some turner's pitch and lying over the ground, the drawing is made on the paper and shadowed with the black-lead pencil. The action of the pencil thus detaches the ground which adheres to the paper, according to the degree to which the finishing is carried; the paper being then removed, the work is bit in the ordinary way. *Stippling* is also executed on the etching ground by dots instead of lines made with the etching needle, which, according to the intensity of the shadow to be represented, are made thicker and closer. The work is then bit in. *Etching on Steel* is executed much in the same way as in the process on copper. The plate is bedded on common glazier's putty, and a ground of Brunswick black is laid in the usual way, through which the needle scratches. It is then bit in, in the way above described. —*Etching on Glass.* The glass is covered with a thin ground of beeswax; and the design being drawn with the etching needle, it is subjected to the action of sulphuric acid sprinkled over with pounded flour or Derbyshire spar. After four or five hours this is removed, and the glass cleaned off with oil of turpentine, leaving the parts covered with the beeswax untouched. This operation may be inverted by drawing the design on the glass with a solution of beeswax and turpentine, and subjecting the ground to the action of the acid.

Mezzotinto Engraving.—In this species of engraving the artist, with a knife or instrument made for the purpose, roughs over the whole surface of the copper in every direction, so as to make it susceptible of delivering a uniform black, smooth, or flat tint. After this process the outline is traced with an etching needle, and the lightest parts are scraped out, then the middle tints so as to leave a greater portion of the ground, and so on according to the depth required in the several parts of the work.

Steel Engraving was introduced by our celebrated countryman, Mr. Perkins.

The steel plate is softened by being deprived of a part of its carbon; the engraving is then made, and the plate hardened again by the restoration of the carbon. The great advantage of steel plates consists in their hardness, by which they are made to yield an indefinite number of impressions; whereas a copper plate wears out after 2 or 3000 impressions, and even much sooner if the engraving be fine. An engraving on a steel plate may be transferred, in relief, to a softened steel cylinder by pressure; this cylinder, after being hardened, may again transfer the design, by being rolled upon a fresh steel plate: thus the design may be multiplied at pleasure.

Aquatinta Engraving, whose effect somewhat resembles that of an Indian-ink drawing. The mode of effecting this is (the design being already etched) to cover the plate with a ground made of resin and Burgundy pitch or mastic dissolved in rectified spirit of wine, which is poured over the plate lying in an inclined position. The spirit of wine, from its rapid evaporation, leaves the rest of the composition with a granulated texture over the whole of the plate, by which means a grain is produced by the aquafortis on the parts left open by the evaporation of the spirit of wine. The margin of the plate is of course protected in the usual way. After the aquafortis has bitten the lighter parts they are *stopt out*, and the aquafortis is again applied, and so on as often as any parts continue to require more depth. Formerly the grain used to be produced by covering the copper with a powder or some substance which took a granulated form, instead of using the compound above mentioned; but this process was found to be both uncertain and imperfect. In the compound the grain is rendered finer or coarser, in proportion to the quantity of resin introduced. This mode of engraving was invented by a Frenchman of the name of St. Non, about 1662.

Engraving on Stone, or *Lithography*. —A modern invention, by means whereof impressions may be taken from drawings made on stone. The merit of this discovery belongs to Aloys Senefelder, a musical performer of the theatre at Munich about the year 1800. The following are the principles on which the art of lithography depends:—First, the facility with which calcareous stones imbibe water; second, the great disposition they have to adhere to resinous and oily substances; third, the affinity between each other of oily and resinous substances, and the power they possess of repelling water or a body moistened with water. Hence, when drawings are made on a polished surface of calcareous stone with a resinous or oily medium, they are so adhesive that nothing short of mechanical means can effect their separation from it, and, whilst the other parts of the stone take up the water poured upon them, the resinous or oily parts repel it. Lastly, when over a stone prepared in this manner a colored oily or resinous substance is passed, it will adhere to the drawings made as above, and not to the watery parts of the stone. The ink and chalk used in lithography are of a saponaceous quality; the former is prepared in Germany from a compound of tallow soap, pure white wax, a small quantity of tallow, and a portion of lamp-black, all boiled together, and when cool dissolved in distilled water. The chalk for the crayons used in drawing on the stone is a composition consisting of the ingredients above mentioned, but to it is added when boiling a small quantity of potash. After the drawing on the stone has been executed and is perfectly dry, a very weak solution of vitriolic acid is poured upon the stone, which not only takes up the alkali from the chalk or ink, as the case may be, leaving an insoluble substance behind it, but it lowers in a very small degree that part of the surface of the stone not drawn upon, and prepares it for absorbing water with greater freedom. Weak gum water is then applied to the stone, to close its pores and keep it moist. The stone is now washed with water, and the daubing ink applied with balls as in printing; after which it passed in the usual way through the press, the process of watering and daubing being applied for every impression. There is a mode of transferring drawings made with the chemical ink on paper prepared with a solution of size or gum tragacanth, which being *laid on the stone and passed through the press* leaves the drawing on the stone, and the process above described for preparing the stone and taking the impressions is carried into effect. In Germany many engravings are made on stone with the burin, in the same way as on copper; but the very great inferiority of these to copper engravings makes it improbable that this method will ever come into general use. Perhaps one of the greatest advantages of the art of lithography is the extraordinary number of copies that may be taken from a block. As many as

70,000 copies or prints have been taken from one block, and the last of them nearly as good as the first. Expedition is also gained, inasmuch as a fifth more copies can be taken in the same time than from a copper-plate : and as regards economy the advantage over every other species of engraving is very great.

Zincography.—This art, which is of very recent introduction, is similar in principle to lithography, the surface of the plates of zinc on which it is executed being bit away, leaving the design prominent or in relief.—A species of engraving on copper, called the *medallic*, has been invented within the last twenty-five years. Its object is to give accurate representations of medals, coins, and bassi-relievi of a small size. Some of the impressions are exceedingly accurate and beautiful, and appear so salient, that we can hardly convince ourselves at first that we are looking upon a flat surface.

ENGROSS'ING, the writing of a deed over fair, and in proper legible characters. Among lawyers it more particularly means the copying of any writing upon parchment or stamped paper. In statute law, engrossing means the buying up of large quantities of any commodity in order to sell it again at an unusually high price.

ENHARMON'IC SCALE, in music, a scale in which the modulation proceeds by intervals less than semitones; that is, by quarter tones, having two dieses or signs of raising or lowering the voice.

ENIG'MA, a proposition put in obscure or ambiguous terms to puzzle or exercise the ingenuity in discovering its meaning. In the present day, the enigma is only a jeu d'esprit, or a species of amusement to beguile a leisure hour; but formally it was a matter of such importance that the eastern monarchs used to send mutual embassies for the solution of enigmas. Every one remembers the enigma which Samson proposed to the Philistines for solution; and the still more famous enigma of the Sphinx, the source at once of the elevation and the misfortunes of Œdipus. About the 17th century the enigma, which had been for centuries neglected as a species of literary display, again came into favor; and in France particularly it was cultivated with so much zeal, that several grand treatises were dedicated to its history and characteristics. The best enigmas with which we are acquainted were written by Schiller, and have been incorporated in his works. Even in the present day the periodical literature of France and Germany does not disdain this species of writing; though, as was before observed, it is now employed generally for amusement, and rarely to convey moral instruction.

ENNUI, (*French*,) a word expressive of lassitude, or weariness arising from the want of employment.

ENS, among metaphysicians, denotes entity, being, or existence: this the schools call *ens reale*, and *ens positivum*, to distinguish it from their *ens rationis*, which exists only in the imagination.—*Ens*, among chemists, signifies the essence or virtue of any substance.

ENSEM'BLE, (*French*,) a term used in the fine arts to denote the general effect of a whole work, without reference to the parts. The *ensemble* of a picture, for instance, may be satisfactory to the eye of the spectator, though the several parts may not bear a critical analysis; or, in a drama, the characters may be well drawn, and yet it may be deficient in the *ensemble*, that is, as a whole.

EN'SIFORM, an epithet for that which resembles a sword, (*ensis*;) as an *ensiform* leaf.

EN'SIGN, the flag or banner under which soldiers are ranged, according to the different regiments to which they belong.—*Ensign* is also the officer that carries the colors, being the lowest commissioned officer in a company of infantry.—*Naval ensign*, is a large banner hoisted on a staff, and carried over the poop or stern of a ship.

ENTAB'LATURE, in architecture, the architrave, frieze, and cornice, at the top of a column, and which is over the capital; the horizontal continuous work which rests upon a row of columns.

ENTAIL', in law, an estate entailed, abridged and limited by certain conditions prescribed by the first donor. Estates tail are either *general* or *special*; and are always less estates than a fee simple.—*To entail*, is to settle the descent of lands and tenements, by gift to a man and certain heirs specified, so that neither the donee nor any subsequent possessor can either alienate or bequeath it.

EN'TASIS, in architecture, a delicate and almost imperceptible swelling of the shaft of a column, to be found in almost all the Grecian examples, adopted to prevent the shafts being strictly frusta of cones. This refinement, which is alluded to in the second chapter of the third book of *Vitruvius*, was first observed in execution by Mr. Allason in 1814 in the Athenian edifices.

ENTEL'ECHY, a peripatetic term, invented by Aristotle in order to express an object in its complete actualization, as opposed to merely *potential* existence.

ENTERTAIN'MENT, the pleasure which the mind receives from anything interesting, and which arrests the attention. Also, the hospitable reception of, and amusement we provide for, our guests.—In a dramatic sense, the farce or pantomime which follows a tragedy or comedy.

ENTHU'SIASM, in a religious sense, implies a transport of the mind, whereby a person vainly fancies himself inspired with some revelation from heaven, or that his actions are governed by a divine impulse. Devotion, when it does not lie under the check of reason, is apt to degenerate into enthusiasm; and when once it fancies itself under the influence of a divine impulse, it is no wonder that it should slight human ordinances, and trust to the conceits of an overweening imagination. But enthusiasm, in another sense, when under the control of reason and experience, becomes a noble passion, that forms sublime ideas, and prompts to the ardent pursuit of laudable objects. Such is the enthusiasm of the poet, the orator, the painter, and the sculptor—such is the enthusiasm of the patriot, the hero, the philanthropist, and the truly devout Christian.

EN'THYMEME, among logicians, denotes a syllogism, perfect in the mind, but imperfect in the expression. This is the character under which the universal form of reasoning, or syllogism, generally presents itself in connected writing. For example, the following argument, if drawn out in the correct logical form, would stand thus, "All tyrants deserve death; but Cæsar is a tyrant, therefore Cæsar deserves death." But in the rapid diction of oratory, or poetry, it would probably be expressed either, "All tyrants deserve death, therefore so does Cæsar;" in which case the minor premiss, "Cæsar is a tyrant," is suppressed: or, "Cæsar is a tyrant. therefore he deserves death," by suppressing the major premiss. Instances may be cited in which the enthymeme consists merely of one of the premisses expressed, while both the other premiss and the conclusion are to be supplied by a rapid exercise of thought. Thus in the well-known words, "But Brutus says he was ambitious, and Brutus is an honorable man," the last of these propositions contains a complete argument,—"what honorable men say is to be believed: Brutus is an honorable man, therefore what Brutus says is to be believed."

ENTI'ERTIE, or ENTIRE'TY, in law, the whole of a thing, in distinction from a moiety: thus a bond, damages, &c., are said to be *entire*, when they cannot be apportioned.

ENTRE'METS, small plates, or dainties, set between the principal dishes at table.—In music, the inferior and lesser movements inserted in a composition between those of more importance.

ENTREPAS', in horsemanship, is a short broken pace, nearly resembling an amble.

ENTREPOT', a warehouse or magazine for the deposit of goods.

EN'TRY, in law, the act of taking possession of lands.—In commerce, the act of setting down in an account-book the particulars of trade; as make an *entry* of that sale, debt, or credit. Book-keeping is performed either by *single* or *double entry*.—*Entry*, at the custom-house, the exhibition or depositing of a ship's papers in the hands of the proper officers, and obtaining permission to land the goods.

ENU'CLEATE, to open as a nucleus; to clear from knots or lumps; hence, to explain, or clear from obscurity.

ENUMERA'TION, an account of several things, in which mention is made of every particular article.—*Enumeration*, in rhetoric, is that part of a peroration in which the orator recapitulates the principal points or heads of the discourse or argument.

ENVI'RONS, the parts or places which surround another place; as the *environs* of a city or large town.

EN'VOY, a person deputed by government to negotiate some affair with any foreign prince or state. There are envoys *ordinary* and *extraordinary*, as well as ambassadors; they are equally the same under the protection of the law of nations, and enjoy all the privileges of ambassadors, but, being in rank below them, they are not treated with equal ceremony. The word *envoy* is also sometimes applied to resident ministers.

EN'VY, a feeling that springs from pride or disappointed ambition, excited by the sight of another's superiority or success, accompanied with some degree of malignity, and usually with a desire to depreciate him.

E'PACTS, in chronology, the excesses

of the solar month above the lunar synodical month, and of the solar year above the lunar year of twelve synodical months. The epacts, then, are either *annual* or *monthly*. Suppose the new moon to be on the 1st of January: since the lunar month is 29 days, 12 hours, 44 minutes, 3 seconds, and the month of January contains 31 days; the monthly epact is 1 day, 11 hours, 15 minutes, 57 seconds. The annual epact is nearly 11 days; the Julian solar year being 365 days, 6 hours; and the Julian lunar year 354 days, 8 hours, 48 minutes, 38 seconds. In the ordinary tables of the church calendar the epacts are given only for a single century; but as the Gregorian calendar now in use defines precisely the length of the year, tables, though somewhat more complicated, have been formed, which show the epacts of every future year in all time to come. The epacts were invented by Luigi Lilio Ghiraldi, more frequently styled Aloysius Lilius, a physician of Naples, and author of the Gregorian Calendar, for the purpose of showing the days of the new moons, and thence the moon's age on any day of the year, and consequently of regulating the church festivals. It is only in ecclesiastical computations that the epacts are ever employed; in civil affairs the civilized portion of mankind have long since laid aside the use of the lunisolar year, and regulated time entirely by the sun. In the calendar of the Church of England, Easter and the other movable feasts are determined in the same manner as in the old Romish calendar, excepting that the golden numbers are prefixed to the days of the *full moons*, instead of the days of the new moons. The epacts are consequently not used. It is desirable that the custom of reckoning time by the moon, which had its origin in ignorant ages, were abandoned, and the civil year adopted for every purpose.

EP'ARCHY, the prefecture or territory under the jurisdiction of an *eparch* or governor.

EPAU'LE, in fortification, the shoulder of the bastion, or the angle of the face and flank; which is often called the *angle of the epaule*.

EPAU'LEMENT, in fortification, a work raised to cover sidewise, made of earth, gabions, &c. It also denotes a mass of earth, called a square orillon, raised to cover the cannon of a casement, and faced with a wall.

EPAULETTES', distinguishing ornaments worn both by military and naval officers. In the different armies of the German states ensigns are not allowed to wear epaulettes; and hence the phrase "to obtain epaulettes," is synonymous with "to become a lieutenant." In the British army all officers with the rank of captain upwards wear two epaulettes; all under that rank only one.

EPENET'IC, the laudatory or "encomiastic" species of oratory: a branch of the Epideictic, according to the division of Aristotle's Rhetoric.

EPEN'THESIS, a figure of grammar, by which one or more letters are inserted in the middle of a word; as in the Latin *rettulit* for *retulit*.

EPHEBEI'UM, in ancient architecture, the building appropriated for the wrestling and exercises of youth till they had, on their arrival at manhood, the right to enter the gymnasium.

EPHE'BI, applied particularly to the Athenian youth between the ages of eighteen and twenty years.

EPH'OD, in Jewish antiquity, a part of the sacerdotal habit, being a kind of girdle which was brought from behind the neck over the two shoulders, and hanging down before, it was extended across the stomach, then carried round the waist and used as a girdle to the tunic. They were of two sorts; one of plain linen, and the other embroidered for the high priest. On the part in front were two precious stones, on which were engraven the names of the twelve tribes of Israel. Before the breast was a square piece or breast-plate.

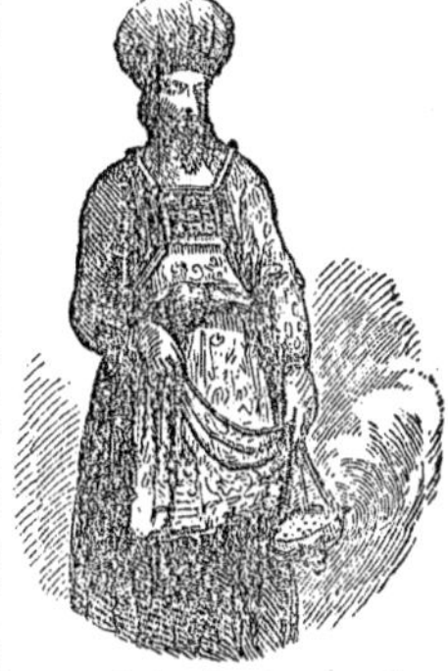

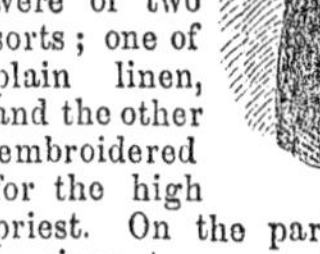

EPH'ORI, in Grecian antiquity, magistrates established in ancient Sparta to balance the regal power. The authority of the *ephori* was very great: they were five in number, presided over shows and festivals, had the care of the public money, specially superintended the education of youth, and were the arbiters of war and peace.

EP'IC, a poem of an elevated character, describing generally the exploits of heroes. This species of poetry claims a very ancient origin, and is universally allowed to be the most dignified and majestic to which the powers of the poet can be directed. There are various theories regarding the character of an epic poem; and while some critics claim this title exclusively for the *Iliad* and *Odyssey* of Homer, the *Æneid* of Virgil, and the *Paradise Lost* of Milton, others—and particularly the Germans—embrace in the catalogue of epic writers Scott, Byron, Pope, Moore, and Campbell. Epic poetry has often been compared to the drama; and the essential difference between them is, that description is the province of the former—action of the latter. The emotions which epic poetry excite are not so frequent and violent as those produced by dramatic composition; but they are more prolonged, and more developed by actual occurrences; for an epic poem embraces a wider compass of time and action than is admissible in the drama. History has generally supplied the best epic writers with themes; but a close attention to historical truth in the development of the story is by no means requisite. Fiction, invention, imagination, may be indulged in to an almost unlimited extent; provided always the poet be careful to preserve what the critics call unity, *i. e.* provided his work embrace an entire action, or have a beginning, a middle, and an end. This is the distinguishing characteristic of the great epic poems. If the epic is the highest, it is also the most difficult style of poetical composition, and that in which mediocrity is least endurable; and hence few of the writers of epics on the classical model have obtained a high reputation as national poets in any language. Virgil is the earliest imitator of Homer whose epic has been preserved, and the most successful. The other Greek and Latin epic poets contain passages of great beauty; but their poems, as wholes, are of an inferior order. In the English language there are only two epics which can be said to form part of the national literature, and those only in part framed on the classical model: the *Paradise Lost* and *Regained* of Milton. French epics, including even the *Henriade* of Voltaire, so famous in its time, have no place among the chefs-d'œuvre of the national literature. Of the great Italian poems, only one (the *Jerusalem Delivered* of Tasso) fulfils the conditions of an epic. The poem of Dante, however sublime in style, has no unity of event or action: those of Ariosto, and the other Romanzieri, form a class distinguished from the epic by the mixture of the serious and ludicrous. The old German and Spanish national poems,—the *Romance of the Cid*, and the *Niebelungen-Lied*, especially the latter, which is closely confined to the conduct of one great action,—although the work of writers unskilled in classical literature, deserve the title of epic as truly as those of Homer.

EP'ICENE, in grammar, an epithet for the gender of such words as are common to both sexes.

EPICHIRE'MA, in logic, a mode of reasoning, which comprehends the proof of one or both the premises of a syllogism, before the conclusion is drawn.

EPICHIROTO'NIA, in Grecian antiquity, the annual ceremony of revising the laws, which was instituted by Solon. They gave their votes by holding up their hands: hence the name.

EPICITHARIS'MA, in the ancient drama, the last part of the interlude, or a flourish of music after the play was over.

EPIC REPRESENTA'TION, the Epos or epic poem, relates a grand event on which important consequences depend. In plastic art, reliefs on walls, and friezes, and encaustic, and fresco-painting which can be executed on large surfaces as well as oil-paintings, by which a considerable space on canvas may be filled, are peculiarly adapted for the representation of an Epos, or of a great action. But the artist has not, like the poet, the power of representing in connection, those consequences of single events, scenes, &c., which form the whole. The limits of connection (with the poet often only single words, clever phrases, or striking transitions) are denied to the artist, and he must therefore limit himself to the means at his command, of showing in the clearest manner possible, the point of the event from which its consequences are developed. The plastic artist can and may depict the moment of an event or a scene, including several events which he may define or suggest. To choose this moment rightly, to draw strikingly, and to execute intelligibly, is the important task, in the performance of which the true master and epic artist are seen. The epic picture, whether it belong to plastic work or painting, is thus the representation of an important action of human life, of ancient or modern times, of distant or neighboring nations, of events which have happened or which have been invented. It must in every case be true or probable, *i. e.*, belonging to history and reality, or possible; in other words, the circumstances to be represented must be brought out conformably to Nature and Art, and have nothing contradictory in themselves. The epic work of Art, is always only a fragment (though an important one) of a classic or romantic, of a more or less historical, or of a pure poetic epos, often the quintessence of an epos, but never the epos itself. The plastic descriptive work of Art is thus limited to the poetical important event, but is in its limitation the utmost concentration of history, while it brings forward a principal action, with a short but clear glance of the most important preceding and succeeding circumstances, so that all forms are arranged in action in their due relation to each other, or to the principal point of the picture. If this be undertaken with genius and happily executed by a masterly hand, the whole will not only attract the eye of the spectator, as a harmonious grouping of different details, rich in references, and finding a centre point of union and conclusion, but will rivet his attention.

EPICTE'TIAN, pertaining to Epictetus, the Stoic philosopher; a man who was held in such high esteem, that it is said his study lamp was sold after his death for three thousand drachmas.

EPICURE'ANS, a numerous sect of philosophers in Greece and Rome: the disciples of Epicurus, who flourished about 300 years B.C. They maintained that sensual pleasure was man's chief felicity; that the world was formed by a concourse of atoms, and not governed by Providence; that the gods resided in the extramundane spaces, in soft, inactive ease, and eternal tranquillity; that future rewards and punishments were idle chimeras; and that the soul was extinguished with the body. They are mentioned in the xviith chapter of the Acts of the Apostles. Epicurus himself maintained a more manly philosophy than the generality of his followers; he held, indeed, that pleasure was the chief end of human pursuit; and this pleasure he placed in an exemption from pain, and a perfect tranquillity of body and mind; but the means which he pointed out as conducive to this end were prudence, temperance, fortitude, and justice, in the union of which perfect happiness consists. He pursued pleasure, therefore, in its most rational acceptation, and his life seems to have been stained with few vices. The precepts and practices of the Epicureans have, however, loaded his memory with unmerited infamy; and an Epicurean, according to the perverted meaning of his doctrine, is one who is devoted to sensual enjoyments, particularly those of the table.

EPIDE'MIA, in Grecian antiquity, festivals kept in honor of Apollo and Diana, at the stated seasons when these deities, who could not be present everywhere, were supposed to visit different places, in order to receive the vows of their adorers.

EPIDEM'IC, a disease which prevails in a place or tract of country only for a temporary period, or that attacks many people at the same season. There are some epidemics which prevail every year, and which are produced by the various changes of the seasons. Thus, the spring is accompanied by inflammatory diseases; summer by complaints in the stomach and bowels; autumn by catarrhs; and winter by intermittents. An epidemic at its commencement is usually mild, and becomes more dangerous as it spreads; but as it goes off, it again generally assumes a mild form. Epidemics are not originally contagious; it is only under particular circumstances, especially if the disorder is a violent one, and many patients are crowded into a small room, so as to form a corrupt atmosphere about the sick, that contagion takes place. That which is frequently ascribed to contagion, is only the consequence of a violent shock of the nervous system at the sight of a sick person, perhaps in a loathsome state, whereby the disease, to which the body was already disposed, is more quickly developed. It is essential to the medical notion of an *epidemic* that it be of a temporary, in contradistinction to a permanent character. It differs from *endemic*, inasmuch as the latter class of diseases are of a permanent nature, and prevail only among certain people, and in certain districts.

EPIG'ONI, the collective appellation of the sons of the seven Greek princes who conducted the first war against Thebes without success. The war subsequently undertaken by the Epigoni to avenge the defeat of their forefathers is celebrated in history. Their capture of Thebes forms the theme of Wilkie's epic poem, the *Epigoniad*, which was published about the middle of the last century, and procured for its author great reputation.

EP'IGRAM, in poetry, a short poem or piece in verse, which has only one subject, and finishes by a witty or ingenious turn of thought; or, to use a more general definition, an interesting thought represented happily in a few words. The first of these definitions, although tolerably correct as to the modern epigram, differs, as it will be seen, widely from the original sense of the word in Greek. The Greek epigram was, in the first instance, a short collection of lines actually inscribed on a monument, statue, fountain, &c.; and the word was thence transferred to such short poems as might serve for inscriptions: of such the collection termed the *Greek epigram* is almost wholly composed. Their general characteristic is perfect simplicity, and the seemingly studied absence of that *point* which characterizes the modern epigram. They are almost wholly in one form of metre, the elegiac. In the poetry of classical Rome, the term epigram was still somewhat indiscriminately used to designate short pieces in verse; but the works of Catullus, and still more the well-known collection of the *Epigrams of Martial*, contain a great number which present the modern epigrammatic character: and Martial has, in fact, afforded the model on which the modern epigram has been framed. In this class of composition, and especially where the turn of thought is satirical, the French writers have been far more successful than those of any other nation; and the term "piquant" seems expressly invented to designate the peculiar force of those epigrammatic sallies of fancy of which their literature is full.

EP'IGRAPH, also termed *motto*. In literature, a citation from some author, or a sentence framed for the purpose, placed at the commencement of a work or of its separate divisions.

EP'ILOGUE, in the drama, a speech addressed to the audience when the play is ended. In the modern tragedy the epilogue is usually smart and lively, intended, probably, to compose the passions raised in the course of the representation; but it has been compared to a merry jig upon the organ, after a good sermon, to wipe away any impression that might have been made by it, and send the congregation away just as they came.—In rhetoric, the conclusion of a speech, containing a recapitulation of the whole.

EPINI'CION, in the Greek and Latin poetry, is a poem or composition celebrating a victory. Also, a festival on account of a victory.

EPIPH'ANY a Christian festival, observed on the sixth of January, (the twelfth day after Christmas,) in honor of the appearance of our Saviour to the magi, or wise men, who came to adore him, and bring him presents. The Greek fathers used the word for the appearance of Christ in the world.

EPIPHONE'MA, in rhetoric, a sententious exclamation or remark, not closely connected with the general tenor of the oration, and generally expressed with vehemence.

EPIPH'ORA, in rhetoric, the emphatic repetition of a word or series of words at the end of several sentences or stanzas. One of the finest instances of this figure in modern oratory occurs in Fox's defence of himself and his measures in the House of Commons after the dissolution of the Coalition ministry.

EPIPLEX'IS, a rhetorical figure, which, by an elegant kind of upbraiding, endeavors to convince.

EPIP'LOCE, a rhetorical figure, by which one aggravation, or striking circumstance, is added to another; as, "He not only spared the rebels, but encouraged them; not only encouraged them, but rewarded them."

EPIS'COPACY, a form of church government by diocesan bishops.

EPISCOPA'LIANS, an appellation given to those who adhere to the episcopal form of church government and discipline.

EP'ISODE, in poetry, a separate incident, story, or action, which a poet invents, and connects with his principal action, that his work may abound with a greater variety of events: though, in a more limited sense, all the particular incidents of which the action or narration is compounded, are called episodes. In epic poetry, there is much more room for the episode than in dramatic, where the poem is confined to a present action. The term *episode* has also been transferred to historical painting, in a sense analogous to that which it bears in poetry.

EPIS'TATES, the title of the presidents of the two great councils of the Athenians, viz., the Ecclesia and the senate of the Five Hundred. They were both respectively elected from the number of the prohedri of the ecclesia and senate, and their office only lasted one day. The latter of these two officers had the post of the greatest trust, as in his hands were placed the keys of the citadel and public treasury.

EPIS'TLE, the use of this word is now

confined to the designation of those written addresses by apostolical writers to their Christian brethren which are contained in the canon of Scripture; a few others, either spurious or of high antiquity, although not recognized among inspired writings, are also so denominated. The epistles of St. Paul, and others contained in the volume of the New Testament, are not arranged according to their date, but, in all probability, according to the views which those who arranged the canon entertained of the relative importance either of the writings themselves, or of the parties to whom they are addressed. Thus, the epistles of St. Paul to the different churches, and the Catholic epistles of St. John (*i. e.* addressed to the universal church,) are ranked before the epistles of those saints to individual Christians. An exception to this rule is to be found in the epistle to the Hebrews, which is placed last among those of St. Paul, and seems to have been admitted into the canon at a comparatively recent period. The practice of reading a portion of an epistle in the service of the church is extremely ancient, and said to be noticed by Justin in his *First Apology*.

EPISTOLOG'RAPHY, the art or practice of writing letters.

EPIS'TROPHE, in rhetoric, a figure of speech in which several successive sentences end with the same word or affirmation, as, "Are they Hebrews? so am I. Are they Israelites? so am I. Are they of the seed of Abraham? so am I," &c.

EP'ISTYLE, in ancient architecture, a term used by the Greeks for what we call the *architrave*, viz., a massive piece of stone or wood laid immediately over the capital of a column.

EP'ITAPH, literally an inscription on a tomb. As has been well observed, inscriptions in honor of the dead are perhaps as old as tombs themselves; though they were by no means bestowed in such profusion in ancient as in modern times. Among the Greeks, for instance, this honor was paid only to the tombs of heroes, as in the case of Leonidas and his gallant comrades. The Romans were the first to deviate from this course. Every Roman family who consecrated a tomb to their relations had the privilege of inscribing an epitaph thereon; and as their tombs were usually situated on the highway, the attention of passers-by was sought to be arrested by the words "sta viator"—the formula with which all their epitaphs were prefaced. But how much soever the epitaphs of the ancient Greeks and Romans differed in point of number, there were three qualities which they possessed in common—brevity, simplicity, and familiarity; qualities which a modern critic, Boileau, has pronounced to be indispensable in this species of writing. At what period sepulchral inscriptions came into use in England has not been precisely ascertained; though there can be little doubt that this practice was introduced by the Romans at the period of their invasion of Britain. During the first twelve centuries of the Christian era, monumental inscriptions were all written in Latin. About the 13th century, the French language was adopted and continued to be used for this purpose till the middle of the 14th century; at which time monumental inscriptions in the vernacular tongue became common, though the clergy and learned of that time, as might have been expected, still preferred the Latin, as their more familiar idiom. The modern English, French, and German epitaphs, of which several collections have been made, are infinitely more numerous than those of any time or nation, and exhibit every variety of style and sentiment; from the most chaste and majestic gravity, impressive tenderness, and laconic terseness, to the most puerile epigrammatic conceits, pointed satire, and heraldic prolixity.

EPITA'SIS, in ancient poetry, the second part or division of a dramatic poem, in which the plot, entered upon in the first part, or *protasis*, was carried on, heightened, and worked up till it arrived at its height, called *catastasis*.—In rhetoric, that part of an oration in which the orator addresses himself most forcibly to the passions.

EPITHALA'MIUM, a nuptial song, sung by a chorus of boys and girls when the bride and bridegroom entered the bridal chamber, and again on the first morning after the marriage. This was the custom in Greece, which was somewhat varied at Rome, where the chorus consisted of girls only, who sang before the door of the nuptial chamber till midnight. The most perfect examples of this species which antiquity has left us are by Theocritus and Catullus.

EP'ITHET, in rhetoric and composition, denotes a term employed in an adjective sense to express an attribute or quality of another substantive term. The abundance and the propriety of epithets form peculiar characteristics of various poetical styles. In the strict rhetorical sense, epithets are only such adjectives as convey a notion already implied in the noun substantive itself, and add nothing to the sense. Thus, the "glorious" sun is a mere epithet; while the "rising" or the "setting" sun would, as conveying some additional idea into the sense of the passage, not be considered as epithets. The former sort, however, are sometimes called in disparagement by writers on rhetoric "otiosa," or idle epithets.

EPITITH'IDES, in architecture, the crown or upper mouldings of an entablature.

EPIT'OME, in literature, an abridgment; a work in which the contents of a former work are reduced within a smaller space by curtailment and condensation. In the later classical period, extending through the declining age of the Western Empire, the practice of epitomizing the writings of older writers, especially in history, became very prevalent; and while some regard the works of Justin, Eutropius, and similar writers, as having preserved to us much historical knowledge which would otherwise have been lost, others have maintained that these laborious compilers have done great disservice to literature, inasmuch as the voluminous works which they abridged being superseded by their more popular and cheaper compendia, in an illiterate age, have, from that cause, for the most part perished.

EPIT'ROPE, or EPIT'ROPY, in rhetoric, a figure of speech, by which one thing is granted, with a view to obtain an advantage; as, "I concede the fact, but this very concession overthrows your own argument."

EPIZEUX'IS, in rhetoric, a figure which repeats the same word, without any other intervening; such is that of Virgil, "nunc, nunc, insurgite remis."

E'POCH, a certain fixed period, or point of time, made famous by some remarkable event, and serving as a standard in chronology and history. The principal are the Creation, 4004 B.C.; the Flood, 2348 B.C.; the birth of Abraham, 1996 B.C.; the conquest of Canaan, 1451 B.C.; the taking of Troy, 1184 B.C.; the finishing of Solomon's temple, 1104 B.C.; the first Olympiad, 776 B.C.: the building of Rome, 753 B.C.; the era of Nabonassar, 747 B.C.; the founding of the Persian Empire, by Cyrus, 559 B.C.; the death of Alexander, 323 B.C; the death of Cæsar, 44 B.C; the birth of Christ, 1, or the commencement of the Christian era; the Hegira of Mahomet, 622 A.D.—The Christian era, used by almost all Christian nations, dates from January 1st, the middle of the fourth year of the 194th Olympiad, in the 753d of the building of Rome, and 4714th of the Julian period. The Christian year, in its division, follows exactly the Roman year, consisting of 365 days for three successive years, and of 366 in the fourth year, which is termed *leap* year. The simplicity of this form has brought it into very general use, and it is customary for astronomers and chronologists, in treating of ancient time, to date back in the same order from its commencement.—*See* CALENDAR.

EP'ODE, in lyric poetry, the third or last part of the ode, the ancient ode being divided into strophe, antistrophe, and epode. The word is now used for any little verse or verses, that follow one or more great ones.

EPOPEE', or EPOPŒ'IA, in poetry, the fable, or subject of an epic poem.

EPOP'TÆ, in antiquity, a name given to those who were admitted to view the secrets of the greater mysteries, or religious ceremonies of the Greeks.

EPOT'IDES, in the naval architecture of the ancients, two thick blocks of wood, one on each side the prow of a galley, for warding off the blows of the rostra of the enemy's vessels.

EPULO'NES, in Roman antiquity, public officers who assisted at the sacrifices, and had the care of the *epulum*, or sacred banquet, committed to them.

EQUAL'ITY, a term of relation between things the same in magnitude, quantity, or quality. Also, the same degree of dignity or claims; as, *equality* of men, in the scale of being; an *equality* of rights, &c.

EQUANIM'ITY, that even and calm frame of mind and temper, under good or bad fortune, which is not easily elated or depressed. A truly great man bears misfortunes with *equanimity*, and carries himself in prosperity without vain exultation or excessive joy.

EQ'UERRY, an officer of state under the master of the horse. There are five equerries, who ride out with her majesty; for which purpose they give their attendance monthly, one at a time, and have a table provided for them.

E'QUES AURA'TUS, a Roman knight, so called because none but knights were allowed to gild their armor.

EQUES'TRIA, a place in the Roman theatres where the knights or *equites* sat

EQUES'TRIAN GAMES, in Roman antiquity, (*ludi equestres,*) horse-races, of which there are five kinds; the *prodromus* or plain horse-race, the chariot race, the decursory race about funeral piles, the *ludi sevirales*, and the *ludi neptunales*.—*Equestrian order*, the second rank in Rome, next to the senators. —*Equestrian statue*, the representation of a person on horseback.

EQUIPAGE', in ordinary language, signifies the carriage, horses, and liveries of any gentleman when he appears abroad.—*Equipage*, in marine affairs, signifies the crew of a ship, together with all a ship's furniture, masts, sails, ammunition, &c. In the art military, it denotes all sorts of utensils and artillery, &c., necessary for commencing and prosecuting with ease or success any military operation.

EQUIPOL'LENCE, in logic, an equivalence, or agreement, either as to the nature of the thing, or as to the grammatical sense of any two or more propositions; that is, when two propositions signify one and the same thing, though they express it differently.

EQUI'RIA, in antiquity, games instituted by Romulus in honor of Mars, and which consisted in horse-racing. They were celebrated on the third of the calends of March.

EQ'UITES, amongst the Romans, were persons of the second degree of nobility, immediately succeeding the senators in point of rank. Every *eques* or knight had a horse kept at the public charge; he received also the stipend of a horseman, to serve in the wars, and wore a ring, which was given him by the state. The *equites* composed a large body of men, and constituted the Roman cavalry; for there was always a sufficient number of them in the city, and nothing but a review was requisite to fit them for service.

EQ'UITY, in a moral sense, is the impartial distribution of justice. So, in an enlarged view, Blackstone observes:—"Equity, in its true and general meaning, is the soul and spirit of all law; positive law is construed, and rational law is made by it. In this, equity is synonymous with justice." In English jurisprudence, a court of equity or chancery, is a court which corrects the operation of the literal text of the law, and supplied its defects, by reasonable construction, and by rules of proceeding and deciding, which are not admissible in a court of law. Equity then, is the law of reason, exercised by the chancellor or judge, giving remedy in cases to which the courts of law are not competent. It will remove legal impediments to the fair decision of a question depending at law. It will prevent a party from improperly setting up, at a trial, some title or claim which would be inequitable. It will compel him to discover, on his own oath, facts which he knows are material to the right of the other party, but which a court of law cannot compel the party to discover. It will provide for the safety of property in dispute pending litigation. It will counteract, or control, or set aside, fraudulent judgments. It will also exercise, in many cases, *exclusive* jurisdiction; particularly in granting special relief beyond the reach of the common law. It will grant injunctions to prevent waste or irreparable injury, or to secure a settled right, or to prevent vexatious litigations, or to compel the restitution of title deeds; it will appoint receivers of property, where it is in danger of misapplication; it will prohibit a party from leaving the country in order to avoid a suit; it will decree a specific performance of contracts respecting real estates; it will, in many cases, supply the imperfect execution of instruments, and reform and alter them according to the real intention of the parties; it will grant relief in cases of lost deeds and securities; and, in all cases in which its interference is asked, its general rule is, that he who asks equity must do equity. In short, its jurisdiction is almost undefined, where the positive law is silent, but substantial justice entitles the party to relief.

EQUITY OF REDEMP'TION, in law, is the advantage allowed to one who mortgages his property, to have a reasonable time allowed him to redeem it; for although the estate, upon non-payment of the money, becomes vested in the mortgagee, yet equity considers it only a pledge for the money, and gives the party a right to redeem, which is called his *equity of redemption.*

EQUIV'OCAL, an epithet for whatever is ambiguous or susceptible of different constructions; as, that man's character is very *equivocal.*

EQUIV'OCAL TERM, in logic, a term which has several significations, applying respectively and equally to several objects. A word is generally said to be employed equivocally where the middle term is used in different senses in the two premisses, or where a proposition is liable to be understood in various senses, according to the various meanings of one of its terms.

EQUIVOCA'TION, the use of equivocal terms, which may be understood by the hearer in a different sense from that in which they are taken by the speaker. He who is guilty of *equivocation*, may be fairly suspected of hypocrisy.

EQ'UIVOQUE, a word or phrase susceptible of different significations.

ERAS'TIANS, the followers of Erastus, a German divine; a sect which obtained some notoriety in England in the time of the civil wars. They referred the punishment of all offences, civil or religious, to the civil magistrate; and asserted that the church had no power to enforce any acts of discipline, nor to refuse the communion of the Lord's Supper to any one who desired it.

ERA'TO, one of the muses, whose name signifies *loving* or *lovely*. She has much in common with Terpsichore—the same attributes, the same dress, and frequently a lyre and *plectrum*. She presides over the songs of lovers.

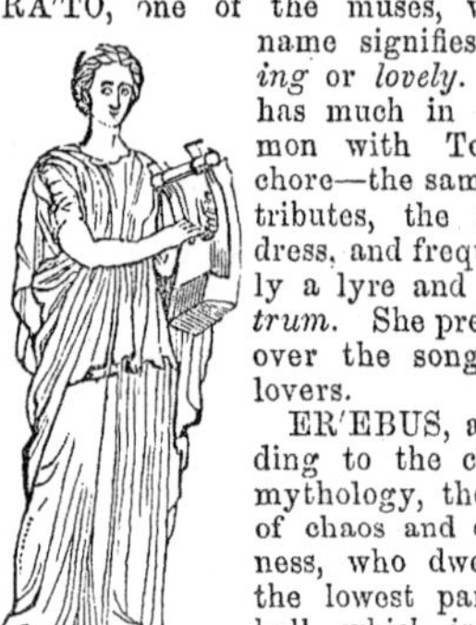

ER'EBUS, according to the classic mythology, the son of chaos and darkness, who dwelt in the lowest part of hell, which is frequently called by his name.

EREMIT'ICAL, (from *eremite*, a hermit,) living in solitude, or in seclusion from the world.

EROT'IC POETRY, a term for amatory poetry. The name of *erotic* writers has been applied particularly to a class of romance writers who belong to the later periods of Greek literature, and whose works abound in sophistical subtleties and ornaments.

EROTOM'ANY, a term employed by some writers to denote that modification of insanity, of which the passion of love is the origin, and in which the love of a particular individual constitutes the predominant idea, occupying the whole attention of the patient. It sometimes passes into perfect delirium, leads to suicide, hysterics, &c. Young people are peculiarly subject to it, who have an excitable nervous system and lively imagination, who give themselves up to an excess in pleasure, or are spoiled by reading romances, and rendered effeminate by an injudicious education and indolence.

ERRAT'IC, wandering, or having no certain course; also, not fixed or stationary; hence the planets are called *erratic stars;* and fevers which observe no regular periods, are denominated *erratic fevers*.

ERRA'TUM, an error of the press; in the plural, *Errata*, a list of which is usually printed at the beginning or end of a book.

ER'ROR, a wandering or deviation from the truth. An error may be either *voluntary* or *involuntary;* when committed through carelessness or haste it is a *blunder*.—*Error*, in law, is a mistake committed in pleading, or in a process; whereupon a *writ of error* is brought to remedy it, which carries the suit to another tribunal for redress.

ERSE, the language of the descendants of the Gaels or Celts, in the highlands of Scotland.—*Erse* is a corruption of *Irish*. The highlanders were supposed by their Gothic neighbors to be an Irish colony, and hence the name given to their language. The highlanders themselves invariably call it *Gaelic*. It first attracted notice after the publication in the English language of the poems of Ossian, said to be derived from it about the middle of the last century. These, it was pretended, were translated from manuscripts in the translator's possession; but such poems in a written form, it is now sufficiently known, never had any existence either in the Irish or Gaelic language. Although not committed to writing, or rather not handed down in writing, these poems, committed to memory and handed down from one bard or story-teller to another, still exist in the Highlands of Scotland, and in a dress not remote from that in which they were rendered by Macpherson into English. Their scene is sometimes laid in Scotland, but more frequently in Ireland. In short, they are the Iliad and Odyssey of the Celtic race of the two islands, handed down by tradition only,—what the poems of Homer were in all likelihood to the Greeks themselves, before the art of writing was known to them. The Erse, although a rude and uncultivated language, is a nervous and manly one, both as to expression and sound, and well suited to poetry, whether sublime or tender. The range of its sounds is very great; for it possesses twelve vowels, and no less than eighteen diphthongs and triphthongs, with forty-one consonants, including aspirates. Many of the consonants are guttural; and of these, as well of the vocalic sounds, there are several utterly unpronounceable by a stranger: the attempts made to express such a variety of sounds by the Roman alphabet are, of course, both awkward and imperfect. As to the grammar, that of the Gaelic is of complex structure, implying a primitive language which has undergone little change by admixture with other tongues.

EQUES'TRIAN STAT'UE, statues of men on horseback, usually formed of bronze, but sometimes of lead and stone. London enjoys the singular eminence of possessing the worst equestrian statues to be found in any city of Europe.

ER'MINE, the fur of the animal of this name. It is an emblem of purity, and of honor without stain. Robes of royal personages are lined with it to signify the internal purity that should regulate their conduct.

ERUDI'TION, the attainment of profound learning and extensive knowledge, obtained by study and instruction; particularly learning in history, antiquity, and languages, as distinct from the useful arts and sciences.

ESCALADE', in the military art, a furious attack made upon a rampart, or scaling the walls of a fortification, by filling up the ditches with bundles of fagots, called fascines, and entering by ladders; without proceeding in form, breaking ground, or carrying on regular works to secure the men—a mode of attack much adopted in the late wars, but generally accompanied with great slaughter.

ESCAL'LOP, an emblem of St. James the Great, which is frequently met with in churches, dedicated to his honor. It is one of the attributes and insignia of pilgrims, adopted by them in their voyages to the sepulchre of this apostle, gathered by them on the sea-shore, and fastened on their hoods or hats as a mark of the pilgrimage.

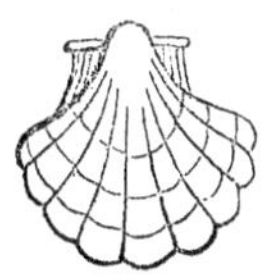

ESCAPE,' in law, is where a person arrested gains his liberty before he is delivered by law. In *civil* cases, after the prisoner has been suffered voluntarily to escape, the sheriff can never after retake him, and must answer for the debt; but the plaintiff may retake him at any time. In the case of a negligent escape, the sheriff, upon fresh pursuit, may retake the prisoner, and the sheriff shall be excused if he have him again before any action is brought against himself for the escape. In *criminal* cases, an escape of a person arrested is an offence against public justice, and the party is punishable by fine and imprisonment.

ESCARP'MENT, or ESCARP', in the military art, the exterior slope facing fortified works; the interior slope being the *counterscarp*.

ESCHEAT', in law, lands or profits that fall to a lord within his manor, either by forfeiture, the death of the tenant, or through failure of heirs.

ES'CORT, a guard or company of armed men attending an officer, or baggage, provisions, or munitions conveyed by land, to protect them from an enemy, &c.

ES'CUAGE, in feudal customs, a kind of knight-service, called service of the shield, by which the tenant was bound to follow his lord to the wars at his own charge.

ESCULA'PIAN, (from *Æsculapius* the physician,) pertaining to the healing art.

ES'CULENT, an epithet for such plants or roots as may be eaten.

ESCU'RIAL, a celebrated palace and monastery in Spain, about twenty miles from Madrid, built by Philip II. It is in the shape of a gridiron, and contains the king's palace. St. Lawrence's church, the monastery of Jerenomites, and the free schools. It was erected in consequence of a vow made by Philip, on the day of the battle of St. Quentin, and dedicated to St. Lawrence, whose festival was on that day. Though the building is immensely large and the most superb in the kingdom, its exterior has rather the austere simplicity of a convent than the elegance of a palace. It is a quadrangle, 740 feet in length by 580 in breadth; and is said to have cost 50 millions of dollars.

ES'DRAS, the name of two apocryphal books, usually bound up with the Scriptures. They were always excluded the Jewish canon.

ESOTER'IC, an epithet applied to the private instructions and doctrines of Pythagoras; opposed to *exoteric*, or public. Much dispute has prevailed among the learned as to the precise import of this distinction. By some it was thought that the ancient philosophers had a set of mysterious doctrines which they communicated only to the more enlightened of their disciples, and another more popular doctrine which they promulgated to the multitude. In the case of Aristotle, to whose writings the distinction properly applied, this opinion is, to a certain extent, well founded; except so far as regards the suspicion of intentional concealment implied in it. The exoteric or *published* writings of that philosopher appear to have been written in the form of dialogues, all of which are lost. His esoteric works, we gather from the synonymous term *acroamatic*, were not intended to supersede the necessity of oral instruction to render them intelligible. This agrees well enough with the brevity, the frequent repetitions, and the perplexed arrangement of the works of Aristotle which survive.

ES'PIONAGE, a system of employing spies, or secret emissaries, either in military or political affairs.

ESPOUS'ALS, in law, a contract or mutual promise of marriage between a man and woman.

ESPLANADE', in fortification, the glacis of the counterscarp, or sloping of the parapet of the covered way towards the country. The word is now also used for a sloping walk or promenade.

ESPRIT' DE CORPS, a French phrase, signifying that species of attachment with which persons, more especially military men, are animated to the corps or service to which they belong.

ESQUIRE', anciently a shield or armor-bearer; the person that attended a knight in time of war, and carried his shield. It is now a title given to the sons of knights, or those who serve the king in any worshipful calling, as officers of the king's courts, counsellors at law, &c. It has, however, become a sort of vague and undefined compliment, placed at the end of a man's name, and may be regarded more as an expression of respect than anything else.

ES'SAY, in literature, an attempt; a species of composition. In general, this title is given to short disquisitions on subjects of taste, philosophy, or common life. In this sense it has been applied to periodical papers, published at regular intervals under a collective name, by one or more writers, containing remarks on topics of the day, or on more serious subjects. From the appearance of the *Tatler*, in the beginning of the last century, which was chiefly written by Sir Richard Steele, this species of literature continued to be a favorite in England for seventy years, and many similar series of essays were produced; the best of which are united in one collection under the name of *The English Essayists*. The most celebrated of these works was the *Spectator*, to which Addison was the best contributor; and next to it the *Rambler*, published and almost wholly written by Samuel Johnson. The title of essay has been also adopted, by way of indicating diffidence in the completeness of their work, by various authors of more extended performances; as, by Locke (*Essay on the Human Understanding*.)

ES'SENCE, in philosophy, a scholastic term, denoting what the Platonists called the idea of a species. The school philosophers give two significations of the word essence: the first denoting the whole essential perfection of a being, and consequently its entity, with all its intrinsic and necessary attributes taken together; the second denoting the principal or most important attributes of anything. The essences of things were held by many to be uncreated, eternal, and immutable.

ESSENES', a sect among the Jews in the time of our Saviour, of whom an account is preserved to us by Josephus and Philo, though they are not mentioned in Scripture. They were few in number, and lived chiefly in solitude, taking no part in public affairs, but devoting their lives to contemplation. There were indeed two classes of them, distinguished as the practical and contemplative, who differed in the degree of strictness and austerity which they observed. They believed in the immortality of the soul, and held the Scripture in the highest reverence; interpreting it, however, after an allegorical system of their own.

ESSENTIAL PROP'ERTIES, in logic, such as necessarily depend upon, and are connected with, the nature and essence of a thing, in distinction from the *accidental*.

ESSOIN', in law, an excuse by reason of sickness or any other just cause for one that is summoned to appear and answer an action, &c.—The first three days of a term are called *essoin days*, as three days are allowed for the appearance of suitors.

ESTAB'LISHMENT, in a military sense, the quota of officers and men in an army, regiment, or company, which being much greater in war than in peace, has given rise to the distinctive terms of War Establishment and Peace Establishment.—The word is also used when speaking of the ministers of a church established by law, as belonging to the *Establishment*.

ESTACADE', in the military art, a French word for a dyke, constructed with piles in the sea, a river, or morass, to oppose the entry of troops.

ESTAFET'TE, a military courier, sent from one part of an army to another; or a speedy messenger who travels on horseback.

ESTATE', in law, the title or interest that a person has in lands, tenements, or other effects; comprehending the whole in which a person has any property. Estates are either *real* or *personal;* otherwise distinguished into freeholds, which descend to heirs; or chattels and effects, which go to executors or administrators. There are also estates for life, for years, at will, &c. — *Estates of the realm* are the distinct parts of any state or government, as the king, lords, and commons, in England.

ES'THER, a canonical book of the Old Testament, containing the history of a Jewish virgin, dwelling with her uncle Mordecai at Shushan, in the reign of Ahasuerus, one of the kings of Persia. Archbishop Usher supposes Darius Hystaspes to be the Ahasuerus of Scripture, and Artystona to be Esther. Scaliger considers him as Xerxes, and his queen Hamestris as Esther. Josephus, on the contrary, asserts that Ahasuerus was Artaxerxes Longimanus; and the Septuagint, throughout the whole book of Esther, translates Ahasuerus by Artaxerxes.

ES'TIMATE, a judgment or opinion formed of the value, degree, extent, or quantity of anything, without ascertaining it. Also a computation of probable value or cost, such as is generally prepared by engineers, architects, and builders, previous to the commencement of any undertaking.

ESTO'VERS, in law, a reasonable allowance out of lands or goods for the subsistence of a man accused of felony, during his imprisonment. But it is more generally taken for certain allowances of wood made to tenants, and called, from the Saxon, *house-bote, hedge-bote, plough-bote,* &c.

ESTRAY', a tame beast found without any owner known, which, by the English law if not reclaimed within a year and a day, falls to the lord of the manor.

ESTREAT', in law, a true copy or duplicate of an original writing, particularly of the penalties or fines to be levied by the bailiff or other officer, of every man for his offence.

ET CÆT'ERA, and the contraction *etc.* or *&c.*, denote the rest or others of the kind; and so forth.

ETCH'ING, a method of engraving on copper or steel, in which the lines and strokes are eaten in with aquafortis. *See* Engraving.

ETER'NITY, everlasting duration, without beginning or end; a term expressive of that perpetuity which can only be imagined, on account of the impossibility of conceiving when time was not, or will not be; hence many have concluded that there has been an eternity of past time, and must be an eternity of future time.

ETH'ICS, the doctrine of manners, or science of moral philosophy, which teaches men their duty and the springs and principles of human conduct.

ETHNOG'RAPHY, the science which treats of the particularities of nations, describing their customs, peculiarities, &c. Although a peculiar name has been given to it, it is in general considered as a branch of the sciences of geography and history.

ETIOL'OGY, an account of the causes of anything, particularly of diseases.

ET'IQUETTE, is the ceremonial code of polite life, more voluminous and minute in each portion of society according to its rank. The word is derived from the custom of arranging places at processions, &c. by tickets delivered beforehand to applicants. The Byzantine court appears to have carried the practice of ceremonial observations to the most inconvenient and ludicrous extent. But of modern courtly etiquette, Philip the Good, Duke of Burgundy, is regarded by some as the founder. His desire to conceal his inferiority in rank, as a great feudatory only, to the great sovereigns of Europe, whom he equalled in power, induced him to surround his presence with a multitude of officers and numberless formalities. At no time, probably, was the spirit of etiquette so predominant and so tyrannical as in the court of Louis XIV.; and the *Memoirs of St. Simon* are full of the most extraordinary proofs of the subjugation of the minds of men of sense, wit, and even independent character in other respects, to its engrossing influence,—their pride in attaining any little point of precedence, and their mortification in failing of it. The smaller courts of Germany caricatured the ceremonial of that of the Great Monarch, and carried its strictness to an absurd extent. At the present day the ancient etiquette of courts is continually losing something of its strictness.

ETYMOL'OGY, a branch of philology, which teaches the origin and derivation of words, with a view to ascertain their radical or primary signification. In grammar, it comprehends not only the derivation of words, but their various inflections and modifications. One who is well versed in the deduction of words from their originals, is called an *etymologist*.

EU'CHARIST, the sacrament of the Lord's Supper; so called because the death of our Redeemer is thereby commemorated with thankful remembrance, and bread and wine are taken as emblems of his flesh and blood.

EUCHOL'OGY, a book of prayers; synonymous, in the phraseology of the Roman Catholic church, with *missal* or *breviary*.

EU'CRASY, an agreeable, well-proportioned mixture of qualities, by which a body is said to be in good order, and disposed for a good state of health.

EUHARMON'IC, in music, producing harmony or concordant sounds.

EU'LOGY, in a general sense, an encomium pronounced on any person for his meritorious or virtuous qualities; but, in a more restricted meaning, it was used in ecclesiastical history to denote any present bestowed on the church after having been *blessed* or *hallowed*.

EU'NOMY, equal law, or a well-adjusted constitution of government.

EUPA'TRIDÆ, in ancient history, the nobles of Attica, in whose hands in early times all the power of government was vested, in consequence of which the lower orders sunk into a low state of degradation, being particularly oppressed by their debts which the pressure of their circumstances compelled them to incur, and which, if not paid, gave the creditor power over the bodies and liberties of the debtor and his family. These evils were remedied by the legislation of Solon, who reduced the interest of debts, and deprived the creditor of his power over the body of the debtor, and at the same time threw the judicial and much of the legislative power into the hands of the people at large. The alterations in the constitution of Athens, subsequent to the time of Solon, by degrees deprived the Eupatridæ of all their political privileges, and finally established an unmixed democracy.

EU'PEPSY, in medicine, good concoction in the stomach; perfect digestion.

EU'PHEMISM, in rhetoric, a figure by which things in themselves disagreeable and shocking, are expressed in terms neither offensive to good manners nor repulsive to "ears polite."

EU'PHONY, an easy and smooth enunciation of words. A grammatical license, whereby a letter that is too harsh is converted into a smoother, contrary to the ordinary rules, for the purpose of promoting smoothness and elegance in the pronunciation.

EU'RITHMY, in architecture, painting, and sculpture, is a certain majesty, elegance, and ease in the various parts of a body, arising from its just proportions.—In medicine, *eurithmy* signifies a good disposition of the pulse.

EUSTA'THIANS, a sect of Christians, the followers of Eustathius, an Armenian bishop in the fourth century, who, under pretence of great purity and severity, introduced many irregularities.

EU'STYLE, in architecture, a sort of building in which the columns are placed at the most convenient distances from each other, most of the intercolumniations being just two diameters and a quarter of the column.

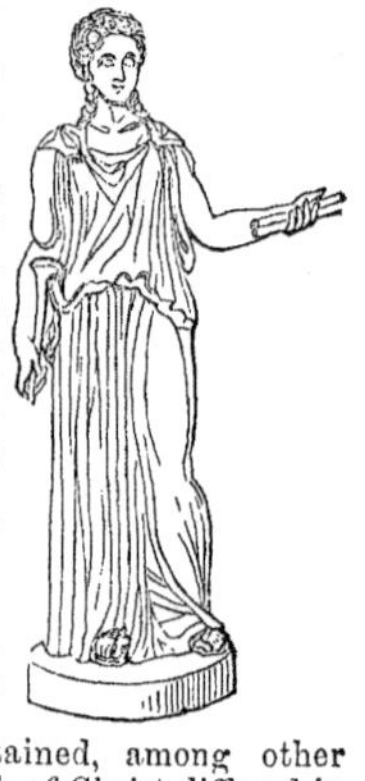

EUTER'PE, one of the muses, considered as presiding over music, because the invention of the flute is ascribed to her. She is usually represented as a virgin crowned with flowers, having a flute in her hand, or with various instruments about her. As her name denotes, she is the inspirer of pleasure.

EUTY'CHIANS, a religious sect in the fifth century, called after one Eutychus, who maintained, among other things, that the flesh of Christ differed in its nature from that of mankind.

EUTHANA'SIA, or EUTHAN'ASY, a gentle, easy, happy death.

EVAN'GELIST, a general name given to those who write or preach the gospel of Jesus Christ. The word is of Greek origin, signifying one who publishes glad tidings, or is the messenger of good news. But it is applied principally to the writers of the four Gospels, or *Evangelia*, viz. Matthew, Mark, Luke, and John.—The word also denotes certain ministers in the primitive church, who assisted the Apostles in diffusing the knowledge of the Gospel, and travelled about to execute such commissions as they were entrusted with, for the advancement of Christianity.

EVAN'GELISTS, in the Fine Arts, on the earliest sculptures the EVANGELISTS are symbolized by four scrolls, or, with reference to the four streams of Paradise, by four rivers flowing down from a hill, on which stands a Cross and the Lamb, the MONOGRAM of Christ. They were afterwards represented as the forms out of Ezekiel, vii. 1–10, viz., a man, a lion, a bull, and an eagle, which are mentioned as supporting the throne of God (Rev. iv. 6–7.) After the fifth century, the Byzantine artists, keeping strictly to biblical terms, represented the Evangelists (at first in mosaic) as miraculous animals, half *men* and half *beasts;* they had wings like the CHERUBIM, and were either in the act of writing or had a scroll before them. The human face was given only to Matthew or Mark, to which of these two was doubtful, even to the time of Jerome, with whom originated the present appropriation of the attributes; the other three had the heads of a lion, an ox, and an eagle, with corresponding feet. This representation was customary for some time in the Greek Church. In the latter part of the middle ages the Western Church began to separate the human figure from that of the animal, and to represent the Evangelists only in the former manner, generally as writing, and three of them with the animals by their sides as attributes. The four animals are often represented with scrolls, anciently inscribed with the initial sentences of each Gospel. In later examples the names of the Evangelists are inscribed on the scrolls. In sepulchral brasses the Evangelistic symbols are found variously arranged, but they are most frequently placed so as to follow the same order. According to St. Jerome's arrangement St. Matthew had a man or angel by his side, because his Gospel begins with a genealogy showing the human descent of Christ. St. Mark has a lion, the symbol of the royal dignity of the Saviour, and referring to the desert (Mark i. 13) in which he was with wild beasts. St. Luke has the ox, the symbol of the high priesthood, because his Gospel begins with the history of Zacharias serving in the temple. St. John has the eagle, the emblem of the divinity of Christ, and referring to the doctrine of the *Logos*, with which his Gospel commences. Christ was thus symbolized by the Evangelists, as Man, King, High Priest, and God. The EVANGELISTIC SYMBOLS are found variously employed in Christian edifices and ornaments of every period in the history of Art, and they are introduced in Christian design under a great variety of place and circumstance, *e. g.* most appropriately on books of the Holy Gospels, enamelled in silver and set on the angles of the covers; on crosses, as being the four great witnesses of the doctrine of the Cross. For the same reason, on the four gables of Cruciform Churches; also in cross frontals for altars; at the four corners of monumental stones and brasses in testimony of the faith of the deceased in the Gospel of Christ; around images of the Majesty, the Holy Trinity, Agnus Dei, Crucifixion, Resurrection, whether painted on glass, or ceilings and wall, or embroidered on vestments or altar-cloths, as the sacred mysteries represented are described in the Holy Gospels.

EVA'SION, the act of eluding or escaping from the pressure of an argument, or from an accusation, charge, or interrogatory.

EVA'TES, a branch of the Druids, or ancient Celtic philosophers. Strabo divides the British and Gaulic philosophers into three sects, Bards, Evates, and Druids. He adds, that the Bards were the poets and musicians; the Evates, the priests and naturalists; and the Druids were moralists as well as naturalists.

EVE'NING, or EVE, the precise time when evening begins is not ascertained by usage. In strictness, *evening* commences at the setting of the sun, and continues during twilight, and *night* commences with total darkness. But it sometimes includes a portion of the afternoon; as in the phrase, "the morning and evening service of the church;" and in customary language it extends to bedtime; as "I spent the evening with a friend."—Figuratively, we use it for the decline of life, or old age; as "the *evening* of life."

EV'IDENCE, in its most general sense, means the proofs which establish, or have a tendency to establish, any facts or conclusions. It may be divided into three sorts, mathematical, moral, and legal. The first is employed in the demonstrations which belong to pure mathematics; the second is employed in the general affairs of life, and in those reasonings which are applied to convince the understanding in cases not admitting of strict demonstration; the third is that which is employed in judicial tribunals for the purpose of deciding upon the rights and wrongs of litigants. According to our system of jurisprudence in common law trials, it is the peculiar province of a jury to decide all matters of fact. The verdict of the jury is, however, to be given, and the trial is to be had, in the presence of a judge or judges, who preside at the trial, and are bound to decide all matters of law, arising in the course of the trial. Whenever, therefore, a question arises, whether anything offered as proof at such trial is or is not proper to go before the jury as evidence, that question is to be decided by the court, and, unless permitted by the court, it can never legally come before the consideration of the jury. Hence, whatever is so permitted to be brought before the jury, for the purpose of enabling them to decide any matter of fact in dispute between the parties, is in a legal sense, *evidence*, and is so called in contra-distinction to mere argument and comment. This gives rise to a very important distinction, at the common law, as to the *competency* and the credibility of evidence. It is *competent*, when by the principles of law, it is admissible to establish any fact, or has any tendency to prove it. It is *credible*, when, being introduced, it affords satisfactory proof of the fact. It follows, therefore, that evidence may be *competent* to be produced before a jury, when it may nevertheless not amount to *credible* proof, so as to satisfy the minds of the jury; and, on the other hand, it may be such as, if before them, would satisfy their minds of the truth of the fact, but yet, by the rules of law, it is not admissible. Whether there is *any evidence* of a fact, is a question for the court; whether it is *sufficient*, is a question for the jury.

E'VIL, in philosophy, &c. is either *moral* or *natural*. Moral evil is any deviation of a moral agent from the rules of conduct prescribed to him. Some make the essence of moral evil consist in the disagreement of our manners to the divine will, whether known by reason or revelation; others, in being contrary to reason and truth; and others, in being inconsistent with the nature, faculties, affections, and situation of mankind.

EVOCA'TI, soldiers among the Romans, who having served their full time in the army, went afterwards volunteers at the request of some favorite general; on which account they were called by the honorable names of *Emeriti* and *Beneficiarii*.

EVOCA'TION, in Roman antiquity, a solemn invitation or prayer to the gods of a besieged town, to forsake it and come over to the besiegers.

EVOLU'TION, in military tactics, the complicated movement of a body of men when they change their position by countermarching, wheeling, &c.

E'VOVÆ, in music, the vowels used with the ending notes of the ecclesiastical tones: it is a word, for brevity's sake, formed of the six vowels in the words *sæculorum amen*, which are subjoined to the notes in Antiphonaries, &c., to indicate that those are the ending notes.

EXAGGERA'TION, in rhetoric, a kind of hyperbole, whereby things are augmented or amplified, by saying more than the strict truth will warrant.—In painting, a method of giving a representation of things too strong for the life.

EXALTA'DOS, in Spanish history, the name of the party attached the *liberal* system of politics, corresponding to the "extreme gauche" of the French, or Whig radicals, in English politics.

EXAMINA'TION, in its primary sense, is a careful and accurate inspection or inquiry, in order to discover the real state of anything.—In judicial proceedings, an attempt to ascertain truth, generally on the oath of the party examined, by interrogatories.—In schools, an inquiry into the acquisitions of the students, by questioning them in literature and the sciences, or by hearing their recitals.

EXAM'INERS, in law, two officers in the court of Chancery, who are appointed on oath, to examine witnesses on either side.

EX'ARCH, in antiquity, an officer sent by the emperors of the East into Italy, as prefect or governor.—*Exarch* also denotes an officer still subsisting in the Greek church, who visits the provinces, in order to see whether the bishops and clergy do their duty.

EXAUCTORA'TION, or EXAUTHORA'TION, in Roman antiquity, temporary dismission from service: thus the *exauctori milites* were deprived of their pay and arms, without being absolutely discharged.

EXCALCEA'TION, among the Hebrews, was a law, whereby a widow, whom her husband's brother refused to marry, had a right to summon him to a court of justice, and, upon his refusal, might *excalceate* him, that is, pull off one of his shoes, and spit in his face; both of which were considered actions of great ignominy.

EX CA'THEDRA, a Latin phrase; originally applied to decisions rendered by prelates, chiefly popes, from their cathedra or chair: *i. e.* in a solemn judicial manner. Hence applied to every decision pronounced by one in the exercise of his peculiar authority: a professor in his lecture room, a judge from the bench, &c.

EX'CELLENCY, a title of honor formerly given to kings and emperors, but now given to governors, ambassadors, &c. who are elevated by virtue of particular offices. The title of excellency is in no case hereditary, or transferable from one member to another, but always belongs to the office, and is only borne, on the European continent, by ministers in actual service, by the highest court and military dignitaries, and by ambassadors and plenipotentiaries. Foreign ministers are addressed by the title of *your excellency*, by way of courtesy, even if they have no rank which entitles them to this distinction; but *chargé d'affaires* never receive the title.

EXCHANGE', in commerce, traffic by permutation, or the act of giving one thing or commodity for another. The receipt or payment of money in one country for the like sum in another, by means of *bills of exchange*. Thus, *A* in London, is creditor to *B* in New York, to the amount of 100*l*. *C* in London is debtor to *D* in New York, in a like sum: by the operation of the bill of exchange, the London creditor is paid by the London debtor, and the New York creditor is paid by the New York debtor; and, consequently, two debts are paid, though no specie is sent from London to New York, or from New York to London. This is the principle of a bill of exchange; and the great convenience here represented is the foundation of exchange itself. That variation *above* and *below par*, which is called the course of exchange, results from the same causes that act upon the price of commodities of every other kind. If bills upon New York be scarce, that is, if New York is but little indebted to London, the London creditor, who wants bills on New York to remit to that city, is obliged to purchase them dearly; then the course of exchange is *above par*: if, on the other hand, London owes less to New York than New York owes to London, New York bills will be proportionably plenty, and the exchange with that city *below par*. Hence, it is a maxim that, when the course of exchange rises *above par*, the balance of trade runs against the country where it rises. In London, bills of exchange are bought and sold by brokers, who go round to the principal merchants, and discover whether they are buyers or sellers of bills. A few of the brokers of most influence, after ascertaining the state of the relative supply of and demand for bills, suggest a price at which the greater part of the transactions of the day are settled, with such deviations as particular bills, from their being in very high or low credit, may be subject to. In London and other great commercial cities, a class of middlemen speculate largely on the rise and fall of the exchange, buying bills when they expect a rise, and selling them when a fall is anticipated.—*Exchange*, in arithmetic, is the finding what quantity of the money in one place is equal to a given sum of another, according to a certain course of exchange.—*Course of exchange* is the current price betwixt two places, which is always fluctuating and unsettled.—*Arbitration of exchange* is a calculation of the exchanges of different places to discover which is the most profitable.—*Exchange of prisoners*, in war, the act of giving up men on both sides, upon certain conditions agreed to by the contending parties.

EXCHANGE', (often contracted into CHANGE,) signifies a building or other place in considerable trading cities, where the merchants, agents, bankers, brokers, and other persons concerned in commerce, meet at certain times, to confer and treat together of matters relating to exchanges, remittances, payments, adventures, assurances, freights, and other mercantile negotiations both by sea and land.

EXCHEQ'UER, in British jurisprudence, an ancient court of record, in which all causes concerning the revenues and rights of the crown are heard and determined, and where the crown-revenues are received. It took this name from the cloth that covered the table of the court, which was party-colored or chequered. This court is said to have been erected by William the Conqueror.—The public Exchequer is under the control of the lords of the Treasury, and of a minister called the chancellor of the exchequer.—To institute a process against a person in this court, is called to *exchequer* him.

EXCHEQ'UER-BILLS, bills for money, or promissory notes, issued from the exchequer, under the authority of government, and bearing interest.

EXCISE', an inland duty, paid in some

instances upon the commodity consumed, or on the retail, which is the last stage before consumption; but in others this duty is paid at the manufactories. The excise was first introduced in England by the parliament which beheaded Charles I. and its great founder was Mr. Pym; and is now one of the most considerable branches of the national revenue. It was formerly farmed out, but is at present managed for the government by commissioners. who receive the whole product of the excise, and pay it into the exchequer.—The officer who inspects excisable commodities and rates the duties on them is called an *exciseman.*

EXCLAMA'TION, emphatical utterance; or the sign by which emphatical utterance is marked: thus (!).—In grammar, a word expressing some passion, as wonder, fear, &c.

EXCOMMUNICA'TION, an ecclesiastical censure, whereby a person is excluded from communion with the church, and deprived of some civil rights. In the present state of church-government in England, excommunication is seldom used but as a sort of writ of outlawry on contempt of the bishop's court, in the several descriptions of causes that belong to ecclesiastical jurisdiction. It is published in the church, and if the offender does not submit in forty days, the civil magistrate interposes, and the excommunicated person is imprisoned till he submits, and obtains absolution.—The Roman Catholics use the phrase *fulminating an excommunication,* to signify the solemn pronouncing of an excommunication after several admonitions. This fulmination principally consists of curses, execrations, and other ceremonies; and is called *anathema.*—*Excommunication* amongst the Jews was of three kinds or degrees. The first was called *Niddui*, and was a separation for a few days. The second was *Cherem*, and was a separation attended with execration and malediction; the third was *Shammatha*, and was the last and greater excommunication.—*Excommunication* amongst the Greeks and Romans excluded the person, on whom it was pronounced, from the sacrifices and temples, and delivered him over to the *Furies.*

EXCU'BIÆ, in antiquity, the watches and guards kept in the day by the Romans, in distinction from *vigiliæ*, which were kept at night.

EX'EAT, in ecclesiastical history, a term employed in the permission which a bishop grants to a priest to go out of his diocese.

EXECU'TION, in law, the completing or finishing some act, as of judgment or deed, and it usually signifies the obtaining possession of anything received by judgment of law. Also, the carrying into effect a sentence or judgment of court; as the infliction of capital punishment.—*Execution*, in painting, is the term given to the peculiar mode of working for effect—the manipulation peculiar to each individual artist; where it predominates over finish, or where execution exhibits a studied eccentricity, it degenerates into mannerism, which, when it merely exhibits the manual dexterity of the artist, is usually the exponent of mediocrity: at the same time it must be admitted, that good execution is always aimed at by the true artist. All qualities of execution, properly so called, are influenced by, and in a great degree dependent on, a far higher power than that of mere execution —knowledge of truth. For exactly in proportion as an artist is certain of his end, will he be swift and simple in his means; and as he is accurate and deep in his knowledge, will he be refined and precise in his touch.

EXECU'TIONER, the officer who inflicts capital punishment in pursuance of a legal warrant; the common hangman.

EXEC'UTIVE, in politics, that branch of the government which executes the functions of governing the state. The word is used in distinction from *legislative* and *judicial.* The body that deliberates and enacts laws, is *legislative;* the body that judges or applies the laws to particular cases, is *judicial;* and the body that carries the laws into effect, or superintends the enforcement of them, is *executive.* In all monarchical states this power rests in the prince.

EXEC'UTOR, in law, a person appointed by another's last will and testament, to have the execution of the same after his decease, and the disposing of the testator's goods and effects, according to the intent of the will.

EXEC'UTORY, in law, signifies that which is to take effect on a future contingency; as an *executory* devise or remainder.

EXE'DRÆ, in antiquity, a general name for such buildings as were distinct from the main body of the churches, and yet within the limits of the consecrated ground.

EXEGE'SIS, a discourse intended to explain or illustrate a subject. The term is applied most usually to the exposition or interpretation of the Holy Scriptures.

This department of biblical learning has been most assiduously cultivated in modern times, especially by the Germans, as the writings of Michaelis, Schleusner, Rosenmüller, Gesenius, &c., amply testify.

EXEM'PLAR, a pattern or model; the ideal model which an artist attempts to imitate. That which serves as a model for imitation, or as a warning for others, is termed *exemplary;* as, *exemplary* justice; *exemplary* punishment.

EXEQUA'TUR, an official recognition of a person in the character of consul or commercial agent, authorizing him to exercise his powers.

EX'ERCISE, the exertion of the body, for health, amusement, labor, or the attainment of any art. Exercise increases the circulation of the blood, attenuates and divides the fluids, and promotes a regular perspiration, as well as a due secretion of all the humors; for it accelerates the animal spirits, and facilitates their distribution into all the fibres of the body, strengthens the parts, creates an appetite, and helps digestion. Whence it arises, that those who accustom themselves to exercise are generally very robust, and seldom subject to diseases. It should never be forgotten by those of studious habits, that the delicate springs of our frail machines lose their activity, and the vessels become clogged with obstructions, when we totally desist from exercise; from which consequences arise which necessarily affect the brain; a mere studious life is therefore equally prejudicial to the body and the mind. We may further observe, that an inclination to study ought not to be carried to the extent of aversion to society and motion. The natural lot of man is to live among his fellows; and whatever may be his situation in the world, there are a thousand occasions wherein his physical energies may be rendered serviceable to his fellow-creatures, as well as to himself. Many rational causes have therefore given rise to the practice of particular exercises; and those legislators who deserve to be called the most sagacious and benevolent, have instituted opportunities for enabling youth who devote themselves to study, to become expert also in laudable exercises.—*Mental exercise* is the exertion of the mind or faculties for improvement, as in the various branches of literature, art, and science.—*Military exercise* consists in the use of arms, in marches, evolutions, &c.—*Naval exercise* consists in the management of artillery, and in the evolutions of fleets.

EXER'GUE, a term used by medallists to denote the little space around and without the work or figures of a medal for an inscription, &c.

EXHEREDA'TION, in the civil law, a father's excluding a child from inheriting any part of his estate.

EXHIB'IT, any paper produced or presented to a court or to auditors, referees, or arbitrators, as a voucher, &c. — In chancery, a deed or writing produced in court and sworn to, and a certificate of the oath endorsed on it by the examiner or commissioner.

EXHIBI'TION, a public display of whatever is interesting either as a matter of art or curiosity. Also, a benefaction settled for the benefit of scholars in the universities, that are not on the foundation. The person receiving this is called an *exhibitioner.*—*Exhibition* was anciently an allowance for meat and drink, such as the religious appropriators made to the poor depending vicar.

EXHUMA'TION, the digging up of a dead body that has been interred.

EX'IGENT, in law, a writ or part of the process of outlawry. The *exigent* or *exigi facias* requires the defendant to be proclaimed in five courts successively, to render himself; and if he does not, he is outlawed.

EX'ILE, a state of banishment or expulsion from one's country by authority; or it may be an abandonment of one's country, for a foreign land, from disgust or any other motive, which is called *voluntary exile.*

EXIST'ENCE, the state of being, or having an actual essence. Mr. Locke says, that we arrive at the knowledge of our own existence, by intuition; of the existence of God, by demonstration; and of other things, by sensation. As for our own existence, continues he, we perceive it so plainly, that it neither needs, nor is capable of, any proof. I think, I reason, I feel pleasure and pain; can any of these be more evident to me than my own existence? If I doubt of all other things, that very doubt makes me perceive my own existence, and will not suffer me to doubt. If I know I doubt, I have as certain a perception of the thing doubting, as of that thought which I call doubt: experience then convinces us, that we have an intuitive knowledge of our own existence.

EX'IT, a departure; a term used to denote the action of quitting the stage by a player after he has performed his part. Figuratively, the act of quitting this mortal existence.

EXO'DIA, amongst the Romans, were a sort of after-pieces, performed by young gentlemen when the play was concluded. They bore no relation to the drama before exhibited; but were intended to revive, or rather improve the Fescennine verses, which had fallen into disuse. Professional actors never performed any part in the *Exodia*.

EX'ODE, in the Greek drama, the concluding part of a play, or that part which comprehends all that occurs after the last interlude.

EX'ODUS, a canonical book of the Old Testament; being the second of the Pentateuch, or five books of Moses. It contains a history of the departure of the children of Israel from Egypt; from which it received its name.

EX OFFI'CIO, in law, the power a person has, by virtue of his office, to do certain acts without special authority.

EXO'MIS, in Grecian costume, a garment worn chiefly by the working classes, without sleeves, or with only one sleeve for the left arm, leaving the right and part of the breast exposed and free. It varied much in form, sometimes it was a chiton, at others a pallium, serving the purposes of each. In works of Art it is usually applied to representations of the Amazons, and to Charon, Vulcan, and Dædalus. It was also the dress of old men in the comic plays of Aristophanes and others.

EX'ORCISM, the solemn adjuration by which those endowed with certain powers were believed to be able to subject evil spirits to their obedience: more particularly to compel them to leave the bodies of those supposed to be subject to demoniacal possession. The exorcists form one of the minor orders in the church of Rome.

EXOR'DIUM, in oratory and literature, the opening part of an oration; which, according to ancient critics, should be drawn either from the subject itself or from the situation of the speaker; presenting either brief remarks on the general character of the topic on which he is about to deliver himself, or insinuations, (according to the advice of Cicero,) calculated to prejudice the audience in favor of the speaker, and against his adversary.

EXOTER'IC, in rhetoric, a term applied to such of Aristotle's lectures as were open to all persons. *See* Esoteric.

EXOT'IC, an appellation for the produce of foreign countries. Exotic plants are such as belong to a soil and climate entirely different from the place where they are raised, and therefore can be preserved for the most part only in greenhouses.

EX-PAR'TE, in law, on one side, as *ex-parte* statement, a partial statement, or that which is made on one side only.

EXPATRIA'TION, the forsaking one's own country, with a renunciation of allegiance, and with a view of becoming a permanent resident and citizen in another country.

EXPECT'ANCY, in law, a state of waiting or suspension. An *estate in expectancy* is one which is to take effect or commence after the determination of another estate.—Estates of this kind are *remainders* and *reversions*.

EXPECT'ANT, in law, an epithet for whatever has a relation to, or dependence upon another.

EXPECTA'TION, in the doctrine of chances, is applied to any contingent event, upon the happening of which some benefit is expected.—*Expectation* differs from *hope* in this: hope originates in desire, and may exist with little or no ground of belief that the desired event will arrive; whereas expectation is founded on some reasons which render the event probable.—*Expectation*, of life, is a term used to express the number of years, which, according to the experience of bills of mortality, persons at any age may be expected to live.

EXPE'DIENT, a temporary means of effecting an object, without regard to ulterior consequences.

EXPEDI'TION, the march of an army, or the voyage of a fleet, to a distant place for hostile purposes; as, the *expedition* of the English to Holland; the *expedition* of the French to Egypt.

EXPE'RIENCE, the source of knowledge arising from the faculty of memory, and the power of reasoning by analogy. Thus, we learn the instability of human affairs by observation or by *experience*.

EXPER'IMENT, an act or operation designed to discover some unknown truth, principle, or effect.—In chemistry, a trial of the results of certain applications and motions of natural bodies, in order to discover something of their laws, nature, &c.—*Experimental* knowledge is the most valuable, because it is most certain, and most safely to be trusted.

EXPERIMEN'TAL PHILOS'OPHY, those branches of science, the deductions in which are founded on experiment, as contrasted with the moral, mathematical, and speculative branches of knowledge

The principal experimental science is Chemistry: but there are many others, as, Optics, Pneumatics, Hydrostatics, Electricity, Magnetism, &c.

EXPERIMEN'TUM CRU'CIS, a leading or decisive experiment.

EXPIA'TION, a religious ceremony, by which satisfaction is made for sins of omission or commission, accidental or intentional. The chief mode of expiation among the Jews and Pagans was by sacrifice.—*Expiation*, in a figurative sense, is applied by divines to the pardon procured to men's sins, by the obedience and death of Christ.

EXPORTA'TION, that part of foreign commerce which consists in sending out goods for sale, and which is therefore the *active* part of trade, as importation, or the purchasing of goods, is the passive.—We apply the word *exports* to goods or produce which are sent abroad or usually exported.

EXPOS'ITOR, one who explains the writings of others; it is applied particularly to those who profess to expound the Scriptures.

EX POST FACTO, (literally, for something done afterwards,) as an *ex post facto* law, a law which operates upon a subject not liable to it at the time the law was made.

EXPOSTULA'TION, in rhetoric, a warm address to a person, who has done another some injury, representing the wrong in the strongest terms, and demanding redress.

EXPRESS', a messenger or courier sent to communicate information of an important event, or to deliver important dispatches.

EXPRES'SION, in painting, the distinct and natural exhibition of character or of sentiment in the characters represented. The term expression is frequently confounded with that of passion, but they differ in this, that *expression* is a general term, implying a representation of an object agreeably to its nature and character, and the use or office it is to have in the work; whereas *passion*, in painting, denotes a motion of the body, accompanied with certain indications of strong feeling portrayed in the countenance; so that every passion is an expression, but not every expression, a passion. —*Expression*, in rhetoric, the elocution, diction, or choice of words suited to the subject and sentiment.—In music, the tone and manner which give life and reality to ideas and sentiments.—*Theatrical expression*, is a distinct, sonorous, and pleasing pronunciation, accompanied with action suited to the sentiment.

EXPROPRIA'TION, the surrender of a claim to exclusive property.

EXPUR'GATORY, serving to purify from anything noxious or erroneous; as the *expurgatory* index of the Roman Catholics, which directs the expunging of passages of authors contrary to their creed or principles.

EX'TANT, an epithet for anything which still subsists or is in being; as a part only of the writings of Cicero are *extant*.

EXTEM'PORE, without previous study or meditation; as he writes or speaks *extempore*. Though an adverb, it is often unnecessarily and improperly used as an adjective; as an *extempore* sermon, instead of an *extemporary* or *extemporaneous* sermon, &c.—To *extemporize* well, requires a ready mind well furnished with knowledge.

EXTENT', in law, is used in a double sense; sometimes it signifies a writ or command to the sheriff for the valuing of the lands or tenements of a debtor; and sometimes the act of the sheriff, or other commissioner, upon this writ; but most commonly it denotes an estimate or valuation of lands.—*Extent in aid*, a seizure made by the government, when a public accountant becomes a defaulter, and prays for relief against his creditors.

EXTENUA'TION, the act of representing anything less faulty or criminal than it is in fact; it is opposed to *aggravation*.

EXTIN'GUISHMENT, in law, the annihilation of an estate, &c. by means of its being merged or consolidated with another.

EXTOR'TION, the unlawful act of any person in authority, who, by color of his office, takes money or any other thing when none is due. Whenever property of any kind is wrested from a person by menace, duress, violence, authority, or by any illegal means, it is *extortion*. The word *extort* has a very wide signification. Conquerors *extort* contributions from the vanquished; officers often *extort* illegal fees; confessions of guilt are *extorted* by the rack; promises which men are unable to perform are sometimes *extorted* by duress, &c.

EX'TRA, a Latin preposition denoting beyond or excess; as *extra-work*, *extra-pay*, &c. It serves as a prefix to numerous English words.

EX'TRACT, in literature, some selec-

matter or sentence taken from a book.—In law, a draught or copy of a writing.

EXTRAJUDI'CIAL, out of the ordinary course of legal proceedings.

EXTRAMUN'DANE, beyond the limit of the material world.

EXTRAORDINA'RII, in Roman antiquity, a chosen body of men, consisting of a third part of the foreign horse, and a fifth of the foot, which was separated from the rest of the forces borrowed from the confederate state, with great policy and caution; to prevent any design that they might possibly entertain against the natural forces.

EXTRAVAGAN'ZA, in music, the Italian for a kind of composition remarkable for its wildness and incoherence.—Irregular dramatic pieces, generally of the burlesque cast, are also sometimes called extravaganzas.

EXTREME', the utmost point, or furthest degree; as the *extremes* of heat and cold; the *extremes* of virtue and vice.—In logic, the extreme terms of a syllogism are the predicate and subject. Thus, "Man is an animal: Henry is a man, therefore Henry is an animal;" the word animal is the greatest extreme, Henry the less extreme, and man the medium.—In music, a word employed in describing those intervals in which the diatonic distances are increased or diminished by a chromatic semitone.

EXTREME' UNC'TION, one of the seven sacraments of the Romish church, founded upon the passage in the Epistle of St. James in which he says, "If any be sick among you, let him call upon the elders of the church, and let them pray over him, anointing him with oil in the name of the Lord." The performance of this ceremony is supposed to purify the soul of the dying person from any sins that he may have committed, and which have not been previously expiated by participation in the other means of grace.

EXTREM'ITY, in its primary sense, signifies the utmost point or border of a thing. It also denotes the highest or furthest degree; as the *extremity* of pain or suffering; or the Greeks have endured oppression in its utmost *extremity*.—In painting and sculpture, the *extremities* of the body, are the head, hands, and feet.

EYE, the eye is the most active feature in the countenance, the first of our organs to awake, and the last to cease motion. It is indicative of the higher and holier emotions, of all those feelings which distinguish man from the brute. In the eye we look for meaning, sentiment, and reproof; it is the chief feature of expression. A large eye is not only consistent with beauty, but essential to it. Homer describes Juno as "ox-eyed." The eye of the gazelle illustrates the Arab's idea of woman's beauty, when he compares the eye of his beloved to that of this animal. The timidity, gentleness, and innocent fear in the eyes of all the deer tribe, are compared with the modesty of a young girl. In a well-formed face the eye ought to be sunk, relatively to the forehead, but not in reference to the face; that would impart a very mean expression. It is the strong shadow produced by the projecting eyebrow which gives powerful effect to the eye in sculpture.—The word *eye* is used in a great variety of senses, both literal and figurative.—*Eye*, in architecture, is used to signify any round window, made in a pediment, an attic, the reins of a vault, &c.—*Eye of a dome*, an aperture at the top of a dome, as that of the Pantheon at Rome, or of St. Paul's at London; it is usually covered with a lantern.—*Eye of the volute*, is the centre of the volute, or that point in which the helix, or spiral of which it is formed, commences.

EY'RIE, or EY'RY, the place where birds of prey construct their nests.

EZE'KIEL, one of the four principal prophets. Like them, he bears a book; but his own peculiar attribute is a closed gate with towers, which is either placed in his hand or standing by his side, and which referring to his vision of the new temple, is the type of the heavenly Jerusalem, mentioned by St. John in Revelation. It is one of the oldest symbols of Christianity, and also alludes to the mystery of the miraculous conception; for we find it together with Moses and the burning bush, Aaron's rod, Gideon's Angel and Fleece, on the volets of a picture of the Virgin by Van Eyck, of which only a copy at Bruges is in existence. The subjects usually chosen by the painter in which Ezekiel appears are—his Vision of the Almighty, and his Vision of the Resurrection of the Dead, and in a group with the three other great prophets.

F.

F, the sixth letter of the alphabet, is a labial articulation, formed by placing the upper teeth on the under lip, and accompanied with an emission of breath. Its kindred letter is *v*, which is chiefly distinguished from *f* by being more vocal. The Romans for some time used F inverted thus, Ⅎ, for V consonant, as DIℲI, for DIVI. Some have supposed that this was one of the three letters invented by Claudius, but many inscriptions belonging to periods much anterior to the time of Claudius exhibit this singular use of this letter. F, as a numeral, with the Romans, signified 40, with a dash over it, 40,000. On medals, monuments, &c., F stands for *Fabius*, *Furius*, *Felix*, *Faustus*, &c.—With merchants, *f* signifies *folio* (page.) *F* often stands in medical prescriptions and on documents for *fiat* (let it be made or done.) F also stands for *fellow*, as F.A.S. *Fraternitatis Antiquariorum Socius*, or Fellow of the Antiquarian Society.—*Fl.* is the abbreviation for *florin*, or guilder; and *fr.* for *franc*.—In music, *f* over a line means *forte; ff*, *molto forte;* and F is the nominal of the fourth note in the natural diatonic scale of C.

FA, in music, one of the syllables invented by Guido Aretine, to mark the fourth note of the modern scale, which rises thus, *ut*, *re*, *mi*, *fa*.

FA'BIAN, an epithet signifying that line of military tactics which declines the risking of a battle in the open field, but seeks every opportunity of harassing the enemy by countermarches, ambuscades, &c. It is so called from Q. Fabius Maximus, the Roman general opposed to Hannibal.

FA'BLE, a fictitious narration, or species of didactic allegory, which may be described as a method of inculcating practicable rules of worldly prudence or wisdom, by imaginary representations drawn from the physical or external world. It consists, properly, of two parts: symbolical representation, and the application of the instruction intended to be deduced from it, which latter is called the *moral* of the tale, and must be apparent in the fable itself, in order to render it poetical. The satisfaction which we derive from fables does not lie wholly in the pleasure that we receive from the symbolical representation, but it lies deeper, in the feeling that the order of nature is the same in the spiritual and material world; and the fabulist, whose object is not merely to render a truth perceptible by means of a fictitious action, chooses his characters from the brute creation.—Some fables are founded upon irony; some are pathetic; and some even aspire to the sublime; but, generally speaking, a fable should possess unity, that the whole tenor of it may be easily seen; and dignity, since the subject has a certain degree of importance.—We find that fables have been highly valued, not only in times of the greatest simplicity, but among the most polite ages of the world. Jotham's fable of the trees is the oldest that is extant, and as beautiful as any that have been made since. Nathan's fable of the poor man is next in antiquity, and had so good an effect as to convey instruction to the ear of a king. We find Æsop in the most distant ages of Greece; and in the early days of the Roman commonwealth, we read of a mutiny appeased by the fable of the belly and the members. To which we may add that although fables had their rise in the very infancy of learning, they never flourished more than when learning was at its greatest height.—*Fable* is also used for the plot of an epic or dramatic poem, and is, according to Aristotle, the principal part, and, as it were, the soul of a poem. In this sense the fable is defined to be a discourse invented with art, to form the manners by instruction, disguised under the allegory of an action.

FA'BLIAUX, in French literature, the metrical tales of the Trouvères or early poets of the Langue d'Oil, or dialect of the north of France; composed, for the most part, in the 12th and 13th centuries.

FAB'RIC, in general, denotes the structure or construction of anything; but particularly of buildings, as a church, hall, house, &c. It is also applied to the texture of cloths, or stuffs; as, this is cloth of a beautiful *fabric*.

FAB'ULOUS AGE, that period in the history of every nation in which supernatural events are represented to have happened. The fabulous age of Greece and Rome is called also the *heroic* age.

FACADE' (pron. *fassade'*,) in architecture, the front or external aspect of an edifice. As in most edifices only one side is conspicuous, viz., that which faces the street, and usually contains the principal entrance, this has been denominated, *par eminence*, the façade.

FACE, in anatomy, the front part of the head, and the seat of most of the senses, comprising the forehead, the eyes and eye-lids, the nose, cheeks, mouth, and chin. The human face is called the image of the soul, as being the place whence the ideas, emotions, &c. of the soul are chiefly set to view. Nor can it be denied that the character of each individual is often strongly marked by the conformation of the countenance; physiognomy, therefore, in a certain degree, always has existed.—*Face*, among painters and artists, is used to denote a certain dimension of the human body, adapted for determining the proportion which the several parts should bear to one another; thus the different parts of the body are said to consist, in length, of so many *faces*.—We also use the word *face* in speaking of the surface of a thing, or the side presented to the view of a spectator; as, the *face* of the earth; the *face* of the sun; the *face* of a stone, &c.

FA'CETS, the name of the little faces or planes to be found in brilliant and rose diamonds.

FA'CIAL LINE OR ANGLE, these terms are used in describing the conformation that exists in the bones of the face, &c,. and which so strikingly characterizes the varieties of the human race. On the relation of the jaw to the forehead is founded the *facial line*, discovered by Peter Camper. Suppose a straight line drawn at the base of the skull, from the great occipital cavity across the external orifice of the ear to the bottom of the nose. If we draw another straight line from the bottom of the nose, or from the roots of the upper incisor teeth to the forehead, then both lines will form an angle which will be more acute the less the shape of the face, in brutes, resembles that of men. In apes, this angle is only from 45° to 60°; in the ourang-outang, 63°; in the skull of a negro, about 70°; in a European, from 75° to 85°. In Grecian works of statuary, this angle amounts to 90°: in the statues of Jupiter, it is 100°.

FA'CIES HIPPOCRAT'ICA, in medicine, that death-like appearance which consists in the nostrils being sharp, the eyes hollow, the temples low, the tips of the ears contracted, the forehead dry and wrinkled, and the complexion pale and livid. It is so called from Hippocrates, by whom it has been so justly described in his prognostics.

FACSIM'ILE, an imitation of an original in all its traits and peculiarities. The object of fac-similes is various; but in all cases their perfect accuracy is indispensable.

FAC'TION, in ancient history, an appellation given to the different troops or companies of combatants in the games of the circus. Of these factions there were four,—the green, blue, red, and white; to which two others were said to have been added by the emperor Domitian.—the pruple and the yellow. In the time of Justinian 40,000 persons were killed in a contest between two of these factions; so that they were at last suppressed by universal consent. The term faction is applied, also, in a more general sense, to any party in a state which attempts without adequate motives to disturb the public repose, or to assail the measures of government with uncompromising opposition. In the ancient Greek republics, faction was carried to an extent unparalleled in modern times. The middle ages were distinguished chiefly by two factions, the Guelfs and Guibelins, who long kept Italy in a state of alarm. In the present day, in England, the term *faction* is bandied about between the three great parties of the country, the Whigs, Tories, and Radicals, being applied indiscriminately by the adherents of one party to those of another.

FAC'TOR, in commerce, an agent or correspondent residing in some remote part, commissioned by merchants to buy or sell goods on their account, to negotiate bills of exchange, or to transact other business for them. It is universally held in courts of law and equity, that the principal is held liable for the acts of his agent, provided that the conduct of the latter be conformable to the common usage and mode of dealing; but an agent cannot delegate his rights to another so as to bind the principal, unless expressly authorized to nominate a sub-agent. Establishments for trade, in foreign parts of the world, are called *factories*.—The word *factory* is now also used for a manufactory on an extensive scale.

FAC'TORAGE, the allowance or percentage given to factors by the merchants and manufacturers, &c. who employ them; and which is usually fixed by special agreement between the merchant and factor.

FAC'ULTY, a term used to denote the powers or capacities of the human mind, viz. understanding, will, memory, imagination, &c.—If it be a power exerted by the body alone, it is called a *corporeal* or animal faculty; if it belong to the mind, it is called a *rational* faculty. And it may further be distinguished into the *natural* faculty, or that by which the body is nourished; and the *vital*, or that by which life is preserved, &c.—*Faculty*, a term applied to the different members or departments of an university, divided according to the arts and sciences taught there. In most foreign universities there are four faculties; of arts, including humanity and philosophy; of theology; of physic; and of civil law. The degrees in the several faculties are those of bachelor, master, and doctor.—*Faculty*, in law, a privilege granted to a person, by favor and indulgence, or doing that which, by the strict letter of the law, he ought not to do.—*Faculty of advocates*, a term applied to the college or society of advocates in Scotland, who plead in all actions before the court of session, judiciary and exchequer.

FAI'ENCE, or IMITATION PORCELAIN, a kind of pottery, superior to the common sort in its glazing, beauty of form, and richness of painting. It derived its name from the town of Faenza, in Romagna, where it is said to have been invented in 1299. It reached its highest perfection in the 16th century; and some pieces were painted by the great artists of the period, which are highly valued as monuments of early art.

FAIR, (either from the Latin feriæ or forum,) a meeting held at stated times of the year in particular places, for the purposes of traffic, to which merchants resort with their wares. Fairs, in Christian countries, were usually held on particular festivals; and are so still in England, unless where they have been fixed to particular days in the month by later grants or privileges. By the English law, the king's authority only is supposed to confer the privilege of holding a fair. Fairs are considered free, unless toll is due to the owners by special grant, or by custom which supposes such grant. The most important fairs now held are probably those of Germany, and particularly the Leipsic fairs, where books form so important a branch of its commerce. But in no country can they have the importance they formerly had, because the communication between different parts of a country has become so easy, that merchandise may now be readily obtained direct from the places where it is produced or manufactured.

FAI'RIES, imaginary beings, who occupied a distinguished place in the traditional superstitions of the nations of Western Europe, and especially in these islands. Their English name is probably derived from "fair," or has the same etymology with that word; and, although some similarity has been traced between them and the Peris of the Persians (pronounced Feri by the Arabians,) it is not probable that the resemblance of name is more than accidental. There is also a distinction between the fairy of the English and the Fata or prophetic sibyl of the Italians, from which last the French Fée is derived; although the French, in their romantic mythology, have somewhat mingled the characteristics of the two. The British fairies, also, although they have something in common with the Dwergas or Gnomes of the Scandinavian mythology, are not identical with them; they are in fact peculiar to people of Celtic race, and the notions respecting them prevalent among the Celtic population in Scotland, Wales, and Ireland tally to a remarkable degree. The popular belief, however, was nowhere invested with so poetical a character as in the Lowlands of Scotland, where it forms a main ingredient in the beautiful ballad poetry of the district. The fairies of the Scottish and English mythology are diminutive beings, who render themselves occasionally visible to men, especially in exposed places, on the sides of hills, or in the glades of forests, which it is their custom to frequent. They have also dealings with men, but of an uncertain and unreal character. Their presents are sometimes valuable; but generally accompanied, in that case, with some condition or peculiarity which renders them mischievous: more often they are unsubstantial, and turn into dirt or ashes in the hands of those to whom they have been given. Mortals have been occasionally transported into Fairy-land, and have found that all its apparent splendor was equally delusive. One of the most ordinary employments of fairies, in vulgar superstition, is that of stealing children at nurse, and substituting their own offspring in place of them, which after a short time perish or are carried away. The popular belief in fairies has been made the subject of poetical amplification in the hands of so many of the greatest writers, from Shakspeare to Scott, that it is not easy to disentangle the embellishments with which it has been invested from the original notions on which they are founded. The Fata of the Italians, who figures in their romantic epics, and from whom the French have made the Fée of their fairy tales, is quite a different personage: a female magician, sometimes benevolent, and sometimes malevolent, partaking herself of the supernatural character, and peculiarly gifted with the spirit of prophecy. Such is the Fata Morgana, to whom the celebrated optical delusion occasionally produced in the Straits of Messina was formerly attributed by popular belief.—*Fairy of the mine*, an imaginary being supposed to inhabit mines, wandering about in the drifts and chambers, always employed, yet effecting nothing.—*Fairy ring or circle*, a phenomenon frequently seen in the fields, consisting of a round bare path with grass in the middle, formerly ascribed to the dances of the fairies. It has been supposed by some, that these rings are the effect of lightning; but a more rational theory ascribes them to a kind of fungus which grows in a circle from the centre outwards, destroying the grass as it extends, while the interior of the circle is enriched by the decayed roots of the fungi.

FAITH, in divinity and philosophy, the firm belief of certain truths upon the testimony of the person who reveals them. The grounds of a rational faith are, that the things revealed be not contrary to, though they may be above natural reason; that the revealer be well acquainted with the things he reveals; that he be above all suspicion of deceiving us. Where these criterions are found, no reasonable person will deny his assent. Whatever propositions, therefore, are beyond reason, but not contrary to it, are, when revealed, the proper matter of faith.—*Justifying*, or *saving faith*, signifies perfect confidence in the truth of the Gospel, which influences the will, and leads to an entire reliance on Christ for salvation.—*Public faith*, is represented on medals, sometimes with a basket of fruit in one hand, and some ears of corn in the other: and sometimes holding a turtle-dove. But the most usual symbol is with her two hands joined together.—*Faith*, (Fides) in ancient Art, is represented as a matron wearing a wreath of olive or laurel leaves, and carrying in her hand ears of corn, or a basket of fruit. In Christian Art, by a female carrying a cup surmounted by a cross, emblematical of the Eucharist, "the Mystery of Faith."

FA'KIR, or FA'QUIR, a devotee, or Indian monk. The fakirs are a kind of fanatics in the East Indies, who retire from the world, and give themselves up to contemplation. Their great aim is to gain the veneration of the world by their absurd and cruel penances, outdoing even the mortifications and severities of the ancient Christian anchorets. Some of them mangle their bodies with scourges and knives; others never lie down; and others remain all their lives in one posture. There is also another kind of fakirs, who do not practise such severities, but make a vow of poverty, and go from village to village, prophesying and telling fortunes.

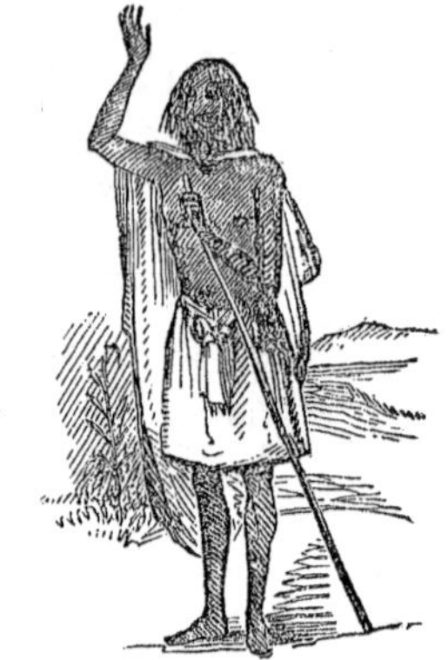

FAL'CON, a bird nearly allied to the hawk, about the size of a raven, and capable of being trained for sport, in which it was formerly much employed. It is usually represented in coats of arms with bells on its legs, and also decorated with a hood, virols, rings, &c.—*Falcon*, the attribute of St. Jerome, and of the holy hermit Otho of Ariano; the former has a hooded falcon on his hand, while the latter has it sitting on his head.

FAL'CONET, a small cannon, or piece of ordnance.

FAL'CONRY, the art of training all kinds of hawks, but more especially the larger sort, called the gentle falcon, to the exercise or sport of hawking. This sport was much practised in Europe and Asia in the chivalric ages, and continued in favor till the 17th century; but the invention of fire-arms gradually superseded it. In France, England, and Germany, falconry was at one time in such high esteem, that during the reign of Francis I. of France, his grand falconer received an annual revenue of 4000 livres; had under him fifteen noblemen and fifty falconers; and enjoyed the privilege of hawking through the whole kingdom at pleasure. The whole establishment, which cost annually about 40,000 livres, attended the king wherever he went, and those who were distinguished for their skill in the sport were loaded with royal favors. In England, falconry was also in high esteem, and there is to this day an hereditary grand falconer (the duke of St. Alban's,) who, by virtue of his office, presents the king, or queen regnant, with a cast of falcons on the day of the coronation. A similar service is performed by the representative of the Stanley family in the Isle of Man. The origin of this celebrated sport has given occasion to much controversy. It has been said that it was unknown to the Greeks; it is, however, described by Ctesias and Aristotle as practised in their time in India and Thrace. Martial and Apuleius present us with plain indications of the knowledge of this pastime among the Romans. In modern Europe, it appears to have been practised earliest, or at least with most ardor, in Germany: the title of the emperor, Henry the Fowler (A.D. 920,) is said to be derived from an anecdote respecting his fondness for it. In the 12th century, it was the favorite sport of nobles and knights throughout Europe; and in that which followed its rules were reduced into a system by the Emperor Frederic II., (Barbarossa,) and by Demetrius, physician to the Greek Emperor Palæologus. In that court the grand falconer was an officer of distinction; and the title was borrowed from it by the western sovereigns. According to the opinion of Strutt, the sport was not known so early in England as on the Continent; yet there are traces of it as early as the 8th century.

FALD'STOOL, a kind of stool placed at the south side of the altar, at which the kings of England kneel at their coronation; also a folding stool or desk, provided with a cushion, for a person to kneel on during the performance of certain acts of devotion; also a small desk, at which, in cathedrals, churches, &c., the litany is enjoined to be sung or said. It is sometimes called a *litany stool.*

FAL'LACY, in logic and rhetoric, has been defined "any argument, or apparent argument, which professes to be decisive of the matter at issue, while in reality it is not." Fallacies have been divided into those "in dictione," in the words: and "extra dictionem," in the matter. The latter of these it is not the province of logic to discover and refute; they being, strictly, instances in which the conclusion follows from the premisses, and which therefore depend on the unsoundness of these premisses themselves, which can only be detected by a knowledge of the subject-matter of the argument. Logical fallacies, or fallacies in dictione, are those in which the conclusion appears to follow, but in reality does not, from the premisses; and which, consequently, can be detected by one unlearned in the subject-matter of the argument, but acquainted with the rules of logic.

FALSE, contrary to the truth or fact: the word is applicable to any subject physical or moral.—*False*, in music, an epithet applied by theorists to certain chords, because they do not contain all the intervals appertaining to those chords in their perfect state. Those intonations of the voice which do not truly express the intended intervals are also called *false*, as well as all ill-adjusted combinations.—*False*, an epithet used also in law, as *false imprisonment*, the trespass of imprisoning a man without lawful cause.—In mineralogy, as *false diamond*, a diamond counterfeited with glass.—It is also a word much used in military affairs; as, a *false* alarm, a *false* attack, &c.—*False flower*, in botany, a flower which does not seem to produce any fruit. —*False roof*, in carpentry, that part of a house which is between the roof and the covering.

FALSET'TO, in music, an Italian term, denoting that species of voice in a man, the compass of which lies above his natural voice, and is produced by artificial constraint.

FAMILIAR SPIRITS, demons, or evil spirits, supposed to be continually within call and at the service of their masters, sometimes under an assumed shape; sometimes compelled by magical skill, and sometimes doing voluntary service. In Eastern stories, nothing is more common than the mention of magic gems, rings, &c., to which are attached genii, sometimes good, sometimes bad; but in modern Christian Europe the notion of *familiars* has always been restricted to evil spirits.

FANAT'IC, one who indulges wild and extravagant notions of religion, and sometimes exhibits strange motions and postures, and vehement vociferation in religious worship. — The ancients called those *fanatici* who passed their time in temples, (*fana*,) and being often seized with a kind of enthusiasm, as if inspired by the divinity, exhibited wild and antic gestures. Prudentius represents them as cutting and slashing their arms with knives: shaking the head was also common among the *fanatici;* hence the word was applied to different religious sects, who, on their first appearance amongst us, sought notoriety by the extravagance of their actions, and by pretending to inspirations.

FANDAN'GO, an old Spanish dance,

which proceeds generally from a slow and uniform to the most lively motion. It is seldom danced but at the theatre, and in the parties of the lower classes; nor is it even then customary to dance it with those voluptuous looks and attitudes which distinguish the true fandango. There is another species of fandango, called the *bolero*, the motions and steps of which are slow and sedate, but grow rather more lively towards the end. In these dances the time is beat by castanets.

FANFARE', (*French*,) a short, lively, loud, and warlike piece of music, composed for trumpets and kettle-drums. Also, small, lively pieces performed on hunting-horns, in the chase. From its meaning is derived *fanfaron*, a boaster, and *fanfaronade*, boasting.

FANTA'SIA, in music, the name generally given to a species of composition, supposed to be struck off in the heat of the imagination; and in which the composer is allowed to give free range to his ideas, unconfined by the rules of the science. Some limit the term to mere extemporaneous effusions, which are transitive and evanescent: differing from the *capricio* in this, that though the latter is wild, it is the result of premeditation, and becomes permanent; whereas the *fantasia*, when finished, no longer exists.

FANTOCCI'NI, dramatic representations in which puppets are substituted in the scene for human performers.

FARCE, a dramatic piece or entertainment of low comic character. It was originally a droll, or petty show exhibited by mountebanks and their buffoons in the open streets, to gather the people together. It has, however, long been removed from the street to the theatre; and instead of being performed by merry-andrews to amuse the rabble, is acted by comedians, and become the entertainment of a polite audience. As the aim of a farce is to promote mirth, the dialogue is not refined, nor is there any opportunity lost to excite laughter, however wild or extravagant the plot, or however ridiculous the characters. The original term seems to signify a miscellaneous compound or mixture of different things. In modern languages it has borne various significations. Certain songs which were sung between the prayers on the occasion of religious worship are said to have been denominated farces in Germany, during the middle ages; whence the word appears to have denoted simply an interlude of any kind. In England, the farce appears to have risen to the dignity of a regular theatrical entertainment about the beginning of the last century; since which time it has formed one of the most popular exhibitions, and is usually performed, by way of contrast, after a tragedy at the national theatres. The farce is restricted to three acts as its limit, but frequently consists only of two or one. Of all the pieces of this class which have successively amused English audiences, none have acquired a permanent literary reputation except those of Foote,—performances in which the license of the theatre in satirizing living persons was carried to the utmost height. The *Fabulæ Atellanæ* of the Romans, which appears to have been short dramatic entertainments of a miscellaneous character, sometimes pastoral, sometimes tragi-comic, &c., but not so coarse in plan or diction as the *Mimes* and their *Exodia*, which were satirical dialogues in verse between some set characters or stage-buffoons, appear to have filled in some respects the place of the modern farce. On the French stage the vaudeville answers to the English farce.

FAS'CES, in Roman antiquity, bundles of rods with an axe in the centre of each bundle, carried before the consuls as a badge of their office. The use of the fasces was introduced by the elder Tarquin

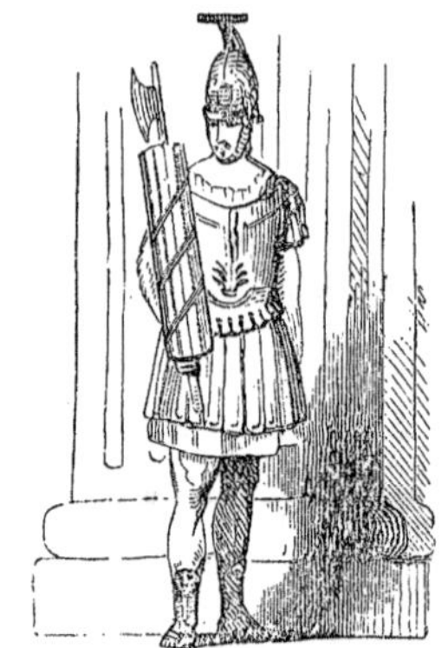

as a mark of sovereign authority: in after-times they were borne before the consuls, but by turns only, each having his day. These latter had twelve of them, carried by so many lictors.

FAS'CIA, in architecture, a flat member in an entablature or elsewhere, like a flat band or broad fillet. The architrave, when subdivided for instance, has three bands, called fasciæ; of which the lower is called the first fascia, the middle one the second, and the upper one the third.—*Fascia*, a bandage employed in various ways, 1. As a diadem, worn round the head as an emblem of royalty, the color being white, that worn by women was purple. 2. Fastened round the legs, especially of women, from the ankle to the knee, serving the purpose of leggings, as a protection to the legs of the wearer, a practice that was adopted in Europe during the middle ages.

FASCINA'TION, a kind of witchcraft or enchantment supposed to operate by the influence of the eye. A belief in fascination appears to have been very generally prevalent in most ages and countries. It has been till very recently, and in some remote districts is even yet, prevalent among the Scotch Highlanders, and the inhabitants of the Western islands, where the fear of the evil eye has led to various precautions against its influence; and in Turkey, when a child is born, it is immediately laid in the cradle and loaded with amulets, while the most absurd ceremonies are used to protect it from the noxious fascination of some invisible demon.

FASH'ION, a term used to signify the prevailing mode or taste in any country, the only recognized quality which it possesses being mutability. It may safely be averred that in proportion to the influence which fashion exercises in any country may its claim to civilization be vindicated, nothing being so characteristic of a rude and barbarous state of existence as a rigid adherence to the customs of antiquity. The term *fashion* has generally been considered as applicable chiefly to the adornment of the person, in conformity with the prevailing taste as introduced by some individual of consideration in society; but it has a much wider signification, being applied to the most trivial kind of conventional usages, a disregard or ignorance of which is sufficient in the eyes of the votaries of this tyrannical goddess to banish the offender beyond the pale of civilized society.

FAS'TI, in ancient history, the records of the Roman state, in which all public matters, military and civil, were registered by the high priest, according to the days on which they took place. The *Fasti* of Ovid is a poem giving an account of the Roman year, and the ceremonies attached to the different days, with their historical or mythological origin. The first six books, containing the first six months of the year, beginning with January, have come down to us; the rest are lost.

FASTS, occasional abstinence from food, on days appointed by public authority to be observed in fasting and humiliation. Solemn fasts have been observed in all ages and nations, especially in times of mourning and affliction. Among the Jews, besides their stated fast days, they were occasionally enjoined in the time of any public calamity. They were observed upon the second and fifth days of the week, beginning an hour before sunset, and continuing till midnight on the following day. On these occasions they always wore *sackcloth* next their skins, rent their clothes, which were of coarse white stuff; sprinkled ashes on their heads; went barefoot; and neither washed their hands nor anointed their bodies as usual. They thronged the temple, made long and mournful prayers, and had every external appearance of humiliation and dejection. In order to complete their abstinence, at night they were allowed to eat nothing but a little bread dipped in water, with some salt for seasoning, except they chose some bitter herbs and pulse. The practice of fasting is recommended in the New Testament by the example of the Apostles and early Christians, who are frequently represented as fasting, especially on solemn occasions, such as when Paul and Barnabas are sent forth by the Apostles to preach to the Gentiles. The observance of stated fast days prevailed very early and universally in the church.

FA'TALISM, the belief of an unchangeable destiny, to which everything is subject, uninfluenced by reason, and independent of a controlling cause; the doctrine, in short, which teaches that all things take place by an inevitable necessity.

FA'TA MORGA'NA, a singular aerial phenomenon seen in the straits of Messina. When the rising sun shines from that point whence its incident ray forms an angle of about 45° on the sea of Reggio, and the bright surface of the water in the bay is not disturbed either by the wind or current, when the tide is at its height, and the waters are pressed up by currents to a great elevation in the middle of the channel, the spectator being placed on an eminence, with his back to the sun and his face to the sea, the mountains of Messina rising like a wall behind it, and forming the back-ground of the picture,—on a sudden there appears in the water, as in a catoptric theatre, various multiplied objects—numberless series of pilasters, arches, castles, well-delineated regular columns, lofty towers, superb palaces, with balconies and windows, extended alleys of trees, delightful plains, with herds and flocks, armies of men on foot, on horseback, and many other things, in their natural colors and proper actions, passing rapidly in succession along the surface of the sea, during the whole of the short period of time while the above-mentioned causes remain. All these objects, which are exhibited in the Fata Morgana, are proved by the accurate observations of the coast and town of Reggio, to be derived from objects on shore. If, in addition to the circumstances before described, the atmosphere be highly impregnated with vapor, and dense exhalations, not previously dispersed by the action of the wind and waves, or rarified by the sun, it then happens, that in this vapor, as in a curtain extended along the channel to the height of above forty palms, and nearly down to the sea, the observer will behold the scene of the same objects not only reflected from the surface of the sea, but likewise in the air, though not so distinctly or well defined as the former objects of the sea. Lastly, if the air be slightly hazy and opaque, and at the same time dewy, and adapted to form the iris, then the above-mentioned objects will appear only at the surface of the sea, as in the first case; but all vividly colored or fringed with red, green, blue, and other prismatic colors.

FATE, destiny depending on a superior cause and uncontrollable. According to the Stoics, every event is determined by Fate; and in the sense in which the moderns use the word, it implies the order or determination of Providence.

FATES, in mythology, the three sister goddesses named Clotho, (spinster,) Lachesis, (allotter,) and Atropos, (unchangeable,) whose office it was to spin the destinies of men, and break the threads when their appointed hours of death came. They were also called Parcæ by the Latins. Their Greek name was Μοῖραι, *i. e.*, "the dispensers."

FAUNA'LIA, three Roman festivals annually observed in honor of the god *Faunus*. The first was kept on the ides of February, the second on the 16th of the calends of March, and the third on the nones of December. The sacrifices on these occasions were lambs and kids. It is supposed that the Roman Faunus was the same with the Greek Pan.

FAUNS, rural deities, among the Romans, represented with horns on their heads, sharp pointed ears, and the rest of their bodies like goats. They were the mythological demi-gods of woods and forests, thence called *sylvan* deities. The figure is taken from an antique statue in the Florentine museum, and represents a young faun as a flute-player.

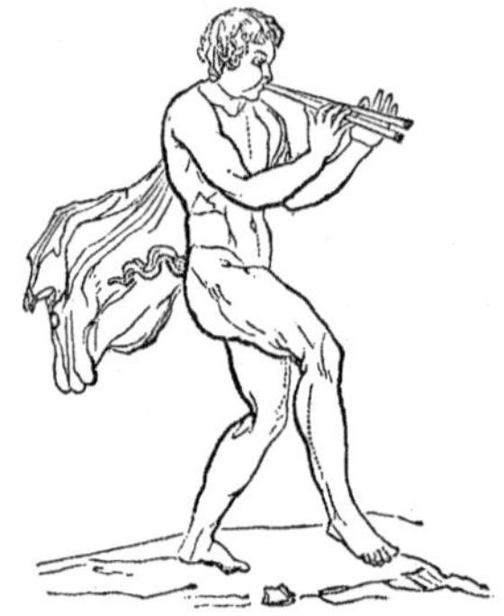

FAUX JOUR, (French,) *false light;* a term used in the Fine Arts, signifying that a picture is placed so that the light falls upon it from a different side from that which the painter has represented the light in the picture as falling upon objects, or that it is covered with a bright glare, so that nothing can be properly distinguished.

FAVIS'SÆ, large vaults under ground in the area of the Roman capitol, where the Romans carefully lodged and deposited with a degree of religious care the old statues, and other sacred utensils, when they happened to be broken; such a superstitious veneration did they pay to everything belonging to the capitol.

FE'ALTY, in feudal law, an oath taken on the admittance of any tenant to be true to the lord of whom he held his land. Under the feudal system of tenures, every vassal or tenant was bound to be true and faithful to his lord, and to defend him against his enemies: the tenant is called a liege man; the land a liege fee; and the superior, a liege lord.

FEASTS, or FESTIVALS, in a religious sense, are aniversary times of feasting and thanksgiving, such as Christmas Easter, &c. Feasts were of divine institution; intended by the Deity to perpetuate among his chosen people, the Jews, the memory of his mercies and miracles; as well as to keep alive the friendship betwixt the different tribes and families, by bringing them together on solemn occasions, and offering up their thanksgivings in the holy city.—Among Christians, *movable feasts* are those which, depending on astronomical calculations, do not always return on the same days of the year. Of these, the principal is Easter, which fixes all the rest, as Palm-Sunday, Good Friday, Ash-Wednesday, Sexagesima, Ascension-day, Pentecost, and Trinity Sunday. *Immovable feasts*, those which are constantly celebrated on the same day; of these, the principal are Christmas day, or the Nativity, the Circumcision, Epiphany, Candlemas or the Purification, Lady-day or the Annunciation, All Saints, and All Souls, and the days of the several apostles. The four quarterly feasts, are Lady-day, or the annunciation of the Virgin Mary, on the 25th of March; the nativity of St. John the Baptist, on the 24th of June; the feast of St. Michael, the archangel, on the 29th of September; and Christmas, or rather of St. Thomas the apostle, on the 21st of December.—The *feasts of the ancients* were conducted with great ceremony. The guests wore white garments, decorated themselves with garlands, and often anointed the head, beard, and breast with fragrant oils. The banqueting room was also often adorned with garlands and roses, which were hung over the table, as the emblem of silence: hence the common phrase, to communicate a thing *sub rosa* (under the rose.) The luxurious Romans drank out of crystal, amber, and the costly *murra* (a kind of porcelain introduced by Pompey,) as well as onyx, beryl, and elegantly wrought gold, set with precious stones. After the meal was ended, flute players, female singers, dancers and buffoons of all kinds, amused the guests, or the guests themselves joined in various sports and games.

FEB'RUARY. in chronology, the second month of the year, reckoning from January, first added to the calendar of Romulus by Numa Pompilius. February derived its name from *Februa*, a feast held by the Romans in this month, in behalf of the *manes* of the deceased, at which ceremony sacrifices were performed, and the last offices were paid to the shades of the defunct. February in a common year consists only of 28 days, but in the bissextile year it has 29, on account of the intercalary day added that year.

FE'CIALES, a college of priests instituted at Rome by Numa, consisting of twenty persons. selected out of the best families. Their business was to be arbitrators of all matters relating to war and peace, and to be the guardians of the public faith.

FED'ERAL GOVERNMENT, such a government as consists of several independent provinces or states, united under one head; but the degree to which such states give up their individual rights may be very different, although as relates to general politics they have one common interest, and agree to be governed by one and the same principle. Of such kind is the government of the United States of America.

FED'ERALIST, an appellation in the United States, given to those politicians who wanted to strengthen the *fœdus*, or general government compact, in opposition to others who wished to enfeeble it by extending the separate authority of the several states. Hamilton was a chief *federalist*, Jefferson a leading *anti-federalist*.

FEE, a reward or recompense for professional services; as the *fees* of lawyers, physicians, &c. Public offices have likewise their settled *fees*, for the several branches of business transacted in them.

FEE-ESTATE, in law, properly signifies an inheritable estate in land, held of some superior or lord; and in this sense it is distinguished from *allodium*, which is the absolute property in land. It is the *theory* of the English law that all the lands of the kingdom, except the royal domains, are held in fee, or by a tenure, of some superior lord, the absolute or allodial property being only in the king, so that all the tenures are strictly feudal. The most ample estate a person can have is that of *fee-simple*; and such an estate can be had only in property that is inheritable, and of a permanent nature.—*Fee-farm*, a kind of tenure without homage, fealty, or other service, except that mentioned in the feoffment; which is usually the full rent. The nature of this tenure is, that if the rent is in arrear or unpaid for two years, then the feoffer and his heirs may have an action for the recovery of his lands.

FEEL'ING, one of the five external senses, by which we obtain the ideas of solid, hard, soft, rough, hot, cold, wet, dry, and other tangible qualities. This sense is the coarsest, but at the same time it is the surest of the five; it is besides the most universal. We see and hear with small portions of our body; but we feel with all. Nature has bestowed that general sensation wherever there are nerves, and they are everywhere where there is life. Were it otherwise, the parts divested of it might be destroyed without our knowledge. All the nervous solids, while animated by their fluids, have this general sensation; but the papillæ in the skin, those of the fingers in particular, have it in a more exquisite degree. Like every other sense, feeling is capable of the greatest improvement; thus we see that persons, born without arms, acquire the nicest feeling in their toes; and, in blind people, this sense becomes so much developed, that individuals born blind, and acquiring the faculty of sight in after life, for a long time depend rather on their feeling than on their sight, because they receive clearer ideas through the former sense.

FEET, in Christian Art, the feet of our Lord, also of angels and of the apostles, should always be represented naked, without shoes or sandals.

FEINT, in military tactics, a mock attack, made to conceal the true one.

FELI'CITAS, the appellation of a Roman goddess, a Christian martyr, and a traditional empress, mentioned in romantic poetry only.—1. *Felicitas*, a divine being, agreeing with the Eudæmonia (felicity) and the Eutychia (good fortune) of the Greeks, in whom was personified the idea of happiness arising from blissful occurrences. Thus, *Felicitas* (Eutychia) means more than Fortuna or Tyche, by which was meant chance or luck. The Felicitas of the Greeks, Eutychia, is represented on many earthen vessels as announcing to the spectator the desired result of the action intended. We also meet with it as illustrative of success in arms, and of happiness in marriage. On Roman coins she is represented with the modius on her head, the staff of Hermes in her hand, and resting on a cornucopia; but her attributes differ according to circumstances. 2. St. Felicitas, a Christian lady of Rome, who is depicted with a palm-branch and cross; she is the patroness of male children. She had seven sons, who with her suffered martyrdom at Rome, A.D. 160. Felicitas was thrown into a cauldron of boiling oil, while her sons' heads were cut off and exhibited before her. 3. The empress Felicitas, a principal character in the romance of Count Octavian; her two children, who, with herself, were cast into a forest, were nursed by a lioness.

FEL'LOW, the member of a college or of a corporate body.—This word has a very wide and opposite meaning; for though we say, in speaking of a skilful artist, this man has not his *fellow*, we also apply it in the most ignoble sense, and say, such a one is a mean or worthless *fellow*.

FE'LO DE SE, in law, a person that, being of sound mind, and of the age of discretion, wilfully causes his own death.

FEL'ONY, in law, generally includes all capital crimes below treason, such as murder, burglary, &c.; and is punished with death or transportation, according to the enormity of the offence.

FELUC'CA, a light open vessel with six oars, much used in the Mediterranean. It has this peculiarity, that its helm may be used either at the head or the stern.

FEME COV'ERT, in law, a married woman, who is under covert of her husband. By the common law of England, the legal capacity of a woman to contract, or sue and be sued, separately, ceases on marriage; and her husband becomes liable to her debts existing at that time.—*Feme-sole*, a single woman.—*Feme-sole merchant*, a woman who carries on trade alone, or without her husband.

FEMINA'LIA, a kind of short pantaloons or closely-fitting breeches, reaching a short distance below the knees, worn by the Roman soldiers in their expeditions to cold countries; they are seen depicted on the Column of Trajan, and on the Arch of Constantine at Rome.

FEM'ININE, in grammar, denoting the female gender.

FEN'CING, the art of using skilfully a sword or foil either in attack or defence. In the exercise of this art, foils or thin swords are used, which, being blunted at the points, and bending readily, are rendered harmless.

FEN'GITE, a kind of transparent alabaster or marble, sometimes used for windows as in the church of St. Miniato at Florence.

FEO'DUM, FEOD, or FEUD, in feudal law, the right which the vassal had in land, &c., to use the same, and take the profits thereof, rendering unto his lord such fees, duties, and services, as belonged to military tenure.

FEOFF'MENT, in law, is a gift or grant of any manors, messuages, lands, or tenements to another in *fee*, that is, to him and his heirs forever, by delivery of seisin, and possession of the estate granted. The giver is called the *feoffer*, and the person who is thus invested is called the *feoffee*.

FERA'LIA, in antiquity, a festival observed among the Romans on the 21st of Feruary, or, according to Ovid, on the 17th, in honor of the *manes* of their deceased friends and relations. During the ceremony, which consisted in making presents at their graves, marriages were forbidden, and the temples of the divinities shut up; because they fancied that during this festival, departed spirits suffered no pains in hell, but were permitted to wander about their graves and feast upon the meats prepared for them.

FERENTA'RIA, in ancient Rome, a sort of light-armed soldiers.

FER'ETORY, this term is applied to the bier or shrine containing the reliques of saints, borne in processions. The type of a feretory is a coffin, but the form is usually that of a ridged chest, with a roof-like top, usually ornamented by pierced work, with the sides and top engraved and enamelled, and sometimes with images in high relief. They were made of various metals. 1. Of solid gold and silver adorned with jewels. 2. Of copper, gilt and enamelled. 3. Of wood overlaid with plates of metal, or richly painted and gilt. 4. Of ivory, or of crystal, mounted in metal and gilt. 5. Of wood, covered with precious stuffs and embroidery.

FE'RIA, in the Romish breviary, is applied to the several days of the week; thus, Monday is the *feria secunda*, Tuesday the *feria tertia*, and so on.

FE'RIÆ, in Roman antiquity, holidays, or days upon which they abstained from business. The *feriæ* were of several kinds, namely, *Feriæ stativæ*, or stated festivals; *feriæ conceptivæ*, or movable feasts; *feriæ imperativæ*, or occasional festivals enjoined by the consuls or other magistrates on some public occasion; and *feriæ denicales*, for private occasions. There were also the *feriæ Latinæ*, kept by the fifty Latin towns on Mount Albanus; and the *feriæ mundinæ*, festivals kept for nine days on the appearance of any prodigy.—It was a pollution of the *feriæ*, according to Macrobius, if the *rex sacrorum* or *flamines* saw any work done on them, and therefore they ordered proclamation to be made by the herald, that every one might abstain from work; and whoever transgressed the order was fined.

FE'RINE, an epithet for such beasts as are wild and savage, as lions, tigers, wolves, bears, &c.

FE'RIO, in logic, a mode in the first figure of syllogisms, consisting of a universal negative, a particular affirmative, and a particular negative.—A similar mode in the third figure of syllogisms, is termed *ferison*.

FER'ULA, in ecclesiastical history, signifies a place separated from the church, wherein the *audientes* were kept, as not being allowed to enter the church.—Under the eastern empire, the *ferula* was the emperor's sceptre, as is seen on a variety of medals; it consisted of a long stem or shank, and a flat square head.

FES'CENNINE VERSES, so called from Fescennia, an Etrurian town, where they first had their origin, were rude extemporaneous pieces of poetry recited by the youth of Latium and Etruria at rustic festivals, especially at harvest home, with gestures adapted to the sense. They consisted principally of raillery and playful rustic abuse; a species of humor very much in vogue with the Grecian and Egyptian country people also. The Fescennine verses are chiefly remarkable from having given rise to satire, the only class of poetry of native Italian growth.

FESTI'NO, in logic, a mood of syllogisms in the second figure, in which the first proposition is a universal negative, the second a particular affirmative, and the third a particular negative.

FESTOON', a carved ornament in wood, stone, &c., usually in the form of a garland or wreath, composed of flowers, fruits, leaves, &c., bound together, and suspended by the ends. It was employed by the architects of the middle ages frequently with much success in their friezes of the composite order. It is usefully and aptly employed in decoration. The

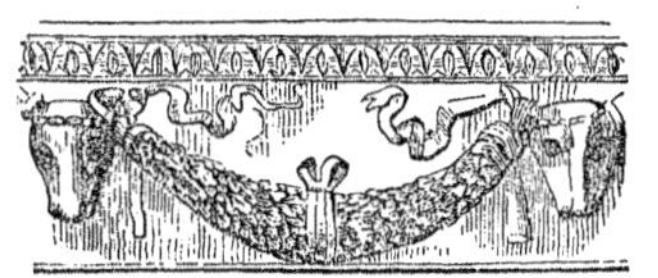

garland is of greatest size in the middle, and diminishes gradually to the points of suspension from which the ends generally hang down. The festoon in architecture is sometimes composed of an imitation of drapery, similarly disposed, and frequently of an assemblage of musical instruments, implements of war, or of the chase and the like, according to the purpose to which the building it ornaments is appropriated.

FE'TICH, FETICHISM, the word fetich

is said to be derived from the Portuguese, and appears to have been brought into usage from the writings of some travellers on the western coast of Africa. It is now comprehensively employed to signify any object of worship not representing a living (or rather, perhaps, a human) figure; thus excluding idols, properly so called. This perverted form of religion prevails very extensively among barbarous nations, and especially those of the Negro race. Among the latter, tribes, families, and individuals have their respective fetiches; which are often objects casually selected, or chosen under the influence of some occasional superstition, as stones, weapons, vessels, plants, &c., &c.

FEUD, an inveterate quarrel between families or parties in a state. The word is not applicable to wars between different nations, but to intestine wars and animosities between families, clans, or tribes.

FEU'DAL SYSTEM, a form of government anciently subsisting in Europe, and which, about twelve centuries ago, was so universally received, that Spelman calls it "the law of nations in our western world." The origin of this system, is to be found in the military policy of the Celtic or northern nations, known by the names of Goths, Vandals, Franks, Huns, and Lombards, who overran Europe on the declension of the Roman empire, and brought it with them from the countries out of which they emigrated. According to the feudal scheme, a victorious leader allotted considerable portions of land, called *feoda*, *fiefs*, or *feuds*, to his principal officers, who in their turn, divided their possessions among their inferiors; and the condition upon which these rewards were given, was that of faithful military service both at home and abroad. To this they engaged themselves by an oath of fealty; in the event of a breach of which, either by not performing the service agreed upon, or by deserting their lord in time of battle, &c., the lands were to return to their original possessor. Every person, therefore, who was a feudatory, *i. e.* who had received lands, was bound to do everything in his power to defend the lord of his fee; while, on the other hand, the latter was no less subordinate to his immediate superior; and so on up to the prince himself. Thus the several orders of vassals formed a system of concentric circles, of which each was under the influence of the next, and all moved around a common centre, the king, as the supreme feudal lord. As there was a graduated scale from the lowest vassal to the prince or lord paramount of the territory, every man's interest was involved in the security of the whole; and every man was a pledge of security to his neighbor. In the midst of that disinterestedness of sentiment which belongs to a rude state of society, the connection of the lord and his vassal was of a salutary nature; and, as is the end of all social combinations, each individual contributed to support that strength by which he was protected. But besides these feudal grants, which were held only on the terms of military service above mentioned, there were others called *allodial*, which were given upon more enlarged principles. To these every free man had a title, and could not only claim his territory as well as the rest, but dispose of it at his pleasure. A part of their freedom consisted in liberty to go to the wars; for this, in the times to which we are referring, was the only way to acquire any degree of renown. Only the serfs or villeins, were destined to follow the arts of peace. The feudal vassals, properly so called, constituted the army; while the national militia was composed of the allodial proprietors. It has, however, often been argued, that the bare theory of feudal government, as a permanent institution, however fair-seeming, is hollow; that the family connection it supposes could be but a source of minute, domestic tyranny; and that in their best period, the customs enumerated must have been liable to the grossest abuse. In process of time, the evil increased to an enormous height; and even the political value of the system decayed. In its vigor, it had at least constituted a regular, powerful, and compact system of government; a unanimity had pervaded the various departments of the state; and while the power was internally diffused, it presented to foreign nations a united and formidable front. As the ideas engendered by property advanced, and the great grew more avaricious of money than of glory; and when, it ought perhaps to be added, man's notions of right and order became more correct, nothing was heard of but the enormities of the powerful, and the sufferings of the humbler classes; and the strength of feudal government declined amidst a spirit of disaffection too universal to be checked—Mr. Hallam in his work on the Middle Ages, ably exhibits a picture of the advantages and disadvantages of the feudal system. If, says he, we look at the feudal polity as a scheme of civil freedom, it bears a noble countenance. To the feudal law it is owing, that the very names of right and privilege were not swept away, as in Asia, by the desolating hand of power. The tyranny which, on every favorable moment, was breaking through all barriers, would have rioted without control, if, when the people were poor and disunited, the nobility had not been brave and free. So far as the sphere of feudality extended, it diffused the spirit of liberty, and the notions of private right. The bulk of the people, it is true, were degraded by servitude; but this had no connection with the feudal tenures. As a school of moral discipline, the feudal institutions were perhaps most to be valued. Society had sunk, for several centuries after the dissolution of the Roman empire, into a condition of open depravity; where, if any vices could be selected as more eminently characteristic than others, they were falsehood, treachery, and ingratitude. In slowly purging off the lees of this extreme corruption, the feudal spirit exerted its ameliorating influence. Violation of faith stood first in the catalogue of crimes most repugnant to the very essence of feudal tenure, most severely and promptly avenged, most branded by general infamy. The feudal law-books breathe throughout a spirit of mutual obligation. The feudal course of jurisdiction promoted, what trial by peers is peculiarly calculated to promote, a keener feeling and a readier perception of moral as well as of legal distinctions. And as the judgment and sympathy of mankind are seldom mistaken in these great points of veracity and justice, except through the temporary success of crimes or the wants of a definite standard of right, they gradually recovered themselves, when law precluded the one and supplied the other. In the reciprocal services of lord and vassal, there was ample scope for every magnanimous and disinterested energy. The heart of man when placed in circumstances which have a tendency to excite them, will seldom be deficient in such sentiments. No occasions could be more favorable, than the protection of a faithful supporter, or the defence of a beneficent suzerain, against such powerful aggression, as left little prospect except of sharing in his ruin. From these feelings, engendered from the feudal relation, has sprung up the peculiar sentiment of personal reverence and attachment towards a sovereign, which we denominate loyalty; alike distinguishable from the stupid devotion of eastern slaves, and from the abstract respect with which free citizens regard their chief magistrate. Men who had been used to swear fealty, to profess subjection, to follow, at home and in the field, a feudal superior and his family, easily transferred the same allegiance to the monarch. It was a very powerful feeling which could make the bravest men put up with slights and ill-treatment at the hands of their sovereign; or call forth all the energies of disinterested exertion for one whom they never saw, or in whose character there was nothing to esteem. In ages when the rights of the community were unfelt, this sentiment was one great preservative of society; and though collateral or even subservient to more enlarged principles, it is still indispensable to the tranquillity and permanence of every monarchy.

FEUIL'LANS, an order of bare-footed monks, who observe the same rules with the Benardines.

FI'AT, in law, a short order or warrant signed by a judge, for making out and allowing certain processes.—*Fiat justitia* are the words written by the king on his warrant to bring a writ of error in parliament, &c.

FIB'ULA, a brooch, buckle, or clasp, used for fastening together various parts of male and female attire, as well as for ornament. They were made of ivory, gold, bronze, precious stones set in gold, and sometimes of silver, and of every variety of form, upon which the most elaborate ornament was frequently bestowed. In ancient Art we see the fibula employed to pin together the two parts of a cloak or scarf, (*chlamys*, *pallium*, &c.,) so as to fasten them over the right shoulder. Sometimes, but rarely, we see it on the breast. In female costume it is seen worn on both shoulders, and sometimes on the sleeves, breast, and to fasten the tunic when tucked up at the knee.

FICTI'LIA, TESTA, the term applied to all ancient pottery, from domestic utensils to architectural ornaments, coarse or fine, burnt, or only hardened by exposure to the air. The most plastic species of clay for the finer kinds of pottery was found in Etruria, and the earthen table vessels of Arretium maintained their superiority even to the time of Pliny. Among the Greeks, the pottery of Athens, and of the island of Samos, was the most famed, the finest, and of the most carefully washed earth; it was called *Samian clay*, and produced the hardest ware.

FIC'TION, in law, a supposition that a thing is true without inquiring whether it is or not, so that it may have the effect of truth, as far as is consistent with equity.

FIC'TOR, a term applied to any artist who works in wax, clay, or other plastic material, as contradistinguished from one who works in bronze, marble, wood, ivory, or other solid substances.

FIEF, a fee; an estate held of a superior on condition of military service.—*See* FEUDAL SYSTEM.

FIELD, in heraldry, the whole surface of the shield or escutcheon.—*Field*, in military tactics, the ground chosen for any battle.—*Field*, in painting, the ground or blank space on which anything may be drawn.

FIELD-MAR'SHAL, the highest military officer in England.—*Field-officer*, a military officer above the rank of a captain, as a major or colonel.—*Field-colors*, in war, are small flags of about a foot and a half square, which are carried along with the quarter-master general, for marking out the ground for the squadrons and battalions.—*Field-pieces*, small cannons, from three to twelve pounders, carried along with an army in the field.—*Field-staff*, a weapon carried by the gunners, about the length of a halbert, with a spear at the end; having on each side ears screwed on, like the cock of a match-lock, where the gunners screw in lighted matches, when they are upon command.—*Field-works*, in fortification, are those thrown up by an army in besieging a fortress, or by the besieged to defend the place.

FI'ERI FA'CIAS, in law, a judicial writ commanding the sheriff to levy the debt or damages on the goods of one against whom judgment has been had in an action of debt.

FIFE, a small wooden musical wind instrument of the flute species played by holes, exceedingly shrill in tone, and rarely used except in military bands.

FIF'TEENTH, an ancient tribute or tax laid upon cities, boroughs, &c., through all England, and so termed because it amounted to a fifteenth part of what each city or town had been valued at; or it was a fifteenth of every man's personal estate according to a reasonable valuation. In doomsday-book, there are certain rates mentioned for levying this tribute yearly.

FIFTH, in music, one of the harmonical intervals or concords. It is the second in order of the concords, the ratio of the chords that afford it being as 3 : 2. It is called the fifth, as containing five terms or sounds between its extremes and four degrees; so that in the natural scale of music it comes in the fifth place or order from the fundamental. The ancients called it *diapente*, and the Italians at present call it *quinta*. The *imperfect*, *defective* or *false fifth*, called by the ancients *semi-diapente*, is less than the fifth by a lesser semitone.

FIFTH-MON'ARCHY-MEN, a fanatical sect, who formed a principal support of Cromwell during the Protectorate They considered his assumption of power as an earnest of the foundations of the fifth monarchy, which should succeed to the Assyrian, the Persian, the Grecian, and the Roman, and in which Jesus Christ should reign with the saints on earth for the space of a thousand years. Upon the restoration of the royal family, and the return of the kingdom to its former principles in church and state, a party of these enthusiasts, headed by a man of the name of Venner, made a desperate insurrection in the streets of London, which was put down with the slaughter of a great number of them.

FIG'URE, in physics, denotes the surface or terminating extremities of any body; and, considered as a property of body affecting our senses, is defined, a quality which may be perceived by two of the outward senses—touch and sight.—*Figure*, in dancing, denotes the several steps which the dancer makes in order and cadence, considered as they mark certain *figures* on the floor.—*Figure*, in rhetoric, a mode of speaking or writing in which words are deflected from their ordinary signification, thereby expressing a passion with more emphasis and beauty than by the ordinary way. Rhetorical figures are often highly serviceable as well as ornamental, and serve to awaken and fix attention; but they are to be used with prudence and caution; for whatever is described in a multitude of words, or is carried on to a disproportionate length, fails of the end proposed, and grows tiresome rather than pleasing. The principal figures of rhetoric are the metaphor, allegory, simile, and personification; which, with their further divisions into hyperbole, climax, antithesis, &c., will be found under their respective heads.—*Figure*, in painting and designing, denotes the lines and colors which form the representation of any animal, but more particularly, of a human personage. Thus a painting is said to be full of figures, when there are many representations of men; and a landscape is said to be without figures, when there is nothing but natural scenery.

FIL'ACER, an officer of the common pleas, so called from his filing the writs on which he makes out processes. There are fourteen of these officers, who are severally allotted to particular divisions and counties, and make out all original processes, real, personal, and mixed.

FIL'LAGREE WORK, or FIL'IGRANE, a delicate and elaborate manufacture, primarily executed in threads of gold and silver, but lately imitated with colored and gilt paper. In Sumatra, manufactures of fillagree-work are carried to very great perfection. In China also, where the fillagree is mostly of silver, many beautiful articles are produced.

FIL'LET, in architecture, a little square member, ornament, or moulding, used in various places, but generally as a corona over a great moulding.—Among painters and gilders, a little rule or line of leaf-gold, drawn over certain mouldings, or on the edges of frames, panels, &c.

FIL'LIBEG, } PHIL'LIBEG, } A dress reaching

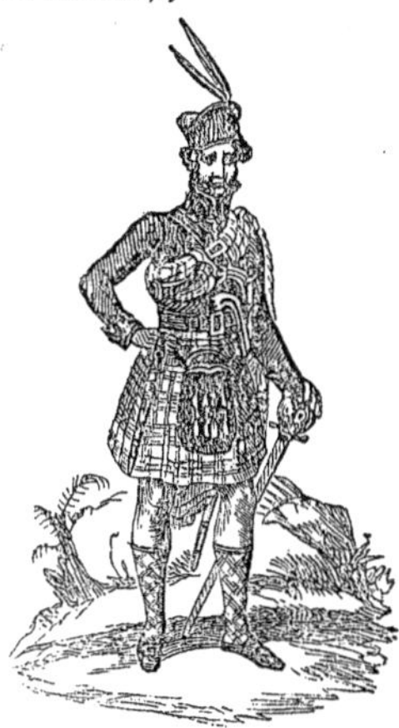

only to the knees, worn in the Highlands of Scotland.

FIM'BRIA, Fringe, by the Greeks and Romans, fringes and tassels were ornaments but little worn, except on the garments of females, by whom they were sometimes attached to the tunic. The extremities of the threads of the warps (*thrums*) formed the usual fringes, to which an ornamental appearance was given by twisting and crossing the threads, and the production of a net-like form. Fringes were also made of gold thread and other materials, which were attached to the garments, &c.

FI'NAL CAUSES, the purposes or ultimate ends in view. The *efficient* cause is that which produces the event or effect; the *final* cause is that for which anything is done.

FINA'LE, the concluding part of a musical composition. In instrumental pieces, it has mostly a character of vivacity, and requires a quick movement and lively performance.

FINE, in law, a penalty or amends made in money for an offence; also, money paid for the renewal of a lease, and a conveyance of lands or tenements, in order to cut off all controversies.

FINE ARTS, a term somewhat indefinite in its meaning, but generally applied to those arts which depend on the mind and imagination: opposed to the mechanical.

FINESSE', may be defined simply as a peculiar aptitude of discovering, in any business, the best means of attaining the object in view; or as the power of embracing in one comprehensive glance the various interests of any subject, together with ingenuity to devise and tact to carry out the plan best calculated to obtain success.

FINE STUFF, in architecture, plaister used in common ceilings and walls for the reception of paper or color. It is composed of lime, slaked and sifted through a fine sieve, then mixed with a due quantity of hair and fine sand. A mixture of lime and hair, used in the *first coat* and floating of plastering, is called *coarse stuff*.

FIN'GER BOARD, in music, the black board attached to the neck of instruments of the viol class, on which the strings are pressed by the fingers for the purpose of adjusting their lengths, so as to produce the different sounds.

FIN'GERING, in music, the act of disposing of the fingers in a convenient, natural, and apt manner, in the performance of any instrument, but more especially the organ and piano-forte. Good fingering is one of the first things to which a judicious master attends; for to a facility in this branch of the performer's art must a pupil look, as the means of acquiring a facile and graceful execution, and the power of giving passages with articulation, accent, and expression.

FIN'IAL, an ornament employed in Gothic architecture, as a termination to pinnacles, pediments, canopies; it consists of a bunch of foliage, and therein closely resembles the crocket: and sometimes finials are composed of four or more crockets, united together. Church spires, when perfect, are frequently terminated with finials.

FIN'ISH, the last touches applied to a picture or other work of Art. It always constitutes the difference between excellence and mediocrity. Small pictures require the most careful finish, but in larger works, too much attention to high finish detracts from the boldness and vigor demanded by works on a large scale.

FIN'ISHING COAT, in architecture, the best coat of stucco work when three coats are used. When in the third coat fine stuff is used for paper, it is called setting.

FIN'TO, in music, a feint or an attempt to do something and not to do it; as *cadenza finto*, when having done everything proper for a true character, instead of falling on the right final, a higher or a lower note is taken.

FIRE, in former times, fire obtained a place among the elements, and was for a long time considered to be a constituent part in the composition of all bodies, and to require only the concurrence of favorable circumstances to develop its activity. Its all-consuming energy, the similarity of its effects to those of the sun, its intimate connection with light, its terrible and yet beneficent power,—easily explain how it happened that, in times when cause and effect, form and essence, were not yet distinctly separated, fire became an object of religious veneration, a distinguished element in mythology, an expressive symbol in poetry, and an important agent in the systems of cosmogony. When natural philosophy was treated in the schools, theories were adopted to which little attention is paid in the present age, when all science is founded on facts and observations. Caloric, be it a material agent or the consequence of vibratory motion, is at present considered the cause of the phenomena which were formerly ascribed to fire; and though its nature is as unknown to us as that of fire was to the ancients, the substitution of one of these terms for the other has introduced a greater precision of language, and cause and effect are no longer confounded under the same name.—*Fire, flame*, the attribute of St. Florian, the protector against conflagration; of the hermit Anthony, because the tempter appeared to him from the fire; of Bishop Basil, who saved a poor boy, by burning his compact with the devils; of St. Bridget of Scotland, over whose head a flame was seen from childhood; of St. Columba of Cordova, who saved an angel from death by fire; of St. Patrick, before whom fire sprung out of the earth, upon his drawing a cross upon it with his staff; of the Dominican, Peter Gonzales, called St. Elmo, who enveloped in a mantle, lay upon burning coals, whence the expression *St. Elmo's fire*; and of many Christian martyrs condemned to die by fire.

FIRE-ARMS, a general designation for all sorts of guns, fowling-pieces, blunderbusses, pistols, &c., which effect their discharge by the combustion of gunpowder.

FIRE, GREEK, a destructive composition, used in war from the 7th to the 13th century. When the Arabs besieged Constantinople in 668, the Greek architect Callinicus of Heliopolis, deserted from the caliph to the Greeks, and took with him a composition, which, by its wonderful effects, struck terror into the enemy, and forced them to take to flight. Sometimes it was wrapped in flax attached to arrows and javelins, and so thrown into the fortifications and other buildings of the enemy, to set them on fire. At other times it was used in throwing stone balls from iron or metallic tubes against the enemy. The receipt for the composition of the *Greek fire* was long supposed to be lost; but the baron Von Aretin of Munich has, it is said, discovered in a Latin MS. of the 13th century, in the central library in that city, a dissertation on the Greek fire, which contains the receipt.

FIR'MAMENT, in Scripture, denotes the great arch or expanse over our heads, in which are placed the atmosphere and the clouds, and in which the stars *appear* to be placed, and are *really* seen.—In the Ptolemaic astronomy, the firmament is the eighth heaven or sphere, with respect to the seven spheres of the planets which it surrounds. It is supposed to have two motions; a diurnal motion, given to it by the *primum mobile*, from east to west about the poles of the ecliptic; and another opposite motion from west to east, which last it finishes, according to Tycho, in 25,412 years; according to Ptolemy, in 36,000; and according to Co pernicus, in 25,800; in which time the fixed stars return to the same points in which they were at the beginning. This period is commonly called the Platonic, or great year.

FIR'MAN, in the Persian language, signifies a command, and is the name given in Turkey, Persia, and India to mandates or certificates of the sovereign, issued for various purposes. Those best known to Europeans are given to travellers, and serve as passports. The fermân has placed at its head in Turkey the cipher of the reigning sultan, written in a complicated manner, affixed by the chief secretary of the sign manual.

FIRST-FRUITS, offerings made to God by the Hebrews, or part of the fruit of their harvest, as an acknowledgment of his sovereign dominion. They were called first-fruits because they were offered in the temple before any part of the crop was touched.—*First-fruits*, in the church of England, are the profits of every spiritual benefice for the first year, according to the valuation in the king's books.

FISC, or FIS'CUS, the treasury of a prince, or state. It differs from the *ærarium*, which was the treasury of the public, or people: thus, when the money arising from the sale of condemned persons' goods was appropriated for the use of the public, their goods were said to be *publicari;* but when it was destined for the support of the prince, they were called *confiscari.*

FIS'CAL, in the civil law, something relating to the pecuniary interest of the prince or people. The officers appointed for the management of the fisc, were called *procuratores fisci*, and *advocati fisci.*

FISH, a fish has been employed as a symbol of our Lord from the earliest times, (it is found depicted in the tombs of the Roman catacombs,) by whom St. Peter was called a "fisher of men;" and the faithful were sometimes represented by fish, with reference to the waters of baptism in which they were born, and fish were therefore frequently carved on the baptismal fonts. Fish are used as emblems of Chastity; it is an attribute of the Apostle Simon. The VESICA PISCIS is a symbolical figure, consisting of two intersecting segments of circles, employed also as an emblem of the Saviour from the fourth century. The seals of abbeys, colleges, and other religious establishments were all invariably made of this form.

FITCH, among the brushes used in painting, some are made of the hair of the sable, a kind of weasel; others of the badger, and of white hog's bristles; but among the best are those of the fitch or polecat, which are black in color, elastic and firm, though soft. They are made both flat and round, and are used also for varnishing.

FLAG, a general name for colors, standards, bearers, ensigns, &c.—*To strike or lower the flag*, is to pull it down upon the cap in token of respect or submission.—*To strike the flag* in an engagement, is the sign of surrendering.—*To hang out the white flag*, is to ask quarter; or in some cases, it denotes that the vessel has no hostile intention, but comes to trade, &c. The *red* flag is a sign of defiance and battle.—*To hang the flag half-mast high*, is a token or signal of mourning.

FLAGEL'LANTS, a sect of enthusiasts who first appeared in the middle of the 13th century, and being then repressed, sprang up again with renewed violence in the 14th. Beginning first at Cremona in Italy, the contagion of the example spread in a few years throughout Europe; and every city was infested by multitudes who went naked from the loins upward, and inflicted upon themselves several daily flagellations, with the idea of obtaining thereby merit in the eyes of God. They formed themselves into a society, and at first were at least innocent in their behavior; but as their numbers increased, they gave way to great excesses, and were eventually suppressed by a holy war proclaimed against them by Pope Clement VI.

FLA'GEOLET, a wooden musical wind instrument, played with a mouthpiece, the holes and keys whereof are stopped with the fingers, in the same way as the flute.

FLAKE WHITE, a white pigment extensively used in oil-painting; like nearly all the other white pigments, it is prepared from the carbonate of the oxide of lead, obtained by exposing sheets of lead to the vapor of acetic and carbonic acids. It derives its name from the form in which it appears in commerce—that of flakes or scales. As a pigment it possesses great body, and enters largely into numerous compound tints.

FLAMBOYANT, FLAME-LIKE, a term applied to those contours of which the inflexions have a resemblance to those of flame; and by antiquaries of France to that style of architecture which was contemporary in that country with the perpendicular in England, from the flame-like wavings of its tracery. It is regarded by some as a vitiated decorated rather than a distinct style: in rich works, the intricacy and redundancy of the ornaments are frequently truly surprising.

FLA'MEN, in Roman antiquity, the name of an order of priests, instituted by Romulus or Numa; authors not being agreed on this head. Originally there were three priests so called; the *Flamen Dialis*, consecrated to Jupiter; *Flamen Martialis*, sacred to Mars; and *Flamen Quirinalis*, who superintended the rites of Quirinus or Romulus.

FLAMME'UM, the yellow veil worn on the wedding-day by Roman brides. It was sufficiently large to cover the wearer from head to foot. It was removed by the husband upon their arrival at their home.

FLANK, the side of an army, or a battalion encamped on the right and left.—In fortification, that part of a bastion which reaches from the curtain to the face; or any part of a work that defends another work along the outside of its parapet.

FLAT, in music, a character of this form ♭, which depresses the note before which it is placed a chromatic semitone. Flats and sharps were originally contrived to remedy the defects of musical instruments whereon temperament was required, the natural scale of music being limited to certain fixed sounds, and adjusted to an instrument in many points defective; for we can only proceed from one note to another by a particular order of degrees. Hence, from one note to another, upwards or downwards, we cannot find any interval at pleasure. To supply or remedy this defect, musicians have had recourse to a scale proceeding by twelve degrees, making therefore thirteen notes to an octave, including the extremes, which, though it does not make the instrument perfect, leaves little room for complaint. In instruments whose sounds are fixed, a sound or note dividing it into two unequal parts, called semitones, is placed between the extremes of every tone of the natural scale; so that we have twelve semitones between thirteen notes in the compass of an octave. In order, then, to keep the diatonic series distinct, the inverted notes answer for the name of the natural note next below, with this character ♯, called a sharp; or the name of the natural note next above it, with this character ♭, called a flat. Thus D ♭ signifies a semitone below D natural (♮.) On keyed instruments the short keys are the representatives of these flats and sharps. The system, however, does not strictly produce what it represents: it is only an approximation.

FLAT FIFTH, in music, an interval of a fifth depressed by a flat, called by the ancients *semidiapente*.

FLEECE, ORDER OF THE GOLDEN, one of the most distinguished among European orders of knighthood. It was founded by Philip III., duke of Burgundy, in 1430; and as by its foundation his successors were declared to be hereditary grand masters, that title passed, with the Burgundian inheritance, to the house of Austria; thence after the death of Charles V., to the Spanish line of that house: but when the monarchy of Spain passed to the Bourbons and the Spanish Netherlands to Austria, the archdukes of Austria claimed the grand mastership; and claims are made on it at present both by the emperor of Austria and king of Spain; the order is consequently conferred both at Vienna and Madrid, and is, in both courts, the highest in point of rank. As its nominal object is the protection of religion, it is rarely conferred on any Protestants, with the exception, by courtesy, of Protestant sovereigns.

FLEET, a squadron of ships of war, belonging to any prince or state. It also denotes any number of trading ships, employed in a particular branch of commerce. Merchant-fleets generally take their denomination from the place they are bound to, as the Turkey-fleet, East-India-fleet, &c. These, in times of peace, go in fleets for their mutual aid and assistance: in time of war, besides this security, they procure convoys of men of war, either to escort them to the places whither they are bound, or to a certain place or latitude.—It is also the name of a prison in London, where debtors are confined; and to which persons are committed by the courts of chancery and common-pleas.

FLEM'ISH SCHOOL, in painting, the school formed in Flanders. The works of this school are distinguished by the most perfect knowledge of chiaro-scuro; high finishing without dryness; by an admirable union of colors well blended and contrasted, and by a flowing, luxurious pencil. Its defects are somewhat similar to those of the Dutch school. The Flemish painters, like the Dutch, represented nature as they found her, and not as she should be. Rubens and Vandyke, (the glory of this school,) though men of the greatest genius, were not free from this defect, and the former especially. Teniers was another great master of the school in question; to it also belongs Snyders, Steenwick, Nefs, Schwaneveldt, Van Eyck, &c.

FLESH, Flesh Tints, the colors which best represent the human body, sometimes termed the *carnations*, but employed in a more extended sense than this latter term, which better expresses the more delicate portions of the body, such as the face, bosom, and hands.

FLE'TA, the title of an ancient treatise on English law, attributed to the reign of Edward I., and named (according to tradition) from its composition by a judge in the Fleet prison.

FLEUR DE LIS, the royal insignia of France. Its origin is disputed; by some it is supposed to represent a lily, by others, the iron head of some weapon. It is of frequent occurrence in English armory.

FLORA'LIA, a feast kept by the Romans in honor of the goddess Flora. This feast began April the 25th, and continued till the 1st of May, during which time the *Ludi Florales* were celebrated.

FLOR'ENTINE FRES'CO, Fresco Secco, a kind of painting first practised at Florence during the flourishing period of Italian Art for decorating walls. Like common fresco the lime is used wet, but in this case it can be moistened and kept damp and fit for painting on.

FLOR'ENTINE LAKE, a pigment prepared from cochineal; it is now obsolete; the greater durability in oil-painting of the lakes prepared from madder having entirely superseded those prepared from cochineal.

FLOR'ENTINE MOSA'IC, the term applied to the art of inlaying tables and other plane surfaces with *pietra dura*, carried on principally at Florence. Very beautiful patterns are thus produced by the combination of precious stones, forming the most difficult branch of mosaic art.

FLOR'ID STYLE, in literary composition, that which is too much enriched with figures and flowers of rhetoric. Longinus uses the terms *florid* and *affected style* indifferently, and describes them as quite contrary to the true sublime.—The *florid style* of architecture, or *florid Gothic*, an elaborate kind of Gothic architecture, filled with points, ramifications, mullions, &c.—*Florid*, in music, any composition or performance of a rich and embellished kind.

FLOR'IN, a coin of different value; the silver florin of Holland is worth about 1*s*. 8*d*. Most of the gold florins are of a coarse alloy, weighing variously from about fourteen to seventeen carats.

FLO'TA, a name given by the Spaniards to the ships that formerly sailed together, or under convoy, from Cadiz and the other ports of the peninsula, authorized to trade directly with the transatlantic possessions of Spain.

FLOTIL'LA, literally a little fleet; in which sense, however, it is seldom used, being applied almost invariably to a fleet, how large soever, composed of small vessels. Thus the term flotilla was given to the immense naval force with which Napoleon meditated the invasion of Great Britain, and which consisted of 2365 vessels of every description, was manned by about 17,000 sailors, and carried 160,000 soldiers, and 10,000 horses. In Spain, the name flotilla is given to a number of vessels appointed to announce to the home government the departure and nature of the cargo of the flota or mercantile ships from foreign ports on their homeward voyage.

FLOT'SAM, in law, a term for goods lost by shipwreck, but which are floating on the sea.—There are two other uncouth terms made use of to describe wrecked goods, viz., *jetsam* and *lagan;* the former, when the goods are sunk; and the latter, when they are sunk, but tied to a cork or buoy to be found again.

FLOUR'ISH, in music, a prelude or preparatory air, without any settled rule; also the decorative notes which a singer or instrumental performer occasionally introduces.—In military language, it is the sounding of trumpets on receiving an officer or other person of distinction.

FLOW'ERS. Flowers are employed in Art as attributes. 1st. Of mythological persons—Aphroditè, the Hours, and Zephyr. 2d. Among legendary personages—of St. Dorothea, who is represented with flowers and fruits by her side, or in a basket; also with a branch of roses in her hand, or crowned with those flowers; of St. Sophronia, upon whose corpse birds and flowers are strewed; of St. Rosa de Lima, who was named Rosa on account of her beauty, and has a rose with a broken crown of thorns; of St. Rosa of Viterbo, who holds roses in her hand or in her apron; of St. Elizabeth of Hungary, who has roses in her lap or in a basket; of St. Casilda, who generally wears a wreath of white roses on her head; of the holy pair Ascylus and Victoria, both crowned with roses; of St. Angelus, from whose mouth fall roses and lilies; and of St. Hugo, who holds three flowers in his hand. For the lily, the attribute of many saints.

FLUTE, *the common or English*, a musical wind instrument, consisting of a tube about eighteen inches in length, furnished with holes at the side for the purpose of varying its sounds by stopping and opening them with the fingers.—The *German flute* is formed of several joints or pieces screwed into each other, with holes at the side, and the addition of several brass or silver keys, to temper the tones to the various flats and sharps.

FLUTES, or FLU'TINGS, in architecture, perpendicular channels, or cavities, cut along the shaft of a column or pilaster. They are chiefly effected in the Ionic order, where they had their first rise; though they are also used in the richer orders, as the Corinthian and Composite, but seldom in the Doric, and scarcely ever in the Tuscan. Each column has twenty-four flutes, and each flute is hollowed in exactly a quadrant of a circle. The Doric, however, has but twenty. Between the flutes are little spaces that separate them, called *stria*, or *lists;* though in the Doric, the flutes are frequently made to join to one another, without any intermediate space at all; the list being sharpened off to a thin edge, which forms a part of each flute. Fluted columns are sometimes, though improperly, termed *reeded.*

FLUX'IONS, a method of calculation invented by Sir Isaac Newton. In this branch of mathematics, magnitudes of every kind are supposed to be generated by motion. This science is employed in the investigation of curves, in finding the contents of solids, and computing their surfaces; in finding the centres of gravities and oscillation of different bodies; the attractions of bodies under different forms; the direction of wind, which has the greatest effect on an engine; and in the solution of many other interesting and important problems.

FLY'ERS, in architecture, stairs that do not wind, but are made of an oblong square figure, and go straight forward, the second standing behind the first, and so on.

FO, the name given by the Chinese to Buddha, by one of those phenomena in literature whereby appellations are introduced from one language into others with which it has little or no affinity. Originally the name Buddha was expressed in the Chinese language with sufficient exactness by the term Fô-thau, pronounced Fôudah; but, as is usual in China with proper names, the last syllable was subsequently dropped.

FOIL, among jewellers, a thin leaf of metal placed under precious stones, to increase their lustre and improve their color. Hence anything of a different color or quality, which serves to adorn or set off another thing to advantage, is termed a *foil.*—In fencing, an elastic piece of steel, or sword without a point, to fence with by way of exercise. The *foil* usually has a button or piece of cork at the end, covered with leather.

FOLD, in painting, the doubling or lapping of one piece of drapery over another.

FO'LIAGE, in architecture and sculpture, a group of leaves of plants and flowers, so arranged as to form architectural or sculptural ornaments; as in friezes, panels, and also in the capital of the Corinthian order.

FO'LIO, in account books, denotes a page, or rather both the right and left hand pages, these being expressed by the same figure.—*Folio*, a book of the largest size, the leaves of which are formed by once doubling a sheet of paper.

FOLK'MOTE, a word used in England before the Norman conquest to denote an annual assembly of the people, answering in some measure to a modern parliament. Some authors, however, allege that the folkmote was an inferior court, or common council of a city or borough.

FONT, the vessel used to contain the consecrated water in baptism, usually constructed of stone and lined with lead; and in the earlier ages of the church were always large enough to allow of the complete immersion of infants. The forms of fonts have generally varied in different ages, and often exhibit exquisite richness both of design and ornament. Fonts were required to be covered and locked; originally these covers were simply flat, movable lids, but they were subsequently very highly ornamented, assuming the form of spires, and enriched with various decorations in the form of pinnacles, buttresses, &c.—*Font* or *Fount*, a complete assortment of printing types of one size, including a due proportion of all the letters, points, figures, accents, &c.

FONTINA'LIA, in Roman antiquity, a religious feast celebrated Oct. 13, in honor of the nymphs of wells and fountains. The ceremony consisted in throwing nosegays into the fountains, and putting crowns of flowers upon the wells.

FOOL, in ordinary language, signifies one who is deficient in intellect, or who pursues a course contrary to the dictates of reason. In Scripture, the word *fool* is often used for a wicked or depraved person. But in its most legitimate sense, the term *fool* means one who is destitute of reason; either from having been born an idiot; or become idiotic from some injury done to the brain.—*To play the fool*, to act the buffoon; to occupy one's time in absurd trifling.

FOOLS, we frequently meet in ancient churches, especially under the seats of choir-halls, representations of men in grotesque costume, and in various postures, with a fool's cap and bells. The introduction of these and other ludicrous, or even indecent images, in the very buildings dedicated to the solemn worship of God, has long been a subject of inquiry among the learned, and of surprise and scandal to the generality of persons. The source of many of these representations may be traced to the pagan orgies of the Saturnalia and Lupercalia. It is necessary to draw a great distinction between the *burlesque* figures, and symbolical representations of the vices and virtues, which are often introduced under the guise of animals whose nature corresponds to the passion or virtue represented; hence human beings may be depicted with heads of beasts and birds, such as foxes, lions, or hawks, to denote cunning, courage, or rapacity. Again, animals are frequently introduced with the same intention, and most admirable moral lessons are imparted under the same types as have been selected by Æsop and his imitators.

FOOLS, FEAST OF, a festival anciently celebrated in almost every church and monastery of France, on New Years' Day, in which every absurdity and even indecency was practised. It was equivalent to the Saturnalia, among the Romans, whence indeed it is said to be derived. This festival received some modifications in the different districts where it was celebrated, and acquired various designations according to the multifarious ceremonies of which it consisted. Several bishops and councils attempted, though in vain, to abolish this festival; but at length about the 15th century it became less generally observed, and soon after fell into almost total disuse, though its characteristic absurdities are still maintained in the Carnival of the present times.

FOOT, in poetry, a certain number of syllables, constituting part of a verse; as, the iambus, the dactyl, and the spondee.

FOR'AGE, all kind of provender for cattle, especially for horses in time of war. —*A foraging party*, those who are sent out by the general in order to collect provisions either for the horses or for the troops.

FORCE, in mechanics, the energy or impulse with which one body affects another, with reference to the direction of motion, and the centres of the masses. It consists in the transfer of the motion of one body to another.—*Physical force*, is the force of material bodies.—*Moral force*, is the power of acting on the reason in judging and determining.—*Force*, in law, signifies any unlawful violence offered to persons or property.—*A forcible entry*, is a violent and actual entry into houses, or lands; and a *forcible detainer*, is a violent withholding the possession of lands, &c., so that the person who has a right of entry is hindered therefrom.—The word *force* has numerous other meanings; as strength or power for war—virtue—efficacy—validity—destiny—necessity, &c.

FORECLOSE', in law, to exclude or bar the equity of redemption on mortgages, &c.

FORE-SHORT'ENING, the art of representing objects on a plane surface as they appear to the eye, depending upon a correct knowledge of form, perspective, and chiaroscuro. It is one of the most difficult studies in the art of design, and when executed with skill constitutes the excellence of the master. Michael Angelo, Rubens, and Correggio, were distinguished among other rare qualities for their skill in fore-shortening. They practised modelling for assistance in attaining this art.

FORE'STALLING, the act of buying or bargaining for any provisions or merchandise, before they reach the market to which they were going, with an intent to sell the same again at higher prices.

FOR'FEITURE, in law, the loss of some right, privilege, or estate, goods, lands, or employments, &c., for neglecting to do one's duty, or for some crime committed.

FOR'GERY, in law, the fraudulent making or altering any deed, or writing, &c., to the prejudice of another man's right, particularly the counterfeiting the signature of another with intent to defraud.

FORLORN-HOPE, in military affairs, a detachment of men appointed to lead in an assault, to storm a counterscarp, enter a breach, or perform any other service attended with great and imminent peril.

FORM, the external appearance of objects; the quality that distinguishes one thing from another.—*Form*, in painting, signifies especially the human body. The study of forms, and the changes they undergo by muscular contractions, require on the part of the artist the utmost attention and assiduity. The conscientious artist ought scrupulously to avoid any tendency to exaggerate the superficial forms of the body: nothing is more simple, more calm; nothing shows a grander breadth of design than the human body; the muscles assist by their reunion in the production of general forms; the special forms are scarcely visible.—*Form*, in physiology, the essential and distinguishing modification of the matter of which any body is composed.—*Form*, in a moral sense, the manner of being or doing a thing according to rules: thus we say, a *form* of government, a *form* of argument, &c.—*Form*, in law, the rules established and requisite to be observed in legal proceedings.—*Form*, in mechanics, a kind of mould in which anything is wrought.—*Essential form* is that mode of existence which constitutes a thing what it is, and without which it could not exist.—*Form*, in printing, pages or columns of type, properly arranged, and enclosed and locked in an iron frame called a chase, for the purpose of being put to press. There are two forms required for every sheet, one for each side; and each form consists of more or fewer pages, according to the size of the books. —In schools, a *class*.

FORM'ALIST, one who observes the outward forms and ceremonies of worship, for appearance' sake, without possessing the life and spirit of pure religion.

FORM'ATIVE ARTS, those arts which, independently of external wants and aims, yet, on the other hand, bound to the imitation of nature, represent life by means of the forms naturally connected.

FOR'MULA, in mathematics, a general theorem or literal expression for resolving any part of a problem.—*Formula*, in theology, a profession of faith.

FORT, in the military art, a small fortified place, surrounded with a moat, rampart, and parapet; or with palisades, stockades, and other means of defence.

FORTE, in music, a direction to the performer to execute the part loudly to which the word is affixed. It is indicated by the single letter F. If two F F's, thus, are used, the part is to be played or performed *fortissimo*, very loud.

FORTIFICA'TION, the art or science of fortifying a place, or of putting it in such a posture of defence, that every one of its parts defends, and is defended, by some other parts, by means of ramparts, parapets, moats, and other bulwarks; so that a small number of men within may be able to defend themselves for a considerable time against the assaults of a numerous army without.—*Ancient fortification*, at first consisted of walls or defences made of the trunks and large branches of trees, mixed with earth, to secure them against the attacks of the enemy. This was afterwards altered to stone-walls, on which were raised breastworks, behind which they made use of their darts and arrows in security.—*Modern fortification*, is that which is flanked and defended by bastions and out-works, the ramparts of which are so solid, that they cannot be beat down but by the continual fire of several batteries of cannon. The principal works belonging to a fortification are, the ditch or trench made round each work; the rampart, or elevation of earth, raised along the faces of any work, to cover the inner part; the parapet, or that part of a rampart which serves to cover the troops planted there; the bastion, that part of the inner enclosure of a fortification making an angle towards the field; the counterscarp, the slope of the ditch facing the body of the place; the covert way, the space extending round the counterscarp; and the glacis, the part beyond the covert way, to which it serves as a parapet. In recent times, however, fortification has undergone important changes, and engineers have adopted different systems; but those which have acquired the greatest reputation in Europe, are the systems of Count Pagan, the Baron de Coehorn, Von Scheiter, and Marshal Vauban.

FOR'TITUDE, the basis or source of coolness and intrepidity in danger, of patience in suffering, of forbearance under injuries, and of magnanimity in all conditions of life. In fine, fortitude is the virtue of a rational and considerate mind, founded on a sense of honor and a regard to duty. The motives to fortitude are many powerful, and this virtue tends much to the happiness of the individual, by giving composure and presence of mind, and keeping the other passions in due subordination.

FORTU'NA, in mythology, the goddess who presided over the destinies of mankind, and, generally speaking, over all the events of life. She was represented as blind, with winged feet, and resting on a wheel. The goddess was not known in the more ancient systems of the Greek theogony: all the guidance of human affairs, for instance, is entrusted by Homer to destiny; but in Italy, and chiefly at Rome, Actium, and Præneste, her worship was most assiduously cultivated.

FO'RUM, in Rome, a public place where causes were judicially tried, and orations delivered to the people. There were six of these forums, viz., the *Romanum*, *Julianum*, *Augustum*, *Palladium*, *Trojanum*, and *Salustii* forum. The chief of these was the *forum Romanum*, called, by way of eminence, *the forum*. In this was an apartment called the rostra, where the lawyers pleaded, and the orators harangued the people, &c. Here was also the *comitium*, or hall of justice, with the sanctuary of Saturn, the temple of Castor, &c., altogether forming a most splendid place. The word *forum* was also applied to a place of traffic, or market-place: of these there were vast numbers, as the *forum piscarium*, *olitorium*, &c. These were generally called *fora venalia*, in distinction from the former, which were called *fora civilia*.—In the law, *forum* signifies a court of justice, the place where disputed rights are settled; hence *forum competens*, a competent jurisdiction; *forum incompetens*, a court not authorized to try the cause, &c.

FOUNDA'TION, in architecture, the lower part of a wall, on which the insistent wall is raised, and always of much greater thickness than such insistent wall. A practice has lately been introduced of laying foundations (if not in water) on a bed of what is called *concrete*, which is a mixture of rough small stones or large gravel stones with sand and stone, lime and water, with just enough of the lime to act as a cementitious medium, with the best effect.

FOUNDA'TIONS, in political economy, the generic name given to institutions established and endowed by individuals, associations, or the public, for the promotion of what is believed to be, at the time when the foundation is made, some useful or benevolent purpose. In most old-settled and rich countries there are foundations for a vast variety of objects. During the Middle Ages, it was very common to bequeath property for the foundation of monastic institutions and scholastic establishments. The two great universities of Oxford and Cambridge are noble examples of the last species of foundations; and by far the greater number of the grammar and free schools in most parts of England, and indeed of Europe, owe their origin to the same source. A great deal of property has also been bequeathed by benevolent individuals in this and other countries for the erection and endowment of hospitals, or foundations of various descriptions, for the relief and assistance of the poor; and not unfrequently also property is appropriated, or foundation instituted for the amusement and recreation of the public.

FOURTH, in music, one of the harmonical intervals; so called because it contains four sounds or terms between its extremes, and three intervals; or as being the fourth in order of the natural or diatonic scale from the fundamental.

FRANC, a French coin, worth twenty sols, or ten-pence sterling.

FRAN'CHISE, in a general sense, signifies some privilege or exemption from ordinary jurisdiction. A franchise may be vested either in bodies politic, or corporations; in borough towns, or in individuals; as the electoral franchise. Corporate liberties being usually held by charter, are all said to be derived from the crown, but some lie in prescription without the help of any charter.

FRANCIS'CANS, Friars-Minor, or Gray-Friars, the religious order of Saint Francis, by whom they were founded about the year 1200.

FRANK'INCENSE, an odoriferous, dry, resinous substance, procured from the juniper-tree in Turkey and the East Indies. It is of a pale yellow color, very inflammable, and is used as a perfume.

FRANKS, an appellation given by the Turks, and other nations of Asia, to all the people of the western parts of Europe, English, French, Italians, &c.

FRATER'NITIES, in the middle ages, consisted of pious laymen who formed societies for the purpose of relieving the sick and destitute, and performing other Christian duties.

FRA'TRAGE, in law, a partition among brothers or co-heirs coming to the same inheritance or succession; also that part of the inheritance that comes to the youngest brothers.

FREE'BOOTERS, a name given to some adventurers of all nations, but especially of France and England, who have obtained a place in history by the courage and intrepidity which they displayed in executing the most difficult enterprises. The origin of their history is merged in obscurity, and it is impossible to ascertain precisely whence their name is derived; but the *flibustiers* of the French naval historians are identical with the *buccaneers* of our own language. The South American islands formed the chief theatre of their depredations; and such was the relentless hostility with which they visited the Spaniards, that during the latter half of the seventeenth century, which embraced the most formidable period of the freebooter's career, their commercial operations in the Indian seas were nearly destroyed. At the commencement of the 18th century, the freebooters sustained in their expedition a series of disasters, which sensibly diminished their numbers; and since that period the designation has been applied indiscriminately to any individual who regards "the universe as his property," and appropriates to himself either furtively or forcibly the possessions of another.

FREE'HOLD, that land or tenement which is held in fee-simple, fee-tail, or for term of life. It is of two kinds; in *deed* and in *law*. The first is the real possession of such land or tenement; the last is the right a man has to such land or tenement, before his entry or seizure. More properly, a *freehold* is an estate in lands or tenements, in fee-simple, or in tail, for the term of the life of the holder, or for the life of another person, in dower or by the courtesy.—*Freehold* is also extended to such offices as a man holds in fee or for life. It is also taken in opposition to villenage. In Scotland, a *freehold* is an estate held of the crown or prince. In the United States, a *freehold* is an estate which a man holds in his own right, subject to no superior nor to conditions.

FREE'HOLDER, one who owns an estate in fee-simple, fee-tail, or for life; the possessor of a freehold. In Scotland, a freeholder is a person holding of the crown or prince; but the title is, in modern language, applied to such as, before the passing of the reform act, were entitled to elect or be elected members of parliament, and who must have held lands, extending to a forty shilling land of old extent, or to £400 Scots of valued rent.

FREE'MAN, in ancient law, one free from servitude, as distinguished from a vassal or bondsman. In Great Britain, a freeman is one who enjoys the freedom of a city or borough.

FREEMA'SONRY, a term applied to the organization of a society calling themselves free and accepted masons, and all the mysteries therewith connected. This society, if we can reckon as one a number of societies, many of which are unconnected with each other, though they have the same origin, and a great similarity in their constitution, extends over almost all the countries of Europe, many parts of America, and some other parts of the globe. According to its own peculiar language, it is founded on the practise of social and moral virtue. It claims the character of charity, in the most extended sense; and brotherly love, relief, and truth are inculcated in it The first societies of antiquity with which *free masonry* appears to stand in historical connection, are the corporations of architects, which, with the Romans, existed under the names of Collegia and Corpora, first established in the time of Numa. Our distinct historical information on the subject merely amounts to this, that the fraternity of architects or builders in the middle ages extended over all Catholic countries, and was especially patronized by the see of Rome. It is to this craft that we owe the magnificent Gothic edifices dedicated to religion, which contrast so strongly with the barbarous efforts of those ages in most other departments of art. It is said that this association was introduced into Scotland in the 13th century, and about the same time into England, it being ascertained that the Abbey of Kilwinning in the former country was raised by this fraternity; and it is believed to have continued to exist, although small in number, in these two countries after it had disappeared from the Continent. The Kilwinning and York lodges are respectively the most ancient in either country. But the mode and period in which the association became changed from a mere professional fraternity to a society of persons of all descriptions connected by secret symbols, is unknown. It certainly excited great attention, and numbered individuals of high rank as honorary members, as early as the 15th century. The Scottish masons appointed St. Clair of Roslin as their hereditary grand-master in 1630; and the office was resigned by his descendant in 1736, when the grand lodge of Scotland was instituted. In 1725, the first French lodge was established; in 1730, the first American; in 1735, the first German. Pope Clement XII. excommunicated the freemasons in Spain and Portugal: until recent events, their name was synonymous with that of deists and revolutionists. But the most singular chapter in the history of the society relates to its fortunes in America; where it has given origin to two political parties. The story of the abduction and murder of William Morgan, suspected of having revealed the secrets of the fraternity, made a great sensation in the Union, and is not cleared up at this day.

FREE-THINK'ER, a term applied to those who reject the ordinary modes of thinking in matters of religion. It is almost synonymous with *deist*. *Free-thinking*, in England, first appeared in the form of opposition to abuses in the church, which were attacked in the reign of James II. and William III.

FREIGHT, in navigation and commerce, the hire of a ship, or a part thereof, for the conveyance and carriage of goods from one place to another; or the sum agreed on between the owner and the merchant, for the hire and use of a vessel. In a more extended sense, it means the burden of such ship.

FRENCH-HORN', a musical wind instrument made of copper. It possesses a range of three octaves, and is capable of producing tones of great sweetness.

FRES'CO PAINT'ING, a method of painting by incorporating the colors with plaster before it is dry, by which it becomes as permanent as the wall itself. This method of painting is executed with mineral and earthy pigments upon a freshly laid stucco ground of lime or gypsum. Vegetable pigments cannot be used for fresco-painting even when mixed with mineral pigments; and of the latter, only those are available which resist the chemical action of the lime. Burnt pigments are the best for this style of painting; they are generally ground with clean water, and rendered so thin, that they can be worked with the brush; to some are added lime, milk, &c. The pigments unite with the lime or gypsum ground, and are therefore extremely durable; but as this ground, after standing a night, is unfit for painting on, there must be only a sufficient quantity for one day prepared. Fresco-painting is therefore difficult, as it cannot be retouched. This art, which is employed generally for large pictures on walls and ceilings, was understood by the ancients, but first made of real importance by the Italians in the sixteenth century.

FRET, in architecture, an ornament consisting of two lists or small fillets variously interlaced or interwoven, and running at parallel distances equal to their breadth.—*Fret-work* is sometimes used to fill up and enrich flat empty spaces, but is mostly practised in roofs, which are fretted over with plaster-work. —*Frets*, in music, certain short pieces of wire fixed on the finger-boards of guitars, &c. at right angles to the strings, and which, as the strings are brought into contact with them by the pressure of the fingers, serve to vary and determine the pitch of the tones. Formerly, these frets or stops consisted of strings tied round the neck of the instrument.

FRIAR, (from the French *frere*, a brother,) a term common to monks of all orders; there being a kind of fraternity, or brotherhood, between the several religious persons of the same monastery. Friars are generally distinguished into four principal branches, viz., 1. Minors, gray friars, or Franciscans; 2. Augustines; 3. Dominicans, or black friars; 4. White friars, or Carmelites.

FRI DAY, the sixth day of the week, so called from Frea, or Friga, a goddess worshipped by the Saxons on this day.

FRIEND'SHIP, a noble and virtuous attachment between individuals, springing from a pure source; this is *true* friendship. *False* friendship may subsist between bad men, as between thieves—a temporary attachment springing from interest, which may change in a moment to enmity and rancor.

FRIEZE, in architecture, the member in the entablature of an order between the architrave and the cornice. It is always plain in the Tuscan; ornamented with triglyphs and sculpture in the Doric; in the Ionic it is occasionally, in modern or Italian architecture, swelled; in which case it is called a *pulvinated* or *cushioned* frieze; and in the Corinthian and Composite it is variously decorated, according to the taste of the architect.

FRIG'ATE, a ship of war, light built, and a good sailer. Frigates have two decks, and generally mount from twenty to forty-four guns.

FRIGATOON', a Venetian vessel built with a square stern, without any foremast; it is used in the Adriatic.

FRONDE', WAR OF THE, that maintained by the malcontent partisans of the parliament in France, under the regency of Louis XIV., against the government of Cardinal Mazarin. The name of Fronde (*sling*) was given to this war in consequence of some incidents of a street quarrel, which have been differently represented. The party opposed to government was called that of the Fronde; and the word Frondeurs has hence acquired in the French language the signification of discontented politicians.

FRON'TAL, in architecture, a little pediment or front-piece over a small door or window.—*Frontal*, the hangings or ornamental panel in front of an altar, were of three kinds: 1st, of precious metals, adorned with enamels and jewels; 2d, of wood, painted, gilt, embossed, and often set with crystals; 3d, of cloth of gold, velvet, or silk embroidered, and occasionally enriched with pearls.

FRONTIER', the border, confine or extreme part of a kingdom or province, bordering on another country. Frontiers were anciently called marches.

FRON'TISPIECE, in architecture, the face or fore front of a house; but more usually applied to the decorated entrance of a building.—This term is also used for the ornamental first page of a book, being, as the derivation imports, that part which first meets the eye.

FRUIT-PAINTING, may be considered to have originated with Zeuxis, who painted a bunch of grapes so naturally that the birds came and pecked at them. Since the introduction in modern times of pictures of *still life*, fruit and flower-painting has become a distinct branch of art, cultivated principally in the Netherlands.

FRUIT-WORK, this branch of art attained some excellence in antiquity, although used only for architectural ornaments. Workers in clay and bronze also imitated fruits, and in the time of Marcus Varro, there lived at Rome a clay-modeller who imitated apples and grapes so exactly, that at first sight they were not to be distinguished from nature. Festoons of fruit were also carved in stone for the decoration of temples. The most celebrated specimen in bronze is a colossal pine-apple, formerly on the tomb of the Emperor Hadrian, but now in the great Bramanhe niche, at the end of the garden of the Belvedere at Rome. We find the capitals and friezes of buildings of the middle ages, carved with grapes, and in the age of the *Renaissance* we meet with festoons of fruits, which afterwards, in the age of *Rococo*, were employed too frequently in decoration. At Florence, beautiful imitations of richly colored fruits, such as purple grapes, &c., were made in *Pietra dura*, or Florentine Mosaic.

FU'GITIVE, in literature, short and occasional compositions either in poetry or prose; written in haste or at intervals, and considered to be fleeting and temporary.

FU'GLEMAN, or FLU'GELMAN, a non-commissioned officer, appointed to take his place in front of a regiment as a guide to the soldiers in their movements of the drill. The word is derived from the German flügel, *a wing*.

FU'GUE, in music, a piece of composition in which the different parts follow each other, each repeating in order what the first had performed.

FUNC'TION, any office, duty, or employment belonging to a particular station or character; as the *functions* of a judge, a bishop, &c.—*Functions*, applied to the actions of the body, are divided into vital, animal and natural. The *vital* functions are those necessary to life, and without which the individual cannot subsist; as the motion of the heart, lungs, &c. The *natural* functions are such as we cannot subsist any considerable time without; as the digestion of the aliment, and its conversion into blood. Under animal functions are included the senses of touching, tasting, &c., memory, judgment, and voluntary motion, without which an animal may be said to exist, though under great privations. In short, all parts of the body have their own functions, or actions, peculiar to themselves. Life consists in the exercise of these functions, and health in the free exercise of them.

FUNDS, a term adopted by those who speak of the public revenue of nations, to signify the several taxes that have been laid upon commodities, either by way of duties of custom, or excise, or in any other manner, to supply the exigencies of the state, and to pay interest for what sums it may have occasion to borrow.—The capital stock of a banking institution, or the joint stock of a commercial or manufacturing house, constitutes its *funds;* and hence the word is applied to the money which an individual may possess, or the means he can employ for carrying on any enterprise or operation.—The *Funding system* commenced in England shortly after the Revolution of 1688, and as the sums were at first borrowed for short periods, and partially repaid, the first transaction which assumed the character of a permanent loan was when, at the establishment of the Bank of England, in 1693, its capital, then amounting to 1,200,000*l.*, was advanced to the government.—A *sinking fund* is a sum of money appropriated to the payment of the public stock, or the payment of the public debt.

FU'NERAL GAMES, the celebration of these games among the Greeks, mostly consisted of horse-races; the prizes were of different sorts and value, according to the quality and magnificence of the person that celebrated them. The garlands, given to victors on this occasion, were usually of parsley, which was thought to have some particular relation to the dead. Among the Romans, the funeral games consisted chiefly of processions; but sometimes also of mortal combats of gladiators, around the funeral pile.

FU'NERAL PALLS, the palls in ancient use, especially at the funerals of persons of distinction, were of the most costly materials and beautifully ornamented, being constructed of velvet or cloth of gold, embroidered with heraldic devices and imagery. The form was usually square, sometimes with lappets, with a cross extending the whole length and width, formed of a different material from the pall itself, and generally enriched with ornaments or appropriate inscriptions. The color of the palls varied at different periods. In the sixteenth century, and perhaps earlier, black was used; they were frequently made of red, purple, green and blue velvet, or cloth of gold, with reference to the heraldic tinctures that were peculiar to the deceased.

FU'NERAL RITES, ceremonies accompanying the interment or burial of any person. These rites differed among the ancients according to the different genius and religion of each country. The ancient Christians testified their abhorrence of the pagan custom of burning the dead, and always deposited the body entire in the ground; and it was usual to bestow the honor of embalming upon the martyrs, at least, if not upon others.

FU'RIES, in mythology, called by the Greeks Erinnyes and Eumenides, were the avenging deities, who punished gods and men for their transgressions against those whom they were bound to esteem and reverence. Their number was not fixed, though sometimes they were considered to be three sisters. The Athenians, who, according to Plutarch, were particularly addicted to this art of *euphemism*, called them also the *venerable goddesses*, their true names being considered ominous. By this name they were mentioned in the oaths taken at the Areopagus.

FUR'LOUGH, leave granted to a non-commissioned officer or soldier to be absent for a given time from his regiment.

FUSILEER', a soldier belonging to what is termed the light infantry: they were formerly armed with a *fusil;* but they are not now so distinguished, their muskets being like the rest.

FUS'TIAN, in literature, an inflated style of writing, in which high-sounding and bombastic terms are used, instead of such as are natural, simple, and suited to the subject.

FYL'FOT, a cross of peculiar form, frequently introduced in decoration and embroidery during the middle ages. It occurs on monumental brasses anterior to the accession of Richard II., being found on the girdle of a priest of the date A.D. 1011. It is considered to have been in use at a very remote period as a mystic symbol amongst religious devotees in India and China, whence it was introduced into Europe about the sixth century.

G.

G, the seventh letter in the English alphabet; but in the Greek, and all the oriental languages, it occupies the third place. It is a mute, and cannot be sounded without the assistance of a vowel. It has a hard and a soft sound, as in *game*, and *gesture;* and in many words, as in *sign*, *reign*, &c., the sound is not perceived. As a numeral it formerly stood for 400, and with a dash over it, for 400,000.—G, in music, is the nominal of the fifth note in the natural diatonic scale of C, and to which Guido applied the monosyllable *sol*. It is also one of the names of the highest cliff.

GA'BIONS, in fortification, baskets made of osier-twigs, of a cylindrical form, six feet high, and four wide; which, being filled with earth, serve as a shelter from the enemy's fire.

GA'BLE, in architecture, the vertical triangular piece of wall at the end of the roof, from the level of the eaves to the summit.

GA'BRIEL, ST., one of the three archangels, the "messenger;" the "angel of the annunciation;" in pictures representing this mystery, he is frequently represented in royal robes, bearing a sceptre, or a lily, and kneeling. In some instances, he is represented floating in the air, with his hands crossed over his breast.

GADS, or GADLYNGS, in armor, are the bosses or small spikes of steel with which the knuckles were armed. The gads of the gauntlets of Edward the Black Prince are of brass, and made in the shape of lions or leopards.

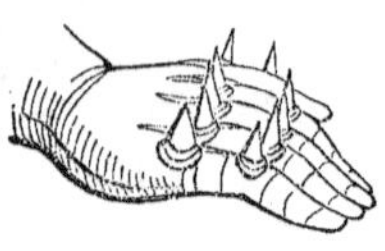

GAE'LIC, is the name of that dialect in the ancient Celtic language, which is spoken in the Highlands of Scotland. It is a generally received opinion, that the Celtic, at the time of the Roman invasion, was universally spoken over the west of Europe; for, although divided into a variety of dialects, yet they all show the clearest proofs of a common origin. The Gaelic, which, from a variety of causes, has retained much of its original purity, is bold, expressive, and copious. It derives no assistance from the languages either of Greece or Rome, from which it differs in its structure and formation. More than two thirds of the names of places in Great Britain and Ireland are of Celtic origin, which, if other proofs were wanting, would establish the fact of its once having been the language of the country.—*See* ERSE.

GAIL'LIARDE, an ancient Italian dance, of a sportive character and lively movement. It was sometimes called *Romanesque*, because it was said to have come originally from Rome.

GAL'AXY, in astronomy, the *Via Lactea*, or *Milky Way;* a long, white, luminous track, which seems to encompass the heavens like a girdle; forming nearly a great circle of the celestial sphere. This, like every other phenomenon of nature, has supplied the poet with many a fantastic, and many a beautiful dream. The invention of the telescope has confirmed the conjecture of science, that it consists in a multitude of stars, too remote to be separately distinguished by the naked eye.

GALL, the gall of the ox is used in water-color painting, mixed with the pigments to make them flow freely upon paper which has a greasiness of surface. To fit it for this purpose, the gall is strained and exposed to a gentle heat until nearly solidified; it is then of a dark olive-brown color, scarcely fit to mix with the pure blue or red pigments. Colorless ox-gall should be prepared by boiling the crude gall with animal charcoal, and filtering the liquid.

GAL'LEON, vessels of war formerly used by the Spaniards and Portuguese. In more recent times, those vessels were called *galleons*, in which the Spaniards transported treasures from their American colonies.

GAL'LERY, in architecture, a long, narrow room, the width of which is at least three times less than its length; by which proportion it is distinguished from a *saloon*. Corridors are sometimes also called *galleries*.—*Gallery*, in fortification, a covered walk across a ditch in a besieged town, made of strong planks and covered with earth. It was formerly used for carrying a mine to the foot of the ramparts.—*Gallery*, (*of a mine*,) a narrow passage, or branch of a mine carried on underground to a work designed to be blown up.—*Gallery*, (*in a ship*,) a balcony, projecting from the stern of a ship of war, or of a large merchantman.—*Gallery*, in the Fine Arts, a term applied to a collection of works in painting or sculpture. The earliest gallery of which there is any record was that of Verres. It is described by Cicero, and was rich in pictures as well as sculpture. In Europe, at the present day, the gallery of the Louvre, though much reduced in 1815 by the restoration of many works of art which conquest had enabled the French to acquire, is the finest in Europe, if taken as a whole. That founded at Florence by Cosmo II. long enjoyed the first rank, but must be now considered secondary to the French collection. The other principal galleries of Europe are those at Munich, Dresden, Berlin, and, though last not least both in size and importance, that of the Vatican at Rome; which, however, is more generally called the Museum of the Vatican.

GAL'LEY, a naval vessel of large size, long and narrow, usually propelled by oars, with occasionally the addition of sails. Most of the ships employed by the ancients may be termed galleys, and according to the number of banks of rowers were *biremes* when with two banks, *triremes* when with three, and so on, up to as many as forty, but those with more than four or five banks must be regarded as curiosities. Galleys were in use in the Mediterranean until the close of the eighteenth century, for coast navigation, the largest of which were about 160 feet long and 30 feet wide, with 52 oars. Among the Venetians there was in use a kind of large galley, with a very lofty poop, called *galeazza*. The state galley of the Doges was termed BUCENTAUR.—The punishment of the *galleys*,

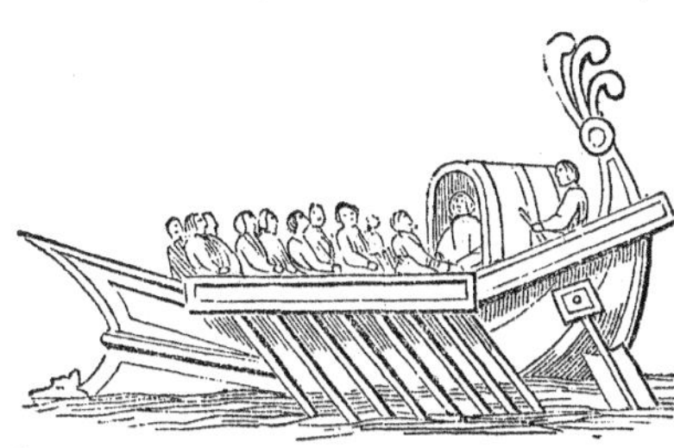

i. e. the employment of condemned criminals in the toilsome employment of rowing them, is said to have originated under the Greek empire; as well as the name Γαλκαροι, or galley slaves—in French galériens. It was used by all the nations bordering on the Mediterranean. In France, under the old jurisprudence, the punishment of the galleys was the severest after that of death. About the end of the reign of Louis XIV., when galleys themselves began to be disused, the galley slaves were employed in hospitals, public works, &c.: and the name of the punishment was changed by the constituent assembly (1798) to *travaux forcés*, compulsory labor, whence the word *forçat* for a criminal so condemned. Under the code of the empire the punishment was accompanied with forfeiture of property, infamy, and branding. By an alteration of the law effected in 1832, the brand was abolished; and the criminals, who had hitherto been intermingled in the three penal fortresses (Toulon, Rochefort, and Brest,) were classified. Toulon was appropriated to those condemned for 10 years and under; Brest, to those from 10 to 20; Rochefort, to the condemned for life.

GAL'LI, the priests of Cybele were so named at Rome from the country (Galatia or Gallo-Græcia) in which Pessinus, the head-quarters of her worship, was situated: also termed Curetes, Corybantes, and Idæi Dactyli. Cybele, the mother of the gods, was introduced to Rome from Asia on the occasion of a pestilence by the advice of the Sybilline oracles, and her worship became in time one of the most popular in the city.

GAL'LICAN, anything belonging to France: thus the term gallican church denotes the church of France, or the assembly of the clergy of that kingdom.

GAL'LICISM, an idiom or phrase of the French language, introduced in speaking or writing another language.

GAL'LIOT, a small galley or Dutch vessel, carrying a main and mizenmast, and a large gaff-mainsail; built very slightly, and designed only for chase. It can both sail and row, and has sixteen or twenty oars. All the seamen on board are soldiers, and each has a musket by him on quitting his oar.

GALLOPADE', in the manege, a sidelong or curveting kind of gallop. Also the term for a sprightly and active kind of dance.

GALL-STONE, a concretion found in the gall-bladder of the ox, which is employed as a pigment in water-color painting. It yields a fine golden-yellow color, similar to Indian yellow. It is not permanent.

GAL'LY, in printing, a wooden or metal frame, into which the compositor empties the lines out of his *composing-stick*, and in which he ties up the page when it is completed.

GAL'VANISM, electrical phenomena, in which the electricity is developed without the aid of friction, and in which a chemical action takes place between certain bodies. It includes all those electrical phenomena arising from the chemical agency of certain metals with different fluids. Volta discovered the means of multiplying those effects; hence the science has also been called *voltaism*, or *voltaic electricity*; and, from its action on the muscles of animals newly killed, *animal electricity*. The galvanic battery or pile, is an instrument of vast power, and admits of extensive application in the wide field of chemical research, and accordingly the acquisition of it has led to important discoveries. The electricity produced by the galvanic battery is much less intense than that produced by an ordinary electrical machine, but it possesses this great advantage, that its action may be kept up for any length of time, in a continuous manner; whereas, in a highly charged electric battery, the whole of the electric power is expended as soon as the circuit is completed. The effects of galvanism may be distinguished into the three classes of physiological, chemical, and physical. With respect to the physiological effects, we may refer to the marvellous cures said to have been effected by currents of electricity—to the facts recorded of animals recently killed, exhibiting many of the signs of life, so long as they are placed between the poles of the pile. Animals stupefied by breathing the fumes of charcoal, may be brought at once to life by placing them between the poles of the pile. Among the chemical effects produced by the galvanic pile, the decomposition of water, of oxydes, and the alkalies, are the most remarkable. Among the physical effects we may remark the production of heat, light and magnetism. This last effect, and the mutual action which the currents exert on each other, constitutes the science of electro-magnetism. Galvanism is heat, light, electricity, and magnetism, united in combination or in simultaneous action; sometimes one and sometimes another of them predominating, and thus producing more or less all the effects of each—usual means of excitement, contact of dissimilar bodies, especially of metals and fluids.

GALVANOG'RAPHY, ELECTROGRAPHY, this is one of the most beautiful and successful inventions of modern times, as by its means plastic objects, *e. g.*, wood, stone, coins, plaster casts, &c., and copper plates for engravings, may be exactly copied in copper, and bronzed or gilt. The invention is especially valuable for copper-plate engraving, as by its means any number of duplicates of the original plate may be obtained. Galvanography, after many experiments, has produced works of Art far surpassing the expectations at first entertained, and the uses to which it may be applied are multifarious, for since the first galvanic plate was taken, it has been used in all branches of engraving, having been found to unite all the known methods of the graver and etching needle, aqua tinta, scraper, and roulette work, &c., and, moreover, is very easy of execution.

GAMBE'SON, or WAMBEYS, in armor, a body-covering stuffed with wool and padded in parallel lines of needle-work.

GAM'BOGE, a gum-resin brought from the East, which yields a fine yellow pigment, very useful in water-color painting. The finest quality is the *pipe-gamboge*, brought from Siam. It dissolves readily in water, is very transparent and glossy when dry. It is indispensable in water colors, forming, with the various blues, excellent compound greens. This pigment would be useful in oil painting, as it resists for a long time the action of strong light, provided the resinous part could be separated from the other parts.

GAME, all sorts of birds and beasts that are objects of the chase.—*Game laws.* In England, laws have been enacted to secure to certain privileged classes the right of hunting and shooting wild birds and animals, and preventing their being destroyed or sold in the market; and it is believed that nothing has been so fertile a source of crime, among the lower orders, as these enactments.

GAMES, in antiquity, were public diversions, or contests, exhibited on certain occasions, as spectacles for the gratification of the people. Such, among the Greeks, were the Olympic, Pythian, Isthmian, and Nemæan games; and, among the Romans, the Apollinarian, Circensian, Capitoline, &c. The Romans had three sorts of games, viz., sacred, honorary, and ludicrous. The first were instituted in honor of some deity or hero; the second were those exhibited by private persons, to please the people; as the combats of gladiators, the scenic games, and other amphitheatrical sports. The ludicrous games were much of the same nature with the games of exercise and hazard among us; such were the *ludus Trojanus, tesseræ*, &c. By a decree of the Roman senate, it was enacted that the public games should be consecrated, and united with the worship of the gods as a part thereof: whence it appears, that feasts, sacrifices, and games, made up the greatest part, or rather the whole, of the external worship offered by the Romans to their deities.

GAM'UT, or GAM'MA UT, in music, a scale whereon the musical notes are disposed in their several orders, and marked by the monosyllables ut, re, mi, fa, sol, la. Its invention is attributed to Guido Aretino, a monk of Tuscany; it is also called the harmonical hand, from Guido having made use of the figure of the hand to demonstrate the progression of his sounds.

GANT'LET, or GAUNT'LET, a large kind of glove, made of iron, and the fingers covered with small plates, formerly worn by cavaliers, armed at all points.—*To throw the gantlet*, is a proverbial phrase, signifying to challenge or defy. The expression derives its origin from the days of chivalry, when he that challenged an opponent in the lists threw down his glove, and he that accepted the challenge took it up.

GANT'LOPE, or GANT'LET, in military affairs, an old punishment in which the criminal, running between the ranks, received a lash from every man. A similar punishment is used on board of ships; but it is seldom inflicted, except for such crimes as are calculated to excite general antipathy among the seamen.

GAN'YMEDE, great-grandson of Dardanus, who founded the city of Troy, son of Tros and of Callirrhoe, a daughter of the Scamander. Jupiter, in the shape of an eagle, carried him off from Mount Ida to the seat of the gods, where he discharged the office of cup-bearer to the immortals, Hebe having rendered herself unworthy of this office. This fiction has afforded, both to poets and artists, an inexhaustible supply of subjects. Numerous paintings, statues, cameos, and intaglios, master-works of ancient Art, have descended to us, upon which this youth, scarcely passed the years of boyhood, is represented as of great beauty. The representations of Ganymede are to be recognized by the Phrygian cap, and the eagle, which is either standing beside him, or carrying him in its talons to Olympus.

GAOL DELIV'ERY, a term in law for the clearing of a prison by a judicial condemnation or acquittal of the prisoners; also a commission from the king to deliver or clear the gaols.

GARD DE BRAS, in armor, the plate attached to the cuff of the gantlet or the coudiere.

GAR'DENING, that branch of cultivation which teaches us how to dispose fruit-trees, flowers, and herbs, to the best advantage, whether for profit or pleasure; and directs us how to prepare the soil for sowing the different kinds of seeds, as well as how to treat the plants, during their various stages of vegetation, till they repay our care by the produce they yield when arrived at maturity. The art embraces the following heads: Horticulture, which comprehends the culture of culinary vegetables and fruits; floriculture, which includes the culture of ornamental and curious flowers, shrubs, and trees; aboriculture, which implies the culture of trees or shrubs used for various purposes in the arts and in general economy; and landscape gardening, or the general disposition of the scenery or landscape about a country residence. Horticulture includes the culture of the kitchen garden and orchard; floriculture, the culture of flower gardens, botanic gardens, shrubberies, and pleasure-grounds; aboriculture, the culture of nurseries for fruit and forest trees and shrubs; and landscape gardening, the formation and management of lawns, roads, walks, lakes, ponds, and artificial rivers, of rock work, and of every description of objects in artificial scenery which come under the denomination of ornamental or picturesque.

GARGOYLE', this term is derived from the French *gargouille*, a dragon or monster. It is applied to the spouts in the form of dragons that project from the roof-gutters in ancient buildings.

GAR'LANDS, of various descriptions, are used in the ceremonies, &c., of the Catholic Church. 1. Of flowers, suspended over altars, and in churches on festival days. 2. Of roses, and other flowers, worn round the heads of the assistant clergy and others in certain processions. 3. Of silver, set with jewels, or of natural flowers, and placed on images. 4. Of artificial flowers and other ornaments carried at the funerals of virgins.

GAR'NISHMENT, in law, a warning or notice given to a party to appear in court or give information; a technical term, used only in one or two instances.

GAR'RISON, a body of forces disposed in a fortress to defend it against the enemy, or to keep the inhabitants of the town where it is situated in subjection. The term *garrison* is sometimes used synonymously with *winter quarters*, viz. a place where a number of troops are laid up in the winter season without keeping the regular guard.

GARROTE', THE, a mode of capital punishment employed in Spain. The criminal is seated on a stool with his back to a stake. A tight collar is passed round his throat, of which the ends nearly meet; the executioner standing behind him, twists them closer by means of a screw: the death is instantaneous.

GAR'TER, ORDER OF THE, a military order of knighthood, said to have been first instituted by Richard I. at the siege of Acre, where he caused twenty-six knights, who firmly stood by him, to wear thongs of blue leather about their legs. It is also understood to have been perfected by Edward III., and to have received some alterations, which were afterwards laid aside, from Edward VI.; but the number of knights remained as at first established, till the year 1786, when it was increased to thirty-two. This order is never conferred but upon persons of the highest rank. The habit and ensigns of this order are the garter. mantle, cap and collar The badge of the order is the image of Saint George, called the George; and the motto is *Honi soit qui mal y pense*, or "Evil to him that evil thinks hereof." A vulgar story (says Hume) prevails, but it is not supported by any ancient authority, that, at a court ball, Edward the Third's mistress, commonly supposed to be the Countess of Salisbury, dropped her garter; and the king, taking it up, observed some of the courtiers to smile, as if they thought he had not obtained this favor by accident; upon which he called out *Honi soit qui mal y pense.*

GAS'TROMANCY, a kind of divination practised among the ancients by means of words issuing or seeming to issue from the belly. This term is applied also to a species of divination performed by means of glasses or other round transparent vessels, in the centre of which certain figures appear by magic art.

GASTRON'OMY, the science of eating and drinking. The gastronomy of the Romans was the most gross and luxurious, as that of the French is the most refined and delicate, combined with the rules of health and social merriment.

GAUZE, a very thin, slight, transparent kind of stuff, woven sometimes of silk, and sometimes only of thread; and frequently with flowers of silver or gold on a silk ground. It is said to have been invented in Gaza, a city of Palestine.

GAV'EL-KIND, a tenure in England, by which land descended from the father to all his sons in equal portions, and the land of a brother, dying without issue, descended equally to his brothers. This species of tenure prevailed in England before the Norman conquest, in many parts of the kingdom, perhaps in the whole realm; but particularly in Kent, where it still exists.

GA'VOT, in music, an air for a dance, which has two strains; the first having usually four or eight bars, and the second eight or twelve more, each of which are played twice over. It is of a brisk nature.

GAZETTE', a periodical paper, published at short intervals, containing articles of general intelligence. In Europe such sheets were generally termed *Mercuries* in the first times of their invention, and appeared only occasionally; the earliest were published during the general apprehensions from the presence of the Spanish armada, but some doubt has been lately thrown on the authenticity of the specimens preserved in the British Museum. The first gazette produced in France (under that title) was in 1631: the first in England in 1665, when the court resided at Oxford on account of the plague in London. From that period the Gazette has regularly appeared twice a week, containing such notifications as are either published by the court or the government, or such as are authoritatively required by law in private transactions The name Gazette is said to be derived from Gazetta, a small Venetian coin, being the price that was paid for one of the flying sheets of commercial and military information (notizie scritte,) which were first published by that republic in 1563.

GAZETTEER', a topographical work, alphabetically arranged, containing a brief description of empires, kingdoms, cities, towns, and rivers. It may either include the whole world, or be limited to a particular country. The first work of this kind, with which we are acquainted, is that of Stephen of Byzantium, who lived in the beginning of the sixth century.

GAZONS', in fortification, pieces of fresh earth, covered with grass, and cut in form of a wedge, to line the outsides of works made of earth, as ramparts, parapets, &c.

GEHEN'NA, a term in Scripture, adopted from the usage of the Jews to signify hell or the place of eternal punishment. The word is a slight corruption of Gehinnon, or the Valley of Hinnom in the neighborhood of Jerusalem, wherein, at a place named Tophet, it was recorded that certain idolatrous Jews had sacrificed to Moloch. The sewers of the city were emptied into this hollow, and perpetual fires were kept up to consume the noxious matter, and prevent pestilential effluvia. Hence, it is said, the name of the place came to be used metaphorically in the sense above described. From this word seems to be derived the old French gehenne, *torture;* and from thence the common word gêne, *constraint.*

GELOS'COPY, a kind of divination drawn from laughter; or a method of knowing the qualities and character of a person, acquired from the consideration of his laughter.

GEMAR'A, the second part of the Talmud or commentary on the Jewish laws.

GEMO'NIÆ SCA'LÆ, in Roman antiquity, a place for executing criminals, situated on the Aventine mount, or tenth region of the city.

GEMS, the name given to *precious stones* in general, but more especially to such as by their color, brilliancy, polish, purity, and rarity, are sought after as objects of decoration. Gems of the most valuable kinds form the principal part of the crown jewels of sovereign princes, and are esteemed not merely for their beauty, but as comprising the greatest value in the smallest bulk. Gems are remarkable for their hardness and internal lustre. Under this name are comprehended the diamond, ruby, sapphire, hyacinth, beryl, garnet, emerald, topaz, chrysolite, &c. To these have been added rock crystals, the finer flints of pebbles, the cat's eye, the oculus mundi, the chalcedony, the moon-stones, the onyx, the cornelian, the sardonyx, agate, &c. Of most of these species there are some of an inferior class and beauty; these are commonly called by jewellers *occidental stones*. They are mostly the produce of Europe, and found in mines or stone quarries; and are so named in opposition to those of a higher class, which are always accounted *oriental*, and supposed to be only produced in the east.—*Gem-engraving*, or *gem-sculpture*, called also *lithoglyptics*, is the art of representing designs upon precious stones, either in raised work, as *cameos*, or by figures cut below the surface, as *intaglios*. This art is of great antiquity, and was probably practised by the Babylonians. Some think the art originated in India; but wherever it originated, we have ample evidence that among the Greeks and Romans it was in high esteem. The merit of cameos and intaglios depends on their erudition, as it is termed, or the goodness of the workmanship, and the beauty of their polish. The antique Greek gems are the most highly prized; and, next to them, the Roman ones of the times of the higher empire.—*Artificial gems*. In order to approximate as near as possible to the brilliancy and refractive power of native gems, a basis, called a *paste*, is made from the finest flint glass, composed of selected materials, combined in different proportions, according to the preference of the manufacturer. This is mixed with metallic oxydes capable of producing the desired color.—The *imitation of antique gems* consists in a method of taking the impressions and figures of antique gems, with their engravings, in glass, of the color of the original gems. Great care is necessary in the operation, to take the impression of the gem in a very fine earth, and to press down upon this a piece of proper glass, softened or half melted at the fire, so that the figures of the impression made in the earth may be nicely and perfectly expressed upon the glass.

GENDARMES', or GENS D'ARMES, in the history of France, an appellation given to a select body of troops, who were destined to watch over the interior public safety, and consequently much employed by the police. They were so called on account of their succeeding the ancient gendarmes, who were completely clothed in armor, and commanded by captain-lieutenants, the king and the princes of the blood being their captains. At the revolution this body was broken up, and the name was given to a corps which was employed in the protection of the streets. August 16th, 1830, a royal ordinance abolished the *gens d'armes*, and established a new body called the *municipal guard* of Paris, to consist of 1443 men, under the direction of the prefect of police.

GEN'DER, in grammar, a distinction in nouns to mark the sexes; genders are either masculine, for the male sex; feminine, for the female sex; or neuter, for those which are of neither sex. The English language has very few terminations by which the genders are distinguished, such as *count* and *countess*, but generally supplies distinct words; as *boy*, *girl;* whereas, in the Latin and French, the terminations always mark the distinction, as *bonus equus*, a good horse; *bona equa*, a good mare; *un bon citoyen* a good citizen; *une bonne citoyenne*, a good female citizen.

GENEAL'OGY, a history of the descent of a person or family from a series of ancestors. In various chapters and military orders, it is required that the candidates produce their genealogy, to show that they are noble by so many descents.—The Jews were anxious to preserve their genealogies entire and uninterrupted; and this care on their part affords an argument of considerable importance with respect to the accomplishment of those prophecies that pertain to the Messiah: accordingly, in their sacred writings, we find genealogies carried on for above 3500 years.

GEN'ERAL, in the army, is, next to field marshal, the highest military title adopted by the European states. Like most military designations, it owes its origin to the French, who, about the middle of the 15th century, conferred the title of lieutenant-general on the individual to whom the monarch (by virtue of his birth the commander or general of the national forces) intrusted the superintendence of the army. The title of general is conferred either on the commander-in-chief of the forces of a nation, or on the commander of an army or grand division; it is also given to the officers next in rank to the general, who, besides performing functions peculiar to their own offices, frequently act as the sub stitutes of their superior, with the designation of lieutenant-general and major-general.—A particular beat of drum which in the morning gives notice to the infantry to be in readiness to march, is also called the *general.*

GENERALIS'SIMO, a title conferred, especially by the French, on the commander-in-chief of an army consisting of two or more grand divisions, each under the superintendence of a general. According to Balzac, this dignity was first assumed by Cardinal Richelieu on the occasion of his leading the French army into Italy; but the term does not appear to have found favor among the other European states.

GENERALIZA'TION, in logic, has been defined as the act of comprehending under a common name several objects agreeing in some point which we abstract from each of them and which that common term serves to indicate.—Ex. Copernicus *generalized* the celestial motions, by merely referring them to the moon's motion. Newton generalized them still more, by referring this last to the motion of a stone through the air.

GEN'ERAL IS'SUE, in law, that plea which denies at once the whole declaration or indictment, without offering any special matter by which to evade it. This is the ordinary plea upon which most causes are tried, and is now almost invariably used in all criminal cases. It puts everything in issue, that is denies everything, and requires the party to prove all that he has stated In many cases, for the protection of justices, constables, excise officers, &c., they are allowed to plead the general issue, and give the special matter for their justification, under the act, in evidence.

GEN'ERATOR, in music, the principal sound or sounds by which others are produced. Thus the lowest C for the treble of the pianoforte, besides its octave, will strike an attentive ear with its twelfth above, or G in alt., and with its seventeenth above, or E in alt. Hence C is called their *generator*, the G and E its products or harmonics.

GENER'IC, or GENER'ICAL, an epithet pertaining to a genus or kind. It is a word used to signify all species of natural bodies, which agree in certain essential and peculiar characters, and therefore all of the same family or kind; so that the word used as the *generic* name, equally expresses every one of them, and some other words expressive of the peculiar qualities of figures of each are added, in order to denote them singly, and make up what is called the *specific* name. Thus the word *rosa*, or rose, is the generic name of the whole series of flowers of that kind, which are distinguished by the specific names of the red rose, the white rose, the moss rose, &c. Thus also we see *Canis* is the *generic* name of animals of the dog kind; *Felis*, of the cat kind; *Cervus*, of the deer kind, &c.

GEN'ESIS, a canonical book of the Old Testament, and the first of the Pentateuch, or five books of Moses. The Greeks gave it the name of Genesis, from its beginning with the history of the creation of the world. It includes the history of 2369 years, and besides the history of the creation, contains an account of the original innocence and fall of man; the propagation of mankind; the general defection and corruption of the world; the deluge; the restoration and re-peopling of the earth; and the history of the first patriarchs down to the death of Joseph.

GENETH'LIAC, an ode or other short poem composed in honor of the birth of an individual.

GE'NII, called by the Eastern nations Genn or Gien, are a race of beings created from fire, occupying an intermediate place between man and angels, and endowed with a corporeal form, which they are capable of metamorphosing at pleasure. They are said to have inhabited this earth many ages before the creation of man, and to have been at last driven thence for rebellious conduct against Allah. Their present place of abode is *Ginnistan*, the Persian Elysium; but they are represented as still interesting themselves deeply in the affairs of this earth, over which they exercise considerable influence. Every one is aware of the important part which the genii perform in the interesting stories of the East; and indeed a more correct idea may be formed of their origin, characteristics, and history, from a perusal of the *Arabian Nights' Entertainments*, than can be conveyed by the most elaborate dissertation.

GEN'ITIVE CASE, the second case in Latin and Greek nouns, which denote possession: it is marked in English by s with an apostrophe, thus ('s).

GE'NIUS, an aptitude for a particular pursuit, founded on some stimulus in youth, by which the mind and faculties are directed to excellence. It combines opposite intellectual qualities; the deepest penetration with the liveliest fancy; the greatest quickness with the most indefatigable diligence. To what is old it gives a new form; or it invents new; and its own productions are altogether original. We estimate it higher than *talent*, in the common acceptation of that term, which in the capacity for originating in extent and energy is inferior to *genius*. Where ordinary powers advance by slow degrees, genius soars on rapid wings. But genius does not assume its distinctive character in every exercise of its powers. A gifted poet, for instance, is not necessarily an ingenious philosopher, nor does the statesman's genius include that of the soldier. We distinguish this genius, therefore, into various kinds, as poetical, musical, mathematical, military, &c.; thus, for example, Milton possessed a genius for poetry, Mozart for music, Newton for mathematics, &c. Yet, although the union of great excellence in different walks of art and science is but rarely found in one man, some, like Michael Angelo, who was equally celebrated as a statuary, architect, and painter, are found possessing genius of a most comprehensive character.—By the ancients the word *genius* was used to express a supposed invisible spirit which directs a course of events. According to the belief of the Romans, every person had his own genius, that is, a spiritual being, which introduced him into life, accompanied him during the course of it, and again conducted him out of it at the close of his career. This belief was no doubt a consequence of their idea of a divine spirit pervading the whole physical world; and was probably a personification of the particular structure or bent of mind which a man receives from nature. The guardian spirit of a person (a purely Italian idea, which in modern language has been wrongfully transferred to Grecian Art,) is generally represented as a veiled figure in a toga, holding a patera and cornucopia, or as a beautiful youth, nude or nearly so, with the wings of a bird on his shoulders. The guardian spirits of the female sex, junones, are represented as young maidens with the wings of a butterfly or a moth, and draped. The Romans also gave a genius to edifices, towns, armies, and kingdoms. The Roman genius of a place was depicted as a serpent devouring fruits, which lay before it; there are, however, many exceptions to these rules. The modern world comprises under the term genii, the angels or messengers of heaven, and those emblematical figures, which, as everything was personified in ancient Art, are regarded as the deification of ideas. The most common idea of Christian genii are the patron angel of childhood and of youth, the angel of baptism, those of poverty and mercy, of religion and virtue, and the genii of the three Christian graces, faith, hope, and charity. In modern times we find the genii of countries often personified: the greatest work of this kind is the genius of Bavaria, a bronze female statue of colossal size by Schwanthaler, recently completed and placed in front of the *Walhalla*, near Munich. Modern representations of river gods are only to be regarded as genii when they are executed in the romantic and not in the antique style.

GENS, in ancient history, a clan or sect, forming a subdivision of the Roman people next in order to the curia or tribe. The members and houses composing one of these clans were not necessarily united by ties of blood, but were originally brought together by a political distribution of the citizens, and bound by religious rites, and a common name, derived probably from some ancient hero.

GEN'TILES, a name given by the Jews to all who were not of the twelve tribes of Israel. Among Christians, it is the name of all heathens who did not embrace the Christian faith.

GEN'TLEMAN, in the modern languages of western Europe, we generally find a word to signify a person distinguished by his standing from the laboring classes, *gentiluomo*, *gentilhomme*, *hidalgo*, &c. In the German language, the term which most nearly expresses the same idea, is *gebildet*, which includes not only gentlemanly manners, but also a cultivated mind. The English law-books say, that, under the denomination of *gentlemen*, are comprised all above yeomen; so that noblemen are truly called *gentlemen;* and further, that a *gentleman*, in England, is generally defined to be one, who, without any title, bears a coat of arms, or whose ancestors have been freemen: the coat determines whether he is or is not descended from others of the same name. In the highest sense, the term *gentleman* signifies a man who not only does what is just and right, but whose conduct is guided by a true principle of honor, which springs from that self-respect and intellectual refinement which manifest themselves in easy and free, yet delicate manners.

GENRE-PAINT'ING, pictures of life

and manners. Under this title are comprised the grave episodes of life, which are to history what a single scene is to a drama, or a lyric to an epic poem. Also comic scenes of every kind; a comic subject is seldom placed in the highest category of art, because it is the nature of comedy to overstep the strict line of beauty and to become caricature. The principal genre pictures consist of scenes of every-day life, and may be classified. Those of the Netherlands are the best, and deserve to live; though far from the ideal of art, they show a skilful execution and lead to higher thoughts. Another kind are the low attempts at coloring called *costume* or *portrait* genre pictures, which are merely studies. In taking for its subject the events of daily life, genre-painting (unless the subject is eminently suited to the idea) avoids religious themes as high and lasting, as well as historical subjects, which, though transitory, ought never to appear so. A view of an open house, into which the sun is shining, a peasant lighting his pipe,—all the passing events of life, its characters and aims, offer fitting subjects for genre-painting. Pure nature, true humanity, national character, as revealed by domestic manners, &c., form the circle of true genre-painting, the boundary being more clearly defined than is the case in historical or religious art. The distinction between history and genre-painting cannot be too clearly drawn. Transitions from one to the other are admissible, and such pictures belong to the happiest productions of art; and there are also circumstances under which the advantages of both styles may be united. We meet with specimens of genre-painting among the ancients. As the character of ancient worship changed, a freer space was offered to Art, which, by degrees, overstepped the ideal circle of the mythic-normal, withdrew the mystic veil with which the Saga covered everything, and revealing nature, assumed an individual character from which a genre-like style of art arose tending towards the mythic. This style was, however, very different from what we now call genre-painting, which may be explained by the plastic character pervading art. Still we see by the mural paintings at Herculaneum and Pompeii, that in later Roman art there were colored pictures of the genre kind. These were certainly imperfect attempts, but they prove, nevertheless, that mere manual artists turned to domestic painting. The introduction of a new religion, in the service of which art was enrolled, delayed the progress of life-painting for more than a thousand years, but when that which was unnatural in Christian Art gave place to a free Germanic spirit, genre-painting arose refreshed. This spirit inclining towards the poetry of real life employed genre-painting for ecclesiastical purposes, but so many pleasing effects were developed, that religion was soon neglected and cast aside. The carpenter's workshop became popular, although it was not that of Joseph; the landscape was beautiful, even without the procession of the three kings; and the nosegay riveted the eye, although not placed in the oratory of the Virgin.

GENRE-SCULP'TURE, we have evidences of this branch of Art having been attempted by the ancients. After the time of Alexander the Great, religion, and consequently Art, underwent a great change; there was more room for individuality, and a style of art was developed which corresponded to the wants of the age, and which produced many works of a genre character. We know that genre-painting was very popular during the last ages of Grecian art, from the descriptions extant of the kitchen—scenes, &c., painted by Pyreicos, who finished these little pictures so exquisitely that they fetched a much higher price than large paintings by other artists. There are several specimens of genre-sculpture extant, the most remarkable of which is the *Venus Callipygos*, in the Museum at Naples. We find this style very often employed in Etruscan art, of which we have some specimens in the collection of bronzes in London, viz., a circular vase, the handle of which is formed by the figures of two struggling gladiators, a handle formed by two jugglers, also a rare bronze, formed of an Etruscan slave, kneeling, whose physiognomy betrays his descent; he is employed in cleaning a shoe, and holds a sponge in one hand. We meet with genre-sculpture among the biblical and legendary subjects in the middle ages; and it was carried on in the Germanic period, though only in small works, and those of a secular nature, viz., ivory carvings, and illuminations in books. Many critics affect to treat such works slightingly, but whoever looks at them with an unprejudiced eye, will be delighted at the union of nature with grandeur of conception, and will reasonably expect to see such subjects chosen for the highest efforts of the artist.

GE'NUS, in natural history, a subdivision of any class or order of things, whether of the animal, vegetable, or mineral kingdoms. All the species of a genus agree in certain characteristics.—In music, a distribution of the *tetrachord*, or the four principal sounds, according to their quality.

GEOG'RAPHY, properly, a description of the earth or terrestrial globe, particularly of the divisions of its surface, natural and artificial, and of the position of the several countries, kingdoms, states, cities, &c. As a science, geography includes the doctrine or knowledge of the astronomical circles or divisions of the sphere, by which the relative position of places on the globe may be ascertained; and usually treatises of geography contain some account of the inhabitants of the earth, of their government, manners, &c., and an account of the principal animals, plants, and minerals.—*General or universal geography*, the science which conveys a knowledge of the earth, both as a distinct and independent body in the universe, and as connected with a system of heavenly bodies.—*Mathematical geography*, that branch of the general science which is derived from the application of mathematical truths to the figure of the earth, and which teaches us to determine the relative position of places, their longitudes and latitudes, the different lines and circles imagined to be drawn upon the earth's surface, their measure, distance, &c.—*Physical geography*, that branch which gives a description of the principal features of the earth's surface the various climates and temperature, showing how these, together with other causes, affect the condition of the human race, and also a general account of the animals and productions of the globe.—*Political geography*, that branch which considers the earth as the abode of rational beings, according to their diffusion over the globe, and their social relations as they are divided into larger or smaller societies.—*Sacred* or *biblical geography*, the geography of Palestine, and other oriental nations mentioned in Scripture, having for its object the illustration of sacred history.

GEOL'OGY, the doctrine or science of the structure of the earth or terraqueous globe, and of the substances which compose it; or the science of the compound minerals or aggregate substances which compose the earth, the relations which the several constituent masses bear to each other, their formation, structure, position, and direction. It also investigates the successive changes that have taken place in the organic and inorganic kingdoms of nature; it inquires into the causes of these changes, and the influence which they have exerted in modifying the surface and external structure of our planet. It is a science founded on exact observation and careful induction, and is intimately connected with all the physical sciences. The geologist, in order that he may conduct his investigations with success, ought to be well versed in chemistry, mineralogy, zoology, botany, comparative anatomy; in short, every branch of science relating to organic and inorganic nature Within the memory of the present generation the science of geology has made immense progress. Aided not only by the higher branches of physics, but by recent discoveries in mineralogy and chemistry, in botany, zoology, and comparative anatomy, it has extracted from the archives of the interior of the earth, records of former conditions of our planet, and deciphered documents which were a sealed book to our ancestors. It extends its researches into regions more vast and remote than come within the scope of any other physical science except astronomy, of which it has emphatically been termed the sister science.

GE'OMANCY, a kind of divination by means of figures or lines, formed by little dots or points, either on the earth or on paper, and representing the four elements, the cardinal points, the planetary bodies, &c. This pretended science was flourishing in the days of Chaucer, and was deeply cultivated by Dryden at the time of his *rifaccimento* of the Knight's Tale. Cattan, who wrote a book on geomancy in the sixteenth century, absurdly enough observes, that it is "no art of inchaunting, as some may suppose it to be, or of divination, which is made by diabolicke invocation; but it is a part of natural magicke, called of many worthy men the daughter of astrologie, and the abbreviation thereof."

GEOM'ETRY, originally and properly, the art of measuring the earth, or any distances or dimensions on it. But geometry now denotes the science of magnitude in general, comprehending the doctrines and relations of whatever is susceptible of augmentation and diminution; as the mensuration of lines, surfaces, solids, velocity, weight, &c., with their various relations. Geometry is the most general and important of the mathematical sciences; it is founded upon a few axioms or self-evident truths, and every proposition which it lays down, whether it be theorem or problem, is subjected to the most accurate and rigid demonstration. Its usefulness extends to almost every art and science. Astronomy, navigation, surveying, architecture, fortification, engineering, perspective, drawing, optics, mechanics, &c., all depend upon it.—*Geometry* has been distinguished into theoretical or *speculative* and *practical*. The former treats of the various properties and relations of magnitudes, with demonstrations of theorems, &c.; and the latter relates to the performance of certain geometrical operations, such as the construction of figures, the drawing of lines in certain positions, and the application of geometrical principles to the various measurements in the ordinary concerns of life.—*Theoretical geometry* is again divided into *elementary* or *common geometry*, and the higher geometry; the former being employed in the consideration of lines, superficies, angles, planes, figures, and solids; and the latter, in the consideration of the higher order of curve lines and problems.

GEOPON'ICA, the name of a Greek compilation of precepts on rural economy, extracted from ancient writers. The name of the compiler is unknown; but the authorities which he quotes are numerous and deservedly celebrated.

GEOPON'ICS, the art or science of cultivating the earth.

GE'ORAMA, an instrument or machine which exhibits a very complete view of the earth, invented in Paris. It is a hollow sphere of forty feet diamater, formed by thirty-six bars of iron representing the parallels and meridians, and covered with a bluish cloth, intended to represent seas and lakes. The land, mountains, and rivers are painted on paper and pasted on this cover.

GEORGE, St., a saint or hero whose name is famous throughout all the East, and by which several orders, both military and religious, have been distinguished. St. George is usually represented on horseback, in full armor, with a formidable dragon writhing at his feet. His sanctity is established in the Latin as well as the Greek church; and England and Portugal have chosen him for their patron saint. According to ancient legends, this renowned saint was a prince of Cappadocia; whose greatest achievement was the conquest of an enormous dragon, by which he effected the deliverance of Aja, the daughter of a king. The legend belongs to the age of the crusades. The ancient Christian emperors bore the knight upon their standards. To these sacred banners the crusaders attributed a miraculous power, and were sure of conquest while they floated above their heads. Many, however, deny his very existence; and reduce his effigy to a mere symbol of victory gained by the crusaders over the Mussulman nation. The legend of his life is one of the most familiar and popular of the Christian mythology. He is usually represented as a knight clothed in armor, mounted on horseback, and combating with a dragon. The variations are so slight, that the subject can be easily recognized. As patron saint, he stands in armor, holding a lance, sometimes with a banner with a red cross, and a palm branch. Sometimes the lance is broken and the dragon dead at his feet.

GEOR'GICS, a poetical composition treating of husbandry, after the manner of Virgil's poems on rural subjects, which are called Georgics.

GER'MAN SCHOOL, in painting. In this school we find an attention to individual nature, as usually seen, without attempt at selection, or notion of ideal beauty. The German painters seem to have set a particular value on high finishing, rather than on a good arrangement and disposition of the subject. Their coloring is far better than their drawing, but their draperies are generally in bad taste. Though among the painters of this school some are free from the application of these observations, they are not sufficient in number to change the general judgment that must be passed upon it. Wohlgemuth, Holbein, and Albert Durer are the heads of it. These observations do not apply to a school which seems now rising in Germany, and which, with such leaders as Retsch and others, seems likely to put the school of painting there on a level with its highly splendid intellectual powers in all other branches of the arts and sciences.

GEROCO'MIA, that part of medicine which prescribes a regimen for old age.

GER'RA, in antiquity, a sort of square shield, used first by the Persians and afterwards by the Greeks.

GER'UND, in grammar, a verbal noun of the neuter gender, partaking of the nature of a participle, declinable only in the singular number, through all the cases except the vocative; as, nom. *amandum*, gen. *amandi*, dat. *amando*, accus. *amandum*, abl. *amando*.

GERU'SIA, in ancient history, the senate of Sparta. The number of this council was thirty, including the two kings; and the qualifications of its members were, pure Spartan blood, and an age not below sixty years. The election was performed in a primitive manner by acclamation, the candidates being brought forth one by one before the people. He who was greeted with the loudest applause was held to receive the highest honor next the throne. The functions of the gerusia were partly deliberative, partly judicial, and partly executive. It prepared measures which were to be laid before the popular assembly; it exercised a criminal jurisdiction, with power of capital punishment; and also wielded a kind of censorial authority for the correction of abuses.

GES'TURE, any action or posture intended to express an idea or passion, or to enforce an argument or opinion: hence propriety of gesture is of the first importance to an orator.—The interpretation of the proper significance of gesture is very important for the understanding of works of art. Much of this is common to humanity, and seems to us necessary; on the other hand there are also qualities of a positive nature, that is derived from the particular views and customs of the nation. Here there is very much indeed to be learned and guessed at, as well by the artist in studying life, as by the scientific in works of art.

GEY'SERS, the celebrated spouting fountains of boiling water in Iceland. The Geysers are situated about 30 miles from the volcano Hecla, in plains full of hot springs and steaming fissures. Their jets are intermittent, and the height to which they rise appears to vary much at different times.

GHAUTS, a term applied originally to the narrow and difficult passes in the mountains of Central Hindostan, but which has been gradually extended to the mountains themselves. They consist of two great chains extending along the east and west coasts of the Deccan, parallel to each other, or rather diverging, and leaving between them and the sea only a plain of forty or fifty miles in breadth.

GHOST, the soul or spirit separate from the body. The ancients supposed every man to be possessed of three different ghosts, which, after the dissolution of the human body, were differently disposed of. These they distinguished by the names of *Manes*, *Spiritus*, *Umbra*. The *Manes*, they fancied, went down into the infernal regions; the *Spiritus* ascended to the skies, and the *Umbra* hovered about the tomb, as being unwilling to quit its old connections.—*To give up the ghost*, a phrase frequently used in Scripture for—to yield up the breath, or expire.

GHOST, HOLY, the third person in the Holy Trinity; but according to some theologians, a biblical metaphor, to designate the divine influence. All Christians who subscribe to the doctrine of the Athanasian creed, believe the Holy Ghost to have proceeded from the Father and the Son; yet the Son and the Holy Ghost are both eternal, since they are co-eternal with the Father. The Greek church maintains that the Holy Ghost proceeds from the Father only; and this difference is one of the main points of distinction between that church and the Roman Catholic.—A military order in France under the old *regime*, which was abolished by the revolution, but revived by the Bourbons.

GI'ANTS, history, both sacred and profane, makes mention of giants, or people of extraordinary stature. Nations, as well as individuals, in their infancy, love the miraculous; and any event which deviates from the common course of things, immediately becomes a wonder on which poetry eagerly seizes; hence the Cyclops and Læstrygons of the ancients, and the ogres of romance. Instances, however, are by no means wanting of uncommonly large persons, hardly needing the exaggeration of a lively imagination to make them objects of wonder. The giants spoken of in Scripture might be men of extraordinary stature; but not so much above the ordinary measure as they have fancied, who describe them as three or four times larger than men are at present. And when we find the Israelites describing themselves as appearing like grasshoppers before the Anakites, we must bear in mind the universal practice among the nations of the East to express their astonishment in the most extravagant style of hyperbole. The giants of Greek mythology are believed by some to represent the struggle of the elements of nature against the gods, that is, against the order of creation. They were said to hurl mountains and forests against Olympus, disdaining the lightnings of Jupiter, &c. Giants, indeed, make a very considerable figure in the fabulous history of every nation; but, like ghosts and fairies, they have always vanished at the approach of science and civilization. The fossil bones which gave currency to the belief of their existence, have, upon minute inquiry, been found generally to belong to elephants, whales, &c.

GI'ANT'S CAUSE'WAY, a vast assemblage of basaltic crystallized rocks, on the northern coast of Ireland. This magnificent production of nature extends two miles in length along the coast of Antrim, and probably runs under the sea as far as the coast of Scotland, since something of the same kind is met with there, and known by the name of Fingal's Cave. It consists of many hundred thousands of columns of a black kind of rock, hard as marble, of about twenty feet in height, and a pentagonal or five-sided figure.

GIAOUR, a word literally signifying *dog* in the Turkish language; and commonly applied by the Turks to designate the adherents of all religions except the Mohammedan, but more particularly Christians.

GIB'ELINES, or GHIB'ELINES, a faction in Italy, in the 13th century, who were the opponents of another faction, called the *Guelfs* [which see.]

GIL'BERTINE, one of a religious order, so named from Gilbert, lord of Sempringham in Lincolnshire.

GIL'DA MERCATO'RIA, in law, mercantile meetings, assemblies, or corporate bodies.

GILD'ING, the art of covering anything with gold, either in a foliated or liquid state. The beauty of gold has induced many attempts to imitate its appearance, and hence several methods of gilding have been invented. The art of gilding, at the present day, is performed either upon metals or upon wood, leather, parchment, or paper; and there are three distinct methods in general practice; namely, *wash*, or *water gilding*, in which the gold is spread, whilst reduced to a fluid state, by solution in mercury; *leaf gilding*, either burnished or in oil, performed by cementing thin leaves of gold upon the work, either by size or by oil; and *japanner's gilding*, in which gold dust or powder is used instead of leaves. Gold is also applied to glass, porcelain, and other vitrified substances, of which the surfaces, being very smooth, are capable of perfect contact with the gold leaves.

GILES, St., the Hermit, Saint Gilles, (*Fr.*,) Sant. Egidio, (*Ital.*) This saint has obtained great popularity both in England and Scotland, as well as in France. He is usually represented as an old man with a flowing white beard, naked, or clothed in white, (the color of the habit of the Benedictines,) and accompanied by a hind wounded by an arrow.

GIM'BAL, a brass ring by which a sea compass is suspended in its box, by means of which the card is kept in a horizontal position, notwithstanding the rolling of the ship.

GIP'SIES, or GYP'SIES, a wandering tribe, or race of vagabonds, spread over the greater part of Europe, and some parts of Asia and Africa; strolling about and subsisting mostly by theft, low games, and fortune-telling. The name is supposed to be corrupted from *Egyptian*, as they were formerly thought to have come from Egypt; but it is now believed they are of Indian origin, and that they belonged to the race of the Sindes, an Indian caste, which was dispersed, in 1400, by the expeditions of Timour. Their language is the same throughout Europe with but little variation, and even now resembles the dialect of Hindostan. The late Bishop Heber relates in his Narrative of a Journey through the Upper Provinces of India, that he met with a camp of gypsies on the banks of the Ganges, who spoke the Hindoo language as their mother tongue; and he further observes, that he found the same people in Persia and Russia. Gypsies are remarkable for the yellow brown, or rather olive color of their skin; the jet black of their hair and eyes; the extreme whiteness of their teeth; and for the symmetry of their limbs, which distinguishes even the men, whose general appearance, however, is repulsive and shy. Though some occasionally follow a trade or honest calling, they rarely settle permanently anywhere. Wherever the climate is mild enough, they are found in forests and deserts, in companies. They seldom have tents, but seek shelter from the cold of winter in grottoes and caves, or they build huts, sunk some feet in the earth, and covered with sods laid on poles. They are fond of instrumental music, which they chiefly practise by the ear, and their lively motions are remarkable in their own peculiar dances. The youthful gypsies traverse the country, the men obtaining their living by gymnastic feats, tricks, &c., while the women invariably practise fortune-telling and chiromancy. They are not nice in their food, but eat all kinds of flesh; even that of animals which have died a natural death. Brandy is their favorite beverage; tobacco their greatest luxury; both men and women chew and smoke it with avidity, and are ready to make great sacrifices for the sake of satisfying this inclination. As for religion they have no settled notions or principles: amongst the Turks they are Mohammedans; in Christian countries, if they make any religious profession at all, they follow the forms of Christianity, without, however, caring for instruction, or having any interest in the spirit of religion. They marry with none but their own race, but their marriages are formed in the rudest manner, and when a gypsy becomes tired of his wife, he will turn her off without ceremony.

GIR'DER, in architecture, a principal beam in a floor for supporting the binding or other joists, whereby their bearing or length is lessened. Perhaps so called, because the ends of the joists are inclosed by it.

GIR'DLE, a belt or band of leather or some other substance used in girding up the loins. The girdle was in use among the Hebrews, Greeks, and Romans, for various purposes more or less important. By the Hebrews it was worn chiefly upon a journey, and sometimes as a mark of humiliation and sorrow; and by the Greeks and Romans it was used as a military ornament. To deprive a soldier of his girdle was the deepest mark of ignominy with which he could be branded; and even among the civilians, who always wore a girdle over the tunic to render their motions unembarrassed, the want of this appendage was considered strongly presumptive of idle and dissolute propensities. *Zonam solvere virgineam* was a well-known phrase appropriated to the marriage ceremony. To Venus was attributed by the poets the possession of a particular kind of girdle, called *cestus*, which was said to have the power of inspiring love.

GIRONDE', THE, in French history, a celebrated political party during the revolution; its members were termed Girondists or Girondins. The name was derived from that of the department La Gironde, (in which Bordeaux is situated,) which sent to the legislative assembly of 1791, among its representatives, three men of eloquence and talent, (Gaudet, Gensonné, Vergniaud,) who were among the chief leaders of the party. Its principles were republican. During the continuance of that assembly the Girondists formed a powerful, but not always consistent party. Out of these Louis XVI. chose his republican ministers in the beginning of 1792. But after the massacres of September in that year the party in general withdrew from all connection with the Jacobins, and approximated towards the Constitutionalists. In the Convention the Girondists at first commanded a majority, but on the king's trial they were much divided; and, being pressed by the violence of the sections of Paris, they were at length expelled from the assembly: thirty-four of them were outlawed, and finally twenty-two of their leaders guillotined (7th and 31st October, 1793,) while a few escaped, and others put an end to themselves. Perhaps the most celebrated member of the Gironde party was a lady, Madame Roland, the wife of the minister of that name, who was executed when the party fell.

GIROUETTE, (*French*, weathercock,) a term applied to numerous public characters in France, who, during the revolutionary era, turned with every political breeze. To mark these, a *Dictionnaire des Girouettes* was published, containing their names, &c., with a number of weathercocks against each, corresponding to the number of changes in the individual's political creed.

GIV'EN, a term much used by mathematicians, to denote something supposed to be known. Thus, if a magnitude be known, it is said to be a *given* magnitude, if the ratio between two quantities be known, these quantities are said to have a *given* ratio, &c., &c.

GLA'CIERS, immense masses or fields of ice which accumulate in the valleys between high mountains, from the melting of the snow at their top, and which, owing to their elevation, generally remain solid. The ice of the glaciers is entirely different from that of the sea and river water. It is not formed in layers, but consists of little grains of congealed snow; and hence, though perfectly clear, and often smooth on the surface, it is not transparent. As glaciers, in some positions, and in hot summers, decrease, they often also increase for a number of years so as to render a valley uninhabitable. Their increase is caused partly by alternate thawing and freezing; their decrease, by the mountain rivers, which often flow under them, and thus form an arch of ice over the torrent. In the Tyrol, Switzerland, Piedmont, and Savoy, the glaciers are so numerous that they have been calculated to form altogether a superficial extent of 1484 square miles.

GLA'CIS, in fortification, a mass of earth serving as a parapet to the covered way, having an easy slope or declivity towards the champaign or field.

GLA'DIATORS, in antiquity, combatants who fought at the public games in Rome, for the entertainment of the spectators. They were at first prisoners, slaves, or condemned criminals; but afterwards freemen fought in the arena, either for hire, or from choice. The games were commenced by a *prœlusio*, in which they fought with weapons of wood, till, upon a signal, they assumed their arms, and began in earnest to fight in pairs. In case the vanquished was not

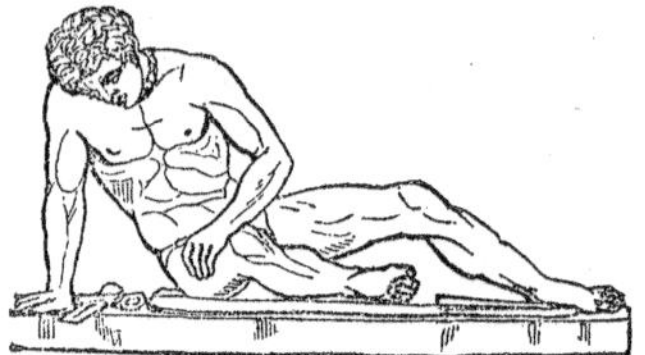

killed in the combat, his fate was decided by the people. If they wished to save the life of the vanquished gladiator, they signified the same by clenching the fingers of both hands between each other, and holding the thumbs upright, close together; the contrary was signified by bending back their thumbs. The first of these signals was called *pollicem premere*, the second *pollicem vertere*. The victors were honored with a palm branch, a sum of money, or other marks of the people's favor; and they were not unfrequently released from further service, and received as a badge of freedom, the *rudis*, or wooden sword. The cut represents the celebrated statue of the Dying Gladiator.

GLASS PAINTING, in painting, the method of staining glass in such a manner as to produce the effect of representing all the subjects whereof the art is susceptible. A French painter of Marseilles is said to have been the first who instructed the Italians in this art, during the pontificate of Julius II. It was, however, practised to a considerable extent by Lucas of Leyden, and Albert Durer. The art of glass-painting is practised under three systems, which may be distinguished as the *mosaic method; the enamel method;* and a method compounded of these two, or the *mosaic-enamel method.* There is yet another mode of ornamenting glass, which consists in applying pigments mixed with copal varnish. But this is of a perishable nature, and should not be regarded as true glass-painting, which is only perfected by the aid of fire, and is as durable as the glass itself. Most true glass-paintings are formed by combining the two processes of enamelling and staining, since, although it would not be possible to execute a glass-painting by staining the glass merely, yet it can be entirely formed of painted glass By the *mosaic* method, each color of the design must be represented by a separate piece of glass, except yellow, brown, and black; these colors are applied upon *white* glass, and for shadows. In the *enamel* method, colored glass is not used, the picture being painted upon white-glass with enamel fragments. The *mosaic-enamel* method consists of a combination of the two other processes; white and colored glass, as well as every variety of enamel color, being employed in it.

GLAU'CUS, in Grecian mythology, the name of a marine deity, the son, according to some of the genealogists, of Neptune and one of the Naiads; according to others, of Polybius and Alcyone. He enjoyed the power of prophecy.

GLAZ'ING, is that part of the practice of oil-painting which consists in the application of an extremely thin layer of color over another, for the purpose of modifying its tone. The pigments employed are generally transparent, although, in some instances, such as in the representation of clouds, dust, smoke, &c., opaque pigments are admissible when mixed in minute quantities with a large proportion of oil. By glazing, the painter can produce certain effects, such as transparency and mellowness, impossible with the aid of solid pigments alone, the intention being to give a natural and agreeable harmony and mellowness to the execution of a picture such as would be produced by a colored varnish. The color employed in glazing should be of a darker tint than the solid pigment over which it is laid. Glazing formed a very important part in the practice of the Venetian school, and in those derived from it. Those who paint *alla prima* can produce the desired effect without glazing.

GLEAN'ING, the practice of collecting corn left in a harvest field after the harvest has been carried, which appears by the Mosaic law to have been allowed to the poor. The right of the poor to glean is, however, not admitted in the English common law.

GLEBE, in law, church land; usually taken for that which is annexed to a parish church of common right.

GLEE, in music, a composition for voices in three or more parts. The subjects of the words are various, being gay, grave, amatory, pathetic, or bacchanalian. It may consist of only one movement, but usually has more.

GLEE-MAN, itinerant minstrels were so called by the Saxons: their appellation is translated joculatores by the Latin writers of the middle ages. The name appears to have been supplanted by the Norman minstrel, shortly after the conquest.

GLOBE, in practical methematics, an artificial spherical body, on the convex surface of which are represented the countries, seas, &c. of our earth; or the face of the heavens, with the several circles which are conceived upon them. That with the parts of the earth delineated upon its surface, is called the *terrestrial globe;* and that with the constellations, &c. the *celestial globe.* Their principal use, besides serving as maps to distinguish the earth's surface, and the situation of the fixed stars, is to illustrate and explain the phenomena arising from the diurnal motion of the earth. They are consequently of the highest importance in acquiring a knowledge of geography and astronomy.

GLOB'ULAR CHART, a name given to the representation of the surface, or of some part of the surface of the terrestrial globe upon a plane, wherein the parallels of latitude are circles, nearly concentric, the meridian curves bending towards the poles, and the rhumb-lines are also curves.

GLOB'ULE, a small particle of matter of a spherical form; a word particularly applied to the red particles of blood, which swim in a transparent serum, and may be discovered by the microscope.

GLO'RY, in painting and sculpture, a circle, either plain or radiated, surrounding the heads of saints, &c., and especially of our Saviour. The term glory is used in the sacred writings in various senses, all of which, however, may be easily deduced from the original meaning of its Hebrew equivalent, which signifies *weight.* Thus *the glory of God* means all those attributes and qualities which give him *weight* in our eyes, or inspire us with reverence.

GLOSS, in the rhetoric of Aristotle, this word is used in the sense of a foreign, obsolete, or otherwise strange idiom; which, judiciously employed, he reckons among the ornaments of style. From the sense of "something requiring interpretation" the word came to mean the interpretation itself; strictly, of a single word or phrase. In the twelfth century, the comments or annotations of learned jurists on passages in the text of the Roman law were denominated glosses; when these extended to a running commentary, they were termed an apparatus. The glosses were collected by Accursius in the 13th century, and from that period they formed for a long time a body of authority reckoned equal or even superior to the text itself.

GLOS'SARY, a dictionary of difficult words and phrases in any language or writer; sometimes used for a dictionary of words in general.

GLOVES, well-known articles of dress used for covering the hands. The practice of covering the hands with gloves has prevailed among almost all the nations of the earth from time immemorial, and is common at once to the rude Tartar, who seeks by their means to protect himself from cold, and to the refined European, with whom their use is an emblem of luxury. In the middle ages, gloves constituted a costly article of dress, being often highly decorated with embroidery and richly adorned with precious stones. In the age of chivalry it was usual for the soldiers who had gained the favor of a lady to wear her glove in his helmet; and, as is well known, the throwing of a glove was the most usual mode of challenging to duel. This latter practice prevailed so early as the year 1245.

GLYCO'NIAN, or GLYCON'IC, a kind of verse in Greek and Latin poetry, consisting of three feet, a spondee, a choriamb, and a pyrrhic.

GLYPH, in sculpture and architecture, any channel or cavity intended as an ornament.

GLYPTOG'RAPHY, a description of the art of engraving on precious stones.

GLYPTOTHE'CA, a building or room for the preservation of works of sculpture; a word adopted by the Germans, as in the instance of the celebrated Glyptothek at Munich.

GNOMES, spirits with which the imagination of certain philosophers has peopled the interior parts of the earth, and to whose care mines, quarries, &c. are assigned.

GNO'MIC POETS, Greek poets, whose remains chiefly consist of short sententious precepts and reflections, are so termed in classical bibliography. The principal writers of this description, of whom a few fragments are extant, are Theognis and Solon, who lived in the 6th century before the Christian era. With them Tyrtæus and Simonides are joined by Brunck in his edition, although these writers have little of a gnomic character. The metre of these poets is elegiac.

GNOS'TICS, a sect of philosophers that arose in the first ages of Christianity, who pretended they were the only men who had a true knowledge of the Christian religion. They formed for themselves a system of theology, agreeable to the philosophy of Pythagoras and Plato, and fancied they discovered deeper mysteries in the Scriptures than were perceived by those whom they considered as simple and ignorant. They held that all natures, intelligible, intellectual, and material, are derived by successive emanations from the Deity. In process of time, the name designated sectarians of various descriptions, but who all agreed in certain opinions; and the tenet which seems most particularly to distinguish the Gnostic name, was the existence of two first principles, or deities, the one the author of good, and the other of evil.

GOBELINS, or HOTEL-ROYAL DE GOBELINS, a celebrated academy for tapestry-drawing, and manufactory of tapestry, erected in the suburb of St. Marcel, at Paris, by Louis XIV. in the year 1666. The place was previously famous on account of the dyeing manufactory established there by Giles and John Gobelins, in the reign of Francis I. These eminent dyers discovered a method of producing a beautiful scarlet, which has ever since been known by their name; and so extensive has been their fame, that not only the color, but the house in which their business was carried on, and the river they made use of, are called *gobelins*.

GOD, the appellation which we give to the Creator and Sovereign of the universe; the Supreme Being.—The words *god* and *goddess* are also the appellatives common to the heathen deities; which they divided into *dii majorum gentium*, and *dii minorum gentium;* that is, into the superior and inferior gods. Another division was taken from their place of residence; thus there were celestial, terrestrial, infernal, marine, and sylvan gods. They were also divided into animal and natural gods: the animal gods were mortals, who had been raised to divinity by ignorance and superstition; and the natural gods, the parts of nature, such as the stars, the elements, mountains, rivers, &c. There were also deities, who were supposed to preside over particular persons: some had the care of women in child-birth; others, the care of children and young persons; and others were the deities of marriage. Each action, virtue, and profession had also its particular god: the shepherds had their Pan; the gardeners, their Flora; the learned, their Mercury and Minerva; and the poets, their Apollo and the Muses.

GOD'FATHER, and GOD'MOTHER, the man and woman who are sponsors for a child at baptism; who promise to answer for his future conduct, and solemnly promise that he shall follow a life of piety and virtue, by this means laying themselves under an indispensable obligation to instruct the child and watch over his conduct. This practice is of great antiquity in the Christian church, and was probably instituted to prevent children being brought up in idolatry, in case their parents died before they arrived at years of discretion.

GOLD, this metal, which in purity and firmness surpasses all others, is employed both in the plastic arts, and to a limited extent in painting. The most varied and beautiful objects extant are the vessels used in religious services; and as it was most properly employed in the sacred vessels and sanctuary of the Old Temple, so the chalices and tabernacles of the Catholic church, and the shrines of the saints have been moulded of this precious metal; and in ecclesiastical ornament of all kinds, with its multiplied fibres, and mingled with silk and purple, it enriches the sacerdotal vestments and the hangings of the altar. Gold signifies purity, dignity, wisdom, and glory, and it is used in painting for the Nimbi which surround the heads of the saints, and it frequently forms the ground on which sacred subjects are painted, the better to express the majesty of the mystery depicted. It is a proper emblem of brightness and glory.

GOLD'EN-FLEECE, in the mythological fables of the ancients, signified the skin or fleece of the ram upon which Phryxus and Hella are supposed to have swum over the sea to Colchis; which being sacrificed to Jupiter, its fleece was hung upon a tree in the grove of Mars, guarded by two brazen-hoofed bulls, and a monstrous dragon that never slept; but was at last taken and carried off by Jason and the Argonauts.

GOLD'EN NUM'BER, in chronology, is that number which indicates the year of the lunar cycle, for any given time. It

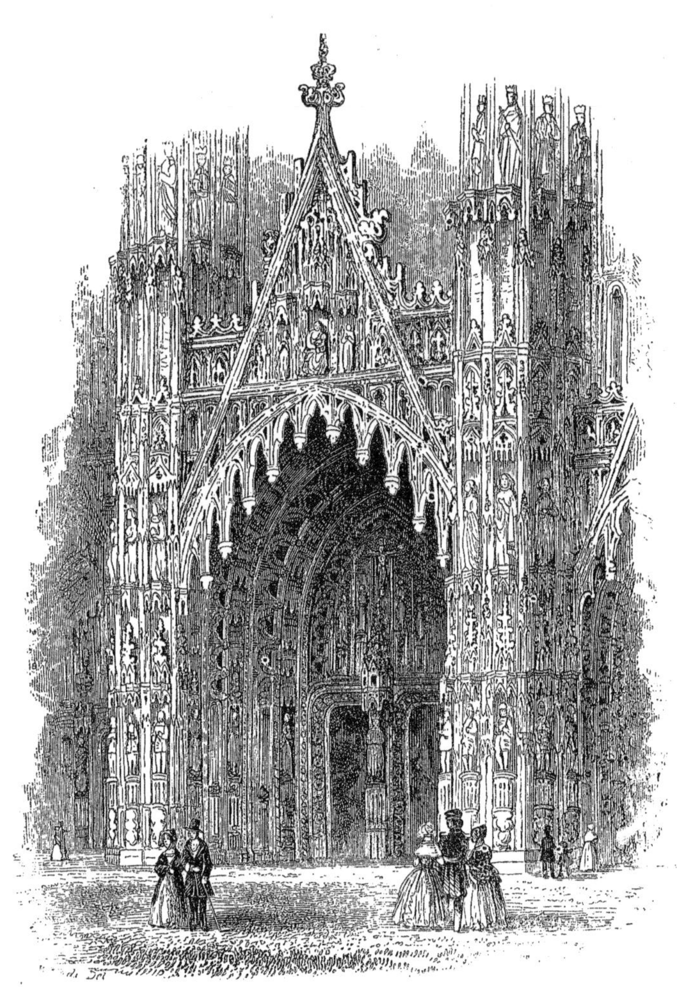

GOTHIC ARCHITECTURE.

(Cathedral at Troyes, France) p. 273

was called the Golden Number, because in the ancient calendar it was written in letters of gold, on account of its great usefulness in ecclesiastical computations, especially in fixing the time of Easter. It was likewise called the Prime, because it pointed out the first day of the new moon, *primum lunæ*. To find the Golden Number, add 1 to the year of our Lord, divide the sum by 19, and the remainder is the Golden Number, the quotient at the same time expressing the number of cycles which have revolved from the beginning of the year preceding the birth of Christ.

GON'DOLA, the name given to the pleasure boats used at Venice, where the numerous canals with which it is intersected generally render it necessary to substitute boats for carriages. The gondola is from 25 to 30 feet long, and five

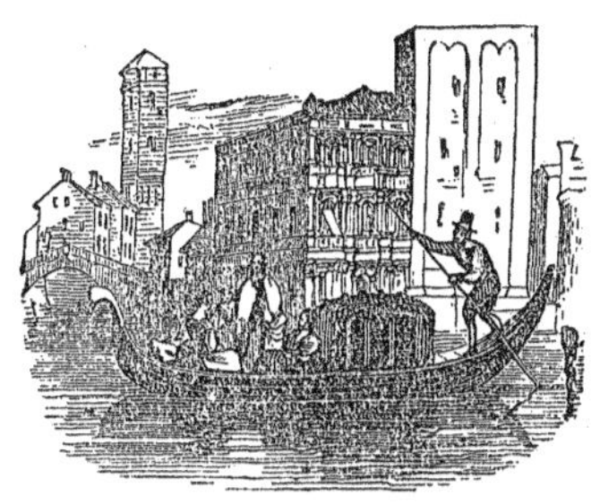

feet wide in the centre, in which a sort of cabin is constructed for passengers. They are sharp-pointed both at the prow and stern, and are rowed by two men called *gondolieri*. The cabins are always furnished with black curtains, which give a sombre appearance to the gondola at a distance.

GOOD FRI'DAY, the name given in England to the anniversary of our Saviour's crucifixion. The French and most other European nations substitute the epithet *holy* for *good*. From the first dawn of Christianity, Good Friday has been regarded as a solemn festival by the great body of the Christian world.

GOOD-WILL, in law, the custom of any trade or business. A contract to transfer it is, in general, good at law, though not usually enforced in equity. In what cases the good-will of a partnership can be claimed as property by the representatives of a deceased partner appears doubtful.

GOR'DIAN KNOT, in antiquity, a knot made in the harness of the chariot of Gordius, king of Phrygia, so very intricate, that there was no finding where it began or ended. An oracle had declared that he who should untie this knot should be master of Asia. Alexander having undertaken it, and fearing that his inability to untie it should prove an ill augury, cut it asunder with his sword, and thus either accomplished or eluded the oracle. Hence, in modern language, *to cut the Gordian knot* is to remove a difficulty by bold or unusual means.

GORGE, in architecture, the narrowest part of the Tuscan and Doric capitals, lying between the astragal, above the shaft of the column and the annulets.—In fortification, the entrance of a bastion, ravelin, or other outwork.

GOR'GET, in plate-armor, the piece covering the neck attached to the helmet. The old covering for the neck was called *camail*, made of leather or cloth, and attached to the hood; on this plates of steel were riveted; and thus the gorget was formed, about the time of Edward II. The name is supposed to have originated in Lombardy.

GORGONEI'A, in architecture, carvings of masks imitating the Gorgon or Medusa's head.

GOR'GONS, in mythology, three sister deities, fabled by the Greeks to dwell near the Western Ocean. Their heads, which were twined with serpents instead of hair, had the power of turning all who beheld them to stone; of which property Perseus made use after he had, by the help of Minerva, cut off the head of Medusa.

GOS'PEL, is used to signify the whole system of the Christian religion, and more particularly, as the term literally implies the good news of the coming of the Messiah. The word was also originally applied to the books which contained an account of the life of Christ, many of which were in circulation in the first century of the Christian era; though only four, those of Matthew, Mark, Luke and John, were considered canonical by the fathers.

GOTH'IC, pertaining to the Goths; as Gothic customs; Gothic barbarity. In architecture, a term at first applied opprobriously to the architecture of the middle ages, but now in general use as its distinctive appellation. By some the term Gothic is considered to include the Romanesque, Saxon, and Norman styles which have circular arches, but it is only appropriately applied to the styles which are distinguished by the pointed arch. Gothic architecture so restricted has been divided into three distinct periods: the first period is named the Early English, it prevailed in the thirteenth century; the second period or style, of the fourteenth century, is named the decorated style; and the third period is called the perpendicular style. The chief characteristics of Gothic architecture are:—the predominance of the arch and the subserviency and subordination of all the other parts to this chief feature; the tendency of the whole composition to vertical lines; the absence of the column and entablature of classic architecture, of square edges and rectangular surfaces, and the substitution of clustered shafts, contrasted surfaces, and members multiplied in rich variety. The Gothic style is that best adapted for ecclesiastical edifices.

GOV'ERNMENT, that form of fundamental rules and principles by which a nation or state is governed. If this power be vested in the hands of one, it is a *monarchy;* if in the hands of the nobility, an *aristocracy;* and if in the hands of the people, or those chosen by them, a *democracy.*—The *executive government* is the power of administering public affairs; the *legislative government*, that of making the laws.—*Government* is also a post or office which gives a person the power or right to govern or rule over a place, a city, or province, either supremely or by deputation. Thus, the government of Ireland is vested in the lord-lieutenant.—*Government*, in grammar, the influence of a word in regard to construction, as when established usage requires that one word should cause another to be in a particular case or mood.

GRACE, in objects of taste, a certain species of beauty, which appears to consist in the union of elegance and dignity.—In theology, the free unmerited love and favor of God; or the divine influence in restraining from sin.—*Days of grace*, in commercial law, three days allowed for the payment of a bill after it has become due.—The word *grace* is also used in speaking of or to a duke or duchess, as your Grace, his or her Grace. —*The Graces*, among the heathen world, were female beauties deified: they were three in number; Aglaia, Thalia, and Euphrosyne, the constant attendants of Venus.—In music, *graces* are turns, trills, and shakes, introduced for the purpose of embellishment.

GRADA'TION, in general, the ascending step by step, or proceeding in a regular and uniform manner. It also means a degree in any order or series. Thus we say, there is a *gradation* in the scale of being; or we observe a *gradation* in the progress of society from a rude state to civilized life.—*Gradation*, in logic, is an argumentation, consisting of four or more propositions, so disposed, as that the attribute of the first is the subject of the second; and the attribute of the second, the subject of the third; and so on, till the last attribute come to be predicated of the subject of the first proposition.

GRAD'UATE, one who has obtained a degree at a university, or from some professional incorporated society, after a due course of study, and suitable examination.

GRAM'MAR, the art which analyzes and classes the words in a language, which details its peculiarities, and furnishes rules, recognized by the best authorities, for its construction. General grammar teaches the principles which are common to all languages; and the grammar of any particular language teaches the principles peculiar to that language.

GRAND, in the Fine Arts, a quality by which the highest degree of majesty and dignity is imparted to a work of art. Its source is in form freed from ordinary and common bounds, and to be duly felt requires an investigation of the different qualities by which great and extraordinary objects produce impression on the mind.

GRANDEE', the highest title of Spanish nobility. The collective body of the higher nobility in Spain is termed *la grandeza.* They were originally the same with the *ricos hombres.* Grandees bear different titles—duke, marquis, &c.; but there is no essential difference of rank between these titles: all are equal among themselves. Grandeeships descend through females, and thus become accumulated in families.

GRAN'DEUR, in a general sense, greatness; that quality or combination of qualities in an object, which elevates or expands the mind, and excites pleasurable emotions in him who views or contemplates it. Thus the extent and uniformity of surface in the ocean constitute *grandeur;* as do the extent, the elevation, and the concave appearance or vault of the sky. So we speak of the *grandeur* of a large and well-proportioned edifice, of an extensive range of lofty mountains, of a large cataract, of a pyramid, &c.

GRAND JU'RY, a jury whose duty is to examine into the grounds of accusation against offenders, and if they see just cause, then to find bills of indictment against them to be presented to the court.

GRANT, in law, a gift in writing of such things as cannot conveniently be passed or verbally conveyed.

GRAPE'-SHOT, in artillery, a combination of small shot put into a thick canvass bag, and corded so as to form a kind of cylinder.

GRA'VER, called also BURIN, the sharp tool, whose extremity is a triangular form, for cutting the lines of an engraving on the copper.—*See* ENGRAVING.

GRAVITA'TION, the force by which bodies are pressed or drawn, or by which they tend toward the centre of the earth or other centre, or the effect of that force. Thus the falling of a body to the earth is ascribed to *gravitation*. The attraction of *gravitation* exists between bodies in the mass, and acts at sensible distances. It is thus distinguished from chemical and cohesive attractions which unite the particles of bodies together, and act at insensible distances, or distances too small to be measured.—*Terrestrial gravitation*, that which respects the earth, or by which bodies descend, or tend towards the centre of the earth. All bodies, when unsupported, fall by gravitation towards the earth, in straight lines tending to its centre.—*General* or *universal gravitation*, that by which all the planets tend towards one another, and, indeed, by which all the bodies and particles of matter in the universe tend towards one another. The theory of *universal gravitation* was established by Newton. He proved that the moon gravitates towards the earth, and the earth towards the moon, all the secondaries to their primaries; and these to their secondaries; also the primaries to the sun, and the sun to the primaries. It is also highly probable, that the bodies of the solar system, and those of other systems, gravitate mutually towards each other. The terms *gravitation* and *gravity* are generally used synonymously.

GRAY, is compounded of black and white in various proportions, or of the three primary colors, red, blue, and yellow; according to the predominance of either of these, there are produced blue grays, purple grays, green grays; but when the red or yellow predominate, there are produced the various hues of brown.

GRAZIO'SO, in music, an instruction to the performer that the music to which this word is affixed is to be executed elegantly and gracefully.

GREAVE, a piece of armor defending the shin. The greave was a piece of steel hollowed to fit the front of the leg, and fastened with straps behind. The greave common among the Greeks was used in some instances by the Roman soldiery, but only on one leg, the other being covered with the buckler. It is said to have been discontinued in the armies of the Greek empire, under the emperor Maurice, (about the end of the 6th century,) and again brought into use in those armies of the middle ages, about 1320. They were also called *jambs*, *beinbergs*, &c. They were originally of leather, quilted linen, &c. The *clavons* were a species of greaves made of cloth.

GREEK CHURCH, that portion of Christians who conform, in their creed, usages, and church government, to the views of Christianity introduced into the former Greek empire, and perfected, since the fifth century, under the patriarchs of Constantinople, Alexandria, Antioch, and Jerusalem. Like the Roman Catholic, this church recognizes two sources of doctrine, the bible and tradition, under which last it comprehends not only those doctrines which were orally delivered by the apostles, but also those which have been approved of by the fathers of the Greek church. It is the only church which holds that the Holy Ghost proceeds from the Father only, thus differing from the Catholic and Protestant churches, which agree in deriving the Holy Ghost from the Father and the Son. Like the Catholic church, it has seven sacraments—baptism, chrism, the eucharist preceded by confession, penance, ordination, marriage, and supreme unction; but it is peculiar in holding that full purification from original sin in baptism requires an immersion three times of the whole body in water, whether infants or adults are to be baptized, and in joining chrism (confirmation) with it as the completion of baptism. It rejects the doctrine of purgatory, has nothing to do with predestination, works of supererogation, indulgences, and dispensations; and it recognizes neither the pope nor any one else as the visible vicar of Christ on earth. In the invocation of the saints, in their fasts, relics, &c., they are as zealous as the Romanists; it may be said, indeed, that the services of the Greek church consist almost entirely of outward forms. This is the religion of Russia; the ecclesiastical establishment of which consists in a holy synod, four metropolitans, eleven archbishops, nineteen bishops, 12,500 parish churches, and 425 convents, fifty-eight of which are connected with monastic schools for the education of the clergy. The Greek church, under the Turkish dominion, remained, as far as was possible under such circumstances, faithful to the original constitution. The patriarch of Constantinople exercises the highest ecclesiastical jurisdiction over the Greeks in the whole Turkish empire; but they labor under many disabilities, among which is a heavy poll-tax, under the name of "exemption from beheading."

GREEK FIRE, a combustible composition invented by the Greeks in the middle ages, during their wars with the Arabs and Turks. It consists of naphtha, bitumen, sulphur, gum, &c.

GREEK LAN'GUAGE, the language of the primitive inhabitants of Greece, the Pelasgi, was already extinct in the time of Herodotus, who asserts that it was different from the Hellenic, and adds, that it is probable the Hellenes have retained their original language. From the great number of Hellenic tribes of the same race, it was to be expected that there would be different dialects, the knowledge of which is the more necessary for becoming acquainted with the Greek language, since the writers of this nation have transmitted the peculiarities of the different dialects in the use of single letters, words, terminations, and expressions, and that not merely to characterize more particularly an individual represented as speaking but even when they speak in their own person. It is customary to distinguish three leading dialects, according to the three leading branches of the Greeks, the Æolic, the Doric, and the Ionic, to which was afterwards added the mixed Attic dialect. At what time this language first began to be expressed in writing, has long been a subject of doubt. According to the general opinion, Cadmus, the Phœnician, introduced the alphabet into Greece. His alphabet consisted of but sixteen letters; four are said to have been invented by Palamedes in the Trojan war, and four more by Simonides of Ceos. As the Ionians first adopted these letters, and the Athenians received them from them, the alphabet with twenty-four letters is called the *Ionic*. Those who have most carefully studied the subject, believe that the use of the alphabet became common in Greece about 550 years before Christ, and about as long after Homer. In Homer's time, all knowledge, religion, and laws were preserved by memory alone, and for that reason were put in verse, till prose was introduced with the art of writing. The Greek language, as preserved in the writings of the celebrated authors of antiquity, as Homer, Hesiod, Demosthenes, Aristotle, Plato, Xenophon, &c., has a great variety of terms and expressions, suitable to the genius and occasions of a polite and learned people, who had a taste for arts and sciences. In it, proper names are significative; which is the reason that the modern languages borrow so many terms from it. When any new invention, instrument, machine, or the like, is discovered, recourse is generally had to the Greek for a name to it; the facility wherewith words are there compounded, affording such as will be expressive of its use; such are barometer, hygrometer, microscope, telescope, thermometer, &c. But of all sciences medicine most abounds with such terms; as, diaphoretic, diagnosis, diarrhœa, hemorrhage, hydrophobia, phthisis, atrophy, &c.—*Modern Greek*, or *Romaic*. The Greek language seems to have preserved its purity longer than any other known to us; and even long after its purity was lost, the echo of this beautiful tongue served to keep alive something of the spirit of ancient Greece. All the supports of this majestic and refined dialect seemed to fail, when the Greeks were enslaved by the fall of Constantinople, (A.D. 1543.) All the cultivated classes who still retained the pure Greek, the language of the Byzantine princes, either perished in the conflict, or took to flight, or courted the favor of their rude conquerors by adopting their dialect. In the lower classes only did the common Greek survive the vulgar dialect of the polished classes. But the Greek spirit, not yet extinguished by all the adversities the nation had undergone, finally revived with increasing vigor, and even the love of song kept alive some sparks of patriotic sentiment. From the beginning of the present century, external circumstances have greatly favored the progress of education in Greece; schools have been established; and the language itself, which in its degradation was not destitute of melody and flexibility, gained energy and vivacity from the efforts of several patriotic individuals, who endeavored to bring it nearer the ancient classic dialect.

GREEN, a secondary color, compounded of the primaries blue and yellow: if the blue predominates, the compound is a blue-green; if the yellow predominates, it is a yellow-green; or a *warm green.*—*Green*, in blazonry, *sinople*, signified love, joy, and abundance. Among the Greeks green symbolized victory, and among the Moors it had the same signification: it also designated hope, joy, youth, and spring, (the youth of the year,) which gives the hope of harvest.

GREEN'-CLOTH, in British polity, a board or court of justice held in the counting-house or the British monarch's household, and composed of the lord-steward and inferior officers. To this court is committed the charge and supervision of the royal household in matters of justice and government, with power to correct all offenders, and to maintain the peace of the verge, or jurisdiction of the court-royal, which extends every way two hundred yards from the gate of the palace. Without a warrant first obtained from this court, no servant of the household can be arrested for debt.—It takes its name from a green-cloth spread over the board at which it is held.

GREEN PIG'MENTS, are derived chiefly from the mineral world, and owe their color to the presence of copper. Among the most valuable to the painter are malachite or mountain green, terra verde, Veronese green, native carbonate of copper, cobalt green, and chrome green. The only vegetable green is *sap green*, which is employed occasionally in water-color painting.

GREEN-ROOM, in the theatre, the name given to the actors' retiring room; so called, in all probability, from its being originally painted or otherwise ornamented with green.

GREGO'RIAN, the *Gregorian year*, in chronology, is a correction of the Julian year. In the latter, every secular or hundredth year is bissextile: in the former year every one in four. This reformation, which was made by pope Gregory XIII., A.D. 1582, is also called the *New-style*.

GRENADE', a hollow shell or globe of iron, filled with combustibles, and thrown out of a howitzer. There is also a smaller kind, thrown by hand, which are called *hand-grenades*. These were originally used by soldiers, who, from long service and distinguished bravery, were selected for the service; and hence the name of *grenadiers*, who now form the first company of a battalion.

GRIF'FIN, a fabulous animal of antiquity represented with the body and feet of a lion, the head of an eagle or vulture, and as being furnished with wings and claws. The griffin is one of those imaginary creatures to which the ancients were so confessedly partial, but it belongs more to the romantic than the classical mythology. It plays a prominent part in the fairy tales and romances of the middle ages; and, like the dragon which was fabled to guard the golden apples of the Hesperides, its chief duties consisted in watching over hidden treasures, and in guarding captive princesses, or the castles in which they were confined. The griffin is at once the symbol of strength and swiftness, courage, prudence, and vigilance—qualities which its form is well calculated to represent; and hence it has been adopted into the language of heraldry, where it constitutes a prominent feature in the armorial bearings of many princely and noble families.

GRIMACE', in painting and sculpture, an unnatural distortion of the countenance, from habit, affectation, or insolence.

GRISA'ILLE, in gray; a style of painting employed to represent solid bodies in relief, such as friezes, mouldings, ornaments of cornices, bas-reliefs, &c., by means of gray tints. The objects represented are supposed to be white; the shadows which they project, and the lights, from those most vividly reflected, to the least, are properly depicted by the various gray tints produced by the mixture of white with black pigments, or sometimes by brown. Many painters make the frotté, or first sketch of their pictures in a brown tint, to which the term *en grisaille* is sometimes misapplied.

GROAT, a silver coin, first struck in the reign of Edward I., before whose time the English had no silver coin larger than a penny. It has since been used as a money of account equal to fourpence.

GROIN'ED CEILING, or GROINED ROOF, a ceiling formed by three or more intersecting vaults, every two of which form a groin at the intersection, and all the groins meet in a common point called the apex or summit. The curved surface between two adjacent groins is termed the sectroid. Groined roofs are common to classic and medieval architecture, but it is in the latter style that they are seen in their greatest perfection. In this style, by

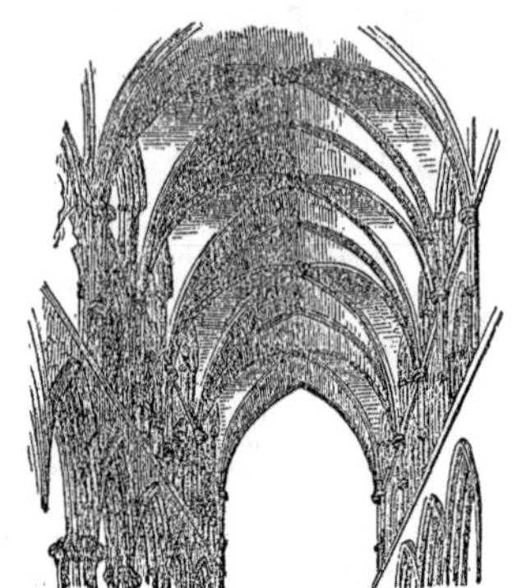

increasing the number of intersecting vaults, varying their plans, and covering their surface with ribs and veins, great variety and richness were obtained, and at length the utmost limit of complexity was reached in the fan groin tracery vaulting.

GROTESQUE', in the Fine Arts, a term applied to capricious ornaments, which as a whole have no type in nature; consisting of figures, animals, leaves, flowers, fruits, and the like, all connected together.—*Grotesque*, in architecture, artificial grotto-work decorated with rock-work, shells, &c.

GROT'TO, the name given to subterraneous natural excavations formed in the heart of mountains or other places. Many of these cavities are famed for the mephitic exhalations that issue from them, and to this class belongs more especially the Grotto del Cane, near Naples; but there are others not less celebrated for their beauty and grandeur, of which the grottoes of Antiparos and Fingal, are well-known examples. In picturesque gardening, the term is applied to an artificial or ornamental cave or low building intended to represent a natural grotto. The best specimen of this kind is the grotto attached to the Colosseum, which may be considered a model for all similar designs.

GROUND, in the Fine Arts, a word of various application. In painting, it is the first layer of color on which the figures or other objects are painted; of sculpture, it is the surface from which, in *relievi*, the figures rise, and in architecture, it is used to denote the face of the scenery or country round a building.

GROUP, in painting, an assemblage of objects, whose lighted parts form a mass of light, and their shaded parts a mass of shadow: the word is also used to denote any adjoining assemblage of figures, animals, fruits, flowers, &c. In speaking also of objects of different sorts, it is usual to say that one object *groups* with another. Lights in groups should, as well as shadows, be connected together, or the

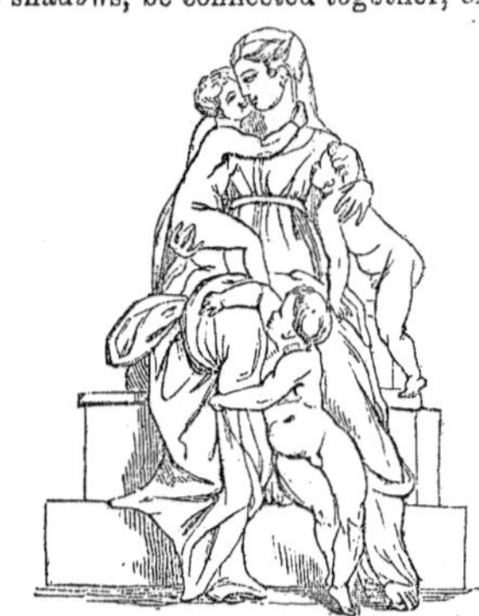

necessary repose will be wanting. In sculpture, the word *group* is applied to a design in which there are two or more figures. In music, *group* signifies a number of notes linked together at the stems.

GUAR'ANTOR, one who engages to see that the stipulations of another are performed; also one who engages to secure another in any right or possession.

GUAR'ANTY, or GUARANTEE', an undertaking or engagement by a third party, that the stipulations of a treaty, or the engagement or promise of another shall be performed.

GUARD, the duty of guarding or defending any post or person from an attack or surprise. Also, the soldiers, who do this duty.—*Guard*, in fencing, a posture or action proper to defend the body.—*Van-guard*, in military affairs, a body of troops, either horse or foot, that march before an army or division, to prevent surprise or give notice of danger. —*Rear-guard*, a body of troops that march in the rear for a like purpose.—*Life-guards*, a body of select troops, whose especial duty is to defend the person of a prince or chief officer.

GUARD'IAN, in law, a person appointed by will, or otherwise, to superintend the education and property of a minor, to whom the guardian is bound to account, after the child is of age, under responsibility for the just performance of the trust.

GUARDS, in a particular sense, the troops that are designed to guard the royal person and palace; and which consist both of horse and foot. In Britain, the household troops or guards consist of the life-guards, the royal regiment of horse-guards, and three regiments of foot-guards.—*Yeomen of the Guards*, a band of body-guards instituted by Henry VIII. in the year 1545. Their dress is similar to that of the time of their founder. One hundred are by rotation on duty, and there are seventy more, out of whom the place of any of the hundred who die is supplied.—*National Guards*, a military body which has acquired historical importance in the politics of France, originated with the revolution, but underwent many changes both during Napoleon's sway and under the restored Bourbons. It was abolished in April, 1827, for having demanded the removal of Villele's ministry; but was revived at Paris during the popular commotion in July, 1830, which ended in seating Louis Philippe on the throne.—*Guard-ship*, a vessel of war appointed to superintend the marine affairs of a harbor or river, to see that the ships not in commission have their proper watch-word kept duly, by sending her guard-boats round them every night; and to receive seamen who are impressed in time of war.

GUE'BRES, a Persian sect, who still worship fire as an emanation or emblem of the Deity.

GUELFS, or GUELPHS, the name of a family, composing a faction formerly in Italy, whose contests with a rival faction, called the Ghibelines, was the cause of much misery and bloodshed.—The wars of the Guelfs and Ghibelines became the struggle between the spiritual and secular power. The popes, who endeavored to reduce the German emperors to acknowledge their supremacy, and the cities of Italy, struggling for independence, and deliverance from the oppressive yoke of these same emperors, formed the party of the Guelfs. Those who favored the emperors were called Ghibelines.—A branch of the Guelf family was in the 11th century transplanted from Italy to Germany, where it became the ruling race of several countries; and the memory of this ancient name has lately been revived by the institution of the Hanoverian Guelfic order.

GUERRIL'LA, the plan of harassing the French armies by the constant attacks of independent bands, acting in a mountainous country, was adopted in the north of Spain during the Peninsular war. It was first reduced into a kind of system in 1810. The bands which conducted this desultory warfare were called Partidas: the name of Guerrilla is, by a misapplication of the term, frequently applied to them.

GUIDE, in music, the leading part in a canon or fugue.

GUILD, a company, fraternity, or corporation, associated for some commercial purpose; of which every member was to pay something toward the common charge. The ancient guilds were licensed by the king, and governed by laws and orders of their own.

GUILD'HALL, the chief hall of the city of London, for holding courts, and for the meeting of the lord-mayor and commonalty, in order to make laws and ordinances for the welfare and regulation of the city.—*Guild-rents* are rents paid to the crown by any guild or fraternity: or those that formerly belonged to religious houses, and came to the crown at the general dissolution of monasteries.

GUIL'LOCHE, in architecture, an ornament composed of curved fillets, which, by repetition, form a continued series.

GUILLOTINE', the name given to the instrument of capital punishment used in France; so called from Joseph Ignace Guillotin, by whom it was introduced into that country. This person was born at Saintes, and, established as a physician at Paris, obtained a certain celebrity in the early period of the Revolution by the strong part which he took in favor of the rights of the Tiers-Etat. He was elected in consequence a deputy to the National Assembly. When that body was occupied in its long discussions relative to the reform of the penal code (in 1790) Guillotin proposed the adoption of decapitation—up to that time used only for nobles—as the only method of capital punishment. From sentiments of humanity he recommended the employment of a machine which had been long known in Italy under the name of "mannaja," and in other countries also; for something much resembling it had been used in Scotland and in England within the jurisdiction of the borough of Halifax. The Assembly applauded the idea, and the machine was adopted, to which the Parisians have given the name of "Guillotine," of which Guillotin is most erroneously supposed to have been the inventor. It consists of two upright pieces of wood fixed in a horizontal frame; a sharp blade of steel moves up and down by means of a pulley in grooves in the two uprights; the edge is oblique instead of horizontal in shape, which gives it the mechanical power of the wedge. The criminal is laid on his face, his neck immediately under the blade, which severs it at a blow from his body. It is equally a vulgar error that Guillotin perished by the instrument which bears his name. He was imprisoned during the Reign of Terror, but released at the revolution of July, 1794; and died in 1814, after founding the association termed the Academy of Medicine.

GUIN'EA, an English gold coin, first coined in the reign of Charles II., and till lately current for 21*s*. It was so called because it was made from the gold that was brought from Guinea, on the coast of Africa.

GUITAR', a musical stringed instrument, rather larger than a violin, and played with the fingers. It is much used in Spain and Italy, more especially in the former country, where there are few, even of the laboring class, who do not solace themselves with its practice.

GUN, a fire-arm, or weapon of offence, which forcibly discharges a ball, shot, or other offensive matter, through a cylindrical barrel, by means of gunpowder. The larger species of guns are called cannon; and the smaller kinds are called muskets, carbines, fowling-pieces, &c. The gun is supposed to have been used in Asia at a very early date; but it was not invented in Europe before the 14th century. Roger Bacon, about the year 1280, suggested the possibility of applying the preparation since called gunpowder to the purposes of war; but the idea of blowing a body to a distance by its power was produced by its accidentally doing so, in the laboratory of Bartholomew Schwartz, a German monk. Guns were originally made of iron bars, soldered together, and strengthened with iron hoops, an example of which is still preserved in the Tower of London.

GUN'NERY, the science of using artillery against an enemy judiciously, and to the greatest effect. Besides an accurate acquaintance with the management of ordnance of all kinds, the range and force of every kind, the charge and direction necessary for different distances, their materials, the fabrication and effect of gunpowder, &c.; the artillerist must be able to instruct his men in their several exercises, and be thoroughly acquainted with all the tactics necessary in the art of attack and defence; he must be practically skilled in throwing up batteries and other field-works: he must understand mathematics, (particularly the doctrine of curves, to calculate the path of the balls;) and have some knowledge of mechanics.

GUN'POWDER, a composition of nitre, sulphur, and charcoal, mixed and reduced to fine powder, and usually granulated. It is in the highest degree combustible, and, by means of its elastic force, explodes with great intensity. The discoverer of this compound, and the person who first thought of applying it to the purposes of war, are unknown. It is certain, however, that it was used in the fourteenth century. From certain archives quoted by Wiegleb, it appears that cannons were employed in Germany before the year 1372. No traces of it can be found in any European author previously to the thirteenth century; but it seems to have been known to the Chinese long before that period. There is reason to believe that cannons were used in the battle of Cressy, which was fought in 1346. They seem even to have been used three years earlier, at the siege of Algesiras; but before this time they must have been known in Germany, as there is a piece of ordnance at Amberg, on which is inscribed the year 1303. Roger Bacon, who died in 1292, knew the properties of gunpowder; but it does not follow that he was acquainted with its application to fire-arms.

GUN'POWDER PLOT, in English history, the celebrated conspiracy of certain disappointed Roman Catholics to destroy the king, James I., and the two Houses of Parliament, by gunpowder, which was detected on the 4th of November, 1605.

GUS'TO, that which excites pleasant sensations in the palate or tongue. Figuratively this word is used for intellectual taste.

GUT'TURALS, letters pronounced by a peculiar effort of the throat. There are no gutturals properly so called in the English language, although the guttural sound may often be heard in some provincial pronunciations of the letter *r*. Nor are there in the pure French or Italian, although they are frequent in the dialects: *e. g.* the letter *c* hard (as in *casa*) has in the Tuscan a strong guttural sound. In the Spanish language alone, of those derived from the Latin, gutturals are common. In German, the guttural *ch* is largely used. In the Celtic language, *gh* and *ch* are also sounded with much variety of guttural intonation.

GYMNA'SIARCH, an Athenian officer who had the charge of providing the oil and other necessaries for the gymnasia. This was one of the offices at Athens, the expenses of which were defrayed from the private pocket of the individual on whom they devolved, and who received no salary from the state.

GYMNA'SIUM, originally a space measured out and covered with sand for the exercise of athletic games. Afterwards, among the classical Greeks, the gymnasia became spacious buildings or institutions for the mental as well as corporeal instruction of youth. They were first built at Lacedæmon, whence they spread through the rest of Greece, &c., into Italy. They did not consist of single edifices, but comprised several buildings and porticoes, used for study and discourse, for baths, anointing rooms, palæstras in which the exercises took place, and for other purposes. Two of the Athenian gymnasia, viz., the Lyceum and Academy, were rendered famous by being the scenes of the lectures of Aristotle and Plato respectively. The term gymnasium has descended to modern times. In Germany the higher schools, intended to give immediate preparation for the universities, are termed gymnasia. In Prussia the scholars undergo examination on leaving them: their compositions at this examination are sent to the minister of instruction and ecclesiastical affairs; and they receive testimonials of fitness, No. 1, 2, or 3, according to their degree of proficiency. Persons who have fitted themselves for the universities without passing through the gymnasia are examined by a committee appointed by government, which sits half-yearly for the purpose.

GYMNAS'TICS, under this name were comprised by the ancients all those games and exercises which were performed with the body partly naked; such as wrestling, boxing, running, throwing the quoit, playing at ball, &c. They were first instituted at Lacedæmon, where they were not confined to men, but were also considered a necessary part of the education of females. In the rest of Greece, where they subsequently spread, they were also held of the highest importance, and as such were conducted under the superintendence of the government, and entered conspicuously into the political schemes of the philosophers. In this respect the Greeks offered a remarkable contrast to their Asiatic neighbors, among whom it was considered a great disgrace even for a man to be seen naked. At Rome gymnastics were principally exercised by the mercenary athletes.

GYMNOS'OPHISTS, a sect of Indian philosophers who lived naked in the woods, whence they derived their name, and submitted to other strange austerities. They believed in the immortality of the soul and its migration into several bodies. They enjoyed great reputation for astronomical and physical science. There was likewise an African sect of philosophers bearing the same name, who are said to have lived in Æthiopia, near the sources of the Nile, whose habits differed from those of the Indian sect, inasmuch as they lived as anchorites, while the latter congregated in societies.

GYMNO'TUS, the name of an eel, remarkable for its power of affecting the nervous system, in the manner of electricity. This animal and the torpedo, on dissection, appear to have an arrangement of muscular plates not unlike a galvanic trough, and well adapted to produce the effect.

GYNÆCE'UM, among the ancients the apartment of the women, a separate room in the inner part of the house, where they employed themselves in spinning, weaving and needle-work.

GYNÆCON'OMI, certain magistrates amongst the Athenians, who had an eye upon the conduct of the women, and punished such as forsook the line of propriety and modesty. A list of such as had been fined was put up by them upon a palm-tree in the *Ceramicus*. The *gynæconomi* were ten in number, and differed from the *gynæcocosmi*; for the former were inspectors of manners, the latter of dress.

GYN'ARCHY or GYNÆCOC'RACY, government by a woman: or a state where women are legally capable of the supreme command. Of this Great Britain and Spain are familiar examples.

GYR'OMANCY, a kind of divination performed by walking round in a circle or ring.

H.

H, the eighth letter and sixth consonant of the English alphabet. It is not strictly a vowel, nor an articulation; but the mark of a stronger breathing than that which precedes the utterance of any other letter. It is pronounced with a strong expiration of the breath between the lips, closing, as it were, by a gentle motion of the lower jaw to the upper, and the tongue nearly approaching the palate. H is sometimes mute, as in *honor*, *honest;* also when united with *g*, as in *right, fight, brought*. In *which, what*, and some other words where it follows *w*, it is sounded before it, *hwich hwat*, &c. H, among the Greeks, as a numeral, signified 8; in the Latin of the middle ages, 200, and with a dash over it, 200,000.—In music, *h* is the seventh degree in the diatonic scale, and the twelfth in the chromatic.

HA'BEAS-COR'PUS, in law, a writ for delivering a person from false imprisonment, or for removing a person from one court to another. By the action of this writ, of which there are several kinds, adapted to different occasions, relief from all unjust imprisonment may be obtained, causes removed from one court to another for the promotion of justice, and prosecutors compelled to bring the prosecuted to open trial, instead of prolonging his imprisonment. Thus it not only protects the citizen from unlawful imprisonment at the suggestion of the civil officers of the government, but also against groundless arrests at the suit or instigation of individuals. The right is, however, liable to be suspended; it being sometimes necessary to clothe the executive with an extraordinary power, as the Romans were in the habit of choosing a dictator in emergencies, when the public was in danger.

HABEN'DUM, in law, a word of form in a deed or conveyance, which must consist of two parts, viz. the *premises* and *habendum* (to have and to hold.)

HABER'GEON, a coat of mail formerly worn to defend the neck and breast. It was formed of little iron rings united, and descended from the neck to the middle of the body.

HAB'IT, in philosophy, an aptitude or disposition either of mind or body, acquired by a frequent repetition of the same act: thus virtue is called a habit of the mind; strength, a habit of the body. All natural habits, whether of body or mind, are no other than the body and mind themselves considered as either acting or suffering; or they are modes of the body or mind wherein either perseveres till effaced by some contrary mode. —*Habit*, in medicine, denotes the settled constitution of the body; or a particular state formed by nature, or induced by extraneous circumstances.

HA'DES, in classical mythology, the abode of the dead. According to Hesiod the mortals of the brazen age were the first who descended to Hades. Hades was also an appellation of the god Pluto; in which sense alone, it is said, Hesiod uses it. The word occurs frequently in the Septuagint, and in the Greek New Testament, and almost invariably signifies the state of the dead in general, without regard to the virtuous or vicious characters of the persons, their happiness or misery.

HADJ, the Mohammedan pilgrimage to Mecca and Medina; whence Hadji, a pilgrim, or one who has performed this pilgrimage; Hedjaz, the Holy Land, where these cities are situated. By far the most authentic description of it is that of Burkhardt, who performed it in the guise of a Mohammedan, in 1814. It is fixed to a particular lunar month, and consequently takes place in every season of the year. It was a custom long anterior to the establishment of Islamism, when the famous "black stone" of the Caaba at Mecca was an object of idolatrous veneration. Every year a black silk stuff is now sent by the sultan to cover the Caaba. There are usually five or six caravans; from Syria, Egypt, Barbary, the East, and the North. In 1814, the number of pilgrims was about 70,000, and this was considered small. The pilgrims go through several ceremonies at Mecca, of which the principal are the *towaf*, or procession round the Caaba, and drinking of the well of Zemzen; they then proceed to the summit of Mount Ararat; and lastly to Medina, the place of the prophet's burial.

HAGIOG'RAPHY, sacred writings. The Jews divide the books of the Scriptures into three parts; the Law, which is contained in the first five books of the Old Testament; the Prophets, or Nevim; and the Cetuvim, or *writings*, by way of eminence. The latter class is called by the Greeks *Hagiographa*, comprehending the books of Psalms, Proverbs, Job, Daniel, Ezra, Nehemiah, Ruth, Esther, Chronicles, Canticles, Lamentations, and Ecclesiastes.

HAIL, the small masses of ice or frozen vapor, falling from the clouds in showers or storms. These masses consist of little spherules united, but not all of the same consistence; some being as hard and solid as perfect ice; others soft, like frozen snow. Hailstones assume various figures; some are round, others angular, others pyramidical, others flat, and sometimes they are stellated with six radii, like crystals of snow. Hail occurs chiefly in spring and summer, and is always accompanied with electrical phenomena, and not unfrequently with thunder. It usually precedes storms of rain, sometimes accompanies them; but never, or very rarely, follows them, especially if the rain is of any duration. The time of its continuance is always very short, generally only a few minutes. The usual size of hailstones is about a quarter of an inch in diameter, but they are frequently of much larger dimensions, sometimes even 3 and 4 inches in diameter. Hail-storms are very destructive to crops, particularly in hot climates. The phenomena attending the formation and fall of hail are not well understood; but it is supposed that the cold necessary for its formation is produced by the wind; and that when hailstones are formed they are also carried along through the atmosphere by currents of wind, in a direction very oblique to the horizon, by which means they may be kept suspended a sufficient length of time to acquire the dimensions they possess, by congealing the particles of humid vapor with which they successively come in contact. The electricity with which hail is always accompanied, is only the effect of the passage of the particles of water from the liquid to the solid state. Hail-rods, upon the same principle as lightning-rods, have been erected in Germany and Switzerland, with the view of subtracting the superabundant electricity from the clouds, and preventing the formation of hail; but they have not been attended with the success which was expected.

HAIR, in physiology, slender, oblong, and flexible filaments, growing out of the pores of animals, and serving most of them as a covering. It consists of the bulb, situated under the skin, which is a nervous vesicle, and a trunk which perforates the skin and cuticle, and is covered with a peculiar vagina or sheath. The color of human hair depends on the medullary juice; but there are also general differences of it, peculiar in some degree to the climates. In the hottest countries it is very black; in the colder it is yellowish, brown, or inclining to red; but in all places it grows gray or white with age. In quadrupeds it is of the most various conformation, from the finest wool to the bristles of a hog. The principal constituent parts of hair are animal matter, oil, silex, sulphur, carbonate of lime, &c. Among the ancients, from the earliest times, the hair of the head was an object of especial care and attention. Among the Greeks, it at first was worn long by adults; boys, especially those of Sparta, until the age of puberty, wore their hair cropped close. At a later period, it was customary for men to wear their hair cut short. The Athenian custom was the opposite of the Spartan; the hair was worn long in childhood, and cut upon arriving at manhood. The cutting of the hair was an act of solemnity, and performed with many ceremonies. The Roman youth, before the age of puberty, wore their hair in ringlets upon their shoulders; but about the time of putting on the *toga virilis*, they cut it short; such of them, at least, as wished to distinguish themselves from the maccaronis and effeminate coxcombs. The hair thus cut off was consecrated to Apollo, who is always represented with flowing hair, or to some other god, under whose protection they supposed themselves to be more immediately placed. In works of Art, the *Ephebi* (youth who had attained the age of 18,) and the *Athletæ* are always represented with short hair. Among the females, it was the custom to confine the hair with a band, or with network, sometimes richly ornamented with gold and other metals, examples of which are seen in the paintings found at Pompeii. In other representations we find the hair inclosed in a kind of bag, made of various textile materials. The color which was most prized was *blonde*, although *black* was the most common. In times of mourning the hair was cut short.

HAIR PEN'CILS, in painting, are composed of very fine hairs, as of the minever, the marten, the badger, the polecat, &c., which are mounted in a quill when they are small or of moderate size, but when larger than a quill they are mounted in white-iron tubes. The most essential quality of a good pencil is to form a fine point, so that all the hairs may be united when they are moistened by drawing them through the lips.

HAIR'S BREADTH, a measure of length, equal to the forty-eighth part of an inch.

HAL'BERD, or HAL'BERT, an ancient military weapon, intended for both cutting and thrusting, formerly carried by sergeants of foot and artillery. It was a kind of combination of a spear and a battle-axe, with a variously formed head, and a shaft about six feet long. It is now rarely to be seen in use, except in Scotland in the hands of town-officers (counterparts of English javelin-men)

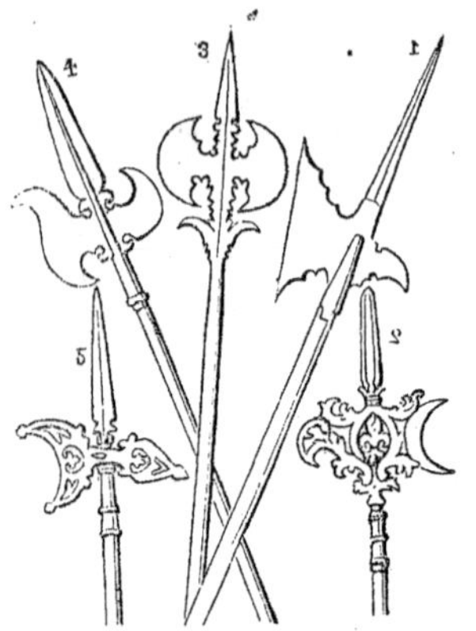

1. Halbert, time of Henry VIII. 2 do., with fleur de lis, Henry VII. 3. Double-axed halbert, Charles I. 4. Halbert, Charles II. 5 do., William III.

when attending the magistrates of a borough.

HAL'CYON DAYS, a name given by the ancients to the seven days that precede and follow the winter solstice, from the circumstance of the halcyon or alcedo selecting that period for incubation. While this process was going on, the weather was generally remarkable for its calmness; and hence the expression has passed into a proverb, signifying days of peace and tranquillity.

HALL, in architecture, a large room at the entrance of a house or palace. In the houses of ministers of state, magistrates, &c., it is the place where they give audience and despatch business. In magnificent edifices where the hall is very large and lofty, and placed in the middle of the edifice, it is called a *saloon*. An edifice, in which courts of justice are held; as Westminster *Hall*, which was originally a royal palace; the kings of England formerly holding their parliaments and courts of judicature in their own dwellings, as is still the practice in Spain. It is perhaps a term improperly applied, as now, to the entrance of a dwelling-house, though not so to a servants' hall. At Oxford an unendowed college is styled a *hall;* but at Cambridge the term is used indiscriminately for *college*, whether endowed or not.

HALLELU'IAH, a word signifying *praise the Lord*, or *praise ye Jehovah.* It is met with in the beginning of some Psalms, and the end of others. It is a word of such liquid fluency and harmonious softness, that it is retained in our hymns without translation. In conformity with the German and other continental languages in which *j* has the sound of *y*, we often see it written *Hallelujah;* but to pronounce the word with the English sound of *j* destroys its beauty, and it ought never to be so written.

HALLUCINA'TION, in medicine, erroneous imagination. *Hallucinations of the senses* arise from some defect in the organs of sense, or from some unusual circumstances attending the object; and they are sometimes symptoms of general disease, as in fevers. *Maniacal hallucinations* arise from some imaginary or mistaken idea.

HA'LO, a circle appearing round the body of the sun, moon, or stars, but more especially about the body of the sun and moon, called also corona, or crown. Haloes are sometimes white and sometimes colored. Sometimes one only appears, and sometimes several concentric circles appear at the same time. Haloes are at times accompanied with other phenomena, such as *parhelia*, or mock-suns; *paraselenes*, or mock-moons; *anthelia*, or glories. All these appearances are occasioned by the refraction, reflection, or inflection of light falling upon, or passing near thick vapor floating in the atmosphere.

HAMADRY'ADS, certain nymphs or inferior deities supposed by the Greek and Roman poets to preside over woods and forests, and, as their name implied, to live and die with the particular trees to which they were attached.

HAND, in anatomy, an important member of the human body, which, from the facilities it affords in all operations, and accuracy in ascertaining the magnitude, &c. of extraneous objects, is justly considered as contributing very essentially to all that is either ingenious or scientific in the human character.—In Christian Art a hand is the indication of a holy person or thing, and frequently occurs in pictures representing martyrdoms, as extended from a cloud over a saint. A hand in the act of benediction is frequently met with in early Christian Art, and generally represents the Almighty Father. Previous to the twelfth century, the Supreme was always represented by a hand extended from a cloud, sometimes open, with rays proceeding from the fingers, but generally in the act of benediction, viz., with two fingers raised and the rest open. The hands of our Saviour pierced, were frequently represented in sculpture.

HAND'LING, in painting, management of the pencil by touch. Handling should be bold, with freedom, firmness, and spirit.

HANSEAT'IC, pertaining to the Hanse towns, or to their confederacy. The Hanse towns in Germany were certain commercial cities which associated for the protection of commerce as early as the 12th century. To this confederacy acceded certain commercial cities in Holland, England, France, Spain, and Italy, until they amounted to seventy-two, which for centuries commanded the respect and defied the power of kings. From the middle of the 15th century, the power of the confederacy, though still very formidable, began to decline. This, however, was not owing to any misconduct on the part of its leaders, but to the progress of that improvement it had done so much to promote. The civilization, which had been at first confined to the cities, gradually extended over the contiguous country; and feudal anarchy was everywhere superseded by a system of subordination and the progress of the Arts. At present it only consists of the cities of Hamburgh, Lubeck, and Bremen; and they, indeed, possess merely the shadow of their former state.

HAP'PINESS, the agreeable sensations which spring from the enjoyment of good. It consists in the possession not only of the goods of the body, as health, strength, &c., but also of the more refined goods of the mind, as knowledge, memory, taste, and especially the moral virtues, magnanimity, fortitude, benevolence, &c. That state is mostly to be sought after, in which the fewest competitions and disappointments can happen, which least of all impairs any sense of pleasure, and opens an unexpected source of the most refined and lasting enjoyments. That state which is attended with all those advantages, is a state or course of virtue: therefore, a state of virtue, in which the moral goods of the mind are attained, is the happiest state; and he only can be esteemed really and permanently happy, who enjoys peace of mind in the favor of the Almighty.

HARANGUE', a popular oration, generally implying loudness or declamation; and not a deliberate and argumentative address or discourse.

HAR'BOR, a port, haven, or inlet of the sea, in which ships can moor, and be sheltered from the fury of winds and a heavy sea.

HARD'WARE, instruments and utensils of every kind manufactured from metals, comprising iron, brass, steel, and copper articles of all descriptions. Birmingham and Sheffield are the principal seats of the British hardware manufactures; and from these immense quantities of knives, razors, scissors, fire-arms, gilt and plated goods, &c. are supplied to an extent almost incredible. The total aggregate value of the iron and other hardware manufactures of England and Scotland may be estimated at not less than 17,500,000*l.* a year; affording direct employment, in the various departments of the trade, for at least 360,000 persons.

HA'REM, the apartments in which Mussulman princes confine their women, who are prohibited from the society of others. They are waited on by female slaves, and guarded by black eunuchs: the head of the latter is called *Kizlar-aga*. There are two kizlar-agas, one of the old, the other of the new palace, each of which has its harem. The one is occupied by the women of former sultans, and those who have incurred the displeasure of the reigning prince; the other by such as still enjoy his favor. The lady who first presents him with a male heir, is styled the *sultana*, by way of eminence. She must then retire into the old palace; but if her son ascends the throne, she returns to the new palace, and has the title of *sultana valide*. She is the only woman who is allowed to appear without a veil; none of the others, even when sick, are permitted to lay aside the veil, in the presence of any one except the sultan. When visited by the physician, their bed is covered with a thick counterpane, and the pulse felt through gauze. The life of the ladies of the imperial harem is spent in bathing, dressing, walking in the garden, witnessing the voluptuous dances performed by their slaves, &c. The women of other Turks enjoy the society of their friends at the baths, or at each other's houses, appear in public accompanied by slaves and eunuchs, and enjoy a degree of liberty which increases as they descend in rank. But those of the sultan have none of these privileges. It is, of course, only the richer Moslems who can maintain harems: the poorer classes have generally but one wife.

HAR'LEQUIN, the principal character in pantomime, clad in a party-colored dress, with a half-mask, and who is perpetually dancing, leaping, or performing tricks with his wonder-working wand. This character was first introduced into Italian comedy, where he united extravagant buffoonrey with great corporeal agility.

HARMAT'TAN, the name given to a prevailing wind on the coast of Africa, which is of a peculiarly dry and parching character.

HARMON'ICA, or ARMON'ICA, a musical instrument, in which the sound is produced from glasses, blown as near as possible in the form of hemispheres, having each an open neck or socket in the middle. The diameter of the largest glass is nine inches, and that of the smallest three inches. Between these there are twenty-three different sizes, differing from each other a quarter of an inch in diameter. The largest glass in the instrument is G, including three complete octaves; and they are distinguished by painting the apparent parts of the glasses within side, every semitone white, and the other notes of the octave with the seven prismatic colors; so that glasses of the same color, (the white excepted,) are always octaves to each other. The method of extracting exquisite tones, by rubbing the finger on the brim of drinking-glasses, filled with water in different proportions, was an old discovery; but it remained for Dr. Franklin to construct the *harmonica*. "The advantages of this instrument," says Dr. Franklin, "are, that its tones are incomparably sweet beyond any other; that they may be swelled and softened at pleasure, by stronger or weaker pressures of the finger, and continued to any length; and that the instrument, once well tuned, never again wants tuning." Its disadvantages are, the difficulty of adjusting the tones by grinding; the extreme skilfulness necessary in the player; and the impracticability of performing upon it many of the ordinary operations of the musical art; for however much it excels all others in the delicacy and duration of its tones, yet it is confined to those of a soft and plaintive character, and to slow solemn movements.

HARMON'ICS, that branch of music which considers the differences and proportions of sound. This science was by the ancients divided into seven parts; viz. of sounds, of intervals, of system, of the genera, of the tones or modes, of mutation, and of melopæia.

HARMON'IC TRIAD, in music, the chord of a note consisting of a third and perfect fifth, or, in other words, the common chord.

HAR'MONY, in music, the agreeable result or union of several musical sounds heard at one and the same time. *Natural harmony* consists of the harmonic triad or common chord.—*Artificial harmony* is a mixture of concords and discords.—*Figured harmony* is that in which, for the purpose of melody, one or more of the parts of a composition move, during the continuance of a chord, through certain notes which do not form any of the constituent parts of that chord.—*Harmony*, as applied to nature, the necessary reciprocal accordance of causes and effects, by which the existence of one thing is dependent on that of another.—In matters of literature, we use the word *harmony* for a certain agreement between the several parts of the discourse. In architecture, *harmony* denotes an agreeable relation between the parts of a building. In painting, it signifies the union or connection between the figures, with respect to the subject of the piece; and also denotes the union or agreeable mixture of different colors.—*Harmony of the spheres*, a favorite hypothesis of Pythagoras and many other ancient philosophers, according to which, celestial music, imperceptible by the ears of mortals, was supposed to be produced by the sweetly tuned motions of the stars and planets. This harmony they attributed to the various proportionate impressions of the heavenly globes upon one another, acting at proper intervals.

HAR'MONY OF THE SCRIP'TURES, GOSPELS, &c., the correspondence of the several writers of different parts of the Scriptures in their respective narratives, or statements of doctrine. The earliest Harmony of the Gospels was composed by Tatian, in the second century, with the title *Diatessaron*.

HAR'MONY PRE-ESTAB'LISHED, a hypothesis invented by Leibnitz, to explain the correspondence between the course of our sensations and the series of changes actually going on in the universe, of which, according to that philosopher and many others, we have no direct knowledge. This hypothesis is connected, in the Leibnitzian system, with the doctrine of monads,—certain spiritual powers or substances, one of which constitutes the principle of vitality and consciousness in every living being. Each of these, is, in its degree, a mirror, in which the changes going on in the universe are reflected with greater or less fidelity. But between simple substances, such as spirit and matter, soul and body, no real reciprocal action can take place. The Author of the universe has consequently so ordained that the series of changes going on in any particular conscious monad, corresponds precisely to those of the monads in contiguity to which it is placed. Hence arises our belief that mind is acted on by matter, and vice versa; a belief which leads to no practical errors in virtue.

HARMOS'TES, in ancient history, a Spartan magistrate, called also sometimes *sophronistes*, who was appointed to superintend a conquered state. Other Greek states which made conquests afterwards borrowed the name.

HARP, a musical stringed instrument, of a triangular figure. It stands erect, and, when used, is placed at the feet of the performer, who produces its tones by the action of the thumb and fingers of both hands on the strings. Its origin is very variously ascribed; but whatever it may have been, its invention is manifestly very ancient; for it appears to have been in use (under various forms) with the Egyptians, Hebrews, Greeks, and Romans. The Anglo-Saxons excelled in playing on the harp. The Irish, Scots, and Welsh also made much use of this instrument; and with the Anglo-Normans it was equally popular. By the Welsh laws, a harp was one of the things that were necessary to characterize a freeman or gentleman; and none could pretend to this rank, who had not a harp, and was not able to play upon it. By the same laws, to prevent slaves from pretending to be gentlemen, it was expressly forbidden to teach, or to permit, them to play upon the harp; and none but the king, the king's musicians, and gentlemen, were allowed to have harps in their possession. The modern harp forms one of the most elegant objects to the eye, while it produces some of the most agreeable effects to the ear, of any instrument in use. There are generally 35 strings, but sometimes the number is extended to 43: and the compass usually extends from double A of the bass clef, to double G in the G clef.

HAR'PIES, in mythology, three rapacious winged monsters, supposed to be the goddesses of storms, and called Aello, Ocypete, and Celœno. They are so differently described by the poets, that it is difficult to say anything definite concerning them. Hesiod represents them as young virgins, of great beauty; Vossius supposes them to be three winds; but both poets and artists appear generally to vie with each other in depicting them under the most hideous forms.

HARPOON', an iron instrument, formed at one end like a barbed arrow, and having a rope at the other, for the purpose of spearing the whale. As soon as the boat has been rowed within a competent distance of the whale, the harpooner launches his instrument; and the fish being wounded, immediately descends under the ice with amazing rapidity, carrying the harpoon along with him, and a considerable length of the line, which is purposely let down, to give him room to dive. Being soon exhausted with the fatigue and loss of blood, he re-ascends, in order to breathe, where he presently expires, and floats upon the surface of the water.—*Harpoon gun*, an instrument for discharging harpoons at whales in preference to the common method of the hand. It consists of a kind of swivel, having a barrel of wrought iron, about two feet long, and is furnished with two locks, which act simultaneously, for the purpose of diminishing the liability of the gun missing fire.

HARP'SICHORD, a musical instrument with strings of wire, played on by means of keys, the striking of which moves certain little jacks, which also move a double row of chords or strings, stretched over four bridges on the table of the instrument. Since the invention of that superior instrument, the grand piano-forte, the use of the harpsichord is greatly diminished.

HAR'USPICE, in Roman history, a person who pretended to foretell future events by inspecting the entrails of beasts sacrificed, or watching the circumstances attending their slaughter, or their manner of burning and the ascent of the smoke.

HAR'VEST MOON, an epithet applied to those moons which, in the autumnal months, rise on successive nights, soon after sunset, owing to the oblique ascension of the signs of the Zodiac, through which the moon is then passing.

HASTA'TI, among the Romans, were soldiers armed with spears, who were always drawn up in the first line of battle. These were picked out the next in age to the *velites*. At last they laid aside the spear, but still retained their name.

HATCH'WAY, in ships, a square or oblong opening in the deck, affording a passage from one deck to another, or into the hold or lower apartments.

HAT'TI-SHERIFF, in Turkish polity, an order which comes immediately from the Grand Signior, who subscribes it usually with these words:—"Let my order be executed according to its form and import." These words are generally edged with gold, or otherwise ornamented; and an order given in this way is irrevocable.

HAU'BERK, in armor, a tunic of ringed mail, with wide sleeves reaching a little below the elbow, and descending below the knees; being cut up before and behind a little way, for convenience in riding, it had the appearance of terminating in short trowsers. It was introduced in the twelfth century, and is supposed to have been introduced from Germany.—Hauberk is the name given to this vestment by the Normans, signifying a protection for the throat, but the term could only have been appropriate when the capuchin or cowl formed a component part of it.

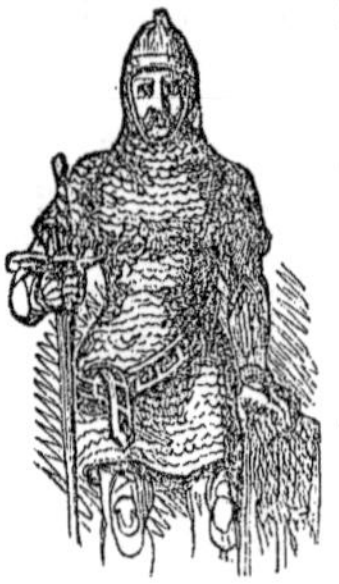

HAUT'BOY, a musical wind instrument, shaped somewhat like the flute, but spreading and widening at the bottom, and sounded through a reed.

HAV'ERSACK, a kind of bag of strong coarse linen, to carry bread and provisions on a march.

HEALTH, that condition of the body, in which all the vital, natural, and animal functions, are performed easily and perfectly, and unattended with pain. The most perfect state of health is generally connected with a certain conformation and structure of the bodily organs, and well marked by certain external signs. To preserve health, it is necessary to be temperate in food, exercise, and sleep; to pay strict attention to bodily cleanliness; to abstain from spirituous liquors, and to guard against excess of all kinds. The Greeks and Romans deified health, representing it under the figure of a woman, whom they supposed to be the daughter of Æsculapius. We find the name of the goddess Salus, or Health, on many medals of the Roman emperors, with different inscriptions, as *Salus publica*, *Salus reipublicæ*, *Salus Augusti*, &c.

HEAV'EN, literally the sky, or azure vault which spreads above us like a hollow hemisphere, and appears to rest on the limits of the horizon. Modern astronomy has taught us, that this blue vault is, in fact, the immeasurable space in which our earth, the sun, and all the planets, revolve. In metaphorical language, this space is called the abode of the Deity, and the seat of the souls of the just in the life to come. In these latter senses, it is sometimes called the empyrean, from the splendor by which it is characterized. It is also sometimes called the firmament. The word which, in the first chapter of Genesis, is translated *firmament*, was corrupted, it is said, by the Septuagint translators, and should be rendered *expanse* or *extension*. St. Paul speaks of the *third heaven;* and the orientals always describe seven heavens, or more. The foundation of the doctrine of several heavens was this: the ancient philosophers assumed there were as many different heavens as they saw bodies in motion; they considered them solid, although transparent, and supposed the blue space extended over our heads firm as a sapphire. They could not conceive that otherwise they could sustain those bodies; and they deemed them spherical, as the most proper form for motion. Thus, there were seven heavens for the seven planets, and an eighth for the fixed stars. Ptolemy discountenanced this system. He said, the deities (by which name he calls the stars, for they were adored in his time,) moved in an ethereal fluid. It was, however, by very slow degrees that men became acquainted with the true science which instructs us in the laws of celestial motion, and the magnitudes, distances, &c., of those effulgent orbs which deck the vast expanse. The heavens, then, to follow the path of the Newtonian or true system, are filled with a fluid much finer and thinner than this air, and extending beyond all limits of which we have any conception. There being nothing visible to us in the remote part of the heavens, we can only consider them as the places of the stars. We shall have a vast idea of this space if we consider that the largest of the fixed stars, which are probably the nearest to us, are at a distance too great for the expression of all that we can conceive from figures, and for all means of admeasurement. The sun, which in that little space of the heavens that makes the system of which our world is a part, is in reality nothing more than a fixed star.

HEBDOM'ADARY, a member of a chapter or convent, whose duty it is to officiate in the choir, rehearse the anthems and prayers, and perform other services, which, on extraordinary occasions, are performed by the superiors.

HEBDOM'ARY, a solemnity of the ancient Greeks, in which the Athenians sung hymns in honor of Apollo, and carried in their hands branches of laurel. It was observed on the seventh day of every lunar month; hence the name.

HE'BE, in Grecian mythology, was the goddess of youth, whose office it was to hand round the nectar at the banquets of the gods. She was the daughter of Jupiter and Juno.

HE'BRAISM, an idiom or manner of speaking peculiar to the Hebrew language.

HE'BREW, the language spoken by the Jews, and which appears to be the most ancient of all the languages in the world. The books of the Old Testament are the only pieces to be found, in all antiquity, written in pure Hebrew; and the language of many of these is extremely sublime. But Hebrew literature, independently of its containing the records of a divine revelation, possesses a peculiar scientific interest. It surpasses in antiquity, general credibility, originality, poetic strength, and religious importance, that of any other nation before the Christian era, and contains most remarkable memorials and trustworthy materials for the history of the human race, and its mental development.—The *Epistle to the Hebrews*, a canonical book of the New Testament. The Hebrews, to whom this epistle was addressed, were the believing Jews of Palestine, and its design was to convince them of the insufficiency and abolishment of the ceremonial and ritual law. In order to which the apostle undertakes to show, first, the superior excellency of Christ's person above that of Moses; secondly, the superiority of Christ's priesthood above the Levitical; and thirdly, the mere figurative nature, and utter insufficiency, of the legal ceremonies and sacrifices.

HEC'ATE, in mythology, a Grecian goddess, daughter of the Titan Perses and Asteria. She presided over popular assemblies, war, the administration of justice, and the rearing of children. There is a good deal of obscurity attached to this goddess, who is often confounded with Artemis or Diana, and Proserpine; whence she is sometimes considered the patroness of magic and the infernal regions. She was called the triple goddess, and was supposed to wander along the earth at night. Statues were set up to her in market-places, and especially at cross roads.

HECATE'SIA, in Grecian antiquity, a public entertainment given by the Athenians every new moon, in honor of Hecate.

HEC'ATOMB, amongst the Greeks, was a sacrifice consisting of a hundred oxen offered upon some very extraordinary occasion.—*Hecatomb*, in its most general sense, signifies no more than a sacrifice of a hundred animals; but the ox being the chief of animals used in sacrifice, gave derivation to the word.

HEGI'RA, the epoch of the flight of Mahomet from Mecca, July 10, 622, whence Eastern nations date the year of 354 days; which is found by subtracting 622 from our year, and then multiplying by 365 52, and dividing by 354.

HEI'GHTEN, in painting, a verb signifying to make prominent by means of touches of light or brilliant colors, as contrasted with the shadows.

HEIR, in law, the person who succeeds another by descent to lands, tenements, and hereditaments, being an estate of inheritance, or an estate in fee; because nothing passes by right of inheritance but in fee. We give the title to a person who is to inherit after the death of an ancestor, and during his life, as well as to the person who has actually come into possession.—*Heir-apparent*, is a person so called in the lifetime of his ancestor, at whose death he is heir at law.—*Heir-presumptive*, one who, if the ancestor should die immediately, would, in the present circumstances of things, be his heir; but whose right of inheritance may be defeated by the contingency of some nearer heir being born.

HEIR'-LOOM, any furniture or personal chattel, which by law descends to the heir with the house or freehold.

HELIX, HELICES, in architecture, the curling stalks or volutes under the flowers in each face of the abacus of the Corinthian capital.

HELLE'NIC, the name given to the common dialect which prevailed very generally among the Greek writers after the time of Alexander. It was formed with very slight variations, from the pure Attic of the age preceding its introduction.

HELLENIS'TIC, the name given to that dialect of the Grecian language that was used by the Jewish writers. Its peculiarities consisted in the introduction of foreign words very little disguised, but more especially of oriental metaphors and idioms; but not at all in the inflexions of words, which were the same as in the Hellenic. In this dialect, it is said, the

Septuagint was written, and also the books of the New Testament; and that it was thus denominated to show that it was Greek filled with Hebraisms and Syriacisms.

HEL'LENISTS, the name by which the Jews who from their foreign birth or travel used the Greek (Hellenic) language, are distinguished in the Acts of Apostles. The word is derived, according to a common method of formation in the Greek language, from the verb ἑλληνίζειν, *to Hellenize*, or adopt the manners of a Greek. There were great numbers of Jews scattered throughout the Roman empire at this period, more especially in the Asiatic and East African provinces, where the Greek was the current language; and as they were in the habit of making frequent journeys to and from Jerusalem, they heard the preaching of the Apostles, and became efficacious instruments in conveying the knowledge of the word throughout all lands. From their long sojourn in foreign countries they were distinguished from the Hebraists, or native Jews, by the greater liberality of their views with respect to the nature of the promises of the Old Testament. It appears from Acts, vi. 1, that these Jews retained the distinctive name of Hellenists after their conversion to Christianity, and that there continued to subsist some jealousy between them and the native Christians.

HEL'MET, defensive armor for the head: a word of Scandinavian derivation. The armor of the ancients, which particularly guarded the head, was known by the general denominations of head-piece, casque, and helmet. Helmets were anciently formed of various materials, but chiefly of skins of beasts, brass, and iron. An open helmet covers only the head, ears, and neck, leaving the face unguarded. Some open helmets have a bar or bars from the forehead to the chin, to guard against the transverse cut of a broad-sword; but it affords little defence against the point of a lance or sword. A close helmet entirely covers the head, face, and neck; having on the front perforations for the admission of air, and slits through which the wearer may see the objects around him; this part, which is styled the visor, (from the French word *viser*, to take aim,) lifts up by means of a pivot over each ear. Some helmets have a bever, (from *buveur*, drinker, or from the Italian *bevere*, to drink,) which, when closed, covers the mouth and chin, and either lifts up by revolving on the same pivots as the visor, or lets down by means of two or more pivots on each side near the jaws. The use of the bever was to enable the wearer to eat and drink more commodiously than could be done in a helmet with a visor only. The helmets of the Greeks and Romans were mostly

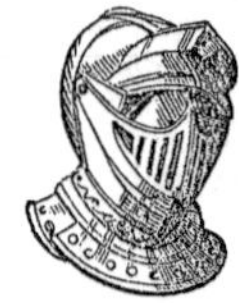

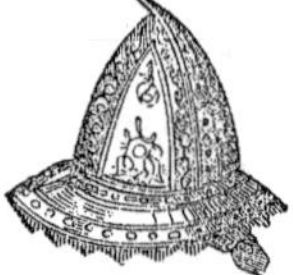

open, not unlike skull-caps, as formerly worn by modern dragoons. Montfaucon says he never saw an ancient helmet with a visor to raise or let down, although he is of opinion that they had those contrivances. It seems as if the Romans, at least those of which Pompey's army was composed at Pharsalia, had open helmets, as Cæsar directed his soldiers to strike them in the face, which order, had their faces been covered, he would not have given.

HE'LOTS, in ancient history, the slaves of the Spartans, who consisted originally of the Achæan inhabitants of Laconia, who were subdued by force of arms by the Dorian invaders. The name was derived from Helos, a town of Laconia, of which the inhabitants were thus reduced to servitude; but to this class were afterwards added the Messenians, who still clung to their native soil after its subjugation by the Spartans. They were employed either as domestic slaves, cultivators of the land, or in the public works; and though they do not appear to have been treated ordinarily with much severity, yet the recollection of their former state urged them frequently to revolt, while their numbers rendered them so formidable to their masters as to drive the latter to schemes of the most abominable treachery for their repression.

HELVET'IC, an epithet designating what pertains to the *Helvetii*, the ancient inhabitants of Switzerland, or to the modern states and inhabitants of the Alpine regions; as the *Helvetic* confederacy, &c.

HEM'I, a Greek word used in the composition of several terms borrowed from that language. It signifies *half*, the same as *semi*, and *demi*: thus, *hemiplegia* is a palsy of one *half* of the body; *hemistich*, *half* a verse: *hemicycle*, a *semi*-circle.

HEM'ISTICH, in poetry, denotes half a verse, or a verse not completed. In reading common English verse, a short pause is required at the end of each hemistich.

HENDECASYL'LABLES, in poetical composition, a verse of eleven syllables. Among the ancients it was particularly used by Catullus, and is well adapted for elegant trifles.

HEP'TACHORD, in ancient poetry, verses sung or played on seven chords or different notes; in which sense the word was applied to the lyre when it had but seven strings.

HEP'TARCHY, a government exercised by seven persons; or, a nation divided into seven governments.—*Saxon heptarchy*, the seven kingdoms existing in England, between the fifth and ninth centuries. These kingdoms were severally named, 1. Kent; 2. Sussex; 3. Wessex; 4. Essex; 5. Northumberland; 6. East-Angleland; 7. Mercia. The *heptarchy* was formed by degrees; but it may be said to have commenced in 449, when Hengist arrived on the island. In 827 Egbert was enabled, by a combination of circumstances, to assume the title of King of England; but, in reality, three of the kingdoms, Northumberland, East Angleland, and Mercia, were still governed by their own kings, though those kings were his vassals and tributaries. The kingdoms he actually governed were Kent, Sussex, Wessex, and Essex.

HERACLI'DÆ, the return of the Heraclidæ into Peloponnesus, in chronology, constituted the beginning of profane history; all the time preceding that period being accounted fabulous. This return happened in the year of the world 2682, a hundred years after they were expelled, and eighty after the destruction of Troy.

HER'ALD, the title of an officer in England whose duty it anciently was to declare war, to challenge in battle and combat, to proclaim peace, and to execute martial messages; but who is, at present, to conduct royal processions, the creations of nobility, and the ceremonies of knighthood; to publish declarations of war, not to the enemy, but at home; to proclaim peace; to record and blazon armorial bearings; and to regulate abuses in arms, under the authority of the earl-marshal, by whom he is created. The heralds were formed into a college by Richard the Third. The three chief heralds are called kings at arms, the principal of which is Garter; the next is called Clarencieux, and the third Norroy; these two last are called provincial heralds. Besides these there are six other inferior heralds, viz., York, Lancaster, Somerset, Richmond, Chester, and Windsor; to which, on the accession of king George I. to the crown, a new herald was added, styled Hanover herald; and another styled Gloucester king at arms.—*Heralds*, amongst the ancient Greeks and Romans, were held in great estimation, and looked upon as sacred. Those of Greece carried in their hands a rod of laurel, round which two serpents, without crests, were twisted as emblems of peace.

HER'ALDRY, is the art, practice, or science of recording genealogies, and blazoning arms or ensigns armorial; or it is the science of conventional distinctions impressed on shields, banners, and other military accoutrements. It also teaches whatever relates to the marshalling of cavalcades, processions, and other public ceremonies.—*Heraldry* has been divided into *personal* and *national*. The first of these divisions treats of bearings belonging to individuals, either in their own or in hereditary right. The second treats of distinctive emblems adopted by civil communities.

HERBA'RIA, collections of dried plants, such as the old botanists called *horti sicci*, or dry gardens. They are formed by gluing to sheets of paper branches and other parts of plants pressed flat, and dried in the sun or otherwise. If well prepared, they are as useful to the botanist as plants alive; but it is necessary to have some practical skill to be able to employ them advantageously. The largest public herbaria are those of the Museum at Paris; the Imperial collection of Vienna; the Royal of Berlin; and that of the British Museum, formerly Sir Joseph Bank's. Nothing certain is known of the extent of these collections, but they probably contain, in some cases, as many as 60,000 species. The herbarium is an unattractive part of public museums; but a very important one for numerous purposes of science, both practical and speculative.

HERCULA'NEUM, an ancient city of Naples, overwhelmed by an eruption of Mount Vesuvius in the reign of Titus; it was discovered in the year 1689, since which time many manuscripts, paintings, statues, and other relics of antiquity, have been discovered. From the excavations that have been made from time to time, the ancient streets and buildings have been, as it were, again thrown open, and the domestic affairs of the ancients revealed to the eyes of modern archæologists. Since 1828 new excavations have taken place, and a splendid private house has been discovered, with a suite of chambers, and a court in the centre. There is a separate part of the mansion allotted to females, a garden surrounded by arcades and columns, and also a grand saloon, which probably served for the meeting of the whole family. Another house, also discovered, was very remarkable, from the quantity and nature of the provisions in it, none of which had been disturbed for eighteen centuries, for the doors remained fastened, in the same state as they were at the period of the catastrophe which buried Herculaneum. The family which occupied this mansion was, in all likelihood, when the disaster took place, laying in provisions for the winter. The provisions found in the store-rooms consist of dates, chestnuts, large walnuts, dried figs, almonds, prunes, corn, oil, pease, lentils, pies, and hams. The internal arrangement of the house, the manner in which it was ornamented, all, in fact, announced that it had belonged to a very rich family and to admirers of the Arts; for there were discovered many pictures, representing Polyphemus and Galatea; Hercules and the three Hesperides, Cupid and a Bacchante, Mercury and Io, Perseus killing Medusa, and others. There were also in the same house, vases, articles in glass, bronze and terra cotta, as well as medallions in silver, representing in relief Apollo and Diana.

HERCU'LEAN, an epithet expressive of the great labor necessary to execute any task; such as it would require the strength or courage of Hercules to encounter or accomplish.

HER'CULES, in mythology, one of the most celebrated personages of antiquity, believed to be the son of Jupiter and Alcmæna, the daughter of Electryon, king of Mycenæ. The history and wonderful exploits of this hero are so well known, that it would be superfluous to dwell upon them here. There is, perhaps, no subject connected with antiquity to the right comprehension of which such formidable difficulties are presented; and hence the numerous attempts that have been made to separate truth from fiction in the history of Hercules, by divesting it of the mythological traditions with which it had been encumbered by all the writers of antiquity. In some shape or another, all the profane nations of antiquity seem to have possessed a divinity to whom they attributed an extraordinary degree of bodily strength, combined with indomitable perseverance and moral energy in prosecuting and overcoming difficult achievements. The reader will at once recognize, as belonging to this class, the Baal of the Syrians, the Melkarth of Phœnicia, and the Rama of Hindostan; who, like the Grecian Hercules, outstripping in bodily and intellectual endowments the great mass of the people of the rude era in which they lived, achieved a multiplicity of deeds which were looked upon as altogether miraculous, and which procured for their authors empire and dominion during their lives, and after death a place among the gods.

HEREDIT'AMENTS, in law, lands, tenements, and whatever immovable things a person may have to himself and his heirs, by way of inheritance; and which, if not otherwise bequeathed, descend to him who is next heir, and not to the executor, as chattels do.

HERED'ITARY, an appellation given to whatever belongs to a family by right of succession, from heir to heir. Some monarchies are hereditary, and others elective; and some hereditary monarchies descend only to the heirs male, as in France; but others, to the next of blood, as in Spain, England, &c.—*Hereditary* is also applied to offices and posts of honor annexed to certain families; thus in England the office of earl-marshal is hereditary in the family of Howard. It is also figuratively applied to good or ill qualities, supposed to be transmitted from a parent to a child; as, hereditary bravery, hereditary pride.

HER'ESY, a fundamental error in religion, or an error of opinion respecting some fundamental doctrine of religion. But in countries where there is an established church, an opinion is deemed *heresy*, when it differs from that of the church. The Scriptures being the standard of faith, any opinion that is repugnant to its doctrines, is *heresy;* but as men differ in the interpretation of Scripture, an opinion deemed heretical by one body of Christians, may be deemed orthodox by another. In Scripture and primitive usage, *heresy* meant merely sect, party, or the doctrines of a sect, as we now use *denomination* or *persuasion*, implying no reproach.

HER'ETOCH, among the ancient Saxons, signified the leader or commander of an army, or the commander of the militia in a country or district.

HER'IOT, in law, the fine paid to the

lord of the manor, by copyholders, on the death of the tenant.

HER'ISSON, in fortification, a beam or bar armed with iron spikes pointing outwards, and turning on a pivot; used to block up a passage.

HERMENEU'TICS, the art of finding the meaning of an author's words and phrases, and of explaining it to others. The word is seldom used except in reference to theological subjects.

HERMET'IC ART, the imaginary art or science of alchemy; so termed from Hermes Trismegistus, a personage of questionable reality, looked up to by the alchemists as the founder of the art. Some spurious works bearing his name are still extant.

HER'MITS, or ER'EMITES, persons who, in the early ages of Christianity, secluded themselves from the world for devotional purposes, betaking themselves to solitary and desert places (ἐρημός,) whence their name. In the first five centuries of our era this class of persons was extremely numerous; nor have individuals been wanting in latter ages who have undergone the same privations with the same mistaken views, and have acquired great reputation for sanctity in consequence.

HE'RO, in pagan mythology, an illustrious mortal, but supposed by the populace to partake of immortality, and after his death to be placed among the gods.—*Hero* is also used in a more extensive sense for a great, illustrious, and extraordinary personage; particularly one eminent for valor, courage, intrepidity, and other military virtues.—*Hero*, in a poem or romance, is the principal personage, or the one who has the principal share in the actions related; as Achilles in the Iliad, Ulysses in the Odyssey, &c. —*Heroic verse*, hexameter verse, so called because it is used by poets in their heroic poems.—*Heroic age*, that age or period of the world wherein the heroes, or demigods, are supposed to have lived. The heroic age coincides with the fabulous age.

HERRN'HUT, an establishment in Upper Lusatia, comprising, it is said, at present 120 houses, and 1500 inhabitants, which was founded by a few Moravians about the year 1722, under the patronage of Count Zinzendorf. The principles of the society thus formed are seclusion from the world, the enjoyment of a contemplative life, and the possession of all goods in common. Its members are bound together, under the title of Moravian Brethren, by strict laws and observances. Accusations have been thrown out against them of their indulging, in their retirement, in many licentious practices; but it is certain that their industry supplies many of the markets of Germany with various useful and ornamental articles of handiwork; that their zeal has prompted them to establish affiliated societies in many parts of Europe and America; and that in religious matters they are neither extravagant themselves, nor intolerant of others.

HER'THA, (sometimes written Aertha, Aortha, and Eorthe.) In German mythology, the name generally assigned in modern times to the chief divinity of the ancient German and Scandinavian nations. She was worshipped under a variety of names, of which the chief were exactly analogous to those of Terra, Rhea, Cybele, and Ops, among the Greeks and Romans. Long before the Christian era the knowledge of Hertha appeared to have been extended over a great portion of northern Europe. Tacitus speaks of the wonderful unanimity which tribes that had no other feature in common displayed in worshipping this goddess, whom he designates Herthus, or *Mother Earth*. Her chief sanctuary was situated, according to the same authority, in a sacred grove in an island of the ocean, *in insula oceani*, which, by some writers, has been supposed to be Riga, and by others Zetland or Heligoland; but no modern researches have been able accurately to fix its locality.

HESPER'IDES, in Greek mythology, the daughters of Night, or the granddaughters of Hesperus the brother of Atlas, three or seven in number, possessors of the fabulous garden of golden fruit watched over by an enchanted dragon at the western extremities of the earth. Such at least is the most ordinary form of the fable, but it is very variously represented.

HET'EROCLITE, in grammar, a word which is irregular or anomalous, either in declension or conjugation, or which deviates from the ordinary forms of inflection in words of a like kind.

HEX'ACHORD, in music, a progression of six notes, to which Guido attached the syllables *ut*, *re*, *mi*, *fa*, *sol*, *la*. The hexachord is also called a sixth; and is twofold, greater and less. The former is composed of two greater, two less tones, and one greater semitone, making five intervals; the latter of two greater tones, one lesser and two greater semitones.

HEXAM'ETER, in ancient poetry, a verse consisting of six feet, the first four of which may be either dactyls or spondees, the fifth must regularly be a dactyl, and the sixth always a spondee. Hexameter verse was employed on almost every topic to which poetry can be applied. In modern times several poets of France, England, and Germany have attempted to introduce this measure into the language of their respective countries. The few specimens we have seen of it in French appeared to us wholly unsuccessful. The little countenance given to the attempts made by Dr. Southey and others to introduce it into English literature, is conclusive, we think, against its ever being generally adopted in that country; but, on the other hand, it has been cultivated in Germany with great success, as the *Hermann and Dorothea* of Goethe, and many other examples that might be cited, abundantly prove. One of the most successful specimens of modern hexameter is the admirable poem of *Evangeline*, by our countryman, Longfellow.

HEX'APLE, the combination of six versions of the Old Testament by Origen, is so called: viz., the Septuagint, Aquila, Theodotian, Symmachus, one found at Jericho, and another at Nicopolis.

HEX'ASTYLE, in architecture, that species of temple or other building having six columns in front.

HIA'TUS, a word which has passed into several modern languages. In diplomatics and bibliography, it signifies a deficiency in the text of an author, as from a passage erased, worn out, &c. In grammar and prosody, it properly signifies the occurrence of a final vowel, followed immediately by the initial vowel of another word, without the suppression of either by an apostrophe. This, in Greek and Latin poetry, was only admissible in certain excepted cases; as where, in Greek, a final long vowel is succeeded by an initial short vowel, and becomes sometimes short by position: or in Latin, where the *cæsura* gave an additional force to the first vowel, as in the celebrated line,

"Ter sunt conatī īmponere Peliŏ Ossam."

which affords an instance of both, the first hiatus being occasioned by the cæsura; the second, an imitation of the Greek prosody. In French the hiatus is carefully avoided: in English less so, although by the more accurate poets still regarded as a blemish, except in some instances where a long vowel is followed by a short one. The worst species of hiatus is where the same vowel sound is repeated.

HI'ERARCHY, a term literally signifying *holy government*, and applied sometimes to the supposed polity, or social constitution, among angels. Also, ecclesiastical government, or the subordination of rank among the different orders of clergy.

HIEROGLYPH'ICS, in antiquity, mystical characters or symbols used in writings and inscriptions, particularly by the Egyptians, as signs of sacred, divine, or supernatural things. The hieroglyphics were figures of animals, parts of the human body, &c., containing a meaning which was intelligible only to the priests, and those who were initiated in their mysteries. In a general sense, a hieroglyphic is any symbol or figure which may serve to represent an object and convey a meaning.

HIEROGRAM'MATISTS, in antiquity, priests amongst the Egyptians who presided over learning and religion. Their duty was to take care of the hieroglyphics, and expound religious mysteries and opinions. They were also skilled in divination, and were honored with many exemptions from civil duties and taxes.

HIEROM'ANCY, in Grecian antiquity, a species of divination, which predicted future events by observing the appearances of the various things offered in sacrifice.

HIEROM'NEMON, in ancient Greece, a magistrate who presided over the sacred rites and solemnities.

HIERON'ICES, in antiquity, a conqueror at the Olympic, Pythian, Isthmian, and Nemean games.

HIEROPHAN'TES, in Grecian antiquity, the priests and priestesses who were appointed by the state to have the supervisal of sacred rites, and to take care of the sacrifices.

HIEROPH'YLAX, an officer in the Greek church, who was guardian or keeper of the holy utensils, vestments, &c., answering to our sacristan or vestry-keeper.

HIGH'NESS, a title of honor given to princes. The kings of England before James I. were not saluted with the title of "majesty," but that of highness only. At present the children of crowned heads are generally styled *royal highness*. Those of the emperors of Austria and Russia are styled *imperial highness*.

HIGH-PRIEST, the head of the Jewish priesthood. Moses conferred this dignity upon his orotner, in whose family it descended without interruption. After the subjugation of the Jews by the Seleucidæ, the Ptolemies, and the Romans, it was often arbitrarily conferred by the foreign masters. The importance of this officer is indicated by the splendor and costliness of his garment, which was among the most beautiful works of ancient art.

HILA'RIA, in antiquity, a festival celebrated by the Romans on the 8th of the calends of April, in honor of the god Pan.

HINDOOS', the primitive inhabitants of the East Indies ; a people distinguished for their humanity, gentleness, industry, and knowledge of the polite arts, at a time when most of their Asiatic neighbors were yet only in the first stages of civilization, when the Greeks lay in obscurity, and the nations of Europe were in a state of barbarism. They have preserved their national character from the most distant ages, even under the dominion of foreigners, and have retained to the present day their language, their written characters, their government, religion, manners, customs, and habits of life. They possess great natural talents, but are at present deprived of opportunities for their development, though they are still largely engaged in manufactures and commerce. In earlier times, before they were oppressed by a foreign yoke, they had reached a higher degree of civilization, and their country has been considered as the cradle of the arts and sciences. They are divided into four distinct classes, or *castes*, which, to the great disadvantage of cultivation, are essentially and perpetually separate from each other, so that no transition from one to another is possible. But the most extraordinary custom of the Hindoos is the burning of widows at the funeral of their husbands.

HIPPOCEN'TAUR, in ancient fable, a supposed monster, half man and half horse. The *hippocentaur* differed from the *centaur* in this, that the latter rode on an ox, and the former on a horse, as the name imports.

HIP'POCRENE, a celebrated fountain at the foot of Mount Helicon, supposed to have been produced by the horse Pegasus having struck his foot against the mountain. It was regarded in antiquity with peculiar veneration, as it was believed to be a favorite haunt of the Muses, and was consequently looked upon as one of the chief sources whence the poets drew their inspiration.

HIP'PODROME, in antiquity, a course for chariot and horse races. There are in England some vestiges of similar courses, the most remarkable of which is that near Stonehenge. This hippodrome occupies a tract of ground extending about two hundred druidical cubits, or three hundred and fifty feet, in breadth, and six thousand druidical cubits, or more than a mile and three quarters, in length. It runs directly east and west, and is completely inclosed with a bank of earth. The goal and career are at the east end. The goal is a high bank of earth, raised with a slope inwards, on which the judges are supposed to have sat. There is one about half a mile to the southward of Leicester; another near Dorchester ; and a third on the banks of the Lowther, near Penrith in Cumberland. But these must have been humble imitations indeed of the splendid structures erected in ancient times, as may be seen in the description of the one at Olympias, as given by Pausanias, or of that which was finished by Constantine, and which still fills the traveller who visits the Turkish capital with astonishment. It is surrounded by two ranges of columns, extending farther than the eye can reach, raised one above the other, and resting on a broad foundation, and is adorned by an immense quantity of statues, in marble, porphyry, and bronze.

HISTOR'ICAL PAINTING, in painting, that department of the art which comprehends all representations whereof history furnishes the subject. But under this head are generally included subjects from fabulous history, and those founded on allegory.

HISTORIOG'RAPHER, a professed historian, or writer of histories. It has been a common, although not uniform practice in European courts, to confer the place of public historiographer on some learned man as a mark of royal favor. Voltaire had at one period the title of Royal Historiographer of France.

HIS'TORY, an account of facts, particularly of facts respecting nations or states ; a narration of events in the order in which they happened, with their causes and effects. History differs from annals. Annals relate simply the facts and events of each year, in strict chronological order, without any observations of the annalist. History regards less strictly the arrangement of events under each year, and admits the observations of the writer. This distinction, however, is not always regarded with strictness. History is of different kinds, or treats of different subjects; as, a history of government, or political history; history of the Christian church, or ecclesiastical history; history of the affairs of nations, empires, kingdoms, and states, their rise, progress, and decline, or civil history; history of religion as contained in the bible, or sacred history.—*Profane history* is another name for civil history, as distinguished from sacred history; history of war and conquests, or military history; history of law; history of commerce; history of the crusades; history of literature, history of science, &c. In these and similar examples, history is written narrative or relation. The divisions of history in relation to periods of time have been reckoned three. 1. Ancient history, which includes the Jewish history, and that of the nations of antiquity, and reaches down to the destruction of the Roman empire, A.D. 476. 2. History of the middle ages, which begins with 476, and comes down to the discovery of America in 1492, or to the reformation. 3. Modern history, from either of these eras to our own times.—*Classical history*, properly so called, is the history of the national affairs and conquests of the Greeks and Romans.—The uses of history are as varied as they are important. To become acquainted with the characters of men, the marks, sources, and effects of their passions and prejudices, the power and changes of their customs, and the like, is an essential and necessary step to prudence; and all this knowledge is considerably improved by history, which teaches us to make other men's experience our own, to profit by it, and to learn wisdom from their misfortunes. Persons who read history merely for amusement, or, having in view some particular branch of learning, attend only to certain branches of history, are not confined to that order and connection which is absolutely requisite for obtaining a proper knowledge of history; the most regular, as well as successful way of studying which, is to begin with an epitome of universal history, and afterwards apply to the history of particular nations and commonwealths; for the study of particular histories is only extending the knowledge of particular parts of universal history. Unless this be our plan, we shall only fill the memory with some events; which may be done without applying to history, or pretending to the knowledge of it.

HISTRION'IC ART, that of acting in dramatic representation. *Histrio*, in ancient Rome, signified an actor or comedian; but more especially a pantomimist, whose talents were exerted in gesticulations and dancing.

HOCK'DAY, or HOKE'DAY, a day of feasting and mirth, formerly held in England the second Tuesday after Easter, to commemorate the destruction of the Danes in the time of Ethelred.

HO'LINESS, a title of quality given to the pope, who is styled, "your holiness," or, "holy father:" in Latin, *sanctissime*, or *beatissime pater*.

HOL'OCAUST, a burnt offering or sacrifice, wholly consumed by fire: of this kind was the daily sacrifice in the Jewish church. This was done by way of acknowledgment, that the person offering, and all that belonged to him, were the effects of the divine bounty. The pagan nations, who also offered holocausts, probably considered them in the same light.

HOL'OGRAPH, a deed or testament wholly written by the hand of the testator.

HO'LY ALLI'ANCE, THE, a league formed between certain of the principal sovereigns of Europe, after the defeat of Napoleon at Waterloo; on the proposal, it is said, of the Emperor Alexander. It arose from the religious enthusiasm which was prevalent at that period of deliverance from French domination, and with which the Russian emperor was just then considerably imbued. The act of this alliance is said to have been sent in his handwriting to the emperor of Austria and king of Prussia, and signed by them. It is not supposed that the original terms of the league were other than indefinite; for the maintenance of justice, religion, &c., in the name of the Gospel. But it was subsequently connected with the determination of those monarchs to support, in conjunction with England and France, existing governments throughout Europe, by the Declaration of November, 1819: afterwards the congresses of Troppau, Laybach, and Verona established the character of the alliance; to which the war of France against Spain, in 1823, gave additional illustration. Since the secession of England and France, the alliance can scarcely be said to have any active existence.

HO'LY ROOD, or HOLY CROSS, a festival kept on the 14th of September, to commemorate the exaltation of the Holy Cross. It is from this circumstance that the royal palace in Edinburgh has derived its appellation.

HO'LY THURSDAY, or ASCENSION

DAY, in the Romish calendar, the 39th day after Easter Sunday. A festival in commemoration of Christ's ascension.

HO'LY-WATER, in the Roman Catholic and Greek churches, water which has been consecrated by prayers, exorcisms, and other ceremonies, to sprinkle the faithful and things used for the church. It is contained in a particular kind of vases, at the doors of churches, and also within them at certain places, from which the Catholics sprinkle themselves before prayer. The Protestants renounce the use of holy-water probably from a fear that it would be considered, like amulets or relics, as something efficacious in itself, without the repentance commanded by the church.

HO'LY-WEEK, the week before Easter, in which the passion of our Saviour is commemorated.

HO'MÆOMERI'A, the name given to the physical theory of Anaxagoras, a Grecian philosopher of Clazomenæ, who flourished in the fifth century B.C. According to this hypothesis, every material substance is made up of infinitely small parts similar to itself. Hence the growth and nourishment of animals and vegetables was accounted for, by supposing the alimentary substance to be analyzed into its various component parts corresponding to the parts of the substance nourished. For instance, corn was supposed to contain particles of blood, bone, flesh, skin, &c., which by the process of digestion were separated from each other, and added to the corresponding parts of the animal body. This theory bears some resemblance to that of the *monads* of Leibnitz in modern times.

HOM'AGE, in law, the oath of submission and loyalty, which the tenant, under the feudal system, used to take to his lord when first admitted to his land.

HOMER'IC, pertaining to Homer, the great poet of Greece, or to his poetry.

HOM'ICIDE, in law, the killing of one human being by another. It is of three kinds, *justifiable*, *excusable*, or *felonious; justifiable*, when it proceeds from unavoidable necessity, without an intention to kill, and without negligence; *excusable*, when it happens from misadventure, or in self-defence; *felonious*, when it proceeds from malice, or is done in the prosecution of some unlawful act, or in a sudden passion. Homicide committed with premeditated malice, is *murder*. Suicide also, or self-murder, is felonious homicide.—The lines of distinction between felonious and excusable or justifiable homicide, and between manslaughter and murder, are, in many cases, difficult to define with precision. But, in general, the accused has the advantage of any uncertainty or obscurity that may hang over his case, since the presumptions of law are usually in his favor.

HOM'ILY, a sermon or discourse upon some point of religion, delivered in a plain manner, so as to be easily understood by the common people. In the primitive church, homily rather meant a conference or conversation by way of question and answer, which made part of the office of a bishop, till the fifth century, when the learned priests were allowed to preach, catechize, &c., in the same manner as the bishops used to do. There are still extant several fine homilies, composed by the ancient fathers.—*Homiletic or pastoral theology*, a branch of practical theology, which teaches the manner in which ministers of the gospel should adapt their discourses to the capacities of their hearers, and pursue the best methods of instructing them by their doctrines and examples.

HOMŒOP'ATHY, a mode of treating diseases, which consists in the administration of a medicine which is capable of exciting in healthy persons symptoms closely similar to those of the disease which it is desired to cure.

HOMOGE'NEOUS, or HOMOGE'NEAL, an appellation given to things, the elements of which are of similar nature and properties.—*Homogeneous light*, that whereof the rays are all of one color and degree of refrangibility, without any mixture of others.

HOMO'NYMS, words which agree in sound, but differ in signification; as the substantive "bear" and the verb "bear."

HOMOOU'SIANS, and HOMOIOU'SIANS, names by which the Orthodox and Arian parties were distinguished in the great controversy upon the nature of Christ in the fourth century; the former word signifying that the nature of the Father and Son is the *same*, the latter that they are *similar*. Homoousian (Gr. ὁμοουσιος) is derived from ὁμος, *the same*, and ουσια, *being;* Homoiousian (ὁμοιουσιος) from ὁμοιος, *similar*, and ουσια.

HOMOPHO'NOUS, in music, of the same pitch, or unisonal. Two or more sounds are said to be homophonous when they are exactly of the same pitch.

HOMOPH'ONY, homophonous words or syllables, in language, are words or syllables having the same sound, although expressed in writing by various combinations of letters. Languages which abound in homophonies are, 1. Some Oriental monosyllabic tongues, namely, the Chinese and its kindred dialects, in which very few sounds comprise the whole vocabulary, and the same sound is expressed by a variety of ideographic characters, (in Chinese there are only 400 such sounds, multiplied by the distinctions of tone and accent to 1600 or 2000;) and, 2. Some European tongues in which, according to the genius of the dialect, the syllables of the original languages from which the words are chiefly derived have been contracted in speaking, and part of their sounds dropped, while the greater part of the letters is retained. Thus in English, and still more in French, which is peculiarly a dialect of Latin abounding in contractions, homophonies are numerous, (in the latter tongue the number of syllables differently spelt, all having nearly the sound of our broad A, amounts to more than a hundred;) while in Italian, in which the original proportions of the Roman language are preserved, they are scarcely to be found at all.

HONG, the Chinese name for the foreign factories situated at Canton. The hong merchants are those persons who are alone legally permitted to trade with foreigners. They are ten in number, and are always held responsible by the government for paying all duties, whether on imports or exports in foreign vessels. No foreign ship that enters the Chinese ports can commence unloading until she has obtained a hong merchant as security for the duties.

HON'OR, a testimony of esteem or submission, expressed by words, actions, and an exterior behavior by which we make known the veneration and respect we entertain for any one, on account of his dignity or merit. The word *honor* is also used in general for the esteem due to virtue, glory, and reputation. It moreover means, that dignified respect for character, which springs from principle or moral rectitude, and which is a distinguishing trait in the character of good men. It is also used for virtue and probity themselves, and for an exactness in performing whatever we have promised: and in this last sense we use the term, *a man of honor*. But honor is more particularly applied to two different kinds of virtue, bravery in men, and chastity in women. Virtue and honor were deified among the Greeks and Romans, and had a joint temple consecrated to them at Rome; but afterwards they had separate temples, which were so placed, that no one could enter the temple of Honor, without passing through that of Virtue; by which the Romans were continually put in mind, that virtue is the only direct path to true glory. The first temple to honor was erected by Scipio Africanus, and another afterwards was built by Claudius Marcellus. We find a personification of this quality on several medals of Galba and of Vitellius. She is represented half naked, holding in one hand a spear, and in the other a cornucopia: upon others, a long robe envelops the figure, and the spear is exchanged for an olive branch.—*Honor*, in law, a superior seignory, to which other lordships and manors owe suit and service, and which, itself, holds of the king only—*Honors of war*, honorable terms granted to a vanquished enemy, when he is permitted to march out of a town with all the insignia of military honors.—*Laws of honor*, among persons of fashion, signify certain rules by which their social intercourse is regulated, and which are founded on a regard to reputation. These laws require a punctilious attention to decorum in external deportment, but often lead to the most flagrant violations of moral duty.—*Court of honor*, an ancient court of civil and criminal jurisdiction, having power to redress injuries of honor, and to hold pleas respecting matters of arms and deeds of war.—*Maids of honor*, ladies in the service of European queens, whose business it is to attend the queen when she appears in public. In England, they are six in number, with a salary of £300 each.

HON'ORABLE, a title prefixed to the Christian names of the younger sons of earls, and to those of all the children, both sons and daughters, of viscounts and barons. It is also conferred on persons filling certain offices of trust and dignity such as the maids of honor of the queen and queen dowager; and collectively on certain public bodies or institutions, as the House of Commons, the Congress of the United States, the East India Company, &c., &c. The title of *right honorable* is given to all peers and peeresses of the United Kingdom; to the eldest sons and all the daughters of peers above the rank of viscount; to all privy counsellors; and to some civic functionaries, as the lord mayors of London and Dublin, the lord provosts of Edinburgh and Glasgow, &c.

HONORA'RIUM, a term used almost synonymously with *fee*, and applied at present chiefly to the fees tendered to professors in universities, and to medical or other professional gentlemen for their services. It was originally applied solely to the salaries of the great officers of state, whose services it was considered, by a perhaps pardonable euphemism, were remunerated only, as it were, *honoris causa;* a shade of meaning which is still perceptible in the present use of the term.

HON'ORS. Greece, in the heroic times, rendered to all her great generals and captains some liberal reward as a proof of the public approbation and respect. This was sometimes offered in the shape of a vase of gold, or of a silver tripod, or some other valuable article either of utility or of mere ornament. Similar rewards were conceded to the victorious Roman leader in the shape of a triumph or ovation. Nor was it to military merit alone that the ancients decreed honors: the Fine Arts were made objects of national regard and encouragement. Philosophy, eloquence, painting, poetry, music, sculpture, architecture, were each enabled to aspire to the highest distinctions. The Lacedæmonians, even although their education was decidedly warlike, erected statues to the poet Tyrtæus. At the celebrated public games in Sparta, prizes were distributed to the most successful amongst the poets and musicians. Athens erected statues to Solon, to Socrates, and an infinity of others. To Homer temples were raised; and various poets and artists received crowns, prerogatives, and often the rights of citizenship. The Athenians inscribed upon the front of their temples the names of the able architects who had designed them. The town of Pergamus purchased with the public funds a palace for the reception of the works of Apelles. The Eleans, for whom Phidias executed the statue of Jupiter Olympus, in honor for the memory of the artist, and in respect for the surpassing beauty of his work, erected, in favor of his descendants, a lucrative office, of which the only duty consisted in taking care of, and keeping free from blemish, that celebrated piece of art. In the times of the republic, by the Romans, amongst whom the use of arms constituted the chief, nay, almost the only species of merit, few testimonies of esteem were awarded to the practisers of the Fine Arts. They affixed no honorable distinctions to the successful architect, painter, or sculptor, inasmuch as these peaceful avocations were, for the most part, cultivated either by slaves or freedmen. It was not until the reign of Augustus Cæsar that the Arts were duly honored. On the revival of intellectual energy, after the darkness of the middle ages, the Arts were liberally encouraged. Michael Angelo was high in favor with the fierce Julius II. Raphael was greatly beloved by Leo X.; and the emperor Maximilian became the warm patron of Albert Durer, whom he ennobled. Leonardo da Vinci died in the arms of Francis I. Rubens enjoyed the highest consideration, and was entrusted with important negotiations both by Philip IV. of Spain and Charles II. of England. Even the stern Henry VIII. was a mild and kind master to Holbein; and the illustrious name of Medici will at once recall the zeal of that princely family for the cultivation of the Fine Arts.

HOOD, an article of dress designed to cover the head and shoulders, and sometimes signifying, among the ancients, a mantle, which served likewise to envelop the whole body. In this sense we find it alluded to, as serving to conceal from observation the persons of the Roman youth during their nocturnal rambles. In such a habit is usually depicted Telesphorus, the son of Esculapius.

HO'PLITES, the heavy-armed infantry of Grecian antiquity. According to the Athenian regulations (similar, probably, to those of other states), the higher classes of citizens only, as estimated by the census, were liable to this expensive form of military service; in process of time, however, it seems that the Thetes or inferior classes also served as hoplites. The hoplites were armed in early times with the spear, heavy defensive armor, and large shield; the latter were exchanged after the time of Iphicrates for the light cuirass and target.

HORDE, a company of wandering people, who have no settled habitation, but stroll about, dwelling under tents, to be ready to shift, as soon as the provisions of the place fail them.

HORI'ZON, is the plane of a great circle of the sphere, dividing the visible from the invisible hemisphere. The horizon is either *sensible* or *rational*. The sensible horizon is a plane which is a tangent to the earth's surface at the place of the spectator, extended on all sides till it is bounded by the sky; the rational horizon is a plane parallel to the former, but passing through the centre of the earth. Both the sensible and rational horizon are relative terms, and change with every change of the spectator's position on the surface of the earth; in all cases they are perpendicular to the direction of gravity.—*Artificial* or *painter's horizon*. In every picture the *artificial eye*, or *point of sight*, is supposed to be at a certain height from the base line; as high as a human figure would be, represented as standing there. To this point everything in the picture tends, as everything in a *real* view tends to the *natural* eye. The picture then, as far as this circumstance is concerned, is perfect, if the *artificial eye* and the *artificial horizon* go together; for these always bear the same relation to each other, wherever the picture may be placed.

HOR'OSCOPE, a representation of the aspect of the heavens and positions of the celestial bodies at a particular moment, drawn according to the rules of the imaginary science of astrology. Thus the aspect of the heavens at the moment of the birth of an individual is his horoscope, and supposed to indicate his future destinies.

HORSE'-POWER, the power of a horse, or its equivalent; the force with which a horse acts when drawing. It is compounded of his weight and muscular strength, and diminishes as his speed increases. The mode of ascertaining a horse's power is to find what weight he can raise, and to what height in a given time, the horse being supposed to pull horizontally. From a variety of experiments of this sort, it is found that a horse, at an average, can raise 160 pounds weight at the velocity of 2 1-2 miles per hour. The power of a horse exerted in this way, is made the standard for estimating the power of a steam-engine. Thus we speak of an engine of 60 or 80 horse-power, each horse-power being estimated as equivalent to 33,000 pounds, raised one foot high per minute.

HOR'TICULTURE, the cultivation of a garden; or the art of cultivating gardens. It includes in its most extensive signification the cultivation of esculent vegetables, fruits, and ornamental plants, and the formation and management of rural scenery, for the purposes of utility and embellishment, but in a more restricted sense, it is employed to designate that branch of rural economy which consists in the formation and culture of gardens. Its results are culinary vegetables, fruits, and flowers.

HOR'TUS SICCUS, literally, a dry garden; an appellation given to a collection of specimens of plants, carefully dried and preserved. The old name of *herbarium*.

HOSAN'NA, was a form of supplication amongst the Hebrews, signifying, *save, I beseech you*, or *help him God!* This acclamation was so much used at the feast of tabernacles, that the solemnity was called *Hosanna rabba*. It was used at the inauguration of kings to express their good wishes for the prosperity of their princes. At the feast of tabernacles it was continually echoed, both as expressive of gratitude for former deliverances, and of their joyful expectation of a future one by the Messiah.

HO'SEA, a canonical book of the Old Testament, and the first of the minor prophets. His prophecies are chiefly directed to the ten tribes before their captivity, threatening them with destruction in case of disobedience, but comforting the pious with the promise of the Messiah, and of the happy state of the church in the latter days.

HOS'PITAL, a place or building properly endowed, or otherwise supported by charitable contributions, for the reception and support of the poor, aged, infirm, sick, or helpless. Also, a house for the reception of disabled seamen or soldiers, foundlings, &c., who are supported by public or private charity, as well as for pauper lunatics, infected persons, &c.—Hospitals for the sick and wounded, and also those for the poor and infirm, were wholly unknown among the ancients. In Sparta, where all the citizens ate together, there was no institution for the sick. In Rome, neither under the consuls nor emperors did they ever think of making any provision for the infirm or the poor. The first establishment of hospitals must be ascribed to Christians. After the establishment of Christianity, the emperors at Constantinople built many hospitals for poor infants, the aged, orphans, and strangers. Piety impelled many individuals to appropriate a part of their funds to religious and charitable purposes; and this good example being followed, from patriotic and benevolent motives, hospitals of various kinds were founded in most of the civilized nations of Europe.

HOS'PITALLERS, an order of religious knights, who built a hospital at Jerusalem for pilgrims. They are now known by the title of knights of Malta.

HOSPI'TIUM, a term used in old writers either for an inn or a monastery, built for the reception of strangers and travellers. In the more early ages of the world, before public inns were thought of, persons who travelled lodged in private houses, and were obliged, if need required, to return the favor to those that entertained them. This was the occasion of the most intimate friendship betwixt the parties, insomuch that they treated one another as relations. Hence the word *hospitium*, which properly signifies lodging or entertainment at the house of another, is used for friendship, founded upon the basis of hospitality.

HOS'PODAR, a title borne by the princes of Wallachia and Moldavia, who receive the investiture of their principalities from the grand seignior. He gives them a vest and standard: they are under his protection, and obliged to serve him, and he even sometimes deposes them; but in other respects they are absolute sovereigns within their own dominions.

HOST, in church history, a contraction of *hostia*, a Latin word, signifying a victim, or sacrifice offered to the Deity. In a general sense, the term is used to Jesus Christ, as an *hostitia* offered to the Father for the sins of mankind.—In the church of Rome, the *host* is the consecrated wafer used in the sacrament of the Eucharist; which wafer, or bread, being transubstantiated, as is taught, into the real body and blood of Christ, is in that rite offered up a sacrifice anew. The elevation of the host is a ceremony prevalent in all Catholic countries, in which the consecrated elements are raised aloft and carried in procession through a church, or even through the streets of a city. On these occasions the people fall on their knees and worship the host. The origin of the custom is dated from the 12th century, when, it is said, it was thought necessary to make this public and conspicuous declaration of the Eucharist on the occasion of the promulgation of the opinions of Berengarius against transubstantiation.

HOS'TAGE, a person given up to an enemy as a security for the performance of the articles of a treaty; on the performance of which the person is to be released.

HOTEL', signifies, in a general sense, a large inn for the reception of strangers; but in a particular sense, especially in France, it is applied to the residences of the king, nobility, or other persons of rank: or it is used synonymously with hospitals, as the *Hotel Dieu*, *Hotel des Invalides*, &c.

HOTTE, a basket of wicker-work, much used in France, for carrying burthens on the back. It is slung over the arms by means of straps, and great weights are thus carried with much facility.

HOT'TENTOTS, natives of the southern extremity of Africa; a race of people whose appearance, habits, and general ignorance, show in the most striking manner to what a degraded condition mankind may be reduced, when wholly destitute of the blessings of civilization.

HOUR, a space of time equal to one twenty-fourth part of a day and night, and consisting of 60 minutes, each minute being 60 seconds.—The ancient *Hebrews* did not divide their day into hours. Their division of the day was into four parts, morning, high day or noon, the first evening, and the last evening; and their night was divided into three parts, night, midnight, and the morning watch. But afterwards they adopted the manner of the *Greeks* and *Romans*, who divided the day, *i. e.*, the space of time from sun rising till sun-set, into twelve equal parts, which consequently differed in length, at the different seasons of the year, though still equal to each other.

HOU'RIS, the name given by the Europeans to the imaginary beings whose company in the Mohammedan paradise is to form the principal felicity of the *believers*. The name is derived from hûr al oyûn, signifying *black-eyed*. They are represented in the Koran as most beautiful virgins, with complexions like rubies and pearls, and possessed of every intellectual and corporeal charm. They are not created of clay, as mortal women, but of pure musk; and are endowed with immortal youth, and immunity from the diseases and defects of ordinary beings.

HOURS, in mythology, divinities regarded in two points of view—as the goddesses of the seasons, and hours of the day; and their number is stated in different ways accordingly. Their duty was to hold the gates of heaven, which they opened to send forth the chariot of the sun in the morning, and receive it again in the evening. No classical poet has described them with greater beauty than Shelley, in a celebrated passage of his *Prometheus Unbound*. These goddesses are often depicted as forming the train of Venus.

HOURS, CANON'ICAL, the seven hours of prayer, observed, it is said, by the Catholic church since the 5th century; chiefly in monasteries. The number seems before that time to have varied, although some peculiar seasons of the day and night were always set apart for this observance. They became finally fixed at seven by the rule of St. Benedict; a number, perhaps, recommended by the literal acceptation of the words of David, (Psalm cxix.,) "Seven times a day will I praise thee." These hours are termed, in the language of the Latin church, matins, prima, tertia, nona, vespers, completa or completorium, which last takes place at midnight. At the time of the Reformation the canonical hours were reduced in the Lutheran church to two, morning and evening; the "reformed" church never observed them.

HOUSE, a human habitation, or place of abode of a family. Among the Eastern nations, and those to the south, houses are flat on the top, with the ascent to the upper story by steps on the outside. As we proceed northward, a declivity of the roof becomes requisite to throw off the rain and snow, which are of greater continuance in higher latitudes. Among the ancient Greeks, Romans, and Jews, the houses usually enclosed a quadrangular area or court, open to the sky. This part of the house was by the Romans called the *impluvium*, or *cavædium*, and was provided with channels to carry off the waters into the sewers. The word *house* is a term used in various ways; as, in the phrase, "a religious house," either the buildings of a monastery, or the community of persons inhabiting them, may be designated. In the Middle Ages, when a family retired to the lodge connected with the mansion, or to their country-seat, it was called "keeping their secret house."—*House*, among genealogists, a noble family, or an illustrious race, descended from the same stock; as the house of Austria; the house of Hanover.—When speaking of a body of men united in their legislative capacity, and holding their place by right or by election, we also use the word *house;* as the House of Lords or the House of Commons.

HOUSE'-BREAKING, in law, the breaking open and entering of a house by daylight, with the intent to commit a felony. The same crime committed at night is denominated a *burglary*.

HOUSE'HOLD, the whole of a family considered collectively, including the mistress, children, and servants. But the household of a sovereign prince includes only the officers and domestics belonging to his palace.

HOWAD'JI, the Arabian name for merchant or shopkeeper, and applied by the Orientals to all travellers.

HOW'ITZER, a kind of mortar, mounted upon a carriage like a gun. The howitzer is used to throw grenades, case-shot, and sometimes fire-balls; their principal use, however, is in the discharge of grenades.

HUE AND CRY, in law, the common law process of pursuing a felon. The original signification of the phrase evidently was, that the offender should be pursued with a loud outcry, in order that all might hear and be induced to join in the pursuit.

HU'GUENOT, a French word used after the year 1560, as an appellation for a Protestant. Its origin, and consequently its *literal* meaning, has received various explanations. Their history forms an important feature in the annals of persecution. The religious prejudices of the people were kept alive by contending political factions, till France was nearly desolated by what was termed "religious wars;" and at length a dreadful massacre of the Huguenots took place on St. Bartholomew's day, 1572. Henry IV., 1598, protected them by the edict of Nantes; but Louis XIV., 1685, revoked this edict, in consequence of which 500,000 Huguenots fled to Switzerland, Germany, Holland, England, and America, where their industry and wealth found a welcome reception.

HUISSIERS', civil officers in France, whose attendance is necessary at every judicial tribunal, from that of a justice of the peace to the court of cassation. There are different degrees of them, answering in some respects to the sheriffs, clerks, and criers of our courts.

HULK, in naval architecture, the body of a vessel, or that part which is, in truth, the vessel itself; the masts, sails, and cordage, composing only the apparatus for its navigation.—*Hulk* is also an old ship; so called because such ship being no longer intended for navigation, the masts are taken away. Such old vessels are employed in the business of raising sand or ballast; and the criminals that are condemned to this work in the way of punishment, are said to be condemned *to the hulks*.

HUMAN'ITIES, a term used in schools and colleges, to signify polite literature, or grammar, rhetoric, and poetry, including the study of the ancient classics, in distinction from philosophy and science.

HUR'RICANE, a most violent storm of wind, generally accompanied by thunder and lightning, and rain, or hail. Hurricanes prevail chiefly in the East and West Indies, the Isle of France, and in some parts of China. A hurricane is distinguished from every other kind of tempest by the extreme violence of the wind, and by its sudden changes; the wind often veering suddenly several points, sometimes a quarter of the circle and even more. Hurricanes appear to have an electric origin; the velocity of the wind exceeds that of a cannon ball, sometimes 300 feet in a second. Corn, vines, sugar-canes, forests, houses, everything is swept away by it. What are called hurricanes in more northern latitudes are only whirlwinds occasioned by the meeting of opposite currents of air.

HUS'BANDRY, the practical part of the science of agriculture, or the business of cultivating the earth and rearing animals. Husbandry is the proper term for that which is commonly called farming; and, accordingly, in law, a man of this profession is not to be styled a farmer, but a husbandman. It includes agriculture, breeding, grazing, dairying, and every other occupation by which riches may be drawn from the superficial products of the earth. For a long time past it has been progressively rising in estimation; and the present age beholds the descendants of feudal chieftains seeking honorable renown in that pursuit which was once abandoned to the meanest of their ancestors' vassals. Late improvements in agriculture consist in the lessening the quantity of labor, by means of implements, machines, and methodical arrangements.

HUSSARS', the name by which certain cavalry regiments are distinguished. It is a word of Hungarian origin, and was originally given to the cavalry of that country, raised in 1458, when Mathias I. ordered the prelates and nobles to assemble, with their cavalry, in his camp. Every twenty houses were obliged to furnish a man; and thus from the Hungarian words *husz* (twenty,) and *ar* (pay,) was formed the name *huszar* or *ussar*.

HUSS'ITES, the disciples of John Huss, a Bohemian, and curate of the chapel of Bethlehem at Prague; who, about the year 1414, embraced and dedefended the opinion of Wickliff of England, for which he was cited before the council of Constance and, refusing to renounce his supposed errors, he was condemned to be burnt alive, which sentence was accordingly excuted upon him at Constance. This gave rise to a rebellion of the Hussites, who avenged his death by one of the fiercest and most terrible civil wars ever known.

HUS'TINGS, (from the Saxon word, *hustinge*, a council, or court,) a court held in the guildhalls of several English cities, as London, Westminster, Winchester, and York, by the principal officers of their respective corporations. Here, deeds may be enrolled, outlawries sued out, and replevins and writs of error determined. Here, also, the elections of officers and parliamentary representatives take place. In a popular sense, the word *hustings* is used for a place raised for the candidates at elections of members of parliament.

HUTCHINSO'NIANS, the name given to those who embraced the opinions of John Hutchinson, a well-known philosopher and naturalist of the 18th century. Though the followers of Hutchinson have never constituted a sect, they have reckoned among their number several distinguished divines both of the established churches of England and Scotland, and of dissenting communities. The number of professed Hutchinsonians is rapidly decreasing, though the principles and views of their founder are still entertained by many. The chief characteristics of Hutchinson's philosophy consist in his rejection of Newton's doctrine of gravitation; and in his maintaining the existence of a plenum on the authority of the Old Testament, which, according to him, embraces a complete system of natural philosophy as well as of religion.

HY'ACINTH, a genus of pellucid gems, whose color is red with an admixture of yellow. The hyacinth, though less striking to the eye than any other red gems, is not without its beauty in the finest specimens. Its structure is foliated; its lustre, strong; its fracture, conchoidal; and it is found of various sizes, from that of a pin's head to the third of an inch in diameter. Like common crystal, it is sometimes found columnar, and sometimes in a pebble form; and is always hardest and brightest in the larger masses.

HYACIN'THUS, in Grecian mythology, the son of Amyclas, king of Laconia, and of the muse Clio, accidentally killed by Apollo while they were playing at quoits. The story is thus related:—Zephyr, enraged at the preference displayed by Hyacinthus for Apollo, caused the wind of which he was the god to turn from its course a quoit thrown by Apollo, which, hitting him on the forehead instantaneously caused his death. The latter immortalized his favorite by causing the flower which still bears his name to spring from his blood, and inscribed the word AI (Gr. *αι*, *alas*) on its leaves, to indicate the deep grief of the god for his loss. An annual festival, named Hyacinthia, was celebrated at Amyclæ in honor of Hyacinthus. It continued three days, on the first of which all was lamentation, and mourning, and woe; but on the second and third days they danced and sung hymns to Apollo, offered sacrifices, exhibited spectacles, treated their friends, and enjoyed themselves with much festivity.

HY'BRID, an epithet for any animal whose sire is of one kind, and dam of another kind.

HY'DRA, a celebrated monster which infested the neighborhood of the lake Lerna in Peloponnesus. It was the fruit of Echidna's union with Typhon. It had a hundred heads, according to Diodorus: but accounts vary much on this point, and no wonder; since, as soon as one of these heads was cut off, two immediately grew up, unless the wound was stopped by fire. It was one of the labors of Hercules to destroy this monster, which he easily effected with the assistance of Iolas, who applied burning iron to the wounds as soon as each head was cut off. The ancient artists differ in their representations of the hydra. Sometimes it is a serpent branched out into several others; and sometimes has a human head, with serpents upon it instead of hair, and descending less and less in serpentine folds. —The term *hydra* is sometimes used in a metaphorical sense for any manifold evil.

HY'DROMANCY, a method of divination by water, amongst the ancients, performed by holding a ring in a thread over the water, and repeating, along with the question to be solved, a certain form of words. If the question was answered affirmatively, the ring of its own accord struck the sides of the bowl.

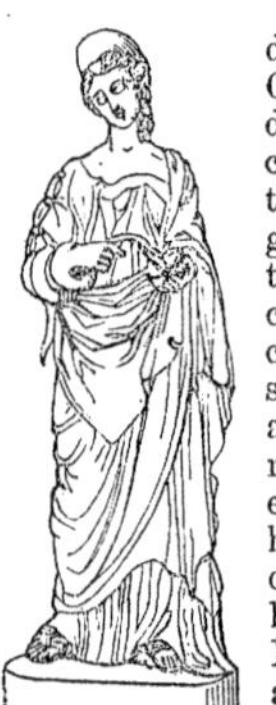

HYGE'IA, the goddess of health, in the Greek mythology; the daughter or wife of Æsculapius, according to the different recitals of genealogists. Her statues (of which the most celebrated was at Sicyon) sometimes represented her attended by a large serpent coiled round her body, and elevating its head above her arm to drink of a cup which she held in her hand. Isis, in Egyptian monuments, appears sometimes in a similar attitude. The employment of the serpent as a mythological symbol of life and health has been by some derived from the history contained in the first chapter of Genesis.

HY'GEINE, that branch of medicine which relates to the means of preserving public health.

HYLOZO'ISM, in philosophy, strictly the doctrine that matter lives. Some writers have confined this name to the tenet of the *anima mundi*, or soul of the world; others to the theory of a peculiar life residing in the whole of nature, approaching, therefore, in its sense to pantheism. This life is either merely organic or actually sentient: the latter notion has been also called *hylopathism*.

HY'MEN, among the ancients, the god of Marriage. The origin of the worship of this divinity is attributed to the following story:—A young Athenian, named Hymenæus, in humble circumstances, having become enamored of a rich and noble lady, from whose presence he was debarred, attired himself in female habiliments, and joined a religious procession to Eleusis, in which his mistress took part. On their way thither the parties who composed it were attacked by pirates, who carried them into captivity; but Hymenæus seized the opportunity, when they were asleep, of putting them to death, and departing immediately for Athens, engaged to restore all the ladies to their families on condition of his obtaining permission to marry the object of his affection. The Athenians consented; the nuptials of Hymenæus were crowned with happiness; and from that period the Greeks instituted festivals in his honor, and invoked him at the celebration of their marriages. The formula employed on these occasions was, "O Hymenæe Hymen, Hymen O Hymenæe." —*Hymeneal* is used to signify a song or ode composed in celebration of a marriage.

HYMN, an ode in praise of the Deity, or some divine personage. The earliest Greek hymns are those attributed, probably without foundation, to Homer: imitated by Callimachus. They are in heroic verse, except one of Callimachus in hexameters and pentameters; and their contents, for the most part, are narrations of the events in the mythological history of the respective gods and goddesses to whom they are dedicated, related in an encomiastic strain. The choric strains of some of the tragedians in honor of deities, introduced into their dramas, appear also to have the character of hymns; especially as dramatic performances among the Greeks, had something of a religious solemnity attached to them. The Theurgic hymns were strains of a higher character, and intended only for those who were initiated into certain mysteries supposed to have for their object the diffusion of more exalted notions of the divinity. Those which are falsely attributed to Orpheus, and pass by his name, are said to be of this class; but, except from their obscurity, it is difficult to say from what reason. Philosophical hymns, intended for the use of the followers of a still higher species of worship, are mentioned in the division of ancient hymns; but we have no genuine examples of such compositions. In modern literature, hymns are pieces of sacred poetry intended to be sung in churches, of which the Psalms of David, the most ancient pieces of poetry, properly so called, on record, (except the book of Job,) furnish the chief example and model. St. Hilary, bishop of Poitiers, is said to have been the first who composed hymns to be sung in churches. The Latin hymns of the Roman Catholic church are well known from the exquisite music to which they have been united.

HYPÆ'THRAL, in architecture, a building or temple uncovered by a roof. The temples of this class are arranged by Vitruvius under the seventh order, having six columns in front and rear, and surrounded by a *dipteral* or double portico. The famous temple of Neptune at Pæstum, still remaining, is an example of this species of building.

HYPAL'LAGE, in grammar, a figure consisting of a mutual change of cases: a species of hyperbaton.

HY'PER, a Greek word signifying *over*, which is used in English composition to denote excess, or something *over* or beyond what is necessary.

HYPER'BATON, in grammar, a figurative construction inverting the natural and proper order of words and sentences. The species are the *anastrophe*, *hypallage*, &c.; but the proper hyperbaton is a long retention of the verb which completes the sentence.

HYPER'BOLE, in rhetoric, a figure by which expressions are used signifying more than is intended to represent to the hearer or reader; as when thoughts and sentiments are clothed in tumid language, or ideas brought forward which in themselves are incredible, in order to induce a belief of something less than that which is offered. Exaggeration is hyperbole applied to narrative, when false assertions are added to true, in order to increase the impression made by them.

HYPERBO'REANS, the name given by the ancients to the unknown inhabitants of the most northern regions of the globe, who were reported always to enjoy a delightful climate, being, according to their notions, situated beyond the domain of Boreas or the north wind; but, in fact, they were the Laplanders, the Samoiedes, and the most northern of the Russians.

HY'PERCATALEC'TIC, in Greek and Latin poetry, a verse exceeding its proper length by one syllable.

HY'PERCRIT'ICISM, consists in viewing the works of an author in an ungenerous spirit, exaggerating minor defects, and overlooking or undervaluing such merits or beauties as might fairly be considered to outweigh the former.

HYPER'METER, a verse containing a syllable more than the ordinary measure. When this is the case, the following line begins with a vowel, and the redundant syllable of the former line blends with the first of the following.

HY'PHEN, a mark or character in grammar, implying that two words are to be connected; as pre-established, five-leaved, &c. Hyphens also serve to show the connection of such words as are divided by one or more of the syllables coming at the end of a line.

HYPOB'OLE, in rhetoric, a figure in which several things are mentioned that seem to make against the argument or in favor of the opposite side, and each of them is refuted in order.

HYPOCAUS'TUM, in ancient architecture, a vaulted apartment from which the fire's heat is distributed to the rooms above by means of earthen tubes. This method, first used in baths, was afterwards adopted in private houses, and diffused an agreeable and equable temperature throughout the different rooms.

HYPOCHONDRI'ASIS, an affection characterized by dyspepsia; languor and want of energy; sadness and fear, arising from uncertain causes; with a melancholic temperament. The principal causes are sorrow, fear, or excess of any of the passions; too long-continued watching; and irregular diet. *Hypochondriacs* are continually apprehending future evils; and in respect to their feelings and fears, however groundless, there is usually the most obstinate belief and persuasion.

HYPOS'TASIS, in theology, a term used to denote the subsistence of the Father, Son, and Holy Spirit, in the Godhead, called by the Greek Christians, three *hypostases*. The Latins more generally used *persona*, and this is the modern practice: hence it is said the Godhead consists of three *persons*.

HYPOTHECA'TION, in the civil law, an engagement by which the debtor assigns his goods in pledge to a creditor as a security for his debt, without parting with the immediate possession; differing in this last particular, from the simple pledge.

HYPOTH'ESIS, a principle taken for granted, in order to draw a conclusion therefrom for the proof of a point in question. Also, a system or theory imagined or assumed to account for what is not understood.

HYSTEROL'OGY, or HYSTERON PROTERON, in rhetoric, a figure by which the ordinary course of thought is inverted in expression, and the last put first: as, where objects subsequent in order of time are presented before their antecedents, cause before effect, &c.; as, *Valet atque vivet*, (he is well and lives.)

I.

I, the ninth letter in the alphabet, and the third vowel. Its sound varies; in some words it is long, as *high, mind, pine;* in some it is short, as *bid, kid;* and in others it is pronounced like *y*, as *collier*, *onion*, &c.; in a few words its sound approaches to the *ee* in *beef*, as in *machine*, which is the sound of the long *i* in all European languages except the English. In all Latin words of Latin origin, *i* preceding a vowel (unless it follows another vowel,) is a consonant, as *Ianus* (*Janus*,) *coniicio* (*conjicio*;) but in words of Greek origin, it is a vowel, as *iambus*, *iaspis*. No English word ends with *i*, but when the sound of the letter occurs at the end of a word, it is expressed by *y*. I, used as a numeral, signifies no more than one, and it stands for as many units as it is repeated times; thus II stands for 2, and III for 3. When put before a higher numeral it subtracts itself, as IV, four; and when set after it, the effect is addition, as XII, twelve.

IAM'BIC, or IAM'BUS, in poetry, a foot consisting of two syllables, the first short and the last long, as in *declare*, *adorn*. Thus, verses composed of short and long syllables alternately are termed *iambics*: as,

If ty | rant fac | tion dare | assail | her throne,
A peo | ple's love | shall make | her cause | their own.

IAM'BICS, a species of verse consisting of short and long syllables alternately, used by the Greek and Latin poets, and especially by the Greek tragic poets. The iambics of the Greek tragic poets were originally composed of a succession of six iambi, but at a later period various other feet were admitted. In most modern European languages the verse of five iambic feet is a favorite metre. According to Aristotle, the iambic measure was first employed in satirical poems, called *iamba*, which appear to have been represented or acted.

ICE'BERG, a hill or mountain of ice, or a vast body of ice accumulated in valleys in high northern latitudes, or floating on the ocean. This term is applied to such elevated masses as exist in the valleys of the frigid zones; to those which are found on the surface of fixed ice; and to ice of great thickness and height in a floating state. These lofty floating masses are sometimes detached from the icebergs on shore, and sometimes formed at a distance from any land. They are found in both the frigid zones, and are sometimes carried toward the equator as low as 40°.

ICH DIEN, (Germ.,) literally, *I serve:* the motto of the Prince of Wales, which was originally adopted by Edward the Black Prince in proof of his subjection to his father Edward III., and has been continued without interruption down to the present time.

ICHNOG'RAPHY, in architecture, the transverse section of a building, which represents the circumference of the whole edifice; the different apartments; the thickness of the walls; the distribution of parts; the dimensions of doors, windows, chimneys; the projection of columns and door-posts; and, in short, all that can come into view in such a section.

ICH'THYS, (Gr. *a fish*,) a word found on many seals, rings, urns, tombstones, &c., belonging to the early times of Christianity, and supposed to have a mystical meaning, from each character forming an initial letter of the words Ιηςους Χριστος, Θεου Υἱος, Σωτηρ; *i. e.*, Jesus Christ, the Son of God, the Saviour. This interpretation is not unlikely, when we consider at once the universal reverence with which the fish was symbolically regarded among most ancient nations, and the many signs and ceremonies adopted by the Christians, with some change of meaning, from the religious rites of the surrounding nations.

I'CONISM, in rhetoric, a figure of speech which consists in representing a thing to the life.

ICON'OCLASTS, that party of Christians which would not tolerate images in their churches, much less the adoration of them. Images and paintings were unknown in the Christian church till the fourth century; and the opposition to them was long continued with great violence.

ICONOG'RAPHY, the description of images or ancient statues, busts, semi-busts, paintings in fresco, mosaic works, &c.

IDE'A, in general, the image or resemblance of a thing, which, though not seen, is conceived by the mind; whatever is held or comprehended by the understanding or intellectual faculties. In logic, *idea* denotes the immediate object about which the mind is employed, when we perceive or think of anything. Locke used the word *idea*, to express whatever is meant by phantasm, notion, species, or whatever it is which the mind can be employed about in thinking. Darwin, in his *Zoonomia*, uses *idea* for a notion of external things which our organs bring us acquainted with originally, and he defines it a contraction, motion, or configuration of the fibres which constitute the immediate organ of sense; synonymous with which he sometimes uses *sensual motion*, in contradistinction to *muscular motion*. By *idea* Kant eminently designated every conception formed by the reason, (as distinct from the understanding,) and raised above all sensuous perception. These ideas he subdivides into, 1st, empirical, which have an element drawn from experience, for instance, organization, a state, a church; and 2d, pure, which are totally free from all that is sensible or empirical, such as liberty, immortality, holiness, felicity, Deity. Another division of the Kantian ideas, is into theoretical and practical, according to a similar division of the reason itself. Thus the idea of truth is a theoretical, that of morality a practical idea.

IDE'AL, that which considers ideas as images, phantasms, or forms in the mind; as, the *ideal* theory of philosophy.—*Beau ideal*, or *ideal beauty;* an expression in the Fine Arts, used to denote a selection for a particular object, of the finest parts from different subjects, united in that one so as to form a more perfect whole than nature usually exhibits in a single specimen of the species; or, in other words, the divesting nature of accident in the representation of an individual.

IDE'ALISM, a term applied to several metaphysical systems, varying in its signification according to the meaning attached in each particular scheme to the word *idea;* from which it is derived. In England the best known system of idealism is that of Berkeley. In reference to this philosopher's doctrines, the word is used in its empirical sense for the object of consciousness in sensation. In its Platonic or transcendental sense, the term *idealism* has been applied to the doctrines of Kant and Schelling; neither of whom is an idealist in the way in which Berkeley may be so called. The system of Berkeley may be thus expressed:—The qualities of supposed objects cannot be perceived distinct from the mind that perceived them; and these qualities, it will be allowed, are all that we can know of such objects. If, therefore, there were external bodies, it is impossible we should ever know it; and if there were not, we should have exactly the same reason for believing there were as we have now. All, therefore, which really exists is spirit, or the thinking principle—ourselves, our fellow-men, and God. What we call ideas are presented to us by God in a certain order of succession, which order of successive presentation is what we mean by the laws of nature.

IDEN'TITY, sameness, as distinguished from similitude and diversity; the sameness of a substance under every possible variety of circumstances. Among philosophers, *personal identity* denotes the sameness of the conscious subject *I*, throughout all the various states of which it is the subject.—*System of identity*, in philosophy, (otherwise called *identism*,) a name which has been given to the metaphysical theory of the German writer Schelling. It rests on the principle that the two elements of thought, the objects respectively of understanding and reason, called by the various terms of matter and spirit, objective and subjective, real and ideal, &c., are only relatively opposed to one another, as different forms of the one *absolute* or *infinite:* hence sometimes called the two poles of the absolute.—In a secondary sense the term *identity* denotes a merely relative sameness, which may be also called logical, or abstract. Thus, in logic, whatever things are subjects of the same attribute, or collection of attributes, are considered the same; for example, dog and lion are the same relatively to the common notion quadruped, under which they are both contained. Again, in physics, a tree may be assumed to be the same in relation to all the rights of property, notwithstanding the physical change which it undergoes from the constant segregation of old, and aggregation of new particles. Lastly, it is only in this logical use of the term, that we can be said in memory to be conscious of the identity of the reproduced, and the original idea, for if they were absolutely identical, it would be impossible to distinguish between the first appearance, and the recurrence of an idea.

IDEOGRAPH'IC CHAR'ACTERS, in philology, characters used in writing which express figures or motions, instead of the arbitrary signs of the alphabet. The Chinese characters are ideographic, although the symbols, at first intended to represent distinct objects, have become by use merely conventional. The hieroglyphical characters of the ancient Egyptians were of the same description. Ideographical writing is opposed to phonetic.

IDEOL'OGY, literally, the science of mind, is the term applied by the latter disciples of Condillac to the history and evolutions of human ideas, considered as so many successive modes of certain original or transformed sensations. The writings of this school are characterized by an unrivalled simplicity, boldness, and subtlety; and the different phases of its doctrines are admirably exhibited in the physiological researches of Cabanis, the moral dissertations of Garat and Volney, and the metaphysical disquisitions of Destutt de Tracy.

IDES, one of the three epochs or divisions of the ancient Roman month. The *calends* were the first days of the different months; the *ides*, days near the middle of the months; and the *nones*, the ninth day before the ides. In the months of March, May, July, and October, the ides fell on the 15th; in the other months on the 13th. The Romans used a very peculiar method of reckoning the days of the month. Instead of employing the ordinal numbers first, second, third, &c., they distinguished them by the number of days intervening between any given day and the next following of the three fixed divisions. For example, as there were always eight days between the nones and the ides, the day after the nones was called the eighth *before* the ides, the next the seventh day *before* the ides, the next the sixth day before the ides, and so on. In leap years, when February had twenty-nine days, the extra day was accounted for by calling both the twenty-fourth and twenty-fifth days of that month the sixth day before the calends of March; whence the leap year got the name of bissextile, (from bis, *twice*, and sextus, *sixth*.)

ID'IOM, in philology, a mode of speaking or writing foreign from the usages of universal grammar or the general laws of language, and restricted to the genius of some individual tongue. Thus, a sentence or phrase consisting of words arranged in a particular manner may be a Latin idiom; the same, arranged in a different manner, an English idiom, &c. The use of a particular inflexion of a word may also be an idiom. We also use the term idiom in a more general sense, to express the general genius or character of a language. We have a number of subordinate words to express the idioms of particular tongues: thus, a Latin idiom is a Latinism, a French idiom a Gallicism, &c. The word idiom is also not uncommonly, but incorrectly, used in the same sense with the French *idiome;* a dialect or variety of language. *Idiotisme* is the French term expressing the correct signification of the English "idiom."

IDIOPATH'IC, a disease which does not depend upon any other disease, and which is thus opposed to those diseases which are *symptomatic*. Thus, an epilepsy is *idiopathic*, when it happens merely through some fault in the brain; and *sympathetic*, when it is the consequence of some other disorder.

IDIOSYN'CRASY, a peculiar temperament or organization of body, whereby it is rendered more liable to certain disorders, than bodies differently constituted usually are.

IDOL'ATRY, in its literal acceptation, denotes the worship paid to idols. It is also used to signify the superstitious adoration paid to other objects. Soon after the flood, idolatry seems to have been the prevailing religion of all the world; for wherever we cast our eyes at the time of Abraham, we scarcely see anything but false worship and idolatry. The heavenly bodies appear to have been the first objects of idolatrous worship; and, on account of their beauty, their influence on the productions of the earth, and the regularity of their motions, the sun and moon were particularly so, being considered as the most glorious and resplendent images of the Deity; afterwards, as their sentiments became more corrupted, they began to form images, and to entertain the opinion, that by virtue of consecration, the gods were called down, to inhabit or dwell in their statues. But history plainly teaches us, that before the idea of one infinite and true God was properly comprehended by men, their imaginations created rulers and deities, to whom they ascribed the direction of all outward events, and every tribe or family had its peculiar object of adoration. The selfish and cunning turned this frailty to their own advantage; and hence originated seers, oracles, and all the numerous superstitions which have disgraced the world.

I'DYL, a short pastoral poem. The Greek word is derived from εἶδος, *form*, or *visible object;* and hence the object, or, at least, the necessary accompaniment of this species of poem, has been said to be a vivid and simple representation of ordinary objects in pastoral nature. But in common usage the signification of this word is hardly different from that of eclogue. The poems of Theocritus are termed Idyls, those of Virgil Eclogues; but it would be difficult to assign a distinction between the two, except what arises from the greater simplicity of language and thought which characterizes the former. Many critics, however, aver that the eclogue requires something of epic or dramatic action; the idyl only picturesque representation, sentiment, or narrative. In English poetry, among this class may be ranked, *The Seasons* of Thomson, Shenstone's *Schoolmistress*, Burn's *Cottager's Saturday Night*, Goldsmith's *Deserted Village*, &c., &c.

IG'NIS FAT'UUS, a kind of luminous meteor, which flits about in the air a little above the surface of the earth, and appears chiefly in marshy places, or near stagnant waters, or in churchyards, during the nights of summer. There are many instances of travellers having been decoyed by these lights into marshy places, where they perished; and hence the name *Jack-with-a-lantern*, *Will-with-a-wisp:* some people ascribing the appearance to the agency of evil spirits, who take this mode of alluring men to their destruction. The cause of the phenomenon does not seem to be perfectly understood; it is generally supposed to be produced by the decomposition of animal or vegetable matters, or by the evolution of gases which spontaneously inflame in the atmosphere.

IGNORA'MUS, in law, the endorsement of a grand jury on a bill of indictment, equivalent to "not found." The jury are said to *ignore* a bill when they do not find the evidence such as to make good the presentment.

I. H. S. an abbreviation for *Jesus Hominum Salvator*, Jesus the Saviour of Mankind.

IL'IAD, the oldest epic poem in existence; commonly attributed to Homer, but according to some modern hypotheses, the work of several hands. The theme of the poem is the siege of Ilium (whence its name) or Troy; or, more properly speaking, the quarrel of Achilles with Agamemnon, general of the Grecian army before that city. It consists of twenty-four books. The first book relates the origin of the quarrel; and the residue of the poem contains an account of the efforts made by Agamemnon and the chiefs who adhered to his party to conquer the Trojans without the aid of Achilles, their defeat, the pacification of Achilles, his resumption of arms in the common cause, and the death of Hector by his hand. Neither the landing of the chieftains, nor the conclusion of the war and capture of Troy, come within its range.

ILLATIVE CONVER'SION, in logic, is that in which the truth of the converse follows from the truth of the exposita or proposition given. Thus the proposition "no virtuous man is a rebel," becomes, by illative conversion, "no rebel is a virtuous man." "Some boasters are cowards;" therefore, a converse, "Some cowards are boasters."

ILLUMINA'TI, or THE ENLIGHTENED, a secret society formed in 1776, chiefly under the direction of Adam Weishaupt, professor of law at Ingolstadt, in Bavaria. Its professed object was the attainment of a higher degree of virtue and morality than that reached in the ordinary course of society. It numbered at one time 2000 members. It was suppressed by the Bavarian government in 1784. It has been supposed that this and some other secret societies were actively engaged in preparing the way for the French revolution; but of this no satisfactory proof has been adduced. Among the early Christians, the term *Illuminati* was given to persons who had received baptism; in which ceremony they received a lighted taper, as a symbol of the faith and grace they had received by that sacrament.

ILLU'MINATING, the art of laying colors on initial capitals in books, or otherwise embellishing manuscript books, as was formerly done by artists called *Illuminators.* These manuscripts, containing portraits, pictures, and emblematic figures, form a valuable part of the riches preserved in the principal libraries in Europe.

ILLUSTRA'TION, in rhetoric, appears to differ from comparison or simile in this only, that the latter is used merely to give force to the expression : the former to throw light upon an argument. The term illustration is, however, sometimes used in a wider sense, in which it seems to comprehend example, which is the recital of a particular fact or instance evincing the truth of a general proposition laid down in the argument; and parable, which is a species of symbolical narrative, in which the actors and events are intended to represent certain other actors and events in a typical manner.

IM'AGE, in rhetoric, a term somewhat loosely used; but which appears generally to denote a metaphor dilated, and rendered a more complete picture by the assemblage of various ideas through which the same metaphor continues to run, yet not sufficiently expanded to form an allegory.

IM'AGES, in sculpture. This word was used among the ancients, more particularly to denominate the portraits of their ancestors, either in painting or sculpture. The Greeks and Romans entertained for these images the greatest veneration, and even rendered them a sort of worship. The Romans preserved with especial care the images of their ancestors, and had them carried both in their funeral pomps and in their triumphs. This honor, however, was restricted to figures of such as had held important offices in the state; as for instance, those of ædile, prætor, or consul. These images were often made of wax, sometimes of marble, and were occasionally adorned with pearls. The atrium or porch of those families who had for a long time held the principal magistracies, were filled with an infinite number of these images. They became smoke-dried, in course of time, by the fire which was always kept lighted in the atrium, in honor of the lares, or household gods. In order to prevent this, they were sometimes deposited in the chests or presses. On days of solemnity or rejoicing, they drew these statues forth, crowned them with laurel, or decked them with the habits which characterized the public offices of the parties whom they depicted. The ancients were likewise habituated to engrave upon their rings the images of their friends, with which they also ornamented their cups and vases. The disciples of Epicurus did not content themselves with depositing the image of their master in their inner or sleeping apartments, where they rendered it a species of worship, but bore it, in like manner, on their rings, and had it engraven on their vases. The Roman emperor Claudius permitted not his subjects indiscriminately to wear his figure on their rings, but those alone who had made public entry of them—thus, in fact, forming a kind of tax thereon. It was also customary, among the ancients, to place at the stern of a vessel the images of certain deities or animals, which thence acquired the title of *tutelæ navis*, the guardian of the ship. Another custom was to set up, both in public and private libraries, the images or busts of the most celebrated writers. Both Greeks and Romans offered in the temples of their gods, not only images of themselves, but of other personages also. Thus Diogenes Laertius informs us, that Mithridates, son of Rodobates, dedicated to the Muses the statue of Plato. According to another ancient author, Romulus dedicated to Vulcan certain chariots of gold, together with his own statue ; and we read in Tacitus, that Julia dedicated to Augustus the image of Marcellus. Since the introduction of Christianity, the use of images has been preserved in the Greek and Roman Catholic churches.

IMAGINA'TION, the faculty of the mind which forms images or representations of things. It acts either in presenting images to the mind of things without, or by reproducing those whose originals are not, at the moment, present to the mind or the sense. We therefore distinguish—(1.) original imagination, or the faculty of forming images of things in the mind—that is, the faculty which produces the picture of an object which the mind perceives by the actual impression of the object—from the (2.) reproductive imagination, or the faculty which recalls the image of an object in the mind without the presence of the object. Besides the power of forming, preserving, and recalling such conceptions, the imagination has also the power (3.) to combine different conceptions, and thus create new images. In this case, it operates involuntarily, according to the laws of the association of ideas, when the mind is abandoned to the current of ideas, as in waking dreams or reveries. The association of ideas is either directed to a definite object by the understanding, or it operates only in subjection to the general laws of the understanding. In the former case, the imagination is confined; in the latter, its operations are free, but not lawless, the general law of tendency to a definite end fixing limits to its action, within which it may have free play, but which must not be overstepped. The free and yet regulated action of the imagination alone can give birth to the productions of the Fine Arts. In this case, it forms images according to ideas. It composes, creates, and is called the *poetical faculty*. From the twofold action of the imagination, we may distinguish two spheres, within which it moves—the prosaic and the poetical. In the former, it presents subjects on which the understanding operates for the common purposes of life. Here it is restricted by the definite object for which we put it in action. In the latter, it gives life to the soul, by a free, yet regulated action, elevates the mind by ideal creations, and representations above common realities, and thus ennobles existence. Imagination operates in all classes, all ages, all situations, all climates, in the most exalted hero, the profound thinker, the passionate lover, in joy and grief, in hope and fear, and makes man truly man.

IM'AM, or IM'AN, a Mahometan priest, or head of the congregations in their mosques. In ecclesiastical affairs they are independent, and are not subject to the mufti, though he is the supreme priest.

IMBRO'GLIO, (a word borrowed from the Italian brogliare, *to confound or mix together;* whence the French brouiller and English embroil.) In literary language, the plot of a romance or a drama, when much perplexed and complicated, is said to be an "imbroglio." The small burlesque theatrical pieces so termed by the Italians derive their ludicrous character from a similar species of absurdity.

IMITA'TION, the act of following in manner, or of copying in form; the act of making the similitude of anything, or of attempting a resemblance. By the *imitation* of bad men, or of evil examples, we are apt to contract vicious habits. In the *imitation* of natural forms and colors, we are often unsuccessful.—*Imitation*, in music, is a reiteration of the same air, or of one which is similar, in several parts where it is repeated by one after the other, either in unison, or at the distance of a fourth, a fifth, a third, or any interval whatever.—*Imitation*, in oratory, is an endeavor to resemble a speaker or writer in the qualities which we propose to ourselves as patterns. A method of translating, in which modern examples and illustrations are used for ancient, or domestic for foreign, or in which the translator not only varies the words and sense, but forsakes them as he sees occasion.

IMMOLA'TIO, a ceremony used in the Roman sacrifices; it consisted in throwing upon the head of the victim some sort of corn and frankincense, together with the *mola* or salt cake, and a little wine.

IMMORTAL'ITY, the quality of endless duration, as the immortality of the soul. The idea that the dissolution of the body involves the annihilation of existence, is so cheerless, so saddening, that the wisest and best of men, of all ages, have rejected it, and all civilized nations have adopted the belief of its continuation after death, as one of the main points of their religious faith. The Scriptures afford numerous evidences of the soul's immortality; the hope of it is a religious conviction; man cannot relinquish it, without abandoning, at the same time, his whole dignity as a reasonable being and a free agent; and hence the belief in immortality becomes intimately connected with our belief in the existence and goodness of God.

IMMU'NES, in Roman history, an epithet applied to such provinces as had obtained an exemption from the ordinary tribute. The term is also applied to soldiers who were exempt from military service.

IMMU'NITY, in jurisprudence, legal freedom from any legal obligation. Thus the phrase "ecclesiastical immunities" comprehends all that portion of the rights of the Church, in different countries, which consists in the freedom of its members, or of its property, from burdens thrown by law on other classes.

IMPALE'MENT, the putting to death by thrusting a stake through the body, the victim being left to perish by lingering torments. This barbarous mode of torture is used by the Turks, as a punishment for Christians who say anything against the law of the prophet, who intrigue with a Mohammedan woman, or who enter a mosque.

IMPARISYL'LABIC, in grammar, an epithet for words having unequal syllables.

IMPAR'LANCE, in law, a privilege or license granted, on petitioning the court for a day to consider or advise what answer the defendant shall make to the plaintiff's declaration.

IMPASTA'TION, the mixture of various materials of different colours and consistencies, baked or bound together with some cement, and hardened by the air or by fire.

IMPEACH'MENT, the accusation and prosecution of a person for treason, or other high crimes and misdemeanors. In England the house of lords has an original jurisdiction in criminal matters, exercised over either peers or commons, upon impeachment by a member of the lower house. Any member of the house of commons may not only impeach one of their own body, but also any lord of parliament. When any person is impeached, articles, containing the accusation, are exhibited on behalf of the commons, who appoint managers to conduct the prosecution. These articles are carried to the lords, and if they find the accused guilty upon sufficient evidence, no pardon under the Great Seal can be pleaded to such impeachment. Till the house of commons demand judgment on an impeachment exhibited by them, the lords cannot pass sentence. In the United States, it is the right of the house of representatives to impeach, and of the senate to try and determine impeachments. The senate of the United States, and the senates in the several states, are the high courts of impeachment.

IMPER'ATIVE, in grammar, one of the moods of a verb, used when we would command, exhort, or advise; as *go, attend*, &c.

IMPERA'TOR, in Roman antiquity, a title of honor conferred on victorious generals, by their armies, and afterwards confirmed by the senate. After the overthrow of the republic, *imperator* became the highest title of the supreme ruler; and in later times it had the signification which we attach to the word *emperor*.

IMPER'FECT CON'CORDS, in music, such as are liable to change from major to minor, or the contrary, as are thirds and sixths; still, however, not losing their consonancy.

IMPER'FECT TENSE, in grammar, that modification of a verb which expresses that the action or event of which we speak was, at a certain time to which we refer, in an unfinished state. This is in English designated by the auxiliary "was," joined with the present participle.

IMPE'RIAL, in architecture, a species of dome whose profile is pointed towards the top and widens towards the base, thus forming a curve of contrary flexure.—*Imperial*, pertaining to an empire. Thus the *imperial chamber*, means the sovereign court of the German empire; an *imperial city*, a city in Germany which has no head but the emperor; the *imperial diet*, an assembly of all the states in the German empire.

IMPE'RIALIST, a subject or soldier of an emperor. The denomination *imperialists* is often given to the troops or armies of the emperor of Austria.

IMPER'SONAL VERB, in grammar, a verb used only in the third person singular, with *it* for a nominative in English, as *it rains;* and without a nominative in Latin, as *pugnatur*.

IMPETRA'TION, in law, the obtaining anything by request or prayer: but in old statutes, it is taken for the pre-obtaining of church benefices from the court of Rome, which belonged to the disposal of the king and other lay-patrons of the realm.

IMPOSE', in printing, to put the pages on the *imposing stone*, and fit on the chase, and thus prepare the form for the press.—In legislation, to lay on a tax, toll, duty, or penalty.—*To impose on*, to mislead by a false pretence.

IMPOSI'TION *of hands*, a religious ceremony, in which a bishop lays his hand upon the head of a person, in ordination, confirmation, or in uttering a blessing. This practice is also generally observed at the ordination of congregational ministers, while one prays for a blessing on the labors of him they are ordaining. Imposition of hands was a Jewish ceremony, introduced not by any divine authority, but by custom; it being their practice, whenever they prayed for any person, to lay their hands on his head. Our Saviour observed the same ceremony both when he conferred his blessing on the children, and when he cured the sick.

IMPOS'SIBLE, that which cannot be done or effected. A proposition is said to be *impossible*, when it contains two ideas, which mutually destroy each other, and which can neither be conceived nor united together in the mind: thus, it is impossible that a circle should be a square, or that two and two should make five. A thing is said to be *physically impossible*, that cannot be done by any natural powers, as the resurrection of the dead; and *morally impossible*, when in its own nature it is possible, but attended with difficulties or circumstances which give it the appearance of being impossible.

IM'POST, any tax or tribute imposed by authority; particularly a duty or tax laid by government on goods imported.—In architecture, that part of a pillar in vaults and arches, on which the weight of the building rests; or the capital of a pillar, or cornice which crowns the pier and supports the first stone or part of an arch.

IM'POTENCE, or IM'POTENCY, want of strength or power, animal, intellectual, or moral. The first is a want of some physical principle, necessary to an action; the last denotes the want of power or inclination to resist or overcome habits or natural propensities.

IMPRESCRIP'TIBLE RIGHTS, such rights as a man may use or not at pleasure, those which cannot be lost to him by the claims of another founded on prescription.

IMPRES'SION, in the Arts, is used to signify the transfer of engravings from a hard to a soft substance, whether by means of the rolling-press, as in copper-plate and lithographic printing, or by copies in wax, &c., from medals and engraved gems. The word is also used to denote a single edition of a book; as, the whole *impression* of the work was sold in two months.

IMPRIMA'TUR, (*Latin*, let it be printed,) the word by which the licenser allows a book to be printed, in countries where the censorship of books is rigorously exercised. This formula was much used in English books printed in the 16th and 17th centuries; and this permission is even still vested in some of the British universities, especially in Scotland, where it is nothing unusual to find on the title-page of some works recommended to public favor by the senatus academicus the "imprimatur" of the principal.

IMPRI'MIS, (*Latin*,) in the first place; first in order.

IM'PRINT, the designation of the place where, by whom, and when a book is published, are always placed at the bottom of the title. Among the early printers it was inserted at the end of the book, and is styled the colophon.

IMPROMP'TU, in literature, any short and pointed production supposed to be brought forth on the spur of the moment; generally of an epigrammatic character.

IMPROPRIA'TION, in law, the act of appropriating or employing the revenues of a church living to one's own use.—*Lay impropriation* is an ecclesiastical living in the hands of a layman. Before the destruction of the monasteries by Henry VIII., in 1539, many livings were in the possession of *impropriators;* the great tithes they kept themselves, allowing the small tithes to the vicar or substitute who served the church. On the suppression of the monasteries, Henry disposed of the great tithings among his favorites.

IM'PROVISATORE, an Italian word, signifying a person who has the talent of composing and reciting a suite of verses on a given subject immediately and without premeditation. This peculiar talent, thus restricted, appears to belong, almost exclusively, to the Italian language and people. Much, no doubt, of the facility of these improvisatori, which appears almost preternatural to one unaccustomed to hear them, arises from the peculiar ease and flexibility of their language, and its richness in rhymes. But this circumstance will not wholly account for so singular a national faculty; for, about the time of the revival of letters, Italy possessed improvisatori in Latin as well as Italian. Many poets have enjoyed considerable celebrity in their day from their success in this mode of composition; but we are not aware that any of their poems have acquired a permanent celebrity, although often taken down from their recitation. Tuscany and the Venetian states have been most famous for the production of improvisatori, especially Sienna and Verona; in which latter city the talent seems to have been perpetuated by succession. The chevalier Bernardino Perfetti, the most famous of all these reciters, was of Sienna: he flourished in the first half of the 17th century. He is said to have possessed unbounded erudition, and to have been able to pour forth extempore poetical essays on the most abstruse questions of science. There have been many distinguished females possessed of this talent, (improvisatrici.) Corilla, the most celebrated of them, was of Pistoia in Tuscany. She was the original of Madame de Staël's *Corinne.* She received in 1776 the laureate crown at Rome, an honor which had also been accorded to Perfetti. Germany is said to have produced one noted improvisatrice, Anna Louisa Karsch. There appears no reason why the term improvisation should not also be applied to the delivery of unpremeditated discourses in prose. It is the exertion of a very similar faculty, perfected in the same manner by habits to a degree almost inconceivable by those not accustomed to witness its exercise. It is, however, much more general. The North American Indians are represented to possess it in a high degree. In Europe, it is most generally to be found in the pulpit. Public secular oratory of this unpremeditated description is far more common in England, and the power much more sedulously cultivated, than in any continental country.

INA'LIENABLE, an epithet applied to such things as cannot be legally alienated or made over to another: thus the dominions of a sovereign, the revenues of the church, the estates of a minor, &c. are *inalienable*, otherwise than with a reserve of the right of redemption.

INAUGURA'TION, was originally applied to the Roman ceremony of admission to the college of augurs, or soothsayers, or to the selection of a proper site for the erection of temples or other national edifices; but it afterwards received a more extended signification, and is now used in a sense nearly synonymous with the *consecration* of a prelate, or the *coronation* of a king or emperor. It means also an introduction to any office with certain ceremonies.

INCA, or YNCA, a name given by the Indians of ancient Peru to their kings and princes of the blood. The empire of the Incas, founded, according to tradition, by the celebrated Manco Capac, extended over the table-land of the Andes, from Pasto to the neighborhood of Chili, as well as the low lands on the coast. It was destroyed by the Spaniards under Pizarro and Almagro. The blood royal of the Incas is preserved, or believed to be so, among the Indians of the present day, and Tupac Amaru, who carried on a long and nearly successful insurrection against Spain in the latter part of the last century, professed to be descended from them.

IN CÆNA DOMINI, (Lat. *at the Lord's Supper*,) the name of a celebrated papal bull, containing a collection of extracts from different constitutions of the pope, comprising those rights which, since the time of Gregory VII., have been uninterruptedly claimed by the Roman see, and a proclamation of anathema against all who violate them. It was annually read on Holy Thursday, whence it receives its name; but lately on Easter Monday. The sects of heretics are cursed in it by their several designations. A copy of the bull is hung up at the door of the churches of St. Peter and St. John Lateran: and all patriarchs, primates, bishops, &c., are required to have it read once or more annually in their churches.

INCARNA'TION, a word in common use among the theologians to express the union of the Godhead with the Manhood in Jesus Christ. The real manner of this union, or indwelling of the God in the Man, is allowed to be a mystery such as cannot be fully apprehended by the human intellect.

IN'CENSE, in the materia medica, a dry resinous substance, known by the name of *thus* and *olibanum*. The burning of incense made part of the daily service of the Jewish temple; and in the Romish church it is the deacon's office to *incense* the officiating priest or prelate, and the choir. In the religious rites of heathen nations, too, the odors of spices and fragrant gums were burnt as incense.

INCEP'TIVE, in grammar, an epithet for verbs which express a proceeding by degrees in an action.

INCOG'NITO, (abbreviated to *incog*.,) unknown, or so disguised as not to be recognized; a mode of travelling without any mark of distinction, which is sometimes adopted by princes and great people who do not wish to be recognized.

INCOMPAT'IBLE, in a general sense, morally inconsistent; or that cannot subsist with another, without destroying it: thus, truth and falsehood are essentially *incompatible:* so cold and heat are *incompatible* in the same subject, the strongest overcoming and expelling the weakest. In a legal sense, that is *incompatible* which cannot be united in the same person, without violating the law, or constitution.

INCORPORA'TION, in law, the formation of a legal or a political body, with the quality of perpetual existence or succession, unless limited by the act of incorporation.

IN'CUBUS, or *Nightmare*, the name of a disease which consists in a spasmodic contraction of the muscles of the breast, usually happening in the night, and attended with a very painful difficulty of respiration and great anxiety. The most obvious symptom of this disease is a sensation of some great weight laid upon the breast. Sometimes the sufferer finds himself in some inextricable difficulty, endeavoring to escape from a monster, or, perhaps, in imminent danger of falling from a precipice, while his limbs refuse to do their office, until he suddenly awakens himself by starting from his recumbent posture, or by a cry of terror.

INCUM'BENT, the person who is in present possession of an ecclesiastical benefice.

INCUNAB'ULA, in bibliography, a term applied to books printed during the early period of the art; in general confined to those which appeared before the year 1500.

INDECLI'NABLE, in grammar, a word admitting of no declension or inflexion. Adverbs, prepositions, particles, conjunctions, are all indeclinable. In classical languages, indeclinable nouns are those few (chiefly borrowed by the Greeks and Latins from foreign languages) of which the termination is not altered in the several cases.

INDEFEA'SIBLE, in law, an epithet for an estate, or any right which cannot be defeated or made void.

INDEF'INITE, or INDETER'MINATE, that which has no certain bounds; or to which the human mind cannot affix any. Descartes makes use of this word in his philosophy instead of *infinite*, both in numbers and quantities, to signify an inconceivable number, or a number so great as not to be capable of any addition.—*Indefinite*, is also used to signify a thing that has but one extreme; for instance, a line drawn from any point and extended infinitely.—*Indefinite*, in grammar, is understood of nouns, pronouns, verbs, participles, articles, &c. which are left in an uncertain indeterminate sense, and not fixed to any particular time, thing, or other circumstance.

INDEM'NITY, in law, a writing to secure one from all damage and danger that may ensue from any act.—*Act of Indemnity*, an act passed every session of parliament for the relief of those who have neglected to take the necessary oaths, &c.

INDENT'URE, in law, a writing containing an agreement or contract made between two or more persons; so called because it was indented or cut scollopwise, so as to correspond with another writing containing the same words. But *indenting* is often neglected, while the writings or counterparts retain the name of *indentures*.

INDEPEN'DENTS, a sect of Protestants, distinguished, not by doctrine, but discipline. They regard every congregation of Christians, meeting in one building for the purpose of public worship, as a complete church, *independent* of any other religious government; and they reject the use of all creeds, as impious substitutes for the letter of the Scripture. The direction of each church is vested in its elders. The *Independents* arose in the reign of Elizabeth; and during the civil wars of England, in the 17th century, they formed a powerful party.

IN'DEX, in arithmetic and algebra, the number that shows to what power the quantity is to be raised; the exponent.—*Index*, in literature, an alphabetical table of the contents of a book.—*Expurgatory index*, a catalogue of prohibited books in the church of Rome.

IN'DIAN, a general name of any native of the Indies; as, an East *Indian*, or West *Indian*. It is particularly applied to an aboriginal native of the American continent.

IN'DIAN ARCHITEC'TURE, the architecture of India, in its details, bears a striking resemblance to that of Persia and Egypt, and they are considered to

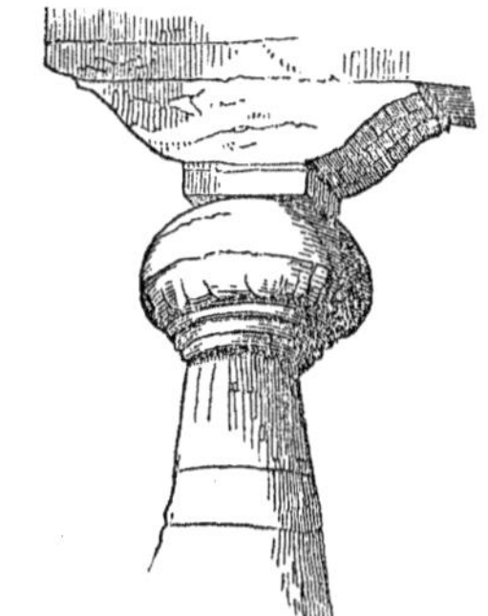

Indian Capital Elephantal.

have a common origin. Its monuments may be divided into two classes, the *excavated*, which is either in the form of a cavern, or in which a solid rock is sculptured into the resemblance of a building; and the *constructed*, in which it is actually a building, or formed by the aggregation of different materials. The first class is exemplified in the caves of Elephanta and Ellora, and the sculptured pagodas of Mavalipouram, and the second class in the pagodas of Chillimbaram, Tanjore, and others. The architecture of India, it is said, resembles in its details that of Egypt, but its differences are also very striking. In the architecture of Egypt, massiveness and solidity are carried to the extreme; in Indian architecture these have no place. In the former, the ornaments are subordinate to the leading forms, and enrich without hiding them. In the latter, the principal forms are overwhelmed and decomposed by the accessories. In the one grandeur of effect is the result, while littleness is the characteristic of the other.

IN'DIAN INK, a substance brought

from China, used for water-colors. It is in rolls or in square cakes, and is said to consist of lamp-black and animal glue.

INDIC'ATIVE, in grammar, the first mood, or manner, of conjugating a verb, by which we simply affirm, deny, or indicate something; as, he *writes; they run.*

INDIC'TION, CYCLE OF, in chronology, a mode of computing time by the space of fifteen years, instituted by Constantine the Great; originally the period for the payment of certain taxes. The popes, since the time of Charlemagne, have dated their acts by the year of the indiction, which was fixed on the 1st of January. At the time of the reformation of the calendar, the year 1582 was reckoned the tenth year of indiction. Now this date, when divided by 15, leaves a remainder, 7, that is, three less than the indiction, and the same must necessarily be the case in all subsequent cases; so that, in order to find the indiction for any year, divide the date by 15, and add 3 to the remainder. It has no connection with the motions of the heavenly bodies.

INDICT'MENT, in law, a written accusation of one or more persons for a crime or misdemeanor, preferred to, and presented on oath by a grand jury. In determining whether there is a reasonable cause to put the accused upon his trial, the grand jury hear evidence only of the charge; and if twelve of them are satisfied of the truth of the charge, the indictment is then said to be found, and is publicly delivered into court. If the grand jury think the accusation groundless, the accused is discharged; but a new bill of indictment may be preferred to a subsequent grand jury. By the constitution of the United States, no person is held to answer for a capital or otherwise infamous crime, unless on a presentment or indictment by a grand jury, except in cases arising in the land or naval forces; and the same principle is adopted in several of the states.

INDORS'ER, he who writes his name on the back of a bill of exchange. That which is written on the back is called the *indorsement;* and the person to whom the bill is assigned by indorsement, is the *indorsee.*

INDUC'TION, the counter-process in scientific method to deduction, implies the raising individuals into generals, and those into still higher generalities; deduction being the *bringing down* of universals to lower genera or to individuals. Every deduction, therefore, to be valid, must rest on a prior induction, which, in order that we may obtain logical certainty, must be a *complete* induction; that is to say, must include *all* the individuals which constitute the genus. This, it is evident, is impossible, so long as we assume the only power necessary to induction to be the observation of particulars; for these are infinite in number: we can never be sure that we have observed them all. We are therefore compelled, if we are to admit the possibility of science properly so called, to allow the necessity of some spontaneous action of the understanding in every inductive process; of a faculty, in short, which takes occasion from experience to arrive at the knowledge of truths not contained in that experience.

INDUL'GENCE, a power claimed by the Roman Catholic church of granting to its contrite members remission for a certain term, either on earth or in purgatory, of the penalty incurred by their transgressions. The practice was first instituted in the eleventh century by Popes Gregory VII., Victor, and Urban II., as a recompense to those who embarked in the perilous enterprise of the Crusades; but its benefits in process of time extended to all who, either by donations or other services, contributed to the well-being of the church. It was the profligate sale of indulgences that first excited Luther to commence his warfare against the see of Rome; and although the traffic in indulgences has been reprobated by many councils, and some minor corruptions have been partially reformed, still the Council of Trent decreed the usefulness and validity of such instruments, and left the whole control of their nature and manner of issuing them entirely in the discretion of the pope for the time being.

INDUL'TO, in ecclesiastical affairs, an Italian term for a dispensation granted by the pope, to do or obtain something contrary to the common law.

IN ES'SE, (*Latin,*) actually existing; distinguished from *in posse*, which denotes that a thing is not, but may be.

IN'FAMY, in law, that total loss of character or public disgrace which a convict incurs, and by which a person is rendered incapable of being a witness or a juror.

IN'FANCY, the period physically considered, from birth to seven years, and legally, till 21, previously to which no one can inherit or execute any obligation, or incur any responsibility except for necessaries.

INFANT'E, and INFANT'A, appellations severally given to all the sons and daughters of the kings of Spain and Portugal, except the eldest. The dignity of the title consists in the pre-eminence implied by styling the children of the king, *the* children.

IN'FANTRY, the general name for soldiers who serve on foot. The term is in all probability derived from the Italian word *fante*, signifying a child or young person; and was originally conferred on the young Italian peasantry, who served in the wars on foot, the nobles being usually mounted. There are, however, various other accounts of the origin of the term. Among the ancient Greeks and Romans, the infantry constituted the chief strength of an army; and, with the exception of that period in European history during which the institutions of chivalry prevailed, when the tournament with its gay appendages engaged the attention of all the powerful nobles and otherwise distinguished persons, who thus imparted to the *cavalry* a factitious importance, it has generally been regarded as the principal military arm. Since the institution of standing armies this has been peculiarly the case.

INFEC'TION, the act or process of infecting, or the act by which poisonous matter, morbid miasmata, or exhalations, produce disease in a healthy body.—The thing which infects. The terms *infection* and *contagion* are used as synonymous in a great majority of cases. Different writers proposed and attempted to make a distinction between them, but there has been a great disagreement as to what the distinction should be; and in general no regard is paid to the proposed distinctions. *Infection* is used in two acceptations; first, as denoting the effluvium or infectious matter exhaled from the person of one diseased, in which sense it is synonymous with *contagion;* and secondly, as signifying the act of communication of such morbid effluvium, by which disease is transferred. The atmosphere and other inert substances are often contaminated by the deleterious or offensive qualities of malaria, the matter of contagion, effluvia from putrid animal or vegetable substances.

INFEODA'TION *of tithes*, in law, the granting of tithes to mere laymen.

INFE'RIÆ, in Roman antiquity, sacrifices offered to the infernal deities for the souls of the departed.

IN'FINITE, in mathematics, *infinite quantities* are such quantities as are either greater or less than assignable ones. And *infinite series*, a series considered as infinitely continued as to the number of its terms.

INFINITES'IMAL, a term denoting an indefinitely small quantity.

INFIN'ITIVE, in grammar, a mood expressing the action of the verb, without limitation of person or number, as *to love*.

INFIN'ITY, a term applied to the vast and the minute, to distances and spaces too great to be expressed in any numbers of measures, or too small to be expressed by any fraction; and one of the incomprehensible, but necessarily existing wonders of the universe. We apply *infinity* to God and his perfections. We speak of the infinity of his existence, his power, and his goodness.

INFIR'MARY, a charitable establishment where the poor may receive medical advice and medicine gratis.

INFLEC'TION, in grammar, in strictness of language is any change which takes place in a word from a modification of its sense between the *root* and the *termination*. The inflection must, therefore, not be confounded with the termination itself. Thus, the syllable *am* is the root of all the words employed in the conjugation of the Latin verb amo, *I love:* in the imperfect tense, the inflection is the syllable *ab*. The termination varies according to the person; amabam, amabas, amabat.

INFLUEN'ZA, an epidemic catarrh which has in various times spread more rapidly and extensively than any other disorder, and this universality of its attacks, together with the greater severity of its symptoms, principally distinguishes it from common catarrh. It attacks all ages and conditions of life, but is seldom fatal, except to the aged, or to those previously suffering, or having a tendency to pulmonary disease. The epidemics of 1831-2, and of 1836-7, were nearly universal throughout the civilized world.

INFORMA'TION, in law, an accusation or complaint exhibited against a person for some criminal offence. An information differs from an indictment, inasmuch as the latter is exhibited on the oath of twelve men, but the information is only the allegation of the individual who exhibits it.—He who communicates to a magistrate a knowledge of the violations of law, is an *informer;* but he who takes a trade of laying informations is termed a *common informer* and is generally held in disesteem by society.

INFRALAPSA'RIANS, in church history, an appellation given to such predestinarians as think the decrees of God, in regard to the salvation and damnation of mankind, were formed in consequence of Adam's fall.

INFU'LA, in Roman antiquity, a broad kind of fillet, made of white wool, which the priests used to wear round their heads. At later periods, the imperial governors wore *infula* as a sign of dignity, and, as such, it was adopted, in the 7th century, by the bishops of the Roman Catholic church, who continue to wear it on solemn occasions. It is, in fact, the *mitre;* which the bishops of the church of England have in their coat of arms, but never wear on their head.

IN'GOT, a small bar of metal made of a certain form and size, by casting it in moulds. The term is chiefly applied to the small bars of gold and silver, intended either for coining or for exportation to foreign countries.

IN'GRESS, E'GRESS, and RE'GRESS, in law, words frequently used in leases of lands, which signify a free entry into, a going out of, and returning from some part of the premises leased to another.

INGRES'SU, in law, a writ of entry, termed also a *præcipe quod reddat.*

INGRESS'US, in law, a duty which the heir at full age formerly paid to the chief lord for entering upon lands which had fallen to him.

INHAB'ITANT, a dweller; one who dwells or resides permanently in a place, or who has a fixed residence, as distinguished from an occasional lodger or visitor; as the *inhabitant* of a house or cottage; the *inhabitants* of a town, city, county, or state. So brute animals are *inhabitants* of the regions to which their natures are adapted; and we speak of spiritual beings, as *inhabitants* of heaven. —In *English law*, the term *inhabitant* is used in various technical senses. Thus a person having lands or tenements in his own possession, is an inhabitant for the purpose of repair of bridges, wherever he may reside; but for purposes of personal services, the *inhabitant* must necessarily be a resident. For the purpose of the poor rate, the word means a person residing permanently, and sleeping in the parish. Where the right of voting is in *inhabitant* householders, it is generally understood that an inhabitant is one who keeps a house in his own occupation, either personally residing in it, or having it occupied by servants and ready for his residence, he having what is termed the *animus revertendi,* or intention to return.

INHE'RENT, that which is inseparable, distinguished from the accidental and acquired; as the *inherent* qualities of the magnet. &c.

INHER'ITANCE, an estate derived from an ancestor to an heir by succession or in course of law; or an estate which the law casts on a child or other person, as the representative of the deceased ancestor. An estate, or real property which a man has to himself and heirs, or the heirs of his body, &c., is termed a *freehold of inheritance.*

INHIBI'TION, in law, a writ to forbid a judge's proceeding in a cause that lies before him. This writ generally issues out of a higher court to an inferior, and is of much the same nature as a prohibition.

INI'TIATIVE, in politics. In legislative assemblies constituted so as to comprise more than one chamber, or more than one distinct and co-ordinate power, that branch of the legislature to which belongs of right the power to propose measures of a particular class is said to have the initiative with respect to those measures. Thus in England all propositions for taxing the subject, whether directly or indirectly, must begin in the Commons; a usage which has been adopted in most modern constitutions. On the other hand, there are some private bills which by custom originate in the Lords; and one bill, that, namely, for a general pardon, is proposed in the first instance by the crown.

INJUNC'TION, in law, a writ or prohibition granted in several cases; and for the most part grounded on an interlocutory order or decree, made in the court of chancery or exchequer, for staying proceedings either in courts of law, or ecclesiastical courts. When the reason for granting an injunction ceases, the injunction is dissolved.

IN'JURY, in a legal sense, any wrong or damage done to another, either in his person, rights, reputation, or goods. Whatever impairs the quality or diminishes the value of goods or property, is an *injury;* so also whatever impairs the health, weakens the mental faculties, or prejudices the character of a person, is an *injury.*

IN'LAND, in law, that part of any land or mansion which lay next to the mansion-house, and was used by the lord himself.—In geography, that which is situated in the interior of a country remote from the sea-coast.—*Inland bills*, in commerce, bills payable in the country where they are drawn.

INLAY'ING, the art of diversifying cabinet-work, or working in wood or metal with several pieces of different colors, curiously put together.

IN LIM'INE, (*Latin*,) in the outset; before anything is said or done.

INN, in England, a college of municipal or common law professors and students; formerly, the town-house of a nobleman, bishop, or other distinguished personage, in which he resided when he attended the court.—*Inns of court*, colleges or corporate societies in which students of law reside and once were instructed. The principal are the Inner Temple, the Middle Temple, Lincoln's Inn, and Gray's Inn. Every candidate for the rank of barrister-at-law is obliged to be admitted a member of one of these societies, and to submit to its regulations as a student.—*Inns of Chancery*, colleges in which young students formerly began their law studies. These are now occupied chiefly by attorneys, solicitors, &c.

IN'NATE IDE'AS, principles or ideas supposed to be stamped on the mind from the first moment of its existence, and which it constantly brings into the world with it: a doctrine which has given rise to much discussion, and which the celebrated Locke took great pains to refute.

IN'NOCENTS' DAY, a festival observed in the church on the 28th of December, in memory of the children that were slain by command of Herod.

INOCULA'TION, the insertion of poisonous or infectious matter into any part of the body; but in this country the phrase is commonly used to signify the insertion of the virus of the common small-pox, the insertion of the virus of the cow-pox being called *Vaccination*. Inoculation was introduced into general notice by Lady Mary Wortley Montague, whose son was inoculated at Constantinople about the year 1721, and whose daughter was the first who underwent the operation in England. A milder disease is thus propagated than when it is received in the natural way.

IN PRO'PRIA PERSO'NA, (*Latin*,) in one's own person or character.

IN'QUEST, judicial inquiry. It may either be a jury to decide on the guilt of an accused person, according to fact and law; or to examine the weights and measures used by shopkeepers; decide on the cause of any violent or sudden death; or to examine into accusations before trial.

INQUI'RY, *writ of*, in law, a writ that issues out to the sheriff to summon a jury to inquire what damages a plaintiff has sustained in an action upon the case where judgment goes by default.

INQUISI'TION, the title given to a court armed with extensive criminal authority in various European countries; especially instituted to inquire into offences against the established religion. The first of these tribunals of faith was that established in the south of France after the conquest of the Albigenses in the 13th century. They were established in Spain in the middle of the same century, not without much opposition on the part of the bishops and secular clergy, who, in Castile, long maintained their exclusive spiritual jurisdiction. In 1480, the supreme general inquisition was founded at Seville by Queen Isabella, with the aid of the Cardinal Pedro Gonzalez de Mendoza. This great court, commonly known by the name of the Holy Office, had far more extensive authority than those local tribunals of the same name which had previously been established. Thomas de Torquemada, prior of a Dominican convent, was its first president, with the title of inquisitor-general. The process of the inquisition was widely different from that of all other courts of justice. The kings named the grand inquisitor, who appointed his assessors, some of whom were secular, but the greater part regular ecclesiastics: the counsellors were six or seven in number, of whom one, by the ordinance of Philip III., must be a Dominican. A party who was brought under cognizance of the court by secret accusation was immediately seized by its officers, (termed officials or familiars,) and his property put under sequestration. If the accused was fortunate enough to absent himself, and did not appear at the third summons, he was excommunicated, and in some cases burnt in effigy. The subsequent process of the court by imprisonment, secret examination, and torture, is well known. Penitent offenders were subjected to imprisonment, scourging, confiscation, and legal infamy. Those convicted, who were sentenced to death, were burnt at the Autos da Fe, which usually take place on some Sunday between Trinity and Advent. During the 18th century, the chief officers of the inquisition were for the most part men of intelligence and moderation, and its proceedings chiefly directed against parties guilty of such offences against decency or religion as would have been punishable in most European countries, although not by an equally arbitrary process. But there were exceptions to this general character; and by the provincial courts of inquisition, of which Spain contained sixteen, some acts of barbarous injustice were committed. According to a common calculation, 340,000 persons had been punished by the inquisition from 1481 to 1808, of whom nearly 32,000 were burnt. In that year it was abolished by Napoleon. It was afterwards re-established by Ferdinand III. in 1814; but having been again abrogated by the Cortes in 1820, it has not been since reconstituted. In Portugal, the supreme court of inquisition was established in 1557. Its history in many respects resembles that of the Spanish court; but in the 18th century its power was greatly curtailed by ordinances which required a certain degree of publicity in its procedure. It was abolished by the Cortes of 1821. There were courts of inquisition in various southern provinces of France, the principal that of Languedoc, established at Toulouse, which was first founded after the war against the Albigenses; but their power was limited not long after their creation, and fell into desuetude long before their final abolition. In several Italian states courts of inquisition have been established; but the institution has never taken much hold on the sentiments or habits of the people of that country. It was restored at Rome by Pius VII. after the expulsion of the French, but had jurisdiction only over the faith and conduct of the clergy.

INQUIS'ITOR, in law, any officer, as the sheriff and the coroner, having power to inquire into certain matters.—*Grand inquisitor* is the name given to a judge of the Inquisition.

INSAN'ITY, mental derangement of any degree, from slight delirium to raving madness. It is, however, rarely used to express temporary delirium occasioned by fever, &c.

INSCRIBE', to engrave on a monument, pillar, &c.; or to commend by a short address, less formal than a dedication; as, to *inscribe* an ode or book to a prince.

INSCRIP'TI, in Roman antiquity, a name given to those who were branded with any ignominious mark after the manner in which slaves were treated.

INSCRIP'TION, any monumental writing, engraved or affixed to a thing, to give a more distinct knowledge of it, or to transmit some important fact to posterity. The inscriptions mentioned by Herodotus and Diodorus Siculus, sufficiently show that this was the first method of conveying instruction to mankind, and transmitting the knowledge of history and sciences to posterity: thus the ancients engraved upon pillars both the principles of sciences, and the history of the world. Pisistratus carved precepts of husbandry on pillars of stone; and the treaties of confederacy between the Romans and Jews were engraved on plates of brass. Antiquarians have accordingly been very curious in examining the inscriptions on ancient ruins, coins, medals, &c.

INSOLV'ENCY, inability of a person to pay all his debts; or the state of wanting property sufficient for such payment. *Insolvency* is a term in *mercantile law*, applied to designate the condition of all persons unable to pay their debts according to the ordinary usage of trade. A bankrupt is an insolvent, but persons may be in a state of insolvency, without having committed any of the specific acts which render them liable to a commission of bankruptcy.

INSPIRA'TION, the infusion of ideas into the mind by the Holy Spirit; the conveying into the minds of men, ideas, notices, or monitions by extraordinary or supernatural influence.—*Inspiration of the sacred writers*, is defined an influence of the Holy Spirit exercised on the understandings, imaginations, memories, and other mental powers of the writers, by means of which they were qualified for communicating to the world divine revelation, or the knowledge of the will of God, without error or mistake. Writers on theology have enumerated several kinds or degrees of inspiration, which are founded upon the supposition that God imparted to the sacred writers that measure and degree of assistance which was just suited to the nature of the subjects which they committed to writing, and did not supersede the use of their natural powers and faculties, and of their acquired knowledge where these were sufficient. The measure of divine assistance which enabled Moses to give an account of the creation; Joshua to record with exactness the settlement of the Israelites in Canaan; David to mingle prophetic information with the varied effusions of gratitude, contrition, and piety; Isaiah to deliver predictions respecting the Messiah; and the Evangelists to record, in their own several styles and ways, the life and transactions of Jesus Christ, has been termed *inspiration of direction*. In some cases inspiration only produced correctness and accuracy in relating past occurrences, and preserved the writers generally from relating anything derogatory to the revelation with which it was connected. This has been termed *inspiration of superintendency*. Where indeed it not only communicates ideas, new and unknown before, but has also imparted greater strength and vigor to the efforts of the mind than the writers could otherwise have attained, this divine assistance has been called *inspiration of elevation*. Further, when the prophets and apostles received such communications of the Holy Spirit, as suggested and dictated minutely every part of the truths delivered; this, which is the highest degree of divine assistance, has been termed *inspiration of suggestion*. The infusion or communication of ideas or poetic spirit, by a superior being or supposed presiding power; as, the *inspiration* of Homer or other poet.

INSTALLA'TION, the ceremony of inducting, or investing with any charge, office, or rank; as, the placing a dean or prebendary in his stall or seat, or a knight into his order.

INSTAL'MENT, in commercial transactions, the payment of a certain portion of a gross sum, which is to be paid at different times, or, as the phrase is, by *instalments*. In constituting a capital-stock by subscriptions of individuals, it is customary to afford facilities to subscribers by dividing the sum subscribed into instalments, or portions payable at distinct periods. In large contracts also, it is not unusual to agree that the money shall be paid by instalments.

IN'STANT, a part of time or duration in which no succession is perceived. There are three kinds of instants distinguished by the schoolmen; a *temporary*, a *natural*, and a *rational* instant. The first is a part of time immediately preceding another; the second is what is otherwise termed a *priority of nature*, which obtains in things subordinated in acting, as first and second causes, or causes and their effects; and the third is not any real instant, but a point which the understanding conceives to have existed before some other instant, founded on the nature of the things which cause it to be conceived.

INSTAN'TER, in law, instantly; without the least delay; as, the party was compelled to plead *instanter*.

INSTAN'TIÆ CRUCIS, in philosophy, *crucial* instances or examples; a phrase invented by the fancy of Bacon. The use of crucial examples or experiments is to facilitate the process of induction. For example, A and B, two different causes, may produce a certain number of similar effects; find some effect which the one produces and the other does not, and this will point out, as the direction-post at a point where two highways meet, (crux,) which of these causes may have been in operation in any particular instance. Thus, for example, many of the symptoms of the Oriental plague are common to other diseases; but when the observer discovers the peculiar *bubo* or boil of the complaint, he has an *instantia crucis*, which directs him immediately to its discovery.

IN STATU QUO, (*Latin*,) a term signifying that condition in which things were left at a certain period; as when belligerent parties agree that their mutual relations should be *in statu quo*, or as they were before the commencement of a war; and the like.

INSTAURA'TA TER'RA, in archæology, land ready stocked or furnished with all things necessary to carry on the employment of a farmer.

INSTAU'RUM ECCLE'SIÆ, the vestments, plate, and all utensils belonging to a church.

IN'STINCT, that power of volition or impulse produced by the peculiar nature of an animal, which prompts it to do certain things, independent of all instruction or experience, and without deliberation, where such act is immediately connected with its own individual preservation, or with that of its kind Indeed, it is manifest that instinct not only makes animals perform certain actions necessary to the preservation of the species, but often altogether foreign to the apparent wants of the individual; and often, also, extremely complicated. We cannot attribute these actions to intelligence, without supposing a degree of foresight and understanding infinitely superior to what we can admit in the species that perform them. The actions performed by instinct are not the effects of imitation, for the individuals that execute them have often never seen them done by others; they bear no proportion to the common intelligence of the species, but become more singular, more skilful, more disinterested, in proportion as the animals belong to the less elevated classes. They are so much the property of the species, that all the individuals perform them in the same manner, without any improvement. The duckling hastens to the water, the hen remains the proper time on her eggs during incubation, the beaver builds his curious habitation with a skill peculiar to the species, and the bees construct, with architectural accuracy, their waxen cells. Instinct, then, is the general property of the living principle, or the law of organized life in a state of action.

IN'STITUTE, or INSTITU'TION, any society instituted or established according to certain laws, or regulations, for the furtherance of some particular object, such as colleges or seminaries for the cultivation of the sciences, Literary Institutes, Mechanics' Institutes, and others. We apply the word *institution* to laws, rites, and ceremonies, which are enjoined by authority as permanent rules of conduct or of government; as, the institutions of Moses or Lycurgus. Also, a society of individuals for promoting any public object, as a charitable or benevolent *institution*.

IN'STRUMENT, Musical, a machine or sonorous body, artificially constructed for the production of musical sounds. They are divided into three kinds, wind instruments, stringed instruments, and instruments of percussion.—*Mathematical instruments*, a common case of, contains,—a pair of plain compasses; a pair of drawing compasses; a drawing pen; a protractor; a parallel ruler; a plain scale; and a sector; besides black lead pencils.—*Instrument*, in law, a deed or writing drawn up between two parties, and containing several covenants agreed between them.

INSTRUMEN'TAL MU'SIC, music produced by instruments, as distinguished from *vocal* music; particularly applied to the greater compositions, in which the human voice has no part. Until the middle of the last century, the Italian composers used no other instruments in their great pieces than violins and bass-viols; at that time, however, they began to use the haut-boy and the horn; and even to this day, the Italians use wind instruments much less than the French and Germans. In general, symphonies and overtures, solos, duets, terzettos, quartettos, &c., sonatas, fantasias, concerts for single instruments, dances, marches, &c., belong to instrumental music.

IN'SULATED, in architecture, an appellation given to such columns as stand alone, or free from any contiguous wall, &c., like an island in the sea; whence the name.

INSUR'ANCE, in law and commerce, the act of providing against a possible loss, by entering into contract with one who is willing to give assurance; that is, to bind himself to make good such possible loss, upon the contingency of its occurrence. In this contract, the chances of the benefit are equal to the insurer and the assurer. The first actually pays a certain sum, and the latter undertakes to pay a larger, if an accident should happen. The one, therefore, renders his property secure; the other receives money, with the probability that it is clear gain. The instrument by which the contract is made, is denominated a *policy*, and the stipulated consideration is called the *premium*. These are generally for protection against losses by fire, or risks at sea. Policies on *lives* are another description of this contract, whereby a party, for a certain premium, agrees to pay a certain sum, if a person, to whose life it relates, shall die within a time specified, or to pay the executors of the insured a certain sum at the time of his death. These policies, however, usually make an exception of death by suicide. According to general practice, a life insurance is seldom made by the payment of a single sum when it is effected, but almost always by the payment of an *annual premium* during its continuance, the first being paid down at the commencement of the insurance. An individual, therefore, who has insured a sum on his life, would forfeit all the advantages of the insurance, were he not to continue regularly to make his annual payments.

INTA'GLIOS, precious stones on which are engraved the heads of eminent men, inscriptions, &c., such as are set in rings, &c.

IN'TELLECT, that faculty of the human soul or mind, which receives or comprehends the ideas communicated to it by the senses, or by perception, or by other means; the faculty of thinking; otherwise called the *understanding*. It is applied to the mind when only its rational powers are considered, apart from the animating principle, or the *will*, and from the source of the passions. A clear *intellect* receives and entertains the same ideas which another communicates with perspicuity. In the philosophy of Kant, the intellect is distinguished into two faculties, understanding and reason. The understanding, acting on experience, merely compares, judges, and measures its representations, and is conversant solely with their mutual limits and relations, classifying them according to certain schemes of its own which are called categories. While, however, the understanding is thus limited, the activity of the reason is unbounded, and as the principle of principles, it is the base and the verification of every special principle and reasoning.—

INTEND'ANT, a word much used in France, denoting a person who has the charge, direction, or management of some office or department; as an *intendant* of marine, an *intendant* of finance, &c.

INTER'CALARY DAY, in the calendar, a day inserted out of the usual order to preserve the account of time. Thus every fourth year containing 366 days, while the other years contain only 365, one of the months in that year must have an additional day, which is called the intercalary day. The additional day was given to February, as being the shortest month, and in the ancient Roman calendar was inserted between the 24th and 25th days. In the ecclesiastical calendar it still retains that place; but in the civil calendar it is the 29th.

INTERCES'SION, in Roman antiquity, the act of a tribune of the people, whereby he inhibited the act of another magistrate, or prevented the passing of a law in the senate, which was usually done by the single word *veto*.

INTERCOLUMNIA'TION, in architecture, the space between two columns, which is always to be proportioned to the height and bulk of the columns. It is one of the most important elements in architecture, and on it depend the effect of the columns themselves, their proportion, and the harmony of an edifice.

IN'TERDICT, in ecclesiastical history, a spiritual weapon, by which the popes used in former times to reduce individuals or whole states to the most abject submission to their power. In the middle ages it was the most terrible blow which could be inflicted on the people or the prince. When an interdict was laid on a kingdom all spiritual services ceased; the churches were shut up; the sacraments were no longer administered; no corpses were buried with funeral rites; and all the ministry of the church which was then believed to be the only channel of salvation was forbidden to be exercised. The first memorable occasion on which this method of warfare was adopted was the marriage of King Robert of France with Bertha his cousin, when Gregory V. in 998 issued interdicts against the whole country, and compelled the sovereign to dissolve his union. It had, however, been often used before by bishops; an instance is quoted by Moreri as early as A.D. 870. The ban under which England was laid in the reign of John by Innocent III. is well known in the history of that country. The latest pretensions to the exercise of this power were assumed by Pius VII., when he issued an inefficient decree against Napoleon in 1809.

IN'TERIM, in modern European history, the name given to a decree of the Emperor Charles V., after the overthrow of the Protestant League of Smalcalde, in which he attempted to reduce to harmony the conflicting opinions of the Protestants and Romanists. The use of the cap, however, and the marriage of the clergy, were the only points which he conceded to the Reformers; and it became a question among them, and gave rise to many serious disputes, whether they could conscientiously submit even to a temporary decree of such a nature. The enactments of the *interim* were intended only to remain in full force till some definitive settlement could be made; whence it derives the name by which it is generally known. It received the force of law at the Diet of Augsburgh, in 1548. Its provisions against the Protestants were however, in most respects, set aside by the treaty of Passau, 1552.

INTERJEC'TION, in grammar, an indeclinable part of speech, serving to express some passion or emotion of the mind; as, "Alas! my fondest hopes are now forever fled!"

INTERLACING ARCHES, in architecture, circular arches which intersect each other, as in the figure. They are frequent in arcades in the Norman style of the twelfth century, and from them Dr. Milner supposed the pointed arch to have had its origin.

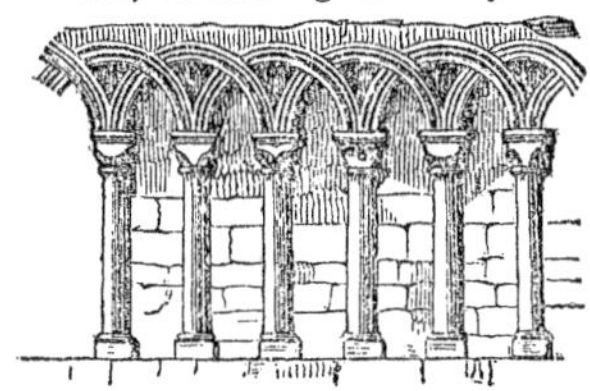

Interlacing Arcade, Norwich Cathedral.

INTERLOC'UTOR, in literary phraseology, a person who is introduced as taking part in a dialogue; in dramatic literature, termed *dramatis persona:* the latter name, however, comprehends such as appear on the stage but take no part in speaking, termed by the Greeks mute personages.

INTERLOC'UTORY *Order or Decree*, in law, an order that does not decide the cause, but only some matter incident thereto, which may happen in the intermediate stage of a cause; as when, in chancery, the plaintiff obtains an order for an injunction until the hearing of the cause; which order, not being final, is called interlocutory.

IN'TERLUDE, in the drama, a light entertainment exhibited on the stage between the principal performance and the afterpiece. At present, the term *interlude* is applied principally to small comic operas, written for two or three persons. In ancient tragedy, the chorus sung the interludes between the acts.

IN'TERMEDE, or INTERMEZ'ZO, in dramatic literature, nearly the same with interlude. A short musical piece, generally of a burlesque character; but many, not intended merely for introduction between the acts of a more serious performance, are comprised under these names by the French and Italians.

INTERNUN'CIO, an envoy of the pope, sent to small states and republics, distinguished from the nuncio who represents the pope at the courts of emperors and kings. Also a species of diplomatic officers, who ranked, according to the old practice, between ambassadors and plenipotentiaries.

INTERPOLA'TION, in philological criticism, the insertion of spurious passages in the writings of some ancient author.

INTERREG'NUM, the time during which a throne is vacant in elective kingdoms; for in such as are hereditary, like that of England, there is no such thing as an *interregnum*.

INTERROGA'TION, in grammar, a character or point (?) denoting a question, as, Do you love me?—*Interrogation*, in rhetoric, a figure containing a proposition in the form of a question.

INTERROG'ATORY, in law, a question in writing demanded of a witness in a cause who is to answer it under the solemnity of an oath.

IN'TERVAL, in music, the difference between the number of vibrations, produced by one sonorous body of a certain magnitude and texture, and of those produced by another of a different magnitude and texture, in the same time. The ancients divided the *intervals* into simple or uncomposite, which they call *diastems*, and composite intervals, which they call *systems*. Modern musicians consider the *semitone* as a simple interval, and only call those composite which consist of two or more semitones.

INTONA'TION, in music, the act of sounding the notes in the scale with the voice, or any other given order of musical tones. It consists, in fact, in giving to the tones of the voice or instrument that occasional impulse, swell, and decrease, on which, in a great measure, all expression depends.

INTOXICA'TION, the state produced by the excessive use of alcoholic liquids. It may be called *progressive madness*. Its first stage is marked by an increased circulation of the blood; the consciousness is not yet attacked, the fancy is more lively, and the feeling of strength and courage is increased. In the second stage, the effect on the brain is more decided: the peculiarities of character, and the faults of temperament, which in his sober moments the individual could control and conceal, manifest themselves without reserve. Consciousness, in the next stage, becomes more weakened; the balance of the body cannot be kept, and dizziness attacks the brain. In the next degree, the soul is overwhelmed in the tumult of animal excitement; consciousness is extinguished; the organs of speech refuse to perform their office, or the tongue pours forth an incoherent jargon; the face is red and swollen; the eyes are protruded and meaningless; and the drunkard falls into a state of stupor and insensibility.

INTRAN'SITIVE, in grammar, an epithet for a verb that expresses actions that do not *pass over* to an object, as I *go*, I *come*, I *sleep*, &c.

IN TRAN'SITU, a Latin expression, signifying, during the passage from one place to another.

INTRENCH'MENT, in fortification, any work that shelters a post against the attacks of an enemy.

IN'TROIT, in ecclesiastical antiquities, the verses chanted or repeated at the first entering of the congregation into the church; a custom as old as the fourth century: called "ingressa" in the Ambrosian ritual.

INTRU'SION, in law, a violent or unlawful seizing upon lands or tenements.

INTUI'TION, the act by which the mind perceives the agreement or disagreement of two ideas, or the truth of things, immediately, or the moment they are presented, without the intervention of other ideas, or without reasoning and deduction. Intuition is the most simple act of the reason or intellect, on which, according to Locke, depends the certainty and evidence of all our knowledge; which certainly every one finds to be so great, that he cannot imagine, and therefore cannot require, greater. In the philosophy of Kant, the term *intuition* is used to denote the single act of the sense upon outward objects according to its own laws.

INTU'ITIVE, perceived by the mind immediately, without the intervention of argument or testimony; exhibiting truth to the mind on bare inspection; as, *intuitive* evidence. The different species of *intuitive evidence*, according to Dugald Stewart, are, 1. The evidence of axioms; 2. The evidence of consciousness; of perception and of memory; 3. The evidence of those fundamental laws of human belief which form an essential part of our constitution, and of which our entire conviction is implied, not only in all speculative reasonings, but in all our conduct as active beings. Of this class is the evidence for our own personal identity; for the existence of the material world; for the continuance of those laws which have been found, in the course of our past experience, to regulate the succession of phenomena. Such truths no man ever thinks of stating to himself in the form of propositions; but all our conduct and all our reasonings proceed on the supposition that they are admitted. Every step which the reason makes in demonstrative knowledge has *intuitive* certainty; and, consequently, the power of reason presupposes that of intuition.

IN'VALIDS, those soldiers or sailors who, either on account of wounds or length of service, are admitted into hospitals, and there maintained at the public expense. The practice of making provision for soldiers worn out or disabled in the public service dates from high antiquity. The liberality of Pisistratus to the Athenian soldiers is known to every scholar; and the history of ancient Rome is replete with instances of the veterans of the legions being rewarded with grants of land. It must be admitted, however, that in ancient times such recompenses had not their origin in that high philanthropic feeling by which the moderns are actuated in making provision for military and naval invalids; for they were granted only after victory, and emanated more from individual power or favor than from any general or established principles of benevolence. In modern times there is no civilized country without institutions for the maintenance of invalids; but the most magnificent are, without question, the Greenwich and Chelsea hospitals in England, and in France the Hôtel des Invalides.

INVEN'TION, the action or operation of finding out something new; the contrivance of that which did not before exist; as, the invention of logarithms; the invention of the art of printing; the invention of the orrery. Invention differs from discovery. Invention is applied to the contrivance and production of something that did not before exist. Discovery brings to light that which existed before, but which was not known. We are indebted to invention for the thermometer and barometer. We are indebted to discovery for the knowledge of the islands in the Pacific ocean, and for the knowledge of galvanism, and many species of earth not formerly known. This distinction is important, though not always observed.—That which is invented. The cotton gin is the invention of Whitney; the steamboat is the invention of Fulton. The Doric, Ionic, and Corinthian orders are said to be inventions of the Greeks; the Tuscan and Composite are inventions of the Latins.—In painting, the finding or choice of the objects which are to enter into the composition of the piece.—In poetry, it is applied to whatever the poet adds to the history of the subject.—In rhetoric, the finding and selecting of arguments to prove and illustrate the point in view.

INVER'SION, in rhetoric and philology, the transposition of words out of their natural order. Every language has a customary arrangement of its own to regulate the order of succession in which words forming part of the same sentence, member, or proposition follow each other. On the other hand, there is undoubtedly a natural or philosophical order of words following each other in the same analytical succession in which ideas present themselves to the mind, varied occasionally by that produced by the succession of sentiments or emotions; and as in every language many customary phrases, if not the general arrangement of the words, are contrary to this primitive order, every language has customary inversions of its own. Deviations from the *customary* order of words are more commonly called transpositions; but each word has, of course, a relative and somewhat arbitrary signification. As an instance of ordinary inversion, it may be observed that, according to the metaphysical or analytical order, the subject of a proposition precedes the predicate, being the first idea which presents itself to the mind. Thus, in the construction of a sentence containing a proposition, "Solon is wise," or "Alexander reigns," we habitually follow the order of nature. But when a substantive and adjective in connection form part of a sentence, *i. e.*, a subject or predicate, or a part of either, the substantive is that which seems naturally to present itself first to the mind; whereas in most modern languages it follows the adjective, while in the Greek and Latin its ordinary although not its necessary place was before it: "Who is a wise man?" "Vir bonus est quis?" "The end of a long silence." "Finis silentii diuturni." It is in general to be observed, that modern languages admit far less readily than ancient of transposition; but there are considerable differences in this respect between modern languages themselves. German admits much latitude, French very little. In our own language we are frequently able to vary the analytical order by following what may be termed the order of emotion, where a French writer could not do so: thus in the proposition, "Great is Diana of the Ephesians," it would be impossible, in French, to give the force which is added to the expression by the transposition of the predicate to the beginning without violating the habitual rules of construction. A similar instance of inversion is to be found in the Swedish and some kindred languages, in which the article follows instead of preceding the noun.—*Inversion*, in music, the change of place between two notes of an interval; that is, placing the lower note an octave higher, or the higher note an octave lower.

INVERT'ED ARCH, in architecture, one wherein the lowest stone or brick is

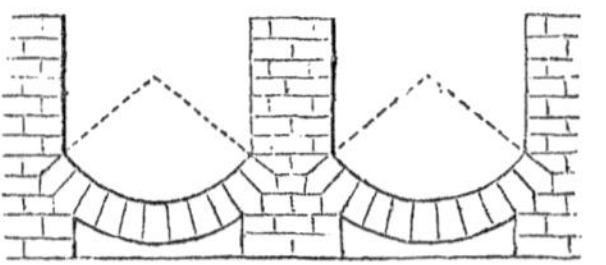

the key-stone. It is used in foundations, to distribute the weight of particular points over the whole extent of the foundation, and hence its employment is frequently of the first importance in constructive architecture.

INVES'TITURE, in feudal law, the delivery of a fief by a lord to his vassal, accompanied by peculiar ceremonies. The investiture of a bishop was, properly speaking, his endowment with the fiefs and temporalities of the see. Hence it became a subject of contest between the popes and emperors, and one of the principal grounds of the great quarrel of Guelfs and Ghibellines. It was conceded by the emperors to the Roman see in 1122; but the question was ended by a substantial compromise, which left the nomination in reality in the hands of the temporal prince in European monarchies under the Roman Catholic religion.

INVOCA'TION, in literature, signifies, in a general sense, an address at the commencement of a poem, preferred to the Muses or some other being supposed capable of giving inspiration. Thus, while the ancient poets generally addressed their invocations to some particular muse or divinity, Milton invokes the "Heavenly Muse" and the "Holy Spirit;" and, in his *Henriade*, Voltaire calls to his aid "auguste Verité."

IN'VOICE, in commerce, a written account of the particulars of merchandise shipped or sent to a purchaser, factor, &c. with the value or prices and charges annexed.

ION'IC DIALECT, the most euphonious of the four written varieties of the Greek language, was spoken by the inhabitants of the Ionian Islands, and in their colonial possessions in Asia Minor. It was originally the same as the Attic dialect, at least they boasted of a common origin; but from the extensive commercial intercourse of the Ionians with the eastern nations, their language gradually imbibed a portion of Asiatic effeminacy, which at length became its chief characteristic, forming a striking contrast to that combination of strength and harmony which distinguished the dialect of Attica. The chief writers in the Ionic dialect are Herodotus, Hippocrates, and Galen: but it is in the writings of the first that the most complete specimen is to be found.

ION'IC ORDER, one of the five orders of architecture. The distinguishing characteristic of this order is the volute of its capital. In the Grecian Ionic, the volutes appear the same on the front and rear; being connected on the flanks by a baluster-like form; through the external angles of the capitals of the corner columns, however, a diagonal volute is introduced. The Romans gave their Ionic four diagonal volutes, and curved the sides of the abacus. The Greek volute continues the fillet of the spiral along the face of the abacus, whereas in the Roman, its origin is behind the ovolo. In the modern Ionic capital, the volutes are placed diagonally, and the abacus has its sides hollowed out. The shaft, including the base, which is half a diameter, and the capital to the bottom of the volute, generally a little more, is about 9 diameters high, and may be fluted in 24 flutes, with fillets between them; these fillets are semi-circular. The pedestal is a little taller and more ornamented than the Doric. The bases used to this order are very various. The Attic base is very often used, and with an astragal added above the upper torus, makes a beautiful and appropriate base. The cornices of this order may be divided into three divisions, the plain Grecian cornice, the dentil cornice, and the modillion cornice. The best examples of this order are the temple on the Ilissus, of Minerva Polias, and Erichtheus in the Acropolis, and the aqueduct of Adrian at Athens; the temple of Fortuna Virilis, and the Coliseum at Rome. The boldness of the capital, with the beauty of the shaft, makes it eligible for porticoes, frontispieces, entrances to houses, &c.

ION'IC PHILOSOPHERS, the earliest among the Greek schools of philosophy. Speculation arose in Greece, as elsewhere, in the attempt to discover the laws of outward phenomena, and the origin and successive stages of the world's development. Such an attempt, it is needless to say, must at first have been extremely rude. To the student of philosophical literature, however, no such undertaking, however unsuccessful, can possibly be otherwise than interesting; and in this instance in particular we are able to discover the manifest traces of that liveliness of thought and systematic spirit which distinguish the later Greek speculations. The fathers of the Ionic school were Thales and his disciple Anaximenes. They were succeeded in the same line of thought by Diogenes of Apollonia, and Heraclitus of Ephesus. The characteristic mark which distinguishes the speculations of these thinkers is the endeavor to refer all sensible things to one original principle in nature. The two first named were satisfied with a very simple solution of the problem. Water with the one, and air with the other, were made the original materials out of which all things arose, and into which they were finally resolved. In their successors the germs of a more philosophical doctrine are apparent. They retain, indeed, the simplicity of an original element; but the *air* of Diogenes and the *fire* of Heraclitus are apparently only sensible symbols which they used only in order to present more vividly to the imagination the energy of the one vital principle which is the ground of all outward appearances. It would indeed be a mistake to regard these philosophers as *materialists*. The distinction between objective and subjective, between a *law* operating in the universe, and the corresponding apprehension of that law by reason, however obvious it may seem at the present day, seems to have required the deep meditation of numerous powerful thinkers to bring it into clear consciousness. But we meet also with a class of thinkers in whom the contrary tendency prevailed. Anaximander (B.C. 590) and Anaxagoras, the master of Pericles, agree in this respect, that they consider the world to be made up of numberless small particles, of different kinds and of various shapes, by the change in whose relative position all phenomena are to be accounted for. This hypothesis is combined by Anaxagoras with a Supreme Reason, the author of all that is regular and harmonious in the disposition of these elementary atoms. Anaxagoras may indeed be considered as the first philosopher who clearly and broadly stated the leading distinctions between mind and matter.

I'RONY, a mode of speech, or writing, expressing a sense contrary to what the speaker or writer means to convey. When irony is uttered, the dissimulation is generally apparent from the manner of speaking, which may be either accompanied by an arch look or by affected gravity.

ISA'IAH, or *the Prophecy of* ISAIAH, a canonical book of the Old Testament. Isaiah is the first of the four great prophets, the other three being Jeremiah, Ezekiel, and Daniel. The style of Isaiah is noble, sublime and florid. Grotius calls him the Demosthenes of the Hebrews. He had the advantage, above the other prophets, of improving his diction by conversing with men of the greatest learning and elocution; and this added a sublimity, force, and majesty to what he said. He boldly reproved the vices of the age in which he lived, and openly displayed the judgments of God that threatened the Jewish nation; at the same time denouncing vengeance on the Assyrians, Egyptians, Ethiopians, Moabites, Edomites, Syrians, and Arabians, who were instrumental in inflicting those judgments. He foretold the deliverance of the Jews from their captivity in Babylon, by the hands of Cyrus, king of Persia, a hundred years before it came to pass; but the most remarkable of his predictions are those concerning the Messiah, in which he not only foretold his coming in the flesh, but many of the great and memorable circumstances of his life and death. The whole, indeed, bears the stamp of genius and true inspiration.

I'SIS, one of the chief deities in the Egyptian mythology. By the Egyptians she was regarded as the sister or sister-wife of Osiris, who concurred with her in the endeavor to polish and civilize their subjects; to teach them agriculture and other necessary arts of life. Among the higher, and more philosophical theologians, she was made the symbol of pantheistic divinity. By the people she was worshipped as the goddess of fecundity. The cow was sacred to her. She is represented variously, though most usually as a woman with the horns of a cow, and sometimes with the lotus on her head, and the sistrum in her hand.

IS'LAMISM, the practical as well as the doctrinal tenets of the Mohammedan religion, embracing the whole of their civil and religious polity.

ISLANDS OF THE BLESSED, according to the Grecian mythology, the Happy Islands, supposed to lie westward in the ocean, whither after death, the souls of the virtuous were transported. In the early mythology of the Greeks, the Islands of the Blessed, the Elysian fields, and the infernal regions, were generally confounded with each other.

ISOTOM'IC, in music, consisting of intervals, in which each concord is alike tempered, and in which there are twelve equal semitones.

IS'SUE, in law, the legitimate offspring of parents. Also, the profits arising from lands, tenements, fines, &c.—The point of matter *at issue* between contending parties in a suit, is when a thing is affirmed on the one side, and denied on the other.

IST'HMIAN GAMES, so called because they were celebrated in the Isthmus of Corinth, which joins the Peloponnesus to the Continent, at the temple of Isthmian Neptune, which was surrounded with a thick forest of pine. They were originally held in the night, and had perhaps fallen into disuse, when Theseus restored them, and ordered them to be celebrated in the day. The contests were of the same kind as at the Olympic games; and so great was the concourse at these games, that only the principal people, of the most remarkable cities, could have place.

ITAL'IAN, a native of Italy, or the language spoken by its inhabitants. The origin of this beautiful and most harmonious tongue, is involved in great obscurity.

ITAL'ICS, in printing, characters or letters (first used in Italy) which stand inclining; thus—*Italic;* and which are often used by way of distinction from Roman letters, for emphasis, antithesis, or some peculiar importance attached to the words in which they are employed.—*Italicize*, to write or print in Italic characters.

ITAL'IC SCHOOL OF PHILOSOPHY, comprehends properly the Pythagorean and Eleatic systems taken together; but sometimes it is used as synonymous merely with the school of Pythagoras. Under the several heads will be found the chief features of these philosophical systems, which, comprising as they do all that can be said in reference to the Italic school, it would seem unnecessary in this place further to advert to. The Italic school has been so designated from the fact that its founder, Pythagoras, taught in Italy, spreading his doctrine among the people of Tarentum, Metapontum, Heraclea, Naples, etc.

I'VORY, the tusks and teeth of the elephant, and of the walrus or sea-horse; a hard, solid substance, of a fine white creamy color, and greatly esteemed for the fineness of its grain, and the high polish it is capable of receiving. That of India loses its color and becomes yellow; but that of Achem and Ceylon is free from this imperfection. Ivory is extensively used by cutlers in the manufacture of handles for knives and forks; by miniature painters for their tablets; by turners, in making numberless useful and ornamental objects, as well as for chess-men, billiard balls, toys, &c.; also by musical and philosophical instrument makers; comb-makers; and by dentists for making artificial teeth; for which last-mentioned purpose the ivory of the walrus is preferred. The western and eastern coasts of Africa, the Cape of Good Hope, Ceylon, India, and the countries to the eastward of the straits of Malacca, are the great marts whence supplies of ivory are derived. Ivory articles are said to be manufactured to a greater extent, and with better success, at Dieppe, than in any other place in Europe; but the preparation of this beautiful material is much better understood by the Chinese than by any other people. No European artist has hitherto succeeded in cutting concentric balls after the manner of the Chinese; and their boxes, chess-men, and other ivory articles, are all far superior to any that are to be met with anywhere else. The use of ivory was well known in very early ages. We find it employed for arms, girdles, sceptres, harnesses of horses, sword-hilts, &c. The ancients were also acquainted with the art of sculpturing in ivory, of dying and encrusting it. Homer refers to the extreme whiteness of ivory. The coffer of Cypselus was doubtless the most ancient monument of this kind in basso-relievo, and we meet with similar instances in the temple of Juno, at Olympius, in the time of Pausanias—that is to say, seven hundred years after it had been built. Antiquity possessed numerous statues of ivory, particularly in the temples of Jupiter and of Juno at Olympius. In these statues there was very frequently a mixture of gold. The most celebrated are stated to have been the Olympian Jupiter and the Minerva of Phidias: the former was covered with a golden drapery, and seated on a throne formed of gold, of ivory and cedar-wood, and enriched with precious stones. In his hand the god held a figure of Victory, alike of ivory and gold. The Minerva was erected in the Parthenon at Athens during the first year of the eighty-seventh Olympiad, the year which commenced the Peloponnesian war. Pausanias, likewise, makes mention of an ivory statue of Juno, on her throne, of remarkable magnificence, by Polycletes, together with an infinity of others.

I'VY, in mythological painting and sculpture, a plant, the leaves of which were made very plentiful use of by ancient artists on vases, pedestals, altars, &c. It was also, in the shape of a crown, the constant attribute of Bacchus, probably because, being evergreen, it implied, in an allegorical and at the same time elegant manner, the eternal youth of that deity.

J.

J, this letter, although very ancient, has been added to the English alphabet only in modern days. Its form was originally identical with that of I, and it is only within the last century that any distinction was made between them. The separation of these two letters in English dictionaries is of still more recent date. It seems to have had the sound of *y* in many words, as it still has in the German. The English sound of this letter may be expressed by *dzh*, or *edzh*, a compound sound coinciding exactly with that of *g*, in *genius;* the French *j*, with the articulation *d* preceding it. It is the tenth letter of the English alphabet, and the seventh consonant.

JA'COBINS, in French history, a political club, which bore a well-known part in the first revolution. It was first formed by some distinguished members of the First Assembly, particularly from Brittany, where revolutionary sentiments ran high. They took, at first, the name of Friends of the Revolution; but as, at the end of 1789, they held their meetings in the hall of a suppressed Jacobin monastery in the Rue Saint Honoré, the name of Jacobins, at first familiarly given them, was finally assumed by themselves. The history of the Jacobin club is, in effect, the history of the Revolution. It contained at one time more than 2,500 members, and corresponded with more than 400 affiliated societies in France. The club of the Cordeliers, formed by a small and more violent party out of the general body of Jacobins, was reunited with the parent society in June, 1791; but continued to form a separate section within its limits. The Jacobin club, which had almost controlled the first assembly, was thus, during the continuance of the second, itself divided between two contending parties; although the name of Jacobins, as a political party, is commonly given to that section which opposed the Girondists or less moderate in the club no less than in the assembly. After the destruction of the latter under the Convention, the club was again exclusively governed by the more violent among its own members, until the downfall of Robespierre. After that period it became unpopular; and its members having attempted an insurrection on behalf of the subdued Terrorists, November 11, 1794, the meeting was dispersed by force, and the club finally suppressed. Some wri ters, such as Barruel, have seen in the first formation of this and similar societies, the long-concocted operations of a conspiracy against legitimate government and religion throughout Europe. The Jacobins, and the other principal clubs of the Revolution, adopted all the forms of a legislative assembly. In the constitution of 1792, their legal existence was recognized. See the historians of the French Revolution, especially Carlyle, Mignet, and Thiers, for general views; Buchez et Roux, *Histoire Parlementaire de la Revolution Française*, for the most complete series of details respecting the Jacobins and their meetings which has yet been made public.—*Jacobins*, in ecclesiastical history, the religious of the order of St. Dominic were so called in France, from the situation of the principal convent at Paris, near the Rue St. Jacques.

JAC'OBITES, in English history, that party which, after the Revolution of 1688, adhered to the dethroned monarch James II., and afterwards to his descendants. In Scotland and Ireland, where the revolution was not effected except with the assistance of arms, the Jacobite party formed one of the two great divisions of each nation; and although crushed in the latter country by conquest, they continued in the former to comprise a large proportion of the population until long after the last rebellion in 1745. But in England the revolution was effected at first with the consent of all parties; the adherents to the exiled monarch were silenced: yet in a year or two, the Jacobite faction rose into strength, and continued to harass the government of William throughout his reign. Its immediate cause was to be found in the refusal of a portion of the bishops and clergy to take the oaths to the new government, which gave, as it were, a certain consistency and tangible ground of opposition to the friends of the dethroned monarch in general. At the same time many of William's chief advisers and officers maintained a secret correspondence with James II. at the French court, less from any attachment to his cause than with a view to secure their own interest in case of his return. After the death of James II. in France, and accession of Anne in England the efforts of the party languished for a time; but towards the close of her reign they revived, on the prospect of a change in the succession. In 1715, on the arrival of George I., broke out the unsuccessful first rebellion in Scotland: its ill conduct and failure proved a considerable check to the hopes of the English Jacobites. Bishop Atterbury, the last of their bolder intriguers and adherents, was banished in 1722: after which time it is probable that no extensive conspiracy took place on their part. In Scotland, however, the party maintained its strength unabated, until the second rebellion of 1745, by its complete failure, put an end to its political existence.—*Jacobites*, in ecclesiastical history, the monophysite Christians of Syria are so called, from Jacob Baradzi, who revived their belief and form of worship in that country and Mesopotamia, in the middle of the 6th century. Many unsuccessful attempts have been made at various times to unite them with the church of Rome.

JAC'OBUS, a gold coin in the reign of James I. of the value of 25*s*.

JAC'QUERIE, in history, the name popularly given to a revolt of the French peasantry against the nobility, which took place while king John was a prisoner in England, in 1356. *Jacques Bonhomme* was a term of derision applied by the nobles to the peasants, from which the insurrection took its name. It began in the Beauvoisis, under a chief of the name of Caillet, and desolated Picardy, Artois, and Brie, where savage reprisals were executed against the nobility for their oppressions. It was suppressed after some weeks by the dauphin and Charles the Bad, king of Navarre. A similar spirit in England produced, not many years afterwards, the rebellion of Wat Tylor.

JACTITA'TION *of Marriage*, a suit in the ecclesiastical court, when one of the parties declares that he or she is married, which if the other party deny, and no adequate proof of the marriage be brought, the offending party is enjoined silence on that head.

JAMBS, in architecture, the side or vertical pieces of any opening in a wall, which bear the piece that discharges the superincumbent weight of such wall.

JAN'IZARIES, or JAN'ISSARIES, the appellation given to the grand seignior's guard, or the soldiers of the Turkish infantry. They became turbulent, and rising in arms against the sultan, in May, 1826, were attacked, defeated, and subsequently abolished, and their places supplied by troops trained after the European manner.

JAN'SENISTS, a denomination of Roman Catholics in France, who followed the opinon of Jansen, bishop of Ypres, and formed a considerable party in the latter half of the 17th century. The Jansenists were Calvinistic in many of their sentiments, and in several respects approximated to the reformed opinions. They did not, however, separate themselves from the Catholic church; nor did they long survive the decree of Alexander VII., by which certain propositions extracted from their writings are condemned as heretical. The Jansenists are chiefly celebrated for the contest they maintained with the Jesuits, by whom they were at last overcome, and subjected to the enmity both of Louis XIV. and the pope.

JAN'UARY, the first month of the year. By some the name is derived from Janus, a Roman divinity; by others from janua, *a gate*. The months of January and February were inserted in the Roman year by Numa Pompilius. The Roman feast of the kalends of January seems to have been converted in the 6th century into the Christian festival of the circumcision.

JA'NUS, a Latin deity, originally the same as the sun. He was represented with two faces looking opposite ways, and holding a key in one hand, a staff in the other. He presided over the commencement of all undertakings, whence the first month in the year was named after him. His temple at Rome was kept open in the time of war, and shut in peace. The warlike disposition of the Romans is manifest from the fact that this temple was only shut six times in 800 years: viz., once in the reign of Numa; at the conclusion of the first Punic war; thrice in the reign of Augustus; and once again under Nero.

JEAL'OUSY, that passion or peculiar uneasiness which arises from the fear that a rival may rob us of the affection of one whom we love, or the suspicion that he has already done it; or it is the uneasiness which arises from the fear that another does, or will enjoy some advantage which we desire for ourselves. A man's jealousy is excited by the attentions of a rival to his favorite lady. A woman's jealousy is roused by her husband's attentions to another woman. The candidate for office manifests a jealousy of others who seek the same office. The jealousy of a student is awakened by the apprehension that his fellow will bear away the palm of praise. In short, jealousy is awakened by whatever may exalt others, or give them pleasures and advantages which we desire for ourselves. —*Jealousy* is nearly allied to envy, for jealousy, before a good is lost by ourselves, is converted into envy, after it is obtained by others.

JEHO'VAH, one of the Scripture names of God, signifying the Being who is self-existent, and gives existence to others. This is the awful and ineffable name of the God of Israel, which was revealed to Moses; denoting Him who is, who was, and who is to come.

JEM'IDAR, in military affairs, a black officer, who has the same rank as a lieutenant in the East India Company's service.

JES'UITS, or *the Society of Jesus*, the most celebrated of all the Romish religious orders; founded by Ignatius Loyola, a Spaniard, in the year 1534, when he, with Francis Xavier and four or five other students at the university of Paris, bound themselves to undertake the conversion of unbelievers. As a religious body, the Jesuits differ from their predecessors, inasmuch as, their principle being to conform as much as possible with the manners of the age, they have never adopted the austere observances and exclusive spiritual character upon which all earlier orders had grounded their claims to notoriety. They are divided into different classes; of which only *the professed* take the religious vows of poverty, chastity, and obedience to their superior. Among the novices are frequently enrolled influential laymen, as was Louis the XIV. himself in his latter years; and this is one of the means which the order has employed to extend its efficiency where it would be least liable to observation. The professed are of several ranks, the whole body being under the absolute control of the general, whose abode is fixed in Rome, and whose council consists of an admonitor and five assistants or counsellors, who represent the five principal Catholic states—Italy, Germany, France, Spain, and Portugal. To Rome, as the central seat of the order, are sent monthly communications from the superiors of the different provinces through which its members are distributed.

JEU D'ESPRIT', (*French*,) a witticism or unexpected association of ideas

JEWS, the descendants of Abraham, once an independent tribe in Palestine, but dispersed by the Romans; yet still distinguished by their religion, peculiar pursuits, and primitive customs. They are the negotiators of money between all nations, and everywhere distinguished for their successful enterprise and accumu lations of wealth. They have, however, lost the distinction of twelve tribes, though perhaps more numerous than at any period.—*See* JUDAISM.

JEW'S'-HARP, an instrument of music, of a very imperfect character, which, placed between the teeth and by means of a spring struck by the finger, gives a sound which is modulated by the breath. By some it has been called the *jaw's-harp*, because the place where it is played upon is between the jaws.

JOB, or *the book of Job*, a canonical book of the Old Testament, containing the narrative of a series of misfortunes which happened to a man named Job, as a trial of his patience and fortitude, together with conferences which he held with his several friends on the subject of his misfortunes, and the manner in which he was restored to happiness. Many of the Jewish Rabbins pretend that this relation is purely a fiction ; others think it a simple narrative of a matter of fact; while a third class of critics acknowledge that the ground-work of the story is true, but that it is written in a poetical style, and decorated with peculiar circumstances. to render the narration more profitable and interesting. Such is the opinion of Grotius, who supposed that the events recorded in it happened in Arabia, while the Hebrews wandered in the desert. The whole narrative is characterized by simplicity of manner and intensity of feeling, combined with pure and lofty sentiments, illustrating in a striking manner, the nature of man and the providence of God.

JOHN BULL, the well-known collective name of the English nation, was first used in Arbuthnot's satire, *The History of John Bull*, usually published in Swift's works ; in which the French are designated as Lewis Baboon, the Dutch as Nicholas Frog, &c.

JOHN (ST.) THE EVANGELIST, the author of the Gospel which bears his name, of the book of Revelations, which he wrote while an exile in the isle of Patmos, and of three Epistles. He was emphatically called "the disciple whom Jesus loved ;" and he was one of the most pure and estimable characters mentioned in the New Testament.

JOHN THE BAPTIST, the inspired harbinger of the Messiah. His zeal, as one who came to "prepare the way" of a greater and more glorious prophet, was equalled only by his self-denial and humility. He at last fell a victim to his independence and severe virtues, being beheaded by order of Herod Antipas, tetrarch of Galilee, to gratify a vindictive woman. His disciples are said to have been the founders of the sect of *Sabians*.

JOINT-STOCK, stock held in company. *Joint-Stock Companies*, associations of a number of individuals for the purpose of carrying on a specified business or undertaking. They are generally formed for the accomplishment of extensive schemes of trade or manufacture, or the completion of some object of national and local importance, such as railways, bridges, canals, &c. They have also been found well adapted for the formation of banks.

JOINT-TEN'ANCY, in law, a tenure of estate by unity of interest, title, time, and possession.

JOINT'URE, in law, a wife's separate estate, secured by will, or by marriage settlement. In other cases the wife inherits one third.

JO'NAH, *prophecy of*, a canonical book of the Old Testament, in which it is related that Jonah, about the year 771, B.C., was ordered to go and prophesy the destruction of the Ninevites, on account of their wickedness. But instead of obeying the divine command, he embarked for Tarshish, when a tempest arising, the mariners drew lots to determine who was the cause of it, and as the lot fell to him he was thrown into the sea, and was swallowed by a great fish, which after three days, cast him on the shore. After this he boldly preached to the people of Nineveh, and predicted their destruction ; but which, on account of their repentance, was averted. Jonah, dreading the suspicion which might attach to him as a false prophet, retired to a mountain at a distance from the city, where he learnt the folly and unreasonableness of his own discontent. It may be observed that some critics consider this book as a collection of traditions, collected after the destruction of Nineveh, while others treat it as a mere allegorical poem.

JOSH'UA, a canonical book of the Old Testament, containing a history of the wars and transactions of the person whose name it bears. This book is divisible into three parts, the first of which is a history of the conquest of Canaan ; the second, which begins with the 12th chapter, is a description of that country, and the division of it among the tribes : and the third, comprised in the last two chapters, contains the renewal of the covenant which he caused the Israelites to make, and the death of their victorious leader.

JOUR'NAL, a diary; an account of daily transactions and events; or the book containing such account.—Among merchants, a book in which every particular article or charge is fairly entered from the waste book or blotter.—In navigation, a daily register of the ship's course and distance, the winds, weather, and other occurrences.—A paper published daily, or other newspaper; also, the title of a book or pamphlet published at stated times, containing an account of inventions, discoveries, and improvements in arts and sciences; as, the Journal des Savans; the Journal of Science.—A narrative, periodically or occasionally published, of the transactions of a society, &c., as the Journals of the Houses of Congress.

JU'BILEE, a grand festival celebrated every fiftieth year, by the Jews, in commemoration of their deliverance out of Egypt. At this festival, which was a season of joy, all debts were to be cancelled; all bond-servants were set free; all slaves or captives were released; and all estates which had been sold reverted to the original proprietors or their descendants.—In imitation of the Jewish jubilee, the Romish church instituted a year of jubilee, during which the popes grant plenary indulgences, &c.

JU'DAISM, the religious doctrines and rites of the Jews, a people of Judah, or Judea. These doctrines and rites are detailed in the five books of Moses, hence called *the law*. The *Caraites* acknowledge no other; but the *Rabbinists*, the second of the two sects of Jews, add those inculcated by the *talmud*. The following is a summary of the religious creed of the Jews: 1, that God is the creator and active supporter of all things; 2, that God is ONE, and eternally unchangeable; 3, that God is incorporeal, and cannot have any material properties; 4, that God shall eternally subsist; 5, that God is alone to be worshipped; 6, that whatever has been taught by the prophets is true: 7, that Moses is the head and father of all contemporary doctors, and of all those who lived before and shall live after him; 8, that the law was given by Moses; 9, that the law shall always exist, and never be altered; 10, that God knows all the thoughts and actions of man; 11, that God will reward the observance and punish the breach of his law; 12, that the Messiah is to come, though he tarry a long time; and 13, that there shall be a resurrection of the dead when God shall think fit. These doctrines, commonly received by the Jews to this day, were drawn up about the end of the eleventh century by the famous Jewish rabbi Maimonides.

JUDG'ES, THE BOOK OF, a canonical book of the Old Testament, so called from its relating the state of the Israelites under the administration of many illustrious persons who were called judges, from the circumstance of their being both the civil and military governors of the people. The power of the judges extended to affairs of peace and war. They were protectors of the laws, defenders of religion, avengers of all crimes; but they could make no laws, nor impose any new burthens upon the people. They lived without pomp or retinue, unless their own fortunes enabled them to do it; for the revenues of their office consisted in voluntary presents from the people. They continued from the death of Joshua till the beginning of the reign of Saul.

JUDG'MENT, in metaphysics, a faculty of the soul, whereby it compares ideas, and perceives their agreement or disagreement.—In law, the sentence or doom pronounced in any cause, civil or criminal, by the judge or court by which it is tried. Judgments are either interlocutory, that is, given in the middle of a cause on some intermediate point, or final, so as to put an end to the action.

JU'DICES SELEC'TI, in Roman antiquities, were persons summoned by the prætor, to give their verdict in criminal matters in the Roman courts, as juries do in ours. No person could be regularly admitted into this number till he was twenty-five years of age. *Sortitia Judicum*, or impanelling the jury, was the office of the *Judex Quæstionis*, and was performed after both parties were come into court, for each had a right to reject or challenge whom they pleased, others being substituted in their room.

JUDI'CIUM DEI, the term formerly applied to all extraordinary trials of secret crimes, as those by arms, single combat, ordeals, &c., in which it was believed that heaven would miraculously interfere to clear the innocent and confound the guilty.

JU'LIAN PE'RIOD, in chronology, signifies a revolution of 7980 years, which arises from multiplying the solar cycle, the cycle of the moon, and the cycle of indiction into one another. This period is of great use, as the standard and general receptacle of all other epochas, periods, and cycles: into this as into a large ocean, all the streams of time discharge themselves, yet so as not to lose their peculiar characters; and had historians remarked the number of each cycle in each year respectively, there could have been no dispute about the time of any action or event in past ages.—When the Christian era commenced 4713 years of the Julian period were elapsed, 4713 therefore being added to the year of our Lord, will give the year of the Julian period.

JULY', the seventh month of the year. It was the fifth month of the old Roman year, and known by the name of *Quintilis;* but received the name of July in compliment to Julius Cæsar, who reformed the calendar, in such a manner, that this month stood as it does now with us, the seventh in order.

JUNE, the sixth month of the year, in which is the summer solstice. It was the fourth month of the old Roman year, but the sixth of the year as reformed by Numa and Julius Cæsar. Some suppose it received its name in honor of Junius Brutus. It was looked upon as under the protection of Mercury.

JU'NO, the Latin name of the divinity called by the Greeks Hera. She was the sister and consort of Jupiter, and was held to preside over marriage, and protect married women. She was represented as the model of majestic beauty, in royal

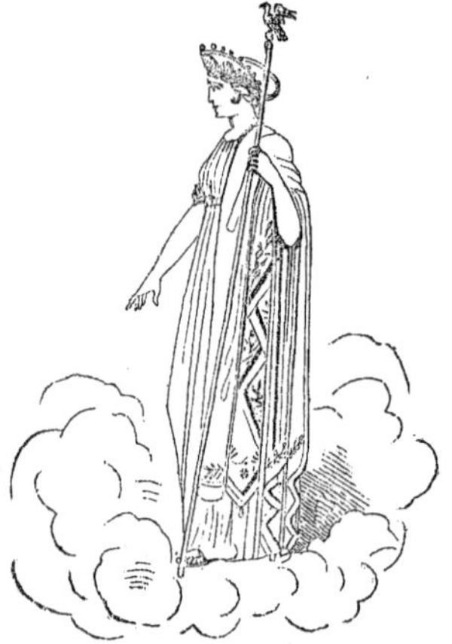

attire, and attended by her favorite bird the peacock. Her principal temples in Greece were at Samos and Argos. She was also the patroness of Veii, whence she was invited to Rome on the occasion of the last siege of the former city.

JUN'TA, a grand Spanish council of state. Besides the assembly of the states or *cortes*, there were two juntas: one which presided over the commerce, the mint, and the mines; and the other forming a board for regulating the tobacco monopoly. The assembling of a junta by Napoleon in 1808, and the part they subsequently played in Spanish history, are sufficiently known to the reader. In English the term *junto* (evidently of Spanish origin) is used almost synonymously with cabal or faction.

JU'PITER, the supreme deity among the Greeks and Romans. He was called by the Greeks Zeus (Ζευς,) and appears originally to have been worshipped as an elemental divinity who presided over rain, snow, lightning, &c. He was the son of Saturn, whom he deposed from his throne, and thence became the supreme monarch of gods and men. He married his sister Juno, by whom he had Vulcan

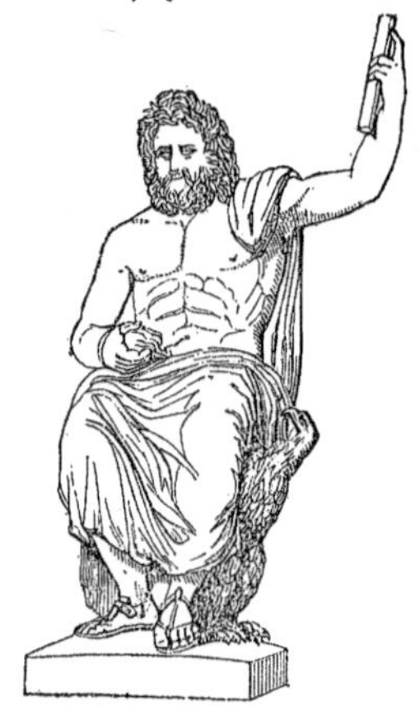

but he had a numerous progeny besides, the chief of whom was Minerva. His most celebrated Grecian temple was at Olympia in Elis, and his chief oracle was at Dodona in Epirus. He is usually represented as seated on an ivory throne with a sceptre in his left hand and a thunderbolt in his right. The eagle, his favorite bird, is generally placed by the side of the throne.

JURISCON'SULT, a master of Roman jurisprudence, who was consulted on the interpretation of the laws.

JURISDIC'TION, in its most general sense, is the power to make, declare, or apply the law; when confined to the judiciary department, it is what we denominate the *judicial power*, the right of administering justice through the laws. Inferior courts have jurisdiction of debt and trespass, or of smaller offences; the supreme courts have jurisdiction of treason, murder, and other high crimes.

JURISPRU'DENCE, the science which gives a knowledge of the laws, customs, and rights of men in a state or community, necessary for the due administration of justice.

JU'RIS U'TRUM, in law, a writ in behalf of a clergyman whose predecessor has alienated the lands belonging to his church.

JU'RY, a certain number of men sworn to inquire into or to determine facts, and to declare the truth according to the evidence legally deduced, and they are sworn judges upon evidence in matters of fact. When the object is inquiry only, the tribunal is sometimes called an inquest or inquisition; but when facts are to be determined by it for judicial purposes, it is always termed a jury. Trial by jury, in popular language, signifies the determination of facts in the administration of civil or criminal justice by twelve men, sworn to decide facts truly according to the evidence produced before them. Grand juries are exclusively incident to courts of criminal jurisdiction; their office is to examine into charges of crimes brought to them, and if satisfied that they are true, or at least that they deserve more particular examination, to return a bill of indictment against the accused, upon which he is afterward tried by a petty jury. A grand jury must consist of twelve at the least, but in practice a greater number usually serve, and twelve must always concur in finding every indictment. Petty or common juries consist of twelve men only. They are appointed to try all cases both civil and criminal, and to give their verdict according to the evidence adduced.

JUS, (*Latin*,) in its general acceptation, signifies that which is right or conformable to law.—*Jus accrescendi*, in law, the right of survivorship between two joint tenants.—*Jus coronæ*, signifies, in general, the rights of the crown. These are a part of the laws of the kingdom, though they differ in many things from the general laws relating to the subject.—*Jus duplicatum*, is a double right, and is used when a person has the possession of a thing, as well as a right to it.—*Jus divinum*, is that which is ordered by a revelation, in contradistinction to that which is ordered by reason: but it is evident that the distinction exists only in the form, and not in the essence, because that which is ordered by our reason is to be referred to God, as its origin, equally with that which is decreed by revelation.—*Jus gentium*, the law of nations, or the laws established between different kingdoms and states, in relation to each other.—*Jus hereditatis*, the right or law of inheritance.—*Jus patronatus*, in the canon law, is the right of presenting to a benefice; or a kind of commission granted by the bishop to inquire who is the rightful patron of a church.—*Jus possessionis*, is a right of seisin or possession, as *jus proprietatis* is the right of ownership of lands, &c.—*Jus quiritium*, in antiquity, the fullest enjoyment of Roman citizenship. This is also called *Jus civile* and *Jus urbanum*.—*Jus imaginis*, the right of using pictures and statues, similar to the modern right of bearing coats of arms, which was allowed to none but those whose ancestors or themselves had borne some curule office.

JUSTICE OF THE PEACE, the word *justice* is applied to judicial magistrates; as justices of such a court, and, in the English laws, justices of the forest, hundred, or the laborers, &c.; and hence the appellation justice of the peace—that is, a judicial magistrate intrusted with the conservation of the peace. A great part of the civil officers, are, in fact, the conservators of the peace, as their duty is to prevent or punish breaches of the peace. Thus the judges, grand-jurymen, justices of the peace, mayors and aldermen of municipal corporations, sheriffs, coroners, constables, watchmen, and all officers of the police, are instituted for the purpose of preventing, in different ways, crimes and disturbances of the peace of the community, or for arresting, trying and punishing the violators of the laws and good order of society. In England and the United States, the justice of the peace, though not high in rank, is an officer of great importance, as the first judicial proceedings are had before him in regard to arresting persons accused of grave offences; and his jurisdiction extends to trial and adjudication for small offences. In case of the commission of a crime or a breach of the peace, a complaint is made to one of these magistrates. If he is satisfied with the evidence of a commission of some offence, the cognizance of which belongs to him, either for the purpose of arresting, or for trying the party accused, he issues a warrant directed to a constable, or other executive officer designated by the law for this purpose, ordering the person complained of to be brought before him, and he thereupon tries the party, if the offence be within his jurisdiction, and acquits him or awards punishment. If the offence charged be of a graver character, the adjudication upon which is not within the justice's jurisdiction, the question then is, whether the party complained of is to be imprisoned, or required to give bonds to await his trial before the tribunal having jurisdiction, or is to be discharged; and on these questions the justice decides according to his view of the law and the facts. In the United States, the office is held only by special appointment, and the tenure is different in different states, the office having been held, in one state at least, during good behavior; but the commission is more usually for seven years, or some other specific limited period. These magistrates have usually also a civil jurisdiction, of suits for debts, on promises, or for trespasses, (where the title to real estate does not come in question, and with some other exceptions,) to an amount varying, in the different states, from $13.33 to $100. In some states, a party may appeal from the decision of the justice to a higher tribunal, whatever may be the amount in question, in a civil suit, and whatever may be the judgment. In other states, no appeal is allowed, except in case of an amount in question exceeding four dollars, or some other certain, but always inconsiderable sum. So an appeal is usually allowed to the accused party in a criminal prosecution before a justice of the peace, in case of the judgment being for a penalty over a certain specified and small amount, or an imprisonment over a certain number of days. It is evidently of the greatest importance to the peace and good order of a community, that the justices should be discreet, honest and intelligent.

JUSTIFICA'TION, in law, the showing good reason in a court, why one has done the thing for which he is called to answer. *Pleas in justification* must set forth some special matter: thus, on being sued for a trespass, a person may justify it by proving that the land is his own freehold; that he entered a house, in order to apprehend a felon; or by virtue of a warrant, to levy a forfeiture; or, in order to take a distress.—In theology, *justification* signifies remission of sin and absolution from guilt and punishment, or an act of free grace by which God pardons the sinner and accepts him as righteous, on account of the merits of Christ.

JUVENA'LIÆ, in Roman antiquity, a feast instituted for youth by Nero, when his beard was first shaven.

K.

The eleventh letter of the English alphabet, is borrowed from the Greeks, being the same character as the Greek *kappa*, answering to the Oriental *kaph*. It represents a close articulation, formed by pressing the root of the tongue against the upper part of the mouth, with a depression of the lower jaw and opening of the teeth. It is usually denominated a guttural, but is more properly a palatal. Before all the vowels, it has one invariable sound, corresponding with that of *c*, before *a*, *o*, and *u*, as in *keel*, *ken*. In monosyllables, it is used after *c*, as in *crack*, *check*, *deck*, being necessary to exhibit a correct pronunciation in the derivatives, *cracked*, *checked*, *decked*, *cracking*, for without it, *c*, before the vowels *e* and *i* would be sounded like *s*. Formerly, *k* was added to *c*, in certain words of Latin origin, as in *musick*, *publick*, *republick*. But in modern practice, *k* is very properly omitted, being entirely superfluous, and the more properly, as it is never written in the derivatives, *musical*, *publication*, *republican*. It was till lately retained in *traffick*, as in monosyllables, on account of the pronunciation of the derivatives, *trafficked*, *trafficking*, but we now write *traffic*. *K* is silent before *n*, as in *know*, *knife*, *knee*. As a numeral, K stands for 250; and with a stroke over it thus, $\overline{\text{K}}$, 250,000. As a contraction, K stands for *knight*, as K.B., Knight of the Bath; K.G., Knight of the Garter; K.C.B., Knight Commander of the Bath; K.T., Knight of the Thistle; and K.H., Knight of Hanover. This character was not used by the ancient Romans, and rarely in the later ages of their empire. In the place of *k* they used *c*, as in *clino*, for the Greek κλινω. In the Teutonic dialects, this Greek letter is sometimes represented by *h*.

KA'LAND, a lay fraternity instituted in Germany in the 13th century, for the purpose of doing honor to deceased relatives and friends. The term is probably derived from kalendæ, the first day of any month, as the members of this society chose that day for the observance of their ceremonies. These consisted originally of prayers, followed by a slight repast, in which all the members participated; but in process of time the religious purposes of the society became wholly merged in the festivities, so that it eventually was found necessary to abolish the fraternity on account of its excesses.

KA'MI, spirits or divinities, the belief in which appears to have characterized the ancient religion of Japan before it became intermingled with foreign doctrines, and still constitutes its groundwork. These spirits are partly elemental, subordinate to the gods of the sun and moon, and partly the spirits of men; but, in fact, every natural agent or phenomenon has its spirit or genius. The human spirits survive the body, and receive happiness or punishment for the actions of the individual in life. Distinguished benefactors of their species, or men renowned for purity of life, are deified; and their *kami* become objects of worship, like the heroes of antiquity. The number of them is said at present to be above 3,000. They are worshipped in temples in which no images are retained, each particular divinity being merely typified by a mirror, the emblem of purity; and all the rites of the worship appear to be symbolical of purification.

KAM'SIN, the name given to a hot and dry southerly wind, common in Egypt and the deserts of Africa, which prevails more or less for fifty days. On the approach of this wind the sky becomes dark and heavy, the air gray and thick, and filled with a dust so subtile that it penetrates everywhere. It is not remarkably hot at first, but increases in heat the longer it continues, during which time it causes a difficulty of breathing, and when at its highest pitch, will sometimes cause suffocation.

KAN'TIAN PHILOS'OPHY, (known also by the name of the Critical Philosophy,) a system which owes its existence to Immanuel Kant, professor of logic and metaphysics in the university of Königsberg in the latter half of the 18th century. The promulgation of Kant's doctrines forms a very marked era in the history of philosophy. Our limits will prevent us from giving an explanation of this system in any degree adequate to its importance. We must confine ourselves to a brief outline of its leading features. At the time when Kant commenced his metaphysical labors the philosophical world was divided between the sensualism of the French followers of Locke on the one hand, and the dogmatic rationalism of the disciples of Wolf and Leibnitz on the other. The former, by a species of analytical legerdemain, resolved all our mental powers into modifications of sense; while the latter, in an equally indiscriminating spirit, though with far more laudable intentions, sought to construct a system of real truth out of the abstract conceptions of the understanding. Against both of these schools Kant declared open warfare. Withdrawing himself from all ontological speculation, he sought, by a stricter analysis of our intellectual powers, to ascertain the possibility and to determine the limits of human knowledge. He divides the speculative part of our nature into three great provinces—sense, understanding, and reason. Our perception of the outward world is representative merely: of things as they are in themselves it affords us no notices. In order to render human experience possible, two ground-forms, under which all sensible things are contemplated, are assumed—time and space. To these he assigns a strictly subjective reality. The truth of the fundamental axioms of geometry rests on the necessity and universality of our intuitions of space in its three dimensions—intuitions which are not derived from any one of our senses, or from any combinations of them, but lie at the ground and are the condition of all sensible human experience. The understanding, or the faculty which combines and classifies the materials yielded by sense, Kant subjects to a similar analysis. All its operations are generalized into four fundamental modes or forms of conception; which, after the example of Aristotle, he names categories. These are four in number: 1. Quantity, including unity, multeity, totality; 2. Quality divided into reality, negation, and limitation; 3. Relation, viz. substance and accident, cause and effect, action and reaction; and 4. Modality, also subdivided into possibility, existence, and necessity. These form, as it were, the moulds in which the rude material of the senses is shaped into conceptions, and becomes knowledge properly so called. The categories in themselves are the subject-matter of logic, which is so far forth a pure science, determinable à priori. The third and highest faculty, the reason, consists in the power of forming ideas—pure forms of intelligence, to which the sensible world has no adequate correspondents. Out of these ideas no science can be formed; they are to be regarded as regulative only, not as constitutive. The existence of God, immortality, freedom, are the objects after which the reason is perpetually striving, but concerning which it can decide nothing either one way or the other. Thus far Kant's system may be regarded as one of pure skepticism. The deficiencies of our speculative reason he conceives to be supplied by the moral faculty, to which he has given the name of practical reason, the object of which is to determine, not what is, but what ought to be. As the former determines the form of our knowledge, so the latter prescribes the form of our action. Obligation is not a mere feeling; it has a pure form under which the reason is compelled to regard human conduct. The personality of man, which lies at the ground of speculative knowledge, becomes, in relation to action, freedom of the will. It is in our moral nature that we must seek for the only valid foundation of the belief in God, the immortality of the soul, and a future state in which the demands of the practical reason shall be realized.

KEEL, the lowest piece of timber in a ship, running her whole length from the lower part of her stem to the lower part of her stern post, and supporting the whole frame. Sometimes a second keel, or *false keel*, as it is called, is put under the first.

KEEL'-HAULING, among seamen, a punishment of offenders at sea by letting them down from the yard-arm with ropes, and drawing them under the keel from one side to the other.

KEEL'SON, or KEL'SON, in naval architecture, a principal timber in a ship, laid withinside across all the timbers over the keel, and fastened with long bolts; so that it forms the interior or counterpart of the keel.

KEEP, a strong tower in old castles, where the besieged retreated in cases of extremity. It is also called the *donjon* or *dungeon*.

KEEP'ER, in English law, an officer of different descriptions, as the *keeper of the great seal*, a lord by his office, and one of the privy council, through whose hands pass all charters, commissions, and grants of the king under the great seal; the *keeper of the privy seal*, through whose hands pass all charters, &c., before they come to the great seal. There is also the *keeper of the forests*, the *keeper of the touch*, an officer of the mint, &c.

KEEP'ING, a term used in various branches of the Fine Arts, to denote the just proportion and relation of the various parts.—In painting, it signifies the peculiar management of coloring and *chiaro oscuro*, so as to produce a proper degree of *relievo* in different objects, according to their relative position and importance. If the lights, shadows, and half tints be not in proper *keeping*, that is, in their exact relative proportion of depths, no rotundity can be effected, and without due opposition of light, shade, and colors, no apparent separation of objects can take place.

KE'RI-CHE'TIB, in philology, the name given to various readings in the Hebrew Bible. Keri signifies *that which is read*, and chetib *that which is written*. When any such various readings occur, the false reading or chetib is written in the text, and the true reading or keri is written in the margin. These corrections, which are about 1000 in number, have been generally attributed to Ezra; but as several keri-chetibs are found in the sacred books the produce of his own pen, it is more probable that they are of later date.

KEY, in music, the name of the fundamental note or tone, to which the whole piece is accommodated, and in which it usually begins and always ends. There are but two species of keys; one of the major, and one of the minor mode, all the keys in which we employ sharps or flats being deduced from the natural keys of C major and A minor, of which they are mere transpositions.—The *keys* of an organ or pianoforte, are movable projecting levers, made of ivory or wood, so placed as conveniently to receive the fingers of the performer, by which the mechanism is set in motion and the sounds produced.

KEY'STONE, in architecture, the highest central stone of an arch; that placed on the top or vertex, to bind the

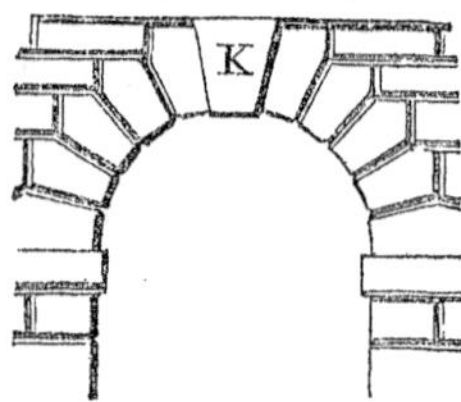

K, the Keystone.

two sweeps together. In some arches the keystone projects from the face. In vaulted Gothic roofs, the keystones are usually ornamented with a boss or pendant.

KHAN, an Asiatic governor. In the north of Asia this title expresses the full regal dignity; but there are also *khans* of provinces, cities, &c. "This is the word," says Sir William Jones, "so variously and so erroneously written by Europeans. The sovereign lord of Tartary is neither the *cham*, as our travellers call him, nor the *han*, as Voltaire will have it; but the *khán*, or *cán*, with an aspirate on the first letter."—Khan is frequently used to signify an Eastern caravansera, in which travellers find a gratuitous lodging, provided their stay be limited to a single night.

KING, the chief magistrate or sovereign of a nation; a man invested with supreme authority over a nation, tribe, or country. Kings are absolute monarchs, when they possess the powers of government without control, or the entire sovereignty over a nation: they are called *limited* monarchs when their power is restrained by fixed laws. Kings are *hereditary* sovereigns, when they hold the powers of government by right of birth or inheritance, and *elective*, when raised to the throne by choice. The person of the king of England is sacred. He cannot, by any process of law, be called to account for any of his acts. His concurrence is necessary for every legislative enactment. He sends embassies, makes treaties, and even enters into wars without any previous consultation with parliament. He nominates the judges, and the other high officers of state, the officers of the army and navy, the governors of colonies and dependencies, the bishops, deans, and some other dignitaries of the English Church. He calls parliament together, and can at his pleasure prorogue or dissolve it. He is the fountain of honor; all hereditary titles are derived from his grant.—*King at arms*, an officer in England of great antiquity, and formerly of great authority, whose business is to direct the heralds, preside at their chapters, and have the jurisdiction of armory. There are three kings at arms, viz., garter, clarencieux, and norroy (*northroy*.) The first of these is styled *principal king at arms*, and the two latter *provincial kings*, because their duties are confined to the provinces; the one (*clarencieux*,) officiating south of the Trent, and the other (*norroy*,) north of that river. There is also a *Lyon king at arms* for Scotland, and an *Ulster king at arms* for Ireland, whose duties are nearly analogous to those of England.

KINGS, BOOKS OF, two canonical books of the Old Testament, so called because they contain the history of the kings of Israel and Judah, from the beginning of the reign of Solomon, down to the Babylonish captivity, for the space of near six hundred years.

KING'S BENCH, BANCUS REGIUS, so called because the king used formerly to sit there in person. It is the supreme court of common law in England, consisting of the Lord Chief Justice, and three puisne or inferior judges, who hear and determine, for the most part, all pleas which concern the crown.

KI'OSK, (a Turkish word,) a kind of summer-house, or open pavilion, with a tent-shaped roof, and supported by pillars. *Kiosks* have been introduced from Turkey and Persia into European gardens, which they greatly serve to embellish.

KIRK, in Scotland, a church.—*Kirkman*, one of the church of Scotland.—*Kirk sessions*, an inferior church-judicatory, in Scotland, consisting of the ministers, elders, and deacons of a parish.

KIT-CAT CLUB, the name of a celebrated association in London, instituted about 1688 by some young men, originally for convivial purposes; but as its most distinguished members were whigs in politics, it gradually assumed a political character, till in the reign of Queen Anne it came to be regarded as exclusively political in its objects. At that period it comprised above forty noblemen and gentlemen of the first rank and quality, merit and fortune, firm friends to the Hanoverian succession; among whom were Addison, Steele, Marlborough, Walpole, &c. &c. It was originally formed in Shire Lane, and derived its name from one Christopher (Kit) Kat, who supplied the members with mutton pies. The fame of this club has been transmitted chiefly by the collection of the portraits of the members painted by Sir Godfrey Kneller, himself a member, who was obliged to invent a new-sized canvass accommodated to the height of walls; whence has originated the application of the epithet *kit-kat* to any portrait about three quarters in length. It was dissolved in the year 1720.

KNIGHT. Originally, a knight was a youth; and young men being employed as servants, hence it came to signify a servant. But among our warlike ancestors, the word was particularly applied to a young man after he was admitted to the privilege of bearing arms. The admission to this privilege was a ceremony of great importance, and was the origin of the institution of knighthood. Hence, in feudal times, a *knight* was a man admitted to military rank by a certain ceremony. This privilege was conferred on youths of family and fortune, and hence sprung the honorable title of knight, in modern usage, which in dignity ranks next to nobility. Knighthood is the highest rank of a commoner, but a knight is still a commoner. A knight has the title of *Sir* before his Christian name, as, *Sir* John, *Sir* William. Anciently, when the Christian name was not known, the style was *Sir* Knight.

KNIGHT'ED, created a knight.

KNIGHT-ER'RANT, or *wandering Knight*, one who in the generous enthusiasm of chivalry, set out, attended by his esquire or shield-bearer, with the design of exposing his life wherever wrong was to be redressed. The chivalrous age in which this profession was taken up, demanded such exertions; and though poetry has given an air of fiction, to the adventures of knights-errant, they are founded on truth.

KNIGHT'HOOD, the order or fraternity of knights. The order of knighthood, as now existing, appears to have originated in the eleventh and twelfth centuries, and it was introduced into England from France. It was a military institution, but there appears to have been something of a religious character belonging to it, and the order of knighthood, like the orders of the clergy, could be conferred only by persons who were themselves members of the order. In early times some knights undertook the protection of pilgrims; others were vowed to the defence or recovery of the holy sepulchre; others roved about as knights-errant, seeking adventures. It was common to create knights on various occasions. The most honorable species of knighthood was that conferred on the field and after a battle; but the more common fashion, especially in France, was to make knights when a battle was expected. In the age of chivalry, the youth who aspired to the honor of knighthood, was first educated, in general, as a page attached to the family, and especially to the ladies of some noble house, during which period he was also trained to the use of arms, riding, &c. When properly qualified for arms he became an esquire, or squire, in which capacity he attended on some knight, and was his shield-bearer. The third, and highest rank of chivalry, was that of knighthood, which was not conferred before the twenty-first year, except in the case of distinguished birth or great achievements. The candidate, when the order was conferred with full solemnity, had to go through various imposing preliminary ceremonies, and was then admitted with religious rites. Knighthood was conferred by the *accolade*, which

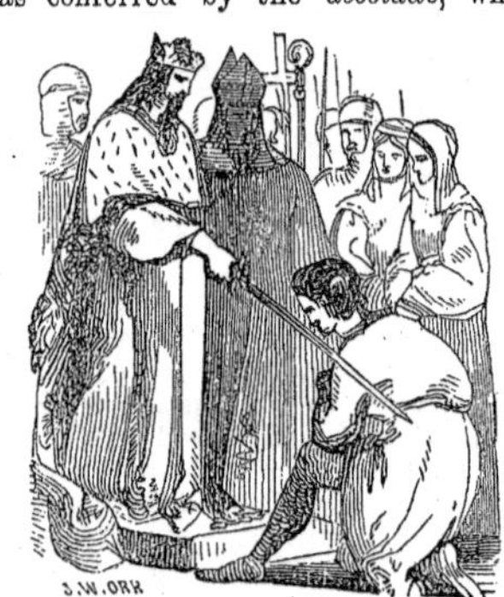

Conferring Knighthood.

from the derivation of the name, should appear to have been originally an embrace, but afterwards consisted, as it still does, in a blow of the flat of a sword on the neck of the kneeling candidate. The oath of knighthood was previously administered. Knighthood is now conferred in England by the king, (or queen when the throne is filled by a female,) by simple verbal declaration, attended with a slight form, without any patent or other written instrument. It gives to the party precedence over esquires and other untitled gentlemen. *Sir* is prefixed to the baptismal name of knights and baronets, and their wives have the legal designation of *Dame*, which is ordinarily converted into *Lady*. The chief distinction of rank which subsisted between knights in France and England, was that of *knights bachelors*, and *knights bannerets*. The knight bachelor was of the lower order, and obtained his honor without any reference to a qualification of property, and many of this rank were mere adventurers, who offered their services in war to any successful leader. The knight banneret was one who possessed fiefs to a considerable amount, and was obliged to serve in war with a greater attendance, and carried a banner. The orders of knighthood are of two classes; either they are associations, or fraternities, possessing property and rights of their own, as independent bodies, or they are merely honorary associations, established by sovereigns within their respective dominions. To the former class belonged the three celebrated religious orders founded during the Crusades—Templars, Hospitallers, and Teutonic Knights. The other class, consisting of orders merely titular, embraces most of the existing European orders; such as the order of the Golden Fleece, the order of the Holy Ghost, the order of St. Michael. The three great British orders are the Garter, the Thistle, and St. Patrick. The Garter is the most ancient and illustrious of the three. It was founded by Edward the Third. The knights, twenty-five in number, are the most eminent persons of the English nation, together with many illustrious foreigners, chiefly sovereign princes. The order of the Thistle was instituted in 1540, by James the Fifth of Scotland. The number of knights is sixteen, all of whom are nobility of Scotland. The order of St. Patrick was instituted in 1783. The number of knights is twenty-two, who are peers of Ireland. The order of the Bath differs in some respects from those spoken of. It is now composed of three classes, military, and civil knights, grand crosses, knights commanders, and knights companions. All these orders have particular badges. There are also knights of the Guelphic order, knights of the Ionian order, of St. Michael and St. George.

KNOUT, a mode of punishment in Russia, which at one time was exercised with the greatest possible barbarity, but which is now less cruel, though it at present consists of a severe scourging on the back with a leather strap, in the point of which wire is interwoven. Formerly, in addition to this, the nose was slit up, and the ears were cut off.

KNOWL'EDGE, that information which the mind receives, either by its own experience, or by the testimony of others. The beneficial use of knowledge is *wisdom*. That portion of knowledge, the truth of which can be demonstrated, is *science*.

KRAAL, the name given to the villages of the Hottentots.

KRA'KEN, a name applied in the fabulous epoch of zoology to a marine monster of gigantic size.

L.

L, the twelfth letter of the English alphabet. It is a semi-vowel, formed in the voice by intercepting the breath between the tip of the tongue and the forepart of the palate, with the mouth open. There is something of aspiration in its sound, and therefore our British ancestors usually doubled it, or added an *h* to it; as in *llan*, or *lhan*, a temple. In English words of one syllable it is doubled at the end, as in *all*, *wall*, *mill*, *well*, &c., but not after diphthongs and digraphs, as *foul*, *fool*, *prowl*, *growl*, *foal*, &c.; words of more syllables than one, as *foretel*, *proportional*, &c., are written with a single *l*. In some words *l* is mute, as in *half*, *calf*, *talk*, *chalk*. It may be placed after most of the consonants, as in *blue*, *clear*, *flame*, &c., but before none of them. As a numeral letter L denotes 50; and with a dash over it, 50,000.

LA, in music, the syllable by which Guido denotes the last sound of each hexachord: if it begins in C, it answers to our A; if in G, to E; and if in F, to D.

LAB'ADISTS, a sect who lived in the 17th century, the followers of Jean de Labadie, who held that God can and does deceive men, that the observance of the Sabbath is not required, and other heretical opinions.

LA'BARUM, in Roman antiquity, the standard borne before the emperors; being a rich purple streamer, supported by a spear. It was the name given to the imperial standard, upon which Constantine, after his conversion, blazoned the monogram of Christ.

LA'BORED, in the Fine Arts, a term applied to works of art wherein are apparent the marks of constraint in the execution; and used in opposition to the term *easy* or *free*.

LAB'YRINTH, literally a place, usually subterraneous, full of inextricable windings. Ancient history gives an account of four celebrated labyrinths; the Cretan, Egyptian, Lemnian, and Italian. The first was built by Dædalus at the instigation of Minos, to secure the Minotaur; the second is said to have been constructed by Psammetichus, king of Egypt; the third was on the island of Lemnos, and was supported by columns of great beauty; and the fourth was designated by Porsenna, king of Etruria, as a tomb for himself and his successors. Of these labyrinths the Cretan is most celebrated in the historical and mythological writings of antiquity; but the Egyptian was by far the most important, both in extent and magnificence. The latter, which was built on the isle of Meroe, was a vast edifice, composed of twelve palaces, all contained within the compass of one wall, and communicating with each other. It had only one entrance; but the innumerable turnings and windings of the terraces and rooms of which it consisted rendered it impossible for those who had once entered within its walls to get out without a guide. It is said to have been designed either as a burial-place for the Egyptian kings, or for the preservation of the sacred crocodiles, the chief objects of Egyptian idolatry. It was partly demolished between the reigns of Augustus and Titus; but even at the period of Pliny's visit, its ruins were magnificent. With regard to the labyrinth of Crete, no doubt can now remain, after the statements of Cockerell and Tournefort, that its existence was a reality, and not merely a fabulous creation of the Grecian imagination. According to these travellers the island of Crete abounds even at the present day in extensive caverns, one of which, consisting principally of many long windings and narrow passages that can only be safely explored by means of a clue, exhibits a wonderful similarity in all essential particulars to the famous labyrinth of Dædalus. It is impossible, at this distant period, to pronounce with certainty on so difficult a question; but the substantial coincidences that exist between the ancient and modern labyrinths seem to leave little doubt as to their identity.

LACHRYMATO'RY, in antiquity, a vessel in which were collected the tears of a deceased person's friends, and preserved along with the ashes and urn. It was a small glass bottle or phial, many of which have been found in the tombs and sepulchres of the ancients.

LA'CONISM, a short and pointed saying; so termed from the celebrity which the Lacedæmonians enjoyed in antiquity for their belief and sententious mode of expressing themselves produced by the severe discipline of their institutions, and the gravity which it engendered. When they became famous for this quality, they appear to have begun to aim at the exhibition of it in rather an affected manner, of which some curious instances are contained in Herodotus. None of the many Laconisms recorded in ancient history are more noble than the expression of the Spartan mother to her son, when presenting him with his buckler: ἢ ταν ἢ ἐπι ταν—"either bring it back, or be brought home dead upon it."

LA'DING, a term applied to the goods in a ship, whose quantity is limited by her own tonnage, when the specific gravity of the goods is greater than water.

LA'DY, this word originally appertained only as a title to the daughters of earls; but now, by custom, it belongs to any woman of genteel manners and education.

LA'DY-DAY, the 25th of March, so called because it is the day of the Annunciation of the Virgin Mary.

LAGOON', a name given to those creeks, or shallow lakes, which extend along the coast, and which contain numerous small islands; Venice, for instance, is built on sixty of them. Towards the sea the islets are secured by dams, natural or artificial.

LAIR, among sportsmen, the place where the deer harbor by day. This term is also used to signify a place where cattle usually rest under shelter; also the bed or couch of a wild beast.

LAIRD, a title of honor in the Highlands, equivalent to that of *Lord*.

LA'ITY, the great body of the faithful, as opposed to those who are set apart for the ministration of the services and sacraments—the clergy. This distinction is plainly observed in the writers of the third century—Origen, Cyprian, and Tertullian; and is generally supposed to have prevailed from the first foundation of Christianity. The word laity is properly a general name for the people: in the writings of the Fathers βιωτικοὶ, seculars, ἰδιῶται, private men, and λαικοὶ; laymen, are used indifferently to express this class.

LA'MA, a pretended delegate of heaven, or pontiff of Tartary and Thibet. He is worshipped as a supernatural being by his subjects, and is never to be seen but in the secret recesses of his palace, where he sits cross-legged on a cushion. The people believe that the supreme divinity lives in him, that he knows and sees everything in the deepest recesses of the heart, and that he never dies, but on the dissolution of his mortal frame his soul enters into the body of a new-born child. The worship of his followers consists in clamorous songs and prayers, in splendid processions, in the solemnization of certain festivals, and in personal austerities.

LAMENTA'TIONS, a canonical book

of the Old Testament, written by the prophet Jeremiah. The first four chapters of the Lamentations are an *abecedary*, every verse or couplet beginning with one of the letters of the Hebrew alphabet, in the alphabetical order.

LAMPADEPHO'RIA, a torch race, which it was customary to exhibit at certain sacred festivals at Athens. The performers were three young men, to one of whom, chosen by lot, was given a lighted torch, which he was to carry to the goal unextinguished; or if he failed, to deliver it to the second; who, if he failed also, gave it to the third: whence a metaphor is sometimes derived by ancient writers, to be applied to persons who anxiously wait for the deaths of others. If the runners slackened their pace, they were driven on by the blows of the spectators.

LANCE, a weapon consisting of a long shaft with a sharp point, much used by the nations of antiquity, and also by the moderns before the invention of gunpowder. The Macedonian phalanx and the Roman infantry, as well as the most barbarous nations, all considered the lance as one of the most effective weapons; and even at the present day it is still considered of great value, though it is now almost universally borne by cavalry. Almost all the armies of Europe have now regiments of *lancers*, so called from the lance being the chief offensive weapon with which they are armed. The lances in use among the European cavalry have a shaft of ash or beech wood, eight, twelve, or in some cases even sixteen feet long, with a steel point eight or ten inches in length, adorned by a small flag, the waving of which is said to frighten the enemy's horses. The ancient lancea was a general term for missile weapons or javelins.

LAN'DAMMAN, in Switzerland, the president of the diet of the Helvetic republic. The highest magistrate in ten of the cantons also bears the title of landamman; in the others he is designated by various appellations.

LAN'DAU, the name given to a peculiar kind of carriage, which opens and closes at the top; so called from Landau in Germany, where they were originally made.

LAND'FALL, the first land seen after a voyage is so called. A *good* landfall is when the land is seen as expected.

LAND'GRAVE, a title taken by some German counts in the twelfth century, who wished to distinguish themselves from the inferior counts under their jurisdiction; and thus assumed the designation of land-graf, or count of the whole country. This was the origin of the landgraves of Thuringia, of Lower and Higher Alsace, the only three who were princes of the empire.

LAND'SCAPE, the scenery presented to the eye in the country; as also, in its more common acceptation, a picture representing such scenery. A landscape in the latter sense may, however, become allegorical and historical, in the meaning applied by artists to those terms. The chief study of the landscape painter is the vegetable world, air, water, rocks, and buildings. To these he may impart an ideal beauty, and thus elevate his art above mere topographical painting; which may be applied to his work, if he merely copies without refinement what is presented to his eye.

LAND'SCAPE GAR'DENING, the art of laying out grounds so as to produce the effect of natural landscape. Its principles are the same as those upon which the landscape painter proceeds in composing a picture.

LAN'GUAGE, human speech; the expression of ideas by words or significant articulate sounds, for the communication of thoughts. *Language* consists in the oral utterance of sounds, which usage has made the representatives of ideas. When two or more persons customarily annex the same sounds to the same ideas, the expression of these sounds by one person communicates his ideas to another. This is the primary sense of *language*, the use of which is to communicate the thoughts of one person to another through the organs of hearing. Articulate sounds are represented by letters, marks, or characters which form words. Hence, language consists also in words duly arranged in sentences, written, printed, or engraved, and exhibited to the eye.—The speech or expression of ideas peculiar to a particular nation. Men had originally one and the same *language*, but the tribes or families of men, since their dispersion, have distinct *languages*. Many philologists have included all known languages under three great divisions:—1. Languages composed of monosyllabic roots without any forms of grammar. To this class belong the Chinese idioms. 2. Languages composed of monosyllabic roots, but with a great abundance of grammatical forms, as the Indo-Germanic, Armenian, and other languages. 3. Languages whose verbal roots consist in their present form of two syllables, and require three consonants for the expression of their fundamental meaning. This class is limited to the Schemitic languages, including the Aramæan, the Hebrew, and Arabic. The Indo-Germanic languages are divided into—1. The Indian branch, comprising the Sanscrit, and its derivatives. 2. The Medo-Persic or Arian branch, at the head of which stands the Zend. 3. The Teutonic branch, with the Gothic at its head, and comprising the different German dialects, the Anglo-Saxon, the Icelandic, Swedish, Danish, &c. 4. The Græco-Latin branch, comprising the two ancient classical languages. 5. The Slavonic branch, including the Lithuanian, the ancient Prussian, the Russian, the Polish, and Bohemian. 6. The Celtic branch, including the Welsh, Cornish, Armorican, the Irish or Erse, the Gaelic or Highland Scotch, and the Manx.

The comparative perfection of a language, as an instrument for the communication of thought, depends mainly on its copiousness. In order to estimate this, it must be borne in mind that the classes of words employed in a language are all reducible into two, which have been termed by some *notional* and *relational*. The former express distinct ideas or notions; the latter serve to display the relation, connection, and order of ideas. Nouns and verbs belong to the first class; prepositions, adverbs, &c., and the signs denoting the inflections of verbs and nouns, to the latter. With respect to the former class, all languages, to be serviceable for the purposes of life, must be sufficiently copious to express all distinct notions. But the comparative richness of a language is mainly shown by the manner in which this is done. As nations advance from barbarism towards civilization, new notions, and new varieties of notions, are constantly requiring utterance. In those in which this can easily be done by composition, (as in Greek and German,) great facilities are afforded for the easy expression of thought, comparatively with those in which it can only be effected by the laborious process of borrowing and adopting words from the vocabularies of more advanced nations.

But it is in the *relational* words, or modes in which relations of ideas are expressed, that the genius of different languages most varies. The Chinese, in their singular and obscure tongue, seem never to have reached beyond the process of varying the collocation of their unchangeable roots in the sentence, in order to express varieties of meaning. The next process should appear to be that of using auxiliary words. In many languages (our own among the number) relations are almost wholly expressed in this manner. But in others the auxiliary words have, in course of time, coalesced with the principal; so that many relations are expressed by varying the beginning, termination, &c., of the principal word. This, at least, is the most probable origin of those forms termed in grammar *inflections*, or forms of declension and conjugation, in which Greek, Latin, Sanscrit, German, and their derivative languages are more or less rich; the Greek, for example, being more copious than the Latin or modern German, in having the dual form and additional tenses (the aorists, and the paulo-post futurum.) And some languages (especially among the American Indians) are so curiously constructed as to carry the power of inflection far beyond this point. A complex idea, which in English would require to be expressed by a pronoun, an adverb, and an auxiliary verb, (or, perhaps, a second auxiliary verb also, *e. g.*, "I desire," or "I ab stain,") together with the principal verb, would in some American languages be expressed merely by a variety of the form of the principal verb itself.

As a general rule, the power of inflection adds greatly to the copiousness of a language; and although some enthusiasts, in their admiration of our own, have maintained that the process of conjugating or declining by auxiliary words and particles is more convenient, and affords more variety and harmony than that by changes in the termination of the verb or noun, it is probable that few candid reasoners will hold the same opinion. But there are distinctions in language, arising out of relations simply imaginary, which may be pronounced unnecessary and cumbersome. Such are the genders, common to almost all languages of the Indo-European family except our own, but for which it would be difficult to assign either utility or beauty.

Another and a more substantial disadvantage of language rich in inflections, if the fact be true, is to be found in the greater difficulty which common people are supposed to have in framing their speech grammatically and accurately under this system than the other. The greater the niceties of a language, it has been urged, the greater the difference must inevitably be between the variety spoken and written by educated men and that in use among the uneducated; and it has been contended that in ancient Italy, for instance, the rustic language was altogether different from the written Latin. But the facts on which this reasoning rests may be pronounced extremely controvertible. There are certainly some grounds for the suspicion that there was an unusual difference between the vulgar and the polished Roman tongue, at least in the later times of the empire; but if this was always the case, it is singular that Plautus and Terence should nowhere furnish us, by way of heightening the ludicrous, with instances of ungrammatical locution. The language of ancient Greece was more refined and inflective than that of Rome; and there is no appearance that there was a greater diversity between the speech of the peasant and the philosopher and rhetorician than in any modern country. In Attica the very reverse seems to have been the truth, since its most elegant writers and orators appear carefully to have modelled their language on the common dialect of their countrymen. And, finally, the wild Indians of America speak with purity a language often surpassing in variety of inflections those of the most civilized and illustrious nations of the Old World.

LANGUEN'TE, in music, a direction to the performer, when prefixed to a composition denoting that it is to be performed in a languishing or soft manner.

LAO'COON, in fabulous history, the priest of Apollo or Neptune during the Trojan war. While he was engaged in sacrificing a bull to Neptune, two enormous serpents sent by Minerva, in revenge for his having endeavored to dissuade the Trojans from admitting the famous wooden horse within their walls, issued from the sea; and having fastened on his two sons, whom he vainly endeavored to save, at last attacked the father himself, and crushed him to death in their complicated folds. This story has gained immortal celebrity from its forming the subject of one of the most beautiful groups of sculpture in the whole history of ancient Art. The composition is pyramidal, and represents Laocoon and his two sons writhing and expiring in the convulsions of the serpents. Agony in an intense degree is exhibited in the countenance and convulsed body of Laocoon, who is attempting to disengage himself from the serpents; and the sons are represented as imploring assistance from their helpless parent. This famous group of sculpture was discovered at Rome among the ruins of the palace of Titus, at the beginning of the 16th century, and afterwards placed in the Farnese palace, whence it found its way to the Vatican. It was executed by Polydorus, Agesander, Athenodorus, the three celebrated artists of Rhodes.

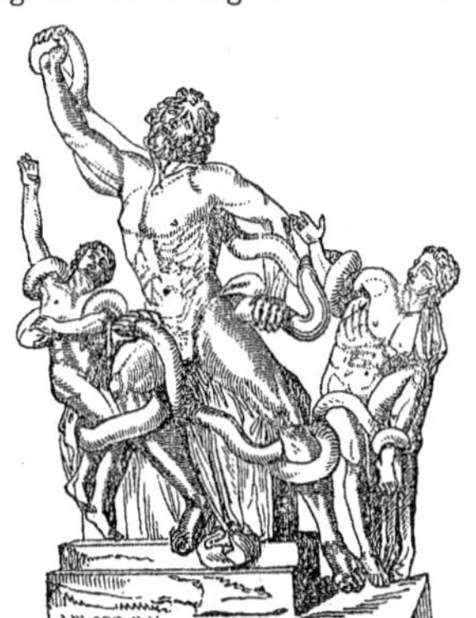

LAP'IDARY, one who polishes and engraves stones. This is effected by means of friction produced by wheels of various metal, according to the nature of the stone to be worked. Thus diamonds require wheels of soft steel; rubies, sapphires, and topazes, copper wheels; emeralds, amethysts, &c., leaden wheels—worked with oil and various powders.—The term *lapidary* is also used for a virtuoso skilled in the nature, kinds, &c. of precious stones, or a merchant who deals in them.—*Lapidary-style*, denotes that which is proper for monumental or other inscriptions.

LA'PIS LA'ZULI, in painting, a stone of an azure or blue color, of which the paint called *ultramarine* is made. It is a combination of silex, the blue fluate of lime and sulphate of lime, and iron; is very compact and hard, and is found in lumps of a beautiful blue color, richly variegated with clouds of white, and veins of shining gold color.

LA'PIS MARMO'REUS, in archæology, a marble stone in Westminster Hall, in the midst of which stood a chair wherein the English kings anciently sat at their coronation. The courts of Chancery and King's Bench were erected over this stone.

LA'PITHÆ, in ancient geography, a people of Thessaly, chiefly known to us from their fabled contests with the Centaurs. The battle between the Centaurs and the Lapithæ has been described by Hesiod, and by Ovid with great minuteness. To the Lapithæ has been attributed the invention of bits and bridles for horses.

LAPSE, in ecclesiastical law, an omission on the part of the patron to present to a benefice within six months after it is vacant, upon which default the ordinary has a right to collate to the said benefice.—*Lapsed Legacy*, one which falls or is lost by a lapse; as where the legatee dies before the testator, or where a legacy is given upon a future contingency, and the legatee dies before the contingency happens.

LAR'CENY, is the fraudulent taking by a person of the goods of another, without his consent, with the intent, on the part of the taker, to appropriate them to his own use. Larceny was formerly divided, in England, into two kinds, *grand* and *petty;* the former being the stealing of an article over the value of one shilling, the latter, that of an article not over that value. The same division of the kinds of the offence, according to the value of the thing stolen, is made in some of the United States. But this distinction is abolished in England by a statute. In that country, the punishment for grand larceny was death; but, most frequently of late years, it has been commuted for transportation; and, now, the punishment of all simple larceny, of whatever value, is, the imprisonment or transportation. In the United States, the punishment is usually imprisonment in the common jail, or penitentiary, for a longer or shorter period.

LA'RES, in antiquity, the domestic or household gods among the Romans, which the family honored as their protectors. They were images of wood, stone, or metal, and generally stood upon the hearth in a kind of shrine.

LAR'GO and LARGHET'TO, (*Italian,*) musical terms, directing to slow movement. *Largo* is one degree quicker than *grave*, and two degrees quicker than *adagio*.

LAR'VA, spectres of the deceased were so termed by the Romans: mere empty forms or phantoms, as their name indicates; yet endowed with a sort of existence resembling life, since they were to be propitiated by libation and sacrifice. The larva of Caligula, according to Suetonius, was often seen in his palace after his decease. The larvæ are described by Seneca, and often represented in paintings and on gems under the figure of a skeleton; sometimes under those of old men, with shorn locks and long beards, carrying an owl on their hands.

LA'RYNX, an organ of the voice, being a cartilaginous cavity connected with the windpipe, and on the size and flexibility of which depend the powers and tones of the human voice. The superior opening of the larynx is called the *glottis*.

LASCAR', in the East Indies, a native seaman, or a gunner.

LAT'ERAN, a church at Rome, the Pope's see, and the metropolitan or the whole world, dedicated to St. John Lateran. The name is derived from the Roman family of the Laterani, who possessed a palace on this spot, which was seized by Nero, and became from his time an imperial residence. The Lateran palace was given by Constantine to the popes, who continued to inhabit it until their retirement to Avignon, when it was exchanged for the Vatican. The building was then converted into a church. Eleven councils have been held in the Basilica of this name (hence styled Lateran councils in ecclesiastical history,) of which four are considered by the Roman Catholics to be general. The last of these (or the 12th General, according to the same computation) is the most celebrated. It was held in 1215 by Innocent III., and is principally famous as establishing the Roman Catholic doctrine of the Eucharist, using for the first time the term transubstantiation for the change of the elements. This council was convoked on the occasion of the heresy of the Albigenses, and its exposition of the Catholic faith is directed principally against them. It established also some canons for the maintenance of discipline among the clergy, and that which enforces confession and communion upon all the faithful at least once a year.

LAT'ICLAVE, in antiquity, an ornament of dress worn by Roman senators.

LAT'IN, the language spoken by the ancient Romans, or the inhabitants of Latium, from which it derives its name. The Latin tongue was, for a while, confined almost wholly within the walls of Rome; nor would the Romans allow the common use of it to their neighbors, or to the nations they subdued: but, by degrees, they in time became sensible of the necessity of its being generally understood for the convenience of commerce; and accordingly used their endeavors that all the nations subject to their empire, should be united by one common language, so that at length they imposed the use of it by an express law.

LATITUDINA'RIANS, in ecclesiastical history, a class of English divines in the reign of Charles II., opposed alike to the high tenets of the ruling party in the church, and the fanaticism which then distinguished so many of the Dissenters. Henry More, and the other Platonizing divines of the time, were sometimes comprehended under this appellation. The word has been since very generally used to designate those who hold opinions at variance with the more rigid interpretation of Scripture and church traditions, or merely as a term of party vituperation.

LA'TRIA, the highest kind of worship, or that paid to God: distinguished by the Catholics from *dulia*, or the inferior worship paid to saints.

LAU'REATE, literally crowned with laurels; applied at present to a well-known officer in the royal household. At the Certamina, or gymnastic and other contests celebrated under the Roman emperors, especially at the Quinquatria, or Feast of Minerva, poets also contended, and the prize was a crown of oak or olive leaves. But it was from some traditionary belief respecting the coronation of Virgil and Horace with laurel in the Capitol, (of which, however, no record is extant,) that the dignity of poet laureate was invented in the 14th century, and conferred on Petrarch at Rome by the senator or supreme magistrate of the city. It was intended to confer the same honor on Tasso, who, however, died on the night before the proposed celebration. In 1725 and 1776 it was granted to two celebrated improvisatori, the Signor Rufetti and the Signora Morelli, better known by the name of Corilla. In most European countries the sovereign has assumed the privilege of nominating a court poet with various titles. In France and Spain these have never been termed poets laureate; but the imperial poet, or Poeta Cesareo, in Germany, was invested with the laurel. This crown, however, was customarily given at the universities in the middle ages to such persons as took degrees in grammar and rhetoric, of which poetry formed a branch; whence, according to some authors, the term Baccalaureatus has been derived. In England traces of a stipendiary poet royal are found as early as Henry III., and of a poet laureate by that name under Edward IV. Skelton, under Henry VII. and VIII., was created poet laureate by the universities of Oxford and Cambridge, and appears to have held the same dignity at court; but the academical and court honor were distinct until the extinction of the university custom, of which Henry VIII.'s reign exhibits the last instance. Royal poets laureate are supposed not to have begun to write in English until after the Reformation. The office was made patent by Charles I., and the salary fixed at £100 annually, and a tierce of Spanish Canary wine. Under Queen Anne it was placed in the control of the lord-chamberlain. In the reign of George III. the annual tierce of wine was commuted for an increase of salary, and at the close of the same reign the custom of requiring annual odes from the lord-chamberlain was discontinued. The most distinguished poets in recent times who have held the office are Southey, Wordsworth, and Tennyson.

LAUREA'TION, in the Scotch universities, signifies the act of taking the degree of master of arts, which the students are permitted to do after four years' study.

LAURENTA'LIA, in antiquity, a festival kept by the Romans on the 23d of December, in memory of Acca Laurentia, the nurse of Romulus and Remus. She was called *Lupa* by way of nick-name; hence the story of the wolf that suckled the royal twins.

LAW, an established or permanent rule, prescribed by the supreme power of a state to its subjects, for regulating their social actions. Laws may be divided into the following classes: declaratory laws; directory laws; remedial laws; and prohibitory and penal laws. *Declaratory laws* only declare what the law shall be, not what it has been, or is. *Directory laws* are those which prescribe rules of conduct, or limit or enlarge rights, or point out modes of remedy. *Remedial laws* are those whose object it is to redress some private injury, or some public inconvenience. *Prohibitory and penal laws* are those which forbid certain things to be done or omitted, under a penalty, or vindicatory sanction. The legislation of no country, probably, ever gave origin to its whole body of laws. In the very formation of society, the principles of natural justice, and the obligations of good faith, must have been recognized before any common legislature was acknowledged. Debts were contracted, obligations created, personal property acquired, and lands cultivated, before any positive rules were fixed as to the rights of possession and enjoyment growing out of them. The first rudiments of jurisprudence resulted from general consent or acquiescence; and when legislation began to act upon it, it was rather to confirm, alter, or add to, than to supersede, the primitive principles adopted into it. The formation of codes, or systems of general law, for the government of a people, and adapted to their wants, takes place only in advanced stages of society, when knowledge is considerably diffused, and legislators have the means of ascertaining the best principles of policy and the best rules for justice, not by mere speculation and theory, but by the results of experience, and the reasoning of the learned and the wise.—We shall now proceed to give separate definitions of the word *law*, as it is variously applied.—*Municipal* or *civil law*, is a rule of civil conduct prescribed by the supreme power of a state, commanding what its subjects are to do, and prohibiting what they are to forbear.—The *law of nature*, otherwise called ethics, or morals, comprehends those rules of right and wrong, of which the sentiment is in every man's breast, and of the justice of which reflection affords sufficient conviction. The *divine law* is that which, not being naturally felt, nor discovered by reflection, is found only in inspired writings.—The *law of nations* is that rule of conduct which nations are to observe toward each other. This is founded upon the law of nature; but either ascertained or modified by usage, or by mutual compacts.—The *written law*, those laws or rules of action prescribed or enacted by a sovereign or state, and promulgated and recorded in writing. *Unwritten* or *common law*, a rule of action which derives its authority from long usage, or established custom, which has been immemorially received and recognized by judicial tribunals.—*Ecclesiastical* or *canon law*, a rule of action prescribed for the government of a church.—*Martial law*, the rules ordained for the government of an army or military force.—*Marine laws*, rules for the regulation of navigation, and the commercial intercourse of nations.—*Physical laws*, the invariable tendency or determination of any species of matter to a particular form with definite properties, and the determination of a body to certain motions, changes, and relations, which uniformly take place in the same circumstances.—The *Mosaic law*, the institutions of Moses, or the code of laws prescribed to the Jews, as recorded in the Old Testament. That part which relates to the mere external rites and ceremonies to be observed by them, as distinct from the moral precepts, is called the *ceremonial law*.

LAY, the lyric poems of the old French minstrels, or trouvères, were termed lais; but the title appears, in modern usage, to be peculiarly appropriate to narrative poems, or serious subjects of moderate length in simple style and light metre.

LAY BROTH'ERS, persons received into convents of monks, under the three vows, but not in holy orders. The introduction of this class of devotees appears to have begun in the 11th century. They are dressed somewhat differently from the other monks or *brothers of the choir*, and often employed in the manual exercises necessary for the uses of the community. The Carthusian and Cistercian orders are said to have first recognized the distinction, and their example was followed by the other orders. The same distinction exists in monasteries of females between the nuns, properly so called, and the lay sisters, or sisters converse.

LAY EL'DERS, in Presbyterian churches, ministers of ecclesiastical jurisdiction, not ordained as clergymen, who assist the pastor in each congregation. The divines of that persuasion rest the appointment of lay elders in some measure on that of presbyters "in every city," by Paul and Barnabas, who, they imagine, from the manner in which they are mentioned, could not have been all preachers.

LAY'MAN, the appellation by which the rest of the community are distinguished from the clergy.—*Layman or lay-figure*, among painters, signifies a small statue, whose joints are so formed that it may be put into any attitude for the purpose of adjusting the drapery of figures.

LA'ZAR-HOUSE, or LAZARET'TO, a public building in the southern European states of the nature of an hospital, for the reception of the poor and those afflicted with contagious disorders. In some places lazarettoes are set apart for the performance of quarantine; in which case only those are admitted who have arrived from countries infested by the plague, or suspected of being so.

LAZARISTS, in ecclesiastical history, a body of missionaries, founded by St. Vincent de Paul in 1632; so termed from occupying the priory of St. Lazarus, at Paris, as their head-quarters. Their primary object was to dispense religious instruction and assistance among the poorer inhabitants of the rural districts of France. They were dispersed at the time of the revolution, but have since re-established a congregation at Paris; and the French Government has lately projected entrusting them with the spiritual care of the colony at Algiers.

LAZ'ARUS, SAINT, ORDER OF, a military order of religious persons, originally an association of knights, for the purpose of maintaining lepers, &c., in lazar-houses or hospitals, especially in the Holy Land. Being driven out of Palestine in 1253, they followed St. Louis to France. In 1490, their order was suppressed by Pope Innocent VIII., and united with that of St. John; but the bull was not universally received. In 1572, they were united in Italy with the order of St. Maurice; in 1608, in France, with that of Our Lady of Mount Carmel. The knights of these united orders were allowed to marry.

LAZZARO'NI, a name given to the poorer classes at Naples, from the hospital of St. Lazarus, which served as a refuge for the destitute in that city. Forty years ago two large sections of the people were generally comprehended under this name, the fishermen, and the lazzaroni, properly so called, who lived in the streets, and performed no other labor but that of errand porters and occasional servants. These alone were estimated at 40,000. These lazzaroni formed a powerful community, which under Masaniello, accomplished the revolution of Naples; and, in later times overthrew the popular government, under the influence of Cardinal Ruffo and the English party. But during the French occupation of Naples they ceased to exist as a distinct class; and the name is now only used to designate, in general language, the mob or populace of that great city.

LEAD'ING NOTE, in music, the sharp seventh of the scale.

LEADS, or SPACE LINES, are pieces of type metal cast to specific thickness and lengths, lower than types, so that they do not make any impression in printing, but leave a white space where placed. Their general use is to be placed between the lines when a work is not closely printed, which is considered to look better than when printed solid, and also to branch out the heads of pages and titles.

LEAGUE, in politics, an alliance between two or more powers, in order to execute some common enterprise. It is more active, and less durable, than an alliance or a confederacy; both of which have some permanent object, while neither necessarily requires active co-operation. In the middle ages, the word league was used nearly in the sense now attached to these latter terms: hence we read of the Hanseatic league, and of the three leagues still subsisting in the canton of the Grisons in Switzerland; both of which were more properly confederacies. The word is of Spanish origin; and it has been said that the period of its commonest use in political language was commensurate with that during which the Spanish government exercised the greatest influence among those of Europe—the 16th and 17th centuries.

LEASE, in law, a demise of lands or tenements, or a conveyance of them, generally in consideration of rent or other annual recompense, for term of years, for life, or at will, provided it be for a shorter term than the lessor has in the premises. The party letting the lands, &c. is called the *lessor*, and the party to whom they are let, the *lessee*. Any one of the conditions of a lease not being complied with, the proprietor may resume possession.

LEC'TERN or LET'TERN, a reading desk or stand for the larger books, used in the service of the Roman Catholic church. The *lectern* was sometimes a fixture of stone or marble, but it was oftener constructed of wood or brass, and movable. It was of various forms, sometimes highly decorated and enriched; a frequent form of the brass *lettern* was that of a pelican or an eagle, with its wings expanded to receive the book.

LECTI'CA, a sort of couch used by the Romans for the same purpose as the sedan chair, or rather the palanquin, is employed by the moderns, with this difference, that the person carried on the lectica reclined. It was used also for the conveyance of dead bodies to the funeral pile. The persons who carried the lectica were called *lecticarii*, whose number in the Lower Empire is said to have amounted to 11,000.

LEC'TISTER'NIUM, a religious festival or ceremony among the ancient Romans, celebrated during times of public calamity, and remarkable as a singular relic of barbarous superstition, retaining the impression of a very rude age. In this festival the gods themselves were invited to the entertainment; their statues were taken from their pedestals, laid on couches with pillows and pedestals, and placed at the table, while the servants used gravely to convey the viands to the idols' lips. The first festival of this sort, according to Livy, which took place, was held in the year of Rome 354, on the occasion of a contagious disease which committed frightful ravages among their cattle, and lasted for eight successive days. On the celebration of this festival enemies were said to forget their animosity, and all prisoners were liberated.

LEC'TOR, in the early church, a person set apart for the purpose of reading parts of the Bible and other writings of a religious character to the people. They were consecrated by prayers and ceremonies for this office, and in the third century appear to have formed proper officers of the church.

LEC'TURE, a discourse read or pronounced on any subject; usually, a formal or methodical discourse, intended for instruction; as, a lecture on morals, philosophy, rhetoric, or theology: but the term is applied in a more extended sense to every species of instruction communicated *vivâ voce.* In the Scotch and continental universities, as well as those recently established in England, the great business of teaching is carried on by means of public lectures delivered at stated periods, and embracing the different subjects included in the curriculum of study.—*Pulpit lectures* have for their object some portion of Scripture, which is explained, and the doctrines therein contained stated and enforced.

LEG'ACY, in law, a bequest or gift by will of any personal effects; the person bequeathing is called the *testator*, and he to whom it is bequeathed the *legatee.* There is also a *residuary legatee*, or one to whom, after the several devises or bequests made by will, the residue of the testator's estate and effects are given.

LEG'ATE, the pope's ambassador to foreign countries; either a cardinal or a bishop. The power of a legate is sometimes given without the title. It was one of the ecclesiastical privileges of England from the Norman conquest, that no foreign legate should be obtruded upon the English, unless the king should desire it upon some extraordinary emergency, as when a case was too difficult for the English prelates to determine.

LEGA'TION, a term denoting the body of official persons attached to an embassy. Hence *secretary of legation.*

LEGA'TO, (*Italian,*) in music, a word used in an opposite sense to *staccato*, and implying that the notes of a movement or passage to which it is affixed are to be performed in a close, smooth, and gliding manner.

LE'GEND, a book used in the ancient Roman churches, containing the lessons that were to be read. The word was afterwards used to denote a chronicle or register of the lives of saints. As these histories were often nothing more than pious fictions, the name of a *legend* was given to the incredulous fables which make pretensions to truth.—*Legend*, in Roman antiquity, signifies the motto engraved upon medals, which differs from the inscription properly so called. The *inscription* signifies words placed on the reverse of a medal in lieu of figures; but the legend is the word made use of round the head or other figure.

LEG'ER, the principal book used in merchants' accounts, wherein every man's particular account is kept; the book into which a summary of the journal is carried.—*Leger-lines*, in music, those lines added to the usual stave of five lines, when more are wanted for notes ascending or descending.

LEGERDEMAIN', tricks, which, from the dexterity of the performer, are made to deceive the observer, and are called *sleight of hand.*

LE'GION, in Roman antiquity, a body of soldiers in the Roman army, consisting of different numbers at different periods of time. In the time of Romulus the legion consisted of 3,000 foot and 300 horse; though after the reception of the Sabines, it was augmented to 4,000. In the war with Hannibal it was raised to 5,000; after this it sunk to 4,000 or 4,500, which was the number in the time of Polybius. The number of legions kept in pay together, also differed according to times and occasions. Each legion was divided into ten cohorts, each cohort into ten companies, and each company into two centuries. The chief commander of the legion was called *Legatus* (lieutenant.) The principal standard of a legion was a silver eagle; and the legions were named from their commanders, (as the *Claudian legion.*) or from the place where they were stationed, &c. The word *legion* was revived in the time of Napoleon; and has since been commonly applied to a body of troops of an indefinite number, and usually of different kinds; as the *English-German legion*, the *British legion* in Spain, &c.

LE'GION OF HONOR, an order instituted by Napoleon, while consul, (May 19, 1802,) for military and civil merit. It consisted of different grades of merit, as grand crosses, crosses, commanders, officers, and legionaries; all of whom receive pensions with this mark of distinction.

LEG'ISLATOR, one who frames or establishes the laws and polity of a state or kingdom. The term is chiefly applied to some distinguished persons of antiquity, such as Moses among the Jews; Theseus, Draco, Solon, among the Athenians; Lycurgus among the Spartans; and Numa among the Romans.

LEG'ISLATURE, the supreme power of a state.

LEGIT'IMACY, a word which, in a political sense, is variously defined, according to the bias of the party by whom it is used. But in its most commonly received acceptation, it denotes the lawfulness of the government, in an hereditary monarchy, where the supreme dignity and power pass by law from one regent to another, according to the right of primogeniture.—*Legitimate* means, *according to law;* hence, children born in wedlock are called legitimate, and those born out of wedlock are styled illegitimate.

LE'MURES, among the ancient Romans, spectres or ghosts, believed to be the souls of the dead, which tormented men in the night. In order to lay them, a ceremony called *lemuria* was observed on the nights of the 9th, 11th, and 13th of May.

LENT, a solemn time of fasting and abstinence in the Christian church, observed as a time of humiliation before Easter, the great festival of our Saviour's resurrection. It begins on Ash-Wednesday, and continues forty days.

LE'ONINE VERSE, a kind of Latin verse, consisting of hexameters and pentameters, of which the final and middle syllables rhyme. Some say it derived its name from pope Leo I. (A.D. 680,) others from Leonius, a poet of the 12th century.

LES'SONS, are certain portions of the Scriptures read in most Christian churches during divine service, the performance of which in the ancient church devolved, among other duties, on the catechumen. In the English church, the course of lessons begins with the year at the book of Genesis, and, with the omission of the two books of Chronicles, continues through the Old Testament, including portions of the Apocrypha. In the *second* lessons, as they are called, the same course is followed with the New Testament. In the Presbyterian church, the word *lesson*, in this sense, is unknown, though the practice of reading a portion of Scripture is almost universally adopted; but the selection of the passage is left to the choice of the officiating clergyman.

LE'THE, in Greek mythology, the River of Oblivion: one of the streams of the infernal regions. Its waters possessed the quality of causing those who drank them to forget the whole of their former existence. In the sixth book of *Virgil's Æneid*, the shades of the departed, after fulfilling their various destinies in the infernal regions during a thousand years, are brought to drink of the water of Lethe, as a preparation for their transmigration into new bodies.

LET'TER, a mark or character, written, printed, engraved, or painted; used as the representative of a sound, or of an articulation of the human organs of speech. By sounds, and articulations or closures of the organs, are formed syllables and words. Hence a letter is the first element of *written* language, as a simple sound is the first element of *spoken* language or speech. As *sounds* are audible and communicate ideas to others by the ear, so *letters* are visible representatives of sounds, and communicate the thoughts of others by means of the eye. Letters are distinguished by grammarians into vowels, and consonants (which latter are again subdivided into mutes, and liquids) and diphthongs, according to the organ employed in their pronunciation.

LEVANT', in geography, is applied in a general sense to any country situated to the eastward of us, or in the eastern part of any continent or country; but, in a more contracted signification, it is given to that part of the Mediterranean Sea bounded by Asia Minor on the north, Syria and Palestine on the east, Egypt and Barca on the south, and by the island of Candia and the rest of the Mediterranean on the west.

LEV'EE, in court phraseology, a ceremonial visit of the nobility, gentry, &c., who assemble to pay their respects to the queen (or king.) It consists of gentlemen only, by which it is distinguished from what is termed a *drawing-room*, where ladies as well as gentlemen attend.

LEV'EE-EN-MASSE, a military expression for the patriotic rising of a whole people, including all capable of bearing arms, who are not otherwise engaged in the regular service; and is the most formidable obstacle an enemy can encounter. In Germany it is called the *land-*

sturm, in distinction from the *landwehr*, or militia. In 1813 the governments of Northern Germany called it forth in every part of the country.

LEVI'ATHAN, a word which, in the Hebrew, signifies a great fish. Some suppose, from the description of it in the book of Job, it means a whale, while others have presumed it is a crocodile. In Isaiah, however, it is called the crooked serpent.

LE'VITES, a term applied in Scripture to such of the tribe of Levi as were employed in the lower offices and ministries of the temple. In this particular, they were distinguished from the priests, who, being descended from Aaron, were likewise of the tribe of Levi. The Levites bore some resemblance in the tabernacle, and temple of the Jews, to the deacons among Christians. They were employed in bringing wood, water, and other necessaries for the sacrifice, and they sung and played upon instruments in the temple. They also applied themselves to the study of the law, and were the ordinary judges of the country, though always subordinate to the priests. Their subsistence was the tithes of corn, fruit and cattle throughout Israel; but the priests were entitled to a tenth of their tithes, by way of first-fruits to the Lord.

LEVIT'ICUS, a canonical book of the Old Testament, so called from its containing the laws and regulations relating to the priests, Levites, and sacrifices. These duties, rites and ceremonies, formed what is termed the *Levitical law.*

LEXICOL'OGY, or LEXICOG'RAPHY, a word used by some writers to express that branch of philology which treats of words alone, independently of their grammatical and rhetorical uses; considering their senses, their composition and their etymology.

LEX'ICON, a dictionary of words, or vocabulary; originally, and still usually, confined to dictionaries of the Greek or Hebrew tongues. The oldest Greek lexicon is the *Onomasticon*, which was written 180 years before Christ: the oldest Hebrew lexicon belongs to the 9th century.

LEZE-MAJ'ESTY, in jurisprudence, any crime committed against the sovereign power in a state. The name is derived from the Roman phrase, "crimen læsæ majestatis," which denoted a charge brought against a citizen for acts of rebellion, usurpation of office, and general misdemeanors of a political character, which were comprehended under the title of injuries to the "majesty of the Roman people." The emperors transferred to all offences against themselves the same criminal character; and offences of leze-majesty were multiplied under their arbitrary governments.

LIBA'TION, among the Greeks and Romans, was an essential part of solemn sacrifices. It was also performed alone, as a drink offering, by way of procuring the protection and favor of the gods, in the ordinary affairs of life. At sacrifices, after the libation had been tasted by the priest, and handed to the bystanders, it was poured upon the victim. At entertainments a little wine was generally poured out of the cup, before the liquor began to circulate.

LI'BEL, in law, the malicious defamation of any person, either written or printed, in order to provoke him to anger, or to expose him to public hatred, contempt, or ridicule. Any book, pamphlet, writing, or picture, containing such representations, although only communicated to a single person, is considered in law a publication of it; and libellers may be brought to punishment by a prosecution, or be compelled to make reparation by a civil action. The civil action is grounded upon the injury which the libel is supposed to occasion to the individual; the public prosecution upon its tendency to provoke a breach of the peace. In a civil action, the plaintiff recovers damages, the amount of which is settled by the jury: but, upon an indictment, the jury has merely to acquit the defendant, or to find him guilty, after which the court passes judgment.—*Libel*, in the ecclesiastical and admiralty courts, is the name given to the formal written statement of the complainant's ground of complaint against the defendant.

LI'BER, in Roman mythology, a surname of Bacchus, in reference, perhaps, to the idea of his being a liberator or deliverer. Liber was originally an old divinity, who presided over fertility, and who was worshipped in connection with Libera (a name of Proserpine,) and Ceres.

LIB'ERAL, in politics, a conventional name given to that party in a country which advocates progressive reform of abuses in the state, real or supposed.

LIB'ERAL ARTS, such as depend more on the exertion of the mind than on manual labor, and regard intellectual improvement and amusement, rather than the necessity of subsistence.

LIBERA'LIA, a sacred festival, with games; so called from Liber, a Latin name of Bacchus, in honor of which god they were celebrated at Rome. It was on occasion of this festival that the Roman youths who attained the age of seventeen assumed the manly dress, or *toga*.

LIBER'TAS, in the mythology of the Greeks and Romans, was a goddess worshipped with peculiar veneration. By the former she was invoked by the synonymous title Eleutheria; and throughout all parts, both of Greece and Italy, statues, temples, and altars were erected in honor of her. At Rome, her most famous temple, built by T. Gracchus, was situated on the Aventine Mount. She was represented under the figure of a woman, holding in one hand a cap, the symbol of liberty, and two poniards in the other. In modern times a cap is also used as a symbol of liberty; thus, in France a red cap formed the badge of the Jacobin club. In England a blue cap with a white border is used as a symbol of the constitutional freedom of the nation, and Britannia sometimes bears it on the point of her spear.

LIBER'TUS, in Roman antiquity, a person who from being a slave had obtained his freedom. The *liberti* were such as had been actually made free themselves; the *libertini* were the children of such persons.

LIB'ERTY, freedom from restraint, in a general sense, and applicable to the body, or to the will or mind. The body is at liberty, when not confined; the will or mind is at liberty, when not checked or controlled. A man enjoys liberty, when no physical force operates to restrain his actions or volitions.—*Natural liberty*, consists in the power of acting as one thinks fit, without any restraint or control, except from the laws of nature. It is a state of exemption from the control of others, and from positive laws and the institutions of social life. This liberty is abridged by the establishment of government.—*Civil liberty*, is the liberty of men in a state of society, or natural liberty, so far only abridged and restrained, as is necessary and expedient for the safety and interest of the society, state, or nation. A restraint of natural liberty, not necessary or expedient for the public, is tyranny or oppression. Civil liberty is an exemption from the arbitrary will of others, which exemption is secured by established laws, which restrain every man from injuring or controlling another. Hence the restraints of law are essential to civil liberty.—*Political liberty*, is sometimes used as synonymous with civil liberty. But it more properly designates the liberty of a nation, the freedom of a nation or state from all unjust abridgment of its rights and independence by another nation. Hence we often speak of the political liberties of Europe, or the nations of Europe.—*Religious liberty*, is the free right of adopting and enjoying opinions on religious subjects, and of worshipping the Supreme Being according to the dictates of conscience, without external control.—*Liberty*, in metaphysics, as opposed to *necessity*, is the power of an agent to do or forbear any particular action, according to the determination or thought of the mind, by which either is preferred to the other.—*Liberty of the press*, is freedom from any restriction on the power to publish books; the free power of publishing what one pleases, subject only to punishment for abusing the privilege, or publishing what is mischievous to the public or injurious to individuals.

LI'BRARY, a collection of books belonging to a private person, or to a public institution or a company.—An apartment, or suite of apartments, or a whole building appropriated to the keeping of books. The most celebrated library of antiquity was the Alexandrian in Lower Egypt. The principal libraries of modern times are the Royal library at Paris, the Bavarian State library at Munich, the Imperial library at Petersburg, the Imperial library at Vienna, the University library at Göttingen, the Royal library at Dresden, the Royal library at Copenhagen, the Royal library at Berlin, the Vatican library at Rome, the Ambrosian library at Milan, the Bodleian library at Oxford, the University library at Cambridge, the library of the British Museum in London, the Advocates' library in Edinburgh, and that of Trinity College in Dublin.

LI'CENSE, in law, an authority given to a person to do some lawful act. A license is a personal power, and therefore cannot be transferred to another. If the person licensed abuse the power given him, he becomes a trespasser. A license may be either verbal or written; when written, the paper containing the authority is called a *license*.

LICEN'TIATE, in law, one who has full license to practise any art or faculty; generally, a physician who has a license to practise, granted by the college of physicians.

LIC'TORS, in Roman antiquity, officers or beadles who carried the fasces before the chief magistrates whenever they appeared in public. It was also a part of their duty to be the public executioners in beheading, scourging, &c. A dictator was attended by twenty-four lictors; a consul by twelve; the master of the horse, six; a prætor, six; and each vestal virgin had one.

LIEGE, in law, a term used either as *liege lord*, signifying one that acknowledges no superior, or the chief lord of the fee; or as *liege man*, he who owes homage and allegiance to the liege lord. By the term *liege people* is meant the subjects of a monarch, because they owe him their allegiance.

LI'EN, in law, the right which one person, in certain cases, possesses of detaining property belonging to another, when placed in his possession, until some demand, which the former has, is satisfied. Liens are of two kinds: *particular liens*, that is, where the person in possession of goods may detain them until a claim which accrues to him from those identical goods is satisfied; and *general liens*, that is, where the person in possession may detain the goods, not only for his claim accruing from them, but also for the general balance of his account with the owners. Some liens also are created by express agreement, and some by usage.

LIEUTEN'ANT, this word, like *captain*, and many others, has received gradually a much narrower meaning than it had originally. Its true meaning is a deputy, a substitute, from the French *lieu*, (place, post,) and *tenant*, (holder.) A *lieutenant général du royaume* is a person invested with almost all the powers of the sovereign. Such was the count d'Artois (afterwards Charles X.) before Louis XVIII. entered France, in 1814.—*Lieutenant-general* was formerly the title of a commanding general, but at present it signifies the degree above major-general.—*Lieutenant-colonel* is the officer between the colonel and major.—*Lieutenant*, in military language, signifies the officer next below a captain. There are first lieutenants, and second, or *sous-lieutenants*, with different pay.—A lieutenant in the navy is the second officer next in command to the captain of a ship.—In England, the *lord-lieutenant* of a county has the authority to call out the militia in case of invasion or rebellion. The governor of Ireland is also called *lord-lieutenant of Ireland.* In some English colonies, jointly under a *governor-general*, the chief magistrate of each separate colony is called *lieutenant-governor*. Many of the United States choose lieutenant-governors to act in case of the governor's death.

LIG'ATURE, in music, the tie which binds several notes of like length together, by which they appear in groups. Thus four quavers, by means of a ligature at the top or bottom, assume the form , the line connecting them being the ligature.

LIGHT, that imponderable ethereal agent or matter which makes objects perceptible to the sense of seeing, but the particles of which are separately invisible. It has been believed that light is a fluid or real matter, existing independent of other substances, with properties peculiar to itself. Its velocity is astonishing, as it passes through a space of nearly twelve millions of miles in a minute. Light, when decomposed, is found to consist of rays differently colored; as, red, orange, yellow, green, blue, indigo, and violet. The sun is the principal source of light in the solar system; but light is also emitted from bodies ignited, or in combustion, and is reflected from enlightened bodies, as the moon. Light is also emitted from certain putrefying substances. It is usually united with heat, but it exists also independent of it. The intensity of light, at different distances from a luminous body, is inversely as the squares of those distances, so that in this respect it follows the same law as heat, sound, and the force of gravity. Light acts a very important part in the vegetable economy. The green color of plants and the hues of flowers entirely depend upon it. It is also found to assist in developing the forms of some of the lower classes of animals. There are two theories respecting the nature of light. Some maintain that it is composed of material particles, which are constantly thrown off from the luminous body; while others suppose that it is a fluid, diffused through all nature, and that the luminous body occasions waves or undulations in this fluid, by which the light is propagated in the same manner as sound is conveyed through the air. The first is called the *corpuscular*, the second the *undulatory theory;* the latter is now more generally entertained, several facts being wholly inexplicable on the former theory. The language, however, which is employed in treating of light is, for the most part, accommodated to the former.—*Light*, in painting, the medium by which objects are discerned. In a picture it means the part the most illuminated. This may happen from *natural light*, as the sun or moon; or from *artificial light*, as a fire, candle, &c. The principal light is generally made to fall on the spot where the principal figures are placed, and generally near the centre of the picture. A reflected light is that which a body in shadow receives from a contiguous light object.

LIGHT'NING, a sudden discharge of electricity from a cloud to the earth, or from the earth to a cloud, or from one cloud to another, that is, from a body positively charged to one negatively charged, producing a vivid flash of light, and usually a loud report, called thunder. Sometimes lightning is a mere instantaneous flash of light without thunder, as *heat-lightning*, lightning seen by reflection, the flash being beyond the limits of our horizon. When the flash of lightning takes a zigzag course, or when it branches out, it is termed *forked lightning;* when it has the appearance of a sudden and wide illumination, it is called *sheet-lightning*.

LIM'BO, a region, supposed by some of the school theologians to lie on the edge or neighborhood of hell. This served as a receptacle for the souls of just men, not admitted into purgatory or heaven. Such were, according to some Christian writers, the patriarchs and other pious ancients who died before the birth of Christ: hence the limbo was called Limbus Patrum. These, it was believed, would be liberated at Christ's second coming, and admitted to the privileges of the blessed in heaven. Though some have asserted that, when our Saviour went down into hell, he liberated these souls, and carried them away with him into heaven. This latter idea is probably an adorned representation of the remarkable passage in St. Peter's epistle, (i. 3, 19,) where he says that Christ preached to the spirits in prison; and, being held by certain of the later fathers, seems to have given some influence to the growing opinion in favor of a purgatory. The limbus puerorum, or infantum, was a similar receptacle allotted by some of the schoolmen to the souls of infants who die unbaptized. Dante has fixed his limbo, in which the distinguished spirits of antiquity are confined, as the outermost of the circle of his hell. The use which Milton has made of the same superstitious belief is well known.

LIMITA'TION, in law, a certain time prescribed by statute, within which an action must be brought.

LINE, in fortification, whatever is drawn on the ground of the field, as a trench, or a row of gabions, &c.—*Lines* are most commonly made to shut up an avenue, or entrance to some place, and are distinguished into *lines of approach*, of *defence*, of *communication*, &c.—*Line*, in genealogy, a series or succession of relations, from a common progenitor. *Direct* line, is that which goes from father to son; being the order of ascendants and descendants. The *collateral* line, is the order of those who descend from a common father related to the former, but out of the line of ascendants and descendants: in this are placed uncles, aunts, nephews, &c.—*A ship of the line*, in naval affairs, any vessel of war large enough to be drawn up in the line of battle.—In military affairs, regular troops, in distinction from the militia, volunteers, &c., are called troops of *the line*.

LIN'EN, cloth made of flax, being much finer than that which is made of hemp. In common linen the warp and woof cross each other at right angles; if figures are woven in, it is called *damask*. The species of goods which come under the denomination of linen, are tablecloths, sheeting, cambric, lawn, shirting, towels, &c. The chief countries in which linens are manufactured are Russia, Germany, Switzerland, Holland, Scotland, and Ireland. In several parts of Germany, Switzerland, Flanders, and France, linens are frequently embellished with painting; and in England the produce of the Irish linen manufacture is beautifully printed in the manner of calicoes.—In the middle ages, linen and woollen cloth formed the only materials for dress and fine linen was held in very high estimation. In more ancient times linen formed the dress of the Egyptian priests, who wore it at all their religious ceremonies.

LIPOGRAMMAT'IC WORKS or WRITINGS, compositions in which a particular letter is omitted throughout. The ancients produced many ingenious trifles of this description. In the *Odyssey* of Tryphiodorus there was no A in the first book, no B in the second, and so on. There are other pieces of modern invention, such as the *Pugna Porcorum*, in which all the words begin with the letter P. Odes in Spanish, containing only one of the vowels, are refinements on the same invention.

LIST, the enclosed field of ground wherein the ancient knights held their jousts and tournaments; so called from its being encircled with pales, barriers, or stakes, as with a list. Some of these were double, one for each cavalier, which kept them apart, and prevented them from coming nearer each other than a spear's length. Hence the expression *to enter the lists* is synonymous with engaging in contest.

LIT'ANY, signifies a general supplication; and was applied by the Eastern church in early ages to a special form of prayer which was introduced into the ritual, or used on particular occasions. The term passed over into the Western church, where the words *rogatio* and *supplicatio* have been used in the same technical sense. It is supposed that the change of term was occasioned by the frequency of processional supplications from the Eastern to the Western churches, beginning in the fourth century. The litany of the English Church is mostly translated from the forms of the Western litanies previously used in that country; those of the breviary of Salisbury and York. The direction in the prayer-book is, that the litany shall be read on Wednesdays, Fridays, and Sundays: on the two former, as fast-days in the primitive Church; the one as the day in which Christ was sold by Judas, the other as that of the crucifixion, and therefore periods of peculiar humiliation: on the Sunday, as the day appointed for the most complete and solemn service in the week.

LITERA'TI, in general, denotes men of learning.—In antiquity, those who were branded with any letters by way of ignominy, were so called.

LIT'ERATES, in ecclesiastical affairs, a name given to those who are admitted to ordination by the bishop without having taken a university degree.

LIT'ERATURE, in the general sense of the word, comprises the entire results of knowledge and mental activity expressed in writing; but in a narrower sense, it is used to denote the department of elegant letters, excluding works of abstract science and mere erudition. In this limited view it comprehends languages, particularly Greek and Latin, grammar, etymology, logic, rhetoric, poetry, history, criticism, bibliography, and a description of the attainments of the human mind in every sphere of research and invention. The history of literature represents the development and successive changes of civilization, so far as these are exhibited in written works, and embraces the history of the literature of special ages or countries, and of the separate branches of literature, as poetry, rhetoric, philology, and so forth. A brief sketch of the literature of different nations, in ancient and modern times, will be given in the present article.

I. Ancient Literature.

1. *Chinese Literature.*—The antiquity of Chinese literature is proportionate to that of the language, and its development has been greatly promoted by the early invention of the art of printing, which has been known in China for at least nine hundred years. The Chinese language presents a remarkable specimen of philological structure, which for ingenuity of arrangement and copiousness of expression, is not surpassed in any written literature. It belongs to that class of idioms which are called monosyllabic. Every word consists of only one syllable. The roots or original characters of the Chinese are only 214 in number, and it is supposed that a minute analysis would reduce them to a still smaller amount. Each of these characters represents one word, and each word an idea. Their various combinations form the whole language. Taken singly, they express the principal objects or ideas that are suggested in the common intercourse of life; and combined, according to obvious analogies, they are made to comprehend the entire field of thought. Thus the character, which originally represents the word *hand*, is so modified and combined with others, as to denote every variety of manual labor and occupation. The Chinese characters are written from top to bottom, and from right to left. The lines are not horizontal, but perpendicular and parallel to each other. Much importance is attached by the Chinese to the graphic beauty of their written characters, which in picturesque effect, it must be owned, are superior to most forms of alphabetic symbols. The grammar of the language is very limited. The nouns and verbs cannot be inflected, and hence the relation of words to each other in a sentence can be understood only from the context, or marked by their position.

The Chinese literature is rich in works in every department of composition, both verse and prose. Their scholars are fond of discussions in moral philosophy, but they have also numerous books of history, geography, voyages, dramas, romances, tales, and fictions of all kinds. The labors of various European travellers and students have given us specimens of almost every description of Chinese literature. In legislation, we have a translation of the Penal Code of the Empire; in politics and morals, the sacred books of Confucius, and his successor Meng-Tsew; in philology and belles-lettres, a well-executed dictionary of the language; several translations and abstracts of history; and selections from the drama, criticism, and romance. Among the most successful explorers of the field of Chinese literature, we may mention Staunton, Davis, Morrison, Klaproth, and Remusat, who have followed up the earlier researches of the Jesuits at Pekin, and greatly elucidated a subject which had been supposed to be inaccessible.

2. *Greek Literature.*—The language which we call Greek, was not the primitive language of Greece, for that country was originally inhabited by the Pelasgi, whose language had become extinct in the time of Herodotus. With regard to its origin, there is a diversity of opinion among the learned, although it evidently forms a branch of the extensive family of languages, known by the name of Indo-Germanic. It has existed as a spoken language for at least three thousand years, and with the exception of the Arabic and the English, has been more widely diffused than any other tongue. Out of Greece, it was spoken in a great part of Asia Minor, of the south of Italy and Sicily, and in other regions which were settled by Grecian colonies. The Greek language is divided into four leading dialects, the Æolic, Ionic, Doric, and Attic, beside which there are several secondary dialects. The four principal dialects may, however, be reduced to two, the Hellenic-Doric, and the Ionic-Attic, the latter originally spoken in the northern part of Peloponnesus and Attica, the former in other parts of Greece. In each of these dialects, there are celebrated authors. To the Ionic dialect, belong in part the works of the oldest poets, Homer, Hesiod, Theognis; of some prose writers, especially Herodotus and Hippocrates; and the poems of Pindar, Theocritus, Bion, and Moschus. The Doric dialect was of the greatest antiquity. We have few remains of Doric prose, which consists chiefly of mathematical or philosophical writings. After Athens became the centre of literary cultivation in Greece, the works of Æschylus, Sophocles, Euripides, Aristophanes, Thucydides, Xenophon, Plato, Isocrates, Demosthenes, and so forth, were regarded as standards of style, and made the Attic the common dialect of literature. Poetry, however, was not written in the Attic dialect. The peculiarities of Homer were imitated by all subsequent poets, except the dramatists, and even they assumed the Doric to a certain degree in their choruses, for the sake of the solemnity of expression which belonged to the oldest liturgies of the Greeks. According to the general tradition, Cadmus the Phœnician, was the first who introduced the alphabet into Greece. His alphabet consisted of but sixteen letters; four are said to have been invented by Palamedes in the Trojan war, and four more by Simonides of Ceos. It has been maintained however by some persons, that the art of writing was practised by the Pelasgi before the time of Cadmus. On the other hand, many of the most sagacious critics, place the origin of writing in Greece at a much later period.

The origin of Greek literature, or the intellectual cultivation of the Greeks, by written works, dates at a period of which we have few historical memorials. The first period of Grecian cultivation, which extends to 80 years after the Trojan war, is called the ante-Homeric period, and is destitute of any literary remains, properly deserving the name. Of the poets previous to Homer, nothing satisfactory is known. The most ancient was Olen, who is mentioned by Pausanias. He was followed by Linus, Orpheus, Musæus, and others, but the poems which are circulated under their names cannot be regarded as their genuine productions. It was in the Greek colonies of Asia Minor, that the first great impulse was given to the development of literature; and among them we find the earliest authentic specimens of Greek poetry and historical composition. Situated on the borders of a noble sea, enjoying a climate of delicious softness and purity, abounding in the most nutritious and tempting products of nature, whose fertility was not inferior to its beauty, these colonies possessed a character of refined voluptuousness, which, if not favorable to the performance of great deeds, allured the dreamy spirit to poetical contemplations, and was manifested in noble creations of the fancy, which have not been surpassed in the progress of cultivation. Living near the scene of the Trojan war, the bards devoted their first poems to the celebration of Grecian heroism. With them, commenced the second period of Greek literature, which we call the Epic age. Of these, Homer alone has survived. We have from him the two great poems, the Iliad and Odyssey, with several hymns and epigrams. He gave his name to the Homeridæ, an Ionian school of minstrels, who preserved the old Homeric and epic style, and who are probably the authors of much that has been ascribed to Homer himself.

Next to the Homeridæ, come the Cyclic poets, whose works embrace the whole circle of mythology and tradition, describing the origin of the gods and of the world, the adventures of the Heroic times, the Argonautic expedition, the labors of Hercules and Theseus, the principal events of the Theban and Trojan wars, and the fortunes of the Greeks after the fall of Troy. A transition between these historic-poets and the later school of Ionian minstrelsy, is formed by Hesiod, who conducted poetry back from Asia Minor into Greece. Of the sixteen works ascribed to him, we have the Theogony, the Shield of Hercules, and Works and Days, the last, an agricultural poem, interspersed with moral reflections and prudential maxims.

The third period commences with the growth of lyric poetry, of apologues and philosophy, with which history gained a new development and a higher degree of certainty. Lyric poetry sprung up on the decline of the Epic school, and was much cultivated from the beginning of the epoch of the Olympiads (776 B.C.,) to the first Persian war. The poems of this period are considered among the most valuable productions of Grecian literature. Many of them resembled the epic, and contained the subjects of heroic song. They were sung by bands of youths and maidens, accompanied by instrumental music. Among the most celebrated of the lyric poets were Archilochus of Paros, the inventor of the Iambus; Tyrtæus, Terpander, and Alcman, whose martial strains enkindled the valor of the Spartans; Callimachus of Ephesus, inventor of the elegiac measure; Simonides and Anacreon of Ceos; the impassioned Sappho of Mitylene; Stesichorus, Hipponax, and Pindar. Many didactic poems, fables, and proverbs were written during this period, and served to prepare the way for prose composition.

The philosophy of this age was marked by its constant reference to practical affairs. Among its expounders, we may consider the seven wise men of Greece, as they are called, (Periander, or according to some, Epimenides of Crete, Pittacus, Thales, Solon, Bias, Chilo, and Cleobulus,) of whom six acquired their fame, not by the teaching of speculative abstractions, but by their admirable wisdom in the affairs of life, and their skill in the offices of state. Their celebrated sayings are the maxims of experience, applied to the practical relations of life. But with the progress of intellectual culture, a taste for speculative inquiries was unfolded. This resulted in the establishment of the Ionic philosophy by Thales, the Italian, by Pythagoras, and the older and later Eleatic. With the development of these schools, we are brought to the scientific period of Greek literature. The Ionic school ascribed a material origin to the universe. Its principal followers were Pherecydes, Anixamander, Anaxamines, Anaxagoras, Diogenes of Apollonia, and Archilaus of Miletus. Of the Pythagorean school, which explained the organization of the world by number and measure, were Ocellus Lucanus, Timæus of Locris, Epicharmus, Theages, Archytas, Philolaus, and Eudoxus. To the older Eleatic school, which cherished a more sublime, but less intelligible conception of the origin of the world, assuming the fact of a pure necessary existence, belonged Xenophanes and Parmenides; to the later Eleatic, Melissus and Diagoras. Until about the commencement of the 90th Olympiad, the philosophers and their disciples were dispersed throughout the various Grecian cities. Athens subsequently became their chief residence, where the class of men called Sophists first rose into importance as public teachers. Of these, the most distinguished names that have been preserved to us are Gorgias of Leontium, Protagoras of Abdera, Hippias of Elis, Prodicus of Cos, Trasimæus and Tisias. They were especially devoted to the subjects of politics and eloquence, but also made a study of the natural sciences, mathematics, the theory of the fine arts, and philosophy. Professing the art of logic as a trade, they were less earnest in the pursuit of truth, than in the construction of plausible arguments. Their fallacious pretences awakened the honest indignation of Socrates, who not only became their zealous antagonist, but gave a vigorous and original impulse to the progress of philosophy. This shrewd and subtle reasoner opened a new direction to philosophical research, turning it to the study of human nature, and of the laws of psychology and ethics instead of barren speculations and theories. Without leaving any written record of his genius, he is known at the present day by the affectionate and beautiful memorials which have been consecrated to his character in the productions of his disciples. Among these, Plato was pre-eminent by the force and comprehensiveness of his reason, the marvellous keenness of his insight in the region of transcendental ideas, the vigor and acuteness of his logical faculties, and the winning sweetness and grace of expression, which lend a charm to his writings that has never been equalled in philosophical literature. The masterly conversations of Socrates, in which he expounded the principles of his philosophy in the streets and market-place of Athens, are reproduced with admirable dramatic effect, in the glowing pages of his eloquent disciple.

The progress of history kept pace in Grecian cultivation with the development of philosophy. Among the oldest historical prose writers, are Cadmus, Dionysius, and Hecatæus of Miletus, Hellanicus of Mitylene, and Pherecydes of Scyros. After them appears Herodotus, who has received the name of the Homer of history. He was followed by Thucydides, the grave, condensed, and philosophical historian of the Peloponnesian War. Strongly contrasted with his sternness and energy, is Xenophon, whose limpid narrative flows on with the charming facility of a graceful stream, presenting a delightful specimen of the tranquil beauty of Greek prose in its most simple form. These three historians distinguished the period from 550 to 500 B.C., during which time we have to notice the introduction of a new class of poetical creations.

The popular festivals, which were celebrated after the vintage, with rude songs and dances, led to the gradual creation of the drama. A more artistic form was given to the wild choruses in honor of Bacchus; the recitation of fables by an intermediate speaker was introduced into the performances; and soon the games of the vintage festival were repeated on other occasions. The spirit of the drama was thus cherished, until the appearance of Æschylus, who may be deemed the author of the dramatic art in Greece. He divided the story into different portions, substituted the dialogue for recitation by a single person, and assigned the various parts to skilful actors. The three great tragic writers are Æschylus, Sophocles and Euripides, while the most distinguished rank in comedy is held by Cratinus, Eupolis, Crates, and especially Aristophanes.

During this period we find several didactic and lyric poets, while the sister art of eloquence was illustrated by the names of Lysias, Demosthenes, Æschines, Antiphon, Gorgias, and Isocrates.

The succeeding period, which is usually called the Alexandrine, was characterized by the prevalence of a critical spirit; the luxuriant bloom of the earlier Greek literature had passed away; and the fresh creative impulses of genius were made to yield to the love of speculation and the influence of erudition. The glowing imaginative philosophy of Plato was succeeded by the more rigid system of Aristotle, who founded the Peripatetic school, and gave order and precision to the principles of reasoning. With the passion for subtle analysis, which was the characteristic of his mind, he drew a sharp line of distinction between logic and rhetoric, ethics and politics, physics and metaphysics, thus enlarging the boundaries of philosophy, and establishing a system which exercised an undisputed supremacy for ages. The dogmatic tendencies of Aristotle found their counterpart in the skeptical principles of which Pyrrho of Elis was the most distinguished advocate. The same principles prevailed to a certain extent in the Middle and New Academies founded by Arcesilaus and Carneades, while the Socratic philosophy was modified by the disciples of the Stoic school, established by Zeno, and of the Epicurean, which bears the name of its celebrated founder. At length the intellectual sceptre which had been so long wielded by the philosophers and poets of Greece, passed from Athens to Alexandria; the nation itself was absorbed in the progress of Roman conquest; Greek literature ceased to give birth to original productions; and its brilliant career became the subject of history.

Hebrew Literature.—The language and literature of the ancient Hebrews, apart from its religious character and claims, presents a curious and important subject of investigation. It is the oldest literature of which any remains have come down to modern times. With a rich poetical coloring, a profound sentiment of humanity, and a lofty religious faith, it sustains a most intimate relation to the development of the intellect and the moral and political history of the race. The Hebrew language is one of the oldest branches of the numerous family of languages which have received the name Shemitic, on account of the supposed descent of the nations by which they were spoken, from Shem, the son of Noah. These are the Chaldaic, the Aramæan, the Hebrew, the Syriac, the Arabic, the Phœnician, and the Ethiopian. The history of the language has been divided by many critics into four periods. I. From Abraham to Moses. II. From Moses to Solomon. III. From Solomon to Ezra. IV. From Ezra to the end of the age of the Maccabees, when it was gradually lost in the modern Aramæan and became a dead language. The differences, however, which can be traced in the language are so slight, that a sounder division would be into only two periods, the first extending from the time of Moses to the reign of Hezekiah, and the second from the reign of Hezekiah to its final extinction as a spoken language. The written characters or letters, which date from the time of Solomon, were the same as the Phœnician. During the Babylonish captivity, the Hebrews received from the Chaldees the square character in common use, and in the time of Ezra, the old Hebrew manuscripts were copied in these characters. The punctuation of the language was not settled until after the seventh century of the Christian era. The accents, vowels, points, and divisions into words, were also introduced at a later period.

The poetical and religious sentiment was the foundation of Hebrew literature. Lyric poetry received a rich development under David, to whom are ascribed several noble specimens of song and elegy. The fragments of didactic poetry which bear the name of Solomon are stamped with a character of practical wisdom, and often exhibit an energy of expression, which authorize us to class them among the most extraordinary productions of ancient literature. After the division of the kingdom, the prophets became the great teachers of the people, and have left various collections of their writings, none of which have come down to us with completeness. Upon the return of the exiled people from the Babylonish captivity, the remains of Hebrew literature were collected by a college of learned men under the direction of Ezra, and from their labors we have received the books of the Old Testament in their present form.

Roman Literature.—The language of the ancient Romans is usually called Latin, for though Rome and Latium were originally separate communities, they always appear to have spoken the same language. The Latins, as far as we can decide on such a question at the present day, seem to have formed a part of that great race which overspread both Greece and Italy under the name of Pelasgians. It is supposed that the Pelasgians who settled in Italy originally spoke the same language with the Pelasgians who settled in Greece. The Greek and Latin languages accordingly have many elements in common, though each has its own distinctive character.

The history of Roman literature may be divided into four periods. I. From the earliest times till Cicero. II. To the death of Augustus, A.D. 14. III. To the death of Trojan. IV. To the conquest of Rome by the Goths. During the first five hundred years of the Roman history, scarcely any attention was paid to literature. Its earliest attempts were translations and imitations of the Greek models. The Odyssey was translated into Latin by Livius Andronicus, a Greek captive of Tarentum, and the earliest writer of whom we have any account. His tragedies and comedies were taken entirely from the Greek. He was followed by Nævius, who wrote an historical poem on the first Punic war, by the two tragic writers Pacuvius and Attius, and by Ennius, B.C. 239, the first epic poet, and who may be regarded as the founder of Roman literature. Being a Greek by birth, he introduced the study of his native language at Rome, and had among his pupils Cato, Scipio Africanus, and other distinguished citizens of that day. At the same time, he taught the Romans the art of easy and graceful writing in their own language, and helped to inspire them with a love of literature by his refined taste and elegant cultivation. Contemporary with Ennius was Plautus, whose dramatic pieces, in imitation of the later comedy of the Greeks, were remarkable for their vivacity of expression and their genuine comic humor. He was followed by Cecilius and Terence, of whom the latter has left several admirable comedies, fully imbued with the Grecian spirit. The first prose writers were Quintus Fabius Pictor and Lucius Cincius Alimentus, who lived in the time of the second Punic war, and wrote a complete history of Rome. Their style was meagre and insipid, aiming only at brevity, and entirely destitute of ornament or grace.

With the age of Augustus, in which some earlier writers are usually reckoned, a new spirit is exhibited in Roman literature. In didactic poetry, Lucretius surpassed his Grecian masters, by the force of thought and the splendor of diction, which characterize his great philosophical poem on the origin of the universe. Catullus attempted various styles of poetry, in all of which he obtained eminent success. His lyric and elegiac poems, his epigrams and satires, are marked by singular versatility of feeling, frequent flashes of wit, and rare felicity of expression. Among the elegiac poets, of whose genius we still possess the remains, the highest distinction was gained by Tibullus, Propertius and Ovid. The former of these poets was pronounced by Quinctilian to be the greatest master of elegiac verse; Ovid possessed an uncommon fertility of invention and ease of versification; while Propertius tempers the voluptuous cast of his writings with a certain dignity of thought and vigorous mode of expression. The great lyric poet of the Augustan age is Horace, whose graceful and sportive fancy, combined with his remarkable power of delicate and effective satire, continues to make him a favorite with all who have the slightest tincture of classical learning. The noblest production of this period, however, is the Æneid of Virgil, which, with his elaborate poem on rural affairs, the Georgics, and his sweet and tender pastorals, or Eclogues, fairly entitles him to the position which has been given him by universal consent, of the most gifted epic and didactic poet in Roman literature.

The prose writings of the Latin authors, taken as a whole, betray a higher order of genius and cultivation than the works of the poets. In this department, the preeminence belongs to Cicero, whose various productions in eloquence, philosophy, and criticism, are among the most valuable treasures of antiquity. In history, Cesar, Sallust, and Livy, are the most prominent names, who, each in his own peculiar style, have left models of historical composition, which have been the admiration of every subsequent age. The literature of the Augustan period partook of the general character of the Roman people. Devoted to the realization of practical objects, with slight tendencies to the ideal aspect of things, and absorbed in the exciting game of politics and war, the Romans had little taste either for abstract speculation or for the loftiest flights of poetical fancy. Hence no new system of philosophy was produced in their literature; their best poets were essentially imitative; and of all branches of study, those connected with popular eloquence were held in the greatest esteem.

With the death of Augustus commenced the decline of Roman literature. Among the poets of this period, are Phædrus, an ingenious fabulist, the satirists, Juvenal and Persius, whose works are more important for their illustrations of the manners of the age, than for their poetical merit, and Lucan, who describes the wars of Cesar and Pompey in an insipid historical epic. In prose, we have the sombre, but condensed and powerful histories of Tacitus, and the quaint and artificial treatises on ethics and philosophy by Seneca. Subsequent to the reign of Trajan, we meet with no writers, who have any claim upon our attention, and the literature of Rome, after a brief interval of splendor, during the golden age between Cicero and Augustus, passes into unimportance and obscurity.

Sanscrit Literature.—Until the close of the last century, the Sanscrit literature was almost wholly unknown to the learned of Europe. The Roman Catholic missionaries in India, had, to a certain extent, engaged in the study of the language at an earlier period, but it is only since the year 1790, that it has attracted the attention of eminent scholars. Among those who have given an impulse to the study of Sanscrit, and who have themselves pursued it with distinguished success, are Sir William Jones, Wilkins, Forster, Colebrooke, Wilson, Haughton, Rosen, Chezy, Burnouf, A. W. Schlegel, and Bopp. We are indebted to their labors for a knowledge of this rich and curious literature, which, on many accounts, may be considered as one of the most remarkable products in the history of intellectual culture.

The Sanscrit language is a branch of the Indo-Germanic family of languages, and is supposed to bear the greatest resemblance to the primitive type. In its construction, it is in the highest degree ingenious and elaborate, and the variety and beauty of its forms are well adapted to illustrate the laws of the formation of language. It is the sacred language of the Bramins, and contains the Vedas, the oldest records of their religion. The last century before the Christian era, was the period of its richest blossoming, although it extends back to a far more remote antiquity. It appears in its most ancient form in the Vedas, which date from the thirteenth century before Christ, and in that state exhibits many striking analogies with the Zend, the ancient language of Persia. These writings are the foundation of Sanscrit literature, and diffuse their influence through the whole course of its development.

The Vedas are divided into four classes, the first being in poetry, the second in prose, the third consisting of lyrical prayers, and the fourth of devotional pieces, intended to be used in sacrifices and other religious offices. Each Veda is composed of two parts, the prayers and the commandments. The Sanscrit possesses a variety of other works in sacred literature, which contain not only a copious exposition of religious doctrines, but numerous discussions of philosophical and scientific subjects, and an extensive collection of poetical legends.

The two oldest and most interesting epic poems are "The Ramayana," describing the seventh great incarnation of Vishnu, and "The Mahabharata," devoted to the wars of two rival lines descended from the ancient Indian monarch, Bharata. An episode from this work called "Bhagavat Gita" has been translated by Wilkins, Herder, Schlegel and others, and has excited no small interest as an illustration of the early Oriental philosophy.

A new character was given to Sanscrit poetry about one hundred years before the Christian era, by the introduction of themes connected with courts and princes. It lost the popular and national tendency which appears in the two great epics, alluded to above, and assumed a more artificial form. With a manifest improvement in the mere externals of style, the new poetry shows a degeneracy in point of thought, and an entire absence of original invention. In the principal works of this class we find labored descriptions of natural objects, and many curious artifices of composition, but they are destitute both of brilliancy of imagination and depth of reflection. The most fertile author of the new school is undoubtedly Calidasa, who attempted almost every species of poetical composition, and whose epic, lyric, and dramatic productions, must be allowed to possess considerable merit. His best descriptive poem, entitled "Meghaduta," is a model of simplicity and elegance. It exhibits a highly ideal character, tracing out the spiritual significance of visible phenomena, and striving to penetrate into the hidden life of the universe. The drama called "Sacontala" or the "Fatal Ring," by this author, has received the warmest commendation from modern critics. "All its scenes," says the genial Herder, "are connected by flowery bands, each grows out of the subject as naturally as a beautiful plant. A multitude of sublime as well as tender ideas are found in it, which we should look for in vain, in a Grecian drama." A valuable translation of this poem has been made by Sir William Jones.

The influence of religious speculation in India early gave birth to numerous philosophical writings. With the love of contemplation, to which the natives are so strongly inclined, and the progress of thought in opposition to the doctrines of the Vedas, a variety of philosophical systems was the natural consequence. The oldest of these is called the "Sankhya." It teaches the duality of matter and spirit, which are essentially different in their nature, though found in such intimate union. The problem of life, is the emancipation of the soul from the dominion of the senses, and the attainment of blessedness by the supremacy of the intellect. Another system of transcendental speculation is named the "Nyaya." This is constructed from strict logical deductions, which it applies to the interpretation of nature, and arrives at a theory of materialism, the reverse of the Sankhya ideality. The Nyaya school has produced a multitude of writings. Opposed to each of these systems is the "Mimansa," which maintains the doctrines of the Vedas in their original strictness, and strives to reconcile them with the suggestions of philosophy.

The Sanscrit literature, moreover, abounds in works on various other branches of learning. Its philological treatises, especially, are of great value. The Indian grammarians surpass those of any other ancient people. No less important are the Sanscrit works on rhetoric, criticism, music, astronomy, and jurisprudence. They well deserve the attention of the scholar, not only on account of their intrinsic character, but as precious memorials of the early development of the intellect, and significant illustrations of the history of the race.

II. Modern Literature.

An interval of eight centuries separates the period of the decline of Roman literature from that of the first dawn of modern literature in Europe. The successive invasions of the barbarians during the rapid dismemberment of the ancient empire of Rome, for a time destroyed all languages, and centuries elapsed before the new tongues were sufficiently matured for the cultivation of letters. In the Eastern Empire, during the third, fourth, and fifth centuries after Christ, nothing was produced except some works of theology, by the Fathers of the Church. The Arabs first began to cultivate literature in the sixth, and the Persians in the ninth century after Christ. The Provençal, or language of the Troubadours, in the south of France, first attained a stable character towards the close of the ninth century, and the *Langue d'Oil*, or Romance-tongue of Normandy, about fifty years later. Nearly all of the living languages of Europe date the first beginnings of their literature as far back as the tenth century, though, except to gratify a philological taste, there is little that will repay the student of modern literature for going beyond the twelfth century. The following sketches of the literature of civilized nations, since the decline of classic literature, have been arranged nearly in the order of time:

Arabic Literature.—Literature, after its final decay and extinction in the Eastern and Western Roman Empires, revived first among the Arabic tribes in the East. Even before the era of Mahomet, there were renowned poets and story-tellers in Arabia. In the fifth century, during the great fairs of Mecca, poetical contests frequently took place, the victorious productions being lettered with gold and hung up in the Caaba. Among the most renowned poets of this period were Amralkeis, Tharafa, and Antar. Their works are distinguished by imaginative power, richness of illustration, and great skill in depicting the passions of love and revenge. With Mahomet commenced a memorable epoch in Arabic literature. Through the Koran, which was arranged from Mahomet's teachings, by Abubekr, the first caliph, the method of writing and the literary style of the nation were determined. The reigns of Haroun Al-Raschid and Al-Mamun in the seventh and eighth centuries, were the most enlightened period of the Arabic dominion, though for two centuries afterwards the nation produced many eminent geographers, philosophers, jurists and historians. Under the government of Al-Mamun, excellent universities were established at Bagdad, Bussora and Bokhara, and extensive libraries in Alexandria, Bagdad and Cairo. The dynasty of the Abbassides in Bagdad emulated that of the Ommanides in Spain; during the tenth century the University of Cordova was almost the only refuge of literature in Europe. The labors of the Arabic scholars and travellers contributed greatly to the spread of geographical knowledge. Ibn Batuta, who in the thirteenth century visited Africa, India, China, and Russia, ranks with Marco Polo and Rubruquis. In the twelfth century Abu'l Kasein wrote the history of the Arabs in Spain; Bohæddin, a biography of Sultan Saladin; Ibn Arabschah described the exploits of Tamerlane, and Hadji Khalfa, in later times, has produced an encyclopedia of Arabic, Persian, and Turkish literature. The style of the Arabian historians is clear, concise, and unincumbered with imagery. The most renowned philosopher was Avicenna, who flourished in the eleventh century. Averrhoes, whose name is also familiar to scholars, was famous as an expounder of the system of Aristotle. In the departments of medicine, astronomy, geometry, and arithmetic, there are many Arabic works which exhibit great research and scientific knowledge.

The number and variety of the works produced by the Arabian poets, is most remarkable, and their influence on the modern literature of Europe was greater than is generally suspected. In picturesque narration they have rarely been excelled, and the "Thousand and One Nights," which first appeared in its collected form during the reign of Caliph Mansur in the ninth century, has been naturalized in all modern languages. Only half of this, however, is Arabic; the remainder having been translated from the Sanscrit and Persian. The Arabian poets left many poetic chronicles, the most celebrated of which are: "The Deeds of Antar," "The Deeds of the Warriors," and "The Deeds of the Heroes." Of late years, several eminent French and German scholars have given their attention to the study of Arabic literature, the best works of which are now accessible through their translations.

Persian Literature.—The modern literature of Persia succeeded that of Arabia. After the conquest of the country by the caliphs, about the middle of the seventh century, the arts and sciences of the Arabs, together with the religion of Mahomet, were transplanted upon Persian soil, but the fruits of this new culture did not appear for several succeeding generations. The first Persian books, both of poetry and history, were written in the early part of the tenth century, and for several centuries there was no interruption in the list of renowned authors. Literature was encouraged and rewarded, whatever might be the political convulsions that affected the empire. Persian poetry consists for the most part of small lyrics, arranged in *divans*, or collections. There are also several voluminous historical, romantic, and allegorical poems, besides legends and narratives told in a mixture of prose and verse. The first Persian poet is Rudegi, who flourished about the year 952. Firdûsi, the great epic poet of Persia, died in the year 1030, at the age of seventy. He wrote the "*Schahnameh*," or "Kings' Book," describing the deeds of the Persian rulers, from the creation of the world to the downfall of the Sassanide dynasty in 632. He was thirty years in the composition of this work, which contains sixty thousand verses. The most celebrated portion is that recounting the adventures of the hero Rustem. Nisâmi, at the close of the twelfth century, wrote extensive romantic poems, the most remarkable of which were "Medjnoun and Leila," and "*Iskander-Nameh*," an epic on Alexander the Great. Chakâni was a celebrated writer of odes in the thirteenth century. Saadi, one of the most celebrated Persian authors, was born in 1175, and lived till 1263. His poems are principally moral and didactic, but rich with the experience of a fruitful life, and written in a very simple and graceful style. His best works are the *Gulistan*, or "Garden of Roses," and the *Bostan*, or "Garden of Trees." Hâfiz, the Oriental poet of love, was born at Schiraz, in the beginning of the fourteenth century, where he lived as a dervish in willing poverty, resisting the invitations of the caliphs to reside in Bagdad. In the year 1388, he had an interview with Tamerlane, by whom he was treated with much honor. His poems consisted of odes and elegies, which have been collected into a "Divan." His lyrics, devoted to the praise of love and wine, are full of fire and melody.

Djami, who died in 1492, was one of the most prolific of Persian writers. His life was spent at Herat, where, in the hall of the great mosque, he taught the people the precepts of virtue and religion. He left behind him forty works, theological, poetical, and mystical. Seven of his principal poems were united under the title of "The Seven Stars of the Bear." His history of mysticism, entitled "The Breath of Man," is his greatest prose work. Among the later Persian poems are the *Schehinscheh-Nameh*, a continuation of the Book of Kings, and the *George-Nameh*, an account of the conquest of India by the British. The Persian is the only Mahometan literature containing dramatic poetry. Its dramas strikingly resemble the old French mysteries. Of the collections of tales, legends, and fairy-stories, the most celebrated are the *Anwâri soheili*, or "Lights of the Canopy," and the *Behâri danisch*, or "Spring of Wisdom." The historical works in the Persian language are very numerous and valuable. They embrace the history of the Mohammedan races, from Mongolia to Barbary. The principal works are the Chronicle of Wassâf, a history of the successors of Genghis Khan, which appeared in 1333; the "Marrow of the Chronicles," by Khaswini, in 1370, and the *Rauset Essafa*, a great universal history, of which modern historians have made good use. It was written by Mirchond, about the year 1450. In the departments of ethics, rhetoric, theology, and medicine, the Persian scholars are only second to the Arabic. They also excelled in translation, and have reproduced in Persian, nearly the entire literature of India.

Italian Literature.—The Italian language assumed a regular and finished character at the court of Roger I., king of Sicily, in the twelfth century. Several poets arose, who, borrowing the forms of verse from the Provençal troubadours, gave the people songs in their native language in place of the melodies of the Moors and Arabians. The Italian soon became the court language of Italy, and Malespina's History of Florence, which was written in the year 1280, is scarcely inferior, in elegance and purity of style to any Italian prose works which have since been produced. The first genuine poet of Italy, however, was her greatest, and one of the greatest of all time Dante commenced his great poem of the "Divina Commedia" in the year 1304, just before his exile from Florence, and completed it during his many years of wandering from one court of Italy to another. Out of the rude and imperfect materials within his reach, he constructed an epic which places his name beside that of him whom he humbly called his master—Virgil. Taking the religious faith of his time as the material, he conducts the reader through the sad and terrible circles of Hell, the twilight region of Purgatory, and the fair mount of Paradise, showing him all forms of torture and punishment for the vile, all varieties of supreme happiness for the pure and good. The poem takes a fierce and gloomy character from the wrongs and persecutions which the poet endured in his life. Dante died in 1321, at which time Petrarch, who was born in 1304, had commenced those studies which led to the restoration of classic literature to Italy. As an enthusiastic admirer of antiquity, he imparted to his contemporaries that passion for the study of the Greek and Roman authors which preserved many of their masterpieces at a moment when they were about to be lost to the world. His songs and sonnets, most of which were inspired by his unfortunate love for Laura de Sade, give him a worthy place after Dante, in Italian literature. He died in 1374. Contemporary with Petrarch was the great master of Italian prose—Boccaccio, who was born in 1313. He early devoted his life to literature, and in 1341, assisted at the celebrated examination of Petrarch, previous to his coronation in the capitol. His principal work is the Decamerone, a collection of one hundred tales, which, notwithstanding the impurities with which they are disfigured, are models of narration, and exhibit the most varied powers of imagination and invention. Boccaccio is considered as the inventor of romances of love—a branch of literature which was wholly unknown to antiquity.

For a century following the death of Boccaccio, the literature of Italy shows no great name, though several scholars distinguished themselves by their attainments and the aid which they rendered to the cause of classic literature. The most noted of these were John of Ravenna; Lionardo Aretino, who wrote a history of Florence in Latin; Poggio Bracciolini, a most voluminous writer, who enjoyed the patronage of Cosmo de'Medici, at Florence; Francesco Fileflo and Lorenzo Valla, both men of great erudition, whose labors contributed to bring on a new era of Italian literature. Lorenzo de'Medici, called the Magnificent, towards the close of the fifteenth century, gave the first impulse to the cultivation of the Italian tongue, which had been lost sight of in the rage for imitating Latin poets. Besides being the author of many elegant songs and sonnets, his court was the home of all the authors of that period. Among these were Politiano, who wrote *Orfeo*, a fable formed on the myth of Orpheus, which was performed at the court of Mantua, in 1483; Luigi Pulci, the author of *Morgante Maggiore*, and Boiardo, author of the *Orlando Innamorato*. Both the last-named poems are chivalrous romances, written in the *ottava rima*, and full of a quaint humor, which before that time had only appeared in the prose of Boccaccio. But the master of the gay and sparkling poetic narrative was Ariosto, wh` was born in 1474, and first appeared as a a author about the year 1500. Five years later he commenced his *Orlando Furioso*, which was not completed till 1516. This is a romantic poem in forty-six cantos, celebrating the adventures of Roland, the nephew of Charlemagne. It is one of the classics of Italy, and has been translated into all modern languages. After the death of Ariosto in 1533, no literary work of any prominence appeared until Torquato Tasso published his *Jerusalem Delivered*, in 1581. Alamanni, Trissino and Bernardo Tasso flourished in the interval and produced labored poems, which are no longer read. The subject of Tasso's poem is the rescue of the Holy Sepulchre from the Moslems, by the Crusaders, under Godfrey of Bouillon. The wrongs and persecutions heaped upon Tasso clouded his mind and shortened his days; he died in Rome, in 1595, on the day before that appointed for his coronation. Three other Italian authors of the sixteenth century are worthy of mention: Cardinal Bembo, the most finished scholar of his day, and author of a history of Venice; Nicolo Machiavelli, whose name has become synonymous with all that is sinister and unscrupulous in politics, from his treatise entitled "The Prince," for which, after his death, an anathema was pronounced against him; and Pietro Aretino, one of the most infamous and dissolute men of his time. Machiavelli wrote an admirable History of Florence, which is still a standard work.

In the half-century following the death of Tasso, there are but two poets who have attained any renown; Guarini, the author of *Pastor Fido*, and Tassoni, who wrote the *Secchia Rapita* (Rape of the Bucket.) Filicaja, whose impassioned lyrics are still the revolutionary inspiration of Italy, belongs to the latter part of the seventeenth century; he died in 1707. After another long interval arose Frugoni, a lyric poet of some celebrity, who died in 1768, and Metastasio, the author of plays, operas and ballets innumerable. He is remarkable for his wonderful command of the language, and the free and spirited movement of his dialogue. He died in Vienna, in the year 1782. During this same period, Italian dramatic literature received a new accession in Goldoni, whose comedies are still the glory of the Italian stage. He had a rival in Count Gazzi, whose works, nevertheless, are far inferior to Goldoni's in humor and brilliancy. What Goldoni did for comedy, Alfieri accomplished for Italian tragedy. This author justly stands at the head of modern Italian literature. His tragedies, odes and lyrics exhibit an eloquence and fervor of thought which is scarcely reached by any other author. His principal works are *Saul*, *Myrrha*, *Octavia*, *Brutus the Second*, and *Philip* II. Since the commencement of this century, Italy has not been barren of authors. Pindemonte, who has published several volumes of dramatic poetry; Ugo Foscolo, author of a poem called "The Sepulchres;" Manzoni, who wrote *I Promessi Sposi*, (The Betrothed,) a charming romance of life on the shores of Lake Como; Silvio Pellico, whose *Le Mie Prigione* is a narrative of his sufferings in the prison at Spielberg, and Niccolini, equally celebrated as a poet and prose writer. Mazzini, Triumvir of Rome during the brief period of the Republic, and Gioberti, are the most distinguished Italian authors of the present generation.

Spanish Literature.—The earliest essay in Spanish literature is the Chronicle of the Cid, which is supposed to have been written about the middle of the twelfth century. In form the poem is sufficiently barbarous, though the language is remarkably spirited and picturesque. It has been the fount of numberless songs and legends, through the later centuries. It narrates the adventures of Ruy Diaz de Bivar, the Cid Campeador. In the following century, Gonzales de Berceo, a monk, wrote nine voluminous poems on the lives of the saints. Alfonso X. of Castile, whose reign terminated in 1284, was the author of a poem entitled *The Philosopher's Stone*, besides several prose works. The first author of the fourteenth century was Prince Don John Manuel, who wrote a prose work entitled *Count Lucanor*, a collection of tales embodying lessons of policy and morality. He was followed by Pedro Lopez de Ayala, and Mendoza, Marquis de Santillana; though the latter belongs properly to the next century. He produced a number of works, both prose and poetry, all of which were remarkable for the erudition they displayed. Some of his lighter poems are very graceful and melodious.

Under the reign of Charles V. Spanish literature first reached its full development. After the union of Arragon and Castile and the transfer of the seat of the government to Madrid, the Castilian became the court language, and thus received a new polish and elegance. The first author of this period was Boscan, an imitator of Petrarch in some respects, but a poet of much native fervor and passion. Garcilaso de la Vega, the friend of Boscan, surpasses him in the sweetness of his verses and in their susceptibility and imagination. He was a master of pastoral poetry, and his eclogues are considered models of that species of writing. His life was actively devoted to the profession of arms. He fought under the banner of Charles XI. in Tunis, Sicily, and Provence, and was finally killed while storming the walls of Nice. Don Diego de Mendoza, one of the most celebrated politicians and generals of that period, is generally awarded a place next to Garcilaso. He was a patron of classical literature, and the author of a history of the Moorish Revolt in the Alpuxarra, and a History of the War of Grenada, but a man of cruel and tyrannical character. Montemayor, who flourished at the same time, attained much celebrity from his pastoral of Diana. These authors during the reign of Charles V. gave Spanish poetry its most graceful and correct form, and have since been regarded as models of classic purity. The great masters of Spanish literature, however, were reserved for the succeeding generation. Herrera and Ponce de Leon, lyrical poets, fill the interval between the age of Garcilaso de la Vega and Cervantes. Herrara is considered the first purely lyrical poet of Spain. Ponce de Leon, who was imprisoned five years by the Inquisition for having translated the song of Solomon, was the author of several volumes of religious poetry.

Two of the brightest stars of Spanish literature, Cervantes and Lope de Vega, were contemporaries, and were followed in the next generation, by the third, Calderon. Cervantes was born in 1549. He travelled through Italy, lost a hand at the battle of Lepanto, and was five years a slave in Barbary. He commenced his literary career by the writing of comedies and tragedies, the first of which, *Galatea*, was published in 1584. Thirty of his comedies have been entirely lost. His great work, Don Quixote, was published in 1605, and was immediately translated into all the languages of Europe. From this time until his death in 1616, he wrote many novels and comedies. The tragedy of *Numantia*, and the comedy of *Life in Algiers*, are the only two of his plays which have been preserved. To this same period belongs Don Alonzo de Ercilla, whose epic of *La Aracuana* was written during the hardships of a campaign against the Aracuanian Indians in Chili. Lope de Vega was born in 1562, and after a life of the most marvellous performances died in 1635. He was a prodigy of learning, imagination, and language. Out of *eighteen hundred* dramas which he wrote, one hundred were each produced in the space of a single day. His detached poems have been printed in 27 volumes in quarto. Very few of his plays are now read or performed. The only remaining authors of eminence during this period are Quevedo, who wrote several moral and religious works and three volumes of lyrics, pastorals, and sonnets; Villegas, an anacreontic poet; and the Jesuit Mariana, author of a History of Spain. The life of Calderon de la Barca, the illustrious head of the Spanish drama, extended from 1600 to 1687. His plays are of four kinds: sacred dramas, from Scriptural sources; historical dramas; classic dramas; and pictures of society and manners. The most celebrated are *The Constant Prince*, *El Secreto a Voces* and *El Magico prodigioso*. A number of small dramatists were contemporary with Calderon, but with his death Spanish literature declined, and has since produced few eminent names. Luyando, counsellor of state, published two tragedies in 1750, and in 1758 appeared *The Life of Friar Gerund*, by Salazar—a work in the style of Don Quixote, but directed against the clergy instead of the chivalry. It abounds with wit and satire, and is perhaps the best Spanish prose work of the last century. Towards the close of the century Huerta achieved considerable reputation by his attempts to revive the Spanish drama. Tomas de Yriarte published in 1782 his *Literary Fables*, and a few years later Melendez appeared as the author of two volumes of idyls and pastorals. Both of these authors display considerable lyric genius; but since their death, in the early part of the present century, Spain has produced no new name in literature.

Portuguese Literature.—Portugal first acquired its position as an independent kingdom after the battle of Ourigue, in 1139. The date of the origin of its literature is nearly coeval with that of the monarchy. Hermiguez and Moniz, two knights who flourished under Alfonso I., wrote the first ballads. King Dionysius, who reigned from 1279 to 1325, and his son, Alfonso IV. were both renowned as poets, but few vestiges of their writings remain. It was not until the fifteenth century, however, that Portuguese literature attained any considerable merit. Macias, a Portuguese knight engaged in the wars with the Moors of Grenada, was called *El Enamorado*, on account of the tender and glowing character of his amatory poems. The first distinguished poet of the country was Bernardin Ribeyro, who flourished under the reign of Emmanuel the Great, in the beginning of the sixteenth century. His most celebrated productions are his eclogues, the scenes of which are laid on the banks of the Tagus and the sea-shores of Portugal. His lyrics of love, the origin of which is attributed to an unholy passion for the king's daughter, are wonderfully sweet and melodious. The first prose work in Portuguese worthy of note, is a romance entitled *The Innocent Girl*, which appeared about this period. Saa de Miranda, who also attained celebrity as a Spanish author, was born in Coimbra in 1495, and wrote many sonnets, lyrics and eclogues in his native tongue. He also wrote a series of poetical epistles, after the manner of Horace. Antonio Ferreira, who was born in 1528, followed the example of Miranda in his sonnets and eclogues, but surpassed him in entering the field of dramatic literature. His *Inez de Castro*, founded on the tragic story of that lady, displays much power and pathos in the delineation of the characters. The other poets of this generation were Andrade Caminha, Diego Bernardes and Rodriguez de Castro, all of whom wrote lyrics, sonnets and pastorals, few of which have survived them.

The sole star of Portuguese literature, who is now almost its only representative to other nations, was Luis de Camoëns, who was born in 1525. After studying at Coimbra, where he was coldly treated by Ferreira, he embraced the profession of arms, and lost an eye in the siege of Ceuta. Sailing for India in 1533, he reached Goa in safety, participated in an expedition against the king of Cochin-China, spent a winter in the islands of Ormuz, and afterwards, on account of a satire entitled *Follies in India*, directed against the Portuguese governor, was banished to Macao, on the coast of China. During his residence of five years in that place, he wrote his great epic of *The Lusiad*, devoted to celebrating the passage of the Cape of Good Hope by Vasco de Gama, and the triumph of Portuguese arms and commerce in the Orient. On his return to Portugal he was shipwrecked on the coast of Cambodia, and escaped by swimming, with the Lusiad in his hand, held above the waves. He died in great poverty, in 1579. He left behind him many sonnets, songs and pastorals, but most of them are penetrated with a vein of deep and settled melancholy. Among the successors of Camoëns, the most noted are Gil Vicente, a dramatic writer, who is supposed to have served as a model to Lope de Vega and Calderon; and Rodriguez Lobo, who was at one time considered a rival of Camoëns. He wrote the *Winter Nights*, a series of philosophical conversations, *Spring*, a romance, and numberless pastorals. Cortereal also described in a ponderous epic the adventures of Manuel de Sousa Sepulveda, a distinguished Portuguese.

The age of Camoëns also gave rise to a new branch of literature. John de Barros, born in 1496, is esteemed by his countrymen as the Livy of Portugal. He commenced his career by a romance entitled *The Emperor Clarimond*, but after his return from service on the coast of Guinea, he devoted himself to the preparation of a grand historical work on the Portuguese empire. Only one fourth of this, entitled *Portuguese Asia*, which was published in 1552, appeared. This is one of the most comprehensive, accurate and interesting historical works of that age. Alfonso D'Albuquerque, one of the most distinguished contemporaries of Barros, wrote a series of *Commentaries*, and Couto and Castanheda undertook to complete the work which Barros had left unfinished. Bernardo de Brito, born in 1570, designed to give a universal History of Portugal, but, commencing with the Creation, he died by the time he reached the Christian Era. Osorio, Bishop of Sylvez, who died in 1580, wrote the History of King Emmanuel, describing the religious troubles of that time in a most liberal and enlightened spirit. Manuel de Faria, born in 1590, almost rivalled Lope de Vega in the amount of his works; his dissertations on the art of poetry are held in most value. He also wrote a History of Portugal and a Commentary on Camoëns. After the subjugation of Portugal by Philip II. of Spain, the literature of the country declined, and presents no distinguished name for nearly a century following. The first author of the last century is the Count of Ericeyra, born in 1673. He was a general in the army, and a scholar of splendid attainments. His chief work was the *Henriqueide*, a epic poem, describing the adventures of Henry of Burgundy, the founder of the Portuguese monarchy Towards the close of the last century, Antonio Garçao and the Countess de Vimieiro acquired some celebrity by their dramatic productions. The only Portuguese authors of note, whom the present century has brought forth, are Antonio da Cruz e Silva, who imitated Pope and other English poets, and J. A. da Cunha, an eminent mathematician and elegiac poet. The Portuguese colonies have produced a few writers, the most noted of whom are Vascencellos and Claudio Manuel da Costa.

French Literature.—The literature of France was later in its development than that of the other nations of Southern Europe. It was necessary to wait the decline of the two romance-tongues of Normandy and Provence before the language could take a settled form, and a still further time elapsed before it was sufficiently matured for the purposes of the scholar and the author. During the thirteenth and fourteenth centuries the kingdom produced many romances, in which the influence of the literature of the Trouvères and Troubadours was manifest. Gilbert de Montreuil, Castellan de Coucy and some others were noted for this species of composition; many sacred dramas and mysteries were written in the north of France, and about the middle of the fifteenth century, several romantic epics appeared. The only remarkable name of this early period is the renowned chronicler, Froissart, who was born in 1337, and in the course of his travels and sojourn at all the courts of Europe, was witness of many of the chivalrous events he describes in his "Chronicles of France, Spain, Italy, England

and Germany." Philip de Comines, who died in 1509, passed his life in the service of Louis IX., and left behind him the "Memoirs" of his time. The latter part of the fifteenth century produced many small writers of satires, odes, songs, &c., among whom, Charles, Duke of Orleans, takes the first rank. The sacred mysteries, the first attempt at theatrical representation, gradually gave place to a rude form of drama and comedy, and a very successful comedy of French life appeared in 1475.

With the reign of Francis I. the study of the classics became popular in France, and from that time till the age of Louis XIV. the progress of French literature was rapid and uninterrupted. The sixteenth century produced a few great names. Scaliger and Casaubon were renowned for their scholastic acquirements; Clement Marot and Theodore Beza cultivated poetry under Francis I., whose sister, Margaret of Valois, published a collection of novels, called the *Heptameron;* Ronsard was the first French poet who showed strong original genius, and, with Regnier, gave the national poetry a freer and more characteristic tone. The drama was improved by Etienne Jodelle, who imitated the Greek tragedians; Claude de Seyssel wrote the History of Louis XII.; and Brantôme and Agrippa d'Aubigné left behind them many memoirs and historical essays. But the boast of the age is the names of Malherbe, Rabelais and Montaigne. Malherbe, born in 1554, is considered the first French classic, in poetry; his language is most inflexibly pure and correct. Rabelais was born in 1483, and his romance of "Gargantua and Pantagruel" was first published in 1533. Notwithstanding its grossness it is one of the most lively, humorous and brilliant books in the language. It satirizes the clerical and political characters of his time. Montaigne, whose life extended from 1533 to 1592, wrote three volumes of Essays, on moral, political and religious subjects, which on account of their elegant style no less than the treasures of thought they contain, have always held their place among French classics.

The seventeenth century is the glory of French literature. Under the auspices of Richelieu, Colbert and Louis XIV. all departments of letters, science and art reached a height unknown before. The French Academy was founded by Richelieu in 1635, and the language, at that time unrivalled in clearness, perspicacity and flexibility, gradually became the polite tongue of Europe. Dramatic poetry, especially, founded on the principles of the Greek theatre, attained a character it has never since reached. Corneille, born in 1606, was the father of the classic French drama. His first play, *The Cid*, belongs rather to the romantic drama, but through the influence of the Academy his later works, the most eminent of which are *Les Horaces*, *Cinna*, *Polyeucte* and *Mort de Pompée* are strictly classical. His dramatic works amount to thirty-three. Racine, who was born in 1639, brought the classic drama to perfection. His language is the most elegant and melodious of all French dramatists, while he is inferior to none in his knowledge of nature and his command of the sentiments and passions. His plays, though constructed on the classic model, are not confined strictly to classic subjects. The most celebrated are: *Andromaque*, *Bajazet*, *Mithridate*, *Phèdre*, *Esther* and *Athalie*. After these two authors ranks Molière, the father and master of French comedy. His *Tartuffe* has a universal celebrity. He died in 1673. Crébillon, sometimes called the French Æschylus, was a writer of tragedies. Legrand, Regnard, and Scarron distinguished themselves as dramatists of secondary note. To this age belong Le Sage, the author of *Gil Blas*; La Fontaine, the greatest fabulist since Esop; and Boileau, the satirist and didactic poet, whose *Art poétique* and *Lutrin* or "Battle of the Books" have been made classic. Mademoiselle de Scudery wrote many chivalrous romances, and Perrault's fairy tales soon became household words. The *Télémaque* of Fenelon was also produced during this period. This author, with Bourdaloue, Bossuet and Massillon, were celebrated as theological writers and pulpit orators. Madame de Sevigné's letters are unsurpassed as specimens of graceful, polished and spirited epistolary writing. As historians, Rollin is the most distinguished, but Mezeray, author of the national Chronicles, the Jesuit D'Orleans, author of Histories of Revolutions in England and Spain, and Bossuet's theological histories, are worthy of notice.

During the eighteenth century, when the literature of Spain, Italy and Portugal were on the decline, and England and Germany remained stationary, France still maintained her supremacy. In 1694 was born Voltaire, who in the course of his life made himself master of nearly every department of literature. His first play, *Œdipe*, was successfully performed in 1718, though his epic of the *Henriade*, written at the same time, was not published till 1729. Many of his succeeding plays were unsuccessful, and his satires and philosophical essays produced only banishment. His principal plays are *Zaire*, *Alzire*, *Brutus*, *Oreste*, *Mahomet* and *Tancrède*. After his return from Germany, he settled at Ferney on the Lake of Geneva, where for twenty years he devoted himself to literature. His principal works are: *History of Charles XII. of Sweden; History of Russia under Peter the Great; Pyrrhonisme de l'histoire*, *Droits de l'homme* and the *Dictionnaire Philosophique*. Jean Jaques Rousseau, born in 1712, exercised scarcely less influence on French literature, than Voltaire. His first work, a dissertation on Modern Music, appeared in Paris in 1743, about which time he wrote several comedies and tragedies and composed an opera. His romance entitled *Nouvelle Heloise*, was published in 1760, and his *Contrât Social* and *Emile* in 1762. His most remarkable work, the *Confessions*, was completed in 1770, and he died in 1778. As bold and independent as Voltaire in his philosophical views, he had nothing of his cynicism. His works, the style of which is absolutely fascinating, express a sincere sympathy with humanity. Montesquieu, whose *Spirit of Laws* is a standard work on jurisprudence, belongs to the first half of the eighteenth century. Among the historians contemporary with Voltaire were Condorcet, author of a *History of Civilization*, and Barthélemy, who also wrote the *Voyage du jeune Anacharsis*. La Bruyère, La Harpe and Madame d'Epinay distinguished themselves by their didactic and epistolary writings. The most noted novelists were Marmontel, Bernardin de St. Pierre, author of *Paul and Virginia*, and Louvet. Marivaux attained distinction as a writer of comedies, and Beaumarchais as a dramatist and writer of operas. The well-known *Barber of Seville* is from his pen. France produced few lyric poets during the last century. Lebrun, Delille and Joseph Chénier are the most worthy of mention, but the *Marseillaise* of Rouget de Lisle is the finest lyric of the century, if not of all French literature. Mirabeau, Barnave, Sieyes and the leaders of the Revolution gave a new and splendid character to French oratory, towards the close of the century.

Chateaubriand, de Staël and Béranger connect the age of Rousseau and Voltaire with the modern literature of France. Chateaubriand was born in 1769, and published his first work, the *Essay on Revolutions*, in London, in 1797, while in exile. His *Atala*, the subject of which was derived from his adventures among the Natchez tribe of Indians, on the Mississippi, appeared in 1801, and his *Génie du Christianisme* in 1802. He also published *Les Martyrs* in 1807, and an account of his travels in the East. He filled many diplomatic stations under the Bourbons, and was made peer of France. After his death, which took place in 1848, his autobiography was published, under the title of *Mémoires d'outre Tombe*. Madame de Staël, the daughter of M. Neckar, afterwards minister under Louis XVI., was born in 1766, and first appeared as an author in 1788, when she published a series of letters on the life and writings of Rousseau. During the French Revolution she remained in Switzerland and England, where she wrote several political pamphlets, dramas, and essays on life and literature. Her romance of *Corinne* was published in 1807, and her *De l'Allemagne*, which directed attention to the literature of Germany, in 1810. Her work entitled *Ten Years of Exile*, was written in Sweden; she died in Paris in 1817. Béranger, who still lives at Passy, near Paris, is the first song-writer of France. Many of his lyrics and ballads have become household words with the common people. Casimir Delavigne, who died in 1843, was among the first restorers of that lyric school, which Lamartine, Victor Hugo and Alfred de Musset have since carried to a high degree of perfection. The most renowned names in cotemporary French literature, are, as poets: Alphonse de Lamartine, author of *Meditations Poëtiques*, *Harmonies Poëtiques* and *La Chute d'un Ange;* Victor Hugo, author of three volumes of lyrical romances and ballads; Alfred de Musset; Jean Réboul, a disciple of Lamartine; and Auguste Barbier, who mingles with his poems a vein of keen satire. Jasmin, a barber of Agen, has obtained much celebrity by his poems in the Gascon dialect. The new school of French romance has infected the modern literature of all countries. Balzac, who died in 1850, is unequalled as a painter of society and manners; Eugene Sue, whose *Mysteries of Paris* and *Wandering Jew* have been so widely read, delights in exciting subjects and the most intricate and improbable plots; Alexander Dumas, best known by his *Count of Monte Christo*, and his romances of travel, is a master of picturesque narrative; Victor Hugo is best known as a novelist by his *Notre Dame de Paris*, a brilliant historical fiction, and Paul de Kock, as a lively though unscrupulous painter of Parisian life, enjoys a remarkable popularity. The most striking and original writer of fiction is Madame Dudevant, better known as "George Sand," whose *André*, *Lettres d'un Voyageur* and *Consuelo*, have placed her in the first rank of French authors. As dramatists, Scribe, Léon Gozlan, Etienne Arago, Germain Delavigne and Felix Pyat have distinguished themselves. The most prominent historical and political writers are Lamartine, Thiers, Michelet, Guizot, Louis Blanc and Thibaudeau; while Cousin and Comte are the founders of the new schools of philosophy. French oratory now occupies a higher position than ever before; its most illustrious names are Guizot, Thiers, Berryer, Lamartine, Odilon Barret and Victor Hugo.

German Literature.—The first period of German literature commenced with the reign of Charlemagne in the eighth century, and extends to the time of the Suabian emperors, at the close of the twelfth century. The first learned society was instituted by Alcuin, the greatest scholar of Charlemagne's time. In the succeeding period, Einhard, Rithard, and Lambert von Aschaffenburg distinguished themselves as historical and theological writers. About this time also originated those epic ballads and fragments which were afterwards collected under the title of the *Niebelungen-Lied*, or "Lay of the Nibelungen," and the "Song of Hildebrand." The Neibelungen-Leid, which has been called the German Iliad, received its present form about the year 1210. Its subject is the history of Siegfried, son of the King of the Netherlands, his marriage with Chriemhild, sister of Günther, King of the Burgundians, and the revenge of Brunhild, Queen of Ireland, who married Günther.

The second period terminates with the close of the fifteenth century. It includes the *Minnesingers*, or German Troubadours, who were the result of the intercourse of Germany with Italy and France, which made German scholars acquainted with the amatory literature of Provence. The most renowned Minnesingers were Wolfram von Eschenbach, who wrote *Parcival*, Walter von der Vogelweide, the most graceful and popular of all, and Heinrich von Ofterdingen. Otto von Friesingen achieved renown for his histories, which were written in Latin.

The third period, dating from the commencement of the fifteenth century, at which time the German language was fully developed and subjected to rule, extends to the present time. It has been subdivided by German critics into three parts, viz.: 1. to the commencement of the Thirty Years' War; 2. to Klopstock and Lessing; 3. to our own day. The progress of the Reformation in the fifteenth century operated very favorably upon German literature. Melancthon, Luther, Ulric von Hutten and the other leaders of the movement were also distinguished scholars. The celebrated Paracelsus, the naturalist, Gesner, the painter, Albert Dürer, and the astronomers Kepler and Copernicus, flourished also in the fifteenth century. The most distinguished poet of this period was Hans Sachs, the shoemaker poet of Nuremberg. He was the master of a school or guild of poetry, which was then considered as an elegant profession. In the number of his works he rivals Lope de Vega, as he is said to have written 6048, 208 of which were comedies and tragedies. He died in 1576. Martin Opitz, who marks the commencement of a new era in German poetry, was born in 1597. He first established a true rhythm in poetry, by measuring the length of the syllables, instead of merely counting them, as formerly. His principal poems are *Vesuvius*, *Judith*, and a number of lyrics. He was followed by Paul Flemming and Simon Dach, who wrote in the low German dialect. As prose writers of the seventeenth century, Puffendorf, a writer on jurisprudence and international law, Leibnitz, the distinguished philosopher and the Brothers Baumgarten, are most prominent. There is no great name in German literature, however, from Opitz till the middle of the last century, when Gellert, Gessner, Klopstock and Hagedorn were the inauguration of a new life. Under these authors, and others of less note, the language attained a richness of expression, a flexibility of style, and a harmony of modulation which it never possessed before. Gellert, born in 1715, is distinguished for his "Spiritual Songs and Odes," his letters and his romance of *The Swedish Countess*, which is the first domestic novel written in the German language. Gessner is best known through his idyls, in which he followed the classic models. Hagedorn, who died in 1754, wrote many poems; he is supposed to have exercised considerable influence on Klopstock in his earlier years. As prose writers, Forster, Mendelssohn, the philosopher, and Musäus, who made a collection of German legends and traditions, are worthy of note.

With Klopstock commenced the golden age of German literature, and the list of renowned names continues unbroken until the present time. Klopstock was born in 1724. In his odes and lyrical poems he struck out a new and bold path, casting aside the mechanical rules of the older schools of German poetry. His greatest work is the *Messias*, a sacred epic, which was commenced in 1745, and finished in 1771. Lessing, born in 1729, stands by the side of Klopstock as a poet, while he is also distinguished as a prose writer. He may be considered as the first successful German dramatist, his plays of *Emilia Galotti*, *Minna von Barnhelm*, and *Nathan the Wise*, still keeping their place on the stage. As a critical writer on all branches of the Fine Arts, he is also distinguished. Wieland follows next in the list of German classics. Born in 1733, he is the link between the age of Gellert and Klopstock, and that of Schiller and Goëthe. He died in 1813. His principal works are *The New Amadis*, which illustrates the triumph of spiritual over physical beauty, the heroic epic of *Oberon*, a romance of the middle ages, the drama of *Alceste*, the *History of the Abderites*, a satirical romance, besides many letters, satires, and criticisms on literature and art. Herder, his cotemporary, in addition to his fame as a poet, is celebrated for his philosophical and theological writings, and his *Spirit of Hebrew Poetry*. He died in 1803. At the commencement of this century, Wieland, Herder, Goethe, and Schiller, were gathered together at the Court of Weimar—the most illustrious congregation of poets since Shakspeare, Spenser, Ben Johnson, and Fletcher, met together in London. Goethe was born in 1749, and from his boyhood displayed a remarkable talent for literature, science, and art. His first romance, *The Sorrows of Werter*, produced a great sensation throughout all Europe. His tragedy of *Götz von Berlichingen*, written at the age of 22, established his fame as a poet. After his settlement at Weimar, in 1776, his works followed each other rapidly. He produced the tragedies of *Iphigenia*, *Egmont*, *Tasso*, and *Clavigo*, the pastoral epic of *Hermann und Dorothea*, the philosophical romances of *Wilhelm Meister* and *Die Wahlverwandschaften*, the *West-Ostliche Divan*, a collection of poems founded in his studies of Oriental litarature, and the first part of his greatest work, *Faust*. He also published narratives of travel in France and Italy, and *Wahrheit und Dichtung*, an autobiography of his life. His philosophic and scientific writings, especially his theory of color, are scarcely less celebrated than his literary works. He is equally a master in all departments of literature, and is generally acknowledged as the greatest author since Shakspeare. He died in 1832. Schiller, born in 1759, exercised scarcely less influence on German literature, than Goethe. His tragedy of the *Robbers* produced nearly as great a revolution as the *Sorrows of Werter*. On account of this and other works he was obliged to fly from his native Wurtemberg, and after many vicissitudes, settled in Weimar, with his great colleagues. After a brief but intense and laborious life, he died in 1805. After the *Robbers*, he wrote the following dramatic works: *Fiesco*, *Cabal and Love*, *Don Carlos*, *The Maid of Orleans*, *Marie Stuart*, *William Tell*, *The Bride of Messina*, and *Wallenstein*. The last is the greatest drama in the German language. His lyrical poems are unsurpassed. His principal prose works are the *History of the Netherlands* and *History of the Thirty Years' War*. This period, so glorious for German literature, produced also the poets, Bürger, author of *Lenore* and *The Wild Huntsman;* Count Stolberg; Voss, author of *Luise;* Salis and Matthisson, elegiac poets; Tiedge, author of *Urania;* and the hero Körner, the Tyrtæus of the wars of 1812 and 1813. The department of prose was filled by many distinguished writers of philosophy, history, and romance, some of whom are still living. Kant, who lived from 1724 to 1804, is the father of modern German philosophy, and exercised a great influence on all his cotemporaries. Schlegel, in the department of literary criticism, and Winckelmann, in that of art, are renowned names. Hegel and Fichte succeeded Kant as philosophers, and Alexander von Humboldt became the leader of a new and splendid company of writers on cosmical science. The name of Tieck heads the school of modern German romance. He was born in 1773, and early attracted attention by his *Bluebeard* and *Puss in Boots*. In addition to a great number of plays, romances, and poems, he produced, in conjunction with

Schlegel, a German translation of Shakspeare, which is the most remarkable work of its kind in all literature. Jean Paul Richter, the most original and peculiar of all German authors, was born in 1763, and died in 1825. His first work was a humorous and satirical production, entitled *The Greenlandic Lawsuit*, followed by "*Selections from the Devil's papers.*" His works are distinguished by a great knowledge of human nature, a bewildering richness of imagination, and a style so quaint and involved, as almost to form a separate dialect. His best works are *Titan*, *Hesperus*, *Die unsichtbare Loge*, and *Flower, Fruit and Thorn Pieces.* E. T. A. Hoffman is scarcely less original, in his romances, which have a wild, fantastic, and supernatural character Among other German authors, the brothers Grimm are celebrated for their *Kinder und Haus Mährchen*, the notorious Kotzebue for his plays, and Wolfgang Mentzel for his History of Germany and German literature.

Since the commencement of the present century Germany has been prolific of authors, but the limits of this sketch prohibit us from much more than the mere mention of their names. Baron de la Motte Fouqué is known as the author of *Undine*, one of the most purely poetical creations of fiction, *Sintram* and *Thiodolf, the Icelander.* Börne attained celebrity as a satirist, critic, and political writer. Uhland stands at the head of the modern generation of poets. His ballads, romances, and his epic of *Ludwig der Baier*, are among the best German poems of the day. After him rank Rückert, also renowned as an Oriental scholar; Hauff, a lyric poet, and author of the romance of *Lichtenstein;* Gustav Schwab, Justinus Kerner, author of the *Seeress of Prevorst;* Arndt, author of the *German Fatherland*, the national lyric; Anastasius Grün, (Count Auersperg,) author of the *Pfaff von Kahlenberg;* Nicholas Lenau, author of *Savonarola;* Ferdinand Freiligrath, a vigorous political poet; Heinrich Heine, author of many popular songs and ballads; Chamisso, who also wrote the romance of *Peter Schlemihl;* Gutzkow, distinguished as a dramatist; Halm, also a dramatist, and author of *Der Sohn der Wildniss;* and, as lyric poets, Herwegh, Geibel, and Beck. Among the distinguished prose writers are Schlosser, author of a Universal History; Neander, author of a History of the Church, and a Life of Christ; Prince Pückler-Muskau and the Countess Hahn-Hahn, critics and tourists; Zschokke, (a Swiss,) distinguished as a novelist, and Feuerbach; Schelling, as a philosopher; Strauss, author of a Life of Christ and head of the German "Rationalists:" Müller, as a historian, and Krummacher, a writer of fables and parables. As historians, Rotteck, Niebuhr, and Ranke, are among the most distinguished of the present century. One of the most popular living prose writers is Adalbert Stifter, whose *Studien* are unsurpassed for exquisite purity and picturesqueness of style.

Scandinavian Literature.—Under this head we have grouped the literature of the three nations of Scandinavian origin. —Sweden, Norway, and Denmark. The old Scandinavian Eddas, or hymns of gods and heroes, may be traced back to the seventh or eighth century. The earlier Edda, which was collected and arranged by Sämund in the year 1100, consists of legends of the gods, most of which were probably written in the eighth century. The latter Edda, collected by Snorre Sturleson in the first half of the thirteenth century, contains fragments of the songs of the Skalds who flourished in the ninth and tenth centuries, especially in the latter, when their genius reached its culmination in Norway and Iceland. Among the most renowned works of the Skalds were the *Eiriksmal*, the apotheosis of King Eric, who died in 952, and the *Hakonarmal*, describing the fall of Jarl Haco. A celebrated Skald was Egill Skalagrimsson, who wrote three epic poems, and two *drapas*, or elegiac poems. The power of the Skalds declined through the eleventh and twelfth centuries, and after the fourteenth, when the Christian element first began to appear in Icelandic poetry, wholly disappeared. Many sagas were written in prose, and the *Heimskringla* of Snorre Sturleson, who died in Iceland in 1238, contains the chronicles of Scandinavian history from its mythic period to the year 1177.

Previous to the establishment of the University of Upsala, in 1476, the only literature of Sweden was a few rhymed historic legends. The two centuries succeeding this period have left no great names, and few distinguished ones. Saxo-Grammaticus made a collection of legends in the fifteenth century; Olaus Magni wrote a history of the North in Latin; Messenius, who died in 1637, wrote comedies and a historical work entitled *Scandia illustrata;* Axel Oxenstierna, the celebrated minister, was also a theologist and patron of literature; Olof Rudbeck, a distinguished scholar, published in 1675 his *Atlantica*, wherein, from the study of the old Sagas, he endeavored to show that Sweden was the Atlantis of the ancients. George Stjernhjelm, who died in 1672, was the author of a poem called *Hercules*, whence he is named the father of Swedish poetry. Swedenborg, the most striking character in Northern literature, was born in 1688. After several years of travel in England and on the continent, he established himself in Sweden, where he devoted his attention to science, and produced a number of works on natural philosophy, mineralogy, zoology, and other kindred subjects. The close of his life was entirely occupied with his religious studies, and the production of his *Arcana Cœlestia*, which contains his revelations of the future life, and his theory of the spiritual universe. These writings gave rise to a new religious sect, the numbers of which, in the United States, are supposed to number about 6000 He professed to be visited by the Holy Spirit, and his works are considered by his disciples as equally inspired with those of the Apostles. He died in London in 1772. Dalin and Madame Nordenflycht, were the first noted poets of the last century. They were succeeded by a multitude of lyric and didactic poets; but Swedish poetry did not attain a high character before the commencement of the present century. Among the authors most worthy of note are Lidner, Bellman, and Thorild. A grand history of Sweden, by Professors Geijer, Fryxell, and Strumbolm, is nearly completed. The present century produced Atterbom and Dahlgren, poets of considerable celebrity, and Tegner, the first of Swedish poets, whose *Frithiof's Saga* has been translated into English, French, and German. Longfellow has translated his *Children of the Lord's Supper*. In the glow of his imagination, his fine artistic feeling and his wonderful command of rhythm, Tegner ranks among the first of modern poets. He died in 1850. Geijer and Runeberg are at the head of the living poets of Sweden. As writers of fiction, Count Sparré, author of *Adolf Findling*, Fredrika Bremer, whose fame as a painter of Swedish life, has extended over both hemispheres, and Madame Flygare-Carlen, author of the *Rose of Thistle Island*, have attained an honorable place. The most celebrated works of Miss Bremer are *The Neighbors*, *The Home*, and *Strife and Peace*.

There are few names in Danish literature before the last century. Ludwig von Holberg, born in 1685, was the first who achieved a permanent reputation as poet and historian. Towards the close of the last century, Denmark produced many distinguished scholars and men of science. Rafn and Finn Magnusen rescued the old Icelandic sagas from oblivion, and established the fact of the discovery of New England by Björne in the tenth century; Petersen became renowned as a classical scholar and critic; Oersted is a well-known name in science and philosophy; and Müller and Allen successfully labored in the department of history. Nearly all these authors first became known in the present century. At the head of Denmark's poets is Œhlenschläger, who died in 1850. His national tragedies, epics, and lyrics were written partly in German and partly in Danish. He is considered the originator of the artist-drama, of which his *Coreggio* is a masterpiece. Baggesen, who commenced his career in the last century, is one of the first Danish lyric poets. Heiberg devoted himself to vaudeville and the romantic drama, and Hauch to tragedy, in which he is justly distinguished. Hertz is known through his *King René's Daughter*, which has been successfully produced on the English stage. One of the most distinguished of modern Danish authors is Hans Christian Andersen, known alike as poet, novelist, and tourist. His romances of Danish life are the most characteristic of his works, though he is better known out of his native country by his *Improvisatore* and *The True Story of my Life*.

Russian Literature—The first fragments of Russian Literature belong to the tenth and eleventh centuries. They consist principally of rude songs and legends, the hero of which is Wladimir the Great, who first introduced Christianity into the country. Nestor a monk in the monastery of Kiev, who died in the year 1116, left behind him a collection of annals, beginning with 852, which throw much light on the early history of Russia. After the empire was freed from the Mongolian rule by Ivan I. in 1478, the progress of literature and the arts was more rapid. The first printing-press was established in Moscow in 1564, though the Academy in that city was not founded until a century later. Peter the Great devoted much attention to the Russian language and literature. At his command, the characters used in printing were greatly simplified and improved. The first Russian newspaper was printed in 1705, in this character.

From 1650 to 1750, Russia produced several authors, but principally among the clergy, and their works are dissertations on theology or lives of the saints. Tatitschev wrote a *History of Russia*, which still retains some value. The only poet of this period was Kantemir, son of the Hospodar of Moldavia, who entered the Russian service, devoted himself to study, and obtained much reputation from his satires. Towards the close of the last century, and especially during the reigns of Elizabeth and Catharine II. the establishment of universities and academies of science and art, contributed greatly to the development of the language and the encouragement of literature. The distinction between the old Slavic and modern Russian dialects is strongly exhibited in the works of Lomonosow, and the predominance of the latter was still further determined by Sumarakow, the first Russian dramatist, whose plays were performed on the stage. Cheraskow, who belongs to the last half of the eighteenth century, wrote a long epic poem on the Conquest of Kazan, and another on Wladimir the Great. He was considered the Homer of his time, but is now never read. Among his cotemporary poets were Prince Dolgoruki, who wrote philosophic odes and epistles, and Count Chvostow, the author of some of the best lyric and didactic poetry in the language.

The first Russian poet whose name was known beyond the borders of the empire, was Derzhavin, who was born at Kazan in 1743, and after filling important civil posts under the Empress Catharine, died in 1816. Many of his most inspired odes were addressed to his imperial patroness. His ode "To God," has been translated into nearly all languages, and a Chinese copy, printed in letters of gold, hangs upon the walls of the palace at Pekin. The prose writers of this period were Platon, Lewanda and Schtscherbatow, who wrote a History of Russia. Under Alexander I. in the commencement of the present century, Russian literature made rapid advances. Karamsin, who stood at the head of Russian authors during this period, first freed the popular style from the fetters of the classic school, and developed the native resources of the language. Prince Alexander Schakowski wrote many comedies and comic operas, and Zukowski, following in the path of Karamsin, produced some vigorous and glowing poetry. Count Puschkin, one of the most celebrated Russian authors, was born in 1799. His first poem published at the age of fourteen, attracted so much attention that he resolved to devote himself to literature. An "Ode to Freedom," however, procured him banishment to the south of Russia, where his best poems were written. His works are: *Russlan and Ljudmilla*, a romantic epic of the heroic age of Russia; the *Mountain Prisoner*, a story of life in the Caucusus; the *Fountains of Baktschissarai*, and *Boris Godunoff*, a dramatic poem. In his invention, the elegance of his diction and the richness of his fancy, Puschkin excels all other Russian authors. He was killed in a duel, in 1837. His cotemporary Baratynski, who stood nearest him in talent, died in 1844. Other poets of the present generation are Lermontow, Podolinski and Baron Delwig. Russian romance is not yet fairly developed. The first names in this department are Bestuzew, who suffered banishment in Siberia and met death in the Caucusus, where his best work, *Amaleth-Beg*, was written—and Bulgarin, author of *Demetrius* and *Mazeppa*. The only histories written in Russia are Histories of Russia. The best of these, which have been produced by the present generation of authors, are those of Ustrialow, Pogodin, Polewoi and Gen. Michailowski-Danilewski.

Polish Literature.—The Polish language has received a more thorough development and boasts a richer literature than any other language of Slavic origin. It first reached a finished and regular form in the sixteenth century, though a fragment of a hymn to the Virgin remains, which was supposed to have been written by St. Adalbert, in the fifteenth century. The first bloom of Polish literature happened during the reigns of Sigismund I. and Augustus, from 1507 to 1572. Michael Rey, the father of Polish poetry, was a bold, spirited satirist. He died in 1586, and was followed by the brothers Kochanowski, Miaskowski and Szymonowicz, who, for his Latin odes, was called the Latin Pindar. Bielski wrote the *Kronika*, a collection of Polish legends, and Górnicki, Secretary to Sigismund, a History of the Crown of Poland. Orzechowski, one of the most distinguished orators of his day, wrote in the Latin language, the *Annales Poloniæ*.

After the commencement of the seventeenth century, Polish letters declined, and as the kingdom came under the ascendency of the Jesuits, a corresponding change came over the character of the literature. Kochowski, who died in 1700, was historiographer to King John Sobieski, and accompanied him against the Turks. Opalinski, the Woiwode of Posen, published in 1652 his *Satyres*, a lively and characteristic work, and a number of Jesuit historians undertook histories of the country, in which few of them were successful.

Through the influence of French authors, Polish literature made another advance, at the close of the first half of the last century. The first poet who served to concentrate the scattered elements of Polish poetry, was Krasicki, who was born in 1734, and in 1767 was made Bishop of Ermeland. He wrote a mock-heroic poem, *Myszeis*, (The Mousead,) an epic entitled *Woyna Chocimska*, (The War of Chocim,) and many fables in verse. The most prominent of the later poets are Godebski, Wezyk, author of romances and dramas, Félinski, author of *Barbara Radziwill*, and Gen. Kropinski, who wrote *Ludgarda*. Tropinski, who died in 1825, was the author of many admirable lyrics and idyls, and a tragedy called *Judyta*. Niemcewicz, his contemporary, wrote the *Historical Lives of Poland*, a History of the reign of Sigismund III., and a romance : *Johann v. Tenczyn*. The university of Wilna, which in 1815 was the seat of Polish learning, witnessed a revolution in the character of the literature. Several young authors, with Mickiewicz at their head, determined to free themselves from the classic spirit of the language, and imitate the later English and German schools. From this time Polish fiction took a freer, bolder and more varied form. Mickiewicz, born in 1798, published his first volume of poetry in 1822. Banished to the interior of Russia, on account of political troubles, he wrote a series of sonnets which attracted the attention of Prince Galizin, under whose auspices his epic poem, *Konrad Wallenrod*, was published in 1828. He is now Professor of Slavic literature in the College of France. His polish epic of *Pan Tadeusz* first appeared in Paris, in 1834. Among his contemporary authors, the most noted are: Odyniec, author of the drama of *Izora;* Korsak, a lyric and elegiac poet; Garczynski, who wrote many fiery battle-songs; and Czajkowski, a noted writer of Slavic romances. The later prose writers of Poland are the historical Lelewel, and Count Plater. It is to be feared that Polish literature will expire with the present generation.

English Literature.—The English language, like other composite modern tongues, such as the French and Italian, passed through several phases before reaching its present form and character. During the prevalence of the Anglo-Saxon tongue, from the fifth century to the Norman conquest, England boasted several authors, whose names and works have in part descended to us. The venerable Bede, born in Northumberland, in 672, is distinguished for his scholarship. He left an Ecclesiastical history of the Angles, which forms the basis of early English history. The monk Cædmon, who flourished in the seventh century, wrote a paraphrase of Genesis and some fragments which are supposed to have given Milton the first idea of "Paradise Lost." The song of Beowulf, which belongs to the eighth century, is a spirited and stirring heroic. King Alfred's poems belong to the best specimens of Anglo-Saxon literature. The Norman conquest introduced the French language and the literature of the Trouvères, while the Anglo-Saxon was left to the peasants and thralls. Out of these elements, however, the English language was gradually formed, and under the reign of Edward III., in the fourteenth century, was made the language of the court. It then assumed a character which is intelligible to the educated English of the present day, and that period, therefore, may be considered as the first age of English literature.

The earliest English author is Chaucer, "the morning-star of English song," who was born in 1328, and produced his first poem, *The Court of Love*, in 1347. During his life he enjoyed the favor of Edward III. and his son, John of Gaunt. He filled various diplomatic stations, among others that of ambassador to Genoa. During his residence in Italy, he became familiar with the works of Dante, Boccaccio, and Petrarch, and is supposed to have visited the latter. He also wrote *Troilus and Cressida*, *The House of Fame*, and *The Canterbury Tales*, his most famous work, an imitation, in poetry, of the Decameron. He died in 1400. The first prose works in the English language were translations of the gospels and of some of the classics. Wickliffe, the Reformer, who first made an English version of the Bible, was a contemporary of Chaucer. Sir Thomas Wyatt, and Henry Howard, Earl of Surrey, who flourished under the reign of Henry VIII., in the beginning of the sixteenth century, are the next English poets of note. They wrote principally songs and odes. Surrey was beheaded on charge of treason in 1547.

The reign of Elizabeth, at the close of the sixteenth century, was the golden age of English literature. Shakspeare, Spenser, Raleigh, Sidney, Ben Jonson, Beaumont and Fletcher, formed a constellation of poets and dramatists, such as no other age or country ever produced. Spenser, born in 1553, became early associated with Sir Philip Sidney, to whom, in 1579, he dedicated his first work, the *Shepherd's Calendar*, a pastoral. From 1586 to 1598, he was sheriff of the county of Cork, in Ireland, and resided at Kilcolman Castle, where his greatest work, *The Faery Queen*, was composed This is an allegory in 12 books, written in stanza of his own invention, (modelled, however, on the Italian *ottava rima*,) and which now bears his name. He died in 1599. Sidney, who was born in 1554, is best known as the author of *Arcadia*, a pastoral romance, and the *Defence of Poetry*. He is the first writer who gave an elegant and correct form to English prose. Shakspeare, the greatest dramatic poet of any age, was born in 1564. He commenced his career by preparing for the stage the plays of some of his predecessors, and this fact has thrown some doubt about the authenticity of two or three of the plays included among his works. The order in which his own plays appeared has never been satisfactorily ascertained. The following, however, are known to have been written before 1598 : *The Two Gentlemen of Verona ; Love's Labor Lost; The Comedy of Errors; Midsummer Night's Dream ; Romeo and Juliet ; Merchant of Venice; Richard II.; Richard III.; Henry IV.*, and *King John*. *The Tempest*, which appeared in 1611, is believed to be his last dramatic work. He also wrote the poems of *Venus and Adonis*, and *The Rape of Lucrece*, a lyric called *The Passionate Pilgrim*, and a great number of sonnets, some of which are the finest in the language. He died in 1616. Ben Jonson was born in 1574, and published his first dramatic work, the comedy of *Every Man in his Humor*, in 1596. In addition to other comedies, the best of which are *Volpone, the Fox*, and *The Alchymist*, he wrote many exquisite songs and madrigals. Sir Walter Raleigh is more distinguished as a gallant knight and daring adventurer than as an author, yet his lyrics and his *History of the World*, written during twelve years' imprisonment in the Tower, give him full claim to the latter title. He was born in 1552 and was beheaded by order of James I. in 1617. Beaumont and Fletcher, contemporaries and in some degree imitators of Shakspeare, deserve the next place after him, among the dramatists of that period. Beaumont is supposed to have been the inventive genius of their plays, and Fletcher to have supplied the wit and fancy. The Faithful Shepherdess is the work of Fletcher alone. Many dramatists flourished during this and the succeeding generation, whose works are now but little read, but who would have attained eminence but for the greater lights with which they are eclipsed. The most noted of them are Marlowe, Marston, Chapman, Decker, Webster, Ford and Massinger.

Between Shakspeare and Milton, the only name which appears in English literature is Cowley, the author of the *Davideis*, a forgotten epic. Milton was borne in 1608, and in his early boyhood exhibited the genius which afterwards made him the first English poet, and one of the great masters of English prose. His *Hymn on the Nativity*, was written in his twenty-first, and his mask of *Comus*, in his twenty-third year. *L'Allegro, Il Penseroso*, and *Lycidas* soon afterwards appeared. After his return from Italy, he devoted his attention to theology and politics. His treatise on *Marriage* was published in 1643, his *Areopagitica* in 1644, and his famous reply to Salmasius in 1651. In the following year he lost his sight, and was obliged to retire from public service. His *Paradise Lost* appeared in 1665, and was followed by *Paradise Regained* in 1671, and *Samson Agonistes*. He died in 1674. Dryden, who, born in 1631, was known as a poet during Milton's life, introduced a new school of poetry—the narrative and didactic. His first noted poem, the *Annus Mirabilis*, was produced in 1666, his satire of *Absalom and Achitophel* in 1681, and shortly afterwards his *Hind and Panther*, a religious satire. He also wrote several rhymed tragedies and an Essay on *Dramatic Poesy*. Defoe, born in 1663, wrote the world-renowned narrative of *Robinson Crusoe*, which was first published in 1719. The seventeenth century was also an important epoch for

English philosophical literature. Lord Bacon, born in 1561, published his *De dignitate et augmentis Scientarum* in 1605, and his celebrated *Novum Organum* in 1620. These, although written in Latin, are the most important philosophical works which have ever emanated from an English author. Hobbes, a writer on politics, jurisprudence and moral philosophy, died in 1679. Locke, born in 1632, first published his *Essay on the Human Understanding*, in 1690.

The commencement of the last century brings us to a group of authors of very different character. The influence of French literature began to be felt, and the characteristics of the English writers of this period are elegance and grace. This is properly the age of English prose, which was enriched, successively, by Addison, Horace Walpole, Swift, Sterne, Richardson, Smollett, Fielding, Hume, Gibbon, Chesterfield, and Robertson. The first poet who rose to eminence in the last century, was Pope, who was born in 1688, and published his *Essay on Criticism* in 1711. His most celebrated poetical works are the *Rape of the Lock*, the *Essay on Man*, and *The Dunciad*. Thomson, author of *The Seasons* and the *Castle of Indolence*, lived and died in the first half of the century. Gay, a contemporary poet, is distinguished for his Fables. Gray ranks as one of the finest lyric poets of England. The few odes he has left, and his *Elegy in a Country Churchyard*, belong to the classics of the language. Goldsmith was born in 1728, and died in 1774. His poems of *The Traveller*, and *The Deserted Village*, and his romance of the *Vicar of Wakefield*, will live as long as his native tongue. Cowper closes the list of the poets of the last century. He died in 1800, after a life darkened by religious melancholy. His *Task*, *Table-talk*, and ballad of *John Gilpin*, are his best poetical works. Returning to the prose writers, Addison is first in point of time, having been born in 1672. His best works are his essays, contributed to *The Spectator*, which he established in 1711, in conjunction with his friend Steele. His English has rarely been excelled for purity and elegance. Chesterfield, Lady Montague, and Horace Walpole, are distinguished as epistolary writers. Dean Swift, born in 1667, was a politician and satirist, but is now best known by his *Tale of a Tub*, published in 1704, and *Gulliver's Travels*, in 1726. Sterne, in his *Tristram Shandy* and *The Sentimental Journey*, displayed a droll mingling of wit and pathos, in a style exceedingly lively and flexible. Richardson, one of the first English romance-writers, was born in 1689. His principal novels, which are of immense length, are *Pamela, Clarissa Harlowe*, and *Sir Charles Grandison*. Smollett, his successor, published his *Roderick Random*, in 1748, and *Humphrey Clinker*, his last work, in 1771. Hume, in addition to political and philosophical works, wrote the *History of England*, from the invasion of Cæsar to the rebellion of 1688, which was published in 1673–4. Smollett wrote four volumes in continuation of the history. Gibbon, born in 1737, completed, after twenty years' labor, his *History of the Decline and Fall of the R[illegible]an Empire*, which appeared from 1782 to 1788. Robertson, the contemporary of Gibbon, published his *History of Scotland* in 1759, and his *History of the Reign of Charles V.* in 1769. Dr. Johnson, whose *Rasselas*, *Lives of the Poets*, and contributions to *The Rambler*, exercised such a salutary influence on the popular taste of his time, died in 1784. His *Dictionary of the English Language*, was first published in 1755. Edmund Burke, one of the most finished and powerful of English orators, published, in 1756, his *Essay on the Sublime and Beautiful*, which is a model of philosophical writing. He died in 1797.

With the present century commenced a new era in English literature. The reign of the drama and the epic were over; the reign of romance, in both prose and poetry, and the expression of a higher and more subtle range of imagination, now commenced. The language lost something, perhaps, of its classic polish and massive strength, but became more free and flowing, more varied in style, and richer in epithet. The authors in whom this change is first apparent, are Coleridge and Wordsworth, in poetry, and Scott in prose. Nearly coeval with the two former, but different in character, were Byron and Moore; the latter are the poets of passion, the former of imagination. Scott, in his Waverley novels, first developed the neglected wealth of English romance. Burns, although his best songs are in the Scottish dialect, stands at the head of all English song-writers. Campbell, in the true lyric inspiration of his poems, is classed with Gray. Rogers and Southey can scarcely be ranked among those poets who assisted in developing the later English literature. The former imitates the old models; the latter, more daring in his forms of verse, and more splendid in his imagination, has never been able to touch the popular heart. Coleridge's prose works contain probably the most important contributions to English philosophical literature, since the time of Bacon. The department of history has been amply filled by Scott, Alison, author of a *History of Europe*, Gillies and Grote, celebrated for their *Histories of Greece*, Napier, in his *History of the Peninsular War*, Hallam, in his *History of the Middle Ages*, and Macaulay in his *History of England*. Most of these writers are now (1851) living. Those who have died since the beginning of the century, are Keats, in 1820; Shelley, in 1822; Byron, in 1824; Scott, in 1832; Coleridge, in 1834; Southey, in 1843; Campbell, in 1844; Thomas Hood, in 1848; and Wordsworth, in 1850. Rogers and Moore are still living, at an advanced age; Leigh Hunt, the author of *The Rimini*, survives his friends, Shelley and Keats. The field of historical romance, opened by Sir Walter Scott, has been successfully followed by Sir Edward Bulwer Lytton and G. P. R. James. As novelists of English life and society, under all its aspects, Dickens and Thackeray—and of late years, Miss Bronte, author of *Shirley* and *Jane Eyre*—stand preëminent. As essayists and critics, the names of Lords Jeffrey and Brougham, Sidney Smith, Macaulay, Professor Wilson, De Quincey, Carlyle and Stevens, surpass even the group who produced *The Tatler* and the *Spectator*. Carlyle, in his *Sartor Resartus*, *Past and Present*, and *Heroes and Hero-Worship*, has made use of an idiom of his own—a broken, involved, Germanesque diction, which resembles that of no other English author. The most prominent living English poets, are Thomas Moore, Leigh Hunt, Rogers, Alfred Tennyson, the present poet-laureate, Milnes, Barry Cornwall, Robert Browning, a lyric and dramatic poet, his wife, Elizabeth Barrett Browning, probably the most impassioned and imaginative of English female authors, Walter Savage Landor, Mary Howitt, R. H. Horne, author of *Orion*, Croly, Philip James Bailey, author of *Festus*, and T. N. Talfourd, author of the tragedy of *Ion*. As prose writers, there still remain Hallam, Macaulay, Grote, Professor Wilson, Brougham, Bulwer, Dickens, Thackeray, Miss Bronte, Miss Martineau, James, Howitt, Stevens, and a number of others. All English works of any merit are now immediately reprinted in this country, and the English literature of the present century is as familiar to most Americans as their own.

American Literature.—The literature of the United States belongs almost exclusively to the present century. The language being that of England, and all the treasures of English literature the common inheritance of our countrymen, whatever American authors produce is necessarily measured by the English standard. The language comes to us finished and matured, while the means of intellectual cultivation—until a comparatively recent period—have been limited, and our abundant stores of legend and history are still too fresh to be made available for the purposes of poetry and fiction. The present generation, however, has witnessed the growth of a national literature, if not peculiarly American in language, at least in style and the materials it has chosen. Our most eminent poets and prose writers are still living, and almost every year adds to the list of younger authors, and to the regard in which American literature is held abroad.

The seventeenth century boasted two or three authors, but none, we believe, native to the soil. Mrs. Anne Bradstreet, wife of a governor of Massachusetts, published in 1640, a poem on the Four Elements, smoothly versified, but of little poetical merit. Cotton Mather, born in 1663, is almost the only prose writer worthy of note. His "Magnalia" contains some valuable historical matter. The last century produced some distinguished prose writers and some accomplished versifiers, though no poet in the true sense of the title. Franklin, born in 1706, was master of a singularly clear, compact, and vigorous style. Jonathan Edwards, who flourished during the last century, wrote a celebrated treatise on the Will, which is one of the first metaphysical works in the language. The Revolutionary struggle, and the circumstances which preceded and succeeded it, produced a number of bold and brilliant writers and speakers, among whom were Jefferson, Hamilton, the Adamses, Richard Henry Lee, and Patrick Henry. The diplomatic correspondence of the Revolution has rarely been surpassed. Philip Freneau, who has been called the first American poet, wrote many patriotic songs, which were sung during the struggle, but none have retained their original vitality. Trumbull was the author of a Hudibrastic poem entitled McFingal, in which the Tories were held up to ridicule; the first part was published in 1775. Joel Barlow, who aspired to the rank of an epic poet, published in 1787, his "Vision of Columbus," which, in 1808, was expanded into the "Columbiad," and printed in what was then a style of unusual magnificence.

Dana, Bryant, Washington Irving, Cooper, Paulding, and Everett, all born towards the close of the last century, are still living. Dana may be considered as the first genuine poet the United States has produced. His "Buccaneer" is a picturesque and striking poem, founded on a legend of the pirates who formerly frequented the American coast. Irving's "Knickerbocker's History of New York" appeared in 1809, and instantly gave him a position, as a writer of the purest style and of exquisite humor and fancy. His latest production, a Biography of Goldsmith, to whom he has been compared, was published in 1849. Many of his works—among them the "Sketch Book," "Bracebridge Hall," "The Alhambra," and the "Life of Columbus," were first published in England, where he lived many years. Cooper's first essay in literature was a novel of society entitled "Precaution," but he subsequently confined himself to the two fields in which he has earned his best fame—the forest and the ocean. His most successful novels are: "The Spy," the "Pioneers," the "Deerslayer," the "Pilot," and the "Pathfinder." Bryant first attracted noticed by his poem of "Thanatopsis," written in his nineteenth year. His first volume, "The Ages," was published in 1825. The most distinguished authors who have died since the commencement of the century are Dr. Channing, whose essays, criticisms, and moral, religious, and political writings have won him much celebrity as a prose writer; William Wirt, author of the "British Spy," a collection of letters written in a chaste and elegant style; Charles Brockden Brown, the earliest American novelist, author of "Wieland;" Richard Henry Wilde, author of a "Life of Tasso;" Chief Justice Marshall, who compiled a voluminous "Life of Washington;" Henry Wheaton, author of standard works on law and political economy; Judge Story, author of several celebrated legal works; Edgar A. Poe, a most original and strongly marked character, who wrote the poem of "The Raven," and a number of weird and fantastic prose stories; Margaret Fuller, a lady of remarkable acquirements, who has left behind her much admirable descriptive and critical writing; and of poets of lesser note, Robert C. Sands, author of "Yamoyden;" J. G. C. Brainard; Pinckney, a very graceful song-writer; P. P. Cooke, author of the "Froissart Ballads;" and Mrs. Osgood, a female writer, who gave evidence of possessing a brilliant and inexhaustible fancy. The most eminent living authors, many of whom are still young, and have scarcely reached the maturity of their powers, are Irving, Cooper, Bryant, Dana, Paulding, author of a number of humorous stories; Miss Sedgwick, who chose for the objects of her fictions the early history of New England; N. P. Willis, whose poems, stories, and records of travels in Europe and the East, are unsurpassed in point and brilliancy; Longfellow, the most popular poet of the country; Ralph Waldo Emerson, the essayist and poet, and the founder of a new school of philosophy; Nathaniel Hawthorne, author of the "Scarlet Letter" and the "House of the Seven Gables;" E. P. Whipple, an essayist and critic; W. Gilmore Simms, J. P. Kennedy, and Dr. Bird, all of whom have written novels relating to the early history of the South; Halleck, the author of the magnificent poem of Marco Bozzaris; Prescott, the historian, author of the "Conquest of Mexico," "Conquest of Peru," and "Lives of Ferdinand and Isabella;" Bancroft, who is now engaged in publishing a complete history of the United States; Herman Melville, author of "Typee," "Omoo," and "Whitejacket;" Mrs. Kirkland, and C. F. Hoffman, both of whom have admirably sketched the wild life of the West; Whittier, a fiery and earnest poet, who strikes unhesitatingly at what he deems oppression; Lowell, one of the youngest and most encouraging of American poets; and Donald C. Mitchell, who has lately achieved an honorable reputation as a prose writer. It is unnecessary to carry the enumeration further, since all the remaining authors are young, and every day adds something to their intellectual stature and relative positions.

LITHOG'RAPHY, the art of tracing letters, figures, or other designs on stone, and of transferring them to paper by impression; an art invented in 1793 by A. Sennefelder at Munich, in Bavaria. The principles upon which this art is founded, are—1. The quality which a compact granular limestone has of imbibing grease or moisture; and 2. The decided antipathy of grease and water for each other. A drawing being made upon the stone with an ink or crayon of a greasy composition, is washed over with water, which sinks into all parts of the stone not defended by the drawing. A cylindrical roller, charged with printing ink is then passed all over the stone, and the drawing receives the ink, whilst the water defends the other parts of the stone from it on account of its greasy nature. Impressions of the drawing may then be taken upon paper, by means of a lithographic press. The most convenient and useful way, however, of proceeding, is to write with proper ink on a prepared paper, and then transfer the writing to the stone by passing it through the press.

LIT'URGY, an office at Athens, by which persons of considerable property were bound to perform certain public duties, or supply the commonwealth with necessaries at their own expense. The persons on whom this office was imposed were usually among the richest inhabitants; and if any one selected to fill it could find another more wealthy than himself who was exempt from public duty, he could insist on being released from his charge, which then devolved on the party denounced. This obnoxious institution was abolished on the proposition of Demosthenes. It is from this term that the English *liturgy*, in ecclesiastical meaning, has been derived; the sense having been contracted from public *ministry* or service in general to the ceremonies of religious worship.—LITURGY, the ritual according to which the religious services of a church are performed. In the writings of the ancients, the name is restricted to the service of the Eucharist, which afterwards came to be distinguished in the Western church by the term of *missa*, or mass. There still exist in Greek, Latin, and some Oriental languages, various rituals by which the Eucharist was celebrated in very early ages. Some have supposed that all these may be referred to one original liturgy, which may have been universally adopted in the primitive church. Palmer, the latest English writer on this subject, conceives that the number of original liturgies may be reduced to four, but not lower. These he entitles the great Oriental liturgy, the Alexandrian, the Roman, and the Gallican; each of which was extensively used from the Apostolic age in the quarters from which he assigns them their names, and became the parents of many other rituals, such as were used, with constantly diverging variations, in the different patriarchates of the empire. The earliest period at which any liturgical forms were consigned to writing is the end of the third or beginning of the fourth century; at least the liturgy called of St. Basil can be traced as high as the latter period. This practice, also, seems frequently to have been applied only to certain parts of the service. We find, therefore, great differences in the MSS. which now exist; and it becomes very difficult to ascertain what the contents of the primitive rituals were, and trace the periods at which many rites and ceremonies have been introduced into the service. The liturgy of the Church of England is a liturgy in the wider and more usual acceptation of the term, comprehending the whole of the various services used on ordinary and extraordinary occasions throughout the year.

LIV'ERY, a suit of clothes made of different colors and trimmings by which noblemen and gentlemen have their servants distinguished; supposed to have originated in the practice followed by cavaliers at tournaments, who used to distinguish themselves by wearing the livery or badge of their mistresses. Persons of distinction formerly gave liveries to persons unconnected with their own household or family, to engage them in their quarrels for the time being. The Romish church has also *liveries* for confessors, virgins, apostles, martyrs, penitents, &c. A particular dress or garb, appropriate or peculiar to particular times or things; as, the *livery* of May; the *livery* of autumn. *Livery of seisin*, in law, signifies delivering the possession of lands, &c. to him who has a right to them.

LIV'ERYMAN, a freeman of the city of London, admitted member of some one of the city companies, by which he enjoys certain powers and privileges. From among their number are elected the common council, sheriff, and other superior officers of the city.

LLOYD'S LIST, a London periodical publication, in which the shipping news received at Lloyd's coffee-house is published. On account of the extensive information which it contains, it is of great importance to merchants. *Lloyd's Coffee-house* has long been celebrated as the resort of eminent merchants, under-writers, merchants, insurance brokers, &c., and the books kept there are replete with valuable maritime intelligence.

LO'CUM TE'NENS, a deputy or

substitute; one who supplies the place of another, or executes his office.

LOCUS IN QUO, in law, the place where anything is alleged to be done in pleadings, &c.—*Locus partitus*, a division made between two towns or counties, to make trial where the land or place in question lies.

LODGE, in architecture, a small house situated in a park or domain, subordinate to the mansion; also, the cottage situate at the gate of the avenue that leads to the mansion.

LODG'MENT, in military affairs, is a work raised with earth, gabions, fascines, &c., to cover the besiegers from the enemy's fire, and to prevent their losing a place which they have gained, and are resolved, if possible, to keep.

LOG'IC, various definitions have been given of logic, some including too little, and others too much. Logic has been called the Art of Reasoning; this definition has been properly amended by calling it the Science as well as the Art of Reasoning: meaning by the former, the analysis of the mental process which takes place whenever we reason; and, by the latter, the rules grounded upon that analysis for conducting the process correctly. But the word Reasoning, again, is ambiguously used. In one of its acceptations it means syllogizing, or that mode of inference which may be called concluding from generals to particulars. The better definition of this term, however, and that which accords more with the general usage of the English language, makes it signify the inferring of any assertion from assertions already admitted. But the province of logic is wider than reasoning even in this extensive sense, for it undoubtedly includes, for instance, precision of language and accuracy of classification; in other words, definition and division. These various operations might be brought within the compass of the science, by defining logic as the science which treats of the operations of the human understanding in the pursuit of truth. This definition, however, includes too much. Truths are known to us in two ways: some are known directly and of themselves; some through the medium of other truths. It is only with the latter that logic has to do. Logic is not the science of belief, but the science of proof. But as the far greatest portion of our knowledge, whether of general truths, or of particular facts, is avowedly matter of inference, our definition of logic is in danger of including the whole field of knowledge; unless we qualify it by some further limitation, showing where the domain of the other arts and sciences, and of common prudence ends, and that of logic begins. The distinction is, that the science or knowledge of the particular subject matter furnishes the evidence, while logic furnishes the principles and rules of the estimation of evidence: logic points out what relations must subsist between data, and whatever can be concluded from them. "Logic, then, is the science of the operations of the understanding which are subservient to the estimation of evidence: both the process itself of proceeding from known truths to unknown, and all intellectual operations auxiliary to this." Logic was highly valued, perhaps overvalued, among the ancient philosophers. The Stoics in particular were celebrated for their application of its principles to their own favorite metaphysical discussions. From the abuse of logical knowledge arose the celebrated fallacies of the Sophists. Zeno is called the father of logic or dialectics; but it was then treated with particular reference to the art of disputation, and soon degenerated into the minister of sophistry. It is to Aristotle, however, that the science owes, not only its first exposition, but its complete development. His logical writings were called *Organon* in later ages, and for almost two thousand years after him maintained authority in the schools of the philosophers, and in the middle ages it became the foundation of the scholastic philosophy, which was little better than a revival under another form, of the logic of the Athenian Sophists.

LOGIS'TÆ, in antiquity, Athenian magistrates, ten in number, whose office it was to receive and pass the accounts of magistrates when they went out of office.

LOGOG'RAPHY, a system of taking down the words of an orator without having recourse to short-hand, which was put in practice during the French revolution. Twelve or fourteen reporters were seated round a table. Each had a long slip of paper, numbered. The writer of No. 1 took down the first three or four words, and as soon as they were spoken gave notice to his neighbor by touching his elbow, or some other sign; No. 2 passed the sign to No 3, and so on, until the first line of each slip was filled; No. 1 then began the second line: thus all the 12 or 14 slips, when filled, being arranged parallel to each other, formed a single page. This mode required great attention and quickness, and was not found to answer well in practice. It was introduced in the National Assembly in October, 1790, the expenses being paid by the civil list; and continued until the 10th of August, 1792, when Louis XVI. and his family, taking refuge from insurrection in the assembly, occupied the box of the logographe. After that time it was not used.—*Logography* is also used to denote a method of printing in which whole words in type are used instead of single letters. This method was at one time introduced into the printing of a daily London newspaper; but after a short trial was abandoned as inconvenient.

LOG'OGRIPH, a kind of riddle, which consists in some allusion or mutilation of words, being of a middle nature between an enigma and a rebus. The word is used by Ben Jonson.

LOK, in Northern mythology, the name of a malevolent deity; corresponding to the Ahriman of the Persians, who is represented to be at war with both gods and men, and originating all the evil with which the universe is desolated. In the *Edda* (the great poem of the Norwegian nations) he is described as the great serpent which encircles the earth (supposed to be emblematical of sin or corruption,) and as having given birth to Hela, or Death, the queen of the infernal regions.

LOL'LARDS, a class of persons in Germany and the Netherlands, who professed, in the 14th century, to undertake spiritual offices in behalf of the sick and dead, and succeeded in attracting the attention and love of the mass of the people when they were, in a great measure, alienated from the secular and regular clergy by their general indifference and neglect. The origin of the name has been much disputed; but the inquiries of Mosheim seem to lead to the result that it is compounded of the German words *lallen* (identical with the *lallare* of the Romans, and the *lull* of our own language, signifying to sing in a murmuring strain) and *hard*, a common affix, as in the somewhat similar word *beghard*. A Lollard, therefore, meant one in the habit of singing to the praise of God, or funeral dirges and the like, as was the custom of the early professors of this holy manner of life. The Lollards, however, were accused—probably through the envy and spite of the mendicant friars and others whose neglected duties they so zealously performed—of holding many heretical opinions. It is not impossible that there might have been some degree of enthusiasm mixed up with so ardent and unworldly a devotion; but the charges of violent reforming views, still more those of practical vice, appear to rest upon no authentic grounds. In process of time the term was applied by the partisans of the church to the heretics and schismatics of the day generally; and the followers of Wicliffe in England are frequently stigmatized under the name of Lollards.

LOM'BARD, a term anciently used in England for a banker or money-lender. The name is derived from the Italian merchants, the great usurers or money-lenders of the middle ages, principally from the cities of Lombardy, who are said to have settled in London in the middle of the 13th century, and to have taken up their residence in a street in the city which still bears their name.

LONGEV'ITY, length or duration of life, generally designating great length of life. Lord Bacon observes, that the succession of ages, and of the generation of men seems no way to shorten the length of human life, since the age of man from the time of Moses to the present has stood at about eighty years, without gradually declining, as one might have expected; but doubtless there are times wherein men live to a longer or shorter age in every conntry; and it has been remarked that those generally prove longest-lived who use a simple diet, and take most bodily exercise; and shortest-lived who indulge in luxury and ease; but these things have their changes and revolutions, whilst the succession of mankind holds on uninterrupted in its course. There are, however, several essential circumstances which must combine to give any individual a chance of exceeding the usual period assigned to human existence. These may be comprehended under the following heads: a proper configuration of body; being born of healthy parents; living in a healthy climate and good atmosphere; having the command of a sufficient supply of food; constant exercise; a due regulation of sleep; a state of marriage; and due command of the passions and temper.

LOOP'HOLES, in fortification, apertures formerly made in the battlements, or in the walls of fortified places, for discharging arrows and javelins against the assailants. Since the invention of gunpowder and the substitution of cannon for such missiles, loopholes have necessarily been discontinued in the construction of fortresses, the assailants of which are now sought to be driven back by guns fired through apertures of a different character, designated *embrasures*, which see.

LORA'RIUS, in antiquity, one who stimulated the gladiators to continue the fight by exercising the scourge upon them. Also, a slave who bound and scourged others at his master's pleasure.

LORD, a title of courtesy given to all British and Irish noblemen, from the *baron* upwards; to the eldest sons of earls; to all the sons of marquesses and dukes; and, as an honorary title, to certain official characters; as the *lord* mayor of London, the *lord* chamberlain of the king's household, the *lord* chancellor, the *lord* chief justice, &c. *Lord* is also a general term, equivalent with *peer*.—*Lord*, in law, one who possesses a *fee* or *manor*. This is the primitive meaning of the word; and it was in right of their feofs that *lords* came to sit in parliament.—In Scripture, a name for the Supreme Being. When LORD, in the Old Testament, is printed in capitals, it is the translation of the Hebrew word for JEHOVAH, and might with great propriety be so rendered. It is also applied to Christ, to the Holy Spirit, to kings, and to prophets.

LORDS, HOUSE OF, is composed of the five orders of nobility, viz.—dukes, marquesses, earls, viscounts, and barons, who have attained the age of 21 years, and labor under no disqualification; of the 16 representative peers of Scotland; of the 28 representative peers of Ireland; of 2 English archbishops and 24 bishops, and 4 representative Irish bishops.

LORD'S SUPPER, a ceremony among Christians by which they commemorate the death of Christ, and make at the same time a profession of their faith. The blessed founder of our religion instituted this rite when he took his last meal with his disciples; breaking the bread, after the oriental manner, as a fitting symbol of his body, which was soon to be broken, while the wine was significant of that blood which was about to be shed.

LORI'CA, in Roman antiquity, a cuirass, a brigandine, or coat of mail, which was made of leather, and set with plates of various forms, or rings like a chain.

LOTOPH'AGI, a name given to a people of ancient Africa who inhabited the Regio Syrtica, so called from the lotus berry forming their principal food. They were represented as a mild, hospitable race of men. The food with which they were nourished, among other peculiar qualities, is said to have had the power of obliterating all remembrance of one's native country.

LOT'TERY, a game of hazard in which small sums are ventured for the chance of obtaining a larger value, either in money or other articles. In general, lotteries consist of a certain number of tickets drawn at the same time with a corresponding number of blanks and prizes, by which the fate of the tickets is determined. This species of gaming has been resorted to at different periods by most of the European governments, as a means of raising money for public purposes. Both state and private lotteries were entirely abolished in England in 1823, on the ground that they tended to foster a spirit of gambling in the great body of the people, and gave rise to many delusive and fraudulent schemes. In 1836 they were suppressed in France. They have been prohibited in most of the United States, but still exist in several of the states of Germany.

LOUIS-D'OR, a French gold coin, which received its name from Louis XIII., who first coined it in 1631. The value of the old *Louis-d'or* was equal to 24 francs; the new *Louis* is of the value of 20 francs.

LOU'IS, ST., KNIGHTS OF, the name of a military order in France instituted by Louis XIV. in 1693.

LOU'VRE, one of the most ancient palaces of France. It existed in the time of Dagobert as a hunting seat, the woods then extending all over the actual site of the northern portion of Paris down to the banks of the Seine. The origin of its name has not been satisfactorily ascertained. It was formed into a stronghold by Philip Augustus, who surrounded it with towers and fosses, and converted it into a state prison for confining the refractory vassals of the crown. It was then without the walls of Paris; but, on their extension in the latter part of the 14th century, it was included within their circuit. Charles V. made additions to it. That part of the palace now called the *Vieux Louvre* was commenced under the reign of Francis I., after the designs of Pierre L'Escot, abbot of Clugny. When Charles IX resided in the Louvre, he began the long gallery which connects it with the Tuilleries, and in which is now deposited the celebrated collection of pictures. It was finished under Henry IV. Louis XIV., from the designs of Lemercier, erected the peristyle which forms the entrance to the Vieux Louvre from the side of the Tuilleries. That monarch also gave a beginning to the remainder of the present modern edifice, from the designs of Claude Perrault. The edifice has never been finished; though, under the reigns of succeeding monarchs, and especially during that of Napoleon, it has slowly advanced towards completion. The eastern front, though not finished even now, exhibits a façade of surpassing beauty—perhaps, in its kind, never equalled. The quadrangle of the Louvre is a perfect square on the plan. Three of its sides were from the designs of Perrault, above mentioned. Besides the gallery above adverted to, which contains some of the finest pictures in the world, the Louvre contains a museum of sculpture, antiquities, and other specimens of art, equally valuable.

LOVE, an affection of the mind excited by beauty and worth of any kind, or by the qualities of an object which communicate pleasure, sensual or intellectual. It is opposed to hatred. Love between the sexes, is a compound affection, consisting of esteem, benevolence, and animal desire. Love is excited by pleasing qualities of any kind, as by kindness, benevolence, charity, and by the qualities which render social intercourse agreeable. In the latter case, love is ardent friendship, or a strong attachment springing from good-will and esteem, and the pleasure derived from the company, civilities, and kindnesses of others. Between certain natural relatives, love seems to be in some cases instinctive. Such is the love of a mother for her child, which manifests itself toward an infant, before any particular qualities in the child are unfolded. This affection is apparently as strong in irrational animals as in human beings. We speak of the love of amusement, the love of books, the love of money, and the love of whatever contributes to our pleasure or supposed profit. The love of God is the first duty of man, and this springs from just views of his attributes or excellencies of his character, which afford the highest delight to the pious heart. Esteem and reverence constitute ingredients in this affection, and a fear of offending him is its inseparable effect.

LU'DI, in antiquity, the shows or public exhibitions which were made among the Greeks and Romans, for the display of skill and the entertainment of the people.

LUKE, or *Gospel of St. Luke*, a canonical book of the New Testament, distinguished for fulness, accuracy, and traces of extensive information. Some think it was properly St. Paul's gospel, and when that apostle speaks of his gospel, he means what is called St. Luke's. Irenæus says, that St. Luke digested into writing what St. Paul preached to the gentiles; and Gregory Nazianzen tells us, that St. Luke wrote with the assistance of St. Paul.

LU'NACY, a species of insanity or madness, supposed to be influenced by the moon, or periodical in the month. In law, strictly, the condition of an insane person who has lucid intervals; but, for convenience, the term is commonly used as embracing the condition of all those who are under certain legal disabilities on account of mental deficiency; such as idiots, fatuous persons, &c.; in short, all who are of unsound mind. By the law of England, the sovereign has the custody of lunatics. This is, in practice, delegated to the keeper of the great seal, to whom applications for a commission of lunacy are directed.

LUPERCA'LIA, a Roman festival in honor of Pan, celebrated in February; when the Luperci ran up and down the city naked, having only a girdle of goat's skin round their waist, and thongs of the same in their hands, with which they struck those they met, particularly married women, who were thence supposed to be rendered prolific. The name is derived from lupus, *a wolf;* because Pan protected cattle from that animal. The indecencies and excesses attending the processions of the Lupercals, which had degenerated from high religious rites to vulgar superstitions, provoked the indignation of Christians in the 4th and 5th centuries.

LUPER'CI, the Roman priests of Pan, and most ancient religious order in the state, having been instituted, according to tradition, by Evander, king of Pallantium, a town that occupied the Palatine Hill before Rome was built. There were three companies of them; viz. the Fabiani, Quintiliani, and Julii—the last of whom were founded in honor of Julius Cæsar.

LU'SIAD, the name given to the great epic poem of Portugal, written by Camoens, and published in 1571. The subject of this poem is the establishment of the Portuguese empire in India; but whatever of chivalrous, great, beautiful, or noble, could be gathered from the traditions of his country, has been interwoven into the story. Among all the heroic poets, either of ancient or modern times, there has never, since Homer, been any one so intensely national, or so loved or honored by his countrymen, as Camoens. It seems as if the national feelings of the Portuguese had centered and reposed themselves in the person of this poet, whom they consider as worthy to supply the place of a whole host of poets, and as being in himself a complete literature to his country. The great defect of the *Lusiad* consists in its preposterous mythological machinery, and its clumsy management; but in all the qualities of versification and beauty of language it is perfect, and may be regarded as the "well, pure and undefiled," of the Portuguese language. Few modern poems have been so frequently translated as the *Lusiad*. Mr. Adamson, in his *Memoirs of the Life and Writings of Camoens*, notices one Hebrew translation of it, five Latin, six Spanish, four Italian, three French, four German, and two English. Of the two English versions one is that of Sir R. Fanshawe, written during Cromwell's usurpation, and distinguished for its fidelity to the original; the other is that of Mickle, who, unlike the former, took great liberties with the original, but whose additions and alterations have met with great approbation from all critics—except, as indeed was to be expected, from the Portuguese themselves.

M.

M, the thirteenth letter of the English alphabet, is a liquid and labial consonant, pronounced by slightly striking the under lip against the upper one. It is sometimes called a semi-vowel, as the articulation or compression of the lips is accompanied with a humming sound through the nose. M. as a numeral stands for *mille*, a thousand; and with a dash over it, 1,000,000. M. A. *magister artium:* M. D. *medicinæ doctor:* MS. *manuscript*, and MSS. *manuscripts*. M. also stands for *noon*, from the Latin *meridies:* hence P.M. *post meridiem* (afternoon;) and A.M. *ante meridiem* (morning.) M, in French, stands for *Monsieur;* MM. for *Messieurs*.

MAB, in northern mythology, the queen of the imaginary beings called fairies; so fancifully described by the sportive imagination of Shakspeare, in Romeo and Juliet.

MACARON'IC or MACARO'NIAN, an appellation given to a burlesque kind of poetry, made up of a jumble of words of different languages, of Latin words modernized, or of native words ending in Latin terminations. Drummond's *Polemo-Middinia*, a Scottish burlesque, is, perhaps, the best known macaronic form of our language.

MAC'CABEES, two apocryphal books of Scripture, containing the history of Judas and his brothers, and their wars against the Syrian kings in defence of their religion and liberties. The first book is an excellent history, and comes nearest to the style of the sacred historians. The second book of the Maccabees begins with two epistles sent from the Jews of Jerusalem to the Jews of Egypt and Alexandria, to exhort them to observe the feast of the dedication of the new altar erected by Judas on his purifying the temple.

MACH'IAVELISM, the principles inculcated by Machiavelli, an Italian writer, secretary and historiographer to the republic of Florence. Hence the word *Machiavelian* denotes political cunning and artifice, intended to favor arbitrary power.

MACHICOLA'TIONS, in architecture, openings made through the roofs of portals to the floor above, or in the floors of projecting galleries, for the purpose of defence, by pouring through them boiling lead, pitch, &c., upon the enemy. In the galleries they are formed by the parapet or breast-work B being set out beyond the face of the wall C on corbels D; the spaces E between the corbels, being open throughout, are the machicolations.

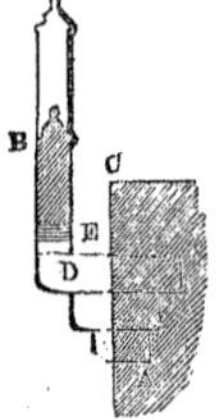

MAC'ROCOSM, the universe, or the visible system of worlds; opposed to *microcosm*, or the world of man.

MADON'NA, a term of compellation, equivalent to *madam*. It is given to the Virgin Mary; and pictures of the Italian schools, representing the Virgin, are generally called *madonnas*.

MAD'NESS, a dreadful kind of delirium, without fever, in which the patient raves or is furious. Melancholy and madness may very justly be considered as diseases nearly allied; for they have both the same origin, that is, an excessive congestion of blood in the brain: they only differ in degree, and with respect to the time of appearing; melancholy being the primary disease, of which madness is the augmentation.

MAD'RIGAL, one of the lesser kind of poems, usually consisting of fewer verses than the sonnet or roundelay. In its composition the fancy and convenience of the poet are not subjected to very strict rules, rhymes and verses of different species being often intermixed. The subjects are mostly of a tender and gallant nature; the character often quaint, the expression marked with great simplicity. Grassineau, in his *Musical Dictionary*, describes the madrigal as "a little piece of poetry, the verses whereof are free and easy, usually unequal: it borders on a sonnet and an epigram, but has not the briskness of the one, nor the poignancy of the other."

MÆSTO'SO, in music, an Italian word signifying *majestic*, and used as a direction to play the part with force and grandeur.

MAGAZINE', in literature, a pamphlet periodically published, containing miscellaneous papers or compositions. The first publication of this kind in England, was the *Gentleman's Magazine*, which first appeared in 1731, under the name of *Sylvanus Urban*, by Edward Cave, and which is still continued. A magazine differs from a newspaper and review; the peculiar province of a newspaper is to communicate information on politics and passing events, both foreign and domestic; and that of the review is to communicate information on literary and scientific subjects, and to give a critical survey of these. The magazine, while it embraces all the features of the newspaper and review, is of a more miscellaneous character, containing, in the form of tales, sketches, poetry, &c., a great variety of matter of an original character which would be foreign to the others.

MAGGIO'RE, in music, an Italian epithet signifying *greater*.

MA'GI, or MA'GIANS, an ancient religious sect in Persia, and other eastern countries, who maintained that there were two principles, the one the cause of all good, the other the cause of all evil; and, abominating the adoration of images, worshipped God only by fire, which they looked upon as the brightest and most glorious symbol of the Deity. This religion was reformed by Zoroaster, who maintained that there was one supreme independent being; and under him two principles or angels, one the angel of goodness and light, and the other of evil and darkness. The priests of the *Magi* were the most skilful mathematicians and philosophers of the ages in which they lived, insomuch that a learned man and a magician became synonymous terms.

MAG'IC, properly signifies the doctrine of the Magi; but the Magi being supposed to have acquired their extraordinary skill from familiar spirits or other supernatural information, the word *magic* acquired the signification it now bears, viz. a science which teaches to perform wonderful and surprising acts, by the application of certain means, which procure the assistance and interposition of demons. The *magicians* of antiquity were generally acquainted with certain secret powers, properties and affinities of bodies, and were hence enabled to produce surprising effects, to astonish the vulgar; and these surprising effects, produced by natural causes, procured them the credit in their pretensions to supernatural and miraculous power — Astrology, divination, enchantments and witchcraft, were parts of this fanciful science; which, from being truly respectable once, as having had for its object mathematics and natural philosophy, by these means became contemptible, its professors opprobrious, its productions ridiculous, and its illusions mere juggler's tricks.

MAG'ISTRATE, a public civil officer, invested with the executive government or some branch of it. In this sense, the president of the United States is the highest or first magistrate. But the word is more particularly applied to subordinate officers, to whom the executive power of the law is committed, either wholly or in part; as, governors, mayors, justices of the peace, and the like.

MAG'NA CHARTA, the Great Charter of Liberties, obtained by the English barons from king John, in 1215. The barons consisted of the whole nobility of England; their followers comprehended all the yeomanry and free peasantry, and the accession of the capital was a pledge of the adherence of the citizens and burgesses. John had been obliged to yield to this general union, and conferences were opened, on the plain called Runnymede, on the banks of the Thames, near Staines, in sight of the forces of each other. At length the preliminaries being agreed on, the barons presented heads of their grievances and means of redress; and the king directed that the articles should be reduced to the form of a charter, in which state it issued as a royal grant. To secure the execution of this charter, John was compelled to surrender the city and Tower of London, to be temporarily held by the barons, and consented that the barons should choose twenty-five of their number, to be guardians of the liberties of the kingdom, with power, in case of any breach of the charter, or denial of redress, to make war on the king, to seize his castle and lands, and to distress and annoy him in every possible way till justice was done. Many parts of the charter were pointed against the abuses of the power of the king as lord paramount; the tyrannical exercise of the forest laws was checked, and many grievances incident to feudal tenures were mitigated or abolished. But besides these provisions, it contains many for the benefit of the people at large, and a few maxims of just government, applicable to all places and times.

MAG'NATES, in Hungary at this day, and formerly also in Poland, the title of the noble estate in the national representation. The Hungarian magnates are divided into greater and lesser; certain high state officers belonging to the first class, the counts and barons of the kingdom to the second. The title is of Latin derivation.

MAGNIF'ICO, the title given by courtesy to a nobleman of Venice.

MAGNIL'OQUENCE, a lofty manner of speaking; tumid, pompous words or style; language expressive of pretensions greater than realities warrant.

MAHA'BARATA, the name of one of the great Indian epic poems, the subject of which is a long civil war between two dynasties of ancient India, the Kurus and Pandus. This poem embraces the whole circle of Indian mythology; but it is still more valuable as embodying an immense number of historical fragments, which will be of great importance to the future historian of India. Many episodes from the *Mahabarata* have been ably translated by some of the most celebrated Orientalists; and parts of the original have been published at different periods in Germany. The period at which the *Mahabarata* was written is wholly unknown, and it has no less baffled all the researches of the learned to discover the date at which it assumed its present methodical form.

MA'HADO, a name of one of the Indian deities, from whom the sacred Ganges is fabled to spring.

MAHOM'ETANS, or MOHAMMEDANS, believers in the doctrines and divine mission of Mahomet, the warrior and prophet of Arabia, whose creed maintains that there is but one God, and that Mahomet is his prophet, and teaches ceremonies by prayer, with washings, &c., almsgiving, fasting, sobriety, pilgrimage to Mecca, &c. Besides these they have some negative precepts and institutions of the Koran, in which several things are prohibited, as usury, the drinking of wine, all games that depend upon chance, the eating of blood and swine's flesh, and whatever dies of itself, is strangled, or is killed by a blow or by another beast. These doctrines and practices Mahomet established by the sword, by preaching, and by the alcoran or koran, which contains the principles of his religion; and he and his followers met with such success, as in a few years to subdue half the known world.

MA'HOUND, formerly a contemptuous name for Mohammed and the devil, and thence applied to any character of seeming power and great wickedness. In Scotland Mahoun was formerly used, as meaning Satan.

MAI'A, in Grecian mythology; 1, the daughter of Atlas and Pleione, one of the Pleiads, who became mother of Mercury by Jupiter: 2, a daughter of the god Faunus, and wife of Vulcan; frequently confounded by mythologists with the former personage.

MAIN'PRIZE, in law, the receiving a person into friendly custody who might otherwise be committed to prison, on security given for his forthcoming on a day appointed.

MAIN'TENANCE, in law, is an unlawful maintaining or supporting a suit between others, by stirring up quarrels, or interfering in a cause in which the person has no concern. Thus if any person disinterested in a cause officiously gives evidence, without being called upon for that purpose, or acts the part of counsel by speaking in the cause, or retains an attorney for the party, he is guilty of maintenance, and is liable to be prosecuted by indictment. But it is no maintenance, where a person gives a poor man money out of charity to carry on a suit.

MAIN'TENANCE, CAP OF, a cap of dignity, anciently belonging to the rank of a duke; termed by the French *bonnet ducal*.

MAJ'ESTY, this title of honor is derived from the Romans, among whom it stood for the collective power and dignity of the sovereign body; as *majestas populi Romani.* Hence treason was termed *crimen læsæ majestatis*, an injury offered to majesty. Majesty was the attribute of consuls, prætors, &c., only as representing the public; and hence, in later times, when it was transferred to the emperors along with the sovereign power, inferior magistrates were entitled, in ceremonial language, by the appellation of dignitas. Majesty is now the conventional title of European emperors and kings.

MA'JOR, the title of several military officers, as major-general, major of a brigade, major of a regiment, &c.—In logic, the Major term is, in a syllogism, the predicate of the conclusion. The major premise is that which contains the major term. In hypothetical syllogisms, the hypothetical premise is called the major.—In music, an epithet applied to the modes in which the third is four semitones above the tonic or key-note, and to intervals consisting of four semitones. The *major* mode takes a major or sharp 3d, and is thus distinguished from that having a minor or flat one. The *major* mode has always a greater 3d, that is, a third consisting of two tones, and the minor mode has always a minor third; that is, a 3d consisting of a tone and a semitone.

MAJORAT', in modern legal phraseology, as employed by several European nations, the right of succession to property according to age.

MAJOR'ITY, in law, in the United States, the age of twenty-one, at which time the male citizen is allowed to exercise the right of suffrage.—In politics, the age at which the sovereign, in hereditary monarchies, becomes capable of exercising supreme authority.

MALADMINISTRA'TION, bad management of public affairs, or a misdemeanor in public employments, particularly of executive and ministerial duties, prescribed by law.

MA'LUM IN SE, (Latin,) in law, an offence at common law, in distinction from *malum prohibitum;* such as playing at unlawful games, &c., which are only *mala prohibita* under certain circumstances.

MALVERSA'TION, in law, misbehavior in an office, employ, or commission, as breach of trust, extortion, &c.

MAM'ELUKE, (Arabic, memalik, *a Slave*,) a name applied to the male slaves imported from Circassia into Egypt by the master of that country. In the 13th century, when the countries in the vicinity of Mount Caucasus were ravaged by Genghis Khan, Nojmedden, sultan of Egypt, purchased several thousands of the natives of those regions, especially Turks, and formed them into an armed body of guards. These guards, or Mamelukes, in the sequel, seized on all the power of the country, murdered the sultan, Touran Shah, A.D. 1258, and made Ibeg, one of their own number, his successor. After that period the Mamelukes, whose numbers were continually enriched by importations from their own country, governed Egypt 263 years. This military sovereignty was destroyed by Selim I., the Turkish sultan, who took Cairo in 1517. Nevertheless, the Mamelukes, under their 24 beys, continued for 200 years more to exercise a power scarcely inferior to that of the Turkish pachas, whom, in the 18th century, they reduced to mere ciphers in the government. Their power was again considerably broken by the French invasion under Bonaparte, to which they offered a determined opposition. After the abandonment of Egypt by the French, the struggle between the beys and the pachas was renewed: finally, in 1811, the present pacha, Mohammed Ali, having invited the principal leaders of the Mamelukes to a banquet, slew 470 of them by treachery, and compelled the remainder to submission.

MAM'MON, in the Syriac language, signifies riches. It is used Matt. vi. 24, and Luke xvi. 13, and is there called the *mammon* of unrighteousness, intimating that riches are frequently the instruments of iniquity, or acquired by unrighteous means.

MAN, mankind; the human race; the whole species of human beings; beings distinguished from all other animals by the powers of reason and speech, as well as by their shape and dignified aspect. When opposed to *woman*, *man* sometimes denotes the male sex in general. It sometimes bears the sense of a male adult of some uncommon qualifications; particularly, the sense of strength, vigor, bravery, virile powers, or magnanimity, as distinguished from the weakness, timidity, or impotence of a boy, or from the narrow-mindedness of low-bred men So, in popular language, it is said, he is no *man.* Play your part like a *man.* He has not the spirit of a *man.* An individual of the human species. Under this phraseology, females may be comprehended. So a law restraining *man*, or *every man* from a particular act, comprehends women and children, if of competent age to be the subjects of law. One who is master of his mental powers, or who conducts himself with his usual judgment, we say, he is not his own *man*. It is sometimes used indefinitely, without reference to a particular individual; any person; one. This is as much as a *man* can desire.

MANDA'MUS, in law, a writ issued from a court of law, and directed to any person, corporation, or inferior court, commanding the performance of some special thing.

MANDARIN', the magistrates and governors of provinces in China, who are chosen out of the most learned men, and whose government is always at a great distance from the place of their birth.

MAN'DUCI, in antiquity, hideous figures introduced at the public representations of the Romans, which served as bugbears.

MAN'EGE, the art of breaking in and riding horses, or the place set apart for equestrian exercises.

MA'NES, in the pagan system of theology, a general name for the infernal deities. The ancients comprehended under the term *manes* not only Pluto, Proserpine, and Minos, but the souls of the deceased were likewise included. It was usual to erect altars and offer libations to the *manes* of deceased friends and relations, for the superstitious notion that the spirits of the departed had an important influence on the good or bad fortune of the living, made people very cautious of offending them. When it was not known whether a corpse had been buried or not, a cenotaph was erected, and the manes were solemnly invited to rest there, from fear that otherwise they would wander about the world, terrifying the living, and seeking the body which they had once inhabited.

MAN'GONEL, an engine formerly used for throwing stones and battering walls.

MAN'HOOD, the state of one who is a man, of an adult male, or one who is advanced beyond puberty, boyhood, or childhood; virility. The qualities of a man; courage; bravery; resolution.

MANICHEES', in church history, a sect of Christian heretics in the third century, the followers of Manes, who made his appearance in the reign of the emperor Probus; pretending to be the Comforter whom our Saviour promised to send into the world. He taught that there are two principles, or gods, coeternal and independent of each other; the first principle, or *light*, the author of all good: the second principle, or *darkness*, the author of all evil—a doctrine which he borrowed from the Persian magi.

MAN'IFEST, an invoice of a cargo of goods, imported or laden for export, to be exhibited at the custom-house by the master of the vessel, or the owner or shipper.

MANIFES'TO, in politics, a declaration of motives publicly issued by a belligerent state, or by a general acting with full powers, previously to the commencement of hostilities. They are in the form of letters, with a superscription or heading addressed to the public in general, and signed with the name of the authority who sends them forth. The usage of issuing manifestoes is said to date so far back as the 14th century. The term is probably derived from the Latin words "manifestum est," with which such documents usually commenced.

MANIP'ULUS, in Roman antiquity, a body of infantry, consisting of two hundred men, and constituting the third part of a cohort.

MAN'NER, in the Fine Arts, a peculiarity of treating a subject, or of executing it, by which individual artists are distinguished: the latter arising out of a particular mode of using the media and implements of art, the former out of a singular method of observing nature.

MAN'OR, an ancient royalty or lordship, formerly called a barony, consisting of demesnes, services, and a court-baron; and comprehending in it messuages, lands, meadow, pasture, wood, rents, an advowson, &c. It may contain one or more villages, or hamlets, or only a great part of a village, &c. In these days, a *manor* rather signifies the jurisdiction and royalty incorporeal, than the land or site; for a man may have a manor in gross, as the law terms it, that is, the right and interest of a court-baron, with the perquisites thereto belonging. Some estates in the United States still retain the name of manor, from the times of the colonies.

MANSARD-ROOF, in architecture, a roof of peculiar construction, named after its first practicer Julius, or as some say, Francis Mansard, who used it upon all his principal buildings. Before the time of either of these architects, however, this kind of roof was employed by the Abbé de Clugny in the old palace of the Louvre.

MAN'SLAUGHTER, in a general

sense, the killing of a man or of men; destruction of the human species; murder. In law, the unlawful killing of a man without malice, express or implied. This may be voluntary, upon a sudden heat or excitement of anger; or involuntary, but in the commission of some unlawful act. Manslaughter differs from murder in not proceeding from malice prepense or deliberate, which is essential to constitute murder. It differs from homicide excusable, being done in consequence of some unlawful act, whereas excusable homicide happens in consequence of misadventure.

MAN″TELET, in fortification, a kind of movable parapet, or wooden penthouse, used in a siege. Mantelets are cased with tin and set on wheels, so as to be driven before the pioneers, to protect them from the enemy's small shot.

MAN′TLE, in architecture, the piece lying horizontally across from one jamb of a chimney to the other. In malacology, the external fold of the skin of the mollusks.

MAN′UAL, was applied originally to the Roman Catholic service book, from its convenient size, (being such as might be carried in the hand;) but it now signifies any small work used chiefly for the purpose of reference.

MANUMIS′SION, among the Romans, the solemn ceremony by which a slave was emancipated, or liberated from personal bondage.

MAN′USCRIPTS, literally writings of any kind, whether on paper or any other material, in contradistinction to such as are printed. Books were generally written upon vellum, after the papyrus used in classical times had become obsolete, until the general introduction of paper made from rags, about the 15th century after Christ; and the finest and whitest vellum is generally indicative of great age in a manuscript. The dearness of this material gave rise to the practice of using old manuscript books on which the writing had been erased, and also to that of abbreviations. These were carried to excess in the 12th century, and from that time until the invention of printing; and for a long period subsequent to that invention, abbreviations were still in common use: in Greek printing they were usual until within the last fifty years. Of Latin MSS., those prior to the reign of Charlemagne (A.D. 800) are considered ancient. Manuscripts of the early classical age were written on sheets rolled together.—*Illuminated manuscripts* are such as are embellished with ornaments, drawings, emblematical figures, &c., illustrative of the text. This practice was introduced at a very early period; for we find the works of Varro, Pomponius Atticus, and others adorned by illuminations. But it was chiefly employed in the breviaries and prayer-book of the early Christian church. The colors most employed for this purpose were gold and azure. Illuminations were in a high state of perfection between the 5th and 10th centuries; after which they seemed to have partaken of the barbarism of the middle ages, which threw their chilling influence over every description of art. On the revival of the arts in the 15th and 16th centuries many excellent performances were produced; but the art did not take deep root, and became extinct with the invention of printing.

MAP, a delineation of a country according to a scale, in which the proportion, shape, and position of places are exactly preserved. The top is usually the north, and the right hand the east, and, when otherwise, distinguished by a *fleur de lis* pointing to the north. It is called a universal map when it represents the whole surface of the earth, or the two hemispheres; and a particular map when it only represents particular regions or countries. A map is properly a representation of land, as distinguished from a chart, which only represents the sea or sea-coast. In maps, three things are essentially requisite: 1, that all places have the same situation and distance from the great circles therein, as on the globe, to show their parallels, longitudes, zones, climates, and other celestial appearances; 2, that their magnitudes be proportionable to their real magnitudes on the globe; 3, that all places have the same situation, bearing and distance, as on the earth itself. The degrees of longitude are always numbered at top and bottom, and the degrees of latitude on the east and west sides.

MAR′ABUTS, or MAR′ABOOTS, in Northern Africa, among the Berbers, a kind of saints or sorcerers who are held in high estimation. They distribute amulets, affect to work miracles, and are thought to exercise the gift of prophecy. They live with a good deal of pomp, and maintain a numerous train of wives and concubines. They make no pretensions to abstinence or self-denial.

MARANA′THA, amongst the Jews, was a form of threatening, cursing, or anathematizing, and was looked upon as the most severe denunciation they had. The word is said to signify *the Lord comes, or is come:* which taken as a curse or threat may be thus paraphrased, "the Lord come quickly to take vengeance on thee for thy crimes."

MARCH, the third month of the year, according to the calendar of Numa and Julius Cæsar; but in the calendar of Romulus it stood first, in honor of his reputed father, Mars. This month seems to have a strong claim to the first place in the series, because in March the sun enters into the sign Aries, which is reckoned the first sign of the zodiac.—*March*, in music, a military air, played by inflatile and pulsatile instruments, to regulate the steps and to animate the minds of soldiers. The march, however, has long been adapted to every species of musical instrument, and some of the most celebrated compositions of the greatest masters are in this style; as the March of the Priests in Mozart's *Zauber-flöte*, the Peasant's March in Weber's *Freischutz*, and, above all, Beethoven's Funeral Marches. In most Dictionaries of musical terms, it is truly said that a march should always be composed in common time, with an odd crotchet or quaver at the beginning. It is usually quick for ordinary marching, and slow for grand occasions; but no general rules can be laid down for its composition. —*March of the Deities.*—The ancients, in all their representations of the superhuman powers, and even of heroic men or demigods, paid great attention to their step or gait. They held a grave, steady, and at the same time light step to be indicative of dignity and even of a spiritual nature. Occasionally, as on a medal of Antoninus representing the advance of Mars to Sylvia, the figure appears rather to glide over the surface of the earth than to tread upon it. The Belvidere Apollo has a similar character of step or walk. The foot of the deity scarcely presses the ground.

MARCHES, borders or confines, particularly the boundaries between England and Wales. The office of "lords marchers" was originally to guard the frontiers.

MARCO'SIANS, a sect of Christian heretics in the second century, so called from their leader Marcus, who represented the Deity as consisting not of a trinity, but a quaternity, *viz.* the Ineffable, Silence, the Father, and Truth.

MAR'GIN, in printing, is the arrangement of the pages in a sheet at proper distances from each other, according to the size of the paper; so that when the sheet is printed and folded, the border of white paper round them shall be regular and uniform in every leaf of the book. In architecture, that part of the upper side of a course of slates which appears uncovered by the next superior course.

MAR'GRAVE, or, more properly, MARKGRAVE, a title of rank formerly used in Germany, and equivalent to the English marquis. Both words spring from a common origin.

MARI'A THERE'SA, ORDER OF, a military order of Austria, consisting of grand crosses, commanders, and knights; founded in 1757.

MARINES', a corps of men enlisted to serve as soldiers on board of ships-of-war in naval engagements, and on shore under certain circumstances. They sometimes assist, particularly in the British service, in performing some naval duties on board of ship.

MAR'ITIME LAW, signifies the laws relating to harbors, ships, and sailors. It forms an important branch of the commercial law of all trading nations, and embraces an infinite variety of subjects, most of which have been defined under their respective heads. The most celebrated codes of maritime law have been, in classical times, that of Rhodes; in modern times, the *Consolato del Mare*, a compilation supposed to have been framed at Barcelona as early as the 9th century; the laws of the Isle of Oleron, in the time of Richard I. of England; the laws of Wisby, in the island of Gothland, to which some northern jurists have assigned an earlier origin than the laws of Oleron, but which there can be little doubt were merely a compilation from those above specified. But by far the most complete and well-digested system of maritime jurisprudence that has ever appeared is that comprised in the *Ordonnance de la Marine*, issued by Louis XIV. in 1681, by which maritime law was elevated to the rank of a regular system, and has formed the basis of many of the subsequent decisions of American, English, and foreign courts. This excellent code was compiled under the direction of M. Colbert, by individuals of great talent and learning, after a careful revision of all the ancient sea laws of France and other countries, and upon consultation with the different parliaments, the courts of admiralty, and the chambers of commerce of the different towns. It combines whatever experience and the wisdom of ages had shown to be best in the Roman laws, and in the institutions of the modern maritime states of Europe.

MARK, or *the Gospel of* St. Mark, a canonical book of the New Testament, the second in order. St. Mark wrote his gospel at Rome, where he accompanied St. Peter, in the year of Christ 44. Tertullian, and others, pretend that St. Mark was no more than an amanuensis to St. Peter, who dictated this gospel to him; others assert that he wrote it after St. Peter's death. Nor are the learned less divided as to the language this gospel was written in; some affirming it to have been in Greek, and others in Latin. It however seems plainly intended for Christian converts from paganism, and is distinguished from the other evangelical writings by its brevity, passing over much that relates to the character of Christ as Messiah.

MAROONS', the name given to revolted negroes in the West Indies, and in some parts of South America. In many cases, by taking to the forests and mountains, they have rendered themselves formidable to the colonies, and sustained a long and brave resistance to the white population.

MARQUE, *letter of*, a power granted by a state to its subjects, to make reprisals on the subjects of a state with whom it is at war.

MAR'QUETRY, in architecture, inlaid work consisting of different pieces of divers colored woods of small thickness glued on to a ground usually of oak or fir, well dried and seasoned, which, to prevent casting and warping, is composed of several thicknesses. The early Italian builders used it in cabinet work, and John of Vienna, and others of his period, by its means represented figures and landscapes; but in the present day it is chiefly confined in its use to floors, in which the various pieces of wood are usually disposed in regular geometrical figures, and are rarely of more than three or four species.

MAR'QUIS, or MAR'QUESS, a title of honor, next in dignity to that of duke, first given to those who commanded the marches, or borders and frontiers of a kingdom. Marquises were not known in England till Richard II. in the year 1337, created Robert de Vere marquis of Dublin. The marquis's coronet is a circle of gold set round with four strawberry leaves, and as many pearls on pyramidal points of equal height alternate.

MAR'RIAGE, the act of uniting a man and woman for life; wedlock; the state or condition of being married; the legal union of a man and woman for life. Marriage is regarded by the law as a civil contract binding the parties to certain reciprocal obligations, and the general principle of law respecting this, as well as other civil contracts, is, that it is to be held valid according to the usage of the country wherein it is made. Although among protestants marriage has ceased to be regarded as a sacrament, yet in most protestant countries the entrance into the married state has continued to be accompanied with religious observances. These are not, however, in the eye of the law, essential to the constitution of a valid marriage, any further than the legislative power may have seen it proper to annex them to and incorporate them with the civil contract. The laws concerning marriage are different, in the separate states of the Union. By the laws of most of the states, as well as that of Scotland, a marriage is valid, when contracted by any form of ceremony without the proclamation of banns, or the aid of a clergyman, provided the parties on the occasion express a solemn acceptance of each other as man and wife. It is also contracted by the writing of the parties without any ceremony, provided the writing express their acceptance of each other as man and wife. Also by a verbal acceptance of each other as man and wife in the presence of witnesses, or by a promise followed by intercourse.

MARSEILLAISE HYMN, the name popularly, though erroneously, given to the national anthem of the French. The origin of this song, which has played so important a part in the revolutions not only of France but other continental states, was long involved in obscurity; but the following statement respecting it may be relied on as authentic: The *Marseillaise Hymn* was the production of Rouget de Lille, a French officer of engineers, who was quartered at Strasburg in the year 1791, when Marshal Luckner commanded the army, at that time entirely composed of young conscripts. The marshal was to march the following morning of a certain day; and, late in the evening previous, he inquired if there were any men of a musical or poetical genius in the army who could compose a song to animate his young soldiers. Some one mentioned Captain Rouget de Lille, who was immediately ordered into the presence of the marshal to receive his commands on the subject; which having been given, and a promise made by De Lille that a song would be ready the following morning, he went to his quarters, and during the night he not only wrote the song in question, but also set it to music; and next morning the army marched to its tune, and carried everything before it with an enthusiasm only to be equalled by absolute phrensy. The song is said to have been styled the *Marseillaise Hymn* from a body of troops, on their march from Marseilles, having entered Paris playing that tune at a time when it was little known in the capital. The original of the *Marseillaise* is said to be in the possession of Louis Philippe.

MARS, or MA'VORS, the Latin names of the deity called by the Greeks *Ares*. He was fabled to be the son of Juno, conceived by means of the virtue of a certain plant; and was worshipped as the God of War. At Rome he was honored as the progenitor of Romulus, the founder of the city, of which he was held to be the protector; and it was to the honor of this divinity that the Latin husbandmen used to offer up a peculiar sacrifice, called *suovetaurilia*, which, as the derivation of the word implies, consisted of a pig, a sheep, and a bull.

MAR'SHAL, a title of honor in many European countries, applied to various dignities and high offices. The derivation of the word, and its early use, are extremely uncertain. The title of Marshal of England is now hereditary in the family of the Dukes of Norfolk. William Fitz-Osborn and Roger de Montgomery are said to have been marshals to William the Conqueror. The earl marshal is eighth in rank among the great officers of state in England. He has the same jurisdiction over the court of chivalry which was formerly exercised by the constable and marshal jointly. Marshal of France is the highest military rank in the French army. This officer appears first in history under the reign of Philip Augustus, as commander-in-chief of the royal armies. The number of marshals was increased by several successive sovereigns: in the reign of Henry IV. the states of Blois limited it to four, but this restriction was not observed; and, in the reign of Louis XIV., there were at one period no less than twenty. After the deposition of Louis XVI. the dignity of marshal ceased; but was revived by Napoleon, with the title of Marshal of the Empire.

MARTEL'LO TOWERS, the name given to the circular buildings of masonry which were erected along different parts of the British coasts at the commencement of the present century, intended as a defence against the meditated invasion of Napoleon. The origin of the name is usually supposed to be derived from a fort in Mortella (Myrtle) Bay, Corsica, which, after a determined resistance, was at last captured by the British in 1794. These towers were provided with vaulted roofs, and consisted of two stories—the lower for the reception of stores, the upper, which was shell-proof, for the casement of troops; and the wall of the building terminated in a parapet, which secured the men in working the pieces of artillery, which, besides, were constructed on moving pivots, so as to be fired in any direction. In most places of England these towers have been dismantled; those that remain either serve as stations for the coast blockade force, or, like that near Leith, are not employed for any purpose.

MARTINET', a cant phrase for a severe military disciplinarian: probably derived from a certain Colonel Martinet, who served in the French army under Louis XIV., who was the inventor of a peculiar whip, called by his name, for the purpose of military punishment, and also (if Voltaire may be believed) of the bayonet.

MAR'TYR, any innocent person who suffers death in defence of a cause, rather than abandon it. In the Christian sense of the word, it is one who lays down his life for the gospel, or suffers death for the sake of his religion. The Christian church has abounded in martyrs, and history is filled with surprising accounts of their singular constancy and fortitude under the most cruel torments human nature was capable of suffering. The primitive Christians believed that the martyrs enjoyed very singular privileges: that upon their death they were immediately admitted to the beatific vision, while other souls waited for the completion of their happiness till the day of judgment; and that God would grant chiefly to their prayers the hastening of his kingdom, and shortening the times of persecution. The festivals of the martyrs are of very ancient date, and may be carried back at least till the time of Polycarp, who suffered martyrdom about the year of Christ 168. On these days the Christians met at the graves of the martyrs, and offered prayers and thanksgivings to God for the examples they had afforded them; they celebrated the eucharist, and gave alms to the poor; which, together with a panegyrical oration or sermon, and reading the acts of the martyrs, were the spiritual exercises of these anniversaries.

MARTYROL'OGY, a catalogue or list of martyrs, including the history of their lives and sufferings.

MA'SONS, or FREE AND ACCEPTED MASONS, a term applied to a fraternity of great antiquity, and so called probably because the first founders of that society were persons of that craft or occupation. It is generally understood that they are bound by an oath of secresy not to reveal anything that passes within the society, and the members throughout the whole world are known to each other by certain secret signs.

MAS'ORA, a Hebrew work on the bible, by several Rabbins. It is a collection of remarks, critical, grammatical, and exegetical, on the books of the Old Testament by the Jewish doctors of the third and succeeding centuries. It is divided into the great and little; the former contains the whole collection in separate books; the little is an extract from the observations which were written in the margins of the biblical manuscripts.

MASQUE, or MASK, a species of drama. It originated from the custom in processions, and other solemn occasions, of introducing personages in masks to represent imaginary characters. Many of these characters, even in the religious shows of Italy, &c., were of a grotesque description, and the performance often intermixed with dancing and buffoonery. By degrees, in England, something of a dramatic character was added to these exhibitions. At first, as in the well-known progresses of Queen Elizabeth, monologues or dialogues in verse were put into the mouths of the masked performers; and in the reign of James I., they had ripened into regular dramatic performances; sometimes, as in the *Tempest* of Shakspeare, introduced by way of interlude in regular plays; at other times acted as separate pieces, with much machinery and decoration. Ben Jonson was the first, and indeed almost the only classical English writer (with the exception of Milton, in the solitary and noble specimen of *Comus*) who devoted much labor and taste to this department of the drama. His masques were represented at court; the Queen of James I., and after her the accomplished Queen Henrietta Maria, did not disdain to take part, at least as silent dramatis personæ, in some of these pageants. The taste for them died away in the reign of Charles I., and after the interruption given to the progress of dramatic art and literature by the civil wars, they were not again brought into fashion.

MASQUERADE', (Ital. mascherata,) an amusement practised in almost every civilized country of modern times, consisting of a ball and other festivities in which only those who are masked or disguised can participate. This species of amusement had its origin in Italy, where, according to *Hall's Chronicle*, they had become fashionable so early as the beginning of the 16th century.

MASS, in the church of Rome, the prayers and ceremonies used at the celebration of the eucharist; or, in other words, consecrating the bread and wine into the body and blood of Christ, and offering them so transubstantiated, as an expiatory sacrifice for the quick and the dead. As the mass is believed to be a representation of the passion of our blessed Saviour, so every action of the priest, and every particular part of the service, is supposed to allude to the particular circumstances of his passion and death. It consists of three parts: the offertorium, or offering the elements on the altar; the consecration, by which they are supposed to undergo the transubstantiation into the real body and blood of Christ; and the sumption, or actual participation in them by the communicants. These ceremonies are accompanied by the recitation of various prayers; and the priest goes through numerous evolutions, which are supposed to represent the circumstances attending the passion of our Lord. The general division of masses consists in high and low; *high mass* is sung by the choristers, and celebrated with the assistance of a deacon and sub-deacon; *low masses* are those in which the prayers are barely rehearsed without singing. There are a great number of different or occasional masses in the Romish church, many of which have nothing peculiar but the name: as the masses of the saints, &c.

MAS'SIVE, in architecture, sculpture, &c., heavy, full, solid. This term is one of commendation, or otherwise, according to the nature of the work respecting which it is used. Thus in speaking of an abutment, a wall, the pier of a bridge, &c., the architect is complimented by the application of this term; whereas, the precise contrary is generally the case, when it is employed in speaking of a portico, an arch, column, or a roof.

MAS'TER, a man who rules, governs, or directs either men or business. A man who has servants is their *master;* he who has apprentices is their *master*, as he has the government and direction of them.—In *commercial navigation*, the person intrusted with the care and navigation of a ship; otherwise called *captain*.—In *ships of war*, an officer who takes rank immediately after the lieutenants, and navigates the ship under the direction of the captain.—The director of a school; a teacher; and instructor. In this sense the word is giving place to the more appropriate words, teacher, instructor, and preceptor.—A title of dignity or a degree in colleges and universities; as, *Master* of Arts. In the American and English universities this degree follows that of Bachelor; it is the highest in the faculty of arts, but subordinate to that of doctor of divinity.—*In all the arts.* A professor of either of the fine arts, who gives lectures thereon to students. In another, and more general sense, any distinguished practiser of art, whose works are sufficiently excellent to have attained him an undying reputation, and to render his performances referred to as models for style and execution by the young artist. Without the existence of the works of the great masters, the arts would still be in their infancy.

MA'STER-SING'ERS, a class of poets who flourished in Germany during the 15th and part of the 16th century. They were confined to a few imperial towns, and their chief seat was the city of Nuremberg. They were generally of burgher extraction; and formed regular corporations, into which proficients were admitted by the ordinary course of apprenticeship. Their poetry (generally confined to devotional or scriptural pieces, legendary tales, with some admixture of satire and amatory lyrics) was subjected to a peculiar and pedantic code of laws, both composition and versification; and a board of judges (styled merker) assembled to hear the poems recited, and *mark* the faults which might be committed in either particular: he who had the fewest faults received the prize. Hans Sachs, the famous cobbler of Nuremberg, was a member of these societies; although his genius was of too independent a character to submit to the trammels of their poetical regulations.

MAT'ADOR, in Spanish bull-fights, the name given to the person who gives the death wound to the bull. After the *banderilleros* have goaded the animal to madness by fastening squibs upon him and discharging them, the *matador* (*el matador*, the killer,) advances with a naked sword and aims a fatal blow at him. If this is effectual, the slaughtered animal is dragged away and another is brought forward.

MATE'RIALISM, the doctrine held by those who maintain that the soul of man is not a spiritual substance distinct from matter, but that it is the result or effect of the organization of matter in the body. This theory, however, does not explain how matter can think, and how physical motion can produce mental changes, which we do not observe in so many organic beings. In decided opposition to materialism, is our consciousness of the identity and liberty of man, which would be annihilated by it, because matter is governed by the necessity of nature, and free will therefore excluded.

MAT'INS, the first part of the daily service, particularly in the Romish church.

MATRA'LIA, in antiquity, a Roman festival celebrated by the matrons, in honor of the goddess Mater Matula, on the third of the ides of June.

MATRIC'ULATE, to enter or admit to membership in a body or society, particularly in a college or university, by enrolling the name in a register.

MATRONA'LIA, a Roman festival instituted by Romulus, and celebrated on the calends of March, in honor of Mars. It was kept by matrons, to whom presents were made by the men, as by husbands to their wives, &c. Bachelors were entirely excluded from any share in the solemnity.

MAT'THEW, or *Gospel of St. Matthew*, a canonical book of the New Testament. St. Matthew wrote his gospel in Judea, at the request of those he had converted, and it is thought he began it in the year 41, eight years after Christ's resurrection. It was written, according to the testimony of all the ancients, in the Hebrew or Syriac language, which was then common in Judea: but the Greek version of it, which now passes for the original, is as old as the apostolical times. St. Matthew's view in writing his gospel, was chiefly to show the royal descent of Jesus Christ, and to represent his life and conversation among men.

MAUN'DAY THURSDAY, the Thursday in passion-week, or next before Good Friday. The word is supposed by some to be derived from the Saxon *mand*, a basket; because on that day princes used to give alms to the poor from their baskets. Others think it was called *Maunday* or *Mandate* Thursday, from the *dies mandati*, (the day of command,) the command which Christ gave his disciples to commemorate him in the Lord's supper, which he this day instituted; or from the new commandment that he gave them to love one another, after he had washed their feet as a token of his love to them.

MAUR, SAINT, CONGREGATION OF, a learned body of religious of the Benedictine order; so called from a village near Paris, where they were established in 1618. On the request of Louis XIII., Gregory XV. gave this order his approval by an apostolic brief, dated 17th of May, 1621; and it obtained new privileges from Urban VIII., by a bull dated 21st of January, 1627. The fame of this body attracted the attention of many other religious orders, several of which were induced to submit to its rules; and at last it numbered upwards of a hundred religious houses. The literary world owes to them a series of very valuable editions of ancient Greek authors, chiefly fathers, during the 17th century. Among the most eminent of its members during that period may be mentioned Jean Mabillon, Thierri Ruinart, Hugh Menard, and Bernard de Montfaucon, &c. &c. (See Mosheim, *Eccl. Hist.*, vol. v.)

MAUSOLE'UM, a general designation of any superb and magnificent monument of the dead, adorned with rich sculpture, and inscribed with an epitaph. In a more confined acceptation it signifies the pompous monument in honor of some emperor, prince, or very illustrious personage; but it properly and literally signifies that particular monument built by Artemisia, to the memory of her husband Mausolus, king of Caria, whence it derives its name. This monument was so superb that it was reckoned one of the wonders of the world.

MAX'IM, an established proposition or principle; in which sense, according to popular usage, it denotes nearly the same as *axiom* in philosophy and mathematics. Maxims are self-evident propositions, and the principles of all science; for on these, and definitions, all demonstrative knowledge depends.—In music, the longest note formerly used, equal to two longs, or four breves.

MAY, the fifth month of our year, but the third of the Roman. The name is supposed to be derived from Maia, the mother of Mercury, to whom the Romans offered sacrifices on the first day of the month; but various other derivations have been assigned to it.—*See* CALENDAR.

MAY-DAY. The 1st of May is usually so called in England, by way of eminence, in commemoration of the festivities which from a very early period were till recently, and in many parts of the country are still observed on that day. It would be out of place in this work to give any detailed account of them, as they are universally known; but a few words as to their origin may not be out of place. In looking at the nature of these rites, which are, to a certain extent, common to every place in which they are observed, it is evident that they had their origin in the heathen observances practised in honor of the Latin goddess Flora; but it is impossible to fix with accuracy the precise period at which they were introduced into England. The earliest notice of the celebration of May-day may be traced to the Druids, who on May-eve were accustomed to light large fires on eminences in gratitude and joy for the return of Spring. At a later period the observance of this day appears not to have been peculiar to any class of society, for the most exalted as well as the lowest persons took part in it. In his *Court of Love* Chaucer says, that on this day "forth goeth all the Court, most and least, to fetch the flowers fresh, and braunch and bloom;" and it is well known that Henry VIII. and Katherine, and all the court partook in their diversion. The custom has been but partially introduced into the United States.

MAY'HEM, in law, a wound or hurt, by which a man loses the use of any member. It originally applied to such corporeal injuries as rendered a man less fit for war.

MAYOR, (Lat. major, meaning the first or senior alderman,) the title of the chief municipal officer of a borough, to whom it appears to have been first given by charters granted some time after the conquest. In France, the first municipal officer of each commune, according to a general system established by the law of 14th December, 1789, which created municipalities. The maire has one or more *adjuncts* or assessors, according to the population of the commune, chosen in the same manner.

MEAS'URE, in music, the interval or space of time between raising and depressing the hand in a movement; being the same as *bar*. The measure is regulated according to the different values of the notes of a piece, by which the time assigned to each note is expressed. Semibreves, for instance, occupy one rise and one fall, called a whole measure. In *poetry*, the measure or metre is the manner of ordering and combining the quantities, or the long and short syllables. Thus hexameter, pentameter, iambic, Sapphic verses, &c., consist of different *measures*.—In dancing, the interval between steps, corresponding to the interval between notes in the music.

MED'AL, a piece of metal in the form of a coin, intending to convey to posterity the portrait of some great person, or the memory of some illustrious action. The parts of a medal are the two sides, one of which is called the face or head, and the other the reverse. On each side is the area, or field, which makes the middle of the medal; the rim, or border; and the exergue, or plain circular space just within the edge: and on the two sides are distinguished the type, or the figure represented, and the legend, or inscription. Egyptian medals are the most ancient; but the Grecian medals far excel all others in design, attitude, strength, and delicacy. Those of the Romans are beautiful, the engraving fine, the invention simple, and the taste exquisite. They are distinguished into consular and imperial; the consular medals are the most ancient, though the copper and silver ones do not go farther back than the 484th year of Rome, and those of gold no farther than the year 546. Among the imperial medals, a distinction is made between those of the upper and lower empire. The first commenced under Julius Cæsar, and continued till A.D. 260: the lower empire includes a space of nearly 1200 years, and ends with the taking of Constantinople. The use of medals is very considerable: they often throw great light on history, in confirming such passages as are true in old authors, in reconciling such as are variously narrated, and in recording such as have been omitted. In this case a cabinet of medals may be said to be a body of history. It was, indeed, an excellent way to perpetuate the memory of great actions, thus to coin out the life of an emperor, and to put every exploit into the mint—a kind of printing before the art was invented. Nor are medals of less use in architecture, painting, poetry, &c.; for a cabinet of medals is a collection of pictures in miniature, and by them the plans of many of the most considerable buildings of antiquity are preserved.

MEDAL'LIONS, are medals of a larger size, and supposed to have been struck by the different emperors for their friends, or for foreign princes and ambassadors. That the smallness of the number of these, however, might not put to hazard the loss of the devices they bore, the Romans generally took care to stamp the subjects of them upon their ordinary coins. Medallions, in respect to other coins, resembled what modern medals, properly so speaking, are in respect to money, having had no current value, but merely an arbitrary one.

ME'DIANT, in music, the chord which is a major or minor third higher than the key note, according as the mode is major or minor.

ME'DIATIZA'TION, the annexation of the smaller German sovereignties to larger contiguous states, which took place, on a large scale, after the dissolution of the German empire in 1806. The same thing had been done on various occasions during the continuance of the empire; and the dominions so annexed were said to be mediatized, *i. e.*, made mediately instead of immediately dependant on the empire. The term was retained when the abolition of the German union had rendered it in strictness inappropriate. A few more were mediatized after the peace of 1815.

MEDIA'TOR, a term applied to Jesus Christ, as interceding between God and man, and obtaining for the latter the remission of the punishment due to original and contracted sin. The divinity of our Saviour is argued from his mediatorial character: it seeming impossible that a mere man could efficaciously intercede by the sacrifice of himself for the sins of his fellow-men. Those reasoners, therefore, who have arrived at the conclusion of the mere humanity of Christ, either expressly deny or essentially modify the idea of his mediatorial character.

MED'ICINE, the art which treats of the means of preserving health when present, and of restoring it when lost: an art that assists nature in the preservation of health by the use of proper remedies. It is founded on the study of man's physical and moral nature, in health and in disease. It has struggled at all times, and continues to struggle, with favorite theories; and has, with the slowness which marks all the important advancements of mankind, but lately emerged from some of the prejudices of many centuries, and will doubtless long continue subject to others. Hippocrates, who lived about the middle of the fifth century before the Christian era, is the earliest author on medicine whose writings have been preserved. He was a man of very superior medical acquirements, and, by the consent of posterity, he has been styled the Father of Medicine.

MEDI'ETAS LIN'GUÆ, in law, a jury consisting of half natives and half foreigners, which is impanelled in cases where the party to be tried is a foreigner.

MEDIE'VAL, relating to the middle ages.—*Medieval architecture*, the architecture of Europe during the middle ages, including the Norman and early Gothic styles.

ME'DIUM, in philosophy, the space or region through which a body in motion passes to any point, in logic, the mean or middle term of a syllogism, being an argument or reason for which we affirm or deny anything.—*Medium* also denotes the means or instrument by which anything is accomplished, conveyed, or carried on. Thus money is the *medium* of commerce; bills of credit or bank-notes are often used as mediums of trade in the place of gold and silver; and intelligence is communicated through the medium of the press.

MEDU'SA, in mythology, the chief of the Gorgons; according to Hesiod, the eldest daughter of Celo and the sea-god Phorcus. Various stories are related of this mythological personage; but her chief peculiarity was the power she possessed of turning all who looked upon her into stone. She was slain by Perseus, who placed her head in the shield of Minerva, where it continued to retain the same petrifying power as before.

MEGALE'SIAN GAMES, one of the most magnificent of the Roman exhibitions of the circus; in honor of Cybele, the mother of the gods.

MEGA'RIAN SCHOOL OF GREEK PHILOSOPHY, founded at Megara by the disciples of Socrates, who retired thither after his death, and distinguished in later times by its logical subtlety. Its most celebrated names were those of Euclides, Eubulides, and Stilpo.

MEL'ODRAME, or MEL'O-DRAMA, a dramatic performance in which music is intermixed; or that species of drama in which the declamation of certain passages is interrupted by music. If only only one person acts, it is a *monodrama;* if two, a *duodrama*. It differs from the opera and operetta in this, that the performers do not sing, but declaim, and the music only fills the pauses, either preparing or continuing the feelings expressed by the actors. Melo-dramas are generally romantic and extravagant.

MEL'ODY, in music, the agreeable effect of different sounds, ranged and disposed in succession; so that melody is the effect of a single voice or instrument, by which it is distinguished from harmony. "Melody," says an eminent French musician, "is for music, what thought is for poetry, or drawing for painting."

MELPO'MENE, the muse who presides over tragedy; represented usually with a mask in one hand, a club or dagger in the other, and with buskins on her feet.

MELUSI'NE, in the mediæval mythology of France, a beautiful nymph or fairy, whose history occupies a large space in the popular superstitions of that country. She is represented as the daughter of Helmas, king of Albania, and the fairy Persine; and as having married Raymund, count of Toulouse, who built her the magnificent castle of Lusignan (originally called Lusineem, the *anagram* of Melusine). Like most of the fairies of that period, she was doomed to a periodical metamorphosis, during which the lower part of her body assumed the form of a fish or a serpent. On these occasions she exerted all her ingenuity to escape observation; but having been once accidentally seen by her husband in this condition, she swooned away, and soon afterwards disappeared, none knew whither. But her form is said to be seen from time to time on the tower of Lusignan, clad in mourning, and uttering deep lamentations; and her appearance is universally believed to indicate an impending calamity to the royal family of France.

MEM'BER, a limb: a part appendant to the body. We say of a figure, in the arts of design, that its different members are exact and well proportioned.—In architecture, this word is applied to each of the different parts of a building, to each separate portion of an entablature, or to each different moulding of a cornice.

MEM'OIRS, a species of history, written by persons who had some share in the transactions they relate; answering to what the Romans called *commentarii* (commentaries.) They furnish the reader with interesting individual anecdotes, and often expose the most secret motives, or disclose the whole character of events, which may be barely hinted at in books of general history. These qualities, when the writer is to be relied on for his veracity and judgment, give them an advantage over the other kinds of historical writings, since they satisfy the mere reader for amusement as well as the student. The French were the earliest, and have always been by far the most successful writers, in this branch of literature. Their historical memoirs, partly autobiographical, and partly the works of authors who had access to the papers and memorials of those whose lives they illustrated, form a complete series from the sixteenth century to the present time, and throw the greatest light on some portions of history; while their memoirs of celebrated individuals in the ranks of literature and fashion are still more numerous and interesting. In the last century, this branch of literature became so popular, that any distinguished individual who did not leave authentic memoirs of himself was sure to become the subject, after his death, of fabricated memoirs, published under his name; and this species of falsification, of which Voltaire then complained, appears to be now carried on as extensively as at any former period. The collections of historical memoirs recently edited in Paris contain three series of historical memoirs relating to French history, and one of English memoirs, translated, illustrating the period of the civil war and revolution. The latter undertaking was conducted by M. Guizot.

MEMORABIL'IA, things remarkable and worthy of remembrance.

MEMO'RIAL, in diplomacy, a species of informal state of paper much used in negotiation. Memorials are said to be of three classes. 1. Memorials in the form of letters, subscribed by the writer, and speaking in the second person as addressed to another. 2. Memorials proper, or written representations, subscribed by the writer, and with an address, but not speaking in the second person. 3. Notes, in which there is neither subscription nor address. Species of the first class of memorials are, circulars from the bureau of foreign affairs sent to foreign agents; answers to the memorials of ambassadors; and notes to foreign cabinets and ambassadors.

MEM'ORY, is defined to be the power or capacity of having what was once present to the senses or the understanding suggested again to the mind, accompanied by a distinct consciousness of past existence. The term is also employed, though more rarely, to denote the act or operation of remembering, or the peculiar state of the mind when it exercises this faculty, in contradistinction to the faculty itself. Various opinions have been propounded by metaphysicians respecting the nature and origin of the faculty of memory. Upon this point, however, it is not our intention to enter into any details, as this question is so mixed up with that of other faculties of the mind, such as perception and association, and such metaphysical questions, as personal identity, &c., as to be inseparable from them; and to these heads we must refer the reader for information. We may, however, remark, that the ancient Platonists and Peripatetics ascribed the faculty of memory to the common theory of ideas; that is, of images in the brain or in the mind, of all the objects of thought; and in this opinion they were supported, with slight modifications, by many other philosophers of antiquity. But Dr. Reid, who has examined this question with great acuteness, has satisfactorily demonstrated the theory of the ancients to be very defective. The more modern theories of Locke, Hume, and other philosophers, also meet with little consideration from the same acute metaphysician, who, after exposing their fallacies, sums up in these words: "Thus, when philosophers have piled one supposition on another, as the giants piled the mountains in order to scale the heavens, it is all to no purpose—memory remains unaccountable; and we know as little how we remember things past as how we are conscious of the present." The word *memory* is not employed uniformly in the same precise sense, but it always expresses some modification of that faculty which enables us to treasure up, and preserve for future use the knowledge which we acquire; a faculty which is obviously the great foundation of all intellectual improvement. The word *memory* is sometimes used to express a capacity of retaining knowledge, and sometimes a power of recalling it to our thoughts when we have occasion to apply it to use. The latter operation of the mind, however, is more properly called *recollection.* Hence a distinction is made between *memory* and *recollection. Memory* retains past ideas without any, or with little effort; *recollection* implies an effort to recall ideas that are past. Memory depends upon attention, without which even the objects of our perceptions make no impression on the memory, and the permanence of the impression which anything leaves in the memory is proportioned to the degree of attention which was originally given to it. There is also a strong connection between memory and the association of ideas.

MEM'PHIAN, pertaining to Memphis; a term expressive of something very obscure: a sense borrowed from the intellectual darkness of Egypt in the time of Moses.

MEN'DICANTS, a term applied to several orders of monks who live on alms, or beg from door to door.

MEN'NONITES, or MENNONISTS, a sect founded by a German, named Simon Menno, in 1645, the leading tenet of which is, that Jesus Christ's nature did not partake of that of his mother.

MENOL'OGY, in the Greek church, a brief calendar of the lives of the saints, or a simple remembrance of those whose lives are not written.

MEN'SA, in archæology, denotes all patrimony or goods necessary for a livelihood.

MENSA'LIA, in law, such parsonages or spiritual livings as were united to the tables of religious houses, called by the canonists mensal benefices.

MENSA'RII, in Roman antiquity, officers appointed to manage the public treasury.

MENSO'RES, in antiquity, those officers who were sent onward to provide lodgings for the Roman emperors in their routes, and to the domestics who waited at table.—*Mensores frumentarius*, distributors of the corn.

ME'NU, INSTITUTES OF, the name given to the most celebrated code of Indian civil and religious law; so called from Menu, Menou, or Manu, the son of Brama, by whom it is supposed to have been revealed. The Hindoos themselves ascribe to this system the highest antiquity; and many of the most learned Europeans are of opinion that of all known works there is none which carries with it more convincing proofs of high antiquity and perfect integrity. Sir W. Jones assigns the date of its origin somewhere between Homer and the Twelve Tables of the Romans; and Schlegel asserts it as his belief that it was seen by Alexander the Great in a state not materially different from that in which we possess it. The Institutes of Menu are of a most comprehensive nature: they embrace all that relates to human life; the history of the creation of the world and man; the nature of God and spirits; and a complete system of morals, government, and religion. The work, says Sir W. Jones, contains abundance of curious matter, interesting both to speculative lawyers and antiquaries, with many beauties which need not to be pointed out, and with many blemishes which cannot be justified or palliated: it is a system of despotism and priestcraft; both, indeed, limited by law, but artfully conspiring to give mutual support.

MERCA'TOR'S CHART, a chart, in which the parallels of latitude and the meridians are represented by straight lines.

MER'CHANT, one who exports the produce of one country, and imports the produce of another; or, according to popular usage, any trader who deals wholesale.

MER'CY-SEAT, in scripture antiquities, a table, or cover, lined on both sides with plates of gold, and set over the ark of the covenant, on each side of which was a cherubim of gold with wings spread over the mercy-seat.

MER'CURY, the Latin name of the Grecian Hermes. He was the son of Jupiter and Maia, and discharged the office of the messenger of the gods. Part of his duty was also to conduct the shades of the dead to the infernal regions. He presides over eloquence, profit, good fortune, and theft; in which he was himself so great a proficient that, on the day of his birth, he

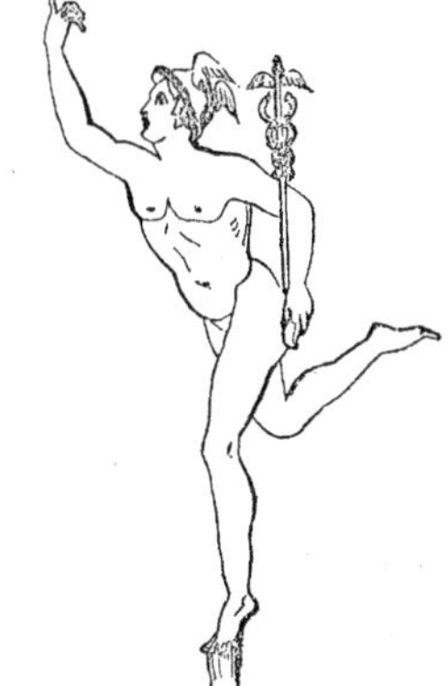

stole fifty kine from the herds of Apollo, whom he repaid by the gift of his invention, the lyre.

MER'GER, in law, is the destruction of a lesser estate in lands and tenements by the acquisition of a greater estate in the same immediately succeeding by the same party and in the same right. Thus an estate for years is said to merge, or sink, in an estate for life, if there be no other estate vested in another person intervening between the two; and an estate for life in an estate of inheritance. There is no merger of an estate tail.

MER'LON, in fortification, is that part of a parapet which is terminated by two embrasures of a battery.

MER'MAID, an imaginary or fabulous creature, which seamen have described as having the head and body of a woman, with the tail of a fish. *Mermen* also have been seen, if we might trust the same authority. It is not, however, any recent fiction; ancient writers having given full credence to it.

MES'MERISM, the doctrine of animal magnetism, so named from its author, Frederic Anthony Mesmer, a German physician. In 1778, Mesmer propounded a theory, according to which all the phenomena of life are referred to the motion and agency of a certain universal magnetic fluid, which admits of being influenced by external agents, and especially by magnetic instruments. Wonderful effects were said to have been produced by him and others who co-operated with him, upon animal bodies, and many cures performed by the agency of a certain magnetical apparatus. The use of magnetic instruments is now quite exploded, and the principal means used to produce the effects of mesmerism are such as touching and stroking with the hands, according to rule, breathing on a person, fixing the eye upon him, &c. The mesmerized person must always be of a weaker constitution than the mesmerizer, and, if possible, of a different sex, and must also believe devoutly in the science. The effects produced upon the person to whom mesmerism is communicated, or the *mesmeree*, as he is called, consist partly in bodily sensations, as chilliness, heaviness, flying pains, &c.; partly in a diminished activity of the external senses; partly in fainting, convulsions, sleep, with lively dreams, in which the mesmeree is transported to higher regions, observes the internal organization of his own body, prophesies, gives medical prescriptions, receives inspired views of heaven and hell, purgatory, &c.; reads sealed letters laid on his stomach, and when awakened is totally unconscious of what he has experienced. Six stages or degrees of mesmerism have been enumerated, viz.—the *walking stage*, the stage of *half-sleep*, *mesmeric sleep* or *stupor*, *somnambulism*, *self-contemplation* or *clairvoyance*, *universal illumination*, in which the patient knows what is going on in distant regions, and all that has happened or will happen to those persons with whom he is brought into mesmeric relation, and so forth. More latterly mesmerism has been associated with phrenology, so that by touching certain organs, the patient, when mesmerized, is made to dance, sing, fight, or steal, &c.

MESNE, in law, a lord of a manor who has tenants holding under him, though he holds the manor of a superior.—*Mesne process*, an intermediate process which issues pending the suit, upon some collateral interlocutory matter. Sometimes it is put in contradistinction to *final process*, or *process of execution*, and then it signifies all such processes as intervene between the beginning and end of a suit.

MESS, in military language, denotes a sort of ordinary, or public dinner, for the maintenance of which every officer, who takes his meals there, gives a certain proportion of his pay. In a British military mess-room the young subaltern and the veteran field-officer meet on equal terms, a soldierlike frankness prevails, and the toils of service are, as they ought to be, forgotten during the moments devoted to social hilarity.—In naval language, the *mess* denotes a particular company of the officers or crew of a ship, who eat, drink, and associate together: hence the term *messmate* is applied to any one of the number thus associated.

MES'SAGE, an official communication sent by a President or King to the congress of the nation.

MES'SENGERS, certain officers employed in the secretary of state's department to convey despatches, either at home or abroad.

MESSI'AD, the name given to the only modern epic poem of Germany; the subject of which is, as the name implies, the sufferings and triumphs of the Messiah. It is written in hexameter verse, for which, as we have elsewhere observed, the German is better fitted than any modern language, and consists of 20 books. The publication of this poem procured for its author unbounded reputation; but posterity does not appear to sanction the high award pronounced on it by contemporaneous writers. Schlegel, indeed, maintains that the modern literature of Germany may be said to date from the *Messiad;* but this high praise must be understood as referring chiefly to its having been among the first productions in which the power and resources of the German language were developed, rather than to its innate merits as an epic poem, or to the influence it has exercised over the national poetry of

Germany. The reputation of Klopstock among his own countrymen rests chiefly on his Odes; and it must be admitted that in all those parts of his epic into which a lyric spirit could be infused—in other words, whenever the feelings or the sympathies were to be excited—there are few poets, either ancient or modern, to whom he deserves to be postponed; but, on the other hand, the dignity and sublimity of his sentiments are not unfrequently disfigured by the pedantry and affectation of his style, and the tediousness of his episodes.

MESSI'AH, a Hebrew word signifying *the anointed;* a title which the Jews gave to their unexpected great deliverer, whose coming they still wait for: and a name which Christians apply to Jesus Christ, in whom the prophecies relating to the Messiah were accomplished. Among the Jews, anointing was the ceremony of consecrating persons to the highest offices and dignities; kings, priests, and sometimes prophets were anointed: thus Aaron and his son received the sacerdotal, Elisha the prophetic, and David, Solomon, and others, the royal unction. The ancient Hebrews being instructed by the prophets, had very clear notions of the Messiah; these, however, were changed by degrees; insomuch that when Jesus Christ appeared in Judea, they were in expectation of a temporal monarch, who should free them from their subjection to the Romans. Hence they were greatly offended at the outward appearance, the humility, and seeming weakness of our Saviour; which prevented their acknowledging him to be the Christ they expected.

MES'SUAGE, in law, is said to be properly a dwelling-house with a small portion of land adjacent, or the site of the manor. It is now one of the general words used in the legal description of dwelling-houses with the land attached.

MESTI'ZO, in Spanish America, the child of a Spaniard or creole and a native Indian.

METAB'ASIS, in rhetoric, transition; a passing from one thing to another.

METACAR'PUS, in anatomy, that part of the hand between the wrist and the fingers. The inner part of the metacarpus is called the palm, and the other the back of the hand.

METACH'RONISM, an error in chronology, by placing an event after its real time.

METALEP'SIS, in rhetoric, the continuation of a trope in one word through a succession of significations, or the union of two or more tropes of a different kind in one word, so that the several gradations or intervening senses come between the word expressed and the thing intended by it.

METAMOR'PHOSIS, the changing of something into a different form; in which sense it includes the transformation of insects, as well as the mythological changes related by the poets of antiquity.

MET'APHOR, in rhetoric, is the application of a word in some other than its ordinary use, on account of some applicability or resemblance between the two objects: thus, if we call a hero a *lion;* a shrewd, crafty fellow, a *fox;* a minister, *a pillar of the state*, &c., we speak *metaphorically*. Brevity and power are the characteristic excellencies of the metaphor; novelty shows the original wit: but metaphors indulged in merely for the sake of unexpected contrast, frequently prove more allied to the ridiculous than the sublime, and ought to be but rarely used. Metaphors have been divided by writers on rhetoric into several classes; but the most appropriate are those which are termed analogical, and which derive their force, not from any actual resemblance between two objects, but from a resemblance between the relations which they bear respectively to certain other objects. Thus "the sea of life" is a common and appropriate metaphor; not from any resemblance between the idea of the visible sea and the complex notion of that abstraction which we term human life, but because there is a fancied similarity between the position of navigators in an uncertain voyage and that of human beings engaged in the manifold scenes of life.

METAPH'RASIS, a bare or literal translation out of one language into another.

METAPHYS'ICS, that branch of philosophy which inquires into the science of the mind, or spiritual existence. With respect to animals, it takes them up where physiology leaves them; and, proceeding higher, ventures to speak of Deity itself. The end of this science is the search of pure and abstracted truth. It casts a light upon all the objects of thought and meditation, by ranging every being with all the absolute and relative perfections and properties, modes and attendants of it, in proper ranks or classes; and thereby it discovers the various relations of things to each other, and what are their general or special differences from each other; wherein a great part of human knowledge consists. It has been very pertinently remarked that "a man who contemns metaphysics must think his own nature unworthy of examination. Metaphysical inquiries, indeed, have often been disfigured with overstrained subtilty and revolting sophistry, and too often arbitrary analogies, bold comparisons, and unmeaning mysticism have claimed and received homage as having unlocked the long-hidden truth; but the same has taken place in regard to religion and politics, and all the great subjects which strongly stir the soul of man."

MET'APLASM, in grammar, a transmutation or change made in a word by transposing or retrenching a syllable or letter.

METATH'ESIS, in literature, a figure by which the letters or syllables of a word are transposed.—In medicine, a change or removal of a morbid cause, without expulsion.

METEMPSYCHO'SIS, the doctrine of transmigration, which supposes that the soul of man, upon leaving the body, becomes the soul of some other animal. This was the doctrine of Pythagoras and his followers, and such is still the prevailing doctrine in some parts of Asia, particularly in India and China. The Indian doctrine of metempsychosis rests on the supposition that all beings derive their origin from God, and are placed in this world in an altogether degraded condition, from which they all, but more particularly the human race, must either decline into still lower degradation, or rise gradually to a higher state more accordant with their divine original, according as they give ear to the vicious or the virtuous suggestions of their nature. It must be remarked, however, that the Indians make a wide distinction between the future destiny of those who have passed through life tainted by the usual vices and infirmities of human nature, and those whose lives have been spent in the constant discharge of religious duties. In the latter case, the soul does not pass through different stages of existence, "but proceeds directly to reunion with the Supreme Being, with which it is identified, as a river at its confluence with the sea merges therein altogether. His vital faculties, and the elements of which his body consists, are absorbed completely and absolutely; both name and form cease; and he becomes immortal, without parts or members."

METEMP'TOSIS, a term in chronology expressing the solar equitation necessary to prevent the new moon from happening a day too late, or the suppression of the bissextile once in 134 years.

METEOROM'ANCY, a species of divination by thunder and lightning, held in high estimation by the Romans.

METH'OD, a suitable and convenient arrangement of things or ideas. In logic and rhetoric, the art or rule of disposing ideas in such a manner that they may be easily comprehended, either in order to discover the truth, or to demonstrate it to others. Method is essential to science; and without method, business of any kind will fall into confusion. In studying a science, we generally mean by *method*, a system of classification, or arrangement of natural bodies according to their common characteristics; as the method of Ray, the Linnæan method. The difference between *method* and *system* is this: *system* is an arrangement founded, throughout all its parts, on some one principle; *method* is an arrangement less fixed and determinate, and founded on more general relations.

METHOD'IC SECT, a name given to certain ancient physicians, who conducted their practice by rules after the manner of Galen and his followers, in opposition to the *empiric sect.*

METH'ODISTS, the body of Christians to whom this name is chiefly applied are the followers of the late John Wesley, the founder of this numerous sect; hence called Wesleyan Methodists. But the term bears a more extensive meaning, being applied to several bodies or sections of Christians who have seceded or withdrawn from the Wesleyan denomination. The origin of the Methodist Society took place at Oxford in 1729. After the Revolution, when the principles of religious toleration were recognized amid the progress of free inquiry, the clergy of the Established Church were thought by some to have sunk into a state of comparative lukewarmness and indifference. This alleged degeneracy was observed with pain by John Wesley and his brother Charles, when students at the University of Oxford; and being joined by a few of their fellow-students who were intended for the ministry in the Established Church, they formed the most rigid rules for the regulation of their time and studies, for reading the Scriptures, for self-examination, and other religious exercises. The ardent piety and rigid observance of system in everything connected with the new opinions displayed by the Wesleys and their adherents, as well as in their college studies, which they never neglected, attracted the notice and excited the jeers of various members of the University, and gained for them the appellation of *Methodists;* in allusion to the *methodici*, a class of physicians at Rome who practised only by theory.

METŒ'CI, the resident aliens, who formed a large class of the inhabitants of Athens. They were distinguished from the few full citizens by many disabilities and burdens. They had no share in the administration of the state, and were precluded from the power of possessing landed estates. Each was compelled to purchase the shelter he received from the state by the payment of a small annual sum, and to place himself under the guardianship of a citizen, who was his formal representative in the courts of law. They were generally engaged in mercantile and mechanical business.

METON'IC CY'CLE, in chronology, the period of nineteen years, in which the lunations of the moon return to the same days of the month; so called from its discoverer Meton, an Athenian, who lived about 400 B.C. From its great use in the calendar, this is called the *golden number*.

METONYM'IA, or MET'ONYMY, in rhetoric, a figure of speech whereby one thing is put for another, as the cause for the effect, the part for the whole, and the like; as, "my friend keeps a good *table*," instead of good *provisions;* "that boy has a clear *head*," meaning *intellect*.

METO'PA, in architecture, the square space in the frieze between the triglyphs of the Doric order. It is left either plain or decorated, according to the taste of the architect. In the most ancient examples of this order, the metopa is left quite open, as is manifest from a passage alluded to in the art.

METOPOS'COPY, the art of divination by inspecting the forehead, treated of especially by the famous Cardanus. The signs of the forehead are chiefly its lines; but moles and spots are also supposed to have their particular meaning. The lines are under the dominion of their several planets.

ME'TRE, in the classical sense of a word, a subdivision of a verse. The Greeks measured some species of verses (the dactylic, choriambic, antispastic, Ionic, &c.) by considering each foot as a metre; in others (the iambic, trochaic, and anapæstic,) each *dipodia*, or two feet, formed a metre. Thus, the dactylic hexameter (the heroic verse) contains six dactyls and spondees: the iambic, anapæstic, and trochaic *trimeter*, six of those feet respectively. A line is said to be *acatalectic* when the last syllable of the last foot is wanting; *brachycatalectic*, when two syllables are cut off in the same way; *hypercatalectic*, when there is one superfluous syllable.

METROMA'NIA, a rage for composing verses, which is said (upon the authority of a respectable medical work) to have once seized a person in a tertian fever, who was otherwise by no means gifted with poetical powers, but who, when the fit was off, became as dull and prosaic as the most unimaginative of human beings could desire. We apprehend that fits of this kind are more frequent than the public have any idea of.

MET'RONOME, an instrument for measuring musical time. It is contrived on the principle of a clock, having a short pendulum, whose bob being movable up and down on the rod, is thus capable of increasing or decreasing the length of a note or bar as required by the character of the music. The length or duration of a note is often expressed at the head of a piece of music by stating that a pendulum of a given length in inches will vibrate a minim, crotchet, or other note, as the case may be.

METROP'OLIS, the capital or principal city of a country or province: as London or Paris. The term metropolis is also applied to archiepiscopal churches, and sometimes to the principal or mother church of a city. The Roman empire having been divided into thirteen dioceses, and one hundred and twenty provinces, each diocese and each province had its metropolis, or capital city, where the proconsul had his residence. To this civil division, the ecclesiastical was afterwards adapted, and the bishop of the capital city had the direction of affairs, and the pre-eminence over all the bishops of the province. His residence in the metropolis gave him the title of *metropolitan*.

METROPOL'ITAN, in early ecclesiastical history, was a title applied to the archbishop, or chief ecclesiastical dignitary, resident in a city. The establishment of metropolitans took place at the end of the third century, and was confirmed by the council of Nice. In some of the Protestant states of Germany the title exists to the present time, and the person in possession of it has rank equivalent to the bishops of the English church.

MEZ'ZANINE, in architecture, an entresole, or little window, less in height than in breadth, serving to give light to an attic.

MEZ'ZO, in music, an Italian word, signifying *half*. Thus *mezzo forte*, *mezzo piano*, *mezzo voce*, imply a middle degree of piano or soft. By *mezzo soprano* is understood, a pitch of voice between the soprano or treble and counter-tenor.

MEZZOTIN'TO, a particular manner of engraving, so called from its resemblance to drawings in Indian ink. To perform this, the smooth surface of the copper or steel plate is furrowed all over with an instrument made for the purpose, till the whole is of a regular roughness throughout; so that if a paper were to be worked off from it at the copper-plate press it would be black all over. When this is done, the plate is rubbed with charcoal, black chalk, or black lead, and then the design is drawn with white chalk; after which the outlines and deepest shades are not scraped at all, the next shades are scraped but little, the next more, and so on, till the shades gradually falling off, leave the paper white, in which places the plate is perfectly burnished. By an artificial disposition of the shades, and different parts of a figure on different plates, mezzotintos are printed in colors, so as to represent actual paintings.

MI'CAH, a canonical book of the Old Testament, written by the prophet Micah; in which the writer censures the reigning vices of Jerusalem and Samaria, and denounces the judgments of God against both kingdoms. The birthplace of our Saviour is thus designated by him: "But thou, Bethlehem Ephrata, little among the thousands of Judah, out of thee shall come forth a ruler in Israel, whose generation is of old, from everlasting."

MICH'AELMAS, or *Feast of St. Michael*, a festival of the Romish church, observed on the 29th of September. In England, Michaelmas is one of the regular periods for settling rents; and an old custom is still in use of having a roast goose for dinner on that day, probably because geese are at that period most plentiful, and in the highest perfection.

MI'CROCOSM, man has been called so by some fanciful writers on natural philosophy and metaphysics, by reason of a supposed correspondence between the different parts and qualities of his nature and those of the universe.

MICROG'RAPHY, the description of objects which are too minute to be seen without the help of a microscope.

MIDDLE AGES, a term used by historians to denote that period which begins with the final destruction of the Roman empire, and ends with the revival of letters in Europe, or, as some writers have it, with the discovery of America; *i. e.* from the eighth to the fifteenth century. In general, it may be said, the middle ages embrace that period of history in which the feudal system was established and developed, down to the most prominent events which necessarily led to its overthrow.

MID'SHIPMAN. Midshipmen are young gentlemen ranking as the highest of the class of petty officers on board a ship of war; their duty is to pass to the seamen the orders of the captain or other superior officer, and to superintend the performance of the duties so commanded.

MID'SUMMER, the summer solstice. The 24th of June is Midsummer-day, which is also quarter day.

MILIEU, (JUSTE,) PARTY OF THE, a French party nickname, arising, it is said, out of a casual expression of King Louis Philippe, but which has obtained a notoriety rather greater than such ephemeral phrases usually acquire. It has served to denote the great party opposed to the Carlists, or Legitimists, on the one hand, and to the extreme left section of the Chamber of Deputies, with its allies the Republicans, on the other. After the overthrow of the feeble ministry of Lafitte, in March, 1831, Casimir Périer was authorized to form a new cabinet; and his administration seems to have realized more than any other the ideal of a government of the Juste Milieu. After a short interval he was succeeded by Soult; who has been perhaps, since that time, more identified with the Juste Milieu party than any other minister: Molé, Guizot, Dupin, Thiers, Barrot, the most eminent statesmen of France, having each of them adopted a line and formed to a certain extent a party of his own, alternately aided and opposed by the great body of the partisans of the Juste Milieu.

MILI'TIA, a body of soldiers, regularly enrolled and trained, though not in constant service in time of peace, and thereby distinguished from *standing armies*. In England the origin of this national force is generally traced back to Alfred.

MILLENA'RIANS, or CHIL'IASTS, a name given to those who, in the prim itive ages, believed that the saints will one day reign on earth with Jesus Christ a thousand years. The former appellation is of Latin original, the latter of Greek. The Millenarians held, that after the coming of Antichrist, and the destruction of all nations which shall follow, there shall be a first resurrection of the just alone; that all who shall be found upon earth, both good and bad, shall continue alive—the good, to obey the just who are risen as their princes—the bad to be conquered by the just, and to be subject to them; that Jesus Christ will then descend from heaven in his glory; that the city of Jerusalem will be rebuilt, enlarged, embellished, and its gates stand open night and day.

MILLEN'NIUM, the reign of Christ with his saints upon earth for the space of a thousand years; an idea derived from a passage in the 20th chap. of the Apocalypse, and not uncommonly entertained by Christians in all ages, but especially in the times of the primitive church. The opinion seems to be traced as far back as to Papias, a father of the second century. It is the subject of much discussion among the writers of that and the succeeding ages; was maintained by Justin Martyr, Irenæus, Tertullian, and many others, and powerfully refuted by Origen.

MIME, the name given by the ancient Greeks and Romans at once to a species of dramatic entertainment, and to the authors and actors by whom it was respectively composed and performed. It consisted chiefly of a rude representation of common life, and resembled the modern farce or vaudeville in its character and accompaniments. Sophron of Syrracuse, who lived about 400 years before the Christian era, is considered the inventor of this species of composition. His pieces were read even with pleasure by Plato, who is said to have introduced this kind of dramatic entertainment into Athens.

MIME'SIS, in rhetoric, imitation of the voice and gestures of another person.

MIND, the intellectual or intelligent power in man. "When the mind," says Mr. Locke, "turns its view inward upon itself, thinking is the first idea that occurs; wherein it observes a great variety of modifications, whence it frames to itself distinct ideas. Thus the perception annexed to any impression on the body by an external object, is called sensation; when an idea recurs without the presence of the object, it is called remembrance; when sought after by the mind, and again brought into view, it is recollection; when the ideas are taken notice of, and, as it were, registered in the memory, it is attention; when the mind fixes its view on any one idea, and considers it on all sides, it is called study.

MINER'VA, the Latin goddess corresponding to, and confounded with, the Grecian Pallas or Athena. She was fabled to have sprung in full armor from the forehead of her father Jupiter. Minerva was worshipped as the goddess of wisdom, and the patroness of industry and the arts. Athens, the city to which she gave name, was her favorite spot; and there her worship was celebrated with great splendor, and the magnificent temple, the Parthenon, erected to her honor.

MINERVA'LIA, in Roman antiquity, festivals celebrated in honor of Minerva, in the month of March; at which time the scholars had a vacation, and usually made a present to their masters, called from this festival *minerval.*

MIN'IATURE, a representation of nature on a very small scale. *Miniature painting* is generally executed on ivory; and is, as to composition, drawing, and finishing, subject to the same laws as Painting.

MIN'IM, in music, a note equal to two crotchets, or half a semibreve.

MIN'IMS, a religious order in the church of Rome, founded by St. Francis de Paula, towards the end of the 15th century.

MIN'ISTER, the pastor of a church, duly authorized to perform religious worship in public, administer the sacraments, &c.—In politics, one to whom a sovereign prince intrusts the administration of the government; as, a *minister of state;* the *prime minister;* or a *foreign minister.* —In the United States, no minister (or secretary, in the language of our government) can be chosen either representative or senator.—*Foreign minister*, a person sent from one government to another, and accredited to the latter, in order to transact public business in the name of his government

MIN'NEHOFE, the name given by the Germans to the courts of love, so famous in the history of chivalry. The subjects brought before these courts were chiefly connected with the Romantic gallantry of the period, and consisted either of questions proposed with the view to entrap the judges into some awkward decision; or of serious complaints, resulting from affairs of the heart which were discussed and decided upon with all the formality of a court of law. These minnehöfe were for a long period looked upon as forming an indispensable part in all chivalrous exercises. Knights, ladies, and poets participated alike in their proceedings; and large collections of their decisions are still extant. A certain number of ladies, remarkable at once for personal and mental attractions, acted as judges in these courts: the fair sex also conducted the proceedings as counsel, attorneys-general, and solicitors-general, &c.; and they were attended by a numerous train of nobles, knights, and others, who were invested by the court with gradations of rank and precedency analogous to those conferred by the sovereign.

MIN'NESINGERS, the most ancient school of German poets, whose name is derived from the old German word minne (*love.*) The songs and fame of the Provençal troubadours appear to have penetrated into Germany under the first emperors of the house of Hohenstauffen; in whose time the crusades and the frequent Italian wars combined to bring their nation, seated as it is in the centre of Europe, to closer communication with those surrounding it. The minnesingers imitated in German the strains of those early poets, and, like them, made love their principal subject; which was celebrated with much of pedantry and false conceits, but, at the same time, not without generous and chivalric feeling. The verses of the minnesingers are in the old Swabian dialect of the high German, which, under the Hohenstauffens, themselves of Swabian race, was the court language. As was the case with the troubadours, the minnesingers belonged to two different classes: there were among them many knights, princes, and even sovereigns; while there was also another class of more professional poets—wandering minstrels, who attached themselves to the persons of the distinguished chiefs, or wandered from court to court. The oldest of the minnesingers known to us is Henry of Veldeck, about 1170. During the remainder of the 12th and first half of the 13th century, this school of poets flourished; afterwards it gradually declined, and was succeeded by the less chivalrous and homelier school of the master-singers. We possess the names of more than 300 poets, and pieces of the composition of a large proportion of them, who sang during the short period in question.

MI'NOR, in law, an heir male or female, under the age of twenty-one.—In logic, the second proposition of a regular syllogism.—In music, signifies *less*, and is applied to certain concords or intervals which differ from others of the same denomination by half a tone.

MINOR'ITY, in law, a state of being under age. Also the smaller number of persons who give their votes on any questions, particularly in parliament: opposed to *majority*.

MI'NOS, in mythological history, was son of Jupiter and Europa, and king of Crete, and so celebrated as a lawgiver on earth that after his death he was appointed judge of the infernal regions, in which office he was associated with Æacus and Rhadamanthus.

MIN'OTAUR, a fabled monster of classical antiquity, half man and half bull, frequently mentioned by the poets.

MIN'STER, was anciently applied only to the church of a monastery or convent; and forms the termination of the name of many places in England in which such churches formerly existed, as Westminster, Leominster, &c. It is sometimes, but incorrectly, used in common language to signify a cathedral church.

MIN'STRELS, defined by Percy as an order of men in the middle ages who subsisted by the arts of poetry and music, and sang to the harp verses composed by themselves or others. They appear to have been the successors of the minnesingers, scalds, and bards of different European nations, who, even after the age of chivalry had passed, attempted to gain a subsistence by practising those arts which at an earlier period had procured fame and honor for their predecessors. In the piping times of peace, the minstrel sang of mimic war to the dull barons of dungeon castles, who had ears, although they could not read; who, doubly steeped in the ennui of wealth and want of occupation, listened greedily, like other great men, to their own praises. Minstrelsy supplied the lack of a more refined intellectual entertainment and of rational conversation, as professional gentlemen do now at civic banquets: their harpings lulled the rude Sauls to sleep, which is now done by quarto epics. The person of the minstrel was sacred; his profession was a passport; he was "high placed in hall a welcome guest;" the assumption of his character became the disguise of lovers of adventure.

MIN'UET, a dance in slow time and with short measured steps, which requires great dignity and grace of carriage.

MIN'UTE, an architectonic measure; the lower diameter of a column, being divided into sixty parts, each part is called a minute.

MI'QUELETS, in modern history, a species of partisan troops raised in the north of Spain, and chiefly in Catalonia. The miquelets became first known in the wars between Spain and France in the 17th century. At several periods (in 1689, 1789, and again in the wars of Napoleon) the French have endeavored to organize similar corps, to oppose to the miquelets in the mountain warfare of those districts.

MIR'ACLE, an event or effect produced in a manner different from the common and regular method of Providence, by the interposition either of God himself, or some superior agent to whom He delegated the power. Lord Bacon observes, that a miracle was never wrought by God to convert an atheist, because the light of nature might have led him to confess a God: but miracles, says he, are designed to convert idolaters, and the superstitious, who have acknowledged a deity, but erred in the manner of adoring him; because no light of nature extends so far as fully to declare the will and true worship of God.

MIR'ZA, the common style of honor in Persia, when it precedes the surname of an individual. When appended to the surname it signifies prince.

MISAN'THROPY signifies a general dislike or aversion to man and mankind; in contradistinction to *philanthropy*, which means the love of our species.

MIS'CELLANY, a word usually applied to a collection of literary works or treatises. The most celebrated collection of works known by this name is *Constable's Miscellany*.

MISCH'NA, or MIS'NA, the code or collection of the civil law of the Jews. The Jews pretend, that when God gave the written law to Moses, he gave him also another not written, which was preserved by tradition among the doctors of the synagogue, till through their dispersion they were in danger of departing from the traditions of their fathers, when it was judged proper to commit them to writing.

MISDEMEAN'OR, in law, a minor offence, or one of less magnitude than that which is generally designated a crime, the latter being, in common usage, made to denote an offence of a more atrocious character.

MISERE'RE, the 50th Psalm, 4th of the Penitential Psalms, is that designated by the Roman Catholic church under this word, on account of its first words (in the Vulgate translation, "miserere mei Deus, secundum magnam misericordium tuam.") It is the usual psalm appointed for acts of penitence and mortification.

MISNO'MER, in law, a misnaming or mistaking a person's name. The Christian name of a person should always be perfect, but the law is not so strict in regard to surnames, a small mistake in which will be overlooked.

MISPRIS'ION, in law, any high offence under the degree of capital, but bordering thereon.—*Misprision of treason* consists in a bare knowledge and concealment of treason, without assenting to it. Misprisions are called *negative*, when they consist in the concealment of something that ought to be revealed; and *positive*, when they consist in the commission of something which ought not to be done.

MIS'SAL, in the Romish church, the book which contains the prayers and ceremonies of the Mass. Some early missals are beautifully executed, and are objects of bibliomania.

MISSA'LIA, the money paid to a Catholic priest for a mass read for the dead.

MISSIL'IA, in antiquity, were a certain kind of largesses thrown among the Roman people, such as small coins of gold or silver, sweetmeats, &c.

MIS'SIO, among the Romans, was a full discharge given to a soldier after twenty years' service, and differed from the *exauctoratio*, which was a discharge from duty after seventeen years' service. —*Missi* also signified a rescue sent by the emperor or person who exhibited the games, to a wounded gladiator.

MIS'SIONARIES, all religious communities, from the earliest ages of Christianity, have endeavored to propagate their tenets, not by the force of arms, but by the persuasive precepts of the Gospel; and there is scarcely a corner of the habitable globe which has not been penetrated by men expressly sent out to carry its glad tidings to pagan nations. Foremost among the Protestant countries which have thus distinguished themselves are the United States and England.

MIS'SIONS, stations of missionaries in infidel countries. In geography, the extensive districts formerly under the control of missionaries of the church of Rome, on the borders of the Spanish and Portuguese settlements in America, were so called. These missionaries chiefly belonged to the orders of the Capuchins, Dominicans, and Jesuits; but the latter were the most celebrated and the most successful. Their settlements in Paraguay comprehended a vast province, which they governed with independent authority: in Brazil they had also extensive districts under their control. The downfall of the order was followed by the destruction of these settlements.

MITH'RAS, the grand deity of the Persians, supposed to be the sun or god of fire, to which they paid adoration as the purest emblem of the divine essence.

MI'TRA, in antiquity, a cap or covering for the head, worn by the Roman ladies, sometimes by the men, but it was looked upon as a mark of effeminacy in them, especially when it was tied upon their heads. Amongst the Greeks, *mitra* was a piece of defensive armor made of brass, lined with wool, and worn next to the skin, under the coat of mail.

MI'TRE, a sacerdotal ornament worn on the head by bishops and certain abbots on solemn occasions; being a sort of cap, pointed and cleft at top. The high priest among the Jews wore a mitre or bonnet on his head.

MIT'TIMUS, in law, a precept or command in writing under the hand and seal of a justice of the peace, or other proper officer, directed to the gaoler or keeper of a prison, for the receiving and safe keeping of an offender charged with any crime until he be delivered by due course of law.

MNEMON'ICS, the art of assisting the memory—an art which, when founded on a simple system, is of incalculable use to all persons, but more especially to those who wish to study history and the sciences to advantage. The ancients were well acquainted with mnemonics; according to some, the science came from the East to the Greeks; others consider the poet Simonides as the inventor of them.—The principal difficulty in attaining a competent knowledge of history, consists in retaining the dates of the several epochas, eras, &c., to which the principal occurrences in history belong; but this difficulty is considerably obviated by the employment of modern systems of mnemonics.

MNEMOS'YNE, in classical mythology, the goddess of memory: daughter, according to the genealogists, of Uranus (Heaven) and Gaia (Earth,) and mother, by Jupiter, of the Nine Muses. Her statues usually have the figure enveloped in long and ample drapery, and the right hand raised towards the chin.

MOAT, a ditch made round the old castles, and filled with water. The moat surrounding a military fortress of modern construction (or the ditch) is left dry; but where it is capable of inundation at pleasure, this circumstance is considered an advantage to the system of defence.

MODE, a term used by Locke to denote "such complex ideas, which, however compounded, contain not in them the supposition of subsisting by themselves, but are considered as dependences on, or affections of, substances. Of these modes there are two kinds, simple and mixed. Simple modes are "only variations or different combinations of the same simple idea, without the mixture of any other, as a dozen or a score, which are nothing but the ideas of so many distinct units added together." Mixed modes are those "compounded of simple ideas of several kinds put together to make one complex one— e. g., *beauty;* and consisting of a certain composition of color and figure, causing delight in the beholder." The term is now universally laid aside by writers on mental philosophy.—In music, a regular disposition of the air and accompaniments relative to certain principal sounds, on which a piece of music is formed, and which are called the essential sounds of the *mode.* In the earliest Greek music there were only three modes, but various new modes were afterwards added. The moderns, however, only reckon two modes, the major and minor. The major mode is that division of the octave by which the intervals between the third and fourth, and seventh and eighth, become half-tones, and all the other intervals whole tones. The minor mode is that division by which the intervals between the second and third, and fifth and sixth, become half-tones, and all the others whole tones.—In logic, the form or manner of a syllogism with respect to the quantity and quality of its constituent propositions.

MOD'EL, in the Fine Arts, that which is an object of imitation.—In painting and sculpture, it is the individual whom the artist procures for getting up his proportions, details, play of the muscles, &c.—Also in sculpture, it is the term applied to the small sketch in wax or clay for a work of art.—In architecture, it is a small pattern in relief, either of wood, plaster, or other material, of the building proposed to be executed.

MOD'ELLING, in the Fine Arts, the

art of making a mould from which works in plaster are to be cast; also used for the forming in clay of the design itself.

MOD'ERATES, the name given to a party in the Church of Scotland which arose early in the eighteenth century, claimed the character of moderation in doctrine, discipline, and church government, and which has continued to exist in a greater or less degree of vigor down to the present time.

MOD'ERATOR, a person who presides at a public assembly, to propose questions, preserve order, and regulate the proceedings.

MOD'ERNS, those who have lived in times recently passed, or are now living; opposed to the ancients. The term is especially applied to those of modern nations, or of nations which arose out of the ruins of the Greek and Roman empires, the people of which are called the ancients.

MODIFICA'TION, in philosophy, that which modifies a thing, or gives it this or that manner of being. Quantity and quality are accidents which modify all bodies. According to Spinosa's system, all the beings that compose the universe are only so many different modifications of one and the same substance; and it is the different arrangement and situation of their parts, that make all the difference between them.

MODIL'LION, in architecture, an ornament sometimes square on its profile, and sometimes scroll-shaped, with the intervention of one or two small horizontal members placed at intervals under the corona in the richer orders. They should stand centrally over columns when the latter are employed. They are simplest in the Ionic and Composite orders, more carving being bestowed on them in the Corinthian order.

MODULA'TION, in music, the art of composing agreeable to the laws prescribed by any particular key, or of changing the mode or key. Also the regular progression of several parts through the sounds that are in the harmony of any particular key, as well as the proceeding naturally and regularly from one key to another. In pieces of a mild and quiet character, it is not proper to modulate so often as in those which have to express violent and great passions. Where everything relating to expression is considered, modulation also must be so determined by the expression, that each single idea in the melody shall appear in the tone that is most proper for it.

MOD'ULES, in architecture, a measure equal to the semi-diameter of a Doric column. It is a term only applied in the Doric order, and consists of thirty minutes.

MO'DUS OPERAN'DI, a Latin phrase, signifying the way or method by which an operation or performance of any kind is effected.

MOGRA'BIANS, or MEN OF THE WEST, a name formerly given to a species of Turkish infantry, composed of the peasants of the northern parts of Africa, who sought to ameliorate their condition by entering into foreign service.

MO'GUL, GREAT, the name by which the chief of the empire so called, founded in Hindostan by Baber, in the 15th century, was known in Europe. The last person to whom this title of right belonged was Shah Allum; and the Mogul empire having terminated at his death in 1806, his vast possessions fell chiefly into the hands of the East India Company.

MOLE, a mound or massive work formed of massive stones laid in the sea by means of coffer-dams, extended in a right line or as an arch of a circle, before a port, which it serves to defend from the violent impulse of the waves; thus protecting ships in a harbor. The word is sometimes used for the harbor itself. Among the Romans, a kind of mausoleum, built like a round tower on a square base, insulated, encompassed with columns, and covered with a dome.

MO'LINISM, in Roman Catholic theology, a system of opinions on the subjects of grace and predestination somewhat resembling that advocated by the Arminian party among Protestants. It derived its name from the Jesuit Louis Molina, professor of theology in the university of Evora in Portugal.

MOL'LAH, the title of the higher order of judges in the Turkish empire. After the three first magistrates of the empire follow fourteen mollahs, who preside over the fourteen principal seats of justice in the empire; among these, the mollahs of Mecca and Medina have the highest rank.

MO'LOCH, the name of the chief god of the Phœnicians, frequently mentioned in Scripture as the God of the Ammonites, and probably the same as the Saturn of the Syrians and Carthaginians. Human sacrifices were offered at the shrine of this divinity; and it was chiefly in the valley of Tophet, to the east of Jerusalem, that this brutal idolatry was perpetrated.

MOLOS'SUS, in Greek and Latin poetry, a foot consisting of three long syllables, as *churchyard-wall.*

MO'MIERS, the name by which certain religionists of the so-called Evangelical party have been designated in Switzerland, and some parts of France and Germany, since 1818.

MO'NAD, in metaphysics, this word has been used by Leibnitz and his followers, partisans of what has been called the Monadic Theory. "After studying," says Stewart, "with all possible diligence what Leibnitz has said of his *monads* in different parts of his works, I find myself quite incompetent to annex any precise idea to the word as he employed it." He then quotes the following as "some of his most intelligible attempts to explain his meaning:" "A simple substance has no parts: a compound substance is an aggregate of simple substances, or of monads." "Monads, having no parts, are neither extended, figured, nor divisible. They are the real atoms of nature; in other words, the elements of things."

MON'ARCHY, the government of a single person. Monarch and monarchy are equivalent in common speech to king and kingdom: so that we often read of the Spartan monarchs, &c., although the government of Sparta was under a double race of kings reigning at the same time. Monarchies are usually said to be of four kinds—*absolute*, *limited*, *hereditary*, and *elective*, which are self-explanatory terms. The only elective monarchy in Europe was that of Poland. All absolute and limited monarchies have adopted the hereditary principle.

MON'ASTERY, the general name for those religious houses appropriated to the reception and maintenance of monks and nuns, but especially of the former.

MON'DAY, the second day of the week is so called, and means, literally, the *day of the moon.* Its equivalents in Fr. and Germ. are respectively Lundi and Montag, signifying also *day of the moon.*

MON'EY, in political economy, the name given to the commodity adopted to serve as the universal equivalent of all other commodities, and for which individuals readily exchange their surplus products or services.

MONK, a man who retires from the ordinary temporal concerns of the world, and devotes himself to religion. Monks usually live in monasteries, on entering which they take a vow to observe certain rules. Some, however, live as hermits in solitude, and others have lived a strolling life without any fixed residence. Monks are distinguished by the color of their habits into black, white, gray, &c.

MON'OCHORD, a musical instrument originally having but one string as its name imports; but it is now generally constructed with two, by means of which the musician is better enabled to try the proportions of sounds and intervals, and judge of the harmony of two tempered notes.

MON'OCHROME, an ancient mode of painting in which only one color is used. The most numerous monuments existing of this kind of painting are on terra cotta.

MON'ODY, a species of poem of a mournful character, in which a single mourner is supposed to bewail himself; thus distinguished from those pastoral elegies which are in the form of dialogues.

MONOG'AMY, the state or condition of those who have only been once married, and are restrained to a single wife.

MON'OGRAM, in archæology, a character or cipher composed of one, two, or more letters interwoven, being an abbreviation of a name; anciently used as a seal, badge, arms, &c. Printers, engravers, &c., formerly made use of monograms to distinguish their works.

MON'OGRAPH, a treatise on a single subject in literature or science.

MON'OLITH, a term recently introduced into the language, to signify a pillar or other large substance consisting of a single stone. Some remarkable monoliths have been found in Egypt; of these, the zodiac of Denderah, and the obelisk of the Luxor, both of which have been removed to Paris, are well-known examples.

MON'OLOGUE, a dramatic scene, in which a person appears alone on the stage, and soliloquizes.

MONOMA'NIA, the name given by some physicians to that form of mania in which the mind of the patient is absorbed by one idea.

MONOPH'YSITE, one who maintains that Jesus Christ had but one nature, or that the human and the divine nature were so united as to form one nature only.

MONOP'OLY, an exclusive right, secured to one or more persons, to carry on some branch of trade or manufacture, or the sole power of vending any species of goods, obtained either by engrossing the articles in market by purchase, or by a license from the government. The most frequent monopolies formerly granted, were the right of trading to certain foreign countries, the right of importing or exporting certain articles, and that of exercising particular arts or trades. There is, however, one species of monopoly, sanctioned by the laws of all countries that have made any advances in the arts—the exclusive right of an invention or improvement for a limited number of years.

MON'OTHEISM, the doctrine or belief of the existence of one God only: opposed to *polytheism*, or a plurality of gods.

MON'OTONE, in rhetoric, a sameness of sound, or the utterance of successive syllables on one unvaried key, without infliction or cadence.

MONSEIG'NEUR, a title of courtesy in France, which was prefixed to the titles of dukes and peers, archbishops, bishops, and some other exalted personages, and used in addressing them. *Monseigneur* simply was, before the Revolution, the title given to the dauphin. *Monsieur* is now the common title of courtesy and respect in France.

MONT DE PIETE, the name given on some parts of the Continent to certain benevolent institutions, established for the purpose of lending money to the poor at a moderate rate of interest. They originated under the papal government in the 15th century, and were intended to countervail the exorbitant usurious practices of the Jews, who formed at that period the great money-lenders of Europe.

MON'UMENT, in architecture, a building or erection of any kind, destined to preserve the memory or achievements of the person who raised it, or for whom it was raised; as a triumphal arch, a mausoleum, a pyramid, a pillar, a tomb, &c.

MOOD, (sometimes written *mode*,) in grammar, the manner of forming a verb, or the manner of the verb's inflections, so as to express the different forms and manners of the action, or the different intentions of the speaker.

MOOT'-CASE, or MOOT'-POINT, an unsettled point or question to be mooted or debated.

MORAL'ITY, the duties of men in their social character; or that rule of conduct which promotes the happiness of others, and renders their welfare accordant with our own. This implies, that our acts must proceed from a motive of obedience to the divine will.—The term *moralities* was given to a kind of allegorical plays, formerly in vogue, and which consisted of moral discourses in praise of virtue and condemnation of vice. They were occasionally exhibited as late as the reign of Henry VIII., and after various modifications, assumed the form of the masque, which became a favorite entertainment at the court of Elizabeth and her successor.

MORAL PHILOSOPHY, the science of manners and duty; the science which treats of the nature and condition of man as a social being, of the duties which result from his social relations, and the reasons on which they are founded. It is denominated a science, as it deduces the rules of conduct and duty from the principles and connections of our nature, and proves that the observance of them is productive of our happiness. It is likewise called an art as it contains a system of rules for becoming virtuous and happy; and whoever practises these rules attains an habitual power or facility of becoming virtuous and happy. It is an art and a science of the highest dignity, importance, and use. Its object is man's duty, or his conduct in the several moral capacities and connections which he sustains. Its office is to direct our conduct, to show whence our obligations arise, and where they terminate. Its use or end is the attainment of happiness, and the means it employs are rules for the right conduct of our moral powers. Like natural philosophy, it appeals to nature or fact; it depends on observation, and it builds its reasonings on plain incontrovertible experiments, or upon the fullest induction of particulars which the subject will admit. The terms, *moral philosophy*, *moral science*, and *morals*, are synonymous, though some writers have employed them improperly to denote the whole field of knowledge, relating primarily to the mind of man, thus giving them a signification co-extensive with the word *metaphysics*.

MORAL SENSE, an innate or natural sense of right and wrong; an instinctive perception of what is right or wrong in moral conduct, which approves some actions and disapproves others, independent of education or the knowledge of any positive rule or law. But the existence of any such moral sense is very much doubted.

MORA'VIANS, otherwise called HERNHUTTERS, or UNITED BRETHREN, a sect of Christians, among whom social polity makes a figure as conspicuous, at least, as religious doctrine. The United Brethren are much attached to instrumental as well as vocal music; celebrate agapæ or love feasts; and cast lots, to discover the will of the Lord. These people live in communities, and provide for their poor; but do not make a common stock of their property. They wear a plain, uniform dress, and are extremely methodical in all their concerns.

MORBIDEZ'ZA, delicacy or softness of style, as opposed to anything harsh, hard, or angular. This word is more particularly applicable, in painting and sculpture, to representations of human flesh and its characteristics.

MOR'DENTE, in music, a grace in use by the Indian school, which is effected by turning upon a note without using the note below.

MORESQUE', in painting, a species of ornamental painting, in which foliage, fruits, flowers, &c., are combined, by springing out of each other, without the introduction of the human figure, or that of any animals; and receiving its name from having been much used by the Moors, who, however, were not the inventors of it.

MORGANAT'IC MAR'RIAGE, or *Left-handed Marriage*, a marriage between a man of superior and a woman of inferior rank, in which it is stipulated that the latter and her children shall not enjoy the rank or inherit the possessions of her husband. Such marriages are not uncommon in the families of sovereign princes, and of the higher nobility in Germany; but they are restricted to personages of these exalted classes.

MOR'ION, a kind of helmet copied by the Spaniards from the Moors.

MOR'PHEUS, in ancient mythology, the god of dreams; the son of Somnus, who presided over sleep, with whom he is frequently confounded. The chief distinction between them appears to be this: Morpheus had the power of assuming only the human shape, while the transformations of Somnus were unlimited. He is generally represented as a beautiful youth, with a bunch of poppies in his hand,

MORTAL'ITY, BILLS OF. Bills of Mortality are extracts from official registers, showing the numbers who have died in some fixed period of time, as a year, a month, or a week; and hence they are called yearly, monthly, or weekly bills.

MORT'GAGE, literally, a dead pledge; the grant of an estate in fee as security for the payment of money, and on the condition that if the money shall be paid according to the contract, the grant shall be void, and the mortgagee shall reconvey the estate to the mortgager.

MORT'MAIN, in law, an alienation of lands, tenements, or hereditaments, to any corporation, sole or aggregate, guild, or fraternity. The foundation of the statutes of mortmain is Magna Charta; by which it was rendered unlawful for any one to give his lands to a religious house, &c. in order to take them back again to hold of the same house; which was extended, by interpretation, so as to annul gifts of lands which religious houses did not give back to the donor to his own use, but kept in their own hands after taking.

MOSA'IC, in painting, a species of representation of objects by means of very minute pieces of stones or pebbles of different colors, carefully inlaid upon a ground generally of metal. In St. Peter's at Rome are to be seen some works of this sort on a magnificent scale. This art was practised at a very early period, and was re-introduced to Italy by the Byzantine Greeks.

MOSQUE, a Mahometan temple, or place of religious worship. All mosques are square buildings, generally constructed of stone, in the Moresque or Saracenic style of architecture. Before the chief-gate is a square court paved with white marble, and surrounded with a low gallery whose roof is supported by marble pillars. In these galleries the Turks wash themselves before they enter the mosque.

MOTET', in music, a composition consisting of from one to eight parts, of a sacred character.

MO'TION, in painting and sculpture, the change of place or position which from certain attitudes a figure seems to be making in its representation in a picture. It can be only implied from the attitude which prepares the animal for the given change, and differs from action, which see. Upon motion in art, depends that life which seems to pervade a picture when executed by a master.—In music, the manner of beating the measure so as to hasten or retard the pronunciation of the words or notes.

MO'TION IN COURT, in law, an occasional application to the court, by the parties or their counsel, for the purpose of obtaining some rule or order of court which becomes necessary in the progress of a cause. Motions are either of a criminal nature, as motions for an attachment for a misbehavior; or of a civil nature. Motions are accompanied by affidavits stating the facts on which they are grounded, and generally preceded by a notice to the opposite party. In any public assembly, the proposing of any matter for the consideration of those present.

MOT'TO, is used to signify a word or sentence added to a device ; and when put upon a scroll, it is commonly employed as an external ornament of coat armor. The use of mottoes for this purpose is very ancient. The term motto is also applied as a sentence or quotation prefixed to any writing or publication.

MOULD'INGS, in architecture, certain projections beyond the bare wall, column, &c., an assemblage of which forms a cornice, or other decoration.

MOUNT'ING, the act of straining a print or drawing upon canvass, or of placing it upon an ornamental frame.

MOV'ABLE FEASTS, certain festivals held in commemoration of different events recorded in the Gospels and the Acts of the Apostles, and connected with the personal circumstances of Christ during the last year of his earthly life, and after his death. As they are reckoned backward and forward from his resurrection, and as the celebration of that day depends on the time of new moon, which varies at different times through the space of a month, these dependent festivals also vary in the same way. Easter is always the first Sunday after the first new moon after the 21st of March ; and from this all the others are reckoned for each year.

MOVE'MENT, in politics, an expression that has been adopted of late years into the political vocabulary of most European nations, signifying that party in a state whose principles consist in a restless endeavor to obtain such concessions in favor of popular rights as will ultimately place the chief functions of government in the hands of the people. It is opposed to the Conservative party.

MUCK, RUNNING A, a phrase which has been adopted into the English language to signify an indiscriminate attack upon friends and enemies. This expression is derived from the Javan word amok, which means *to kill*; the inhabitants of Java, and many other of the Asiatic islands, being remarkable for an irresistible phrensy resulting from a desire of vengeance, which leads them to aim at indiscriminate destruction, and thus to subject themselves to be treated like wild beasts which it is impossible to take alive.

MUEZ'ZIN, or MUED'DIN, among the Mahometans, the crier who announces the hour of prayer from the minaret, and reminds the faithful of their duty.

MUF'TI, the chief priest among the Mussulmans, appointed by the grand seignior himself. He is the oracle in all doubtful questions of their law.

MUGGLETO'NIANS, a religious sect which arose in England, about the year 1657 ; so denominated from their leader Ludowic Muggleton, a tailor, who, with his associate Reeves, asserted that they were the two last witnesses of God mentioned in the Revelations.

MULAT'TO, a term in general use in American countries, in which there exists a mixed population of different races and colors, for the offspring of a union between a white and a negro.

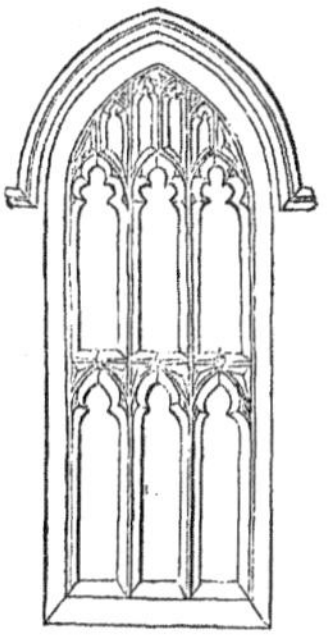

MUL'LION, in architecture, a vertical division between the lights of windows, screens, &c., in Gothic architecture. Mullions are rarely found earlier than the early English style. Their mouldings are very various. Sometimes the styles in wainscoting are called mullions.

MU'LIER, in law, a married woman, in distinction from a concubine. Also, a name for lawful issue born in wedlock, who are preferred before an elder brother of illegitimate birth.

MULTO'CA, the name given to the code of laws by which the Turkish empire is governed, consisting of the precepts contained in the Koran, the oral injunctions of Mohammed, and the decisions of the early caliphs and doctors. It relates to every subject of life, and comprises various matters appertaining to government, the sultan being the sole judge of its application to particular cases.

MUNI'CIPAL, in the Roman civil law, an epithet which signifies, invested with the rights and privileges of Roman citizens. Thus the municipal cities were those whose inhabitants were capable of enjoying civil offices in the city of Rome ; though the greater part of them had no suffrages or votes there.——In modern times, *Municipal law* pertains solely to the citizens and inhabitants of a state, and is thus distinguished from *political* law, *commercial* law, and the *law of na-*

tions. And those are called *municipal officers* who are elected to defend the interest of cities, to maintain their rights and privileges, and to preserve order and harmony among the citizens; such as mayors, sheriffs, aldermen, &c.

MU'NIMENTS, in law, the writings relating to a person's inheritance, by which he is enabled to defend his title to his estate: or, in a more general sense, all manner of evidences, such as charters, feofments, releases, &c.

MU'RAL CROWN, among the ancient Romans a golden crown or circle of gold, indented and embattled, bestowed on him who first mounted the wall of a besieged place and there planted a standard.

MUR'DER, in law, the wilful and felonious killing a person from premeditated malice; provided the party wounded or otherwise hurt, die within a year and a day after the fact be committed. To constitute murder, in law, the person killing another must be of sound mind or in possession of his reason, and the act must be done with malice prepense and aforethought; but malice may be implied, as well as expressed.

MUR'ZAS, the name given to the hereditary nobility of the Tartars, or, more strictly, perhaps, to the second class of their nobility, the first or principal class being designated beys.

MU'SES, in the poetry of the ancients, personifications of the various branches of delightful exercises in which human genius displays itself. They were beautifully said to be the daughters of Jove and Mnemosyné, or Memory; and they were represented as companions of Apollo upon Parnassus. As the subject was wholly dependent upon the fancy of the poet, it was not always treated of alike. Thus according to some, all the functions of the Muses were united in three persons; Mnemé, Aœde, and Meleté; that is, Memory, Song, and Meditation; but it was more usual to reckon nine, and to name them as follows: Clio, to whom they attributed the invention of history; Melpomene, the inventor of tragedy; Thalia, of comedy; Euterpe, of the use of the flute; Terpsichore, of the harp; Erato, of the lyre and lute; Calliope, of heroic verse; Urania, of astrology; and Polyhymnia, of rhetoric.

MUSE'UM, a place set apart as a repository for curious, valuable, and interesting objects connected with the arts and sciences, more especially such as relate to natural history. The term was originally applied to a study or a place set apart for learned men in the royal palace of Alexandria, by Ptolemy Philadelphus, who founded a college, and gave salaries to the several members, adding also an extensive library, which was one of the most celebrated in the world.

MU'SIC, is the science of sounds, considered as capable of producing melody, and agreeably affecting the mind by a due disposition, combination, and proportion. It treats of the number, time, division, succession, and combination of sounds. It is divided into *theoretical* music, which inquires into the properties of concords and discords, and explains their combinations and proportions for the production of melody and harmony; and *practical* music, which is the art of applying the theory of music in the composition of all sorts of tunes and airs. Music is also either vocal or instrumental. *Vocal* music is the melody of a single voice, or the harmony of two or more voices in concert; *instrumental* music is that produced by one or more instruments. As civilization advances, music, as a science, gains new advocates; and the day is evidently fast approaching when few will decry music on the ground that its effects are merely sensual. It is addressed to the ear, indeed; but all the influences which we receive from without are conveyed through the medium of the senses; and the tones of music often speak a language to the soul richer in meaning than words could express. Nothing is merely sensual which makes a lasting spiritual impression upon us; and those who deny to music such a power, have not heard its sublimest strains, or have not the capacity to appreciate them. With regard to the antiquity of music, it appears to have been almost coeval with man. Moses tells us that Jubal, who lived before the flood, was the inventor of the kinnor and the hugah, *i. e.* the harp and the organ. The Jews were fond of music in their religious ceremonies, their feasts, their public rejoicings, their marriages and their mournings. Kings and great men among the Jews studied music, and David made a very great proficiency in it. In their time, indeed, music had reached its highest perfection among the Hebrew nation, and part of their religious service consisted in chanting solemn psalms, with instrumental accompaniments.—The invention of the lyre is ascribed to Hermes Trismegistus, the Mercury of the Egyptians, which is a proof of its antiquity: but a still greater proof of the existence of musical instruments amongst them at a very early period, is drawn from the figure of an instrument said to be represented on an obelisk, erected, as is supposed, by Sesostris at Heliopolis. The Greeks, we know, were exceedingly fond of music. It had a considerable share in their education; and so great was its influence over their bodies as well as their minds, that it was thought to be a remedy for many disorders.

MU'SICAL GLASSES, a musical instrument consisting of a number of glass goblets, resembling finger glasses, which are tuned by filling them more or less with water, and played upon with the end of a finger damped.

MUS'SULMAN, or MOS'LEM, a follower of Mahomet. This word signifies, in the Turkish language, a true believer.

MUSTER-ROLL, a specific list of the officers and men in every regiment, troop, or company, made out by the adjutant, and delivered to the inspecting field-officer or pay-master, &c., by which they are paid, and their strength and condition known.

MUTE, in law, a person that stands speechless when he ought to answer or plead.—In grammar, a letter that represents no sound. Mutes are of two kinds: the *pure mutes* which entirely intercept the voice, as *k*, *p*, and *t*, in the syllables, *ek*, *ep*, *et*: and the *impure mutes*, which intercept the voice less suddenly, as *b*, *d*, and *g*, in the syllables *eb*, *ed*, *eg*.

MUTES, in the grand seignior's seraglio, dumb officers who are sent to strangle, with the bow-string, bashaws or other persons who fall under the sultan's displeasure.—*Mutes*, among undertakers, men who are employed to stand at the door of the deceased, until the body is carried out.

MU'TINY, an insurrection of soldiers or seamen, or open resistance to the authority of their commanders. Any attempt to excite opposition to lawful authority, or disobedience, of commands, is by the laws of most nations declared to be mutiny, and is punishable by the sentence of a court-martial.

MU'ZARAB, Christians living under the government of the Moors in Spain; so called, it is said, from an Arabic werd signifying imitators or followers of the Arabs.

MYOL'OGY, the doctrine of the muscles. In the Fine Arts, the term is applied to a description of the muscles of animals.

MYRIORA'MA, a movable picture, capable of forming an almost endless variety of picturesque scenes, by means of several fragments or sections of landscapes on cards, which may be placed together in numberless combinations.

MYR'MIDONS, in classical mythology, a people on the southern borders of Thessaly, who accompanied Achilles to the Trojan war.

MYS'TERY, something secret or concealed, impossible or difficult to comprehend. All religions, true or false, have their mysteries. In the religions of Pagan antiquity, the secret rites and ceremonies performed by a select few in honor of some divinity were so called. "Each of the Pagan gods," says Bishop Warburton, "had, besides the public and open, a secret worship paid them, into which none were admitted but those who had been selected by preparatory ceremonies, called initiation; and this secret worship was termed *the mysteries*." The first mysteries of which we have any account were those of Isis and Osiris in Egypt; whence they were introduced into Greece and Italy, and in process of time disseminated through the northern and western nations of Europe. The religion of the *Jews* was likewise full of mysteries; their laws, nay, their whole constitution and nation, were mysterious; but the mysteries of the Old Testament were generally types or shadows of something in the New. The Christian religion has also its mysteries; but, in the scripture language, the word mystery is used with some latitude, and denotes whatever is not to be known without a divine revelation.

MYS'TERIES, in modern literature, a species of dramatic composition, with characters and events drawn from sacred history. Saint Gregory Nazianzen composed the earliest sacred dramas extant, on the model of the Greek tragedies, but with Christian hymns substituted for the ancient chorus. The mysteries of the middle ages are thought by some to have been first introduced by pilgrims returning from the Holy Land. They originated among, and were probably first performed by, ecclesiastics.

MYS'TICISM, in religion, a word of very vague signification, applied, for the most part, indiscriminately to all those views or tendencies in religion which aspire towards a more direct communication between man and God, not through the medium of the senses, but through the inward perception of the mind, than that which is afforded us through revelation.

MYS'TICS, a religious sect distinguished by their professing a pure, sublime, and perfect devotion, with an entire disinterested love of God, free from all selfish considerations, and by their aspiring to a state of passive contemplation.

MYTHOL'OGY, the history of the fabulous gods and heroes of antiquity, with the explanations of the fables or allegories couched therein. According to the opinion of most writers, among whom is that profound thinker, Lord Bacon, a great deal of concealed instruction and allegory was originally intended in most part of the ancient mythology: he observes, that some fables discover a great and evident similitude, relation, and connection with the thing they signify, as well in the structure of the fable, as in the meaning of the names whereby the persons or actors are characterized. He also takes a more enlarged and higher view of the subject, and looks on them not as the product of the age, nor the invention of the poets, but as sacred relics, or, as he terms them, "gentle whispers, and the breath of better times, that from the tradition of more ancient nations, came at length into the flutes and trumpets of the Greeks."

N.

N, the fourteenth letter and eleventh consonant of the English alphabet, is an imperfect mute or semi-vowel, because part of its articulation may be continued for any length of time; it is also a liquid, and a nasal letter, the sound being formed by forcing the voice strongly through the mouth and nostrils, which, at the same time, is intercepted by applying the tip of the tongue to the fore part of the palate, with the lips open. It has one sound only, and after *m* is silent, or nearly so, as in *hymn*, *condemn*. Among the ancients, N stood as a numeral for 900; and, with a dash over it, for 9000. N. or No. stands as an abbreviation for *numero*, number; also for north.

NA'BOB, an Indian word for a deputy; a title of dignity and power applied to those who act under the soubahs or viceroys. The term, however, has become proverbial, of late years, to signify a person who has acquired great wealth, and lives in great splendor.

NA'HUM, or *the prophecy of Nahum*, a canonical book of the Old Testament. Nahum, the seventh of the twelve minor prophets, was a native of Elkoshai, a little village of Galilee. The subject of his prophecy is the destruction of Nineveh, which he describes in the most lively and pathetic manner; his style being bold and figurative.

NA'IADS, in mythology, water-nymphs, or deities that preside over brooks and fountains. They are represented as beautiful women, with their heads crowned with rushes, and reclining against an urn from which water is flowing.

NAIVETE', naturalness; absence of artifice. The essential meaning of the word is a natural, unreserved expression of sentiments and thoughts, without regard to conventional rules, and without weighing the construction which may be put upon the language or conduct.

NAME, a word whereby men have agreed to express some idea; or which serves to signify a thing or subject spoken of. Names are either proper or appellative. Proper names are those which represent some individual thing or person, so as to distinguish it from all other things of the same species; and are either called Christian, as that given us at baptism, or surnames; the first imposed for the distinction of persons, answering to the Roman *prænomen;* the second for the distinction of families, answering to the *nomen* of the Romans, and the *patronymicum* of the Greeks. The ancient Britons, says Camden, generally took their names from colors, because they painted themselves. When they were subdued by the Romans, they took Roman names; the Saxons introduced the German names; the Danes brought with them their names; and the Normans introduced theirs.

NARRA'TION, in rhetoric, the term usually applied to the second division of an oratorical discourse, in which the facts of the case are set forth from which the orator intends to draw his conclusions. This part of a discourse should be characterized by the greatest simplicity of style, as well as by absence of all rhetorical ornaments.

NARCIS'SUS, in mythology, the beautiful son of Cephesus and the nymph Liriope, whose history formed one of the most favorite topics with the poets of classical antiquity. Though beloved by all the Grecian nymphs, he treated them with contemptuous indifference; but having accidentally seen his own image reflected in a fountain, he became so enamored of it that he languished till he died, and thus realized the prophecy of

Tiresias, that he should live until he saw himself. After his death the gods, moved with compassion for his fate, changed him into the flower which bears his name.

NATA'LIS, or NATALIS DIES, properly signifies a birth-day; but it was used by the ancients more particularly to signify the feast held on the anniversary of the birth-day of an emperor: hence in time it served to denote any sort of feast; and the primitive Christians used it in this sense.

NA'TION, a collective appellation for a people inhabiting a certain extent of territory under the same government. The word is also used in some universities by way of distinguishing students of different districts or countries, as the case may be. This latter meaning is borrowed from the custom that was adopted in the University of Paris previously to the institution of faculties, when those who resorted to it from different countries lived under the same institutions and masters, a *common country*, however, being the only bond of union.

NATIONAL GUARD (OF FRANCE,) a military institution composed of citizens, and not incorporated with the standing army. It may in fact be considered the army of the people, in opposition to the standing force, considered as the army of the state. It is, therefore, not liable to be sent across the frontiers, except by the consent of the individuals composing it; but when the country is attacked, it is expected to act, with or without the aid of the regulars; also to concur with the latter in preserving the public peace. The officers are elected by their comrades, and not appointed by the public authorities.

NATIV'ITY, the day of a person's birth. The word nativity is chiefly used in speaking of the saints, as the nativity of St. John the Baptist, &c. But when we say *the Nativity*, it is understood to mean that of Jesus Christ, or Christmas Day.

NAT'URAL, in music, a character marked thus ♮, whose office is to contradict the flats or sharps placed at the beginning of a stave or elsewhere, and by the use of which the note to which it is prefixed returns to the diatonic scale.

NATURALIZA'TION, in law, the act of naturalizing an alien, or placing him in the condition (that is, investing him with the rights and privileges) of a natural subject.

NA'TURE, a word of vast and comprehensive signification, embracing as it were, the whole universe—all that is comprised under the superintending care of the great Creator. Thus when we say, Nature is benevolent and wise, we understand either the Deity himself, or a power performing the will of the Deity, and conducting everything in this world under his order: a notion supported by some ancient systems of philosophy, adopted by poets, and most easy to popular idea. Independently of this, however, we often say Nature herself, &c. in a merely figurative sense; personifying the laws of nature, that is, the properties of matter. When, therefore, we say, that nature covers the earth with abundance, we mean that God covers the earth with abundance; when we say that nature is magnificent and inexhaustible, we mean that creation is magnificent and inexhaustible. When we speak of the study of nature, we mean the study of creation; which embraces first the knowledge of things, and secondly the knowledge of the properties of things. Nature (meaning thereby the whole body of created things) presents an assemblage of objects in every respect worthy of the attention of mankind. Nature is made to conform in some degree to the hand of man, and resist only when his ignorance violates its essential order. It yields its secrets to his inquiries; to his sensibility it presents the most engaging images; and remains, to all ages, a picture perpetually renewed of the primitive creation of God.—There is another sense, too, in which the word *nature* is of continual occurrence; viz., the *nature* of man; by which we understand the peculiar constitution of his body or mind, or the qualities of the species which distinguish him from other animals. So also we express by this word, the essential qualities or attributes of any other thing; as the *nature* of blood, of a metal, of plants, &c. Again, when we allude to the established or regular course of things, we say, this or that event is not according to *nature*.—In the Fine Arts, *nature* often means the successful imitation of nature; but, with artists of a higher order, *nature* does not signify a *mere copy*, but as it were, the expression of the *ideal* of nature, at which she aims in all her formations, yet without ever absolutely attaining it.—By the *law of nature* is understood, that system of principles which human reason has discovered to regulate the conduct of man in all his various relations. In its most extensive sense, it comprehends man's duties to God, to himself, and to all mankind.

NA'VAL AR'CHITECTURE, or SHIP-BUILDING, the art of constructing vessels for the purposes of navigation, was, in all probability, anterior to the deluge, and is generally admitted to have been handed down by Noah to his posterity. That, in a rude state, it was practised in Egypt, there is no question; and the Greeks are supposed to have derived their knowledge of it from the Carthaginians. But neither in Greece nor in Rome, did naval architecture rise to what may be termed a scientific knowledge of the art of ship-building. The crusades first gave the impulse to improvements in ship-building. In modern times the United States and England excel in naval architecture. The American vessels in elegance of form and speed in sailing, surpass those of all other nations.

NAVA'LIS CORO'NA, a crown among the Romans, given to him who first boarded an enemy's ship; it was a circle of gold representing the beaks of ships.

NAVE, in architecture, that part of a temple enclosed by the walls. The part in front of it was called *pronaos*, and that in the rear *posticum*. In modern architecture, it is the middle part or alley of a church, between the aisles or wings.

NAVIGA'TION, the art and science by which, in open seas, ships are conducted from port to port. This is effected by charts of the seas, and by keeping a journal of the courses from hour to hour, and the distance on each by means of the log line, each knot on which corresponds to a mile of distance. Also by observations on the sun, moon, and stars, made with instruments, and checked by tables and almanacs.

NAVIGA'TION LAWS, a branch of maritime law, defining the peculiar privileges to be enjoyed by British ships, and the way in which they shall be manned; as also the conditions under which foreign ships shall be allowed to engage in the trade of this country, either as importers or exporters of commodities.

NA'VY, the whole naval establishment of any country, including the collective body of ships, officers, men, stores, &c.

NAZ'ARITE, among the Jews, one who had laid himself under the obligation of a vow to observe the rules of Nazariteship, either for his whole life as was the case with Samuel, and John the Baptist, or only for a specified time. The rules of Nazariteship, during the time specified in the vow, obliged the man or woman to more than ordinary degrees of purity.

NECES'SITY, the cause of that which cannot be otherwise, or whatever is done by a power that is irresistible; in which sense it stands opposed to freedom. The schools distinguish a physical necessity and a moral necessity; and a simple or absolute necessity, and a relative one. *Physical necessity*, is the want of a principle, or of a natural means necessary to act, which is otherwise called a physical or natural impotence. *Moral necessity*, is only a great difficulty, such as that arising from a long habit, a strong inclination, or violent passion. *Simple* or *absolute necessity*, is that which has no dependence on any state or conjuncture, or any particular situation of things, but is found everywhere, and in all the circumstances in which the agent can be supposed. *Relative necessity*, is that which places a man in a real incapacity of acting or not acting in those circumstances, and that situation he is found in, though in other circumstances, and in another state of things, he might act or not act. When a man's actions are determined by causes beyond his control, he acts from *necessity*, and is not a free agent.

NECROL'OGY, a register of the deaths of benefactors in a monastery. Formerly, also, what is now called *martyrology* was called *necrology*.—A register of distinguished persons who die within a certain period (not a record of their lives and actions, for that is *biography*) is also known by this term.

NEC'ROMANCY, a sort of magic practised by the Jews, Greeks, and Romans, by which they attempted to raise the dead or make them appear. The witch of Endor is a striking example of a bold and artful deception of this kind.

NECROP'OLIS, in antiquity, the name given to some ancient cemeteries in the vicinity of large cities. It has also been given to some of our modern ones.

NEC'TAR, in mythology, the supposed drink of the gods, and which was imagined to contribute much towards their eternal existence. It was, according to the fables of the poets, a most beautiful and delicious liquor, far exceeding anything that the human mind can imagine. It gave a bloom, a beauty and a vigor, which surpassed all conception, and together with *ambrosia* (their solid food,) repaired all the decays or accidental injuries of the divine constitution.

NEFAS'TI DI'ES, an appellation given by the Romans to those days wherein it was not allowed to administer justice or hold courts.

NEGA'TION, in logic, a declaration that something is not, or the affirming one thing to be different from another; as, the soul is *not* matter.

NEG'ATIVE, in general, something that implies a negation: thus we say, negative quantities, negative signs, negative powers, &c. "Our words and ideas," says Dr. Watts, "are so unhappily linked together, that we can never know which are positive, which negative ideas, by the words that express them: for some positive terms denote a negative idea, as *dead;* and there are both positive and negative terms invented to signify the same and contrary ideas, as *unhappy* and *miserable.*" If we say, such a thing is "not a man," or "not white," nothing is determined; the thing may be a dog, and it may be black: something of a positive character is necessary to express what it is.—*Negative pregnant*, in law, a negative which implies an affirmation; as when a person denies having done a thing in a certain manner or at a certain time, as stated in the declaration; which implies that he did it in some manner.

NEHEMI'AH, a canonical book of the Old Testament, so called from the name of its author. Nehemiah was born at Babylon during the captivity, and succeeded Ezra in the government of Judah and Jerusalem. He was a Jew, and was promoted to the office of cup-bearer to Artaxerxes Longimanus, king of Persia; when the opportunities he had of being daily in the king's presence, together with the favor of Esther the queen procured him the favor of being authorized to repair and fortify the city of Jerusalem, in the same manner as it was before its destruction by the Babylonians.

NE INJUS'TE VEX'ES, in law, a writ that lies for a tenant who is distrained by his lord for more services than he is obliged to perform, being a prohibition to the lord not to distrain or vex his tenant.

NEMÆ'AN GAMES, in antiquity, celebrated games in Greece, deriving their name from Nemæa, a village between the cities of Cleonæ and Philus, where they were celebrated every third year. They were instituted in memory of Archemorus or Opheltes; but, after some intermission, were revived by Hercules, in honor of Jupiter, after his victory over the Nemæan lion. The exercises were chariot races, and all the parts of the Pentathlon.

NEM. CON. for *Nemine contradicente*, (no one opposing,) a term chiefly used in parliamentary bodies when anything is carried without opposition.—*Nemine dissentiente*, (no one dissenting,) are terms similarly applied.

NEM'ESIS, a Greek divinity, worshipped as the goddess of vengeance. According to Hesiod, she was the daughter of Night, and was represented as pursuing with inflexible hatred the proud and insolent. The reluctance of the Greeks to speak boastfully of their good fortune, lest they should incur a reverse, is well known; and from various passages in the *Anthologia*, and other ancient writings, it is clear that this feeling originated in a desire to propitiate this divinity. The worship of this goddess was very extensive. Temples were erected to her honor, not only in Greece, but throughout the Roman empire. Nowhere, however, was her worship so pompously celebrated as at Rhamnus, a town of Attica, where she had a statue 10 cubits high of a single stone, and so exquisitely beautiful as to equal even the finest productions of Phidias.

NEOL'OGY, a new phrase or word introduced into a language, or any innovation on ordinary modes of expression. Most European tongues have their classical diction fixed by precedent and authority; and words introduced by bold or careless writers, since this standard was established, go by the name of neologisms until usage has added them at last to the received national vocabulary. *Neology*, in the last century, was the name given by orthodox divines in Germany, to the novel system of interpretation which then began to be applied by many to the records of revealed religion.

NEOME'NIA, in antiquity, a festival observed at the beginning of a lunar month in honor of all the gods, but particularly Apollo.

NE'OPHYTE, in the primitive church newly converted Christians were so termed; and the same appellation is still given, in the Roman Catholic church, to converts made by missionaries among the heathen, to any person entering on the priestly office, and to those persons newly received into the communion of the church.

NEOPLATON'ISTS, in ancient literature, the mystical philosophers of the school of Ammonius Saccas and Plotinus are commonly so called, who mixed some tenets of ancient Platonism with others derived from a variety of sources, and particularly from the demonology of the East. They flourished in the 4th and 5th centuries of the Christian era.

NEORA'MA, an invention of Allaux, a Frenchman, in 1827, for representing the interior of a large building in which the spectator appears to be placed. Everything is exhibited to the life by means of groups and shading.

NEPEN'THE, a species of magic potion, mentioned by the Greeks and Romans, which was supposed to have the power of obliterating all pain and sorrow from the memory of those who partook of it. It is now used figuratively to express any efficient remedy in giving rest and consolation to an afflicted mind.

NEPHA'LIA, Grecian festivals or sacrifices instituted in honor of various deities, as Aurora, Venus, &c. They were so called because no wine was offered during their celebration. It was chiefly at Athens that these festivals were observed.

NE PLUS ULTRA, *i. e.* no farther, the extremity or utmost extent to which anything can go.

NEPTUNA'LIA, in antiquity, feasts observed by the Romans in honor of Neptune. They differ from the *Consualia*, in which that god was considered as presiding over horses and the manege; whereas, the *Neptunalia* were feasts of Neptune, in his more general character as god of the sea.

NEP'TUNE, a Roman divinity, whose attributes are nearly the same as those of the Greek Poseidon. He was the brother of Jupiter, and presided over the

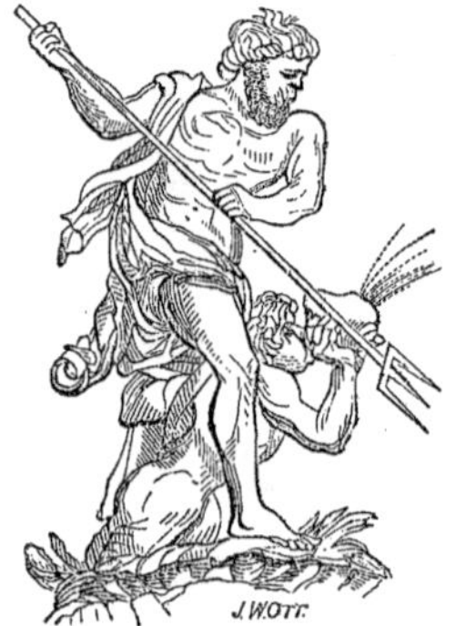

sea. He is represented similar in appearance to Jupiter, but his symbols are a trident and the dolphin.

NEPTUN'IAN, or NEPTUN'IST, one who adopts the theory that the substances of which the earth is composed were formed from aqueous solution; opposed to the *Plutonic* theory, which attributes the earth's formation to the action of fire.

NE'REIDS, in mythology, sea-nymphs, daughters of Nereus and Doris, and celebrated for their beauty. In ancient monuments the Nereids are represented as riding upon sea-horses, sometimes with the human form entire, and at others with the tail of a fish.

NE'REUS, a marine Grecian deity, son of Ocean and Earth. He possessed the gift of prophecy, and was distinguished for his knowledge and love of truth and justice.

NESS, the termination of several names of places in Great Britain, where there is a headland or promontory, as Inverness, Sheerness. The word is probably derived from the Fr. nez, or the Germ. nase, *nose.*

NESTO'RIANS, the followers of Nestorius, patriarch of Constantinople, in the first half of the fifth century. This prelate agitated the Christian world, after the Arian controversy had been quietly settled, by the introduction of certain subtle disputations concerning the incarnation of Christ, from whence debates and contentions arose which harassed the church for the space of more than two centuries. He affected to distinguish with peculiar precision between the divine and human natures united in Christ; and, in guarding over-carefully against the propensity which he discovered in the Christians of his own day to confuse the two, and look upon them as absorbed into one compound substance, he forbade men to entertain any combined notion at all, and kept constantly before their eyes both the god and the man.

NEUTRAL'ITY, the state of being unengaged in disputes or contests between others; the state of taking no part on either side.—In *international law*, that condition of a nation or state in which it does not take part directly or indirectly in a war between other states. A neutral state has the right of furnishing to either of the contending parties all supplies which do not fall within the description of *contraband of war*, which signifies in general, arms and munitions of war, and those out of which munitions of war are made. All such articles are liable to be seized. A neutral state has also the right to conclude such treaties with either belligerent party, as are unconnected with the subject of the war.

NEW'EL, in architecture, the space, either solid or open, round which the steps of a staircase are turned about.

NEWS, literally, fresh information. This word has been fancifully derived from the initial letters of the four cardinal points of the compass, *n*orth, *e*ast, *w*est, and *s*outh.

NEWS'PAPERS, publications in numbers, consisting commonly of single sheets, and published at short and stated intervals, conveying intelligence of passing events. In Rome, under the government of the emperors, periodical notices of passing events (diurna, acta diurna) were compiled and distributed for general reading; but our accounts of these ancient newspapers, derived from classical sources, are somewhat obscure and uncertain. In modern Europe, the earliest occasional sheets of daily intelligence seem to have appeared at Venice, during the war of 1563 against the Turks; and the earliest regular paper to have been a monthly one, published in the same city by the state: but these were distributed in manuscript, and, owing to the jealousy of the government, continued to be so down to very late times. Extraordinary gazettes are said to have been published in England by authority, during the time when the arrival of the Spanish Armada was apprehended; but the specimens preserved in the British Museum, and so long regarded as authentic, seem now to be demonstrated forgeries. The *Mercuries*, *Intelligencers*, &c. of the civil wars, seem to have been the first English papers which appeared regularly. The *Gazette de France* appeared regularly from 1631 to 1792, forming a collection of 163 volumes; it was continued, also, but with some interruptions, through the period of the revolution; and the name still exists, the journal so called being at present, however, but a second-rate paper. From their first imperfect beginning, newspapers have gradually increased in number, matter, and consequence, until they form, in many countries, one of the most important features in the social economy of the people; exercising a marked influence on domestic manners, literature, and usages, but more especially powerful as a great political instrument.

NEW STYLE, the method of reckoning the days of the year in accordance with the Gregorian Calendar, which adjusts the odd hours and minutes, by which the earth's revolution exceeds 365 days, and renders celestial phenomena and terrestrial reckoning equal.

NEW TES'TAMENT, the name given to that portion of the Bible which comprises the writings of the apostles and their immediate disciples. It consists of five historical books, viz., the respective Gospels of Matthew, Mark, Luke, and John, and the Acts of the Apostles (attributed to Luke;) of twenty-one apostolical epistles, of which the early fathers have unanimously ascribed fourteen to St. Paul, three to St. John, two to St. Peter, one to St. James, and one to St. Jude; and of the book known by the name of the Apocalypse or the Revelation of St. John.

NEWTO'NIAN SYS'TEM, or *Newtonian Philosophy*, a phrase often applied to the Copernican or Solar system, which was generally adopted before Newton's time; and by others applied to the laws of planetary motion, first promulgated by Kepler and Hooke; but strictly applicable only to certain geometrical and analytical demonstrations of those known laws, as developed by the genius and industry of Sir Isaac Newton. The chief parts of the Newtonian philosophy are explained by the author in his "Principia.'

NEW YEAR'S DAY. The celebration of the commencement of the new year dates from high antiquity. The Jews regarded it as the anniversary of Adam's birth-day, and celebrated it with splendid entertainments—a practice which they have continued down to the present time. The Romans also made this a holiday, and dedicated it to Janus with rich and numerous sacrifices; the newly-elected magistracy entered upon their duties on this day; all undertakings then commenced were considered sure to terminate favorably; the people made each other presents of gilt dates, figs, and plums; and even the emperors received from their subjects new year's gifts, which at a later period it became compulsory to bestow.

NIBELUN'GEN, LAY OF THE, the name given to the most ancient existing monument of German epic poetry. The origin of this poem is veiled in great obscurity; it is supposed to have existed, in substance at least, two centuries before the reign of Charlemagne, and, like the early compositions of poets in all ages, to have consisted originally of detached ballads and poems, which were afterwards gradually collected, and at length moulded into the complete form in which they at present exist. The last of the modifications which it underwent took place towards the end of the 12th century, and is attributed to the Minnesinger Henrich von Ofterdingen. The story turns upon the adventures of Chrimhild of Burgundy, who is first won by the valiant Siegfried, and after he is treacherously murdered gives her hand to Attila, king of the Huns, chiefly in the hope that through his power and influence she may be revenged on the murderers of her former lord. The *Nibelungen Lied* formed for many centuries the chief traditionary record of the romantic deeds and sentiments of the German nation, but at the era of the Reformation it sank wholly into oblivion; from which, however, it has within the last thirty years been rescued, and permanently placed by the labors and commentaries of Hagen, Zeune, Simrock, and Schlegel, among the most conspicuous monuments of human genius. All the questions relating to its origin, nature, and characteristics are discussed with great interest by the German literati, to many of whom, indeed, it forms a distinct branch of study. In the *Nibelungen Lied*, in the same manner as in the legends of Troy and of Iceland, the interest turns on the fate of a youthful hero, who is represented as invested with all the attributes of beauty, magnanimity, and triumph, but dearly purchasing all these perishable glories by the certainty of an early and predicted death. In his person, as is usual, we have a living type both of the splendor and the decline of the heroic world. The poem closes with the description of a great catastrophe borrowed from a half-historical incident in the early traditions of the north. In this respect also, as in many others, we cannot fail to perceive a resemblance to the *Iliad*. If the last catastrophe of the German poem be one more tragical, bloody, and litanic than anything in Homer, the death of the German hero, on the other hand, has in it more solemnity and stillness, and is withal depicted with more exquisite touches of tenderness than any similar scene in any heroic poem with which we are acquainted. The *Nibelungen Lied* is, moreover, a poem abounding in variety; in it, both sides of human life, the joyful as well as the sorrowful, are depicted in all their reality.

NICE, COUN'CIL OF, the first, and, according to most writers, the most important, œcumenical council held in the Christian church. It was convened, A.D. 325, at Nicæa, by the emperor Constantine, in order to settle the differences that had arisen in the Christian church in respect to the doctrines of Arius. This council was attended by upwards of 250 bishops, of whom a great majority came from the East, by presbyters, deacons, and others from all parts of the Christian world. The chief question, as was remarked above, was the Arian heresy; and the council issued in the excommunication of Arius. The decision of this council had not the effect of restoring tranquillity to the Eastern church, for the Arian controversy was still warmly carried on; but it has supplied that mode of stating the doctrine of the Divinity (as far as relates to the Father and Son) in which it has ever since been received by the orthodox sects.

NI'CENE CREED, in ecclesiastical affairs, a particular creed, or confession of faith, drawn up by the clergy in the council of Nice, and since adopted by the church of England.

NICHE, in architecture, a hollow or recess in a wall, for the reception of a statue or bust.

NICOLA'TIANS, one of the earliest Christian sects, mentioned in the Revelations of St. John, where the angel of God reproaches the church of Pergamos with harboring persons of this denomination. They are there characterized as inclining to the licentious and pagan practices of the Gentiles.

NIM'BUS, a circle or disk, of a luminous nature, which, on sundry ancient medals and other monuments, environs the heads of divinities or sovereigns: the primitive Christian artists adopted this usage, and applied it to their personifications of the great Founder of their religion, and also to the saints and martyrs of the holy church. There can be little doubt but that the origin of this custom arose from a desire on the part of the people of remote antiquity to compliment their kings and heroes by decorating them with a resemblance to the rays of the sun, the great apparent source of life, heat, and fertility.

NI'OBE, in classical mythology, daughter of Tantalus, and one of the Pleiades, married to Amphion, king of Thebes. Proud of her numerous and flourishing offspring, she provoked the anger of Apollo and Diana, who slew them all: she was herself changed by Jupiter, in Phrygia, into a rock, from which a rivulet, fed by her tears, continually pours. The subject of Niobe and her children was a great favorite with the poets of antiquity.

NIZAM', the title of great officers of state in the Asiatic governments.

NOBIL'ITY, the general appellation for a privileged order of society which exists in every civilized country, with the exception of the United States and Norway. In Roman antiquity persons were not noble by birth, but in consequence of the public offices held by their ancestors, who had the sole right to bequeath their images to their descendants. An hereditary nobility is found in the infancy of most nations, ancient and modern. Its origin is to be attributed to various causes; for the most part to military despotism; in some cases, to the honors paid to superior ability, or to the guardians of the mysteries of religion. The priestly nobility of the remotest antiquity has everywhere yielded to the superiority of military chieftains. In France and Germany, the first hereditary nobility begins with the downfall of the Carlovingian dynasty; in England, with the conquest of the Normans, in the tenth and eleventh centuries; and was afterwards spread over all Europe; for, since that time, dignities, as well as lands, have become hereditary. — A contemporary writer has remarked, that "it is a curious particular in the history of nobility, that among the natives of Otaheite, rank is not only hereditary, but actually descends to the son, to the degradation of the father while yet alive: thus, he who is a nobleman to-day, if a son be born to him, is a commoner to-morrow, and his son takes his rank."

NO'BLE, in numismatics, a gold coin value 6*s*. 8*d*. which was struck in the reign of Edward III., and stamped with the impression of a ship, which emblem is supposed to have been commemorative of a naval victory obtained by Edward over the French at Sluys, in 1340.

NO'MADS, or NO'MADES, a name given to nations whose chief occupation consists in feeding their flocks, and who have no fixed place of abode, but shift their residence according to the state of pasture. Nomadic tribes are seldom found to quit their wandering life, until they are compelled to do so by being surrounded by tribes in settled habitations, or unless they can make themselves masters of the settlements of a civilized nation.

NO'MANCY, the art or practice of divining the destiny of persons by the letters which form their names.

NOM DE GUERRE, a French term commonly used to denote an assumed or fictitious name.

NOMENCLA'TOR, in Roman antiquity, was usually a slave who attended upon persons that stood candidates for offices, and prompted or suggested to them the names of all the citizens thèy met, that they might address them by their names; which, among that people, was esteemed an especial act of courtesy.

NOMENCLA'TURE, was originally applied to a catalogue of the most ordinary words in any language, with their significations, &c., drawn up for the purpose of facilitating their use and retention to those who are endeavoring to acquire a language. But, in a more general sense, this term is employed to denote the language peculiar to any science or art: thus we speak of the nomenclature of chemistry, botany, &c.

NO'MINALISTS, a term originally applied to a scholastic sect which arose in the 11th century. Its founder was John Roscelin, a churchman of Compiegne, who asserted that general terms have no corresponding reality either in or out of our minds, being, in truth, words, and nothing more. This doctrine naturally excited great consternation among the schoolmen, with whom, hitherto, all that was real in nature was conceived to depend on these general notions or *essences*. Its promulgator underwent much persecution for his opinions, and was ultimately compelled to retract them, as inconsistent with the doctrine of the Trin ity as it was then stated. He found, however, an able successor in the person of Peter Abelard, who attracted numerous disciples by his dialectical skill and eloquence, and, with his followers, whom he led in a body to Paris, was the occasion of founding the celebrated university of that city. After his death, the ancient realism was restored to its supremacy; nor do we meet with a nominalist until the 13th century, when William of Occam revived his doctrines under some modifications.

NON'AGE, the time of life before a person, according to the laws of his country, becomes of age to manage his own concerns.

NON-ASSUMP'SIT, in law, is a general plea in a personal action, by which a man denies that he has made any promise.—The following legal terms or phrases, beginning with *non*, properly follow in this place; viz.—*Non compos mentis*, a phrase to denote a person's not being of sound memory and understanding. A distinction is made between an idiot and a person *non compos mentis*, the former being constitutionally destitute of reason, the latter deprived of that with which he was naturally endowed: but, to many purposes, the law makes no distinction between the two.—*Non distringendo*, a writ granted not to distrain. —*Non est inventus*, that is, literally, "He has not been found;" the answer made by the sheriff in the return of the writ, when the defendant is not to be found in his bailiwick.—*Non liquet*, "it does not appear;" a verdict given by a jury, when a matter is to be deferred to another day of trial.—*Non pros*, or *Nolle prosequi*, is a term made use of to signify that the plaintiff will proceed no farther in his action. In criminal cases it can only be entered by the attorney-general.

NONCONFORM'IST, one who refuses to conform to the rites and worship of the established church. The name was at first particularly applied to those clergymen who were ejected from their livings by the act of uniformity in 1662.

NONES, in the Roman calendar, the fifth day of the months January, February, April, June, August, September, November, and December; and the seventh of March, May, July, and October; these four last months having six days before the nones, and the others only four. March, May, July, and October had six days in their nones; because these alone, in the ancient constitution of the year by Numa, had thirty-one days apiece, the rest having only twenty-nine, and February thirty; but when Cæsar reformed the year, and made other months contain thirty-one days, he did not allot them six days of nones. The nones, like the calends and ides, were reckoned backwards.

NON'SUIT, in law, the default or non-appearance of the plaintiff in a suit, when called in court, by which the plaintiff is presumed to signify his intention to drop the suit; he is therefore *nonsuited*, that is, his non-appearance is entered on the record, and this entry amounts to a judgment of the court that the plaintiff has dropped the suit.

NON'JURORS, the adherents of James II. who refused to take the oath of allegiance to the government and crown of England at the Revolution, when James abdicated, and the Hanoverian family was introduced.

NOR'MAL, an adjective signifying that the ordinary structure peculiar to a family, a genus, or a species, is in no wise departed from.

NOR'MAN AR'CHITECTURE, a style of architecture imported into England immediately from Normandy, at the time of the Conquest. It is readily distinguished from the styles which succeeded to it by its general massive character, round-headed doors and windows, and low square central tower.

NORNES, in Scandinavian mythology, the three fates, equivalent to the Moira, of the Greeks. Their names were Urd, Wörand, and Sculd; or Past, Present, and Future. They were represented as endowed with great beauty, but of a melancholy and sombre disposition; they were consulted even by the gods, and their decrees were sure and irrevocable.

NO'TABLES, in French history, the deputies of the states under the old régime, appointed and convoked on certain occasions by the king. In 1786 this assembly was summoned, 160 years after its last meeting, and proposed various reforms in different branches of the government. It again met, for the last time, in 1788.

NO'TARIES, APOSTOL'ICAL AND IMPE'RIAL, public notaries appointed by the popes and emperors, in virtue of their supposed jurisdiction over other powers, to exercise their functions in foreign states. Edward II. forbade the imperial notaries to practise in England. Charles VIII. of France, in 1490, abolished both these classes of notaries, and forbade his lay subjects to employ them.

NO'TARY, or NO'TARY PUB'LIC, in modern usage, an officer authorized to attest contracts or writings, chiefly in mercantile matters, to make them authentic in a foreign country; who protests foreign bills of exchange, and inland bills and notes: and in particular, to note the non-payment of an accepted bill.

NOTE, in music, a character which, by its place on the staff, represents a sound, and by its form, determines the time or continuance of such sound. There are six notes in ordinary use, viz., the semibreve, minim, crotchet, quaver, semiquaver, and demisemiquaver. To these may be added the breve, yet met with in sacred music, and the half demisemiquaver, much used by the moderns.

NOTTUR'NO, in music, originally synonymous with serenade; but applied at present to a piece of music in which the emotions chiefly of love and tenderness are developed. Of modern composers Chopin, Field, and Herg are the most distinguished in this department.

NOVA'TIANS, the followers of Novatian, a presbyter of Rome, who was stigmatized as a schismatic and heretic, and founded a sect of this name in the 3d century, which continued to flourish to the end of the 5th. The aim of Novatian was to deny readmission into the church to all persons who, in the time of persecution, or on other accounts, had once lapsed from the faith.

NOV'EL, in literature, a fictitious tale, or imaginary history of real life, generally intended to exhibit the operation of the passions, foremost among which is love. "In the novel," says Goethe, "sentiments and events are to be chiefly represented; in the drama, character and actions. The hero of the novel must be passive, or, at least, not in a high degree active; but we expect of the dramatic hero action." The Italian novella, of which the best and earliest specimens are those contained in the *Decameron* of Boccaccio, was rather a short tale, turning on an event, or on a series of adventures of humor, pathos, or intrigue, than a novel in the modern acceptation of the term. In its present signification in the English language, it seems to express a species of fictitious narrative somewhat different from a romance; yet it would be difficult to assign the exact distinction, and, in the French language, the same name (roman) is used for both; while it differs from a tale merely in the circumstance that a certain degree of length is necessary to constitute a novel. Although, in fact, the terms novel and romance are often used indifferently, yet they have also often been treated as distinct classes of composition in English literature. Perhaps, if we seek to draw the distinction with as much of accuracy as the subject will admit, we may say that the proper object of a novel is the delineation of social manners, or the development of a story founded on the incidents of ordinary life, or both together. Thus will be excluded from the class of novels, on the one hand, tales of which the incidents are not merely improbable, (for this may be the case in a novel,) but occurring out of the common course of life, and such as are founded on imaginary times and imaginary manners, tales of supernatural incidents, chivalrous romances, pastoral romances, &c.; and, on the other hand, we must exclude from the same class fictitious narratives, in which the author's principal object is neither the story nor the costume, but which are obviously written with an ulterior view, although their incidents and character may perhaps, in other respects, fall under the definition suggested above. Thus, political, philosophical, and satirical fictions are clearly not to be ranked as novels. But it is obvious that no definition can be drawn which shall, on this subject, entirely satisfy the caprices of popular language. Of the novel, in this confined sense, the works of Richardson, and those of Fielding and Smollett, afforded, perhaps, the first examples in English literature. The first of these authors gave birth to the sentimental novel, the latter two to the comic or humorous. Marivaux, Prévost, &c., spread the former style of composition in France; where, as well as on the Continent generally, it attained a high degree of vogue. The novel of manners, whether comic or serious, has, perhaps, been always a more popular species of fiction in England. It may be doubted whether the historical fiction, to which Sir Walter Scott has given such universal popularity, belongs strictly to the class of novel or romance. By aiming at the delineation of real, although past manners, and by the general turn of the story, it seems to resemble the former; while the romantic character of many of its incidents seems to assimilate it to the latter.

NOVEM'BER, the eleventh month of the Julian year, consisting only of thirty days. It is the first winter month in the northern hemisphere, and the first summer month of the southern. Its name, November, originates in its being the ninth month of the Roman reckoning.

NOV'ICE, a person not yet skilled or experienced in an art or profession. *Novice* is more particularly used in monasteries for a religious person, in his or her novitiate, or year of probation, and who has not made the vows.

NOVI HOM'INES, among the Romans, were such persons as, by their own personal merit, had raised themselves to curule dignities without the aid of family connections. This reproach, as is well known, was addressed by Catiline to Cicero.

NOVI'TIATE, the term appointed for the trial of those who are to enter a monastery, in order to ascertain whether they have the qualifications necessary for living up to the rule to which they are to bind themselves by vow. The novitiate is generally very severe; the novice generally having to perform many menial offices about the convent, and to give account of the most trifling actions to the master of the novices.

NOX, in mythology, the goddess of

night. In the Grecian mythology, she was the daughter of Chaos, the sister of Elpen and Erebus, and the mother of Æther, Hemera, Manatas, Momus, the Fates, &c., &c.; which were all personifications of the natural phenomena life, sleep, death, &c.

NUDE COM'PACT, in law, a contract made without any consideration, and therefore not valid.—*Nude matter*, a bare allegation of something done.

NUDIPEDA'LIA, in antiquity, a festival in which all were obliged to walk barefooted. This was done on account of some public calamity; as the plague, a famine, &c., &c. It was likewise usual for the Roman matrons, when any supplication and vows were to be made to the goddess Vesta, to walk in procession to her temple barefooted.

NU'DITIES, in painting and sculpture, those parts of the human figure which are not covered with drapery. The gods, demigods, and heroes of antiquity are generally represented either entirely naked, or with a slight mantle only thrown across the shoulders. Figures of fauns, satyrs, &c., also have this distinction. An exception must, however, be made with respect to Jupiter, who is very seldom found without an ample robe enveloping different parts of his body. Perhaps the reverence entertained by the ancients for this their principal deity, prevented them from exhibiting him in a state of absolute nudity.

NUI'SANCE, in law, that which incommodes or annoys; something that produces inconvenience or damage. Nuisances are public or private: *public*, when they annoy citizens in general, as obstructions of the highway; *private*, when they affect individuals only, as when one man erects a house so near his neighbor's as to throw the water off the roof upon his neighbor's land or house, or to intercept the light that his neighbor before enjoyed.

NUM'BERS, the title of the fourth book of the Pentateuch, so called because it contains an account of the numbering of the people. The book comprehends a period of the Israelitish history of about thirty-eight years.—*Numbers*, in poetry, oratory, music, &c. are certain measures, or cadences, which render a verse, period, or song, agreeable to the ear. —*Poetical numbers* consist in a certain harmony in the order and quantity of syllables constituting feet.—*Rhetorical numbers* are a sort of simple, unaffected harmony, less apparent than that of verse, but such as is perceived and affects the mind with pleasure.

NU'MERAL LET'TERS, the Roman capital letters which stand as substitutes for figures; as I for 1; X for 10; L for 50; C for 100, &c.

NUMISMAT'ICS, the science of coins and medals, principally those struck by the ancient Greeks and Romans. The word *coin* is in modern times applied to those pieces of metal struck for the purpose of circulation as money; while the word *medal* signifies pieces of metal similar to coins not intended for circulation as money, but struck and distributed in commemoration of some person or event. Ancient coins, however, are often termed in common language *medals*. The parts of a coin or medal are, the *obverse* or *face*, containing generally the head, bust, or figure of the sovereign or person in whose honor the medal was struck, or some emblematic figure relating to him; and the *reverse*, containing various figures or words. The

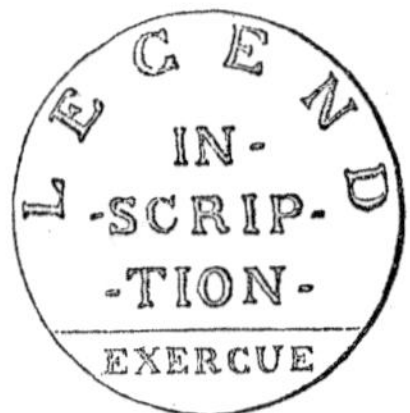

words around the border form the *legend*, those in the middle or field the *inscription*. The lower part of the coin separated by a line from the figures or the inscription, is the *basis* or *exergue*, and contains the date, the place where the coin was struck, &c. The metals of which coins and medals have been chiefly composed are gold, silver, brass or copper. The earliest coins are Phœnician, and were struck or imprinted from dies unreversed, so that the inscription was reversed; but those struck by the ancient Greeks and Romans are most deserving our attention. The study of coins and medals is indispensable to archæology, and to a thorough acquaintance with the Fine Arts. They indicate the names of countries and cities, determine their position, and present pictures of many celebrated places. They fix the period of events, and enable us to trace series of kings. In short, they serve to make us acquainted with whatever relates to ancient usages, civil, military, and religious, while they enable us to trace the epochs of different styles of art, and are of great assistance in our philological researches.

NUN'CIO, an ambassador from the pope to some Catholic prince or state, or who attends some congress or assembly as the pope's representative. The nuncio is generally a prelate of the court of Rome; if a cardinal, he is styled legate. Since the time of the council of Trent the nuncios have acted as judges of appeal from the decisions of the respective bishops in those countries which are subject to the decretals and discipline of the council of Trent. In other Catholic kingdoms and states holding themselves independent of the court of Rome in matters of discipline, the nuncio has merely a diplomatic character like the minister of any other foreign power.

NUN'CUPATIVE WILL, in law, a will or testamentary desire expressed verbally, but not put into writing. It depends merely on oral testimony for proof, though afterwards reduced to writing. Nuncupative, in a general sense, signifies something that exists only in name.

NUN'DINÆ, in antiquity, days set apart by the Romans for the country people to expose their wares and commodities to sale, very similar to the large markets or fairs. They were called *Nundinæ*, because they were kept every ninth day.

NUN'NERY, in the Romish church, a religious house for nuns, or females who have bound themselves by vow to a single life.

NYCHTHEM'ERON, among the ancients, signified the whole natural day, or day and night, consisting of twenty-four hours, or equal parts. This way of considering the day was particularly adopted by the Jews, and seems to owe its origin to that expression of Moses, in the first chapter of Genesis, "the evening and the morning were the first day."

NYMPHÆ'A, certain public baths at Rome, of which there were twelve in number, adorned with curious statues of the Nymphs, to whom they were consecrated, furnished with pleasant grottoes, and supplied with cooling fountains, which rendered them exceedingly delightful, and drew great numbers to frequent them. Silence was particularly required there, as appears by this inscription, *Nymphis loci, bibe, lava, tace.*

NYMPHS, female beings, in Grecian mythology, partaking of the nature of gods and men. They peopled all the regions of earth and water, and were variously designated, according to the places of their abode. Thus, the Naiades inhabited the streams, the Oreiades the mountains, the Dryades the woods, the Hamadryades trees, with which they were born and died. They are represented as very beautiful; they constituted the attendants of various of the higher female divinities, especially Diana, and were also considered as having been the nurses of many of the gods, as Jupiter and Pan.

O.

O, the fourth vowel and the fifteenth letter in the alphabet, is pronounced by projecting the lips, and forming an opening resembling the letter itself. The English language designates not less than four sounds by the character *o*, exemplified in the words *no*, *prove*, *for*, *not*. The French indicate the sound *o* (pronounced as in *no*) by various signs. The use of *o* is next in frequency to that of *a*. With an apostrophe after it, *O* signifies *son* in Irish proper names; as O'Neil, (the *son of Neil*,) like the prefix *Mac*. Among the ancients, O was a mark of triple time, from the notion that the ternary, or number 3, is the most perfect of numbers, and properly expressed by a circle, the most perfect figure. O is often used as an interjection or exclamation to express a wish, admiration, warning, pity, imploring, and sometimes surprise; but when language expressive of strong emotion is used the introductory exclamation is properly Oh! Shakspeare uses O for a circle or oval.

OAN'NES, in ancient mythology, the most celebrated divinity of the Babylonians. He was represented as a sea-monster, with human feet and hands; and was said to dwell in the abysses of the Red Sea, whence he was in the habit of issuing daily, and proceeding to Babylon, where he communicated instruction on religion, the science of government, and the useful arts. It has been generally supposed that Oannes was identical with the god Dagon.

O'ASIS, a fertile spot, watered by springs, and covered with verdure, situated in the midst of the uninhabited deserts of Northern Africa; the name is also applied to a cluster of verdant spots. In the desert of Sahara there are several of these. They serve as stopping-places for the caravans, and often contain villages. In Arabic, they are called *wadys*

OATH, a solemn affirmation or declaration, made with an appeal to God for the truth of what is affirmed. The appeal to God in an oath, implies that the person imprecates his vengeance and renounces his favor if the declaration is false; or if the declaration is a promise, the person invokes the vengeance of God if he should fail to fulfil it. A person who is to be a witness in a cause may have two oaths administered to him; the one to speak the truth, in relation to what the court shall think fit to ask him, concerning himself or anything else that is not evidence in the cause; and the other purely to give evidence in the cause wherein he is produced as a witness. The laws of all civilized states have required the security of an oath for evidence given in a court of justice; and the Christian religion, while it utterly prohibits profane and needless swearing, does not seem to forbid oaths duly required, or taken on necessary occasions. But the Quakers and Moravians,—swayed by the sense which they put upon that text of Scripture in St. Matthew, which says, "Swear not at all," and St. James's words, ch. v. 12,—refuse to swear on any occasion, even at the requisition of a magistrate, and in a court of justice. Any believer in a definite form of religion can be a witness, and the oath may be administered "according to such forms and ceremonies as he may declare to be binding." But persons who cannot take an oath are incapable of being witnesses; such, therefore, as will not declare their belief in God, in a future state of rewards and punishments, and that perjury will be punished by the Deity, are excluded; as well as those who, from their years of ignorance, are incapable of comprehending the nature of an oath.—Oaths to perform illegal acts do not bind, nor do they excuse the performance of the act. Perjury is the wilful violation of an oath administered by a lawful authority to a witness in a judicial proceeding. Different formalities have been customary in different countries in taking oaths. The Jews sometimes swore with their hands lifted up, and sometimes placed under the thigh of the person to whom they swore. This was also the custom among the Athenians and the Romans. The ancients guarded against perjury very religiously; and for fear they might fall into it through neglect of due form, they usually declared that they bound themselves only so far as the oath was practicable; and lest the obligation should lie upon their ghosts, they made an express obligation, when they swore, that the oath should be cancelled at their death. Perjury they believed could not pass unpunished, and expected the divine vengeance to overtake the perjured villain even in this life.

OBADI'AH, or THE PROPHECY OF OBADIAH, a canonical book of the Old Testament, which is contained in one single chapter, and is partly an invective against the cruelty of the Edomites, and partly a prediction of the deliverance of Israel, and of the victory and triumph of the whole church over her enemies.

O'BEAH, a species of witchcraft practised among the negroes, the apprehension of which operating upon their superstitious fears, is frequently attended with disease and death.

OBE'DIENCE, PAS'SIVE, in politics, signifies the unqualified obedience which, according to some political philosophers, is due from subjects to the supreme power in the state; insomuch that not only its lawful, but its unlawful commands, may not be forcibly resisted without sin.

OB'ELISK, a lofty quadrangular monolithic column, "diminishing upwards, with the sides gently inclined, but not so as to terminate in an apex at the top; neither is it truncated or cut off at the summit, but the sides are sloped off so as to form a flattish pyramidal figure, by which the whole is suitably finished off and brought to a point, without the upper part being so contracted as to appear insignificant." Egypt was, properly speaking, the land of obelisks; and they are unquestionably to be reckoned among the most ancient monuments of that extraordinary people. Much learning and ingenuity has been expended in endeavoring to ascertain their origin, and the purposes for which they were erected; but it does not appear that any satisfactory solution of the problem has hitherto been given. It has been frequently asserted that obelisks were originally erected in honor of the sun, of which they were said to be symbolical, and that they served the purposes of a gnome or sundial; but this opinion is now almost totally rejected, and it is generally believed that obelisks were nothing more than monumental structures, serving as ornaments to the open squares in which they were generally built, or intended to celebrate some important event and to perpetuate its remembrance. They were usually adorned with hieroglyphics; and we learn from the testimony of Diodorus and Strabo that the inscriptions with which they were charged declared the amount of gold and silver, the number of troops, and the quantity of ivory, perfumes, and corn which all the countries subject to Egypt were required to furnish. The two largest obelisks were erected by Sesostris in Heliopolis. They were formed of a single block of granite, and measured 180 feet in height.

OB'ELUS, in diplomatics, a mark so called from its resemblance to a needle; usually thus — or thus ÷ in ancient MSS. The common use of the line — in modern writing is to mark the place of a break in the sense, where it is suspended, or where there is an ungrammatical transition; but a paragraph introduced where the sense is suspended, is more properly marked by the sign of a parenthesis.

O'BERON, in mediæval mythology, the king of the fairies. Wieland's beautiful poem, and Weber's romantic opera of this name, the *Midsummer Night's Dream*, and innumerable other poems and tales of which he is the hero, have made the name of Oberon so familiar, that it will be unnecessary to do more in this place than to state the origin of the fable. The name Oberon first appears in the old French *fabliaux* of Huon of Bordeaux; it is identical with Auberon, or Alberon, the first syllable of which is nothing more than the old German word Alb, *elf* or *fairy*. He was represented as endowed with magic powers, and with the qualities of a good and upright monarch, rewarding those who practised truth and honesty, and punishing those who acted otherwise. His wife's name was Titania, or Mab, whose powers have been so beautifully depicted in *Romeo and Juliet*.

O'BIT, a funeral solemnity, or office for the dead, most commonly performed when the corpse lies in the church uninterred. It likewise signifies an annual commemoration of the dead, performed on the day of their death, with prayers, alms, &c.

OBIT'UARY, a register in which are enrolled the names of deceased persons for whom obits are to be performed, and the days of their funeral. It is also used for the book containing the foundation or institution of the several obits in a church or monastery. In the former sense it is synonymous with *necrology*, in the latter with *martyrology*.

OB'JECT, that about which any power or faculty is employed, or something apprehended or presented to the mind by sensation or imagination. Thus that quality of a rose which is perceived by the sense of smell, is an *object* of perception. When the *object* is not in contact with the organ of sense, there must be some medium through which we obtain the perception of it. The impression which *objects* make on the senses, must be by the immediate application of them to the organs of sense, or by means of the medium that intervenes between the organs and the *objects*.

OB'LATE, in ecclesiastical antiquities, 1. A person who, on embracing the monastic state, had made a donation of all his goods to the community. 2. One dedicated to a religious order by his parents from an early period of his life. 3. A layman residing as an inmate in a regular community to which he had assigned his property either in perpetuity or for the period of his residence. 4. A layman who had made donation, not only of his property, but his person, as bondsman to a monastic community. In France the king possessed, in ancient times, a privilege of recommending a certain number of *oblati*, chiefly invalided soldiers, to monasteries, whom they were bound to maintain.

OBLA'TION, a sacrifice, or offering made to God. In the canon-law, oblations are defined to be anything offered by godly Christians to God and the church, whether movables or immovables. Till the fourth century, the church had no fixed revenues, the clergy wholly subsisting on voluntary oblations.

OBLIGA'TION, in general, denotes any act whereby a person becomes bound to another to do something. Obligations are of three kinds, viz. natural, civil, and mixed. Natural obligations are entirely founded on natural equity; civil obligations, on civil authority alone, without any foundation in natural equity; and mixed obligations are those which being founded on natural equity, are further enforced by civil authority.—In a legal sense, *obligation* signifies a bond, wherein is contained a penalty, with a condition annexed for the payment of money, &c.

OBLIGA'TO, in music, a term applied to a movement or composition written for a particular instrument. It sometimes means that a movement is restrained by certain rules to give particular expression to a passage, action, &c.

OB'OLUS, a small Grecian silver coin, equal to one penny farthing. It was this coin which they placed in the mouth of the dead, to pay Charon for their passage over the Styx.

OBSECRA'TIO, in Roman antiquity, a solemn ceremony performed by the chief magistrates of Rome, to avert any impending calamity. It consisted of prayers offered up to the gods whom they supposed to be enraged. So exact were they in observing the prescribed form on these occasions, that a person was appointed to read it over to the man who was to pronounce it, and the most trifling omission was held sufficient to vitiate the whole solemnity.

OBSECRA'TION, in rhetoric, a figure in which the orator implores the assistance of God or man.

OB'SEQUIES, were solemnities performed at the burials of eminent persons. The term is now used for the funeral itself.

OBSES'SION, the state of a person vexed or besieged by an evil spirit. In the language of exorcists, demoniacal obsession differed from demoniacal possession: in the latter, the demon had possession of the patient internally; in the former he attacks him from without. Well-known marks of obsession were the being miraculously hoisted or elevated in the air, speaking languages of which the patient had no knowledge, aversion to the offices of religion, and so forth.

OBSID'IONAL CROWN, in Roman antiquities, a crown granted by the state to the general who raised the siege of a beleaguered place. It was formed of grass growing on the rampart. *Obsidional* coins, in numismatics, are pieces struck in besieged places to supply the place of current money. They are of various base metals, and of different shapes. Some of the oldest known are those which were struck at the siege of Pavia, under Francis I.

OB'VERSE, or FACE, in numismatics, the side of the coin which contains the principal symbol: usually, in the coins of monarchical states, ancient and modern, the face in profile of the sovereign; in some instances, the full or half length figure.

OCCA'SIONALISM, or *the System of Occasional Causes*, in metaphysics, a name which has been given to certain theories of the Cartesian school of philosophers, especially Arnold Geulinx, of Antwerp, by which they accounted for the apparent action of the soul on the body; *e. g.* in the phenomena of voluntary motion. According to these theories, (which were more or less clearly developed by different writers,) the will was not the *cause* of the action of the body; but whenever the will required a motion, God caused the body to move in the required direction.

OCCULT', something secret, hidden or invisible, as the occult quality of matter. —The *occult sciences* are magic, necromancy, &c.

OCE'ANUS, in Greek mythology, the oldest of the Titans: according to some, the son of Ouranos and Gaia. His consort was Tethys, his daughters the Oceanides. In Homer, the word ocean merely designates the "river," or stream, which, according to his notion, encompassed the earth.

OCHLOC'RACY, a word coined to express the condition of a state in which the populace have acquired an immediate illegal control over the government; and, by a figure commonly used in the exaggeration of political speakers and writers, a government in which the power of the lower classes predominates, either for a time or permanently.

OC'TAVE, in music, an eighth, or an interval of seven degrees or twelve semitones. The octave is the most perfect of the chords, consisting of six full tones and two semi-tones major. It contains the whole diatonic scale. The most simple perception that we can have of two sounds, is that of unisons; the vibrations there beginning and ending together. The next to this is the octave, where the more acute sound makes precisely two vibrations, while the grave or deeper makes one; consequently, the vibrations of the two meet at every single vibration of the more grave one. Hence, unison and octave pass almost for the same concord; hence, also, the ratio of the two sounds that form the octave is as 1 to 2. The octave may be doubled, tripled, and multiplied at pleasure, with changing its nature, but a double octave is less agreeable to the ear than a single one; a triple octave, still less agreeable than a double one, and so on.

OCTA'VO, in printing, the form of a page which is made by folding a sheet into eight leaves, or sixteen pages. It is often written 8vo.

OCTO'BER, in chronology, the tenth month of the Julian year, consisting of thirty-one days: it obtained the name of October from its being the eighth month in the calendar of Romulus.

OCTASTY'LOS, in architecture, a temple or other building having eight columns in front.

OC'TROI, an old French term (from *auctoritas*) signifying a grant or privilege from government, is particularly applied to the commercial privileges granted to a person or to a company. In a like sense the term is applied to the constitution of a state granted by a prince, in contradistinction to those which are derived from a compact between a ruler and the representatives of the people. It also signifies a tax levied at the gates of some cities in France upon all articles of food.

O'DALISQUES, properly ODALIKS, (Turkish, oda, a *chamber*,) female slaves employed in domestic service about the persons of the wives, female relatives, &c. of the sultan.

ODD'FEL'LOWS, persons affiliated to certain associations that originated, about the year 1820; but now oddfellow societies form parts of an important system, widely ramified in Great Britain and the United States. The oddfellows are in many respects similar to freemasons, as to initiatory rites, secret oaths, &c.; and hold frequent meetings, ostensibly for philanthropic purposes.

ODE, among the Greeks and Romans, was a short lyric composition, usually intended to be sung, and accompanied by some musical instrument, generally the lyre; hence the expression lyric verse. In the modern sense of the word, the ode appears to be distinguished from the song by greater length and variety, and by not being necessarily adapted to music. It is distinguished also from the ballad, and other species of lyric poetry, by its being confined to the expression of sentiment, or of imaginative thought, on a given subject, not admitting of narrative, except incidentally. The odes of Pindar, Anacreon, and Horace, are, in fact, the models on which the modern notion of the ode is formed, and which have been imitated in similar compositions in modern times. Until the science of Greek metres was so accurately explored as it has recently been, the Pindaric ode was supposed to admit of an excessive irregularity in the length and measure of lines. In point of fact, however, a scheme of perfect metrical irregularity pervaded the Greek ode. the Anacreontic ode consists of a number of lines of the same metrical length and arrangement. The Horatian ode, again, consists of an indefinite number of stanzas, precisely similar to each other, each forming a complete metrical whole. The Dithyrambic ode was a bacchanalian song; and as, from the attributes of the divinity to which it was dedicated, it admitted great irregularity and license, the name has been transferred in modern times to all odes partaking of a wild and impetuous character.

ODE'UM, or ODE'ON, in ancient architecture, a building wherein the poets and musicians contended for the prizes, both in vocal and instrumental music. Pericles, who was the first person to erect one of these buildings at Athens, instituted it for the choragi of the different tribes to rehearse their performances; but these buildings in the end were used for far different purposes from those for which they were originally destined. An odeum was to be found in all the principal cities of antiquity. The word odeon has been preserved in most modern languages: thus, there is an odeon in Paris, appropriated to theatrical and other similar purposes.

O'DIN, a Scandinavian deity, who seems, like the Jupiter of the Greeks, to have formed the connecting link between the ancient and more recent systems of their mythology. The conqueror Odin appears to have been a chieftain who led the Asi (the Goths) from the confines of Asia to northern Europe. But, when deified by public adoration, the attributes of an earlier deity seem to have been transferred to him. Odin is the chief of the gods; by his wife Freya he has two chief sons, Thor and Balder: the death of the latter (for the Scandinavian gods are not all immortal) furnishes many legends to the northern mythology.

OD'YSSEY, an epic poem, attributed, in general, to Homer, but, according to some modern hypotheses, not by the hand of the author of the *Iliad*. The subject of the poem is the return of Ulysses from Troy to his native island, Ithaca.

ŒCON'OMY, in architecture, the harmonious and skilful combination of the parts of the building, which renders them suitable to their several purposes, and tends to connect them conveniently with each other.

ŒCUMEN'ICAL, in the Greek language applied to ecclesiastical matters in the sense of universal. Several patriarchs of Constantinople and Rome assumed the title of œcumenical (particularly John, A.D. 590, and Cyril, his successor,) apparently in opposition to the pretensions of the bishop of Rome. Œcumenical councils are those to which prelates resorted from every part of Christendom under the jurisdiction of the Roman empire.

OFFENCE', in law, the violation of any law; this is termed *capital* if punished with death, and not capital if visited with any other punishment.

OF'FERINGS, literally, gifts presented at the altar in token of acknowledgment of the Divine goodness. Offerings constituted a large portion of the Jewish worship. They consisted chiefly of bread, salt, fruits, wine, and oil, and had different names according to the purposes for which they were employed. A distinction has often been made between offerings and sacrifices; the former being said to refer only to the fruits of the earth, the latter to animals; but this can scarcely have been the case, for both the burnt and the sin offering required animals to be sacrificed. Among the Greeks, Romans, and other nations, the same practice prevailed of offering at their altars wheat, flour, and bread. In a modern sense, the term *offering* is applied to certain dues payable by custom to the Church, as the Easter offerings, &c. This latter custom has obtained from the first period of Christianity, when those who officiated at the altar had no other maintenance or allowance than the free gifts or offerings (oblations) of the people.

OF'FERTORY, the first part of the Mass, in which the priest prepares the elements for consecration. In the English communion service, it denotes the sentences which are delivered by the officiating priest while the people are making their oblations or offerings.

OF'FICER, is used generally to signify any person in the enjoyment of a post or office, whether civil or military, under the crown. Under their different heads will be found a notice of the chief civil and military officers; to these the reader is referred.

OFF'SET, in architecture, the superior surface left uncovered by the continuation upwards of a wall where the thickness diminishes, forming a ledge.

OGEE, or O. G., in architecture, a moulding, consisting of two members, the one concave, the other convex; or, of a round and a hollow, somewhat like an S.

O'GIVE, in architecture, an arch or branch of a Gothic vault; which, instead of being circular, passes diagonally from one angle to another, and forms a cross with the other arches. The middle, where the ogives cross each other, is called the key. The members or mouldings of the ogives are called nerves, branches, or reins; and the arches which separate the ogives, double arches.

O'GRES, the well-known name of those imaginary monsters with which the nursery tales of England abound. They are usually represented as cannibals of malignant dispositions, and as endowed with gigantic height and power. It is difficult to speak with certainty of the origin of these fabulous creations; but it is probable that the term ogre is derived from Oegir, one of the giants in the Scandinavian mythology; though it has been alleged, with perhaps more probability, that it has been borrowed from the Ogurs, or Onogurs, a desperate and savage Asiatic horde, which overran part of Europe about the middle of the 5th century.

OIL-PAINT'ING, the art of painting with oil colors, which are the kind most commonly used for large pictures. This art has the pre-eminence above all other kinds of painting on account of its liveliness, strength, agreeableness, and natural appearance; on account of the variety and mixture of tints; in short, on account of the charm of the coloring. The various colors chiefly used in oil painting are, white lead, Cremnitz white, chrome, king's yellow, Naples yellow, patent yellow, the ochres, Dutch pink, terra da Sienna, yellow lake, vermilion, red lead, Indian and Venetian red, the several sorts of lake, brown, pink, Vandyke brown, burnt and unburnt amber, ultramarine, Prussian and Antwerp blue, ivory black, blue black, asphaltum. The principal oils are those extracted from the poppy, nut, and linseed, the latter being used for the ground work. Oil paintings are made upon wood, copper, and other metals; also upon walls and thick silk, but now most commonly upon canvas, stretched upon a frame, and done over with glue or gold for a ground, and by some with white water colors.

OL'IGARCHY, a state in which the sovereign power is lodged in the hands of a small, exclusive class, is so called. It differs from aristocracy, in that the latter term appears to designate a government in which the whole of a particular class or interest, *e. g.*, the noble, the wealthy, &c., share directly or indirectly in the management of public affairs; while, in an oligarchy, it is a party or section formed out of one of these classes which enjoys the advantages of government.

O'LIO, a miscellany; a collection of various pieces. It is chiefly applied to musical collections.

OL'LA PODRI'DA, the name given to a favorite dish of all classes in Spain; consisting of a mixture of all kinds of meat cut into small pieces, and stewed with various kinds of vegetables. The epithet *podrida* is applied to this dish, in consequence of the poorer classes being obliged to serve it up so often that the odor arising from long keeping is far from agreeable. The phrase *olla podrida* is often used metaphorically in England for any incongruous mélange.

OLYMP'IAD, in chronology, a Grecian epoch of four years, being the interval between the celebration of the Olympic games.

OLYMP'IC GAMES, the greatest of the national festivals of Greece, celebrated once every four years at Olympia, or Pisa, in Elis, in honor of Olympian Jupiter. Their institution is variously attributed to Jupiter, Pelops, and Hercules; but it appears that they had fallen into disuse for some time, till they were revived by Iphitus, 776 B.C. From this period it is that the Olympiads are reckoned. Like the other public festivals, the Olympian games might be attended by all who bore the Hellenic name; and such was their universal celebrity, that spectators quaternially crowded to witness them, not only from all parts of Greece itself, but from every Grecian colony in Europe, Asia, and Africa. In these games, none were allowed to contend but those who could prove that they were freemen of genuine Hellenic origin, and unstained by crime or immorality.

OME'GA, the name for the Greek long *o*. It was the last letter in the Greek alphabet, as *alpha* was the first; and from the expression in Revelations, "I am Alpha and Omega, the beginning and the ending, saith the Lord, which is, and which was, and which is to come, the Almighty," the characters of alpha and omega became with the Christians symbolical hieroglyphics.

O'MENS, casual indications, from which men believe themselves enabled to conjecture or foretell future events. The essential characteristic of all omens is their happening by accident; and it is this which distinguishes them from all other modes of divination. This branch of superstition seems nearly as ancient as the world itself; and in none do we find such remarkable indications of sameness of origin. Many external circumstances appear to be received in almost all countries as ominous. The omens in which the Thugs or secret murderers of India, believe with peculiar devotion, are almost the very same which an ancient Roman would have observed with equal attention; especially the appearance of animals on the right or left hand. Omens, among the Greeks (and, we may add, among almost all nations in periods of ignorance, and among the vulgar of the present day,) may be divided into three classes: those derived from natural occurrences, relating to inanimate objects, lightning, earthquakes, phosphoric appearances, &c.; those derived from animals, especially birds, the region of their appearance, their voices, &c.; and those which the individual drew from sudden sensations of his own. Sneezing, in most times and countries, has been a peculiarly ominous occurrence. The Romans, as is well known, carried the science of omens to a very profound depth: the flight of birds was the main element in *augury;* the omens afforded by the entrails of sacrificed animals, in the learning of *extispicium*. One remarkable variety between Greek and Roman divination has often been noticed; the right hand in the former generally denoted good luck, and the left the contrary. Among the Romans this rule was reversed, although their writers in later times often adopt the Greek mode of expression.

ONE'IROCRIT'ICS, the science of interpreting dreams: treated of by Artemidorus, Macrobius, and other classical writers; by Thomas Aquinas, and others of the schoolmen; and, among many other moderns, by Cardanus, and Maio, a Neapolitan philosopher. According to all these writers, the secret of one irocritical science consists in the relation supposed to exist between the dream and the thing signified; but they are far from keeping to the relations of agreement and similitude, and they frequently have recourse to others of dissimilitude, and contrariety.

ONOM'ATOPE, or ONOMATOPŒ'IA, in grammar and rhetoric, a figure in which words are formed to resemble the sound made by the thing signified, or in which words are formed or supposed to be formed in imitation of natural sounds; as, to *buzz*, as bees; to *crackle*, as burning thorns or brushwood; to *creak*, as a door on its hinges, &c.—A word whose sound corresponds to the sound of the thing signified, or which expresses by its sound the thing represented; as, to *neigh*, to *murmur*, to *bleat*. Greek and German are rich in words of this description.

ONTOL'OGY, the doctrine of being; a name formerly given to that part of the science of metaphysics which investigates and explains the nature and essence of all beings, their qualities and attributes. It investigates the nature, 1. of things in general, their possibility, reality, and necessity; 2. of substance and accidence, cause, effect, and mutual operation; 3. of quantity, quality, similarity, and equality of things; 4. of space and time; and 5. of the simple and compound.

O'NUS PROBAN'DI, in law, the burden of proving what has been alleged against another.

O'PENINGS, in architecture, the piercings or unfitted parts in a wall, left for the purpose of admitting light, air, &c.

O'PERA, a musical drama in which the music forms an essential part, and not merely an accompaniment. The whole dramatic art of the ancients possessed much of an operatic character. The choric parts were sung; and if the dialogue was not carried on in the musical tone termed *recitative* in modern times, it was certainly delivered in an artificially raised and sustained key, very different from the ordinary or oratorical speech. The first operas in modern times were performed in Italy, about the end of the 15th century. The *Orpheo* of Poliziano has been cited as the first complete piece of this sort. According as the serious or the comic character prevails in the opera, it is termed *opera seria*, or *opera buffa*. The name of *grand opera* is given to that kind which is confined to music and song; of which the *recitativo* is a principal feature. An *operetta* is a short musical drama of a light character; to which species of composition the French *vaudeville* belongs. The opera, properly speaking, admits only of singing and recitation, although, in some of the German operas, dialogue is also introduced. The romantic opera, which is considered as a German invention, is a compound between the two Italian species. Metastasio in Italy, and Goethe in Germany, have both written for the opera; but these are splendid exceptions, and the poetry has, in most instances, been held entirely subservient to the music.

O'PHIOMANCY, the art of divination from serpents. Thus, the seven coils of the serpent seen on the tomb of Anchises were held to indicate the number of years of Æneas's future wanderings.

O'PHITES, the name of an early sect of Christian heretics, who emanated from the Gnostics, so called from their worshipping the serpent that tempted Eve. They considered the serpent as the father of all the sciences, which, but for the temptation of our first parents, would never have been known.

OPIN'ION, the judgment which the mind forms of any proposition, for the truth or falsehood of which there is not sufficient evidence to produce absolute belief. Some things are known to be scientifically correct, or capable of mathematical demonstration; but other things depend on testimony. When one or two men relate a story including many circumstances to a third person, and another comes who positively contradicts it, either in whole or in part, he, to whom those jarring testimonies are given, weighs all the circumstances in his own mind, balances the one against the other, and lends an assent more or less wavering, to that side on which the evidence appears to preponderate. This assent is his *opinion* respecting the facts of which he has received such different accounts.

OPISTHOG'RAPHUM, in classical antiquity, a set of tickets, or roll of parchment or paper, answering the purpose of a memorandum book, or commonplace book, to enter notes and other extemporary matters to be revised afterwards: so called from being written over both on the front and back. Any ordinary MS. in which the transcriber had employed both the front and back of the papyrus was indeed an opisthograph, strictly so called.

OPPOSI'TION, in politics, a word well understood in free representative governments, but nowhere else: denoting that intelligent and independent spirit in the members of the legislative assembly, which induces them to persevere in opposing whatever legislation is injurious to the state, but which does not so far influence them as to oppose what is beneficial. A temperate and consistent opposition is therefore an essential element of good government; for though it may struggle against an existing administration, it contributes at the same time to the soundness and vigor of the body politic.—*Opposition*, in logic, the disagreement between propositions which have the same subject and the same predicate.—In rhetoric, a figure whereby two things are joined, which seem incompatible.

OP'TATIVE, in grammar, a mode or form of a Greek verb, by which is expressed the wish or desire to do a thing.

OPTE'RIA, in antiquity, presents made by the bridegroom to the bride when he first saw her.

OPTI'MATES, in Roman antiquity, one of the divisions of the Roman people, opposed to the *Populares*. It does not certainly appear what were the characteristic differences betwixt these two parties. Some say the *Optimates* were warm supporters of the dignity of the chief magistrate, and sticklers for the grandeur of the state; caring little for the other classes; whereas the *Populares* boldly stood up for the rights of the people, pleaded for larger privileges, and labored to bring matters nearer to a level. Tully says, that the Optimates were the best citizens, who wished to deserve the approbation of the better sort; and that the Populares courted the favor of the populace, not so much considering what was right, as what would please the people and gratify their own thirst of vain glory.

OPTI'ME, a scholar in the first class of mathematics at Cambridge.

OP'TIMISM, that philosophical and religious doctrine which maintains that this world, in spite of its apparent imperfections, is the best that could have been devised, and that everything in nature is ordered for the best.

OP'TION, in ecclesiastical law, a prerogative of the archbishops of the church of England. Every bishop is bound, immediately after his confirmation, to make a legal conveyance to the archbishop of the next avoidance of any one benefice or dignity belonging to his see which the archbishop may choose (whence the name.)

OR'ACLE, the name primarily given to the response delivered by the ancient heathen divinities to those who consulted them respecting the future, but afterwards applied both to the place where responses were given as well as to the divinities from whom the responses were supposed to proceed. To the desire so natural to man to obtain a glimpse into futurity, coupled with the ennobling belief that his destiny was predetermined in a higher sphere, is doubtless to be traced the origin of the art of divination, which has in all, but more especially in the earlier stages of society, exercised so powerful an influence over the human mind. But, of all the modes of divination, that by consulting the oracle was the most popular. In other cases, as the interpretation of events depended on man alone, there might be mistake or deception; but in the oracle, when the deity was believed to pronounce either in his own voice or in that of a consecrated agent, it was supposed there could be none. Hence oracles obtained such credit and celebrity in antiquity, but more especially among the Greeks, that they were resorted to on every occasion of doubt and emergency, both by princes and states, as well as by private individuals. The general characteristics of oracles were ambiguity, obscurity, and convertibility; so that one answer would agree with several various and sometimes directly opposite events. Thus, when Crœsus was on the point of invading the Medes, he consulted the oracle of Delphi as to the success of the enterprise, and received for an answer that by passing the river Halys he would ruin a great empire. But whether it was his own empire or that of his enemies that was destined to be ruined was not intimated; and in either case, the oracle could not fail to be right.

OR'ANGEMEN, the name given by the Catholics in Ireland to their Protestant countrymen, on account of their adherence to king William (of the house of Orange,) while the former party supported the cause of James II.

ORA'TION, in modern usage, an oration differs from a sermon, from an argument at the bar, from a speech before a deliberative assembly, and from a popular harangue, though all these are orations in the generic sense. The word is now applied chiefly to discourses pronounced on special occasions, as a funeral oration, an oration on some anniversary, &c., and to academic declamations.

OR'ATOR, in modern usage, signifies an eloquent public speaker; or a person who pronounces a discourse publicly on some special occasion. In ancient Rome *orators* were advocates of a superior kind, differing from the *patrons:* the latter were allowed only to plead causes on behalf of their *clients;* whereas the former might quit the *forum* and ascend the *rostra* or *tribunal*, to harangue the senate or the people. The *orators* had rarely a profound knowledge of the law, but they were eloquent, and their style was generally correct and concise.

ORATO'RIO, a sacred musical composition, consisting of airs, recitatives, duets, trios, choruses, &c., the subject of which is generally taken from Scripture. The text is usually in a dramatic form, as in Handel's *Samson;* but it sometimes takes the form of a narrative, as in *Israel in Egypt;* occasionally it is of a mixed character, as in Haydn's *Creation;* and sometimes it consists merely of detached passages from Scripture as in the *Messiah*. The origin of oratorios has been variously ascribed; but the most prevalent opinion regards them as originally founded upon the spiritual songs and dialogues which were sung or recited by the priests of the oratory. The more recent introduction of this species of musical drama is on all sides attributed to St. Philippo Neri, about the middle of the 16th century; but oratorios, properly so called, were not produced till about a century afterwards. At first the persons introduced were sometimes ideal, sometimes parabolical, and sometimes, as in the latter oratorios, taken from sacred history; but this species of drama soon assumed a more regular form, and oratorios became great favorites in Italy; where they were constantly performed during the Carnival; and they have since given birth to some of the noblest and most elaborate compositions of the great masters both of that and other countries.

OR'ATORY, the art of speaking well, or of speaking according to the rules of rhetoric, in order to persuade. To constitute oratory, the speaking must be just and pertinent to the subject; it must be methodical, all parts of the discourse being disposed in due order and connection; and it must be embellished with the beauties of language and pronounced with eloquence. Oratory consists of four parts, invention, disposition, elocution, and pronunciation. Diction, manner, gesture, modulation, a methodical arrangement of the several topics to be introduced, and a logical illustration of them, are all essential requisites in oratory; and, as Cicero has observed, "the action of the body ought to be suited to the expressions, not in a theatrical way, mimicking the words by particular gesticulations, but in a manner expressive of the general sense, with a sedate and manly inflection."

OR'ATORY, signifies, commonly, a room in a private house set apart for prayer. It differs from a chapel, inasmuch as it does not contain an altar, nor may mass be celebrated in it.—*Oratory, Priests of the*, a religious order founded by Philip Nevi, in 1574, for the study of theology, and for superintending the religious exercises of the devout; but they are not bound by monastic vows. This order still exists in Italy.

OR'CHESTRA, the space in theatres between the stage and the seats of the spectators. It was appropriated by the Greeks to the chorus and musicians, by the Romans to the magistrates and senators, and by moderns to the musicians. The word is also used to denote the whole instrumental band performing together in modern concerts, operas, or sacred music.

ORDE'AL, an ancient mode of trial, in which an appeal was made to God to manifest the truth, by leaving nature to its ordinary course, if the accused were guilty; by interposing a miracle if innocent. This mode of distributing justice in criminal charges prevailed, during the middle ages, throughout almost the whole of Europe; and it is still practised in some parts of the East Indies. In England it existed from the time of the Confessor to that of Henry III., who abolished it by declaration: while it lasted, the more popular modes of resorting to it were those of *fire* (or the hot iron,) and of *water;* the former for freemen and people of rank, the latter for peasants. The method of administering the ordeal by fire, in England, was by placing nine red-hot plough-shares in a line, at certain distances from each other, and requiring the person accused to walk over them barefoot and blindfold. If his feet always alighted in the spaces between the shares, so that he passed over them unhurt, his success was deemed a divine assertion of his innocence; if on the contrary, he was burnt, the disaster was an oracular proof of his guilt. The *ordeal by water* was of two kinds; either by plunging the bare arm to the elbow in boiling water, or by casting the person suspected into a river or pond of cold water, and if he floated without an effort to swim, it was an evidence of guilt, but if he sunk he was acquitted. There were also ordeals by lot, as by the casual choice between a pair of dice, one marked with a cross and the other blank, mentioned in the laws of the Frisons. The famous trial of the bier, in which the supposed perpetrator was required to touch the body of a murdered person, and was pronounced guilty if the blood flowed, may be regarded as a species of ordeal, although founded more on usage than legal enactment; as this form of superstition did not become prevalent until later times, when ordeals were no longer a recognized part of the law. To the same head may be referred the various absurd and cruel methods which were adopted in different countries to try suspected witches. Ordeals are of common use in the judicial practice of various heathen nations, especially of the Hindoos.

ORDER OF THE DAY, in parliamentary usage, one method of superseding a question already proposed to the House is by moving "for the order of the day to be read." This motion, to entitle it to precedence, must be for the order generally, and not for any particular order; and, if this is carried, the orders must be read and proceeded on in the course ir which they stand. But it can be in its turn superseded by a motion "to adjourn."

OR'DERS, or HO'LY OR'DERS, denote the character and office peculiar to ecclesiastics, whereby they are set apart for the ministry. Since the Reformation, there are three orders of the clergy acknowledged, namely, bishops, priests, and deacons; whence the phrase, "to be in orders," is the same as to be of the clerical order.—*Religious orders*, associations, or societies of monastics, bound to lead strict and devotional lives, according to the prescribed rules of their respective communities. An order, in fact, consists in the rules to be observed by those who enter it; thus some orders are more austere than others, and one order dresses in white, while another is habited in gray or black.—*Military Orders* are societies established by princes, the members of which are distinguished by particular badges, and consist of persons who have done particular service to the prince and state, or who enjoy, by the privileges of birth, the highest distinctions in the state. They originated from the institutions of chivalry and the ecclesiastical corporations, and were, in the beginning, fraternities of men, who, in addition to particular duties enjoined by the law of honor, united for the performance of patriotic or Christian purposes. Free birth and an irreproachable life were the conditions of admission. During the time of the crusades numerous military orders arose, and were an example for all future orders. The oldest of the religious military orders is that of St. John of Jerusalem; and on their model the secular military orders were formed in later times, which united religious with military exercises. But the original pious object of these orders was changed, and they acquired by degrees their present character.—*Orders*, in law, rules made by the court in causes there depending.

OR'DINAL, or ORDER, the name given in England to an old work containing the ritual or religious ceremonies necessary to be performed before the ordination of a priest. It was composed in the reign of Edward VI., and revised by the English clergy in 1552.

OR'DINANCE, in law, a temporary act of parliament, not introducing any new law, but founded on some act formerly made; consequently, such ordinances might be altered by subsequent ones.

OR'DINARY, in general signifies *common* or *usual;* thus an ambassador or envoy *in ordinary*, is one sent to reside constantly at some foreign court, in order to preserve a good understanding, and watch over the interest of his own nation. —*Ordinary*, in the common and canon law, one who has ordinary or immediate jurisdiction. In which sense, archdeacons are ordinaries; though the appellation is more frequently given to the bishop of the diocese, who has the ordinary ecclesiastical jurisdiction.

ORDINA'TION, the conferring holy orders, or initiating a person into the priesthood. In the church of England the first thing necessary on application for holy orders, is the possession of a *title*, that is, a sort of assurance from a rector to the bishop, that, provided the latter finds the party fit to be ordained, the former will take him for his curate, with a stated salary. The candidate is then examined by the bishop or his chaplain, respecting both his faith and his erudition; and various certificates are necessary, particularly one signed by the clergyman of the parish in which he has resided during a given time. Subscription to the thirty-nine articles is required, and a clerk must have attained his twenty-third year before he can be ordained a deacon; and his twenty-fourth to receive priest's orders.—The ceremony of ordination is performed by the bishop by the imposition of hands on the person to be ordained. In the English church, and in most Protestant countries where the church is connected with the state, ordination is a requisite to preaching; but in some sects ordination is not considered necessary for that purpose, although it is considered proper previous to the administration of the sacraments by the preacher.—In the Presbyterian and congregational churches, *ordination* means the act of settling or establishing a licensed preacher over a congregation with pastoral charge and authority: or the act of conferring on a clergyman the powers of a settled minister of the gospel, without the charge of a particular church, but with general powers wherever he may be called to officiate.

ORD'NANCE, a general name for artillery of every description.—*Ordnance Office*, or *Board of Ordnance*, an office kept within the tower of London, which superintends and disposes of all the arms, instruments, and utensils of war, both by sea and land, in all the magazines, garrisons, and forts in Great Britain. The Board of Ordnance is divided into two distinct branches, the civil and the military; the latter being subordinate to, and under the authority of the former.

ORD'ONNANCE, in architecture, the right assignment, for convenience and propriety, of the measure of the several apartments, that they be neither too large nor too small for the purposes of the building, and that they be conveniently distributed and lighted.

O'READS, in Greek mythology, nymphs of the mountains, companions of Diana, and usually invoked along with that goddess.

OR'GAN, in music, a wind instrument, of ancient invention, blown by bellows, and containing numerous pipes of various kinds and dimensions, which, for its solemnity, grandeur, and rich volume of tone, is particularly fitted for the purpose for which it is commonly employed. Organs are sometimes of an immense size. St. Jerome mentions an organ with twelve pair of bellows, which might be heard at the distance of a thousand paces, or a mile; and another at Jerusalem, which might be heard at the Mount of Olives. The organ in the Cathedral church at Ulm, in Germany, is said to be 93 feet high and 28 broad, its largest pipe being 13 inches in diameter, and it having 16 pair of bellows.

ORGA'NIC LAWS, in modern political phraseology, the name given to laws directly concerning the fundamental parts of the constitution of a state. According to the distinction taken by some French writers, fundamental laws are merely declaratory, containing the principles or theory of government. Organic laws are those which apply those principles to the actual condition of society, by positive enactment, and add the sanction of punishment.

ORGA'NISTS, the old name given in the Roman Catholic church to those priests who organized or sang in parts. The name *organists of the hallelujah* was applied in the 13th century, to certain priests who assisted in the performance of the mass. They were generally four in number, and derived their name from singing in parts, or organizing the melody appropriated to the word hallelujah.

ORGANIZA'TION, the processes by which an organized body is formed: also, the totality of the parts which constitute, and of the laws which regulate an organized body.

OR'GANON, in philosophical language, nearly synonymous with *method*, and implying a body of rules and canons for the direction of the scientific faculty, either generally or in reference to some particular department; as, the *organon* of Aristotle; the *organon* of Bacon. The *organon* of Aristotle is his System of Logic, and contains his Categories, his treatise on Interpretation, or the nature of Propositions, his former and latter Analytics, and his eight books of Topics; to which may be added, his book on Sophisms. The *Novum Organon* of Bacon contains the development of his system of philosophy, or the inductive system.

ORGAN POINT, in music, a succession of chords, in some of which the harmony of the fifth is taken unprepared on the bass as a holding note, whether preceded by the tonic or by the harmony of the fourth of the key.

OR'GIA, in antiquity, feasts and sacrifices performed in honor of Bacchus, instituted by Orpheus, and chiefly celebrated on the mountains by wild, distracted women, called *bacchæ*.—These feasts were held in the night: hence the term, "nocturnal orgies."

OR'GUES, in fortification, long and thick pieces of wood shod with iron, and suspended each by a separate rope over a gate so as to be ready to let fall and stop it up upon the approach of an enemy. The term also denotes a machine composed of arquebuses, or musket-barrels, linked together so that they may be discharged all at once, and used to defend breaches.

O'RIEL, a large bay or recessed window in a hall, chapel, or other apartment. It usually projects from the outer face of the wall, either in a semi-octagonal or semi-square plan, and is of various kinds and sizes. When not on the ground-floor it is supported on brackets or corbels.

O'RIENT, the east or eastern part of the horizon. In surveying, *to orient* a plan signifies to mark its situation or bearing with respect to the four cardinal points.

ORIEN'TALS, the natives or inhabitants of the Eastern parts of the world. It is common to give this appellation to the inhabitants of Asia from the Hellespont and Mediterranean to Japan.—An *orientalism* is an idiom of the eastern languages.—An *orientalist*, one versed in the eastern languages and literature.

O'RIFLAMME, the ancient royal standard of France. It was the banner of the abbey of St. Dennis, which was presented by the abbot to the lord-protector of the convent, whenever engaged in the field on its behalf. This protectorship was attached to the countship of

Vexin; and when that county was added to the possessions of the crown by Philip I., this banner, which he bore in consequence, became, in time, the great standard of the monarchy. By some it is said to have been lost at Agincourt, but, according to others, its last display in the field was in the reign of Charles VII.

OR'IGENISTS, in the history of the church, followers of Origen of Alexandria, a celebrated Christian father, who held that the souls of men have a pre-existent state; that they are holy intelligences, and sin before they are united to the body, &c.

ORIG'INAL, in the Fine Arts, a work not copied from another, but the work of the artist himself. When an artist copies his own work, it is called a duplicate. A certain freedom and ease are always discernible in an original, which in a copy are looked for in vain; though copies have sometimes been executed which it is almost impossible to detect, and which have deceived even excellent judges. In its more obvious and general sense, the word is used as an adjective, and applied to such productions as possess the principles of novelty or invention, as distinguished from that of imitation or mannerism; but as a substantive, it means such works as are the undoubted performances of the great masters in any given art or branch of art, a distinction which it is often very difficult to award justly, and which has been consequently given, over and over again, through want of complete evidence, to successful and spirited copies.

ORIL'LON, in fortification, a round mass of earth faced with a wall, raised on the shoulder of those bastions that have casements to cover the cannon of the retired flank.

ORI'ON, in Greek mythology, the son of Hyrieus; according to Homer a youth slain by Diana, on account of the love borne to him by Aurora; but according to others, a king and a mighty hunter. Antiquity is full of contradictions respecting the origin, character, and fate of this mythological personage, and the only point in which it agrees respecting him is in his elevation to the stars after his death.

OR'LO, in architecture, the plinth to the base of a column or a pedestal.

OR'MOLU, bronze or copper, gilt, usually goes under this name. The French are celebrated in this branch of manufacture.

ORNITH'OMANCY, divination by the flight of birds. The Etruscans were the most celebrated practisers of it.

OROMAS'DES, in Persian mythology, the principle of Good, created by the will of the great eternal spirit Zeruane Akherene, simultaneously with Ahriman, the principle of evil, with whom he is in perpetual conflict. Oromasdes is the creator of the earth, sun, moon, and stars, to which he originally assigned each its proper place, and whose various movements he continues to regulate. According to the Persian myths, the world which is to last 12,000 years, during which the war between the Good and Evil principle is to go on increasing, is at length to be consumed, the Evil principle exterminated, and a new world be formed.

OR'PHAN, a fatherless child or minor; or one that is deprived both of father and mother. The lord chancellor is the general guardian of all orphans and minors throughout the realm.—In London the lord-mayor and aldermen have the custody of the orphans of deceased freemen, and also the keeping of their lands and goods: accordingly, the executors or administrators of freemen leaving such orphans, are to exhibit inventories of the estates of the deceased, and give security to the chamberlain of London for the orphan's part.

OR'PHANS' COURT, a court in some states of the United States of America, having jurisdiction of the persons and estates of orphans.

OR'PHEAN MYS'TERIES, the mysteries of which Orpheus was the founder were so called. These mysteries were at a remote period in the highest estimation, and exercised an important influence over the intellectual development of mankind. Their nature is involved in an impenetrable veil of obscurity; but there can be no doubt that they partook of the general character of all mysteries, inculcating a purer knowledge of religion than was compatible with the superstitious observances then prevalent. On the union of these mysteries with the Bacchanalian orgies they fell into merited contempt, and were at length gradually disused. The initiated in these mysteries, as well as the persons employed to initiate candidates in them, were called, in some cases, *Orpheotelestæ*.

OR'PHEUS, a mythological personage; according to the common story, a son of the Thracian river Æagrus and the muse Calliope. His power of moving inanimate things by music, the share he bore in the Argonautic expedition, his descent into the Shades to recover his wife Eurydice, and his death by the violence of the Thracian women, are well-known circumstances in ancient romantic fable. Moderns have imagined that his name is a general mythic designation for the earliest bards who came with their art from Thrace to Greece. Whether any fragments of poetry either of the real Orpheus or of this supposed school, existed in Grecian classical ages, has been doubted. What passed as the poetry of Orpheus in the time of Aristotle seems to have been decidedly supposititious, as much so as the poems which we possess under the same name, some of which are thought to be as recent as the 4th century after Christ. According to modern theories, the Orphic poetry of ancient times contained the whole body of Grecian esoterical religion and import of the Mysteries.

OR'THODOX, or OR'THODOXY, these terms are restricted in application to right judgments in matters of religious faith; and although every sect maintains of course the exclusive correctness of its own views, yet the title of orthodoxy is appropriated by ecclesiastical historians to the standard maintained by the Catholic or universal church. The term orthodox is generally restricted also to those principal tenets which have been always held by the great mass of professing Christians: large bodies of dissenters in England are allowed by the church to be orthodox, inasmuch as they hold the three creeds, and therefore profess the principal articles of the Christian faith in common with those who differ from them in matters of church authority and discipline.

OR'THOEPY, the art of uttering words with propriety; a correct pronunciation of words.

ORTHOG'RAPHY, that part of grammar which teaches the nature and properties of letters, and the proper spelling or writing of words.—In architecture, the elevation or representation of the front of a building.—The *internal orthography*, called also a *section*, is a delineation of a building, such as it would appear if the external wall were removed.—In perspective, the right side of any plane, *i. e.* the side or plane that lies parallel to a straight line which may be imagined to pass through the outward convex points of the eyes, continued to a convenient length.

O'RUS, an Egyptian god, son of Isis and Osiris, according to Herodotus; answering to the Greek Apollo. He frequently appears in Egyptian paintings sitting on the lap of Isis.

OSIAN'DRIANS, in ecclesiastical history, a sect among the Lutherans; so called from their founder Osiander, a celebrated divine. They differed from the followers of Luther and Calvin as to the efficient cause of the justification.

OSI'RIS, in mythology, one of the chief Egyptian divinities, the brother and husband of Isis, and, together with her, the greatest benefactor of Egypt, into which he introduced a knowledge of religion, laws, and the arts and sciences. After having accomplished great reformations at home, he visited the greater part of Europe and Asia, where he enlightened the minds of men by teaching them the worship of the gods and the arts of civilization. He was styled "the Manifester of Good;" and to this title he had an undisputed right, for he appeared on earth to benefit mankind; and after having performed the duties he had come to fulfil, and fallen a sacrifice to Typhon the evil principle (which was at length overcome by his influence after his leaving the world,) he "rose again to a new life," and became the "judge of mankind in a future state." Other titles of Osiris were, "President of the West," "Lord of the East," "Lord of Lords," "Eternal Ruler," "King of the Gods," &c. Osiris has been identified with many of the Grecian divinities; but more especially with Jupiter, Pluto, and with Bacchus, on account of his reputed conquest of India. Osiris was particularly worshipped at Philae and Abydus: so sacred was the former that no one was permitted to visit it without express permission; and the latter was regarded with such veneration that persons living at a distance from it sought, and with difficulty obtained, permission to possess a sepulchre within its necropolis.

OS'SIAN'S POEMS, the name given to a collection of poems, alleged to have been the production of Ossian, the son of Fingal, a Scottish bard, who lived in the third century. They were first given to the world in an English version by James M'Pherson, Esq., in 1760, with the assurance that they were translations made by himself from ancient Erse manuscripts which he had collected in the Highlands of Scotland; and such was the enthusiasm which their appearance excited, that they may be almost said to have given a new tone to poetry throughout all Europe. There were not, however, wanting many distinguished persons who, from the first, denied their authenticity; foremost among whom was Dr. Johnson, who boldly pronounced the whole of the poems ascribed to Ossian to be forgeries; and his opinion was corroborated by Hume, Gibbon, and many others, who defied M'Pherson to produce a manuscript of any Erse poem of earlier date than the sixteenth century. On the other hand, M'Pherson's assertions as to the genuineness of the poems found warm supporters in Dr. Blair, Dr. Henry, Lord Kaimes, and many other distinguished names, and almost to a man in the whole body of the Highlanders. In this unsettled state the controversy remained till the year 1800, when Malcolm Laing, so well known for his historical labors, in a Dissertation appended to the second volume of his *History of Scotland*, endeavored to establish, from historical and internal evidence, that the so called poems of Ossian are absolutely and totally spurious. The sensation created by this Dissertation was unprecedented. Many converts were made to the opinions therein set forth; but the general disbelief in the authenticity of the poems was not complete till 1805, when a committee of the Highland Society of Edinburgh, which had been appointed in 1797 to inquire into their nature and authenticity, reported to the effect "that they had not been able to obtain any one poem the same in title and tenor with the poems of Ossian." Since that period the controversy, so far as it regards their translation from Erse manuscripts, may be said to be terminated. But although these poems had never been committed to writing, or rather have not been handed down in writing, there can be, we believe, but little doubt that many of them still exist in the Highlands of Scotland, in a dress not very different from that in which they were rendered by M'Pherson into English, having been committed to memory, and transmitted from one bard or storyteller to another in regular succession; and consequently their pretensions to be regarded as historical authority on many points can scarcely be denied. Their scene is sometimes laid in Scotland, but more frequently in Ireland; and they may be justly considered the *Iliad* and *Odyssey* of the Celtic race of the two islands, handed down by tradition only—what the poems of Homer were, in all likelihood, to the Greeks themselves before they were acquainted with the art of writing.

OSSILE'GIUM, in antiquity, the act of collecting the bones and ashes of the dead after the funeral-pile was consumed, and which was performed by the friends or near relations of the deceased, who first washed their hands and ungirt their garments. When all the bones were collected, they were washed with wine, milk, perfumes, and the tears of friends; after this ceremony was over, the relics were put into an urn, and deposited in a sepulchre.

OS'TRACISM, in Grecian antiquity, a kind of popular judgment or condemnation among the Athenians, whereby such persons as had power and popularity enough to attempt anything against the public liberty were banished for a term of ten years. This punishment was called *ostracism*, from a Greek word which properly signifies a shell; but, when applied to this object, it is used for the billet on which the Athenians wrote the names of the citizens whom they intended to banish, which was a piece of baked earth, or tile, in the form of a shell. If 6000 of the shells deposited in the place appointed were in favor of the banishment of the accused, it took effect; otherwise he was acquitted. After the expiration of ten years, the exiled citizen was at liberty to return to his country, and take possession of his wealth, and all his civil privileges. To this sentence no disgrace was attached; for it was never inflicted upon criminals, but only upon those who had excited the jealousy or suspicion of their fellow-citizens, by the influence they had gained by peculiar merit, wealth, or other causes. Aristotle and Plutarch called ostracism the "medicine of the state."

OTTA'VA RI'MA, an Italian form of versification, consisting of stanzas of two alternate triplets and a couplet at the end: the verses being, in the proper Italian metre, the heroic of eleven syllables. It is a happy metre, in the hands of an able versifier, for the expression of feelings varying from the sublime and pathetic to the humorous; although rather deficient in variety, and possessing too little repose and solemnity for the sustained majesty of epic poetry. It has been adopted by the Germans, who have given it something of an elegiac turn; and, of late, by English poets, of whom the most distinguished is Lord Byron, who has employed it in his *Beppo* and *Don Juan*, works belonging to a mixed class of poetry, between the serious and the burlesque.

OT'TOMAN, an appellation given to what pertains to the Turks or their government; as, the *Ottoman* power or empire. The word originated in Othman, the name of a sultan who assumed the government about the year 1300. The finest countries of the old world have been ruled for five hundred years by the Turks, or Ottomans, a mixed people, composed of Tartars, robbers, slaves, and kidnapped Christian children.

OUT'LAWRY, the putting a man out of the protection of the law, or the process by which a man is deprived of that protection. A defendant is outlawed in Great Britain, upon certain proceedings being had, when he does not appear to answer to an indictment or process. On an outlawry for felony, the person forfeits his lands, goods, and chattels. In personal actions, the goods and chattels only are liable; and they are forfeited to the king, with the profits of the lands; for the party being without the law, is incapable of taking care of them himself. In an indictment for treason or felony, an outlawry of the party indicted is equivalent to a conviction. But in the case of either treason or felony, an outlawry may be reversed by a writ of error, or plea; and the judgment upon the reversal is, that the party shall be restored to all that he lost, &c.; he must, however, plead to the indictment against him.

OUT'LINE, contour; the line by which a figure is defined; the exterior line. In drawing, the representation of an imaginary line circumscribing the boundary of the visible superficies of objects, without indicating by shade or light the elevations or depressions, and without color. The study of contour or outline is of the greatest importance to the painter, and in recent times great attention has been paid to it.—The first sketch of a figure. —First general sketch of any scheme or design.

OUT'WORKS, in fortification, all those works of a fortress which are situated without the principal wall, within or beyond the principal ditch. They are designed not only to cover the body of the place, but also to keep the enemy at a distance, and prevent his taking advantage of the cavities and elevations usually found in the places about the counterscarp, which might serve them either as lodgments, or as rideaux, to facilitate the carrying on their trenches, and planting their batteries against the place: such are ravelins, tenailles, horn-works, crown-works, &c.

OVA'TION, an inferior kind of triumph which, according to the ancient Roman custom, was granted to distinguished military leaders. Some antiquaries imagine the distinction between the triumph and the ovation to have originally consisted, not in the greater or less degree of honor, but in the latter being strictly appropriated to successes by which peace was obtained, or to distinguish brilliant achievements in time of peace. Thus we find that ovations were permitted, though triumphs were not, in civil wars. An ovation was celebrated by Mark Antony and Octavius to solemnize their reconciliation.

O'VERT ACT, in law, an open or manifest act from whence criminality is implied. No indictment for high treason is good unless some *overt act* is alleged in it.

O'VERTURE, the introductory piece of music prefixed to an opera or oratorio. Its movements in works of the modern school generally contain snatches of the more prominent and leading airs in the opera, and introduce the audience to a general notion of the emotions which it is the desire of the author to excite. The word *overture* also signifies a *proposal;* in which sense it is always used in the Presbyterian church to indicate those resolutions proposed by presbyteries and synods, and afterwards laid before the General Assembly, either for its sanction or rejection.

O'VOLO, in architecture, a moulding whose profile is the quadrant of a circle; though in Grecian architecture there is a deviation from that exact form, which is most apparent at the upper portion, where it resembles the form of an egg, whence this moulding derives its name.

OWL, THE, among the ancients, generally was considered as an omen of misfortune or death. As, however, according to Philostratus, the Egyptians represented Minerva under the form of an owl, the Athenians, so peculiarly under the care of this goddess, looked upon the appearance of this bird as a favorable omen. From this circumstance it formed upon ancient coins, the symbol of Athens and her foreign possessions.

OWL'ING, so called from its being usually carried on in the night, is the offence of transporting wool or sheep out of England, contrary to the statute.

OX'GANG, in English antiquities, was used to signify as much land as a single ox could *ear* or plough in a season. The *oxgang* was contracted or expanded according to the quality of the land; forty acres constituting the *maximum* and six the *minimum* of the measure.

OXYMO'RON, a rhetorical figure, in which an epithet of a quite contrary signification is added to a word; as, *tender cruelty*.

O'YER AND TER'MINER, in law, a court by virtue of the king's commission, to hear and determine all treasons, felonies, and misdemeanors.

O YES, in law, corrupted from the French "*oyez*, hear ye;" the expression used by the crier of a court, in order to enjoin silence when any proclamation is made.

P.

P, a consonant of the labial series. As was to be expected from the approximation of this letter in sound to *b*, it is susceptible of interchange with the latter in nearly all the languages of which we have any knowledge, but more especially in the German. P. M. stands for *post meridiem*, afternoon; P. S. for *postscript*. As a numeral, P, like C, stands for one hundred, and with a dash over it, $\bar{P}$, for four hundred thousand. P, in music, an abbreviation of the Italian word *piano*, soft, denoting that the force of the voice or instrument is to be diminished. P.P. means *piu piano*, or more soft; and P.P.P. *pianissimo*, as soft as possible.

PACA'LIA, a feast among the Romans in honor of the goddess Pax, or peace, who was worshipped as a deity with great solemnity, and honored with an altar and a magnificent temple.

PACHA', or PASHAW', the military governor of a Turkish province. The most distinguished of them have three horse tails carried before them; the inferior, two. Though the pacha is appointed and removed at the will of the sultan, his power is very great, and the provincial administration is in his hands. This word is also written *bashaw*.

PA'CHACA'MAC, the name given by the idolaters of Peru to the being whom they worshipped as the creator of the universe; this divinity was held in the highest veneration. In the fruitful valley of Pachacama (whence the name) the incas dedicated to his honor a temple of such splendor and wealth, that notwithstanding the rapacity of the Spanish soldiers, by whom it was plundered previously to the arrival of Pizarro, that general is said to have drawn from it treasures to the amount of 900,000 ducats. The ruins of this temple which still remain, furnish a high notion of its former magnificence.

PACIFICA'TION, EDICTS OF, the term usually applied to the edicts issued by the French monarchs in favor of their Protestant subjects, in the view of allaying the commotions occasioned by their previous persecutions. The first edict of this nature was promulgated by Charles IX. in 1562; but the most celebrated was the edict of Nantes issued by Henry IV. in 1598, and revoked by Louis XIV. in 1685.

PAC'TIO, among the Romans, was a temporary cessation from hostilities; a truce or league for a limited time. It differed from *Fœdus*, which was a perpetual league, and required one of those heralds called *Feciales*, to confirm it by solemn proclamation; neither of which conditions were necessary in the truce called *Pactio*.

PAD'ISHAH, a title assumed by the Turkish sultan. Formerly the Ottoman Porte applied that name only to the king of France, calling the other European sovereigns *koral;* but it has since been applied to other foreign princes of Europe.

PA'DUAN COINS, in the Fine Arts, coins forged by the celebrated Paduans, Cavino and Bassiano; who were also the artists employed on the pope's medals, from Julius III. to Gregory XIII. (1571.) These coins hold the first rank in imitations of ancient medals for their masterly execution.

PÆ'AN, among the ancients, a song of rejoicing in honor of Apollo, chiefly used on occasions of victory and triumph. Such songs were named Pæans, because the words *Io Pæan!* frequently occurred in them, which alluded to Apollo's contest with the serpent.—*Pæan*, in ancient poetry, a foot of four syllables, of which there are four kinds, the *pæan primus, secundus, &c.*

PÆ'DOBAP'TISTS, those who hold that baptism should be administered during infancy. The great majority of Christian churches which allow the baptism of infants are thus denominated from that circumstance, and are thereby distinguished from the Antipædobaptists, *i. e.*, those who deny the validity of infant baptism.

PÆDOTHY'SIA, the inhuman custom of sacrificing children, which prevailed among the heathens.

PAGANA'LIA, in antiquity, certain festivals observed by the Romans in the month of January. They were instituted by Servius Tullius, who appointed a certain number of villages (*pagi,*) in each of which an altar was to be raised for annual sacrifices to their tutelar gods, at which all the inhabitants were to assist, and give presents in money according to their sex and age, by which means the number of country-people was known.

PA'GANISM, the religion of the heathen world, in which the Deity is represented under various forms, and by all kinds of images or idols; it is therefore called idolatry or image worship. The theology of the pagans was of three sorts, fabulous, natural, and political or civil. The first treats of the genealogy, worship, and attributes of their deities, who were for the most part the offspring of the imagination of poets, painters, and statuaries. The natural theology of the pagans was studied and taught by the philosophers, who rejected the multiplicity of gods introduced by the poets, and brought their theology to a more rational form. The political or civil theology of the pagans was instituted by legislators, statesmen, and politicians to keep the people in subjection to the civil power. This chiefly related to their temples, altars, sacrifices, and rites of worship. In its origin paganism, as a system, was simple. A few great divinities were placed in heaven to guide the affairs of the visible and invisible worlds. By degrees each great planet, each law of nature, each region and city, nay each river, fountain, wood, tree, mineral, had its tutelary divinity. The laws of nature were often inexplicable; what more obvious than to infer that each was subject to a superior power? As the ideas of men became more precise and refined, gods were placed over human faculties and passions: thus the understanding and the will, love and revenge, were the offspring of certain deities. Mere abstractions were similarly personified; until the empire of reason, of sentiment, and of morals, was as much pervaded as earth, air, and ocean with these visionary beings. In all countries we find instances of deification of individuals. Thus he who during life, proved himself a benefactor to his countrymen, who taught them useful arts, or freed them from some impending evil, would be regarded with affectionate admiration by his contemporaries; and time, which so constantly increases every object, would convert a great exploit, a shining virtue, into a divine effort. But it not unfrequently happened that men were often deified for brute strength, unaccompanied by those elevated mental qualities which form the noblest distinction of the hero. It may, however, be observed, that in such cases men were always reverenced for the quality most wanted in a state. If a district were infested by wild beasts, or by predatory savages, a Hercules arose to free it. If a country required laws, a Minos established them. If the culture of the grape was unknown, a Bacchus appeared to teach it. Such benefactors, it was believed, deserved, as they certainly obtained, the peculiar favor of heaven—rewards which far transcended those bestowed on other men. In most cases, however, each was held to be a divinity, or at least the offspring of one. As the generation of the gods was a received tenet, and their union with mortals of constant occurrence, imagination had little difficulty in the filiation of a benefactor. Most nations were eager to proclaim a god as their founder; and when one laid claim to the honor, the example was speedily followed by others with equal appearance of justice. Hence the prodigious number of divinities; heaven and hell, the earth and the planets, air and ocean, the whole frame of nature, every part of the universe, visible and invisible, even the realms of imagination, being pervaded by them; and hence idolatry became a complicated system, endless in its forms of worship as in its objects.

PA'GEANT, in its general sense, a public representation or exhibition of a showy and splendid character. It was a very early custom in the middle ages, both in England and on the Continent, to celebrate festive occasions of a public nature, as royal visits, marriages, &c., by some ornamental show in the public streets of cities. During the period of chivalry these shows began to be exhibited with the addition of masked figures, representing allegorical personages, with appropriate scenery; and as, in process of time, speeches in verse or prose were put into the mouths of these figures, and sometimes a kind of dramatic entertainment performed between them, the pageant consequently holds a place in early English literature.

PAGO'DA, a Hindoo place of worship, divided, like our churches, into an open space, a place for worship, and an interior or chancel. The most remarkable pagodas are those of Benares, Siam, Pegu, and particularly that of Juggernaut, in Orissa. In the interior of these buildings, besides altars and statues of the gods, there are many curiosities. The statues, which are likewise called *pago-*

das, and which are often numerous, are usually rude images of baked earth, richly gilt, but without any kind of expression. Pagoda is also the name of a gold or silver coin current in Hindostan, of different values in different parts of India, from $2.00 to $2.25.

PAINS AND PEN'ALTIES, in law, an act for the infliction of pains and penalties beyond or contrary to the common law, in the particular cases of great public offenders.

PAINT'ING, the art of representing objects in nature, or scenes in human life, with fidelity and passion. It was coeval with civilization, and practised, with success by the Greeks and Romans; obscured for many centuries, but revived in Italy in the 15th century, where it produced the Roman, Venetian, and Tuscan schools; afterwards, the German, Dutch, Flemish, French and Spanish schools; and, finally, the English school, which equals, and bids fair to transcend them all, in correctness of drawing, effect of coloring, and taste of design. It is distinguished into historical painting, portrait painting, landscape painting, animal painting, marine painting, &c.; and as regards the form and the materials, into painting in oil, water colors, fresco, miniature, distemper, mosaic, &c. Historical painting is the noblest and most comprehensive of all branches of the art; for in that the painter vies with the poet, embodying ideas, and representing them to the spectator. He must have technical skill, a practised eye and hand, and must understand how to group his skilfully executed parts so as to produce a beautiful composition; and all this is insufficient without a poetic spirit which can form a striking conception of an historical event, or create imaginary scenes of beauty. The following rules of criticism in painting have been laid down:—1. The subject must be well imagined, and, if possible, improved in the painter's hands; he must think well as an historian, poet, or philosopher; and more especially as a painter, in making a wise use of all the advantages of his art, and in finding expedients to supply its defects. 2. The expression must be proper to the subject, and the characters of the persons; it must be strong, so that the dumb-show may be perfectly and readily understood; every part of the picture must contribute to this end; colors, animals, draperies, and especially the attitudes of the figures. 3. There must be one principal light, and this and all the subordinate ones, with the shadows and reposes, must make one entire and harmonious mass; while the several parts must be well connected and contrasted, so so as to make the whole as grateful to the eye as a good piece of music is to the ear. 4. The drawing must be just; nothing must be out of place, or ill-proportioned; and the proportions should vary according to the characters of the persons drawn. 5. The coloring, whether gay or solid, must be natural, and such as delights the eye, in shadows as well as in lights and in middle tints; and the colors, whether they are laid on thick, or finely wrought, must appear to have been applied by a light and accurate hand. 6. Nature must be the obvious foundation of the piece; but nature must be raised and improved, not only from what is commonly seen to what is rarely met with, but even yet higher, from a judicious and beautiful idea in the painter's mind.

PAIR'ING, in parliamentary language, that practice by which two members of a legislative body, of opposite political opinions, agree to absent themselves from divisions of the house during a stated period.

PAL'ACE, a magnificent house in which a sovereign or other distinguished person resides; as a royal palace; a pontifical palace; a ducal palace.—*Palace-Court*, a court in England which administers justice between the domestic servants of the crown.

PAL'ADIN, a name formerly given to the knights-errant, who travelled from place to place to give proofs of their valor and their gallantry; extolling their own mistresses as unrivalled in beauty, and compelling those who refused to acknowledge the truth of their panegyrics to engage with them in mortal combat. Of this kind the most famous were Amadis of Gaul and the brave Roland or Orlando.

PALÆOG'RAPHY, a description of ancient writings, inscriptions, characters, &c.

PALÆS'TRA, in Grecian antiquity, a public building where the youth exercised themselves in wrestling, running, playing at quoits, &c. Some say the palæstra consisted both of a college and an academy, the one for exercises of the mind, the other for those of the body; but most authors describe the palæstra as a mere academy for bodily exercises.

PALANQUIN', or PALANKEEN', a sort of litter or covered carriage, used in the East Indies, and borne on the shoulders of four porters, called *coolies*, eight of whom are attached to it, and who relieve each other. They are usually provided with a bed and cushions, and a curtain, which can be dropped when the occupant is disposed to sleep. The motion is easy, and the travelling in this way safe and rapid.

PALA'RIA, in antiquity, an exercise performed by the Roman soldiers, to improve them in all their necessary manœuvres.

PAL'ATINE, an epithet applied originally to persons holding an office or employment in the palace of a sovereign; hence it imports—possessing royal privileges, as the counties *palatine* of Lancaster, Chester, and Durham, in England, which have particular jurisdictions. —On the continent a *palatine*, or *count palatine*, is a person delegated by a prince to hold courts of justice in a province, or one who has a palace and a court of justice in his own house. All the princes of the German empire were originally servants of the imperial crown. In course of time they acquired independent authority, and secured that authority to their heirs: among these was the count palatine, or of the palace, in the German language denominated the *pfalzgraf*. This officer was a president who decided upon appeals made to the emperor himself, from the judgment of provincial courts. All titles, except that of lord, which is complimentary, and belonged to territory, were originally official, as are those of judge, general, &c., at this day.

PALEOL'OGY, a discourse or treatise on antiquities, or the knowledge of ancient things.

PAL'FREY, a word seldom used except in novels and romances to signify a small or gentle horse, such as is fit for a lady's use. It is also used by the old poetical writers for a horse used by kings or noblemen, or on state occasions.

PALI'CI, in Grecian mythology, twin divinities worshipped in Sicily, and especially in the neighborhood of Ætna; sons, according to some, of Jupiter and Thalia, the daughter of Vulcan; according to others, of Vulcan and Ætna, daughter of Ocean. Their heads appear on coins of Catania.

PA'LIMPSEST, the name given to a sort of parchment, from which whatever was written thereon might be erased, so as to admit of its being written on anew. The term means, literally, *twice rubbed*.

PAL'INDROME, in composition, a verse or line which reads the same either forwards or backwards; *e. g.* that which is put in the mouth of Satan—*Signa te, signa, temere me tangis et angis* (cross thyself, cross thyself, you touch and torment me in vain;) or, *Roma tibi subito motibus ibit amor.*

PALINGENE'SIA, in philosophy, a new or second birth—regeneration. The doctrine of the destruction and reproduction of worlds and living beings is Oriental; but the word in question appears to be of Stoical origin.

PAL'INODE, or PAL'INODY, a recantation, particularly a poetical one, of anything dishonorable or false uttered against another person.

PAL'LET, among painters, a little oval tablet of wood or ivory, on which a painter places the several colors he has occasion to use. The middle serves to mix the colors on, and to make the tints required. It is held by putting the thumb through a hole made at one end of it.

PAL'LIUM, an upper garment or mantle worn by the Greeks, as the *toga* was by the Romans. Each of these was so peculiar to the respective nations, that *Palliatus* is used to signify a Greek, and *Togatus* a Roman.—*Pallium*, or *Pall*, also the woollen mantle which the Roman emperors were accustomed from the fourth century, to send to the patriarchs and primates of the empire, and which was worn as a mark of ecclesiastical dignity. Since the 12th century it has consisted of a white woollen band or fillet, which is thrown over the shoulders outside of the sacerdotal vestments; one band hanging over the back, and another over the breast, and both ornamented with a red chaplet.

PALM'ER, a pilgrim bearing a staff; or one who returned from the Holy Land, bearing branches of palm: he was distinguished from other pilgrims by his profession of poverty, and living on alms as he travelled.

PALM'ISTRY, a mode of telling fortunes by the lines of the hand; a trick of imposture much practised by gipsies.

PALM SUN'DAY, the sixth Sunday in Lent, the next before Easter, commemorative of our Saviour's triumphal entrance into Jerusalem, when palm branches were strewed in the way.

PAN, the chief rural divinity of the Greeks, who presided over flocks and herds. He was said by some to be the son of Mercury; and his birthplace was Arcadia, to which province his worship seems to have been confined in early times. The introduction of his worship into the other Grecian states is thus accounted for. He was represented with the head and breast of an elderly man, while his lower parts were like the hind quarters of a goat, whose horns he likewise bore on his forehead. His emblems were the shepherd's crook and pipe of seven reeds, his own invention,

PANATHENÆ'A, in Grecian antiquity, an ancient Athenian festival, in honor of Minerva, who was the protectress of Athens, and called *Athena*. There were two solemnities of this name, one of which was called the *greater panathenæa*, and celebrated once in five years. These were distinguished from the *less* (which were celebrated every third year) not only by their greater splendor and longer continuance, but particularly by the solemn procession, in which the *peplus*, a sacred garment, consecrated by young virgins, and made of white wool, embroidered with gold, was carried from the Acropolis into the temple of the goddess, whose ivory statue was covered with it. This festival was so holy, that criminals were released from the prisons on the occasion of its celebration, and men of distinguished merit were rewarded with gold crowns.

PANCRA'TIUM, among the ancients, a kind of exercise which consisted of wrestling and boxing. In these contests it was customary for the weaker party, when he found himself pressed by his adversary, to fall down, and fight rolling on the ground.

PAN'DECTS, the name of a volume of the civil law, digested by order of the emperor Justinian.

PAN'DIT, or PUN'DIT, a learned Brahmin; or one versed in the Sanscrit language, and in the sciences, laws, and religion of the country.

PANDOURS', a kind of light infantry, formerly organized as separate corps in the Austrian service; raised from the Servian and Rascian inhabitants of the Turkish frontier, and originally under leaders of their own, styled Harumbachas. Since 1755, they have been included in the regular army.

PANEGY'RIC, in oratory, an eulogy or harangue, written or spoken, in praise of an individual or body of men. Among the ancients, orations were recited in praise of the departed on various occasions, before solemn assemblies: hence the name. Among the later Romans, the baser practice prevailed of reciting panegyrical orations on distinguished living persons in their presence. Among the moderns panegyrical oratory has been chiefly confined to funeral discourses from the pulpit.

PAN'EL, in law, a schedule or roll of parchment on which are written the names of the jurors returned by the sheriff. *Impanelling* a jury, is returning their names in such schedule.

PAN'IC, an ill-grounded terror inspired by the misapprehension of danger. The origin of the word is said to be derived from Pan, one of the captains of Bacchus, who with a few men routed a numerous army, by a noise which his soldiers raised in a rocky valley favored with a great number of echoes. Hence all ill-grounded fears have been called *panic* fears.

PAN'OPLY, literally all the armor that can be worn for defence: complete armor.

PANORA'MA, a picture in which all the objects of nature that are visible from a single point are represented on the interior surface of a round or cylindrical wall, the point of view being in the axis of the cylinder. The rules according to which the different objects are represented in perspective are easily deduced from the consideration that the lines on the panorama are the intersections of the cylindrical surface of the picture, with one or more conical surfaces having their summits at the point of view, and of which the bases are the lines of nature which the artist proposes to represent. In executing this kind of perspective, the artist divides the horizon into a considerable number of parts, twenty, for example, and draws, in the ordinary way, on a plane surface, a perspective view of all the objects comprised in each of these portions of the horizon. He then paints on a canvass, representing the development of the cylindrical surface, the twenty drawings, in as many vertical and parallel stripes; and the picture is completed by stretching the canvas on the cylindrical wall of the rotunda which is to contain the panorama. When a painting of this kind is well executed, its truth is such as to produce a complete illusion. No other method of representing objects is so well calculated to give an exact idea of the general aspect and appearance of a country as seen all round from a given point.

PANTHE'A, in antiquity, statues composed of the figures or symbols of several divinities.

PAN'THEISM, in metaphysical theology, the theory which identifies nature, or the universe in its totality with God. This doctrine differs from atheism in the greater distinctness with which it asserts the unity and essential vitality of nature, parts of which all animated beings are. The most ancient Greek philosophers were pantheists in this sense, Anaxagoras being the first who distinctly stated the coexistence with nature of a reasonable creator—" a mind, the principle of all things." In this sense, too, Spinosa may be called a pantheist. The pantheism of Schelling, and many modern German philosophers, is of a different stamp. According to these thinkers, God is conceived as the absolute and original Being, revealing himself variously in outward nature, and in human intelligence and freedom.

PANTHE'ON, in Roman antiquity, a temple of a circular form, dedicated to all the heathen deities. It was built on the *Campus Martius*, by Agrippa, son-in-law to Augustus; but is now converted into a church and dedicated to the Virgin Mary and all the martyrs. It is, however, called the *rotunda*, on account of its form, and is one of the finest edifices in Rome. The well-preserved portico seems to be of a later period than the temple itself; it consists of sixteen columns of oriental granite, each of which is 15 feet in circumference. The interior was formerly adorned with the most beautiful statues of the various deities, but they were removed by Constantine to Constantinople; at present there are in the eight niches, eight fine columns, placed there by the emperor Adrian. What is very remarkable, and shows the alteration which has taken place at Rome, is, that the entrance is now twelve steps below, though heretofore it was twelve steps above the surface of the ground.

PAN'TOMIME, in the modern drama, a mimic representation by gestures, actions, and various kinds of tricks performed by Harlequin and Columbine as the hero and heroine, assisted by Pantaloon and his clown.—*Pantomimes*, among the ancients, were persons who could imitate all kinds of actions and characters by signs and gestures. Scaliger supposes they were first introduced upon the stage to succeed the chorus and comedies, and divert the audience with apish postures and antic dances. In after times their interludes became distinct entertainments, and were separately exhibited.

PA'PACY, the office of pope, or, historically, the succession of popes in the see of Rome. The origin of the term is oriental. The word papas was used in lower Greek, with the signification of father, and is still applied by the Greek church to the priests of that communion. In the Western Church, the title was not uncommonly given to bishops in general, and was not confined to the Roman pontiff for several centuries.

PA'PER-MONEY, or PA'PER CUR'-RENCY, bank notes or bills issued by the credit of government, and circulated as the representative of coin. In a more extensive sense, these terms may denote all kinds of notes and bills of exchange.

PA'PIST, one that adheres to the doctrines and ceremonies of the church of Rome; a Roman Catholic.

PAPY'RUS, an Egyptian sedge-like plant, or reed-grass, which has acquired an immortal fame in consequence of its leaves having furnished the ancients with paper. It grows in the marshes of Egypt or in the stagnant places of the Nile. Its roots are tortuous, and in thickness about four or five inches; its stem, which is triangular and tapering, rises to the height of ten feet, and is terminated by a compound, wide spreading, and beautiful umbel, which is surrounded with an involucre composed of eight large sword-shaped leaves. The uses of the papyrus were, however, by no means confined to the making of paper. The inhabitants of the countries where it grows, even to this day, manufacture it into sail-cloth, cordage, and sometimes wearing apparel.

PAR, (Latin, *equal*,) in commerce, is said of any two things equal in value; and in money-affairs, the equality of one kind of money or property with another: thus, when $100 stock is worth exactly $100 specie, the stock is said to be *at par;* that is, the purchaser is required to give neither more nor less of the commodity with which he parts, than he receives of that which he acquires: thus, too, the *par* of exchange is the equal value of money in one country and another.

PA'RA, a Turkish coin, very small and thin, of copper and silver, the fortieth part of a Turkish piaster.

PAR'ABLE, a fable or allegorical representation of something real or apparent in life or nature, from which a moral is drawn for instruction. Parables are certainly a most delicate way of impressing disagreeable truths on the mind, and in many cases have the advantage of a more open reproof, and even of formal lessons of morality: thus Nathan made David sensible of his guilt by a parable;

and thus our Saviour, in compliance with the customs of the Jews, who had a kind of natural genius for this sort of instruction, spoke frequently in parables, most beautifully constructed, and calculated to convince them of their errors and prejudices.

PARACEL'SIAN, a name given to a physician who follows the practice of Paracelsus, a celebrated Swiss physician and alchymist who lived at the close of the 15th century, and who performed many extraordinary cures by means totally unknown to the generality of medical practitioners of his time.

PARACH'RONISM, an error in chronology, by which an event is related as having happened later than its true date.

PAR'ACLETE, a name attached to the Holy Spirit, as an advocate, intercessor, or comforter of mankind. It was not an uncommon opinion of the early heretics, that the Paraclete, whose mission was promised by Christ, was to appear corporeally upon the earth, and complete the dispensation announced by our Lord and the apostles; and they drew a distinction between the person of the Comforter and the effusion of his grace upon the disciples on the day of Pentecost. Accordingly, several of them, Simon Magus, Manes, and others, gave themselves out as this expected Paraclete; and Tertullian himself was at one period infatuated by the claims advanced by Montanus to this personification.

PARACROS'TIC, a poetical composition in which the first verse contains, in order, all the letters which commence the remaining verses of the poem or division. According to Cicero, the original sibylline verses were paracrostics.

PAR'ADIGM, in grammar, an example of a verb conjugated in the several moods, tenses and persons.

PAR'ADISE, a region of supreme felicity; generally meaning the garden of Eden, in which Adam and Eve were placed immediately after their creation. The locality of this happy spot has been assigned, by different writers, to places the most opposite. In truth there is scarcely any part of the world where Paradise has not been sought for. The most probable opinion is, that it was situated between the confluence of Euphrates and Tigris, and their separation; Pison being a branch arising from one of them after their separation,—and Gihon, another branch arising from the other, on the western side.—When Christians use the word, they mean that celestial paradise, or place of pure and refined delight in which the souls of the blessed enjoy everlasting happiness. In this sense it is frequently used in the New Testament: our Saviour tells the penitent thief on the cross, "This day shalt thou be with me in Paradise;" and St. Paul, speaking of himself in the third person, says, "I knew a man who was caught up into Paradise, and heard unspeakable words, which it is not lawful for a man to utter."

PAR'ADOX, in philosophy, a tenet or proposition seemingly absurd, or contrary to received opinion, yet true in fact.

PAR'AGOGE, a figure in grammar by which the addition of a letter or syllable is made to the end of a word.

PAR'AGON, a model by way of distinction implying superior excellence or perfection: as, a *paragon* of beauty or eloquence.

PAR'AGRAM, a play upon words. Hence *paragrammatist*, an appellation for a punster.

PAR'AGRAPH, any section or portion of a writing which relates to a particular point, whether consisting of one sentence or many sentences. Paragraphs are generally distinguished by a break in the lines; or, when a great quantity of print is intended to be compressed into a small space, they may be separated by a dash, thus ——. A paragraph is also sometimes marked thus, ¶.

PARALEP'SIS, or PAR'ALEPSY, a figure in rhetoric by which the speaker pretends to pass by what at the same time he really mentions.

PARALIPOM'ENA, in matters of literature, denotes a supplement of things omitted in a preceding work.

PAR'ALLEL, is often used metaphorically, to denote the continued comparison of two objects, particularly in history. Thus we speak of drawing an historical *parallel* between ages, countries, or men. —*Parallel passages*, are such passages in a book as agree in import; as, for instance, the parallel passages in the bible.

PARAL'OGISM, in logic, a fallacious argument or false reasoning; an error committed in demonstration, when a consequence is drawn from principles which are false, or though true, are not proved; or when a proposition is passed over that should have been proved by the way.

PAR'AMOUNT, in Eng. the supreme lord of the fee. The lords of those manors that have other manors under them are styled lords-paramount; and the king, who, in law, is chief lord of all the lands in England, is thus the lord-paramount.—In common parlance, it means superior to anything else; as, a man's private interest is usually *paramount* to all other considerations.

PAR'ANYMPH, among the ancients, the person who waited on the bridegroom and directed the nuptial solemnities. As the *paranymph* officiated only on the part of the bridegroom, a woman called *pronuba* officiated on the part of the bride.—In poetry, the term paranymph is still occasionally used for the *brideman*.

PAR'APEGM, in ancient customs, signified a brazen table fixed to a pillar, on which laws and proclamations were engraved. Also, a table set in a public place, containing an account of the rising and setting of the stars, eclipses, seasons, &c.

PAR'APET, in fortification, a wall, rampart, or elevation of earth for screening soldiers from an enemy's shot. It means literally, a wall breast high.

PA'RAPH, in diplomatics, the figure formed by a flourish of the pen at the conclusion of a signature. This formed, in the middle ages, a sort of rude provision against forgery, like the flourishes in the plates of bank notes. In some countries (as in Spain,) the paraph is still a usual addition to a signature.

PARAPHERNA'LIA, in English law, the goods which a wife brings with her at her marriage, or which she possesses beyond her dower or jointure, and which remain at her disposal after her husband's death. They consist principally of the woman's apparel, jewels, &c., which, in the lifetime of her husband, she wore as the ornaments of her person; nor can the husband devise such ornaments and jewels of his wife, though, during his life, he has power to dispose of them.

PAR'APHRASE, an explanation of some text or passage in a book, in a more clear and ample manner than is expressed in the words of the author; such as the *paraphrase* of the New Testament by Erasmus. A paraphrase partakes of the nature both of a version, if the work paraphrased be in a foreign language, and of a commentary. Its object is to express the full sense contained in the words which are paraphrased, by the introduction of circumlocutions, explanatory clauses, and expansions of the author's meaning.

PAR'ASANG, a Persian measure of length, varying in different ages, and in different places, from thirty to fifty stadia or furlongs.

PARASCE'NIUM, in the Grecian and Roman theatres, was a place behind the scenes whither the actors withdrew to dress and undress themselves. The Romans more frequently called it *postscenium*.

PARASCE'VE, a word signifying *preparation*, given by the Jews to the sixth day of the week, or Friday; because, not being allowed to prepare their food on the sabbath day, they provided and prepared it on the day previous.

PARASI'TI, among the Greeks, were an order of priests, or at least ministers of the gods, resembling the *Epulones* at Rome. Their business was to collect and take care of the sacred corn destined for the service of the temples and the gods; to see that sacrifices were duly performed, and that no one withheld the first fruits, &c. from the deities. In every village of the Athenians, certain *Parasiti*, in honor of Hercules, were maintained at the public charge; but, to ease the commonwealth of this burthen, the magistrates at last obliged some of the richer sort to take them to their own tables, and entertain them at their individual expense: hence the word *parasite*, by which we denote a hanger-on, a fawning flatterer, one who, for the sake of a good dinner at the expense of another person, would be ready to surfeit him with adulation.

PARAVAIL', in feudal law, the lowest tenant holding under a mediate lord, as distinguished from a tenant in *capite*, who holds immediately of the king.

PAR'CÆ, or the FATES, in the heathen mythology, were three goddesses who were supposed to preside over the accidents and events, and to determine the date or period of human life. They were called Atropos, Clotho, and Lachesis, and are represented as spinning the thread of human life; in which employment Clotho held the distaff, Lachesis turned the wheel, and Atropos cut the thread. Their persons are variously described; sometimes they are represented as old women, one holding a distaff, another a wheel, and a third a pair of scissors. Others paint Clotho in a robe of various colors, with a crown of stars upon her head, and holding a distaff in her hand; Lachesis in a garment covered with stars, and holding several spindles; and Atropos they clad in black, cutting the thread with a large pair of scissors.

PAR'CENER, or CO-PAR'CENER, in law, a coheir, or one who holds lands by descent from an ancestor in common with others. The holding or occupation of lands of inheritance by two or more persons, differs from *joint tenancy*, which is created by deed or devise, whereas *parcenary* is created by the descent of lands from a common ancestor.

PAREL'CON, in grammar, the addition of a word or syllable at the end of another.

PAREM'BOLE, a figure in rhetoric, often confounded with the *parenthesis*. The parembole is, in reality, a species of parenthesis; but its specific character is this, that *it relates to the subject;* while the parenthesis is foreign from it.

PA'RENT, a term of relationship applicable to those from whom we immediately receive our being. Parents, by the law of the land as well as by the law of nature, are bound to educate, maintain, and defend their children, over whom they have a legal as well as a natural power: they likewise have interest in the profits of their children's labor, during their nonage, in case the children live with and are provided for by them; yet the parent has no interest in the real or personal estate of a child, any otherwise than as his guardian. The laws relating to the mutual rights and duties of parents and children are a very important part of every code, and have a very intimate connection with the state of society and with civil institutions. In ancient times, when paternity was a great foundation of civil authority, the parental rights were much more absolute than in the modern, extending, in some countries, to the right of life and death, and continuing during the life of the two parties.

PARENTA'LIA, in antiquity, funeral obsequies, or the last duties paid by children to their deceased parents. The term is also used for a sacrifice, or solemn service, offered annually to the manes of the dead.

PAREN'THESIS, in rhetoric, a figure by which a series of words is inserted in a sentence, having no grammatical connection with those which precede or follow, with the object of explaining some detached portion of the sentence. In ancient authors, a parenthetical form of writing is even more common than among moderns; because much which a Greek or Roman author would have conveyed by way of parenthesis is now inserted in separate explanatory notes.

PA'RIAS, a degraded tribe of Hindoos, who live by themselves in the outskirts of towns; and, in the country, build their houses apart from the villages, or rather have villages of their own. They dare not in cities pass through the streets where the Brahmins live; nor enter a temple of the superior castes. They are prohibited from all approach to anything pure, and are doomed to perform all kinds of menial work.

PAR IM'PAR, in antiquity, a game of chance practised among the Greeks and Romans. It was identical with the game of "even or odd" practised by the boys of modern times.

PAR'ISH, the precinct or territorial jurisdiction of a secular priest, or a circuit of ground or district inhabited by people who belong to one church, and are under the particular charge of its minister. In the earliest ages of the church, the name *parish* was applied to the district placed under the superintendence of the bishop, and was equivalent to the diocese. Parishes were originally ecclesiastical divisions, but they now come under the class of civil divisions. In England, their limits cannot be altered but by legislative enactment; and in Scotland it requires the authority of the Court of Session, together with the consent of three fourths of the heritors, to erect new churches and to disjoin parishes. Towns originally contained but one parish, but from the increase of inhabitants, many of them are divided into several parishes. The number of parishes and parochial chapelries in England and Wales is estimated at about 10,700. In Scotland, the number of parishes recognized by law is 948.—In some of the United States, parish is an ecclesiastical society not bounded by territorial limits; but the inhabitants of a town belonging to one church, though residing promiscuously among the people belonging to another church, are called a parish. This is particularly the case in Massachusetts. In Connecticut, the legal appellation of such a society is ecclesiastical society.

PARK, in England, a large piece of ground enclosed and privileged for beasts of the chase. Also, a piece of ground in cities, planted with trees and devoted to public recreation.—*Park of artillery*, a place in the rear of both lines of an army for encamping the artillery, which is formed in lines, the guns in front, the ammunition wagons behind the guns, and the pontoons and tumbrils forming the third line. The whole is surrounded with a rope.

PAR'LIAMENT, the grand assembly of the three estates in Great Britain, or the great council of the nation, consisting of the King, Lords, and Commons, which form the legislative branch of the government. The word *parliament* was introduced into England under the Norman kings. The supreme council of the nation was called by our Saxon ancestors, the *wittenagemote*, the meeting of wise men or sages. A parliament is called by the king's [queen's] writ, or letter, directed to each lord, summoning him to appear; and by writs sent by the lord chancellor under the great seal, commanding the sheriffs of each county to take the necessary steps for the election of members for the county, and the boroughs contained in it. On the day appointed for the meeting of parliament, the king [queen] sits in the house of lords under a canopy, dressed in his [her] robes, as are all the lords in theirs; and, the commons being summoned to the bar of that house, the sovereign addresses both houses on the state of public affairs. The commons are then required to choose a speaker, which officer being presented to and approved by the sovereign, the latter withdraws, the commons retire to their own house, and the business of parliament begins. In the house of lords, the seat of each member is prescribed according to rank; though, except in the presence of the king [queen] this formality is almost wholly dispensed with. The princes of the blood sit on each side of the throne; the two archbishops against the wall on the king's right hand; the bishops of London, Durham, and Winchester below the former, and the other bishops according to priority of consecration. On the king's [queen's] left hand, above all the dukes except those of the blood royal, sit the lord treasurer, lord president, and lord privy-seal; then the dukes, marquises, and earls, the individuals of each class taking precedence according to the date of their creation. Across the room are woolsacks, continued from ancient custom; and on the first of these, immediately before the throne, sits the lord chancellor, as speaker of the house. On the other woolsacks are seated judges, masters in chancery, and the king's counsel, who only give their advice on points of law. In the house of commons there are no peculiar seats for any members. The speaker only has a chair appropriated to him at the upper end of the house, and at a table before him sit the clerk and his assistant. When the parliament is thus assembled, no member is to depart without leave. Upon extraordinary occasions, all the members are summoned; otherwise three hundred of the commons is reckoned a full house, and forty may compose a house for the dispatch of business. The method of making laws is much the same in both houses. In each house the act of the majority binds the whole; and this majority is declared by votes openly given; not privately, or by ballot.

PARLIAMENTA'RIAN, an epithet for those who sided with the English republican parliament in opposition to king Charles I.

PARNAS'SUS, in mythology, a celebrated mountain in ancient Greece, sacred to Apollo and the Muses, and, from the numerous objects of classical interest of which it formed the theatre, considered "holy" by the Greeks. On its side stood the city of Delphi, near which flowed the Castalian spring, the grand source of ancient inspiration; and from this circumstance, in metaphorical language, the word Parnassus has come to signify poetry itself. A good collection of the Italian poets, printed at Milan, bears the title *Il Parnasso Italiano.*

PARO'DY, a kind of writing in which the words of an author or his thoughts are, by some slight alterations, adapted to a different purpose; or it may be defined, a poetical pleasantry in which the verses of some author are, by way of ridicule, applied to another object; or in turning a serious work into burlesque by affecting to observe the same rhymes, words, and cadences.

PAR'OL, in law, anything done verbally, or by oral declaration; as *parol evidence.*—*Parole,* in military affairs, a promise given by a prisoner of war when suffered to be at large, that he will return at the time appointed, unless he shall have previously been discharged or exchanged.—*Parole* also means the watchword given out every day in orders by a commanding officer, in camp or garrison, by which friends may be distinguished from enemies.

PAROMOL'OGY, in rhetoric, a figure of speech by which the orator concedes something to his adversary, in order to strengthen his own argument.

PARONOMA'SIA, a rhetorical figure, by which words nearly alike in sound, but of very different or opposite meanings, are affectedly or designedly used; a play upon words.

PAR'QUETRY, a species of joinery or

cabinet work, which consists in making a *parquet*, or inlaid floor, composed of small pieces of wood, either square or triangular, which, by the manner of their disposition, are capable of forming various combinations of figures. Two sorts of wood are employed for this purpose almost of the same color, or differing only in shade, and these two sorts suffice for the production of a great variety of effects.

PAR'RICIDE, strictly signifies the murder or murderer of a father, as *matricide* does of a mother; yet this word is ordinarily taken in both senses, and is also extended to the murder of any near relation. The word *parricide* is also applied to one who invades or destroys any to whom he owes particular reverence, as his country or patron. By the Roman law it was punished in a severer manner than any other kind of homicide. After being scourged, the delinquents were sewn up in a leathern sack.

PARRICID'IUM, a name given by a decree of the Roman senate to the ides of March, which was the anniversary of Cæsar's assassination. Dolabella the consul proposed a law to change its name to *Natalis Urbis*, as he looked on that day as the birthday of Roman liberty.

PAR'SEE, the name given by English writers to the Persian refugees, driven from their country by the persecutions of the Mussulmans, who now inhabit various parts of India. Their principal emigration to Baroach, Surat, and the neighboring coast, is supposed to have taken place about the end of the eighth century. The sacred fire, the emblem of their religion, called *behrem*, is believed by them to have been brought by the first emigrants from Persia, and, after many changes of place, is now preserved at Odisari and Nausari, near Surat, and at Bombay. In this latter city, under the protection of the British government, they have grown into a colony of considerable numbers and of great opulence. They have become particularly distinguished in the art of shipbuilding, and the dock-yard of Bombay is now almost exclusively in their hands. Their character is variously estimated by different observers; but all agree in attributing to them industry and economy, and attachment to their religion, and to those of the higher class strong sentiments of honor and honesty. Their number is said to equal 700,000; and at Bombay, according to late calculations, at least 20,000.

PARS'ING, in grammar, the resolving a sentence into its elements, by showing the several parts of speech of which it is composed, and their relation to each other according to grammatical rules.

PAR'SON, the rector or incumbent of a parish, who has the parochial charge or cure of souls.—*Parsonage*, a rectory endowed with a house, glebe, lands, tithes, &c., for the maintenance of the incumbent.

PAR'THENON, in ancient architecture, the name given to the celebrated Grecian temple of Minerva, erected during the splendid era of Pericles. It was built of marble upon a spot elevated on all sides above the town and citadel; of the Doric order; 222 Greek feet in length, and 69 in height. This magnificent temple had resisted all the ravages of time; had been in turn converted into a Christian church and a Turkish mosque; but in the year 1687, when the Venetians besieged the citadel of Athens, under the command of general Kœnigsmarck, a bomb fell most unluckily on the devoted Parthenon, set fire to the powder which the Turks had shut up therein, and thus the roof was entirely destroyed, and the whole building almost reduced to ruins.

PARTICEPS CRIM'INIS, in law, an accomplice, or one who has a share in the guilt.

PARTI'CIPANTS, a semi-religious order of knighthood, founded by Pope Sextus V., in 1586, in honor of Our Lady of Loretto. The members of this order were allowed to marry. The order was soon extinguished; and the title of Knights of Loretto is now conferred on some civil servants of the pope.

PARTI'TION, in music, the arrangement of the several parts of a composition on the same page or pages, ranged methodically above and under each other, so that they may be all under the eye of the performer or conductor, and sung or played jointly or separately as the composer intended. It is commonly called a *score*.—In architecture, the vertical assemblage of materials which divides one apartment from another. It is usually, however, employed to denote such division when constructed of vertical pieces of timber called *quarters*.—In politics, the division of the states of a sovereign or prince, after his decease, among his heirs, as was the custom in some of the princely families in the ancient German empire: or among other powers, such as that of the states of the king of Spain, which was in contemplation (against all justice) between William III., Louis XIV., and the Dutch, by the treaties of 1698 and 1699, when Charles II., the reigning monarch, was without near heirs. But the most celebrated partitions in history, to which the name has become almost exclusively attached, were those of Poland by Russia, Prussia, and Austria.

PART'NERSHIP, the association of two or more persons for the prosecution of any trade, manufacture, or commercial enterprise, at their joint expense. In this case the connection is formed by contract; each partner furnishing a part of the capital stock, and being entitled to a proportional share of profit, or subject to a proportional share of loss; or one or more of the partners may furnish money or stock, and the others may contribute their services. A partnership or association of this kind is a standing or permanent company, and is denominated a *firm* or *house*. Though partnerships ought not to be entered into without great circumspection, the benefits of a union of the means and advantages of different persons for the conduct of a business, in many instances, are too obvious to need illustration.

PAR'TY, in politics, a body of men united under different leaders for promoting, by their joint endeavors, the national interest, upon some particular principle in which they are all agreed. The origin of party may be traced to that law of the human mind which is founded in our natural desire of sympathy, and our disposition to afford it. From the earliest ages down to the present time, the principle of mutual co-operation has been adopted with success in executing favorite designs, and in aiming at the accomplishment of certain ends. Among the ancient Romans, for example, "*idem sentire de republica*" formed a principal ground of friendship and attachment; and the same feeling, modified by different forms of government and other circumstances, is at present in full operation in all the civilized states of Europe and America. The benefits of party may be briefly stated to be, increased energy in pursuit of a common object, regular co-operation, mutual control and regulation, and an advantageous division of labor. But, though party or combination may in this manner be productive of good results, like every other principle and feeling in our nature, it is liable to be abused. It involves a frequent sacrifice of individual notions of what is just and proper, and tempts bodies of men to act in a way that would often be deemed discreditable in individuals. Perhaps the worst effect of party is its tendency to generate narrow, false, and illiberal prejudices, by teaching the adherents of one party to regard those that belong to an opposing party as unworthy of confidence; and in making them oppose good measures because they happen to be proposed by a different party, and support bad measures because they are proposed or supported by their own party.

PASIG'RAPHY, the imaginary universal language to be spoken and written by all nations, the invention of which has exercised the ingenuity of so many learned men, has been denoted by this word. Leibnitz seems to have been one of the first who conceived this to be possible. Many writers in Germany (where the name was invented) have followed him in the endeavor to devise schemes for this fanciful object. In England, Bishop Wilkins, in the reign of Charles II., invented a scheme for a universal language, grammar and character.

PASQUINADE', a satirical writing directed against one or more individuals. A mutilated ancient statue of a gladiator dug up at Rome about 300 years ago, which now lies in the court of the Capitol, was popularly termed, by the Romans, "Pasquino," from the name, it is said, of a barber of eccentric and well-known character, opposite to whose house it was originally set up. This statue, and another, called by the populace Marforio, which was situated near it, were used for the purpose of bearing satirical placards, often reflecting on the court and church of Rome, which were affixed to them at night, not unfrequently in the form of a dialogue between the two statues. So annoying did Pasquin often become to the government, that on one occasion a serious design was entertained of throwing him into the river; but the ministers of the reigning pontiff are said to have dissuaded him from it, representing that if this were done "the frogs in the Tiber would croak louder than ever Pasquin had spoken." He has, however, lost his public spirit, and rarely or never ventures to attack the powers that be. But his statue is still the occasional receptacle of jocose comments on private matters. The difference between a *pasquinade* and a *satire* is, that the end of the latter is to correct and reform, while that of the former is only to ridicule and expose.

PAS'SING-BELL, the bell that is

tolled at the hour of death, or immediately after death. The *passing-bell* was originally intended to drive away any demon that might seek to take possession of the soul of the deceased, on which account it was sometimes called the *soul-bell*. Mr. Ellis in his notes to Brand, quotes Wheatley's apology for our retaining this ceremony; "Our church," says he, "in imitation of the saints in former ages, calls on the minister, and others who are at hand, to assist their brother in his last extremity. In order to this, she directs that when any one is passing out of this life a bell should be tolled."

PAS'SION, or THE PAS'SIONS, are strong feelings or emotions of the mind excited by an adequate cause, and existing in such strength as to engross the whole man, and resist the influence of every other cause of sensation. In order to form a clear notion of *the passions*, we must begin with rejecting the phrase that man is possessed of this or that number of passions, and say that he is possessed of *one* quality, that is, susceptibility, which is liable to be acted upon by this or that number of causes. Man, therefore, has not so many feelings, but one feeling, assuming different forms of appearance according to the impression it receives; and the number of passions is exactly that of the circumstances that are important to a sentient creature. Now, these, in a comprehensive point of view, are only of two kinds; those that contribute to its pleasure, and those that are productive of pain. It is for this reason that, according to some, man has only two passions: the desire of happiness, and the aversion to evil; but subdivided, each order has its genera, and each genus its species. The desire of happiness is separated into love, or the wish to possess that which will impart happiness; hope, which is the expectation of possessing it; and joy, which is the assurance of possession. The aversion to evil is separated into fear, which belongs to the dread of evil; grief, which belongs to the presence of it; and anger, which resents it. These, again, to which also other genera may be added, are distinguished into species; as, to fear belong terror and horror; and to anger, envy, jealousy, hatred, and malice. Some think the most natural division of the passions is into pleasurable and painful.—*Passions*, in painting and sculpture, the representation in the countenance and other parts, of the violent emotions of the mind, produced by anger, fear, grief, &c. The expression of the passions is a language without which the painter can never hope for success; it is in this that he has the means of appealing to the sympathy of the spectator. The close observation of nature under similar circumstances is the only mode by which his aim can be accomplished.

PAS'SION-WEEK, the week immediately preceding the festival of Easter; so called, because in that week our Saviour's passion and death happened. The Thursday in this week is called *Maundy Thursday*, and the Friday, *Good Friday*. The "passion of Christ" is celebrated in the Catholic and most Protestant churches on the European continent during Lent, and particularly during Passion-week, by sermons relating to the sufferings of the Saviour; and it is no inconsiderable treat to the lovers of sacred music who may be sojourning at Rome during the time, to hear the compositions of Palestrini, Pergolesi, Allegri, &c., in the purest style, as performed in the Sistine Chapel.

PAS'SIVE, in grammar, a term given to a verb which expresses passion, or the effect of an action of some agent.—*Passive obedience*, in civil polity, denotes not only quiet unresisting submission to power, but implies the denial of the right of resistance, or the recognition of the duty to submit in all cases to the existing government.—*Passive prayer*, among mystic divines, is a suspension of the soul or intellectual faculties, and yielding only to the impulses of grace.—*Passive commerce*, trade in which the productions of a country are carried on by foreigners in their own ships: opposed to *active* commerce.

PASS'OVER, a solemn festival of the Jews, celebrated on the 14th day of the month following the vernal equinox, and instituted in commemoration of their providential deliverance on the night before their departure from Egypt, when the destroying angel, who put to death the first-born of the Egyptians, *passed over* the house of the Hebrews, which were sprinkled with the blood of a lamb.

PASS'PORT, a written license from a king, governor, or other proper authority, granting permission or safe conduct for one to pass through his territories, or to pass from one country to another, or to navigate a particular sea without molestation. Also, a license for importing or exporting contraband goods or movables without paying the usual duties. In all passports it is usual to describe the persons, purposes, and destinations of the traveller, intended to show that their characters are good, and their objects in travelling lawful. The use of passports is abolished in the United States and England.

PASTE, in gem sculpture, a preparation of glass, calcined crystal, lead, and other ingredients, for imitating gems. This art was well known to the ancients, and after being long lost, was restored, at the end of the fifteenth century, by a Milanese painter.

PAS'TEL, in painting, a crayon formed with any color and gum water, for painting on paper or parchment. The great defect of this mode of painting is its want of durability.

PASTIC'CIO, in painting, a picture painted by a master in a style dissimilar to that in which he generally painted. David Teniers could, for instance, imitate, with surprising exactness, the styles of many of the first masters of Italy and Flanders. The same may be affirmed of Luca Giordano, a Neapolitan artist.

PASTOPH'ORI, in antiquity, priests among the Greeks and Romans whose office it was to carry the images along with the shrines of the gods at solemn festivals. The cells or apartments near the temples where the *Pastophori* lived, were called *Pastophoria*.

PAS'TORAL, something descriptive of a shepherd's life; or a poem in which any action or passion is represented by its effects on a country life. The complete character of this poem consists in simplicity, brevity, and delicacy; the two first of which render an eclogue or idyl natural, and the last delightful. As the first strains of poetry must have been heard in the primitive times of the human race, and as a shepherd's life is congenial with this mode of occupation, we naturally consider poetry as having originated in the pastoral period; but the poetic idea of pastoral life, where all is purity and simplicity, is not supported by experience in past or present times.

PASTORA'LE, in ecclesiastical affairs, that part of theology which includes the execution of the duties of the clergyman, or the practical application of his theological knowledge. In the *pastorale* of a Roman Catholic priest, the chief part of the canon law is comprised; while that of the Protestant minister consists of principles addressed merely to his understanding, including certain rules which experience has shown to be important for the execution of clerical duties.

PATAVIN'ITY, a term used by classical scholars to denote a peculiarity of Livy's diction; so denominated from *Patavium* or *Padua*, the place of his nativity; but as authors are not agreed as to what this *patavinity* consists in, it may reasonably be concluded that it is one of those delicacies which are undiscernible when a language is no longer spoken.

PATE, in fortification, a kind of plat form, resembling what is called a horseshoe; not always regular, but generally oval, encompassed only with a parapet, and having nothing to flank it.

PAT'ENTS, or LET'TERS PAT'ENT, (*open* letters,) writings sealed with the great seal, granting a privilege to some person, or authorizing a man to do or enjoy that which he could not of himself. They are called *patent* on account of their form being open, ready to be exhibited for the confirmation of the authority delegated by them. In England and the United States, patents are granted for a term not exceeding fourteen years. The time in England may be prolonged by a private act, and in the United States by act of congress. In France, patents are given for five, ten, or fifteen years, at the option of the inventor; but this last term is never to be prolonged without a particular decree of the legislature.—The *caveat* is an instrument by which notice is requested to be given to the person who enters it, whenever any application is made for a patent for a certain invention, which is therein described in general terms, and must be renewed annually. It simply gives notice that the invention is nearly completed, with a request that, if any other person should apply for a patent for the same thing, the preference may be given to him who entered it.

PA'TERA, in architecture, an ornament frequently seen in the Doric frieze, and in the tympans of arches. The patera was a small dish or vase used by the Romans in their sacrifices, in which they offered their consecrated food to the gods, and with which they made libations; and hence, as the Doric was used for temples, it became an ornament of that order. It was also enclosed in urns with the ashes of the dead, after it had been used in the libations of wine and other liquors at the funeral.

PAT'ERNOSTER, the Lord's prayer, so called from the two first words thereof in Latin. It is also sometimes used for a rosary or string of beads, used by Roman Catholics in their devotions; but more especially for every tenth large bead in the said rosary; for at this they repeat the Lord's prayer; and at the intervening small ones, only an *Ave Maria.*—In architecture, the same term is used for an ornament cut in the form of beads, either oval or round, for astragals, &c.

PA'THOS, language capable of moving the tender passions, and of exciting the finest emotions of the soul.

PA'TIENCE, the quality of enduring affliction, pain, persecution, or other evil, without murmuring or fretfulness.

PAT'IN, in the Romish church, the cover of the chalice, used for holding particles of the host.

PA'TOIS, a word in general use in most European countries, signifying the dialect peculiar to the lower classes.

PA'TRES CONSCRIP'TI, a name given to the Roman senators in general, though at first it was applied to a particular part of that body. The hundred appointed by Romulus were called simply *Patres;* a second hundred added by Romulus and Tatius upon the union of their people, were denominated *Patres Minorum Gentium;* a third hundred being afterwards added by Tarquinius Priscus, the two latter classes were called *Patres Conscripti*, because they were written down or put upon the list with the original hundred of Romulus.

PA'TRIARCH, properly signifies the head or chief of a family. The name of patriarchs is generally confined to the progenitors of the Israelites who lived before Moses, Abraham, Isaac, Jacob, &c.; or to the heads of families before the flood, as the antediluvian *patriarchs.* The appellation has from hence been transferred to the bishops of the first churches of the East; as, the patriarchs of Antioch, Alexandria, Jerusalem, Constantinople.

PATRI'CIAN, in Roman history, a title given at first to the descendants of the senators whom Romulus created, and called *patres*, "fathers." It was afterwards enjoyed by those who became senators by other channels than that of hereditary claim: but the dignity of the patricians was lessened by the fall of the republic, the civil wars, and the establishment of the imperial dignity.—The word *patrician*, in its general and modern acceptation, signifies noble; senatorial; not plebeian.

PAT'RICK, St., *Order of*, an Irish order of knighthood, instituted by George III. in 1783, which is the only one belonging to Ireland, but it is the most splendid of any.

PA'TRIOT, one who sincerely loves his country, and who, as a proof of that love, exerts his best energies in contributing to his country's welfare. In the Latin of the middle ages, *patriota* signified a native, in contradistinction to *peregrinus*, a foreigner, that is, one who did not enjoy the rights of citizenship. As the native, or citizen, was considered to be attached by his interests to the commonwealth, the word gradually received the meaning of a citizen who loves his country. Like many other words, its true meaning has at times been sadly perverted, or irreverently used.

PAT'RIOTISM, the love of one's country—the noblest passion that animates the breast of a true citizen, either in defending it from foreign enemies, or in protecting its rights and maintaining its laws and institutions in vigor and purity when assailed by domestic foes.

PATROL', in war, a round or march made by the guard in the night-time, to observe what passes, and to secure the peace and safety of a city or camp, or other place. The patrol generally consists of a body of five or six men detached from a body on guard, and commanded by a serjeant.

PA'TRON, in its most general sense, signifies one that specially countenances and supports another, or lends his aid to advance the interests of some undertaking; as a patron of the Fine Arts; the patrons of a charitable institution, &c.—*Patron*, (*patronus*,) among the Romans, was an appellation given to any person in power, under whose protection a few inferiors put themselves, under certain conditions of obedience and personal service. The persons protected were called *clients.* The duty of the patrons was to be their clients' counsellors in difficult cases, their advocates in judgments, their advisers in matters of doubt, and their overseers in all their affairs.—*Patron* was also a title conferred on a master who had freed his slave; the relation of patron commencing when that of master expired. The patron was legal heir to his freedmen, if they died intestate, or without lawful issue born after their freedom commenced. By the Papian law, if a freedman's fortune amounted to ten thousand sesterces and he had three children, the patron was entitled to a child's portion.—*Patron* in the English canon and common law, a person who, having the advowson of a parsonage, vicarage, or other spiritual promotion belonging to his manor, has the gift and disposition of the benefice, and may present to it whenever it becomes vacant.—*Patron*, in the church of Rome, a guardian or saint, whose name a person bears, or under whose protection he is placed, and whom he invokes: or a saint, in whose name a church or order is founded.—*Lay-patronage* is a right attached to a person either as founder or as heir of the founder, or as possessor of the see to which the patronage is annexed.—*Ecclesiastical patronage* is that which a person is entitled to by virtue of some benefice which he holds.

PATRONYM'IC, a term applied to such names of men and women as are derived from those of their parents or ancestors; as Tydides, the son of Tydeus.

PAULI'CIANS, in ecclesiastical history, a branch of the ancient Manichees, so called from their founder, one Paulus, an Armenian. For several centuries they suffered great persecution, and were at length wholly exterminated.

PAUSA'NIA, in Grecian antiquity, a festival, in which were solemn games, wherein nobody contended but free-born Spartans. It was instituted in honor of Pausanias, the Spartan general, under whose conduct the Greeks overcame Mardonius, in the celebrated battle at Platæa.

PAUSE, a character of time in music, marked thus 𝄐, denoting that the note over which it is placed is to be drawn out to a greater length than usual, or to be embellished with appoggiatures, shakes, or other graces.

PAVIL'ION, in architecture, a kind of turret or building, usually insulated and contained under a single roof: sometimes square, and sometimes in form of a dome. Sometimes a pavilion is a projecting part in front of a building; sometimes it flanks a corner.—In military affairs, a tent raised on posts. The word is also sometimes used for a flag, ensign, or banner.

PAWN'BROKER, a species of banker, who advances money at a certain rate of interest upon the security of goods deposited in his hands; having power to sell the goods if the principal sum, and the interest thereon, be not paid within a specified time. The practice of advancing money to the poor, either with or without interest, seems to have been occasionally adopted in ancient times; but the first public establishments of this kind were founded in Italy, under the name of Monti di Pietà, in the 14th and 15th centuries, and were intended to countervail the exorbitant usurious practices of the Jews, who formed at that period the great money-lenders of Europe. From Italy these establishments gradually spread over the Continent, in many parts of which they still exist.

PAX, an allegorical divinity among the ancients, worshipped as the goddess of peace. She had a celebrated temple at Rome, which was built by Vespasian, and was consumed by fire in the reign of Commodus. This term is sometimes applied to a small image of Christ, because, in former times, the kiss which the people gave it before leaving church was called the kiss of peace.

PEACE, in a general sense, signifies a state of tranquillity or freedom from disturbance. In a political sense, freedom from war with a foreign power, or from internal commotion. It likewise denotes a calm and tranquil state of the mind, which is the effect of a clear conscience. Also, that quiet, order, and security which is guaranteed by the laws.

PEC'ULATOR, one who defrauds the public by appropriating to his own use money entrusted to his care.

PECU'LIAR, in the English canon law, a parish or church that has jurisdiction within itself, and is competent to the granting probates of wills and letters of administration, exempt from the ordinary or bishop's court.—*Court of Peculiars*, a branch of the court of arches, belonging to the archbishop of Canterbury, which takes cognizance of matters relating to parishes that have a peculiar jurisdiction.

PED'AGOGUE, among the ancient Greeks, a slave charged with the personal care of a boy from the earliest age after infancy (from the milk, in the loose phrase of Plutarch; from about the age of seven, as it is more accurately stated by Æschines) until he became a youth, *i. e.*, until the seventeenth or twentieth year. The pedagogue's duty was to attend his charge on all occasions when he left his father's house; to the lecture-rooms, of masters, the theatres, &c. He was also entrusted with the duty of instructing and disciplining the child in all the inferior branches of education and ordinary manners. He was, consequently, of a very superior order of common slaves.

PED'ALS, in music, the keys played by the feet, (hence the name,) by which the deepest bass pipes of an organ are put in motion. A *pedal* is also used under a piano, in order to strengthen and prolong the tones. In a harp, the pedal serves to elevate the notes half a tone.

PED'ESTAL, in architecture, the lowest part of a column, being that which serves as its stand. It consists of three parts, viz., a trunk or dye, which forms the body; a cornice, the head; and a base, the foot of the pedestal.

PED'IMENT, the triangular finishing above the entablature at the end of buildings or over porticoes. The mouldings of the entablature bound the inclined sides of the pediment. Also the triangular finishing over doors and windows. In the debased Roman style the same name is given to these same parts, though not

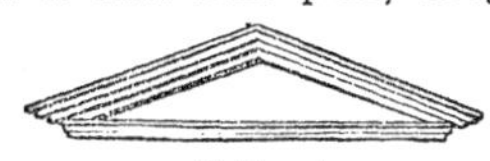

Pediment.

triangular in their form, but circular, elliptical, or interrupted. In the architecture of the middle ages, small gables and triangular decorations over openings, niches, &c., are called pediments. These have the angle at the apex more acute than the corresponding decoration of classic architecture.

PEER, in England, a nobleman or peer of the realm. The lords of parliament are the peers of each other; for whatever formality of precedence may attach to the title of duke, earl, marquis, or viscount, it is a *barony* which conveys the right to a seat in parliament, and confers every privilege annexed. It is as a baron, not as a duke, bishop, &c. that a peer sits in parliament; and the parliamentary rights are, at the present day, the essence of nobility. In compliance with an ancient practice, peers are sometimes still created by titles which convey the idea of local rights to which they have in reality no pretension; but though this is a mere form, the rank they gain is not an empty one; it is that of an hereditary legislator of the realm. A peer is not to be put upon any inquest, even though the cause have relation to two peers; and where a peer is a defendant in a court of equity, he is not to be sworn to his answer, which is to be received upon the faith of his honor; but when he is to answer to interrogatories, or to make an affidavit, or to be examined as a witness, he is to be sworn.—There are two peculiarities attending the trial of a peer: 1st, the number of jurors is greater than ordinary, every peer having a right to sit; 2dly, unanimity is not required, but the decision depends upon the majority, which, however, must amount to twelve.

PEER'ESS, a woman who is noble by descent, creation or marriage. If a peeress by descent or creation marries a person under the degree of nobility, she still continues noble; but if she has obtained the dignity by marriage only, by a subsequent marriage with a commoner she loses it; though by the courtesy of England, she always retains her title.

PEG'ASUS, in Greek mythology, a winged horse, produced by Neptune; or according to some authors, which sprung from the blood of Medusa when Perseus cut off her head.

PEINE FORTE ET DURE, a special punishment inflicted in ancient times on those who, being arraigned of felony, refused to put themselves on the ordinary trial, but stood mute. It was vulgarly called *pressing to death*.

PELA'GIANS, a Christian sect who appeared about the beginning of the fifth century. Pelagius, the founder of it, was born in Wales, and his real name was Morgan, which in the Welsh language signifies *sea born;* whence the Latin name Pelagius. Some of our ancient historians pretend that he was abbot of Bangor; but this is impossible, because the British monasteries were of a later date. St Austin gives him the character of a very pious man, and a person of superior birth. Among other tenets of belief, the Pelagians denied original sin, maintaining that Adam would have died, whether he had sinned or not; while they asserted the doctrine of free will, and the merit of good works.

PE'NAL LAWS, laws made for the punishment of criminal offences.

PEN'ALTY, (in law,) a fine or forfeiture by way of punishment, which is a *pecuniary* penalty; but the word *penalty* is not confined to this; for imprisonment, whipping, transportation, &c. are equally penalties, though in the shape of personal punishments.

PEN'ANCE, in ecclesiastical law, the infliction of some pain or bodily suffering, as fasting, flagellation, &c.; as an exercise of repentance for some sin, either voluntary or imposed.—*Penance* is one of the seven sacraments of the Romish church.

PENA'TES, in Roman antiquity, tutelar deities, either of countries or of particular houses, in which last sense they were the same with the *lares*. The Penates were originally the tutelar gods of the Trojans; but being adopted by the Romans, they were thus named.

PEND'ANT, in gothic architecture, an ornamented polygonal piece of stone or timber hanging down from the vault or roof of a building. Of stone pendants some exquisite examples may be seen in Henry VII.'s chapel at Westminster. In ancient writers the springers of arches, which rest on shafts or corbels, are called *pendants.*—In painting, &c. a picture or print which from uniformity of size and subject seems to hang up as a companion to another. The term may also be applied to bassi relievi of similar sizes.

PENETRA'LE, was a sacred room or chapel in private houses, set apart for the worship of the household gods among the Romans. In temples also there were *penetralia*, or apartments of peculiar sanctity, where the images of the gods were kept, and certain solemn ceremonies peformed.

PENITEN'TIARY, in the ancient Christian church, a name given to certain presbyters, appointed in every church to receive the private confessions of the people, in order to facilitate public discipline, by acquainting them what sins were to be expiated by public penance, and to appoint private penance for such crimes as it might be deemed unadvisable to censure publicly.—*Penitentiary*, at the court of Rome, an office in which are examined and delivered out the secret bulls, graces, or dispensations relating to cases of conscience, confessions, &c.—The title of *penitentiary* was also given to an officer in some cathedrals, who was vested with power from the bishop to absolve in cases reserved to him.—*Penitentiary*, the name of prisons where felons are kept to hard labor.

PEN'ITENTS, an appellation given to certain fraternities in Catholic countries, distinguished by their different habits, and generally employed in charitable acts.

PEN'NON, in heraldry, a small pointed flag, borne by a gentleman. When knighthood was conferred upon him, the point was cut off, and the square flag that remained bore the name of *banner.*

PEN'SION, an annual allowance of a sum of money to a person by government, in consideration of past services, civil or military; or, at least, such a pension ought to be.

PEN'SIONER, one who receives an annuity from another, whether in consideration of service past or present, or merely as a benevolence.

PENTAM'ETER, in Latin and Greek poetry, a verse consisting of five feet or metres. The two first may be either dactyls or spondees; the third is always a spondee, and the two last anapæsts. A pentameter verse subjoined to an hexameter constitutes what is called *elegiac.* The pentameter has not been generally introduced into any modern language with which we are acquainted: though Goethe and Schiller have left us some excellent specimens of the facility with which it might be engrafted on the German language. The hexameter and pentamer distich is beautifully described in the lines of Schiller, which are thus rendered by Coleridge, who was long considered as the original author:

> In the hexameter rises the fountain's silvery column:
> In the pentameter aye falling in melody back.

Every page of Ovid's *Heroides* or *Tristia*, illustrates the manner in which the hexameter breaks, as it were, and falls back in the pentameter, thereby adding a most exquisite grace to the rhythm; indeed the secret genius of the metre appears to consist in this play.

PEN'TASTICH, in poetry, a composition consisting of five verses.

PEN'TASTYLE, in architecture, a building in which there are five rows of columns.

PEN'TATEUCH, an appellation given to the first five books of the Old Testament, viz. Genesis, Exodus, Leviticus, Numbers, and Deuteronomy.

PENTATH'LUM, in antiquity, a general name for the five exercises performed at the Grecian games, namely, wrestling, boxing, leaping, running, and playing at the discus.

PENTECON'TER, in antiquity, a Grecian vessel of fifty oars; smaller than a trireme.

PEN'TECOST, a solemn festival of the Jews, instituted in memory of the promulgation of the law, and so named because that event took place on the fiftieth day after their departure from Egypt. It is retained by us in the Christian church (and by us called Whitsuntide) on account of the miraculous descent of the Holy Ghost on the apostles, which happened on one of the annual returns of its celebration.

PENUL'TIMA, PENULT', or PENULTIMATE SYLLABLE, in grammar, the last syllable but one of a word; and hence the *anti-penultimate* syllable is the last but two, or that immediately before the penultima.

PEO'PLE, the body of persons who compose a community, town, city, or nation. We say, the *people* of a town; the *people* of New York or Paris; the American *peo-*

ple. In this sense, the word is not used in the plural, but it comprehends all classes of inhabitants, considered as a collective body, or any portion of the inhabitants of a city or country.

PERCEP'TION, the act of perceiving or of receiving impressions by the senses; or that act or process of the mind which makes known an external object. In other words, the notice which the mind takes of external objects. We gain a knowledge of the coldness and smoothness of marble by *perception.* — In philosophy, the faculty of perceiving; the faculty or peculiar part of man's constitution, by which he has knowledge through the medium or instrumentality of the bodily organs, or by which he holds communication with the external world. It is distinguished from *conception* by the circumstance that its objects are in every instance supposed to have an actual existence. We may *conceive* things that have no reality, but we are never said to *perceive* such things. Perception differs from *consciousness* in that it takes cognizance only of objects without the mind. We *perceive* a man, a horse, a tree; when we think or feel, we are conscious of our thoughts and emotions. It is further supposed in *perception* that the objects of it are present. We can *remember* former objects of perception, but we do not perceive them again until they are once more present. The term *perception,* however, is sometimes analogically employed in common speech in reference to truths, the evidence of which is certain. Thus we may *perceive* the truth of a mathematical proposition. Various theories of perception have arisen among philosophers. These have been designated by the terms *idealism* and *realism.*

PERFECTIBIL'ITY, the capability of arriving at perfection. This word, which is entirely modern, and scarcely as yet admitted in our language on classical English authority, is commonly used in reasoning on the social condition of mankind.

PERFEC'TION, in the highest sense to which this word can be applied, means an inherent or essential attribute of supreme or infinite excellence. If we speak of *physical perfection,* we mean that a natural object has all its powers, faculties, or qualities entire and in full vigor, and all its parts in due proportion. — *Moral perfection* is the complete possession of such moral qualities and virtues as the thing spoken of is capable of possessing.

PE'RI, in Persian mythology, are the descendants of fallen spirits, excluded from paradise until their penance is accomplished.

PERIB'OLOS, in architecture, a court or enclosure entirely round a temple, surrounded by a wall. One of the most extraordinary examples of a peribolos is at Palmyra, where the great temple is surrounded by a wall with two rows of interior columns, each side whereof is from 700 to 800 feet long.

PER'IDROME, in ancient architecture, the space in a peripteral temple between the walls of the cell and the columns. It is a term that may be applied to any gallery of communication round an edifice.

PE'RIOD, in rhetoric, has been defined "a passage, *i. e.*, series of words, developed in properly connected parts." In a stricter sense, a period is a sentence so framed that the grammatical construction will not admit a close, and the meaning remains suspended until the end of it. A sentence in which the sense would permit of a stop before its completion is, in this sense, not a period. The Greek and Latin languages were much more periodic than most modern tongues; that is, they admitted of the construction of sentences so that a single grammatical connection should run through a great series of words, while a similar series, in a modern language, would be so arranged as to form several distinct grammatical wholes.

PERIOD'ICALS, in literature, comprise the whole of those publications which appear at regular intervals, whether devoted to general information, or especially intended for some particular class of readers. They consequently include all the newspapers, reviews, and magazines, as well as such works on science and art as are published in a series of volumes, parts, or numbers; and while they have contributed greatly to the diffusion of general knowledge, they have done much towards promoting the cause of truth, and facilitating the progress of science.

PERIPATET'ICS, the followers of Aristotle, whose doctrines are distinguished by the name of *peripatetic philosophy.* He also was called the Peripatetic because he delivered his lectures *walking* in the Lyceum at Athens.

PERIPH'RASIS, or PER'IPHRASE, in rhetoric, circumlocution; or the use of more words than are necessary to express an idea.

PERIP'TEROUS, in architecture, an epithet for a place encompassed about with columns.

PER'ISTYLE, a range of columns surrounding anything, as the cella of a temple, or any place, as a court or cloister. It is frequently but incorrectly limited in signification to a range of columns surrounding the interior of a place.

PER'JURY, in law, is a wilful false oath taken in a court of justice, by a witness lawfully required to depose the truth in a matter of some consequence to the point in question. A false oath therefore, taken before no court, or before a court incompetent to try the issue in question, does not constitute the offence of perjury. Perjury is a misdemeanor at common law, and punishable by fine and imprisonment.—*Subornation of perjury* is the offence of procuring a man to commit perjury.

PER'MIT, a note given by the officers of customs to authorize the landing, delivery or transfer, of imported merchandize.

PERORA'TION, the concluding part of an oration, in which the speaker recapitulates the principal points of his discourse or argument, and urges them with greater earnestness and force, with a view to make a deep impression on his audience. The main excellence of a peroration consists in vehemence, pathos, and brevity.

PERPETU'ITY, in the doctrine of Annuities, is the sum of money which will purchase a certain annuity to continue forever. This is equal to the product of the annuity into the number of years in which the simple interest of any sum will equal the principal. For example, if the rate of interest be 4 per cent., the simple interest of any sum will amount to a sum equal to the principal in twenty-five years. The value, therefore, of the perpetuity of $100 per annum is $2500. The number of years is equal to unit divided by the rate of interest, or 100 divided by the rate per cent.

PERSECU'TION, the infliction of pain, punishment, or death upon others unjustly, more especially for adhering to a religious creed or mode of worship. The history of the world is full of persecutions; and there is scarcely any dominant sect or party, religious or political, which has not at times disgraced humanity by inflicting unjust punishment or penalties upon their fellow-men, for adhering to principles which their consciences dictated and their judgment approved.

PER'SEUS, son of Jupiter, and Danae, one of the most distinguished heroes of the Grecian mythology. His history is too well-known to be recapitulated here. His chief exploit was the conquest of Medusa.

PERSEVE'RANCE, in theology, the continuance of the elect in a state of grace to the end of their lives, which, according to some theologians, must always be the case with him who has once been truly called into such a state. Since God is represented as the image of perfection and immutability in himself, so, it is argued, having once begun the preparation of a human being for a blessed eternity, he will not leave his work unfinished; but the person concerned must necessarily persevere to the end in a state of acceptance, under the absolute decree of which he was originally elected unto life.

PER'SONAL, in law, belonging to the person and not to the thing; as *personal goods*, opposed to *real* property or estates; *personal action*, an action against the person, wherein a man claims satisfaction in damages for an injury to his person or property.—*Personal identity*, in metaphysics, sameness of being, of which consciousness is the evidence.

PER'SONAL PROP'ERTY, according to the division recognized by our law, is best defined negatively, as including everything which may be made the subject of property, and which is not legally considered as appertaining to land. The original distinction was undoubtedly between things movable and immovable.

PERSONIFICA'TION, the giving to an inanimate object the sentiments and language of a rational being; or the representation of an inanimate being with the affections and actions of a person. The more the imagination prevails among a people, the more common are personifications; and as reflection acquires the ascendancy personifications are less used.

PERSPEC'TIVE, the science which teaches the representation of an object or objects on a definite surface so as to affect the eye when viewed from a given point, in the same manner as the object or objects themselves. Correctly defined, a perspective delineation is a section, by the plane or other surface, on which the delineation is made, of the cone of rays proceeding from every part of the object to the eye of the spectator. It is intimately connected with the arts of design, and is indispensable in architecture, engineering, fortification, sculpture, and generally all the mechanical arts; but it is particularly necessary in the art of painting, as without a correct observance of the rules of perspective no picture can have truth and life. Perspective alone enables us to represent foreshortenings with accuracy, and it is requisite in delineating even the simplest positions of objects. Suppose we view a point situated beyond an upright transparent plane, as a glass window, the spot where a straight line from the eye to this point will go through the window is the *perspective representation* of it: for the eye views all objects by means of rays of light, which proceed from it, to the different points of the object, in straight lines. Let us then imagine a spectator to be looking at a prospect without doors, from within, through a glass window; he will perceive not only the vast extent which so small an aperture will admit to be seen by his eye, but also the shape, size, and situation of every object upon the glass. If the objects are near the window, the spaces which they take upon the glass will be proportionably larger than when they are at a greater distance; if they are parallel to the window, then their shapes upon the glass will be parallel also; but if they are oblique, then their shapes will be oblique, and so on. And he will always perceive, that as he alters the situation of his eye, the situation of the objects upon the window will be altered also: if he raises his eye, the objects will seem to keep pace with it, and rise higher upon the window; and the contrary if he lowers it. And so in every situation of the eye, the objects upon the window will seem to rise higher or lower; and consequently the depth of the whole prospect will be proportionably greater or less, as the eye is elevated or depressed: and the horizon will, in every situation of the eye, be upon a level with it: that is, the imaginary line which parts the earth and sky will seem to be raised as far above the ground upon which the spectator stands as his eye is. Now suppose the person at the window, keeping his head steady, draws the figure of an object seen through it upon the glass with a pencil, as if the point of the pencil touched the object: he would then have a true representation of the object in perspective, as it appears to his eye: for as vision is occasioned by pencils of rays coming in straight lines to the eye from every point of the visible object, it is plain that, by joining the points in the transparent plane through which all those pencils of rays respectively pass, an exact representation must be formed of the object, as it appears to the eye in that particular position, and at that determined distance. And were pictures of things to be always first drawn on transparent planes, this simple operation, with the principle on which it is founded, would comprise the whole theory and practice of perspective. Perspective is divided into two branches, *linear* and *ærial*. *Linear perspective* has reference to the position, form, magnitude, &c. of the several lines or contours of objects, &c. The outlines of such objects as buildings, machinery, and most works of human labor which consist of geometrical forms, or which can be reduced to them, may be most accurately obtained by the rules of linear perspective, since the intersection with an interposed plane of the rays of light proceeding from every point of such objects may be obtained by the principles of geometry.

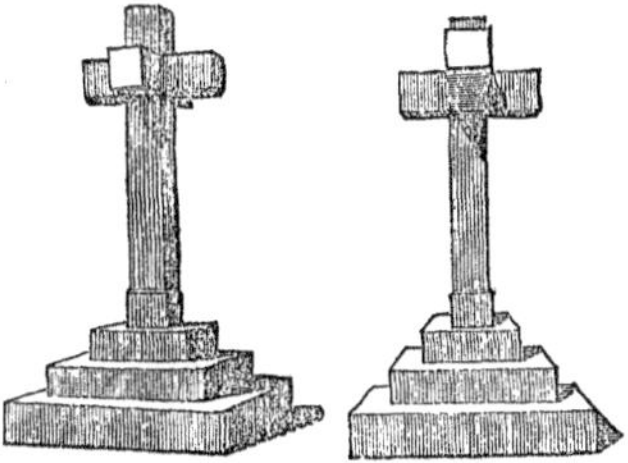

Oblique perspective. Parallel perspective.

Linear perspective includes the various kinds of projection; as scenographic, orthographic, ichnographic, stereographic projections, &c.—*Aerial perspective* teaches how to give due diminution to the strength of light, shade, and colors of objects according to their distances, and the quantity of light falling on them, and to the medium through which they are seen.—*Perspective plane*, the surface on which the object or picture is delineated, or it is the transparent surface or plane through which we suppose objects to be viewed; it also termed the plane of projection, and the plane of the picture.—*Parallel perspective* is where the picture which is supposed to be so situated, as to be parallel to the side of the principal object in the picture; as a building, for instance.—*Oblique perspective*, is when the plane of the picture is supposed to stand oblique to the sides of the object represented; in which case the representations of the lines upon those sides will not be parallel among themselves, but will tend toward their vanishing point. —*Isometrical perspective*, a kind of perspective on the principles of orthographic projection invented by Professor Farish of Cambridge, by which solids, of the form of rectangular parallelopipeds, or such as are reducible to this form, can be represented with their three pair of planes in one figure, which gives a more intelligible idea of their form than can be done by a separate plan and elevation. At the same time, this method admits of their dimensions being measured by a scale as directly as by the usual mode of delineation. As applied to machinery, it gives the elevation and ground plan in one view. It is considered for such purposes, to be preferable to the methods in common use, as it is easier and simpler in its application.

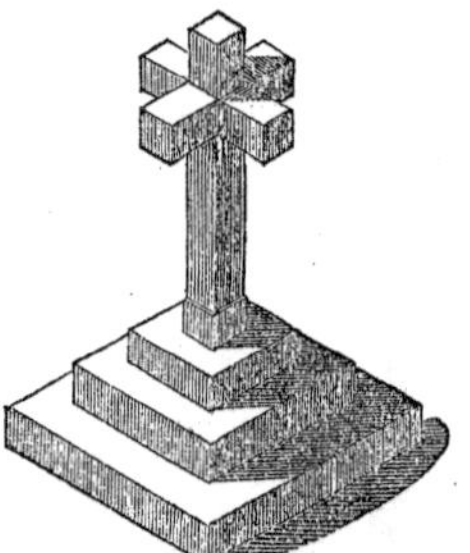

Isometrical Perspective.

PES'TILENCE, any contagious or infectious disease that is epidemic and mortal.—It is also used to denote any moral disease or corruption destructive of happiness.

PET'ALISM, in antiquity, a form of proscription or banishment practised at Syracuse, by writing the person's name on a leaf; whence the name. It differed from the Athenian *ostracism* merely in being for five years instead of ten, and the name being written on leaves instead of shells or tiles.

PETARD', in fortification, a hollow engine shaped like a sugar-loaf, to be loaded with powder and fixed on a plank; made for breaking open gates, drawbridges, &c.

PET'ASUS, in antiquity, a covering for the head, similar to a broad-brimmed hat, used to keep off the heat of the sun.—In architecture, the cupola of a house, in the form of a petasus.

PETAURIS'TÆ, in antiquity, a name given to certain athletæ, who threw themselves from a machine called a *petaurum*, which was hung high in the air, and descended to the earth by means of a rope.

PE'TER-PENCE, the popular name of an impost, otherwise termed "the fee of Rome," or, in the Anglo-Saxon, "Romescot:" originally a voluntary offering by the faithful to the see of Rome; afterwards a due levied in various amounts from every house or family in a country. Peter-pence were paid in France, Poland, and other realms. In England this tax is recognized by the Norman laws of William the Conqueror. Edward III. discontinued the payment when the popes resided at Avignon; but it was afterwards revived, and finally ceased in the reign of Henry VIII.

PET'IT, or PET'TY. The former word occurs in our law books in such phrases as *petit jury*, *petit treason*, *petit larceny*, *&c.*; but the practice is giving way to the use of the English *petty*.—*Petit treason*, the crime of killing a person to whom the offender owes duty or subjection. Thus the crime of murder, when a wife kills her husband, or a servant his master, has this appellation.—*Petit larceny*, the stealing of goods of the value of twelve pence, or under that amount.—*Petit jury*, a jury of twelve freeholders who are empanelled to try causes in a court; so called in distinction from the grand jury, which tries the truth of indictments.

PETI'TION, a formal supplication or request made by an inferior to a superior, especially to one having some jurisdiction Also, a paper containing a supplication or solicitation.

PETI TIO PRINCIP'II, in logic, the taking a thing for true, and drawing conclusions from it as such; when it is either false, or at least requires to be proved before any inferences can be deduced from it. In common parlance this is called "begging the question."

PHA'ETON, in mythology, the son of Apollo and Clymenes, one of the Oceanides, according to most writers. The fable of his adventures is well known. Taunted with his doubtful origin, he asked his father to lend him the chariot of the sun for a day, as a proof of his filial rights. Unable to guide the fiery steeds, he was dashed to the ground by Jupiter with a thunderbolt, to prevent his consuming the heavens and earth.

PHALANSTE'RIANISM, the system of Charles Fourier, the French socialist; who, as a remedy for the evils of society, as at present constituted, advocated its reorganization into so many *phalansteries*, containing each from 500 to 2000 persons, upon principles similar to those of joint-stock companies ; the members to live in one spacious edifice, cultivating a common domain; the proceeds to be shared according to the amount of capital, skill, or labor invested by each.

PHA'LANX, in the military affairs of Greece, a square and compact battalion or body of soldiers, formed in ranks and files compact and deep, with their shields joined and pikes crossing each other, so as to render it almost impossible to break it. At first the phalanx consisted of 4000 men, but was afterwards doubled and even quadrupled. The Macedonian phalanx is thus described by Polybius. It was a square of pikemen, consisting of sixteen in flank and five hundred in front; the soldiers stood so close together that the pikes of the fifth rank extended three feet beyond the front: the rest, whose pikes were not serviceable owing to their distance from the front, couched them upon the shoulders of those that stood before them, and so locking them together in file, pressed forward to support and push on the former rank, by which means the assault was rendered more violent and irresistible.—The word *phalanx* is likewise used for any combination of people distinguished for firmness or solidity of union.

PHAR'ISEES, a sect among the Jews, who distinguished themselves by their zeal for the traditions of the elders, which they derived from the same fountain with the written word itself, pretending that both were delivered to Moses on Mount Sinai, and were therefore both of equal authority. From their rigorous observance of these traditions they considered themselves as more holy than other Jews, and therefore separated themselves from them; and hence, from the Hebrew word *pharis*, which signifies to separate, they had the name of *pharisees* or *separatists*. The pharisees numbered in their ranks the most distinguished lawyers and statesmen in Judæa; and as persons of all conditions were admitted into their society, they gained a political influence which often decided the fate of the Jewish nation under the Maccabees, and brought into their hands the power which had been left to the great council by the Romans in the time of Christ. They believed in a resurrection from the dead, and the existence of angels; but, according to Josephus, their belief extended to no more than a Pythagorean resurrection, that is, of the soul only, by its transmigration into another body and being born anew with it. From this resurrection they excluded all who were notoriously wicked, being of opinion that the souls of such persons were doomed to a state of everlasting woe.

PHA'ROS, a light-house or lofty building near the sea, where a fire is kept burning during the night to serve as a beacon to vessels. The Pharos of Alexandria, built in the reign of Pharos, was one of the most celebrated works of antiquity, and from this circumstance the name is supposed to have been given to edifices of a similar description. The tower of king Pharos stood at the mouth of the Nile; it consisted of several stories or galleries, surmounted with a lantern, and was seen for many leagues at sea, as well as all along the coast.

PHELLOPLAS'TICS, the art of representing works of architecture on a reduced scale in cork, which affords very fine models, and are cheaper than those in wood, stone, gypsum, &c.

PHIDI'TIA, in antiquity, Lacedemonian festivals, remarkable for the frugality of the entertainment, and the charitable intention of the meeting. They were held in public places, and in the open air. Those who attended made contributions of flour, wine, cheese, and figs. Rich and poor assisted alike at this feast, and were upon the same footing; the design of the institution being, like that of the Roman Charistia, to reconcile differences, and to cultivate peace, friendship, and a good understanding among all the citizens, of every rank and degree.

PHIGA'LIAN MARBLES, (so called from having been discovered near the site of Phigalia, a town of Arcadia,) the name given to a series of sculptures in alto relievo, now deposited in the British Museum, where they form part of the collection known by the name of the *Elgin Marbles*. They originally formed the fringe round the interior of the cella of the temple dedicated to Apollo the Deliverer; a title conferred on him by the Phigalians in gratitude for his having delivered them from a pestilence. They represent the combat of the Centaurs and the Lapithæ, and that of the Greeks and Amazons. The similarity, both in design and execution, which they bear to the decorations on the Parthenon leaves no doubt that they are the workmanship of the same master minds which designed, constructed, and adorned that splendid monument of the golden age of art.

PHILANTHRO'PINISM, a name given in Germany to the system of education on natural principles, as it is termed, which was promoted by Basedow and his friends in the last century, and mainly founded on the notions of Locke and Rousseau. An institution for the purposes of education founded under the protection of the Duke of Dossau, in 1774, was the first so called "Philanthropin." It was dissolved in 1793; and of the similar institutions afterwards founded, only one, it is said, has continued to maintain itself. But the influence of the labors of the Philanthropinists has undoubtedly entered largely into the modern system of education.

PHILAN'THROPY, good-will and benevolence towards the whole of mankind. It differs from *friendship*, inasmuch as it has no limits to its sphere of action, whereas friendship may be confined to an individual; but a true *philanthropist* so loves his fellow-men that he is continually exerting himself for their welfare.

PHILIP'PIC, a word used to denote any discourse or declamation full of acrimonious invective. It is derived from an oration made by Demosthenes against Philip of Macedon, in which the orator inveighs against the indolence of the Athenians. The fourteen orations of Cicero against Mark Antony are also called *philippics*.

PHILOL'OGY, in its usual acceptation, is that branch of literature which comprehends a knowledge of the etymology or origin and combination of words, and whatever relates to the history, affinity, and present state of languages. In a wider sense it signifies an assemblage of sciences, consisting of grammar, rhetoric, poetry, antiquities, history, criticism, &c., usually understood by the French term *belles lettres*. Of late years, however, a new and very extensive province has been added to the dominion of philology; namely, the science of language in a more general sense, considered philosophically with respect to the light it throws on the nature of human intellect and progress of human knowledge; and historically, with reference to the connection between different tongues, and the connection thus indicated between different nations and races. Some attempts have recently made to confine the use of the word philology to this particular branch of learning. It comprehends, 1. *Phonology*, or the knowledge of the sounds of the human voice; which appears to include orthography, or the system to be adopted when we endeavor to render, by our own alphabet, the sounds of a foreign language; 2. *Etymology;* 3. *Ideology*, or the science of the modification of language by grammatical forms, according to the various points of view from which men contemplate the ideas which words are meant to express.

PHILOS'OPHER'S STONE, a stone or preparation which the alchymists formerly sought, as the instrument of converting the baser metals into pure gold. The alchymists held that the baser metals were all convertible into silver and gold by a long series of processes, and the instrument by which it was supposed that this mighty change was to be effected, was a certain mineral to be produced by these processes, which being mixed with the base metal would transmute it, and this was called the *philosopher's stone*.

PHILOS'OPHY, literally, the love of wisdom. But in modern acceptation, *philosophy* is a general term denoting an explanation of the reasons of things; or an investigation of the causes of all phenomena both of mind and of matter. When applied to any particular department of knowledge, it denotes the collection of general laws or principles under which all the subordinate phenomena or facts relating to that subject, are comprehended. Thus, that branch of *philosophy* which treats of God, &c., is called *theology;* that which treats of nature is called *physics*, or *natural philosophy;* that which treats of man is called *logic* and *ethics*, or *moral philosophy;* that which treats of the mind is called *intellectual* or *mental philosophy*, or *metaphysics*. The term *philosophy* is often used, apparently with no great precision, though it is not difficult to deduce from the use of this term the general meaning or notion which is attached to it. We speak of the philosophy of the human mind as being of all philosophies that to which the name philosophy is particularly appropriated; and when the term philosophy is used absolutely, this seems to be the philosophy that is spoken of. Other philosophies are referred to their several objects by qualifying terms: thus we speak of natural philosophy, meaning thereby the philosophy of nature, or of material objects. We also speak of the philosophy of positive law, understanding thereby the philosophy of those binding rules, properly called laws. The terms philosophy of history, philosophy of manufactures, and other such terms are also used. All objects then which can occupy the mind may have something in common, called their philosophy; which philosophy is nothing else than the general expression for that effort of the mind whereby it strives, pursuant to its laws, to reduce its knowledge to the form of ultimate truths or principles, and to determine the immutable relations which exist between things as it conceives them. The philosophy which comprises within itself all philosophies is that which labors to determine the laws or ultimate principles in obedience to which the mind itself operates. Thus, every kind of knowledge, the objects of which are things external, has its philosophy or principles, which, when discovered and systematized, form the science of the things to which they severally belong. But we must assume that the mind also has its laws and powers which may be discovered by observation, as we discover by observation the laws or principles which govern the relations of things external to the mind, or conceived as external. Accordingly the human mind, by the necessity imprinted on it, seeks to discover the ultimate foundation of all that it knows or conceives; to discover what itself is, and what is its relation to all things, and so it strives to form a system out of all such ultimate laws or principles. Such a system may be called a philosophy in the proper and absolute sense of the term, and the attempt to form such a system is to philosophize. Systems of philosophy have existed in all nations. The objects of philosophy are to ascertain facts or truth, and the causes of things or their phenomena; to enlarge our views of God and his works, and to render our knowledge of both practically useful and subservient to human happiness.—*Pythagorean philosophy*, the system taught by Pythagoras, who flourished 500 years before the Christian era. He described the Deity as one incorruptible, invisible being; and differed from some of the ancients, as Epicurus, in conceiving a connection between God and man; that is, in teaching the doctrine of a superintending providence. He asserted the immortality of the soul; but in a sense essentially peculiar, and which appears to have been adopted by Plato, as it is in part at this day by the Hindoos. In the cosmogony of Pythagoras, spirit, however diffused through all animals, was part of the Divinity himself, separated only by the gross forms of matter, and ready, whenever disengaged, to unite itself with the kindred essence of God; but God was only purity; and the mind recoiled from the idea of uniting with him a portion of spirit soiled with the corruption of a sinful life. The soul, therefore, once tainted, could never return to the Deity whence it emanated, till it had again recovered its innocence. After having animated a human body by which crimes had been committed, it was denied the great object of its desire, a union with its God, and forced to enter into other bodies, till at length it filled a righteous one. To this theory was added another, by means of which punishments, proportioned to its offences, were awarded: according to this, the soul of a negro-driver would pass into the body of an infant negro; and that which in one existence plied the whip, in the other would receive the lash: the soul of the wicked would occupy the body of some animal exposed to suffering; and that of a being of few foibles undergo a sentence proportionably mild.—Such is the doctrine of the metempsychosis or transmigration of souls, a leading feature in the Pythagorean system.—*Socratic philosophy*, or the doctrines of Socrates, who flourished at Athens about 400 years B.C., and died a martyr in the cause of natural religion against paganism. He is said to have opened the career of moral philosophy in Greece, where he preceded Plato, from the writings of which latter the philosophy of Socrates is chiefly known, for he wrote nothing himself. While other philosophers boasted of their knowledge, he laid the greatest stress upon his ignorance, asserting that he knew nothing but this, that *he knew nothing*. Socrates led men from the contemplation of universal nature to that of themselves; a branch of philosophy which was inculcated in that famous inscription, *Know thyself!* The Socratic method of argument was that of leading an antagonist to acknowledge a proposition himself, by dint of repeated questions, in preference to that of laying it down authoritatively.—*Platonic philosophy*, a system of theology and morals, delivered by Plato about 350 years B.C. Plato, it is said, labored to reestablish natural religion by opposing paganism. The existence of the one God was zealously inculcated by him; and also the immortality of the soul, the resurrection of the dead, the everlasting reward of righteousness, and punishment of sin. It was Plato, too, who taught that the world was created by the *Logos* or *Word;* and that through knowledge of the word men live happily on earth and obtain eternal felicity hereafter. From him, also, came the doctrine of *grace*, and the inducements to monastic life; for he pressed upon his disciples that the world is filled with corruption; that it is the duty of the righteous to fly from it and to seek a union with God, who alone is life and health; that in the world the soul is continually surrounded with enemies: and that, in the unceasing combat through which it has to struggle, it can conquer only with the assistance of God or of his holy angels. "A happy immortality," said Plato, "is a great prize set before us, and a great object of hope, which should engage us to labor in the acquirement of wisdom and virtue all the time of our life." In morals, he taught that there is nothing solid and substantial but piety, which is the source of all virtues and the gift of God; that the love of our neighbor, which proceeds from the love of God as its principle, produces that sacred union which makes families and nations happy; that self-love produces that discord and division which reigns among mankind, and is the chief cause of our sins: that it is better to suffer wrong than to do it; that it is wrong to hurt an enemy or to revenge an injury received; that it is better to die than to sin; and that man ought continually to learn to die, and yet to endure life with all patience and submission to the will of God.—The *Aristotelian philosophy*, which succeeded the Platonic, is characterized by a systematic striving to embrace all the objects of philosophy by cool and patient reflection.—The *Epicurian philosophy*, or the system of Epicurus, an Athenian. This teacher laid down, as the basis of his doctrine, that the supreme good consists in pleasure; a proposition that soon suffered a two-fold abuse. On the one hand, by misconstruction, it was regarded as a barefaced inculcation of sensuality; on the other, adopted by the luxurious, the indolent, and the licentious, as a cloak and authority for their conduct; and hence it has happened that the name Epicurean is now used in an absolute sense to designate one minutely and luxuriously attentive to his food. Epicurus is reported to have written three hundred books, but of these none are extant; and the particulars of his philosophy, which have come down to posterity, are chiefly found in the writings of Lucretius, Diogenes, Laertius, and Cicero. His system, for which he is said to have been almost wholly indebted to Democritus, consisted of three parts: canonical, physical, and etherial. Soundness and simplicity of sense, assisted with some natural reflections, constituted all the method of Epicurus. His search after truth proceeded only by the senses, to the evidence of which he gave so great a certainty that he considered them as the first natural light of mankind. It is in the meanings allowed to the words pleasure and pain that everything which is important in the morals and doubtful in the history of the Epicurean system is contained. According to Gassendus, the *pleasure* of Epicurus consisted in the highest tranquillity of mind, united with the most perfect health of body; blessings enjoyed only through the habits of rectitude, benevolence, and temperance; but Cicero, Horace, Plutarch, and several of the fathers of the Christian church represent the system in a very different point of view. The disagreement, however, is easily reconciled, if we believe one side to speak of what Epicurus *taught*, and the other of what many of his followers, and still more of those who took shelter under his name, were accustomed to *practise*.—To the foregoing we must add the *Stoic philosophy*, or the doctrines of Zeno the stoic, whose morality was of a magnanimous and unyielding kind, formed to resist temptation to evil, and to render men callous to adversity: thus they maintained, among other things, that a man might be happy in the midst of the severest tortures;—the *Cynic philosophy*, the followers of which affected a great contempt of riches and of all sciences except morality;—and the *Skeptical philosophy*, under Pyrrho, who affected to doubt everything.—In glancing at the *history of philosophy*, the student has abundant opportunities of observing its gradual development as a science, and tracing the progress and aberrations of the human mind—in themselves subjects most important and instructive. Departing from, or only partially retaining, the conflicting dogmas of the Greek and Roman philosophers, we find the scholastics of the middle ages engaged in a struggle for the attainment of intellectual excellence, under the influence of principles derived from the Christian faith and doctrine; yet the progress of philosophic truths was for a long time feeble, irregular, and vacillating. During the 15th century, there arose a freer and more independent spirit of inquiry, penetrating deeper into ultimate causes; till at length, the cool and searching energy of Bacon enabled him to produce his *Novum Organum*, and to give a more substantial basis to the efforts of the intellect, by making observation and experience the predominant character of philosophy. Some there were, however, who disputed his laws, and hence new theories occasionally obtained a temporary distinction; but his doctrines, in a great measure, ultimately prevailed; and, at no distant period, the calm reasoning of Locke introduced into the study of the human mind the method of investigation which his great predecessor had pointed out. The subject, however, presents so wide and tempting a field for observation, that we dare not venture on it, lest, by unduly extending one article, we may be compelled to curtail others which equally demand our attention; and enough, perhaps, has been already said to direct the inquiring mind towards a study which, as it were, embraces all nature in its mighty grasp.

PHŒ'NIX, in fabulous history, a wonderful bird which the ancients describe as of the size of an eagle; its head finely crested with a beautiful plumage, its neck covered with feathers of a gold color; its tail white, and its body purple. By some authors this bird is said to come from Arabia to Egypt every five hundred years, at the death of his parent bringing the body with him, embalmed in myrrh, to the temple of the sun, where he buries it. According to others, when he finds himself near his end, he prepares a nest of myrrh and precious herbs, in which he burns himself; but from his ashes he revives in the freshness of youth. The several eras when the phœnix has been seen are fixed by tradition. The first, we are told, was in the reign of Sesostris; the second in that of Amasis; and in the period when Ptolemy, the third of the Macedonian race, was seated on the throne of Egypt, another phœnix directed its flight towards Heliopolis. From late mythological researches, it is conjectured that the phœnix is a symbol of a period of 500 years, of which the conclusion was celebrated by a solemn sacrifice, in which the figure of a bird was burnt.

PHONET'IC WRI'TING, that writing in which the signs used represent sounds; in opposition to *ideographic*, in which they represent objects, or symbolically denote abstract ideas, as in the figurative part of the Egyptian hieroglyphics. The signs representing sounds are usually arbitrary, or at least have become so in process of time; as in the ancient Roman alphabet, of which the letters are for the most part derived from the Hebrew or Phœnician, in which languages they may have originally partaken of a symbolical character. But, in a species of phonetic writing which is intermixed with the figurative hieroglyphics in Egyptian inscriptions, every letter is denoted by a figure representing some object, the name of which begins with that letter.

PHONOL'OGY, the science or doctrine of the elementary sounds uttered by the human voice, including its various degrees of intonation.

PHOTOGEN'IC DRAW'ING, the name given by Mr. H. F. Talbot, the inventor or discoverer of it, to a "new art," which, though not identical, is very similar to that of M. Daguerre. The outline of the process is as follows: A piece of copper is plated in the usual way with silver by passing the metals together through a rolling mill, and is then cut into pieces of a proper size. The silver surface is carefully polished, and cleansed by wiping it over with a piece of cotton dipped in dilute nitric acid, washing, and drying. When thus duly prepared—and much depends upon the manner in which these preliminary operations are performed and the materials used—the plate is subjected to the diffused vapor of iodine, which forms a slightly brown or yellow film upon the silver; it is then ready to be subjected to the action of the image to be represented, which is thrown upon it, care being taken to exclude all other light, by an instrument upon the principle of the camera obscura. In the course of a few seconds or minutes, the requisite time depending upon the intensity of the light, the plate is removed; and though nothing is as yet visible upon it it has received the image, which is brought out and rendered evident by subjecting it, inclined at an angle of about 45°, to the vapor of mercury. This operation is performed in a box with a glass side, at the bottom of which is a basin of mercury, heated to about 170°, so that the operator may see the progress of the appearance of the image, and remove the plate when it is perfect; but light must be as far as possible excluded, and more especially daylight. The plate is then washed by cautious immersion in a solution of hypo-sulphite of soda, and lastly with boiling distilled water, and allowed to dry: it is now perfect, may be exposed to light without injury; but must be carefully protected from all friction by covering it with a glass. The action of the various shades of light upon the film of iodine, and the subsequent influence of the mercurial vapor upon which the visibility of the picture depends, have not been satisfactorily explained, and require further experimental elucidation. The perfection of the drawing, and the extraordinary manner in which the minutest details are represented, we have noticed in our former article; they must, however, be seen to be accurately judged of and duly appreciated.

PHRASE, a short sentence or expression; said to be complete when it conveys complete sense, as "to err is human;" and incomplete when it consists of several words without affirming anything. Any peculiar sentence or short idiomatic expression is also denominated a phrase.—In music, any regular symmetrical course of notes which begin and complete the intended expression.

PHRENOL'OGY, a modern science, which professes to teach, from the conformation of the human skull, the particular characters and propensities of men, presuming that the powers of the mind and the sensations are performed by peculiar parts of the brain: the front parts being intellectual, the middle sentimental, and the hinder parts governing the animal propensities: the degree being in proportion to the projection or bulk of the parts. It was long ago observed by physiologists, that the characters of animals were determined by the formation of the forehead, and that the intelligence of the animal, in most cases, rose or fell in proportion to the elevation or depression of the skull. But it was reserved to Drs. Gall and Spurzheim to expand this germ of doctrine into a minute system, and to map out the whole cranium into small sections, each section being the dwelling-place, or workshop, of a certain faculty, propensity, or sentiment, in all amounting to thirty-six, and to which certain names have been given in order to mark their specific qualities, their uses and abuses.

PHYLAC'TERY, among the ancients, a general name given to all kinds of spells, charms, or amulets, which they wore about them, to preserve them from disease or danger. It is more particularly used to signify a slip of paper on which was written some text of Scripture, especially of the Decalogue, which the more devout Jews wore on the forehead, breast, or neck, as a badge of their religion.—Among the primitive Christians, a *phylactery* was a case in which they inclosed the relics of their dead.

PHY'LÆ, the tribes into which the whole of Attica was divided in antiquity. Originally there were but four phylæ, which were frequently remodelled, but remained the same in number till soon after the expulsion of the Pisistradidæ, when Cleisthenes caused their number to be increased to ten. What the precise nature of the change effected on this occasion was is not known, but it is probable that the new tribes embraced a large number of citizens that had been excluded from the former. The phylæ were afterwards increased to twelve, by the addition of two in honor of Antigonous and his son Demetrius. The Athenian senate was composed of fifty delegates from each of these tribes.

PHY'LARCH, an Athenian officer appointed for each phyle or tribe, to superintend the registering of its members and other common duties. The title answers to that of the Roman tribune, but its functions never reached the same importance.

PHYS'ICAL, an epithet denoting that which relates to nature or natural productions, as opposed to things moral or imaginary. We speak of physical force or power, with reference to material things: thus armies and navies are the *physical* force of a nation; whereas knowledge, skill, &c., constitute *moral* force.—*A physical body* or substance, is a material body or substance, in distinction from spirit or metaphysical substance.—*Physical education*, the education which is directed to the object of giving strength, health, and vigor to the bodily organs and powers.

PHYSIOGNOM'ICS, among physicians, signs in the countenance which serve to indicate the state, disposition, &c., both of the body and mind: and hence the art of reducing these signs to practice is termed physiognomy.

PHYSIOG'NOMY, the art of discovering the predominant temper or other characteristic qualities of the mind by the features of the face or external signs of the countenance. Whatever be thought of the possibility of laying down strict rules for such judgments, it is a fact of every-day occurrence, that we are, almost without reflection on our part, impressed favorably or unfavorably in regard to the temper and talents of others by the expression of their countenances. No study, says Lavater, mathematics excepted, more justly deserves to be termed a science than physiognomy. It is a department of physics, including theology and belles-lettres; and in the same manner with these sciences may be reduced to rule. It may acquire a fixed and appropriate character; it may be communicated and taught. Physiognomy, he adds, is a source of pure and exalted mental gratification. It affords a new view of the perfection of Deity; it displays a new scene of harmony and beauty in his works; it reveals internal motives, which, without it, would only have been discovered in the world to come. We all have some sort of intuitive method by which we form our opinions; and though our rules for judging of men from their appearance may often fail, we still continue to trust in them.

PHYSIOG'NOTYPE, a machine for taking an exact imprint or cast of the countenance, lately invented by a Parisian. This instrument is a metallic, oval plate, pierced with a large quantity of minute holes very closely together, and through each of which a wire passes with extreme facility. These needles have the appearance of a brush. The whole is surrounded with a double case of tin, which contains warm water, in order to keep the instrument of a proper temperature with the blood. If any figure be applied against this brush of needles, it will yield to the slightest pressure, and leave an exact mould, taking up only about two seconds.

PIANO-FORTE, a musical stringed instrument, the strings of which are extended over bridges rising on the sounding-board, and are made to vibrate by means of small covered hammers, which are put in motion by keys. It has been gradually improved, till it has become one of the most important instruments in all domestic musical entertainments.

PIAS'TRE, a variable denomination of money. In the West, its use is nearly confined to Italy, and Spain with its colonies; in which it generally means a dollar, or the largest silver coin of those regions; but the term is there obsolescent. The old *rose* piastre of Tuscany contains 10 pauls, or about $1.05; the old *two-globed* piastre of Spain, whether Mexican or Sevillan, is worth about $1.03. Both pass in the United States for a dollar. In the East, on the other hand, *piastre* means a coin of scarcely 1-20th the value of the foregoing; namely, worth about five cents.

PIAZ'ZA, an Italian name for a portico or covered walk. The word literally signifies a broad open place or square; whence it came to be applied to the walks or porticos surrounding them.

PI'BROCH, martial music produced by the bag-pipe of the Highlanders. It is said to signify also the instrument itself; but the former meaning, if, indeed, there are *any* instances of the latter to be found in any classical writer, has received the sanction of the two most celebrated poets of their time, Lord Byron and Sir Walter Scott. The connoisseurs, says the latter writer, in pipe-music, affect to discover, in a well-composed pibroch, the imitative sounds of march, conflict, flight, pursuit, and all the "current of a heady fight."

PICARDS', the name of a fanatical and immoral sect of Christians, who sprang up in Bohemia in the fifteenth century. They derived their name from Picard, a native of Flanders, who styled himself the New Adam, and attempted to revive the absurdities of the Adamites of the second century in imitating the state of primeval innocence. They were completely annihilated by Zisca, the great general of the Hussites, who, struck with their abominable practices, had marched against them.

PICK'ET, or PIC'QUET, in military discipline, a certain number of men, horse or foot, who do duty as an outguard, to prevent surprises. Also, a punishment which consists in making the offender stand with one foot on a pointed stake.—*Pickets*, in fortification, sharp stakes, sometimes shod with iron, used in laying out ground, or for pinning the fascines of a battery. In the artillery, pickets five or six feet long are used to pin the park lines; in the camp, they are used about six or eight inches long to fix the tent cords, or five feet long in the cavalry camp to fasten the horses.

PICTS' WALL, an ancient wall began by the emperor Adrian, A.D. 123, on the northern boundary of England, from Carlisle to Newcastle, to prevent the incursions of the Picts and Scots. It was first made only of turf, strengthened with palisades till the emperor Severus coming in person into Britain, had it built with stone; and Aetius, the Roman general, rebuilt it with brick, A.D. 430. Some remains of this wall are still visible in parts of Northumberland and Cumberland.

PICTURESQUE', an epithet denoting that peculiar kind of beauty which, either in a prospect, a painting, or a description, strikes the mind with great power, or imparts to it agreeable sensations. In the theory of the Arts, the word *picturesque* is used as contradistinguished from *poetic* and *plastic*. The *poetical* has reference to the fundamental idea to be represented—to the painter's conception of his subject; whilst the *picturesque* relates to the mode of expressing the conception, the grouping, the distribution of objects, persons, and lights. The poetical part of a picture, as well as its mechanical execution, may be without fault, and yet the picture be a total failure as regards the picturesque.

PIER, a very strong stone wall or mass of solid stone-work running into the water, to resist the force of the sea, to support the arches of a bridge, or the quay of a wharf, and to withstand the dashing of waves.—Also, a part of the wall of a house between windows.

PIE'RIAN, an epithet given to the muses, from Mount Pierus, in Thessaly, which was sacred to them; or from their victory over the nine daughters of the Macedonian king, Pierus.

PI'ETIST, a person belonging to a sect of Protestants which sprung up in Germany, in the latter part of the 17th century. They professed great strictness and purity of life, affecting to despise learning and ecclesiastical polity, as also forms and ceremonies in religion, and giving themselves up to mystic theology.

PI'ETY, that holy principle which consists in veneration accompanied with love for the Supreme Being; and which manifests itself, in practice, by obedience to God's will, and a pure devotion to his service.—Piety both towards God and man was one of the virtues held in most esteem by the ancients, and is therefore commemorated on innumerable medals, sometimes under the figure of a female carrying children, or of Æneas bearing his father, &c., but more frequently under that of a female standing at an altar.

PIG'MENTS, preparations of various kinds used in painting and dyeing, to impart the colors required. They are obtained from animal, vegetable, and mineral substances.

PIG'MY, by ancient authors on natural history, this name was applied to a fabulous race of dwarfish and deformed human beings; it is now restricted to a species of ape, the Chimpanzee. Ancient fable described a nation of pigmies dwelling somewhere near the shores of the ocean, and maintaining perpetual wars with the cranes; of which Athenæus gives the mythological origin. Ctesias the Greek historian, as quoted by Photius, represented a nation of them as inhabiting India, and attending its king on his military expeditions. Other ancients believed them to inhabit the Indian islands.

PILAS'TER, a debased pillar; a square pillar projecting from a pier, or from a wall, to the extent of from ¼ to ⅛ of its breadth. Pilasters originated in the Grecian antæ. In Roman architecture they were sometimes tapered like columns, and finished with capitals modelled after the order with which they were used.

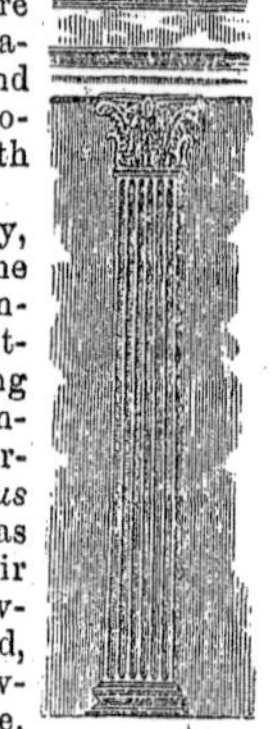

PILE'US, in antiquity, a hat or cap worn by the Romans, during any indisposition which prevented them from appearing safely with their heads uncovered, as was the general custom. The *Pileus* was also worn by such as had lately received their freedom, because on having their liberty granted, they were constantly shaved: the *Pileus*, therefore, being necessary on this account, was also esteemed a badge of liberty; hence *pileo donari* signifies to be made free.

PIL'GRIM, one that travels to a distance from his own country to visit a holy place for devotional purposes. In the middle ages, kings, princes, bishops, and others made *pilgrimages* to visit the holy sepulchre at Jerusalem, in pious devotion to the Saviour. This was permitted while Palestine was held by the Saracens; but when the Turks obtained possession of that country, the Christian pilgrims were visited with the greatest indignities, and their repeated complaints occasioned the excitement which led to the crusades. In subsequent times pilgrimages to Rome, Compostella, Loretto, Tours, and other places where the relics of martyrs and saints attracted the notice of devotees, have been common; and pilgrims to this day travel to Rome, where they are provided for in establishments founded especially for their reception and entertainment. But pilgrimages are not confined to Christian nations. According to a command in the *Koran*, every good Mussulman is enjoined once in his lifetime to repair to Mecca; and there are many other places, especially in Persia, endowed with sufficient sanctity to attract multitudes of pilgrims. The Hindoos have also their pilgrimages, the most celebrated of which is to the city of Juggernaut, where stands the temple erected in honor of the deity of the same name; a full account of which will be found in the *Geo. Dict.*, art. "Juggernaut." Among existing Christian pilgrimages, the most celebrated is that of Marianzell, in Austria.

PIL'LAR, a kind of irregular column, either too massive or too slender for regular architecture; the parts and proportions of which, not being restricted to any rules, are arbitrary.

PIL'LORY, an instrument of punishment, consisting of a frame of wood erected on posts, made to confine the head and hands of a criminal, in order to expose him to view, and to render him publicly infamous.

PI'LUM, a missile weapon used by the Roman soldiers, and in a charge darted upon the enemy. Its point was so long and small, that after the first discharge it was generally so bent as to be rendered useless.

PINA'CIA, among the Athenians, were tablets of brass inscribed with the names of all the citizens in each tribe, who were duly qualified and willing to be judges of the court of Areopagus. These tablets were cast into one vessel provided for the purpose, and the same number of beans, a hundred being white and all the rest black, were thrown into another. Then the names of the candidates and the beans were drawn out one by one; and they whose names were drawn out together with the white beans were elected judges or senators.

PINACOTHE'CA, in ancient architecture, the apartment in a house for the reception of paintings.

PINDAREES', the name given in British India to the hordes of mounted robbers who, for several years, (since 1812,) infested the possessions of the East India Company. These freebooters have existed since 1761, but made themselves particularly formidable in the 19th century. They were descended mostly from the caste of Mohammedan warriors, which formerly received high pay from the Indian princes; and these latter, after becoming tributary to the British, secretly excited the Pindarees to attack the company. In 1817 the marquis of Hastings, then governor-general, determined on their destruction, and being attacked on all sides, they were conquered and dispersed.

PINDAR'IC, an ode in imitation of the odes of Pindar, the prince of Greek lyric poets.

PIN'-MONEY, gifts by a husband to his wife for the purchase of apparel, ornaments for her person, or for private expenditure. Usually, however, a sum of money for that purpose is secured by the husband to his wife by settlement, or by articles executed before the marriage, and such a provision cannot be attached for the husband's debts.

PIN'NACE, a small vessel navigated with oars and sails, and having generally two masts which are rigged like those of a schooner; also one of the boats belonging to a man of war, usually with eight oars, and used to carry the officers to and from shore.

PIN'NACLE, in architecture, the top or roof of a building, terminating in a point. Among the ancients the pinnacle was appropriated to temples; their ordinary roofs being all flat. It was from the pinnacle that the *pediment* took its rise.

PIONEER', in military tactics, a military laborer, or one whose business is to attend an army in its march, to clear the way, by cutting down trees and levelling roads; as also to work at intrenchments, or form mines for destroying an enemy's works.

PI'RACY, the crime of robbery or taking of property from others by open violence on the high seas without authority. It includes all acts of robbery and depredation committed at sea, which, if occurring upon land, would amount to felony. The word *pirate* signifies literally an adventurer.—*Piracy* is also frequently used to signify any infringement on the law of copyright. It is extremely difficult to lay down any general principle on which to decide as to what is and what is not piracy. Generally it is held, that one writer may borrow the ideas or theories of another: but that he must dress them up and explain them in a different way, and in his own language. This, however, is often done so as merely to evade the law: and it were well, in order to make greater attention be paid to originality, were the law as to piracy less lax than it is at present.

PIROGUE', a kind of canoe, used in the Southern and Eastern seas, made from a single trunk of a tree hollowed out. Pirogues are generally small, and worked by paddles; they are, however, sometimes large, decked, rigged with sails, and furnished with out-riggers.

PIROUET'TE, in dancing, a rapid circumvolution upon one foot, which on the stage is repeated by the dancers many times in succession.—In riding, it is the sudden short turn of a horse, so as to bring his head suddenly in the opposite direction to where it was before.

PIS'CARY, in our ancient statutes,

the right or liberty of fishing in another man's waters.

PITCH, in music, the degree of acuteness or graveness of a note. It may be the key-note, or the note on which any air or part begins. Any sound less acute than some other sound, is said to be of a lower pitch than that other sound, and *vice versa*.—*Concert pitch*, in musical performances, the degree of acuteness or gravity generally adopted for some one given note, and by which every other note is governed. It is not regulated by any fixed standard. The *opera pitch* is higher than the concert pitch.—*Pitch of a roof*, in architecture, the inclination of the sloping sides of the roof to the horizon, or the vertical angle formed by the sloping sides. It is usually designated by the ratio of its height to its span.

PIU', in music, Italian for *a little more*. It is prefixed to words to increase their force, as *piu allegra*, a little brisker; *piu piano*, a little softer, &c.

PIX, a covered vessel used in Roman Catholic countries for holding the consecrated host. Pixes are most frequently made of gold or silver, and sometimes are in form like a chalice with merely the addition of a lid.

PLAC'ARD, properly a written or printed paper posted in a public place. It seems to have been formerly the name of an edict, proclamation, or manifesto issued by authority, but this sense is, I believe, seldom or never annexed to the word. A *placard* now is an advertisement, or a libel, or a paper intended to censure public or private characters or public measures, posted in a public place. In the case of libels or papers intended to censure public or private characters, or the measures of government, these papers are usually pasted up at night for secrecy. It is also used for any paper posted to give public notice, as an advertisement.

PLA'CITA, (Lat.,) in the middle ages, were public courts or assemblies, in which the sovereign presided when a consultation was held upon the affairs of the state.

PLAFOND', the ceiling of a room whether flat or arched; also the under side of the projection of the larmier of the cornice, generally any soffit.

PLA'GAL MEL'ODIES, in music, such as have their principal notes lying between the fifth of the key and its octave or twelfth.

PLA'GIARISM, (from the Latin legal term plagium, which signified the offence of stealing a slave, or kidnapping a free person into slavery.) A plagiary, in the modern sense of the word, is one who borrows without acknowledgment, in literary composition, the thoughts or words of another; and the theft itself is styled plagiarism.

PLAGUE, a malignant and contagious disease that often prevails in Egypt, Syria, and Turkey. It generally proves fatal to nations and great cities, but is arrested by cleanliness, or the avoiding of putrid fermentations of which it seems to be an extension.

PLAIN-SONG, a term in ancient ecclesiastical music signifying the plain, unvaried chant of churches; so called in contradistinction from the prick-song, or variegated music sung by note. It is an extremely simple melody and admits but one measure, the duple, and only notes of equal value. It is rarely allowed to extend beyond the compass of an octave. It is still used in the Romish church.

PLAIN'TIFF, in law, the person who commences a suit before a judicial tribunal, for the recovery of a claim; opposed to *defendant*.

PLAN, the representation of something drawn on a *plane;* as a map, chart, or ichnography. It is, however, more particularly used for a draught of a building, as it appears, or is intended to appear on the ground; showing the extent, division, and distribution of its area, or ground plot, into apartments, rooms, passages, &c.—A *perspective plan* is that which is exhibited according to the rules of perspective. The word *plan* also signifies a scheme or project; the form of something to be done existing in the mind, with the several parts adjusted in idea. A *plan*, in this sense, may be expressed in words or committed to writing; as a *plan* of a constitution of government, the *plan* of a military expedition, &c.

PLANTA'GENET, the surname of the royal family of England from Henry II. to Richard III. inclusive. The origin of the name is involved in deep obscurity. The best antiquaries derive it from the well-known story of the Earl of Anjou, the ancestor of the royal race, who having made a pilgrimage to Rome, where he was scourged with broom twigs, assumed the name of *Plantagenista*, (literally, a *broom twig*,) which his descendants retained. The name Plantagenet belongs to the noble house of Buckingham.

PLANTA'TION, in the United States and the West Indies, a cultivated estate; a farm. In the United States, this word is applied to an estate, a tract of land occupied and cultivated, in those states only where the labor is performed by slaves, and where the land is more or less appropriated to the culture of tobacco, rice, indigo, and cotton, that is, from Maryland to Georgia inclusive, on the Atlantic, and in the western states where the land is appropriated to the same articles, or to the culture of the sugar-cane. From Maryland, northward and eastward, estates in land are called farms.—An original settlement in a new country; a town or village planted.

PLAS'TIC ART, a branch of sculpture, being the art of forming figures of men and animals in plaster, clay, &c.—The word plastic signifies having power to give form or fashion to a mass of matter; as, the plastic hand of the Creator, &c.—*Plastic nature*, a certain power by which, as an instrument, many philosophers, both ancient and modern, supposed that the great motions in the corporeal world, and the various processes of generation and corruption were perpetually carried on.

PLAT'BAND, in architecture, a square moulding projecting less than its height or breadth. The fillets between the flutes of columns are sometimes called, but improperly, by this name. It is also sometimes used to denote the lintel of a door.

PLATE, in architecture, a piece of timber lying horizontally on a wall for the reception of the ends of girders, joints, rafters, &c.

PLAT'FORM, in architecture, a row of beams which support the timber-work of a roof; also any erection consisting of boards raised above the ground for an exhibition or any other temporary purpose.—*Platform*, in the military art, an elevation of earth on which cannon are mounted to fire on an enemy.

PLATON'IC, pertaining to Plato, his school, philosophy, opinions, &c. The leading characteristic of the mind of Plato is its comprehensiveness. This quality discovers itself equally in the form in which his philosophy is communicated, and in that philosophy itself. The form to which we allude is, it is well known, that of the dialogue. The Dialogues of Plato are at once vivid representations of Athenian life and character, and constituent parts of a system of universal philosophy; the harmonious productions of a genius which combined the dramatic imagination with the scientific intellect in a degree which has never before nor since been equalled. It is in this circumstance that we must seek alike for the influence which Plato's writings have exerted, and for the difficulty of rightly apprehending their meaning. What has been said of history in general may with equal truth be applied to the Platonic dialogues—that they are "philosophy teaching by examples." In place of a formal refutation of sophistry, we are introduced to living sophists; in the room of an elaborate system of philosophy, we meet the greatest philosophers of his day, reasoning and conversing with disciples eager in the pursuit of knowledge—with Athenians full of national prejudices, with men abounding with individual peculiarities.—*Platonic love* denotes a pure spiritual affection, for which Plato was a great advocate, subsisting between the different sexes, unmixed with carnal affections, and regarding no other object but the mind and its excellencies. It is also sometimes understood as a sincere disinterested friendship subsisting between persons of the same sex, abstracted from any selfish views, and regarding no other object than the individual so esteemed.—*Platonic year*, or the great year, a period of time determined by the revolution of the equinoxes, or the space of time in which the stars and constellations return to their former places in respect to the equinoxes. This revolution, which is calculated by the precession of the equinoxes, is accomplished in about 25,000 years.

PLA'TONIST, one that adheres to the philosophy of Plato.

PLATOON', in the military art, a small square body of forty or fifty musketeers, drawn out of a battalion of foot, and placed between the squadrons of horse to sustain them; or a small body acting together, but separate from the main body; as, to fire by platoons.

PLEA, in law, that which is alleged by a party for himself in court, in a cause there depending; but in a more limited sense, the defendant's answer to the plaintiff's declaration and demand. That which the plaintiff alleges in his declaration is answered and repelled, or justified by the defendant's *plea*.

PLEAD'ING, in law, a speech delivered at the bar in defence of a cause: but, in a stricter sense, *pleadings* are all the allegations of the parties to a suit, made after the declaration, till the issue is joined. In this sense they express whatever is contained in the bar, replication, rejoiner, &c. till the question is brought to issue, that is, to rest on a single point.

—*Pleading*, amongst the Greeks and Romans, was limited as to its duration, by a *clepsydra* or hour-glass of water; and to see that the orators had justice done them, in this respect, an officer was appointed to distribute the proper quantity of water to each.

PLEAS'URE, the gratification of the senses or of the mind; agreeable sensations or emotions; some enjoyment or delight lasting for a time and then ceasing; the excitement, relish, or happiness produced by enjoyment or the expectation of good; opposed to *pain*. We receive *pleasure* from the indulgence of appetite; from the view of a beautiful landscape; from the harmony of sounds; from agreeable society; from the expectation of seeing an absent friend; from the prospect of gain or success of any kind.—*Pleasure*, bodily and mental, carnal and spiritual, constitutes the whole of positive happiness, as *pain* constitutes the whole of misery.—*Pleasure* is properly positive excitement of the passions or the mind; but we give the name also to the absence of excitement, when that excitement is painful; as when we cease to labor, or repose after fatigue, or when the mind is tranquillized after anxiety or agitation.—*Pleasure* is susceptible of increase to any degree; but the word, when unqualified, expresses less excitement or happiness than *delight* or *joy*.

PLEAS'URE-GROUND, that portion of ground adjoining a dwelling in the country which is exclusively devoted to ornamental and recreative purposes. In the ancient style of gardening, the pleasure-ground was laid out in straight walks, and regular or symmetrical forms, commonly borrowed from architecture; but, in the modern style, it is laid out in winding walks, and in forms borrowed direct from nature. A portion of lawn or smooth grassy surface may be considered as essential to the pleasure-ground under both styles.

PLEBE'IANS, the free citizens of Rome who did not come under the class of the patricians or clients. Though always personally independent, they had in early times no political power, the government being entirely in the hands of the patricians, who, with their clients and the king, formed the original people. The class of plebeians was of after-growth, and probably drew its numbers from various sources, as from clients whose obligations were dissolved by the decay of the houses of their patrons, and the inhabitants of conquered states who where admitted to rights of citizenship. The plebeian families with patrician names are supposed to have arisen from marriages of disparagement contracted between the higher and lower classes. As this body, from its constitution, naturally grew in vigor while the patricians became weaker, it soon formed the main strength of the Roman armies, and became desirous of sharing in the advantages of the conquests made by its prowess; while the patricians, on their part, tenaciously clung to all their privileges, and, far from yielding to the demands of the other party, exercised the severe rights which as creditors they possessed over the liberties of many of its members. This state of things produced a continued series of collisions between the two orders, in which the latter gradually gained ground, till, in the last ages of the republic, it was admitted to a full share of all the powers and privileges before confined to one order.

PLEDGE, something left in pawn; that which is deposited with another as security for the repayment of money borrowed, or for the performance of some agreement or obligation.—In law, bail; surety given for the prosecution of a suit, or for the appearance of a defendant, or for restoring goods taken in distress and replevied.—*To pledge*, in drinking, is to warrant a person that he shall receive no harm while drinking, or from the draught; a practice which originated with our ancestors in their rude state, and which was intended to assure the person that he would not be stabbed while drinking, or poisoned by the liquor. Notwithstanding the reason has long since ceased, the custom still continues—a remarkable instance of the force of habit.

PLENIPOTEN'TIARY, a person invested with full power to transact any business; generally, an ambassador from a prince, invested with full power to negotiate a treaty or conclude peace with another prince or state.

PLE'ONASM, redundancy of words in speaking or writing; the use of more words to express ideas, than are necessary. This may be justifiable when we intend to present thoughts with particular perspicuity or force, as "I saw it with my *own* eyes," "I heard it with my *own* ears."

PLETH'RON, or PLETH'RUM, in Grecian antiquity, a square measure, the exact contents of which are not certainly known. Some suppose it to correspond with the Roman *juger*, or 240 feet; others say it was the square of a hundred cubits.

PLINTH, a flat, square member, in form of a brick, which serves as a foun-

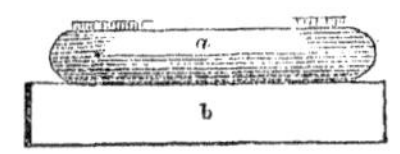

a. Torus. *b*. Plinth.

dation of a column; being the flat square table under the moulding of the base and pedestal, at the bottom of the order.—*Plinth of a statue*, is a base, flat, round, or square.—*Plinth of a wall*, two or three rows of bricks advanced from the wall, in form of a flatband; and, in general, any flat, high moulding, that serves in a front wall to mark the floors, to sustain the eaves of a wall, or the larmier of a chimney.

PLOT, any stratagem or plan of a complicated nature, adapted to the accomplishment of some mischievous purpose; as a *plot* against the government, or against the life of a person.—*Plot*, in dramatic writings, the fable of a tragedy or comedy, but more particularly the knot or intrigue, comprising a complication of incidents which are ultimately unfolded.—*Plot*, in surveying, the plan or draught of any field, farm, &c. surveyed with an instrument, and laid down in the proper figure and dimensions.

PLU'TEUS, the wall sometimes made use of to close the intervals between the columns of a building; it was either of stone or some less durable material when it occurred in the interior of a building. The pluteus was also a kind of podium interposed between two orders of columns, where one was placed above the other.—A movable gallery on wheels, shaped like an arched sort of wagon, used by besiegers for the protection of their archers, who were stationed on it to clear the walls with their arrows.

PLU'TUS, the god of riches, said to have been the son of Jasius and Demeter or Ceres. There are no particulars known as to his worship; but he is introduced as an actor in the play of Aristophanes which bears his name, and he bears a part also in the *Timon* of Lucian.

PLU'TO, in Greek and Roman mythology, the brother of Jupiter and Neptune, and lord of the infernal regions. He is represented as an old man with a dignified but severe aspect, holding in his hand a two-pronged fork. He was generally called by the Greeks Hades, and by the Romans *Orcus* and *Dis*. His wife was

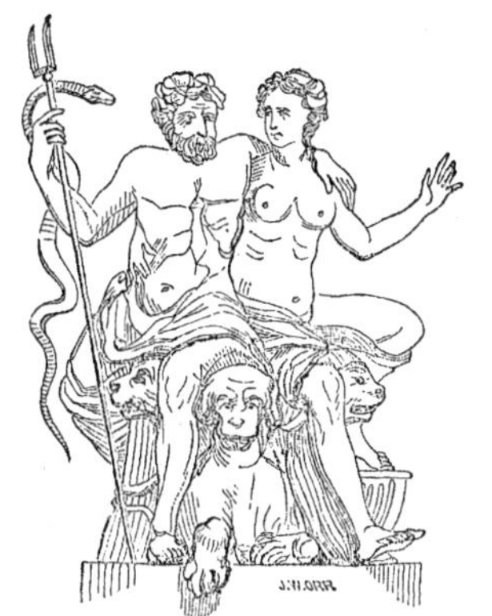

Pluto and Proserpine.

Proserpine, daughter of Jupiter and Ceres, whom Pluto seized in the island of Sicily while she was plucking flowers, and carried to the lower world.

PO'DIUM, (Latin,) in architecture, the part in an amphitheatre projecting over the arena, above which it was raised about 12 or 15 feet: in this part sat the personages of distinction. The word is also used to signify a balcony.

PŒ'CILE, a celebrated portico or gallery at Athens, where Zeno inculcated his doctrines. The Pœcile was adorned with the statues of gods and benefactors; and the picture of Polygnotus, so well-known to the classical reader, which represented Miltiades at the head of the 1000 Greeks at the battle of Marathon, was here suspended for ages.

PO'EM, a metrical composition; a composition in which the verses consist of certain measures, whether in blank verse or in rhyme; as, the *poems* of Homer or of Milton; opposed to *prose*.—This term is also applied to some compositions in which the language is that of excited imagination; as the *poems* of Ossian.

PO'ET, one who has a particular genius for metrical composition, combined with those higher requisites which belong to a lively imagination, and a keen sense of the beauties of nature. Many write verses who have no just claim to the title of *poets*, and yet such writers may be many degrees beyond those versifying scribes who, in derision, are termed *poetasters*.

POET'ICAL JUS'TICE, a term often used in speaking of dramatic writings, to denote a distribution of rewards and punishments to the several characters at the catastrophe or close of a piece.

PO'ET LAU'REATE, the appellation given to a poet whose duty it is to compose birth-day odes, and other poems of rejoicing, for the monarch in whose service he is retained. The laureate's post in England is at present filled by Alfred Tennyson, and the services formerly required are dispensed with. The first mention of a king's poet in England, under the title of poet laureate, occurs in the reign of Edward IV. *Poeta laureatus* was, however, also an academical title in England, conferred by the universities when the candidates received the degrees in grammar (which included rhetoric and versification.) The last instance of a laureated degree at Oxford occurs in 1512. Ben Jonson was court poet to James I. and received a pension, but does not appear to have the title of laureate formally granted him. Dryden was appointed laureate to Charles II., and afterwards to James II., by regular patent under privy seal. Nahum Tate, Rowe, Eusden, Cibber, Whitehead, T. Warton, Pye, Southey, Wordsworth, and Tennyson, (the last of whom was appointed in 1851.)

PO'ETRY. To produce a complete and satisfactory definition of poetry has been, hitherto, unsuccessfully attempted by writers on taste, and by poets themselves. A popular one, sufficiently adapted to general notions, is furnished by the *doyen* of living critics, Lord Jeffrey: "The end of poetry is to please; and the name, we think, is strictly applicable to every metrical composition from which we derive pleasure without any laborious exercise of the understanding." But, in the first place, it has been truly observed that "verse is the limit by which poetry is bounded: it is the adjunct of poetry, but not its living principle." "Poetry," says Coleridge, "is not the proper antithesis to prose, but to science. Poetry is opposed to science, and prose to metre." "The proper and immediate object of science is the acquirement or communication of truth; the proper and immediate object of poetry is the communication of immediate pleasure." It is essentially a creative art: its operation is "making," not transcribing. "Imitation" it is, as Aristotle defines it; not because it copies, but because it has its model in nature, and can never depart far from it without losing its character. Lord Bacon explains this by saying, that poetry "doth raise and erect the mind, by *submitting the shows of things to the desire of the mind.*" The imagination alters these "shows of things" by adding or subtracting qualities, and poetry produces to view the forms which result from the operation.

1. Imagination is, emphatically, the great poetical faculty. It is "the first moving or creative principle of the mind, which fashions out of materials previously existing, new materials and original truths." It is "a complex power, including those faculties which are called by metaphysicians conception, abstraction, and judgment:" the first enabling us to form a notion of objects of perception and knowledge; the second "separating the selected materials from the qualities and circumstances which are connected with them in nature;" the third selecting the materials. Its operations are most various, and it exhibits itself in poetry in very different degrees and forms. It may shine here and there, chiefly in comparison, or in bold and pleasing metaphor, breaking the chain of a narrative, as in Homer and the earlier poetry of most nations; it may hurry image on image, connected only by those exquisite links of thought which are present in the mind of the poet, in daring, compressed, rapid language, as if language were inadequate to its expression, as in the inspired prophets, in Æschylus, and often in Shakspeare; it may predominate in entire sustained conceptions, grasping at general features, as in Milton; it may cling more closely to the "shows of things," dwelling in particulars, reproducing with startling vividness images little altered, graphic, and minute, as in Dante.

2. No distinction has given critics more trouble, in the way of definition, than that between imagination and fancy. "Fancy," it has been said, "is given to beguile and quicken the temporal part of our nature; imagination to incite and support the eternal." "The distinction between fancy and imagination," says another, "is simply that the former altogether changes and remodels the original idea, impregnating it with something extraneous; the latter leaves it undisturbed, but associates it with things to which in some view or other it bears a resemblance."

3. Lord Jeffrey associates with the pleasure of imagination that derived from "the easy exercise of reason." This is produced chiefly by the faculties of thought, wit, and reflection. It may, indeed, be doubted whether the expression of thought, however energetic and acute,

clad in current poetical diction, is really poetry. Certainly it is so, if at all, in a very inferior degree to that of the imagination.

4. The expression of passion, sentiment, or pathos, is the most common and universal of all sources of poetical pleasure. It is the very soul of all early and simple poetry; it pervades no less that of the most civilized communities. Yet this class of poetry is less truly and emphatically poetical than the imaginative, although more popular. The pleasure occasioned by it is of a mixed nature: it arises from the excitement of peculiar sympathies, not produced, but heightened only, by the form in which that excitement is conveyed.

5. The dramatic faculty, of which we have already spoken, seems to consist in acute powers of observation of the varieties of human character, together with the rarer power of delineating it with such force as to bring the imaginary person distinctly before the reader. It is the wonderful and unique characteristic of Shakspeare, in whom all individuality, as has often been observed, seems absolutely lost.

6. The descriptive faculty is of the same kind; that of bringing the objects of external nature, or passing scenes of whatever sort, vividly before the reader's fancy. It is obvious that this also is a faculty common to poets with many others who are not so: but sustained energy of description, as in Homer, forms a magnificent groundwork for strictly poetical ornament. In the poetry of modern times, especially in this country, and in Germany, the description of external nature has been made subservient to the purposes of imagination and reflection by writers of high genius; and this combination peculiarly characterizes the taste of the age.

7. Lord Jeffrey ranks last the pleasure derived from diction as of a secondary order, which it undoubtedly is, and yet almost essential. The highest poetry, without beauty of style, is rarely or never popular. We have no space to characterize minutely this poetical quality; but by way of example, it may suffice to observe that Virgil is, perhaps, of all poets, he of whose charm the greatest proportion is derived from simple beauty and felicity of diction; through a whole range of ill-chosen subjects, always graceful, always equable, and as nearly approaching to faultlessness as human skill can construct.

8. Lastly, we must not omit the pleasure of *melody*: not essential to poetry, since there may be poetry without verse; not always a merit of the poet's own, since much depends on the language; and a Greek or Italian poet, cæteris paribus, will ever be preferable to an English or German one on this account alone; but a grace which heightens the charm of the noblest poetry, and sometimes captivates the sense even in the most indifferent.

Dr. Channing says, "In an intellectual nature, framed for progress and for higher modes of being, there must be creative energies, powers of original and ever-growing thought; and poetry is the form in which those energies are chiefly manifested. It is the glorious prerogative of this art that 'it makes all things new' for the gratification of a divine instinct. It indeed finds its elements in what it actually sees and experiences in the worlds of matter and mind; but it combines and blends these into new forms and according to new affinities; breaks down, if we may so say, the distinctions and bounds of nature; imparts to material objects life, and sentiment, and emotion, and invests the mind with the powers and splendors of the outward creation; describes the surrounding universe in the colors which the passions throw over it, and depicts the mind in those moments of repose or agitation, of tenderness or sublime emotion, which manifests its thirst for a more powerful and joyful existence. To a man of a literal and prosaic character, the mind may seem lawless in these workings; but it observes higher laws than it transgresses, the laws of the immortal intellect; it is trying and developing its best faculties; and in the objects which it describes, or in the emotions which it awakens, anticipates those states of progressive power, splendor, beauty, and happiness, for which it was created. We accordingly believe that poetry, far from injuring society, is one of the great instruments of its refinement and exaltation. It lifts the mind above ordinary life, gives it a respite from depressing cares, and awakens the consciousness of its affinity with what is pure and noble. In its legitimate and highest efforts it has the same tendency and aim with Christianity; that is to spiritualize our nature. True, poetry has been made the instrument of vice, the pander of bad passions: but, when genius thus stoops, it dims its fires, and parts with much of its power; and, even when poetry is enslaved to licentiousness or misan-thropy, she cannot wholly forget her true vocation. Strains of pure feeling, touches of tenderness, images of innocent happiness, sympathies with suffering virtue, bursts of scorn or indignation at the hollowness of the world, passages true to our moral nature, often escape in an immoral work, and show us how hard it is for a gifted spirit to divorce itself wholly from what is good. Poetry has a natural alliance with our best affections. It delights in the beauty and sublimity of the outward creation and of the soul. It indeed portrays with terrible energy the excesses of the passions; but they are passions which show a mighty nature, which are full of power, which command awe, and excite a deep though shuddering sympathy. Its great tendency and purpose is, to carry the mind above and beyond the beaten, dusty, weary walks of ordinary life; to lift it into a purer element, and to breathe into it more profound and generous emotion. It reveals to us the loveliness of nature, brings back the freshness of youthful feeling, revives the relish of simple pleasures, keeps unquenched the enthusiasm which warmed the spring-time of our being, refines youthful love, strengthens our interest in human nuture by vivid delineations of its tenderest and loftiest feelings, spreads our sympathies over all classes of society, knits us by new ties with universal being, and through the brightness of its prophetic visions, helps faith to lay hold on the future life. It is not true that the poet paints a life which does not exist. He only extracts and concentrates, as it were, life's ethereal essence, arrests and condenses its volatile fragrance, brings together its scattered beauties, and prolongs its more refined but evanescent joys; and in this, he does well; for it is good to feel that life is not wholly usurped by cares for subsistence and physical gratifications, but admits, in measures which may be indefinitely enlarged, sentiments and delights worthy of a higher being."

POINT, in music, a mark or note anciently used to distinguish tones or sounds. Hence, *simple counterpoint* is when a note of the lower part answers exactly to that of the upper: and *figurative counterpoint* is when a note is syncopated, and one of the parts makes several notes or inflections of the voice, while the other holds on one.—In modern music, a dot placed by a note to raise its value or prolong its time by one half, so as to make a semibreve equal to three minims; a minim equal to three quavers, &c.—A character used to mark the divisions of writing, or the pauses to be observed in reading or speaking; as the comma, semicolon, colon, and period. The period is called a *full* stop, as it marks the close of a sentence.—Particular; single thing or subject. In what *point* do we differ? All *points* of controversy between the parties are adjusted. We say, in *point* of antiquity, in *point* of fact, in *point* of excellence. The letter in every *point* is admirable. The treaty is executed in every *point.*

POLA'CRE, a vessel with three masts, used in the Mediterranean. The masts are usually of one piece, so that they have neither tops, caps, nor cross-trees, nor horses to their upper yards.

POL'EMARCH, in antiquity, an Athenian magistrate whose duty it was to take care that the children of such as lost their lives in their country's service were maintained out of the public treasury. He had also the care of sojourners and strangers in Athens; his authority over them being equal to that of the archon over the citizens.

POLEM'ICS, controversial writings, particularly applied to controversies on matters of divinity.

POLE'-STAR, or PO'LAR STAR, in astronomy, a star of the second magnitude, the last in the tail of Ursa Minor, which is nearly vertical to the pole of the earth. Owing to its proximity, it never sets; it is therefore of great use to navigators in the northern hemisphere, in determining the latitudes, &c.

POLICE', is a term employed to designate those regulations which have for their object to secure the maintenance of good order, cleanliness, health, &c. in cities and country districts; and it is also used to designate the description of force by which these objects are effected. This force differs from military in its being commanded by civil officers and not being under military law; but it is generally drilled and armed in a half military manner, and has a distinctive uniform. The police force is employed alike to prevent and detect offences; and may be either open or secret. By an open police is meant officers dressed in their accustomed uniform, and known to everybody; while by a secret police is meant officers whom it may be difficult or impossible to distinguish from certain classes of citizens, whose dress and manners they may think it expedient to assume. The latter are employed that they may, without exciting the suspicion of guilty parties, or of those who are projecting some outrage, acquire their confidence, and by making themselves masters of their secrets, secure their apprehension or prevent the outrage.

POL'ICY, in its primary signification, is the same as *polity*, comprehending the fundamental constitution or frame of civil government in a state or kingdom. But by usage, *policy* is now more generally used to denote what is included under *legislation* and *administration*, and may be defined, the art or manner of governing a nation; or that system of measures which the sovereign of a country adopts and pursues, as the best adapted to the interests of the nation. Thus we speak of *domestic policy*, or the system of internal regulations in a nation; *foreign policy*, or the measures which respect foreign nations; *commercial policy*, or the measures which respect commerce.—*Policy*, in commerce, the writing or instruction by which a contract of indemnity is effected between the insurer and the insured; or the instrument containing the terms or conditions on which a person or company undertakes to indemnify another person or company against losses of property exposed to peculiar hazards, as houses or goods exposed to fire, or ships and goods exposed to destruction on the high seas. The terms *policy of insurance* or *assurance*, are also used for the contract between the insurer and the insured. *Policies* are *valued* or *open; valued*, when the property or goods insured are valued at prime cost; *open*, when the goods are not valued, but if lost, their value must be proved.

POLITE'NESS, polished manners, or that conduct towards others which good will in the first place, and good sense in the second, imperiously dictates. It unites gracefulness and gentility of behavior with an obliging willingness to conform to the wants and wishes of others.

POLIT'ICAL ARITH'METIC, the art of making arithmetical calculations on matters relating to a nation, its revenues, value of lands and effects, produce of lands or manufactures, population, and the general statistics of a country.

POLIT'ICAL ECON'OMY, the science of the laws which regulate the production, distribution, and consumption of the products, necessary, useful, or agreeable to man, which it requires some portion of voluntary labor to produce, procure, or preserve. It must be observed, however, that the limits of this department of knowledge are not yet accurately defined; hence much discussion has arisen among different writers as to its extent, object, and the various subjects to be comprehended under it. It is, in general, said of political economy, that its object is to ascertain the circumstances most favorable for the production of wealth, and the laws which determine its distribution, among the different ranks and orders into which society is divided; and this definition seems quite unexceptionable, provided it be clearly understood, that by *wealth*, in this science, is meant only those articles or products which require some portion of human industry for their production, acquisition, or preservation, and which, consequently, possess exchangeable value. The principal topics discussed by political economists are:—1. The definition of wealth; 2. of productive and unproductive labor; 3. on the nature and measures of value; 4. on the rent of land; 5. the wages of labor; 6. the profits of capital; 7. the results of machinery; 8. the circulating medium or currency; 9. the nature and conditions of commerce, or exchange of commodities. Continental writers on political economy not only treat of the principles which govern the production and accumulation of wealth, and its distribution and consumption, but also introduce in their systems inquiries into the principles according to which the governments of states may be organized, so as to promote in the best manner the well-being of those subjected to their authority; but this last subject belongs properly to general politics.

POL'ITICS, the science of government; that part of ethics which consists in the regulation and government of a nation or state, for the preservation of its safety, peace, and prosperity; comprehending the defence of its independence and rights against foreign control or conquest, the augmentation of its strength and resources, and the protection of its citizens in their rights, with the preservation and improvement of their morals.—*Politics*, in its widest extent, is both the science and the art of government, or the science whose subject is the regulation of man, in all his relations as the member of a state, and the application of this science. In other words, it is the theory and practice of obtaining the ends of civil society as perfectly as possible. The subjects which political science comprises have been arranged under the following heads:—1. Natural law; 2.

abstract politics, that is, the object of a state, and the relations between it and individual citizens; 3. political economy; 4. the science of police, or municipal regulation: 5. practical politics, or the conduct of the immediate public affairs of a state; 6. history of politics; 7. history of the European system of states, being the only system in which the modern art of politics has received a practical development; 8. statistics; 9. positive law relating to state affairs, commonly called constitutional law; 10. practical law of nations; 11. diplomacy; 12. the technical science of politics, an acquaintance with the forms and style of public business in different countries. In common parlance we understand by the *politics* of a country the course of its government, more particularly as respects its relations with foreign nations.

POL'ITY, the form or constitution of civil government of a nation or state; and in free states, the frame or fundamental system by which the several branches of government are established, and the powers and duties of each designated and defined. The word seems also to embrace legislation and administration of government.—2. The constitution or general fundamental principles of government of any class of citizens, considered in an appropriate character, or as a subordinate state.

POLL, in elections, the register of those who give their vote, containing their name, place of residence, &c. Also the place where the votes are registered; as "we are going to the *poll;*" "several electors were unable to get to the *poll,*" &c.

POLL TAX, a tax still levied in many of the continental states, and formerly also in England, in proportion to the rank or fortune of the individual. In England this species of tax was first levied in 1378; and, as is well known, it was from the brutality with which the levying of it was accompanied, that the rebellion of Wat Tyler took its rise in 1381. Various poll taxes were levied at different periods in the subsequent history of England; but they were finally abolished in the reign of William III. *See* TAXATION.

POLONOISE', in music, a movement of three crotchets in a bar, with the rhythmical cesura on the last.

POLYANTOG'RAPHY, the act or practice of multiplying copies of one's own hand-writing, by engraving on stone; a species of lithography.

POL'YARCHY, a word sometimes used by political writers in a sense opposed to monarchy: the government of many, whether a privileged class (aristocracy,) or the people at large (democracy.)

POL'YCHROMY, a modern term used to express the ancient practice of coloring statues, and the exteriors and interiors of buildings. This practice dates from the highest antiquity, but probably reached its greatest perfection in the twelfth and thirteenth centuries.

POLYG'AMY, a plurality of wives or husbands at the same time. In some countries, as in Turkey for instance, polygamy is allowed; but by the laws of England, polygamy is made felony, except in the case of absence beyond the seas for seven years. Polygamy prevailed among the Jewish patriarchs, both before and under the Mosaic law; but the state of manners had probably become reformed in this respect before the time of Christ, for in the New Testament we meet no trace of its practice. Polygamy has been allowed under all the religions which have prevailed in Asia. By the laws of Mohammed, every Mussulman is permitted to have a plurality of wives: the Arabs, however, seldom avail themselves of this privilege. The ancient Romans never practised it, though it was not forbidden among them; and Mark Antony is mentioned as the first who took the liberty of having two wives. From that time it became frequent in the Roman empire, till the reigns of Theodosius, Honorius, and Arcadius, who prohibited it A.D. 393.

POL'YGLOT, a word generally applied to such Bibles as have been printed with the text represented in various languages, The most ancient instance of this parallel representation of various texts is the work of Origen, known by the name of the *Hexapla*, in imitation of which several similar editions of the Scriptures have been published since the invention of printing; of which the most important are, 1. *The Complutensian*, or edition of Cardinal Ximenes, printed at Alcala in Spain, 1515, in four languages, comprehended in six vols., folio. 2. *The Antwerp Polyglot*, by Montanus, 8 vols., folio, 1569. 3. *The Paris Polyglot*, by Le Jay, 10 vols., folio, 1628–45. 4. *The English* or *Walton's Polyglot*, London, 1657. These contain among them the Hebrew, Chaldee, Syriac, and Samaritan texts, with Latin versions each: the Septuagint, the Greek of the New Testament the Italic and the Vulgate.

POL'YGRAPH, an instrument for multiplying copies of a writing with ease and expedition.

POLYG'RAPHY, the art of writing in various ciphers, and deciphering the same.

POLYHYM'NIA, among the Greeks and Romans, the muse that presided over lyric poetry, to whom is attributed the invention of mimes and pantomimes. By the Grecian artists she is represented covered with a veil, and in a meditating posture. Her attributes are the lyre and the plectrum. She places the forefinger of her right hand upon her mouth, or holds a scroll.

POLYM'ATHY, the knowledge of many arts and sciences. Hence a person who is acquainted with many branches of learning is styled a *polymath*.

POL'YSTYLE, a term applied to an edifice, the columns of which are too numerous to be readily counted; which reminds us of an old tradition respecting the pillars at Stonehenge—namely, that no two persons ever counted their number alike on the first trial.

POL'YSYLLABLE, in grammar, a word consisting of more syllables than three; for when a word consists of one, two, or three syllables, it is called a monosyllable, dissyllable, and trisyllable.

POLYSYN'DETON, in grammar and rhetoric, a figure in which a redundance of conjunctions, especially copulative ones, is used; as, "we have armies and fleets and gold and stores—all the sinews of war."

POLYTECH'NIC, an epithet denoting or comprehending many arts; as, a *polytechnic school*; the *Polytechnic Gallery*.—The POLYTECHNIC SCHOOL, in France, was established by a decree of the national convention of March 11th, 1794, which was passed by the influence of Monge, Carnot, Fourcroy, &c. It is now established in the buildings of the ancient college of Navarre. Napoleon did much for it, and under him it received considerable modifications. The pupils were obliged to live in the building, and wear a uniform. Its object is to diffuse a knowledge of the mathematical, physical, and chemical sciences, and to prepare the pupils for the artillery service and the various departments of engineering, military, naval, and civil. The number of pupils is limited to 300. The terms for the students not supported on the foundation are 1000 francs a year, independent of the expense of uniform and books. The pupil, at the time of admission, must be more than sixteen and less than twenty years old. The course of studies lasts two years, in certain cases three. A rigorous examination precedes admission, and another examination takes place before the pupils leave the institution, and it is invariably attended by the greater number of the marshals of France, together with many of the most distinguished scholars.

POMŒ'RIUM, in antiquity, a space of ground both within and without the walls, which the augurs consecrated on the first building of any city.

POMO'NA, the Italian goddess of fruit-trees. Her worship was assiduously cultivated at Rome, where there was a *flamen pomonalis*, who sacrificed to her every year for the preservation of the fruit.

POM'PA CIRCEN'SIS, or CEREA'LIS, in antiquity, a procession exhibited at the *Ludi Cereales* of the Romans, consisting of a solemn march of the persons who were to engage in the exercises of the circus, attended by the magistrates and ladies of quality; the statues of the gods and illustrious men being carried along in state on wagons called *thensæ*.

PON'TIFEX, among the Romans, was one of the order of Pontifices, who had the superintendence and direction of divine worship in general. The Pontifices were erected into a college consisting of fifteen persons, of whom the eight first had the title of *Majores*, and the seven others of *Pontifices Minores*. They made together but one body, the chief of which was called *Pontifex Maximus*.

PON'TIFF, the high or chief priest in the Romish and Greek churches. The ancient Romans had a college of *pontiffs;* the Jews had their *pontiffs;* and the pope is called a *sovereign pontiff*.—The word *pontificate* is used for the state or dignity of a pontiff, or high-priest; but more particularly for the reign of a pope.

PONTIFICA'LIA, the robes in which a bishop performs divine service.

PONTOONS', or PONTOON BRIDGE, a floating bridge, formed of flat-bottomed boats, anchored or made fast in two lines, and used in forming bridges over rivers for the passage of armies.—*Pontoon carriage*, a vehicle formed of two wheels only, and two long side pieces, whose fore-ends are supported by timbers.

PONT-VOLANT', in military affairs, a kind of bridge used in sieges for surprising a post or outwork that has but narrow moats. It is composed of two small bridges laid one above the other, and so contrived that, by the aid of cords and pulleys, the upper one may be pushed forward till it reaches the destined point.

POOR, THE, in political economy, the term employed to designate those persons, or that portion of the population of any county, who, being destitute of wealth, are, through age, bodily or mental infirmity, want of employment, or other cause, unable to support themselves, and have to depend for support on the contributions of others.

PO'PÆ, in Roman antiquity, certain officers of inferior rank who assisted the priests at sacrifices.

POPE, the head of the Roman Catholic church. The appellation of *pope* was anciently given to all Christian bishops; but about the latter end of the eleventh century, in the pontificate of Gregory VII. it was adopted by the bishop of Rome, whose peculiar title it has ever since continued. The spiritual monarchy of Rome sprung up soon after the declension of the Roman empire. The bishops of Rome affect to owe their origin to the appointment of St. Peter, who was considered as transferring the keys of heaven (figuratively consigned to his keeping,) to these bishops as his successors; hence they assumed a supremacy which was admitted by all the Western Christians, but resisted by the Eastern ones, who in Greece, Turkey, and Russia, have a separate Greek church. The vices of the clergy led, however, in the 14th and 15th centuries, to schisms; and a personal quarrel between the pope and Henry VIII. induced the latter to assume the title of the Head of the Anglican church, as well as to recognize the principles of the Reformers, which were adopted by many German princes, and the Northern sovereigns. The pope retains his spiritual ascendancy throughout Italy, France, Austria, Spain, and Portugal; and four fifths of the Irish are Catholics. He is also regarded as a sovereign in certain provinces contiguous to Rome.

POP'ULAR, enjoying the favor of the great body of the people; as, a *popular* ministry. Also, whatever pertains to the common people; as the *popular* voice.—In law, a *popular* action is one which gives a penalty to the person that sues for the same.

POPULA'RES, the name of a party at Rome, who struggled to ingratiate themselves with the people, and, by extending *their* influence and power, to increase their own. The *Populares* were opposed to the *Optimates*.

POPULAR'ITY, the state of possessing the affections and confidence of the people in general. "The man whose ruling principle is duty, is never perplexed with anxious corroding calculations of interest and *popularity*."

POPULA'TION, the aggregate number of people in any country. Owing to the increase of births above that of the deaths, the population is continually increasing in most parts of the habitable world. "Countries," says Adam Smith, in his Wealth of Nations, "are populous, not in proportion to the number of people whom their produce can clothe and lodge, but in proportion to that of those whom it can feed." The law of population, or of the increase of the human species, has not, till a comparatively recent period, attracted that attention to which it is eminently entitled. It was formerly taken for granted that every increase of population was an advantage, and it was usual for legislators to encourage early marriages, and to bestow rewards on those who brought up the greatest number of children. But recent researches have shown that every increase in the numbers of a people, occasioned by artificial expedients, and which is not either accompanied or preceded by a corresponding increase of the means of subsistence, can be productive only of misery or of increased mortality; that the difficulty never is to bring human beings into the world, but to feed, clothe, and educate them when there; that mankind do everywhere increase their numbers, till their farther multiplication is restrained by the difficulty of providing subsistence, and the poverty of some part of the society; and that, consequently, instead of attempting to strengthen the principle of increase, we should rather endeavor to strengthen the principles by which it is controlled and regulated.

PORCH, in architecture, a kind of vestibule supported by columns at the entrance of temples, halls, churches, or other buildings.—By way of distinction, a public portico in Athens, where Zeno the philosopher taught his disciples, was called *the porch*. Hence, *the porch*, in classical literature, is equivalent to the *school of the Stoics*.

PORTCUL'LIS, a strong grating of timber or iron, resembling a harrow, made to slide in vertical grooves in the jambs of the entrance gate of a fortified place, to protect the gate in case of assault. The vertical bars, when of wood, were pointed with iron at the bottom, for the purpose of striking into the ground when the grating was dropped, or of in-

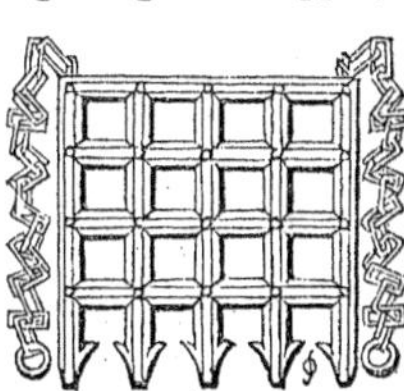

Portcullis.

juring whatever it might fall upon. In general there were a succession of portcullises in the same gateway. It is sometimes called a *portcluse.*

PORTE, THE SUBLIME, the official title of the government of the Ottoman empire: said to be derived from a gate of the palace at Broussa, the original metropolis of that empire, Bâb Humayoor, the sublime gate.

PORT'GREVE, or PORT'REEVE, in former times, a chief magistrate of a port or maritime town. This officer is now styled either mayor or bailiff. According to Camden, the chief magistrate of London was anciently called *portgreve*, but was exchanged by Richard I. for two bailiffs, and these gave place in the reign of John to a mayor.

PORT'HOLES, the openings or embrasures in the sides of ships of war, through which guns are put.

POR'TICO, in architecture, a kind of gallery on the ground, supported by columns, where people may walk under cover. Though this word is derived from *porta*, a gate or door, yet it is used for any arrangement of columns which form a gallery.—The Athenians were curious in their porticoes, and the poets and philosophers recited their works, and held their disputations there. The most famous portico was that called *Pœcile*, which was in fact a picture gallery adorned with the works of the greatest masters.

PORT'LAND VASE, a celebrated cinerary urn or vase, long in possession of the noble family of the Barberini at Rome (whence it was called the Barberini vase;) from whom it came into possession of the Portland family, who deposited it, in 1810, in the British Museum, of which it is one of the most valuable reliques. This beautiful specimen of ancient art was found in the tomb of the Emperor Alexander Severus and his mother Mammæa.

POR'TRAIT, in painting, the representation of an individual, or, more strictly speaking, of a face, painted from real life. Portraits are of full length, half length, &c.; and are executed in oil or water colors, crayons, &c.

PORT ROY'ALISTS, the name popularly given to the members of the celebrated convent of the Port Royal des Champs. It was founded about 1204, by Matthieu de Marli, on the eve of his departure for the Holy Land; and, though originally limited in its means and objects, it gradually acquired such importance as to have secured for it a prominent place in the history of Europe. It would be out of place here to give any details of its varied fortunes, and the religious controversies which it carried on in the 17th century—the period of its greatest importance. It was abolished by Louis XIV., as a nest of Jansenists and heretics. Among the distinguished names connected with Port Royal, are those of Lancelot, Paschal, Arnauld, Nicole de Sacy, and Tillemont. The school books which were published for the use of that institution, were translated into all the languages of Europe, and maintained their reputation long after its abolition.

POSID'IUM, or POSID'EON, in ancient chronology, the seventh month of the Athenian year, which consisted of thirty days, answered to the latter part of December and beginning of January, and had its name from a festival in honor of Neptune Posidonius which was during that month celebrated.

POSI'TION, in painting, the placing of the model in the manner best calculated for the end in view by the artist. Such positions as are most natural and easy, and which exhibit the peculiar habit of the individual, in portrait painting, are preferable.

POS'ITIVE, is used in opposition to *relative* or arbitrary: thus, we say, beauty is no positive thing, but depends on different tastes. It is also used in opposition to *natural:* as, a thing is of *positive* right, meaning that it is founded on a law which depends absolutely on the authority of him who made it.

POS'SE COMITA'TUS, in law, the armed power of the county, or the attendance of all persons charged by the sheriff to assist him in the suppression of riots, &c.

POSSES'SION, in law, the holding or occupying of anything, either *de jure* or *de facto.* Possession *de jure*, is the title a man has to enjoy a thing, though it be usurped and in the actual possession of another; or where lands are descended to a person, and he has not yet entered into them: and possession *de facto*, or actual possession, is where there is an actual and effectual enjoyment of a thing. Long undisturbed possession is presumptive proof of right or property in the possessor.

POST-DATE, to date after the real time; as to *post-date* a bill or a contract, that is, to date it after the true time of drawing the one or making the other.

POST-DILU'VIAN, a person who lived after the flood, or who has lived since that event.

POST-DISSE'IZIN, in law, a writ intended to put in possession a person who has been disseized after a judgment to recover the same lands of the same person, under the statute of Merton.

POS'TEA, in law, is the return of a record of the proceedings in a cause after a trial and verdict by writ of *nisi prius*, into the court of common pleas, after a verdict; and there afterwards recorded.

POS'TERN, in fortification, a small gate, usually in the angle of a flank of a bastion, or in that of the curtain or near the orillon, descending into the ditch.

POS'THUMOUS, born after the death of a father. Also, published after the death of the author; as *posthumous works*.

POS'TIL, a marginal note; originally, a note in the margin of the Bible, so called because written after the text.

POSTLIMIN'IUM, or POSTLIM'INY, among the Romans, was the return of a person to his own country who had gone to sojourn in a foreign country, or who had been banished or taken by an enemy.—In the modern law of nations, the right of *postliminy* is that by virtue of which, persons and things taken by an enemy in war, are restored to their former state, when coming again under the power of the nation to which they belonged. But this cannot extend in all cases to personal effects, on account of the difficulty of ascertaining their identity.

POST'-NOTE, in commerce, a bank note intended to be transmitted to a distant place by the public mail, and made payable to *order;* differing in this from a common bank note, which is payable to the *bearer*.

POST'-OFFICE, an establishment for the reception, conveyance, and delivery of letters, &c. Posts were originally intended to serve merely for the conveyance of public dispatches, and of persons travelling by authority of government. But the great convenience it afforded to individuals, particularly as commercial transactions multiplied and extended, to have a safe, regular, and speedy communication between distant parts of the country, induced the government to convert it into a source of revenue.

POST POSI'TION, in music, retardations of the harmony, effected by placing discords upon the accented parts of a bar not prepared and resolved according to the rules for discords.

POSTSCE'NIUM, in architecture, the back part of the theatre behind the scenes, furnished with conveniences for robing the actors and depositing the machinery.

POST'SCRIPT, an addition made to a letter after it is concluded and signed by the writer. Also, any addition made to a literary performance after it had been supposed to be finished, containing something omitted or something new occurring to the writer.

POS'TULATES, fundamental principles in any art or science, which are too easy and self-evident to need demonstration.

POW'ER, in a philosophical sense, the faculty of doing or performing anything. The exertion of *power* proceeds from the will; and in strictness, no being destitute of will or intelligence can exert power.—*Active power* is that which moves the body; *speculative power* is that by which we see, judge, remember, or, in general, by which we *think*. Power may exist without exertion: we have *power* to speak when we are silent. This word, indeed, has an almost unlimited signification, whether as regards animal strength or mental ability: we speak of the *powers* of genius; the reasoning *powers;* the *power* which a man has of relieving the distressed; his moral *power*, quadrate, &c.—*Power*, in law, the authority which one man gives another to act for him. The instrument or deed by which this is done is called a *power of attorney*.

PRÆCEP'TORIS, in ecclesiastical affairs, certain benefices having their name from being possessed by the more eminent Templars, whom the chief master, by his authority, created and called *Præceptores Templi*.

PRÆCIPE IN CAP'ITE. in law, a writ issuing out of the court of chancery for a tenant who held of the king in chief, as of his crown, and not as of any honor, castle, or manor.

PRÆCOG'NITA, things previously

known in order to understand something else. Thus a knowledge of the structure of the human body is one of the *præcognita* of medical science and skill.

PRÆFEC'TURE, in antiquity, an appellation given to certain towns in Italy, whose inhabitants had the name of Roman citizens, but were neither allowed to enjoy their own laws nor magistrates, being governed by annual prefects sent from Rome. These were generally such places as were suspected, or had some way or other incurred the displeasure of the state.—The title *præfectus* was given to many officers in ancient Rome.

PRÆMUNI'RE, in law, a writ granted against a person for introducing and maintaining the papal power, creating an *imperium in imperio*, and yielding that obedience to the mandates of the pope, which constitutionally belongs to our rightful sovereign.

PRÆNO'MEN, among the Romans, like our Christian name, served to distinguish brothers, &c., from each other: as Caius, Lucius, Marcus, Julius, &c. Care was generally taken, in conferring the *prænomen*, to give that of the father to the oldest, that of the grandfather to the second, and so on. The *prænomen* was not brought into use till long after the *nomen*, or family name.

PRÆ'TOR, a chief magistrate among the Romans, instituted for the administration of justice in the absence of the consuls. The office of *prætor* was instituted in the year of the city 388, to administer justice in the city, instead of the consuls, who were at that time wholly engaged in foreign wars. The institution also was intended to compensate to the nobility the loss of their exclusive right to the consulship, to which honor the commons had now put in their claim, and succeeded. The prætor decreed and proclaimed public feasts, had the power to make and repeal laws, with the approbation of the senate and the people; and kept a register of all the freed-men who were enfranchised at Rome. In the absence of the consuls he had a right to command the armies; he also commanded the *quæstors*, who served him as lieutenants, and were charged with part of the business of his office. He was entitled to the *prætexta*, the curule chair, and two lictors to walk before him in Rome, and six when out of the city.

PRÆTORIA'NI, or *Pretorian Guards*, were the emperor's guards, who in time were increased to ten thousand. The Prætorian bands owe their first institution to Scipio Africanus, who chose for his guards a company of the bravest men in his army; but in time they became very inimical to the liberties of their country.

PRÆTO'RIUM, among the Romans, denoted the hall or court where the prætor administered justice: it was also his palace.

PRAGMAT'IC SANC'TION, in the civil law, is a rescript or answer of the sovereign, delivered by advice of his council to some college, order, or body of people, who consult him in relation to the affairs of their community. A similar answer given to an individual is called simply a rescript.—The term *pragmatic sanction* was given to the settlement made by Charles VI., emperor of Germany, when, having no sons, in 1722 he settled his hereditary dominions on his eldest daughter, the archduchess Maria Theresa.

PRA'TIQUE, in commerce, a license or permission to hold intercourse and trade with the inhabitants of a place, after having performed quarantine, or upon a certificate that the ship did not come from an infected place.

PRAX'EANS, a sect of heretics that sprung up in Asia in the second century; so called from their founder, Praxeas, an Asiatic haeresiarch. The distinguishing characteristics of this sect were their denial of plurality of persons in the godhead, and their belief that it was the Father himself who suffered on the cross. The Monarchici, Sabellians, and Patripassians adopted these sentiments.

PREAD'AMITE, an appellation given to the inhabitants of the earth, who by some are supposed to have lived before Adam.

PRE'AMBLE, in law, the introductory matter to a statute, which contains the reasons for making such an enactment.

PREB'END, the stipend or maintenance a prebendary receives out of the estate of a cathedral or collegiate church. Prebends are *simple* or *dignitary*; a simple prebend has no more than the revenue for its support: but a prebend with dignity, has always a jurisdiction annexed to it.

PREB'ENDARY, an ecclesiastic who enjoys a prebend. The difference between a prebendary and a canon is, that the former receives his prebend in consideration of his officiating in the church; but the latter merely in consequence of his being received into the cathedral.

PRECE'DENCE, by custom and courtesy, the right of taking place before another, which is determined by authority, and followed exactly on all public occasions of processions and the like.

PRE'CEDENT, in law, a judicial decision, which serves as a rule for future determinations in similar or analogous cases: thus the precedents of a court have the force of laws, and no court will reverse a judgment contrary to many precedents.—*Precedent* also frequently denotes an original authentic instrument or writing, which serves as a form to draw others by.

PRECEN'TOR, the chanter or master of the choir in a cathedral.

PRE'CEPT, in law, a command in writing sent by a justice of the peace, &c., for bringing a person, record, or other matter before him.—In a general sense, a *precept* signifies any commandment or order intended as an authoritative rule of action: but applied particularly to commands respecting moral conduct. Hence *preceptor*, a teacher.

PREDESTINA'TION, in theology, a term to denote the pre-ordination of men by the Supreme Being to everlasting happiness or misery. One who believes in this doctrine is called a *predestinarian.*

PREDIC'AMENT, in logic, a category. The school philosophers distribute all the objects of our thoughts and ideas into genera or classes, which the Greeks call *categories*, and the Latin *predicaments.*

PRED'ICATE, in logic, that part of a proposition which affirms or denies something of the subject: thus, in these propositions, "snow is white, ink is not white," whiteness is the *predicate* affirmed of snow, and denied of ink.

PRE-EMP'TION, the right of purchasing before others. Prior discovery of land inhabited by uncivilized tribes is held to give the discoverer the *pre-emption*, or right of purchase before others.

PRE-EXIST'ENCE, in philosophy, the existence of anything before another; commonly used for the existence of the human soul, in some former condition, before it became connected with its present body. It was the doctrine of the Pythagorean school, and connected with their peculiar tenet of the Metempsychosis. It was also the doctrine of Plato; and he uses in support of it arguments which have exercised a strong influence on many minds, and to this day are constantly recurring to those who study the subject on independent principles; particularly the rapidity of learning in early childhood, which he explains as an effort of reminiscence, not acquisition. Others have enlisted into the service those peculiar sensations which are sometimes raised by scenes, persons, sounds, words, though seen or heard, as our reasons would persuade us, for the first time, as if we were conscious of some prior familiarity with men. This poetical, rather than philosophical view of the subject, is beautifully illustrated in a well-known ode of Wordsworth.

PREF'ACE, the observations prefixed to a work or treatise, intended to inform the reader of its plan and peculiarities. There are few subjects which afford so wide a field for the display of skill and address as preface writing; and those who wish to witness an unrivalled exhibition of these qualities may consult some of Dr. Johnson's prefaces, either to his own writings or to the numerous works which he edited.

PRE'FECT, an important political functionary in modern France. Under the old régime, the officers who were sent round to the provinces to superintend the details of administration on behalf of the king were at first styled *maitres des requêtes.* These were made permanent local officers in the reign of Henry II., and afterwards attained many additional powers, with the title of intendants. These were abolished at the revolution, when various attempts were made to establish elective local governments. By a law of the year 1800 prefects were first appointed for the departments, with powers similar in many respects to those of the old intendants, with a council of prefecture, and a general council of the department; which, however, fell into disuse. With slight variations, the prefects retain the same jurisdiction. They are, in some respects, analogous to our sheriffs: but with far greater powers. They possess not the nominal only, but the actual direction of the police establishment, within their respective depart ments, together with extensive powers of municipal regulation; the arrondissements or districts into which the departments are subdivided are under sous-préfets appointed by them. Their power, however, is considerably controlled by that of the council of the prefecture, which acts in some measure as a court of appeal from the prefect, taking cognizance of various cases within the sphere of his administrative interference, if legal disputes arise upon it.

PRE'JUDICE, decision neither founded upon nor consistent with reason, and the error of ignorance, weakness, or idleness. It is the enemy of all truth, knowledge, and improvement; and is the blindness of the mind, rendering its powers useless and mischievous. Innumerable are the prejudices we imbibe in our youth; we are accustomed to believe without reflection, and to receive opinions from others without examining the grounds by which they can be supported.

PRE'LATE, an ecclesiastic raised to some eminent dignity in the church; as a bishop, an archbishop, or a patriarch. The office or dignity of a prelate is called a *prelacy*.

PRELIM'INARY, in general, denotes something to be examined and determined before an affair can be treated of to the purpose. The *preliminaries of peace* consist chiefly in settling the powers of ambassadors, and certain points in dispute, which must be determined previous to the treaty itself.

PRE'LUDE, a short flight of music; the preface or introduction to a movement, and usually consisting of a few bars of harmony in the same key as the movement which it precedes; being, in fact, a preparation to the ear for what is to follow.—Something introductory, or that shows what is to follow; something preceding which bears some relation or resemblance to that which is to follow.

PREM'ISES, in logic, the two first propositions of a syllogism, from which the inference or conclusion is drawn. Also, propositions antecedently proposed or proved.—*Premises*, in law, lands, tenements, &c. before mentioned in a lease or deed.

PRE'MIUM, properly, a reward or recompense; but it is chiefly used in a mercantile sense for the sum of money given to an insurer, whether of ships, houses, lives, &c. Also the recompense or prize offered for a specific recovery, or for success in an enterprise. It is sometimes synonymous with *interest;* but generally it is a sum per cent.; distinct from the interest, as, the bank lends money to government at a *premium* of 2 per cent.

PREMON'STRANTS, a religious order of regular canons or monks of Prémontré, in the isle of France; instituted in 1120.

PREPENSE', in law, premeditation and forethought as applied to bad actions; whence the term *malice prepense*.

PREROG'ATIVE, an exclusive or peculiar privilege.—The *royal prerogative* is that special pre-eminence which a sovereign has not only over other persons, but over the ordinary course of the common law, in right of the legal dignity. Among these are the right of appointing ambassadors, and of making peace and war.—It is the *prerogative* of a father to govern his children. And the right of governing created beings is the *prerogative* of the Great Creator.

PRES'BYTER, in the primitive Christian church, an elder; one who had authority in the church, and whose duty was to watch over the flock. The word is borrowed from the Greek translation of the Old Testament, where it usually signifies a ruler or governor; it being a title of office and dignity, not of age, and in this sense bishops are sometimes called presbyters in the New Testament.

PYESBYTE'RIANS, a sect of Protestants, so called from their maintaining that the government of the church appointed in the New Testament was by *presbyteries;* that is, by ministers and ruling elders, associated for its government and discipline. The presbyterians stand opposed to the *episcopalians*, the latter preferring the hierarchy of bishops; and to *congregationalists* or *independents*, who hold every *pastor* to be as a bishop or overseer of his own congregation, *independent* of any person or body of men.

PRES'BYTERY, is that form of ecclesiastical polity according to which there is no gradation of order in the church, but which vests church government in a society of clerical and lay presbyters, or, in common phraseology, ministers and lay elders, all possessed officially of equal rank and power.

PRESCRIP'TION, in law, a right and title to a thing grounded upon a continued possession of it beyond the memory of man.—*Prescription* differs from a *custom*, which is a local usage. Prescription is a *personal* usage annexed to the person.

PRES'ENCE OF MIND, that calm, collected state of the mind and faculties, which enables a person to speak or act without disorder or embarrassment in unexpected difficulties.

PRESENTA'TION, in ecclesiastical law, the act of a patron offering his clerk to the bishop, to be instituted in a benefice of his gift. An advowson is the right of presentation. A patron may revoke his presentation before institution, but not afterwards.

PRESENT'MENT, in law, a declaration or report made by jurors or others of any offence to be inquired of in the court to which it is presented.

PRES'ENTS, in the *plural*, is used in law, for a deed of conveyance, a lease, or other written instrument; as in the phrase, "Know all men by these *presents;*" that is, by the writing itself, *per presentes*.

PRES'IDENT, an officer appointed to preside over a corporation, company, or assembly of men, to keep order, manage their concerns, or govern their proceedings. Also an officer appointed or elected to govern a province or territory, or to administer the government of a nation. The supreme executive officer of the United States of America is styled president. The qualifications required of a person raised to this dignity are, to be a natural-born citizen of the age of thirty-five years, and to have resided fourteen years within the States. The election is by electoral colleges in every state. These colleges contain, in each state, a number of electors equal to all the senators and representatives of that state in congress; but their appointment varies in different states, and at different times; sometimes it is made by their respective legislatures, sometimes by general election throughout the state, sometimes part of the electors are chosen by district and part by general election. The colleges in each state vote by ballot for a president (and at the same time for a vice-president); and the votes of all the electors, taken in this manner, are counted by the president of the senate: when, if any person have an absolute majority of votes, he is duly elected; if not, the election is made by the house of representatives between the three persons having the highest number; in which case the votes are taken by states, and a majority of all the states is necessary to constitute a choice.

PRESS, is metaphorically applied either to the whole literature of a country, or to that part of it more immediately connected with newspapers, or other periodical publications.

PREST'-MONEY, called *earnest-money*, the sum given to a soldier at the time he enlists, so called because it binds the receiver to be ready for service at all times appointed.

PRESUMP'TIVE EV'IDENCE, in law, is that which is derived from circumstances which necessarily or usually attend a fact, as distinct from direct evidence or positive proof.

PRETEN'SION, a holding out the appearance of right or possession of a thing, with a view to make others believe what is not real, or what, if true, is not yet known or admitted. There are ill-founded pretensions and well-founded pretensions: for instance, a man may make *pretensions*, to rights which he cannot maintain, or to skill which he does not possess; and he may make *pretensions* to acquirements which he really possesses, but is not known to possess.

PRETERI'TION, in rhetoric, a figure by which, in pretending to pass over anything, we make a summary mention of it; as, "I will not say the prince is noble, or that he is as learned as he is accomplished," &c. The most artful praises are those bestowed by way of *preterition*.

PRETERNAT'URAL, an epithet for those events in the physical world which are deemed extraordinary, but not miraculous; in distinction from events which are *supernatural*, which cannot be produced by physical laws or powers, and must therefore be produced by the direct intervention of Omnipotence.

PREVARICA'TION, a deviation from the plain path of truth and fair dealing; a shuffling or quibbling to evade the truth or the disclosure of truth.—In the civil law, the collusion of an informer with the defendant, for the purpose of making a sham prosecution.—In common law, a seeming to undertake a thing falsely or deceitfully, for the purpose of defeating or destroying it.

PREVENT'IVE SERVICE, an appellation for the duty performed by the armed police officers engaged to watch the coasts, for the purpose of preventing smuggling and other illegal acts. The men thus employed are also sometimes termed the *coast blockade force*.

PRIA'PUS, a divinity introduced into Grecian mythology after the time of Alexander. He was the god of fruitfulness, and by the Romans was looked on particularly as the guardian of gardens, in which indecent and rudely sculptured wooden statues of him were usually set up.

PRICE CUR'RENT, in commerce, a published list or enumeration of the various articles of merchandise, with their prices, the duties (if any) payable thereon when imported or exported, with the drawbacks occasionally allowed upon their exportation.

PRIEST, according to the modern acceptation of the word, is a person who is set apart or consecrated to the ministry of the Gospel. In its most general sense the word includes all orders of the clergy duly licensed according to the forms and rules of each respective denomination of Christians: but Protestants are accustomed to apply the word more especially to clergymen of the Roman Catholic persuasion.—In primitive ages, the fathers of families, princes, and kings were priests. In the days of Moses the office of priest was restricted to the tribe of Levi, and the priesthood consisted of three orders, the high-priest, the priests, and the Levites; and the office was made hereditary in the family of Aaron.—Among pagans, priests were persons whose appropriate business was to offer sacrifices and perform other sacred rites of religion.

PRI'MACY, the chief ecclesiastical station or dignity. The archbishop of Canterbury is *primate* of all England.

PRIM'ITIVE COLORS, these are said to be restricted to three—namely, red, yellow and blue, from the mixtures and combinations of which all other colors, tints, and gradations are produced.

PRIMOGEN'ITURE, in law, the right of the first-born. This right is an unjust prerogative, and contrary to the natural right; for since it is birth alone gives children a title to the paternal succession, the chance of primogeniture should not throw any inequality among them. It was not till the race of Hugh Capet, that the prerogative of succession to the crown was appropriated to the first-born. By the ancient custom of gavel-kind, still preserved in Kent, primogeniture is disregarded, the paternal estate being equally shared among the sons.

PRINCE, a general title for all sovereigns or persons exercising the functions of government in an independent manner, even though they are permitted so to do by the will of another.

PRIN'CIPAL, in commerce, is the capital of a sum due or lent, so called in opposition to *interest*. It also denotes the first fund put by partners into a common stock, by which it is distinguished from the calls or accessions afterwards required.—In law, the absolute perpetrator of a crime is called a *principal* in the first degree; a *principal* in the second degree, is one who is present, aiding and abetting; distinguished from an *accessary*.—In architecture, a main timber in an assemblage of carpentry. Thus, in a roof, the strong rafters used for trussing the beams are called principal rafters.—In the Fine Arts, the chief circumstance in a work of art, to which the rest are to be subordinate.

PRIN'CIPLE, in a general sense, the origin, source, or primordial substance of anything.—In science, a truth admitted either without proof, or considered as having been before proved.—In ethics, that which is believed, and serves as a rule of action or the basis of a system; as the *principles* of morality; the *principles* of the Stoics, &c.

PRIN'CIPLES, in the Fine Arts, those general and fundamental truths from which the rules and maxims of art are deduced. To each art particular principles are attached on which its theory is founded. These principles, before they can be said to have stability, must be found to depend on certain truths, which, recognized by every one, and indisputable, oblige the mind to concur in the deductions that result from them. Before a law in any art is laid down, it is necessary to trace it to the principles from which it springs, though there may be causes which prevent those principles being universally admitted; such as ignorance, prejudice, love of novelty, and the like.

PRI'OR, the superior of a convent of monks, or one next in dignity to an abbot.

PRISCIL'LIANISTS, in church history, a Christian sect, so called from their leader Priscillian, a Spaniard by birth, and bishop of Avila. He is said to have practised magic, and to have maintained the principal errors of the Manichees; but his peculiar tenet was, that it is lawful to make false oaths in the support of one's cause and interest.

PRIVATEER', a ship or vessel of war owned and equipped by private persons at their own expense, and who are permitted by the government to seize or plunder the vessels of an enemy in war. The owners of privateers must give bond not to break the stipulations of treaties subsisting with their government, and not to misuse their captives. If a ship be fitted out and act as a privateer without being licensed or commissioned by government, it is a pirate. That the severest restrictions should be enforced on privateering is manifestly for the interest of individuals, to whatever belligerent power they belong. The wish to amass plunder is the only principle by which they are actuated; and such being the case, it would be idle to suppose that they should be very scrupulous about abstaining from excesses.

PRIV'ILEGE, in law, some peculiar benefit granted to certain persons or places, contrary to the usual course of the law, or beyond the common advantages of other citizens. Thus the nobles of Great Britain have the *privilege* of being tried by their peers only; and members of parliament have the *privilege* of exemption from arrests in certain cases.

PRIV'ITY, in law, is a peculiar mutual relation which subsists between individuals connected in various ways; so that, besides those who are actually parties to a transaction, others connected with these parties are said to be privy to the transaction, and are bound by its consequences. Several sorts of privity are enumerated by writers on law; but those of most ordinary occurrence are three: privity of blood, of estate, and of contract. The former subsists between an ancestor and his heir; the second between lessor and lessee, tenant for life and reversioner created by the same instrument; and privity of contracts between those who are parties to a contract, which species of privity is personal only.

PRIV'Y-COUN'CIL, in British polity, an executive body, with whose assistance the crown issues proclamations, which, if not contrary to law, are binding on the subject. Anciently, the *privy council* was a high court of justice; but in modern times it seldom or never interferes with judicial matters, confining itself to the executive branch of government. A privy-council is summoned on a warning of forty-four hours, and never held without the presence of a secretary of state. In debates, the lowest delivers his opinion first; the sovereign, if present, last; and though the privy-councillors thus give their opinions, it is that of the sovereign alone which is decisive.—*Privy-seal*, a seal affixed by the queen, or by the lord keeper of the privy-seal, to instruments that afterwards pass the great seal. The word *privy-seal*, is also used elliptically for the person intrusted with the privy-seal; as, "the qeeen's sign-manual is the warrant to the *privy-seal*, who makes out a writ or warrant thereon to the chancery."

PRIZE, anything captured by a belligerent using the right of war: in common language, only ships thus captured, with the property taken in them, are so called. Prizes taken in war are condemned by the proper judicature in the courts of the captors; such condemnation is held to divest the title of the proprietor and confer a new ownership. In order to give jurisdiction to a court of prize, it is deemed necessary, by the law of nations, that the property captured, should be in possession of the captors in their own ports, those of an ally, or of a neutral; but no belligerent power has a right to capture in the ports of a neutral country, or within a marine league of her shores; nor does a capture made then render the adjudication valid. Subject to capture are hostile property, that is, the property of persons domiciled in a hostile country, and neutral property, contraband of war.

PRO and CON, i. e. *pro* and *contra*, for and against, a phrase frequently occurring in common parlance.

PROBABIL'ITY, that state of a question which falls short of moral certainty, but inclines the mind to receive it as the truth. Demonstration produces certain knowledge; proof produces belief, and *probability* opinion.—If the chance that a thing may happen is less than the chance that it may not happen, it is said to be probable; and the numbers which express these variable chances, when ascertained, constitute what is termed the *science of probabilities.* As applied to human life, founded on tables of mortality, it serves as the foundation of societies which, for certain annual premiums, varied according to age, undertake to pay certain sums to the heirs of the party, whose life is thereby insured for that sum.

PRO'BATE, in law, the proof of the genuineness and validity of a will, or the exhibition of the will to the proper officer, and such other proceedings as the law prescribes, as preliminary to the execution of it by the executor.

PROB'LEM, in logic, a proposition that appears neither absolutely true nor false, and consequently may be asserted either in the affirmative or negative.—In a general sense, a *problem* may be defined, any question involving doubt or uncertainty, and requiring some operation or further evidence for its solution.

PRO'CESS, in law, the whole course of proceedings in any cause, real or personal, civil or criminal, from the original writ to the end of the suit. In a more limited sense, process denotes that by which a man is first called into any temporal court.—*Original process* is the means taken to compel the defendant to appear in court.—*Mesne process* is that which issues, pending the suit, upon some collateral or interlocutory matter.—*Final process* is the process of execution.

PROCE'S VERBAL, in the language of French jurisprudence, an authentic written minute or report of an official act or proceeding, or statement of facts. The term is also used to signify minutes drawn up by a secretary or other officer of the proceedings of an assembly.

PRO'CHRONISM, an error in chronology, when events are dated anterior to the time at which they happened.

PROCLAMA'TION, a public notice or declaration of anything in the name of the supreme magistrate. Proclamation is used for a solemn declaration of war and peace, and in monarchies for the act of notifying the accession of a prince to the throne; also for the public declaration used at the calling of a court; and for various other objects.

PRO CONFES'SO, in law, a term applied to a defendant in chancery who appears and is afterwards in contempt for not answering; wherefore the matter contained in the bill shall be taken *pro confesso*, that is, as though it had been confessed.

PROCON'SUL, a Roman magistrate sent to govern a province with consular authority. The proconsuls were appointed from the body of the senate, and their authority expired at the end of a year from their appointment. Before the proconsul quitted Rome, he went up to the Capitol, offered sacrifice, put on the robe of war called *paludamentum*, and then departed from the city in pomp, preceded by lictors, with rods and axes, and attended by his friends to some distance from Rome. His equipage, consisting of pavilions, horses, mules, clerks, secretaries, &c. was called his *viaticum*, and provided at the public expense.

PROCRUS'TES, in mythology, a famous robber of ancient Greece, who tortured his victims by placing them on an iron bed, which their stature was made to fit by stretching or mutilating them so as to suit its dimensions; whence the well-known metaphorical expression, the *bed of Procrustes*. He was killed by Theseus near Hermione.

PROC'TOR, a person employed to manage another's cause in a court of civil or ecclesiastical law, as in the court of admiralty, or in a spiritual court.—Also the magistrate or superintendent of a university.

PROCURA'TION, in law, a composition paid by an incumbent to the bishop or archdeacon, to commute for the entertainment which was to have been given him at his visitation. Also, the instrument by which a person is empowered to transact the affairs of another.

PROCURATO'RES, under the Roman emperors, were officers sent into the provinces to regulate the public revenue, receive it, and dispose of it as the emperor directed. Such an officer was Pontius Pilate in Judea; but as the Jews were looked upon as a rebellious people, besides his authority over the revenue, he was invested with all the power of a pro-consul, even a power of life and death.—*Procuratores*, in the Roman courts of judicature, were properly such lawyers as assisted the plaintiff in proving, or the defendant in clearing himself from the matter of fact alleged. They are often confounded with the *advocates*.

PROD'IGY, in ordinary modern language, signifies a surprising though natural event; in contradistinction to *miracle*, which is something out of the course of nature. Among the Romans, however, any extraordinary event or appearance to which, from insufficient acquaintance with natural history, they could not assign a cause, was termed a *prodigy*, and regarded as a supernatural event, indicative of favorable or (more generally) of unfavorable dispositions of their gods. Hence the number of recorded prodigies, many evidently false, some real but misunderstood, which Livy has inserted in his annals.

PRO'DUCE, in an enlarged sense, is what any country yields from labor, and national growth, which may serve either for the use of the inhabitants, or be exported to foreign countries. In a more limited sense, we speak of the *produce* of a farm, of a mine, of a tax, &c.; but when we allude to a work either of nature or art, we use the word *production*.

PRO'EM, preface; introduction; preliminary observations to a book or writing.

PROFES'SION, a word which, when applied to a person's vocation or employment, designates an occupation not merely mechanical. We say, the learned *professions;* the *profession* of a clergyman, a lawyer, a physician, a surgeon, a lecturer, or a teacher. In like manner, we use the word *professional* when speaking of literary and scientific studies, pursuits, or duties.

PROFES'SOR, in its original sense, signifies one who makes open declaration of his sentiments or opinions, particularly one who makes a public avowal of his belief in the Christian doctrine and revelation.—In its more modern and common acceptation, a *professor* is one that publicly teaches any science or branch of learning; as a professor of natural history, of mathematics, of theology, &c. In a university, some professors are denominated from the arts they profess, others from the founders of the professorships, or those who assigned a revenue for the support of the professors.

PRO'FILE, in general, the view of an object from one of its chief sides, at which more or less of the other side is hidden from the eye.—*Profile*, in sculpture and painting, a head, portrait, &c., represented sideways, or in a side view. On almost all medals, faces are represented in profile.—*Profile*, in architecture, denotes the outline of a figure, building, or member, also the draught of a building, representing it as if cut down perpendicularly from the roof to the foundation.

PROF'IT, in political economy, means the advantage or gain resulting to the owner of capital from its employment in industrious undertakings. It is the premium, as it were, on accumulation. Were there no profit there would be little or no motive to save and amass; and all the vast advantages that society derives from the formation and employment of capital would be unknown. But without taking into account the security and consequence conferred on the possessors of capital or wealth, and looking only at its tangible results, profit consists of that part of the produce raised by the agency of capital employed in industrious undertakings that remains in the hands of those by whom it is employed after replacing the capital itself, or such portions of it as may have been wasted in the business, and every expense necessarily incurred in superintending its employment. The *rate* of profit is the proportion which the amount of profit derived from an undertaking bears to the capital employed in it.

PROF'IT AND LOSS, in commerce, the gain or loss arising from goods bought and sold; the former of which, in bookkeeping, is placed on the creditor's side: the latter on the debtor's side.—*Net profit* is the gain made by selling goods at a price beyond what they cost the seller, and beyond all costs and charges.—Among the many wise precepts which appear in the pages of the "Rambler," there are few more worthy to be borne in mind than this: "Let no man anticipate uncertain profits."

PRO'GRAMME, a detailed account or advertisement of some public performance. In a university, a billet or advertisement to invite persons to an oration.—In antiquity, an edict posted in some public place.

PRO'HEDRI, certain Athenian officers chosen to superintend the proceedings in the two legislative assemblies; so called because they had the privilege of sitting in the front seats.

PROHIBI'TION, in law, a writ to forbid any court from proceeding in a cause then depending, on suggestion that the cause of it does not properly belong to that court.

PROJEC'TURE, in architecture, the jutting or leaning outwards of the mouldings and other members of architecture beyond the face of a wall, column, &c.

PROLEGO'MENA, in literature, preliminary or introductory observations or dissertations prefixed to any work. The famous dissertation prefixed by D'Alembert to the *Encyclopédie*, and the dissertations prefixed by Dugald Stewart, Playfair, Leslie, and Mackintosh to the last edition of the *Encyclopædia Britannica*, are among the best specimens of prolegomena.

PROLEP'SIS, a figure in rhetoric, by which the speaker anticipates or prevents objections, by alluding to or answering them himself.

PRO'LOGUE, in dramatic poetry, an address to the audience previous to the commencement of the play, delivered by one of the performers. It may either be in prose or verse, but is generally in the latter; and it usually consists of apologetic remarks on the merits of the piece about to be represented. Sometimes it relates to the situation in which the author or actors stand to the public, and sometimes it contains allusions to subjects incidental to neither.

PROLU'SION, in literature, a term formerly applied to certain pieces or compositions made previously to others, by way of prelude or exercise.

PROME'THEUS, according to the most ordinary form of his legend in Greek mythology, one of the Titans, who was exposed to the wrath of Jupiter on account of his having taught mortals the arts, and especially the use of fire; which he was said to have stolen from heaven, concealed in a pipe. According to another story, Prometheus was actually the creator of men; and in the *Protagoras* of Plato he is made not to have created, but to have inspired them with thought and sense. His punishment was to be chained to a rock on Caucasus, where a vulture perpetually gnawed his liver; from which he was finally rescued by Hercules. This legend has formed the subject of the grandest of all the poetical illustrations of Greek supernatural belief, the *Prometheus Bound* of Æschylus. Many have recognized in the indomitable resolution of this suffering Titan, and his stern endurance of the evils inflicted on him by a power with which he had vainly warred for supremacy, the prototype of the arch-fiend of Milton. Others have sought for a recondite analogy, and discovered in the tortures endured by Prometheus as a sacrifice for mankind, whom he had benefited, a foreshadowing of the great mystery of Christianity.

PROM'ISSORY NOTE, a writing or note of hand, promising the payment of a certain sum at a certain time, in consideration of value received by the promiser.

PROOF, in law and logic, that degree of evidence which convinces the mind of the certainty of truth or fact, and produces belief. *Proof* differs from *demonstration*, being derived from personal knowledge or conclusive reasoning; whereas the term demonstration is applicable only to those truths of which the contrary is inconceivable.—*In printing*, an impression on which the errors and mistakes are marked for the purpose of being corrected. Proofs are—first proof, which is the impression taken with all the errors of workmanship. After it is read by the copy, and the errors corrected, which if not many, and carefully done, another impression is printed with more care, to send to the author; this is termed a clean proof. On it he makes his corrections and alterations: when those are altered in the types, another proof is printed, and read over carefully, previously to the whole number being printed off; this is called the press proof.

PROPAGAN'DA, during the French revolution, was a term applied to secret societies whose object was the propagation of democratical principles; and it has since become to signify any kind of institution for making proselytes for political objects.—The name was originally given to those institutions which were erected by the papal court, for the extension of its own power and the Catholic religion among those who were not within its pale. It was called the *congregatio de propaganda fide*, (society for propagating the faith,) and was founded by Gregory XV. in 1622.

PROP'ERTY, a particular virtue or quality which nature has bestowed on some things exclusive of all others: thus color is a *property* of light; extension, figure, divisibility, and impenetrability, are properties of bodies, &c.—*Property*, in law, is defined to be the highest right a person has, or can have, to anything. At this day property in lands, &c., is acquired either by entry, descent, law, or conveyance; and in goods and chattels property may be gained various ways, as by gift, inheritance, or purchase. The labor of inventing, making, or producing anything, constitutes one of the highest and indefeasible titles to *property*. That also is a person's *property* to which he has a legal title, whether in his possession or not.—Much has of late been said respecting the right of an author to his literary productions, as a species of absolute *property*; and why the productions of manual labor should rank higher in the scale of rights than the productions of the intellect—or why the former should be held without limitation, and the latter be limited to a term of years—will require better arguments to substantiate than have yet been advanced.

PRO'PHET, in general, one who foretels future events; but when we speak of *the prophets*, we mean those inspired persons among the Jews who were commissioned by God to declare his will and purposes to that people. Among the canonical books of the Old Testament, we have the writings of sixteen prophets, four of which are denominated the "greater prophets," viz. Isaiah, Jeremiah, Ezekiel, and Daniel; so called from the length or extent of their writings, which exceed those of the others, viz. Hosea, Joel, Amos, Obadiah, Jonas, Micah, Nahum, Habakkuk, Haggai, Zachariah, and Malachi, who are called the lesser "prophets." The deep sense and religious fire of these men, so far before their age, present a phenomenon that can be explained only by the special action of divine influences. They appear, therefore, as messengers of God, divinely inspired seers; and their preachings and songs were preserved by the Hebrews as the word of God, and among them were rendered more impressive by their connection with poetry and music. Their constant object was the preservation of the doctrines of revelation in their purity: and the richness, originality, and sublimity of their writings still awaken the admiration of those who deny them the character of prophecies.—The *prophecies* in general are supposed to have had a double sense, and a double completion; one sense referred to, which had its accomplishment about the time when the prophets wrote; the other sense had a relation to distant times and events, to which it applies in a somewhat allegorical manner.

PROPITIA'TION, in theology, an atonement or sacrifice offered to God to assuage his wrath, and render him propitious. Among the Jews there were both ordinary and public sacrifices, as holocausts, &c., offered by way of thanksgiving; and extraordinary ones, offered by particular persons guilty of any crime, by way of *propitiation*. It was also a feast among the Jews, celebrated on the 10th of the month Tisri, in commemoration of the divine pardon proclaimed to their forefathers through Moses, who, as God's agent, remitted the punishment due to the crime of their worshipping the golden calf. The Romish church believe the mass to be a sacrifice of propitiation for the living and the dead. The reformed churches allow of no propitiation but that one offered by Jesus Christ on the cross.

PROPI'TIATORY, or MERCY-SEAT, the cover or lid of the ark or covenant, lined within and without with plates of gold. This is said to have been a type of Christ.

PROPOR'TION, in the Fine Arts, the most proper relation of the measure of parts to each other and to the whole. The Greeks used the word to express this idea. In many instances, proportion may be considered almost synonymous with fitness, though there is a distinction between them; since every form susceptible of proportion may be considered either with respect to its whole as connected with the end designed, or with respect to the relation of the several parts to the end. In the first case, fitness is the thing considered; in the second, proportion. Fitness, therefore, expresses the general relation of means to an end, and proportion the proper relation of parts to an end. It is hence needless to dwell on the intimate connection that exists between beauty and proportion, in all complex forms.

PROPOSI'TION, in logic, is defined "a sentence indicative;" *i. e.*, a sentence which affirms or denies. Thus, sentences in the form of command or question are excluded from the character of propositions. Logical propositions are said to be divided, first, according to substance, into categorical and hypothetical; secondly, according to quality, into affirmative and negative; thirdly, according to quantity, into universal and particular. 1. A categorical proposition is where the sentence affirms or denies absolutely, as "man is mortal." A hypothetical proposition is defined to be two or more categoricals united by a conjunction, as "if Caius is man, he is mortal." There are several sorts of hypothetical propositions; conditional, disjunctive, casual, &c. 2. An affirmative proposition is one whose copula (or conjunction) is affirmative, as "man is mortal;" a negative proposition has a negative copula, as "man is not immortal." 3. An universal proposition is when the predicate is said of the whole of the subject, as "all men are mortal," "Caius is mortal;" a particular when it is said of part of the subject only, as "some men are rich." To these two species may be added the indefinite proposition, when the subject has no sign of universality or particularity, or is a singular noun, which is either universal or particular according to the matter.

PROPRE'FECT, among the Romans, the prefect's lieutenant, or an officer whom the prætorium commissioned to do any part of his duty.

PROPRÆ'TOR, a Roman magistrate, who, having discharged the office of prætor at home, was sent into a province to command there with his former pretorial authority.

PROPY'LÆUM, in ancient architecture, the vestibule of a house. The vestibules or porticoes of Athens, leading to the Acropolis were thus denominated.

PRO RA'TA, in commerce, a term sometimes used by merchants for *in proportion;* as each person must reap the profit or sustain the loss *pro rata* to his interest, that is, in proportion to his stock.

PRO RE NA'TA, according to exigencies or circumstances.

PROROGA'TION, a term used at the conclusion of a session of parliament, denoting its continuance from one session to another; as an *adjournment* is a continuation of the session from day to day.

PROSCE'NIUM, in the Grecian and Roman theatres, was the stage or place before the scene, where the *pulpitum* stood, into which the actors came from behind the scenes to perform.

PROSCRIP'TION, a punishment in use among the Romans, which had some analogy to our outlawry. The names of the *proscripti*, or persons suffering under proscription, were posted up in tablets at the forum, to the end that they might be brought to justice, a reward being proposed to those who took them, and a punishment to those who concealed them. Under the triumvirate many of the best Roman citizens fell by proscription.

PROSE, in literature, all language not in verse. Prose diction, to be good, or even admissible, in ordinary criticism, must be conformable to the rules of composition as to style, cadence, &c.

PROSECU'TION, in law, the institution and carrying on a suit in a court of law or equity; or the process of exhibiting formal charges against an offender before a legal tribunal, and pursuing them to final judgment.—The person who institutes and carries on a criminal suit is called the *prosecutor*.

PROS'ELYTE, a new convert to some religion, system or party. Thus a pagan converted to Christianity is a *proselyte*; and, although the word primarily refers to converts to some religious creed, we speak familiarly of *proselytes* to the theories of Lavoisier, Black, &c.

PRO'SERPINE, the Latin form of Persephone, the name of a Grecian goddess, sprung from Jupiter and Ceres. She was stolen from her mother by Pluto, who, enamored of her beauty, carried her off from the plains of Enna in Sicily, while sporting with her companions, to the infernal regions, where she became his queen. The wanderings of Ceres in search of her daughter were much celebrated by the ancient poets. When she at last discovered the place of her concealment, a compromise was entered into, by which Proserpine was allowed to spend two thirds of the year with her parents and the rest with Pluto in his empire.

PROS'ODY, the science which treats of quantity, accent, and the laws of harmony, both in metrical and prose composition. In the Greek and Latin languages every syllable had its determinate value or quantity, and verses were constructed by systems of recurring feet, each foot containing a definite number of syllables possessing a certain quantity and arrangement. The versification of modern European languages, in general, is constructed simply by accent and number of syllables. They have, therefore, no prosody strictly so called. The Germans, however, have labored to subject their language to the ancient metrical system, but with indifferent success.

PROSONOMA'SIA, a figure in rhetoric, wherein allusion is made to the likeness of a sound in several names or words: a kind of pun.

PROSOPOG'RAPHY, in rhetoric, a word used by some critical writers to signify the description of animated objects. Of this figure the portraits of the horse and the leviathan in the book of Job are well-known and beautiful examples.

PROSOPOLEP'SY, a premature opinion or prejudice against a person, formed by a view of his external appearance.

PROSOPOPE'IA, a figure in rhetoric by which things are represented as persons, or by which things inanimate are spoken of as animated beings, or by which an absent person is introduced as speaking, or a deceased person is represented as alive and present. It includes *personification*, but is more extensive in its signification.

PROSPEC'TUS, the outline or plan of a literary work, containing the general subject or design, with the necessary particulars as to the mode of publication. The word *prospectus* has recently been adopted in announcing many undertakings and schemes which are not purely literary.

PRO'STYLE, in architecture, a range of columns in the front of a temple.

PRO'TASIS, in grammar and rhetoric, every properly constructed period is said to be naturally divisible into two parts; of which the first is termed protasis, the second apodosis. In the ancient drama, the protasis was the exposition, usually contained in the first part of the piece, either by way of soliloquy or dialogue, serving to make known the characters and the plot to the audience.

PRO'TEST, a formal and solemn declaration of opinion, given in writing, commonly against some act; as, the formal and recorded dissent of a minority against the majority of any public body.—*Protest*, in commerce, a formal declaration made by a notary-public, at the request of the holder of a bill of exchange, for non-acceptance or non-payment of the same, protesting against the drawer and others concerned, for the exchange, charges, damages, and interest. This *protest* is written on a copy of the bill, and notice given to the indorser of the same, by which he becomes liable to pay the amount with charges and interest: also, a similar declaration against the drawer of a note of hand for non-payment to a banking firm, &c.—There is also another kind of *protest*, viz. a writing attested by a justice of the peace or consul, drawn by the master of a vessel, stating the severity of the voyage by which the ship has suffered, and showing that the damage was not occasioned by his misconduct or neglect.

PROT'ESTANT, in church history, a name first given in Germany to those who adhered to the doctrine of Luther: because, in 1529, they protested against a decree of the emperor Charles V. and the diet of Spires, declaring that they appealed to a general council. This name was afterwards extended to the Calvinists, and is now become common to all who belong to the reformed churches.

PROTESTA'TION, in law, a declaration in pleading, by which the party interposes an oblique allegation or denial of some fact, *protesting* that it does or does not exist.

PRO'TOCOL, in the French language, signifies the formulæ or technical words of legal instruments; in Germany, it has been used to denote the minutes or rough draught of an instrument or a transaction. It is in the latter sense that the word has been borrowed by diplomacy, in which it signifies the original copy of any dispatch, treaty, or other document.

PRO'TOMARTYR, a term applied to Stephen, the first Christian martyr; and used also for the first sufferer in any cause, religious or political.

PRO'TOPOPE, the imperial confessor, an officer of the holy directing synod, the supreme spiritual court of the Greek church in Russia.

PRO'TOTYPE, an original or model after which anything is formed.

PROV'ERB, a familiar saying, which has been variously defined. In point of form, there are two species of proverbs; one containing a maxim directly expressed in a concise and familiar style; the other, in which a maxim is expressed metaphorically, *e.g.* "honesty is the best policy," or, rather, allegorically, *e. g.* "strike, while the iron is hot." In point of substance, proverbs are for the most part rules of moral, or, still more properly, of prudential conduct. In dramatic literature, chiefly French, the term has been applied to short pieces, in which some proverb or popular saying is taken as the foundation of the plot. They originated in the fondness of the higher class of France for private theatricals, which became a sort of passion about the middle of the last century. Carmantelli was the most successful writer of proverbs at the time of their highest popularity. Those of M. Theodore Leclercq, at the present time, have met with considerable success.—*Proverbs, the, of Solomon*, one of the canonical books of the Old Testament. According to the arrangement in its present shape, the first nine books form a species of introduction; those from the tenth to the twenty-fourth contain the proverbs of Solomon, properly so called; and the remainder furnishes a kind of appendix; including the thirtieth and thirty-first, which contain the proverbs of Agur, the son of Jakeh, and of king Lemuel.

PROV'IDENCE, in theology, the care and superintendence which God exercises over his creatures. A belief in divine providence is founded on this rational principle, that the same power which caused a thing to exist is necessary to continue its existence.

PROV'INCE, among the Romans, a country of considerable extent, which, being reduced under their dominion, was new modelled according to the pleasure of the conquerors, subjected to the command of annual governors sent from Rome, and obliged to pay such taxes and contributions as the senate thought fit to demand. These provinces had the appellations of *consular* or *prætorian*, according as they were governed by consuls or prætors.—Among the moderns, a country belonging to a kingdom or state, either by conquest or colonization, usually situated at a distance from the kingdom or state, but more or less dependent on and subject to it.

PROVIN'CIALISM, a mode of speech peculiar to a province or district of country remote from the principal country or from the metropolis.

PROVIS'IONAL, provided for present need or for a temporary occasion; as, a *provisional* government, a *provisional* treaty, &c.

PROVI'SO, in law, an article or clause in any statute, agreement, contract, &c., by which a conditional stipulation is introduced.

PROVI'SOR, the title in the ancient French universities, of an officer charged with the management of their external affairs, both spiritual and temporal, and to a certain extent with their discipline also. The provisor of the Sorbonne was an officer of high importance among the clergy. The principals of Napoleon's Lyceum had the title of provisors, and the modern royal colleges retain it for the same functionary.

PROV'OST, in a general sense, a person who is appointed to preside over or superintend; as, the *provost* of a college. —The *provost-marshal* of an army, is an officer appointed to arrest and secure deserters and other criminals, to hinder the soldiers from pillaging, to regulate weights and measures, &c. There is a similar officer in the English navy, who has the charge of the prisoners taken at sea.

PROXI'MATE CAUSE, that which immediately precedes and produces the effect, as distinguished from the *remote* or *predisposing* cause.

PROX'Y, the agency of another who acts as a substitute for his principal.—In England, any member of the house of lords may cause another peer to vote for him as his *proxy* in his absence.

PRYTANE'UM, in Grecian antiquity, the senate-house in Athens, where the council of the *prytanes* assembled, and where those who had rendered any signal service to the commonwealth were maintained at the public expense.—*Prytaneum* was also a name given to all places sacred to Vesta. Hence those widows called *prytanides*, who took care of the sacred fire, received their name.

PSALM, a divine song or hymn; but chiefly appropriated to the hundred and fifty *Psalms of David*, a canonical book of the Old Testament. Most of these psalms have a particular title, signifying either the name of the author, the person who was to set it to music or sing it, the instrument that was to be used, or the subject and occasion of it. Some have imagined that David was the sole author of the Book of Psalms; but the titles of many of them prove the contrary. Some of the psalms were apparently written by Solomon; a few belong to the reigns of the kings immediately succeeding him; and several to the mournful days of the Babylonish captivity and of the return, especially those headed "for the sons of Korah," most of which are probably by the same author. Finally, a few seem to belong to the age of the Maccabees. The "Psalms of David," whether actually composed by him, or merely of his time, probably constituted an earlier collection, which extended to the seventy-second. But, by whomsoever penned, they are among the highest and sublimest efforts of poetry; and the holy light of revelation, the inspiring belief in the eternal true God, spreads over them a bright splendor, and fills them with a deep and holy fervor.

PSAL'TERY, a musical instrument used by the Hebrews, the true form of which is not now known. That which is now used is a flat triangular instrument, truncated at the top, and strung with thirteen chords of wire.

PSEUDEPIG'RAPHY, the ascription of false names of authors to works. This was carried to a great extent among the Christians of the fourth and following centuries.

PSEU'DO, a prefix (from the Greek) used in the composition of many words to denote *false*, or *spurious*; as, a *pseudo*-apostle, or false apostle; a *pseudo*-prophet, or false prophet, &c.

PSY'CHE, in mythology, the daughter of Sol and Constancy. She was so loved as to be taken for Venus herself. This goddess becoming jealous of her rival charms, ordered Cupid to inspire her with love for some contemptible wretch. But Cupid fell in love with her himself. Many were the trials Psyche underwent, arising partly from her own indiscretion, and partly from the hatred of Venus, with whom, however, a reconciliation was ultimately effected. Psyche, by Jupiter's command, became immortal, and was forever united with her beloved.

PSYCHOL'OGY, in its larger acceptation, may be taken as synonymous with mental philosophy. The word is more frequently used in reference to the lower faculties of the mind, and the classification of the phenomena which they present. All psychology is built on experience, either immediate, or revived by the memory and imagination. But, in reflecting on our intellectual faculties, we discover in them certain laws, which, as soon as they are presented to us, we at once recognize as universal and necessary; certain conditions without the fulfilment of which we are sensible that no act of intellection could have taken place. This universality is something very different from the empirical truth, as a matter of fact, which we attribute to the laws of association, which are, indeed, universal, but which might, for aught we can see, have been different from what they are. Corresponding to this distinction, German writers have discriminated between a higher, or rational, and a lower, or empirical psychology; the first, that of Kant, who sought, in all our mental faculties, to determine that only which is necessary and immutable; the second, that of Hartley, who treats all our intellectual acts as alike objects of mere history, dependent for their validity only on the fact that they do really recur in such and such order. The psychology of Aristotle was of the latter description. He, consequently, regarded the science as forming one of the physical sciences, or those which are conversant with the contingent and changeable. Many pregnant psychological truths are discoverable in that philosopher's work on the soul; in particular, the doctrine of association, the master-light of all sound experimental psychology, owes its first enunciation to him. Among later writers who have made valuable contributions to the science may be enumerated Hobbes, Locke, Hartley, and Sir Thomas Brown. The value of these authors' writings in this peculiar province cannot be too highly appreciated. It is only when psychology intrudes upon the domain, or usurps the attributes of the higher philosophy, that its claims need to be resisted. As a preparation for metaphysical and theological thought, and, indeed, as an indispensable requisite for the science of man, whether history, politics, or ethics, it is not easy to exaggerate its importance.

PUB'LICAN, among the Romans, a farmer of the taxes and public revenues, the inferior officers of which class were deemed oppressive; they were consequently regarded by the Jews and other tributary nations with no small degree of detestation. Under the modern term of *publicans* are comprised inn-keepers, hotel-keepers, alehouse-keepers, keepers of wine vaults, &c.

PUB'LICIST, a writer on the laws of nations.

PUCK, in mediæval mythology, the "merry wanderer of the night," whose character and attributes are so beautifully depicted in the *Midsummer Night's Dream*. This celebrated fairy is known by a variety of names; as *Robin Goodfellow* and *Friar Rush* in England; and in Germany, as *Knecht Ruprecht;* but it is by his designation of Puck, that he is most generally known both in England, Germany, and the more northern nations. He was the chief of the domestic tribe of fairies, or *brownies*, as they are called in Scotland; and innumerable stories are told of his nocturnal exploits, among which, drawing the wine, and cleaning the kitchen while the family were asleep, are the most prominent. The word is probably derived from the old Scandinavian pûki, *a boy;* it is also synonymous with pug, or monkey, whose form this fairy is said to have most frequently assumed.

PUL'PIT, an elevated place or inclosed stage in a church, in which the preacher stands. It is called also a *desk*. Pulpits in modern churches are of wood, but in ancient times some were made of stone, others of marble, and richly carved.

PUN, a species of wit which has been gravely pronounced "low;" but surely it is both fastidious and cynical thus to define it. A *pun* is an expression in which two different applications of a word present an odd or ludicrous idea; but it does not necessarily follow that the ideas to which it gives rise shall be *low*, that is, *vulgar*. That they often are so, we admit; but he must be of an incorrigibly saturnine disposition who would declare that all the mirth-inspiring puns which the inimitable Hood draws from his exhaustless quiver are to be accounted *low*. An inveterate punster, who is constantly on the watch for opportunities to torture every expression into a quibble, is not to be tolerated in decent society; but it would be hard indeed if the laws of decorum were so strict, as to debar us from cheering the dull realities of life with an occasional scintillation of wit, even at the hazard of perpetrating a *bad* pun.

PUNCTUA'TION, in grammar, the discriminating use of certain marks adopted to distinguish the clauses of a period, sometimes with reference to the sense, and at others to the grammatical construction. Thus, a full point (.) closes a perfect sentence; a colon (:) indicates an adjunct; a semicolon (;) distinguishes its principal part; and a comma (,) parts subordinate to the semicolon. A sentence, which may include several periods, terminates a branch of the subject or argument. A question is indicated by (?); an exclamation by (!); and it is sometimes convenient to include a collateral circumstance in a parenthesis ( ).—The ancients were altogether unacquainted with *punctuation*.

PU'NIC, pertaining to the Carthaginians or their language.—Also, a term implying treacherous, deceitful; as *punic* faith.

PUN'ISHMENT, the infliction of pain, or personal suffering according to law, for crimes; intended as an example, to deter others and to correct the offender. The punishment of crimes against the laws is inflicted by the supreme power of the state in virtue of the right of government vested in the legislature, and belongs only to persons clothed with authority. Some punishments consist of exile or transportation, others in loss of liberty by imprisonment. Locke observes, "The rewards and punishments of another life, which the Almightly has established as the enforcements of his law, are of weight enough to determine the choice against whatever pleasure or pain this life can show."

PURGA'TION, the act or operation of clearing one's self of a crime; a mode of trying persons accused of any crime, which was formerly in practice.

PUR'GATORY, a place appointed for the satisfaction of temporal punishments, which, according to the Roman Catholic church, are distinguished from the eternal, of which the latter only are remitted to us by the death of Christ. There is none, perhaps, of the peculiar articles of the Romish faith in favor of which so little can be advanced from the language of Scripture; and it may be safely averred that it was not from that source that the opinion ever gained possession of men's minds. It seems to be a natural but too strict an inference from the imperfectly disclosed economy of the divine judgments, which we find to admit of every degree of severity in this life, and are liable to conclude from analogy must be subject to some equivalent adjustment in the next. Accordingly, we discover some imperfect recognitions of the idea in individual writers several centuries before it can be proved that it formed an established article of faith. Augustin is considered the earliest of these; and he speaks vaguely and inconsistently. It was first inculcated as a doctrine by Gregory the Great, who seems to have connected it with the then popular belief that the world was closely approaching to its end.

PURIFICA'TION, in religion, the act or operation of cleansing ceremonially, by removing any pollution or defilement. Purification by washing was common to the Hebrews and to Pagans; and the Mohammedans always use it previous to devotion.

PU'RIM, among the Jews, the feasts of lots, instituted to commemorate their deliverance from the machinations of Haman.

PU'RIST, a name sometimes applied to rigorous critics of purity in literary style.

PU'RITAN, the name by which the dissenters from the church of England were generally known in the reign of Elizabeth, and the first two Stuarts. The name *Puritan* was given (probably in derision) to them on account of the superior purity of doctrine or discipline which the more rigid reformers claimed as their own; maintaining that they followed the word of God alone in opposition to all human inventions and superstitions, of which they believed the English church to retain a considerable share, notwithstanding its alleged reformation. Hume gives this name to three parties: the *political puritans*, who maintained the highest principles of civil liberty; the *puritans in discipline*, who were averse to the ceremonies and government of the episcopal church; and the *doctrinal puritans*, who rigidly defended the speculative system of the first reformers.

PUR'LIN, in architecture, a piece of timber extending from end to end of a building or roof, across and under the rafters, to support them in the middle.

PUR'SER, in the navy, an officer on board a man-of-war, who takes charge of the provisions, and attends to their preservation and distribution among the officers and crew.

PUR'SUIVANT, in heraldry, the lowest order of officers at arms. The pursuivants are properly attendants on the heralds when they marshal public ceremonies.

PU'SEYISM, in the church of England, the name given to certain new doctrines promulgated of late years by Dr. Pusey, in conjunction with other divines of Oxford, in a series of pamphlets, entitled "Tracts for the Times." These doctrines have manifestly a strong tendency towards Romanism, and accordingly many of their advocates have already gone over to the church of Rome; they relate chiefly to the exclusive claim of episcopacy to the apostolical succession; the denial of the validity of ordination or of the administration of the sacraments by all who cannot prove their claim to unbroken apostolical descent in the episcopal line; the alleged virtue of such ordination in conferring efficacy on the sacraments in the simple *opus operatum*, or rite administered; the exclusive authority of the church, as based on tradition; the introduction into the church of England of many of the observances of Romanism; the doctrine of Reserve, (*see* Tract, No. 90,) and such kindred matters, believed by protestants to be contrary to Scripture, and identical with the doctrines of the church of Rome; leading to the same interference between the human conscience and the direct authority of the word of God.

PYC'NOSTYLE, in ancient architecture, a building where the columns stand very close to each other; only one diameter and a half of the column being allowed to each intercolumniation.

PYR'AMID, a solid body standing on a triangular square, or polygonal base, and terminating in a vertex or point at the top. Or, in other words, it is formed by the meeting of three or more planes at a point termed the apex.—The *Pyramids of Egypt* are noble monuments of Egyptian grandeur, about forty in number, near Memphis. The largest is 481 feet in height, measured perpendicularly, and the area of its base includes eleven acres. The object of this kind of monument was, undoubtedly, either to perpetuate the recollection of some memorable event, or to stand as a testimony of the glory and splendor of deceased monarchs. That it was principally sepulchral has been rendered tolerably evident. Among other reasons, because it was held, from its shape, symbolical of immortality.

PYR'OMANCY, among the classical ancients, a species of divination by means of the fire of the sacrifice; in which, if the flames immediately took hold of and consumed the victims, or if they were bright and pure, or if the sparks rose upward in a pyramidal form, success was said to be indicated. If the contrary took place, misfortunes were said to be presaged.

PYR'RHIC DANCE, called by the Romans Pyrrhica Saltatio, a species of war-like dance, said to have been invented by Pyrrhus to grace the funeral of his father Achilles, though this point is involved in obscurity. This dance consisted chiefly in such an adroit and nimble turning of the body as represented an attempt to avoid the strokes of an enemy in battle, and the motions necessary to perform it were looked upon as a kind of training for the field of battle. This dance is supposed to be described by Homer as engraved on the shield of Achilles. Lord Byron describes the Suliotes as still performing this dance.

PYRR'HONISTS, a sect of ancient philosophers, so called from Pyrrho, a native of Elis, in Peloponnesus. The opinions of these philosophers, who were also called *skeptics*, terminated in the incomprehensibility of all things, in which they found reason both for affirming and denying; they accordingly seemed to be always in search of truth, without ever acknowledging that they had found it: hence the art of disputing upon all things, without ever going further than suspending our judgments, is called *pyrrhonism*.

PYTHAGO'REANS, a sect of ancient philosophers, so called from being the followers of Pythagoras of Samos, who lived in the reign of Tarquin, the last king of Rome. The doctrine of *metempsychosis*, or the transmigration of souls through different orders of animal existence, is the main feature by which the Pythagorean philosophy is popularly known. It is, however, by no means certain that the genuine Pythagoreans held this doctrine in a literal sense. It may have been only a mythical way of communicating their belief in the individuality and *post mortem* duration of the soul.

PYTH'IA, or PYTH'ONESS, in antiquity, the priestess of Apollo, who delivered oracular answers at Delphi, in Greece.

PYTH'IAN GAMES, one of the four great national festivals of Greece, celebrated every fifth year in honor of Apollo, near Delphi. Their institution is variously referred to Amphictyon, son of Deucalion, founder of the council of Amphictyons, and Diomed, son of Tydeus; but the most common legend is, that they were founded by Apollo himself, after he had overcome the dragon Python. The contests were the same as those at Olympia, and the victors were rewarded with apples and garlands of laurel.

Q.

Q, the seventeenth letter of the English alphabet, is not to be found either in the Greek, old Latin, or Saxon alphabets; is never sounded alone, but in conjunction with *u*, and never ends any English word. For *qu* in English, the Dutch use *kw*, the Germans *qu*, and the Swedes and the Danes *qv*. It appears, in short, that *q* is precisely *k*, with this difference in use, that *q* is always followed by *u* in English, and *k* is not. As a numeral Q stands for 500, and with a dash over, it stands for 500,000. Q is used as an abbreviation for *question;* it also stands for quantity, or *quantum*, as *q. pl. quantum placit*, as much as you please; and *q. s. quantum sufficit*, *i. e.* as much as is necessary. Among mathematicians, Q. E. D. stands for *quod erat demonstrandum*, that is, which was to be demonstrated; and Q. E. F. *quod erat faciendum*, which was to be done.

QUACK'ERY, the boastful pretensions of an empiric or ignorant quack.

QUADRAGES'IMA, lent; so called because it consists of forty days.

QUAD'RANGLE, in architecture, any

range of houses or buildings with four sides in the form of a square.

QUADRI'GA, in antiquity, a car or chariot drawn by four horses. On the reverses of medals, we frequently see the emperor or Victory in a quadriga, holding the reins of the horses; whence these coins are, among numismatologists, called *nummi quadrigati* and *victoriati*.

QUADRIREME', a species of the *naves longæ* used by the Romans and also by the Greeks, being a galley with four benches or banks of rowers.

QUAD'ROON, the name given in South America to the offspring of a mulatto woman by a white man.

QUÆ'RE, a term expressive of doubt, and calling for further information.

QUÆS'TIO, in logic, the third proposition in a syllogism, which contains the question to be proved.

QUÆS'TOR, an officer among the Romans who had the management of the public revenue or treasury. The *quæstorship* was the first office any person could fill in the commonwealth.

QUA'KERS, or FRIENDS, a religious sect which made its first appearance in England during the protectorate of Cromwell. Their founder was George Fox, a native of Drayton, in Leicestershire. He proposed but few articles of faith, insisting chiefly on moral virtue, mutual charity, the love of God, and a deep attention to the inward motions and secret operations of the spirit. He required a plain simple worship, and a religion without ceremonies, making it a principal point to wait in profound silence the directions of the Holy Spirit. Although at first the Quakers were guilty of some extravagancies, these wore off, and they settled into a regular body, professing a great austerity of behavior, a singular probity and uprightness in their dealings, a great frugality at their tables, and a remarkable plainness and simplicity in their dress. Their system, or tenets, are laid down by Robert Barclay (one of their members,) in a sensible, well-written "apology," addressed to Charles II. Their principal doctrines are,—that God has given to all men, without exception, supernatural light, which being obeyed can save them; and that this light is Christ, the true light, which lighteth every man that cometh into the world:—that the Scriptures were indeed given by inspiration, and are preferable to all the other writings in the world; but that they are no more than secondary rules of faith and practice, in subordination to the light or spirit of God, which is the primary rule:—that immediate revelation has not ceased, a measure of the spirit being given to every one:—that all superstitions and ceremonies in religion, of mere human institution, ought to be laid aside:—that in civil society, the saluting one another by pulling off the hat, bending the body, or other humiliating posture, should be abolished; and that the use of the singular pronoun *thou* when addressing one person, instead of the customary *you*, should be strictly adhered to. They further laid it down as a solemn obligation, not to take an oath, encourage war, engage in private contests, nor even carry weapons of defence.—The society is governed by its own code of discipline, which is enacted and supported by meetings of four degrees, for discipline; namely, preparative, monthly, quarterly, and yearly meetings. The preparative digest and prepare the business for the monthly meetings, in which the executive power is principally lodged, subject however to the revision and control of the quarterly meetings, which are subordinate and accountable to it, and subject to its supervision and direction. Its authority is paramount, and it possesses the sole power to make or amend the discipline. There are at present ten yearly meetings, namely, London, Dublin, New England, New-York, Philadelphia, Baltimore, Virginia, North Carolina, Ohio, and Indiana. The number of Quakers in the United States is about 150,000.

QUALIFICA'TION, any natural endowment, or any acquirement which fits a person for a place, office, or employment.—Also any property or possession which gives one a right to exercise the elective franchise, or furnishes one with any legal power or capacity.

QUAL'ITY, in the philosophy of Kant, the *second* category, (there being four in all,) comprising the notions of existence or reality, non-existence or negation, and limitation.

QUAN'TITY, in prosody, the amount of time in a syllable. Syllables are either short or long; the former being the unit or smallest measure of time, the latter consisting of two times. This distinction is clearly marked in the ancient languages, in which some syllables are necessarily long or short by position, others by the nature of the vowels which they contain; and, in the Latin language, some common, or susceptible of being sounded as long or short, according to certain rules of elegance or convenience.

All the metrical system of the ancient languages is founded on quantity. In most modern languages there is, strictly speaking, no quantity, as distinct from emphasis or accent; the long syllables being those which receive the arsis, the short those which receive the thesis. In the German language, however, critics have endeavored to establish a conventional system of quantity, and thus to adapt that language to regular versification in the ancient Greek and Latin metres.

QUAN'TUM, [Lat.] the quantity.—*Quantum, meruit* (as much as he deserved,) in law, an action grounded on a promise that the defendant would pay to the plaintiff for his service as much as he should deserve.—*Quantum valebat*, an action to recover of the defendant for goods sold, as much as they were worth.

QUAR'ANTINE, the restraint of intercourse to which a ship arriving in port is subjected, on the presumption that she may be infected with a malignant, contagious disease. This is either for forty days, or for any other limited term, according to circumstances. A ship thus situated is said to be *performing quarantine*. The term is derived from the Italian *quaranta*, forty; it being generally supposed that if no infectious disease breaks out within forty days, or six weeks, no danger need be apprehended from the free admission of the individuals under quarantine. During this period all the goods, clothes, &c. that might be supposed capable of retaining the infection, are subjected to a process of purification, which is a most important part of the quarantine system.—In law, the period of forty days, during which the widow of a man dying possessed of land, has the privilege of remaining in the principal messuage or mansion house.

QUARTER-DAYS, the days which begin the four quarters of the year, namely, the 25th of March, or Lady Day; the 24th of June, or Midsummer Day; the 29th of September, or Michaelmas Day; and the 25th of December, or Christmas Day.

QUAR'TER-SES'SIONS, a court of justice, held quarterly, before magistrates of the district to try minor offences by jury, after bills found by a grand jury. The legal powers of these are often very great, but the questions may in many cases be removed to superior courts.

QUARTET'TO, in music, Italian for a piece for four voices or four instruments.

QUAR'TO, in printing and bookbinding, a size made by twice folding a sheet, which then makes four leaves.

QUASH'ING, in law, the overthrowing and annulling of anything: as, to *quash* an indictment.

QUA'SI CON'TRACT, in the civil law, an act which has not the strict form of a contract, but yet has the force of one. Thus, if one person does another's business in his absence, without his procuration, and it has succeeded to the other person's advantage; the one may have an action for what he has disbursed, and the other to make him give an account of his administration; which amounts to a *quasi contract*.

QUATRAIN', in poetry, a piece consisting of four verses, the rhymes usually alternate; sometimes also, especially in French poetry, intermixed, the first and fourth, second and third, rhyming together.

QUA'VER, in music, a measure of time equal to half a crotchet, or an eighth of a semibreve. Also a shake or rapid vibration of the voice.

QUEEN, a woman who holds a crown singly; or, by courtesy, one who is married to a king. The former is distinguished by the title of *queen regnant*; the latter by that of *queen consort*. A queen consort is a subject, though as the wife of the king she enjoys certain prerogatives. The widow of a king is called a *queen dowager*.

QUES'TION, the application of torture to prisoners under criminal accusation, according to the laws of France before the Revolution. The question was of two kinds: one, where strong evidence, but insufficient of itself to justify a condemnation to death, existed against a prisoner on a capital charge; he might then be subjected to torture to produce confession. This was termed the question préparatoire. It was abolished by an ordinance of Louis XVI. in 1780. The other, termed question préalable or définitive, was applied to the prisoner when convicted of a capital offence, in order to make him discover supposed accomplices. It was abolished by the National Assembly.

QUEST'-MEN, in law, persons chosen to inquire into abuses and misdemeanors, especially such as relate to weights and measures.

QUES'TUS, in law, land which does not descend by hereditary right, but is acquired by one's own labor and industry.

QUID PRO QUO, in law, an equivalent, or the mutual consideration and reciprocal performance of both parties to a contract.

QUID'NUNC, one who is curious to know everything that passes, and is continually asking "What now?" or "What news?" one who knows or pretends to know all occurrences; a news gossiper.

QUI'ETISTS, in ecclesiastical history, a sect of mystics, originated by Molino, a Spanish priest, who maintained that religion consists in the internal rest and meditation of the mind, wholly employed in contemplating God and submitting to his will. This doctrine was termed *quietism*. Its leading feature was the description of the happiness of a soul reposing in perfect *quiet* on God, so as to become conscious of His presence only, and untroubled by external things. He even advanced so far as to maintain that the soul, in its highest state of perfection, is removed even beyond the contemplation of God himself, and is solely occupied in the passive reception of divine influences.

QUINDECEM'VIRI, in Roman antiquity, a college of fifteen magistrates, whose business it was to preside over the sacrifices. They were also the interpreters of the Sibyl's books; which, however, they never consulted but by an express order of the senate.

QUINQUAGENA'RIUS, in Roman antiquity, an officer who had the command of fifty men.

QUINQUAGES'IMA, or Shrove Sunday, so called as being about the fiftieth day before Easter.

QUINQUA'TRIA, in Roman antiquity, festivals celebrated in honor of Minerva with much the same ceremonies as the Panathenæa were at Athens.

QUINQUENNA'LIA, in antiquity, Roman games that were celebrated every five years.

QUIN'QUIREME, in antiquity, a galley having five seats or rows of oars.

QUINTI'LIS, in chronology, the month of July, so called because it was the fifth month of Romulus's year, which began in March. It received the name of July from Marc Antony, in honor of Julius Cæsar, who reformed the calendar.

QUIRINA'LIA, in antiquity, a feast celebrated among the Romans in honor of Romulus, who was called *Quirinus*. These feasts were held on the 13th of the calends of March.

QUIRI'TES, in antiquity, a name given to the populace of Rome, as distinguished from the soldiery.

QUI-TAM, in law, a term for an action brought, or information exhibited, at the suit of the king, on a penal statute wherein half the penalty is directed to fall to the suer or informer.

QUIT-RENT, in law, a small rent payable by the tenants of most manors, whereby they go quit and free from all other services.

QUI VIVE, (French,) literally, "*who lives?*" The challenge of the French sentries to those who approach their posts; equivalent to the English "Who goes there?" Hence, *to be on the qui vive*, is to be on the alert; to be all activity.

QUIZ, an obscure question; something to puzzle.—One whom an observer cannot make out; an odd fellow. The more general use of the word, however, is to signify one addicted to mockery and jesting in simulated gravity; and also the act itself. This word and its derivatives are used only in colloquial or vulgar language. It is said to have originated in a joke. Daly, the manager of a Dublin play-house, wagered that he would make a word of no meaning to be the common talk and puzzle of the city in twenty-four hours; in the course of that time the letters *q*, *u*, *i*, *z* were chalked or pasted on all the walls of Dublin, with such an effect that the wager was won.

QUOAD HOC, a term used frequently in law reports to signify that "as to the thing named," the law is so, &c.

QUOD'LIBET, (Lat. *what you please*,) in the language of the schoolmen, questions on general subjects within the range of their inquiries were termed *questiones quodlibeticæ*, or miscellaneous. In French the word quodlibet, or quolibet, is retained, in the sense of a slight jeu d'esprit, pun, &c. What is termed in music a "pot-pourri" was also called in Germany a *quodlibet*.

QUOD PERMIT'TAT, in law, a writ for the heir of him that is disseized of common pasture, against the heirs of the disseizor.

QUO JU'RE, in law, a writ that lies for a person who has lands wherein another claims common of pasture time out of mind; and is brought in order to compel the person to show by what title he challenges it.

QUO'RUM, in law, a word frequently mentioned in our statutes, and in commissions both of justices of the peace and others. By it is generally understood, such a number of justices as are competent by law to transact business. The term is derived from the words of the commission, *quorum* A. B. *unum esse volumus*.

QUOTA'TION, a passage quoted or cited; the part of a book or writing named, repeated, or adduced as evidence or illustration. — In mercantile language, the current price of commodities or stocks, published in prices-current, &c.

QUO WARRAN'TO, in law, the name of a writ which lies against any particular persons, or bodies politic or corporate, who usurp or make an improper use of any franchise or liberty, in order to oblige them to show by what right and title they hold or claim such franchise.

R.

R, the eighteenth letter of our alphabet, is numbered among the liquids and semi-vowels, and is sometimes called the *canine* letter. Its sound is formed by a guttural extrusion of the breath, which in some words is through the mouth, with a sort of quivering motion or slight jar of the tongue. In words which we have received from the Greek language we follow the Latins, who wrote *h* after *r*, as the representative of the aspirated sound with which this letter was pronounced by the Greeks; as in *rhapsody*, *rhetoric*, &c.; otherwise it is always followed by a vowel at the beginning of words and syllables. As an abbreviation, R in English, stands for *rex* and *regina;* as George R.; Victoria R. In the notes of the ancients, R. or RO. stands for *Roma;* R.C. *Romana civitas;* R.G.C. *rei gerendæ causa;* R.F. E.D. *recte factum et dictum;* RG.F. *regis filius;* R.P. *respublica*, or *Romani principes*. As a numeral, R, in Latin authors, stands for 80, and with a dash over it, for 80,000.

RAB'BI, or RAB'BIN, a title assumed by the pharisees and doctors of the law among the Jews, which literally signifies master or lord. There were several gradations before they arrived at the dignity of a rabbin; but it does not appear that there was any fixed age or previous examination necessary; when, however, a man had distinguished himself by his skill in the written and oral law, and passed through the subordinate degrees, he was saluted a rabbin by the public voice. In their schools the rabbins sat upon raised chairs, and their scholars at their feet: thus St. Paul is said to have studied at the feet of Gamaliel. Such of the doctors as studied the letter or text of the scripture were called *caraites*, those who studied the cabballa, *cabbalists*, and those whose study was in the traditions or oral law, were called *rabbinists*. The customary duty of the *rabbins*, in general, was to pray, preach, and interpret the law in the synagogues. Among the modern Jews, the learned men retain no other title than that of *rabbi;* they have great respect paid them, have the first places or seats in their synagogues, determine all matters of controversy, and frequently pronounce upon civil affairs.

RAB'DOMANCY, in antiquity, a sort of divination by means of rods, according to their manner of falling when they were set up.

RA'CA, a Syriac word signifying empty, foolish, beggarly; a term of extreme contempt. The Jews used to pronounce the word with certain gestures of indignation, as spitting, turning away the head, &c. Our Saviour intimates that whosoever should call his neighbor *raca*, should be condemned by the council of the Sanhedrim.

RACE, the lineage of a family, or the series of descendants indefinitely continued. All mankind are called the *race* of Adam; the Israelites are of the *race* of Abraham; and in like manner, we say, the Capetine or the Carlovingian *race* of kings, &c.

RACK, a horrid engine of torture, furnished with pulleys and cords, &c., for extorting confession from criminals or suspected persons. Its use is entirely unknown in free countries.

RACO'VIANS, in ecclesiastical history, the Unitarians of Poland are sometimes so called; from Racow, a small city of that country, where Jacobus a Sienna, its head, erected a public seminary for their church in 1600. Here the "Racovian Catechism," originally composed by Socinus, and revised by his most eminent followers, was published.

RA'DIX, in etymology, a primitive word from which spring other words.

RAF'TERS, the pieces of timber extending from the plate of a building so as to meet in an angle at the top, and form the roof.

RAIL, in architecture, the horizontal part in any piece of framing or panelling. Thus, in a door, the horizontal pieces between which the panels lie, are called *rails*, whilst the vertical pieces between which the panels are inserted are called *styles*.

RA'JAH, one of the ancient hereditary princes of India, before its conquest by the Moguls; some of whom are tributary to Europeans, and some are said to be independent.

RALLENTAN'DO, in music, an Italian term, implying that the tune of the passage over which it is placed is to be gradually decreased.

RAM'ADAN, the name given to the great fast or Lent of the Mohammedans. It commences with the new moon of the ninth month of the Mohammedan year; and, while it continues, the day is spent uninterruptedly in prayers and other devotional exercises. Even the night is passed by the more rigid of the faithful in the mosques, which are splendidly illuminated on this occasion; but, generally speaking, the arrival of sunset is the signal for a more than usually unlimited indulgence in the pleasures of the table; and, on the third evening of the fast, the grand vizier commences a series of official banquets. The Ramadan ends on the day preceding the only other great festival of the Mohammedans—the *Bairum* equivalent to our Easter.

RAMAYA'NA, the oldest of the two great Sanscrit epic poems, describes the life and actions of the hero Rama, and his wife Sita; and especially Rama's expedition to Ceylon, to rescue Sita from the tyrant Rawana. The poem is thought to have been composed before the Christian era; but there is no certain indication of its age.

RA'MISTS, in philosophy, the partisans of Pierre Ramé, better known by his Latin name of Ramus, royal professor of rhetoric and philosophy at Paris, in the reign of Henry II. He perished in the massacre of St. Bartholomew. His system of logic was opposed to that of the Aristotelian party; and during the latter half of the 16th century a vehement contest was maintained between their respective adherents in France, Germany, and other parts of Europe.

RAM'PART, in fortification, an elevation or mound of earth round a place, capable of resisting the cannon of an enemy; and formed into bastions, curtains, &c. Soldiers continually keep guard upon the ramparts, and pieces of artillery are planted there for the defence of the place. —*Rampart*, in civil architecture, is used for the space left between the wall of a city and the nearest houses.

RAN'GER, in England, an officer whose duty it was to walk through the forest, and present all trespassers at the next forest court. The office of ranger is not of the same importance as formerly, but the situation is still filled, and his duties are of a similar kind.

RANK, the degree of elevation which one man holds in respect to another. This is particularly defined in regard to the nobility in monarchical countries, as also in all offices of state, as well as in the officers of the army and navy.—*Rank*, in military tactics, the straight line which the soldiers of a battalion or squadron make as they stand side by side.—*Rank and file*, a name given to the men carrying firelocks, and standing in the ranks, in which are included the corporals.

RAN'SOM, money paid for redeeming a captive, or for obtaining the liberty of a prisoner of war.

RAN'TERS, a sect of dissenters, originating in Staffordshire, England, in 1807, and marked by the extravagance of their religious enthusiasm. They sprang from the Wesleyan Methodists, from whom they separated, and by whom they are disowned. They hold camp meetings annually, and differ from the parent stock in many of their outward ceremonies, but they still assimilate to the original connection in their religious opinions.

RANZ DE VACHE, in music, a favorite national air among the Swiss shepherds, which they play upon their bagpipes while tending their flocks and herds. It consists of a few simple intervals, is entirely adapted to the primitive life of these people and their instrument (the *Alpenhorn*, horn of the Alps,) and has an uncommon effect in the echoes of the mountains. This effect becoming intimately associated with the locality of Switzerland, explains the many anecdotes of the home-sickness caused by the sound of the *Ranz des Vaches*, when heard by the Swiss in foreign countries.

RASKOL'NIKS, the name of the largest and most important body of dissenters from the Greek Church in the Russian dominions. They designate themselves Starowerzi, or *the Orthodox;* but differ from the Greek church only in the outward forms of religion, and in maintaining a more strict ecclesiastical discipline. This body was formerly subjected to persecution; but it is now treated with comparative toleration, though its members are still excluded from the service of the state. Their number is said to be about 300,000.

RATE, in English law, an assessment by the pound for public purposes; as, for the poor, the highways, church repairs, county expenses, &c. In the navy, the order or class of a ship, according to its magnitude or force.

RA'TION, the proportion or fixed allowance of provisions, drink, forage, &c., assigned to each soldier for his daily subsistence, and for the subsistence of horses. Seamen in the navy also have *rations* of certain articles.

RATIONA'LE, the account or solution of any phenomenon or hypothesis, explaining the principles on which it depends, and every other circumstance.

RA'TIONALISM, the interpretation of scripture truths upon the principles of human reason; which has become famous in the present day by the theological systems to which it has given birth in Germany. The history of the progress of the opinions of the reformed churches of that country may be found in Dr. Pusey's essay upon this subject. He conceives the polemical discussions which prevailed throughout those communities in the 17th and first half of the following century to have prepared the way for the reception of the low views of Christianity, as a moral system, which were derived from the writings of the concealed or avowed deists of England. From the middle of the last century there have arisen in Germany a succession of divines—Baumgarten, Michaelis, Semler, Eichhorn, Paulus, Bretschneider, &c., who have endeavored either to affix a lower and more human character to the invisible operations of God upon men through Christianity, or to reduce the accounts which we have of the foundation of our religion to the mixture of truth and error natural to fallible men. They have questioned the genuineness of almost all the separate parts of Scripture, and the accuracy of all their supernatural narratives. The discredit into which these theologians appear to have fallen arises, in a great measure, from the inability they have shown to produce a connected and consistent system of religion upon the low ground which they have taken up. Of later years a much more spiritual conception of the nature of Scripture promises and Christian assistances is observable in the writings of German divines, under the operation of which their theological criticism has already assumed a more dignified and exalted tone. The sensation created by Strauss's *Life of Christ*, the latest, and in some respects the most remarkable production of the Rationalist school, may probably have aided in this reaction

RAV'ELINS, in fortification, detached works composed of two faces, forming salient angles, and raised before the counterscarp.

RE, in grammar, a prefix or inseparable particle at the beginning of words, to repeat or otherwise modify their meaning; as in *re*-action, *re*-export, &c.

REACH, in sea language, signifies the distance between any two points of land, lying nearly in a right line.

REA'DER, in ecclesiastical matters, one of the five inferior orders in the Romish church. In the Church of England, a reader is a deacon appointed to do divine service in churches and chapels of which no one has the cure. There are also readers (priests) attached to various eleemosynary and other foundations.

RE'ALISM, in philosophy, is the opposite of *idealism*, and is that philosophical system which conceives external things to exist independently of our conception of them; but realism becomes materialism if it considers matter, or physical substance, as the only original cause of things, and the soul itself as a material substance.

RE'ALISTS, in philosophy, a sect of school philosophers formed in opposition to the Nominalists, who held that words, and not things, were the objects of dialectics.

REALM, a royal jurisdiction or extent of a king's dominions.

REAL PRES'ENCE, in the Romish church, the actual presence of the body and blood of Christ in the Eucharist, or the conversion of the substance of the bread and wine into the real body and blood of Christ.

REAR, a military term for behind.—*Rear-guard*, a body of men that marches in the rear of the main body to protect it.—*Rear-rank*, the last line of men that are drawn up two or more deep.—The *rear* is also a naval term applied to the squadron which is hindermost.

REA'SON, that particular faculty in man of which either the exclusive or the more intense enjoyment distinguishes him from the rest of the animal creation. Like most of the terms in the science of mind, that of reason has been employed in a great variety of significations. Dugald Stewart takes it in its widest sense, and comprises under it all the operations of the intellect upon the materials of knowledge which are furnished in the first instance by sense and perception. Its office is to distinguish the true from the false, right from wrong, and to combine means for the attainment of particular ends. According to this definition, therefore, the province of reason is coextensive with the range of human activity, and it directs itself to the three supreme objects of desire to man—the good, the beautiful, and the true. Mr. Hume, however, withdraws the discernment of right and wrong, and of the beautiful and its contrary, from the domain of reason; and, on the other hand, also, denies the certainty of the truth which it enunciates, and limits its convincing force merely to a certain weight of probability. Locke's usage of the term, again, partaking as it does of the general looseness of his phraseology, is very different. In one passage reason is declared to be the faculty which finds out the means, and rightly applies them, to discover either the certain agreement or disagreement of two ideas, or their probable connection. But, in another place, it is said to be conversant with certainty alone, while the discovery of what, as probable, enforces a contingent assent or opinion, is ascribed to an especial faculty, which is called the judgment. Bird, on the other hand, confines the latter term to the apprehension of intuitive truth; but agrees so far with Locke as to make it one part of reason, whose other part is reasoning, both demonstrative and moral. On the whole, however, it is clear that in the mind of Locke the terms reasoning and reason were nearly, if not quite equivalent. But reasoning and deduction are evidently not the source either of the dignity or the authority of the human intellect. The discursive faculty can never establish any other than a conditional truth, which predisposes some anterior and pre-established verity as its basis and verification. If there were not in the human mind something primary, unconditional, and absolute, to which all reasonings might be referred, as to their source and foundation, the discursive process would proceed into infinity, and its conclusions be, as Hume asserts that they are, without any power to enforce assent. But there are unquestionably in the human mind certain necessary and universal principles, which, shining with an intrinsic light of evidence, are themselves above proof, but the authority for all mediate and contingent principles. That which is thus above reasoning is the reason. In the language of English philosophy, the terms reason and understanding are nearly identical, and are so used by Stewart; but in the critical philosophy of Kant a broad distinction has been drawn between them. Reason is the principle of principles; either speculatively verifies every special principle, or practically determines the proper ends of human action. Approximately, it may be called the sum of what, in Scotch philosophy, has been denominated the laws of man's intellectual constitution. The understanding, on the other hand, is coextensive with the vernacular use of reason. It is that which conceives of sensible objects under certain general notions, which again it compares one with another, or with particular representations of them, or with the objects themselves. It is, therefore, the faculty of reflection and generalization. But the act of comparison is called a judgment; and the understanding, when it enunciates its conceptions, becomes also the faculty of judging. But the truth of a proposition which is not identical, or the enunciation of a primary truth, cannot be immediately certain. To prove it, recourse must be had to other propositions previously admitted; the understanding, that is, must deduce one judgment from another, and so becomes the discursive faculty, or reasoning. Farther, in discovering these mediate truths, and in the regular and methodical disposition of them for the purpose of conclusion, as well as in the selection of means for the accomplishment of its ends, it exhibits itself as a power of adaptation.

RE'BEC, a Moorish word, signifying a stringed instrument somewhat similar to the violin, having three strings tuned in fifths, and played with a bow. It was introduced by the Moors into Spain. It appears to have been much used at festive entertainments.

REB'EL, one who revolts from the government to which he owes allegiance, either by openly renouncing the authority of that government, or by taking arms and openly opposing it.

REBEL'LION, an open and avowed renunciation of the authority of the government to which one owes allegiance. *Rebellion* differs from *insurrection;* for insurrection may be a rising in opposition to a particular act or law, without a design to renounce wholly all subjection to the government. It may lead to, but is not necessarily in the first instance rebellion. Rebellion differs also from *mutiny*, that being an insurrection of soldiers or sailors against the authority of their officers.—*Rebellion, the great*, the revolt of the Long Parliament against the authority of Charles I., in English history, is commonly so denominated.

RE'BUS, an enigmatical representation of some name, &c. by using figures or pictures instead of words.—Camden tells us the rebus was in great esteem among our forefathers, and he was nobody who could not hammer out of his name an invention by this wit-craft, and picture it accordingly.—In heraldry, a coat of arms which bears an allusion to the name of a person.

REBUT'TER, in law, the defendant's answer to the plaintiff's sur-rejoinder, in a cause depending in the court of chancery, &c.

RECAP'TION, in law, the taking a second distress of one formerly distrained for the same cause during the plea grounded upon the former distress. It is also the name of a writ which lies for the party thus distrained, to recover damages, &c.

RECEIPT', in commerce, an acquittance or discharge in writing for money received, or other valuable consideration.

RE'CHABITES, a religious order among the ancient Jews, instituted by Jonadab, the son of Rechab, from whom they derived their name. It comprised only the family and posterity of the founder, who was anxious to perpetuate among them the nomadic life; and with this view prescribed to them several rules, the chief of which were—to abstain from wine, from building houses, and from planting vines. These rules were observed by the Rechabites with great strictness. In recent times, a branch of the Temperance society has assumed the name of Rechabites.

RECIP'ROCAL, in general, something that is mutual, or which is returned equally on both sides, or that affects both parties alike.—*Reciprocal terms*, in logic, are those which have the same signification; and consequently are convertible and may be used for each other.

RECITATIVE, language delivered in musical tones; or, as the Italians define it, speaking music. It is used in operas, &c. to express some action or passion, or to relate a story or reveal a secret or design. It differs from an air in having no fixed time or measure; and it is not governed by any principal or predominant key, though its final cadence or close must be in some cognate key of the air which follows, or, at least, in no very remote key. There are two kinds of recitative, *unaccompanied* and *accompanied*. The first is when a few occasional chords are struck by the piano-forte or violoncello to give the singer the pitch, and intimate to him the harmony. The second is when all, or a considerable portion, of the instruments of the orchestra accompany the singer, either in sustained chords or florid passages, in order to give the true expression or coloring to the passion or sentiment to be expressed.

RECK'ONING, in navigation, an account of the ship's course and distance calculated from the log-board without the aid of celestial observation. This is called the *dead-reckoning*.

RECOG'NIZANCE, in law, a bond or obligation acknowledged in some court, or before some judge, with condition to do some particular act, as to appear at the assizes, to keep the peace, &c. The person who enters into such bond is called the *recognizor;* the person to whom one is bound is the *recognizee.*

RECOLLEC'TION, the act of recalling to the memory, as ideas that have escaped; or the operation by which ideas are recalled to the memory or revived in the mind. *Recollection* differs from *remembrance*, as it is the consequence of volition, or an effort of the mind to revive ideas; whereas *remembrance* implies no such volition. We often *remember* things without any voluntary effort. *Recollection* is called also *reminiscence.*

REC'OLLECTS, monks of the order of St. Francis under a reformed rule. The first separation from the original body seems to have taken place towards the end of the 14th century, when some religious persons, desirous of returning to stricter discipline, assumed the title of Brothers of the Observance. From these originated the Recollects, (living in a state of *recollection*, or reclusion,) first established in Spain by the Count de Belalcazar, about 1484, and afterwards introduced into Italy. After much opposition, they acquired the possession of great wealth and court favor in France, during the 16th and 17th centuries.

RECONNOI'TRE, in military language, means to inform one's self by ocular inspection of the situation of an enemy, or the nature of a piece of ground. It is one of the most important departments of the military art, and must precede every considerable movement. Reconnoitering not unfrequently brings on engagements, and considerable bodies of troops march out to cover the reconnoitering party, and to make prisoners if possible, in order to obtain information from them.

REC'ORD, a register; an authentic or official copy of any writing, or account of any facts and proceedings whether public or private, entered in a book for preservation; or the book containing such copy or account; as, the *records* of statutes or of judicial courts; the *records* of a town or parish; the *records* of a family.—In a popular sense, the term *records* is applied to all public documents preserved in a recognized repository; but, in the legal sense of the term, *records* are contemporaneous statements of the proceedings of those higher courts of law which are distinguished as courts of record, written upon rolls of parchment. Records are said to be of three kinds:—1. judicial records; 2. ministerial records on oath, being offices or inquisitions found; 3. records made by conveyance or consent, as fines, recoveries, or deeds enrolled.—In the court of session, a *record* is a judicial minute subscribed by the counsel of the parties in a cause, and by the lord ordinary, whereby the parties mutually agree to hold certain pleadings, as containing their full and final statement of facts and pleas in law. This record forms the basis of the future argument, and of the decision of the cause.—The term *records*, in Scotch law, is usually applied to public registers for decrees of courts, deeds, instruments, and probative writings of every kind.—Authentic memorial; as, the *records* of past ages.—*Court of record*, is a court whose acts and judicial proceedings are enrolled on parchment or in books for a perpetual memorial; and their records are the highest evidence of facts, and their truth cannot be called in question.—*Debt of record*, is a debt which appears to be due by the evidence of a court of record, as upon a judgment or a recognizance.—*Trial by record* is where a matter of record is pleaded, and the opposite party pleads that there is no such record. In this case, the trial is by inspection of the record itself, no other evidence being admissible.

RECORD'ER, a person whom the mayor and other magistrates of a city or corporation associate with them for their better direction in matters of justice, and proceedings in law. He also speaks in their name, upon public occasions.

RECOV'ERY, in law, the obtaining a right to something by a verdict and judgment of court from an opposing party in a suit; as, the *recovery* of debt, damages, and costs, by a plaintiff; the *recovery* of land in ejectments, &c.

REC'TOR, in Great Britain, a term applied to the possessors of several official situations; as, 1. a clergyman who has the charge and cure of a parish, and the property of the tithes, &c.; 2. the chief elective officer in several universities; 3. the head master of large public schools in Scotland; 4. the governor in several convents; 5. the superior of a seminary or college of the Jesuits.

REC'TUS IN CU'RIA, in law, one who stands at the bar, no person objecting anything against him. Also, one who has reversed an outlawry, and can therefore partake of the benefit of the law.

RECUR'RENT VERSES, in poetry, verses that read the same backwards as they do forwards.

RECU'SANT, in English history, one who refuses to acknowledge the kingly supremacy in matters of religion; as a popish *recusant*, who acknowledges only the supremacy of the pope.

RED'DIDIT SE, a law term, used in cases where a man renders himself in discharge of his bail.

REDEMP'TION, in law, the liberation of an estate from a mortgage; or the purchase of the right to re-enter upon it by paying the principal sum for which it was mortgaged, with interest and costs; also, the right of redeeming and re-entering.—In war and in commerce, the act of procuring the deliverance of persons or things from the possession and power of captors by the payment of an equivalent; as, the *redemption* of a ship and cargo.—In theology, the ransom or deliverance of sinners from the bondage of sin and the penalties of God's violated law by the atonement of Christ.

REDEMP'TORISTS, a religious order founded in Naples by Liguori, in 1732, and revived in Austria in 1820. They are bound by the usual monastic vows, and devote themselves to the education of youth and the propagation of Catholicism. They style themselves members of the order of the Holy Redeemer, whence their name; but they are also often called *Liguorists*, from the name of their founder.

REDONDIL'LA, formerly a species of versification used in the south of Europe, consisting of a union of verses of four, six, and eight syllables, of which generally the first rhymed with the fourth, and the second with the third. At a later period, verses of six and eight syllables in general, in Spanish and Portuguese poetry, were called *redondillas*, whether they made perfect rhymes or assonances only. These became common in the dramatic poetry of Spain.

REDOUBT′, in fortification, a small square fort without any defence but in front: used in trenches, lines of circumvallation, contravallation, and approach, to defend passages, &c.

REDUCE′, to copy a picture, a drawing, or print, diminishing its size, and at the same time carefully preserving its proportions. This is done either by the artist adopting himself a smaller scale, or by the employment of mechanical instruments, such as the pantograph.

REDUC′TIO AD ABSUR′DUM, in logic, a mode of argument by which the truth of a proposition is proved by showing the absurdity of the contrary.

REDUPLICA′TION, in logic, a kind of condition expressed in a proposition indicating or assigning the manner wherein the predicate is attributed to the subject.

REFEC′TION, among certain ecclesiastics, a spare meal or repast just sufficing for the support of life; hence the hall in convents, and other communities, where the monks, nuns, &c., take their refections or meals in common, is called the *refectory*.

REFEREE′, one to whose decision a thing is referred; particularly, a person appointed by a court to hear, examine, and decide a case between parties, pending before the court, and make report thereon.

REF′ERENCE, in law, the act of referring a matter in dispute to the decision of an arbitrator. Also, in the court of chancery, the referring a matter to a master.—*Reference*, in printing, a mark in the text of a work referring to a similar one in the side or at the bottom of the page.

REFEREN′DARIES, in the early monarchies of Europe, after the fifth century, public officers charged with the duty of procuring, executing, and despatching diplomas and charters. The office of great referendary, in the French monarchy, became merged in that of chancellor.

REFLEC′TION, the operation of the mind by which it turns its views back upon itself and its operations; the review or reconsideration of past thoughts, opinions, or decisions of the mind, or of past events.

RE′FLEX, in painting, is a term used to denote those places in a picture which are supposed to be illuminated by a light reflected from some other body, represented in the same piece.

REFORM′, PARLIAMEN′TARY, a change to some considerable extent in the representative part of the English constitution, by an extension of the elective franchise to modern large towns, such as Manchester, Birmingham, &c., which heretofore sent no members to parliament and by taking away the franchise from places which had long since become insignificant.

REFORMA′TION, the term applied by Protestants, universally, to denote the change from the Roman Catholic to the Protestant religion, which was first set on foot in Germany by Luther, A.D. 1517, but had been begun in England by Wickliffe, and was afterwards completed by Henry VIII. who assumed the title of Head of the Church. Of all the errors, frauds, and superstitions of the church of Rome, the one which proved most injurious to religion and morals, and that which was most deplored by enlightened and conscientious men, was the facility with which riches were allowed to purchase salvation! Wealth was invested in monasteries, shrines, and chantries; and few persons who had any property at their own disposal went out of the world without bequeathing some of it to the clergy for saying masses, in number proportioned to the amount of the bequest, for the benefit of their souls. Thus were men taught to put their trust in riches; their wealth, being thus invested, became available to them beyond the grave; and in whatever sins they indulged, provided they went through the proper forms and obtained a discharge, they might purchase a free passage through purgatory, or, at least, an abbreviation of the term and a mitigation of its torments while they lasted. But purgatory was not the only invisible world over which the authority of the church extended; for to the pope, as to the representative of St. Peter, it was pretended that the keys of heaven and hell were given; a portion of this power was delegated to every priest, and they inculcated that the soul which departed without confession and absolution, bore with it the weight of its deadly sins to sink it to perdition. To this let us add, that the arrogance of the priests had exasperated the princes; the encroachments of the mendicant friars did injury to the secular ecclesiastics; and a thousand innocent victims of the inquisition called for vengeance. Other causes also conspired to bring on the day of religious freedom : the means of information were vastly increased by the art of printing; materials for thinking were laid before the people by instructive works in the vulgar tongues; the number of learned men increased; and the intelligence for which the Reformation was to open a way began to act generally and powerfully. The centre of Europe, together with the north, which had long submitted with reluctance to Rome, was ready to countenance the boldest measures for shaking off the priestly yoke, of which the best and most reflecting men had become impatient. But no one anticipated the quarter whence the first blow would be struck. Leo X. was created pope in 1513; and, little affected by the universal desire for reformation in the church, he seemed placed at its head merely to employ its revenues in the gratification of his princely tastes. Albert, elector of Mentz and archbishop of Magdeburg, a prince of a similar character, received from Leo, in 1516, permission to sell *indulgences* within his own jurisdiction, on condition of sharing the profits with the pope. In this traffic, Albert employed, among others, John Tetzel, a Dominican monk of Leipsic, who went about from place to place, carrying on his trade with the most unblushing impudence, and extolling his certificates above the papal bulls (which required repentance,) as unconditional promises of the forgiveness of sins in time and eternity. Luther, an Augustine monk of Erfurt,—a man of powerful mind, and distinguished more for his deep piety and strong love of truth, than for deep erudition,—set his face against this abuse, first in his sermons, and afterwards in ninety-five theses, or questions, which he affixed to the door of the church, Oct. 31, 1517. This led to several public disputations, in which he had such a decided advantage over his antagonists, that this man, who was hardly known before, became the public champion of all enlightened men who lamented the degeneracy of the church of Christ. The respect for the Roman court, which was perceptible in his earlier writings, he now discarded, as the injustice of the papal pretensions had become clear to him. The most complete success attended his endeavors; and wherever the reformed religion found its way, the worship of God recovered that simplicity, and warmth, and sincerity, which had characterized it among the first Christians. Religion was no longer a mere subject of the imagination, but appealed to the reason and feelings of men, and invited close investigation. The reformation also had an important influence on morals. While the reformers abolished the principle of blind obedience to the pope and other ecclesiastical dignitaries, denied the merit of penances, fasts, and alms, and rejected the possibility of acts of supererogation, by which saints had enriched the treasury of the church, they again awakened the smothered moral feelings of men, and introduced that more elevated morality which requires holiness of heart and purity of conduct.

REFORM'ED CHURCH, comprises in a general sense, all those bodies of Christians that have separated from the church of Rome since the era of the Reformation; but it is applied in a restricted sense to those Protestant churches which did not embrace the doctrines and discipline of Luther, and more particularly to the Calvinistic churches on the Continent.

REFUGEE', in political history, a term applied to the French protestants, who, on the revocation of the edict of Nantes, fled from the persecution of France. The same term was also applied to the French priests and other royalists who sought an asylum in this country at the commencement of the revolution.

REGA'LIA, in law, the rights and prerogatives of the sovereign power; also the ensigns of royalty, the crown, sceptre, &c., worn by our kings and queens at their coronation.—*Regalia of the church*, are the rights and privileges which cathedrals, &c. enjoy by royal grants. This term is particularly used for such lands and hereditaments as have been given by different sovereigns to the church.

REGARD'ER, in England, an ancient officer of the king's forest, whose business is to inquire into all offences and defaults committed within the forest, and to observe whether the other officers execute their respective duties.

REGAT'TA, a name given to yacht and boat races. The word is adopted from the *regatta* in Venice, where boats, containing one person only, contest for prizes on the canals that intersect that city. It is generally a very gay and attractive spectacle, from the number of spectators present in ornamented gondolas.

REGENERA'TION, in theology, the new birth of man unto righteousness, following on the abolition of the original corruption of his nature. Similar language was used respecting the admission of proselytes to the privilege of Judaism: so, also, in other religions. The Sanscrit name for a Brahmin is said to signify "twice-born;" and Tertullian says that the heathens used baptism in their mysteries, "in regenerationem." When our Saviour admonished Nicodemus not to marvel at his words, "Ye must be born again," he added, with reference, doubtless, to the doctrines already taught among the Jews, "Art thou a master of Israel, and knowest not these things?" But whether the new birth to which allusion is made in these solemn passages of Scripture, actually takes place by and through baptism; whether baptism, duly administered by those authorized, is in itself an "opus operatum," in the language of the schools; or whether the regeneration spoken of as the condition of our salvation takes place after, and independent of baptism, by the operation of the Spirit on the inner man—this is a question on which Protestants have never agreed among themselves, and which divides the English church at this day. The former is the commonly received or Catholic doctrine; and has been so from very early times, as far as we can conclude from the language of the fathers and ancient forms of the church. But it does not appear to be positively declared by the Church of England, though inferred from various passages in the baptismal service.

RE'GENT, one who governs a kingdom during the minority or absence of the rightful monarch.—In English universities, a master of arts under five years' standing, and a doctor under two.—A member of a board or corporate body in the state of New York, who have power to grant acts of incorporation for colleges, and to visit and inspect all colleges, academies, and schools of the state.

REG'ICIDE, the offence of slaying a king or other sovereign. The early Greek republics, unaccustomed to the legitimate rule of monarchs, saw, in the occasional subjugation which they underwent from successful partisans, a mere usurpation, or tyranny; and tyrannicide was with them only the slaying of a public enemy.

REG'IMEN, the regulation of diet, or, in a more general sense, of all the non-naturals, with a view to preserve or restore health.—In grammar, that part of syntax, or construction, which regulates the dependency of words, and the alterations which one occasions or requires in another in connection with it.

REG'IMENT, in military affairs, a body of troops, either horse, foot, or artillery; the infantry consisting of one or more battalions, and commanded by a colonel or lieutenant-colonel.—*Regimentals*, the uniform clothing of the army.

REG'ISTER, an official account of the proceedings of a public body, or a book in which are entered and recorded memoirs, acts, and minutes, to be had recourse to occasionally, as well as for preserving and conveying to future times an exact knowledge of transactions.—*Register*, in printing, such an accurate arrangement of the lines and pages, that those printed on one side of the sheet shall fall exactly on those of the other.

RE'GIUS PROFES'SOR, in literature, a title given to each of the five readers or lecturers in the university of Oxford, so called from king Henry VIII., by whom these professorships were founded.

REG'LET, or RIG'LET, in architecture, a flat narrow moulding, used chiefly in pannels and compartments, to separate the parts or members from each other, and to form knots, frets, and other ornaments.—In printing, a ledge or thin slip of wood exactly planed, used to separate lines and make the work more open.

REG'NUM ECCLESIAS'TICUM, in law, the absolute and independent power which was possessed and exercised by the clergy previous to the reformation, in all spiritual matters; in distinction from the *regnum seculare*.

REGRA'TER, one who buys and resells in the same fair or market; a *forestaller* being one who buys on the road to the market.

REG'ULA, in archæology, the book of rules or orders of a monastery.

REG'ULARS, in military affairs, that part of the army which is entirely at the disposal of government.—In ecclesiastical history, *regulars* are such as live under some rule of obedience, and lead a monastic life.

REHABILITA'TION, in foreign criminal law, is the reinstatement of a criminal in his personal rights which he has lost by a judicial sentence. Thus, in Scotland, a pardon from the king is said to rehabilitate a witness laboring under *infamia juris*. In France, persons condemned to imprisonment or compulsory labor may demand their rehabilitation five years after the expiration of their penalty: the demand is considered by the cour royale of the district, and pronounced upon by the king in his privy council. Various singular forms were attached to the process of rehabilitation in ancient times. There are extant letters of Charles VI., given in 1383, permitting a criminal whose hand had been cut off for homicide to replace it by another made in such fashion as he may choose.

REHEAR'SAL, the recital in private of an opera, oratorio, or, in short, any dramatic work, previously to public exhibition.

REI'NECKE, (the fox,) the name of a celebrated popular German epic poem, which, during the latter part of the middle ages and early centuries of modern times, enjoyed an almost European reputation. It became first known through the medium of a Low German version in the 15th century; and it has, with few interruptions, ever since involved the German literati in discussions as to its origin, which are yet apparently far from being settled. It contains a humorous and satirical account of the adventures of Reinecke (the fox) at the court of King Nodel (the lion;) exhibits the cunning of the former, and the means which he adopted to rebut the charges preferred against him, and the hypocrisy and lies by which he contrived to gain the favor of his sovereign, who loaded him with honors. The king, the officers of his court, and all his subjects are represented, as in *Esop's Fables*, under the names of the animals best suited to their respective characters; and the poem is an admirable satire on the intrigues practised at a weak court. The most successful versions of this poem are those of Goethe, in hexameters; of Soltau, in the measure of the original; and the more recent attempt of Ortlepp. This poem appears, in some form or other, to have been known throughout Europe.

REIS-EFFEN'DI, the name given to one of the chief Turkish officers of state. He is chancellor of the empire and minister of foreign affairs, in which capacity he negotiates with the ambassadors and interpreters of foreign nations.

REJOIN'DER, in law, the defendant's answer to the plaintiff's reply.

RELA'TION, in logic, one of the ten predicaments or accidents belonging to substance.—*Relation, inharmonical*, in music, a term to express that some harsh and displeasing discord is produced in comparing the present note with that of another part.

REL'ATIVE, in general, a term signifying not absolute, but considered as belonging to or respecting something else.—*Relative*, in grammar, a word which relates to or represents another word, called its antecedent, or to a sentence, or member of a sentence, or to a series of sentences, which constitutes its antecedent.—*Relative terms*, in logic, terms which imply relation, as guardian and ward; husband and wife; master and servant.

RELAY', a supply of horses ready on the road to relieve others, in order that a traveller may proceed without delay. In hunting, *relay* signifies fresh sets of dogs, or horses, or both, placed in readiness, in case the game comes that way, to be cast off, or to mount the hunters in lieu of the former.

RELEASE', in law, is a discharge or conveyance of a person's right in lands or tenements, to another who has some former estate in possession. The words generally used therein, are, "remised, released, and forever quit-claimed."

REL'ICS, in the Romish church, are the remains of saints and holy men, or of their garments, &c., which are enjoined to be held in veneration, and are considered, in many instances, to be endued with miraculous powers. They are preserved in the churches, to which they are often the means of attracting pilgrimages, and in very ignorant times and places have been actually made objects of adoration. The virtues which are attributed to them are defended by such instances from Scripture as that of the miracles that were wrought by the bones of Elisha.

RELIEF', (RELIEVO,) in sculpture, that species of sculpture in which the figures are engaged on or rise from a ground. There are three sorts of relievo —*basso-relievo*, in which the figures or

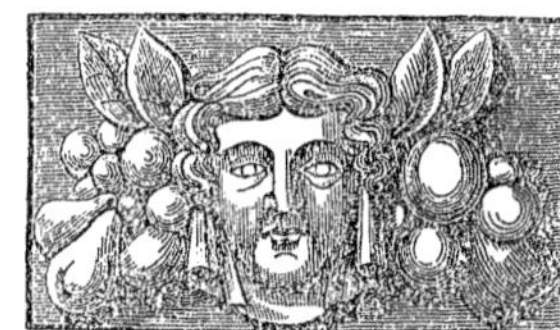

Low Relief.

other objects have but small projection from the ground on which they are sculptured; *mezzo-relievo*, in which the figures stand out about half their natural proportions, the other half appearing immersed in the ground; and lastly, *alto-relievo*, in which the figures stand completely out from the ground, being attached to it only in a few places, and in others worked entirely round like single statues; such are the metopæ of the Elgin marbles in the British Museum, which marbles also, in the Panathenaic

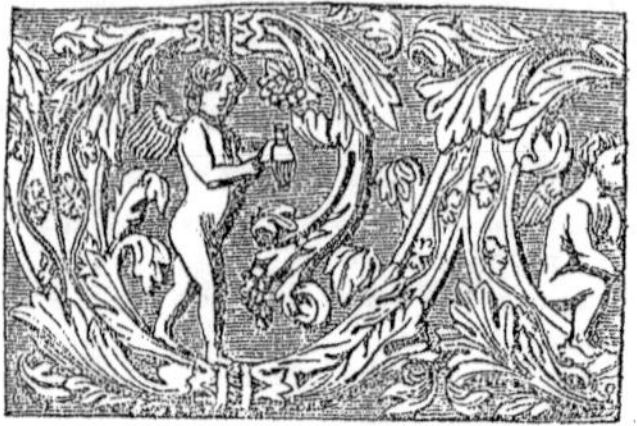

High Relief.

procession, exhibit some exquisite examples of basso-relievo.—*Relief*, in architecture, the projection of a figure or ornament from the ground or plane on which it is sculptured.—In painting, the appearance of projection, or the degree of boldness which a figure exhibits to the eye at a distance.—In feudal law, a fine or composition which the heir of a tenant, holding by knight's service or other tenure, paid to the lord at the death of the ancestor, for the privilege of taking up the estate which, on strict feudal principles, had lapsed or fallen to the lord on the death of the tenant. This relief consisted of horses, arms, money, and the like, the amount of which was originally arbitrary, but afterward fixed at a certain rate by law. It is not payable, unless the heir at the death of his ancestor had attained to the age of twenty-one years.

RELIEF' SYNOD, a respectable body of Presbyterian dissenters in Scotland, whose ground of separation from the established church was the violent exercise of lay patronage which obtained in the latter. Though patronage, or the appointment of clergymen to church benefices by presentations had been established by act of Parliament in 1712, yet a minority of the clergy were opposed to that measure; or at least to the intrusion of a minister into parochial charge contrary to the sentiments of the people. The majority of the church, however, entertained different views, and rigorously enforced the provisions of the act of 1712. With this state of things the people generally, but particularly in rural districts, were dissatisfied; and hence the origin of the Secession church, and the Relief.

RELI'GION, that worship and homage which is due to God, considered as our creator, preserver, and most bountiful benefactor. It is divided into natural and revealed. By *natural religion* is meant, that knowledge, veneration, and love of God, and the practice of those duties to him, our fellow-creatures, and ourselves, which are discoverable from the right exercise of our rational faculties, from considering the nature and perfections of God, and our relation to him and to one another. By *revealed religion* is meant, natural religion explained, enforced, and enlarged, from the express declarations of God himself, from the mouths or pens of his prophets, &c.—Religion, in a more contracted sense, is used for any system of faith and worship; and even for the various sects into which each religion is divided. Religion is different from *theology*, inasmuch as the latter is speculative and the former practical. Religion is a system of duties; theology a system of opinions. Theology inquires into the nature of the power or powers to whom all visible things are in subjection; religion is the sentiment which springs from that inquiry. The slightest knowledge of history is sufficient to inform us that religion has ever had a powerful influence in moulding the sentiments and manners of men. In one region or age it has been favorable to civilization and refinement; in another it has been so directed as to fetter genius or warp the human mind. That, however, depends on the purity of the doctrine and the liberality of its teachers.

RELI'GIOUS HOUSES, different asyla or habitations for priests, nuns, and poor, still existing in Catholic countries, and before the Reformation abounding in England. They consisted of abbeys, monasteries, priories, hospitals, friaries, and nunneries, supported by lands and bequests left them by pious persons, which became enormous. Nearly the whole (above 3000) were dissolved, and their wealth seized by Henry the Eighth; the monks, nuns, and officers being allowed pensions.

RELIQ'UÆ, in Roman antiquity, the ashes and bones of the dead, remaining after burning their bodies; which were gathered up, put into urns, and afterwards deposited in tombs.

RE'LIQUARY, the receptacle for the relics venerated in Roman Catholic churches. The difference between a *reliquary* and a *case* used for the same purpose is, that the former is smaller in dimensions, and contains only small fragments; the latter, in many instances, entire bodies.

REMAIN'DER, in law, an estate in

lands, tenements, or rents, not to be enjoyed till after a term of years or another person's decease. There is this difference between a *remainder* and a *reversion;* in case of a reversion, the estate granted, after the limited time, reverts to the grantor or his heirs; but by a remainder it goes to some third person or a stranger.

REMINIS'CENCE, that faculty of the mind by which ideas formerly received into it, but forgotten, are recalled or revived in the memory.

REMON'STRANCE, a strong representation of reasons against a measure, either public or private; and when addressed to a public body, prince or magistrate, it may be accompanied with a petition or supplication for the removal or prevention of some evil or inconvenience.

REMON'STRANTS, in ecclesiastical history, the appellation given to the Arminians who remonstrated against the decisions of the Synod of Dort, in 1618.

REM'PHAN, an idol worshipped by the Israelites while in the wilderness, according to the language of St. Stephen, as recorded in the acts, "Ye took up the tabernacle of Moloch, and the star of your god Remphan." In this passage commentators are agreed that St. Stephen quotes the words of Amos, "Ye have borne the tabernacle of your Moloch and Chiun, your images." Chiun and Remphan are, therefore, the same, and both are thought to be personifications of Sirius, the Dog-star.

RENT, in law, a sum of money issuing yearly from lands and tenements; a compensation or return, in the nature of an acknowledgment, for the possession of a corporeal inheritance.—*Rack-rent,* is a rent of the full value of the tenement, or near it.—A *fee-farm rent,* is a rent charge issuing out of an estate in fee, of at least one-fourth of the value of the lands at the time of its reservation.

RENT'AL, a schedule in which the rents of manors are set down. It contains the lands let to each tenant, with their names, and the several rents arising.

RENT CHARGE, in law, a charge of rent upon land, with a clause of distress in case of non-payment.

REPEAT', in music, a character showing that what was last played or sung must be repeated.

REPENT'ANCE, in a religious sense, sorrow or deep contrition for sin, as an offence and dishonor to God, and a violation of his holy law; but to render it acceptable, it must be followed by amendment of life. Legal repentance, or such as is excited by the terrors of legal penalties, may exist without an amendment of life.

REP'ERTORY, a place in which things are disposed in an orderly manner, so that they can be easily found, as the index of a book, a common-place book, &c.

REPLEV'IN, in law, a remedy granted on a distress, by which a person, whose effects are distrained, has them restored to him again, on his giving security to the sheriff that he will pursue his action against the party distraining, and return the goods or cattle if the taking them shall be adjudged lawful.

REPLICA'TION, in logic, the assuming or using the same term twice in the same proposition.

REPOSE', in the Fine Arts, the absence of that agitation which is induced by the scattering and division of a subject into too many unconnected parts, in which case a work is said to want repose. Where repose is wanting from this cause, "the eye," says Sir Joshua Reynolds, "is perplexed and fatigued, from not knowing where to rest, where to find the principal action, or which is the principal figure; for where all are making equal pretensions to notice, all are in danger of neglect."

REPORT'ING, the act of giving account of anything, of relating, or of making statements of facts or of adjudged cases in law.—*Newspaper reporting,* the name given to that system by which the Congressional debates and proceedings, and the proceedings of public meetings, &c., are promulgated throughout the country.

REPRESENTA'TION, in politics, the part performed by a deputy chosen by a constituent body to support its interests, and act in its name on a public occasion. Thus a plenipotentiary represents the sovereign or the state which delegates him at a foreign court. But the most ordinary use of the word is to express the principal function of the delegate of a constituency in a legislative assembly. Representation, in this sense, was unknown to the political systems of the ancients, and seems to have originated in the necessities and usages of feudal times; the lord not being able to levy aid from his vassals without their consent, it became customary for these to delegate powers to individuals from among their numbers to attend his summons, and confer with him respecting the aid required. Hence, in our own country, the representation of county freeholders by knights, of communities by their chosen burgesses, in parliament. The most complete early model of a representative feudal assembly is to be found in the parliament of the Sicilies under the Suabian kings; but England is the only country in which it has expanded regularly into a legislature.

REPRESEN'TATIVE, one who lawfully represents another for the performance of any duty, according to the wishes of the other and to his own honest judgment. A member of the house of commons is the *representative* of his constituents and of the nation. In matters concerning his constituents only, he is supposed to be bound by their instructions; but in the enacting of laws for the nation, he is supposed not to be bound by their instructions, as he acts for the whole nation. Any other construction of his duty would be derogatory to him as a free and independent member of the senate.

REPRIEVE', in law, a warrant for suspending the execution of a malefactor.

REPRI'SALS, LETTERS OF, in national law, the capture of property belonging to the subjects of a foreign power in satisfaction of losses sustained by a citizen of the capturing state. Letters of reprisal are granted by the law of nations, where the subject of one state has been oppressed or injured by the subjects of another, and where justice has been refused on application by letters of request.

REPRI'SES, in law, deduction or payments out of the value of lands; such as rent-charges, or annuities.

REPROBA'TION, in theology, is a term commonly applied to the supralapsarian tenet of the consignment of all mankind to eternal punishment, with the exception of those whom God has arbitrarily selected for eternal happiness.

REPUB'LIC, that form of government in which the supreme power is vested in the people. A republic may be either an aristocracy or a democracy: the supreme power, in the former, being consigned to the nobles or a few privileged individuals, as was formerly the case in Venice and Genoa; while, in the latter, it is placed in the hands of rulers chosen by and from the whole body of the people, or by their representatives assembled in a congress or national assembly. The free towns of the Continent, Hamburg, Frankfort, Lübeck, and Bremen, are instances of this latter form of government; but the most perfect example of it is to be found in the United States, and in some of the South American confederations which have shaken off the Spanish yoke. In Switzerland, aristocracy is partially blended with democracy in the form of government.

REQUESTS', COURT OF, in law, a convenient court for the recovery of small debts, held by commissioners duly qualified, who try causes by the oath of parties and of other witnesses.

RE'QUIEM, in music, a prayer in the Romish church, which begins with *Requiem æternam dona eis domine;* whence, "to sing a *requiem*," is to sing a mass for the rest of the souls of deceased persons.

RE'SCRIPT, the answer of an emperor, when consulted by particular persons on some difficult question. This answer serves as a decision of the question, and is therefore equivalent to an edict or decree.

RES'CUE, in law, the forcible retaking of a lawful distress from the distrainor, or from the custody of the law: also, the forcible liberation of a defendant from the custody of the officer.

RESERVA'TION, in law, a clause or part of an instrument by which something is reserved, not conceded or granted.—*Mental reservation*, is the withholding of expression or disclosure of something that affects a proposition or statement, and which if disclosed would materially vary its import.

RESERVE', or CORPS DE RESERVE, in military affairs, the third or last line of an army drawn up for battle; so called because they are reserved to sustain the rest, as occasion requires, and not to engage but in case of necessity.

RESIDEN'TIARY, a canon or other ecclesiastic installed into the privileges and profits of a residence.

RESID'UARY LEGATEE', in law, the legatee to whom the residue of a personal estate is given by will, after deducting all debts and specific legacies.

RESOLU'TION, the operation or process of separating the parts which compose a complex idea or a mixed body.—The determination or decision of a legislative body; or a formal proposition offered for legislative determination.—*Resolution*, in music, the writing out of a canon or fugue in partition from a single line.—*Resolution of a discord*, the descent by a tone or a semitone, according as the mode may require, of a discord which has been heard in the preceding harmony.

RES'ONANCE, in music, the returning

of sound by the air acting on the bodies of stringed musical instruments.

RESPOND'ENT, in law, one that answers in a suit, particularly a chancery suit.—In the schools, one who maintains a thesis in reply, and whose province is to refute objections or overthrow arguments.

RESPONSE', an answer; but more particularly used to denote the answer of the congregation to the priest, in the litany and other parts of divine service.—In the Romish church, a kind of anthem sung after the morning lesson.

RESSEN'TI, a word employed in the arts connected with drawing, to signify whatever is pronounced or expressed with force. Thus we speak of muscles *ressenti*, or a manner *ressenti*. Nature exhibits all the varieties of form, but these are only occasionally to be so denominated. Women, children and men of delicate habits or profession, display only muscles lightly shaped and unmarked by strenuousness, while, on the other hand, men exercised to robust employments present this style of person. Who is not struck with the contrast between the Farnese Hercules and the Belvedere Apollo or the Antinous? Among the moderns, Raffaelle is perhaps the greatest painter to be cited for the precision and variety of the shapes which he has adapted to different figures, as well as for superiority in the art in general.

REST, in music, a pause or interval of time, during which there is an intermission of the voice or sound. A rest may be for a bar, or more than a bar, or for a part of a bar only. The pause or cessation of sound is equal in duration to the note represented by the rest. As there are six musical characters called notes, so there are as many rests.

RESTORA'TION, renewal; revival; re-establishment. In England, the return of King Charles II., in 1660, is by way of eminence called *the Restoration;* and the 29th of May is kept as an anniversary festival, in commemoration of the re-establishment of monarchy.

RESURREC'TION, the history of the resurrection of our Saviour is detailed in the separate narration of each of the four Evangelists, and is also referred to and insisted on in the Acts of the Apostles, and in every one of the Epistles. The importance of this history, as an evidence of the truth of Christianity, is pointed out in a peculiar manner by Paley; namely, that it was alleged from the beginning by all the propagators of Christianity, and relied on as the great test of the doctrines which they taught: consequently, if the fact be untrue, they must all have been either deceivers, or deceived in a point on which it is morally impossible they could be so.

RETAIN'ER, in old English law, a servant not dwelling in the master's house or employed by him in any distinct occupation, but wearing his *livery* (*i. e.*, hat, badge, or suit,) and attending on particular occasions; an important relic of the times of private warfare. The giving liveries, or *retaining* this class of servants, was forbidden by many statutes with little effect.—In the language of the bar, a fee given to a counsel to secure his services: or rather, as it has been said, to prevent the opposite side from engaging them. A *special* retainer is for a particular case expected to come on. A *general* retainer is given by a party desirous of securing a priority of claim on the counsel's services for any case which he may have in any court which that counsel attends. The effect of it is merely this, that if a counsel having a general retainer receive a special retainer on the other side, he cannot accept it until twenty-four hours after notice shall have been given of its arrival to the party so generally retaining him; when, if he does not receive a brief or a special retainer from the latter, he is bound to accept it. The same word in its strict legal acceptation signifies the engagement of an attorney by his client, which enhances the mutual duties implied by the law between them.

RETIA'RIUS, the name of a class of Roman gladiators armed in a peculiar way. The retiarius was furnished with a trident and net, with no more covering than a short tunic; and with these implements he endeavored to entangle and despatch his adversary, who was called secutor (from sequi, to *follow*,) and was armed with a helmet, a shield, and a sword.

RET'ICENCE, or RET'ICENCY, in rhetoric, a figure by which a person really speaks of a thing, while he makes a show as if he would say nothing on the subject.

RETIC'ULATED WORK, in architecture, that wherein the stones are square and laid lozengewise, resembling the meshes of a net. This species of masonry is scarcely ever practised in the present day: but it was very common among the ancients.

RETIRADE', in fortification, a kind

of retrenchment in the body of a bastion or other work, which is to be disputed inch by inch, after the defences are dismantled.

RETRAX'IT, in law, the withdrawing or open renunciation of a suit in court, by which the plaintiff loses his action. A *retraxit* is a bar to any future action, which a *nonsuit* is not.

RETRENCH'MENT, in the art of war, any kind of work raised to cover a post and fortify it against the enemy, such as fascines loaded with earth, gabions, sandbags, &c.

RE'TRO, a prefix to many words, as in retrocession, retrogradation, &c.: implying a going backward.

RE'TURN, in law, a certificate from sheriffs and bailiffs of what is done in the execution of a writ.—*Return days*, certain days in term time for the return of writs.—In military and naval affairs, an official account, report, or statement rendered to the commander; as, the *return* of men fit for duty; or the *return* of provisions, ammunition, &c.—*Returns*, in commerce, that which is returned, whether in goods or specie, for merchandise sent abroad. Also, the return of money laid out in the way of trade; as, "small profits bring quick returns."—*Returns of a mine*, in fortification, the windings and turnings of a gallery leading to a mine.—*Returns*, in military affairs, statements given in by the officers of regiments, companies, &c., of the number, condition, &c., of their men, horses, &c.

REVE'ILLE, in military affairs, the beat of drum about break of day, to give notice that it is time for the soldiers to rise and for the sentinels to forbear challenging.

REVELA'TION, the act of revealing, or making a thing public that was before unknown. It is also used for the discoveries made by God to his prophets, and by them to the world; and more particularly for the books of the Old and New Testament. The principal tests of the truth of any revelation are, its being worthy of God, and consistent with his known attributes; and in its having a tendency to refine, purify, and exalt the mind of man to an imitation of the Deity in his moral perfections.

REV'ELS, MASTER OF THE, or LORD OF MISRULE, the name of an officer formerly attached *pro tempore* to royal and other distinguished houses, whose duty it was to preside over the Christmas entertainments. This office was first permanently instituted in the reign of Henry VIII., and appears to have gone out of fashion towards the end of the 17th century.

REVENDICA'TION, a term of the civil law, signifying a claim legally made to recover property, by one claiming as owner. The right of property must, generally speaking, be complete, to proceed to the action of revendication; thus, no such action can be brought for corporeal things until after delivery, by which they pass.

REV'ENUE, in a general sense, is an annual or continual income, or the yearly profit that accrues to a man from his lands or possessions; but in modern usage, *revenue* is generally applied to the annual produce of taxes, excise, customs, duties, &c. which a nation or state collects or receives into the treasury for public use.

REV'EREND, a title of respect given to the clergy. In Roman Catholic countries the members of the different religious orders are styled *reverend*. In England, deans are *very reverend*, bishops *right reverend*, and archbishops *most reverend*. In Scotland, the principals of the universities and the moderator of the General Assembly for the time being are styled *very reverend*.

REV'ERIE, a loose or irregular train of thoughts, occurring in musing or meditation; or any wild, extravagant conceit of the fancy or imagination.

REVER'SION, in law, is when the possession of an estate which was parted with for a time returns to the donor or his heirs. Also the right which a person has to any inheritance, or place of profit, after the decease of another.

REVET'MENT, in fortification, a strong wall on the outside of a rampart, intended to support the earth.

REVIEW', in military tactics, the display of a body of troops, for the purpose of exhibiting the state of their appearance and discipline before some superior officer or illustrious personage.—*Review*, in literature, a critical examination of a new publication. Also a periodical publication containing critical examinations and analyses of new works. The person who performs this duty is called the *reviewer*.—*Review*, (bill of,) in chancery, a bill where a cause has been heard, but some errors in law appearing, or some new matter being discovered after the decree was made, this bill is given for a fresh examination into the merits of the cause.

REVISE', a second proof-sheet of a

work, for the revisal or re-examination of the errors corrected.—The act of *revising* a book or writing for publication, is termed a *revision*.

REVI'VOR, in law, the reviving of a suit which is abated by the death of any of the parties. This is done by a *bill of revivor*.

REVOKE', to reverse or repeal. A law, decree, or sentence is revoked by the same authority which enacted or passed it. A devise may be *revoked* by the devisor, a use by the grantor, and a will by the testator.—A law may cease to operate without an express *revocation*.

REVOLU'TION, in politics, a material or entire change in the constitution of government. Thus the *revolution* in England, in 1688, was produced by the abdication of King James II. the establishment of the house of Orange upon the throne, and the restoration of the constitution to its primitive state. In like manner, though with very different consequences, the *revolution* in France effected a change of constitution. In the United States, the war of 1776, which achieved the independence of the thirteen states, is known as THE REVOLUTION.

REX SACRO'RUM, among the Romans, was a person appointed to preside in certain sacred duties. He generally performed such office as the kings of Rome had reserved to themselves before the abolition of their power. He was chosen by the *augurs* and *pontifices*, at the establishment of the commonwealth, that the name of king might not be wholly extinct; and in order that his power might never be dangerous to civil liberty, he was not permitted to have the least share in civil affairs.

RHAB'DOMANCY, properly, divination by a rod or wand. Some persons have been believed to be endowed by nature with a peculiar sense or perception, by which they are enabled to discover things hid in the earth, especially metals and water. But a more prevalent opinion has been, that the discovery of these substances might be effected by means of a divining rod. A divining rod is a branch of a tree, generally hazel, forked at the end, and held in a particular way, by the two ends, in the hands of the adept; and is supposed to indicate the position of the substance sought by bending towards it with a slow rotatory motion, the adept, according to modern practice, being placed in contact with some metallic or other magnetic substance. The art is said to be occasionally practised in the south of France and Italy, under the names of metalloscopy, hydroscopy, &c.

RHAP'SODI, in antiquity, a name given to such poets as recited or sung their own works, in detached pieces, from town to town. Hence the term *rhapsodies* was particularly applied to the works of Homer, which were so rehearsed. —In modern usage, a collection of passages, composing a new piece, but without necessary dependence or natural connection, is called a *rhapsody*.

RHEN'ISH, pertaining to the river Rhine, or to Rheims, in France: as *Rhenish* wine.

RHE'TIAN, pertaining to the ancient Rhæti, or to Rhætia, their country, as the *Rhetian* Alps, now the country of Tyrol and the Grisons.

RHET'ORIC, the art of speaking with propriety, elegance, and force; or, as Lord Bacon defines it, the art of applying and addressing the dictates of reason to the fancy, and of recommending them there so as to affect the will and desires. Rhetoric and oratory differ from each other as the theory from the practice; the rhetorician being the one who describes the rules of eloquence, and the orator he who uses them to advantage. The parts of rhetoric are, *invention*, *disposition*, and *elocution*. The forms of speech by which propriety and elegance are produced, are denominated *tropes* and *figures*. The general manner in which the orator employs his words for the formation of his speech is called *style*, which is variously distinguished. Rhetoric divides an oration or speech into five parts: the exordium, narration, confirmation, refutation, and peroration. The *exordium* is the part in which the speaker prepares the minds of the auditors for what he is about to advance. It ought to be expressed with considerable care and perspicuity, and the matter and manner should be to the purpose, brief, and modest. The *narration* is the recital of facts or events; and should have the qualities of clearness, probability, brevity, and consistency. The *confirmation* establishes the proofs of a discourse, and arranges them in the manner best adapted to enforce conviction. The *refutation*, or anticipation, furnishes arguments to answer the assertions that may be opposed to the narration. The *peroration*, or conclusion, should recapitulate the whole with condensed force and energy.

RHYME, in poetry, the correspondence of sounds in the last words or syllables of verses. The latter is the true rhyme of modern European languages. There are rhymed verses in the Latin classical poets, where the jingle seems intentional, and more distinct examples of it in the fragments of Roman military songs, &c., which have come down to us. But in the earlier period of the decay of the Latin language, when accent was substituted for metre in the rhythmical arrangement of the verse, rhyme made its way into the composition of church hymns, &c. It has been attempted with little success, to deduce this innovation from the Goths, and from the Arabians; but the former, like the old Teutonic races, probably used alliteration, but no rhyme in their verses; and the latter could not have influenced European literature until a period long after that in which rhyme first appears. A rhyme in which the final syllables only agree (*strain*, *complain*,) is called a male rhyme; one in which the two final syllables of each verse agree, the last being short (*motion*, *ocean*,) female; and the latter is sometimes extended in Italian poetry to three syllables (*femore*, *immemore*,) when the verse is called *sdrucciolo*. In English such a license is hardly permissible, except in burlesque poetry (see *Hudibras* and *Don Juan* for instances.) By the strict rules of French prosody, the male and female species of rhymes must be alternately used, however intricate the disposition of the verse may be; although the last short syllable is generally mute, or very slightly sounded. Rhymes which extend not only beyond the three last syllables, but through the whole structure of the lines, are used in Arabian and Persian poetry. Rhymes in which the consonants of the last syllable in each verse are identical, (*dress*, *address*,) are vicious in English, but rather admired in French poetry. One more singularity of English poetry deserves notice: while, from the irregularity of our spelling, many syllables rhyme with each other, although widely dissimilar in orthography (*woo*, *pursue*,) there are, on the other hand, rhymes which speak to the eye, and not to the ear; *i. e.*, in which the orthography of the rhyming syllables is the same, but the pronunciation different; as, *wind*, *find*; *gone*, *alone*. This is a license only rendered admissible by precedent.

RHYMOPŒ'IA, in ancient music, that part of the science which prescribed the laws of rhyme, or what appertained to, the rhythmic art.

RHYTHM, in music, variety in the movement as to quickness or slowness, or length and shortness of the notes; or rather the proportion which the parts of the motion have to each other.—Metre; verse; number.—Rhythm is the consonance of measure and time in poetry, prose composition, and music, and by analogy, dancing.—In poetry, it is the relative duration of the moments employed in pronouncing the syllables of a verse; and in music, the relative duration of the sounds that enter into the composition of an air. *Prose* also has its *rhythm*, and the only difference (so far as sound is concerned) between verse and prose is, that the former consists of a regular succession of similar cadences, or of a limited variety of cadences, divided by grammatical pauses and emphases into proportional clauses, so as to present sensible responses to the ear, at regular proportioned distances; prose, on the other hand, is composed of all sorts of cadences, arranged without attention to obvious rule, and divided into clauses which have no obviously ascertained proportion, and present no responses to the ear at any legitimate or determined intervals. In *dancing*, the rhythm is recognized in the sound of the feet.

RIDEAU', in fortification, a rising ground commanding a plain: also a trench covered with earth in form of a parapet to shelter soldiers.

RI'DER, or RI'DER-ROLL, in law, a schedule, or small piece of parchment, often added to some part of a record or act of parliament.

RI'DING, in England, one of the three jurisdictions into which the county of York is divided, anciently under the government of a reeve.

RIFACIMEN'TO, an Italian word, of late often used in English, to denote a remaking or furbishing up anew. Its most usual application is to the process of recasting literary works, so as to adapt them to a somewhat different purpose or to a changed state of circumstances.

RIGHT OF PROP'ERTY, in political economy, the right which states, bodies of individuals and individuals have to the exclusive use and enjoyment of such lands, natural powers, and products as have been appropriated or set apart for any peculiar purpose.

RINFORZAN'DO, in music, a direction to the performer, denoting that the sound is to be increased. It is marked thus <; when the sound is to be diminished this mark > is used.

RING'LEADER, the leader of any

association of men engaged in violation of law or an illegal enterprise, as rioters, mutineers, and the like. According to some this name is derived from the practice which men associating to oppose law have sometimes adopted, of signing their names to articles of agreement in a *ring*, that no one of their number might be distinguished as the leader. According to others it signified originally, one who took the lead in forming the *ring* of a dance.

RINGS, FAIRY, a name given to irregular circles in pastures and lawns on which *agarics* spring up, and which become much more verdant than the surrounding grass. They are caused by the centrifugal growth of the spawn of the *agaric*, which radiates from a common centre, and bears the fructification, which is what appears above ground, only at the circumference. The verdure of the grass where these fungi grow seems to be caused either by their manuring the ground when they decay, or by the nitrogen they give off, which is an active stimulant to vegetation. The application of *fairy rings* was given to this phenomenon from their being regarded as the places where the fairies held their nocturnal revels.

RI'OT, in law, is said to be a tumultuous disturbance of the peace by three persons or more assembling together of their own authority in order to assist each other against any one who shall oppose them in the execution of a private purpose, and afterwards executing the same in a violent and turbulent manner. A rout is said to be a disturbance of the peace by persons assembled together to do a thing, which, if executed, would make them rioters, and making some motion towards that object; an unlawful assembly, a similar disturbance by persons who neither execute their purpose, nor make any actual motion towards the execution of it.

RIPIE'NO, in music, a term signifying full, and is used in compositions of many parts, to distinguish those which fill up the harmony and play only occasionally, from those that play throughout the piece.

RITE, a formal act of religion or other solemn duty; the manner of performing divine service as established by law or custom.

RITORNEL'LO, in music, a passage which is played whilst the principal voice pauses: it often signifies the introduction to an air or any musical piece. This *ritornello* is often repeated after the singing voice has concluded; hence the name.

RIT'UAL, a book containing the rites, or directing the order and manner to be observed in celebrating religious ceremonies, and performing divine service in the church.

ROBES, MASTER OF THE, an officer in the royal household of England, whose duty, as the designation implies, consists in ordering the sovereign's robes. Under a queen, this office, which has always been one of great dignity, is performed by a lady, who enjoys the highest rank of the ladies in the service of the queen.

ROB'IN-GOOD'FELLOW, an old domestic goblin, called in Scotland a *brownie*.

ROC, the well-known monstrous bird of Arabian mythology, of the same fabulous species with the simurg of the Persians. In the notes to vol. iii. of Mr. Lane's edition of the *Arabian Nights' Entertainments* are some curious extracts from the writers of old voyages of that nation; showing that the tale was either founded on, or supported by, the wonderful accounts of travellers. Even Sinbad's well-known adventure, when his crew broke the roc's egg, and were attacked in consequence by the enraged pair of birds, is borrowed from the serious narration of Ibn-El-Wardee. The roc is also described by Marco Paulo. The size of this infamous monster is, of course, described with all the luxuriance of oriental imagination. Ibn-El-Wardee makes one of its wings 10,000 fathoms long. Mr. Lane appears to think that this extravagant fiction was suggested by the condor; but the size and power of that bird are much exaggerated, even in the common accounts. The bearded vulture of Egypt seems a better archetype of the roc. In a drawing from an illuminated Persian MS., which Mr. Lane has copied, the roc, or rather simurg, which is represented as performing the slight operation of carrying off three elephants in its beak and claws, is something like a cock, with eagle's wings and an extravagant tail. The simurg is a creature of importance in Persian mythology: it is the phœnix of oriental fable, one only living at a time, and attains the age of 1700 years.

RODOMONTADE', a term that has passed into most European languages; from Rodomont, a boisterous character in *Orlando Furioso*.

RO'GA, in antiquity, a present which

the emperors made to the senators, magistrates, and even to the people. These *rogæ* were distributed by the emperors on the first day of the year, on their birthday, or on the *natalis dies* of the cities.

ROGA'TION, in the Roman jurisprudence, a demand made by the consuls, or tribunes of the people, when a law was proposed to be passed.—*Rogatio* is also used for the decree itself made in consequence of the people giving their assent to this demand, to distinguish it from a *senatus consultum*, or decree of the senate.

ROGA'TION-WEEK, the week preceding Whitsunday, thus called from the three *rogation-days* or feasts therein, viz. Monday, Tuesday, and Wednesday, on each of which extraordinary prayers and processions were made for the fruits of the earth. The word *rogation* is derived "a rogando Deum," "petitioning God."

ROLL', an official writing; a list, register, or catalogue; as a muster *roll*, a court *roll*, &c.—*Roll call*, the calling over the names of the men who compose any part of a military body.—*Rolls of parliament*, the manuscript registers, or rolls of the proceedings of the ancient English parliaments, which before the invention of printing were all engrossed on parchment, and proclaimed openly in every county. In these *rolls* are also contained a great many decisions of difficult points of law, which were frequently in former times referred to the decision of that high court.

ROLL MOULD'ING, in architecture, a round moulding divided longitudinally along the middle, the upper half of which projects over the lower. It occurs often

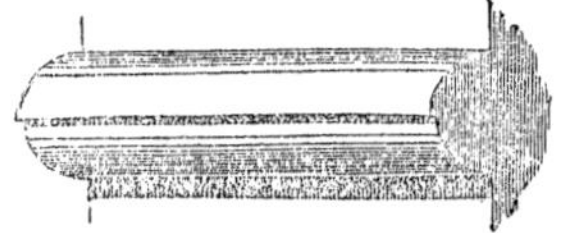

in the early Gothic decorated style, where it is profusely used for drip-stones, string-courses, abacuses, &c.—*Roll and fillet moulding*, a round moulding with a

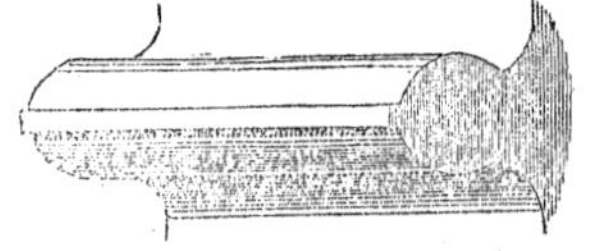

square fillet on the face of it. It is most usual in the early decorated style, and appears to have passed by various gradations into the ogee.

RO'MAN, a native or citizen of Rome; or something pertaining to the place, its people, or their religion.—One of the Christian church at Rome to which St. Paul addressed an epistle, consisting of converts from Judaism or Paganism.—In literature, the ordinary printing char acter now in use, in distinction from the *Italic*.

RO'MAN CATH'OLICS, that society of Christians whose members acknowledge the pope as visible head of the church. The Roman doctors hold that the Scripture is not sufficient for its own interpretation. The books which compose the canon of the New Testament are, they conceive, desultory and incomplete; being many of them written for special occasions, at a period considerably later than the foundation of the religion in various districts, in some of which whole generations of believers may have passed away without having seen or heard of their precious contents. It is not to be supposed, however, that doctrines so important as those shadowed forth in the Epistles of St. Paul, or the Gospel of St. John, could have been left untaught to the churches which flourished before their publication or beyond their reach. It must be admitted, therefore, they argue, that the first preachers of Christianity must have been commissioned and instructed to deliver these same doctrines orally; and it is affirmed that several important doctrines are imperfectly developed in Scripture, and would not be understood, except for some such illustration by the way, the result of which is conveyed in the creeds of the first centuries. It is also affirmed that the practice of the primitive church, the infallibility of which is assumed, authenticates various articles of Roman belief, of which only very slight hints are to be found in Scripture.

ROMANCE', in literature, a tale or fictitious history of extraordinary adventures, intended to excite the passions of wonder and curiosity, and to interest the sensibilities of the heart. The *romance* differs from the *novel*, as it treats of great actions and extravagant adventures, soaring beyond the limits of fact and real life. Romances have of late years given way to historical novels; and even such as are occasionally published are very different from those of the olden time, in which the blandishments of beauty and the enterprises of chivalry were incongruously blended with fictions exceeding all bounds of human credulity. The earliest modern romances were collections of chivalrous adventures, chiefly founded on the lives and achievements of the war-like adherents of two sovereigns, one of whom, perhaps, had only a fabulous existence, while the annals of the other have given rise to a wonderful series of fables—Arthur and Charlemagne. These romances were metrical compositions in that branch of the modern French language termed the *langue d'oil*, which prevailed throughout the north of France, and especially in Normandy. Besides these a great variety of smaller tales, some chivalrous, some marvellous, some simply ludicrous, termed *fabliaux*, exist in the same language. The date of these compositions extend from the 12th to the 15th centuries. From the hands of these rhymers the tales of chivalry passed first into those of prose compilers, who reduced them into a form more resembling that of our modern romances. The French prose romances of chivalry, still confined to the same classes of subjects, belong to the 14th and 15th centuries.

ROMANCE'RO, in Spanish, the general name for a collection of the national ballads or *romances;* so called from the Roman or Romanic tongue, which in the early part of the middle ages, seems to have been the common appellation of all the dialects spoken from the Alps to the western extremity of the Mediterranean. The *Romancero General*, the most celebrated of these collections, was published in 1604–14.

ROMANES'QUE, in painting, appertaining to fable or romance. In historical painting, it consists in the choice of a fanciful subject rather than one founded on fact. The *romanesque* is different from *romantic*, because the latter may be founded on truth, which the former never is.—*Romanesque*, in literature, is applied to the common dialect of Languedoc and some other districts in the south of France, which is a remnant of the old *Romance* language, now nearly extinct. This term must not be confounded with *Romaic*, which is used to signify the language of modern Greece.

RO'MAN LAW, the name given to the law which was founded originally upon the constitutions of the ancient kings of Rome; next upon the twelve tables of the decemviri; then upon the laws or statutes enacted by the senate or by the people; the edicts of the prætor and the responsa prudentum, or the opinions of learned lawyers; and lastly upon the imperial decrees or constitutions of the emperors. The principles of the Roman law are incorporated in a remarkable degree with those of the law of Scotland, and they have exerted an extraordinary influence ever every system of jurisprudence in Europe.

RO'MAN SCHOOL. This school of painting, which, like the Florentine, addressed itself to the mind, is formed upon antique models. Its style was poetical; embellished with all the grandeur, pathos, and freedom from common matters that the happiest imagination could conceive. In touch its masters were easy, correct in drawing, learned and full of grace. In composition it is sometimes whimsical, yet always elegant. The heads of the figures are always drawn with great respect to truth and expression, and it exhibits great intelligence in contrasting attitudes. It is in coloring that it displays the greatest marks of negligence, while in draperies it is eminently successful. At the head of this school was Raffaelle; and among its other principal masters were Giulio Romano, Zuccaro, M. A. Caravaggio, Baroccio, Andrea Sacchi (perhaps the best colorist of this school.)

ROMAN'TIC. By *romantic* is understood that singular intermixture of the wonderful and the mysterious with the sublime and beautiful which introduces us into an enchanted existence, and raises us above the bare realities of life by its dazzling peculiarities. Antiquity was a stranger to this feeling, nor had the classic languages any term to express it. The term *romanticism*—an offshoot of romantic—is of recent invention, and is applied chiefly to the fantastic and unnatural productions of the modern French school of novelists, at the head of which are Victor Hugo, Balzac, "George Sand," &c., and their imitators in France and other countries.

ROMANZIE'RI, in Italian literature, a series of poets who took for the subject of their compositions the chivalrous romances of France and Spain; and, with one or two exceptions only, those relating to the exploits of Charlemagne and his fabulous Paladins. The earliest of these poets flourished in the latter end of the 15th century. Boiardo, although not absolutely the first in order of time, is considered as having laid the groundwork, in his *Orlando Innamorato*, of the edifice of fiction raised by his successors. Pulci, in the *Morgante Maggiore*, was the first who allied the romantic incidents and sentiments of chivalry with light and humorous satire. Berni remodelled the work of Boiardo. Ariosto, in the *Orlando Furioso*, carried this species of poetry to the highest degree of perfection. These are the four principal Romanzieri; but many other poets of the same school flourished until the end of the 16th century. Tasso composed one of his early poems (*Il Rinaldo*) on the common model. In the beginning of the 18th century, the Abate Fortiguerra compiled his *Ricciardetto*, a poem of a semi-burlesque character, intended originally as a parody, but completed as a serious composition; and thus closes the list of the Romanzieri. All these poets adopted the ottava rima, invented by Boccaccio. In their poems the thread of the main narration is frequently interrupted by a multiplicity of minor adventures and intrigues; and this complication of plot appears to have constituted one of the characteristic features of the chivalrous epic.

RON'DEAU, a species of poetry, usually consisting of thirteen verses, of which eight have one rhyme, and five another. It is divided into three couplets, and at the end of the second and third, the beginning of the rondeau is repeated in an equivocal sense, if possible.

RON'DO, in music, either vocal or instrumental, generally consists of three strains, the first of which closes in the original key, while each of the others is so constructed as to reconduct the ear in an easy and natural manner to the first strain.

ROPOROG'RAPHY, a kind of Arabesque style of decoration, found in Pompeii, in which slender columns, formed of parts of plants and animals, are the chief characteristic.

RO'SARY, in the Roman Catholic church, a string of beads, or a chaplet consisting of five or fifteen decades of beads, to direct the recitation of so many *Ave Marias*, or prayers addressed to the Virgin Mary. The rosary serves not only to ascertain the number of recitals, but is intended also to keep the thoughts alive to the act of devotion.

ROSES, FESTIVAL OF, a rural festival of some parts of France, in which the best behaved maiden of the town or village (called *La Rosiere*) is annually crowned with roses in the church, whither she is conducted with great pomp by the villagers. These festivals were originally celebrated on the 8th of June at Salency, a village of Picardy, under Louis XIII., but they were afterwards introduced into Surêne, near Paris, whence they extended to many other places, and have latterly even penetrated to Moravia. The Persians have also an annual festival of roses which consists of bands of youth parading the streets with music, and offering roses, as the Italians during the carnival *confetti*, to all they meet, for which they receive a trifling gratuity.

ROSES, WHITE AND RED, in English history, the well-known feuds that prevailed between the houses of York and Lancaster are so called, from the emblems adopted by their respective partisans; the adherents of the house of York having the white, those of Lancaster the red rose, as their distinguishing symbol. These wars originated with the descendants of Edward III., and after extending over a period of more than eighty years, during which England formed an almost uninterrupted scene of bloodshed and devastation, were at last put an end to by the victory of Henry Tudor, earl of Richmond, over Richard III., in 1485, the victor uniting in his own person the title of Lancaster through his mother, and that of York by his marriage with the daughter of Edward IV. Since that period the rose has been the emblem of England, as the thistle and shamrock (see those terms) are respectively the symbols of Scotland and Ireland.

ROSE WINDOW, in architecture, a circular window divided into compartments by mullions or tracery radiating or branching from a centre. It is called

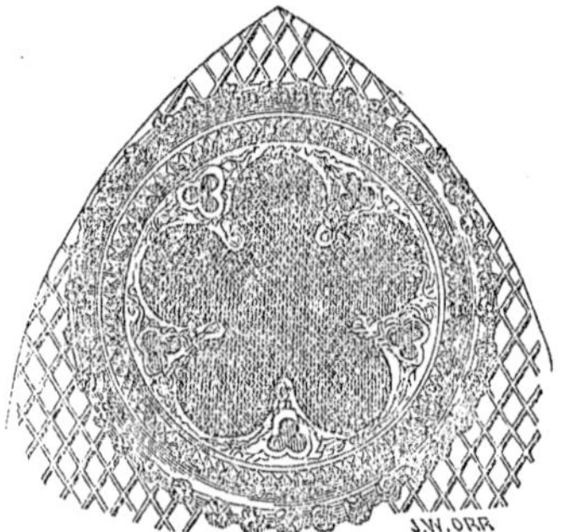

also Catherine Wheel and Mary-gold window.

ROSET'TA STONE, the name given to a stone in the British museum, originally found by the French near the Rosetta mouth of the Nile. It is a piece of black basalt, and contains part of three distinct inscriptions, the first or highest in hieroglyphics, the second in enchorial characters, and the third in Greek. According to the Greek inscription the stone was erected in the reign of Ptolemy Epiphanes, about 193 years before Christ. The inscriptions however are much mutilated, and they have led to no important discovery.

ROSICRU'CIANS, a sect of visionary speculators who existed in Germany about the beginning of the 17th century. They ascribed, indeed, a much higher antiquity to themselves; but it is probable that if any body of philosophers who adopted this title ever existed in reality, they were the alchemists, fire philosophers, or Paracelsists of the 16th century, who adopted this mode of giving vogue and fashion to their tenets. Germany was inundated with tracts, from 1600 to 1630, purporting to come from supporters or from enemies of this sect, in which their opinions and intentions are canvassed, but generally in a wild and unintelligible manner. From one of these, a *Treatise on the Laws of the Rosicrucians*, by Ritter von Maier (1618.) we learn that the fraternity had six fundamental laws:—1. That their chief end and object was to cure the sick without fee or reward. 2. That in travelling they were to change their habits and dress, so as to accommodate themselves to those of the countries in which they sojourned. 3. To meet once a year on a certain day and at a certain place, kept secret from the rest of the world. 4. To fill up vacancies in their body by electing members. 5. To use the letters R C as their common symbol. 6. That the fraternity should remain undivulged for one hundred years from its foundation. It appears probable that the device of the rose issuing out of the cross, which was the same with Martin Luther's seal, was adopted for the purpose of attracting the notice of the religious: the rose was explained to represent the blood of Christ. It would appear from these laws that some species of Freemasonry was intended; and the Rosicrucians have been by some connected with the Freemasons; but there is, in point of fact, no evidence that any such society existed at all, and the name and other circumstances were probably only the device of some alchemists, who usually conveyed their own notions under cover of symbolical language.

ROS'TRA, in antiquity, a part of the Roman forum, where orations, pleadings, funeral harangues, &c., were delivered. It was so called from *rostrum*, the beak of a ship, because it was made of the beaks of the ships taken at Antium.

ROS'TRUM, an important part of the ancient ships of war, which were hence denominated *naves rostratæ*. The *rostrum*, or beak, was made of wood and brass, and fastened to the prow to annoy the enemy's vessels. The first *rostra* were made long and high; but they were afterwards made short and strong, and placed so low as to pierce the enemy's ships under water.—The *rostra* taken by the Romans from their enemies, and hung up as trophies of victory in the forum, occasioned the pulpit, or place for the orators, to be called *rostra*.

RO'TA, the name of an ecclesiastical court at Rome, composed of twelve prelates. This is one of the most august tribunals in Rome, taking cognizance of all suits in the territory of the church, by appeal; and of all matters beneficiary and patrimonial.

ROTUN'DA, a name given to any building that is round both on the outside and inside; but more particularly to a circular building at Rome, which was anciently called the *Pantheon*.

ROUE, a term applied to a person, in the fashionable world, who, regardless of moral principle, devotes his life to sensual pleasures.

ROUN'DELAY, a sort of ancient poem, consisting of thirteen verses, of which eight are in one kind of rhyme, and five in another. It is divided into couplets; at the end of the second and third of which, the beginning of the poem is repeated, and that, if possible, in an equivocal or punning sense.—*Roundelay*, also signifies a song or tune in which the first strain is repeated, and a kind of dance.

ROUND'HEADS, in British history, a name given, during the civil war, to the Puritans or members of the parliament party, from the practice which prevailed among them of cropping the hair round.

ROUND'ROBIN, a term applied to a memorial or remonstrance drawn up by any body of men (though the practice is almost entirely confined to the army and navy,) who have determined to stand by each other in making a statement of their common grievances to the government, or some person high in authority. The term is supposed to be corrupted from *ruban rond*, because their signatures are written round the remonstrance, or in a circular form, so that it cannot be seen who signed it first.

ROUND TABLE, KNIGHTS OF THE, the name given to the famous order of knights that existed in England under the reign of King Arthur, by whom it was founded. The members of this order are said to have been forty in number, and derived their name from a huge round marble table, round which they were accustomed to sit. Their adventures form the themes of much of the early romantic poetry and ballads of England.

ROY'AL, pertaining to or becoming one who is invested with regal power.—Among seamen, a small sail spread immediately above the top-gallant sail; sometimes termed the top-gallant royal. —*Royal Society*, a society incorporated by Charles II. under the name of "The President, Council, and Fellows of the Royal Society, for the Improvement of Natural Philosophy."—*Royal Academy of London*, a corporation instituted by George III. for the advancement of drawing, painting, engraving, sculpture, modelling, and architecture.—*Royal Institution*, a corporation erected in the year 1800; the great object of which is to render science applicable to the comforts and conveniences of mankind.

RU'BEZAHL, the name of a famous spirit of the Riesengebirge in Germany, who is celebrated in innumerable sagas, ballads, and tales, and represented under the various forms of a miner, hunter, monk, dwarf, giant, &c. He is said to aid the poor and oppressed, and shows benighted wanderers their road; but wages incessant war with the proud and wicked. The origin of the name is obscure.

RU'BICON, a small river which separated Italy from Cisalpine Gaul, the province allotted to Cæsar. When Cæsar crossed that stream, he invaded Italy, with the intention of reducing it to his power. Hence the phrase to *pass the Rubicon*, signifies to take a desperate step in an enterprise, or to adopt a measure from which one cannot recede, or from which he is determined not to recede.

RU'BRIC, in the language of the old copies of manuscripts, and of modern printers, any writing or printing in red ink. The date and place on a title-page being frequently in red ink, the word *rubric* has come to signify the false name of a place on a title-page. Many books printed at Paris bear the *rubric* of Genoa, London, &c. But the most common use of the word is in ecclesiastical matters. In MS. Missals, the directions prefixed to the several prayers and offices were written or printed in red ink; and hence, the *rubric* familiarly signifies the order of the liturgy, in Roman Catholic countries as well as in England.

RU'BY, a precious stone, next to the diamond in hardness and value. Its constituent parts are alumina, silica, carbonate of lime, and oxyde of iron. The most esteemed, and, at the same time, rarest color, of the oriental ruby, is pure carmine, or blood red of considerable intensity, forming, when well polished, a blaze of the most exquisite and unrivalled tint. It is, however, more or less pale, and mixed with blue in various proportions; hence it occurs rose-red and reddish white, crimson, peach-blossom red, and lilac blue—the latter variety being named oriental amethyst. A ruby, perfect both in color and transparency, is much less common than a good diamond, and when of the weight of three or four carats, is even more valuable than that gem. The king of Pegu, and the monarchs of Siam and Ava, monopolize the rarest rubies; the finest in the world is in the possession of the first of these kings: its purity has passed into a proverb, and its worth, when compared with gold, is inestimable.

RU'DIMENTS, the first elements or principles of any art or science.—In botany, the germen, ovary or seed-bud, is the *rudiment* of the fruit yet in embryo; and the seed is the *rudiment* of a new plant.

RUDOL'PHINE TA'BLES, a celebrated set of astronomical tables, published by Kepler, and thus entitled in honor of the emperor Rudolph or Rudolphus.

RU'INS, a term peculiarly applied to magnificent buildings fallen into decay by length of time, and whereof there only remains a confused heap of materials. Such are the ruins of the tower of Belus, two days' journey from Bagdat in Syria, on the banks of the Euphrates; which are now no more than a heap of bricks, cemented with bitumen, and whereof we only perceive the plan to have been square. Such also are the ruins of a famous temple, or palace, near Schiras, in Persia, which the antiquaries will maintain to have been built by Ahasuerus, and which the Persians now call Tchelminar, or Chelminar, *q. d.* the Forty Columns, on account of so many columns remaining pretty entire, together with the traces of others, a great quantity of bassi rilievi, and unknown characters, sufficient to show the magnificence of the antique architecture. The most remarkable ruins still existing of entire cities are those of Palmyra and Persepolis, of Herculaneum and Pompeii.

RULE, that which is established as a principle, or settled by authority for guidance and direction. Thus, a statute or law is a *rule* of conduct for the citizens of a state; precedents in law are *rules* of decision to judges.—*Rule*, in monasteries, corporations, or societies, a law or regulation to be observed by the society and its particular members.—In grammar, an established form of construction in a particular class of words.

RUNES, are properly the signs or letters of the ancient alphabet peculiar to the northern nations (Germans and Scandinavians.) Schlegel deduces this alphabet from the Phœnicians. Others have supposed it to have been derived from that of the Romans; but its originally consisting only of sixteen letters has been urged as an argument against this hypothesis. The runen inscriptions found in Germany (especially Northern Saxony,) are thought by some to have tokens of an origin somewhat different from the Scandinavian. The antiquity of both has been much disputed. Of those found in Gothland, it is said that the oldest are not earlier than A.D. 1200, the latest 1449; 1300 stones with Runic inscriptions have, it is said, been discovered in Sweden; many in Denmark; none in Lapland or Finland. Runic staves are massive sticks, generally of willow, inscribed with Runic characters, probably of magical import.

RUNNING-TI'TLE, in printing, the title of a book that is continued from page to page on the upper margin, called, among printers, the *heads*.

RUN'NYMEDE, a celebrated meadow where the conference was held June 15th, 1215, between John and the English barons, in which the former was compelled to sign *Magna Charta* and the *Charta de Foresta*. It is five miles east of Windsor, and is now divided into several enclosures

RUPEE', a coin current in the Mogul empire, and other parts of India. The gold rupee is worth about 2*s.* 6*d.* sterling. Of the silver rupees the new and old are of different values.

RU'RAL ECON'OMY, the general management of territorial property, either by the proprieter or his agent. On a small scale, the agent is termed a bailiff or farm servant; and on a large scale, a land steward or factor. The duties of the latter are to collect the rents, and see that the different clauses in the leases by which the tenants hold their lands are fulfilled; and of the former, to cultivate the land in such a manner as to produce the greatest profit, or to fulfil the intentions of the proprietor as to the kind of produce which he considers it desirable to obtain.

RUS'SIA COM'PANY, a regulated company for conducting the trade with Russia; first incorporated by charter of Philip and Mary, sanctioned by act of parliament in 1566.

RUSTICA'TION, in universities and colleges, the punishment of a student for some offence, by compelling him to leave the institution and reside for a time in the country.

RUS'TIC-WORK, in a building, a term used when the stones, &c., in the face of it are hacked and indented so as to be rough.

RUTH, BOOK OF, a canonical book of the Old Testament, being a kind of appendix to the Book of Judges, and an introduction to those of Samuel. Its title is derived from the person whose story is therein principally related.

RY'OT, in Hindostan, a renter of land by a lease which is considered as perpetual, and at a rate fixed by ancient surveys and valuations. The ryots or peasants may be considered as the cultivators of the soil in India, having a perpetual hereditary and transferable right of occupancy, so long as they continue to pay the share of the produce of the land demanded by the government.

S.

S, the nineteenth letter and fifteenth consonant of our alphabet, is a sibilant articulation; the sound being formed by driving the breath through a narrow passage between the palate and the tongue elevated near it, together with a motion of the lower jaw and teeth towards the upper. The sound of this letter varies, being strong in some words, as in *this*, *thus*, &c., and soft in words which have a final *e*, as *muse*, *wise*, &c. It is generally doubled at the end of words, whereby they become hard and harsh, as in *kiss*, *loss*, &c. In a few words it is silent, as in *isle* and *viscount*. As an abbreviation in music, S stands for *solo*. In books of navigation, and in common usage, S stands for *south*, S.E. for *south-east*, S.W. for *south-west*, S.S.E. for *south-south-east*, S.S.W. for *south-south-west*. In the notes of the ancients, S stands for *Sextus;* Sp. for *Spurius;* and S.P.Q.R. for *senatus populusque Romanus*.

SABÆ'ANS, or SA'BIANS, idolaters of the East, who, in all ages, whether converted in part to Judaism Christianity, or Mohammedanism, or unacquainted with either, have worshipped the stars. Some of the Sabæans, who acknowledge the name of Christ, are distinguished by the title of "Christians of St. John," on account of their attachment to the baptism of that forerunner of the Messiah.—*Sabaism* bears the marks of a primitive religion; to the adoration of the stars, it joins a strong inculcation of respect for agriculture. This belief prevailed in very remote ages in the Asiatic countries between the Euphrates and the Mediterranean; and Chaldæa, the native land of astronomy, was its most celebrated seat. Many allusions are made to this species of worship in the Old Testament, especially in the invectives of the prophets against the various forms of idolatry borrowed by the Jews from their heathen neighbors.

SAB'AOTH, a word of Hebrew derivation, signifying *armies*. It is used, Rom. ix. 29; James v. 4, "the Lord of Sabaoth."

SABA'SIA, in ancient mythology, festivals in honor of various divinities, entitled Sabasii; the origin of which term is not clear. Mithras, the sun, is called Sabasius in ancient monuments, whence the word seems to have some connection with the root of Sabäism; but Bacchus was also thus denominated, according to some, from the Sabæ, a people of Thrace: and the nocturnal Sabasia were celebrated in his name.

SABBATA'RIANS, a sect of baptists who are only remarkable for adhering to the Judaic sabbath, the observance of which they contend was not annulled by the Christian dispensation.

SAB'BATH, the seventh day of the week, a day appointed by the Mosaic law for a total cessation from labor, and for the service of God, according to the divine command, "Remember that ye keep holy the Sabbath day," &c. From the accounts we have of the religious service practised in the patriarchal age, it appears that immediately after the fall, when Adam was restored to favor through a mediator, a stated form of public worship was instituted, which man was required to observe, in testimony, not only of his dependence on the Creator, but also of his faith and hope in the promise made to our first parents, and seen afar off. In the earliest times of Christianity, the desire of distinguishing the Christian from the Jewish observance, gave rise to the celebration of Sunday, the first day of the week, as a sacred festival in commemoration of our Saviour's resurrection—hence emphatically called "the Lord's day." The converts from Judaism, however, retained the celebration of the Sabbath, though they adopted also that of Sunday; and thus in course of time the strict solemnities of the one became blended with the cheerful piety of the other. But independent of the divine injunction, a sabbath, or weekly day of rest and pious meditation, is an institution, on whichever day kept, highly conducive to the happiness and comfort of mankind.—We may here observe, that this septenary division of time has been, from the earliest ages, uniformly observed over all the eastern world. The Assyrians, Egyptians, Arabians, and Persians, made use of a week consisting of seven days. Many futile attempts have been made to account for this uniformity; but a practice so general and prevalent could never have taken place had not the septenary distribution of time been instituted from the beginning, and handed down by tradition.

SABBAT'ICAL YEAR, in the Jewish economy, was every *seventh* year, in which the Israelites were commanded to suffer their fields and vineyards to *rest* or to lie without tillage. The first *sabbatical* year, celebrated by the children of Israel, was the fourteenth year after their coming into the land of Canaan; because they were to be seven years in making themselves masters of it, and seven more in dividing it amongst themselves. This year was reckoned from *Tisri* or September, and for several reasons was called the year of *release:* 1. because the ground remained entirely untilled; 2. because such debts as had been contracted during the six preceding years, were remitted and cancelled; and 3. because all Hebrew slaves were then set at liberty.

SABEL'LIANS, a sect of Christians founded by Sabellius, at Ptolemais, in the third century. Their doctrine taught that the Father, the Son, and the Spirit are names of the one God under different circumstances.

SAC, in law, the privilege enjoyed by

the lord of a manor, of holding courts, trying causes, and imposing fines.

SACK, a wine much esteemed by our ancestors. It was brought from Spain, and is supposed to have been very similar to sherry or canary.

SACK'BUT, a wind instrument of the trumpet species, but differing from the common trumpet in form and size. It is of low or bass pitch, and is drawn out or shortened by means of sliders, according to the acuteness or gravity of the tone to be produced. It is, in fact, the trombone of the Italians.

SAC'RAMENT, in Christian rituals, is defined an outward sign of a spiritual grace annexed to its use. The Roman church recognizes seven sacraments: baptism, confirmation, the eucharist, penance, extreme unction, ordination, and marriage. The Sabæan Christians reduce the sacraments to four; the eucharist, baptism, ordination, and marriage. The Protestant churches acknowledge only two, the eucharist or Lord's supper, and baptism; but they agree with the Roman church in styling the eucharist, pre-eminently, the *holy sacrament.* The eucharist is also known in the Roman church by the name of "the host."

SACRAMENTA'LIA, in ecclesiastical history, certain sacramental offerings formerly paid to the parish priest at Easter, &c.

SACRAMEN'TUM MILITA'RE, in antiquity, the name of the oath taken by the Roman soldiers after the levies were completed.

SAC'RIFICE, a solemn act of religious worship, consisting in the dedication or offering up something animate or inanimate on an altar, by the hands of the priest, either as an expression of gratitude to the Deity for some signal mercy, or to acknowledge our dependence on him, and conciliate his favor. The Jews had two sorts of sacrifices, taking the word in its most extensive signification: the first were offerings of tithes, first-fruits, cakes, wine, oil, honey, &c., and the last, offerings of slaughtered animals. The principal sacrifices of the Hebrews consisted of bullocks, sheep, and goats; but doves and turtles were accepted from those who were not able to bring the other; and whatever the sacrifice might be, it must be perfect and without blemish. The rites of sacrificing were various, all of which are very minutely described in the books of Moses.

SAC'RILEGE, the crime of violating or profaning sacred things; or the alienating to laymen or to common purposes what has been appropriated or consecrated to religious persons or uses.

SAC'RISTY, in architecture, an apartment attached to a church, in which the consecrated vessels of the church, and the garments in which the clergyman officiates, &c., are deposited.

SAD'DER, a work in the modern Persian tongue, comprising a summary of various parts of the *Zendavesta*, or sacred books of the ancient Persians. The authority and character of the Sadder are supposed to be very small; some attribute it to the Parsees, and give it an antiquity of several centuries; others consider it a more modern forgery.

SAD'DUCEES, a sect among the ancient Jews, esteemed as free-thinkers, rather than real Jews, though they assisted at all the ceremonies of worship in the temple. Their origin and name is derived from one Sadoc, who flourished in the reign of Ptolemy Philadelphus, about 263 years B.C. They denied the immortality of the soul, and the existence of all spiritual and immaterial beings. They acknowledged, indeed, that the world was formed by the power of God, and superintended by his providence; but that the soul at death suffered one common extinction with the body. They held the Scriptures alone to be of divine authority, and obligatory upon men, as a system of religion and morals; and paid no regard to those traditionary maxims and human institutions which the Jews in general so highly extolled, and the Pharisees reverenced even more highly than the Scriptures themselves.—The tenets of the Sadducees are called *Sadducism.*

SAFE-CON'DUCT, a pass or warrant of security given by the sovereign under the great seal to a foreigner, for his safe coming into and passing out of the kingdom. Generally speaking, passports have superseded the use of special safe-conducts.

SA'GA, the general name of those ancient compositions which comprise at once the history and mythology of the northern European races. Their language is different from the modern Danish, Swedish, and Norwegian, and is more powerful and expressive than either of these later dialects. Of the mythological sagas the most famous are the saga of Regnar, Lodbrok, the Hervarar saga, the Voluspa saga, and the Wilkina saga. The historical are very numerous; the Jomsvilkingia saga and the Kaflinga saga comprehend much of the early annals of Norway and Denmark; and the Eyrbiggia saga is the chief historical document of ancient Iceland. It is, however, to be remembered, that the chief object of the relators is the interest of the narrative; so that as mere histories they are of imperfect value. Many of them are collected in the great work of Snorre Sturleson called *Heimskringla.* The most classical period of these compositions is considered by antiquaries to fall within the 12th and 13th centuries.

SAGITTA'RII, in the Roman army under the emperors, were young men armed with bows and arrows, who, together with the *Funditores*, were generally sent out to skirmish before the main body.

SAINT, in a limited but the most usual sense of the word, signifies certain individuals whose lives were deemed so eminently pious, that the church of Rome has authorized the rendering of public worship to them. In its widest sense, it signifies the pious, who in this world strictly obey the commands of God, or enjoy, in the eternal world, that bliss which is the reward of such a life on earth.—The doctrine of saints, and the ideas and usages which grew out of it, form one of the main points of difference between the Protestants and Roman Catholics. In all probability, the veneration paid to saints, relics, &c. originated from the virtues displayed by the early Christian martyrs; and it is also very natural to suppose, that in ages when information was transmitted chiefly by tradition, facts easily became exaggerated, without intentional violation of the truth; and many miracles were, accordingly, reported to have been wrought by their relics or intercession.

SAINT JOHN, KNIGHTS OF, or HOSPITALLERS, a military order of religious persons. They derived their name from a church and monastery dedicated to St. John the Baptist, founded at Jerusalem about 1048, by merchants from Amalfi, the brotherhood of its members being devoted to the duty of taking care of poor and sick pilgrims. The order was instituted as a military brotherhood by Raymond du Puy, its principal, early in the 12th century. It was divided into three ranks—knights, chaplains, and servitors; and in its military capacity it was bound to defend the church against the infidels. It possessed various possessions and settlements at different times in different parts of the East. In the 13th century, being driven from Palestine, the knights of this order fixed their principal seat first in Cyprus, and afterwards at Rhodes, where they remained from 1309 to 1522, when the island was captured by Solyman II. After several changes of settlement, they were fixed in 1530 by Charles V. at Malta and its dependent islands, whence they took the name of Knights of Malta. Here they maintained themselves until 1798, when the island was taken by Napoleon. The order, however, continued to subsist, notwithstanding the loss of its sovereign possessions both in Malta and in Tuscany. the seat of the chapter is now at Ferrara. Before the French Revolution the number of knights was estimated at 3000. The temporal powers of the order were chiefly concentrated in the hands of the grand master; but he was, in fact, controlled by the governors of the eight languages. These were, of Provence, Auvergne, France, Italy, Aragon, Germany, Castile, and England. The lands were divided into priories, commanderies, and bailliages. The spiritual power was exercised by the chapter, consisting of eight ballivi conventuales. The knights were under the rules of the order of St. Augustine; but Protestants were not bound to celibacy. They were required to be necessarily of good descent; but those whose proofs of noble ancestry were unquestionable were termed *cavalieri di giustizia*, while others who could not show such proofs might be admitted on account of their merits as *cavalieri di grazia.*

SAINT SIMO'NIANS. Claude Henri, Count de S. Simon, of the ancient family of that name, born in 1760, was engaged during the greater part of his life in a series of unsuccessful commercial enterprises, a traveller, and in the early portion of his life a soldier in America; but having dissipated a considerable fortune, and been unable to draw the attention of the public to a variety of schemes, political and social, which he was constantly publishing, he attempted suicide in 1820; he lived, however, a few years longer, and died in 1825, leaving his papers and projects to Olinde Rodriguez. St. Simon's views of society and the destiny of mankind are contained in a variety of works, and especially in a short treatise entitled the *Nouveau Christianisme*, published after his death by Rodriguez. This book does not contain any scheme for the foundation of a new religion, such as his disciples afterwards invented. It is a diatribe against both the Catholic and Protestant sects for their neglect of the main principle of Christianity, the elevation of the lower classes of society; and inveighs against "l'exploitation de l'homme par l'homme," the existing system of individual industry, under which capitalist and laborer have opposite interests and no common object. The principle of association, and just division of the fruits of common labor between the members of society, he imagined to be the true remedy for its present evils. After his death these ideas were caught up by a number of disciples, and formed into something resembling a system. The new association, or St. Simonian *family*, was chiefly framed by Rodriguez, Bazar, Thierry, Chevalier, and other men of talent. After the revolution of July, 1830, it rose rapidly into notoriety, from the sympathy between the notions which it promulgated and those entertained by many of the republican party. In 1831, the society had about 3000 members, a newspaper (the *Globe*,) and large funds. The views of the St. Simonian family were all directed to the abolition of rank and property in society, and the establishment of association, (such as the followers of Mr. Owen have denominated co-operative,) of which all the members should work in common and divide the fruits of their labor. But with these notions, common to many other social reformers, they united the doctrine, that the division of the goods of the community should be in due proportion to the merits or capacity of the recipient. Society was to be governed by a hierarchy, consisting of a supreme pontiff, apostles, disciples of the first, second, and third order. On the 22d Jan., 1832, the family was dispersed by the government.

SAL'ARY, the stipend or remuneration made to a man for his services—usually a fixed annual sum; in distinction from *wages*, which is for day labor; and *pay*, which is for military service.

SAL'IC, or SAL'IQUE LAW, an ancient and fundamental law of France, usually supposed to have been made by Pharamond, or at least by Clovis, by virtue of which males only can inherit the throne. Though, by this law, the crown of France is prevented from being worn by a woman, the provision was a general one, without particular regard to the royal family; as the crown of England descends to the eldest son, by the *general* right of primogeniture.—The *Salic Franks*, from whom this term was derived, settled in Gaul in the reign of Julian, who is said to have given them lands on condition of their personal service in war. The historian Millot observes, there is no ground for believing that the Salic law expressly settled the right of succession to the crown; it only says that, with relation to the Salic land, women have no share of heritage, without restricting it to the royal family, for all those Salic lands which were held by right of conquest.

SAL'LY, in the military art, the issuing out of the besieged from a town or fort, and falling upon the besiegers in their works, in order to cut them off or harass and exhaust them.—"To cut off a *sally*" is to get between those that made the sally and their town.

SAL'LY-PORT, in fortification, a postern gate, or a passage under ground from the inner to the outer works, such as from the higher flank to the lower, or to the communication from the middle of the curtain to the ravelin.—*Sally-ports* are also doorways on each quarter of a fire-ship, out of which the men make their escape into the boats as soon as the train is fired.

SALOON', a spacious and lofty sort of hall, vaulted at top, and usually comprehending two stories, with two ranges of windows. The saloon is a grand room in the middle of a building, or at the head of a gallery, &c. Its faces or sides should all have a symmetry with each other; and as it commonly takes up the height of two stories, its ceiling should be with a moderate sweep. The saloon is a state-room much used in the palaces of Italy, where the balmy and luxuriant nature of the climate renders airy and spacious apartments desirable; and from thence it travelled into France and England. People of distinction are generally received by the master of a house in the saloon. It is sometimes built square, sometimes round or oval, sometimes octagonal, and sometimes in other forms.

SALUTE', in military discipline, a testimony or act of respect performed in different ways, according to circumstances. In the army, the officers salute by dropping the point of the sword; also by lowering the colors and beating the drums. In the navy, salutes are made by discharges of cannon, striking the colors or top-sails, or by volleys of small arms. Ships always salute with an odd number of guns; and galleys with an even number. The vessel under the wind of the other fires first.

SAL'VAGE, in commerce, allowance or compensation made to those by whose exertions ships or goods have been saved from the dangers of the seas, fire, pirates, or enemies. The crew of a ship are not entitled to salvage for any extraordinary efforts they may have made in saving her, but passengers are entitled to recompense for extraordinary services performed in the hour of danger. If the salvage be performed at sea, or within high or low water mark, the Marine Court has jurisdiction over the subject, and will fix the sum to be paid, and adjust the proportions, which vary according to circumstances. In cases where the party cannot agree, the salvors may retain the property until compensation is made; or they may bring an action or commence a suit in court, against the proprietors for the amount claimed.

SAMAR'ITAN, an inhabitant of Samaria, or one that belonged to the sect which derived their appellation from that city. After the fall of the kingdom of Israel, the people remaining in its territory (consisting of the tribes of Ephraim and Manasseh, mingled with some Assyrian colonists,) were called Samaritans by the Greeks, from the city of Samaria, around which they dwelt. When the Jews, on their return from captivity, rebuilt the temple of Jerusalem, the Samaritans desired to aid in the work; but their offers were rejected by the Jews, who looked upon them as unclean, on account of their mixture with heathens; and the Samaritans revenged themselves by hindering the building of the city and temple. Hence the hatred which prevailed between the Jews and Samaritans, which, in the time of Jesus, when the latter were confined to a narrow strip of country between Judea and Galilee, prevented all intercourse between them, and still continues. In their religious opinions and usages they resemble those Jews who reject the Talmud, and differ from the rabbinical Jews, in receiving only the Pentateuch and book of Joshua, and in rejecting all the other portions of the Bible, as well as the Talmud and rabbinical traditions: but in their manners, rites, and religious ceremonies, they adhere strictly to the Mosaic law.

SA'MIEL, the Arabian name for a hot suffocating wind peculiar to the desert of Arabia. It blows over the deserts in the month of July and August: it approaches the very gates of Bagdat, but is said never to affect a person within its walls. It frequently passes with the velocity of lightning, and there is no way of avoiding its dire effects, but by falling on the ground, and keeping the face close to the earth. Those who are negligent of this precaution experience instant suffocation.

SAMNITES', in antiquity, a sort of gladiators who derived their name from their armor. They are mentioned by Cicero and others.

SAM'UEL, *the books of*, two canonical books of the Old Testament, so called, as being usually ascribed to the prophet Samuel. The books of Samuel, and the books of Kings, are a continued history of the reigns of the kings of Israel and Judah.—The first book of Samuel comprehends the transactions under the government of Eli and Samuel, and under Saul the first king; and also the acts of David while he lived under Saul. The second book is wholly occupied in relating the transactions of David's reign.

SAN-BEN'ITO, a kind of linen garment, painted with hideous figures, and worn by persons condemned by the inquisition. Also a coat of sackcloth used by penitents on their reconciliation to the church.

SANCTIFICA'TION, in an evangelical sense, the act of God's grace by which the affections of men are purified or alienated from sin and the world, and exalted to a supreme love of God.

SANC'TUARY, in a general sense, any sacred asylum; but more especially signifying the SANCTUM-SANCTORUM, the most retired part of the temple at Jerusalem, called also the *Holy of Holies*, in which was kept the ark of the covenant, and into which no person was permitted to enter except the high-priest, and that only once a year, to intercede for the people. From the time of Constantine downwards, certain churches have been set apart in many Catholic countries, to be an asylum for fugitives from the hands of justice. In England, particularly down to the Reformation, any person who had taken refuge in a sanctuary was secured against punishment, if within the space of forty days he gave signs of repentance, and subjected himself to banishment.—In Scotland, the Abbey of Holyroodhouse and its precincts, as having been a royal residence, have the privilege of giving sanctuary to debtors in civil debts. When a person retires to the sanctuary he is protected against personal violence, which protection continues for twenty-four hours; but to enjoy it longer the person must enter his name in the books kept by the baillie of the Abbey. This sanctuary does not protect a crown debtor, nor a fraudulent bankrupt.

SAN'DAL, in antiquity, a kind of costly slipper, worn by the Greek and Roman ladies, made of silk or other precious stuffs, and ornamented with gold or silver.

SANG FROID, [Fr. *cold blood*,] freedom from agitation or excitement of mind.

SAN'GIAC, the title of a provincial governor in Turkey, next in authority to a bey or viceroy.

SAN'HEDRIM, a word said to be derived from the Greek, and signifying the great public council, civil and religious, of the ancient Jewish republic or hierarchy. This council consisted of seventy elders, who received appeals from other tribunals, and had power of life and death.

SANS'CRIT, the learned language of Hindostan. The literal meaning of the word Sanscrita is *polished*, and it is used by grammarians in the sense of "regularly inflected or formed." And it is a question whether, in its present form, it was ever a *spoken* language, although the theory of Schlegel is, that it was imported by the conquering or Brahminical caste. It constitutes the most ancient literature of the Hindoos, and is radically connected with the various dialects of Hindostan, so that they may be regarded as more or less deflected from it. Colebrooke, however, is of opinion that "there seems no good reason for doubting that it was once universally spoken in India;" and he says, that "those who are learned in Sanscrit, at the present day, deliver themselves with such fluency as is sufficient to prove that it may have been spoken in former times with as much facility as the contemporary dialects of the Greek language, or the more modern dialects of the Arabic tongue." Nine tenths of the "Hindustani," it is said, may be traced to the Sanscrit; the remaining tenth is thought to be, perhaps, founded on the old "Hindi" language, which Sir W. Jones thought anterior to it, conceiving the Sanscrit to have been introduced by conquerors in some very distant age. In the Hindoo drama, the gods and saints are made to speak in Sanscrit; while women, benevolent genii, &c., speak another dialect, and the lower personages a third.

SANS-CULOTTES, [from *sans*, without, and *culottes*, breeches,] the name given in derision to the popular party, by the aristocratical, in the beginning of the French revolution of 1789; but though in the first instance applied by way of contempt, yet when the fiercest principles of republicanism prevailed, *sans-culottism* became a term of honor; and some of their bravest generals in their despatches announcing their victories, gloried in the name.

SAP'PHIC, pertaining to Sappho, a Grecian poetess; as *Sapphic* odes, &c The Sapphic verse consists of eleven syllables in five feet, of which the first, fourth, and fifth, are trochees, the second a spondee, and the third a dactyl, in the first three lines, of each stanza, with a fourth consisting only of a dactyl and a spondee.

SAP'PHIRE, a precious stone of a fine blue color. In hardness it is only inferior to the diamond; and the sapphire which is found in the same mines with the ruby, is nearly allied to that gem. They are found in various places; as Pegu, Calicut, Cananor, and Ceylon, in Asia; and Bohemia and Silesia, in Europe. The most highly prized varieties are the crimson and carmine red; these are the oriental ruby of the jeweller: the next is sapphire; and the last is sapphire, or oriental topaz. The asterias, or star-stone, is a very beautiful variety, in which the color is generally of a reddish violet, with an opalescent lustre.

SAP'PING, in sieges, &c., the act of working underground to gain the descent of a ditch, counterscarp, &c.

SAR'ABAND, in music, a composition in triple time very similar to a minuet. When denoting music for the dance, it is to the same measure which usually terminates when the beating hand rises; being thus distinguished from the *courant*, which ends when the hand falls.

SAR'ABITES, a kind of oriental monks or cœnobites, described by Cassian in his *Institutions;* and supposed to be the same with those called Remoboth by St. Jerome and Eust., and characterized as vicious and ignorant. They seem to have been seceders from the ordinary monastic life, which formed a species of society rather resembling that of the Moravians of the present day, and without community of goods.

SARACEN'IC ARCHITEC'TURE. Egypt and Syria present many specimens of Saracenic architecture, which form a striking contrast with the ancient Egyptian and Greek styles. The Saracens, in Egypt, have borrowed but little (if any) of their style from the aborigines of the country. The style called Saracenic, which is justly supposed to have been the parent of the Gothic, is distinguished by the boldness and loftiness of its vaultings; the peculiar mixed form of its curves; the slenderness of its columns; the variety of its capitals; the prodigious multiplicity of its mouldings and ornaments: presenting a strong assemblage of friezes, mosaics, foliage, and arabesques, interlaced with flowers, and disposed altogether with much skill. The *Egyptian Saracenic* differs from the *Spanish* principally in the form of the arch, as may be seen by comparing the gate of Cairo with that of the Alhambra in Grenada, or the great church at Cordova. Among the principal remains of the former style are the walls of Alexandria, built, in 878, by the Caliph Motahwakkel; several arcades of the aqueduct of Alexandria, which are distinguished by the medley of the capitals; the greater and the smaller pharos, the mosque and the ancient palace of the sultans, in the same city: there are also several buildings of the sultan Saladin, whose real name was Joseph or Jussuf, which bear his latter appellation, as the walls at Cairo, the Granaries, &c.

SARCOPH'AGUS, a species of limestone of which ancient coffins were made, and which, according to Pliny, had the power of destroying within forty days the corpses put into them. This quality brought the stone into use for coffins, and thus the name came to be applied to all coffins of stone, though often used for a contrary purpose to that which the name expresses. Of the great number of *sarcophagi* which have come down to us, several are known by particular names; as, the sarcophagus of Homer, in the Besborodko gardens at St. Petersburg; and that of Alexander the Great, in the British museum, once in the mosque of St. Athanasius at Alexandria. It was taken by the British from the French, during their memorable campaign in Egypt.

SARDON'IC LAUGH, (*risus sardonicus*,) so called from the herb *sardonia*, which being eaten is said to cause a deadly convulsive laughter, or spasmodic grin.

SAR'DONYX, a genus of semi-pellucid gems, of the onyx structure, zoned or tabulated, and composed of the matter of the onyx variegated with that of the red or yellow carnelian.

SAS'TRA, among the Hindoos, a book containing sacred ordinances. The six great *Sastras*, in the opinion of the Hindoos, contain all knowledge, human and divine. These are called the Veda, Upaveda, Vedanga, Purana, Dherma, and Dersana.

SA'TAN, a Hebrew word signifying enemy or adversary, and used as such, without any reference to the Evil Power itself, in one or two passages of the Old and New Testaments. The equivalent term in Greek for this word is literally *one who accuses or calumniates;* whence the word *devil* is derived.

SAT'IRE, in literature, a species of writing, generally poetical, the object of which is always castigation. It presupposes not merely much natural wit, but also acute observation, and much variety of life and manners to call this wit into exercise. Satire, in the literary sense of the word, as designating a species of composition, is usually confined to a species of poetry; but prose works, of which the contents are of a satirical character, are often comprehended under the same appellation. Dramatic writings, also, are not satires in the stricter sense of the word, although their contents be of a satirical character. According to their subjects, satires are divided into political and moral, and these again severally subdivided into personal and general. Political satires, in almost every language, have been nearly confined to prose; the moral satire alone has found its appropriate vehicle in verse. The only Greek satirist of whom any fragments have reached us was Archilochus, and his attacks were evidently directed against individuals. Aristophanes possessed a vein of satirical power, both in the indignant and ludicrous strain, which has never been surpassed; and his dramas contain not only sarcasms on individuals, but also political and ethical lessons of the highest value. But the moral satire, properly so called, was invented by the Romans, not only in form, but in substance also, and by them carried to perfection; and it is remarkable that the only species of Roman poetry which has any degree of originality is that which would seem to have accorded the least with the grave and austere turn of the genuine Roman character. In the literature of the modern nations, the fate of satire has been similar to that which has befallen many other species of composition. The name and form of the ancient satire have been preserved by many writers, who have produced, for the most part, little besides cold or exaggerated imitations of antiquity. But the true spirit of satire, in its moral beauty, its humor, and its delicate irony, has been inherited by others, who had too much originality of thought to tie down their genius to an antiquated form of writing.

SAT'URDAY, the last day of the week. The Scandinavians, and from them the Saxons, had a deity named *Seater*, from whom the English name of the *dies Saturnii* of the Romans may be derived; but the subject is by no means clear.

SAT'URN, an Italian deity having many points of similarity with the Grecian Kronos, with whom he is, accordingly, frequently identified. He seems to have been originally the god of earth, (of which his wife Tellus, Ops, or Rhea was the goddess,) and presided over tillage, of which the sickle he carried was the symbol. The treasury at Rome was in his temple. The Grecian Kronos was the youngest son of Heaven and Earth, and the father of Jupiter, Juno, Neptune, and Pluto. He usurped the sovereignty, and was in his turn deposed and imprisoned by Jupiter. His reign was celebrated by the ancient poets as the golden age. The whole history of this deity is probably allegorical. The name itself, with a slight variation signifies time, and his attribute of the sickle, together with the account of his being the son of Heaven, by whose luminaries time is measured, and the husband of Rhea (flowing,) and of his devouring his own progeny, are corroborative of this conjecture.

SATURNA'LIA, in antiquity, feasts in honor of Saturn. The Saturnalia had their origin in Greece, but by whom they were instituted or introduced among the Romans is not known: but they were celebrated with such circumstances as were thought characteristic of the golden age; particularly the overthrow of distinction and rank. Slaves were reputed masters during the three days of this festivity; were at liberty to say what they pleased; and, in fine, were served at table by their owners. These festivities, in which men indulged in riot without restraint, were held annually about the middle of December.

SAT'YRS, in classical mythology, divinities, or rather supernatural personages, represented with the heads, arms, and bodies of men, and the lower parts of goats. They were under the peculiar government of the god Bacchus. Some antiquaries have fancied that the notion of satyrs arose from the introduction of ourang-outangs by the real Bacchus on his return from his conquest of India, and derive the name from the Heb. sahurim, *hairy men;* Bacchus, according to tradition, having remained some time in Palestine during his return. In the same way we may perhaps account for St. Augustin's story, of a satyr having been seen and caught, in his own time, in the deserts of Africa.—In Grecian dramatic literature, the name satyr is applied to a theatrical piece, in which the chorus consisted of satyrs of a semi-burlesque character—to judge of it by the only specimen left to us, the *Cyclops* of Euripides. It was customary for the tragedian to present at the same time three tragic pieces and one satyr, forming a tetralogy.

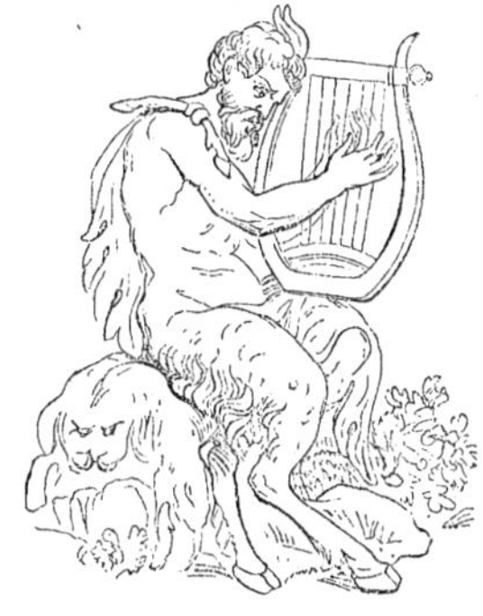

SAU'CISSE, in the art of war, a long pipe or bag, made of cloth well pitched, or of leather, filled with powder, and extending from the chamber of the mine to the entrance of the gallery. It serves to communicate fire to mines, caissons, bomb chests, &c.

SAUCISSONS', in fortification, fagots or fascines, made of great boughs of trees bound together; their use being to cover men, or to make epaulements, &c.

SAX'ON ARCHITEC'TURE, the architecture of England before the Norman conquest. There are some supposed remains of this style in existence, but the characteristics are not satisfactorily determined.

SCAF'FOLDING, in architecture, is the temporary combination of timber-work, by the means of upright poles and horizontal pieces, on which latter are laid the boards for carrying up the different stages or floors of a building, and which are struck or removed as soon as they have answered their purpose.

SCAGLIO'LA, a mixture of fine gypsum and powdered selenite, made into a paste with glue, and serving to form paintings of a stony hardness. The process is as follows:—Upon a tablet of white stucco (consisting of this gypsum paste,) the outlines of the work designed are traced with a sharp instrument, and the cavities thus made are filled up with successive layers of paste, of the same composition, but colored. It takes a very high polish, and, when executed by a skilful workman, is an admirable imitation of marble.

SCALD, signifies in the ancient Norsk language a poet. In the old northern literature, those mythological poems of which the writers are known are properly called songs of the Scalds, while those of unknown authors are termed Eddas. It appears from Tacitus that the ancient Germans had those three classes of poems which were found at a later era in Scandinavia, namely, relating to the gods, to heaven, and to historical subjects. The Scalds whose remains have come down to us are very numerous. Their poems are partly alliterative, and partly rhymed; and this latter circumstance seems to indicate works of comparatively recent date. The historical value of their poems is considerable; but they are written in a peculiar vein of exaggeration, and in a metaphysical and almost enigmatical fashion, which appears to have been characteristic of the poetical art of the north.

SCALE, in music, a progressive series of sounds arising in acuteness or falling in gravity from any given pitch to the greatest practical distance, through such intermediate degrees as create an agreeable and perfect succession, wherein all the harmonical intervals are conveniently divided.

SCAMIL'LI, in ancient architecture, a sort of second plinths or blocks under statues, columns, &c., to raise them, but not, like pedestals, ornamented with any kind of moulding.

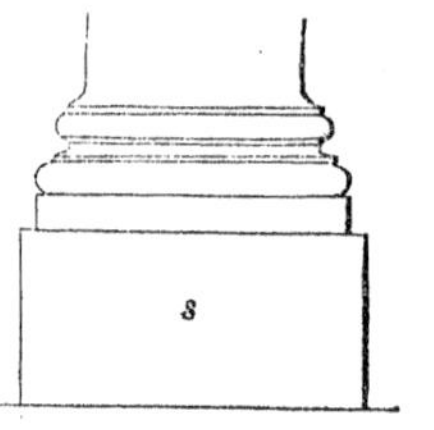

s. Scamilli.

SCANDA'LUM MAGNA'TUM, in law, a defamatory speech or writing made or published to the injury of a person of dignity.

SCAN'NING, in Latin poetry, the examining a verse by counting the feet, to see whether the quantities be duly observed; or, according to modern usage, to recite or measure verse by distinguishing the feet in pronunciation.

SCAPE'-GOAT, in the Jewish ritual, a goat which was brought to the door of the tabernacle, where the high-priest laid his hands upon him, confessing the sins of the people, and putting them on the head of the goat; after which the goat was turned loose into the wilderness.

SCAP'ULARY, a part of the habit of certain religious orders in the Romish church, consisting of two narrow slips of cloth worn over the gown, covering the back and breast, and extending to the feet.

SCAR'AMOUCH, a personage in the old Italian Comedia dell' Arte, dressed in the Spanish or Hispano-Neapolitan costume, and representing a military personage, a poltroon and braggadocio, who always ended by receiving a beating from the hands of Harlequin. The most celebrated Scaramouch of the Italian theatre at Paris was Tiberio Fiurelli, a Neapolitan, who had the honor of making Louis XIV. laugh when an infant; and whose agility was such that he was able, according to his biographers. to give a box on the ear with his foot at the age of 80.

SCARP, in fortification, the interior talus or slope of the ditch next the place at the foot of the rampart.—In heraldry, the scarf which military commanders wear for ornament.

SCENE, in dramatic literature, dramatic representations, having, it is supposed, originally taken place on spots of ground shaded with boughs of trees.—The imaginary place in which the action of the play is supposed to pass; also a division of a drama: properly speaking, whenever the action changes to a new scene or place. But in the French theatre, and those framed on its model, (in which unity of place is observed,) every entry of an actor constitutes a new scene. On the English stage, the subdivision called a scene is extremely arbitrary; the scenes in most plays being far more numerous than the actual changes of scene, while at the same time the French rule is not observed, and actors enter in the middle of a scene. The scenes in a play are numbered as subdivisions of the act.

SCENE PAINT'ING, a department of

painting which forms a walk of art both peculiar and extensive, and has its own laws, its own practical and scientific rules, in the same way as perspective has. The follower of scene painting should, in the first place, be deeply conversant with that particular knowledge, by means of which he is enabled to decide on the effects of those colors he employs by day, when they shall be subjected to a strong artificial light. In the next instance, it is absolutely indispensable that he should be well versed in the rules of both linear and aerial perspective. He traces, by fixed geometrical operations, lines bent or inclined, which the spectator, placed at the proper point of view, imagines to be straight ones. He employs gradual diminutions of plans which give the appearance of an extent and distance existing merely in his own art; thus in a few fathoms to which he is bounded expressing an extent sometimes almost infinite. He uses chiefly water colors, on account of their operating promptly, and presenting no glossy surface. To the scene painter the use of brilliant colors, of skilful *chiaro-scuro*, of striking management of masses of light and shade, is obvious. He addresses less the heart or understanding than the eye. With him *effect* is everything. His fame, as well as his works, is commonly of short duration; and there is consequently the greater reason that he should acquire that promptness and decision of style which would secure immediate approbation.

SCE'NERY, the appearance of the various objects presented to our view; as, the *scenery* on the banks of the Thames at Richmond is diversified and pleasing; or, the landscape scenery presented to the view from the Malvern hills is picturesque and varied.—The paintings representing the scenery of a play.

SCENOG'RAPHY, in perspective, stands opposed to ichnography and orthography. *Ichnography* is the ground-plan; *orthography*, the elevation or a flat view of a front of an object; and *scenography*, is the perspective view, which takes several sides, and represents everything in its apparent proportions.

SCEP'TICISM, also called *Pyrrhonism*, (from its founder, Pyrrho, who lived under Alexander the Great,) the doctrine of a sect of philosophers, who maintained that no certain inferences can be drawn from the senses, and who therefore doubted of everything.—In theology, *scepticism* is a denial of the divine origin of the Christian religion, or of the being, perfections, and truth of God. The most celebrated sceptics of modern times are, Montaigne (A.D. 1580;) Glanville, an Englishman, who flourished about the period of the Restoration; Bayle, and Hume. Of these Mr. Hume has the merit of producing the most systematic and comprehensive scheme of scepticism the world has yet seen. According to this philosopher, all the objects of consciousness may be reduced to two classes—1. the impressions on the senses; and 2. ideas, or copies of those impressions, which differ from their originals only in being less vivid. All knowledge, save that of mathematical relations, consists in the arrangement of these impressions according to the order of their succession. Of the connection between any two links of this succession we know nothing; that to which we give the name of causation being, in fact, nothing more than habitual sequence relatively to the phenomena, and custom, or often-repeated association, in relation to ourselves.

SCEP'TRE, a short staff, the emblem of sovereign power. It is an ensign of royalty of greater antiquity than the crown. It was at first an unornamented staff, or baton, but afterwards became covered with ornaments in ivory, gold, &c. At the present time the sceptre and ball form the two most important emblems of royal and imperial power.

SCHED'ULE, in law, a scroll of paper or parchment appended to a will or any other deed. Also an inventory of goods, &c.

SCHE'RIF, a title given in the East, by prescriptive usage, to those who descend from Mohammed through his son-in-law and daughter, Ali and Fatima. They are also called Emir and Seid, and have the privilege of wearing the green turban. The chiefs of Mecca and Medina, who are always supposed to belong to this sacred family, are styled the scherifs of those cities.

SCHISM, in a theological sense, a division or separation in a church or denomination of Christians; or breach of unity among people of the same religious persuasion. Hence, one who separates from an established church or religious faith is termed a *schismatic*.—In Scripture, the word *schism* seems to denote a breach of charity, rather than a difference of doctrine.

SCHOLAS'TICS, a class of philosophers or *schoolmen*, who arose in the middle ages, and taught a peculiar kind of philosophy, which consisted in applying the ancient dialectics to theology, and intimately uniting both. On account of the excessive subtilty which prevailed in the scholastic philosophy, the expression *scholastic* has been used for the extreme of *subtilty*. After the Reformation and the revival of letters, the system gradually declined, till it gave place to the enlightened philosophy of Lord Bacon and the great men who have followed in his track and carried out his principles.

SCHO'LIA, notes or annotations on an ancient author.—*Scholiast*, one who writes *scholia*, for the purpose of illustrating ancient authors.

SCHOOL, a house or place of rendezvous for pupils or students to receive instruction in various arts and branches of useful and necessary knowledge. In modern usage, the word *school* comprehends every place of education, whether a college, an academy, a primary school, or a school for learning any single art or accomplishment. "The changes which have taken place in science, and in the whole condition of modern nations, who are no longer dependent, like those of the middle ages, for their means of intellectual culture, on the remains of ancient civilization, necessarily make the character of school instruction very different from what it was formerly, when the whole intellectual wealth of Europe was contained in two languages; and though these noble idioms will always retain a high place in a complete system of education, yet their importance is comparatively less, while that of the natural sciences, history, geography, politics, &c. has very much increased. All this has had a great influence upon schools, and will have a still greater. The importance of education, moreover, is now set in strong relief by the general conviction, entertained in free countries, that the general diffusion of knowledge is the only true security for well-regulated liberty, which must rest on a just sense of what is due from man to man; and few results can be attained by the student of history and of mankind more delightful than this of the essential connection of light and liberty; not that great learning necessarily leads to liberty; history affords many instances which disprove this; but that a general diffusion of knowledge always tends to promote a general sense and a love of what is right and just, as well as to furnish the means of securing it." For the foregoing remarks, which are not less forcible than apparent, we are indebted to Blackie's edition of the Conversations Lexicon.—*Schools, Infant*, are said to owe their origin to Mr. Robert Owen of Scotland. They have now been in operation since the year 1820.—*Schools, Normal*, schools for the education of persons intended to become schoolmasters, teachers, or professors in any line. Normal schools form a regular part of the establishments for education in many continental states, especially in Germany. The normal school of Paris was suppressed in 1821, but revived a few years afterwards under the name of preparatory school, and has now (since the event of 1830) resumed its original title.—*Schools, Sunday*, first set on foot by Mr. Robert Raikes of Gloucester. The number of children at present frequenting Sunday-schools in England, varies from 800,000 to 900,000. The education given is almost uniformly confined to reading alone; but many Sunday-schools appear to have evening schools connected with them, open two or three times a week, in which writing and arithmetic are taught. The system of Sunday-school instruction prevails to a great extent in the United States, where it is almost exclusively of a religious character.—*School*, among painters, the style and manner of painting among the great masters of the art at any particular period, as the Italian, Flemish, Dutch, Spanish, and English schools.—*School*, in philosophy, a system of doctrine as delivered by particular teachers, as the *Platonic school*, the *school of Aristotle*, &c.—Also, the seminaries for teaching logic, metaphysics, and theology, which were formed in the middle ages, and which were characterized by academical disputations and subtilties of reasoning. Hence *school divinity* is the phrase used to denote that theology which discusses nice points, and proves everything by argument.

SCIAG'RAPHY, in architecture, a profile or section of a building to exhibit its interior structure.

SCI'ENCE, in a general sense, knowledge, or certain knowledge; the knowledge of many methodically digested and arranged so as to become attainable by one; the comprehension or understanding of truth or facts by the mind. The *science* of God must be perfect.—In philosophy, a collection of the general principles or leading truths relating to any subject.—*Pure science*, as the mathematics, is built on self-evident truths; but the term science is also applied to other subjects founded on generally acknowledged truths, as *metaphysics*; or on experiment and observation, as *chemistry* and *natural philosophy;* or even to an assemblage of the general principles of an art, as the science of *agriculture;* the science of *navigation.* The knowledge of reasons and their conclusions, constitutes *abstract science;* that of causes and effects, and of the laws of nature, *natural* or *physical science.* The term science is often used to signify that which we know inductively, or by the experience of particulars, from which we ascend to general conclusions not necessarily constituted by those particulars, yet warranted by previous experience and by analogies widely observed. This signification of the term is applicable to *physical, moral, and practical science.*—*Physical* or *natural science* is that which is susceptible of experiment, and is therefore said to be founded on experimental evidence.—*Moral science*, is that which, lying in great part beyond the reach of experiment, rests for its certainty on aggregated facts, supported by concurrent testimony, by experience, and by analogy, so as to leave no room for doubt, though not demonstrable.—*Practical science*, is that which consists of general observations arising out of experience, and is otherwise called *theory* in correlation to an art or practice belonging to it. The term *science*, however, is more particularly used in contradistinction to *art* and *literature.* As distinguished from the former, *a science* is a body of truths, the common principles of which are supposed to be known and separated, so that the individual truths, even though some or all may be clear in themselves, have a guarantee that they could have been discovered and known either with certainty, or with such probability as the subject admits of, by other means than their own evidence. As distinguished from *literature*, science is applied to any branch of knowledge which is made the subject of investigation with a view to discover and apply first principles.

SCI'RE FA'CIAS, in law, a judicial writ summoning a person to show cause to the court why something should not be done; as, to require sureties to show cause why the plaintiff should not have execution against them for debt and damages, or to require a third person to show cause why goods in his hands by replevin, should not be delivered to satisfy the execution, &c.

SCLAVO'NIAN, or SCLAVON'IC, pertaining to the *Sclavi*, or their language—a people that anciently inhabited the country between the rivers Save and Drave. Hence the word came to denote the language which is now spoken in Poland, Hungary, Bohemia, &c.

SCORE, in music, a collection of all the vocal and instrumental parts of a composition, arranged on staves one above the other, and bar for bar, presenting at once, to the eye of a skilful musician, the effect of the whole band as the composition proceeds. A composition so arranged is also said to be *in score.*

SCOT, in law, a customary contribution laid upon all subjects according to their ability. Whoever were assessed to any contribution, though not by equal portions, were said to pay scot and lot.

SCO'TIA, in architecture, the name of a hollow moulding, chiefly used between the tori in the bases of columns. It takes its name from the shadow formed by it, which seems to envelop it in darkness. It is sometimes called a casement; and often, from its resemblance to a common pulley, *trochilus.*

SCOT'ISTS, a sect of school-divines and philosophers, thus called from their founder, J. Duns Scotus, a Cordelier, who maintained the immaculate conception of the Virgin, or that she was born without original sin, in opposition to Thomas Aquinas and the Thomists.

SCREEDS, in architecture, wooden rules for running mouldings. Also the extreme guides on the margins of walls and ceilings for floating to, by the aid of the rules. They are always necessary for running a cornice when the ceiling is not floated.

SCREEN, in architecture, a partition usually wrought with rich tracery, placed behind the high altar of a church, and also before small chapels and tombs. Sometimes, as at Easter, they are placed temporarily at the sides of choirs.

SCRIBES, the copyists, and at the same time the interpreters of the law, in the later periods of the Jewish history. They were held in great honor among that people, and ranked with the priests themselves in their estimation. In the New Testament we find them generally referred to in connection with the Pharisees, to which sect they appear generally to have belonged, and with whom they coincided in temper and sentiments. Some ancient writers conceive the scribes to have formed peculiar sects in themselves; but there is no authority to sustain this opinion.

SCRIP'TURE, or the *Holy Scriptures*,

an appellation given, by way of eminence, to the sacred and inspired writings of the Old and New Testaments.

SCRIV'ENER, money scriveners, in old English usage, were parties who received money to place it out at interest, and supplied parties who wished to lend money on security.

SCRU'TINY, in law, an examination of suffrages or votes at an election, for the purpose of ascertaining whether they are good or not.—In the primitive church, an examination of catechumens who were to receive baptism on Easter-day.

SCULP'TURE, the art of giving form and expression, by means of the chisel and other implements, to masses of stone or other hard substances, so as to represent figures of every description, animate and inanimate. It is generally thought that sculpture had its origin from idolatry, as it was found necessary to place before the people the images of their gods to enliven the fervor of their devotion. But to form conclusions concerning the rise and progress of the arts and sciences, without the aid of historical evidence, by analogies which are sometimes accidental, and often fanciful, is a mode of reasoning which, at best, must ever be liable to suspicion. In whatever country the earliest attempts were made, the Egyptians were the first who adopted a certain style of art. Their works were gloomy and grave, but still they were full of deep sentiment, and connected, as would appear by the hieroglyphics which covered them, with poetry and history, and by the mummies, with the belief of immortality. Interesting as the subject would doubtless prove, it is far beyond our limited means to trace the progress of this beautiful art through all its stages in the classic days of Greece, till its decline in Rome, where, though all the treasures of the Grecian sculptors had been carried to deck the Roman capital, the art never became naturalized. During the long and gloomy interval of barbarism that succeeded the downfall of imperial Rome, sculpture, with the sister arts, lay dormant and forgotten. At length, however, through the genius of Michael Angelo Buonarotti, and the skill and perseverance of some of his distinguished successors, seconded by the patronage of the illustrious house of Medici, the treasures of antiquity were collected, and modern art nobly tried to rival the grace and sublimity which existed in the ancient models. Though till within the last century it could hardly be said that a British school of sculpture existed, yet the talent that has been successfully called into action has produced many works of sterling merit. The names of Flaxman, Chantrey, Baily, and Westmacott, are alone sufficient to redeem the national character in this department of art. In the United States, the productions of Greenough, Powers and other distinguished artists, have been received with admiration by the most fastidious connoisseurs. The very essence of sculpture is correctness; and when to correct and perfect form is added the ornament of grace, dignity of character, and appropriate expression, as in the Apollo, the Venus, the Laocoön, the Moses of Michael Angelo, and many others, this art may be said to have accomplished its purpose.—*Sculpture, practice of.* What has been said under the article *Painting*, relative to anatomy, comparative anatomy, symmetry, invention, expression, and drapery, equally applies to the art of sculpture, and need not be here repeated. We shall, therefore, merely state the different methods practised in producing a work in this art. A model as large as the intended figure or group is first made in clay. It is placed on a stand called the sculptor's easel; and the general form is got out with the hand and fingers, small box-wood tools being made use of to touch the parts that the fingers cannot reach. The clay is kept moist, to prevent its shrinking till the model is completed. The model is then moulded in plaster of Paris, before it begins to dry, whence a matrix is formed, into which plaster is introduced; and the matrix being broken away from it, the model in clay is thus transferred into one of plaster. This becomes the standard from which the artist takes all the measurements for the figure he is about to execute. The block of marble and the model being now placed on stands, with a graduated rod, which moves on a frame perpendicular to it, and has a point attached to it which can be made to advance and recede at pleasure, certain prominent points are selected and marked in the model, and their distance measured on the frame longitudinally and vertically, and also the distance that the point of the rod is advanced or receded to touch a given point. This being found on the outside of the rough block, the particular point is drilled down to as great a distance as was measured in the model. This operation being repeated for a great number of points, the surface is worked away to all the several points found as above, till at last it begins to assume the general form of the model. As the sculptor approaches the surface which is to be left when finished, more caution and finer tools become necessary, till at length it is brought into a state for his finishing touches. The process which we have described of bringing the shapeless block into something like the form it is ultimately to bear, and which is an operation purely mechanical, is performed by inferior workmen, by which the artist's labor and time are much spared. It is only with such a genius as Michael Angelo that the making a model could be dispensed with.

SCU'TUM, in antiquity, a sort of buckler of both an oblong and an oval form.

SCYL'LA, a rock in the sea between Sicily and Italy, which was very formidable to the mariners among the ancients. It was opposite to the whirlpool Charybdis.

SEAL, in law, the impression or device printed on wax which is put to any deed by way of ratification.

SEA'MAN, an individual engaged in navigating ships or other vessels upon the high seas. Various regulations have been enacted with respect to the hiring of seamen, their conduct, and the payment of their wages; but these particulars are too numerous for insertion here, and not within the scope of this work.

SEA'MANSHIP, an acquaintance with the art of managing and navigating a ship; applicable both to officers and the men, and indispensably necessary in those who have the ship under their command.

SEA'SONS, the four divisions or portions of the year, namely, Spring, when the sun enters Aries; Summer when he enters Cancer; Autumn, when he enters Libra; and Winter when he enters Capricorn. The diversity of the seasons depends upon the oblique position of the sun's path through the heavens, whereby this luminary rises to different heights above the horizon, making the day sometimes longer, and sometimes shorter than the nights. When the sun rises highest at noon, its rays fall most nearly in the direction of a perpendicular, and consequently a greater number is received upon a given spot; their action also, at the same time, continues the longest. These circumstances make the difference between summer and winter. It is found that the sun does not rise so high in summer, nor descend so low in winter, at the present time as it did formerly; in other words, the obliquity of the ecliptic, which is half the difference between the sun's greatest and least meridian altitudes, is growing less and less continually, and the seasons are thus tending, though slowly, to one unvaried spring.

SEC'OND, in music, an interval of a conjoint degree, being the difference between any sound and the next nearest sound above or below it. There are three kinds of seconds, the minor second or semitone, the major second, and the extreme sharp second.

SEC'OND SIGHT, a superstitious notion, prevalent in the highlands of Scotland, by which certain persons are supposed to be gifted with a kind of supernatural sight, or the power of seeing future or distant events as if they really happened. But the peculiarity of the Highland superstition seems to consist in this, that persons were supposed to be endowed with the faculty who were in no other respect feared or reverenced for their supernatural powers; it was regarded as a mere natural power, like superior sharpness of sight or hearing. The inhabitants of the Western Islands were thought to be peculiarly gifted with it. It could not be exerted at pleasure; the power came on the seer involuntarily, and often to his extreme terror and suffering. Nevertheless, certain rules were in fashion for the interpretation of the visions; such, for instance, as that mentioned by Sir W. Scott, that if a seer saw a figure with his back to him, on altering the position of his own plaid if the figure appeared with its plaid similarly arranged the vision regarded the seer himself.

SEC'RETARY, an officer whose duty it is to write letters and other instruments, for and under the orders and authority of a public body or an individual.—*Secretary of State*, an officer who transacts and superintends the affairs of a particular department of government. In Great Britain, there are three principal secretaries of state. In this country, the secretary of state conducts treaties with foreign powers, and corresponds with the public ministers abroad, and foreign ministers of the United States. He also keeps the seal of the United States, but cannot use it without the authority of the president.

SECT, a collective term for a body of persons adhering to some philosophical or religious system, but constituting a distinct party by holding sentiments different from those of other men. Most *sects* have originated in a particular person, who taught and propagated some peculiar notions in philosophy or religion, and who is considered to have been its founder.

SECTA'RIAN, one of a party in religion which has separated itself from the established church, or which holds tenets different from those of the prevailing denomination in a kingdom or state.

SEC'TION, in general, denotes a distinct part or portion of something which is divided, or the division itself. Such are the subdivisions of a chapter, called also paragraphs and articles.—In architectural drawings, the word *section* is applied to the view of an edifice cut down the middle for the purpose of exhibiting the interior, and describing the height, breadth, thickness, of wall, arches, domes, &c. The drawings relative to an architectural work cannot be said to be complete, unless they comprise plan, elevation, and section.

SEC'ULAR, something that is temporal, in which sense the word stands opposed to *ecclesiastical*: thus we say, secular power, secular jurisdiction, &c. Among Catholics, *secular* is more peculiarly used for an ecclesiastic who lives at liberty in the world, not confined to a monastery, nor bound by vows, or subjected to the particular rules of any religious community; in which sense it stands opposed to *regular*. Thus we say, the *secular* clergy, and the *regular* clergy.—The act of rendering secular the property of the clergy, is called *secularization*.

SEC'ULAR GAMES, in antiquity, solemn games held among the Romans once in an age or century. They lasted three days and three nights, during which time sacrifices were performed, theatrical shows exhibited, with combats, sports, &c., in the circus. The first who had them celebrated at Rome was Valerius Publicolo, the first consul created after the expulsion of the kings. At the time of the celebration of the secular games, heralds were sent throughout all the empire, to intimate that every one might come and see those solemnities which he never yet had seen, nor would ever see again.

SECULARIZA'TION, in politics, the appropriation of church property to secular uses. In most European states such appropriations have taken place on a great scale within the last century. In England, the only great secularization has been that made under Henry VIII.

SECUN'DUM AR'TEM, (Lat.) according to the rules of art.—In medicine, a term frequently used in prescriptions, to denote that the recipe must be made up with particular care.—*Secundum naturam*, according to the course of nature.

SECUTO'RES, in antiquity, a description of gladiators among the Romans, who fought against the *retiarii*. The *secutores* were armed with a sword and a buckler, to keep off the net or noose of their antagonists, and they also wore a casque. This name was also given to such gladiators as took the place of those killed in the combat, or who fought the conqueror.

SE DEFENDEN'DO, in law, a plea used for one who is charged with the death of another, by alleging that he was under a necessity of committing the act in his own defence.

SEDI'TION, in politics, an opposition to the laws, or the administration of justice, and in disturbance of the public peace.—In general, it signifies a local or limited opposition to *civil* authority; a commotion of less extent than an *insurrection*, and consequently less than *rebellion*.

SEE, the name usually given to the diocess of a bishop in England. It was originally applied exclusively to the papal chair at Rome; but it has long been used in its present wide signification.

SEIGN'IORAGE, a royal right or prerogative of the king or queen regnant of England, by which they claim an allowance of gold and silver brought in the mass to be exchanged for coin.—A lord of a manor is sometimes styled a *seignior*, and the lordship a *seigniory*.

SE'IZIN, or SE'ISIN, in law, possession. Seizin in *fact*, or *deed*, is actual or corporal possession; seizin in *law*, is when something is done which the law accounts possession or seizin, as enrolment; or when lands descend to an heir, but he has not yet entered on them. In this case the law considers the heir as *seized* of the estate, and the person who wrongfully enters on the land is accounted a *disseizor*.

SELEU'CIDÆ, a term in chronology designating a particular era. The era of the Seleucidæ, or the Syro-Macedonian era, is a computation of time, commencing from the establishment of the Seleucidæ, a race of Greek kings, who reigned as successors of Alexander the Great, in Syria, as the Ptolemies did in Egypt. This era we find expressed in the book of the Maccabees, and on a great number of Greek medals, struck by the cities of Syria, &c. The Rabbins call it the era of contracts: and the Arabs the era of the two horns. According to the best accounts, the first year of this era falls in the year 312 before Christ, being about eleven or twelve years after Alexander's death.

SELF-COMMAND′, that steady equanimity which enables a man in every situation to exert his reasoning faculty with coolness, and to do what the existing circumstances require. It depends much upon the natural temperament of the body, and much upon the moral cultivation of the mind; and he who from his early youth has been accustomed to make his passions submit to his reason, will, in any sudden emergency, be more capable of acting with a cool and steady resolution, than he who has tamely yielded to or allowed himself to be controlled by the influence of his passions.

SELF-KNOWL′EDGE, a difficult but most important acquisition. It is difficult, because every man is more or less blinded by some fallacy peculiar to himself, and it is disagreeable to investigate our errors, our faults, and our vices. But these difficulties are more than counterbalanced by the advantages of self-knowledge. By knowing the extent of our abilities, we shall be restrained from rashly engaging in enterprises beyond our ability; by investigating our opinions, we may discover those which are based upon false principles; and by examining our virtues and vices, we shall learn what principles ought to be strengthened, and what habits or propensities ought to be abandoned.

SELF-LOVE, an instinctive principle in the human mind which impels every rational creature to preserve his life, and promote his own happiness. It is very generally confounded with selfishness, but their springs of action and their results are very different; for selfishness is the parent and nurse of every vice, while self-love only prompts him who is actuated by it to procure to himself the greatest possible sum of happiness during his whole existence.

SEL′LING OUT, among stockbrokers, a transfer of one's share of stock from one person to another, in distinction from buying in, which is the purchase of the stock held by another.

SEM′IBREVE, in music, the measure note by which all others are regulated. It contains the time of two minims, which are divided either into four crotchets, eight quavers, sixteen semiquavers, or thirty-two demi-semiquavers.

SEM′ICOLON, in grammar and punctuation, the point (;) the mark of a pause to be observed in reading, of less duration than the colon, double the duration of the comma, or half the duration of the period. It is used to distinguish the conjunct members of a sentence.

SEMI-DIAPA′SON, in music, a defective octave, or an octave diminished by a minor semitone.

SEM′INARY, any place of education, in which young persons are instructed in the several branches of learning.

SEMI-PELA′GIANS, a sect of Christians, who hold that God has not by predestination dispensed his grace to one more than to another; that Christ died for all men; that the grace purchased by Christ and necessary to salvation, is offered to all men; that man, before he receives grace, is capable of faith and holy desires; and that man being born free, is capable of accepting grace, or of resisting its influence.

SEM′IQUAVER, in music, a note of half the duration of the quaver, being the sixteenth of the semibreve.

SEMIT′IC LAN′GUAGES, one of the great families of languages. They have been divided thus: 1. Aramæan, (in the north,) including Eastern and Western Aramæan; the Eastern embraces the Assyrian, the Babylonian, from which several dialects originated, as the Chaldaic, the Syro-Chaldaic; and the Samaritan The Western Aramæan includes the Syriac dialect, the Palmyrene, and the Sabian idiom, a corrupted Syriac dialect. 2. Canaanitish languages, which comprise the Phœnician language, with its dialect the Punic, the Hebrew with the Rabbinic dialect. 3. The Arabic language, from which originated the Ethiopian or Abyssinian.

SEM′ITONE, in music, half a tone; an interval of sound, as between *mi* and *fa* in the diatonic scale, which is only half the distance of the interval between *ut* and *re*, or *sol* and *la*. A semitone, strictly speaking, is not half a tone, as there are three kinds of semitones;—greater, lesser, and natural.

SEM′I-VOWEL, in grammar, a half vowel, or an articulation which is accompanied with an imperfect sound; as, *el*, *em*, *en*, which, though uttered with close organs, do not wholly interrupt the sounds.

SEN′ATE, an assembly or council of senators: that is, a body of the principal inhabitants of a state, invested with a share in the government. The senate of ancient Rome was, of all others, the most celebrated: it appointed judges, either from among the senators or knights, to determine processes; it also appointed governors of provinces, and disposed of the revenues of the commonwealth, &c. Yet the whole sovereign power did not reside in the senate, since it could not elect magistrates, make laws, or decide on war and peace; in all which cases the senate was obliged to consult the people. One of the qualifications of a senator was the possession of property to the amount of 80,000 sesterces, about 7000*l.*—In many republican constitutions of modern times, the upper house of the national assembly has been so called. The senate of the United States is composed of two members for each state of the Union. The senators are chosen by the state for six years. The American senate, besides its legislative functions, is also a species of executive council, assisting the president; its consent being necessary for the ratification of treaties, appointment of ambassadors, judges of the supreme court, heads of departments in the administration, &c. It is also the high court of impeachment for public functionaries.—*Senate-house*, a building in which the senate meets, or a place of public council.—*Senate*, in the university of Cambridge, is equivalent to the convocation at Oxford, and consists of all masters of arts, and higher graduates, being masters of arts, who have each a voice in every public measure, in granting degrees, in electing members of parliament, a chancellor, &c.

SENA'TUS AUCTOR'ITAS, a vote of the Roman senate, drawn up in the same form as a decree, but without its force, as having been prevented from passing into a decree by some of the tribunes of the people.

SENA'TUS CONSUL'TUM, a decree of the Roman senate, pronounced on some question or point of law; which, when passed, made a part of the law.

SEN'ESCHAL, an officer in the houses of princes and dignitaries, who has the superintendence of feasts and public ceremonies. In some instances, the seneschal is an officer who has the dispensing of justice, as the high seneschal of England, &c.

SENSE, the faculty of the soul by which it perceives external objects by means of impressions made on certain organs of the body. The external organs of *sense* are usually classed under five heads, viz. those of sight, hearing, feeling, smell, and taste. The nerves and the brain are the organs of *sensation.* If the external organ be destroyed, no sensation can be produced: where there are no nerves there is no sensation: where the nervous branches are most numerous there is most sensation; if the nerve be destroyed, sensation cannot be produced from those parts to which the nerve belongs, which are further from the brain than the injured parts. All the nerves terminate in the brain. If the brain is compressed, sensation is suspended: if the brain is considerably injured, sensation ceases. Sensations are the rudiments and elements of our ideas, that is, of all our thoughts and feelings. In the earliest exercise of the sensative power, sensations are simple, uncompounded with the relics of former corresponding sensations; but the sensations soon become perceptions; that is, they instantaneously recall the relics of other corresponding sensations. The accuracy and extent of the perception depends on the vividness and efficaciousness of the compound sensations, and the number of them received from the same or similar objects in different situations, and through the medium of different senses. The object therefore of earlier education should be to invigorate the organs of sense.—*Common sense* is that power of the mind which, by a kind of instinct, or a short process of reasoning, perceives truth, the relation of things, cause and effect, &c., and hence enables the possessor to discern what is right and expedient, and adopt the best means to accomplish his purpose.—*Moral sense* implies, a determination of the mind to be pleased with those affections, actions or characters of rational agents, which are considered good and conducive to virtue.

SENSIBIL'ITY, acuteness of perception, or that quality of the mind which renders it susceptible of impressions; delicacy of feeling; as *sensibility* to pleasure or pain, shame or praise.

SEN'SUALISM, in mental philosophy, that theory which resolves all our mental acts and intellectual powers into various modifications of mere sensation. The best known, and the most elaborate attempt of this kind which has been made in modern times, is that of Condillac, who conceived that he was following out the principles of Locke into their legitimate consequences. For this belief it cannot be denied that there exists at least plausible ground. Locke does indeed draw a distinction between sensation and reflection, as separate sources of "ideas:" but his account of reflection is so vague, and its existence apparently so unsupported in his system, as to justify the attempt to reduce it to mere revived sensation. The writings of Condillac may be regarded as a fair *reductio ad absurdum* of the theory which attempts to explain the existence of our mental phenomena independently of conditions in the mind itself. The theory opposed to sensualism is called *intellectualism*.

SEN'TENCE, in law, a judicial decision publicly and officially declared in a criminal prosecution. In civil cases, the decision of a court is called a *judgment*.—In grammar, a number of words containing complete sense, and followed by a full pause; a period.

SEN'TIMENT, in its primary sense, signifies a thought prompted by passion or feeling. Also, the decision of the mind, formed by deliberation or reasoning.—*Sentiments*, in poetry, and especially dramatic, are the thoughts which the several persons express, whether they relate to matters of opinion, passion, &c.

SEN'ZA, in music, signifies without; as *senza stromenti*, without instruments; *con è senza violini*, with and without violins.

SEP'ARATISTS, a religious sect which originated in Dublin about the year 1803. Their principle, like that of most sects at their commencement, was to return more nearly to what they conceived to be the primitive form of Christianity. There is nothing very peculiar in their tenets, beyond their withdrawal from the fellowship of other Christian bodies. In the year 1833 an act of parliament was passed for their relief in the matter of oaths.

SE'POYS, the name given to the Hindoo or native troops in the service of the East India Company, of whom there are nearly 200,000, chiefly infantry, though there are several regiments of cavalry and some companies of artillery. They are all disciplined after the European manner, and are hardy, temperate, and subordinate. Their dress consists of a red jacket, with a white cotton vest, trowsers reaching only half-way down the thighs, and a light turban. The character of the Sepoys as soldiers has been the subject of much discussion. According to a modern writer, "the Sepoys have justly been celebrated for excellent qualities; as, for instance, patience and fortitude under difficulties and privations. But, on the other hand, if we analyze the account of the wars in which they have been employed, we shall find that they seem to possess passive rather than active courage; for instance, that in line they will remain steady under fire; in a broken or close country, however, where skirmishers and small detachments are necessarily most employed, they are found wanting." Others, however, disagree even from this modified dispraise.

SEPT, in Irish history, a clan, race, or family, proceeding from a common progenitor.

SEPTEM'BER, so called from its being the seventh month in the Roman year as established by Romulus, which began with March, is the ninth month in the calendar of Numa. Several of the Roman emperors gave names to this month in honor of themselves; but, unlike the month of August, whose ancient name of Sextilis has been quite merged in that of Augustus, the name of September has outlived every other appellation.

SEPTEM'BRISTS, the name given to the agents in the dreadful massacre which took place in Paris on September 2, 1792, during the French Revolution. The numbers that perished in this massacre have been variously given; but the term has become proverbial throughout Europe for all that is bloodthirsty and malignant in human nature.

SEPTEN'NIAL, happening or returning every seven years, as *septennial* parliaments, *i. e.* new parliaments chosen every seven years, as they are at present appointed in England.

SEPTEN'TRION, or SEPTEN'TRIONAL, pertaining to the north or northern regions of the globe.

SEPTUAGES'IMA, in the calendar, the third Sunday before Lent, or before Quadragesima Sunday: supposed to take its name from being about seventy days before Easter.

SEP'TUAGINT, a Greek version of the books of the Old Testament, so called because the translation is supposed to have been made by seventy-two Jews, who, for the sake of round numbers, are usually called the *seventy interpreters*. This translation is said to have been made at the request of Ptolemy Philadelphus, king of Egypt, about 280 years before the birth of Christ. It was in use in the time of our Saviour, and is that out of which all the citations in the New Testament from the Old are taken. It was also the ordinary and canonical translation made use of by the Christian church in the earliest ages; and it still subsists in the churches both of the east and west. It is however observable, that the chronology of the Septuagint makes fifteen hundred years more from the creation to Abraham, than the present Hebrew copies of the Bible.

SEP'ULCHRE, a place destined for the interment of the dead. This term is chiefly used in speaking of the burying places of the ancients, those of the moderns being usually called *tombs*. Sepulchres were held sacred and inviolable, and the care taken of them has always been held a religious duty. Those who have searched or violated them, have been thought odious by all nations, and were always severely punished. The Egyptians called sepulchres *eternal houses*, in contradistinction to their ordinary houses or palaces, which they called inns, on account of their short stay or pilgrimage on earth. The sepulchres of the Hebrews in general were hollow places dug out of rocks. Thus Abraham is said to bury Sarah his wife in the cave of Macpelah. In such sepulchres, also, the bodies of Lazarus and Jesus Christ were buried. And the same custom prevails in the East to this day, according to the account of modern travellers.—*Knights of the holy Sepulchre*, a military order, established in Palestine about the year 1114.

SEPULTU'RA, in archæology, an offering made to the priest for the burial of the dead body.

SE'QUENCE, in music, a regular succession of similar sounds.—In gaming, a set of cards immediately following each other, in the same suit, as a king, queen, knave, &c.; thus we say, a sequence of three, four, or five cards.

SEQUESTRA'TION, in law, the act of taking a thing, in controversy, from the possession of both parties till the right be determined by course of law.—In the civil law, the act of the ordinary, disposing of the goods and chattels of a person deceased, whose estate no one will meddle with.

SE'QUIN, or ZE'CHIN, a gold coin of Venice and Turkey, of different values in different places, but generally about 9*s*.

SERAG'LIO, a Persian word, signifying the palace of a prince or lord; but the term is used, by way of eminence, for the palace of the Grand Seignior at Constantinople, and all the officers and dependents of his court; and in it is transacted all the business of the government. In this building are also kept the females of the harem.

SERAI', a large building for the accommodation of travellers, common in the East. In Turkey they are called *khans*; in Persia, *caravanserais*, which we write *caravansaries*; but in Tartary and India, simply *serais*.

SER'APH, a spirit of the highest rank in the hierarchy of angels; thus called from their being supposed to be most inflamed with divine love, or holy zeal, owing to their more immediate attendance at the throne of God. The Hebrew plural is *seraphim*: the English plural is regularly formed (*seraphs*.)

SERA'PIS, an Egyptian deity. The image and worship of this god were brought from Sinope in Pontus, to Alexandria, in the last year of Ptolemy Soter, in consequence, it is said, of a vision of Ptolemy I. According to some accounts, this image was a statue of Jupiter; but however this may have been, Serapis was clearly, as Sir G. Wilkinson expresses it, "at most a Græco-Egyptian deity," And there is no foundation for the notion entertained by some early Christian fathers, that he represented the patriarch Joseph, (which they supported by an argument drawn from the ornament in the shape of a bushel, which the images of this god usually bore on the head;) or for that of some modern antiquaries, that it was another name for Apis.

SERAS'KIER, a Turkish general or commander of land forces.

SERENADE', signified originally music performed in the open air, on a *serene* evening; but it is now universally applied to a musical performance made by gentlemen in a spirit of gallantry under the windows of ladies whom they admire. This practice, which was formerly very general in Spain and Italy, has latterly fallen greatly into disuse in these countries: but it is still very common in the German university towns, where the students are in the habit of assembling in the evening under the windows of a favorite professor, and offering him a musical tribute.

SERENE' HIGH'NESS, a title of courtesy in European etiquette of considerable antiquity. Before the dissolution of the German empire, Serene and Most Serene Highness were the appropriate addresses of princely houses holding immediately of the empire. Since that period the rules of princely etiquette have become more uncertain.

SERF, a servant, or as is the case in some countries, a peasant slave, attached to the soil and transferred with it.

SER'GEANT, in military affairs, a non-commissioned officer in a company of infantry or troop of cavalry, whose duty is to order and form the ranks, and see discipline preserved.—*Sergeant-at-law*, in England, a barrister who usually pleads in the court of common-pleas, but who is allowed to plead also in other courts. Every judge must first be a sergeant-at-law.—*Sergeant-at-arms*, or *at mace*, an officer appointed to attend the person of the sovereign, arrest persons of quality that offend, &c. A similar sergeant attends the lord chancellor; a third the speaker of the house of commons; and a fourth, the lord mayor of London, on solemn occasions.—*Common sergeant* an officer of the city of London, who attends the lord mayor and court of aldermen on court days, and is in council with them on all occasions. He is, more particularly, to take care of the orphan's estates.—*Sergeantry*, in the old English law, is of two kinds.—*Grand sergeantry*, is a kind of knight service, by which the tenant was bound to do some special honorary service to the king in person, as to carry his banner or sword, or be his champion at his coronation, &c.—*Petit sergeantry* was a tenure by which the tenant was bound to render to the king annually some small implement of war, as a bow, a sword, a lance, &c.

SER'MON, in ecclesiastical usage. The use of the sermon or homily as a portion of the communion service is said to be of remote antiquity. This ancient custom fell into partial disuse during a great part of the middle ages. The homilies of Elfric, archbishop of Canterbury, in the 10th century, were long used in the English church; but these became antiquated; and in the year 1281, preaching seems to have been generally omitted. In that year archbishop Peckham ordered in his Constitutions, that four sermons should be delivered during the year. But for some time prior to the Reformation preaching was again coming more into use; and the publication of homilies by authority, seems to have completely restored the ancient practice. *See* HOMILY.

SER'VICE, in a general sense, labor, whether of body or mind, or of both united, performed in pursuance of duty, or at the command of a superior. The service of persons who spontaneously perform something for another's benefit, is termed *voluntary*, and that of those who work by compulsion *involuntary service*.—Public worship is termed *divine service*.—The duty which a tenant owes to his lord for his fee, is called *personal service*.—The word *service* is also applied to the duty of naval or military men when serving their country; as *home service, foreign service, limited service*, &c.—Various legal processes are also distinguished by the term *service*, as the service of a *writ*, an *attachment*, an *execution*, &c.

SER'VITOR, a poor scholar at Oxford, answering to a *sizer* at Cambridge, who attends on other students for his maintenance and learning.

SES'QUI, in music, a whole and a half; which, joined with *altera, terza, quarta*, &c., is much used in the Italian music to express a set of ratios, particularly the several species of triple time.

SES'SION, in law, a sitting of justices in court upon their commission, as the session oyer and terminer, &c.—The session of a judicial court is called a *term:* thus a court may have two sessions or four sessions annually. The term *sessions*, or *quarter sessions*, is applied to those quarterly meetings of justices of the peace, when minor offences are tried, or business performed which requires the sanction of two or more justices.—*Session of Congress*, the season and space between its meeting and its adjournment.

SES'TERCE, in antiquity, a Roman coin, the fourth part of a denarius in value, or about twopence. The *sestertium*, or *sestertium pondus*, was 250 denarii; about $35. One qualification of a Roman knight was the possession of estate of the value of four hundred thousand sesterces; that of a senator was double this sum.

SET'-OFF, is a term used in law, when the defendant acknowledges the plaintiff's demand, but makes a demand of his own, to *set-off* or counterbalance the debt either wholly or in part.

SET'TLEMENT, in law, the right which an individual acquires to parochial assistance, under the statutes for the relief of the poor, in that parish or district to which he legally belongs, and in which he is said to have the settlement.

SEV'ENTH, in music, an interval; whereof there are four species. First, the defective seventh, consisting of three tones and three greater semitones. Second, the minor seventh, consisting of seven degrees and six intervals, diatonically taken; four being tones, and the rest greater semitones. Third, the major seventh, being only a major semitone less than the octave. Fourth, the extreme sharp seventh, which is only a comma less than the octave.

SEVEN YEARS' WAR, in history, a war carried on in Germany between two alliances, headed respectively by Austria and Prussia, from the year 1756 to 1763, when it was ended by the peace of Hubertsburg. It was signalized chiefly by the extraordinary campaigns of Frederick II., the Great King of Prussia. His principal ally throughout the struggle was England; while he was, at one period, assailed by the forces of Austria, France, the Empire, Sweden, and Russia. When the forces of the Prussian sovereign had been almost annihilated by this coalition, the death of the Russian empress, Elizabeth, caused the withdrawal of Russia from the alliance of his enemies, and brought about the termination of the war without material advantages gained by any party.

SEW'ER, in architecture, a subterraneous conduit, or channel, to receive and carry off the superfluous water and filth of a city. The sewers of Rome have been the models of those of the modern cities of Europe. They are as old as the elder Tarquin. These *cloacæ* had, between the Quirinal, Capitoline, and Palatine hills, many branches, which, joining in the Forum, now the Campo Vaccino, were received for conveyance into the Tiber by a larger one called the *cloaca maxima*. It must be admitted, however, that it is erroneous to designate the Roman cloacæ by the term sewers. They were rather drains, made to carry off the stagnant water of the pestilential marshes which occupied much of the low ground near the Tiber, and the spaces between the Aventine, Palatine, and Capitoline hills. The height and width of the cloaca maxima are equal, each measuring 13 1-2 feet.

SEXAGES'IMA, the second Sunday before Lent, or the next to Shrove Sunday: so called as being about the 60th day before Easter.

SEXHIN'DENI, or SEX'HINDMEN, in Anglo-Saxon history, the middle thanes, who were rated at 600 shillings.

SEX'TAIN, in poetry, a stanza containing six verses.

SEX'TARY-LANDS, in law, lands given to a church or religious house for the maintenance of the sexton or sacristan.

SEXTI'LIS, the sixth month of Romulus's year, but the eighth of the year of Numa. It was under the protection of *Ceres*, and was afterwards called *August*, in honor of Augustus.

SEX'TON, an under officer of the church, whose business it is to take care of the vessels, vestments, &c. belonging to the church, and to attend the officiating clergyman, and perform other duties pertaining to the church. He was anciently called the *sacristan*.

SFORZA'TO, in music, an Italian term signifying that the note over which it is placed must be struck with force.

SFUMA'TO, in painting. This term is applied to the species of painting in which the tints are extremely smooth and blended, so as to present that sort of indefinite contour and outline displayed by natural appearances on a misty day, or at a considerable distance. This style, in the hands of a master, is very agreeable and harmonious. Perhaps Guercino has seized its true spirit better than any other artist of celebrity.

SGRAFIT'TO, in painting, a species of painting in which the ground is prepared with dark stucco, on which a white coat is applied; which last being removed with an iron instrument, the chipping it away opens to the black ground and forms the shadows, giving it the appearance of a chiaro-scuro painting. The principal pictures of Polidoro da Caravaggio are executed in this manner, which is capable of great effect, and is extremely durable, though it must be conceded the appearance is rather harsh.

SHAB'RACK, a military term, of Hungarian origin, used for the cloth furniture of a cavalry officer's troop-horse or charger.

SHAD'OW, in painting, &c. Shadow must not be confounded with obscurity; the latter being an entire *privation* of light, whilst the former is merely a *gradation* of it, the parties in shade being still radiated by the light dispersed through the air. According to Felibien, it may be regarded simply as a light cloud covering the bodies and depriving them of the stronger brilliancy without rendering their colors and shapes imperceptible. It is requisite, in a picture, that there should be different modifications of shadow, as operated on by situation and surrounding objects. The direction of the shades should be diagonal, and the effects triangular, like those of lights. The progression of the latter, in fact, should serve as a model for the former, to the end that the *chiaro-scuro* should be well and naturally balanced.

SHAFT, in architecture, that part of a column between the base and capital, sometimes called the *trunk* of the column. The shaft of a column always diminishes in diameter from about a third of its height. Sometimes it has a slight swelling in the lower part of its height. In the oldest Doric columns, the diminution was so considerable as to give the column a conical appearance. In the Doric edifices at Athens, the upper diameter is not more than a quarter less than the lower diameter.

SHAH, the title given by European writers to the monarch of Persia, who in his own country is designated by the compound appellation of *Padishah*, which see.

SHAH-NAMAH, the most ancient and celebrated poem in the modern Persian language, by the poet who received as a title of honor the name "Firdousi," by which he is known. Its date is supposed to be about A. D. 1000. A complete translation into English, in four volumes, was published by Captain Macan, Calcutta, 1829.

SHAKE, in music, an embellishment, consisting of an alternate reiteration of two notes, comprehending an interval not greater than one whole tone, nor less than a semitone.

SHA'KERS, in ecclesiastical history, a sect said to have originated by a secession from the body of Quakers, in 1747, in Lancashire; who received their nickname from the peculiar contortions of body which they adopted in their religious exercises. Anne Lee, the great female leader of this sect, joined the society in 1758; and, considering herself persecuted in England, went, with a few followers, to New York in 1774, and died ten years afterwards, at which time her sect had made great progress in America. She was considered as the woman spoken of in Revelations. Several flourishing establishments of this sect exist in various parts of the United States.

SHA'MANISM, a general name applied to the idolatrous religions of a number of barbarous tribes, comprehending those of Finnish race, the Ostiaks, Samojeds, and other inhabitants of Siberia as far as the Pacific Ocean. These nations generally believe in a Supreme Being, but to whom they attribute little share in the immediate government of the world: this is in the hands of a number of secondary gods, both benevolent and malevolent towards men. They appear to have very uncertain and fluctuating opinions respecting these last. Thus, those tribes which dwell on the frontier of Russia are said to admit Saint Nicholas among their gods.

SHAM'ROCK, the Irish name for three-leaved grass, or trefoil. According to legendary tradition, when St. Patrick landed near Wicklow, to convert the Irish, in 433, the pagan inhabitants were about to stone him; but having obtained a hearing, he endeavored to explain to them the Trinity in Unity; but they could not understand him, till, plucking a trefoil from the ground, he said, "Is it not as possible for the Father, Son, and Holy Ghost, as for these leaves, to grow upon a single stalk?" Upon which (says the legend) the Irish were immediately convinced.

SHARP'ING, in archæology, a customary present of corn made about Christmas, by farmers in some part of England to the smiths for sharpening their iron implements of husbandry.

SHAS'TER, among the Hindoos, a sacred book containing the dogmas of the religion of the Bramins and the ceremonies of their worship. It consists of three parts: the first containing the moral laws of the Hindoos; the second the rites and ceremonies of their religion; the third the distribution of the people into tribes or classes, with the duties pertaining to each.

SHAWM, in antiquity, an instrument used in the sacred music of the Hebrews.

SHEATH'ING, in naval architecture, sheets of copper nailed all over the outside of a ship's bottom, to protect the planks from the pernicious effects of worms.

SHEIK, an elder or chief of the Arabic tribes or hordes. They are very proud of their long line of noble ancestors; and some of them also take the title of *emir*. The Mohammedans also call the heads of their monasteries *sheiks*, and the Turkish mufti is sometimes called *sheik ulislam*, or chief of the true believers.

SHE'KEL, a Jewish silver coin, worth about 62½ cents. There was also the golden shekel, worth $9.

SHEKI'NAH, the Jewish name for the Divine presence, which rested, in the shape of a cloud, over the "propitiatory," or "mercy-seat," as it is rendered in our translation. The Jews reckon it among the five particulars which were in the first temple, and wanting in the second. On this account God is so often said in Scripture to "dwell between the cherubim;" that is, between the images of the cherubim on the mercy-seat.

SHEMIT'IC, an epithet for anything pertaining to Shem, the son of Noah. What are termed the *Shemitic* languages are the Chaldee, Syriac, Arabic, Hebrew, Samaritan, Ethiopic, and the old Phœnician.

SHER'IFF, an officer appointed in each county, to execute process, preserve the peace, and give assistance to justices and others in doing so. In England, during his office, which is but for a year, he is the first man in his county, and has at his disposal the whole civil force of that county, so as to enable him to preserve the peace. He only executes in person such parts of his office as are either purely honorary, or are of some dignity and public importance, his other functions being performed by a deputy or under sheriff.

SHEW'-BREAD, in the Jewish rites, the loaves of unleavened bread which the priest placed on the golden table in the sanctuary. They were shaped like a brick, and weighed about 8 lbs. The loaves were twelve in number, representing the twelve tribes of Israel; and were to be eaten by the priest only.

SHIB'BOLETH, the name given to a sort of test or criterion by which the ancient Jews sought to distinguish true persons or things from false. The term originated thus: After the battle gained by Jephtha over the Ephraimites, the Gileadites commanded by the former secured all the passes of the river: and on an Ephraimite attempting to cross, they asked him if he was of Ephraim. If he said no, they bade him pronounce the word *Shibboleth*, which the Ephraimites from inability to give the aspirate called *Sibboleth;* and by this means he was detected and instantly thrown into the river. In modern times this word has been adopted into the language of politics, in which it signifies those political opinions on which all the members of a party are agreed, or the watchword by which it is intended to unite them.

SHIELD, a broad piece of defensive armor, formerly borne on the left arm, as a defence against arrows, darts, lances, and other weapons. The shields of the ancients were of different shapes and sizes, and generally made of leather, or wood covered with leather. The surface, or as it is called in heraldry, the *field*, of the shield, or escutcheon, appears to have been in all ages decorated with figures emblematical or historical, serving to express the sentiments, record the honors, or at least distinguish the person of the warrior.

SHI'ITES, that class of the Mohammedans to which the Persians belong. They reject the three first caliphs, and consider Ali as being the only rightful successor of Mohammed. They do not acknowledge the Sunna, or body of traditions respecting Mohammed, as any part of the law, and on these accounts are treated as heretics by the Sunnites, or orthodox Mohammedans.

SHIL'LING, an English silver coin, equal in value to twelve pence. The word is supposed, by some, to be derived from the Latin *silicus*, which signifies a quarter of an ounce, or the 48th part of a Roman pound. In support of this etymology, it is alleged that the Saxon shilling was also the 48th part of the Saxon pound.

SHIP'-BUILDING, the practical branch of naval architecture, or the art of constructing vessels for navigation, particularly ships and other vessels of a large kind, bearing masts; in distinction from *boat-building*. To give an idea of the enormous quantity of timber necessary to construct a ship of war, we may observe that 2,000 tons, or 3,000 loads, are computed to be required for a seventy-four. Now, reckoning fifty oaks to the acre, of 100 years' standing, and the quantity in each tree at a load and a half, it would require forty acres of oak-forest to build one seventy-four; and the quantity increases in a great ratio, for the largest class of line-of-battle ships. A first-rate man-of-war requires about 60,000 cubic feet of timber, and uses 180,000 pounds of rough hemp, in the cordage and sails for it. The average duration of these vast machines, when employed, is computed to be fourteen years. Ship-building made but very slow progress until the introduction of the compass, when the application of astronomy to nautical pursuits at once set the mariner free from the land. Thenceforward the mariner, thrown upon the wide ocean, was brought into contact with unknown perils, to obviate which he was led to untried experiments. The art has since strode forward with giant steps. To the Italians, Catalans, and Portuguese, belong most of the advances in the earlier days of its revival; the Spaniards followed up the discovery of the new world with a rapid improvement in the form and size of their ships, some of which, taken by the cruisers of Elizabeth, carried 2000 tons. In modern times, to Great Britain, France, and the United States belongs the credit of the progress made in this important branch of art. See *Cycl. Useful Arts.*

SHIP'-MONEY, in English history, an ancient impost upon the ports, towns, cities, boroughs, and counties of the realm, for providing ships for the king's service. This demand was revived by Charles I. in the year 1635 and 1636; being laid by the king's writ under the great seal, without the consent of parliament, was held to be contrary to the laws and statutes of the realm, and subsequently abolished.

SHIP'S-PA'PERS, certain papers or documents, descriptive of the ship, its owners, the nature of the cargo, &c. They consist—1st, of the certificate of registry, license, charter-party, bills of lading, bill of health, &c. which are required by law of the country; and 2dly, of those documents required by the law of nations to be on board neutral ships, to vindicate their title to that character.

SHIRE, in English topography, the same with *county.* The word, which was originally spelt *scir* or *scire*, signifies a division. Alfred is said to have made those divisions, which he called *satrapias*, and which took the name of *counties*, after *earls*, *comites*, or *counts* were set over them. He also subdivided the satrapias into *centuries* or *hundreds;* and these into *decennas*, or *tenths of hundreds*, now called *tithings*.

SHIRE-MOTE, the ancient name in England for the county court.

SHIT'TIM-WOOD, in Scripture, a kind of precious wood of which the tables, altars, and boards of the tabernacle were made. The wood is said to be hard, smooth, and very beautiful.

SHORE, in architecture, a piece of timber or other material placed in such a manner as to prop up a wall or other heavy body.—*Dead-shore*, an upright piece fixed in a wall that has been cut or broken through for the purpose of making some alterations in the building—In ma-

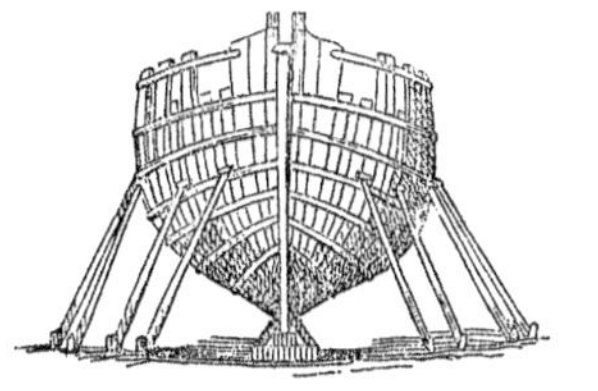

rine language, *shores* are props or stanchions fixed under a ship's side or bottom, to support her on the stocks or when laid on the blocks on the ship.

SHRINE, properly the receptacle of the remains or relics of a saint. Shrines are of two sorts: portable, used in processions, called in Latin *feretra;* and fixed, in churches. The appropriate place for shrines, in the churches of the middle ages, was generally in the eastern part, in the space behind the high altar. Such is the situation of the celebrated shrine of the three kings of Cologne; and such was that of the shrines at St. Alban's, Canterbury, Durham, and Westminster, before the Reformation.

SHROVE-TUES'DAY, the Tuesday after Quinquagesima Sunday, or the day immediately preceding the first of Lent; being so called from the Saxon word *shrive*, to confess; that day having been employed by the people in confessing their sins to the parish priest, and thereby qualifying themselves for a more religious observance of the approaching fast.

SIB'YLS, in antiquity, certain women who pretended to be endowed with a prophetic spirit. They resided in various parts of Persia, Greece, and Italy; and were consulted on all important occasions. They delivered oracular answers, and, as it is pretended, wrote certain prophecies on leaves in verse, which are called *Sibylline verses;* but these Sibylline oracles seem to have been composed to answer political purposes. The number of *Sibyls*, according to Varro, was ten.

SIB'YLLINE BOOKS, documents supposed to contain the fate of the Roman empire. Nine of them are said to have been offered by an old woman, called Amalthæa, to Tarquin the Proud; but Tarquin refusing to give the price she asked, she went away, and burned three of them. Returning with the remainder, she offered them to the king on the same terms as before; and, on his second refusal, departed again, and returned with three, which she still offered at the same price as the original nine. The king, struck with her conduct, at last acceded to her offer, and entrusted the care of the books to certain priests. They were preserved in a stone chest beneath the temple of Jupiter Capitolinus, and were consulted in times of public danger or calamity. They were destroyed by the fire that consumed the Capitol in the Marsic war. After this calamity, ambassadors were sent to collect such fragments of Sibylline prophecies as they could pick up in various countries; and from the verses thus collected Augustus formed two new books, which were deposited in two gilt cases in the temple of the Palatine Apollo. Sibylline verses are often quoted by Christian writers, as containing prophecies of Christianity; but these are spurious a forgery of the second century.

SICIL'IAN VES'PERS, in modern history, the name commonly given to the great massacre of the French in Sicily, in A.D. 1282. They were the soldiers and subjects of Charles of Anjou, who had made himself master of the island after the defeat and death of Conradin. The insurrection broke out on the evening of Easter Tuesday, whence its name. Its consequence was the expulsion of Charles; and the islanders placed themselves under the protection of the king of Arragon.

SIDEROG'RAPHY, the art or practice of engraving on steel, by means of which, impressions may be transferred from a steel plate to a steel cylinder in a rolling press constructed on a peculiar principle. Hence the term *siderographic* art, applied to steel plate engraving.

SID'EROMANCY, in antiquity, a species of divination performed by burning straws, &c. on red-hot iron.

SIEGE, in the art of war, the encampment of an army before a fortified place, with a design to take it. A *siege* differs from a *blockade*, as in a siege the investing army approaches the fortified place to attack and reduce it by force; but in a blockade, the army secures all the avenues to the place to intercept all supplies, and waits till famine reduces the besieged to surrender.—*To raise the siege*, is to give over the attack of a place, and quit the works thrown up against it.

SIER'RA, a term used for a hill, or chain of hills, particularly in Spain, the west coast of Africa, and the coasts of Chili and Peru.

SIGILLA'RIA, feasts in honor of Saturn, celebrated after the Saturnalia. At this festival little statues of gold, silver, &c. were sacrificed to the god instead of men, who had been the usual victims, till Hercules abolished the barbarous custom.

SIGN, in a general sense, a visible token or representation of anything. Also, any motion, appearance, or event which indicates the existence or approach of something else.—*Sign*, in astronomy, the twelfth part of the ecliptic. The signs are reckoned from the point of intersection of the ecliptic and equator, at the vernal equinox, and are named respectively, Aries, Taurus, Gemini, Cancer, Leo, Virgo, Libra, Scorpio, Sagittarius, Capricornus, Aquarius, Pisces. On account of the precession of the equinoxes, the positions of these constellations in the heavens no longer correspond with the divisions of the ecliptic of the same name, but are now considerably in advance of them: the constellation Aries, for example, being in that part of the ecliptic called Taurus.

SIG'NA, in antiquity, standards or ensigns among the ancients: those of the Romans usually bore the figure of an eagle; but the *signa* of the Greeks bore the figures of various animals.

SIG'NALS, certain signs agreed upon between parties at a distance, for the purpose of conveying instantaneous information, orders, &c. Signals are particularly useful in the navigation of fleets, and in naval engagements. They are made by the admiral or commander-in-chief of a squadron, either in the day, or by night, whether for sailing, fighting, or the better security of the merchant-ships under their convoy. They are very numerous and important, being all appointed and determined by the lords of the admiralty, and communicated in the instructions sent to the commander of every ship of the fleet or squadron before their putting to sea.—*Day-signals* are usually made by the sails, by flags and pendants, or guns; *night-signals* are lanterns disposed in certain figures, rockets, or the firing of guns; *fog-signals*, by guns, drums, bells, &c. There are signals of evolution addressed to a whole fleet, to a division, or to a squadron; signals of movements to particular ships; and signals of service, general or particular. Signals used in the army are mostly made by beat of drum or the sound of the bugle.

SIG'NATURE, in printing, is a letter put at the bottom of the first page at least, in each sheet, as a direction to the binder, in folding, gathering, and collating them.—Also, the name of a person written or subscribed by himself.

SIG'NET, CLERK OF THE, an officer, in England, continually in attendance upon the principal secretary of state, who has the royal signet in his keeping for the signing of letters, grants, &c.

SIGN-MAN'UAL, in English polity, the royal signature. In a general sense, it is the signature of any one's name in his own hand-writing.

SIKHS, a religious sect in Hindostan, (founded about A.D. 1500,) which professes the purest Deism, and is chiefly distinguished from the Hindoos by worshipping one only invisible God. The name Sikhs, or lions, was given to the sect, on account of the heroic manner in which they resisted their Mohammedan oppressors, against whom they long fought with varying success. They ultimately subdued Lahore, and established for themselves a country which includes the Punjaub, a part of Mooltan, &c. In 1846 and 1847, they were conquered by the British troops.

SILEN'TIARY, among the Romans, the title of office of a class of slaves attached to wealthy houses. In the court of the emperors, there was a body of officers attached to the household styled silentiaries. Thence the title came to functionaries of higher authority, and was borne by cabinet secretaries in the Lower Empire, and in the courts of Charlemagne and other western potentates who derived their code of ceremonial from Byzantium. Members of the privy council seem to have been sometimes called by this name under the Plantagenets in England.

SILE'NUS, a Grecian divinity, the foster-father and attendant of Bacchus, and likewise leader of the satyrs. This deity was remarkable for his wisdom, his drunkenness being regarded as inspiration. He was represented as a robust old man in a state of intoxication, and riding on an ass, with a can in his hand.

SILHOUET'TE, in the Fine Arts, a name given to the representation of an object filled in of a black color, and in which the inner parts are sometimes indicated by lines of a lighter color, and shadows or extreme depths by the aid of a heightening of gum or other shining medium. This sort of drawing derives its name from its inventor, Etienne de Silhouette, the French minister of finance in 1759. Representations of this sort may be well enough taken from the shadow of a person thrown on a piece of paper placed against a flat surface or wall. The likeness may be still better taken, if on a reduced scale, by means of the instrument called a pantograph. The invention of what is called a *silhouette* is, however, ascribed to a remote period, being said to have been the method whereby the daughter of a Greek potter drew the outline of her lover's portrait on a wall; and has been placed at the time of the renewal of the Olympic games, shortly before the expedition of the Bacchiades from Corinth, about 776 B.C. It is to be observed that Sicyon and Corinth were the first cities in which painting flourished; and that Crato of Sicyon, Philocles of Egypt, and Cleanthes of Corinth, were considered the inventors of *monochromes*, or silhouettes, as they have been more recently called, which were applied to large objects. The Etruscan vases furnish to an amazing extent, and in boundless variety, some of the most beautifully drawn and elegant monochromes or silhouettes that have ever been executed.

SIL'LON, in fortification, a work raised in the middle of a ditch to defend it when it is too wide.

SIM'ILE, in rhetoric, a comparison of two things, which though different in other respects, agree in some strong points of resemblance; by which comparison the character or qualities of a thing are illustrated or presented in an impressive light.

SIMO'NIANS, the name given to the followers of Simon Magus, who pretended to be the great virtue and power of God sent from heaven to earth. Their system was a medley of the philosophy of Plato, the mythological fables of the heathens, and of Christianity. The sum of their doctrines, as enjoined by their founder, was, that from the Divine Being, as a fountain of light, flow various orders of eternal natures, subsisting within the plenitude of the Divine essence; that beyond these in the order of emanation are different classes of intelligences, to the lowest of which belongs the human soul; that matter is the most remote production of the emanative power, which, on account of its infinite distance from the fountain of light, possesses sluggish and malignant qualities, which appear the divine operations, and are the cause of evil; that it is the great design of philosophy to deliver the soul from its imprisonment in matter, and restore it to that divine light from which it was derived; and that for this purpose God had sent us one of the first *æons* into the world. He believed also in the transmigration of souls, and denied the resurrection of the body.

SIM'ONY, in law, the illegal buying or selling ecclesiastical preferment; or the corrupt presentation of any one to a benefice for money or reward. The word is derived from the Chaldæan Magus, Simon, who, according to the Acts of the Apostles, wished to buy of them the power of working miracles.

SIMOON', or SIMOOM', a hot, arid wind which blows in Arabia, Syria, and the adjacent countries, and chiefly about the time of the equinoxes. The simoon, which is identical with the *khamsin* of Syria and the *samiel* of the Turks, and resembles in many respects the *sirocco* and *sorana* of other countries, derives its qualities from blowing over sandy deserts heated intensely by the sun. Sometimes it blows in squalls, bearing along with it quantities of burning sand and dust. In the desert it is greatly dreaded; and the only chance of safety the traveller has, is to fall down with his face close to the ground, and to continue as long as possible without drawing breath. It is described by Bruce, Volney, Charind, Malcolm, and other travellers.

SIM'PLE CON'TRACT, in law, a term applied to debts, where the contract upon which the obligation arises, is neither ascertained by matters of record, nor yet by deed or special instrument.

SIMPLI'CITY, in all the arts. That quality opposed to exuberance or pretension. We say that a work of art possesses a noble simplicity when the effect produced by it is the result of means neither numerous nor complicated. We say also that a form is simply beautiful when, as in the majority of antique vases, it pleases by its agreeable contour alone, without the assistance of any accessories. With regard to an edifice similar remarks apply. It is simply elegant when there is no confused or contradictory diversity of parts, and when the whole is harmonious and graceful. Experience has abundantly proved, that simplicity, as distinguished from meanness or boldness, is always conformable to good taste. This quality may be evidenced in all the different portions of a work, from the general plan even to the execution of the minutest details. The best works of art are always the simplest in point of design. Their projectors sought the principles of grandeur and beauty not in a superfluous quantity of parts, but in unity, in connection, in *tout ensemble*. It is true that the great masters have sometimes produced works the composition of which is extremely rich, but only when the subject necessarily demanded such profusion. When Poussin painted the gathering of manna by the Israelites in the Desert, he could not limit himself to a small number of figures. But often, in the finest specimens of pictorial art, a single group, composed of four or five figures, is found sufficient to tell an interesting story, and to display the most consummate ability in the artist.

SIM'PULUM, in antiquity, a vessel resembling a cruet, used at sacrifices and libations for taking a very little wine at a time.

SIMULA'TION, the assumption of a deceitful appearance or character. It differs from *dissimulation*, inasmuch as the former assumes a false character, while the latter only conceals the true one; but both are truly designated by the word *hypocrisy*.

SI'NECURE, a church benefice without cure or care, or guardianship of souls; as where there is a parish without church or inhabitants. The word is applied to any post that brings profit without labor.

SI'NE DI'E, in parliamentary language, a Latin phrase used for the adjournment of a debate without fixing a day when it shall be resumed.—In law, a term applied to a defendant when judgment is given in his favor, and he is suffered to go *sine die*, or dismissed the court.

SINK'ING FUND, in politics, a term applied to a portion of the public revenue set apart to be devoted to the reduction or diminution of the national debt.

SI NON OM'NES, in law, a writ on association of justices, by which, if all in commission cannot meet at the day assigned, it is allowed that two or more of them may proceed to finish the business.

SI'RENS, melodious divinities, who dwelt on the shores of Sicily, and so charmed passing mariners by the sweetness of their song that they forgot their homes, and remained there till they perished of hunger. Their history has been variously described. According to Homer, in the *Odyssey*, as Ulysses and his companions were on their homeward voyage from Æaca, they came first to the island of the Sirens; but they passed in safety: for, by the directions of Circe, Ulysses stopped the ears of his companions with wax, and had himself tied to the mast before approaching the island; so that, although when he heard the song of the Sirens he made signs for his companions to unbind him, they only secured him the more closely in compliance with his previous instructions. Thus he listened to the songs of the Sirens, and escaped notwithstanding. Hence it was feigned that they threw themselves into the sea from vexation at the escape of Ulysses, an oracle having predicted that they should live only so long as their strains had power to arrest all who heard them. But according to other poets, they threw them selves into the sea from rage and despair on hearing the more melodious song of

Orpheus. Originally there were only two Sirens; but their number was afterwards increased to three, and their names are given with great variety.

SIROC'CO, a periodical wind which generally blows in Italy and Dalmatia every year about Easter. It blows from the southeast by south, and is attended with heat, but not rain; its ordinary period is twenty days, and it usually ceases at sunset. When the sirocco does not blow in this manner, the summer is almost free from westerly winds, whirlwinds, and storms. This wind is prejudicial to plants, drying and burning up their buds; and also causes an extraordinary weakness and lassitude in men. In the summer time, when the westerly wind ceases for a day, it is a sign that the sirocco will blow the day following, which usually begins with a sort of whirlwind.

SIRVEN'TE, in the literature of the middle ages, a species of poem in common use among the Troubadours, usually satirical, and divided into strophes of a peculiar construction.

SIS'TRUM, a kind of timbrel, which the Egyptian priests of Isis used to shake with their hands at the festivals of that goddess.

SIS'YPHUS, in ancient mythology, one of the descendants of Æolus, respecting whom a variety of opinions prevails. By some he is said to have resided at Epyra, in the Peloponnesus; others maintain that he was a Trojan prince, who was punished for betraying state secrets; while others allege that he was a notorious robber, slain by Theseus. Be this as it may, all the ancient poets are agreed that he was distinguished for his craftiness and cunning; and that his punishment in Tartarus for his crimes committed on earth consisted in rolling a huge stone to the top of a high hill, which constantly recoiled, and thus rendered his labor incessant.

SITOPH'YLAX, in Grecian antiquity, an Athenian magistrate, who had the superintendence of the corn, and was to take care that no one bought more than was necessary for the provision of his family.

SI'VA, in Hindoo mythology, a title given to the Supreme Being, considered in the character of the avenger or destroyer. Sir William Jones has compared Siva to Jupiter; but he appears to share many of the attributes of Pluto. Under the name of Mahadeva, he is exhibited also as a type of reproduction: to destroy, according to the Vedantas of India, the Sufis of Persia, and even to many European schools of philosophy, being only to generate or reproduce under another form.

SIXTH, in music, an interval formed of six sounds, or five diatonic degrees. There are four kinds of *sixths*, two *consonant* and two *dissonant*.

SI'ZARS, the lowest class of students at Cambridge, England. At Oxford the same class go in different colleges by the denominations of servitors, &c. They are such as have certain allowances made in their battels (college bills,) through the benefactions of founders or other charitable persons. In college phraseology, a size is a portion of bread, meat, &c. allotted to a student; and hence the name sizar. The sizars at Cambridge are almost entirely on the same footing with independent students; at Oxford they are somewhat lower, and some relics of their former degraded condition still subsist in certain colleges in the customs of bringing up dishes to dinner, dining off the remnants of the fellows' dinners, &c.

SKETCH, an outline or general delineation of anything; a first rough or incomplete draught of a plan or any design: as, the *sketch* of a building; the *sketch* of an essay.—In painting, the first delineated idea of the artist's conception of a subject, in which are usually distinguishable the fire and enthusiasm with which the subject is expressed and felt. Sketches are made either with carbon, with the pen, or the pencil; in general, that method is preferred which seems to present the greatest promptitude and facility.

SLAN'DER, in law, a malicious defamation of a man by words spoken. It is not actionable unless it impute some crime punishable by law; or some infectious disease, such as leprosy or the like, which may have the effect of excluding from society the person slandered; or be uttered concerning him in his trade or business in such a way as to impair his means of livelihood; or, lastly, unless it be attended with special damage. In this case, such special damage must be averred upon the pleadings.

SLA'VERY, bondage; the state of entire subjection of one person to the will of another. *Slavery* is the obligation to labor for the benefit of the master, without the contract or consent of the servant; or it is the establishment of a right which gives one person such a power over another, as to make him absolute master of his life and property. But the condition of a slave is susceptible of innumerable modifications, and there are few nations, whether of ancient or modern times, among whom slavery has been long established, that have not enacted certain laws for limiting the power of a master over his slave. Slavery may proceed from crimes, from captivity, or from debt. Slavery is also *voluntary* or *involuntary; voluntary*, when a person sells or yields his own person to the absolute command of another; *involuntary*, when he is placed under the absolute power of another without his own consent. Slavery no longer exists in Great Britain, nor in any of her colonies, nor in the northern states of America.

SLEEP, one of the most mysterious phenomena in the animal world; a state wherein the body appearing perfectly at rest, external objects act on the organs of sense as usual, without exciting the usual sensations. The voluntary exertion of our mental and corporeal powers being suspended, we rest unconscious of what passes around us, and are not affected by the ordinary impressions of external objects.

SLEIGHT OF HAND, tricks performed by persons who, by great practice, or confederacy with others, perform acts apparently out of the course of nature, which the vulgar and ignorant believe, and even the intelligent admire.

SLUR, in music, a mark connecting notes that are to be sung to the same syllable, or made in one continued breath of a wind instrument, or with one stroke of a stringed instrument.

SMAR'AGD, another name for the emerald. Hence, *smaragdine*, an epithet for anything pertaining to or resembling an emerald; of an emerald green.

SMORZA'TO, in music, a term denoting that the violin bow is to be drawn to its full extent, but gradually lighter till the sound is nearly lost.

SMUG'GLING, the offence of importing goods without paying the duties imposed by law. Smuggling owes its existence, in many cases, to oppressive duties.

SOAVE', in music, a term denoting to the player that the music to which it is prefixed is to be executed with sweetness.

SOBRI'ETY, a word expressive not only of habitual temperance with regard to intoxicating liquors, but also of an habitual freedom from enthusiasm or inordinate passion; as, the *sobriety* of age, a period when calmness and rational views are expected to take the place of an overheated imagination.

SOC'AGE, in law, a tenure of lands by or for certain inferior services of husbandry to be performed by the lord of the fee; a tenure distinct from chivalry or knight's service, in which the render was uncertain.

SO'CIALISM, a social state in which there is a community of property among all the individuals composing it, a state of things in which there are no individual or separate rights in property. It is otherwise termed *agrarianism* and *communism*.

SO'CIALIST, one who advocates a community of property among all the citizens of a state. Some of this sect contend also for a community of females, or a promiscuous intercourse of the sexes; and they have likewise been accused of holding various other heterodox principles. They are also called Owenites from Robert Owen, one of the first promulgators of the social tenets in this country. In France, parties holding similar opinions are called Fourierists, and St. Simonians, from Fourier and St. Simon, two noted socialist leaders. They are also called *communists*.

SOCI'ETY, in its most enlarged sense, signifies the whole race or family of man; as, "the true and natural foundations of *society*, are the wants and fears of individuals." In a narrower sense, it signifies, persons living in the same neighborhood, who frequently meet in company. It is also a name given to any association of persons uniting together, and co-operating to effect some particular object, as the societies or academies for promoting the cause of literature; benevolent societies, for purposes of public charity; missionary societies, for sending missionaries abroad; and various others. In society, a man not only finds more leisure, but better opportunities of applying his talents with success. The *social principle*, in fact, is of such an expansive nature, that it cannot be confined within the circuit of a family, of friends, or a neighborhood; it spreads into wider systems, and draws men into larger communities and commonwealths; since it is in these only that the more sublime powers of our nature attain the highest improvement and perfection of which they are capable. —The purposes for which benevolent and religious societies are formed will be best inferred from the epithets with which they are connected; *temperance* societies are established with a view to promote sobriety, *mendicity* societies for the relief of the indigent, &c. There is no feature, perhaps, which distinguishes a civilized from a savage state more than the establishment of such societies; and in this view England has a right to claim a place in the foremost ranks of civilization, whether we regard the number or the principles of the management of its religious and benevolent institutions.

SO'CII, among the Romans, were such states as were in alliance with the commonwealth of Rome. In the time of Polybius, all Italy was subject to the Romans; yet no state or people in it had been reduced into the form of a province, but retained in general their own laws and governors, and were termed *socii*, or confederates. The *socii* received no consideration for their service, but a distribution of corn. The *auxilia* differed from the *socii*, as being borrowed at a certain pay from foreign princes and states. The name of *socii* in time ceased; all the natives of Italy being accounted Romans, and honored with the *jus civitatis*.

SOCIN'IANS, the followers of Socinus, the uncle and the nephew, both of the same name, and celebrated for similar opinions concerning the nature of Christ. The nephew, Faustus Socinus, was the principal founder of the sect. He was an Italian, born at Sienna, in 1539; who after publishing a treatise on the nature of the Saviour, desired to be admitted into a society of Unitarians already existing in Poland. Their opinions do not appear to have precisely corresponded with his, and admission was refused him; nor did he effect during his lifetime the institution of any distinct congregation; but the views which he disseminated in his writings were gradually referred to and adopted by many ministers and religious communities, especially in Poland, where Crellius, Wolgozenius, and others published a Socinian system of theology, comprised in the *Bibliotheca Fratrum Polonorum*. Since the death of Socinus, the theologians who have asserted the mere humanity of Christ have been generally denominated Socinians. The doctrines, however, to which that appellation can with strictness be applied are not precisely equivalent to those of the modern Unitarians. The Socinian denies the existence of Christ previous to his birth of the Virgin Mary: he allows, however, that that birth was miraculous, and considers the Saviour as an object of peculiar reverence and an inferior degree of worship. By the term Mediator, as applied to Christ, he understands that in establishing the new covenant he was the medium between God and man; and of his sacrifice he says that as the Jewish sacrifices were not made for the payment of sins, but for the remission of them, so also the death of Christ was designed for the remission of sins through God's favor, and not for the satisfaction of them as an equivalent.

SOCIOL'OGY, social science, or the science of society, according to the Positivé Philosophy of M. Compte. It treats of the general structure of human society, the laws of its development, and the progress of actual civilization. Sociology is the most complex of all the sciences, and consists of derivative truths, verified by experience from psychology and the laws of ethology, or the science of the formation of character. The laws of social phenomena are nothing but the laws of the thoughts, feelings, and actions of men united together in the social state; and these laws are approximate generalizations obtained from the past history and present observation of all stages of civilization. And as men's thoughts, feelings, and actions are subject to fixed laws, that is, uniform sequences, so must also the phenomena of society, that is, of aggregates of men. The fundamental problem of society is to discover the laws by which any state of society produces the state which follows it, and takes its place, and to show by deduction that these laws are derivative from those of human nature. The subject matter of the sciences of man, and of society, is peculiar in varying from age to age, and in being progressive. The laws of human nature, and of the external circumstances in which men are placed, form their characters, and men themselves in turn mould and shape circumstances for themselves and their posterity. The institutions of a people are the results of their ideas, and as society advances, mental qualities tend more and more to prevail over bodily, and aggregates of men over individuals. The elements of permanent social union are education through life, which is always a restraining discipline, the feeling of allegiance or loyalty to something fixed and permanent, and a strong and active principle of nationality or union for common interest. Such are some of the leading principles of sociology; but to understand the science aright, it is necessary to have recourse to M. Compte's great work, "*Cours de Philosophie Positive*," and the last book of Mill's System of Logic.

SOCK, the shoe of the ancient actors in comedy. Hence the word is used for comedy, and opposed to *buskin* or tragedy; as, "I have no talents either for the *sock* or *buskin*."

SOC'LE, in architecture, a flat square member under the basis of pedestals of vases and statues, serving as a foot or stand.

SOCRAT'IC PHILOS'OPHY, in a more extensive sense, is used to comprehend the whole development of philosophy of Greece from Socrates to the Neo Platonists. The title is so far just, as all the schools of this period, with the single exception of the Epicurean, called themselves by the name of Socrates, and arrogated to themselves the merit of exclusively propagating the true doctrines of Socrates. But in a narrow and more proper signification, it signifies the peculiar direction and method which Socrates gave to philosophical inquiry. The *Socratic* method of reasoning and instruction was by interrogatories. Instead of laying down a proposition authoritatively, this method led the antagonist or disciple to acknowledge it himself by dint of a series of questions put to him. It was not the object of Socrates to establish any perfectly evolved system of doctrine, so much as to awaken by his discourses a new and more comprehensive pursuit of science, which should direct itself to all that is knowable. To him is ascribed two of the very first principles of science, namely, the inductive method and the definition of ideas.

SOF'FIT, the under part or ceiling of a cornice. Any timber ceiling formed of cross-beams of flying cornices, the square compartments or panels of which are enriched with sculpture, painting, or gilding; such are those in the palaces of Italy, and in the apartments of the Luxembourg at Paris. The term is also employed for the under side or face of an architrave; and more especially for that of the corona or larmier, which the ancients called *lacunaria*, the French denominate *plafond*, and we usually the *drip*. It is enriched with compartments of roses; and in the Doric order has eighteen drops, disposed in three ranks (six in each,) placed to the right of the *guttæ* at the bottom of the triglyphs. The word soffit has likewise been applied to the ceiling of an arch.

SO'FI, a Persian word, which is employed to designate religious persons, otherwise termed Dervishes. It is probably a corruption of the Greek sophos, *wise*. Sofi was the surname borne by the ancestors of the kings of Persia of the race preceding that which now occupies the throne; and Shah Ismael Sofi, the first monarch of that race, also bore it; hence by European writers of the 16th and 17th centuries it was used erroneously as a title of the king of Persia.

SO'FISM, the mystical doctrines of the class of Mohammedan religionists called Sofis. This name is indeed generally applied in the East to persons living together in a monastic way, and professing an ascetic life. But the tenets peculiarly denoted by the name of Sufism are those of a sect which is said to be gaining ground extensively in oriental countries, especially among the educated classes of Mohammedans. These tenets, like those of the Quitetists and other Christian sects of mystics, are founded on a notion of the union of the human soul with the divinity by contemplation and the subjugation of the appetites: but, as has been too frequently the case among Christians also, they have afforded a cover for the most licentious lessons of refined debauchery. The principles of Sufism appear also to have a remarkable affinity, in some respects, with those pantheistic notions which are prominent in the system of the Bramins, and seem to form the very foundation of the still more widely extended religion of Buddha.

SOIREE', the term originally given by the French to certain evening parties held for the sake of conversation only, music, dancing, and similar entertainments being excluded; but the word has been since introduced into all the languages of modern Europe, and is now employed to designate most descriptions of evening parties in which ladies and gentlemen are intermixed, whatever be the amusements introduced. It is frequently applied in England to the public meetings of certain societies held for the advancement of their respective objects, at which tea and other refreshments are dispensed during the intervals of business.

SOKE, in English law, a term which anciently had various significations, viz.: 1. The liberty or privilege of tenants excused from customary burdens and impositions. 2. The power of administering justice. 3. The precinct in which the chief lord exercised his *soc*, or liberty of keeping court within his own jurisdiction

4. A stipulated payment or rent to the lord for using his land, with such liberty and privilege as made the tenant the sokeman or freeholder.—*Soke-men*, those who held by no servile tenure, but paid their rent as a soke, or sign of freedom.

SOLA'RIUM, in antiquity, a place on the tops of houses exposed to the sun, where the Romans used to take air and exercise.

SOL'DAN, a title formerly given to the general who commanded the caliph's army; the epithet was afterwards applied to a governor of Egypt.

SOL'DIER, a man enrolled for military service, or whose occupation is military. It is generally applied to a private, or one in the ranks: but it is also a proper appellation for an officer of any grade who possesses valor, skill, and experience.

SOLDU'RII, in antiquity, a kind of military clients or retainers to the great men in Gaul, who bound themselves to bear all the good or ill fortune of their patrons.

SOL'ECISM, among modern grammarians, any word or expression which does not agree with the established usage of writing or speaking. As customs change, that which may be regarded as a solecism at one time, may at another be considered as correct language. Hence a *solecism* differs from a barbarism, which consists in the use of a word or expression altogether contrary to the spirit of the language.

SOLFEG'GIO, in music, the system of arranging the scale by the names ut, re, mi, fa, sol, la, by which musical students are taught to sing, these notes being represented to the eye by lines and spaces, to which the syllables in question are applied.

SOLI'CITOR, in law, a person authorized and employed to prosecute the suits of others in courts of equity.—*Solicitor-general*, in British polity, an officer of the crown. Till the 13th of Charles II., he, with the attorney-general, had a right, on special occasions, to sit in the house of lords.

SOLIFID'IAN, in theology, one who maintains that faith alone, without works, is necessary to justification.

SO'LO, in music, a passage, or perfect piece in which a single voice or instrument performs without accompaniment. Peculiar freedom, ease, distinctness, and power of execution, are required to perform the solo with correctness, taste, and feeling.

SO'MATIST, one who denies the existence, and consequently the agency, of spiritual substances.

SOMATOL'OGY, the doctrine of bodies or material substances.

SOM'NUS, in classical mythology, the poetical god of sleep, is the son of Erebus and Nox, or of Nox alone. He dwells with his brother Death in a palace at the western extremity of the earth. Homer makes Juno seek him in the isle of Lemnos, whither he had repaired for love of the nymph Pasithea. Ovid makes him dwell in a cavern among the Scythians or Cimmerians; Statius in Æthiopia.

SON, in its primary sense, is the male issue of a parent, father or mother. In a more extended sense, as often used in the Scriptures, sons include descendants in general; as, we are all *sons of Adam*. Also a native or inhabitant of a country; as, the *sons* of America.

SONA'TA, in music, a piece or composition of music, wholly executed by instruments; and which, with regard to the several kinds of instruments, is what the cantata is with respect to vocal performances.

SONG, in general, that which is sung or uttered with musical modulations of the voice, whether of the human voice or that of a bird.—A little poem to be sung, or uttered with musical modulations; a ballad. The term is applied to either a short poetical or musical composition, but most frequently to both in union. As a poetical composition it may be largely defined a short poem divided into portions of returning measure, and turning upon some single thought or feeling. As a union of poetry and music, it may be defined a very brief lyrical poem, founded commonly upon agreeable subjects, to which is added a melody for the purpose of singing it. As denoting a musical composition, *song* is used to signify a vocal melody of any length or character, and not confined to a single movement; but as regards performance, it is confined to an air for a single voice. The songs of a country are characteristic of its manners. Every country has its love *songs*, its war *songs*, and its patriotic *songs*.—A hymn; a sacred poem or hymn to be sung either in joy or thanksgiving, as that sung by Moses and the Israelites after escaping the dangers of the Red Sea and Pharaoh's wrath; or of lamentation, as that of David over the death of Saul and Jonathan. *Songs* of joy are represented as constituting a part of heavenly felicity.

SON'NET, in poetry, a short composition of fourteen or fifteen lines, deca or endecasyllabic, rhymed according to an intricate but not always precisely similar arrangement. It is the oldest form in which the Italian language was used; but was, at a still earlier period, employed, although not commonly, by the Provençal poets. In Italy, Dante, and the Tuscan poets his contemporaries brought the sonnet into public estimation, about the beginning of the 14th century; but by them it was invariably employed as the vehicle of thoughts wrapped in very obscure language, and probably of a symbolical nature, though generally, in their outward signification, breathing the spirit of romantic and chivalrous love. By Petrarch, in the course of the same century, the sonnet was carried to perfection in point of form and polish; although applied by him, as it had been by his predecessors, almost exclusively to the subject of his figurative and mystical passion. Since the time of Petrarch the sonnet has been a favorite form of composition in Italy, especially for the purposes of occasional poetry. In France it has had little success; or rather the French sonnet is a different poem, less regular in its construction than the Italian. In Germany and England the comparative poverty in rhymes of their respective languages has rendered it unusual: but Milton has given to it a dignity peculiarly his own, together with much of the melody and tenderness which characterize his Italian models.—The proper sonnet consists of two quatrains, with four lines and two rhymes each, and two terzines, each with three lines and a single rhyme. The last six lines, however, are susceptible of various arrangements; the one usually adopted in English is the rhyming of the fifth and sixth lines together, frequently after a full pause, so that the sonnet ends with a point, as in an epigram The sonnet generally consists of one principal idea, pursued through the various antitheses of the different strophes. Pieces of a similar metrical structure in octo-syllabic lines are termed by the Italians Anacreontic sonnets. It is sometimes said that there is "hardly an educated Italian who has not composed a sonnet."

SOOTH'SAYING, the foretelling of future events by persons without divine aid or authority, and thus distinguished from *prophecy* by inspiration.

SOPH'ISM, a subtilty in reasoning, the arguments not being logically supported, or in which the inferences are not justly deduced from the premises.

SOPH'ISTS, a name at first given to philosophers, and those who were remarkable for their wisdom: it was afterwards applied to rhetoricians, and lastly to such as spent their time in verbal niceties, logical conundrums, sententious quibbles, and philosophical enigmas. The following, called the *Pseudomenos*, for example, was a famous problem amongst the ancient *sophists:* "When a man says, *I lie*, does he *lie*, or does he *not lie?* If he lies, he speaks truth; and if he speaks the truth, he lies." We find the leading feature of the sophistic doctrine to be a dislike to everything fixed and necessary, in ethics as well as philosophy. Prescription was represented as the sole source of moral distinctions, which must consequently vary with the character and institutions of the people. The *useful* was held to be the only mark by which one opinion could be distinguished from another. An absolute standard of truth is as absurd a notion in speculation as an absolute standard of morals in practice; that only is true which seems so to the individual, and just as long as it so seems "Man is the measure of all things." These and similar doctrines they maintained with great subtlety and acuteness, and found numerous disciples among those who were well prepared for the admission of tenets which swept away at once all the remnants of those prejudices which might still interpose a barrier between their passions and their gratification. Considered as a link in the chain of philosophical development, the Sophists were doubtless the involuntary cause of the greater depth and soundness of the subsequent Grecian philosophy. The success which they had found in demolishing the systems of their predecessors proved the necessity of laying the foundations of human knowledge deeper than heretofore had been done; and it is thus to the Sophists that we may attribute the more critical and cautious spirit which distinguishes the doctrines of Plato and Aristotle from those of Heraclitus or Parmenides.

SOPRA'NO, in music, one of the intermediate portions of the scale, which is a species of the treble, suited to the female voice.

SORBON'NE, the name of a college originally instituted for the education of secular clergymen at the university of Paris, so called after Robert of Sorbon, in Champagne, a theologian of Paris, who founded it during the reign of St. Louis, about 1250, and endowed it with an income which was subsequently much increased. This institution, the teachers in which were always doctors and professors of theology, acquired so much fame, that its name was extended to the whole theological faculty of the university of Paris.

SOR'CERY, magic, or divination by the supposed assistance of evil spirits, or the power of commanding evil spirits.

SORI'TES, in logic, an imperfect syllogism, or an abridged form of stating a series of syllogisms; or it is a species of reasoning in which a series of propositions are so linked together, that the predicate of the one becomes continually the next in succession, till a conclusion is formed by bringing together the subject of the first proposition and the predicate of the last. Thus, all men of revenge have their souls often uneasy. Uneasy souls are a plague to themselves. Now to be one's own plague is folly in the extreme. Therefore all men of revenge are extreme fools. A sorites has as many middle terms as there are intermediate propositions between the first and the last; and, consequently, it may be drawn out into as many syllogisms.

SORTIE', in military language, the issuing of a body of troops from a besieged place to attack the besiegers; a sally.

SOR'TILEGE, divination by lots. A very ancient mode of exploring future events, and which has been supposed by superstitious persons in modern times to derive countenance from various incidents in sacred history, especially the choice of St. Matthias by lot to the place of an apostle.

SOSTENU'TO, in music, a term implying that the notes of the movement or passage or note over which it is placed, is to be held out its full length in an equal and steady manner.

SOT'TO, in music, a term signifying below, or inferior; as, *sotto il soggetto*, below the subject; but *sotto voce* is used to signify with a restrained voice or moderate tone.

SOUL, in metaphysics, the intellectual principle, immaterial and immortal. Various have been the opinions of philosophers concerning the substance of the human soul; but, as Lord Bacon observes, the doctrine concerning the rational soul of man must be deduced from revelation; for as its substance, in its creation, was not formed out of the mass of heaven and earth, but immediately inspired by God; and as the laws of the heavenly bodies, together with those of our earth, make the subject of philosophy, so no knowledge of the substance of the rational soul can be had from philosophy.—By the word *soul*, we also denote the spirit, essence, or chief part; as, charity is the *soul* of all the virtues. Also the animating principle, or that which gives life and energy to the whole; as, an able commander is the *soul* of an army.

SOUTHCOT'TIANS, the followers of Joanna Southcott, a religious fanatic, who was born at Gittisham, in Devonshire, in 1750. She first pretended to a divine mission, and held herself out as the woman spoken of in the book of Revelation. After she had attained her grand climacteric, in 1814, she announced herself as the mother of the promised Shiloh, whose speedy advent she predicted. Her death, in December of that year, did not undeceive her disciples, and the sect continued to exist for many years, nor are we aware that it is yet altogether extinct. Many of her followers wore long beards and a peculiar costume.

SOUTH SEA BUBBLE, a term given to a commercial "scheme" in 1720, which, for a time, produced a kind of national delirium in England. A company for trading to the South Seas, which was entitled the "South Sea Company," had been sanctioned by government, with the specious pretence of discharging the national debt, by reducing all the funds into one. Blunt, the projector, had taken the hint of his plan from Law's celebrated Mississippi scheme, which, in the preceding year, had, in France, entailed ruin upon many thousand families of that kingdom. In the project of Law there was something substantial. It promised an exclusive trade to Louisiana; though the design was defeated by the frantic eagerness of the people. But the South Sea scheme was buoyed up by nothing but the folly and rapaciousness of individuals, which became so blind and extravagant, that Blunt was able to impose upon the whole nation, and make tools of the other directors, to serve his own purpose and that of a few associates. When this projector found that the South Sea stock did not rise according to his expectation, he circulated a report that Gibraltar and Port Mahon would be exchanged for some places in Peru; by which means the English trade to the South Sea would be protected and enlarged. This rumor, diffused by emissaries, acted like a contagion. In five days the directors opened their books for a subscription of 1,000,000*l.* at the rate of 300*l.* for every 100*l.* capital. Persons of all ranks crowded to the house in such a manner, that the first subscription exceeded 2,000,000*l.* of original stock. In a few days this stock advanced to 340*l.*; and the subscriptions were sold for double the price of the first payment. In a little time the stock reached 1,000*l.*, and the whole nation was infected with the spirit of stock-jobbing to an incredible extent. The infatuation prevailed till the 8th of September, when the stock began to fall, and some of the adventurers awoke from their delirium. On the 29th of the same month, the stock had sunk to 150*l.*: several eminent goldsmiths and bankers, who had lent great sums upon it, were obliged to stop payment and abscond; and the ebb of this portentous tide was so violent that it carried everything in its way, and an infinite number of families were overwhelmed with ruin. Public credit sustained a terrible shock; the nation was thrown into a ferment; and nothing was heard but the ravings of grief, disappointment, and despair.

SOV'EREIGN, a supreme ruler, or one who possesses the highest authority without control. A king or queen regnant.—An English gold coin, value twenty shillings.

SPA'HI, one of the Turkish cavalry.

SPAN'DREL, in architecture, the irregular triangular space comprehended between the outer curve or extrados of an arch, a horizontal line drawn from its apex, and a perpendicular line from its springing.—In Gothic Architecture, spandrels are usually ornamented with tracery, foliage, &c.—*Spandrel bracketing*, a cradling of brackets which is placed between curves, each of which is in a vertical plane, and in the circumference of a circle whose plane is horizontal.—*Spandrel wall*, a wall built on the back of an arch filling in the spandrels.

SPEAK'ER, in the parliamentary sense, an officer who acts as chairman during a sitting.—*The Speaker of Congress*, is a member of the house elected by a majority of votes to act as chairman or president, in putting questions, reading bills, keeping order, and carrying into execution the resolutions of the house. The Speaker is not to deliver his sentiments upon any question; but it is his duty to interrupt a member whose language is indecorous; or who wanders from the subject of debate: he may also stop a debate, to remind the house of any standing order, or established mode of proceeding, which he sees about to be violated. He, however, submits everything to the decision of the house. If the number of votes, on the two sides of a question be equal, he may decide it by his own; but otherwise he cannot vote. When the house resolves itself into a committee, the chair is filled by a temporary chairman, and the speaker is then capable of addressing the house on any subject, like a private member.

SPE'CIALTY, in law, a special contract or bond; the evidence of a debt by deed or instrument under seal, thereby differing from what is called *simple contract*.

SPECIFICA'TION, the act of specifying, or designation of particulars: as, the *specification* necessary to be given in taking out a patent; or, the *specification* of a charge against a naval or military officer.

SPEC'TACLE, something that is exhibited to view as extraordinary or deserving especial notice; as, the combats of gladiators in ancient Rome were spectacles at once wonderful and brutal; or, the manager has this season produced a splendid *spectacle*.

SPEC'TRE, a phantom or apparition created, when supposed to be seen, by the mind, through its own fears or guilty recollections.

SPECULA'TION, in commerce, the act or practice of buying articles of merchandise, or any purchasable commodity whatever, in expectation of a rise of price, and of selling the same at a considerable advance. In this it is distinguished from regular trade, in which the profit expected is the difference between the retail and wholesale prices, or the difference of price in the place where the goods are purchased, and the place to which they are to be carried for market. *Speculation* on a large scale, upon the principle of monopolizing, or that kind of speculation which consists in the purchase and sale of shares in public companies, as well as "dabbling" in the stocks, and a variety of other hazardous transactions which might be named, are different species of gambling, and are often no less ruinous.

SPHINX, in antiquity, an emblematical figure, composed of the head and breasts of a woman, the wings of a bird, the legs and claws of a lion, and the body of a dog; and said to have been the Egyptian symbol of Theology.—Also, a fabulous monster of Thebes. According to mythological history, its father was

Typhon the gigantic son of Terra, and it was sent by Juno to afflict the Thebans, which it did by proposing enigmatical questions to persons, whom it killed if they could not expound them. At length, Œdipus having explained its famous riddle on man, it precipitated itself from a rock, and was dashed to pieces. This riddle was as follows: "What creature is that which goes in the morning upon four; at noon, upon two; and in the evening upon three legs." Œdipus answered, "It is man; who, in his infancy, crawls upon all four, walks afterwards on two, till old age brings him to his staff, which constitutes three legs." The Grecian sphinx was probably borrowed from Egypt: where the enormous figure, now half buried in the sand, was probably the archetype of the more elegant monster of Greece. This figure is close to the Pyramids of Ghizeh, and was disinterred by the late Mr. Belzoni, but has been again nearly covered.

SPHRAGIS'TICS, the science of seals, their history, peculiarities, and distinctions, especially with a view to the means which they afford of ascertaining the age and genuineness of documents to which they are affixed. Ancient seals were chiefly impressed on common wax of different colors; sealing-wax came into use in the 16th century. This branch of diplomatics owes its origin to Heineccius, who published a work on the subject in 1709.

SPICCA'TO, in music, a term indicating that every note is to have its distinct sound. When used in relation to instruments played with a bow, it is to be understood that every note is to have a bow distinct from the preceding or succeeding one.

SPIN'ET, a musical stringed instrument, played on by two ranges of keys, the foremost range being in the order of the diatonic scale; and the other range set backward, in the order of the artificial notes or semitones.

SPINO'SISM, in philosophy, the system of Benedict Spinosa, a Jew of Amsterdam, born in 1634, which is developed in his works on ethics. In it he deduces by strictly mathematical reasoning, from a few axioms, the well-known principles, that "there can be no substance but God; whatever is is in God, and nothing can be conceived without God." Hence his scheme is called, with justice, Pantheistic. In fact, as Mr. Hallam observes, "He does not essentially differ from the Pantheists of old. He conceived, as they had done, that the infinity of God required the exclusion of all other substance: that he was infinite *ab omni parte*, and not only in certain senses." "It was one great error of Spinosa," says the same writer, "to entertain too arrogant a notion of the human faculties; in which, by dint of his own subtle demonstrations, he pretended to show a capacity of adequately comprehending the nature of what he denominated God. And this was accompanied by a rigid dogmatism, no one proposition being stated with hesitation; by a disregard of experience, at least as the basis of reasoning; and by a uniform preference of the synthetic mode."

SPIN'STER, in law, the common title by which an unmarried woman, without rank or distinction, is designated.

SPIRE, in architecture, the pyramidal or conical termination of a tower or turret. The earliest spires were merely pyramidal or conical roofs, specimens of which still exist in Norman buildings, as that of the tower of Than church in Normandy. These roofs, becoming gradually elongated, and more and more acute, resulted at length in the elegant tapering spire; among the many existing examples of which, probably, that of Salisbury is the finest. The spires of medieval architecture, to which alone they are appropriate, are generally square, octagonal, or circular in plan; they are sometimes solid, more frequently hollow, and are variously ornamented with bands encircling them, with panels more or less enriched, and with spire lights, which are of infinite variety. Their angles are sometimes crocketted, and they are almost invariably terminated by a finial. In the later styles the general pyramidal outline is obtained by diminishing the diameter of the building in successive stages, and this has been imitated in modern spires, in which the forms and details of classic architecture have been applied to structures essentially medieval. The term spire is sometimes restricted to signify such tapering buildings, crowning towers or turrets, as have parapets at their base. When the spire rises from the exterior of the wall of the tower without the intervention of a parapet, it is called a *broach*.

SPIR'IT, in metaphysics, an incorporeal being of intelligence.—Also, excitement of mind, animation, or whatever has power or energy; the quality of any substance which manifests life and activity; disposition of mind excited and directed to a particular object, &c.—*Holy Spirit*, the third person in the Trinity.

SPIR'ITUAL, mental; intellectual; immaterial. Also, relating to sacred things, or ecclesiastical.—*Spiritually minded*, having the affections refined and elevated above sensual objects, and placed on God and his law.—*Spiritual court*, a court held by a bishop or other ecclesiastic.

SPIR'ITUALISM, as distinguished from Materialism. That system according to which all that is real is spirit, soul, or self; that which is called the external world being either a succession of notions impressed on the mind by the Deity, or else the mere educt of the mind itself. The first is the spiritualism of Berkeley; the second, which may be called pure egotism, that of Fichte.

SPON'DEE, in the Latin and Greek prosody, a poetic foot of two long syllables.—*Spondaic*, pertaining to a spondee.

SPON'SIONS, in international law, acts and engagements made on behalf of states by agents not specially authorized, or exceeding the limits of the authority under which they purport to be made, are so called by writers on this branch of jurisprudence. Such conventions must be confirmed by express or tacit ratification; the latter of which is implied from the fact of acting under it as if bound by its stipulations; but mere silence is not, in general, held equivalent to ratification. Such are the official acts of admirals or generals suspending or limiting hostilities, capitulations of surrender, cartels of exchange, &c.

SPON'SOR, one who binds himself to answer for another, and is responsible for his default. Hence, *sponsor*, in baptism, is a surety for the moral education of the child baptized.

SPONTA'NEOUS, an epithet for things that act by their own impulse, or without any apparent external agency; as, the spontaneous combustion of vegetable substances, which, when highly dried, and closely heaped, will burst into a flame.

SPRING, the season of the year when increasing solar heat restores the energy of vegetation. It comprehends the months of March, April, and May, in the middle latitudes, north of the Equator.

SQUAD'RON, in the art of war, a division or body of troops, which, among the ancients, was always square: whence its name.—A *squadron of ships*, a division or part of a fleet employed on a particular expedition, and commanded by a vice or rear-admiral, or a commodore.

STA'BAT MA'TER DOLORO'SA, the first words of a celebrated Latin hymn of the church, in rhymed lines of eight syllables without metre; said to have been composed by a Franciscan monk named Jacopone, in the 14th century. It has been set to music by nearly all the great composers; but the best known of all their compositions is that of Pergolesi, commenced by him when nearly on his deathbed, and finished by another hand. The stabat mater is performed in the ecclesiastical services of the Roman church during Holy Week.

STACCA'TO, in music, a term denoting that the notes to which it is affixed are to be detached in a striking way from each other, being much like *spiccato*, which see.

STA'DIUM, in ancient architecture, an open area used for exercise by the Grecian youth. With the Romans it was much in the form of the circi, but most of the Grecian stadia were enclosed by merely an earthen mound. Vitruvius informs us that its length was much greater than its breadth; the lists were formed by a bank or terrace. Though the stadium mostly formed part of a gymnasium, it sometimes formed a separate structure, and was built at great cost and with considerable elegance: witness that on the Corinthian Isthmus mentioned by Pausanias, as well as that of Herodie Atticus at Athens, which was of large dimensions, and constructed of Pentelican marble. Besides this, mention is made by that author of several others.

STADT'HOLDER, the name formerly given to the commander-in-chief of the military forces in the republic of the United Netherlands.

STAFF, in military affairs, an establishment of officers in various departments, attached to an army, or to the commander of an army. The staff includes officers not of the line, as adjutants, quarter-masters, chaplain, surgeon, &c. The staff is the medium of communication from the commander-in-chief to every department of an army.—An ensign of authority; a badge of office; as, a constable's *staff*. Also a pole erected in a ship to hoist and display a flag, called a flag-*staff*.

STAGE, in the drama, the place of action and representation, included between the pit and the scenes, and answering to the *proscenium* or *pulpitum*, of the ancients. The word *stage* also often implies the whole dramatic art in composition and performance.—A floor or platform of any kind elevated above the ground or common surface, as for an exhibition to public view; as, a *stage* for a mountebank; a *stage* erected for public speakers.—A place of rest on a journey; as, how far is it to the next *stage?* or the distance between two places of rest on a road; as, it is a twelve mile *stage*. Hence the word *stage-coach*.

STA'GYRITE, an appellation given to Aristotle, from Stagira, a town in Macedonia, the place of his birth.

STAIRS, in architecture, steps for ascending from the lower to the upper part of a house. When these are enclosed with walls or balustrades, with landing-places for communication between the several stories of a building, the whole is called a staircase. Vitruvius makes no mention of staircases in his Treatise on Architecture; and, indeed, with the ancients they formed no feature in the interior, being generally on the outside of the houses. Those of which traces remain are narrow, and so inconvenient that in some cases the steps are a foot in height. In modern architecture, they are often constructed with great display of skill and magnificence, and are no small test of the skill and power of the architect. Those stairs which proceed in a right line of ascent are called *fliers;* when they wind round a solid or open *newel* they are called *winders*. *Mixed stairs* are such as partly wind and partly fly.

STALL, in architecture, a seat raised on the sides of the choir or chancel of a church, mostly appropriated to a dignitary of a cathedral or collegiate church. Sometimes stalls are placed near the high altar, for the priest and deacon or subdeacon to rest while the service in certain parts is carried on by the choristers. In churches of the kinds named there is generally a series of them.

STAMP, in England, a mark set upon things chargeable with duty to government, as evidence that the duty is paid; as, the stamp on a newspaper, the stamp on a bond or indenture, &c.—Any instrument for making impressions on other bodies.—A character of reputation, good or bad, fixed on anything; as, the Scriptures bear the *stamp* of a divine origin; this person bears on his unblushing face the *stamp* of roguery.

STAN'ZA, in poetry, a series or number of verses connected with each other in a poem, of which the metre is constructed of successive series similar in arrangement. The stanza, however, must be understood to form a shorter division than the classical strophe, to which this definition would be equally applicable. The term is of Italian origin, and signifies literally a *station* or *resting-place:* it is so called from terminating with a full point or pause. The *ottava rima*, which consists of six lines in alternate rhyme ended by a couplet, the lines being deca, or rather hendeca-syllabic, is the principal Italian stanza. The Spenserian stanza (which was perhaps invented by the poet from whom it derives its name, but was certainly first applied by him to the construction of a regular poem) consists of eight deca-syllabic verses and an Alexandrine at the end; the first and third verses forming the last rhyme; the second, fourth, fifth, and seventh another; and the eighth and ninth a third rhyme. Lord Byron has given both to the Ottava and the Spenserian stanza in English verse a peculiar and original character.

STAR'-CHAMBER, formerly, a court of criminal jurisdiction at Westminster, England, so called from its roof being ornamented with gilt stars. This court took upon itself to decide upon those cases of offence with regard to which the law was silent; and was in criminal matters what the exchequer is in civil. It passed judgment without the intervention of a jury. It differed from all other judiciary courts in this, that the latter were governed only by the common law, or immemorial custom, and acts of parliament; whereas the former often admitted for law the proclamations of the king in council.

STA'ROST, a title under the Polish republic enjoyed by noblemen who were in possession of certain castles and domains called starosties. These were grants of the crown, and only conferred for life, but generally renewed after the demise of a possessor to his heirs.

STATES, or ESTATES, in modern European history, (French états, German stände,) those divisions of society, professions, or classes of men, which have partaken, either directly or by representation, in the government of their country. Their number has varied in different countries. In France, and most other feudal kingdoms, there have been three estates, (nobles, clergy, commonalty,) members of the ancient national assemblies. Hence the well-known appellation *tiers état* (third estate) for the last. In

Sweden there are at this day four: nobility, clergy, citizens, peasants. In most countries the ancient system of assemblies convoked from separate estates disappeared by the progress of absolute government in the 16th and 17th centuries; and in modern monarchical constitutions the English system of government by king, lords, and commons, or analogous powers, has prevailed. But the states have been reconstituted of late years in some German monarchies and grand duchies, the electorate of Hesse Cassel, &c.

STATES-GENERAL, in French history, assemblies which were first called A.D. 1302, and were held occasionally from that period to the year 1614, when they were discontinued, till they were summoned again at an interesting period, viz., in the year 1789. These states-general, however, were very different from the ancient assemblies of the French nation under the kings of the first and second race. There is no point with respect to which the French antiquaries are more generally agreed than in maintaining that the states-general had no suffrage in the passing of laws, and possessed no proper jurisdiction. The whole tenor of the French history confirms this opinion.

STA'TIONERY, the name given to all the materials employed in the art of writing, but more especially to those of pen, ink, and paper. The term *stationery* is derived from the business of booksellers having been anciently carried on entirely in stalls, or *stations*.

STATIS'TICS, a term of somewhat modern date, adopted to express a more comprehensive view of the various particulars constituting the general and political strength and resources of a country than was usually embraced by writers on political arithmetic. The principal objects of the science of *statistics* are—the extent and population of a state; the occupation of the different classes of its inhabitants; the progress of agriculture, of manufactures, and of internal and foreign trade; the income and wealth of the inhabitants, and the proportion drawn from them for the public service by taxation; their health and longevity; the condition of the poor; the state of schools and other public institutions of utility; with every other subject, the knowledge of which may be useful in ascertaining the moral condition and political strength of a country, its commerce, arts, &c.

STAT'UE, in sculpture, a representation in relief in some solid substance, as marble or bronze, or in some apparently solid substance, of a man or other animal. There are various species of statues: 1. Those smaller than nature. 2. Those of the same size as nature. 3. Those larger than nature. 4. Those that are three or more times larger than nature, and are called *colossal*. The first were by the ancients confined to men and gods generally. The second were confined to the representation of men celebrated for their learning and talents, who had rendered service to the state, and were executed at the public expense. The third were confined to kings, emperors, and, when more than twice the size of nature, to heroes. The fourth species were confined to statues of the gods, or of kings and emperors represented under the form of gods.—*Equestrian statues* are those in which the figure is seated on a horse.

STA'TUS QUO, in politics, a treaty between two or more belligerents, which leaves each party in possession of the same territories, fortresses, &c. as it occupied before hostilities broke out, is said to leave them "in statu quo ante bellum," in the same state as before the war.

STAT'UTES, acts of Congress, which are either public or private.—*Statutes* are distinguished from *common law*. The latter owes its binding force to the principles of justice, to long use, and the consent of a nation. The former owe their binding force to a positive command or declaration of the governing power.

STAVE, in music, the five horizontal and parallel lines on which the notes of tunes are written or printed.

STEE'PLE, in architecture, an appendage erected generally in the western end of churches, to hold the bells. Steeples are denominated, according to their form, either spires or towers: the first are such as ascend continually diminishing either conically or pyramidally: the latter are merely parallelopipeds, and are covered at top platform-wise. The steeple appears to have originated in Gothic architecture.

STEN'CILLING, a method of painting on walls with a stencil, so as to imitate the figures on paper-hangings.

STENOG'RAPHY, the art of writing in short-hand, by using abbreviations or characters for whole words. Some systems are replete with unmeaning symbols and ill-judged contractions; while others are too prolix, by containing a multiplicity of characters, and those characters not simple or easily remembered. No system of arbitrary signs, in fact, however scientific, can, without extensive practice, be of much use to the student; and it is not therefore surprising that many of our most expert reporters neglect or abandon the study of it altogether.

STENTO'RIAN, [from Stentor, a herald in Homer, whose voice was as loud as the united voices of fifty other men,] able to utter a very loud sound. The word *stentorophonic* is also sometimes, though rarely, used.

STERCO'RIANISM, in ecclesiastical history, a nickname which seems to have been applied in the Western church, in the 5th and 6th century, to those who held the opinion that a change took place in the consecrated elements, so as to render the divine body subject to the act of digestion.

STEREOG'RAPHY, the art of drawing the forms and figures of solids upon a plane.

STEREOT'OMY, the science or art of cutting solids into certain figures or sections; as walls or other members in the profiles of architecture.

STER'EOTYPE, an entire solid plate or piece of type cast from an impression in gypsum of a page composed with movable types. Thus we say a book is printed *on* stereotype, or *in* stereotype. In the latter use, the word seems rather to signify the workmanship, or manner of printing, than the plate. See *Cycl. Useful Arts.*

STER'LING, in English commerce, a term which is applied to money, signifying that it is of the fixed, or standard, national value; thus, "a pound sterling" is not indefinitely "a pound," but "an English pound." Camden appears to offer the true etymology of this word, when he derives it from *easterling*, and corroborates, if not demonstrates, the propriety of this suggestion, by quoting old deeds, where English coin is always called *nummi easterlingi.* In explanation, he observes, that in the reign of Richard I. money coined in the eastern part of Germany grew to be much esteemed in England, on account of its purity: this money was called *easterling* money, as all the people of those parts were called easterlings; and in consequence of the partiality related, some of the *easterling* coiners were invited into the kingdom, to perfect its coinage, which was thenceforward denominated *easterling*, *esterling*, or *sterling*. During a considerable period, the only coin in England was one of about the value of a penny: whence it happens, that many ancient writers use the word *easterling* as a substantive, and synonymously with *penny.*—The word *sterling* has also a more general application. We speak of *sterling* value, *sterling* worth, or *sterling* wit; thereby meaning genuine and of good quality.

STEW'ARD, a man who is employed in wealthy families to superintend the household generally, to collect the rents or income, keep the accounts, &c.

STICH'OMANCY, divination by lines or passages in books taken at hazard. Among the Romans verses from the Sibylline books were written on slips of paper, which were thrown into a vessel; and future events were conjectured from the interpretation of one of these slips drawn out at hazard. Of the same kind were the *Sortes Virgilianæ*, *Homericæ*, &c.; a sort of literary superstition by which the works of authors were consulted, and the meaning of a line casually taken assumed as indicative of the fate of the person discovering it. Verses of the Bible selected in this way by chance have been, and are still, frequently taken by the superstitious as oracular. This sort of divination has been called *bibliomancy*, or *sortes biblicæ*. It was condemned by the council of Vannes in 465, and other early synods; but was long afterwards practised in France at the elections of bishops, abbots, &c. The custom of drawing by lots verses from the Bible on such occasions is said to have prevailed as late as 1740, in the cathedrals of Ypres, St. Omer, and Boulogne.

STIFF, constrained, labored, wanting in ease and gracefulness of style. Such, for example, are the Egyptian figures, those of the most ancient Greek style, certain Gothic figures, &c. Stiffness is essentially opposed to beauty of form. Nature, bountiful in almost all her provisions, has given to the limbs and movements of men freedom and suppleness; and it is only through the unworthy affectation which sometimes springs from sophisticated habits of society, that constrained or stiff movements are discernible, except in people out of health.

STIG'MATIZING, in antiquity, the act of affixing a mark upon slaves, sometimes as a punishment, but more usually in order to know them. It was done by applying a red-hot iron, marked with certain letters, to their foreheads, till a fair impression was made, and then pouring ink into the furrows, that the inscription might be the more conspicuous.—*Stigmatizing*, among some nations, was, however, looked upon as a distinguishing mark of honor and nobility.

STIPEN'DIARY, one who performs services for a settled compensation, or stipend, either by the day, month, or year.

STIP'PLING, in the arts, a method of engraving in dots, as distinguished from *etching* in lines.

STIPULA'TION, a contract or bargain; as, the *stipulations* of the allied powers of Europe to furnish each his contingent of troops.

STO'Æ, in antiquity, porticoes in Athens, which were the resort of philosophers, particularly the Stoics.

STOCK, in commerce, any fund consisting of money or goods employed by a person in trade, particularly the sum of money raised by a company for carrying on any trading concern.—*Stock* is a general name for the capitals of trading companies. It is a word also that denotes any sum of money which has been lent to government, on condition of receiving a certain interest till the money is repaid. Hence the price of stocks, or rates per cent., are the several sums for which $100 of those respective stocks sell at any given time.

STOCK'-BROKER, one who deals in the purchase and sale of stocks or shares in the public funds, for others.

STOCK'-JOBBER, one who speculates in the prices of stock from day to day, or by anticipation for future time: a desperate species of gambling, by which thousands are annually ruined.—*Stock-holder*, one who is a proprietor in the public funds, or in the funds of a bank or other company.

STO'IC, a disciple of the philosopher Zeno, who founded a sect. He taught that men should be free from passion, unmoved by joy or grief, and submit without complaint to the unavoidable necessity by which all things are governed. The Stoics are proverbially known for the sternness and austerity of their ethical doctrines, and for the influence which their tenets exercised over some of the noblest spirits of antiquity. Their system appears to have been an attempt to reconcile a theological pantheism, and a materialist psychology, with a logic which seeks the foundations of knowledge in sensible experience, and a morality which claims as its first principle the absolute freedom of the human will. "Live according to nature" is, with the Stoics, the expression of the coincidence which ought to exist between the human will and the universal reason, which they identified with the life and power of nature. This coincidence is virtue, the only good; as vice, its opposite, is the only evil. All things else are in themselves indifferent; being approved or disapproved only by comparison. Virtue, according to them, is the perfect harmony of the soul with itself; vice is, in its essence, inconsistent and self-contradictory. The wise man, the ideal of human perfection, is absolutely and without qualification, free. His actions are determined by his free will, with a power as irresistible as that by which universal nature is guided and animated.

STO'LA, in antiquity, a long robe in use among the Roman ladies, over which they wore a large mantle, or cloak, called the *pallium*.—Also, a sacerdotal ornament worn by the Romish parish priests over their surplice, as a mark of superiority in their respective churches; and by other priests over the alb, while celebrating mass.

STOLE, a long vest or robe, which forms a part of the sacerdotal dress of Roman Catholic parish priests over their surplice, as a mark of superiority in their respective churches, and by other priests over the alb while celebrating mass. It is a long broad white band, of silk or silver stuff, lined with stiff linen, worn by deacons over the left shoulder, and reaching to the right hip; but the priests wear it over both shoulders, and hanging down across the breast. It is marked with three crosses, and not unfrequently has little bells at the end.

STONE'HENGE, in English topography, the remains of a public structure of the ancient Britons, still extant upon Salisbury plain. It consists of many unhewn stones, which with some that are wanting, appear to have originally composed four ranks, one within another. Some of them, especially in the outermost and the third ranks, are twenty feet high and seven broad. The vertical stones sustain horizontal ones, laid across their heads, and fastened by mortises. The whole is supposed to have been once joined together. The purpose of a place of this description, among the generations which, two thousand years ago, peopled the island of Britain, and were not so barbarous or inconsiderable as is commonly supposed, and as the vanity and superior refinement of the Romans contribute to represent, seems to have been that of religious worship. What that religion was can only be conjectured; but judging of these ruins by their similarity to the huge remains of buildings still existing in Egypt—as well as from the circumstance that the heads and horns of oxen and other animals have been found buried in the spot—it has been thought that the rites peculiar to solar worship were there performed; and, consequently, that Stonehenge was once a temple of Baal.

STOP, the instrument by which the sounds of wind music are regulated; as, the *stops* of a flute or an organ. The stops of an organ are a collection of pipes similar in tone and quality, which run through the whole or a great part of the compass of the instrument. In great organs, the stops are numerous and multifarious; but the principal ones are the two *diapasons*, the *principal*, the *twelfth*, the *fifteenth*, the *sesquialtera*, the *mixture* or *furniture*, the *trumpet*, the *clarion*, and the *cornet*. The choir-organ usually contains the *stopt diapason*, the *dulciana*, the *principal*, the *flute*, the *twelfth*, the *bassoon*, and the *vox humana*. The stops of an organ are so arranged, that by means of registers the air proceeding from the bellows may be admitted to supply each stop or series of pipes, or excluded from it at pleasure; and a valve is opened when the proper key is touched, which causes all the pipes belonging to the note, in those series of which the registers are open, to sound at once. Several of the stops are designed to produce imitations of different musical instruments, as the *trumpet*, *clarion*, *cornet* and *flute stops*.

STOR'THING, the parliament of Norway. It is elected once in three years, and sits every year for the despatch of business. The election is double; every qualified person (an owner or life-renter of land paying taxes in the country, and every one possessing land or houses of 150 rix dollars value in towns) joining in the election of councillors, who elect out of their own body the representatives of the country. These must be from 75 to 100 in number. The storthing, when elected, divides itself into two houses: one fourth, chosen by the rest, joining the laything, or upper house; the remainder the odelsthing, or lower house. The storthing has the usual powers of a legislative assembly in a constitutional country, and the king has only a suspensive veto; which, if the storthing passes a law three times in six successive years, becomes of no effect.

STRAPPA'DO, a military punishment formerly practised. It consisted in drawing an offender to the top of a beam and letting him fall, by which means a limb was sometimes dislocated.

STRAT'EGY, properly the science of combining and employing the means which the different branches of the art of war afford, for the purpose of forming projects of operations, and of directing great military movements. It was formerly distinguished from the art of making dispositions and of manœuvring, when in the presence of the enemy; but military writers now, in general, comprehend all these subjects under the denomination of grand and elementary tactics.

STRATH'SPEY, in Scotland, a species of dance in which two persons are engaged. It is so denominated from the country of Strathspey, probably as having been first used there.—A species of dance music in common time, peculiar to Scotland. It probably originated in the same district as the above dance.

STRATOC'RACY, a military government, or that form of government in which the soldiery bear the sway.

STRENGTH, force of writing; vigor; nervous diction. The *strength* of words, of style, of expression, and the like, consists in the full and forcible exhibition of ideas, by which a sensible or deep impression is made on the mind of a hearer or reader. It is distinguished from *softness* or *sweetness*.—*Strength* of language enforces an argument, produces conviction, or excites wonder or other strong emotion; *softness* and *sweetness* give pleasure.

STREPITO'SO, in music, an Italian word denoting that the part to which it is prefixed must be performed in an impetuous and boisterous style.

STRETCH'ING COURSE, in architecture, a course in which the bricks or stones are laid horizontally with their lengths in the direction of the face of the wall.

STRET'TO, in music, a term indicating that the measure to which it is affixed is to be performed short and concise, hence quick. It is the opposite of *largo*.

STRI'Æ, in architecture, the fillets which separate the furrows or grooves of fluted columns.

STRO'PHE, a division of a Greek choral ode answering to a stanza. The name is derived from στρέφειν, *to turn*, because the singers turned in one direction while they recited that portion of the poem; they then turned round and sung the next portion, which was of exactly the same length and metre as the preceding, and was termed the antistrophe. These were sometimes followed by another strophe and antistrophe, sometimes by a single stanza called the epode.

STRUC'TURE, in its usual acceptation, a building of some size and importance. Also, form or construction; as, "we know but little of the *structure* and constitution of the terraqueous globe."

STUC'CO, in building, a fine kind of plaster composed of lime, sand, whiting, and pulverized marble; used for covering walls, &c.

STUD, in building, a small piece of timber or joist inserted in the sills and beams, between the posts, to support the beams or other main timbers.

STUD'IES, in painting, a term applied to those preparatory sketches or exercises made by an artist, consisting of separate parts of a picture, first designed and painted unconnectedly, with a view to their future introduction into the entire work. Thus, entire figures in some instances; in others, human heads, hands, or feet, animals, trees, plants, flowers, and, in short, anything designed from nature, receive the general name of *studies*. The use of studies is to enable a painter to acquire a practical knowledge of his art, and facility of execution. Pieces of instrumental music composed for the purpose of familiarizing the player with the difficulties of his instrument.

STUD'Y, application of the mind to books, to art or science, or to any subject, for the purpose of learning what was not before known; the occupation of a *student*. Also, the apartment devoted to study or literary avocations.

STYLE, in literature, the word style may be defined to mean the distinctive manner of writing which belongs to each author, and also to each body of writers, allied as belonging to the same school, country, or age. It is that which, to use the expression of Dryden, individuates each writer from all others. The style of an author is made up of various minute particulars, which it is extremely difficult to describe, but each of which adds something to the aggregate of qualities which belong to him. Collocation of words, turn of sentences, syntax, rhythm; the relation, abundance, and the character of his usual figures and metaphors; the usual order in which thoughts succeed each other; the logical form in which conclusions are generally deduced from their premises; the particular qualities most insisted on in description; amplification and conciseness, clearness and obscurity, directness and indirectness, exhaustion, suggestion, suppression—all these are features of style, in the largest sense of the expression, in which it seems to comprehend all peculiarities belonging to the manner in which thought is communicated from the writer to the reader. Excellence of style, particularly of the rhetorical parts of style, was more cultivated by the ancients than the moderns; and less, perhaps, at the present day, than at any former period since the English language began to be written in prose with correctness and elegance. Since the period when Bolingbroke, Junius, Johnson, Gibbon, and Burke became established as models, a certain superficial sameness of style, wanting in the roughness and vulgarity, but also in the force and individuality of old English composition, seems to prevail to such an extent as to render modern writing extremely monotonous and artificial. But it should never be forgotten that whatever quality may command a temporary popularity, no work, either in poetry or prose, has ever permanently maintained its hold on public admiration without excellence of style.—*Style*, in the Fine Arts, the mode in which an artist forms and expresses his ideas on and of a given subject. It is the form and character that he gives to the expression of his ideas, according to his particular faculties and powers. Style may be almost considered as the refinement of *manner;* it is a characteristic essence by which we distinguish the works of one master from another. From literature this word has passed into the theoretic language of the Fine Arts; and as in that we hear of the *sublime*, *brilliant*, *agreeable*, *historic*, *regular*, *natural*, *confused*, and other styles, so we have almost the same epithets applied to styles of art. Indeed this is not wonderful, since the principles of taste, in both the one and the other, are founded in nature; and it is a well-known saying, that poetry is a speaking picture. This word is improperly used as applied to coloring and harmony of tints: we speak of the style of a design, of a composition, of draperies, &c.; but not of the style of coloring, but rather the *method* or *manner* of coloring. The definition of this word by Sir Joshua Reynolds is as follows: "Style in painting is the same as in writing—a power over materials, whether words or colors, by which conceptions or sentiments are conveyed."—*Style*, in chronology, the manner of computing time, with regard to the Julian or Gregorian calendar, and termed either *old* style or *new*. By the *old style* the year consisted of 365 days and 6 hours; but the new or Gregorian style was made to correspond more nearly with the period of the sun's revolution, reckoning the year to be 365 days 5 hours 49 minutes 20 seconds, by retrenching 11 days from the old style. The *new style* was introduced into Germany in 1700, and in 1752 into England by act of parliament, whereby the 2d of September in that year was reckoned the 14th.—*Style*, in architecture, a particular mode of erecting buildings, as the Gothic style, the Saxon style, the Norman style, &c.

STY'LITE, the title given to a peculiar class of anchorites from the places on which they took up their solitary abodes, being the tops of various columns in Syria and Egypt. This strange method of devotion took its rise in the second century, and continued to be practised by many individuals for a great length of time. The most famous among them was one St. Simeon, in the 5th century, who is said to have lived thirty-seven years upon various columns of considerable height in the neighborhood of Antioch.

STY'LOBATE, in architecture, in a general sense, any sort of basement on which columns are placed to raise them above the level of the ground or floor; but in its technical sense, it is applied only to a continuous unbroken pedestal, upon which an entire range of columns stand, contradistinguished from pedestals, which are merely detached fragments of a stylobate placed beneath each column.

STYX, in mythology, a nymph: the daughter, according to Hesiod, of Oceanus and Thetis; but other mythologists relate the genealogy differently. She dwelt in a rock palace in the infernal regions, from whence one of the infernal rivers burst forth. This river, Styx, was one of the ten arms or branches of Oceanus. The gods of Olympus swore by the water of Styx; and a deity who took this oath in vain was banished from the heavenly mansions for ten years, to endure various torments.

SUB, a Latin preposition for *under* or *below*; used as a prefix to many English words denoting inferiority of rank or defect in quality; as, subaltern, subordinate, &c.

SU'BAH, in India, a province or viceroyship. Hence, *subahdar*, the governor of a province. *Subahdar* is also used for a native of India, who ranks as captain in the European companies.

SUBAL'TERN, a term for a military officer below the rank of captain.

SUBDOM'INANT, in music, that note which is a fifth below the key-note. It is a species of governing note, inasmuch as it requires the tonic to be heard after it in the plagal cadence. In the regular ascending scale of seven notes it is the fourth; the term, however, has its origin from its relation to the tonic as the fifth below.

SUB'JECT, one that owes allegiance to a government, and is governed by its laws. Men in free governments are *subjects* as well as *citizens*; as citizens, they enjoy rights and franchises; as subjects, they are bound to obey the laws.—*Subject*, that on which any mental operation is performed, or which is treated or discussed.

SUBJEC'TIVE and OBJEC'TIVE, are terms expressing the distinction which in analyzing every intellectual act we necessarily make between ourselves, the conscious *subject*, and that of which we are conscious, the *object*. "I know" and "something is known by me," are convertible propositions; every act of the soul that is not thus resolvable belongs to the emotive part of our nature, as distinguished from the intelligent and percipient. For the distinction between subject and object, all-important in intellectual philosophy, and the neglect of which has been the cause of infinite confusion and perplexity, we are indebted to the schoolmen; from whom it was derived, through Wolf and Leibnitz, by Kant and the modern German philosophers.

SUBLAPSA'RIAN, in theology, one who maintains that the sin of Adam's apostasy being imputed to all his posterity, God in his compassion decreed to send his Son to rescue a great number from their lost state, and to accept of his obedience and death on their account. The word *sublapsarian* is opposed to *supralapsarian*.

SUBLIME', in literature, that style or manner of writing in which a sublime thought, or a fact sublime in its character, is suitably presented to the mind. It has often been said,—but we suspect there is no valid ground for the assertion,—that when men grow philosophical, they can seldom excel in the *sublime*. The sources of the *sublime* in language are well enumerated by Longinus. The first is elevation of mind; the second, ardent sensibility; the third, the proper use of figures; the fourth, grandeur of diction; and the fifth, a dignified harmony of arrangement. The *sublime* in narration is exemplified in the well-known commencement of the book of Genesis: "God said let there be light, and there was light."—*Sublime*, in the Fine Arts, high or exalted in style. That which in art is raised above the higher standard of nature or its prototypes. Sublimity is incompatible with our ideas of elegance, grace, or any of the other sources of beauty, though these may all enter into an object wherein those and many other qualities may be combined with sublimity. They have been, however, not unfrequently considered as some of the sources of the sublime. The nod of Jupiter, in the hands of such a master as Homer, is an indication of sublimity; but when Longinus tells us, that, as applied to literature, the constituent ingredients of sublimity are boldness in thought, the pathetic, proper application of figures, use of tropes and beautiful expressions, and last, musical structure and sounds, we are inclined to think he had very indistinct notions of it himself. We cannot better exemplify the meaning of this term than by referring the reader to the works of Michael Angelo in the Sistine Chapel, wherein, as Fuseli has truly said, "his line is uniformly grand; character and beauty were admitted only as far as they could be made subservient to grandeur. The child, the female, meanness, deformity, were by him indiscriminately stamped with grandeur. A beggar rose from his hand the patriarch of poverty; his infants teem with the man, his men are giants." The *terribile via*; hinted at by Agostino Caracci, is indeed the sublime. *Note.*—The true nature of sublimity is a subject of great interest and importance in mental philosophy, and it has always been a favorite subject of speculation. The term, psychologically considered, has two significations: one that of the quality or circumstance in objects, which raises the emotion named sublimity; the other that of the emotion itself. The invariable condition in objects, either material or moral, is vastness or intensity. The invariable condition of the emotion of sublimity—that which distinguishes this emotion from every other emotion—is a comprehension of this vastness, with a simultaneous feeling of our own comparative insignificance, together with a concomitant sense of present security from any danger which might result from this superior power. The antithesis to the emotion of sublimity is the emotion of contempt. In every case of sublimity in material objects, whatever feelings may simultaneously concur, vastness will be found an invariable condition—vastness either of form or of power; as in the violent dashing of a cataract, in the roar of the ocean, in the violence of the storm, in the majestic quiet of Mont Blanc, preserving its calm amidst all the storms that play around it. In the moral world, the invariable condition of sublimity is intensity—intensity of will. Mere intensity is sufficient to produce the sublime. Lear, who appeals to the heavens, "for they are old like him," is sublime from the very intensity of his sufferings and his passions. Lady Macbeth is sublime from the intensity of her will, which crushes every female feeling for the attainment of her object. Scævola, with his hand in the burning coals, exhibits an intensity of will which is sublime. In all the cases above-mentioned we are moved by a vivid feeling of some greater power than our own; or some will more capable of suffering, more vast in its strength, than our feeble vacillating will.

SUBLIM'ITY, in oratory and composition, loftiness of sentiment or style. Also, moral grandeur; as, "the incomprehensible *sublimity* of God."

SUBME'DIANT, in music, the sixth note, or middle note between the octave and subdominant.

SUBORNA'TION, in law, the crime of procuring a person to take such a false oath as constitutes perjury.

SUBPŒ'NA, in law, a writ commanding the attendance in court of a person on whom it is served; as a witness, &c.

SUBREP'TION, the act of obtaining a favor by surprise or unfair representation, that is, by the suppression of facts.

SUBROGA'TION, in the civil law, the substituting of one person in the place of another, and giving him his rights.

SUBSCRIP'TION, the act of signing or setting one's hand to a paper. Also the giving of a sum of money, or engaging to give it, for the furtherance of some common object in which several are interested, as subscriptions in support of charitable institutions, and the like.

SUB'SIDY, in England, an aid or tax granted to the king, by parliament, upon any urgent occasion, and levied on every subject of ability, according to a certain rate on lands and goods: but the word in some of the statutes, is confounded with that of customs. It signifies, in modern usage, a sum of money given by the government of one nation to that of another, for the immediate purpose of serving the latter, and the ultimate one, of benefiting the former. Thus Great Britain *subsidized* Austria and Prussia, to engage those powers in resisting the progress of the French during the war with Napoleon.

SUB'STANCE, something that we conceive to subsist of itself, independently of any created being, or any particular mode or accident. Our ideas of substances, as Mr. Locke observes, are only such combinations of simple ideas as are taken to represent distinct things subsisting by themselves, in which the confused idea of substance is always the chief. Thus the combination of the ideas of a certain figure, with the powers of motion, thought, and reasoning joined to the substance, make the ordinary idea of a man; and thus the mind observing several simple ideas to go constantly together, which being presumed to belong to one thing, or to be united in one subject, are called by one name, which we are apt afterwards to talk of, and consider, as one simple idea. The word is equally applicable to matter or spirit; we say, "stone is a hard *substance;*" "the soul of man is an immaterial *substance*, endued with thought;" and, "in a good epitome, we may have the *substance* of a large book," &c.

SUB'STITUTE, in law, one delegated to act for another.—In the militia, one engaged to serve in the room of another.

SUB'URBS, the buildings, streets, or parts that lie without the walls, but in the immediate vicinity of a city. Hence *suburban*, inhabiting or being situated near a city.

SUCCEDA'NEUM, that which is used for something else; a substitute. Hence *succedaneous*, being employed for or supplying the place of something else.

SUCCES'SION APOSTOL'ICAL, in theology, by these words is meant the uninterrupted succession of priests in the church by regular ordination, from the first commission given by our Saviour to the Apostles, and recorded in the Gospels, down to the present day. And the doctrine of "the apostolical succession," as it is popularly called, means the belief that the clergy so regularly ordained have a commission from God to preach the gospel, administer the sacraments, and guide the church; that through their ministration only we can derive the grace which is communicated by the sacraments. It follows, of course, that those sects of Christians which have no regular succession, (having seceded from Romanism without retaining ministers regularly ordained, or having subsequently interrupted the succession, that is, all Protestant bodies, except the church of England) have, properly speaking, neither church nor sacraments, since they possess no apostolical authority. This doctrine was, by admission on all hands, of very great antiquity in the church; but whether that antiquity is primitive or not, is a matter of discussion at the present day.

SUCCES'SION, LAW OF, in political economy, the law or rule according to which the succession to the property of deceased individuals is regulated. Generally speaking, this law obtains only in cases where a deceased party has died intestate, or in cases where the power of bequeathing property by will, is limited by the legislature. It is plain that in cases of intestacy, where the deceased either leaves a number of descendants, or where he leaves no direct descendants, the law, in order to prevent endless disputes and litigation, must interfere to regulate the succession to the property; and it will necessarily follow that the succession will be determined in different countries by local circumstances, depending partly on the peculiar state and institutions of each country, and on the views entertained by its legislators of what is just and proper, and most conducive to the public advantage. Hence it is to no purpose in a matter of this kind to look for any general or fixed principles. The succession to the property of those dying intestate, and the power of bequeathing property by will or testament, depend wholly on the rules and regulations enacted in each country; and these necessarily vary with the varying circumstances of different countries and conditions of society.

SUE, to institute legal process against a person; to prosecute in a civil action for the recovery of a real or supposed right; as to *sue* for debt or damages.

SUF'FERANCE, a term in law, applied to tenants; a tenant at *sufferance* being one that continues after his title ceases, without positive leave of the owner.

SUFFE'TES, certain Carthaginian magistrates, whose office bore considerable analogy to that of the Spartan kings and Roman consuls. Their number was two, and they were elected annually from the noblest families of the state. The functions of the suffetes seems principally to have been confined to the management of civil affairs. Thus it was their province to assemble the senate and preside in it, and also to propose the subjects of debate, and collect the votes; but there are instances recorded of suffetes leading the armies of their country. All the cities of note in the Carthaginian dominions had likewise their suffetes; but these, of course, were invested with merely municipal authority.

SUF'FRAGAN, in ecclesiastical polity, a term of relation applied to a bishop, with respect to the archbishop who is his superior; or rather, an assistant bishop.

SUF'FRAGE, a vote given in deciding a controverted question, or in the choice of a man for an office or trust; as, a true patriot deserves the *suffrages* of his fellow-citizens.

SU'ICIDE, the crime of self-murder. Although the practice of self-annihilation, under particular circumstances, was upheld by many of the ancient philosophers, the general lawfulness of suicide was by no means universally received in the ancient pagan world; many of the most considerable names, both Greek and Roman, having expressly declared against that practice. Pythagoras, Socrates, Plato, Tully, have condemned it; even Brutus himself, though he fell by his own hand, yet in his cooler and philosophical hours, wrote a treatise wherein he highly condemned Cato, as being guilty of an act both of impiety and cowardice in destroying himself.—According to modern law, to constitute a suicide, the person must be of years of discretion and of sound mind.

SUIT, in law, an action or process for the recovery of a right or claim.—In a general sense, *suit* denotes a number of things used together, and in a degree necessary to be united, in order to answer the purpose; as a *suit* of curtains, a *suit* of armor, or a *suit* of clothes. We also use the word when speaking of a number of attendants or followers; as, a nobleman and his *suit*. It is right, however, to state, that custom has now pretty generally established the use of the French word *suite* (pronounced *sweet*) in this last named case.

SUIT'OR, in legal phraseology, one who attends a court to prosecute a demand of right in law, as a plaintiff, petitioner or appellant.

SUL'TAN, in Arabic, *mighty*. Various Mohammedan princes are styled by this title besides the Ottoman emperor or grand sultan, to whom it is commonly given by Europeans, but whose peculiar title of Padishah is more dignified. The princes of the deposed family of the khan of the Crim Tartars are also styled sultan: so also the pacha of Egypt in that country, although not by the court of Constantinople.

SUM'MER, one of the four seasons of the year; beginning in the northern hemisphere, when the sun enters Cancer, about the 21st of June, and continuing for three months; during which time, the sun being north of the equator, renders this the hottest period of the year. In latitudes south of the equator, just the opposite takes place, or, in other words, it is summer there when it is winter here.

SUM'MONS, in law, a warning or citation to appear in court; or a written notification signed by the proper officer, to be served on a person, warning him to appear in court at a day specified, to answer to the demand of the plaintiff.

SUMP'TUARY LAWS, those laws which, in extreme cases, have occasionally been made to restrain or limit the expenses of citizens in apparel, food, furniture, &c. Sumptuary laws are abridgments of liberty, and of very difficult execution.

SUN'DAY, the first day of the week, called also the *Lord's-day*, because it is kept holy in memory of the resurrection of Christ; and the *sabbath-day*, because substituted, in the Christian worship, for the sabbath, or day of rest, in the old dispensation. This substitution was first decreed by Constantine the Great, A.D. 321, before whose time both the old and new sabbath were observed by Christians.

SUN'NIAH, the name given to the sect commonly considered as orthodox among the Mussulmans by the followers of Ali. The latter believe that the sovereign imânship, or imaginary dignity which conveys supremacy over all the faithful, belongs of right to the descendants of Ali, son-in-law of Mohammed. The schism between these two sects has subsisted from the earliest times of Mohammedanism; when Ali, having become fourth caliph after the death of Othman, a rebellion was raised against him by Maaniah, founder of the Ommiad race of caliphs about the year 1000 of the Christian era. The division took place between the two parties in the court of the caliph Moli l' Mah, which resulted in the Schiite party becoming pre-eminent in Persia, the

Sunniahites in Turkey and most other Mohammedan countries.

SUPERCAR'GO, a person in a merchant's ship, appointed to manage the sales and superintend all the commercial concerns of the voyage.

SUPEREROGA'TION, in theology, a term applied to such works as a man does which exceed the measure of his duty.

SUPERINTEND'ENT, one who has the oversight and charge of something, with the power of direction; as, the *superintendent* of public works, &c.

SUPERNAT'URAL, being beyond or exceeding the powers or laws of nature; miraculous. A *supernatural* event is one which is not produced according to the ordinary or established laws of natural things. Thus if iron has more specific gravity than water, it will sink in that fluid; and the floating of iron on water must be a *supernatural* event. Now no human being can alter a law of nature; the floating of iron on water therefore must be caused by divine power especially exerted to suspend, in this instance, a law of nature. Hence, *supernatural* events or miracles can be produced only by the immediate agency of divine power.

SUPERNU'MERARY, in military affairs, is an epithet for the officers and non-commissioned officers attached to a regiment for the purpose of supplying the places of such as fall in action, &c.

SUPERSE'DEAS, in law, a writ or command to suspend the powers of an officer in certain cases, or to stay proceedings.

SUPERSTI'TION, a habit of the human mind, attributed to those who are thought to attach religious importance to things of a too trivial nature; or to those who are thought wrong in their ideas of the government of the world, not on the side of excluding supernatural agency, but the reverse. Also, the belief of what is absurd, or belief without evidence.

SUPERSTRUC'TURE, any kind of building raised on a foundation or basis; the word being used to distinguish what is erected on a wall or foundation from the foundation itself.

SUPERTON'IC, in music, the note next above the key-note.

SUP'PLE, in all the Arts. A praiseworthy quality opposed to hardness or inflexibility. It is to be sought in contours, in attitudes, in adjustments, and in fact in all the parts of composition. The contours should be sinuous, flowing; the attitudes easy and unconstrained; the adjustments natural; the compositions various. The term is more strictly applied to the movement of contours, the flow of draperies, &c. than to the general ordonnance of a work.

SUP'PLEMENT, in literature, an addition made to a book or paper, by which it is made more full and complete.

SUPPOSI'TION, in music, the use of two successive notes of equal value as to time, one of which being a discord supposes the other a concord. The harmony, though by rule falling on the accented part of the bar, and free from discords, requires their proper preparation and resolution; and they are called *passing notes.* Discords on the unaccented part of the measure are allowable by conjoint degrees, and it is then not required that the harmony should be so complete on the accented part. This transient use of discords followed by concords is what we, after the French, call *supposition*, whereof there are several kinds.

SUPPRES'SION, a figure in grammar is sometimes so called by which words are omitted in a sentence, which are nevertheless to be understood as necessary to a perfect construction: as, for instance, in most languages, the repetition of a noun is avoided where it is coupled with a pronoun in one branch of the proposition; *e. g.*, "this (horse) is my horse," or "this horse is mine" (horse.)

SUPRALAPSA'RIAN, in theology, one who maintains that God, antecedent to the fall of man, decreed the apostasy and all its consequences, determining to save some and condemn others, and that in all he does he considers his own glory only.

SUPREM'ACY, in English polity, the supreme and undivided authority of the sovereign over all persons and things in this realm, whether spiritual or temporal.—*Oath of supremacy*, in Great Britain, an oath which acknowledges the supremacy of the sovereign in spiritual affairs, and abjures the pretended supremacy of the pope.

SUPREME', highest in authority; holding the highest place in government or power. The parliament of Great Britain is *supreme* in legislation; but the king is *supreme* in the administration of the government. In the United States, the congress is *supreme* in regulating commerce and in making war and peace. In the universe, God only is the *supreme* ruler and judge. His commands are *supreme*, and binding on all his creatures.

SUPRANAT'URALISTS, a name given of late years to the middle party among the divines of Germany, to distinguish them from the *Rationalists*, who exclude all supernatural manifestations from religion; and from the Evangelical party, whose tenets are of a more strict description. Thus many of the supranaturalists have given way to the system of accommodation (as it is termed) in religious matters, so far as to deny the doctrine of original sin, and other tenets which have been considered as fundamental: others approximate to what are regarded as orthodox Protestant opinions.

SUR'CHARGE, in law, any extra charge made by assessors upon such as neglect to make due returns of the taxes to which they are liable.

SURE'TY, in law, one who enters into a bond or recognizance to answer for another's appearance in court, or for his payment of a debt, or for the performance of some act, and who, in case of the principal debtor's failure, is compellable to pay the debt or damages.

SUR'NAME, the family name; the name or appellation added to the baptismal or Christian name. Camden derives it from *sur*, as being added over or above the other, in a metaphorical sense only. The most ancient *surnames* were formed by adding the name of the father to that of the son, in which manner were produced several English *surnames*, ending with the word son; thus, *Thomas William's son*, makes *Thomas Williamson*. The feudal system introduced a second description of *surnames*, derived from the names of places. In short, the greater part of surnames originally designated occupation, estate, place of residence, or some particular thing or event that related to the person.

SUR'PLICE, a white garment worn by clergymen of some denominations over their other dress, in their ministrations. It is particularly the habit of the clergy of the Church of England.

SURREBUT'TER, in law, the replication or answer of the plaintiff to the defendant's rebutter.

SURREJOIN'DER, in law, a second defence, as the *replication* is the first, of the plaintiff's declaration in a cause, and is an answer to the rejoinder of the defendant.

SURREN'DER, in law, a deed testifying that the tenant for life or years of lands, &c. yields up his estate to him that has the immediate estate in remainder or reversion.

SUR'ROGATE, in the civil law, a deputy, or person substituted for another. —A magistrate who presides over the settlement of estates of deceased persons.

SURVEY'OR, in law, one who views and examines for the purpose of ascertaining the condition, value, and quality of a thing; or who surveys or superintends any business, as the surveyor of the highways, a parochial officer who sees that the roads are kept in repair, &c.

SURVI'VOR, in law, the longest liver of joint-tenants, or of any two persons who have a joint interest in a thing; in which case, if there be only two joint-tenants, upon the death of one, the whole goes to the survivor; and if there be more than two, the part of the deceased is divided among all the survivors.

SUSPEN'SION, temporary privation of power, authority, or rights, usually intended as a punishment. A military or naval officer's suspension takes place when he is put under arrest.—In law, prevention or interruption of operation; as the *suspension* of the habeas corpus act.—*Suspension*, in rhetoric, a keeping of the hearer in doubt and in attentive expectation of what is to follow, or what is to be the inference or conclusion from the arguments or observations.—*Suspension of arms*, a short truce agreed on by hostile armies, in order to bury the dead, make proposals for surrender, &c.

SUSPEN'SION-BRIDGE, a structure which is hung and stretched across some chasm, water-course, or other space, over which it is designed to form a passage. In modern structures of this sort, the leading features for the most part consist in fixing securely, in the two opposite banks, the extremities of strong chains, which, being carried over piers or pillars, reach across the space to be passed in such a manner that each portion of chain intercepted between two piers is allowed naturally to assume, by its weight, the figure of the curve named the *catenarian*. From these chains, a platform for the roadway is suspended by means of a series of equidistant vertical rods. The largest suspension bridge in Great Britain, is that over the Menai Strait in Wales, the distance between the points of suspension being 560 feet. A remarkable structure of this kind is over the Niagara river below the Falls, connecting the American and Canadian shores.

SUTTEE', the act of sacrifice to which a Hindoo widow submits, namely, that of immolating herself on the funeral pile of her husband. Though none of the sacred books of the Hindoos absolutely command the *suttee*, they speak of it as highly meritorious, and the means of obtaining eternal beatitude. It is believed also to render the husband and his ancestors happy, and to purify him from all offences, even if he had killed a brahmin. Since the year 1756, when the British power in India became firmly established, upwards of 70,000 Hindoo widows have thus been sacrificed. It is gratifying however, to add, that this shocking perversion of devotion has at length been abolished; and to Lord Bentinck, the governor-general of India, the honor of the abolition is due. Public opinion in England, was greatly divided as to the propriety of interfering with a solemn religious rite of a foreign nation: but the humane decision of the governor-general appears to have been received by the public with heartfelt satisfaction. A short time before Lord Bentinck's order, a rajah in the hill country, who died, had twenty-eight wives burned with his body!

SWAIN'MOTE, in English law, one of the forest courts to be holden before the verderers, as judges, by the steward of the swainmote: the swains, or countrymen, composing the jury.

SWEDENBOR'GIANS, the followers of Emanuel Swedenborg, a Swedish nobleman, who died in 1772. He conceived the society which he founded to be the New Jerusalem spoken of in the Apocalypse; and that he was gifted with peculiar insight into spiritual things, and he professed to hold conversation with spirits, and to be instructed by them in the mysteries of religion. The Swedenborgians interpret Scripture by a system of correspondences, supposing it to have three distinct senses, accommodated respectively to particular classes, both of men and angels. They date the last judgment of the spiritual world and the second advent of Christ from the year 1757. They abound principally in England and in the United States, where they have at the present day several chapels in the large towns. They are distinguished as a body for their intelligence and excellent character.

SWELL, in music, a set of pipes in an organ, acted upon by a key board, and capable of being increased in intensity of sound by the action of a pedal, which allows of its being thereby gradually augmented.

SWIND'LING, the practices of a swindler. When a person by the assumption of a false character, or by a false representation of some sort, obtains the possession of money or other property from another or others, and appropriates it to himself, he is said to be guilty of swindling, and is liable to punishment by law.

SWORD, ORDER OF THE, a Swedish military order of knighthood, instituted by Gustavus Vasa.

SYB'ARITE, a term used metaphorically to designate an effeminate voluptuary; so called from the inhabitants of Sybaris, formerly a town of Italy on the gulf of Tarentum, whom a devotion to sensual pleasures had so enfeebled that they became an easy prey to the Crotonians, a people comparatively insignificant in point of numbers, by whom their city was levelled to the ground B.C. 310.

SYC'OPHANT, an obsequious flatterer or parasite. This word was originally used to denote an informer against those who stole figs, or exported them contrary to law. Hence, in time it came to signify a tale-bearer, or informer in general; thence a flatterer, deceiver, or parasite.

SYL'LABLE, a letter, or a combination of letters, uttered together, or at a single effort or impulse of the voice. A vowel may form a syllable by itself, as *a*, the definite, or in *amen; e* in *even; o* in *over*, and the like. A syllable may also be formed of a vowel and one consonant, as in *go, do, in, at;* or a syllable may be formed by a vowel with two articulations, one preceding, the other following it, as in *can, but, tun;* or a syllable may consist of a combination of consonants, with one vowel or diphthong, as *strong, short, camp, voice.* A syllable sometimes forms a word, and is then significant, as in *go, run, write, sun, moon.* In other cases, a syllable is merely part of a word, and by itself is not significant. Thus *ac*, in *active*, has no signification. At least one vowel or open sound is essential to the formation of a syllable; hence in every word there must be as many syllables as there are single vowels, or single vowels and diphthongs. A word is called according to the number of syllables it contains, viz., monosyllable, a word of one syllable; dissyllable, a word of two syllables: trisyllable, a word of three syllables, polysyllable, a word of many syllables.

SYL'LABUS, an abstract or compendium containing the heads of a discourse.

SYLLEP'SIS, in grammar, a figure

by which we conceive the sense of words otherwise than the words import, and construe them according to the intention of the author. Also, where two nominative cases singular of different persons are joined to a verb.

SYL'LOGISM, a form of reasoning or argument, consisting of three propositions, of which the two first are called the *premises*, and the last the *conclusion*. In this argument, the conclusion necessarily follows from the premises; so that if the two first propositions are true, the conclusion must be true, and the argument amounts to demonstration. Thus, a plant has not the power of locomotion; an oak is a plant; therefore an oak has not the power of locomotion. These propositions are denominated the major, the minor, and the conclusion. The three propositions of a syllogism are made up of three ideas or terms, and these terms are called the *major*, the *minor*, and the *middle*. The subject of the conclusion is called the minor term; its predicate is the major term, and the middle term is that which shows the connection between the major and minor term in the conclusion; or it is that with which the major and minor terms are respectively compared. Syllogisms are divided by some into single, complex, conjunctive, &c., and by others into categorical, hypothetical, conditional, &c. The figure of a syllogism is a proper disposition of the middle term with reference to the major and minor terms. The figures are generally reckoned three. The mood of a syllogism is the designation of its three propositions, according to their quantity and quality. The quantity and quality of propositions, in logic, are marked by arbitrary symbols, as A, E, I, O. Every assertion may be reduced to one of four forms—the universal affirmative marked by A; the universal negative, marked by E; the particular affirmative marked by I; and the particular negative, marked by O. From these, by combination, all syllogisms are derived. In order to remember the figures, certain words have been long used by writers on logic, which make a grotesque appearance; but which nevertheless are of considerable use. Thus, under the first figure, we have Barbara, Celarent, Darii, Ferio; under the second, Cesare, Camestres, Festino, Baroko; and under the third, Darapti, Disamis, Datisi, Felapton, Bokardo, Feriso. Each of these words designates a particular mood. The rules of syllogism may be thus briefly expressed: 1. One at least of the premises must be affirmative, and one at least universal; 2. The middle term must enter universally in one of the premises; and, 3. The conclusion must not speak of any term in a wider sense than it was spoken of in the premise in which it entered. A term universally spoken of is either the subject of universal affirmative, or the predicate of any negative. Syllogisms are nothing else than reasoning reduced to form and method, and all that passes under the name of reasoning, unless it can be made syllogistic, is no reasoning at all, but a mass of words without meaning. The syllogism is the instrument of self-examination, and the last weapon of resort in dispute; and a bad syllogism, with one of the premises implied only, and not expressed, is the first resource of fallacy. To bring forward the suppressed premise, is the visible destruction of every argument which is logically bad.

SYLPH, the name given to the spirits of air in the fantastic nomenclature of the Rosicrucians and Cabalists. The use which Pope has made of this fancy in his *Rape of the Lock* is well known. H. seems to have borrowed it from the enigmatical romance called the *Count de Gabalis*.

SYM'BOL, the emblem, sign or representation of some moral quality by the images or properties of natural things; as the lion is a symbol of courage; the lamb, a symbol of meekness; two hands joined together, a symbol of union, &c. These symbols were much used by the ancients in representing their deities, and are still continued in various ways. In the eucharist, the bread and wine are called *symbols* of the body and blood of Christ.—*Symbolical philosophy*, is the philosophy expressed by hieroglyphics.

SYM'PATHY, the quality of being affected by feelings similar to those of another in whose fate we are interested. This kind of *sympathy* is produced through the medium of organic impression, and is a correspondent feeling of pain or regret. Thus we sympathize with our friends in distress. The word *sympathy* is also used, but less correctly, to denote an agreement of affections or inclinations, or a conformity of natural temperament which makes two persons pleased with each other.

SYM'PHONY, in music, a composition which, from the etymology of the term, evidently implies that the voice anciently formed an essential part of its construction. In the present day, however, the term is otherwise applied, and is ex clusively used for a piece in which instruments only are engaged. It is, in fact, a composition for a perfect instrumental orchestra, which, until the beginning of the eighteenth century, was unknown. The *Concerti grossi* of Corelli were the first of the species, which was carried out to a greater extent in the works of Geminiani and Vivaldi; but it does not seem to us that before the time of Haydn it can be said to have assumed the form which the name now imports. There is, perhaps, no musical composition in which the power of the author is so completely developed as in a symphony. The musician in it becomes a poet, or, perhaps rather, a painter. Scenes and the passions are represented therein by a combination of musical sounds; in illustration of which we need only cite that splendid work of Beethoven, known to all under the name of *Il Pastorale*. The general form of the symphony may be thus described: It opens with a short, serious, slow movement; this is followed by, and forms a contrast to one of spirit and of a lively nature; then comes an andante varied, or an adagio or slow movement; a minuet with its trio follows; and the symphony usually closes with a lively movement.

SYMPO'SIARCH, among the ancients, was the director and manager of an entertainment. This office was sometimes performed by the person at whose expense the feast was provided, and sometimes by the person whom he thought fit to nominate. The feasts of the ancients were called *symposia:* hence the name.

SYNÆ'RESIS, the shortening of a word by the omission of a letter, as *ne'er* for *never*.

SYN'AGOGUE, the religious assemblies of the Jews are so called by Hellenic writers. The Jews had no synagogues, it is thought, before the Babylonish captivity. They were first formed after the return of the Jews to the Holy Land. The rule was, that a synagogue was to be erected in any place where there were ten persons of full age and free condition ready to attend the service of it. Others, however, consider the ten *batelnim*, to use the Hebrew word, to have been ten elders, or stationary men of the synagogue. The service performed in the synagogue consisted, and still consists, of prayers, reading the Scriptures, and preaching and expounding of them. The prayers are contained in liturgies. The reading of the Scriptures consists of three portions: the "Shema," certain selected passages from Deuteronomy and Numbers; the law and the prophets. The third part of the service is mentioned in several places in the narratives of the life of our Saviour, and the Acts. The times of the synagogue service were three days a week (Monday, Thursday, and Saturday,) besides the holy days. The ministration of the synagogue was not confined to the order of priests; the elders, or "rulers of the synagogue" were persons qualified, and duly admitted, of all tribes.

SYNALŒ'PHA, in grammar, a contraction of syllables, performed principally by suppressing some vowel or diphthong at the end of a word, before another vowel or diphthong at the beginning of the next: as, *ill' ego*, for *ille ego*.

SYN'CHISIS, in rhetoric, a confused and disorderly placing of words in a sentence.

SYN'CHRISIS, in rhetoric, a figure of speech in which opposite persons or things are compared.

SYNCHORE'SIS, in rhetoric, a figure of speech wherein an argument is scoffingly conceded to, for the purpose of retorting to it more pointedly.

SYN'CHRONISM, in chronology, concurrence of two or more events in time.—*Synchronal*, simultaneous, or happening at the same time.

SYN'CRETISM, in philosophy, the blending of the tenets of different schools into a system. A party among the Platonists at the revival of letters, to which belonged Ammonius, Pico della Mirandola, Bessarion, and other distinguished men, have received the name of Syncretists.

SYN'CRETISTS, in ecclesiastical history, the partisans of Calixtus, a Lutheran divine of the 16th century, who endeavored to form a comprehensive scheme which should unite the different professors of Christianity. The opinions of Calixtus raised a strong controversy in the Lutheran church. A new confession of faith was drawn up in Saxony for the purpose of excluding his partisans. As doctrines, however, they did not long survive his death, although not without effect on the spirit of the age.

SYN'COPATE, in a primary sense, to contract, as a word, by taking one or more letters or syllables from the middle.—In music, to prolong a note begun on the unaccented part of a bar, to the accented part of the next bar; or to connect the last note of a bar with the first of the following.

SYN'DIC, an officer of government invested with different powers in different countries; generally a kind of magistrate entrusted with the affairs of a city or community. The university of Cambridge has its *syndics;* and in Paris almost all the companies, the university, &c. have theirs.

SYN'DICI, in antiquity, orators appointed by the Athenians to plead in behalf of any law which was to be enacted or abrogated.

SYNEC'DOCHE, in rhetoric, a figure or trope by which the whole of a thing is put for a part, or a part for the whole; as the genus for the species, or the species for the genus, &c.

SYN'OD, in ecclesiastical affairs, a council or meeting to consult on matters of religion. In Scotland, a synod is composed of several adjoining presbyters. The members are the ministers, and a ruling elder from each parish.

SYN'ONYMS, words of the same language which have a similar signification. Strictly speaking, words having exactly the same signification are not to be found in any language, unless one of them has been borrowed from another language; but in this case the shades of difference are often so slight that words may be frequently used for one another, and this interchange produces a pleasing variety in composition, necessary in poetry. Synonyms form an important object of philological study, demanding, on the part of the inquirer, great knowledge of the principles of language.

SYNOP'SIS, a collection of things or parts so arranged as to exhibit the whole or the principal parts in a general view.

SYN'TAX, that division of the grammatical art which analyzes the dependence of parts of speech upon one another and supplies rules for their mutual government. Syntax, as an art, may be divided into two branches: the one common to all languages, and by which words are made to agree in gender, number, case, person, and mood; the other peculiar to each language, and by which one mood is made to govern another, and the consequent variations effected; the first of these is called *concord*, the second *government.* It has been said that the first merit of language is intelligibility; its first grace, purity; and that every other excellence is subordinate. Syntax, then, especially deserves attention: as neither intelligibility nor purity of style can be found where the rules of syntax are violated

SYN'THESIS, in logic, that process of reasoning in which we advance by a regular chain from principles before established or assumed, and propositions already proved, until we arrive at the conclusion. The *synthetical* is therefore opposed to the *analytical* method.

SYNTON'IC, in music, an epithet used by ancient musical writers to distinguish a species of the diatonic genus.

SYR'IAC, pertaining to Syria or its language; as, the *Syriac* version of the Pentateuch.

SYR'IACISM, or SYR'IANISM, a Syrian idiom, or a peculiarity in the Syrian language.

SYR'INX, a nymph of Arcadia, daughter of the river Ladon. Pan became enamored of her and attempted to offer her violence; but Syrinx escaped, and at her own request was changed by the gods into a reed, called *syrinx* by the Greeks. The god made himself a pipe with the reeds into which his favorite nymph had been changed, and upon this pipe he is often introduced playing, in pictures.

SYS'TEM, in science and philosophy, a whole plan or scheme, consisting of many parts connected in such a manner as to create a chain of mutual dependencies; or a regular union of principles or parts forming one entire thing. Thus we say the planetary *system*, or the whole of the bodies supposed to belong to each other; a *system* of botany, or that which comprehends the whole science of plants; a *system* of philosophy, or a theory or doctrine which embraces the whole of philosophy. The great utility of *systems* is to classify the individual subjects of our knowledge in such a way as to enable us readily to retain and employ them, and at the same time to illustrate each by showing its connection with all.—In the Fine Arts, a collection of the rules and principles upon which an artist works.—In music, an interval compounded or supposed to be compounded of several lesser intervals, as the fifth, octave, &c., the elements of which are called *diastems.*

SYS'TYLE, in architecture, the disposition of columns in a building near to each other, but not quite so thick as the *pycnostyle:* the intercolumniation being only two diameters of the column.

SYSY'GIA, in music, any combination of sounds so proportioned to each other as to produce a pleasant effect on the ear.—In grammar, the coupling different feet together in Greek or Latin verse.

T.

T, is the twentieth letter of the English Alphabet, and a close consonant. It represents a close joining of the end of the tongue to the root of the upper teeth, as may be perceived by the syllable, *at*, *et*, *ot*, *ut*, in attempting to pronounce which, the voice is completely intercepted. It is therefore numbered among the mutes, or close articulations, and it differs from *d* chiefly in its closeness; for in pronouncing *ad*, *ed*, we perceive the voice is not so suddenly and entirely intercepted, as in pronouncing *at* and *et*. *T* by itself has one sound only, as in *take*, *turn*, *bat*, *bolt*, *smite*, *bitter*. So we are accustomed to speak; but in reality, *t* can hardly be said to have any sound at all. Its use, like that of all mute articulations, is to modify the manner of uttering the vocal sound which precedes or follows it. When *t* is followed by *h*, as in *think* and *that*, the combination really forms a distinct sound for which we have no single character. This combination has two sounds in English; aspirated, as in *think*, and vocal, as in *that*. The letters *ti*, before a vowel, and unaccented, usually pass into the sound of *sh*, as in *nation*, *motion*, *partial*, *substantiate;* which are pronounced *nashon*, *moshon*, *parshal*, *substanshate*. In this case, *t* loses entirely its proper sound or use, and being blended with the subsequent letter, a new sound results from the combination, which is in fact a simple sound. In a few words, the combination of *ti* has the sound of the English *ch*, as in *Christian*, *mixtion*, *question*. *T* is convertible with *d*. Thus the Germans write *tag*, where we write *day*, and *gut* for *good*. It is also convertible with *s* and *z*, for the Germans write *wasser*, for *water*, and *zahm* for *tame*. T, as an abbreviation, stands for *theologia;* as, S. T. D. *sanctæ theologiæ doctor*, doctor of divinity. In ancient monuments and writings, T is an abbreviature which stands for *Titus*, *Titius*, or *Tullius*.—As a numeral, T, among the Latins, stood for 160, and with a dash over the top, $\bar{T}$, for 160,000.—In music, T is the initial of tenor, vocal, and instrumental.

TABARD', a sort of tunic, or mantle, covering the body before and behind, reaching below the loins, but open at the sides from the shoulders downwards: an ordinary article of dress in England and France in the middle ages. It was at first chiefly used by the military, afterwards by other classes. The tabard, with coats of arms blazoned before and behind, is the state dress of heralds to this day. It is the dress worn by the knaves in cards. Long tabards, which reached to the mid-leg, were a peculiarly English fashion.

TABASHEER', a Persian word signifying a light white porous substance found in the joints of the bamboo: it consists almost entirely of silica. It is said to be used medicinally in the East Indies; but its virtues must be merely imaginary.

TABEL'LION, in the Roman empire, officers who had charge of public documents were so called; they were also secretaries, or registrars, and in some cases judges. The notaries were their assistants. In France, the titles of "Tabellion" and "Greffier" were confounded, and Henry IV. united the functions of tabellion with those of notary; but the old title seems still to be retained (or was until the Revolution) in some few places.

TAB'ERNACLE, a Latin word signifying a *tent* or *cabin*. The tabernacle which was carried from station to station by the Jews during their wanderings in the desert, was a tent of sails and skins stretched upon a framework of wood, and divided into two compartments; the outer, named *the Holy*, being that in which incense was burned, and the shew-bread exhibited; and the inner, or *Holy of Holies*, in which was deposited the ark of the covenant. The Feast of Tabernacles was one of the three principal festivals among the Jews. It commenced on the 15th of the month Tisri, corresponding with the 30th of September, and lasted seven days, during which the people dwelt in booths formed of the boughs of trees. It was instituted in commemoration of the habitation of their ancestors in similar dwellings during the forty years of their pilgrimage in the wilderness.

TAB'LATURE, in music, the use of the letters of the alphabet, or any other character, for expressing the notes or sounds of a composition. It is not now a usual mode of writing. In its stricter and more original sense, it is a mode of writing music for a particular instrument on parallel lines (of which each represents a string of the instrument) by means of certain letters of the alphabet. Thus A denotes that the string is to be struck open, B that one of the fingers is to be put on the first stop, C on the second, D on the third, and so on through the octave.

TA'BLEAUX VI'VANTS, the name given to an amusement in which groups of persons dressed in appropriate costume are made to represent some interesting scene in the works of distinguished painters or authors. It is thus managed: The room in which the spectators are placed being darkened, the group assume their respective attitudes behind a frame (or some other contrivance intended to represent it) covered with gauze; and candles being so placed as to reflect light upon the group from above, the illusion is complete. These representations are not unfrequently resorted to in England; but their home is chiefly in France and Germany, where they form an important feature on all festive occasions. They owe their present popularity to the celebrated M. Händel-Schutz, whose genius for imitation and delineation was unrivalled in Germany. Tableaux are often employed to represent some scene in which a riddle is concealed.

TAB'LETS, in Roman antiquities, pieces of ivory, metal, stone, or other substance, used in judiciary proceedings, or in the passing of laws.

TABOO', a word used by the South Sea islanders to denote something consecrated, sacred, and forbidden to be touched, or set aside for particular uses and persons.

TA'BORITES, the denomination of one of the parties into which the followers of Huss, in Bohemia, separated after the death of their leader. They were so called from Tabor, a hill or fortress of Bohemia, upon which they encamped during the struggle which they maintained against the civil and ecclesiastical power. At their head stood John Ziska von Brockznow, who was distinguished at once for his indomitable courage and his remorseless cruelty. After various fanatical exhibitions, which were met by their adversaries with determined hostility, the better and more quietly disposed portion of the Taborites formed themselves into a religious society under the denomination of the Bohemian Brethren. They established several Christian communities, elected their own bishops, priests, and elders; drew up a rigorous plan of ecclesiastical discipline; and sent forth missionaries to various parts, though with little success. Though harassed by persecutions, they continued to augment their numbers, and at the end of the 15th century they counted about 200 communities of adherents. At the end of this period the distinctive name and opinions of the Taborites were lost among the various assailants of the Romish corruptions, who formed the vanguard of the Reformation in Germany.

TABULA'TUM, in ancient architecture, a term used to denote the floors, ceilings, and other wood-work in a house: occasionally also it was applied to the balconies and other projections of a like nature.

TAC'TICS, a term which, in its most extensive sense, relates to those evolutions, manœuvres and positions which constitute the main-spring of military and naval finesse: tactics are the means by which discipline is made to support the operations of a campaign, and are studied for the purpose of training all the component parts according to one regular plan or system; whereby celerity, precision, and strength are combined, and the whole rendered effective.

TA'GES, an old Italian divinity, who is represented to have sprung as a beautiful boy from the earth, which a Tuscan ploughman had furrowed too deep. The first act of this earth-born god was to foretell from the wings of birds what was to happen to the peasants, by whom he was quickly surrounded; and hence he was worshipped as the inventor of augury. A collection of his prophecies was made and preserved in the sacred records of Etruria.

TAIL, or FEE-TAIL, in law, a limited estate or fee; opposed to fee-simple.

TAILLE, in ancient French jurisprudence, any imposition levied by the king or any other lord on his subjects. There is some obscurity about the derivation of this word. It is commonly deduced from talcæ, *tallies*, little pieces of wood with which reckonings were made. But whether these were not so called from their use in *telling* or counting does not appear. Again, it is apparently connected with the Germ. zoll, Engl. *toll;* but these words are derived by some, through the Ital. tolta, from the Lat. tollere, *to raise.* Perhaps the whole series of words is from the same original root; but it is not easy to trace the affinities. The *Royal Taille*, in old France, which was the impost commonly understood under the general name, was a personal or rather mixed constitution, from persons not noble or ecclesiastical, or enjoying certain other exemptions imposed according to their supposed ability, measured by their goods. In the respect in which it fell on the agricultural class, from which it was chiefly levied, it is described by Adam Smith as "a tax on the supposed profits of the farmer, which they estimate by the stock which he has upon the farm."

TAL'BOTYPE, a photogenic process invented by Mr. H. Fox Talbot, in which paper, prepared in a particular manner, is used instead of the silvered plates of M. Daguerre. The process has also been termed *calotype*.

TAL'ENT, among the ancients, the name of a coin, the true value of which cannot well be ascertained, but it is known that it was different among different nations. Among the Hebrews there was both a talent of gold and a talent of silver; the gold coin weighed only four drachms, and was the same as the shekel of gold: but their talent of silver, called *cicar*, was equivalent to three thousand shekels, or one hundred and thirteen pounds, ten ounces, troy weight. The *Attic* talent is supposed to have been of the value of 193*l*. 15*s*. sterling. The Romans had the great talent and the little talent; the great talent equal to 99*l*. 6*s*. 8*d*., and the little talent to 75*l*. sterling.

TA'LES, in law, additional jurymen, when those impanelled do not appear, or, appearing, are challenged.

TALIO'NIS LEX, (Latin,) a punishment in which a person convicted of a crime suffered exactly in the same manner as he had offended: thus an eye was required for an eye and a tooth for a tooth. This mode of punishment was established by the Mosaic law, and was in some cases imitated by the Romans.

TAL'ISMAN, among the Eastern nations, a figure cut in metal, stone, &c., supposed to have been made with particular ceremonies, and under particular astrological circumstances, and to possess various virtues, but chiefly that of averting disease or violent death from the wearer. In a more general sense, any portable object endowed with imaginary influence in controlling evil spirits, &c. has been so designated. The term is frequently used as synonymous with amulet; but, strictly speaking, the latter is not believed to possess such extensive powers as the talisman.

TAL'LY, a mode of reckoning between buyers and sellers, which before the use of writing was almost universal, and which is even still partially used. The *tally* is a piece of wood on which notches or scores are cut as marks of number. It is customary for traders to have two of these sticks, or one stick cleft into two parts, and to mark or notch them in a corresponding manner; one to be kept by the seller, the other by the purchaser. —In the English exchequer are tallies of loans, one part being kept in the exchequer, the other being given to the creditor in lieu of an obligation for money lent to government.

TAL'MUD, the traditionary or unwritten laws of the Jews. It is called *unwritten*, to distinguish it from the textual or *written* law; and is, in fact, the interpretation which the rabbins affix to the law of Moses, which embodies their doctrine, polity, and ceremonies, and to which many of them adhere more than to the law itself. There are two Talmuds, that of Jerusalem and that of Babylon; not to mention those of Onkelos and Jonathan, which are rather paraphrases than volumes of traditionary doctrines.— The Talmud of Jerusalem consists of two parts—the *Gemara*, and the *Mishna*. The *Mishna* signifies a doubling or reiteration; the *Gemara*, a work brought to perfection or completed—from the Chaldee *gamar*, to finish or complete. The Gemara and the Mishna together, strictly speaking, form the Talmud; but the rabbins are wont to designate the Pentateuch of Moses the *first* part of the Talmud, and which is simply the law. The *second* part is the *Mishna*, which is a more extensive explication or amplification of the law; and the *third* part the *Gemara*, as finishing and completing it. The Mishna is the work of Rabbi Judah Hakkadosh, 120 years after the destruction of the temple of Jerusalem. It is written in a tolerably pure style, and its reasonings are much more solid than those of the Gemara, which the Jewish doctors, it is stated, have stuffed with dreams and chimeras, and many ignorant and impertinent questions and disputations. The Gemara was written about 100 years afterwards by Rabbi Jochanan, the rector of the school at Tiberias. These two works form the Jerusalem Talmud. But the Talmud of Jerusalem is less esteemed than the Talmud of Babylon formed by Rabbi Asa or Aser, who had an acadamy for forty years at a place called Sara, near Babylon, whence it was denominated the Babylonish Talmud. It is this Talmud which the Jews more frequently consult; and it is especially esteemed by those Jews who live beyond the Euphrates, from the circumstance that it was compiled at Babylon. Rabbi Asa was called to his fathers before this celebrated commentary on the Mishna was completed; but it was finished by his disciples (some say his children) about 500 years after Christ. With the exception of the sacred authors, these Talmuds, after the Chaldee paraphrases, are the most ancient books of doctrine possessed by the Jews.

TAL'ON, in architecture, a kind of moulding, which consists of a cymatium, crowned with a square fillet. It is concave at the bottom, and convex at the top; and is usually called by workmen an *ogee*, or O. G.

TAM'BOUR, in fortification, a kind of work formed of palisades or pieces of wood ten feet long, planted close together, and driven firm into the ground.—*Tambour*, in architecture, is applied to a wall of a circular building, surrounded with columns.

TAMBOURINE', one of the most ancient musical instruments, and still used, particularly in Biscay, where a large kind of tambourine, called *tambour de Basque*, is used to accompany all the national songs and dances. In Scripture this instrument is designated a *timbrel;* in profane history we find it was popular among most of the Eastern nations; and in the middle ages it was used by the Troubadours and minstrels. The present tambourine consists of a wooden or brazen hoop, over which a skin is extended, and which is hung with bells. Sometimes the thumb of the right hand is drawn in a circle over the skin; sometimes the fingers are struck against it; while it is supported by the thumb of the left hand. From the performance of it being capable of displaying various graceful movements of the body, the tambourine is generally an attribute of Terpsichore.

TAN'ISTRY, a tenure of lands in Ireland, by which the proprietor had only a life estate, and to this he was admitted by election. The primitive intention seems to have been that the inheritance should descend to the oldest or most worthy of the blood and name of the deceased; but the practice often gave rise to the fiercest and most sanguinary contests between tribes and families.

TAN'TALUS, in Greek mythology, a king of Lydia, Phrygia, or Paphlagonia, according to different authors, whose punishment in the infernal regions is well known to classical readers. He was condemned to be plunged in water, and have delicious fruits continually hanging over his head, without the power of satisfying either thirst or hunger. His crime is differently represented. According to some, he served to the gods at a feast the limbs of his own son Pelops; according to others, he revealed the mystery of the gods, of whom he was high-priest: while others attribute to him the vices of pride and too great wealth.

TARE, in commerce, an allowance for the outside package that contains such goods as cannot be unpacked without detriment; or for paper, bands, cords, &c. When the tare is deducted, the remainder is called the *net* or *neat* weight.

TAR'GUM, in sacred literature, a name given by the Jews to certain glosses and paraphrases of the Scriptures, written in the Chaldaic language: a work which was occasioned by the long captivity of that people.

TAR'IFF, in commerce, a list or table of custom-house and excise duties imposed on goods, with their respective rates.

TARPE'IAN, in Roman antiquity, an appellation given to a steep rock in Rome; whence, by the law of the twelve tables, those guilty of certain crimes were precipitated. It was named after Tarpeia, the daughter of Tarpeius, the governor of the citadel of Rome, who promised to open the gates of the city to the Sabines, provided they gave her their gold bracelets, or, as she expressed it, what they carried on their left hands. The Sabines consented, and, as they entered the gates, threw not only their bracelets, but their shields, upon Tarpeia, who was crushed under the weight. She was buried in the capitol.

TARTU'FFE, a common French nickname for hypocritical pretenders to devotion. It is derived from the celebrated comedy of Molière, of which the hero is so called. Whether Molière invented, or took it from the popular language of the time, does not appear: some say that he intended to attack Louis XIV.'s confessor, Père la Chaise, whom he had once seen eating truffles with peculiar *goût;* and thence the name. The play was written in 1664, but not acted till 1669; great difficulties being thrown in the way of the author by the clergy and the papal legate. On one occasion it was prohibited when the curtain was on the point of rising, and Molière announced to the public its disappointment in the well-known equivocal words, "Monsieur le président ne veut pas qu'on le joue." When at last licensed (through the influence, it is said, of the king himself), it had a run of three months with unparalleled success; and the eager attention and applause which it still excites bear testimony at once to the keenness of the wit, and the peculiar relish of the public for the exposure of the frailties of those who profess a religious character. In England, this play has been made more than once to serve the popular passions of the day. Cibber translated it and made the hero a non-juring churchman; and the play is still acted under the name of *The Hypocrite*, in which the Tartuffe is a methodistical divine.

TASTE, that power of the mind which is conversant about the beautiful, both of nature and of art. In the Latin language, the same metaphor obtained a very wide application, and the term sapient a, was employed to signify quickness and correctness of judgment generally. Shaftsbury's use of the term is nearly as extensive, being applied by him to manners, morals, and government, and to wit, ingenuity, and beauty. In its modern use it is restricted to those objects which fall within the province of imagination. Now, although imagination derives its objects pre-eminently from those of the sight and hearing, and although the epithet *beautiful*, is, for the most part, confined to these, yet the mental power which judges of them borrows its name from a third sense. The reason of this is satisfactorily shown by Coleridge. The senses, he observes, are either purely organic, or mixed. The former present their objects to the mind distinct from its perception of them, while the latter invariably blend the perception of the object with a certain consciousness of the percipient subject. To the latter class belong the touch, the smell, and the taste. Of these, taste and smell differ from the touch, as adding to that reference to our vital being which is common to the three a degree of enjoyment or otherwise; while the taste is distinguished from the smell only by its more frequent and dignified use in human nature. By taste then, as applied to the Fine Arts, we must be supposed to mean an intellectual perception of any object, blended with a distinct reference to our sensibility of enjoyment or dislike. In the same essay Coleridge gives another and a wider definition of taste; as "a metaphor taken from one of the mixed senses, and applied to objects the more purely organic, and of *our moral sense*, when we would imply the co-existence of an immediate personal dislike or complacency." Now, by the constitution of man's nature, every exertion of human activity, in the pursuit of the good, the beautiful, and the true, combines a sense of pleasure, or the contrary, with the perception of their respective objects; and this fact would justify the widest application of the metaphor. While, however, in the case of the true, this co-existent pleasure has not received any distinctive appellation, and while conscience, as comprehending the sense of approbation and disapprobation, is characteristically applied to the moral energy, that of taste has been confined to the perception of beauty and the accompanying gratification. But taste, like all other metaphorical terms, is extremely inaccurate; and by directing attention exclusively to this element of pleasure, it has led to a very inadequate conception of the true nature of the faculty which it designates. Thus Hutcheson maintains that the faculty is peculiar, and a sense which similarly, to the other senses, procures a pleasure totally distinct from a cognition of principles, or of the causes, relations, and usages of an object: that beauty strikes, at first sight, and that knowledge the most perfect will not increase the pleasure which it gives rise to: and lastly, that all the diversity of sentiments excited in different minds by the beautiful, arise solely from the modifications of the sense by association, custom, example, and education. Among the advocates of the theory of a moral taste we may reckon Hume, Akenside, Blair, Lord Kames, and Beattie.

TATTOO′, the beat of the evening drum, giving notice to soldiers to repair to their quarters in garrison, or to their tents in camp.

TAURID′IA, among the Romans, were certain games in honor of the infernal gods. They are sometimes called *taurii ludi.*

TAUTOL′OGY, in rhetoric, a vicious diction, by which the same idea is expressed in two or more different words or phrases, apparently intended to convey different meanings.

TAXA′TION, a tax is a rate or duty laid by government on the incomes or property of individuals, or on the products consumed by them; the produce of such duty or rate being placed at the disposal of government.—A tax may be either general or particular; that is, it may either affect all classes indiscriminately, or only one or more classes.—Taxation is the general term used to express the aggregate of particular taxes. It is also the name given to that branch of the science of political economy which explains the mode in which the revenue required for the public service may be most advantageously raised.

TAX'ES, the assessments imposed by law for the public service, either *direct*, as on persons and necessaries; or *indirect*, as on luxuries and raw materials. Taxes imposed on goods at the time of their importation, are denominated *customs*, *duties*, or *imposts*.

TE'BETH, the tenth month of the Jewish ecclesiastical year, and fourth of the civil. It answers to our month of December.

TECH'NICAL, that method of speaking which is proper, or peculiarly appertaining, to any given art. Artists and amateurs are accustomed, when they talk of matters relating to the arts, to employ many expressions which are not introduced into ordinary language, or at least do not bear the same signification. This species of conversation is not without its advantages. The terms it employs are often arbitrary, but they are much clearer than any other would be to the artist or connoisseur, inasmuch as he has habituated himself to combine with them, and with them alone, the ideas meant to be conveyed; and they besides often save a round-about way of expression. But this stated, we are bound to add that they should never be introduced into books, excepting only such as are addressed *specifically* to the practisers of our art; for in any work designed for the purposes of *general* information, they merely tend to mystify and confuse the reader.

TECHNOL'OGY, a treatise on the Arts; or an explanation of the terms of the Arts. A *technical* word is a word that belongs properly or exclusively to the Arts; and when speaking of the terms of Art, we say *technical* terms, *technical* language, &c.

TE DEUM, (from the first words of the original Latin, "Te Deum laudamus;" *We praise thee, O God.*) The authorship of this sublime hymn has been ascribed by some to Ambrose and Augustine; by others to Ambrose alone, to Hilary, and other less distinguished persons. It is, however, generally thought to have been composed in the Gallican church: the most ancient mention of it being in the rule of Cæsarius, bishop of Arles in the fifth century. The Te Deum, in the office of matins, is always sung after the reading of Scripture; in the English morning service, between the two lessons.

TEM'PERAMENT, in music, the accommodation or adjustment of the imperfect sounds, by transferring a part of their defects to the more perfect ones, to remedy in part the false intervals of instruments of fixed sounds, as the piano, organ, &c.

TEM'PERANCE SOCI'ETIES. The evils of intemperance have long been the subject of much anxious observation in civilized nations, more especially in the United States; and the idea of concentrating public sentiment upon it, in some form, to produce important results, seems to have been first conceived in this country; a meeting, called the General Association of Massachusetts Proper, having been held in 1813, for the express object of "checking the progress of intemperance." The first attempt of the society was to collect facts towards a precise exhibition of the nature and magnitude of the existing evil with the view of drawing public attention to it, and of directing endeavors for its removal. The reports presented from year to year, embraced statements and calculations which were found to make out a case of the most appalling nature, such as to amaze even those whose solicitude on the subject had been greatest. In 1830, from data carefully collected, the Massachusetts society stated in their report, that the number who died annually victims of intemperance was estimated at above 37,000; and that 72,000,000 gallons of distilled spirits were consumed in the country, being about six gallons on an average for every man, woman, and child of the whole population. It also stated that about 400,000 of the community were confirmed drunkards; and that there appeared reason to believe that intemperance was responsible for four fifths of the crime committed in the country, for at least three quarters of the pauperism existing, and for at least one third of the mental derangement. By these exposures, and an unrelaxing perseverance in the course they had commenced; by the circulation of tracts and the addresses of travelling agents; by the formation of auxiliary associations, and by obtaining individual responsibility for the performance of a variety of duties tending to promote the great object in view,—public notice was attracted, and it led to an imitation of the practice in Great Britain and Ireland. Of late years the cause of temperance has made great progress in all parts of the United States.

TEM'PLARS, or *Knights of the Temple*, a military order of religious persons. It was founded by an association of knights, in the beginning of the 12th century, for the protection of pilgrims on the roads in Palestine: afterwards it took for its chief object the protection of the Holy Sepulchre at Jerusalem against the Saracens. Knights were fixed at Jerusalem by King Baldwin II., who gave them the ground on the east of the Temple. Their rules were taken from those of the Benedictine monks: they took the vows of chastity, obedience, and poverty. The classes of the order were knights, esquires, servitors, and chaplains; the universal badge of the order was a girdle of linen thread. The officers of the order were chosen by the chapter from among the knights: they were, for military affairs, marshals, and bannerets: for purposes of government, priors, who superintended single priories or preceptories; abbots, commanders, and grand priors, who governed the possessions of the order within separate provinces; and the grand master, who, in some respects, assumed the dignity of a sovereign prince, being independent in secular matters, and depending solely on the pope in spiritual. The chief part of the 9000 estates, lordships, &c., which the society possessed in the 13th century, was situated in France; and the grand master was usually of that nation. The Templars were driven from Palestine by the Saracens, with the rest of the Christians, and then fixed the chief seat of their order in Cyprus. Their exorbitant power and wealth, and the haughty manner in which they endeavored to keep aloof from the control of European sovereigns, and act as a military republic independent of their authority, were probably the principal reasons which induced Pope Clement V. and Philip the Fair of France to concert their overthrow. The charges of heresy and idolatry, which were preferred against them, were at least unsupported by evidence. In 1307, Jaques de Molay, the grand master, having been enticed into France, was arrested by Philip; the templars' estates were seized; many of them burned alive, after the mockery of a trial; and, in 1312, the order was abolished by a bull of Clement V. Its vast estates fell partly into the hands of the sovereigns of the countries in which they were situated, partly into those of the Hospitallers and other military orders. Detached bodies of the order, however, continued to subsist for some time in different countries.

TEM'PLE, a place of worship, chiefly applied to heathen worship. Originally temples were open places, as Stonehenge, in Wiltshire. In Rome, some of the temples were open, and called *sacella;* others were roofed, and called *ædes.* The most celebrated of the ancient pagan temples were those of Belus in Babylon, Vulcan at Memphis, Jupiter at Thebes, Diana at Ephesus, Apollo in Miletus, Jupiter Olympius in Athens, and Apollo at Delphi. The most celebrated and magnificent temple erected to the true God, was that built by Solomon in Jerusalem.—The *Temples*, in London, are two inns of court, so called because anciently the dwellings of the Knights Templars. They are called the Inner and the Middle Temple, and are situated near the Thames.

TEM'PO, (Italian for *time*,) signifies, in music, the degree of quickness with which a musical piece is to be executed. The different degrees of time are designated by the following terms, *largo*, *adagio*, *andante*, *allegro*, and *presto;* and the intermediate degrees are described by additions.

T E M'P O R A L, belonging to secular concerns; not spiritual; as the *temporal* revenues of the church, called temporalities.—*Temporal courts* are those which take cognizance of civil suits; *temporal power*, civil or political power.

TENAIL', in fortification, an outwork consisting of two parallel sides with a front, in which is a re-entering angle. It is single or double.

TENAIL'LONS, in fortification, works constructed on each side of the ravelins, like the lunettes, but differing in this, that one of the faces of the tenaillon is in the direction of the ravelin, whereas that of the lunette is perpendicular to it.

TEN'ANT, in law, one who holds lands or tenements by any right or title, particularly one who occupies lands or tenements at a yearly rent, for life, years, or at will.—*Tenant in capite*, in England, is one who holds immediately of the king. According to the feudal system, all lands in England are considered as held immediately or mediately of the king, who is styled lord paramount. Such tenants, however, are considered as having the fee of the lands and permanent possession.

TEN'DER, a small vessel employed to attend a larger one for supplying her with provisions or naval stores, or to convey intelligence, &c.—In law, an offer either of money to pay a debt, or of service to be performed, in order to save a penalty or forfeiture which would be incurred by non-payment or non-performance.

TE'NET, any opinion, principle, or doctrine which a person believes and maintains; as, the tenets of Christianity; the tenets of Plato, &c.

TEN'OR, in music, the more delicate of the two voices which belong to the mature age of male singers, it being the second of the four parts reckoning from the bass; and originally the air, to which the other parts were auxiliary. What is called *counter-tenor* (between the treble and the tenor) is in reality only a higher tenor.

TENSE, in grammar, an inflection of verbs by which they are made to signify or distinguish the time of actions or events; as the *present tense*, denoting the time that now is; the *preterite* or *past*, the time that was; and the *future*, the time that will be. Some tenses likewise denote the state of the action, as to its completeness or otherwise, in a certain degree or time, as the *imperfect tense*, which denotes an unfinished action at a certain time; the *perfect*, a finished action at any time; and the *pluperfect*, a finished action before a certain time.

TEN'URE, the feudal relation between lord and vassal in respect of lands. Tenures in capite, or in chief, were those by which land was held immediately of the crown; mesne tenures, of mesne or inferior lords. English tenures under the feudal system are reduced by Blackstone to four: knight-service, or chivalry; free socage; pure villenage; and villein-socage.

TER'APHIM, household deities or images. The teraphim seem to have been either wholly or in part of human form and of small size. They appear to have been superstitiously reverenced as *penates* or household gods, and in some shape or other to have been used as domestic oracles. They are mentioned several times in the Old Testament Scriptures.

TERM, in law, the space of time which the courts are open for the trial of causes. —In universities, &c., the fixed period or time during which students are compelled to reside there previously to their taking a degree. These fall within the four quarters of the year, and are distinguished by the same names as the law terms. —In the Arts, a word or expression that denotes something peculiar to an art: as, a technical *term*.—In contracts, *terms* mean conditions upon which work is agreed to be performed.

TERMINA'LIA, in antiquity, feasts held by the Romans on the 22d and 23d of February, in honor of Terminus, the god of boundaries or land-marks. Cakes and fruit were originally offered, but afterwards animals formed part of the sacrifice.

TER'MINI, in architecture, figures used by the Romans for the support of entablatures, in the place of columns: the upper part consisted of the head and breast of a human body, and the lower of the inverted frustum of a cone. They were so called because they were principally used as boundary marks, and represented their god Terminus, whose altar was on the Tarpeian rock, where he was represented with a human head, without feet or arms, to intimate that he never moved, wherever he might be placed.

TER'MINISTS, in ecclesiastical history, a name given to a class among the Calvinists, whose tenet it is (or was, for such opinions hardly exist at the present day,) that there are persons to whom God has fixed, by a secret decree, a certain *term* before their death, after which he no longer wills their salvation, however long they may live. They instanced the case of Pharaoh, Saul, and Judas, among others.

TERMINOL'OGY, that branch of a science or art which explains the meaning of its technical terms. In some sciences it is of particular importance; in botany, for instance, where not even a leaf can be described without an agreement on certain technical terms.

TER'MINUS, (Lat.) in ancient architecture, a stone raised for the purpose of marking the boundary of a property. Also, a pedestal increasing in size as it rises, or a parallelopiped for the reception of a bust.—Terminus was the name of the god of boundaries among the Romans. Terminus, in more recent times, is applied to the beginning or the end: *i. e.*, to the first and last station of a railroad.

TER'RACE, a platform or bank of earth raised and breasted, particularly in fortifications. Also, a raised walk in a garden, having sloping sides raised with turf.

TER'RA COT'TA, in the Arts, the name given to a very large class of remains of antiquity modelled in clay, many admirable specimens of which have been discovered in Tuscany and Rome. They consist of lamps and vessels of various kinds, besides entire figures and reliefs, some of which display the talents of the sculptor or modeller in no ordinary degree. *Terra cotta* is literally "baked clay;" and the various articles so named, of modern manufacture, (some of which are extremely tasteful,) are modelled or cast in a paste made of pipe or potter's clay and a fine-grained colorless sand, from Ryegate, with pulverized potsherds, slowly dried in the air, and afterwards baked in a kiln.

TER'RÆ FIL'IUS, a scholar at the university of Oxford, England, formerly appointed to make jesting and satirical speeches.

TERROR, REIGN OF, in the history of the French Revolution. This term has been generally applied to the period during which the executions were most numerous, and the country under the sway of the actual terror inspired by the ferocious measures of its governors, who had established it avowedly as the principle of their authority. It seems to be most properly confined to the period between October, 1793, when the revolutionary tribunal, although constituted at an earlier time, was first put in permanent action on the fall of the party of the Gironde, and the overthrow of Robespierre and his accomplices in thermidor (July,) 1794. The agents and partisans of the system have been termed Terrorists.

TER'ZA RI'MA, a peculiar and complicated system of versification, borrowed by the early Italian poets from the Troubadours. The verses are the ordinary Italian heroic lines of eleven syllables (interspersed very rarely with ten-syllable lines.) The rhyme is thus arranged: At the commencement of a poem or portion of a poem, verses 1 and 3 rhyme together; as do verses 2, 4, and 6; the third rhyme begins with verse 5, which rhymes to 7 and 9; the fourth is formed by 8, 10, and 12, and so on; and the poem or canto ends abruptly, the last rhyme, like the first, being on a couplet instead of a triplet. It is obvious that the ryhme is interlaced throughout, and continually in suspense, so that no pause can be found until the end of the poem or canto; as, at the end of every line, there must still be a rhyme incomplete. This continuity gives a very peculiar character to the metre, and renders it highly expressive of sustained narrative or passion, and the abruptness of the conclusion is often turned to good effect by masters of versification. This metre has been rendered celebrated by Dante, who wrote in it his *Divina Commedia*. It has been adopted by his imitators, of whom the latest, Nincenzo Monti, has used it to much advantage; and by Ariosto and other poets for their satires. Byron has adopted it in English, with indifferent success, in his *Prophecy of Dante;* and it has been attempted by various translators.

TERZET'TO, in music, a composition in three parts.

TES'SELLATED PAVE'MENT, in ancient architecture, a pavement formed of small square pieces of stone called *tesseræ* or *dies*. They are frequently, indeed mostly, found inlaid in different colors and patterns, and with a central subject. They are embedded in cement, and rest on prepared hard strata.

TES'SERA, in Roman antiquities, a die, six-sided, like the modern dice; and thus to be distinguished from the talus, which had only three sides. Tickets or tallies used for various puposes were called tesseræ. Thus guards were set at night in their camps by means of a tesseræ with a particular inscription, given from one centurion to another, through the army.

TES'TAMENT, in law, a solemn authentic instrument in writing, whereby a man declares his last will as to the disposal of his estate and effects after his death.—*Testament*, in theology, the name of each of the volumes of the Holy Scriptures, that is, the Old and the New Testament.—The first *Testament* printed in the English language was in 1526. This translation was made by William Tyndale, and was published abroad, after which it was circulated at Oxford and London.

TES'TIMONY, the evidence of facts, oral, as in a court of law, or written, as in the records of history. Testimony is probable and credible when in accordance with general experience, corroborated, and disinterested; but improbable, and unworthy of credit, when contrary to general experience, and uncorroborated.

TE'THYS, in Greek mythology, the daughter of Uranus and Gaia, and wife of her brother Oceanus. The symbol of the sea, and of the element of water; in which character she is sometimes confounded with Thetis, unless indeed the name of the latter goddess be only another form of hers.

TET'RACHORD, in music, a concord consisting of three degrees or intervals, and four terms or sounds; in modern music it is commonly called *a fourth.* The word, in its strictly literal sense, signifies any instrument with four strings, and was applied to the lyre in its primitive state.

TET'RAD, the number four; a collection of four things.

TETRADIAPA'SON, a musical chord, otherwise called a quadruple eighth or twenty-ninth.

TET'RADITES, a word used in several senses, all of them, however, bearing upon its original derivation from *four*.—1. Among the ancients children were so called who were born in the fourth month; and such were believed to be unlucky. 2. The Manichees and others, who believed the Godhead to consist of four instead of three persons, bore this name. And, 3. In ecclesiastical history, different sects of heretics were so called, in consequence of the respect with which they regarded the number four.

TETRAD'ORON, in ancient architecture, a species of brick used by Greek builders in the private dwellings, four palms in length.

TETRADRACH'MA, in ancient coinage, a silver coin worth four drachms, about 75 cents.

TE'TRARCH, a Roman governor of the fourth part of a province. Such originally was the import of the title tetrarch; but it was afterwards applied to any petty king or sovereign. The office, or the territory of a tetrarch, was called a *tetrarchate*.

TETRAS'TICH, a stanza, epigram, or poem consisting of four verses.

TET'RASTYLE, in ancient architecture, a building with four columns in front.

TEUTON'IC, belonging to the Teutones, an ancient people of Germany. The Teutonic language is the parent of the German-Dutch and Anglo-Saxon.—*Teutonic order*, a religious order of knights, established towards the close of the twelfth century, and thus called as consisting chiefly of Germans or Teutones. The original object of the association was to defend the Christian religion against the infidels, and to take care of the sick in the Holy Land. It was at one period immensely rich and powerful.

TEXT, a term signifying an original discourse exclusive of any note or commentary. Also, a certain passage of Scripture, chosen by a preacher to be the subject of his sermon.—*Text-book*, a book containing the leading principles or most important points of a science or branch of learning, arranged in order for the use of students.

THAM'MUZ, the tenth month of the Jewish civil year, containing 29 days, and answering to a part of June and a part of July.

THANE, in early English history, a title of honor belonging to the Anglo-Saxon nobility. In its original meaning, it signified a minister or honorable retainer, and was applied to the followers of kings and chieftains. The thanes in England were formerly persons of some dignity; of these there were two orders, the king's thanes, who attended the Saxon and Danish kings in their courts, and held lands immediately of them; and the ordinary thanes, who were lords of manors, and who had a particalar jurisdiction within their limits. In a later age of the Anglo-Saxon power, the term *thane* seems to have been applied to all landed proprietors who were below the rank of earl, and above that of alderman, and had the privilege of assisting in framing the laws. The rank of thane implied the possession of a certain amount of landed property, and five hides of land is supposed to have been the amount required for a thane of the highest order. After the Conquest, this title was disused, and *baron* took its place. In Scotland, *thane* was a recognized title down to the end of the 15th century, and it appears to have implied from the first a higher dignity than in England, and to have been, for the most part, synonymous with *earl*, which title was generally annexed to the territory of a whole country.

THE'ATINES, a religious order in the Roman Catholic church, the earliest in point of date of the communities of "regular clerks:" it was founded in 1524 by St. Cajetan of Thiene. The members, besides the ordinary monastic vows, bound themselves to the duties of the cure of souls, preaching against heresies, tending the sick and convicts, and to abstain from possessing property or asking for alms.

THE'ATRE, in architecture, a building appropriated to the representation of dramatic spectacles. The theatres of the Greeks and Romans display some of the most extraordinary specimens of their power in the Arts. Bacchus has the reputation of being the inventor of them, which, after their temples, appear to have been the most important public edifices of these people. They seem to have been carried to perfection in the Grecian colonies at an earlier period than they were in the mother country. The first theatre of *stone* at Athens, called the theatre of Bacchus, was built in the time of Themistocles; and as there seems little doubt that the Athenians were the inventors of the drama as a regular scenic action, it is fair to presume that they were the first to regulate the form and proportions which necessity and pleasure dictated in their arrangement. The subjoined diagram shows the general form of the Greek theatre, which differed but little from that of the Romans; and the instructions given by Vitruvius in the eighth chapter of his fifth book, as to the general outline of the plan, are as follows: "Whereas in the Latin theatre the points

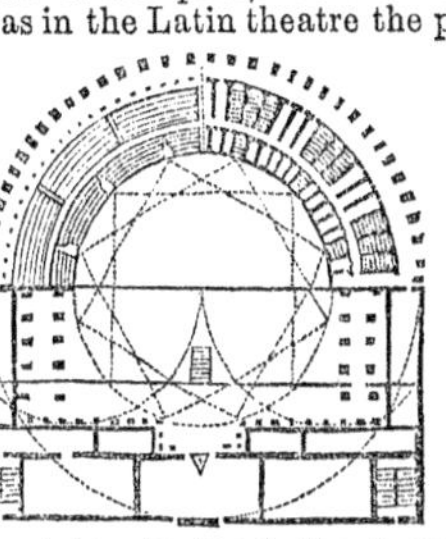

of the four triangles touch the circumference, in the theatres of the Greeks the angles of three squares are substituted; and the side of that square which is nearest to the place of the scene, at the points where it touches the circumference of the circle, is the boundary of the proscenium. A line drawn parallel to this, at the extremity of the circle, will give the front of the scene. Through the centre of the orchestra, opposite to the proscenium, another parallel line is drawn touching the circumference on the right and left; then, one foot of the compasses being fixed on the right-hand point, with a radius equal to the distance from the left point, describe a circle on the right-hand side of the proscenium, and, placing the foot of the compasses on the left-hand point, with the distance of the right-hand interval describe another circle on the left side of the proscenium. Thus describing it from three centres, the Greeks have a larger orchestra, and their scene is further recessed. The pulpitum, which they call λογειον, is less in width; wherefore among them the tragic and comic performers act upon the scene, the rest going through their parts in the orchestra." The ancient theatres were frequently used for the deliberations of the general assembly of the people on political matters, as we find from Tacitus and Ausonius in respect of the theatres at Antioch and Athens. Notwithstanding the use of those buildings in later times as quarries freely used by the inhabitants of the cities in which they stood, there are still considerable ruins at Ephesus, Alabanda, Teos, Smyrna, Hieropolis, Cyzicus, Alinda, Magnesia, Laodicea, Mylassa, Sardis, Miletus, Stratonicea, Telmessus, Jasus, and Patara, all in Asia Minor; in Sicily, at Catana, Taurominium, Syracuse, Argyrium, and Segesta. In Greece, ruins are still extant at Athens, Sparta, in the island of Egina, at Epidaurus, and Megalopolis. According to Pausanias, that at Epidaurus, built by Polycletus, surpassed all the other theatres of Greece in its beauty and proportions; but in grandeur and magnificence the Roman theatres far surpassed those of the Greeks; nor is this surprising, considering the population the former had to accommodate compared with that of the latter. For a very considerable period the theatres of Rome, like those of the Etruscans, were of wood; and Pompey, on his return from the war against Mithridates, was the first who constructed one of stone. This must have been of large dimensions, inasmuch as it would contain 40,000 spectators. The remains of it as some stables of a palace are still visible. There were two other considerable theatres in Rome; the first built in the year 741 of the city, by Cornelius Balbus; and the second which was begun by Julius Cæsar, but not finished till the time of Augustus, who dedicated it to his friend Marcellus. From the remains it appears that it was a specimen of great beauty and purity, as far as relates to the profiles of two of its orders, there being no vestiges of the upper order. The only other remains of Roman theatres are at Saguntum and Oranges, though the Romans usually erected theatres in their newly conquered cities, or at least embellished and improved those they found on the spot. The modern theatres of Rome are, perhaps, the worst in Europe. Italy, however, boasts some beautiful examples; the principal whereof are those at Parma, now in a very dilapidated state, Milan, Verona, Turin, Naples, and Bologna. In France, a very fine theatre at Bourdeaux; the theatre at Versailles; and some elegant theatres in Paris. We subjoin a short table of the width of the stage in a few European and American theatres:

Milan	40 feet
San Benedetto, Venice	40
Theatre Français, Paris	40
Parma	40
Bourdeaux	39
Turin	39
Covent-Garden	37
Argentino, at Rome	36
Theatre Italien, Paris	33
Broadway Theatre, New York	45

THE'BAID, the name given to the heroic poem of Statius, which celebrates the civil war of Thebes waged between the two brothers Eteocles and Polynices. It consists of twelve books.

THE'BAN YEAR, in chronology, the Egyptian year of 365 days 6 hours was so called.

THEFT, in jurisprudence, the general name for the most ordinary class of offences against property; for which English law uses the peculiar designation of larceny. The difficulty of distinguishing between theft, those other species of fraudulent appropriation which are regarded by the laws of most countries as criminal offences, and, finally, that class which is only the subject of civil action, has given rise to a variety of definitions.

THE'ISM, the belief or acknowledgment of the existence of a God, as opposed to *theism*. It has sometimes been defined to be deism; but *theism* differs from *deism*, for although deism implies a belief in the existence of a God, yet it signifies in modern usage a denial of revelation, which *theism* does not.

THEOC'RACY, a term expressing the government of a state immediately by God. The constitution of the Israelites, previous to the appointment of kings, was emphatically a theocracy; their chief magistrates or judges being for the most part occasional officers appointed by the express direction of God. The kingly government may still be considered in a secondary sense as a theocracy, from the general superintendence which Jehovah continued to exercise over it. All politics may in this sense be called theocratic in which the final appeal in matters of moment is made to the will of God, as expressed in oracles, by auguries, or the mouth of the priesthood.

THEOG'ONY, that branch of the heathen theology which taught the genealogy of their gods.

THEOLO'GIUM, in the ancient theatre, a kind of little stage, above that whereon the ordinary actors appeared; being the place where the machinery of the gods was arranged.

THEOL'OGY, the study of religion, or the science which instructs in the knowledge of God and divine things. Theology consists of two branches, *natural* and *revealed*.—*Natural theology* is the knowledge we have of God from his works, by the light of nature and reason.—*Revealed theology* is altogether founded on divine revelation. — There are several other branches into which theology may be divided—as, 1. *Exegetical theology*, which consists in the explanation and interpretation of the Scriptures. 2. *Didactic* or *speculative* theology, by which the several doctrines of religion are stated and explained and their truth established. 3. *Systematic theology*, which arranges methodically the great truths of religion, so as to enable us to contemplate them in their natural connection, and to perceive both the mutual dependence of the parts, and the symmetry of the whole. 4. *Practical theology*, which consists of an exhibition, first, of precepts and directions; and, secondly, of the motives by which we should be excited to comply with these; and both these rules and these motives may be either found expressly revealed in Scripture, or they may be inferences from what it teaches.

THEOM'ANCY, a species of prophecy in which a god himself was believed to reveal future events.

THEOPHILAN'THROPISTS, the title assumed by a deistical society formed at Paris during the French revolution. The object of its founders was to revive public religious ceremonies, which had altogether ceased during the reign of terror, without returning to the rites and ceremonies of Christianity. The revival of the Catholic religion hastened the decline of the society, and in 1802 the consuls prohibited them from holding their meetings in the churches.

THEOR'BO, a musical instrument made in form of a large lute, except that it has two necks. It is used by the Italians for playing a thorough bass.

THE'ORY, in science, properly expresses a connected arrangement of facts according to their bearing on some real or hypothetical law. A *hypothesis* has been distinguished from a theory as an assumption which is conceived to afford a *support* to the discovered law. Thus, some have imagined that the facts of gravitation are explained on the supposition of a subtle and all-pervading ether. Here it is evident that the *facts*, and therefore the *theory* or connected survey of them, are unaffected by the *supposition* in question.—The abstract principles of any science or art, considered without reference to practice.

THEOS'OPHIST, one who pretends to derive his knowledge from divine illumination.

THERAPEU'TÆ, a term applied to those who are wholly employed in the service of religion. This general term has been applied to particular sects of men, concerning whom there have been great disputes among the learned. It is generally supposed that St. Mark established a particular society of Christians about Alexandria, of whom Philo gives an account, and calls them *Therapeutæ*. He speaks of them as a particular sect, retired from the world, who spent their time in reading the writings of ancient authors, in singing hymns and songs composed by some of their own sect, and in dancing together the whole night. Some suppose they were *Essenes;* others imagine they were Jews, residing in Egypt; and Eusebius and others consider them as Christians.

THER'MIDOR, in the French calendar, the name of the 11th month in the year in the French Republic. It commenced on the 19th of July, and ended on the 17th of August. It was the month signalized by the overthrow of Robespierre and the Reign of Terror; thence commonly called the Revolution of Thermidor, and those who boasted of having participated in it called themselves Thermidorians.

THE'SIS, a position or proposition which a person advances and offers to maintain, or which is actually maintained by argument; a theme.

THE'SPIAN ART, that of tragedy or tragic acting is so termed; from Thespis, an Athenian, who lived in the first half of the 6th century before Christ, and introduced the first rudiments of a tragic stage.

THE'URGY, the magician's art; or the power or act of performing supernatural things by invoking the name of God or of subordinate agents.

THIRTY YEARS' WAR, in history, properly a series of wars carried on between the Protestant and Roman Catholic leagues in Germany, in the first half of the 17th century. The house of Austria was, throughout, at the head of the latter party. The Protestant princes of Germany were assisted by various foreign powers; in the earlier part of the war by Denmark and Sweden, and afterwards by France. It is considered to have commenced with the insurrection of the Bohemians in 1618, and ended with the peace of Westphalia in 1648. The celebrated history of this war, by Schiller, is rather a spirited historical essay than an accurate narrative.

THIS'TLE, or SAINT AN'DREW, a Scottish order of knighthood, said to be of great antiquity, but revived by James V. in 1540; again by James II. of England, VII. of Scotland, in 1687; and a third time in 1703, by Queen Anne, who increased the number of knights to twelve, and placed the order on a permanent footing. The thistle, as is well known, is the national emblem of Scotland; and the national motto is very appropriate, being "Nemo me impune lacesset," *nobody shall provoke me with impunity.* This is also the motto of the order of the thistle.

THO'LUS, this word has been variously defined as the middle or centre of an arched or vaulted roof—as the roof itself of a temple or church, or as the lantern or cupola of a large public hall. Pausanias applies the term to several circular edifices with a cupola at top, but which were not considered temples. At Athens was a building of this description, in which were found sundry little silver images, and where the Prytanea offered sacrifices. At Epidaurus was another *tholus*, in the wood sacred to Æsculapius, and behind the temple of that deity. Pausanias speaks of this as a very remarkable structure. It was built of white marble. Polycletes was the architect, and the interior was adorned with paintings. In Sparta was an edifice of a similar kind, in which were found statues of Jupiter and Venus.

THO'MISTS, the followers of Thomas Aquinas, with respect to predestination and grace, in opposition to Scotus.

THOR, in Scandinavian mythology, the son of Odin and Freya, and the divinity who presided over all mischievous spirits that inhabited the elements. His power is represented as irresistible. Many of his deeds are preserved in the *Edda;* but it is probable that the worship of this divinity under the name of Donan, or god of thunder, spread also into Germany, where traces of him are still to be found in numerous local appellations, as Donnersberg, Thorstein, &c. As the worship of this god extended, nothing was more likely than that the Germans should confound him with the Jupiter of the Romans, who were then invading their country; and hence in Germany the day sacred to Jupiter was denominated Donnerstag, while the Scandinavian equivalent of the same deity has been retained by the English in Thursday (Thor's day.)

THOTH, an Egyptian divinity, considered by the Greeks as identical with Mercury. His hieroglyphic represents the beginning of the astronomical year. He was regarded as the inventor of writing and Egyptian philosophy; and is hence paralleled with Mercury by Cicero.

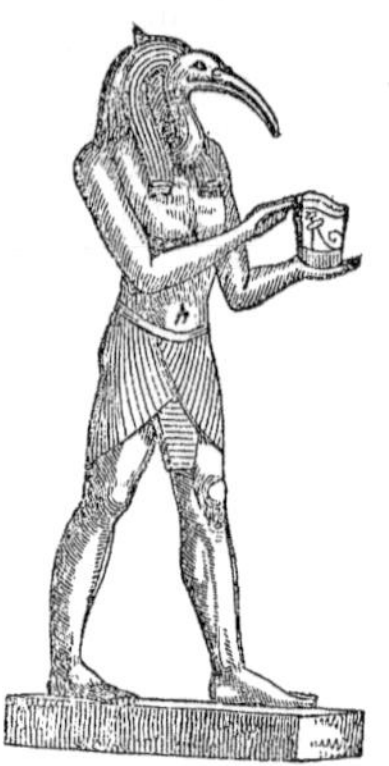

He is represented as a human figure with the head of a lamb or ibis.

THOR'OUGH-BASS, in music, the art by which harmony is superadded to any proposed bass, and includes the fundamental rules of composition. This branch of the musical science is twofold, *theoretical* and *practical*. Theoretical thorough-bass comprehends the knowledge of the connection and disposition of all the several chords, harmonious and dissonant, and includes all the established laws by which they are formed and regulated. Practical thorough-bass supposes a familiar acquaintance with the figures, a facility in taking the chords they indicate, and judgment in the various applications and effects of those chords in accompaniment.

THOUGHT, properly, that which the mind thinks. Thought is either the act or operation of the mind, when attending to a particular subject or thing, or it is the idea consequent on that operation. We say, a man's *thoughts* are employed on government, on religion, on trade, or arts, or his *thoughts* are employed on his dress or on his means of living. By this we mean that the mind is directed to that particular subject or object; that is, according to the literal import of the verb *think*, the mind, the intellectual part of man, is *set* upon such an object, it holds it in view or contemplation, or it extends to it, it stretches to it.

THOU'SAND AND ONE NIGHTS, more commonly called the *Arabian Nights' Entertainments*, from the title adopted in our first translation from Galland's version. A well-known collection of oriental tales, which has acquired in the west a popularity never attained by any other eastern composition. The history of the work has been the subject of much investigation, especially by De Sacy, Von Hammer, and our last learned translator Mr. Lane, from whom we borrow most of this article. It is the opinion of Mr. Lane that the work, in its present form, is the composition of a single author living in Egypt; and that it was most probably "not commenced earlier than the last quarter of the 15th century of our era, and completed before the termination of the first quarter of the next century, soon after the conquest of Egypt by the Osmanlee Turks in 1517." But the origin of the tales is a much more difficult subject of inquiry. It seems to be now established (from the discoveries of De Sacy and Von Hammer) that there was an ancient Persian collection of stories, known by the name of the *Hezar Afzâneh*, (the "Thousand Fanciful Tales,") of unknown antiquity, but certainly older than the 9th century of our era; that the framework of this collection was the same with that of the modern, namely, the story of the cruel king Shakryar and his ingenious queen Chehrazâd; and that this was very early translated into Arabic by the name of the *Thousand Nights*. But Mr. Lane differs from these learned orientalists in still believing that the early work was only a model; that the greater proportion of the modern tales are really Arabian, especially all those founded on the supposed adventures of the Khalif Haroun and his queen Zobeyde, a few only being distinctly of Persian or Indian original.

THREN'ODY, a species of short, occasional poem, composed on the occasion of the funeral of some distinguished personage.

THUGS, a secret and wide-spread association of robbers and murderers in the upper provinces of Hindostan. The existence of this association was scarcely known to the British government before the year 1810, and no combined measures were taken to put it down until about 1830. The Thugs are considered to be a degenerate sect of Kâlî worshippers, and are peculiarly superstitious in their observances. To rob and murder is with them a sacred duty, and they are directed in all their proceedings by auguries, supposed to be vouchsafed by their tutelary goddess Behowanee. They usually move in gangs, consisting of from ten to two hundred or three hundred men, of all races, castes, sects, and religions, yet all joining in the worship of Kâlî, and sacrificing to their tutelary goddess every victim they can seize, and sharing the plunder among themselves. Still they shed no blood unless when forced by circumstances, but strangle their victims by means of a rope or handkerchief. Particular classes, however, are altogether exempt from their attacks; among whom are dancing girls, minstrels, sikhs, fome religious mendicants, tailors, oilmen, blacksmiths, and carpenters. In 1830 vigorous measures were adopted for their suppression, and between 1830 and 1837 upwards of 3000 were brought to justice. In consequence of these measures, the numbers of Thugs have rapidly diminished, and it is to be hoped that they will soon be totally extinct. The system practised by the Thugs is termed *Thugee.*

THULE, a name given by the ancients to the most northern country with which they were acquainted. Some authors imagine it to have been Iceland; others consider it to have been the coast of Norway; while there are many who have not attached to it the idea of any precise country.

THUM'MIM, a Hebrew word denoting perfections. The *urim*, and *thummim*, were worn in the breastplate of the high priest, but what they were has never been satisfactorily ascertained.

THURS'DAY, the fifth day of the week, so named by the Saxons from *Thor*, the old Teutonic god of thunder, answering to the Jove of the Greeks and Romans.

TIA'RA, an ancient crown, which does not appear to have always the same shape. Among the Persians, however, it was a sort of turban, formed like a half-moon, and from this is derived the *tiara* of the pope. Originally the popes wore a common bishop's mitre. The tiara and keys are badges of the papal dignity.—*Tiara*, the well-known ornament with which the ancient Persians adorned their heads. It was in the form of a tower, and adorned with peacocks' feathers. Xenophon says that it was sometimes encompassed with a diadem, at least in ceremonies, and had frequently the figure of a half-moon embroidered upon it.—This was the name also originally given to the mitre of the popes. It was nothing more than a round high cap, at first single instead of double, like that of the other bishops. Nicholas the First added the first gold circle, as the sign of the civil power. The second was added by Boniface about 1300; the third by Urban V. about 1365.

TIERS ETAT, third estate. This term was universally applied in France to the mass of the people under the old *régime.* Before the cities rose to wealth and influence, the nobility and clergy possessed the property of almost the whole country, and the people were subject to the most degrading humiliations; but as trade and commerce began to render men independent, and they were able to shake off their feudal bonds, the *tiers état* gradually rose into importance; and at length the third estate, during the revolution, may be said to have become the nation itself.

TIM'BREL, an ancient musical instrument; a kind of tabor or tambourine, frequently mentioned in Scripture.

TIME, in music, that affection of sound whereby shortness or length is denominated as regards its continuity on the same degree of tune. Time may be considered either with respect to the absolute duration of the notes themselves, measured by motion foreign to music, or with respect to the proportion or quantity of notes compared with each other. The signs or characters by which the time of notes is represented are given under the article MUSIC.

TIMOC'RACY, that form of government whose laws require a certain property to enable a citizen to be capable of the highest offices.

TIRAILLEURS', in the military art, a name given to a species of infantry, seldom intended to fight in close order, but generally dispersed, two and two always supporting each other, and in general to skirmish in front of the line. They must be particularly expert in their movements, to collect quickly into masses at the sound of the bugle, and disperse again with equal expedition; and to act constantly with the whole army. They were introduced by the French during the wars of their revolution, and were soon found so useful as to be indispensable

TIRO'NIAN NOTES, the short-hand of Roman antiquity. According to the received story, they were introduced into Rome by Tiro, the freedman and favorite of Cicero: he is supposed to have imported the art from Greece. MSS., written entirely in what are called the Tironian notes, are not unfrequently of the date of the 7th century and downwards; and they are still common in marginal notes.

TIS'RI, the first Hebrew month of the civil year, and the seventh of the ecclesiastical; answering to a part of our September and a part of October.

TI'TAN, in Grecian mythology, according to the more modern account, the eldest son of Uranus and Gaia, who relinquished the sovereignty of gods and men to his younger brother Saturn, the latter undertaking to destroy all his children, so that the monarchy might revert to those of Titan. He afterwards recovered the sovereignty from Saturn; but Jupiter, the son of the latter, vanquished him, and restored it to his father. This, however, is a tale altogether unknown to the original mythologists. According to them, the Titans were many in number, children of Uranus, and Gaia. Hesiod makes them six. The children of the Titans, Atlas for example, retained the same appellation. The war of these Titans with Jupiter was the subject of many different and contradictory legends. Its scene was laid in Thessaly; by Homer, on the mountains Olympus, Pelion, and Ossa. By some writers Titan is identified with Hyperion; but this point is involved in great obscurity.

TITHES, in English ecclesiastical law, the tenth part of the increase annually arising from the profits of land and stock, allotted to the clergy for their support. The great tithes are chiefly corn, hay, and wood; other things of less value are comprehended under the name of small tithes. Tithes are personal, predial, or mixed; *personal*, when accruing from labor, art, or trade; *predial*, when arising from the earth, as hay, wood, and fruit; and *mixed*, when accruing from beasts, which are fed off the land.—The custom of paying tithes, or of offering a tenth of what a man enjoys, has not only been practised under the Jewish law, and by Christians, but we also find something like it among the heathens. The Babylonians and Egyptians gave their kings a tenth of their revenues. The Romans offered a tenth of all they took from their enemies to the gods; and the Gauls, in like manner, gave a tenth to their god Mars.

TI'THING, a community of ten men, into which all England was divided in the time of the Saxons.

TME'SIS, in grammar, a figure by which a compound word is separated into two parts, and one or more words inserted between them; as, of whom *be* thou *ware* also; 2 Tim. iv. 15, for, of whom *beware* thou also.

TOC'SIN, an old French word of which the derivation seems not to be ascertained. Gregory of Tours uses the word "seing" for the sound of a bell—signifying an alarum bell. The use of the terrible tocsin, during the troubles of the Revolution, to assemble the multitude, has rendered the word almost proverbial.

TO'GA, the name given to the principal outer garment worn by the Romans.

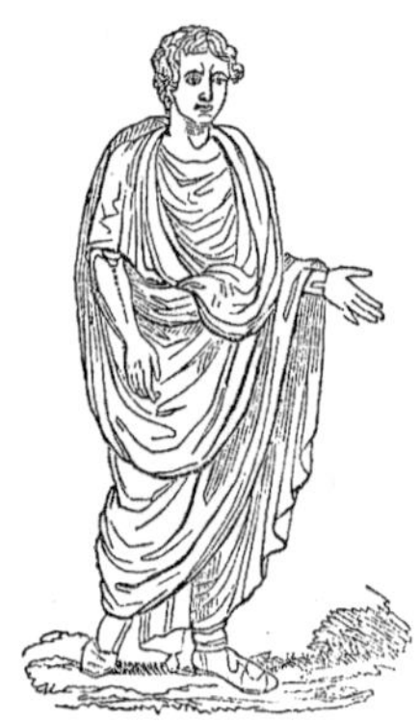

It was a loose flowing garment made of wool and sometimes of silk, the usual color being white. It covered the whole body with the exception of the left arm, and the right of wearing it was the exclusive privilege of every Roman citizen. The *toga virilis*, or manly gown, was assumed by Roman youths when they attained the age of fourteen. The *toga prætexta* was worn by the children of the nobles, by girls until they were married, and by boys until they were fourteen, when they assumed the *toga virilis*. It was also the official robe of the higher magistrates of the city. The *toga picta*, or ornamented toga, was worn by generals in their triumph.

TOLERA'TION, in a general sense, the allowance of that which is not wholly approved; but more especially, the allowance of religious opinions and modes of worship in a state, when contrary to or different from those of the established church or belief.

TOL'MEN, a species of druidical monument, composed of a large stone placed horizontally upon other stones, fixed vertically in the earth, about three or four feet high, and not fewer in number than three, nor more than fifteen. In form it is generally a parallelogram. The tolmen is also at times composed only of a

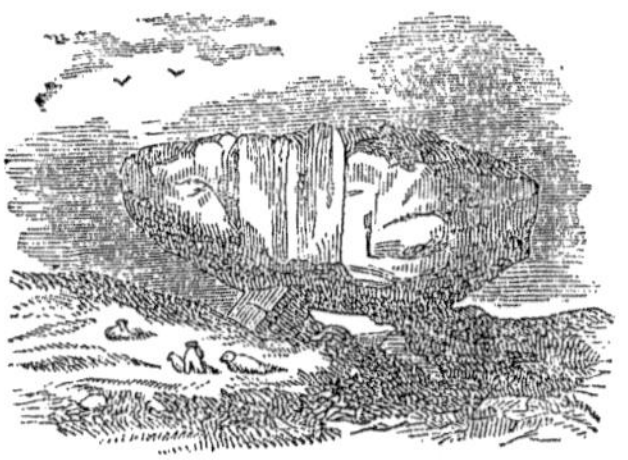

large stone, one end resting on the ground, and the other end supported by a stone placed under it. The large stone or table has generally a hole pierced through. Some have supposed the tolmen to be a kind of druidal oracle, the hole through the stone being an acoustic contrivance, by means of which the priests could return oracular answers. Others suppose the tolmens to have been altars on which victims were sacrificed; the hole being used as a means of dispersing the blood of the victim on those who wished such bloody baptism. A third opinion is, that they indicate, or rather constitute places of sepulture. They are also called *cromlechs*.

TOMB, is used to express both the grave or sepulchre in which the body of a deceased person is interred, and a monument erected in his memory. In many countries it was customary to burn the bodies of the dead, and to collect the ashes into an urn which was deposited in a tomb. The tombs of the Jews were generally hollow places hewn out of a rock. The Greeks constructed their tombs outside the walls of their cities, with the exception of those raised to distinguished personages. The same distinction was observed by the Romans; their sepulchres were in the country near the high roads.

TONE, the degree of elevation which any sound has, so as to determine its acuteness or gravity.—*Musical tones* differ from those of common speech chiefly by being more prolonged, so as to give the ear a more decided perception of their height, formation, and relation to each other. There are two kinds of tones, major and minor. The *tone major* is in the ratio of 8 to 9, which results from the difference between the fourth and fifth. The *tone minor* is as 9 to 10, resulting from the difference between the minor third and the fourth.—*Tone*, in painting, &c., a term used chiefly in coloring to express the prevailing hue. Thus we say, this picture is of a dull tone, of a lively tone, of a soft tone, of a clear tone, &c., and thus it may be also observed—it is requisite to *heighten the tone* of this work, or otherwise, to render the colors more vivid, and, in some instances, the masses more decided and the figures more striking. The word tone, in relation to *chiaro-scuro*, expresses the degree of brightness or intensity. *Tone* is not precisely synonymous with *tint;* the latter relating rather to the *mixture* of colors, and the former to their *effect*.—*Tones, ecclesiastical*, in music, the eight modes now generally called the Gregorian Chant, in which the service of the Catholic church is performed; four whereof are authentic, and four of them plagal. Pope Gregory has been considered the inventor of them. They are the foundation of all music, and will ever be considered stupendous monuments of composition.

TON'IC, in music, the principal note of the key. It is the chief sound upon which all regular melodies depend, and in which they all terminate. Its octaves, both above and below, are equally called by the same name. It is, however, to be understood that the termination here alluded to has relation only to the chief melody, or to its bass, inasmuch as the inner or mean parts of the harmony conclude on the third or mediant, and the fifth or dominant.

TON'TINE, a sort of increasing life annuity, or a loan given by a number of persons with the benefit of survivorship. Thus an annuity is shared among a number, on the principle that the share of each, at his death, is enjoyed by the survivors, until at last the whole goes to the last survivor, or to the last two or three, according to the terms on which the money is advanced.

TO'PAZ, a gem or precious stone, very generally of a fine yellow or gold color. It sometimes occurs in masses, but more generally crystallized in rectangular octahedrons. The *oriental topaz* is most esteemed: its color borders on the orange. The *occidental*, or that found in Peru, is of a softer substance, but its color is nearly the same. There is also the *oriental aqua-marine*, or blue topaz, besides several other kinds, of inferior worth and beauty.

TOOTH OR'NAMENT, in architecture, one of the peculiar marks of the early English style. It consists of a pyramid, having its sides partially cut out, so as to have the resemblance of an inverted flower. It is generally inserted in a hollow moulding.

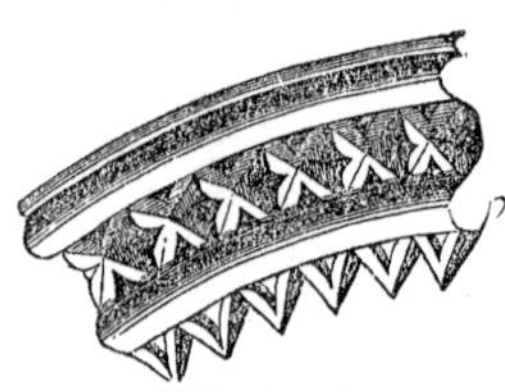

Tooth ornament.

TO'PHET, a polluted unclean place near Jerusalem, into which the Jews used to throw the carcasses of beasts, or the bodies of men to whom they refused burial; and where a fire was perpetually kept up to consume all that was brought. Hence Tophet is sometimes used metaphorically for hell. This place had also been defiled by human sacrifices which had been offered to Moloch. Hence Milton says of this hideous deity, that he

> Made his grove
> The pleasant valley of Hinnom: Tophet thence
> And black Gehenna called, the type of Hell.

The name is derived by some from Heb. toph, *a drum*, on account of the beating of drums and other instruments by which the cries of the children sacrificed to Moloch were stifled.

TOP'ICS, in rhetoric. By abstracting from a proposition which conveys a truth in the concrete (*i. e.*, respecting certain circumstances expressed in the terms of the proposition) a portion of those circumstances denominated accidental, we arrive at the same truth in the abstract, or (in stricter language) more widely applicable, and accommodated to many different sets of accidental circumstances. Thus, for example, in jurisprudence, from an investigation of the truth in various insulated cases in which a too strict application of legal principles has been attended with evil effects, we deduce the general truth that such application is so attended; or, in the proverbial phrase, "summum jus summa injuria." Among the helps employed by the ancients in their favorite study of rhetoric was the collection and arrangement of a great variety of such general truths, according to the several sciences or subjects to which they belonged. These they termed *topoi*, or places; from which the modern term *topic* is derived. They considered it useful for the student in rhetoric to have at hand, by means of his memory, those compendious expressions of universal sentiment, and the general reasonings or declamations applicable to each of them, in order to employ them for particular use by performing the converse of that operation by which they were arrived at; viz. clothing them with the particular circumstances of the case. Thus the topos just cited might be useful to the forensic orator; it affords a subject for reasoning and declamation applicable to a great number of individual instances. Many of these topics answer to what in modern phrase we should term axioms; and, indeed, some of the axioms of pure mathematics are enumerated by Aristotle among the topics which are proper to every species of oratory.

TOPOG'RAPHY, the accurate description or draught of some particular place or tract of land, as of any particular county, city, town, castle, &c. Topography goes into minute details which geography does not enter upon.

TORQUE, in antiquity, a chain or collar formed of a number of small ringlets interlaced with each other, framed of metal, and worn around the neck. No ornament perhaps was of more early or general use. It is mentioned in Genesis, as one of the ornaments conferred by Pharaoh on Joseph. It was in use among the Greeks and Romans, but peculiarly among the Celtic nations. The legends respecting the torques of the Gauls who invaded Rome are well known. It was from his victory over a Gaul that T. Mantius Torquatus derived his surname. And no relic is more commonly found in this country by antiquarian explorers. Boadicea wore a long golden torque.

TOR'SO, the trunk of a statue, mutilated of head and limbs.

TO'RUS, in architecture, a large round moulding in the bases of columns, resembling the astragal in form, but larger.

TO'RY, in British history, a political party opposed to the *Whigs*, and adhering to the ancient constitution of England. The word *Tory* is Irish, and was formerly applied to a class of depredators in that country; but the distinctions of *Tory* and *Whig* (as political partisans) were not known before the year 1678, in the reign of Charles II., when those who believed that the Catholics conspired against the king and state, as deposed by Titus Oates, were called *Whigs*, and those who disbelieved it, *Tories*. Of late years the term *Conservatives* has been adopted by the Tories, as tending to convey the best explanation of their principles. During the American Revolution, those who favored the British were called Tories.

TOUR'NAMENT, a well-known military sport of the middle ages, which without doubt arose from the exercises of military training. A joust or just is, properly speaking, the encounter of two knights in this species of exercise; the tournament, an assembly held for the purpose of exhibiting such justs, or the encounter of several knights on a side. The earlier tournaments were highly dangerous and sanguinary sports. They were performed with the ordinary weapons of warfare, the lance and the sword; and the combatants had only the strength of their armor to rely on for their defence. It was a recognized custom, that whoever slew or disabled an adversary in the tournament was indemnified against all consequences. The account of the tournament given by the Count of Chablais, in Savoy, to Edward I. on his return from Palestine to England, as given by Thomas de Walsingham, represents a sort of violent mêlée, in which knights, esquires, and archers were engaged on both sides, endeavoring to unhorse their riders and overthrow the footmen by every possible means. But in the course of time this chivalric amusement became the subject of minute regulations, which in some degree diminished the danger and insured the fairness of the sport. In tournaments, when under the strict regulation of knightly usage, two sorts of arms were employed: those expressly made for the purpose, viz., lances with blunt heads of iron; and the ordinary arms of warfare, termed, "armes a outrance," which were only employed by such champions as were desirous to signalize themselves in a more than ordinary degree, and frequently were not permitted by the judges of the tournament. Every knight attending was required to show his noble birth and rank, as a title to admission. These were at first proclaimed by the heralds with sound of trumpet; and hence the word blazonry, which signifies the correct deciphering of the heraldic symbols on a coat-of-arms, is derived by some from the German blasen, *to blow*. Afterwards, when armorial bearings became general, the shield of the knight gave token of his rank and family. The attendance of ladies at the tournaments, their distribution of prizes to those who had borne themselves best, arming and unarming the knights, &c., are various romantic circumstances well known to the reader of chivalric legends; but they must not be supposed to have been the necessary, or even usual accompaniments of these knightly sports, at least until a later age, when the taste for gallantry, combining with that for show and spectacle, turned these military exhibitions of skill into little more than gorgeous pageants. The revival of the tournament was recently attempted in the west of Scotland by the Earl of Eglinton; but we scarcely suppose that the success of that attempt was either commensurate with its deserts, or was such as to induce any party to renew it. At the court of Wurtemberg tournaments are not unfrequently exhibited at this day.

TOW'ER, in architecture, a building raised to a considerable elevation, and consisting of several stories. Towers are either round or square, and flat on the top, by which they are distinguished from spires or steeples. Before the invention of guns, places were not only fortified with towers, but attacked with movable towers mounted on wheels, which placed the besiegers on a level with the walls.

TOWN'SHIP, the corporation of a town; the district or territory of a town. —In New England, the counties are divided into townships of five, six, seven, or perhaps ten miles square, and the inhabitants of such townships are invested with certain powers for regulating their own affairs, such as repairing roads, providing for the poor, &c.

TRA'BEA, in Roman antiquities, the robe used at first by the kings, but afterwards by consuls and augurs. The purple *trabea* was used only on the occasion of great sacrifices. The second sort, of purple and white, was commonly worn by consuls on state occasions. A third, of purple and scarlet, was the dress of the augurs.

TRACT, or TREA'TISE, in literature, both originally from the same Latin word tractatus; the latter through the French. It would be difficult to assign any reason for the difference in signification between two words identical in origin and etymological meaning; but the first is now commonly used to describe short compositions, in which some particular subject is "treated," generally in the form of a pamphlet; the latter, more extensive works.

TRADE, the business of buying and selling for money, comprehending every species of exchange or dealing It is, however, chiefly used to denote the barter or purchase and sale of goods, wares, and merchandise, either by wholesale or retail.—*Foreign trade* consists in the exportation and importation of goods, or the exchange of the commodities of the different countries. *Inland* or *home trade* is the exchange or buying and selling of goods within a country.—The word *trade* has also a more limited signification, designating the business which a person has learned, and which he either carries on or is employed in; as, the *trade* of a carpenter, a smith, &c. The liberal arts, learned professions, and agriculture are not included.

TRADI'TION, a truth of doctrine or fact, delivered or handed down to one from another, and received on the faith that the first to whom it was so delivered received it from an authentic source. In common language, the word is used to signify records of facts preserved in the memory of successive persons or generations only, and not committed to writing. In theology, tradition means, generally, that body of doctrine and discipline supposed to have been put forth by our Saviour or his inspired apostles, and not committed to writing; and thus the word is used in a contrary sense from "Scripture." And such traditions are of two sorts; tradition of doctrine (such as that of the Trinity,) which is commonly said to be directly affirmed by tradition and proved by Scripture; and tradition of rites and ceremonies, called by Hooker "traditions ecclesiastical," or "ordinances made in the prime of Christian religion, established with that authority which Christ has left to his church in matters indifferent, and, on that consideration, requisite to be observed till like authority give just cause to alter them."

TRA'GEDY, a species of drama, in which the diction is elevated and the catastrophe melancholy. The name is usually derived from the ancient Greek custom of leading about a goat in procession at the festivals of Bacchus, in whose honor those choral odes were sung which were the groundwork of the Attic tragedy. A Greek tragedy always consisted of two distinct parts; the dialogue, which corresponded in its general features to the dramatical compositions of modern times; and the chorus, the whole tone of which was lyrical rather than dramatical, and which was meant to be sung while the dialogue was intended to be recited. The unity of time:—namely, that the duration of the action should not exceed twenty-four hours: and that of place,—namely, that the scene in which the events occur should be the same throughout, are modern inventions. Eschylus is called the father of *tragedy*.

TRAGI-COM'EDY, in literature, a compound name, invented to express a class of the drama which should partake both of tragedy and comedy. If the mixture of serious with humorous portions in the piece alone entitles it to this name, then all the plays of Shakspeare (with the single exception of the *Merry Wives of Windsor*, to which some add the *Twelfth Night*.) as being pure comedies, belong to this class; as do, indeed, almost all the works of the old English dramatists. But *Troilus and Cressida* alone, of the plays of Shakspeare, bears this title in old editions: on what account we do not know. French critics define the distinction to be, that the *event* of the tragi-comedy is not unhappy or bloody. Dacier condemns them as illegitimate. Guarini, the Italian poet, wrote an essay on the subject.

TRAMON'TANE, lying beyond, or on the farther side of the mountains; applied, particularly by the Italians, to such as live north of the Alps.

TRANCE, a state in which the voluntary functions of the body are suspended, and the soul seems to be rapt in visions.

TRANSAC'TION, the doing or performing of any business; management of any affair.—That which is done; an affair. We are not to expect in history a minute detail of every *transaction*.—In the civil law, an adjustment of a dispute between parties by mutual agreement.—*Philosophical transactions*, the published volumes containing the several papers relating to the sciences, which have been read at the meetings of certain philosophical societies, as the Royal Society of London, and the Royal Society of Edinburgh, and which have been thought worthy of being made public at the expense of such societies. These transactions contain the several discoveries and histories relative to the sciences, such as natural history, mathematics, mechanical philosophy, chemistry, &c., either made by the members themselves, or communicated by them from their correspondents, with the various experiments, observations, &c., made by them or transmitted to them.

TRANSAL'PINE, lying to the north or west of the Alps; as, *Transalpine* Gaul: opposed to *Cisalpine*.

TRANSATLAN'TIC, lying or being beyond the Atlantic. When used by a person in Europe or Africa, *transatlantic* signifies being in America; and *vice versâ*.

TRANSCENDEN'TAL, a word used by German philosophers to express that which *transcends* or *goes beyond* the limits of actual experience. This general meaning is somewhat restricted by Kant, who draws a distinction between the *transcendental* and the *transcendent*. The transcendental he defines to be that which, though it could never be derived from experience, yet is necessarily connected with experience, and which may be shortly expressed as the intellectual *form*, the *matter* of which is supplied by sense. "I call," says he, "all knowledge transcendental, which has regard in general not so much to *objects* as to our mode of knowing or apprehending objects (that is to say, to formal knowledge,) so far as this is conceived to be possible *à priori*. A system of such conceptions would be named transcendental philosophy, as the system of all the principles of pure reason." The *transcendent*, on the contrary, is that which regards those principles as objectively real to which Kant assigns only a subjective or formal reality, and consequently is by him regarded as beyond the limits of the human reason altogether.

TRAN'SCRIPT, a copy of any original writing, particularly that of an act or instrument inserted in the body of another. The title to land must be transferred by deed.

TRAN'SEPT, in architecture, the aisle of ancient churches, extending across the nave and main aisles.

TRANS'FER, in commerce, an act whereby a person surrenders his right, interest, or property in anything to another.

TRANSFIGURA'TION, the supernatural change which is described to have taken place in the appearance of Christ, when, as is recorded, he took Peter, James, and John up into a high mountain with him, and was transfigured before them, his face shining as the sun, and his raiment showing white as light. There appeared in conversation with him Moses and Elias; and the apostles erected three tabernacles or tents to them. An ancient tradition assigns Mount Tabor as the scene of this event, upon which three contiguous grottoes have been fashioned to represent the three tabernacles.

TRANSI'TION, in rhetoric, is of two kinds. The first is when a speech is introduced abruptly; as when Milton gives an account of our first ancestors' evening devotions:

> Both turn'd, and under open sky adored
> The God that made both air, sky, earth and heaven.—
> ——Thou also madest the night,
> Maker omnipotent, and Thou the day.

The second is when a writer suddenly leaves the subject he is upon, and passes to another, from which it seems different at first view, but serves to illustrate it.—In music, a change of key from major to minor, or the contrary.

TRANSLA'TION, in literature, the rendering of a literary work from the original language into another. The peculiar merits and peculiar difficulties of successful translation have often been pointed out by critics, but their judicious directions have been seldom realized by authors. In truth, those difficulties require a talent of so high an order to surmount them, that few writers are fit to undertake the office of translators (we mean of works of any high literary merit,) except those whose genius has more congenial occupation in original composition; for notwithstanding Dryden's sarcastic remark, that "imitation of an author is the most advantageous way for a translator to show himself, but it is the greatest wrong which can be done to the memory and reputation of the dead," we are inclined to doubt whether, in reality, imitation be not the more advantageous method of the two.—"It is the office of the translator to represent the forms of language according to the intention with which they are employed: he will therefore, in his translation, make use of the phrases in his own language to which use and custom have assigned a similar conventional import; taking care, however, to avoid those which, from their form, or any other circumstances, are connected with associations exclusively belonging to modern manners. He will likewise, if he is capable of executing his work upon a philosophic principle, endeavor to render the personal and local allusions into the *genera* of which the local or personal variety employed by the original author is merely the accidental type, and to reproduce them in one of those permanent forms which are connected with the universal and immutable habits of mankind. The *faithful translator* will not venture to take liberties of this sort; he renders into English all the conversational phrases according to their grammatical and logical form, without any reference to the current usage which has affixed to them an arbitrary sense, and appropriated them to a particular and definite purpose. The *spirited translator*, on the contrary, employs the corresponding modern phrases; but he is apt to imagine that a peculiar liveliness and vivacity may be imparted to his performance by the employment of such phrases as are particularly connected with modern manners; and if at any time he feels more than usually anxious to avoid the appearance of pedantry, he thinks he cannot escape from it in any way more effectually than by adopting the slang and jargon of the day. The peculiarities of ancient times he endeavors to represent by substituting in their place the peculiarities of his own time and nation."

TRANSMIGRA'TION, the Pythagorean doctrine of the passing of the soul from one body into another. A belief in this, under various modifications, has existed in different ages of the world, and by various nations. This belief in the transmigration of the soul, as a means of purification and penance, may have been attended with good consequences in certain states of society; but the Christian is content to leave undrawn the veil which the Creator has placed over the particular circumstances of our future condition.

TRANSMUTA'TION, the change of one substance into another of a different nature. The transmutation of base metals into gold was one of the dreams of alchemy.

TRAN'SOM, in architecture, a lintel over a door, or the piece that is framed across a double light window.—In a ship, the beam or timber extended across the stern-post to strengthen the aft part and give it due form.

TRANSPORTA'TION, in English law, a species of punishment. It is not known to the common law of England, and was originally a commutation of punishment, pardon being granted to various descriptions of offenders on condition of undergoing transportation: generally for seven or fourteen years, or for life. It is now a statutable punishment for a great variety of offences. It is said to have been first inflicted as a punishment by a law in the time of Elizabeth, enacting that such rogues as were dangerous to the inferior people should be banished. At that time the English plantations in North America were the receptacles of transported convicts. Virginia, the Jerseys, Delaware, Maryland, &c. are the districts which received the greatest accession to their population from this cause. At the very commencement of the practice, the same arguments were employed against it by Lord Bacon which are urged at this day by many law reformers. "It is," he says, "a shameful and unblessed thing to take the scum of the people, and wicked condemned men, to be those with whom you plant." After the loss of the American colonies, several years elapsed before the government fixed on any place by way of substitute. At length, in 1787, Botany Bay, on the coast of New South Wales, was fixed upon: 760 convicts were despatched that year. But when the expedition arrived, it was discovered that Botany Bay (discovered by Cook in 1770) afforded no practicable site for the colony, which was consequently landed at Port Jackson, where the town of Sydney was founded. From that period to the present, great numbers of convicts have been transported to Port Jackson, and to the later founded colony of Van Diemen's Land—the only two English penal settlements. Much has been done of late years towards regulating the condition of the convicts in the colony, and subjecting the worst part of them to severe privations; in particular, by transporting some of them to particular depots, where they are liable to close inspection and hard labor. Among the writers who have lately contended against the policy of continuing the punishment of transportation, we may particularly mention Archbishop Whately.

TRANSPOSI'TION, in grammar, a change of the natural order of words in a sentence.—*Transposition*, in music, a change in the composition, either in the transcript or the performance, by which the whole is removed into another key.

TRANSUBSTANTIA'TION, in theology, the supposed conversion or change of the substance of the bread and wine in the eucharist, into the body and blood of Jesus Christ. This is a main point in the Roman Catholic religion, and is rejected by the Protestants, the former maintaining the transubstantiation to be real, the latter only figurative; interpreting the text *hoc est corpus meum*, "this signifies my body;" but the council of Trent strenuously contended for the literal sense of the verb *est*, and say expressly, that in *transubstantiation*, the body and blood of Christ are truly, really, and substantially under the species of bread and wine.

TRANSUMP'TION, a syllogism by concession or agreement, used where a question proposed is transferred to another; with this condition, that the proof of the latter should be admitted for a proof of the former.

TRAP'PISTS, the name of a religious order which still exists in Normandy. It was founded in 1140 by a Count de Perche, in a deep valley called La Trappe, whence the name of the order, and has survived all the changes and revolutions of France. The rules of this order are of the strictest kind. It was, however, far less celebrated under its original foundation, than from the reform it underwent under the celebrated Abbé de Rancé, in the reign of Louis XIV.

TRAV'ERSE, in law, a denial of what the opposite party has advanced in any stage of the pleadings.—In fortification, a *traverse* is a trench with a little parapet for protecting men on the flank: also, a wall raised across a work.

TRAV'ESTY, the burlesque imitation of an author's style and composition. Most travesties purposely degrade the subject treated: though they may be intended either to ridicule absurdity, or to convert a grave performance into a humorous one.

TREA'SON, in law, is divided into *high treason* and *petty treason*. High treason is the greatest crime of a civil nature of which a man can be guilty. In general, it is the offence of attempting to subvert the government of the state to which the offender owes allegiance.

TREAS'URER, in law, an officer to whose care the treasure of the government or of any company, is committed.—The *Lord High Treasurer of England* has the charge of all the national revenue.

TREAS'URE-TROVE, in law, money or any other treasure found hidden under the earth.

TREAS'URY, a place or building where wealth or valuable stores are deposited.

TREA'TY. an agreement, league, or contract between two or more nations or sovereigns, formally signed by commissioners properly authorized, and solemnly ratified by the several sovereigns or the supreme power of each state. Treaties are of various kinds, as *treaties* for regulating commercial intercourse, *treaties* of alliance, offensive and defensive, *treaties* for hiring troops, *treaties* of peace, &c. In most monarchies, the power of making and ratifying treaties is vested in the sovereign; in republics, it is vested in the chief magistrate, senate, or executive council; in the United States, it is vested in the president, by and with the consent of the senate; while in the Germanic confederation, the particular states have the right of making treaties of alliance and commerce not inconsistent with the fundamental laws of the confederation. The East India Company enjoys the right of making treaties under certain limitations; but in all cases treaties can only be made by the sovereign power in a state, or by parties upon whom the sovereign power has conferred that right. Hence, in order to enable a public minister or other diplomatic agent to conclude and sign a treaty, he must be furnished with full power by the sovereign authority, and the treaty concluded in this manner is binding on the state, in the same manner as if it had been concluded immediately by the sovereign power. In the United States, it is necessary that the sanction of the legislative body be given to treaties of commerce, or those which impose taxes on the people, entered into by the executive.

TREB'LE, the highest or most acute of the parts in music which is adapted to the voice of females or boys.—*Treble note*, the note in the treble stave, placed on the line with the cliff.

TRENCH'ES, or *lines of approach*, in fortification, ditches cut in oblique zigzag directions, to enable besiegers to approach a fortified place without being exposed to the fire of its cannon. Hence the terms "to open the trenches," to break ground for the purpose of carrying on approaches to a besieged place; "mount the trenches," to mount guard in the trenches, &c.

TRENT, COUN'CIL OF, in ecclesiastical history, was assembled by Paul III. in 1545, and continued, in twenty-five sessions, until 1563, under Julius III. and Pius IV. This celebrated council was convoked at a period when the Christian world was agitated by the early efforts of the reformers; and its most important decrees have therefore reference to the points on which the controversies of the Reformation chiefly turned: *e. g.*, transubstantiation, image-worship, the authority of the pope. There is a certain degree of ambiguity in the expression of some of its decrees, owing to the uncertainty which the doctrines of the reformers caused in the minds of supporters of the Romish faith. But, on the whole, it cannot be denied that they express the general belief of Western Christians at the period when they were drawn up; and that they condemn, although with little decision and firmness, many of the more gross abuses of the church. The authority of these decrees (except so far as the more strictly doctrinal part of them is embodied in the creed of Pope Pius IV.) has been much debated among Romish ecclesiastics. In Germany, Poland, and Italy, they appear to have been adopted from the beginning without restriction; in Spain only with a reservation of the rights of the monarch; in France they have never been solemnly received. But as regards the more important portions of them which contain the rule of faith, they probably accurately express the belief of the Roman Catholic church at the present day.

TRES'PASS, in law, any violation of another's rights; as, the unlawfully entering on his premises; but when violence accompanies the act, it is called a trespass *vi et armis*. — In a moral sense, the transgression of any divine law or command is a *trespass*.

TRI'AD, in music, the common chord, consisting of the third, fifth, and eighth.

TRI'AL, in law, the examination of causes before a proper judge, which, as regards matters of fact, are to be tried by a jury; as regards matters of law, by the judge; and as regards records, by the record itself.

TRIB'UNE, in Roman antiquity, the title of various officers. *A tribune of the people*, was chosen out of the plebeians to protect them against encroachments and oppressions of the patricians, and the attempts of the senate and consuls on their liberty. These tribunes were not, strictly speaking, magistrates, or invested with magisterial powers; but they exercised a great influence upon public affairs. They had the power of putting a negative on the decrees of the senate, and of arresting the proceedings of magistrates by their *veto;* and in process of time their influence was increased to such a degree, that they endangered the safety of the state.— *Military tribune*, an officer in the Roman army, who commanded in chief over a body of forces, particularly the division of a legion, consisting usually of about 1000 men.—The title of *tribune* was also given, as we observed above, to various other officers; as *Tribuni ærarii*, tribunes of the treasury. *Tribuni fabricarum*, those who had the direction of the making of arms. Also, *Tribuni marinorum*, *Tribuni nolanorum*, *Tribuni voluptatum*, mentioned in the Theodosian code, as intendants of the public shows, and other diversions.— *Tribune*, in the French houses of legislature, the pulpit or elevated place from which the members deliver their speeches, which they usually read, if of any considerable length. In general, only short replies are made *extempore*.

TRIB'UTE, a sum of money paid by an inferior sovereign or state to a superior potentate, to secure the friendship or protection of the latter. The *black mail* formerly levied by the Scottish borderers on their less powerful neighbors, for protecting their property from the depredations of caterans, was a species of tribute.

TRICLIN'IUM, in ancient architecture, a room furnished on three sides with couches, the fourth side being left open for facilitating the attendance of the servants, in which company was received and the repasts served. The winter triclinia were placed to the west, and those for summer to the east.

TRI'COLOR, the national French banner of three colors, blue, white, and red, adopted on the occasion of the first revolution. The immediate occasion for adopting them is said to have been that they were the colors worn by the servants of the Duke of Orleans; and they were first assumed by the people when the minister Neckar was dismissed in 1789. But these colors, in combination, appear to have formed a national emblem in France from a very early period. It is also said to have been formed by uniting the three colors successively used in the French standards at different periods; viz. the blue of the banner of St. Martin, the red of the oriflamme, and the white of the white cross, supposed to have been assumed under Philip of Valois. The three colors were given by Henry IV. to the Dutch on their desiring him to confer on them the national colors of his country; and they have since been borne successively by the Dutch republic and the kingdom of the Netherlands. The domestic livery of Louis XIV. was tricolored, as were also the liveries of the Bourbon kings in Spain. At the revolution, when the three colors were assumed on the national flag, they were borne in the same order as the Dutch, but in a different position, viz. the division of colors parallel to the flag-staff; whereas in the Dutch flag it is at right angles with it. Tricolored flags have been adopted in some of the German states, and in Belgium, &c.; and they are often employed as emblematical of liberty.

TRI'DENT, an attribute of Neptune, being a kind of three-pronged sceptre which the fables of antiquity put into the hands of that deity.

TRIERAR'CHIA, an Athenian institution which imposed on a certain body of citizens the duty of fitting out triremes for the use of the state. About 1200 citizens were usually chosen for this purpose from the richest individuals, and these were subdivided into clubs of 12 or 16 to each ship. Demosthenes introduced a new regulation, by which the burden to be borne by each individual was made to bear a given proportion to his property.

TRIET'ERIS, in Grecian chronology, a cycle invented by Thales to connect his year, which consisted of 12 months of 30 days each, amounting to 360 days; this falling short of the true solar year, he inserted a month of 30 days at the end of every three years, by which means he made it exceed the true year by 13 days.

TRIFO'RIUM, (Latin,) in Gothic architecture, an arched story between the lower arches and the clere-story in the aisles, choir, and transepts of a church. An example may be seen in Westminster Abbey, where the triforium affords a communicating gallery entirely round the church.

TRIG'AMY, the state of having three husbands or three wives at the same time.

TRIG'LYPH, in architecture, a member of the Doric frieze, repeated at equal intervals.

TRIL'LO, in music, a term by which it is intimated that the performer is to beat quickly on two notes in conjoint degrees alternately one after another, beginning with the highest and ending with the lowest. It is marked with a single T as well in a vocal as in an instrumental part.

TRI'LOBITES, the name given by Cuvier to an order of Crustaceans, comprehending those remarkable fossil species in which the body is divided into three lobes by two fissures which run parallel to its axis.

TRIL'OGY, the word applied to a series of three dramas, which, although each of them is in one sense complete, yet bear a mutual relation, and form but parts of one historical and poetical picture. All the plays of Æschylus, and the *Henry VI.* of Shakspeare, are examples of a *trilogy*.

TRIN'GLE, in architecture, a little square member or ornament, fixed exactly over every triglyph, under the platband of the architrave, from whence the guttæ or pendant drops hang down.

TRINITA'RIANS, a religious order founded in 1198 under the pontificate of Innocent III. Its members devoted themselves especially to the duty of ransoming captives taken by the Moors and other infidels. Another body of Trinitarians was formed in consequence of a reformation of the order in 1578. There was also a female order of the same name, and dedicated to the same objects.

TRIN'ITY, in theology, the ineffable mystery of three persons in one God—Father, Son, and Holy Spirit.

TRIN'ITY HOUSE, a society so called in England, incorporated by Henry VIII. in 1515, for the promotion of commerce and navigation, by licensing and regulating pilots, ordering and erecting beacons, light-houses, &c. This corporation is governed by a master, four wardens, eight assistants, and thirty-one elder brothers; besides numerous inferior members of the fraternity, named younger brethren. Many valuable privileges are attached to this corporation, and its revenue amounts to about 140,000*l.* per annum.

TRI'O, in music, an instrumental piece of three obligato voices, or two chief voices and an accompanying bass, or of one chief voice and two accompanying parts.

TRIOLETT', a stanza of eight lines, in which, after the third the first line, and after the sixth the first two lines, are repeated, so that the first line is heard three times.

TRIP'LET, in music, a name given to three notes sung or played in the time of two.

TRIP'LE TIME, in music, a time consisting of three measures in a bar.

TRIPLI'CITY, in astrology, the division of the signs according to the number of the elements, each division consisting of three signs.

TRI'POD, in Grecian antiquity, the sacred seat, supported by three feet, on which the priestesses among the ancients used to deliver the oracles.

TRI'POS, at the university of Cambridge, the name given to one who prepares what is termed a *tripos paper*.—A *tripos paper*, also called a *tripos*, is a printed list of the successful candidates for mathematical honors, accompanied by a piece in Latin verse. There are two of these papers, designed to commemorate the two tripos days, or days of examination. The first contains the names of the wranglers, and senior optimes, and the second the names of the junior optimes. The word *tripos* is supposed to refer to the three-legged stool, formerly used at the examinations for these honors.

TRI'REME, in Greek and Roman antiquity, a galley with three tiers or banks of oars, in which the rowers were placed upon seats ascending gradually one above another.

TRISOLYMPON'ICA, in antiquity, one among the Greeks who returned three times victorious from the Olympic games, and on whom special honors were conferred by the state.

TRITHE'IST, in theology, one who believes that there are three distinct Gods in the Godhead, that is, three distinct substances and essences.

TRI'TONE, in music, an interval, now generally called a sharp fourth, consisting of four degrees, and containing three tones between the extremes, on which account the ancients gave it its name. It is, moreover, divisible into six semitones, three diatonic and three chromatic. In dividing the octave, we find on one side the tritone and on the other the false fifth.

TRI'TONS, in the Greek mythology, a kind of demi-gods, half man and half fish, upon whom the Nereids rode.

TRI'UMPH, in Roman antiquity, a public and solemn honor conferred by the Romans on a victorious general, by allowing him a magnificent procession through the city. The triumph was of two kinds, the greater and the less, the latter of which was called an *ovation*. The splendid spectacle was as follows: the whole senate went out to meet the victor, who, being seated in a gilded chariot, usually drawn by white horses, and clad in his triumphal robes, was followed by the kings, princes, and generals whom he had vanquished, loaded with chains. Singers and musicians preceded, followed by choice victims, and by the spoils and emblems of the conquered cities and provinces. Lastly followed the victorious army, horse and foot, crowned with laurel, and adorned with the marks of distinction they had received, shouting *Io triumphe*, and singing songs of victory, or of sportive raillery. Upon the capitol, the general rendered public thanks to the gods for the victory, caused the victims to be slaughtered, and dedicated the crown which he wore and a part of the spoils to Jupiter. All the temples were open, and all the altars loaded with offerings and incense; games and combats were celebrated in the public places; the general gave a costly feast, and the shouts of the multitude rent the air with their rejoicings.

TRIUM'PHAL ARCH, in architecture, an arch erected to perpetuate the memory of a conqueror, or of some remarkable victory or important event. At first it consisted of a single arch, decorated merely with a statue and spoils of the victorious commander; but arches were afterwards erected with two, and then with three passages. Those on the Via Triumphalis in Rome were the most magnificent; and in cases where they served as gates, they were usually constructed with two openings, so that one was appropriated for carriages passing into, and the other for carriages passing out of the city. The following is a list of some of the principal triumphal arches of antiquity: The arch at Rimini, erected in honor of Augustus on the completion of the repairs of the Flaminian Way from Rome to that city. It was one of the noblest as well as most ancient of the arches of the ancients, having a single passage about thirty-three feet wide, and was, contrary to the usual practice, crowned with a pediment. The lesser arch of Septimus Severus at Rome, commonly called the *Arch of the Goldsmiths*, is a curious example, being of a single opening, and crowned with a flat lintel. An extremely elegant arch at Susa, on the Italian side of Mont Cenis, in honor of Augustus. The arches of Aurelian and Janus, which possess more singularity than beauty.

TRIUM'VIRATE, an absolute government administered by three persons, with equal authority; as that of Augustus, Marc Antony, and Lepidus, which gave the last blow to the Roman republic; fer Augustus having vanquished Lepidus and Antony, the triumvirate was soon converted into a monarchy.

TRIUM'VIRS, (*triumviri*,) in Roman history, three men who jointly obtained the sovereign power in Rome.

TRO'CHEE, in the Greek and Latin poetry, a foot consisting of two syllables, the first long, and the second short.

TRO'CHILUS, in architecture, a name used by the ancients for a hollow ring round a column, which the moderns call *scotia.*

TROG'LODYTES, certain tribes in Ethiopia who are represented by ancient writers as living in subterranean caverns, and respecting whom we have many fabulous stories.

TROM'BONE, a deep-toned instrument of the trumpet kind, consisting of three tubes ; the first, to which the mouthpiece is attached, and the third, which terminates in a bell-shaped orifice, are placed side by side; the middle tube is doubled, and slides into the other two like the tube of a telescope. By the side of the tube, every sound in the diatonic and chromatic scales being within its compass, is obtained in perfect tune, and thus the trombone surpasses every other instrument, in admitting, like the violin or the voice, the introduction of the slide. The trombone is of three kinds, the *alto*, the *tenor*, and the *base ;* and in orchestral music, these are generally used together, forming a complete harmony in themselves.

TROOP, in cavalry, a certain number of soldiers mounted, who form a component part of a squadron. It is the same with respect to formation, as *company* in the infantry.—The word *troops* (in the plural) signifies soldiers in general, whether more or less numerous, including infantry, cavalry, and artillery.

TROPE, in rhetoric, a change in the signification of a word, from a primary to a derivative sense, a word or expression used in a different sense from that which it properly signifies ; or a word changed from its original signification to another, for the sake of giving life or emphasis to an idea; as, when we call a stupid fellow an ass, or a shrewd man a fox. Tropes are chiefly of four kinds, metaphor, metonymy, synecdoche, and irony; but to these may be added, allegory, prosopopœia, autonomasia, and perhaps some others. Some authors make figures the genus, of which trope is a species; others make them different things, defining trope to be a change of sense, and figure to be any ornament, except what becomes so by such change.

TRO'PHY, anything taken and preserved as a memorial of victory, as arms, standards, &c. taken from an enemy. It was customary with the ancients to erect their trophies on a spot where they had gained a victory. At first they consisted of the arms they had taken; but afterwards trophies were formed of bronze, marble, or even gold.—In architecture, an ornament representing the stem of a tree, charged or encompassed with military weapons.

TROUBADOURS', poets who flourished in Provence from the 10th to the 13th century. They wrote poems on love and gallantry, on the illustrious characters and remarkable events of the times, &c., which they set to music and sung: they were accordingly general favorites in different courts, diffused a taste for their language and poetry over Europe, and essentially contributed towards the restoration of letters and a love for the Arts. The royal court in Provence, at Arles, was, from the times of Boso I., for nearly two centuries, the theatre of the finest chivalry, the centre of a romantic life. The assembly of knights and Troubadours, with their Moorish story-tellers and buffoons, and ladies acting as judges or parties in matters of courtesy, exhibit a glittering picture of a mirthful, soft, and luxurious life. The knight of Provence devoted himself to the service of his lady-love in true poetic earnest, and made the dance and the sport of the tilt-yard the great business of his life. Each baron, a sovereign in his own territory, invited the neighboring knights to his castle to take parts in tournaments and to contend in song, at a time when the knights of Germany and Northern France were challenging each other to deadly combat. There the gallant knight broke his lance on the shield of his manly antagonist; there the princess sat in the circle of ladies, listening seriously to the songs of the knights, contending in rhymes respecting the laws of love, and at the close of the contest, pronouncing her sentence (*arrêt d'amour.*) Thus the life of the Provençals was lyrical in the highest degree ; but it was necessarily superficial, and would lose its chief value if unaccompanied by music. In the 11th and 12th centuries it had attained its highest bloom : it had spread into Spain and Lombardy, and even German emperors (Frederic Barbarossa,) and English kings (Richard Cœur de Lion,) composed songs in the Provençal dialect. But the poetry of the Troubadours, as in the course of time it became more common, became degraded into mere ballad-singing ; and the few specimens of it that have been preserved, consist of short war-songs and lyrics of pastoral life and love.

TRO'VER, in law, an action which lies against any one who, having the goods of another unjustly in his possession, refuses to deliver them up.

TRUCE, an agreement between states, or those representing them, for the suspension of hostilities. Such an agreement, when made by officers of the state in the general exercise of their duty, and not authorized for the purpose expressly, or by necessary implication, ranks among that class of conventions which jurists term sponsions, and which are binding only if ratified. A general armistice or truce differs from a partial, which is limited to particular places; as between two armies, or between a besieged fortress and the besieging army. The former, in general, requires ratification; power to include the latter is held to be implied in the general authority of military and naval officers.

TRUCE OF GOD, a suspension of arms, which occasionally took place in the middle ages, putting a stop to private hostilities. The right to engage in these hostilities was jealously maintained by the inferior feudatories of the several monarchies of Europe. But it was restrained by the repeated promulgation of these truces, under the authority of the church.

TRUM'PET, the loudest of all portable wind instruments, consisting of a folded tube, generally of brass.—*Speaking trumpet*, a tube, from six to fifteen feet in length, made of tin, perfectly straight and having a very large aperture; the mouth-piece being large enough to admit both lips. By means of this instrument the voice is carried, with distinctness, for a mile or more. It is chiefly used at sea.—*The feast of trumpets*, a festival among the Jews, observed on the first day of the 7th month of the sacred year, which was the first of the civil year, and answered to our September. The beginning of the year was proclaimed by sound of trumpet.

TRUST, in law, is a term commonly used to designate any equitable right or interest, as distinguished from a legal one; properly, that class of equitable rights supposed to be founded in the confidence placed by one party in another; the name *trustee* denoting the person in whom confidence is placed. The origin of conveyances in trust may be traced to the *fidei commissum* of the Romans, which was a gift by will to a person capable of taking in trust for another incapable by the Roman law of taking such benefit, whose claim under such gifts was for a long time precarious, and merely fiduciary, but came at length to be recognized and enforced by law.

TRUSTEE', in law, one to whom is confided the care of an estate, money, or business, to keep or manage for the benefit of another, either by the direction of a body of creditors or at the instance of an individual, &c., or by a legal instrument called a *deed of trust*.

TRUTH, exact accordance with that which is, has been, or shall be.—*Moral truth* consists in relating things according to the honest persuasion of our minds, and is called also veracity. Metaphysical or transcendental truth, denotes the real existence of things conformable to the ideas which we have annexed to their names.

TU'BA, a wind instrument, used by the ancient Romans, resembling our trumpet, though of a somewhat different form.

TU'DOR STYLE, in architecture, a name frequently applied to the latest

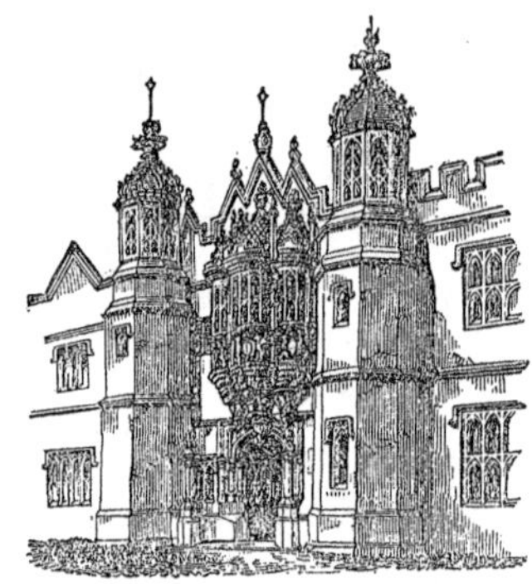

Gothic style in England, called also Florid Gothic. The period of this style is from 1400 to 1537. It is characterized by a flat arch, shallow mouldings, and a profusion of panelling on the walls.

TUES'DAY, the third day of the week, answering to the *dies Martis* of the Romans, but dedicated by the Saxons to *Tuisco*. The peculiar attribute of the deity worshipped under this name is not clearly known.

TUI'LERIES, the residence of the French monarchs, on the right bank of the Seine, in Paris. It was begun by Catharine de Medici, wife of Henry II., in 1564, and the latest additions made to it were by Napoleon, in 1808. The exterior of the Tuileries is deficient in harmony, having been built at different times, and on very different plans, but the interior is magnificent.

TU'MULUS, a barrow or mound of earth in ancient times raised to the memory of the dead. Barrows of loose stones or of dark mould and flints are very common in England; and urns containing the ashes of those who have here been buried, with spears, swords, shields, bracelets, beads, &c., are among the principal contents. We find, indeed, that these rude funeral monuments are met with in most countries.

TUNE, a short air or melody; a series of musical notes in some particular measure, and consisting of a single series, for one voice or instrument, the effect of which is melody; or a union of two or more series or parts to be sung or played in concert, the effect of which is harmony. Thus we say, a merry *tune*, a lively *tune*, a grave *tune*, a psalm *tune*, a martial *tune*.—Correct intonation in singing or playing; the state of giving the proper sounds; as when we say, a harpsichord is in *tune;* that is, when the several chords are of that tension, that each gives its proper sound, and the sounds of all are at due intervals, both of tones and semitones.

TU'NING, the art or operation of adjusting the various sounds of a musical instrument, so that they may be all at due intervals, and the scale of the instrument brought into as correct a state as possible. In tuning an instrument, the first point is to fix upon some one note as a leading note, and then by the pitch of it to determine the relative sounds of all the rest.—The art or operation of adjusting two or more musical instruments, so as to bring them into agreement with each other, as two or more violins, a violin and violoncello, &c. Horns, fifes, flutes, &c., have a permanent relative scale, and only change their pitch by change of temperature.

TU'NING-FORK, a steel instrument consisting of two prongs and a handle; used for tuning instruments, for regulating their pitch, and also the pitch of voices. There are two kinds of tuning forks in use; one of which sounds C major, and the other A minor. The first is used in tuning piano-fortes, and the second in orchestras, for the violins, &c.

TU'NIC, a garment worn within doors by the Romans of both sexes, under the toga: the slaves and common people only appearing in it abroad. The senators wore a tunic with a broad stripe of purple sewed on the breast: the equites had narrow stripes.

TUN'NEL, a subterraneous passage. Some are cut through hills to continue the lines of canals, from half a mile to two or three miles long; others are formed on the lines of railroad, where steep hills render them necessary.

TUR'BAN, a head-dress worn by most Oriental nations, of very various forms, but consisting generally of a piece of fine cloth or linen wound round a cap. The cap is red or green, roundish on the top, and quilted with cotton. The Turkish sultan's turban contains three heron's feathers, with many diamonds and other precious stones. The grand vizier has two heron's feathers; other officers but one.

TUR'BARY, in English law, the right of digging turf on another man's land.—*Common of turbary*, is the liberty which a tenant enjoys of digging turf on the lord's waste.

TURK'ISH AR'CHITECTURE, this style assimilates itself, in a great measure, to that of the Saracenic. In their public buildings they indulge, above all other things, in a great number of towers and minarets. They employ little art, on the other hand, in the construction of private houses, the lower parts of which are generally of cut stone, and the upper of bricks dried in the sun. The dwellings of the rich are surrounded by a courtyard; and in the interior is often a beautiful hall, paved with marble and adorned with fountains. This hall is ordinarily of the whole height of the building, and surmounted by a small dome.

TURN'PIKES, the name given to the toll gates on the public roads, the ancient gate being a mere pole or pike.

TUR'QUOISE, or TURK'OIS, a mineral of a beautiful sky-blue color, occurring in thin layers, or in rounded masses. It is destitute of lustre, but susceptible of a high polish, and is much used in jewellery. It contrasts well with diamonds and pearls set in gold. Some naturalists say that the turquoise is a bone impregnated with cupreous particles, and not a real stone.

TUS'CAN ORDER, in architecture, one of the five orders, and the simplest of them all. It is not found in any ancient example. Palladio has given two examples of this order, from one of which the profile here given is adopted, though by some that composed by Vignola has been preferred. The base, as will be seen on inspection, consists of a simple torus with its fillet, accompanied by a plinth. Sir William Chambers assigns to the column, with its base and capital, a height equal to seven of its diameters. Vitruvius speaks of this order with little praise, but Palladio commends it for its

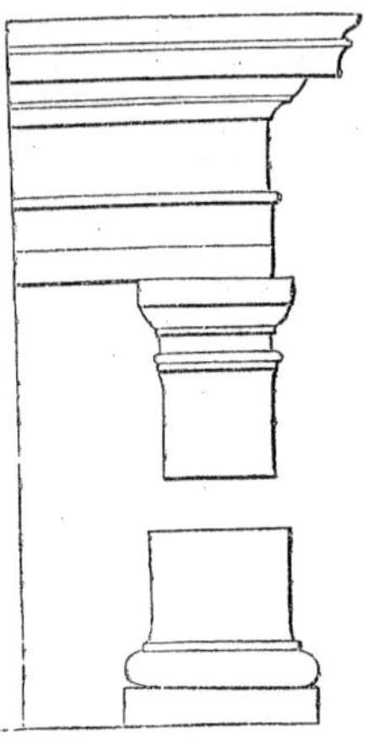

great utility. It does not allow the introduction of ornament; and it is to be observed, that its columns are never fluted. By some architects it has been varied on the shaft with rustic cinctures; but such taste is perhaps very questionable.

TUT'TO, or TUT'TI, in Italian music, a direction for all to play in full concert.

TWELFHIN'DI, among the Anglo-Saxons, men of the highest rank, who were assessed at 1200 shillings; and if any injury were done to such persons, satisfaction was to be made according to their worth.

TYM'PAN, in architecture, that part of the bottom of the pediments which is enclosed between the cornices.—In carpentry, it is applied to the pannels of doors in the same sense.—Among the Greeks and Romans, a *tympanum* was a musical instrument, not unlike the tambourine, beaten wirh the hand.

TYPE, in theology, a sign or symbol; a figure of something to come; as, the paschal lamb was a *type* of Christ. To the word in this sense is opposed *antitype;* Christ, therefore, is the *antitype.*—In natural history, *type* means a general form, such as is common to the species of a genus, or the individual of a species.

TY'PHON, the evil genius of Egyptian mythology. According to Sir G. Wilkinson they seem to have acknowledged two deities, who answered to the description given by the Greeks of Typho. "One who was the brother of Netpe, and opposed to his brother Osiris, as the bad to the good principle; the other bearing the name of Typho, and answering to that part of his character which represents him as the opponent of Horus:" the true evil genius Ombte, whom the Greeks seem to confound with Typho. "He is figured under the human form, having the head of a quadruped, with square-topped ears, which some might have supposed to represent an ass with clipped ears, if the entire animal did not too frequently occur to prevent this erroneous conclusion." In his Egyptian names is "Ombte," in which Sir G. Wilkinson thinks he traces a connection with Antœus, the son of Earth. There appears to have been a general propensity to erase his figure and titles from the monuments at some remote epoch.

TY'RANT, one who exercises arbitrary or excessive power. A monarch or other ruler who, by injustice or cruel punishment, or the demand of unreasonable services, imposes burdens and hardships on those under his control, which law does not authorize, and which are repugnant to the dictates of humanity.—The word *tyrant*, in its original signification, merely meant an *absolute* ruler; but the abuse of the office led to a different application of the word.

U.

U, the twenty-first letter and the fifth vowel of the alphabet, is generally pronounced nearly like *eu* shortened or blended; as in *annuity, enumerate, mute, duke, rule, infuse.* In some words, as in *bull, pull, full,* the sound of *u* is that of the Italian *u*, the French *ou*, but shortened. Its other sound is heard in *tun, run, rub, snub,* &c.

UBIQUITA'RIANS, in ecclesiastical history, a sect of Lutherans who sprung up in Germany about the year 1590, and maintained that the body of Jesus Christ is (*ubique*) omnipresent, or in every place at the same time.

U'KASE, in Russia, a proclamation or imperial order published.

ULE'MA, the college or corporation composed of the three classes of the Turkish hierarchy: the imans, or ministers of religion; the muftis, or doctors of law; the cadis, or administrators of justice. This organization, according to

D'Ohisson was first framed by the caliphs, and adopted, along with the other principles of their government, by the Ottoman sultans. Candidates for admission into the Ulema are educated at the different colleges (medressés) of the empire. The *Sheikh ul Islam*, or mufti of Constantinople, is the president of the whole body.

ULTIMA'TUM, (from *ultimus*, last,) in modern diplomacy, the final conditions offered for the settlement of a dispute, or the basis of a treaty, between two governments. The word is also used for any final proposition or condition.

UL'TRA, a prefix to certain words in modern politics, to denote those members of a party who carry their notions to excess. In 1793, those persons in France were called *ultra-revolutionists*, who demanded much more than the constitution they adopted allowed. When the Bourbons returned to France in 1815, the words *ultra-royalists* and *ultra-liberals* were much used, and have become common wherever political parties exist.

ULTRAMARINE', in painting, a valuable pigment affording a beautiful sky-blue color.—Its name *ultramarine* is derived from being brought from beyond sea, that is to say, from Hindostan and Persia, and it was originally obtained only from the rare mineral *lapis lazuli*.—*Ultramarine ashes*, a pigment which is the residuum of lapis lazuli, after the ultramarine has been extracted.

ULTRAMON'TANE, an epithet applied to countries which lie beyond the mountain: thus France, with regard to Italy, is an ultramontane country.

UM'BER, in painting, a pigment affording a fine dark-brown color. It is a dusky-colored earth, or ore, and was formerly brought from *Umbria*, in Italy. It is used in two states; the first its natural one, with the simple precaution of levigation, or washing; the second, that in which it is found after being burnt. The hues of burnt and unburnt umber greatly differ from each other.

UN, in philology, a particle of negation, giving to words to which it is prefixed a negative signification. *Un* and *in* were formerly used indifferently for this purpose; but the tendency of modern usage is to prefer the use of *in*, in some words, where *un* was before used. It is prefixed generally to adjectives and participles, but sometimes also to verbs, as in *unbend*, *unbind*, &c.

U'NA VO'CE, (Latin,) with one voice; unanimously.

UNBELIEF', in the sense used in the New Testament, signifies a disbelief of the truth of the gospel, and a distrust of God's promises, &c.

UN'CIAL, pertaining to letters of a large size, used in ancient manuscripts.

UNC'TION, the anointing with consecrated oil, a practice among the Jews in consecrating kings and priests; also still in use at coronations: and is one of the seven sacraments of the Catholic church. It is performed, in cases of mortal disease, by anointing the head, hands, and feet with oil consecrated by the bishop, and accompanied with prayers. The anointing of persons who are on their death-bed is called *extreme unction*.

UNDERSTAND'ING, the intellectual faculty, or that faculty of the human mind by which it apprehends the real state of things presented to it, or by which it receives or comprehends the ideas which others express and intend to communicate.

UNDERWRI'TER, one who undersigns a policy of insurance on a ship or its cargo, at a certain rate per cent.

UNDINES', or ONDINES, the name given by the Cabalists to one class of their spirits of the elements, namely, those residing in the waters. The ancient Greeks believed springs and lakes to be haunted by a peculiar race of supernatural nymphs, and this belief passed down unimpaired to the middle ages. The ancient Saxons adored the female deity of the Elbe; and the belief in undines is still scarcely eradicated in that region. The Saxon peasants report that an undine is often met in the market-place of Magdeburg, dressed as a girl of their own class, but always to be known by having one corner of her apron wet. Near Toulouse many objects of value were once discovered on draining a large artificial lake, which are supposed to have been thrown in as offerings to the spirits of the water. The *nixe* of the northern countries is of the same family, and the Scottish *kelpies* are creatures of a similar superstition.

UNIFORM'ITY, ACT OF, the act of the English parliament by which the form of public prayers, administration of sacraments and other rites, is prescribed to be observed in all the churches.

UN'ION, or *Act of Union*, in politics, the act by which Scotland was united to England, or by which the two kingdoms were incorporated into one, in 1707. Also, the legislative union of Great Britain and Ireland, in 1801.—The United States are also called *the Union.*—Among painters, *union* denotes a symmetry and agreement between the several parts of a painting.—In architecture, harmony between the colors in the materials of a building.—In ecclesiastical affairs, the combining or consolidating of two or more churches into one.

U'NISON, in music, a coincidence or agreement of sounds, proceeding from an equality in the number of vibrations made in a given time by a sonorous body. Unison consists in sameness of degree, or similarity in respect to gravity or acuteness, and is applicable to any sound, whether of instruments or of the human organs, &c.

UNITA'RIAN, a name used to designate a religious denomination who hold to the personal unity of God, in opposition to the doctrine of the Unitarian faith. They profess to derive their views from Scripture, and to make it the ultimate arbiter in all religious questions, thus distinguishing themselves from the Rationalists (otherwise called the *Anti-supernaturalists*) of Germany. They undertake to show that, interpreted according to the settled laws of language, the uniform testimony of the sacred writings is, that the Holy Spirit has no personal existence distinct from the Father, and that the Son is a derived and dependent being, whether as some believe, created in some remote period of time, or, as others, beginning to live when he appeared on earth. Three of the passages of the New Testament, which have been relied on to prove the contrary, (1 John v. 7; 1 Tim. iii. 16; and Acts xx. 28,) they hold, with other critics, to be spurious. Others (as John i. 1, &c.; Romans ix. 5,) they maintain to have received an erroneous interpretation. They insist that ecclesiastical history enables them to trace to obsolete systems of heathen philosophy the introduction of the received doctrine into the church, in which, once received, it has been sustained on grounds independent of its merits; and they go so far as to aver that it is satisfactorily refuted by the biblical passages, when rightly understood, which are customarily adduced in its support. The principal Unitarian authorities are Dr. Priestley and Mr. Belsham, who were among the most active teachers of the doctrine in Great Britain, and Dr. William E. Channing in this country, whose writings on the subject have been widely circulated. In the United States, the Unitarian doctrine has prevailed to a considerable extent among the Congregationalists of New England, and is said to number about two hundred and fifty churches in connection with that body.

U'NITIES, in the drama, are three—of time, place, and action. The latter only is strictly adhered to in the dramatic compositions of classical antiquity; but what is termed by moderns the *classical* drama (in opposition to the *romantic*) requires all three.

U'NITY, the state of being one; oneness. *Unity* may consist of a simple substance or existing being, as the soul; but usually it consists in a close junction of particles or parts, constituting a body detached from other bodies. *Unity* is a thing undivided itself, but separate from every other thing.—In poetry, the principle by which a uniform tenor of story and propriety of representation is preserved. In the Greek drama, the three unities required were those of *action*, of *time*, and of *place*; in other words, that there should be but one main plot; that the time supposed should not exceed twenty-four hours, and that the place of the action before the spectators should be one and the same throughout the piece. In the epic poem, the great and almost only *unity* is that of action.—In music, such a combination of parts as to constitute a whole, or a kind of symmetry of style and character.—In all the arts, the correspondence of the various parts of a work, so that they may form one harmonious whole. Unity is indispensable in every work of art.—In law, the properties of a joint estate are derived from its *unity*, which is fourfold; unity of *interest*, unity of *title*, unity of *time*, and unity of *possession*; in other words, joint-tenants have one and the same interest, accruing by one and the same conveyance, commencing at the same time, and held by one and the same undivided possession. Unity of possession is a joint possession of two rights by several titles, as when a man has a lease of land upon a certain rent, and afterwards buys the fee simple. This is a *unity* of possession, by which the lease is extinguished.—*Unity of faith*, is an equal belief of the same truths of God, and possession of the grace of faith in like form and degree.—*Unity of spirit*, is the oneness which subsists between Christ and his saints, by which the same spirit dwells in both, and both have the same disposition and aims; and it is the oneness of Christians among themselves, united under the same head, having the same spirit dwelling in them, and possessing the same graces, faith, love, hope, &c.

UNIVER'SALISTS, those Christians who believe in the final salvation of all men, in opposition to the doctrine of eternal punishment. There is, however, a great difference of opinion, in regard to the future state, among those who are called Universalists: some believe in a remedial punishment of limited duration, which will end in a universal restoration to goodness and happiness; others believe that all men will be happy after the dissolution of the body, but in different degrees until the resurrection; and yet others hold that the future state of all will be alike perfect and happy immediately after death. This denomination has made great progress within a few years in the United States, and numbers about 1200 churches.

UNIVERSAL'ITY, in painting. This quality, though impossible, strictly speaking, to be attained by any individual, should, in a modified sense, be acquired by the artist who enters for fame in the hazardous lists of historical painting. According to the subject which he has to treat, it is requisite that he should know well how to represent both landscape and architecture. He will occasionally find himself obliged to introduce the figures of horses, dogs, tigers, lions, serpents, &c. Warlike arms, utensils devoted to sacred ceremonies, whether ancient or modern, groups of cattle, human figures —in short, almost every object which is susceptible of exhibition on canvass may be regarded as likely to fall in his way, and to demand a faithful delineation. The ancient artists, it is true, mostly disclaimed this *universality;* with them the sole object frequently was, to paint with exactness and expression the human form: but modern art has exploded their exclusive system; and requires at the hand of the painter of history an acquaintance with the extensive range to which we have alluded.

U'NIVERSE, the collective name of heaven and earth: or totality of space, and all its material contents and phenomena, of whose boundless extent and smallest parts finite beings can have no just idea; but, as far as we can discover, it is filled with an ethereal fluid, in which masses of matter are equally disposed throughout space, which masses, like our sun, act as centres of motion, excite luminosity, and transfer motion and momenta to subordinate spheres, like our earth, each centre being millions of millions of miles distant from the others.

UNIVER'SITY, a name applied to an establishment for a liberal education, wherein professors in the several branches of science and polite literature are maintained, and where degrees or honors attached to the attainments of scholars, are conferred. Such an establishment is called a *university* or *universal school,* as intended to embrace the whole compass of study. The universities of Great Britain are seated at Oxford, Cambridge, St. Andrew's, Glasgow, Aberdeen, and Edinburgh. They are governed by chancellors, vice-chancellors, proctors, and beadles; and every college has its master and tutors; there are also public lectures of professors in every established branch of knowledge. The students and all the members wear an ancient costume consisting of trencher-caps and gowns, varied according to their degrees, which are bachelors of arts, divinity, law, music, medicine; masters of arts, and doctors of divinity, law, and physic. The London University and King's College, are two collegiate establishments in the metropolis, of recent foundation, which may probably be the precursors of others. Universities in their present form, and with their present privileges, are institutions comparatively modern. They sprang from the convents of regular clergy or from the chapters of cathedrals in the church of Rome, where young men were educated for holy orders, in that dark period when the clergy possessed all the little erudition which was left in Europe. Probably in every town in Europe where there is now a university, which has any claim to be called ancient, these convents were seminaries of learning from their first institution; for it was not till the more eminent of the laity began to see the importance of literature and science, that universities distinct from convents were founded, with the privilege of admitting to degrees, which conferred some rank in civil society. These universities have long been considered as lay corporations; but as a proof that they had this kind of ecclesiastical origin, it will be sufficient to observe, that the pope arrogated to himself the right of vesting them with all their privileges; and that, prior to the Reformation, every university in Europe conferred its degrees in all the faculties by authority derived from a papal bull. The most ancient universities in Europe are those of Oxford, Cambridge, Paris, Salamanca, and Bologna; and in the two English universities, the first-founded colleges are those of University, Baliol, and Merton, in the former, and St. Peter's in the latter. Oxford and Cambridge however, were universities, or, as they were then called, studies, some hundreds of years before colleges or schools were built in them; for the former flourished as a seminary of learning in the reign of Alfred the Great, and the other, if we may credit its partial historians, at a period still earlier. The universities of Scotland are four, St. Andrews, Glasgow, Aberdeen, and Edinburgh. In Ireland there is but one university, viz., that of Dublin, founded by Queen Elizabeth, and very richly endowed. The University of Oxford, in England, is an establishment for the purposes of education, which corresponds to a federal body united for political purposes. As, in this latter case, the several states have separate jurisdictions, separate duties, and to a certain extent separate interests, so the several colleges and halls which compose the academical body, have each its own private regulations for the education of its members, but all contribute to the university education. This may be brought under the heads of public examinations and college preparation. In its early constitution, and in the gradual additions which for many ages were made to it, the system now followed in the German universities was kept in view, and professorships or readerships in the different arts and sciences were established; but these university officers are no longer the main sources of instruction. The demand for instruction created by the degree examination, is met almost exclusively by lectures delivered in the several colleges and halls, or rather, by private tutors in the colleges and halls; so exclusively indeed, that, although some knowledge of Greek is essential for a degree, and a considerable proficiency for the higher class degrees, the Greek professor has no lectures. What is actually required for a degree of bachelor of arts is, that the student should display some acquaintance with the facts and doctrines of the Christian religion, and especially with the peculiar tenets of the church of England, as set forth in its articles; some proficiency in the Greek and Latin languages, in one or more of the ancient philosophical treatises, or, in lieu of this, in a portion of ancient history; some knowledge also, either of the elements of logic or of the elements of geometry. The statute, however, contemplates the probability of a much higher standard of qualification in a portion of the students; and for these it provides honors additional to that of a mere degree. Their names are printed, arranged in four classes, according to a fixed standard of merit for each class. The candidate is permitted to name the book in which he wishes to be examined: and the examiners are, besides, at liberty to examine in any books which they may select. The mathematical examinations are conducted principally by means of printed questions, answered in writing. A candidate for the first class may be stated generally to have acquired a knowledge of, 1. the elements of analytical geometry and trigonometry; 2. the differential and integral calculus and its applications; 3. mechanics, including the principles of its application to the solar system, embracing the substance of the three first sections of Newton's *Principia*, which are also read in the original forms; 4. the principles of hydrostatics, optics, and plane astronomy. The examinations take place twice a year. Prizes are given for the encouragement of compositions in prose and verse, in Latin and English. There are also public scholarships, which operate as rewards and encouragements of general proficiency or particular acquirements. These include classical literature, mathematics, Hebrew, and the law. The university also affords facilities for the acquirement of various branches which do not enter into the qualifications for a degree. Thus the several professors of geology, chemistry, and many other branches of science, are always provided with classes, often with numerous ones. We now proceed to the college preparation for the public examinations. It is this that really constitutes the Oxford education. The process of instruction in the college is by no means of recitations. Every head of a house appoints a certain number of tutors for this purpose. Questions are put by the tutor, and remarks made by him on the book which is the subject of study. He also gives directions respecting the proper mode of studying. The students usually attend two, three, or four tutors, why thus give instruction in different branches. The college tutor, moreover, has interviews, from time to time, with his pupils, separately, for the sake of ascertaining the individual's state of preparation for the public examination, assisting him in his difficulties, &c. Besides these college tutors, however, there are private tutors, who superintend the studies of individuals, and prepare them for attendance on the exercises of the college tutors. These private tutors are particularly useful to that large class of students who come to college insufficiently prepared. The college instruction closes at the end of each term, with a formal examination of each member separately, by the head and tutors, who attend for this purpose. This summing up of the business of the term is called, in the technical language of the place, *collections* or *terminals*. Each student presents himself in turn, with the books in which he has received instruction during the term, and, in many colleges, with the essays and other exercises which he has written, his analyses of scientific works, abridgments of histories and the like. In some colleges the students are required to present, for their examination, some book also, in which they have not received instruction during the term. Besides the other studies pursued in the colleges, the students write weekly short essays on a given subject, occasionally interchanged with a copy of Latin verses, for those skilled in versification. The liberality of donors has enabled the colleges to provide indirectly for the promotion of study by means of exhibitions, scholarships, and fellowships. Every college and hall examines, if it thinks fit, its own candidates for admission, and pronounces, each according to a standard of its own, on their fitness or unfitness for the university. The first universities founded in Germany were those of Prague, 1348, and Vienna, 1365, both after the model of that of Paris: in both the division into four nations was adopted. This circumstance caused the decline of the former, and the foundation of a new one. The emperor Charles IV. had divided the teachers and students, when the university of Prague was founded, into the Bohemian, Polish, Bavarian, and Saxon nations. The Germans, therefore, (as the Polish nation consisted chiefly of German Silesians,) had the advantage over the Bohemians; and, as these were unwilling to suffer their oppressions, John Huss and Jerome of Prague induced the emperor Wenceslaus to make three nations of the Bohemian and one of the two German. Several thousand students and teachers withdrew immediately, and gave rise to the university of Leipsic, in 1409, where they were divided into four nations, the Misnian, Saxon, Bavarian, and Polish. None of the other German universities, founded in the fifteenth century, adopted the division into nations. Universities were now expressly established, and not left to grow up of themselves, as before. For almost three centuries, the popes continued to erect these institutions, and exercised the right of protecting and of superintending them. Monarchs who wished to establish a university, requested the papal confirmation (which never was denied,) and submitted to the authority which the Roman see arrogated over them. Wittenberg was the first German university which received its confirmation (in 1502,) not from the pope, but from the German emperor; but even this institution eventually requested the papal confirmation. Marburg was established in 1525, without papal or imperial confirmation: the latter, however, was subsequently given. Even Göttingen, founded in 1734, obtained imperial privileges, after the model of those of Halle. The unhappy thirty year's war did much injury to the German universities; but since that period, they have advanced beyond those of any other country; and it may be said that the principal part of the liberty left to the Germans has been academical liberty; hence, also, their abuse of it; hence, too, the fondness with which a German recalls his life at the university; and hence the students' jealousy of their privileges. Germany has more universities than any other country. The general organization of a German university is as follows:—A number of *professores ordinarii* are appointed for the various branches. They divide themselves into four *faculties*, each having a dean annually chosen by themselves from among their number. All these professors generally form the senate, at the head of which is the rector, who is chosen annually. They have jurisdiction over the students, in regard to small offences and matters of police, and make the general provisions respecting instruction, with the consent of the government. Professors in most universities are appointed by the government. Besides these professors, there are an indefinite number of *professores extraordinarii*, for the same branches, or for particular parts of them. They receive small salaries, and are the persons to whom the government look to fill vacancies. They are generally persons who have distinguished themselves, and whose talents the government wishes to secure. In Berlin, there are a great many of these extraordinary professors. The last class of lecturers are the *docentes*, or licentiates, who, after undergoing an examination, have obtained permission to teach (*licentia docendi*.) They receive no salary. Any person can request to be examined by the faculty in this way, and thus capacitate himself to teach. From them the *professores extraordinarii* are ordinarily taken. Every person in these three classes can lecture upon whatever subject he may choose, the professors being only obliged to deliver lectures also on the branches for which they are particularly appointed. Thus we constantly find theologians lecture on politics, philosophers on theological subjects and statistics; theologians on philology, &c. Very often three or four courses are delivered on the same subject. The German student, in the Protestant universities, is left at full liberty to choose the lectures which he will attend. No official examination takes place during his term of study. The only regulation is that, in the case of most sciences, he is required to attend certain lectures, and study full three years, if he wishes to obtain an appointment, practise a profession, &c., if he is not specially exempted from so doing. If he wishes to practise medicine, he must study in Prussia four years. The German student usually divides his term of study among two or more universities; but whilst he is thus left almost at full liberty while at the university, he must go through a severe examination, particularly in Prussia, if he wishes to become a clergyman, statesman, practise as physican, lawyer, or teacher in a superior school. These examinations are both oral and in writing, and the successive steps of promotion are attended with new examinations. In the United States, the word university has been applied to Harvard College at Cambridge, and other smaller literary institutions, but not with exact propriety, as those seminaries are usually devoted to the elementary studies of an academical course.

URA'NIA, in Grecian mythology, the muse of astronomy. She is generally represented with a crown of stars, in a garment spotted with stars, and holding in her left hand a celestial globe or a lyre. *Urania* is likewise the name of the heavenly Venus, or of pure intellectual love. One of the Oceanides, or sea-nymphs, was also called Urania.

U'RIM, the Urim and Thummim, among the Israelites, signify lights and perfections. These were a kind of ornament belonging to the habit of the high priest, in virtue of which he gave oracular answers to the people; but what they were has not been satisfactorily ascertained.

URN, in antiquity, a kind of vase of a roundish form, but largest in the middle, destined to receive the ashes of the dead. The substances employed in the construction of these vessels were numerous. Amongst them are gold, bronze, glass, terra cotta, marble, and porphyry. Many have been discovered bearing inscriptions; others with the name only of the party to whose remains they were devoted.—It was also customary with the Romans to put the names of those who were to engage at the public games, into *urns*, taking them in the order in which they were drawn out. Into such a vessel also they threw the notes of their votes at the elections.—The urn (*urna*) was also a Roman measure for liquids, containing about three gallons and a half, wine measure. It was half the *amphora*.

UR'SULINES, or *Nuns of St. Ursula*, a sisterhood founded by St. Angela of Brescia, in 1537, at first without being bound to the rules of the monastic life, but devoting themselves merely to the practice of Christian charity and the education of children. Many governments, which abolished convents in general, protected the Ursulines on account of their useful labors, particularly in the practice of attending on the sick, and administering to their cure and their comforts.

U'SANCE, in commerce, the time fixed for the payment of bills of exchange, reckoned either from the day on which the bill is accepted, or from that of its date, varying in different countries, and thus called, because wholly dependent on *usage*.

USH'ER, literally a "door-keeper;" being derived from the French "huissier." In Britain, *usher* is the name given to several public officers, in which sense it seems to be synonymous with sergeant. These ushers are in waiting, introduce strangers, and execute orders. Usher is also used as the denomination of an assistant to a school-master; where it seems to refer to his office of introducing the scholars to learning.

USTRI'NUM, in Roman antiquities, a public burning-place, enclosed by walls, in which bodies, mostly of the poorer sort of people, were consumed. An ustrinum, according to Montfauçon, was square, and in compass about 300 feet.

USUCAP'TION, in the civil law, the acquisition of the title or right to property by the undisputed possession and enjoyment of it for a certain term prescribed by law.

U'SUFRUCT, in the civil law, the temporary use or enjoyment of lands or tenements; or the right of receiving the fruits and profits of an inheritance, without a power of alienating the property.

U'SURY, a compensation or reward for money lent. In this sense it is merely equivalent to *interest*. In the common business of life, however, it rarely has this signification; but is chiefly used in an odious sense, to express an exorbitant or illegal compensation for money lent, in contradistinction to legal interest.

UTILITA'RIANS, a name which has been given to a particular sect of modern politicians; those, namely, who profess to try the excellence of modes of government and usages simply by their utility. The celebrated Jeremy Bentham, regarded as the founder of this sect, introduced into the critical department of politics a closer logic than had been commonly applied to it; and aimed at applying his famous principle, "the greatest happiness of the greatest number," as an immediate test by which to affirm or deny the value of institutions. It is evident that all political sects, both of writers and statesmen, profess ultimately the same object. The real characteristic of the Utilitarians consists in the peculiar sense in which they understand it. They confine for the most part the proposed utility, so as to restrict it to that which is useful for the material and economical well-being of the multitude.

UTI POSSIDE'TIS, in politics, a treaty which leaves belligerent parties mutually in possession of what they have acquired by their arms during the war is said to be based on the principle of *uti possidetis* —"as you possess."

UTO'PIA, a term invented by Sir T. More, and applied in his celebrated work called *Utopia* to an imaginary island, which he represents to have been discovered by a companion of Amerigo Vespucci, and as enjoying the utmost perfection in laws, politics, &c., in contradistinction to the defects of those which then existed. The work was first printed in 1516, but Froben's edition, of 1518, is more correct. The word *Utopia* has now passed into all the languages of Europe to signify a state of ideal perfection; and *Utopian* is used synonymously with *fanciful* or *chimerical*.

V.

V, the twenty-second letter of the alphabet, is a labial articulation, nearly allied to *f*, being formed by the same organs; but *v* is vocal, and *f* is aspirate, and this constitutes the principal difference between them. V has one sound only, as in *vain*, *very*, *vote*, *vanity*. Though *v* and *u* have as distinct uses as any two letters in the alphabet, they were formerly considered as one letter; and in some encyclopædias and dictionaries the absurd practice of arranging the words which begin with these letters is still continued. As a numeral, V stands for 5; and with a dash over it, in old books, for 5000.

VA, in music, Italian for "go on," as *va crescendo*, go on increasing.

VACA'TION, in law, the period between the end of one term and the beginning of another: and the same in the universities.

VA'DE IN PACE, (Lat. *go in peace.*) In monastic communities offences were sometimes punished by the dreadful infliction of starving to death in prison; and bones have been occasionally found among the ruins of convents of victims who appear to have perished in this manner. The punishment acquired this name from the words in which the sentence was pronounced. The use which Walter Scott has made of this custom in his poem of *Marmion* is well known. But it is no romantic fiction.

VA'DE-MECUM (from the Latin, signifying *Go with me*,) a favorite book or other thing that a person constantly carries with him.

VA'GRANT, in law, the word *vagrant* has a much more extended meaning than that assigned to it in ordinary language, and in its application the notion of wandering is almost lost. By the law vagrants are divided into three classes—idle and disorderly persons; rogues and vagabonds; incorrigible rogues. Under the first class are included, every person who refuses or neglects to maintain himself and family, he being able to do so; paupers returning without certificate to parishes from which they have been legally removed; pedlars without license, beggars, common prostitutes, &c. Under the second class, are included every person committing any offence which would constitute him an idle or disorderly person, and who has been once already convicted, fortune tellers, and other impostors; persons guilty of indecent exhibitions; persons collecting alms or money under false pretences; wanderers who have no visible means of subsistence, and cannot give a good account of themselves; persons playing at games of chance in public places; reputed thieves; persons having in their possession housebreaking implements or offensive weapons with intent to use them. Under the third class are included persons guilty of the last class of offences, having been already convicted; persons breaking out of legal confinement; every person apprehended as a rogue and vagabond, and violently resisting any constable or other peace officer, so apprehending him. For all these offences the punishment is imprisonment or hard labor for a longer or shorter period, according to the nature of the particular offence. In Scotland, the laws against vagrants, as beggars, fortune tellers, jugglers, minstrels, &c., are of a much less stringent nature, and such persons are seldom apprehended or punished, unless where police regulations are enforced, or where they are entering a parish in the face of an advertised prohibition, or where they are committing or in the notorious habit of committing petty delinquencies.

VAL'ENTINE'S DAY, the 14th of February, a festival in the calendar in honor of St. Valentine, who suffered martyrdom in the reign of the emperor Claudius. He was eminently distinguished for his love and charity; and the custom of choosing valentines, or special loving friends, on this day, is by some supposed to have thence originated. The following solution is, however, the more probable one. It was the practice in ancient Rome, during a great part of the month of February, to celebrate the Lupercalia, which were feasts in honor of Pan and Juno, whence the latter deity was named Februata, or Februalis. On this occasion, amidst a variety of ceremonies, the names of young women were put into a box, from which they were drawn by the men, as chance directed. The pastors of the early Christian church, who by every possible means endeavored to eradicate the vestiges of pagan superstitions, and chiefly by some commutations of their forms, substituted, in the present instance, the names of particular saints, instead of those of the women; and as the festival of the Lupercalia had commenced about the middle of February, they appear to have chosen Valentine's-day for celebrating the new feast, because it occurred nearly at the same time.

VAL'ET, originally, the sons of knights, and afterwards those of the nobility before they had attained the age of chivalry. The name is sometimes written *vasletus*, and seems to be derived from the same root with vassal; probably the Celtic gwâs. Valet in French, and varlet in English, degenerated in later times into the signification of servant.

VALHAL'LA, the palace of immortality, in the Scandinavian mythology, inhabited by the souls of heroes slain in battle.

VALKY'RIUR, the Fates of the Scandinavian mythology: the "choosers of the slain," who conduct heroes killed in battle to Valhalla.

VALLA'RIS CORO'NA, in antiquity, a golden crown which the Roman generals bestowed on him who, in attacking the enemy's camp, first broke in upon the lines or pallisades. It was also called *Corona castrensis*.

VAL'LUM, among the Romans, was the parapet which fortified their encampments.

VALO'REM, or AD VALOREM, according to the value; as, an *ad valorem* duty.

VAL'UE, in commerce, the price or worth of any purchasable commodity. The intrinsic value denotes the real and effective worth of a thing, and is used chiefly with regard to money, the popular value of which may be raised or lowered, but its real or intrinsic value, depending wholly on its weight and purity, is not at all thereby affected.—The value of commodities is regulated principally by the comparative facility of their production, and partly on the relation of the supply and demand. But many other causes operate to raise or depreciate the value of an article; as monopolies, fashion, new inventions, the opening of new markets, or the stoppage of commercial intercourse through war, &c. And, in fact, in all countries where merchants are possessed of large capitals, and where they are left to be guided in the use of them by their own discretion and foresight, the prices of commodities will frequently be very much influenced, not merely by the actual occurrence of changes in the accustomed relation of the supply and demand, but by the mere anticipation of them.—*Value*, in another sense, denotes those properties in a thing which render it useful or estimable: thus, for instance, the *real* or *intrinsic* value of iron is far greater than that of gold.

VAM'PLET, in archæology, a piece of steel, formed like a funnel, placed on tilting spears just before the hand to secure it, but which might be taken off at pleasure.

VAN'DALS, a ferocious race, who, it is believed, were either a Sclavonic tribe, or came from the north of Germany, between the Elbe and the Vistula. During the 4th and 5th centuries they became very powerful, and, under Genseric, their king, overran Spain, Gaul, and Italy. They subsequently established themselves in Africa; but were eventually subdued by Belisarius, the celebrated Roman general in the reign of Justinian, who took their king, Gelimer, prisoner, and carried him to Constantinople in triumph. From the ferocity of their character, and the havoc they made of the finest works of art, the words *Vandalism* and *Vandalic* have been applied to such acts as imply a rude and savage ferocity combined with a disregard of the advantages of civilization.

VA'RIANCE, in law, a difference of statement between two material documents in a cause; as where the plaintiff's declaration differed (formerly) from the writ, or where it differs from a deed on which it is grounded. And, in ordinary language, a departure in the oral evidence from the statement in the pleadings is termed a variance. This variance may be either immaterial or material; and, in the latter case, amendable or not, according to a great variety of distinctions.—*Variation*, in music, the different manner of playing or singing the same air or tune, by subdividing the notes into several others of less value, or by adding graces, &c., yet so that the tune itself may be discovered through all its embellishments.—In grammar, change of termination of nouns and adjectives, constituting what is called case, number, and gender.

VARIO'RUM EDITIONS, in literature, editions of the Greek and Roman classics, in which the notes of different commentators are inserted.

VARRO'NIAN SATIRE, a species of satire so called from the learned Varro, who first composed it. The style was free and unconfined, containing both prose and verse intermixed according to the fancy of the writer.

VAR'TABED, one of an order of ecclesiastics in the Armenian church. They differ from the priests by living in seclusion and celibacy. They also preach, while the priests do not.

VARU'NA, in Hindoo mythology, the god of the waters, the Indian Neptune, and the regent of the west division of the earth. He is represented as a white man, four-armed, riding on a sea animal, with a rope in one of his hands, and a club in another.

VASE, in architecture, an ornament placed on cornices, socles, or pediments, representing such vessels as the ancients used in sacrifices, &c. The Grecian artists gave to every vase the shape best adapted to its use, and most agreeable to the eye. A great number of these vessels have been preserved to the present day, and offer to artists models of the most beautiful forms.—Among florists, the calyx of a plant, as the tulip, is called a *vase*.

VAT'ICAN, the ancient palace of the popes, and the most magnificent in the world, stands at Rome on the right bank of the Tiber, and on the hill anciently called by the same name; derived, according to Aulus Gellius, from Vaticinium, or rather from an ancient oracular deity of the Latins, called by the Romans Jupiter Vaticanus, who was worshipped there. Some say that Pope Symmachus began the construction of the palace. It was inhabited by Charlemagne in 800; and the present irregular edifice has been raised by the gradual additions of a long series of pontiffs. Its extent is enormous, the number of rooms, at the lowest computation, amounting to 4422; and its riches in marbles, bronzes, and frescoes, in ancient statues and gems, and in paintings, are unequalled in the world; not to mention its library, the richest in Europe in manuscripts. The length of the museum of statues alone is computed to be a mile: here are the Sistine Chapel; the Camere of Raphael, painted by himself and pupils; the Museum of Pius VI., peculiarly rich in objects of ancient Italian workmanship; and other deposits of art and antiquity, each of which by itself would suffice to render a city illustrious.

VAU'DEVILLE, in French poetry, a species of light song, frequently of a satirical turn, consisting of several couplets and a refrain or burden, introduced into theatrical pieces. The origin of the word is disputed; some derive it from Vau-de-vire, a village in Normandy. Short comic pieces interspersed with such songs are also termed Vaudevilles.

VAU'DOIS, the inhabitants of some valleys in the Alps between Italy and Provence, from whence they derive their name; and who must be distinguished from the Waldenses, or followers of Peter Waldo, who acquired celebrity in the 12th century, and from whom some writers have deduced both their religious tenets and their appellation also. The Vaudois are celebrated for having maintained the purity of their doctrine for many ages before the Reformation; and it has been asserted by some theologians that the true spirit of the primitive Christianity was kept alive among them throughout the whole period of Romish corruption. This position, however, does not seem susceptible of proof. Another claim that they possess to a place in ecclesiastical history, is derived from the numerous persecutions to which they have been exposed on account of the witness they have so long borne against the erroneous doctrines of the nations by whom they are surrounded. Their extreme antiquity is certain at all events; and the numerous attempts which have been made by Romanist writers to fix on them the stigma of Manicheism seem unsupported by the evidence. For the last three centuries they have been viewed with displeasure by the dukes of Savoy and the kings of Sardinia, their masters, and repeatedly visited with military execution, or more legal forms of violence. One great persecution, in the 17th century, is known to us by Milton's noble sonnet.

VAULT, in architecture, a continued arch, or an arched roof, so constructed that the stones, bricks, or other material

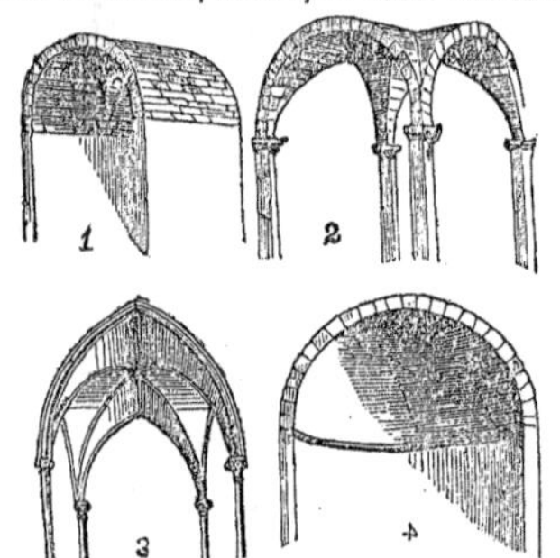

of which it is composed, sustain and keep each other in their places. Vaults are of various kinds, cylindrical, elliptical, single, double, cross, diogonal, Gothic, &c. When a vault is of greater height than half its span, it is said to be *surmounted*, and when of less height, *surbased*. A *rampant vault* is one which springs from planes not parallel to the horizon. One vault placed above another constitutes a *double vault*. A *conic vault* is formed of part of the surface of a cone, and a *spherical vault* of part of the surface of a sphere, as fig. 4. A vault is *simple*, as figs. 1 and 4, when it is formed by the surface of some regular solid, around one axis; and *compound*, as figs. 2 and 3, when compounded of more than one surface of the same solid, or of two different solids. A *groined vault*, fig. 3, is a compound vault, rising to the same height in its surfaces as that of two equal cylinders, or a cylinder with a cylindroid.

VAV'ASOR, an ancient title of nobility in England, said by Camden to be next below a baron.

VEA'DER, the 13th month of the Jewish ecclesiastical year.

VE'DA, the name by which the Hindoos designate the collective body of their Scriptures; sometimes called Vedam, Bedam, &c., according to various provincial pronunciations, by European writers. The four Vedas (Rig, Yajust, Saman, and Atharvan,) are believed, according to the orthodox creed, to have been revealed by Brahma. But the subdivisions are infinite, as are also the connected works—Upavedas, Angas, Upangas, &c.; some of which are considered by Mr. Colebrooke to constitute, according to received opinion, a fifth Veda. The arrangement is ascribed to one Vyasa, a sage of whom nothing positive can be ascertained. The Vedas chiefly consist of prayers, precepts or maxims, and stories; called respectively by different titles. Thus a portion of the mythological histories are called Puranas; but these are not to be confounded with the poems of romantic mythology called by the same name. The genuineness and antiquity of the Vedas have been matter of much dispute among western antiquaries. The chief chronological data are, that they were compiled before the supposed incarnation of Vishnu, as Rama and Kirshna, under which titles he is now so commonly worshipped among the Hindoos; and also before the appearance of Buddha. Sir William Jones gave them a conjectural antiquity of about 3000 years; and Mr. Colebrooke arrives at about the same conclusion.

VEDAN'TA, a sect among the Hindoos, whose theory of philosophy is professedly founded on the revelations contained in the Vedas. Its fundamental tenets appear to have a near connection with the opinions of Epicharmus, Plato, Pyrrho, and what is termed the Berkelian philosophy among ourselves: namely, that matter has no existence independent of mental perception; with the ordinary consequences of that doctrine, of which those practically most important are the maxims of Quietism.

VEDET'TE, in military affairs, a sentinel on horseback detached from the main body of the army, to discover and give notice of the enemy's movements.

VEHM'IC COURTS, criminal courts of justice, established in Germany during the middle ages. These courts are commonly said to have originated in those held by the Missi Dominici, or imperial legates, sent by Charlemagne into the provinces of his empire; but many circumstances denote their descent from the more ancient tribunals of the German tribes, held in the open air in the primitive periods of their history. But the character under which these institutions became formidable and important, about the beginning of the 13th century, arose from the disordered state of northern Germany after the dissolution of the duchy of Saxony. The Vehmic, or as they were called, free courts, were then modelled on a secret system of organization. The president was usually a prince or count of the empire; his assistants were persons affiliated to the society by secret initiation, to the number, it is said, at one time of 100,000. All these were bound to attend the secret meetings of the courts when summoned, and to execute their decrees, if necessary, by taking the life of persons condemned. Westphalia, styled, in the language of the free courts, the Red Land, was the district in which their central authority was seated. These courts exercised a great power, which was occasionally serviceable in repressing the lawless violence of the nobles of that period, but which was also liable to be perverted to the gratification of private malice and tyranny. Various leagues were formed in the fifteenth century, by the nobles of the empire, for the purpose of destroying their influence; which was at last effected, chiefly by the introduction of a better system of public judicature and police in the several states.

VELI'TES, in antiquity, light armed troops in the Roman armies, who derived their name, *a velocitate*, from their swiftness. They seem not to have been divided into distinct bodies or companies, but to have hovered loosely in front of the army. They were disposed sometimes before the front of the *hastati*, sometimes dispersed up and down among the void spaces, and sometimes placed in two bodies in the wings. The *Velites* generally began the combat, skirmishing in flying parties with the first troops of the enemy, and, when repulsed, fell back by the flanks of the army, or rallied again in the rear. Their armor was a javelin, casque, cuirass, and shield, all of a light construction.

VEL'LUM, a fine kind of parchment made of calves' skins, rendered particularly clear and white. The invention of vellum has been usually, though erroneously, ascribed to Attalus, king of Pergamus, now Bergamo: but the art of writing upon skins was known long before the time of Attalus, and is assignable to Eumenes, king of Pergamus, the contemporary with Ptolemy Philadelphus, whose motive for giving his attention to the improvement of vellum is said to be as follows:—The Egyptian monarch was anxiously employed in perfecting his magnificent library at Alexandria; with these feelings and views, he prohibited the exportation of the papyrus from his dominions, that he might not be subjected to the inconvenience of wanting paper for the multitude of scribes, whom he constantly employed to copy the MSS. which he had, by means of skilful emissaries, collected in every part of the known world.

VENEER'ING, the art of inlaying furniture, &c., with different kinds of wood, metal, or other materials. Also, of making representations of flowers, birds, and other figures.

VENE'TIAN SCHOOL, the distinguishing character of this school is coloring, and a consummate intellectual knowledge of chiaro-scuro; in both which, all is grace, spirit, and faithful adherence to nature, so seductive as to lead the spectator away from any consideration of its defects. It is an exquisite bouquet of well-arranged flowers; or a collection of pulpy, juicy, saccharine fruits. But it is not to be inferred that it is altogether wanting in still higher accomplishments: for the head of it was Tiziano de Vecelli; and in its ranks are to be found Tintoretto, Paul Veronese, Giorgione, and many other illustrious masters. *See* PAINTING.

VE'NIAL SIN, in theology, is defined by Roman Catholic theologians, a sin which weakens sanctifying grace, but does not take it away. It is not necessary, although commendable, to mention such sin in confession. Reformed theologians altogether reject the formal distinction between venial and mortal sin.

VENI'RE FA'CIAS, in law, a judicial writ, directed to the sheriff, to cause a jury to *come* or appear in the neighborhood where a cause is brought to issue, to try the same. A *venire facias de nova*, being a writ directing the sheriff to cause a jury to come and try a cause a second time, is granted where there has been a mis-trial; on the ground of irregularity, as, for instance, in summoning the jury; on the ground of misconduct by the jury; and also in certain cases where the verdict given is imperfect by reason of some ambiguity and uncertainty. The great rule of difference between a venire de novo in the latter case and a new trial is, that the former is only granted on matter appearing on the record.

VENI, SANC'TE SPIRI'TUS, (Lat. *Come, Holy Ghost.*) The name given to a mass in the Roman Catholic church to invoke the assistance of the Holy Spirit.

VEN'TIDUCT, in building, a passage for wind or air; a subterraneous passage or spiracle for ventilating apartments.

VENTILA'TION, the act of expelling impure air, and of dissipating noxious vapors. Few persons are aware how very necessary a thorough ventilation is to the preservation of health. We preserve life without food for a considerable time; but keep us without air for a very few minutes, and we cease to exist. It is not, however, enough that we have air; we must have *fresh* air, for the principle by which life is supported is taken from the air during the act of breathing. One fourth only of the atmosphere is capable of supporting life; the remainder serves to dilute the pure vital air, and render it more fit to be respired.

VENTRIL'OQUISM, an art or practice of speaking, by means of which the voice appears to proceed from different places; though the utterer does not change his place, and in many instances does not appear to speak. It has been considered that the sounds were produced independent of the labial and lingual organs, and was supposed to be a natural peculiarity, because few persons have learned it by being taught; but it is certain that practice only is necessary to carry this act of illusion to a high degree of perfection, and that the sound is not produced during inspiration, but proceeds as usual, during expiration, with a less opened mouth. The art of the ventriloquist consists merely in this: after drawing a long breath, he breathes it out slowly and gradually, dextrously dividing the air, and diminishing the sound of the voice by the muscles of the larynx and the palate, moving the lips as little as possible.

VEN'UE, in law, a neighborhood or near place; the place where an action is laid. The county in which the trial of a particular cause takes place, is said to be the *venue* of that cause. Originally jurors were summoned from the immediate neighborhood where a fact happened, to try it by their own knowledge, but they are now summonable from the body of the county. In what are termed *local actions*, the actual place in which the subject matter is situated must be laid as the venue in the action; but in those actions termed *transitory*, that is, actions of debt, contract, for personal injuries, &c., any county may be laid as the venue in the action. In criminal trials, the venue is the county in which the offence charged was actually committed. The courts, however, have a discretionary power of changing the venue, both in civil and criminal cases.

VERBA'TIM ET LITERA'TIM, [Lat.] word for word, and letter for letter.

VER'DICT, in law, the answer of a jury given to the court concerning any matter of fact in any cause, civil or criminal, committed to their trial and examination.

VERGE, in law, the compass or extent of the royal court, within which is bounded the jurisdiction of the lord steward of the royal household.

VER'GERS, certain officers of the courts of the queen's bench and common-pleas who carry white wands before the judges. There are also *vergers* of cathedrals and collegiate churches, who carry a rod tipped with silver before the bishop, dean, &c.

VERMIL'ION, a red pigment, of a hue between scarlet and crimson. There are two kinds of vermilion; the one natural or native, and the other artificial or factitious. Native vermilion is found in several silver-mines, in the form of a ruddy sand, which only requires to be purified. Factitious or common vermilion is made of the red sulphuret of mercury, or, as it was formerly called factitious cinnabar, reduced to a very fine powder.

VER'NAL, appearing in or appertaining to the spring: as, vernal flowers are preparatives to autumnal fruits.—*Vernal signs*, in astronomy, the signs in which the sun appears in the spring.—*Vernal equinox*, the equinox in March; opposed to the autumnal equinox, in September.

VER'SATILE, an epithet for that quality which enables persons to turn readily from one thing to another.

VERSE, in poetry, a line or part of a composition, the cadences of which are similar in each. The harmony of every verse is complete in itself. Verses are made up of feet, the number and species of which constitute the character of the verse, as hexameter, pentameter, &c. In the Greek and Roman versification, a foot was determined by its quantity; in the English, quantity is supplied by accent.—*Blank-verse*, poetry in which the lines do not end in rhymes.—*Heroic verse* usually consists of ten syllables, or, in English, of five accented syllables, constituting five feet.—*Versification* is the art of adjusting the syllables, and forming them into harmonious measure.

VERST, a Russian measure of length, containing 3500 feet; about three quarters of an English mile.

VESI'CA PISCIS, a name given to a symbolical representation of Christ, of a pointed oval or egg-shaped form, made by the intersection of two equal circles cutting each other in their centres. The actual figure of a fish found on the sarcophagi of the early Christians gave way, in course of time, to this oval-shaped ornament, which was the most common symbol used in the middle ages. It is to be met with sculptured, painted on glass, in ecclesiastical seals, &c. &c. The *aureole* or glory, in pictures of the Virgin, &c., was frequently made of this form.

VES'PERS, the evening songs or prayers in the Romish church.—*Sicilian vespers*, in French history, a massacre of all the French in Sicily, in the year 1582. It is so called, because the ring of the bell for vespers was the signal.

VES'TALS, in antiquity, certain virgins consecrated at Rome to the service of the goddess Vesta, and to whom was committed the care of the vestal fire, which was to be kept perpetually burning upon her altar. Their dress was a white vest, with a purple border; a white linen surplice, called *suparum linteum;* and over this a large purple mantle, with a long train. On their heads they wore the *infula*, and from the infula hung ribbons. When a vestal was convicted of unchastity, she was led to the Campus Sceleratus, and stripped of her habit solemnly by the pontiff. She was then put alive into a pit, with a lighted candle, a little water and milk, and thus covered up to pine and languish away the short remainder of her miserable existence.

VES'TIBULE, in architecture, a porch or entrance into a building.—In fortification, that space or covered ground which is in front of a guard-house.

VES'TRY, a place adjoining the church where the vestments of the minister are kept; also where the parishioners assemble for the discharge of parochial business; whence such a meeting is also called a vestry.—*Vestry-clerk*, an officer appointed to attend all vestries, and take account of their proceedings, &c.

VET'ERAN, among the Romans, a soldier who had passed the legal age of military service, which extended from seventeen to forty-six, was termed veteranus; or, in the later times of the republic, one who had served a requisite number of campaigns, generally twenty-five.

VE'TO, in politics, the power enjoyed by a branch of the legislature, which cannot of itself originate or modify a law, to reject the propositions of the other branch or branches. In the Polish diet, every noble who was an independent member could prevent any resolution from passing by his simple dissent (expressed in the words "Nie pozwalam," *I do not permit.*) The privilege of thus arresting the deliberations of the diet was termed the "liberum veto," and proved the fertile source of the disorders and anarchy of that country. In most constitutional monarchies the king has an absolute veto (as in France and England;) in some it is only suspensive. Thus, in Norway, if three successive storthings (assemblies) repeat the same resolution, it becomes law against the will of the king. The president of the United States may return a bill, with his reasons for dissenting from it, to the house in which it originated; but if both houses pass it afterwards by a majority of two thirds in each, it is not in his power again to reject it.

VI'ADUCT, a structure made for conveying a carriage way, either by raising mounds or arched supports across marshes, rivers, &c., as is the case with some of the railroads, or by perforation through hills, &c.

VIAT'ICUM, among the Romans, an allowance or provision made by the republic for such of its officers or magistrates as travelled upon the business of the state into any of the provinces. The term *viaticum* implies not only money for defraying the expenses of travelling, but their clothes, ornaments, baggage, &c.—*Viaticum*, in the church of Rome, an appellation given to the eucharist, when administered to persons at the point of death.

VIA'TOR, in Roman antiquity, an appellation given in common to all officers of any of the magistrates; as lictors, accensi, scribes, criers, &c.

VIC'AR, a particular kind of parish

priest, where the predial tithes are impropriated, that is, belonging to a chapter or religious house, or to a layman, who receives them, and only allows the vicar the smaller tithes as a salary.—*Vicars apostolical*, in the Romish church, are those who perform the functions of the pope in churches or provinces committed to their direction.—The title of *vicar-general* was given by Henry VIII. to the earl of Essex, with power to oversee all the clergy, and regulate all church affairs. It is now the title of an office, which, as well as that of official principal, is united in the chancellor of the diocese. The business of the vicar-general is to exercise jurisdiction over matters purely spiritual.

VICE, (Lat. *vice*, in the turn or place,) is used in composition to denote one *qui vicem gerit*, who acts in the place of another, or is second in authority. Thus we have such words as *vice-chamberlain*, *vice-chancellor*, *vice-resident*, *vicegerent*, *viceroy*, *&c.*—*Vice*, in smithery, an instrument used for holding fast any piece of iron which the artificer is working upon. —Among glaziers, a machine for drawing lead into flat rods for case windows.

VIC'TORY, in classical mythology, a goddess, called by Varro the daughter of Heaven and Earth. Her altar was preserved in the curia or senate-house of Rome; and its destruction was the subject of one of the latest contests between Christians and pagans.

VIDEL'ICET, in law. In pleading, it is usual to state any allegation which forms part of the facts set out, but which it is not intended to prove with precision, with the word "scilicet" (in English, "to wit") preceding it. Thus, numbers and dates, for instance, are frequently laid under a videlicet: as where anything is alleged to have taken place heretofore, "to wit," on such a day; or where, in trespass, the plaintiff charges the defendant with carrying away or injuring divers, "to wit," so many articles, &c. The general rule on this subject is, that where an allegation is in itself material, so that the issue cannot be established without it, there the putting a videlicet before it will not dispense with the proof; but where an allegation is in itself immaterial, there (in general, but not always,) the omission of a videlicet before it will render it material, and make it necessary for the party so alleging it to prove it as stated. But the distinctions on this subject run, as may be supposed, into extreme minuteness.

VI ET AR'MIS, in law, words made use of in indictments and actions of trespass, to show the violent commission of any trespass or crime.

VI'GIL, an ecclesiastical usage, the evening before a feast day, is so termed. The observation of vigils is said by some to be nearly the oldest of Christian ceremonies. According to Lactantius, Jerome, and other ancient authorities, the second advent of our Saviour was expected to take place on the vigil of Easter. They were originally celebrated by meeting together at night (as they are still on some occasions in the Eastern churches,) and are said thus to preserve the memory of the nocturnal assemblies of Christians in times of persecution.

VIGNETTE', originally, a kind of flourish of vine leaves and flowers in the vacant part of the title-page of a book, above the dedication, or at the end of a division. At present, however, the word signifies any small engraved embellishment for the illustration or decoration of a page of any work; and, in a more limited sense, such illustrations as are softened off at the edges, and not terminated by a definite boundary line.—In architecture, ornamental carving in imitation of vine leaves.

VIGORO'SO, in music, a term which, prefixed to a movement, denotes that it is to be performed with strength and firmness.

VIK'ING, a pirate. The *Vikingr* were Northmen who infested the European seas in the 8th, 9th, and 10th centuries. They were generally the sons of Northern kings, who betook themselves to piracy as a means of distinguishing themselves, and of obtaining an independent command.

VIL'LA, in Roman antiquities, originally any country dwelling, farm-house, &c., but in architectural language, the country residences of individuals of the wealthier classes were so called. Many descriptions of ancient villas are here and there scattered in the pages of classical writers; but the two most complete, undoubtedly (besides those contained in the work of Vitruvius,) are the accounts given by Pliny the younger of his Laurentine and Tuscan residences: the first being the complete picture of a marine, and the second of an inland villa. The remains of the first are thought to have been discovered not far from Ostia, in the beginning of the last century. The most important parts of an ordinary villa were the porticoes, one or more, along the front or sides of the mansion; the triclinium or dining-room: the wings forming suits of living apartments, commonly called, in the time of Pliny, diætæ; the baths, with their appurtenances, the hypocausta or vaulted heating-rooms, apodyteria or dressing-rooms, rooms for exercise, &c. Adjacent to the main portico are generally the xystus.

VIL'LAGE, in English legal phraseology, a subdivision of a parish; sometimes a whole parish, and sometimes a manor. Most commonly it means the out part of a parish, consisting of a few houses separate from the rest. In countries where there are peasants attached to the glebe, or possessing distinct rights and obligations from other subjects, a village is properly a place inhabited by peasants only. From the Latin villa was derived the French ville, *city*, originally signifying any residence; and thence a collection of houses which gradually grew around a principal residence. Thus, especially in Normandy, ville is a common termination to the names of towns.

VIL'LEIN, a name given, in ancient times, to persons not proprietors of land, many of whom were attached to the land, and bound to serve the lord of the manor.

VINA'LIA, in antiquity, a festival observed by the Romans, Aug. 19, in honor of Jupiter and Venus.

VI'OL, a stringed musical instrument of the same form as the violin, but larger. Viols are of different kinds; the largest is called the *bass viol*, whose tones are deep, soft, and agreeable.

VIOLIN', the most perfect of all stringed musical instruments played with the bow. The violin consists of three chief parts—the neck, the table, and the soundboard. The violin has four catgut strings of different sizes, of which the largest is wound round with wire. Music for the violin is always set in the G key, which on that account is called the *violin key;* and the excellence of the instrument consists in its purity and distinctness, strength, and fulness of tone.

VIOLONCEL'LO, a musical instrument which comes between the *viola di braccio* (or arm violin) and the double bass, both as to size and tone. It is constructed entirely on the same plan with the violin; and the player holds it between his knees. Its notes are written in the F or bass clef; and it generally accompanies the double bass.

VIOLO'NO, the English *double bass*, a deep-toned musical instrument, the largest of the kind played with a bow, and principally used to sustain the harmony.

VIR'GA, in archæology, the rod or staff which sheriffs, bailiffs, &c. carry as a badge of their office.

VIR'GINAL, in music, a stringed and keyed instrument resembling the spinnet It is now quite obsolete, though former ly in great repute.

VIR'TU, a love of the Fine Arts, and a taste for curiosities.

VIR'TUE, in moral philosophy, is employed both in an abstract and compre hensive sense, to signify the law or laws in which right conduct consists, and also concretely for that quality of actions and persons which arises from their agreement with the rules of morality. By theories of virtue are understood the different explanations which have been given, both of that which distinguishes right from wrong, and of the nature of the feelings with which virtue and vice are contemplated by mankind. The distinction of these two questions, so frequently confounded by ethical writers, is due to Adam Smith, but has since been strongly insisted upon by Mackintosh and Hampden.

VIRTUO'SO, one skilled in antique or natural curiosities; a lover of the liberal arts.

VIS'COUNT, (pron. *vi'count*) in France and England, a nobleman next in degree to an earl. The first viscount was created in the reign of Henry VI.—A *viscount's coronet* has neither flowers nor points raised above the circle, like those of superior degree, but only pearls placed on *Siva*, the circle itself.

VISH'NU, one of the three principal deities of the Hindoo mythology, the other two being Brama and Siva. He is commonly called the Preserver, the other two being respectively the Creator and the Destroyer. The great objects of his providence are brought about by his successive incarnations or avatars, in which he appears and acts on earth. Nine of these have taken place. The last is said to have been the appearance of Buddha, which is supposed by some learned orientalists to have taken place about A.D. 1014; and hence the Buddhists reject the Vedas, which were compiled before that event. The tenth avatar of Vishnu is yet to take place, when he will appear on a white horse, with a blazing scimitar, for the everlasting punishment of the wicked. One of the incarnations of Vishnu is the celebrated Juggernaut, whose temple and worship hold such a prominent place in Indian superstition. On the grand annual festival in his honor, all distinctions of castes and classes are forgotten, and even on that occasion the Brahminical Hindoos and the followers of Buddha cease their religious hostilities. The word Juggernaut signifies literally *Lord of the Universe:* and it is said that on the day he expired, Buddha assumed this appellation, exclaiming "*O Universe, I am thy Lord.*"

VIS'ION, BEATIF'IC, in theology. The doctors of the church distinguish three manners of seeing or knowing God: which they call, 1. *Abstractive vision;* i. e. through the consideration of his attributes. 2. *Beatific* or *intuitive vision;* that which the faithful enjoy in heaven. The belief termed Catholic by the Romanists is, that this vision is accorded to the just, who die without leaving a sin unexpiated, immediately on their departure. The Greek church holds that they do not enjoy it until after the general resurrection. This is one of the opinions condemned by the Council of Florence in 1439; and its decision is confirmed by that of Trent. 3. The third kind of vision, or *comprehension*, is that which belongs to God, who alone can know Himself as He is. Prophetic vision is only the knowledge of future or distant events, given by inspiration.

VISITA'TION, in ecclesiastical polity, an office or act of superintendence, performed by a bishop once in three years, by visiting the churches and their rectors, &c., throughout the whole diocese. Parochial visitation by the archdeacon is annual.

VIS'ITOR, in law, an inspector into the government of a corporation.

VIS'UAL, in perspective, the *visual point* is a point in the horizontal line, in which all the ocular rays unite.

VIT'RIFIED WALLS or FORTIFICATIONS, ancient remains discovered in Scotland, constructed of stones piled rudely upon one another, and firmly cemented together by some matter which has been vitrified by means of fire. They generally surround the top of some steep conical hill. They have been discovered chiefly in the Highlands, but also in Galloway. The vitrification is mostly external, the interior of the walls being a mere heap of loose stones. Daines Barrington considered the vitrification to be accidental, but his explanation of how it took place is not very intelligible. It seems more reasonable to suppose that the art was derived from observation of the ease with which some kinds of earth containing much iron ore are vitrified by fire, and that the process was rendered easy by the quantities of wood which in early days covered the Highlands.

VIVA'CE, in music, an Italian epithet, signifying lively; and *vivacissimo*, very lively.

VI'VARY, a place for keeping living animals, as a park, a warren, a pond, &c.

VI'VA VO'CE, (Latin,) by word of mouth; as, to vote, or to communicate with another person, *vivâ voce.*

VIZIR, (in Arabic, *a porter;* and, by a singular metaphor, the title in various oriental countries of a minister and councillor of state.) The grand khalifs had their vizirs, who attained to the highest rank and consideration in their states, and were often more powerful than their masters; but after the creation of the new dignity of Emir-ul-omrah (commander of commanders,) by Khalif Radhi, the older title lost much of its consideration. In Turkey, the councillors of state who sit in the divan, generally eight in number, are styled vizirs; and the chief among them vizir azem, rendered by us by grand vizir, which is the highest temporal dignity in the empire.

VOCAB'ULARY, a list or collection of the words of a language, arranged in alphabetical order and explained; a word-book; the words of a science; a dictionary or lexicon. We often use *vocabulary* in a sense somewhat different from that of *dictionary*, restricting the signification to the list of words; as when we say, the *vocabulary* of Johnson is more full or extensive than that of Entick. We rarely use the word as synonymous with *dictionary*, but in other countries the corresponding word is so used, and this may be so used in English.

VO'CAL MU'SIC, music produced by the voice, either unaccompanied or accompanied by instruments. Vocal music has many advantages over instrumental, in its endless variety of intonation and expression, and in the support which it derives from its connection with words.

VOCA'TION, in divinity, the grace vouchsafed by God to any man in calling him from death unto life, and putting him into the way of salvation. It is also used for the call of the Holy Spirit, by which persons are supposed to be initiated into the clerical order.

VOICE, the sounds produced by the organs of respiration, especially the larynx. The lungs, the wind-pipe, &c., the finely-arched roof of the mouth, and the pliability of the lips, are each of the greatest importance in producing the different intonations which render the human voice so agreeable and harmonious. A good musical voice depends chiefly upon the soundness and power of the organs of utterance and of hearing; and is much promoted by the practice of singing and gymnastic exercises that expand the chest.

VOIRE DIRE, in law, according to ancient practice, an objection to the competency of a witness, in a trial at common law, could only be taken on a preliminary examination, in which the witness was sworn *to speak the truth*, and then examined touching his interest in the subject matter. The same practice is still followed occasionally, although the objection may now be taken when it arises on the examination in chief.

VOL'TA, in music, an Italian word, signifying that the part is to be repeated, one, two, or more times.

VOL'TIGEUR, a foot-soldier in a select company of every regiment of French infantry. *Voltigeurs* were established by Napoleon during his consulate. Their duties, exercises, and equipment, are similar to those of our light companies.—In the United States, a light horseman.

VOL'TI SU'BITO, in music, a term directing that the leaf is to be turned over quickly.

VOL'UME, properly signifies a roll or book, so called *a volvendo*, because the ancient books were rolls of bark or parchment. This manner lasted till Cicero's time. The several sheets or pieces were glued or pasted end to end, and written only on one side. At the bottom a stick was fastened, called *umbilicus*, round which it was rolled; and at the other end was a piece of parchment, on which the title of the book was written in letters of gold. Of such volumes, Ptolemy's library in Alexandria contained, as some authors say, 700,000.

VOL'UNTARY, in music, a piece played by a musician extemporarily, according to his fancy.

VOL'UNTEER, a person who enters into military or other service of his own free will.

VOLUTE', in architecture, a kind of spiral scroll, used in the Ionic and Composite capitals, of which it is a principal ornament. The number of *volutes* in the Ionic order is four; in the Composite,

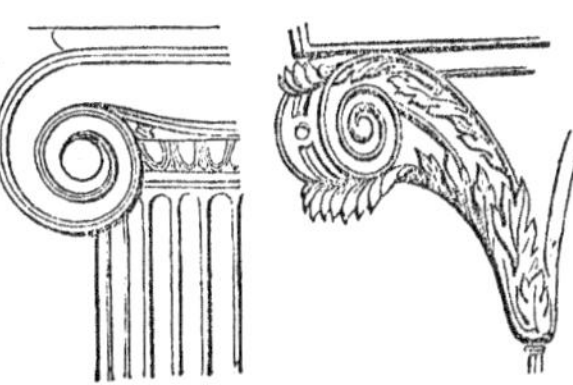

eight. There are also eight angular volutes in the Corinthian capital, accompanied with eight smaller ones, called helices.

VOMITO'RIA, in architecture, the openings, gates, or doors, in the ancient theatres and amphitheatres, which gave ingress and egress to the public.

VOTE, the suffrage of the people of each of the members of an assembly, where any affair is to be carried by a majority assembled in large meetings.

VO'TIVE, in numismatics. Votive medals are such as were struck in grateful commemoration of any auspicious event, such as the recovery from sickness of a prince, &c.; especially those of the Roman emperors, struck every five, ten, or twenty years, on which the public vows on their behalf are recorded. The custom is said to have originated in the repeated continuance of Augustus in his high offices at the prayers of the people. A votive tablet, picture, &c., is one dedicated in consequence of the vow of a worshipper; in classical Europe some deity, in modern Roman Catholic countries, to saints.

VOUCH'ER, one who gives witness or full attestation to anything.—In law, the act of calling in a person to make good his warranty of title.—A book, paper, or document which serves to vouch the truth of accounts, or to confirm and establish facts of any kind. The merchant's books are his *vouchers* for the correctness of his accounts. Notes, bonds, receipts, and other writings, are used as *vouchers* in proving facts.—In Scots law, *voucher* is the technical name for the written evidence of payment.

VOUS'SOIRS, in bridges, are the stones which immediately form the arch, being of the shape of a truncated wedge. Their under sides form the intrados or soffitt. The length of the middle voussoir, or key-stone, ought to be about 1-15th or 1-16th of the span, and the rest should increase all the way down to the imposts. Their joints should be cut perpendicular to the curve of the intrados; consequently the angle of the sides is determined by the curvature.

VOW, a solemn and religious promise, or oath. The use of vows is found in most religions. They make up a considerable part of the pagan worship, being made either in consequence of some deliverance, under some pressing necessity, or for the success of some enterprise. Among the Jews, all vows were to be voluntary, and made by persons wholly in their own power; and if such person made a vow in anything lawful and possible, he was obliged to fulfil it. Among the Romanists, a person is constituted a religious by taking three vows, that of poverty, chastity, and obedience.—Vows, among the Romans, signified sacrifices, offerings, presents, and prayers made for the Cæsars and emperors, particularly for their prosperity and the continuance of their empire.

VOW'EL, in grammar, a letter which can be pronounced alone, thus distinguished from consonants, which require to be sounded with the aid of a vowel. They are divided in ancient prosody into long, short, and common, *i. e.*, either long or short at pleasure. A diphthong consists of two vowels, of which the sounds run (or are supposed to run) into one another.

VUL'CAN, in mythology, the Latin name for the divinity called by the Greeks Hephæstus, the god who presided over the working of metals. He was also called Mulciber. He was the son of Jupiter, who, incensed at his interference on the part of his mother Juno, cast him out of heaven: he fell in the isle of Lemnos, and broke his leg in the fall. His feats as the patron of armorers and workers in metal, his marriage with Venus, and her infidelities, form the subjects of many of the best known classical stories. There is about the character of Vulcan much of the usual confusion belonging to Greek mythology. Cicero mentions three Vulcans, besides the son of Jupiter: one, the child of Uranus; another, of Nilus, who reigned in Egypt; a third, of Mænalius. A peculiarity attending the worship of Vulcan was, that the victims were wholly consumed, in reference to his character as god of fire.—In sculpture, he is represented as bearded, with a hammer and pincers, and a pointed cap. He does not appear lame, as represented by the poets. Cicero, however, praises the sculptor Alcamenes for making his lameness observable without amounting to deformity.

VULCAN'IC THE'ORY, a system which ascribes the changes on the earth's surface to fire, while others ascribe the whole to water, under a theory called Neptunian.

VUL'GATE, a very ancient Latin translation of the Bible, which was translated from the Greek of the Septuagint. It is the only one acknowledged by the Romish church to be authentic.

W.

W, the twenty-third letter of the English alphabet, takes its written form from the union of two V's, and its name of *double u* from the Roman capital V representing that which we call U. In English it is always followed by a vowel, except when followed by *h*, as in *when*, or by *r*, as in *wrong*. The *w*, being a strong breathing, is nearly related to all aspirated sounds, and through them again to the gutturals, so that we find *w* and *g* often interchanged in different languages, as in the words *William*, *Guillaume*, &c.

WAD'SETT, an ancient tenure or lease of land in the Highlands of Scotland, which seems to have been upon a kind of mortgage.

WA'GER OF BAT'TLE, an ancient mode of trial by single combat, where, in appeals of felony, the appellee might fight with the appellant to prove his innocence; and it is but recently that this relic of barbarism and injustice has been abolished. It was also used in affairs of chivalry and honor, and in civil cases upon issue joined in a writ of right.

WA'GER OF LAW, the offer, on the part of the defendant in an action of debt by simple contract, to take an oath in court in the presence of eleven compurgators, that he owes the plaintiff nothing in the manner and form as he has declared, whereupon the law allows him his discharge.

WA'GES, in political economy, are the return made or compensation paid to those employed to perform any kind of labor or service by their employers.—In ordinary language, the term wages is usually employed to designate the sums paid to artisans or laborers employed in manufactures, in household services, and in agriculture, mines, and other manual occupations. Substantially and in fact, however, it has a much more extensive application: the salaries of public functionaries of all sorts, and the fees of lawyers, physicians, and other professional men, are as really wages as the sums paid by them to the menials in their service, and depend on the same laws and principles. "Every man," says Dr. Paley, "has his work. The kind of work varies, and that is all the difference there is. A great deal of labor exists besides that of the hands, many species of industry besides bodily operation, equally necessary, requiring equal assiduity, more attention, more anxiety. It is not true, therefore, that men of elevated stations are exempted from work; it is only true that there is assigned to them work of a different kind; whether more easy or more pleasant may be questioned; but certainly not less wanted, nor less essential to the common good."

WAHA'BEES, a Mussulman sect, of which the founder was a learned Arabian, named Abd el Wahâb, who became persuaded of the corruption, both of doctrine and practice, prevalent among the professors of Islam, especially the Turks. His daughter married Mohammed Ibn Saoûd, the principal person of the town of Derayeh, who became his first convert and leader of the sect, about 1760. Like the original prophet of their faith, Saoûd and his followers propagated their doctrines at once by persuasion and arms. Abd el Aziz and Ibn Saoûd, the son and grandson of the first Saoûd, carried their arms to the utmost extremities of Arabia, and, conformably with the old Mohammedan principle, established a spiritual and temporal leadership united in their persons. The Bedouins, or wandering tribes, formed the bulk of their converts. They acknowledged the Koran and the Sunne, or orthodox tradition, and they professed adherence to the liberal tenets of both; but they accused the other Mohammedans of an idolatrous veneration for the prophet and other saints, and denied the intercession of saints altogether. Like the early Protestants of Europe, their favorite taste was the destruction of the cupolas and tombs of saints. To this the mob of Wahabys added a strong aversion to the rich dress of the Turks, and to the practice of smoking tobacco, which had been prohibited by Abd el Wahâb much on the same bold principle which had induced Mohammed himself to condemn the use of wine. The province of Nedjd became the chief seat of the Wahaby power. Under the last Saoûd (a very handsome man, whom the Arabs called Abou Showareb, or the Father of Mustaches,) it reached its greatest extent. Like the early caliphs, he administered justice in person to great part of Arabia. The Wahabys, in the first twenty years of this century, extended their plundering expeditions to Syria, Irak, and Mesopotamia. In 1803 they took Mekka, and soon conquered the Hidjah. In 1809 Mehemet Ali began hostilities in Arabia; and in 1812 the Hidjah was restored, and the caravans of pilgrims once more arrived with their usual pomp at Mekka; but for some years afterwards the Wahabys maintained their superiority in the rest of Arabia. Saoûd died in 1814, and was succeeded in his political and religious authority by his son Abdallah, under whom the Wahabys were finally subdued by Mehemet Ali; but we possess no authentic account of their conquest, or their present condition.

WAIFS, in law, goods found, of which the owner is not known, and which are claimed by the crown. These were originally such goods as a thief, when pursued, threw away to prevent his being apprehended.

WAIN'SCOT, in architecture, the framed lining in panels wherewith a wall is faced. The wood originally used for this purpose being a species of foreign oak, that wood has acquired the name from the purpose to which it was thus applied.

WAITS, formerly, minstrels or musical watchmen, who attended on great men, and sounded the watch at night. At present the name is given to those itinerant musicians who, in most of the large towns of England and Scotland, especially London go round the principal streets at night for some time before Christmas, play two or three tunes, call the hour, then remove to a suitable distance, where they go through the same ceremony, and so on till four or five o'clock in the morning.

WAI'VER, in law, the passing by, or declining to accept a thing; applied either to an estate, to a plea, &c.

WAI'WODE, in the Turkish empire, the governor of a small province or town.

WAKE, in antiquities and popular usage, the word is of the same meaning as vigil; and the custom originated in the processions which took place early in the morning of feast days to the church, and were not uncommonly followed by revelling and drunkenness. At present most fast days are popularly called wakes by the English peasantry; but the peculiar "wake" or "revel" of county parishes was, originally, the day of the week on which the church had been dedicated; afterwards, the day of the year. In 1536, an act of convocation appointed that the wake should be held in every parish on the same day, namely, the first Sunday in October; but it was disregarded. Wakes are expressly mentioned in Charles the First's *Book of Sports*, among the feasts which it was his majesty's pleasure should be observed. The wake appears to have been also held on the Sunday after the day of dedication: or, more usually, the day of the saint to whom the church was dedicated. —A strange practice of celebrating funeral rites by the lower orders in Ireland, has been thus described by Miss Edgeworth:—"At night the body is *waked;* that is to say, all the friends and neighbors of the deceased collect in a barn or stable, where the corpse is laid upon some boards, or an unhinged door, supported upon stools, the face exposed, the rest of the body covered with a white sheet. Round the body are stuck, in brass candlesticks, which have been borrowed perhaps at five miles' distance, as many candles as the poor person can beg or borrow, observing always to have an odd number. Pipes and tobacco are first distributed, and then, according to the ability of the deceased, cakes and ale, and sometimes whiskey, are *dealt* to the company."

WALDEN'SES, in ecclesiastical history, a remarkable religious sect, said to have derived their name from Peter Waldo, a merchant of Lyons, who preached what he regarded as the pure doctrine of the Scriptures about 1180. Historians have confounded them, on the one hand, with the Vaudois (see that article,) who appear, although their history is involved in much obscurity, to be an older and separate people; and on the other (especially those of the Catholic party,) with the Albigenses; and thus it has been endeavored to throw on them the discredit of the Manichean tracts, which are commonly (but on very doubtful testimony) imputed to the latter. It seems clear, however, that the Waldenses were distinct from these, and probably from the Vaudois also. Their distinguishing character, it has been said, "seems to have consisted in a strict adherence to what they considered to be the doctrine originally delivered by Christ to his apostles." And out of their extremely literal interpretation of the Gospel appears to have arisen most of their peculiarities, whether good or evil. They seem to have rejected an established succession of the priesthood, and the distinguishing characteristics of the priestly office; the high Catholic doctrine of the sacraments, besides the common ecclesiastical abuses of their day; and are said, in addition, to have protested against oaths, warfare, lawsuits, and the accumulation of wealth. Their later history is obscure; and it may be said of them, as well as of other sects of the day, that they had little of the elements of permanence, the same opinions being continually promulgated afresh by new reformers, and then receiving new denominations.

WALPUR'GIS NIGHT, the night of the 1st of May, a festival of St. Philip and St. James. Saint Walpurga was an English lady, sister of Boniface, the apostle of the Germans: her festival falls on the same day with that of the above-mentioned saints, and is a common day in Germany, like Lady-day in England, for the commencement of leases, &c. It is also known as the day on the eve of which, according to popular superstition, the great witch festival is held on the summit of the Brocken, in the Hartz mountains. This superstition is supposed to have originated in the rites performed by the pagan remnants of the Saxons to their gods, when their nation was forcibly converted to Christianity; which, being secretly celebrated in remote places, were supposed by the vulgar to be supernatural orgies.

WALTZ, a national German dance, but now common in England, and other European countries. To waltz with effect, much grace and precision are necessary, or else it becomes a mere vulgar exercise. The waltz of the north of Germany was grave and slow, whilst that of the south is gay, and the quick gay waltz is by far the most prevalent.

WAM'PUM, shells used by the American Indians as money or a medium of commerce. These shells are run on a string, and form a broad belt, which is worn as an ornament or girdle.

WAP'ENSHAW, an exhibition of arms, according to the rank of the individual, made formerly at certain times in every district. These exhibitions or meetings were not designed for military exercises, but only for showing that the lieges were properly provided with arms.

WAP'ENTAKE, in law, a division or district, peculiar to some of the northern counties of England, and answering to the *hundred* or *cantred*, in other counties. This name had its origin in a custom of touching lances or spears when the chief or leading man of the hundred entered on his office.

WAR, a contest between nations or states, carried on by force, either for defence, or for revenging insults and redressing wrongs, for the extension of commerce or acquisition of territory, or for obtaining and establishing the superiority and dominion of one over the other. These objects are accomplished by the slaughter or capture of troops, and the capture and destruction of ships, towns, and property. Among rude nations, war is often waged and carried on for plunder. As war is the contest of nations or states, it always implies that such contest is authorized by the monarch or the sovereign power of the nation. When war is commenced by attacking a nation in peace, it is called an *offensive* war, and such attack is *aggressive*. When war is undertaken to repel invasion or the attacks of an enemy, it is called *defensive*, and a defensive war is considered as justifiable. When war arises between different portions or members of the same nation, or between the established government of a nation, and a portion of the people resisting it, it is called a *civil* war. Very few of the *wars* that have desolated nations and deluged the earth with blood, have been justifiable. Happy would it be for mankind, if the prevalence of Christian principles might ultimately extinguish the spirit of *war*, and if the ambition to be great might yield to the ambition of being good. The "rights of war" are such as arise in times of hostilities—1. between enemies; 2. between neutrals. As between enemies, it is a general law that subjects of a hostile state who are not in arms, or who have submitted, may not be slain. The killing of prisoners is only justifiable in very extreme cases. The usage of exchanging prisoners is now general, but was only firmly established in the 17th century; and it is not now considered obligatory. As to property, that belonging to the government of the vanquished nation belongs to the victorious state, wherever it is found; but private rights are unaffected by conquest, with the remarkable exception of private property when at sea, which is by general usage held lawful prize. Acts of hostility are only lawful, according to modern usage, when committed by those authorized by the express or implied command of the state; such as the regularly commissioned military and naval forces of the nation, and all others called out by the government in its defence, as well as persons spontaneously defending themselves in case of necessity. Irregular bands of marauders are therefore denied the rights of war, and liable to be treated as banditti; and this distinction is generally only observed so far as suits the belligerent's purpose. For private citizens taking up arms, although in obedience to proclamations, are constantly liable to be treated as marauders; as by the French in the Peninsular war, and in numerous other cases.

WARD, in law, a term applied to all infants under the power of guardians.—A certain district, division, or quarter of a town or city.

WAR'DEN, a keeper; as, the warden of a prison.—*Warden of a college*, the head or president.—*Warden of the cinque ports*, an officer or magistrate who has the jurisdiction of certain ports or havens in England.

WARD'MOTE, a court kept in every ward in London, usually called the wardmote court; of this court the inquest has power every year to inquire into all deficiencies with regard to the officers of the ward.

WARD'SHIP, guardianship; care and protection of a ward.—Right of guardianship. Wardship, under the feudal system, was one of the incidents of tenure by knight service. When the tenant died, and his heir was under the age of 21, being a male, or 14, being a female, the lord was entitled to the wardship of the heir, and was called the guardian in chivalry. This wardship consisted in having the custody of the body and lands of such heir, without any account of the profits, till the age of 21 in males, and 14 (which was afterwards advanced to 16) in females, the male heir being then considered capable of performing knight service, and the female capable of marrying. This right of wardship was abolished under the commonwealth.—Pupilage; state of being under a guardian.

WARMTH, in painting, that glowing effect which arises from the use of warm colors, and also from the use of transparent colors, in the process of glazing; opposed to leaden coldness.

WAR'RANT, in law, a precept authorizing an officer to seize an offender and bring him to justice.—*Warrant of attorney*, an authority given to an attorney by his client to appear and plead for him; or in a more general sense, that by which a man appoints another to act in his name, and warrants his transaction.—*Search warrant*, a precept authorizing a person to enter houses, &c. to search for stolen or contraband goods, or to discover whether a criminal be there concealed.—*Warrant officer*, an officer holding a warrant from the navy board, such as the master, surgeon, purser, &c. of a ship.—*Press warrant*, in the navy, a warrant issued by the admiralty, authorizing an officer to impress seamen.

WAR'RANTY, in law, a covenant by deed, made by one party to another, to secure to him the enjoyment of an estate or other thing bargained for. Warranty is *real*, when annexed to lands and tenements granted in fee or for life, &c., and *personal*, when it respects goods sold or their quality. If a man sells goods which are not his own, or which he has no right to sell, the purchaser may have satisfaction for the injury. And if the seller expressly warrants the goods to be sound, and they prove to be otherwise, he must indemnify the purchaser. But the warranty must be at the time of sale.

WAR'REN, a franchise or privileged place for keeping beasts and fowls of the warren, as hares, partridges, and pheasants.

WAS'SAIL-BOWL, a large drinking vessel, in which the Saxons, at their public entertainments, drank health to each other, saying, "Wæs hæl!"—"Health be to you!" or "Your health!" It was also a Saxon custom, to go about with such a bowl, at the time of the Epiphany, singing a festival song, drinking the health of the inhabitants, and, of course, collecting money to replenish the bowl. This custom, from which christmas-boxes, christmas-ale, bell men's verses, and carols, are all, probably, more or less derived, was called *wassailing*, and those who practised it, *wassailers*.

WASTE, in law, an epithet for lands which are not in any man's occupation, but lie common.

WATCH AND WARD, the custom of watching by night, and warding or keeping the peace by day in towns and cities, which was first appointed by Henry III.

WA'TER-COL'ORS, in painting and limning, colors diluted and made with gum-water instead of oil. The principal of the water-colors are as follow: White—Ceruse, white lead, Spanish white, flake white, spodium; Black—Burnt cherry-stones, ivory black, lamp black; Green—Green bice, green verditer, grass green, sap green, verdigris distilled; Blue—Sanders blue, terre blue, blue verditer, indigo, litmus, smalt, Prussian blue, light blue, ultramarine, blue bice; Brown—Spanish brown, Spanish liquorice, umber, bistre, terra de Sienna, burnt and unburnt; Red—Native cinnabar, burnt ochre, Indian red, red lead, minium, lake, vermilion, carmine, red ink, Indian lake; Yellow—English ochre, gall stones, gamboge, masticot, ochre de luce, orpiment, Roman ochre, Dutch pink, saffron water, king's yellow, gold yellow, French berries.

WA'TER-GAVEL, in law, a rent paid for fishing, or any other benefit received from some river.

WA'TER-LINE, a horizontal line supposed to be drawn about a ship's bottom, at the surface of the water. This is higher or lower, according to the depth of water necessary to float her.

WA'TER-LOGGED, is said of a ship when, by leaking and receiving a great quantity of water into her hold, she has become so heavy as to be totally unmanageable.

WA'TERMAN, one who plies with a boat upon a river; a ferryman.

WA'TER-MARK, the utmost limit of the rise of the flood.—The mark visible in paper, which is made in the manufacturing of it.

WA'TER-TABLE, in architecture, a ledge in the wall of a building, about 18 or 20 inches from the ground.

WAX'-WORK, figures formed of wax, in imitation of real persons. Where the likenesses are correct, and the artist has displayed good taste in adjusting the draperies, &c., a collection of wax-work figures, representing public characters, affords an amusing exhibition. But figures of this kind overstep the proper limit of the Fine Arts; and their ghastly fixedness has a tendency to make us shudder even while gratifying our curiosity. At present wax is used for anatomical preparations, or for fruits: it also serves the sculptor for his models and studies.

WAYS AND MEANS, the financial resources to meet the public expenditure, or supplies voted by Congress.

WEDNES'DAY, the fourth day of the week, so called from Wodin, or Odin, a deity or chief among the northern nations of Europe.—*Ash Wednesday*, the first day of Lent. Some think the day received this name, or *Dies cinerum*, from the custom in the early ages of the church, of penitents appearing in sackcloth with ashes on their heads. But, however certain it is that such a practice prevailed, there is no evidence that it was done precisely on that day.

WEEK, a period of seven days, of uncertain origin, but which has been used from time immemorial in eastern countries. The week did not enter into the calendar of the Greeks, who divided the civil month into three periods of ten days each; and it was not introduced at Rome till after the reign of Theodosius. By some writers the use of weeks is supposed to be a remnant of the tradition of the creation; by others, that it was suggested by the phases of the moon; while a third class, with more probability, refer its origin to the seven planets known in ancient times. This opinion explains the circumstance that the days of the week have been universally named after the planets, according to a particular order. In the ancient Egyptian astronomy, the order of the planets, in respect of distance from the earth, beginning with the most remote, is Saturn, Jupiter, Mars, the Sun, Venus, Mercury, the Moon. The day was divided into 24 hours, and each successive hour consecrated to a particular planet in the order now stated; so that one hour being consecrated to Saturn, the next fell to Jupiter, the third to Mars, and so on; and each day was named after the planet to which its first hour was consecrated. Now, suppose the first hour of a particular day to have been consecrated to Saturn, it is evident that Saturn would also have the 8th, the 15th, and the 22d hours. The 23d hour would therefore fall to Jupiter; the 24th to Mars; and the 25th, or the first hour of the following day, would belong to the Sun, from which it would take its name. By proceeding in the same manner, it is found that the first hour of the third day would fall to the Moon, the first of the fourth day to Mars, of the fifth to Mercury, of the sixth to Jupiter, and of the seventh to Venus. The cycle being completed, the first hour of the eighth day would return to Saturn, and all the others constantly succeed in the same order. According to Dio Cassius, the Egyptian week began with Saturday. The Jews, on their flight from Egypt, made Saturday the last day of the week. The Saxons seem to have borrowed the week from some eastern nation, substituting the names of their own divinities for those of the gods of Greece. In England, the Latin names of the days are still retained in legislative and judiciary acts.

WELL, a cylindrical excavation sunk perpendicularly into the earth to such a depth as to reach a supply of water, and walled with stone or brick to support the earth.—*Well*, in the military art, a depth which the miner sinks under ground, with branches or galleries running out from it, either to prepare a mine, or to discover and disappoint the enemy's mine.

WELSH, the language or general name of the people of Wales. The Welsh call themselves *Cymry*, their country *Cymru*, and the name of their language, *Cymraeg*. They are supposed to be the *Cimbri*, of Jutland. It was to Wales that the ancient Britons fled when Great Britain was invaded by the Saxons; and there they long maintained themselves as an independent state, preserving their own language, and being governed by their native kings; till Llewellin, their last prince, being vanquished and slain in 1283, while resisting the forces of Edward I., the country was united to England. The people submitted to the English dominion with extreme reluctance; and Edward, as a conciliatory means, promised to give them for their prince a Welshman by birth, and one who could speak no other language. This notice being received with joy, he invested in the principality his second son, Edward, then an infant, who had been born at Carnarvon. The death of his eldest son, Alphonso, happening soon after, young Edward became heir also of the English monarchy, and united both nations under one government; but some ages elapsed, before the animosity which had long subsisted between them was totally extinguished.

WER'EGILD, in ancient English law, a compensation paid for a man killed by the person who caused his death. Blackstone says it was paid partly as a penalty to the king for the loss of a subject, partly to the lord of the vassal, and partly to the next of kin.

WEST, one of the cardinal points, being that point of the horizon where the sun sets at the equinox, or any point in a direct line between the spectator or other object, and that point of the horizon. In a less strict sense, it is that region of the hemisphere near the point where the sun sets when in the equator.

WEST'ERN EM'PIRE, the name given by historians to the western division of the Roman empire, when divided, by the will of Theodosius the Great, between his sons Honorius and Arcadius, A.D. 395. After the deposition of the emperor Augustulus by Odoacer, A.D. 476, the Western empire was definitely at an end. But when Charlemagne, in the year 800, assumed the imperial crown, it was with the view of reassuming the ancient dignity of the Cæsars in Western Europe; and after him the German emperors were considered by the jurists of their own country, and of their party in Italy, as representing the majesty of ancient Rome, the Italian states being looked on as feudatories of the empire.

WEST'MINSTER ASSEMBLY, a name given to the synod of divines and laymen, who in the reign of Charles I., assembled by authority of parliament, in Henry the Seventh's chapel, Westminster, for the purpose of settling the government, liturgy, and doctrine of the Church of England. The great majority of those who attended this assembly were presbyterians. Those members of episcopalian principles refrained from attending, because the king had declared against the assembly. The Westminster Assembly continued in existence for five years and a half. They signed the solemn league and covenant, drew up the Confession of Faith, a Directory for Public Worship, the Larger and Shorter Catechisms, and some other publications of temporary importance.

WHEEL, BREAK'ING ON THE, a mode of capital punishment, said to have been first employed in Germany; according to some writers, on the murderers of Leopold, duke of Austria, in the 14th century. According to the German method of this savage execution, the criminal was laid on a cart-wheel with his arms and legs extended, and his limbs in that posture fractured with an iron bar. But in France (where it was restricted to cases of assassination, or other murders of an atrocious description, highway robbery, parricide, and rape.) the criminal was laid on a frame of wood in the form of a St. Andrew's cross, with grooves cut transversely in it above and below the knees and elbows; and the executioner struck eight blows with an iron bar, so as to break the limbs in those places, sometimes finishing the criminal by two or three blows on the chest or stomach: thence called *coups de grace*. He was then unbound and laid on a small carriage wheel, with his face upwards, and his arms and legs doubled under him; there to expire, if still alive. Sometimes the sentence contained a *retentum*, by which the executioner was directed to strangle the criminal, either before the first, or after one, two or three blows. This punishment was abolished in France at the Revolution; but it is still resorted to in Germany as the punishment for parricide, the last instance of which took place in 1827 near Gottingen. The assassin of the bishop of Ermeland in Prussia, in 1841, was sentenced to the wheel.

WHIG, one of a political party which had its origin in England in the 17th century, in the reign of the Stuarts, when great contests existed respecting the royal prerogatives. Those who supported the king in his high claims were called *Tories*, and the advocates of popular rights were called *Whigs*. The term is of Scottish origin, and was first used in the reign of Charles II. According to Bishop Burnet, it is derived from *whiggam*, a word which was used by the peasants of the south-west of Scotland, in driving their horses; the drivers being called *whiggamores*, contracted to *whiggs*. In 1648, after the news of the Duke of Hamilton's defeat, the clergy stirred up the people to rise and march to Edinburgh, and they themselves marched at the head of their parishes. The Marquis of Argyle and his party came and headed them. This was called the *whiggamores' inroad*, and ever after that all that opposed the court came, in contempt, to be called *whiggs;* and from Scotland, the word was brought to England, where it has since continued to be used as the distinguishing appellation of the political party opposed to the *Tories*. It was first assumed as a party name by that body of politicians who were most active in placing William III. on the throne of England. Generally speaking, the principles of the whigs have been of a popular character, and their measures, when in power, tending to increase the democratic influence in the constitution. In American history, the friends and supporters of the war and the principles of the revolution, were called *whigs*, and those who opposed them were called *tories* and *royalists*. One of the two great political parties in the United States, is called *whig*.

WHIS'PERING DOMES, or GALLERIES, are places in which whispers or feeble sounds are communicated to a greater distance than under any ordinary circumstances. In order to produce this effect, the form of the roof or walls of the building must be such that sound proceeding from one part is transmitted by reflection or repeated reflections to another. The dome of St. Paul's church in London furnishes an instance.

WHIST, the most perfect game at the card table, requiring great attention and silence, whence its name. This game is played by four persons, who cut for partners; the two highest and the two lowest are together, and the partners sit opposite to each other: the person who cuts the lowest card is to deal first, giving one at a time to each person, till he comes to the last card, which is turned up for the trump, and remains on the table till each person has played a card. The person on the left hand side of the dealer plays first, and whoever wins the trick is to play again, thus going on till the cards are played out. The ace, king, queen, and knave of trumps are called *honors;* whichever side holds three of these honors, reckons two points towards the game, or for the whole of the honors, four points, the game consisting of ten points. The honors are reckoned after the tricks; all above six tricks reckoning also towards the game.

WHITFIELD'IAN METH'ODISTS, the name given to the most numerous body of the Methodists after the Wesleyans; so called from Whitfield, whose early connection with the Methodists will be found noticed under that term. Soon after the return of Mr. Whitfield from America in 1741, he withdrew connection from Wesley on account of religious tenets; the former holding the high doctrine of Calvinism, and differing from the latter chiefly on the subjects of election and general redemption. But though they differed in sentiments, these good men lived and died united in heart. Whitfield devoted his life to itinerant preaching, and was, if possible, more popular as an energetic and eloquent pulpit orator than his former coadjutor. He did not confine his labors to Great Britain and Ireland, but visited North America no fewer than seven different times; and died there at Boston, in 1770, in the fifty-sixth year of his age. But he can scarcely be said to be the founder of a sect: his chief object was itinerating. At several places, indeed, he erected chapels, or *tabernacles*, as he called them; but these he invariably left to the care of any orthodox clergyman, whether in the establishment or among the dissenters, who was prepared to occupy them.

WHIT'SUNTIDE, the fiftieth day after Easter, and which is properly called *Pentecost.* It is said to have received its popular name from the circumstance, that, formerly, people newly baptized came to church between Easter and Pentecost in *white* garments.

WICK'LIFFITES, a religious sect which sprung up in England in the reign of Edward III., and took its name from John Wickliffe, doctor and professor of divinity in the University of Oxford, who maintained that the substance of the sacramental bread and wine remained unaltered after consecration; and opposed the doctrine of purgatory, indulgences, auricular confession, the invocation of saints, and the worship of images. He made an English version of the Bible, and composed two volumes called Aletheia, that is, Truth, from which John Huss learned most of his doctrines. In short, to this reformer we owe the first hint of the reformation, which was effected about two hundred years after.

WIG'WAM, a name given by the English to the huts or cabins of the North American Indians.

WILL, that faculty of the mind by which we determine either to do or forbear an action. The will is directed or influenced by the judgment. The understanding or reason compares different objects, which operate as motives; the judgment determines which is preferable, and the *will* decides which to pursue. The freedom of the will is essential to moral action, and is the great distinction of man from the brute.

WILL or TES'TAMENT, the disposition of a person's estate, to take effect after his or her decease. No person under twenty-one can make a valid will. Wills are to be construed as if made immediately before the death of the testator, unless a contrary intention is expressed; and properties bequeathed in general terms include all property in the possession of the testator at his decease, whether acquired before or after the will was made.

WIN'CHESTER BUSH'EL, the original English standard measure of capacity, given by King Edgar, and kept in the town-hall of the ancient city of Winchester, with other measures both of quantity and length. Until the year 1826, when the imperial standard measure was introduced, the Winchester bushel was the standard for England.

WIN'TER, one of the four seasons of the year, commencing on the day when the sun's distance from the zenith of the place is the greatest, and ending on that when it is at a mean between the greatest and the least. The coldness of winter is therefore owing to the shortness of the days, or time during which the sun is above the horizon, and the oblique direction in which his rays fall upon our part of the globe at that season.

WIS'DOM, the right use of knowledge. It may be considered both as a *faculty* of the mind and as an *acquirement*. In the former sense it is the faculty of discerning or judging what is most just, proper, and useful; in the latter, the knowledge and use of what is best, most just, and most conducive to prosperity or happiness.—In Scripture theology, *wisdom* is the knowledge and fear of God, and sincere and uniform obedience to his commands; in other words, true religion. —*Wisdom of Solomon*, one of the books of the Apocrypha. It is by many thought to have been written after the cabalistic philosophy was introduced among the Jews.

WIT, in its original signification, was synonymous with wisdom. Thus we read of our ancient witenagemot, or Saxon parliament, an assembly of wise men; and so late as the Elizabethan age, a man of great or pregnant wit, meant a man of vast judgment. The word wit, however, like many other words, has in the course of time undergone various mutations. According to Locke, wit lies in the assemblage of ideas, and putting those together with quickness and variety, so that a congruity of associations and pleasant images may be present to the fancy; while Pope defines it to be a quick conception and an easy delivery. It is evident that wit excites in the mind an agreeable surprise, and that this is entirely owing to the strange assemblage of related ideas presented to the mind. Of so much consequence are surprise and novelty, that nothing is more vapid than a joke that has become stale by frequent repetition. For the same reason, a witty repartee is infinitely more pleasing than a witty attack; and a pun or happy allusion thrown out extempore in conversation, will often appear excellent, though it might be deemed execrable in print. Humor and wit are both addressed to the comic passion; but humor aims at the risibility, and wit at the admiration; humor is the seasoning of farce, and wit of comedy; humor judges by instinct; wit by comparison. As a learned divine has well observed, "sometimes it playeth in words and phrases, taking advantage from the ambiguity of their sense, or the affinity of their sound; sometimes it is wrapped in a dress of humorous expression; sometimes it lurketh under an odd similitude; sometimes it is lodged in a sly question, in a smart answer, in a quirkish reason, in a shrewd intimation, in cunningly diverting or cleverly retorting an objection; sometimes it is couched in a bold scheme of speech, in a tart irony, in a lusty hyperbole, in a startling metaphor, in a plausible reconciling of contradictions, or in acute nonsense. Often it consisteth in one knows not what, and springeth up one can hardly tell how." *Note.*—It is difficult to give any strict definition of the term *wit*, its precise boundaries being still too unsettled. It has passed through a greater variety of significations in the course of the last two centuries than most other terms in the English language. Originally, *wit* signified wisdom; and anciently a man of *witte*, was a wise man. In the reign of Elizabeth, a man of pregnant *wit*, or of great *wit*, was a man of vast judgment. In the reign of James I. *wit* was used to signify the intellectual faculties or mental powers collectively. In the time of Cowley it came to signify a superior understanding, and more particularly a quick and brilliant reason. By Dryden it is used as nearly synonymous with talent or ability. According to Locke, it consists in quickness of fancy and imagination. Pope defined *wit* to be a quick conception and an easy delivery; according to which, a man of *wit*, or a *wit*, is a man of brilliant fancy; a man of genius. At present, *wit* is used to designate a peculiar faculty of the mind, connected with the more comprehensive faculty of the imagination: and also the effect produced by this faculty, which consists in the display of remote resemblances between dissimilar objects, or an unexpected combination of remote resemblances; in the exhibition or perception of ludicrous points of analogy or resemblance among things in other respects dissimilar. Hence, a man of *wit*, or a *wit*, is considered to be a man in whom a readiness for such exercise of the mind is remarkable. It is evident that *wit* excites in the mind an agreeable surprise, and that arising, not from anything marvellous in the subject, but solely from the imagery employed or the strange assemblage of related ideas presented to the mind.

This end is effected, 1. by debasing things pompous or seemingly grave; 2. by aggrandizing things little and frivolous; or, 3. by setting ordinary objects in a particular and uncommon point of view, by means not only remote, but apparently contrary. Hence arise a great many kinds of wit. Wit is often joined with humor, but not necessarily so; it often displays itself in the keenest satire; but when it is not kept under proper control, or when it becomes the habitual exercise of the mind, it is apt to impair the nobler powers of the understanding, to chill the feelings, to check friendly and social intercourse, and to break down those barriers which have been established by courtesy. At the same time, when kept within its proper sphere, and judiciously used, it may be rendered very effective in attacking pedantry, pretension, or folly, and may also be employed as a powerful weapon against error.

WITCH'CRAFT, a supernatural power, which persons were formerly supposed to obtain the possession of, by entering into compact with the evil one. Indeed, it was fully believed that they gave themselves up to him body and soul; and he engaged that they should want for nothing, and be able to assume whatever shape they pleased, to visit and torment their enemies! The insane fancies of diseased minds, unusual phenomena of nature, and the artful machinery of designing malignity, ambition, or hypocrisy, were all laid at Satan's feet. Witchcraft was universally believed in throughout Europe till the 16th century, and even maintained its ground with tolerable firmness till the 17th. Vast numbers of reputed witches were convicted and condemned to be burnt. In short, it is recorded, that 500 witches were burned at Geneva in three months, about the year 1515; that 1000 were executed in one year in the diocese of Como; and it has been calculated that not less than 100,000 victims must have suffered, in Germany alone, from the date of Innocent's bull, in 1484, which directed the Inquisition to be vigilant in searching out and punishing witches, to the final extinction of the prosecutions. The number of those put to death in England has been estimated at about 30,000! Much has been said concerning the connection between religious fanaticism and the superstition of witchcraft. It has been seen that the cruelties and absurdities of witch persecution had reached a great height even before the Reformation; but it can scarcely be denied that the strong religious excitement which produced and accompanied that event was in some way connected with the rapid spread and development of that atrocious system. The more intense the belief in the overruling providence of God, and his immediate interference in the course of ordinary events (which especially characterized the revival of religion,) the more does the parallel belief in the agency of evil spirits, and their dealings with man, appear to take root in the imagination. Sir W. Scott observes that, among Protestant sects, the Calvinists (whose views of religion were at once the most gloomy and the most engrossing) seem to have afforded the most terrible examples of this prevailing mania. There seems also to have been a constantly recurring tendency to treat witchcraft and heresy as allied offences. It appears, upon the whole, that the persecutions during the 16th and 17th centuries were most violent in those countries which were the scene of much strife between the two religions, or in which the Calvinist opinions were pushed to an extreme—France, the Netherlands, Northern and Western Germany, Switzerland, Scotland, England under the Commonwealth, and at a still later period New England. A singular example of the contagion of fanaticism suddenly spreading with extraordinary violence, and subsiding again after one terrible outbreak, is to be found in the history of the witch persecutions in Sweden, in the end of the 17th century. In Italy, with the exception of one or two of the northern districts, the superstition was generally less prevalent, or at least less distressing in its effects; and the same may be said of Spain, after the first period of the history of the Inquisition.

WITENAGE'MOTE, literally, an assembly of wise men. Among the Anglo-Saxons, the great national council or parliament, consisting of nobles, or chiefs, the largest landholders, and the principal ecclesiastics. The meetings of this council were frequent; they formed the highest court of judicature in the kingdom; they were summoned by the king in any political emergency; their concurrence was necessary to give validity to laws, and treaties with foreign states were submitted to their approval. They had even power to elect the king, and if the sceptre descended in his race, it was by means of the formal recognition of the new king by the nobles, bishops, &c., in an assembly convened for the purpose.

It seems that in East Anglia the possession of forty hides of land was necessary to entitle a person to rank among those termed in the Latin of the age "proceres," who appear to have been members of the great council. The powers and character of the witenagemote passed to the great council of the early Norman kings, which are called by the same name by Saxon writers.

WIT'NESS, in law, one who gives evidence in a judicial proceeding. In civil cases, witnesses are compelled to attend by the process called *subpœna ad testificandum* (which see,) and punishable if they neglect to do so by attachment or action. In criminal cases, by subpœna or by recognizance taken by the magistrate before whom the information is given.

WO'DEN, or WUOTAN, an Anglo-Saxon divinity, considered to correspond with the Mercury of the ancient Greeks and Romans; from whom Wednesday derives its name. He is sometimes also, though erroneously, considered as identical with Odin.

WOM'AN, the female of the human race, grown to an adult age. In the patriarchal ages women were used agreeably to that simplicity of manners which for a long time after pervaded all nations. They drew water, kept sheep, and fed the cattle; as may be observed in what is related of Rebecca, the niece of Abraham, and Rachel, the daughter of Laban. Among the Greeks and Romans, women were employed in spinning, weaving, embroidery, and all sorts of needle-work; their education being wholly confined to their domestic duties. It is in the Christian home only that woman reigns—the mother, sister, wife, and friend. The influence of Christianity gave woman a new station in society, broke her chains, and released her from the degrading restrictions in which she had almost become the soulless thing which she had been represented to be. As man ceased to be a mere citizen of his own country, and felt himself to be a citizen of the world, so woman was restored to her natural rights. "In every age and country (says Gibbon,) the wiser, or at least the stronger, of the two sexes has usurped the powers of the state, and confined the other to the cares and pleasures of domestic life. In hereditary monarchies, however, and especially in those of modern Europe, the gallant spirit of chivalry, and the law of succession, have accustomed us to allow a singular exception; and a woman is often acknowledged the absolute sovereign of a great kingdom, in which she would be deemed incapable of exercising the smallest employment, civil or military. But as the Roman emperors were still considered as the generals and magistrates of the republic, their wives' mothers, although distinguished by the name of Augusta, were never associated to their personal honors; and a female reign would have appeared an inexpiable prodigy in the eyes of those primitive Romans who married without love, or loved without delicacy and respect."—Born to feel and inspire the kind and tender affections, it is the fault of men if well-educated females become not the grace and ornament of society. This, at least, is the rule; the reverse of this, the exception.

WON'DER, that emotion which is excited by something presented to the senses which is either sudden, extraordinary, or not well understood. The word *wonder* is nearly allied to *astonishment*, though it expresses less, and much less than *amazement*.—Among the ancients, *the seven wonders of the world* were—the Egyptian pyramids—the mausoleums erected by Artemisia—the temple of Diana, at Ephesus—the walls and hanging gardens of Babylon—the colossus at Rhodes—the statue of Jupiter Olympus—and the Pharos or watch-tower at Alexandria.

WOOD-ENGRAV'ING, or wood-cutting, the art of cutting figures in wood, that they may be printed by the same process as common letter-press. The mode of engraving on wood is exactly the reverse of that of copper-plate, the parts intended to appear being raised on the surface. The wood which is used for the purpose of engraving, is that of the box-tree, of which a considerable quantity is imported from Turkey. The design drawn upon the wood is the reverse of the object copied, so that when the impression is taken from the engraving, the object is correctly represented.

WOOD'-GELD, in ancient English customs, the gathering or cutting of wood within the forest; or the money paid for the same to the foresters. Sometimes it also seems to signify an immunity from this payment by the king's grant.

WOOL'SACK, the seat of the Lord Chancellor of England, in the House of Lords, is so called, from its being a large square bag of wool without back or arms, covered with red cloth.

WORDS, are signs, or symbols of ideas and thoughts, produced by sounds, and combinations of sounds, or by letters and their combinations.—In the language of an old writer, who somewhat quaintly expresses himself, "He that has names without ideas, wants meaning in his words, and speaks only empty sounds. He that has complex ideas without names for them, wants despatch in his expression. He that uses his words loosely and unsteadily, will either not be minded or not understood. He that applies names to ideas, different from the common use, wants propriety in his language, and speaks gibberish; and he that has ideas of substances disagreeing with the real existence of things, so far wants the materials of true knowledge."

WORLD, the whole system of created globes; or the orbs which occupy space, and all the beings which inhabit them. The duration of the world is a subject which has given rise to much disputation. Plato, after Ocellus Lucanus, held it to be eternal, and to have flowed from God as rays flow from the sun. Aristotle, who was much of the same opinion, asserts that the world was not generated so as to begin to be a world, which before was none: he lays down a pre-existing and eternal matter as a principle, and thence argues the world eternal. His arguments amount to this, that it is impossible an eternal agent, having an eternal passive subject, should continue long without action; and his opinion was for a long time generally followed, as seeming to be the fittest to end the dispute among so many sects about the first cause. But some of the modern philosophers refute the imaginary eternity of the world by this argument, that if it be *ab eterno*, there must have been a generation of individuals in a continual succession from all eternity, since no cause can be assigned why they should not be generated, viz., one from another.—By the *world* we sometimes understand the things of this world, its pleasures and interests. It also means the customs and manners of mankind; the practice of life.

WOR'SHIP, or DIVINE' WOR'SHIP, the act of paying divine honors to the Supreme Being; or, the reverence and homage offered up to God in prayer, adoration, and other devotional exercises, expressive of pious veneration. If the worship of God, says Paley, be a duty of religion, public worship is a necessary institution; because without it the greater part of mankind would exercise no religious worship at all.

WRANG'LER, Senior, in the university of Cambridge, the student who passes the best examination (especially in mathematical knowledge) in the senate-house, for the first degree or that of bachelor in arts; they who follow next in the same division are respectively termed *second, third, fourth*, &c. *wranglers*.

WRECK, in navigation, the destruction of a ship and the cargo, by being driven ashore, or found floating at sea in a deserted and unmanageable condition. But in order to constitute a legal wreck, the goods must come to land. In former times the most inhospitable and barbarous conduct was exercised against all who had the misfortune to suffer from the perils of the sea; but as commerce and navigation were extended, the law was made to afford the adventurous mariner protection. In England, and other countries, wrecks had been adjudged to the king: but the rigor and injustice of this law was modified so early as the reign of Henry I., when it was ruled, that if any person escaped alive out of the ship, it should be no wreck. And after various modifications, it was decided, in the reign of Henry III. that if goods were cast on shore, having any marks by which they could be identified, they were to revert to the owners, if claimed any time within a year and a day. The plundering of wrecks had, however, become so confirmed by the custom of ages, that various subsequent penal statutes were enacted to repress it.

WREST'LING, a kind of combat or engagement between two persons unarmed, body to body, to prove their strength and dexterity, and try which can throw his opponent on the ground. Wrestling is an exercise of very great antiquity and fame. It was in use in the heroic age; and had considerable rewards and honors assigned to it at the Olympic games.

WRIT, in law, a precept issued by some court or magistrate in the name of the government, and addressed to a sheriff, his deputy, or other subordinate executive officer, commanding him to do some particular thing. Writs are distinguished into *original* and *judicial*, the former being such as a party sues out without any direction of the court in the particular case; the latter, such as are issued in pursuance of a decree, judgment, or order of a court. A writ or summons, is called a *subpœna*, when it requires witnesses to appear; a *latitat*, when it is assumed the party is concealed; of *habeas corpus*, when it is to bring up the body; of *premunire*, when it incurs forfeiture of all property; and of *qui tam*, when to recover a fine, of which the prosecutor is to have a share.

WRI'TING, an art and act of expressing and conveying our ideas to others by letters or characters visible to the eye. Without its aid the experience of each generation would have been almost entirely lost to succeeding ages, and only a faint glimmer of truth could have been discerned through the mists of tradition. The most ancient remains of writing, which have been transmitted to us, are upon hard substances, such as stones and metals, which were used for edicts and matters of public notoriety. Thus we read that the decalogue was written on two tables of stone; but this practice was not peculiar to the Jews, for it was used by most of the Eastern nations, as well as by the Greeks and Romans. The laws penal, civil, and ceremonial, among the Greeks, were engraven on tables of brass, called *cyrbes*. The Chinese, before the invention of paper, wrote or engraved with an iron tool, or style, upon thin boards or on bamboo. Pliny says, that table-books of wood were in use before the time of Homer. In later times these tables were usually waxed over, and written upon with a style. What was written upon the tables which were thus waxed over was easily effaced, and by smoothing the wax new matter might be substituted in the place of what was written before. The bark of trees was also used for writing by the ancients, and is so still in several parts of Asia. The same may be said of the leaves of trees. But the Greeks and Romans continued the use of waxed table-books long after the use of papyrus, leaves, and skins became common, because they were so convenient for correcting extemporary compositions.

X.

X, the twenty-fourth letter of the English alphabet, is borrowed from the Greek. When used at the beginning of a word, it has precisely the sound of *z*, but in the middle and at the end of words, its sound is the same as *ks*; as, *wax*, *luxury*, *taxation*, &c. In French, *x* has the various pronunciations of *s*, *ss*, *gz*, and *z*, according to circumstances. The Italians never use it, on account of its guttural character, but express it by *ss*, as in *Alessandro*; and the Germans generally substitute for it, *ks*, *gs*, or *chs*. X begins no word in our language but such as are of Greek original; and is in few others but what are of Latin derivation. As a numeral, X stands for ten. When laid horizontally, thus, ⋈, it stands for a thousand, and with a dash over it, ten thousand. As an abbreviation, X stands for *Christ*, as in Xn., *Christian*; Xmas., *Christmas*.

XANG'TI in theology, a name among the Chinese for the Supreme Being.

XAN'THICA, in antiquity, a Macedonian festival, so called because it was observed in the month Xanthus, which is supposed to have been the same as April.

XEBEC', a small three-masted vessel, used in the Mediterranean sea, and on the coasts of Spain, Portugal and Barbary. Being generally equipped as a corsair, the xebec is constructed with a narrow floor, for the sake of speed, and of a great breadth, so as to be able to carry a considerable force of sail without danger of overturning. When close hauled, it carries large lateen sails. The Algerine xebecs usually carried from 16 to 24 guns, and from 300 to 450 men, two thirds of whom were soldiers.

XENELA'SIA, in antiquity, a law among the Spartans, by which strangers were excluded from their society, not out of fear lest they should imitate the Spartan manners, but lest the Spartans should be contaminated by foreign vices. It was a barrier set up against contagion; but was not so strict as to exclude deserving men, or any talent worthy of being received.

XE'NIA, among the Greeks and Romans, were presents made by strangers to such persons as had treated them with kindness and hospitality.—*Xenia* was also a name given to the gifts and presents made to the governors of provinces by the inhabitants of them.

XENODO'CHIA, in antiquity, places where strangers were lodged and entertained.

XENOPARO'CHI, in antiquity, Roman officers whose business it was to provide every necessary for ambassadors.

XEROPH'AGY, the name given to a sort of fast which was adopted in the primitive ages of Christianity, and which consisted entirely of dry viands.

XES'TA, in antiquity, an Athenian

measure of capacity, answering to the Roman sextarius.

XYLOCO'PIA, among the Greeks, a sort of punishment inflicted with a cudgel.

XYLOG'RAPHY, wood-engraving; the act or art of cutting figures in wood, in representation of natural objects.

XY'LON, a species of punishment in use among the Greeks, which answered to our putting offenders in the stocks.

XYNOE'CIA, an Athenian festival, observed in memory of Theseus having united all the petty communities of Attica into one commonwealth, whose assemblies were ever after to be held in the Prytaneum at Athens.

XYS'TARCH, an officer in the Grecian gymnasium, who presided over the *xystus*, as lieutenant to the gymnasiarch. His business was to superintend the *athletæ* in their exercises in the two *xysti*.

XYS'TER, in surgery, an instrument used for scraping bones.

XYS'TUS, or XYS'TOS, among the Greeks and Romans, a portico covered at the top, designed for the exercise of the wrestlers when the weather did not permit them to contend in the open air. The Xystus made a necessary part of a gymnasium: and the name given to the athletæ who performed their exercises there, was *Xystici*.

Y.

Y, the twenty-fifth letter of the English alphabet, is sometimes used as a vowel, and at other times as a consonant: as the latter at the beginning of words. In the middle and at the end of words, *y* is precisely the same as *i*; being sounded as *i* long, when accented, as in *reply*, *defy*; and as *i* short, when unaccented, as in *synonymous*, *liberty*, *ability*, &c.—Y, as a numeral, stands for 150, and with a dash over it, for 150,000.—Y, by the Pythagoreans, was made the emblem or symbol of virtue and vice. The broad line at the bottom of the letter, represents the innocency and simplicity of infancy and early youth. The place where it is divided into two parts shows us the years of discretion, when we take the side of wisdom or of folly, and can discriminate what is right from what is wrong. The narrow line on the right exhibits to the fancy the strait path that leads to happiness, and the difficulties which attend a course of virtue. The broad line on the left represents the broad road that leads to destruction, and the seducing blandishments of vice.

YACHT, a sailing vessel, pleasure boat, or small ship with one deck, sufficiently large for a sea voyage. In its original signification it is a vessel of state used to convey princes, ambassadors, and other great personages from one kingdom to another. It is usually fitted with a variety of convenient apartments and suitable furniture. The smaller yachts are generally rigged as sloops.

YA'GERS, or JAGERS, light infantry armed with rifles (*chasseurs*, *riflemen*.) In the Prussian service, the Yagers form a distinct corps with peculiar discipline; in that of Austria, light infantry, generally from the mountain districts. In Germany the term *jager* is applied to a peculiar species of higher servant attached to the families of the aristocracy.

YA'HOO, a name given by Swift, in one of his imaginary voyages, to a race of brutes, having the form of man and all his degrading passions. They are placed in contrast with the *Houyhnhums*, or horses endowed with reason, the whole being designed as a satire on the human race. Chesterfield uses the term *yahoo* for a savage, or one resembling a savage.

YAN'KEE, a word commonly applied to an inhabitant of the United States, as *John Bull* is to an Englishman or *Mynheer* to a Dutchman. It is said to have originated in a corrupt pronunciation of the word *English* by the native Indians of America, who called the early settlers from Great Britain *Yengeese*, but this etymology is doubtful.

YEO'MAN, in English polity, a *commoner*, or a plebeian of the first or most respectable class. In ancient times, it denoted one of those who held *folk-land*; that is, had no *fief*, or book-land, and therefore did not rank among the *gentry*. What he possessed, however, he possessed independently; he was, therefore, no man's vassal. To understand the true condition of the ancient yeomen, it must be observed that there were some lands which never became subject to the feudal system. These were called folk-lands, or the lands of the people. When therefore, it is said that the sovereign is lord of the soil of all England, the assertion is not true. He is certainly the lord paramount of all fiefs; but he has no such reversionary interest in lands that were never held in fee. The collective body of yeomen or freeholders is termed *Yeomanry*. —*Yeomen of the Guard*, a certain description of foot-guards, who attend immediately on the person of the sovereign. They were established by Henry VIII., and their office and dress continue the same.

YEZDEGER'DIAN, noting an era, dated from the overthrow of the Persian empire, when Yezdegerd was defeated by the Arabians, in the eleventh year of the Hegira, A.D. 636.

YEZ'IDEES, a small tribe bordering on the Euphrates, whose religion is said to be a mixture of the worship of the devil, with some of the doctrines of the Magi, Mohammedans, and Christians.

YO'GA, among the Hindoos, a species of asceticism, which consists in a complete abstraction from all worldly objects, by which the Hindoo ascetic expects to obtain final emancipation from further migrations, and union with the universal spirit. Those who practise the Yoga are called *Yogis*, and the horrible tortures which they commit on themselves have been often described.

YOUTH, in painting, sculpture, &c. The most beautiful period of life, and consequently that which the artist will select to display and embody his abstract ideal of corporeal human perfection. The smooth and glowing substance of the skin, the beautifully defined contours of the figure, the firm and well knit muscles of man, and the delicious shapeliness of woman; these qualities, as they are in themselves uniformly amiable in real life, so they cannot fail to draw forth the ability of the artist, and excite the admiration of the beholder, when transmitted to canvass or marble.

YULE, the common Scottish name for Christmas. It appears to be a very ancient Celtic word. In Welsh, wyl or gywl signifies a holiday; whence also the old phrase, "Gule of August," the first day of August, or fast of St. Peter and Vincula, for which various absurd etymologies have been found. Perhaps the old French word "Noel," for Christmas (used also generally as a popular cry of rejoicing,) has the same original. Count de Gebelin, however, derives yule from a supposed primitive word, connected with the idea of revolution or "wheel."

Z.

Z, the last letter of the English alphabet, is a sibillant articulation and semivowel; bearing the same relation to *s*, as *v* does to *f*. In Italian, it is sometimes sounded like our *ts*, sometimes like *ds*; in Spanish, it corresponds to our *th*; and in French, when pronounced at all, it has the sound of a forcibly articulated *s*. As a numeral, Z stands for 2,000, and with a dash over it for 2,000,000.

ZAC'CHO, in architecture, the lowest part of the pedestal of a column.

ZAIMS, a name for certain leaders or chiefs among the Turks, who support and pay a mounted militia of the same name.

ZEAL'OT, one who engages warmly in any cause, and pursues his object with earnestness and ardor. It is generally used in dispraise, or applied to one whose ardor is intemperate and censurable. The fury of *zealots* was one cause of the destruction of Jerusalem.

ZECHARI'AH, one of the minor prophets, who prophesied in the reign of Darius Hystaspes. The design of the first part of Zechariah's prophecy, like that of his contemporary, Haggai, is to encourage the Jews to proceed with rebuilding the Temple, by giving them assurance of God's aid and protection. From this he proceeds to foretel the glory of the Christian church (the true Temple of God,) under its great High-priest and Ruler, Jesus Christ; of whom Zerubbabel and Joshua were figures. He treats of his death, sufferings, and kingdom, in many particulars not mentioned by any other of the minor prophets before him; everything relating to those great events becoming more explicit, in proportion as their accomplishments drew nearer. His style, like that of Haggai, is for the most part prosaic, especially towards the beginning; the last six chapters are more elevated; for which reason, among others, these six chapters are, by many commentators, ascribed to the prophet Jeremiah.

ZEMINDAR', a title introduced into India by its Mohammedan conquerors, conferred in Bengal, and generally throughout the Mogul empire, on the agent employed to collect that share of the produce of the soil which belongs to it. The zemindars were the great landholders of the Mogul empire; but the nature of their tenure has given rise to much dispute. Whether they were hereditary, absolute owners of the soil, or only tenants of the sovereign at a fixed rent by way of land-tax, for which they were personally responsible, was a question much agitated by writers on Indian subjects at the period of the "Permanent Settlement" in 1793. By that settlement the rent was to be fixed in the first instance by custom, and the zemindar was then to give the ryot a lease restricted to himself and his assignees on performance of its conditions; his own share being fixed as before at 10 per cent. of the assessment, and his hereditary right secured. A zemindary, *i. e.*, the district of a zemindar, is liable to be sold by government for arrears of revenue, and existing leases with the ryots to be set aside. At present the land-tax of India is levied in three methods, which prevail in different districts—the "zemindar settlement," by which the zemindar is responsible to government; the "mouzawar" or village settlement, by which the collector contracts with the head man of the village; and the "ryotwar" or cultivator settlement, by which the tax is collected immediately from the peasantry.

ZEND, or ZENDAVES'TA, a book ascribed to Zoroaster, and containing his pretended revelations; which the ancient magicians and modern Persians, called also Gaurs, observe and reverence in the same manner as the Christians do the Bible, and the Mahometans do the Koran, making it the sole rule of their faith and manners.

ZEN'DIK, in Arabic, a name given to those who are charged with atheism, or rather disbelief of any revealed religion; or with magical heresies. The sect of Zendiks opposed the progress of Mohammedanism in Arabia with great obstinacy. It appears to have had many features in common with Sadduceeism among the Jews.

ZEPHANI'AH, a canonical book of the Old Testament, containing the predictions of Zephaniah, the son of Cushi, and grandson of Gedaliah; being the ninth of the twelve lesser prophets. He prophesied in the time of king Josiah, a little after the captivity of the ten tribes, and before that of Judah; so that he was contemporary with Jeremiah.

ZEPH'YRUS, or ZEPH YR, the west wind; a wind blowing from that cardinal point opposite to the east. The poets personify it, and represent Zephyrus as the mildest and most gentle of all the deities of the woods; the character of this personage is youth and gentleness. It is also called Favonius and Occidens.

ZEUG'MA, a figure in grammar by which an adjective or verb which agrees with a nearer word, is, by way of supplement, referred to another more remote.

ZO'HAR, a Jewish book, highly esteemed by the rabbis, and supposed to be of great, though altogether unascertained antiquity. It consists of cabalistical commentaries on Scripture, especially the books of Moses. It has been translated into Latin.

ZOLL'VEREIN, the Prussian or German commercial or customs union, founded, through the example and efforts of the government of Prussia, in the year 1834, and having for its object the establishment of a uniform rate of customs duties throughout the various states joining the union.

ZOOL'ATRY, the worship of animals, which was the characteristic of the ancient Egyptian religion most remarked upon by foreigners.

ZOTHE'CA, in architecture, a small room, or alcove, which might be added to or separated from another, by means of curtains and windows.

FINIS.

www.ingramcontent.com/pod-product-compliance
Lightning Source LLC
LaVergne TN
LVHW021051110826
845150LV00001B/43

* 9 7 8 1 4 2 5 5 6 7 8 2 8 *